**OFFICIAL TOURIST BOARD GUIDE**

# Bed & Breakfast
## 2008

visit**Britain** ™

# Contents

## USEFUL INDEXES

## KEY TO SYMBOLS

Inside back-cover flap

Whinstone Lee Tor,
Peak District, Derbyshire

## VisitBritain

VisitBritain is the organisation created to
market Britain to the rest of the world, and
England to the British.

Formed by the merger of the British Tourist
Authority and the English Tourism Council,
its mission is to build the value of tourism
by creating world-class destination brands
and marketing campaigns.

It will also build partnerships with – and
provide insights to – other organisations
which have a stake in British and English
tourism.

Royal Harbour Marina,
Ramsgate, Kent

# The guide that gives you more

This official VisitBritain guide is packed with information from where to stay, to how to get there and what to see and do. In fact, everything you need to know to enjoy England.

## Quality accommodation

Choose from a wide range of quality-assessed accommodation to suit all budgets and tastes. This guide contains a comprehensive listing of all bed and breakfast establishments participating in VisitBritain's Enjoy England Quality Rose assessment scheme, including guesthouses, farmhouses, inns, restaurants with rooms, hostel and campus accommodation. Just look for the Quality Rose – the official marque of Enjoy England quality-assessed accommodation.

## Regional information

Every region has its own unique attractions – in each section we highlight a selection of interesting ideas for memorable days out. Regional maps show their location as well as National Trails and sections of the National Cycle Network. You'll also find a selection of great events and regional tourism contact details. For even more ideas go online at enjoyengland.com.

## Useful indexes

Indexes at the back make it easy to find accommodation that matches your requirements – and if you know the name of the establishment you can use the property index.

## Tourist information centres

For local information phone or call in to a Tourist Information Centre. Location and contact details can be found at the beginning of each regional section. Alternatively, you can text **INFO** to 62233 to find your nearest Official Partner Tourist Information Centre.

# How to use this guide

In this invaluable bed and breakfast guide, you'll find a great choice of guesthouses, farmhouses, inns, restaurants with rooms, hostel and campus accommodation.

Each property has been visited annually by Enjoy England assessors to nationally agreed standards so that you can book with confidence knowing your accommodation has been checked and rated for quality.

Detailed accommodation entries include descriptions, prices and facilities. You'll also find special offers and themed breaks to suit your tastes, interests and budget.

## Finding accommodation is easy

### Regional entries
The guide is divided into nine regional sections and accommodation is listed alphabetically by place name within each region. Start your search for accommodation in the regional sections of this guide. For an even wider choice, turn to the listing section starting on page 484 where you will find ALL Enjoy England assessed bed and breakfast establishments, including those that have not taken a paid entry.

### Colour maps
Use the colour maps, starting on page 28, to pinpoint the location of all accommodation featured in the regional sections. Then refer to the place index at the back of the guide to find the page number. The index also includes tourism areas such as the New Forest and the Cotswolds.

### Indexes
The indexes, listed on page 701, will help you find the right accommodation if you have a particular requirement, for example, establishments suitable for guests with disabilities or those that offer an evening meal by arrangement.

Kids and weather. They change mood from one moment to the next. Fortunately, that's also one of the most striking things about England's great outdoors and attractions: you just step across the threshold and its landscapes and entertainment venues offer all the varied play potential you need to fill holidays, sunny afternoons or rainy weekends.

So, there you are on the beach building sandcastles, paddling, eating ice cream and basking in the warm memory that you'll take home. You watch the teenagers hanging out with their surfboards, part of the family outing but doing their own thing. There's something for all ages and that's priceless in every sense of the word. Next time, maybe picnicking in woods, leaping through treetops on an aerial adventure, or getting your hands on heritage - whatever makes everyone happy.

Then it rains and you want to stay indoors. London's Science Museum is free, like a good number of England's top attractions, and that pleases Money Bags. Everyone immediately vanishes into one of the galleries: in Who Am I? you're morphing your face older and younger, in another you're discovering how to forecast weather and learning about climate change, which could be useful for planning your next trip!

Anticipate the family's next mood. Animal magic at Chester Zoo, following Harry Potter to Alnwick Castle, or screaming your heads off at Drayton Manor Theme Park in Staffordshire? There's always another boredom-buster just around the corner.

For lots more great ideas visit enjoyEngland.com/ideas

Seaside fun,
Brighton & Hove

# Make fun of England, it runs in the family

# In the cities, it's the buildings that are flowering

River Tyne,
NewcastleGateshead

Cities in England today exude confidence. It's a self-belief that comes from bold investment. And as you gaze up at yet another remarkable new building that demands your attention and sparks your imagination, you realize that nowhere is this confidence more visible than in the architecture of the now.

Architects have done us proud in this country. Many of our cities are studded with gleaming out-of-this-world structures that find the fulcrum between form and function. And today you've taken time out to see the Lowry Museum in Manchester's Salford Quays. Just glimpsing the metal hull of the building from a distance makes you speed your step. Somehow, the thrilling combination of stainless steel and glass makes this inspirational waterside building a fitting home for the world's greatest collection of Lowry works.

It's just the kind of landmark building that you can seek out in many English cities these days. Portsmouth Harbour's 170-metre Spinnaker Tower, in the design of a billowing sail, conjures thoughts of sea breezes. So you take the lift to its Crow's Nest view deck, open to the elements, and see for miles, wind in your hair. Wembley Stadium, Gateshead Millennium Bridge, each one is a vigorous marriage of art and purpose.

Why not set a day aside, fish out your A to Z, and go on a safari of spectacular structures in a city near to (or far from) you.

For lots more great ideas visit
enjoyEngland.com/ideas

Take one of the hundreds of footpaths along the eastern end of Hope Valley in the Peak District and you'll find yourself at Stanage Edge, a bold outcrop of gritstone worshipped throughout the climbing world.

The wind whips the flap of your rucksack, the material snapping like a spinnaker in a force 9, as you pedal up the last few yards of muddy track to where the rock emerges from the stunted bracken. It's only a five-minute walk from the road side car park and an easy drive to find this spot. But make this small effort and you're rewarded with one of the most astounding views in the country.

Out here you feel the full primitive energy of nature. And whether you've packed the crampons and ropes, a pair of hiking boots and a flask or you've brought the Rover and simply come to stretch your legs, it's one of those precious places where you can escape the crowds, taste true freedom and find inner peace.

England boasts an astonishing diversity of natural wonders, from the flat waterscapes of the Norfolk Broads to the jutting peaks of the Lake District, from the ancient woodlands of the New Forest to Dorset's fossil-jewelled Jurassic Coast.

This is our natural heritage, shaped by primeval forces and just waiting to be explored. Do so and you'll return with weary legs, a ravenous appetite and that wonderful tingling sensation you get on your face after a day in the fresh air.

For lot's more great ideas visit enjoyEngland.com/ideas

Whinstone Lee Tor,
Peak District, Derbyshire

# The edge of the world – just a short stroll away

# England a modern diner's haven? It's all waffle

A quiet revolution has been simmering away in England's eateries. Fresh, local and organic ingredients have become the order of the day. As you tuck into a light lunch of crisp salad and garlic mayo (made with free range eggs) you really begin to wonder if Chicken in a Basket wasn't just a bad dream.

Sitting there in the charming Waffle House in St Alban's (the working water wheel on display for all to admire), you can't help but admire the blend of inventiveness, quality produce and sheer dedication that goes into the cooking. Here you'll find waffles of every conceivable shape and size, served with freshly made toppings such as chickpea curry and mango chutney as well as an endless choice of sweet varieties. And, needless to say, every waffle is made with organic stone-ground flour from a mill down the road.

It's just the same in places like Leon in London W1, that dazzling health-conscious take away with a penchant for seasonal ingredients. And let's not forget the gastro pub phenomenon (sparked off and going stronger than ever in The Eagle on Farringdon Road) where high quality cooked-from-scratch bistro meals are served at bar room prices.

And this is the true legacy of the contemporary food revolution in England today: wherever you dine, you'll more than likely be presented with fresh, wholesome food beautifully cooked with passion and care. Enjoy!

For lots more great ideas visit enjoyEngland.com/ideas

# Ratings and awards at a glance

**Reliable, rigorous, easy to use** – look out for the following ratings and awards to help you choose with confidence:

## Ratings made easy

| | |
|---|---|
| ★ | Simple, practical, no frills |
| ★★ | Well presented and well run |
| ★★★ | Good level of quality and comfort |
| ★★★★ | Excellent standard throughout |
| ★★★★★ | Exceptional with a degree of luxury |

For full details of the Enjoy England Quality Rose assessment schemes, go online at
**enjoyengland.com/quality**

## Star ratings

Bed and breakfast establishments are awarded a rating of one to five stars based on a combination of quality of facilities and services provided. Put simply, **the more stars, the higher the quality and the greater the range of facilities and level of service.**

The process to arrive at a star rating is very thorough. Enjoy England professional assessors visit establishments annually and work to strict criteria to check the available facilities and service. A quality score is awarded for every aspect of the experience including the comfort of the bed, the standard of the breakfast (and dinner if offered) and, most importantly, the cleanliness. They also score the warmth of welcome and the level of care that each hotel offers its guests.

From January 2006, all the national assessing bodies (VisitBritain, VisitScotland, Visit Wales and the AA) have operated to a common set of standards, giving holidaymakers and travellers a clear guide on exactly what to expect at each level (see page 702).

## Gold and Silver Awards

If you want a superior level of quality guaranteed seek out accommodation with a Gold or Silver Award. They are only given to bed and breakfast accommodation offering the highest levels of quality within their star rating (see page 22).

## Enjoy England Awards for Excellence

The prestigious and coveted Enjoy England Awards for Excellence showcase the very best in English tourism. Run by VisitBritain in association with England's regions, they include a Bed & Breakfast of the Year category (see page 27).

## National Accessible Scheme

Establishments with a National Accessible Scheme rating have been thoroughly assessed to set criteria and provide access to facilities and services for guests with visual, hearing or mobility impairment (see page 24).

## Welcome schemes

Enjoy England runs four special Welcome schemes: Cyclists Welcome, Walkers Welcome, Welcome Pets! and Families Welcome. Scheme participants actively encourage these types of visitors and make special provision to ensure a welcoming, comfortable stay (see page 20).

## Visitor Attraction Quality Assurance

Attractions achieving high standards in all aspects of the visitor experience, from initial telephone enquiry to departure, receive this Enjoy England award and are visited every year by professional assessors.

# What to expect

All bed and breakfast accommodation that is awarded a star rating will meet the minimum standards – so you can be confident that you will find the basic services that you would expect, such as:

- A clear explanation of booking charges, services offered and cancellation terms
- A full cooked breakfast or substantial continental breakfast
- At least one bathroom or shower room for every six guests
- For a stay of more than one night, rooms cleaned and beds made daily
- Printed advice on how to summon emergency assistance at night
- All statutory obligations will be met.

Proprietors of bed and breakfast accommodation have to provide certain additional facilities and services at the higher star levels, some of which may be important to you:

**THREE-STAR accommodation must provide:**
- Private bathroom/shower room (cannot be shared with the owners)
- Bedrooms must have a washbasin if not en suite.

**FOUR-STAR accommodation must provide:**
- 50% of bedrooms en suite or with private bathroom.

**FIVE-STAR accommodation must provide:**
- All bedrooms with en suite or private bathroom.

Sometimes a bed and breakfast establishment has exceptional bedrooms and bathrooms and offers guests a very special welcome, but cannot achieve a higher star rating because, for example, there are no en suite bedrooms, or it is difficult to put washbasins in the bedrooms (three star). This is sometimes the case with period properties.

# Classifications explained

Bed and breakfast accommodation varies greatly in style and facilities. The following will help you decide which type of establishment is right for you, whether you are seeking a seaside escape for two or family fun on the farm.

| | |
|---|---|
| **Guest Accommodation** | Encompassing a wide range of establishments from one-room bed and breakfasts to larger properties, which may offer dinner and hold an alcohol licence. |
| **Bed and Breakfast** | Accommodating no more than six people, the owners of these establishments welcome you into their home as a special guest. |
| **Guest House** | Generally comprising more than three rooms. Dinner is unlikely to be available (if it is, it will need to be booked in advance). May possibly be licensed. |
| **Farmhouse** | Bed and breakfast, and sometimes dinner, but always on a farm. |
| **Restaurant with Rooms** | A licensed restaurant is the main business but there will be a small number of bedrooms, with all the facilities you would expect, and breakfast the following morning. |
| **Inn** | Pubs with rooms, and many with restaurants as well. |
| **Hostel** | Safe, budget-priced, short-term accommodation for individuals and groups. The Hostel classification includes Group Hostel, Backpacker and Activity Accommodation (all of which are awarded star ratings), and Bunkhouses and Camping Barns. |
| **Campus** | Accommodation provided by educational establishments, including university halls of residence and student village complexes. |

# A special welcome

To help make your selection of accommodation easier there are four special Welcome schemes which accommodation can be assessed to. Owners participating in these schemes go the extra mile to welcome walkers, cyclists, families or pet owners and provide additional facilities and services to make your stay even more comfortable.

## Families Welcome

If you are searching for a great family break look out for the Families Welcome sign. The sign indicates that the proprietor offers additional facilities and services catering for a range of ages and family units. For families with young children, the accommodation will have special facilities such as cots and highchairs, storage for push-chairs and somewhere to heat baby food or milk. Where meals are provided, children's choices will be clearly indicated, with healthy options available.They'll also have information on local walks, attractions, activities or events suitable for children, as well as local child-friendly pubs and restaurants. Not all accommodation is able to cater for all ages or combinations of family units, so do check when you book.

## Welcome Pets!

Want to travel with your faithful companion? Look out for accommodation displaying the Welcome Pets! sign. Participants in this scheme go out of their way to meet the needs of guests bringing dogs, cats and/or small birds. In addition to providing water and food bowls, torches or nightlights, spare leads and pet washing facilities, they'll buy in food on request, and offer toys, treats and bedding. They'll also have information on pet-friendly attractions, pubs, restaurants and recreation. Of course, not everyone is able to offer suitable facilities for every pet, so do check if there are any restrictions on the type, size and number of animals when you book.

## Walkers Welcome

If walking is your passion seek out accommodation participating in the Walkers Welcome scheme. Facilities include a place for drying clothes and boots, maps and books for reference and a first-aid kit. Packed breakfasts and lunch are available on request in hotels and guesthouses, and you have the option to pre-order basic groceries in self-catering accommodation. A wide range of information is provided including public transport, weather, local restaurants and attractions, details of the nearest bank and all night chemists.

## Cyclists Welcome

If you like to explore by bike seek out accommodation displaying the Cyclists Welcome symbol. Facilities include a lockable undercover area and a place to dry outdoor clothing and footwear, an evening meal if there are no eating facilities available within one mile, and a packed breakfast or lunch on request. Information is also provided on cycle hire and cycle repair shops, maps and books for reference, weather and details of the nearest bank and all night chemists and more.

**For further information go online at enjoyengland.com/quality**

# Accommodation entries explained

Each accommodation entry contains detailed information to help you decide if it is right for you. This has been provided by proprietors and our aim is to ensure that it is as objective and factual as possible.

**BATH,** Bath and North East Somerset  Map ref 5C1

★★★
**BED AND BREAKFAST**
**SILVER AWARD**

B&B per room per night
s £52.00-£65.00
d £80.00-£120.00
Evening meal per person
£20.00-£30.00

## Bretherton House

17 Easton Road, Bath BA21 3LN  **t** (01225) 123222  **f** (01225) 123333
**e** bretherton@bath.co.uk  **w** brethertonhouse.co.uk

**open** All year except Christmas and New Year
**bedrooms** 3 double
**bathrooms** 3 en suite
**payment** Credit/debit card, euros

Elegant stone house set in beautiful large garden. Peaceful yet near to the city centre. Spacious, comfortable interior with very attractive bedrooms and modern bathrooms. Ideal for exploring this beautiful Georgian city and the West Country. A warm welcome guaranteed.

⊕ M4, jct 18. A46 to Bath. Right at roundabout, A420 towards Bristol. Left at T-junction. Right at traffic lights. Bretherton House is 200yds on right.

♥ Discounts on stays of 4 or more days (excl Saturdays) – see website for details.

Room 🛏 ♿ 📺 🍴  General 🐾 P 🛎 ✿ 🐕  Leisure ⤴ ▶ 🏛

Sample enhanced entry

1  Listing under town or village with map reference

2  Enjoy England star rating plus Gold or Silver Award where applicable

3  Classification

4  Prices per room for bed and breakfast (B&B) and per person for evening meal

5  Establishment name, address, telephone and fax numbers, email and website address

6  Indicates when the establishment is open

7  Accommodation details and payment accepted

8  Accessible rating where applicable

9  Walkers, cyclists, pets and families welcome where applicable

10  At-a-glance facility symbols

11  Travel directions

12  Special promotions and themed breaks

**A key to symbols can be found on the back-cover flap.
Keep it open for easy reference.**

# Gold and Silver Awards

Enjoy England's unique Gold and Silver Awards are given in recognition of exceptional quality in hotel accommodation.

Enjoy England professional assessors make recommendations for Gold and Silver Awards during assessments. They will look at the quality provided in all areas, in particular housekeeping, hospitality, bedrooms, bathrooms and food, to see if it meets the highest quality for the star level achieved.

While star ratings are based on a combination of quality, range of facilities and level of service offered, Gold and Silver Awards are based solely on quality.

Here we feature bed and breakfast establishments with a Gold Award for which detailed entries are included in the regional pages. Use the property index starting on page 745 to find their page numbers.

An index of all Gold and Silver Award-winning bed and breakfast accommodation can be found at the back of this guide.

## Exceptional properties excelling in outstanding quality

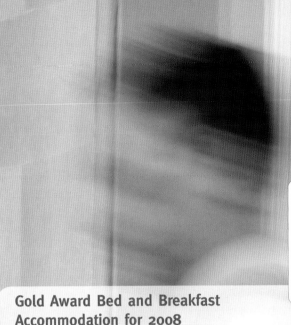

## Gold Award Bed and Breakfast Accommodation for 2008

**17 Burgate,**
Pickering, *North Yorkshire*

**Anchorage House,**
St Austell, *Cornwall*

**Athole Guest House,**
Bath, *Somerset*

**Bays Farm,**
Stowmarket, *Suffolk*

**Brayscroft House,**
Eastbourne, *East Sussex*

**Brookfield House,**
Bovey Tracey, *Devon*

**Burton Mount Country House,**
Beverley, *East Yorkshire*

**Cold Cotes,**
Harrogate, *North Yorkshire*

**Cotteswold House,**
Bibury, *Gloucestershire*

**The Dairy Barns,**
Hickling, *Norfolk*

**Daleside,**
Ampleforth, *North Yorkshire*

**Dolvean House,**
Falmouth, *Cornwall*

**Durrant House,**
Rye, *East Sussex*

**Farnham Farm House,**
Blandford Forum, *Dorset*

**The Galley 'Fish and Seafood' Restaurant & Spa with Cabins,**
Exeter, *Devon*

**Gallon House,**
Knaresborough, *North Yorkshire*

**Giffard House,**
Winchester, *Hampshire*

**Grendon Guest House,**
Buxton, *Derbyshire*

**Hazel Bank Country House,**
Borrowdale, *Cumbria*

**Heatherly Cottage,**
Corsham, *Wiltshire*

**Holmans,**
Burley, *Hampshire*

**Jeake's House,**
Rye, *East Sussex*

**Magnolia House,**
Canterbury, *Kent*

**Moresby Hall,**
Whitehaven, *Cumbria*

**Number One,**
Blackpool, *Lancashire*

**Old Rectory Hopton,**
Diss, *Norfolk*

**The Residence,**
Bath, *Somerset*

**Rock Lodge,**
Stamford, *Lincolnshire*

**The Roundham House,**
Bridport, *Dorset*

**Ryelands,**
Leominster, *Herefordshire*

**The Salty Monk,**
Sidmouth, *Devon*

**Seawards,**
Christchurch, *Dorset*

**Spanhoe Lodge,**
Uppingham, *Rutland*

**Thistleyhaugh Farm,**
Longhorsley, *Northumberland*

**Thorney Mire Barn B&B,**
Hawes, *North Yorkshire*

**The Three Horseshoes Inn,**
High Wycombe,
*Buckinghamshire*

**Throapham House Bed & Breakfast,**
Dinnington, *South Yorkshire*

**Underleigh House,**
Hope, *Derbyshire*

**White Hart Inn,**
Nayland, *Suffolk*

# National Accessible Scheme

Finding suitable accommodation is not always easy, especially if you have to seek out rooms with level entry or large print menus. Use the National Accessible Scheme to help you make your choice.

The criteria VisitBritain and national/regional tourism organisations have adopted do not necessarily conform to British Standards or to Building Regulations. They reflect what the organisations understand to be acceptable to meet the practical needs of guests with mobility or sensory impairments and encourage the industry to increase access to all.

Proprietors of accommodation taking part in the National Accessible Scheme have gone out of their way to ensure a comfortable stay for guests with special hearing, visual or mobility needs. These exceptional places are full of extra touches to make everyone's visit trouble-free, from handrails, ramps and step-free entrances (ideal for buggies too) to level-access showers and colour contrast in the bathrooms. Members of the staff may have attended a disability awareness course and will know what assistance will really be appreciated.

Appropriate National Accessible Scheme symbols are included in the guide entries (shown opposite). If you have additional needs or special requirements we strongly recommend that you make sure these can be met by your chosen establishment before you confirm your reservation. The index at the back of the guide gives a list of bed and breakfast accommodation that has received a National Accessible rating.

For a wider selection of accessible accommodation, order a copy of the Easy Access Britain guide featuring almost 500 places to stay. Available from Tourism for All for £9.99 (plus P&P).

The National Accessible Scheme forms part of the Tourism for All Campaign that is being promoted by VisitBritain and national/regional tourism organisations. Additional help and guidance on finding suitable holiday accommodation can be obtained from:

**Tourism for All**
**c/o Vitalise, Shap Road Industrial Estate, Kendal LA9 6NZ**

**information helpline** 0845 124 9971
**reservations** 0845 124 9973
(lines open 9-5 Mon-Fri)

**f** (01539) 735567

**e** info@tourismforall.org.uk

**w** tourismforall.org.uk

## Mobility Impairment Symbols

 Typically suitable for a person with sufficient mobility to climb a flight of steps but who would benefit from fixtures and fittings to aid balance.

 Typically suitable for a person with restricted walking ability and for those who may need to use a wheelchair some of the time and can negotiate a maximum of three steps.

 Typically suitable for a person who depends on the use of a wheelchair and transfers unaided to and from the wheelchair in a seated position. This person may be an independent traveller.

 Typically suitable for a person who depends on the use of a wheelchair in a seated position. This person also requires personal/mechanical assistance to aid transfer (eg carer, hoist).

  Access Exceptional is awarded to establishments that meet the requirements of independent wheelchair users or assisted wheelchair users shown above and also fulfil more demanding requirements with reference to the British Standards BS8300:2001.

## Visual Impairment Symbols

 Typically provides key additional services and facilities to meet the needs of visually impaired guests.

 Typically provides a higher level of additional services and facilities to meet the needs of visually impaired guests.

## Hearing Impairment Symbols

 Typically provides key additional services and facilities to meet the needs of guests with hearing impairment.

 Typically provides a higher level of additional services and facilities to meet the needs of guests with hearing impairment.

# Quality
# visitor attractions

VisitBritain operates a Visitor Attraction
Quality Assurance Service.

Participating attractions are visited annually by trained,
impartial assessors who look at all aspects of the visit, from
initial telephone enquiries to departure, customer service to
catering, as well as all facilities and activities.

Only those attractions which have been assessed by Enjoy
England and meet the standard receive the quality marque,
your sign of a Quality Assured Visitor Attraction.

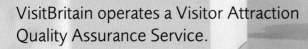

**Look out for the quality marque and visit with confidence.**

# Awards
## for Excellence

enjoy**England**
Awards for
**Excellence**
—2008—

**Enjoy England Awards for Excellence** are all about telling the world what a fantastic place England is to visit, whether it's for a day trip, a weekend break or a fortnight's holiday.

The Awards, now in their 19th year, are run by VisitBritain in association with England's regional tourism organisations. This year there are 12 categories, including Large Hotel of the Year, Small Hotel of the Year, Bed & Breakfast of the Year, Tourist Information Centre of the Year and an award for the best tourism website.

### Winners of the 2007 Bed & Breakfast of the Year Award

- **GOLD WINNER**
  **Number One**, Blackpool, *Lancashire*

- **SILVER WINNERS**
  **The Old School**, Newton-on-the-Moor, *Northumberland*
  **Moorlands Country House**, Pickering, *North Yorkshire*

Winners of the 2008 awards will receive their trophies at a ceremony in April 2008. The day will celebrate excellence in tourism in England.
**For more information about the awards visit enjoyengland.com.**

Number One, Blackpool, Lancashire

Map 1

# Location Maps

Every place name featured in the regional accommodation sections of this Enjoy England guide has a map reference to help you locate it on the maps which follow. For example, to find Colchester, Essex, which has 'Map ref 3B2', turn to Map 3 and refer to grid square B2.

All place names appearing in the regional sections are shown in black type on the maps. This enables you to find other places in your chosen area which may have suitable accommodation – the place index (at the back of this guide) gives page numbers.

Map 1

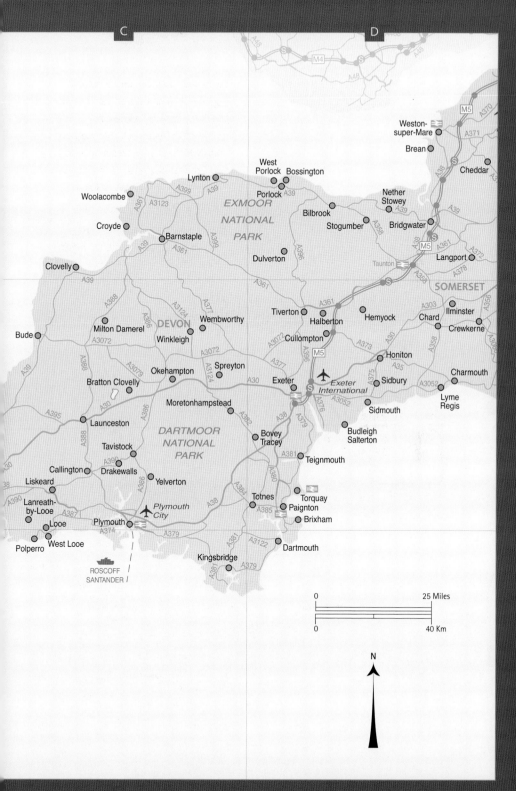

# Map 2

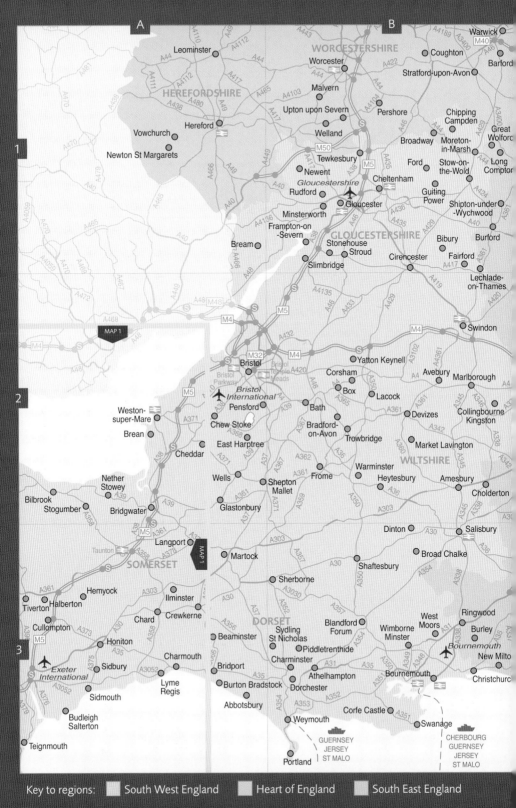

Key to regions: ■ South West England ■ Heart of England ■ South East England

Map 2

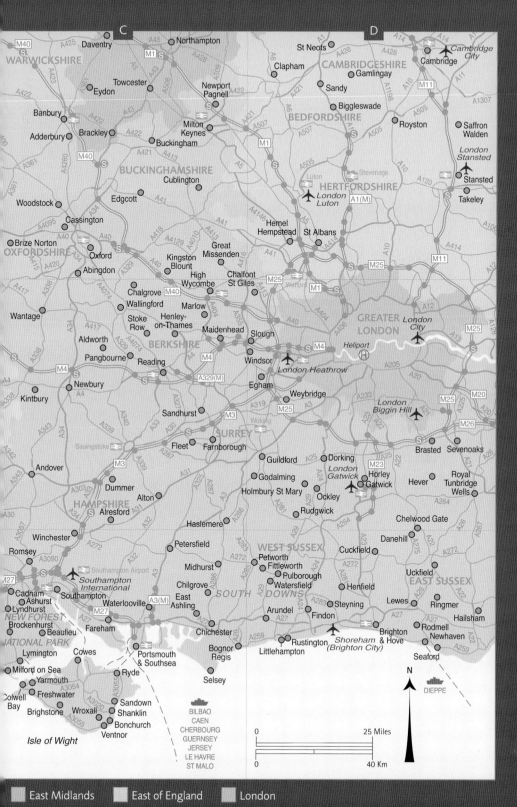

**C**

M40 · Daventry · A425 · A45(M) · Northampton · St Neots · A1 · A428 · Cambridge City · Cambridge · A14 · A14

WARWICKSHIRE · M1 · S · Clapham · CAMBRIDGESHIRE · Gamlingay · M11

A423 · A508 · A509 · Towcester · Newport Pagnell · A422 · Sandy · A10 · A1198 · A1307

Eydon · A5 · A43 · A508 · BEDFORDSHIRE · Biggleswade · Royston · A505 · Saffron Walden

Banbury · A422 · Milton Keynes · A421 · A507 · A505 · London Stansted

Adderbury · Brackley · A422 · Buckingham · M1 · Stevenage · Stansted

M40 · S · A421 · A413 · A5 · A505 · HERTFORDSHIRE · A120 · Takeley

Woodstock · Edgcott · A41 · Cublington · Luton · London Luton · A1(M) · M11

Cassington · Great Missenden · Hemel Hempstead · St Albans · A10 · A414

Brize Norton · Oxford · Kingston Blount · Chalfont St Giles · M25 · Watford · M1 · A12

OXFORDSHIRE · Abingdon · High Wycombe · M25 · GREATER LONDON · London City · M25

Chalgrove · M40 · Marlow · A40 · Heliport · A13

Wantage · Wallingford · Henley-on-Thames · Maidenhead · Slough · M4 · London Heathrow

Aldworth · Stoke Row · Windsor · M4 · A205

Pangbourne · Reading · A329(M) · Egham · London Biggin Hill · M25 · M20

Newbury · Weybridge · M25 · Brasted · Sevenoaks · M26

Kintbury · Sandhurst · M3 · SURREY · Woking

Andover · Fleet · Farnborough · Guildford · Dorking · London Gatwick · Hever · Royal Tunbridge Wells

Dummer · Godalming · Horley · Gatwick

HAMPSHIRE · Alton · Holmbury St Mary · Ockley · A264

Alresford · Haslemere · Rudgwick · Chelwood Gate

Winchester · Petersfield · WEST SUSSEX · Danehill · Cuckfield

Romsey · Midhurst · Petworth · Fittleworth · Uckfield · EAST SUSSEX

Cadnam · Chilgrove · Pulborough · Henfield

Ashurst · Southampton International · Waterlooville · A3(M) · East Ashling · SOUTH DOWNS · Watersfield · Lewes · Ringmer

Lyndhurst · Southampton · Steyning · Hailsham

NEW FOREST · M27 · Fareham · Arundel · Findon · Rodmell

Brockenhurst · Beaulieu · Chichester · Brighton & Hove (Brighton City) · Newhaven

NATIONAL PARK · Cowes · Shoreham

Lymington · Portsmouth & Southsea · Bognor Regis · Rustington · Littlehampton · Seaford

Milford on Sea · Ryde · Selsey · N

Yarmouth · DIEPPE

Colwell Bay · Freshwater · Sandown · Shanklin

Brighstone · Wroxall · Bonchurch · BILBAO · CAEN · CHERBOURG

Ventnor · GUERNSEY · JERSEY · LE HAVRE · ST MALO

*Isle of Wight*

**D**

0 · 25 Miles
0 · 40 Km

☐ East Midlands  ☐ East of England  ☐ London

All place names in black offer accommodation in this guide

Map 3

**Key to regions:** East Midlands    South East England    East of England    London

Map 3

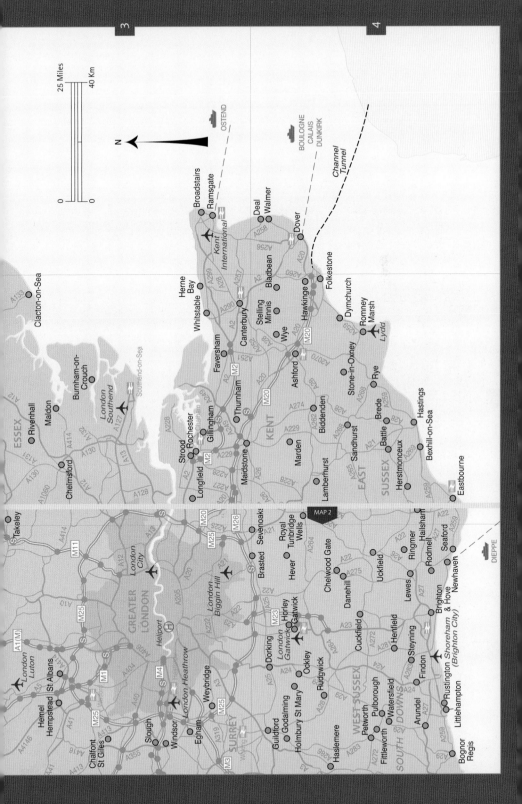

# Map 4

Key to regions: Heart of England | England's Northwest | Yorkshire | East Midlands

Map 4

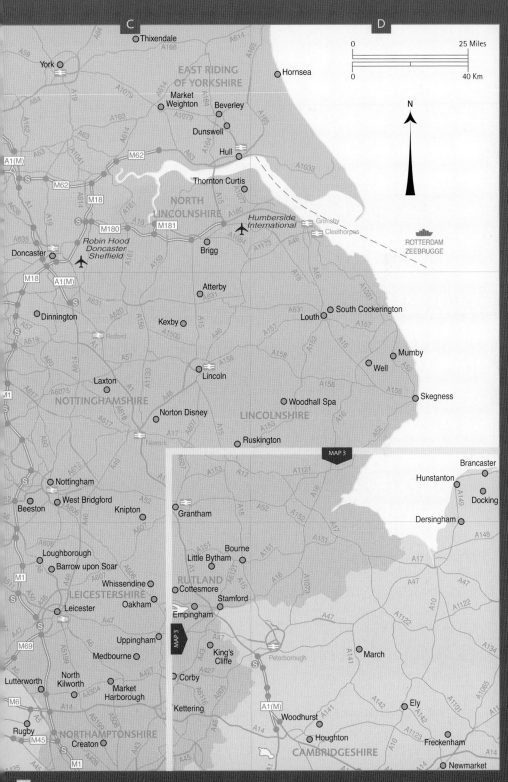

C · D

0 ——— 25 Miles
0 ——— 40 Km

N

Thixendale
Hornsea
York
EAST RIDING OF YORKSHIRE
Market Weighton
Beverley
Dunswell
Hull
A1033
Thornton Curtis
NORTH LINCOLNSHIRE
Humberside International
Grimsby
Cleethorpes
ROTTERDAM ZEEBRUGGE
Robin Hood Doncaster Sheffield
Brigg
Doncaster
Atterby
Dinnington
Kexby
Louth
South Cockerington
Mumby
Well
Laxton
Lincoln
Skegness
NOTTINGHAMSHIRE
Norton Disney
LINCOLNSHIRE
Woodhall Spa
Ruskington
MAP 3
Brancaster
Hunstanton
Docking
Dersingham
Nottingham
West Bridgford
Beeston
Knipton
Grantham
Bourne
Loughborough
Little Bytham
Barrow upon Soar
Whissendine
RUTLAND
Cottesmore
Stamford
LEICESTERSHIRE
Oakham
Leicester
Empingham
March
Uppingham
MAP 3
King's Cliffe
Medbourne
Peterborough
Lutterworth
North Kilworth
Corby
Market Harborough
Ely
Kettering
Freckenham
Rugby
Woodhurst
NORTHAMPTONSHIRE
Creaton
Houghton
CAMBRIDGESHIRE
Newmarket

☐ East of England

All place names in black offer accommodation in this guide

Map 5

Map 5

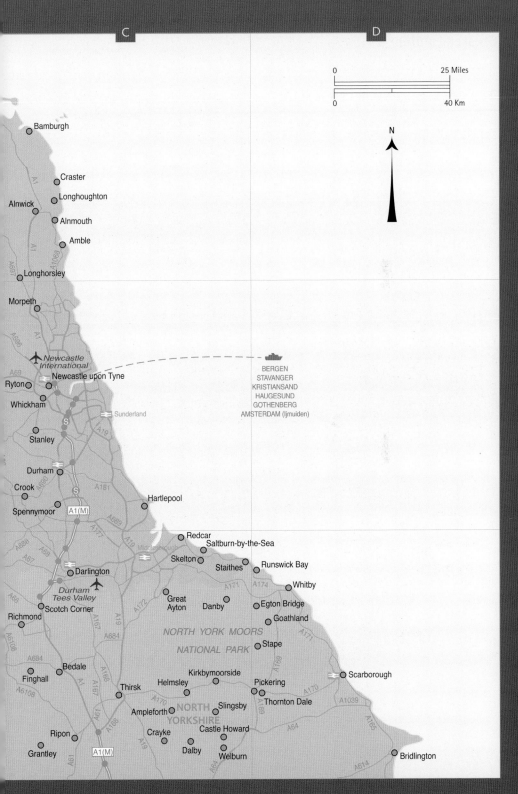

C  D

0                   25 Miles
0                   40 Km

N

Bamburgh

Craster
Longhoughton
Alnwick
Alnmouth

Amble

Longhorsley

Morpeth

Newcastle
International
Ryton
Newcastle upon Tyne
Whickham
Sunderland
S
Stanley

Durham
Crook
S
Spennymoor
A1(M)
Hartlepool

BERGEN
STAVANGER
KRISTIANSAND
HAUGESUND
GOTHENBERG
AMSTERDAM (Ijmuiden)

Redcar
Saltburn-by-the-Sea
Skelton
Staithes
Runswick Bay
Darlington
Whitby
Durham
Tees Valley
Scotch Corner
Great
Ayton
Danby
Egton Bridge
Richmond
Goathland

NORTH YORK MOORS

NATIONAL PARK
Stape

Bedale
Kirkbymoorside
Finghall
Helmsley
Pickering
Scarborough
Thirsk
Slingsby
Thornton Dale
Ampleforth
NORTH
YORKSHIRE
Crayke
Castle Howard
Ripon
Dalby
Grantley
A1(M)
Welburn
Bridlington

# Map 6

## Greater London

Map 6

Map 7

# Central London

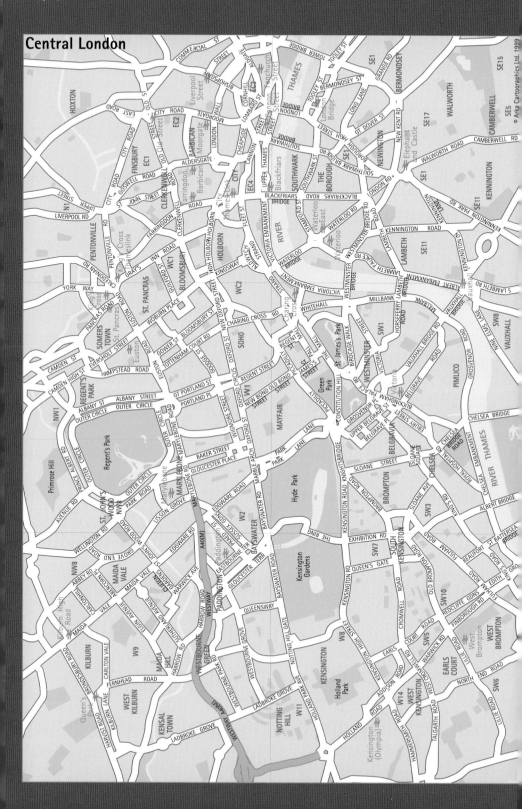

# Finding
# accommodation
## is easy

VisitBritain's official guides to quality accommodation make it quick and easy to find a place to stay. There are several ways to use this guide.

**1**

### PROPERTY INDEX

If you know the name of the establishment you wish to book, turn to the property index at the back where the relevant page number is shown.

**2**

### PLACE INDEX

The place index at the back lists all locations with accommodation featured in the regional sections. A page number is shown where you can find full accommodation and contact details.

**3**

### COLOUR MAPS

All the place names in black on the colour maps at the front have an entry in the regional sections. Refer to the place index for the page number where you will find one or more establishments offering accommodation in your chosen town or village.

**4**

### ALL ASSESSED ACCOMMODATION

Contact details for all VisitBritain assessed accommodation, together with their quality rating, are given in the back section of this guide. Establishments with a full entry in the regional sections are shown in bold. Look in the property index for the page number where their full entry appears.

# England's Northwest

Blackpool and Lancashire, Chester and
Cheshire, Cumbria – The Lake District,
Liverpool and Merseyside, Manchester

# Constant variety and continual delights

England's Northwest is a
region of astonishing
contrasts. Where else can
you travel to four different
worlds – from peak to plain,
from coast to city – in one
short day?

England's Northwest
visitenglandsnorthwest.com

Overlooking Ullswater, Cumbria

Albert Dock, Liverpool    Tatton Park, Cheshire

The Lowry, Manchester

From the Cumbrian peaks to the Cheshire plain, from the seaside thrills of Blackpool to the buzzing energy of Manchester, England's Northwest is bursting with choice for the holidaymaker. Liverpool celebrated its 800th anniversary in 2007 and is an exciting place to be. Fancy a little R&R? Head for Cumbria. This place is a natural wonderland where plunging lakes and swooshing mountains collide in a perfect marriage. Prefer the bright lights to starry skies? Make Manchester your next stop. This glamorous city is a magnet for every designer label and trendy club out there. Or for a peaceful family break, hire a narrow boat in leafy Cheshire and drift along the waterways of the Cheshire Ring.

Experience a sense of déjà vu at Lyme Park in Cheshire – the setting for BBC's Pride and Prejudice. Another must is a visit to Arley Hall, a magnificent Victorian Jacobean stately home with magical gardens. If you find yourself in Chester, book into The Grosvenor Spa – it's the perfect place to escape the hustle and bustle. And no trip to Manchester would be complete without seeing Imperial War Museum North, a powerful exploration of the impact of war on ordinary lives.

If you love mystical places, you'll adore Alderly Edge in Cheshire. Legend has it that this strange place is linked to King Arthur and Merlin. It's also the setting for the classic children's story The Weirdstone of Brisingamen. If you prefer bargain-hunting to wizard-hunting, there's no more colourful and fascinating market than Affleck's Palace in Manchester. And if you want to experience the great outdoors, it doesn't get much grander that in Cumbria – The Lake District.

Whether it's for a night out, day trip or weekend away with the family, England's Northwest has a wealth of attractions to inspire you.

# Destinations

## Blackpool

Britain's favourite holiday resort. Feel the thrill on the Pepsi Max Big One at the Pleasure Beach, take high tea in the magnificent Tower Ballroom, or stroll the seven miles of sandy beaches. Blackpool offers you world-class shows, cosmopolitan restaurants, vibrant nightlife, an active sports scene and breathtakingly beautiful scenery on the doorstep – every ingredient, in fact, for an unforgettable, carefree break.

## Chester

Experience one of Europe's top heritage cities. Walk the unique city walls, complete with surviving Roman sections, then visit the famous Rows, unique two-tiered galleries in black and white 'magpie' style, to shop for everything from antiques to high fashion. Stroll along the banks of the beautiful River Dee, explore the Roman amphitheatre, and don't miss the Grosvenor and Cheshire Military Museums, the beautiful Grosvenor Park and Chester's famous Roodee Racecourse.

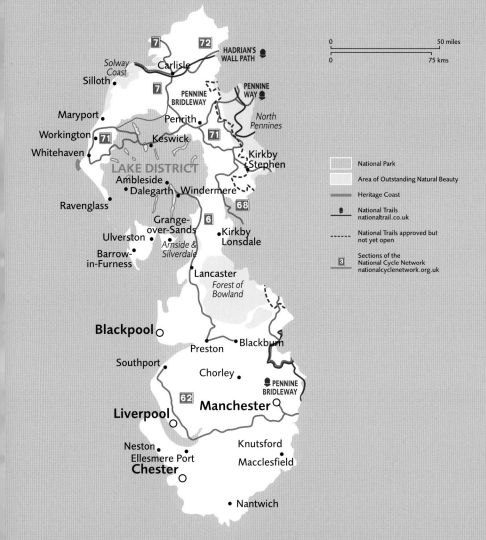

Chester

The Cavern Club, Liverpool

Cumbria – The Lake District

Imperial War Museum North, Manchester

Blackpool

## Cumbria – The Lake District

With breathtaking mountains and 16 sparkling lakes, the unsurpassed scenery of Cumbria – The Lake District has inspired writers and poets across the ages. Explore the best walking and climbing routes that England has to offer. Only five peaks in England are over 900m and they are all in Cumbria. Visit the magnificent World Heritage Site at Hadrian's Wall, the most important Roman monument in Britain. Pull off your hiking boots and relax in high-quality accommodation – you'll be thoroughly spoilt for choice.

## Liverpool

Experience the unique atmosphere of Liverpool. The birthplace of the Beatles and European Capital of Culture 2008 offers you more theatres, museums and galleries than any UK city outside London. Its history as one of the world's great ports has left a remarkable legacy of art and architecture for you to explore, not forgetting, of course, the city's famous sporting pedigree. So if it's Strawberry Fields, Premiership football or Europe's finest culture you're looking for, it has to be Liverpool.

## Manchester

If you haven't been to Manchester, there's never been a better time to visit. Explore a city that has come a long way from its industrial roots and reinvented itself as a truly contemporary metropolis. You'll find modern landmark buildings, a wealth of art and culture, great bars and world-class hospitality. Here there's every experience imaginable, from fine dining and top-class theatre, to major sporting events and year-round festivals. It's a shopping destination in its own right, rivalling that of the capital, with top stores and chic boutiques.

# Places to visit

### Anderton Boat Lift
Northwich, Cheshire
(01606) 786777
andertonboatlift.co.uk
*Sail through the magnificent
Victorian boat lift*

### Arley Hall and Gardens
Northwich, Cheshire
(01565) 777353
arleyhallandgardens.com
*Victorian country house with
splendid gardens*

### Beatles Story
Liverpool, Merseyside
(0151) 709 1963
beatlesstory.com
*The history of the Fab Four*

### Blackwell, The Arts & Crafts House
Windermere, Cumbria
(015394) 46139
blackwell.org.uk
*Elegant Arts and Crafts house and
gardens*

### Bowland Wild Boar Park
Preston, Lancashire
(01995) 61554
wildboarpark.co.uk
*Hand-feed animals in a beautiful
wooded park*

### Chester Zoo
Cheshire
(01244) 380280
chesterzoo.org.uk
*Black Rhinos and 7,000 other
animals in natural enclosures*

### Go Ape! High Wire Forest Adventure
Delamere, Cheshire
0870 444 5562
goape.co.uk
*Rope bridges, swings and zip slides*

### Imperial War Museum North
Large Visitor
Attraction of the Year
– Silver Winner
Manchester
(0161) 836 4000
iwm.org.uk/north
*Spectacular museum with
innovative display techniques*

### Jodrell Bank Visitor Centre
near Macclesfield,
Cheshire
(01477) 571339
jb.man.ac.uk
*Home of the Lovell radio
telescope*

### Lady Lever Art Gallery
Wirral, Merseyside
(0151) 478 4136
ladyleverartgallery.org.uk
*Magnificent collection of fine and
decorative arts*

### The Lowry
Salford, Greater
Manchester
(0161) 876 2000
thelowry.com
*Art and entertainment in stunning
21st century landmark*

### The Manchester Museum
(0161) 275 2634

manchester.ac.uk/museum
*Displays and exhibitions from
around the world*

### Manchester United Museum & Tour
0870 442 1994
manutd.com
*Delve behind the scenes at the
Theatre of Dreams*

### Mirehouse Historic House
Keswick, Cumbria
(017687) 72287
mirehouse.com
*Historic house with literary
connections*

### Muncaster Experience
Lake District National Park,
Cumbria
(01229) 717614
muncaster.co.uk
*Historic castle with ghostly
goings-on*

### The Museum of Science and Industry
Manchester
(0161) 832 2244
msim.org.uk
*Historic buildings packed with
fascinating exhibits*

### The National Football Museum
Preston, Lancashire
(01772) 908442
nationalfootballmuseum.com
*Amazing journey through football
history*

### National Wildflower Centre
Liverpool, Merseyside
(0151) 738 1913
nwc.org.uk
*Wild flowers in a family-friendly
environment*

### Pleasure Beach, Blackpool
Lancashire
0870 444 5566
blackpoolpleasurebeach.co.uk
*Thrills and spills featuring Valhalla
and the Pepsi Max Big One*

### The Rum Story
Whitehaven, Cumbria
(01946) 592933
rumstory.co.uk
*Story of the rum trade*

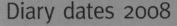

# Diary dates 2008

**South Lakes Wild Animal Park**
Dalton-in-Furness, Cumbria
(01229) 466086
wildanimalpark.co.uk
*The ultimate interactive animal experience*

**Tate Liverpool**
Merseyside
(0151) 702 7400
tate.org.uk/liverpool
*Modern and contemporary art in historic setting*

**Tatton Park (NT)**
Knutsford, Cheshire
(01625) 534400
tattonpark.org.uk
*Historic mansion set in deer park*

**Urbis**
Manchester
(0161) 605 8200
urbis.org.uk
*Multi-media exhibitions of city life*

**Wildfowl & Wetland Trust Martin Mere**
Nr Ormskirk, Lancashire
(01704) 895181
wwt.org.uk
*Feed endangered species straight from your hand*

**World Museum Liverpool**
Merseyside
(0151) 478 4393
worldmuseumliverpool.org.uk
*Treasures from across the world*

**The World of Glass**
St Helens, Merseyside
0870 011 4466
worldofglass.com
*Live glass-blowing and multi-media shows*

**John Smiths Grand National**
Aintree, Merseyside
aintree.co.uk
3 – 5 Apr

**Ullswater Walking Festival**
ullswater.visitor-centre.co.uk
10 – 18 May

**Chester Mystery Plays**
Cathedral Green, Chester
chestermysteryplays.com
28 Jun – 19 Jul

**The British Open (Golf)**
Royal Birkdale, Merseyside
opengolf.com
17 – 20 Jul

**RHS Flower Show at Tatton Park**
Knutsford, Cheshire
rhs.org.uk
23 – 26 Jul*

**Pennine Lancashire Food and Drink Festival**
Various locations, Lancashire
penninelancashirefood.co.uk
4 – 7 Sep*

**Westmorland County Show**
Crooklands, Cumbria
westmorland-county-show.co.uk
11 Sep

**Blackpool Illuminations**
visitblackpool.com
Sep – Nov*

**Manchester Food and Drink Festival**
Various locations, Manchester
foodanddrinkfestival.com
10 – 20 Oct*

**Muncaster Halloween Week**
muncaster.co.uk
27 – 31 Oct

* provisional date at time of going to press

# Tourist Information Centres

When you arrive at your destination, visit an Official Partner Tourist Information Centre for quality assured help with accommodation and information about local attractions and events, or email your request before you go. To search for attractions and Tourist Information Centres on the move just text INFO to 62233, and a web link will be sent to your mobile phone.

| | | | |
|---|---|---|---|
| **Accrington** | Blackburn Road | (01254) 872595 | tourism@hyndburnbc.gov.uk |
| **Altrincham** | 20 Stamford New Road | (0161) 912 5931 | tourist.information@trafford.gov.uk |
| **Ashton-under-Lyne** | Wellington Road | (0161) 343 4343 | tourist.information@tameside.gov.uk |
| **Barnoldswick** | Fernlea Avenue | (01282) 666704 | tourist.info@pendle.gov.uk |
| **Barrow-in-Furness** | Duke Street | (01229) 876505 | touristinfo@barrowbc.gov.uk |
| **Blackburn** | 50-54 Church Street | (01254) 53277 | visit@blackburn.gov.uk |
| **Blackpool** | 1 Clifton Street | (01253) 478222 | tic@blackpool.gov.uk |
| **Bolton** | Le Mans Crescent | (01204) 334321 | tourist.info@bolton.gov.uk |
| **Bowness** | Glebe Road | (015394) 42895 | bownesstic@lake-district.gov.uk |
| **Burnley** | Croft Street | (01282) 664421 | tic@burnley.gov.uk |
| **Bury** | Market Street | (0161) 253 5111 | touristinformation@bury.gov.uk |
| **Carlisle** | Greenmarket | (01228) 625600 | tourism@carlisle-city.gov.uk |
| **Chester (Town Hall)** | Northgate Street | (01244) 402111 | tis@chester.gov.uk |
| **Chester Visitor Centre** | Vicars Lane | (01244) 351609 | tis@chester.gov.uk |
| **Cleveleys** | Victoria Square | (01253) 853378 | cleveleystic@wyrebc.gov.uk |
| **Clitheroe** | 12-14 Market Place | (01200) 425566 | tourism@ribblevalley.gov.uk |
| **Congleton** | High Street | (01260) 271095 | tourism@congleton.gov.uk |
| **Coniston** | Ruskin Avenue | (015394) 41533 | Conistontic@lake-district.gov.uk |
| **Ellesmere Port** | Kinsey Road | (0151) 356 7879 | |
| **Fleetwood** | The Esplanade | (01253) 773953 | fleetwoodtic@btopenworld.com |
| **Garstang** | High Street | (01995) 602125 | garstangtic@wyrebc.gov.uk |
| **Kendal** | Highgate | (01539) 725758 | kendaltic@southlakeland.gov.uk |
| **Keswick** | Market Square | (017687) 72645 | keswicktic@lake-district.gov.uk |
| **Knutsford** | Toft Road | (01565) 632611 | ktic@macclesfield.gov.uk |
| **Lancaster** | 29 Castle Hill | (01524) 32878 | lancastertic@lancaster.gov.uk |
| **Liverpool 08 Place** | Whitechapel | (0151) 233 2459 | contact@liverpool.08.com |
| **Liverpool John Lennon Airport** | Speke Hall Avenue | 0906 680 6886** | info@visitliverpool.com |
| **Lytham St Annes** | 67 St Annes Road West | (01253) 725610 | touristinformation@fylde.gov.uk |
| **Macclesfield** | Town Hall | (01625) 504114 | informationcentre@macclesfield.gov.uk |
| **Manchester Visitor Information Centre** | Lloyd Street | 0871 222 8223 | touristinformation@marketing-manchester.co.uk |
| **Morecambe** | Marine Road Central | (01524) 582808 | morecambetic@lancaster.gov.uk |
| **Nantwich** | Market Street | (01270) 537359 | touristi@crewe-nantwich.gov.uk |
| **Northwich** | 1 The Arcade | (01606) 353534 | tourism@valeroyal.gov.uk |
| **Oldham** | 12 Albion Street | (0161) 627 1024 | ecs.tourist@oldham.gov.uk |
| **Pendle Heritage Centre** | Park Hill | (01282) 661701 | heritage.centre@pendle.gov.uk |

| Penrith | Middlegate | (01768) 867466 | pen.tic@eden.gov.uk |
| Preston | Lancaster Road | (01772) 253731 | tourism@preston.gov.uk |
| Rochdale | The Esplanade | (01706) 864928 | tic@link4life.org |
| Saddleworth | High Street | (01457) 870336 | ecs.saddleworthtic@oldham.gov.uk |
| St Helens | Chalon Way East | (01744) 755150 | info@sthelenstic.com |
| Salford | Salford Quays | (0161) 848 8601 | tic@salford.gov.uk |
| Southport | 112 Lord Street | (01704) 533333 | info@visitsouthport.com |
| Stockport | 30 Market Place | (0161) 474 4444 | tourist.information@stockport.gov.uk |
| Warrington | Horsemarket Street | (01925) 428585 | informationcentre@warrington.gov.uk |
| Whitehaven | Market Place | (01946) 598914 | tic@copelandbc.gov.uk |
| Wigan | 62 Wallgate | (01942) 825677 | tic@wlct.org |
| Wilmslow | Rectory Fields | (01625) 522275 | i.hillaby@macclesfield.gov.uk |
| Windermere | Victoria Street | (015394) 46499 | windermeretic@southlakeland.gov.uk |

** *calls to this number are charged at premium rate*

River Mersey and Liverpool

# Travel info

**By road:**
Motorways intersect within the region which has the best road network in the country. Travelling north or south use the M6, and east or west the M62.

**By rail:**
Most Northwest coastal resorts are connected to InterCity routes with trains from many parts of the country, and there are through trains to major cities and towns.

**By air:**
Fly into Liverpool John Lennon, Manchester or Blackpool airports.

# Find out more

Windermere, Cumbria

There are various publications and guides about England's Northwest available from the following Tourist Boards or by logging on to visitenglandsnorthwest.com or calling 0845 600 6040:

**Visit Chester and Cheshire**
Chester Railway Station, 1st Floor, West Wing Offices, Station Road, Chester CH1 3NT
**t** (01244) 405600
**e** info@visitchesterandcheshire.co.uk
**w** visitchester.com or visitcheshire.com

**Cumbria Tourism**
Windermere Road, Staveley, Kendal LA8 9PL
**t** (015398) 22222
**e** info@cumbriatourism.org
**w** golakes.co.uk

**The Lancashire and Blackpool
Tourist Board**
St George's House, St George's Street
Chorley PR7 2AA
**t** (01257) 226600 (Brochure request)
**e** info@visitlancashire.com
**w** visitlancashire.com

**Marketing Manchester – The Tourist Board for
Greater Manchester**
Churchgate House, 56 Oxford Street
Manchester M1 6EU
**t** (0161) 237 1010
    Brochure request: 0870 609 3013
**e** touristinformation@marketing-manchester.co.uk
**w** visitmanchester.com

**The Mersey Partnership – The Tourist Board for
Liverpool and Merseyside**
12 Princes Parade, Liverpool L3 1BG
**t** (0151) 233 2008 (information enquiries)
**t** 0844 870 0123 (accommodation booking)
**e** info@visitliverpool.com (accommodation enquiries)
**e** 08place@liverpool.gov.uk (information enquiries)
**w** visitliverpool.com

## where to stay in
# England's Northwest

All place names in the blue bands are shown on the maps at the front of this guide.

A complete listing of all Enjoy England assessed accommodation covered by this guide appears at the back.

### Accommodation symbols
Symbols give useful information about services and facilities. Inside the back-cover flap you can find a key to these symbols. Keep it open for easy reference.

**ALDERLEY EDGE,** Cheshire Map ref 4B2

★★★
**BED & BREAKFAST**

B&B per room per night
s  £24.50–£26.50
d  £53.00–£55.00
Evening meal per person
£7.00–£28.00

# Mayfield Bed & Breakfast @ Sheila's
Wilmslow Road, Alderley Edge SK9 7QW  **t** (01625) 583991 & 07703 289663

Bed and breakfast with optional dinner (notice required). If flying from Manchester Airport, car may be left (at owner's risk) with Sheila taking and picking up from the airport. No pets.

**open** All year
**bedrooms** 1 double, 1 twin, 2 single
**payment** Cash/cheques

Room 📺 🐾 🍳  General 🛏 🔥 **P** ⚡ ✕ 🛒 🔌 ◉ ✿

**AMBLESIDE,** Cumbria Map ref 5A3

★★★★
**GUEST HOUSE**

B&B per room per night
s  £30.00–£35.00
d  £30.00–£35.00

# 2 Cambridge Villas
Church Street, Ambleside LA22 9DL  **t** (015394) 32142  **f** (015394) 32755
**e** charles@black475.fsnet.co.uk  **w** 2cambridgevillas.co.uk

Double, twin, family rooms. En suite. TV, tea/coffee all rooms. Central location. Flexible with regard to arrival times. Cycle store and drying facilities available.

**open** All year except Christmas
**bedrooms** 3 double, 2 family
**bathrooms** 3 en suite
**payment** Credit/debit cards, cash/cheques

Room 📺 🐾 🍳  General 🍵 🛏 🔥 ⚡ 🛒 ✿  Leisure 🚲 🏛

# Country Code

always follow the Country Code

- Be safe – plan ahead and follow any signs
- Leave gates and property as you find them
- Protect plants and animals, and take your litter home
- Keep dogs under close control
- Consider other people

## AMBLESIDE, Cumbria Map ref 5A3

★
**BACKPACKER**

Per person per night
B&B £10.00-£17.50

# Ambleside Backpackers

Old Lake Road, Ambleside LA22 0DJ **t** (015394) 32340 **f** (015394) 32340
**e** enquiries@englishlakesbackpackers.co.uk **w** englishlakesbackpackers.co.uk

**open** All year except Christmas
**bedrooms** 12 dormitories
Total no of beds 72
**bathrooms** 5 public
**max group size** 72
**meals** Breakfast available
**payment** Credit/debit cards, cash/cheques

Set in the heart of the beautiful English Lake District. Large traditional lakeland cottage c1871. Walk from the doorstep to Ambleside centre, Lake Windermere or the fells within 5 minutes. Lounge, dining room, fully fitted kitchen, washer/dryer, internet, tea, coffee and light breakfast included. Comfortable, warm, clean and secure.

⊕ Turn into public car park opposite Hayes Garden Centre on A591. At back of car park left up hill, 150yds to Ambleside Backpackers.

♥ Sep-Mar excluding holiday weekends. 5-night Sun-Fri special including light breakfast £50.00 per person.

Room ⬛ General ▦ ◉ 🛏 ⚷ ☎ ⌶ ☼ 🚐 Leisure ♪ 🚲 ⌂

## AMBLESIDE, Cumbria Map ref 5A3

★★★★
**BED & BREAKFAST**

B&B per room per night
**s** £33.00
**d** £64.00
Evening meal per person
£17.00

# Dower House

Wray Castle, Low Wray, Ambleside LA22 0JA **t** (015394) 33211 **f** (015394) 33211

The house overlooks Lake Windermere, three miles from Ambleside. Situated through the main gates of Wray Castle and up the drive. A bird-watcher's paradise.

**open** All year
**bedrooms** 2 double, 1 twin
**bathrooms** All en suite
**payment** Cash/cheques

Room ♿ ☜ General ▨5 P⚷ ✕ 🛏 ☼ Leisure ♪

## AMBLESIDE, Cumbria Map ref 5A3

★★★★
**GUEST ACCOMMODATION
SILVER AWARD**

B&B per room per night
**s** £28.00-£85.00
**d** £56.00-£90.00

# Elder Grove

Lake Road, Ambleside LA22 0DB **t** (015394) 32504 **f** (015394) 32251 **e** info@eldergrove.co.uk **w** eldergrove.co.uk

Our traditional Victorian house is ideally situated for restaurants, shops, walking and sightseeing. All rooms en suite, fantastic Cumbrian breakfasts, relaxing bar with free Internet access, lounge and car park. Non-smoking.

**open** All year except Christmas
**bedrooms** 6 double, 1 twin, 2 single, 1 family
**bathrooms** All en suite
**payment** Credit/debit cards, cash/cheques

Room 🖥 📺 ♿ ☜ General ☖ ▦ 🅟 P⚷ 🍽 🛏 🐾 Leisure ∪▸ 🚲 ⌂

## AMBLESIDE, Cumbria Map ref 5A3

★★★
**GUEST HOUSE**

B&B per room per night
**s** £25.00-£30.00
**d** £50.00-£60.00

# Ferndale Lodge

Lake Road, Ambleside LA22 0DB **t** (015394) 32207 **e** stay@ferndalelodge.co.uk **w** ferndalelodge.co.uk

Small, family-run guesthouse close to the centre of Ambleside offering comfortable accommodation at realistic prices. Excellent breakfasts and a friendly welcome assured. Private car park. An ideal walking base.

**open** All year except Christmas
**bedrooms** 7 double, 2 twin, 1 single
**bathrooms** All en suite
**payment** Credit/debit cards, cash/cheques

Room ⬛ 📺 ♿ ☜ General ☖ ▦ 🅟 P⚷ 🍽 Leisure ∪ ♪▸

**AMBLESIDE,** Cumbria Map ref 5A3

★★★★
**GUEST ACCOMMODATION**

B&B per room per night
s £35.00–£50.00
d £66.00–£100.00

# The Gables

Church Walk, Ambleside LA22 9DJ  t (015394) 33272  e info@thegables-ambleside.co.uk
w thegables-ambleside.co.uk

**open** All year except Christmas
**bedrooms** 6 double, 3 twin, 3 single, 2 family
**bathrooms** All en suite
**payment** Credit/debit cards, cash/cheques

Sharyn and Mark welcome you to The Gables overlooking the bowling green and surrounding fells. Ideally situated in the heart of Ambleside, our guesthouse makes an excellent base for exploring the Lake District. Stylish rooms, all en suite. Hearty breakfasts. Car parking. Drying room. Bike storage. Non-smoking.

⊕ *On arriving in Ambleside on the one-way system, drive alongside the bowling green, bear left and The Gables is directly ahead.*

Room 🛏 📺 ♨ 🍵  General 🛋 🏛 🏃 P 🔌 🍴 📶 🐾  Leisure 🚲 🚣

**AMBLESIDE,** Cumbria Map ref 5A3

★★★★
**GUEST HOUSE
SILVER AWARD**

B&B per room per night
s £35.00–£45.00
d £62.00–£76.00

# Kingswood 'Bee & Bee'

Old Lake Road, Ambleside LA22 0AE  t (015394) 34081  e info@kingswood-guesthouse.co.uk
w kingswood-guesthouse.co.uk

Kingswood Bee & Bee is centrally situated but in a quiet position two minutes' walk from Ambleside's amenities. Traditionally built, centrally heated, well appointed and furnished to a very high standard.

**open** All year
**bedrooms** 2 double, 2 twin, 1 single
**bathrooms** All en suite
**payment** Credit/debit cards, cash/cheques, euros

Room 🛏 📺 ♨ 🍵  General P 🔌 🍴 ℅ ☼  Leisure 🚲 🚣

**AMBLESIDE,** Cumbria Map ref 5A3

★★★
**GUEST ACCOMMODATION**

B&B per room per night
s £28.00–£35.00
d £55.00–£70.00

# Lyndale Guest House

Low Fold, Lake Road, Ambleside LA22 0DN  t (015394) 34244  e alison@lyndale-guesthouse.co.uk
w lyndale-guesthouse.co.uk

Victorian guesthouse providing spacious, comfortable accommodation. Hearty breakfasts and excellent services. Located midway between Lake Windermere and Ambleside. Great for touring and walking. Great value for money.

**open** All year
**bedrooms** 2 double, 2 single, 2 family
**bathrooms** 4 en suite, 2 private
**payment** Credit/debit cards, cash/cheques

Room 📺 ♨ 🍵  General 🛋 🏛 🏃 🔌 🍴 ☼ 🐾

**AMBLESIDE,** Cumbria Map ref 5A3

★★★
**GUEST ACCOMMODATION**

B&B per room per night
s £28.00–£34.00
d £56.00–£68.00

# Meadowbank

Rydal Road, Ambleside LA22 9BA  t (015394) 32710  f (015394) 32710
e enquiries@meadowbank.org.uk

Country house in private garden with ample parking in grounds. Overlooking meadowland and fells, yet a level, easy walk to Ambleside. Good walking base.

**open** All year except Christmas
**bedrooms** 3 double, 2 twin, 1 single, 1 family
**bathrooms** 6 en suite, 1 private
**payment** Credit/debit cards, cash/cheques

Room 🛏 📺 ♨ 🍵  General 🛋 P 🔌 📶 ℅ ☼ 🐾  Leisure 🚲 🚣

## Place index

If you know where you want to stay, the index at the back of the guide will give you the page number listing accommodation in your chosen town, city or village. Check out the other useful indexes too.

## AMBLESIDE, Cumbria Map ref 5A3

★★★★
**GUEST ACCOMMODATION**

B&B per room per night
s Min £100.00
d £100.00–£150.00

# The Old Vicarage

Vicarage Road, Ambleside LA22 9DH  t (015394) 33364  f (015394) 34734
e info@oldvicarageambleside.co.uk  w oldvicarageambleside.co.uk

Quiet central situation. Car park. Pets welcome. Heated indoor swimming pool, sauna and hot tub. Quality accommodation with TV/DVD/VCR, hairdryer, fridge, en suite. Some four-posters, spa baths and some ground-floor rooms.

**open** All year except Christmas
**bedrooms** 4 double, 4 twin, 2 family, 4 suites
**bathrooms** 10 en suite
**payment** Credit/debit cards, cash/cheques, euros

Room 🛏🖨📺♿🕾  General ♿🏬🔥♿P⚲🚭🍴♿📵☼🐾  Leisure ⚲🎣U🎿▶🚲🚠

## AMBLESIDE, Cumbria Map ref 5A3

★★★★★
**BED & BREAKFAST
SILVER AWARD**

B&B per room per night
d £70.00–£80.00

# Red Bank

Wansfell Road, Ambleside LA22 0EG  t (015394) 34637  e info@red-bank.co.uk  w red-bank.co.uk

**open** All year
**bedrooms** 2 double, 1 twin
**bathrooms** All en suite
**payment** Cash/cheques, euros

Elegant, traditionally built Lakeland house in residential fringes of Ambleside. Three tastefully furnished en suite rooms offering spacious, deluxe accommodation. Village centre five minutes. An ideal base for discovering the grandeur of the Lake District National Park. We will do our very best to make your stay as relaxing and comfortable as possible.

Room 📺♿🕾  General ♿9 P⚲🍴♿☼  Leisure 🎿🚲🚠

## AMBLESIDE, Cumbria Map ref 5A3

★★★★
**GUEST ACCOMMODATION**

B&B per room per night
s £25.00–£45.00
d £50.00–£90.00
Evening meal per person
£20.00

# Smallwood House

Compston Road, Ambleside LA22 9DJ  t (015394) 32330  f (015394) 33764
e enq@smallwoodhotel.co.uk  w smallwoodhotel.co.uk

**open** All year
**bedrooms** 4 double, 3 twin, 2 single, 3 family
**bathrooms** All en suite
**payment** Credit/debit cards, cash/cheques, euros

A warm welcome, pleasant rooms (all en suite), some with king-size bed, some with power shower. Fresh home cooking and a friendly, relaxed atmosphere await you here, surrounded by the well-renowned delights of the Lake District. Pets welcome. Private car park. Complimentary use of local leisure club.

⊕ *From south, M6 jct 36 then follow A591 to Ambleside, Compston Road is part of this road. We are situated on right-hand side.*

Room 🖨📺♿🕾  General ♿🏬🔥♿P⚲‼X🍴♿🐾  Leisure ⚲🎣U🎿🚲🚠

# Accessible needs?

If you have special hearing, visual or mobility needs, there's an index of National Accessible Scheme participants featured in this guide. For more accessible accommodation buy a copy of *Easy Access Britain* available online at visitbritaindirect.com.

## AMBLESIDE, Cumbria Map ref 5A3

★★★★
**BED & BREAKFAST
SILVER AWARD**

B&B per room per night
d £75.00–£85.00

# Stepping Stones

Under Loughrigg, Ambleside LA22 9LN  t (015394) 33552  e info@steppingstonesambleside.co.uk
w steppingstonesambleside.co.uk

**open** All year except Christmas
**bedrooms** 2 double, 1 twin
**bathrooms** All en suite
**payment** Cash/cheques

Ideally situated in the heart of the Lake District, Stepping Stones is a beautiful, family-run home from home. The riverside setting provides spectacular views of the fells and open countryside. The spacious bedrooms are superbly appointed with period furnishings and all have the spectacular views. Must-view website.

⊕ 1 mile north of Ambleside on A591, turn left over hump-backed bridge. Continue straight ahead over 2 cattle grids. 100m on right.

Room 🖼 📺 🖐 ᛩ  General P ⅄ 쐐 ✿  Leisure ☇ 🚴 🏊

## AMBLESIDE, Cumbria Map ref 5A3

★★★★
**INN**

B&B per room per night
s £40.00–£70.00
d £80.00–£160.00
Evening meal per person
£15.85–£29.95

# Wateredge Inn

Waterhead Bay, Ambleside LA22 0EP  t (015394) 32332  f (015394) 31878
e stay@wateredgeinn.co.uk  w wateredgeinn.co.uk

**open** All year except Christmas
**bedrooms** 9 double, 6 twin, 3 single, 3 family, 1 suite
**bathrooms** All en suite
**payment** Credit/debit cards, cash/cheques

Delightfully situated family-run inn on the shores of Windermere at Waterhead Bay. Enjoy country-inn-style dining, freshly prepared gourmet bar food, real ales and fine wines, all served overlooking the lake. Pretty bedrooms, many with lake views, offer the best of Lakeland comfort.

⊕ From M6 jct 36 follow A591 through to Ambleside. At Waterhead bear left at traffic lights. Wateredge is on left at end of promenade.

♥ 3-night midweek breaks from £96pp.

Room 🖐 📺 🖐 ᛩ  General 🛏 ▥ ⚹ P ᛩ ✗ ✿ 🐾  Leisure 🚴 🏊

## BACUP, Lancashire Map ref 4B1

★★★★
**GUEST ACCOMMODATION**

B&B per room per night
s £30.00–£40.00
d £50.00–£65.00

# Rossbrook House

New Line, Bacup OL13 0BY  t (01706) 878187  f (01706) 878099  e rossbkhouse@aol.com
w a1touristguide.com/rossbrookhouse

Spacious former vicarage set in own grounds with ample parking. Refurbished to retain the charm of its Victorian past and providing excellent facilities for guests.

**open** All year except Christmas
**bedrooms** 3 double, 1 twin
**bathrooms** All en suite
**payment** Cash/cheques

Room 📺 🖐 ᛩ  General 🛏 ▥ ⚹ P ▨ ✿  Leisure ⚘ 🏊

## It's all quality-assessed accommodation

Our commitment to quality involves wide-ranging accommodation assessment. Rating and awards were correct at the time of going to press but may change following a new assessment. Please check at time of booking.

**BASHALL EAVES,** Lancashire Map ref 4A1

★★★★
GUEST ACCOMMODATION

B&B per room per night
s £50.00–£70.00
d £65.00–£85.00
Evening meal per person
£10.00–£30.00

# The Red Pump Inn

Clitheroe Road, Bashall Eaves, Clitheroe BB7 3DA  t (01254) 826227  e info@theredpumpinn.co.uk
w theredpumpinn.co.uk

**open** All year
**bedrooms** 1 double, 2 twin
**bathrooms** 2 en suite, 1 private
**payment** Credit/debit cards, cash/cheques

This 250-year-old inn in the heart of the beautiful Ribble Valley has spectacular views of surrounding countryside. The inn has a bar, snug with roaring fire, restaurant, cafe and delicatessen and delightful outside dining. A perfect base for walking and exploring the stunning Bowland area. Open all year.

⊕ *Travel to Clitheroe and head north out towards Longridge on the B6243. Pick up signs for Trough of Bowland and Whitewell and Bashall Eaves.*

♥ *Multi-night discounts available. DB&B inclusive rates available. Exclusive fishing on River Hodder by prior reservation.*

Room ⊤⊽ ⛄ ⛨  General ♨ ⓐ P ⚡ ⛾ ⑂ ❀  Leisure ♪ ► ⬡

**BASSENTHWAITE,** Cumbria Map ref 5A2

★★★★
GUEST HOUSE

B&B per room per night
s £30.00–£35.00
d £68.00–£100.00
Evening meal per person
£15.50–£18.50

# Ouse Bridge House

Dubwath, Bassenthwaite Lake, Bassenthwaite CA13 9YD  t (01768) 776322  f (01768) 776350
e enquiries@ousebridge.com  w ousebridge.com

**open** All year except Christmas
**bedrooms** 6 double, 1 twin, 2 single, 2 family
**bathrooms** 9 en suite, 2 private
**payment** Credit/debit cards, cash/cheques

Friendly, family-run small hotel with amazing views over Bassenthwaite Lake and Skiddaw. Recently refurbished deluxe rooms now available with bay windows affording beautiful views. Excellent menu using local produce available in our restaurant. Overall, we offer a relaxed atmosphere, excellent service and delicious food in a stunning and peaceful location.

⊕ *A66 westbound. Bypass Keswick. Right turn signposted B5291 and Castle Inn. Turn immediately right again and the hotel is 50yds on the left.*

♥ *3 nights DB&B È149 – È170pp special anniversary/honeymoon package in deluxe room with lake views, champagne and flowers.*

Room ⌂ ⊤⊽ ⛄ ⛨  General ♨ ⑆ ⓐ P ⚡ ⛾ ✕ ⑂ ℍ ❀  Leisure ∪ ♪ ► ⬡ ⌂

**BLACKBURN,** Lancashire Map ref 4A1

Rating Applied For
GUEST ACCOMMODATION

B&B per room per night
s £50.00–£57.00
d £60.00–£69.00
Evening meal per person
£5.00–£19.50

# The Windmill Hotel and Restaurant

Preston New Road, Blackburn BB2 7NS  t (01254) 812189  e info@windmillatmellor.co.uk
w windmillatmellor.co.uk

A warm and inviting restaurant with seven luxury en suite bedrooms, all with free Wi-Fi Internet and Freeview television. Visit our website.

**open** All year
**bedrooms** 7 double
**bathrooms** All en suite
**payment** Credit/debit cards, cash/cheques, euros

Room ☎ ⊤⊽ ⛄ ⛨  General ♨ ⑆ ⓐ P ⚡ ⛾ ✕ ⑂ ▣ ❀  Leisure ✦ ∪ ♪ ► ⌂

## Key to symbols
Open the back flap for a key to symbols.

## BLACKPOOL, Lancashire Map ref 4A1

★★★
**GUEST HOUSE**

B&B per room per night
s £23.00–£28.00
d £46.00–£70.00
Evening meal per person
£8.00–£10.00

# Ash Lodge

131 Hornby Road, Blackpool FY1 4JG  t (01253) 627637  e admin@ashlodgehotel.co.uk
w ashlodgehotel.co.uk

**open** All year except Christmas
**bedrooms** 1 double, 2 twin, 4 single, 2 family
**bathrooms** 8 en suite, 1 private
**payment** Credit/debit cards, cash/cheques

The Ash Lodge is located in central Blackpool but in a quiet residential area. The hotel is a late Victorian house with many of its original features. However, it has all the modern facilities needed for a comfortable stay. The Ash Lodge has a residential licence.

⊕ *M55 jct 4. Take 3rd left onto A583. Travel approximately 3 miles. At 10th set of lights turn right onto Hornby Road. Ash Lodge is on right.*

Room 📺 ⓦ ⓠ  General ⌂ ▥ ⚲ P ⚹ ⚡ ✕ ⬚ ⍟ ♿

## BLACKPOOL, Lancashire Map ref 4A1

★★★★
**GUEST ACCOMMODATION**

B&B per room per night
s £23.00–£35.00
d £46.00–£60.00
Evening meal per person
Min £9.00

# The Berwick

23 King Edward Avenue, Blackpool FY2 9TA  t (01253) 351496  e theberwickhotel@btconnect.com
w theberwickhotel.co.uk

**open** All year
**bedrooms** 5 double, 3 twin
**bathrooms** All en suite
**payment** Credit/debit cards, cash/cheques

Adjacent to Queen's Promenade and close to Gynn Gardens. Conveniently placed for all Blackpool's attractions. Close to local transport. A friendly home-from-home welcome awaits visitors to our attractively decorated, fully non-smoking hotel. All meals are home cooked and served in our pleasant dining room. Car park at rear.

⊕ *M55 jct 4. A583 to North Shore. Right at lights, Whitegate Drive to North Shore. Left at island to promenade. 3rd right. Hotel 200yds on right.*

♥ *Weekend breaks from £20pppn (excl Bank Holidays). Special rates for over 55s (excl Bank Holidays).*

Room 📺 ⓦ ⓠ  General ⌂5 P ⚹ ⚡ ✕ ⬚ ⍟ ✿  Leisure ♪ ⌖ ⌂

## BLACKPOOL, Lancashire Map ref 4A1

★★★
**GUEST ACCOMMODATION**

B&B per room per night
s £20.00–£33.00
d £40.00–£60.00
Evening meal per person
£6.00

# Hartshead

17 King Edward Avenue, North Shore, Blackpool FY2 9TA  t (01253) 353133 & (01253) 357111
e info@hartshead-hotel.co.uk  w hartshead-hotel.co.uk

**open** All year
**bedrooms** 3 double, 1 twin, 2 single, 3 family, 1 suite
**bathrooms** All en suite
**payment** Credit/debit cards, cash/cheques, euros

Hartshead is ideally situated in the quiet and peaceful North Shore area of Blackpool, 150yds from the promenade. All bedrooms are en suite, with colour Freeview TVs, hospitality trays etc. We are licensed and have a free large car park. We have been awarded 'Welcome to Excellence' status.

⊕ *M55 jct 4, follow signs for North Shore. 250yds past Gynn roundabout on Queens Promenade, turn right into King Edward Avenue.*

♥ *£1 per person per night discount for Senior Citizens, applying to any stay during 2008.*

Room ☎ 📺 ⓦ ⓠ  General ⌂ ▥ ⚲ P ⚡ ⬚ ⍟ ✿

---

**BLACKPOOL,** Lancashire Map ref 4A1

★★★

**GUEST ACCOMMODATION**

B&B per room per night
s £24.00–£28.00
d £44.00–£54.00
Evening meal per person
£7.00–£9.00

## The King Edward

44 King Edward Avenue, Blackpool FY2 9TA  t (01253) 352932  f (01253) 352932
e enquiries@kingedwardhotel.co.uk  w kingedwardhotel.co.uk

open All year
bedrooms 5 double, 1 twin, 3 single, 1 family, 1 suite
bathrooms All en suite
payment Credit/debit cards, cash/cheques

Your hosts Angela and Keith have a first-class reputation for their warm hospitality and offer a high standard of comfort to ensure your holiday is relaxed and carefree. A perfectly located family hotel, no single-sex group bookings.

⊕ Head towards Blackpool North, then Blackpool Promenade, keeping sea to your left. Pass North Promenade, straight on at roundabout, take 2nd right into King Edward Avenue.

♥ Midweek specials throughout the year. £88 B&B Mon-Fri. Special knitting breaks and whisky-tasting. House party at New Year.

Room 📺 ♨ 🖥  General 🛏🪑☕🍽🛎 ❄  Leisure ♪ ▶ 🏛

---

**BLACKPOOL,** Lancashire Map ref 4A1

★★★

**GUEST ACCOMMODATION**

B&B per room per night
s £20.00–£30.00
d £40.00–£50.00
Evening meal per person
£6.00–£10.00

## Kirkstall House

25 Hull Road, Blackpool FY1 4QB  t (01253) 623077  f (01253) 620279  e rooms@kirkstallhotel.co.uk
w kirkstallhotel.co.uk

The Kirkstall is a comfortable, family-run hotel. Because of the excellent service, good home cooking, cleanliness, friendly atmosphere and outstanding value for money, it is very highly recommended.

open All year
bedrooms 2 double, 3 twin, 1 single, 4 family
bathrooms All en suite
payment Credit/debit cards, cash/cheques, euros

Room 📺 ♨ 🖥  General 🛏🪑☕🍽✗🍴🛎

---

**BLACKPOOL,** Lancashire Map ref 4A1

★★★★★
**BED & BREAKFAST**
**GOLD AWARD**

B&B per room per night
s £70.00–£120.00
d £120.00–£140.00

## Number One

1 St Lukes Road, Blackpool FY4 2EL  t (01253) 343901  f (01253) 343901
e info@numberoneblackpool.com  w numberoneblackpool.com

open All year
bedrooms 3 double
bathrooms All en suite
payment Credit/debit cards, cash/cheques, euros

Car park, gardens, putting green and stylishly appointed rooms where king-size bed, 42 inch plasma TV, DVD, CD, PlayStation2 and wireless broadband come as standard. Pristine en suite bathrooms with jacuzzi bath, 17 inch LCD TV, power shower and piped music. Number One is the ultimate boutique B&B experience!

⊕ M6, M55 to end. Roundabout straight on. 2nd mini-roundabout right. 1st lights, left, next lights, left, next lights straight on. St Lukes Road is 3rd on left.

♥ Book 3 or more nights and receive, complimentary, our champagne breakfast hamper on one morning of your choice – usually £15 supplement!

Room 🖥 📺 ♨ 🖥  General 🛏 P ✂ 🍴🛎 ❄  Leisure ▶ 🚲 🏛

---

## Using map references

Map references refer to the colour maps at the front of this guide.

## BLACKPOOL, Lancashire Map ref 4A1

★★★★
**GUEST ACCOMMODATION**

B&B per room per night
s £31.00–£36.00
d £62.00–£72.00
Evening meal per person
£8.95–£10.50

# The Raffles Guest Accommodation

73-77 Hornby Road, Blackpool FY1 4QJ  t (01253) 294713  f (01253) 294240
e enquiries@raffleshotelblackpool.fsworld.co.uk  w raffleshotelblackpool.co.uk

**open** All year
**bedrooms** 12 double, 3 twin, 1 single, 1 family, 3 suites
**bathrooms** All en suite
**payment** Credit/debit cards, cash/cheques

Excellent central location for promenade, shopping centre, Winter Gardens, theatres. All rooms en suite. Licensed bar, English tea rooms, parking and daily housekeeping. Imaginative choice of menus. Listed in the Good Hotel Guide and the Which? Guide to Good Hotels. Three new family apartments each sleeping up to four people.

⊕ Follow coach and car park signs for central car park. Exit onto Central Drive, left and immediately right onto Hornby Road. Through 1st set of lights, on the right.

♥ 3 nights for the price of 2, Mon-Fri (excl Bank Holidays), Jan-Aug.

Room 🛏 📺 ♿  General 🗝 🍳 ♿ P ⛶ ✕ 🍴 🐾 ⚲ ⛤

## BLACKPOOL, Lancashire Map ref 4A1

★★★★
**GUEST ACCOMMODATION**

B&B per room per night
s £22.00–£26.00
d £44.00–£52.00
Evening meal per person
£6.00

# The Sunset

5 Banks Street, Blackpool FY1 1RN  t (01253) 624949  e thesunsethotel@msn.com
w thesunsethotelblackpool.com

Small, friendly, family-run licensed establishment offering bed, breakfast and evening meal. Rooms are clean, comfortable and well equipped. Home cooking a speciality. A warm welcome guaranteed.

**open** All year except Christmas
**bedrooms** 4 double, 1 twin, 1 single, 4 family
**bathrooms** All en suite
**payment** Credit/debit cards, cash/cheques, euros

Room 📺 ♿ ⚲  General 🗝 🍳 ♿ ⛶ ✕ 🍴 🐾 ❄ ⛤

## BLACKPOOL, Lancashire Map ref 4A1

★★★
**GUEST ACCOMMODATION**

B&B per room per night
s £22.50–£42.50
d £45.00–£85.00
Evening meal per person
Min £9.50

# The Vidella

80-82 Dickson Road, North Shore, Blackpool FY1 2BU  t (01253) 621201  f (01253) 620319
e info@videllahotel.com  w videllahotel.com

**open** All year
**bedrooms** 10 double, 8 twin, 5 single, 6 family
**bathrooms** All en suite
**payment** Credit/debit cards, cash/cheques

We believe it is all the little extras that really count to give you the most relaxing and enjoyable stay, from the aroma of fresh flowers to greet you in reception, to help with your luggage and shopping when leaving. Ideally situated close to the North Pier and bus/rail stations.

⊕ M6 jct 32, M55 jct 4. A583, then A5073 to promenade. Right at seafront, left at North Pier, right at 2nd traffic lights. 300yds on left.

♥ Summer senior specials. Discounts for midweek, children, 3+ nights. Christmas package. New Year package. Flexible times for contractors.

Room 🛏 📹 📺 ♿ ⚲  General 🗝 🍳 ♿ P ⛶ ✕ 🍴 🐾 ⛤  Leisure ♦ ∪ ⟩

## B&B prices

Rates for bed and breakfast are shown per room per night.
Double room prices are usually based on two people sharing the room.

## BLACKPOOL, Lancashire Map ref 4A1

★★★

**GUEST ACCOMMODATION**

B&B per room per night
s £22.00–£28.00
d £44.00–£56.00
Evening meal per person
£8.00–£9.00

# The Westcliffe

46 King Edward Avenue, North Shore, Blackpool FY2 9TA  **t** (01253) 352943
**e** westcliffehotel@aol.com  **w** westcliffehotel.com

**open** All year except Christmas and New Year
**bedrooms** 3 double, 1 twin, 2 single, 1 family
**bathrooms** All en suite
**payment** Credit/debit cards, cash/cheques

The Westcliffe is a family-run, no-smoking establishment, splendidly located near the Queen's Promenade. This Victorian terrace has been tastefully refurbished for the comfort of our guests, who enjoy fresh, home-cooked food in friendly and comfortable surroundings. 'Healthier Hotel' award, Gold 'Clean Air' award and Fairtrade products throughout.

⊕ *Follow the A584 along the seafront. At the Gynn roundabout follow the Queen's Promenade. King Edward Avenue is the second turning on the right.*

♥ *Reductions for four or more nights (not incl Sat). Midweek and out-of-season special offers. Ring for full details.*

Room 📺 👜 🍷  General 🛢 👤 🍴 🍷 ✕ 🍳 🗲 ❄

## BOLTON, Greater Manchester Map ref 4A1

★★★

**GUEST HOUSE**

B&B per room per night
s £35.00–£38.00
d £55.00–£60.00
Evening meal per person
£5.00

# Highgrove Guest House

63 Manchester Road, Bolton BL2 1ES  **t** (01204) 384928  **f** 0871 900 1329
**e** thehighgrove@btconnect.com  **w** highgroveguesthouse.co.uk

We are a family-run, welcoming guesthouse. Modern, comfortable, well-appointed rooms, some with DVD. A short walk to the town centre and station. A perfect base for your stay in Bolton.

**open** All year
**bedrooms** 3 twin, 4 single, 3 family
**bathrooms** All en suite
**payment** Credit/debit cards, cash/cheques

Room 🛏 📺 👜 🍷  General 🛢 🏢 👤 P 🗲 ✕ 🍳 ⟲ ♞

## BOLTON-BY-BOWLAND, Lancashire Map ref 4B1

★★★★

**GUEST HOUSE**

B&B per room per night
s £38.00–£48.00
d £60.00–£70.00
Evening meal per person
£23.00–£30.00

# Middle Flass Lodge

Forest Becks Brow, Clitheroe BB7 4NY  **t** (01200) 447259  **f** (01200) 447300
**e** middleflasslodge@btconnect.com  **w** middleflasslodge.co.uk

**open** All year
**bedrooms** 4 double, 2 twin, 1 family
**bathrooms** All en suite
**payment** Credit/debit cards, cash/cheques

Tastefully converted barn/cow byre, set in idyllic countryside location of Forest of Bowland. Ideal touring base on Lancashire/Yorkshire border. Always personal and professional attention with neat and cosy bedrooms. Lounge with stove, dining room with chef-prepared cuisine. Licensed. Gardens and ample parking.

⊕ *From M65 – Clitheroe – Skipton A59. Take Sawley turning. Follow signpost for Bolton-by-Bowland. Just before village take signpost for Settle. Two miles on the right.*

Room 📺 👜  General 🛢 🏢 👤 P 🗲 🍷 ✕ 🍳 🗲 ❄  Leisure 🗡 🚴 🛶

## Check the maps

Colour maps at the front pinpoint all the places you will find accommodation entries in the regional sections. Pick your location and then refer to the place index at the back to find the page number.

## BORROWDALE, Cumbria Map ref 5A3

★★★★★
**GUEST HOUSE**
**GOLD AWARD**

B&B per room per night
s £33.50–£62.50
d £67.00–£125.00
Evening meal per person
Min £32.50

# Hazel Bank Country House

Rosthwaite, Borrowdale, Keswick CA12 5XB  t (017687) 77248  f (017687) 77373
e enquiries@hazelbankhotel.co.uk  w hazelbankhotel.co.uk

**open** All year except Christmas
**bedrooms** 7 double, 1 twin
**bathrooms** All en suite
**payment** Credit/debit cards, cash/cheques

Award-winning, Victorian country house set in four-acre grounds. Peaceful location, superb views of central Lakeland fells. Bedrooms all en suite. Rosette-standard cuisine using local produce. Ideal base for walking. No smokers. No pets. Self-catering cottage for two. Best in Cumbria 2001, 2002 and 2004. Finalist Best in England 2003.

⊕ M6 jct 40 follow A66 (Keswick). B5289 from Keswick (Borrowdale). Before entering village of Rosthwaite turn left up signed drive over hump-back bridge.

♥ Discounts available when bookings are made more than 3 months in advance of arrival.

Room 🛏 📺 👐 🕯  General 🌂12 P ✂ ♟ ✗ 🎱 🎴 🌼  Leisure ∪ ⚓ ▶ 🚲 🏊

## BRAITHWAITE, Cumbria Map ref 5A3

★★★
**INN**

B&B per room per night
s £31.00–£37.00
d £62.00–£74.00
Evening meal per person
£7.95–£11.50

# Coledale Inn

Braithwaite, Keswick CA12 5TN  t (017687) 78272  f (017687) 78416  e info@coledale-inn.com
w coledale-inn.co.uk

Victorian country-house hotel and Georgian inn. Peaceful hillside position away from traffic, with superb mountain views. Families and pets welcome. Fine selection of real ales. Special midweek winter breaks available.

**open** All year
**bedrooms** 11 double, 3 twin, 1 single, 5 family
**bathrooms** All en suite
**payment** Credit/debit cards, cash/cheques

Room 🛏 📺 👐  General 🌂 🎱 🚬 P ♟ ✗ 🎴 🌼 🐾

## BRAMPTON, Cumbria Map ref 5B2

★★★★
**INN**

B&B per room per night
s £40.00–£50.00
d £55.00–£70.00
Evening meal per person
£5.25–£25.00

# Blacksmiths Arms

Talkin, Brampton CA8 1LE  t (01697) 73452  f (01697) 73396  e blacksmithsarmstalkin@yahoo.co.uk
w blacksmithstalkin.co.uk

**open** All year except Christmas
**bedrooms** 6 double, 2 twin
**bathrooms** All en suite
**payment** Credit/debit cards, cash/cheques, euros

Village inn in scenic countryside, three miles south of Brampton and eight miles east of junction 43 on the M6 motorway. Close to Talkin Tarn and within easy reach of Hadrian's Wall, the Lake District, the Borders and Carlisle. Restaurant and bar meals served every day, cask ales, open fire. Closed Christmas day.

Room 🛏 📞 📺 👐 🕯  General 🌂 🎱 🚬 P ♟ ✗ 🎱 🌼  Leisure ∪ ▶ 🏊

# Looking for a little luxury

Gold and Silver Awards are given to establishments achieving the highest levels of quality and service. There's more information at the front of the guide, and an index to all accommodation achieving these awards at the back.

## BROUGHTON IN FURNESS, Cumbria Map ref 5A3

★★★★
**FARMHOUSE**

B&B per room per night
s  Min £28.00
d  Min £28.00

# Low Hall Farm

Kirkby-in-Furness, Broughton in Furness LA17 7TR  **t** (01229) 889220  **e** enquiries@low-hall.co.uk
**w** low-hall.co.uk

**open** All year
**bedrooms** 1 double, 1 twin, 1 family
**bathrooms** All en suite
**payment** Credit/debit cards, cash/cheques

Low Hall is a working farm with stunning views across the Duddon estuary and Lakeland fells. A warm, friendly welcome awaits you. High quality en suite accommodation and a traditional farmhouse breakfast our speciality. Ideal for exploring the South Lakes, beautiful walks with many places of interest on our doorstep.

⊕ *M6 jct 36, follow A590, right at Greenodd (A5092), left at Grizebeck (A595), through Kirkby, pass Soutergate, first left 'Bank House', Low Hall.*

Room 📺 🕯  General ⏱10 P ✂ 🏚 🔌 ✳  Leisure ∪ ⅃ 🚣

## BURNLEY, Lancashire Map ref 4B1

★★★★
**GUEST ACCOMMODATION**

B&B per room per night
s  £30.00
d  £60.00
Evening meal per person
£15.00

# Higher Cockden Barn

Todmorden Road, Briercliffe, Burnley BB10 3QQ  **t** (01282) 831324  **f** (01282) 831324
**e** j.hodkinson_bb@tiscali.co.uk  **w** highercockdenfarm.com

Working farm on edge of Pennine Way Mary Towneley Loop. Ideal for walkers, cyclists, horse-riders. Fishing, clay-pigeon shooting and stabling available. Luggage transfers. Dales and lakes within easy reach. Family room £65.

**open** All year
**bedrooms** 4 double, 4 twin, 1 single, 1 family
**bathrooms** 4 en suite
**payment** Cash/cheques

Room 🔌 📺 🕯 🍵  General ⏱ 🏚 🅰 P ✂ ✗ 🏚 🔌 ✳ 🐕  Leisure ∪ ⅃ ▶ 🚲 🚣

## CALDBECK, Cumbria Map ref 5A2

★★★★

**GUEST HOUSE
SILVER AWARD**

B&B per room per night
s  £25.00–£30.00
d  £50.00

# Swaledale Watch

Whelpo, Caldbeck CA7 8HQ  **t** (01697) 478409  **f** (01697) 478409  **e** nan.savage@talk21.com
**w** swaledale-watch.co.uk

**open** All year except Christmas
**bedrooms** 2 double, 1 twin, 2 family
**bathrooms** 4 en suite, 1 private
**payment** Cash/cheques

A working farm outside picturesque Caldbeck. Enjoy great comfort, excellent food and a warm welcome amidst peaceful, unspoilt countryside. Central for touring, walking or discovering the northern fells. A memorable walk is through 'The Howk', a limestone gorge. Relax 'at home' with open fires.

⊕ *On B5299 1 mile west of Caldbeck village.*

♥ *Honeymoon extras. Special nature walks. Badger-watching evenings.*

Room 🔌 📧 📺 🕯 🍵  General ⏱ 🏚 🅰 P ✂ 🔌 ✳

# It's all in the detail

Please remember that all information in this guide has been supplied by the proprietors well in advance of publication. Since changes do sometimes occur it's a good idea to check details at the time of booking.

## CARNFORTH, Lancashire Map ref 5B3

★★★★
**BED & BREAKFAST**

B&B per room per night
s £27.50–£30.00
d £45.00–£50.00

# Dale Grove

162 Lancaster Road, Carnforth LA5 9EF  t (01524) 733382  e stevenage3@btinternet.com

Delightful Victorian house. Ideally situated for M6 (five minutes), railway station, Lancaster and Morecambe. Lake District 30 minutes away. Opposite the house there are canal and country walks with stunning scenery. RSPB Leighton Moss and golf five miles. Ample off-road parking.

**open** All year
**bedrooms** 2 double, 1 twin
**bathrooms** 1 en suite
**payment** Cash/cheques

Room 📺 ♿ 🍽  General P 🍴 ⛪ 🐾  Leisure ∪ ⏚ ▶ 🚴 🏛

## CASTLE CARROCK, Cumbria Map ref 5B2

★★★★
**RESTAURANT WITH ROOMS
SILVER AWARD**

B&B per room per night
s £79.00–£85.00
d £105.00–£145.00

# The Weary at Castle Carrock

Castle Carrock, Brampton CA8 9LU  t (01228) 670230  f (01228) 670089  e relax@theweary.com
w theweary.com

**open** All year
**bedrooms** 5 double
**bathrooms** All en suite
**payment** Credit/debit cards, cash/cheques

Set in the sleepy village of Castle Carrock, nine miles east of Carlisle. Ideal location for walking, cycling or simply chilling out. The Weary has quickly become a destination for drinkers and diners who wish to enjoy great food in contemporary surroundings in a beautiful part of North Cumbria. Rooms also available for twin/single occupancy.

⊕ *Seven miles east of M6, jct 43 on A69, then B6413.*

♥ *Midweek and weekend breaks. Offers for luxury accommodation throughout the year.*

Room ☎ 📺 ♿ 🍽  General 🛋 🔲 ⚓ P 🍴 🍽 ✕ 🍴 ⛪ 🔥 💻 ✿  Leisure ⏚ ▶ 🏛

## CHESTER, Cheshire Map ref 4A2

★★★
**GUEST ACCOMMODATION**

B&B per room per night
s £35.00
d £55.00

# Homeleigh

14 Hough Green, Chester CH4 8JG  t (01244) 676761  f (01244) 679977  e colin-judy@tiscali.co.uk
w homeleighchester.co.uk

Family run Victorian house, 15 minutes' walk from city centre. Pleasant, award-winning landscaped gardens. Ample parking. Cot available. Winner of Chester in Bloom for the past six years.

**open** All year except Christmas
**bedrooms** 4 double, 1 double/twin, 3 single, 1 family
**bathrooms** All en suite
**payment** Credit/debit cards, cash/cheques

Room 🛗 📺 ♿ 🍽  General 🛋 🔲 ⚓ P 🍴 🍽 ✿ 🐾  Leisure ▶ 🏛

## CHESTER, Cheshire Map ref 4A2

★★★★
**BED & BREAKFAST**

B&B per room per night
s £27.00–£32.00
d £58.00–£64.00

# Laurels

14 Selkirk Road, Curzon Park, Chester CH4 8AH  t (01244) 679682
e howell@ellisroberts.freeserve.co.uk

Quiet residential area near racecourse and river. Within easy walking distance of the city centre. Parking on drive. Key to front door.

**open** All year except Christmas
**bedrooms** 1 double, 1 single, 1 family
**bathrooms** 1 en suite, 2 private
**payment** Cash/cheques

Room 📺 ♿  General 🛋 🔲 ⚓ P 🍴 ⛪ 🐾  Leisure 🏛

## Rest assured

All accommodation in this guide has been rated, or is awaiting assessment, by a professional assessor.

## CHESTER, Cheshire Map ref 4A2

### Lloyd's of Chester

★
**GUEST ACCOMMODATION**

B&B per room per night
s £25.00–£35.00
d £50.00–£65.00

108 Brook Street, Chester CH1 3DU  t (01244) 325838  e lloydsofchesterhotel@hotmail.co.uk

Family-run small hotel and restaurant near city centre and two minutes' walk to train station.

**open** All year
**bedrooms** 6 double, 3 twin, 6 single, 4 family
**bathrooms** All en suite
**payment** Credit/debit cards, cash/cheques, euros

Room   General  Leisure

## CHESTER, Cheshire Map ref 4A2

### Recorder House

★★★★
**GUEST ACCOMMODATION**

B&B per room per night
s £50.00–£70.00
d £70.00–£100.00

19 City Walls, Chester CH1 1SB  t (01244) 326580  f (01244) 326581
e reservations@recorderhotel.co.uk  w recorderhotel.co.uk

High on the walls overlooking the River Dee, the Recorder retains the tranquil atmosphere of its 18th century origins, whilst enjoying a superb location in the centre of the city.

**open** All year except Christmas and New Year
**bedrooms** 8 double, 2 twin
**bathrooms** All en suite
**payment** Credit/debit cards, cash/cheques, euros

Room  General

## CHIPPING, Lancashire Map ref 4A1

### Clark House Farm

★★★★
**FARMHOUSE**

B&B per room per night
s Min £30.00
d £60.00

Chipping, Preston PR3 2GQ  t (01995) 61209  f (01995) 61209  e fpr@agriplus.net
w clarkhousefarm.com

Situated in the heart of Lancashire's Ribble Valley, Clark House Farm offers newly developed en suite rooms decorated to a very high standard.

**open** All year except Christmas and New Year
**bedrooms** 1 double, 1 single, 1 family
**bathrooms** 2 en suite, 1 private
**payment** Cash/cheques

Room  General  Leisure

## CHORLEY, Lancashire Map ref 4A1

### Parr Hall Farm

★★★★
**GUEST ACCOMMODATION**

B&B per room per night
s £35.00–£45.00
d £60.00–£70.00

Parr Lane, Eccleston, Chorley PR7 5SL  t (01257) 451917  f (01257) 453749
e enquiries@parrhallfarm.com  w parrhallfarm.com

**open** All year
**bedrooms** 7 double, 2 twin
**bathrooms** All en suite
**payment** Credit/debit cards, cash/cheques

Georgian farmhouse built in 1721 and tastefully restored. Quiet, rural location within easy walking distance of good public houses, restaurants and village amenities. Conveniently situated for Lancashire coast and countryside, Lake District and Yorkshire Dales. Manchester Airport 45 minutes, M6 junction 27 five miles north on B5250.

⊕ *M6 jct 27, take A5209 to Parbold, turn immediately onto B5250 to Eccleston. Parr Lane is on right after 4.8 miles. Parr Hall Farm 1st property on left.*

Room  General  Leisure

## enjoyEngland.com

Big city buzz or peaceful panoramas? Take a fresh look at England and you may be surprised at what's right on your doorstep. Explore the diversity online at enjoyengland.com

**CLITHEROE,** Lancashire Map ref 4A1

★★★★
INN

B&B per room per night
s £40.00–£55.00
d £70.00–£75.00
Evening meal per person
£8.50–£20.00

## Bayley Arms

Avenue Road, Hurst Green, Clitheroe, Nr Blackburn BB7 9QB **t** (01254) 826478 **f** (01254) 826797
**e** sales@bayleyarms.co.uk **w** bayleyarms.co.uk

16thC country inn, sensational home-cooked food, sensible prices, stylish bedrooms. Close to motorway network, rural village location, ideal for walking, sightseeing, in fact any occasion. A warm welcome is assured.

**open** All year
**bedrooms** 5 double, 2 twin, 1 family
**bathrooms** All en suite
**payment** Credit/debit cards, cash/cheques

Room General Leisure

**COCKERMOUTH,** Cumbria Map ref 5A2

★★★★
GUEST HOUSE

B&B per room per night
s £45.00–£70.00
d £60.00–£85.00
Evening meal per person
£20.00–£25.00

## Rose Cottage

Lorton Road, Cockermouth CA13 9DX **t** (01900) 822189 **f** (01900) 822189
**e** bookings@rosecottageguest.co.uk **w** rosecottageguest.co.uk

**open** All year except Christmas and New Year
**bedrooms** 3 double, 2 twin, 1 single, 2 family
**bathrooms** All en suite
**payment** Credit/debit cards, cash/cheques

In a pleasant position and only a ten-minute walk from the town, this family-run guesthouse is within easy reach of the Lakes and coast. Home cooking. Large, private car park. An ideal base for walking or touring.

♥ *Midweek or weekend breaks available all year (min 2 nights). Family group packages also available all year (min 12 people).*

Room General

**CONISTON,** Cumbria Map ref 5A3

★★★★
GUEST ACCOMMODATION

B&B per room per night
s £30.00
d £60.00

## Oaklands

Yewdale Road, Coniston LA21 8DX **t** (015394) 41245 **f** (015394) 41245
**e** judithzeke@oaklandsguesthouse.fsnet.co.uk **w** oaklandsconiston.co.uk

Spacious 100-year-old Lakeland house, village location, mountain views. Quality breakfast, special diets, owners' personal attention. Parking. Non-smoking.

**open** All year except Christmas
**bedrooms** 2 double, 1 twin, 1 single
**bathrooms** 2 en suite, 1 private
**payment** Cash/cheques, euros

Room General 10 P Leisure

**CONISTON,** Cumbria Map ref 5A3

★★★
INN

B&B per room per night
s £45.00–£55.00
d £60.00–£85.00
Evening meal per person
£8.00–£18.00

## Yewdale Inn

Yewdale Road, Coniston LA21 8DU **t** (015394) 41280 **f** (015394) 41871 **e** mail@yewdalehotel.com
**w** yewdalehotel.com

Small, family-run inn situated in the centre of Coniston, within walking distance of the lake. Ideally positioned for walkers and cyclists. Children and pets welcome.

**open** All year
**bedrooms** 3 double, 4 family
**bathrooms** All en suite
**payment** Credit/debit cards, cash/cheques

Room General Leisure

CYCLISTS WELCOME CYCLISTS WELCOME

A holiday on two wheels

For a fabulous freewheeling break, seek out accommodation participating in our Cyclists Welcome scheme. Look out for the symbol and plan your route online at nationalcyclenetwork.org.

## CROSTHWAITE, Cumbria Map ref 5A3

★★★★
**GUEST HOUSE**

B&B per room per night
s £25.00–£27.50
d £50.00–£55.00
Evening meal per person
£15.00–£17.00

# Crosthwaite House

Crosthwaite, Kendal LA8 8BP  **t** (015395) 68264  **e** bookings@crosthwaitehouse.co.uk
**w** crosthwaitehouse.co.uk

**bedrooms** 3 double, 2 twin, 1 single
**bathrooms** All en suite
**payment** Cash/cheques

Mid-18thC building with unspoilt views of the Lyth and Winster valleys, five miles from Bowness and Kendal. Family atmosphere and home cooking. Self-catering cottages also available. Open March to October.

⊕ M6 jct 36, follow A590/A591 (Barrow). Follow A590 for 3 miles then right onto A5074 (Bowness). After 4 miles right towards Crosthwaite – turn left – house on right.

Room 📺 🚰  General 🛏 🏠 🗄 P ⚡ 🍽 ✕ 🐾 ⛬  Leisure ∪ Ⓟ 🚲 🚣

## DENT, Cumbria Map ref 5B3

★★★
**BED & BREAKFAST**

B&B per room per night
s £35.00–£40.00
d £50.00–£70.00

# Stone Close Tea Room & Guest House

Main Street, Dent, Sedbergh LA10 5QL  **t** (015396) 25231  **e** stoneclose@btinternet.com
**w** dentdale.com

17thC listed building, once two separate cottages. Original features include flagstone floor, cast-iron range and exposed beams. Breakfast served in Tea Room, using local, organic and seasonal produce.

**open** All year
**bedrooms** 1 double, 2 twin
**bathrooms** 1 en suite
**payment** Cash/cheques

Room 📶 📺 🚰 🍵  General 🛏 🗄 🐾 📺 ⛬  Leisure 🚣

## DUFTON, Cumbria Map ref 5B3

★★★★
**FARMHOUSE
SILVER AWARD**

B&B per room per night
s £28.00–£30.00
d £55.00–£60.00

# Brow Farm Bed & Breakfast

Dufton, Appleby-in-Westmorland CA16 6DF  **t** (017683) 52865  **f** (017683) 52865
**e** stay@browfarm.com  **w** browfarm.com

**open** All year except Christmas
**bedrooms** 2 double, 1 twin
**bathrooms** All en suite
**payment** Credit/debit cards, cash/cheques

Situated on the edge of the Pennines, with superb views from every room. Tasteful barn conversion offers rest and relaxation.

⊕ From Appleby take Dufton road for 3 miles. Farm is on right. From Penrith (A66) take Dufton road. Travel through village. Farm on left.

Room 📶 📺 🚰 🍵  General 🛏 🏠 🗄 P ⚡ 🐾 ✳

## DUNSOP BRIDGE, Lancashire Map ref 4A1

★★★★
**FARMHOUSE**

B&B per room per night
d £50.00–£60.00

# Wood End Farm

Dunsop Bridge, Clitheroe BB7 3BE  **t** (01200) 448223

Large spacious 17thC farmhouse with beautifully appointed rooms. Guest lounge with colour TV and large garden. Set in Area of Outstanding Natural Beauty, in the Trough of Bowland.

**open** All year except Christmas and New Year
**bedrooms** 1 double, 1 twin
**bathrooms** All en suite
**payment** Cash/cheques

Room 🚰  General 🛏 ⚡ 🐾 ✳  Leisure ∪

## FOULRIDGE, Lancashire Map ref 4B1

★★★
**INN**

B&B per room per night
s £35.00–£40.00
d £45.00–£55.00
Evening meal per person
£7.50–£20.00

# Hare & Hounds Foulridge

Skipton Old Road, Foulridge, Colne BB8 7PD  t (01282) 864235  f (01282) 865966
e cherylcrabtree@btconnect.com  w hare&houndsfoulridge.co.uk

Personalised country hotel, family-owned, serving breakfast, lunch and dinner seven days per week. Licensed bar and restaurant, five spacious en suite bedrooms.

**open** All year
**bedrooms** 1 double, 3 twin, 1 family
**bathrooms** All en suite
**payment** Credit/debit cards, cash/cheques

Room 📺 🕎 ♒   General 🛋 ♨ P ❗ ✗ 🍽 ✿   Leisure ∪ ♪ ▸ 🕋

## GARSTANG, Lancashire Map ref 4A1

★★★
**GUEST ACCOMMODATION**

B&B per room per night
s £30.00–£32.00
d £42.00–£44.00

# Ashdene

Parkside Lane, Nateby, Garstang PR3 0JA  t (01995) 602676  f (01995) 602676
e ashdene@supanet.com  w ashdenebedandbreakfast.gbr.cc

Small, family-run bed and breakfast. All rooms have en suite facilities. Shops, laundry, public house nearby. On the edge of Garstang, 6 miles from M6 junctions 31 and 32.

**open** All year
**bedrooms** 2 double, 1 twin
**bathrooms** All en suite
**payment** Cash/cheques

Room 📺 🕎 ♒   General 🛋 🏠 P ✂ ⌂ 🐕   Leisure 🕋

## GARSTANG, Lancashire Map ref 4A1

★★★★
**GUEST ACCOMMODATION**

B&B per room per night
s £51.56–£74.00
d £56.12–£80.00
Evening meal per person
£5.00–£30.00

# Guys Thatched Hamlet

Canalside, St Michael's Road, Bilsborrow, Preston PR3 0RS  t (01995) 640010  f (01995) 640141
e info@guysthatchedhamlet.com  w guysthatchedhamlet.com

**open** All year except Christmas
**bedrooms** 48 double, 10 twin, 7 family
**bathrooms** All en suite
**payment** Credit/debit cards, cash/cheques

A canalside haven of thatched-roof buildings, just off the A6 at Bilsborrow near Garstang. Here you will find Guy's Lodge, Owd Nell's Tavern, Guy's Restaurant and Pizzeria, craft shops, bowling green and cricket ground. Guy's Lodge offers rooms from only £52.00. All rooms have Sky TV, tea/coffee etc.

⊕ M55 jct1, just off the A6 at Garstang.

♥ Rooms with spas available. Champagne weekend, from £165. Sunday saver only £65 for 2 people, DB&B.

Room 🛏 ☎ 📺 🕎   General 🛋 🏠 ♨ P ❗ ✗ 🍽 ⌂ ▣ ✿ 🐕   Leisure ♣ ∪ ♪ ▸ 🕋

## GILSLAND, Cumbria Map ref 5B2

★★★★
**GUEST ACCOMMODATION**

B&B per room per night
s £34.00–£39.00
d £60.00–£78.00
Evening meal per person
£9.95–£15.95

# Gilsland Spa

Gilsland, Brampton CA8 7AR  t (016977) 47203  f (016977) 47051  w gilslandspa.co.uk

**open** All year
**bedrooms** 28 double, 49 twin, 13 single, 4 family
**bathrooms** All en suite
**payment** Credit/debit cards, cash/cheques

Situated in the heart of Roman Wall country, commanding spectacular views over the Cumbrian countryside. Many scenic walks to be found in the hotel's 140 acres of park and woodland. No age limit for children.

Room 🛏 ☎ 📺 🕎   General 🛋 ♨ P ✗ 🍽 ⌂ ✿   Leisure ♪ 🕋

★★★★
GUEST HOUSE

B&B per room per night
s £36.00–£39.00
d £64.00–£70.00
Evening meal per person
£20.00–£25.00

# Greenacres Country Guesthouse

Lindale, Grange-over-Sands LA11 6LP  t (015395) 34578  e greenacres_lindale@hotmail.com
w greenacres-lindale.co.uk

**open** All year
**bedrooms** 2 double, 1 twin, 1 single, 1 family
**payment** Credit/debit cards, cash/cheques, euros

Friendly hospitality and quality service our pride. Tea and cakes on arrival. Excellent Cumbrian breakfasts await you in our attractive guesthouse. All bedrooms en suite. Comfortable conservatory and lounges with log fire. Ideal base for Lakeland attractions, ten miles from junction 36 of M6, Lake Windermere six miles, convenient for Morecambe Bay and the Dales.

⊕ At jct 36 of M6 take A590 (Barrow). After 9 miles, at roundabout, 1st exit B5277 (Grange), Greenacres is 250m on right, after Lindale sign.

Room 📺 ♿ 🖵  General 🛏 ▥ ♨ P ⚡ ✕ ▦ ⌂ ⚘  Leisure ♻ ⚓ ▶ 🚲

★★★★
GUEST HOUSE

B&B per room per night
s £36.00–£39.00
d £39.00–£45.00
Evening meal per person
£10.50–£19.95

# The Lymehurst

Kents Bank Road, Grange-over-Sands LA11 7EY  t (015395) 33076  f (015395) 35930
e enquiries@lymehurst.co.uk  w lymehurst.co.uk

**open** All year
**bedrooms** 2 twin, 3 single, 5 family
**bathrooms** All en suite
**payment** Credit/debit cards, cash/cheques

A beautiful Victorian building with a welcoming and peaceful atmosphere retaining many original features, in the centre of Grange-over-Sands, a charming town with many individual shops and cafes. Lymestone restaurant on the lower ground floor open for lunch every day with seasonal menus prepared by Master Chef of Great Britain Kevin Wyper.

⊕ See our website for map.

♥ Competitive rates available for 4 nights or more.

Room ⚲ 🖥 📺 ♿ 🖵  General 🛏 ▥ P ⚡ ♟ ✕ ▦ ⌂ ✿  Leisure ⚓ ▶

★★★
GUEST HOUSE

B&B per room per night
d £68.00–£80.00

# How Foot Lodge

Town End, Grasmere, Ambleside LA22 9SQ  t (015394) 35366  f (015394) 35268
e enquiries@howfoot.co.uk  w howfoot.co.uk

Beautiful Victorian house in peaceful surroundings. Spacious rooms with lovely views. Ideal base for walking and exploring the Lake District. Closed Christmas and second week in January for one month.

**bedrooms** 5 double, 2 twin
**bathrooms** All en suite
**payment** Credit/debit cards, cash/cheques

Room ⚲ 📺 ♿ 🖵  General 🛏 ▥ ♨ P ⚡ ✿

## Take a break

Look out for special promotions and themed breaks. This could be your chance to indulge an interest, find a new one, or just relax and enjoy exceptional value. Offers (highlighted in colour) are subject to availability.

## GREAT ECCLESTON, Lancashire Map ref 4A1

**Rating Applied For**
**INN**

B&B per room per night
s £45.00–£55.00
d £70.00–£100.00
Evening meal per person
£10.00–£25.00

### The Cartford Inn

Cartford Lane, Little Eccleston, Nr Great Eccleston PR3 0YP  t (01995) 670166
e info@thecartfordinn.co.uk  w thecartfordinn.co.uk

**open** All year except Christmas
**bedrooms** 6 double
**bathrooms** All en suite
**payment** Credit/debit cards, cash/cheques, euros

An 18thC coaching inn, nestling on the banks of the river Wyre. Newly refurbished, it combines traditional charm with modern chic. Famous for its real ales, its delightful beer garden overlooks the river and surrounding countryside. Quality food is available in the bar and upstairs in 'Mushrooms' restaurant.

⊕ *Cartford Lane, Little Eccleston, is just off the A586 at Great Eccleston, 15 minutes east of Blackpool and 10 minutes from the M55 (jct 3).*

♥ *For details of our special promotions, please visit our website which will be updated on a regular basis.*

Room 📺 ● General ⚒ ▥ ≛ P ⌿ ♥ ▦ ☿ ✿ Leisure ∪ ♪ ► ⊛ ☂

## HAWKSHEAD, Cumbria Map ref 5A3

★ ★ ★ ★ ★
**INN**

B&B per room per night
s £90.00–£168.75
d £120.00–£225.00
Evening meal per person
£30.00–£50.00

### The Drunken Duck Inn

Barngates, Ambleside LA22 0NG  t (015394) 36347  f (015394) 36781  w drunkenduckinn.co.uk

An old-fashioned inn amidst magnificent scenery, oak-beamed bars, cosy log fires and charming bedrooms. Excellent food and beers. Cumbria Dining Pub of the Year, Good Pub Guide 1999 and 2003.

**open** All year
**bedrooms** 14 double, 2 twin
**bathrooms** All en suite
**payment** Credit/debit cards, cash/cheques

Room ● ℂ 📺 ☿ General ⚒ P ♥ ▦ ✿ Leisure ∪ ♪ ☂

## IRTHINGTON, Cumbria Map ref 5B2

★ ★ ★
**FARMHOUSE**

B&B per room per night
s £35.00
d Min £56.00
Evening meal per person
£8.00–£12.00

### Newtown Farm

Newtown, Irthington, Carlisle CA6 4NX  t (01697) 72768  e susangrice@tiscali.co.uk

Susan and Malcolm welcome you to Newtown Farm bed and breakfast, a family-run working farm located on Hadrian's Wall Path. An ideal resting place for your visit to the Highlands.

**open** All year except Christmas and New Year
**bedrooms** 1 double, 1 family
**bathrooms** All en suite
**payment** Cash/cheques

Room 📺 ● ☿ General ⚒ ▥ P ⌿ ✕ ▦ ☿ ✿ 🐾 Leisure ♪ ☂

# Don't forget www.

Web addresses throughout this guide are shown without the prefix www. Please include www. in the address line of your browser. If a web address does not follow this style it is shown in full.

## KENDAL, Cumbria Map ref 5B3

★★★★
**BED & BREAKFAST**

B&B per room per night
s £30.00–£35.00
d £55.00–£70.00

### Burrow Hall

Plantation Bridge, Kendal LA8 9JR  **t** (015398) 21711  **f** (015398) 21711  **e** burrow.hall@virgin.net  **w** burrowhall.co.uk

**open** All year except Christmas
**bedrooms** 2 double, 1 twin, 1 family
**bathrooms** All en suite
**payment** Credit/debit cards, cash/cheques

Tastefully furnished, 17thC Lakeland house enjoying modern-day comforts. Sits peacefully in idyllic South Lakeland countryside between Kendal and Windermere, on A591. Ideal stopover for Scotland. Ample, safe parking.

Room ♿ TV 🍴 🍷  General 🛇8 ✂ 🛏 ✿  Leisure ♪ ►

## KENDAL, Cumbria Map ref 5B3

★★★★
**GUEST HOUSE**

B&B per room per night
s £35.00–£45.00
d £60.00–£76.00

### The Glen

Oxenholme, Kendal LA9 7RF  **t** (01539) 726386 & 07743 604599  **f** (01539) 724434
**e** greenintheglen@btinternet.com  **w** glen-kendal.co.uk

**open** All year
**bedrooms** 2 double, 1 twin, 2 family, 1 suite
**bathrooms** All en suite
**payment** Credit/debit cards, cash/cheques

Visit the Lakes and Beatrix Potter country but miss the crowds and the hassle – stop at The Glen, in a quiet location under Helm (local walk and view point of Lakeland mountains), but within a short walk of inn and restaurant. Relax in the hot tub and walk on Helm after your day touring.

⊕ *We are 300m up the hill on the right from Oxenholme Lake District railway station.*

Room ♿ 📺 TV 🍴 🍷  General 🛇 🐴 P ✂ 🐾 ✿ 🐕  Leisure 🏊

## KESWICK, Cumbria Map ref 5A3

★★★★
**GUEST ACCOMMODATION**
**SILVER AWARD**

B&B per room per night
d Min £60.00

### Abacourt House

Stanger Street, Keswick CA12 5JU  **t** (017687) 72967  **e** abacourt@btinternet.com  **w** abacourt.co.uk

Victorian town house, lovingly restored to the highest of standards. Beautifully furnished, fully double glazed. Superior en suite in all bedrooms. Central, quiet, cosy and friendly. Brochure available.

**open** All year except Christmas
**bedrooms** 5 double
**bathrooms** All en suite
**payment** Cash/cheques

Room 📺 🍴 🍷  General P ✂ 🍴

# A breath of fresh air

Love the great outdoors? Britain's Camping, Caravan & Holiday Parks 2008 is packed with information on quality sites in some spectacular locations. You can purchase the guide from good bookshops and online at visitbritaindirect.com.

## KESWICK, Cumbria Map ref 5A3

★★★★
**GUEST HOUSE
SILVER AWARD**

B&B per room per night
s £45.00–£60.00
d £62.00–£80.00

# Acorn House

Ambleside Road, Keswick CA12 4DL  **t** (017687) 72553  **e** info@acornhousehotel.co.uk
**w** acornhousehotel.co.uk

**open** All year except Christmas
**bedrooms** 7 double, 2 family/twin
**bathrooms** All en suite
**payment** Credit/debit cards, cash/cheques

Detached Georgian house quietly situated close to town centre with private car park and well-maintained gardens. Friendly and relaxed atmosphere with traditional furniture and individually styled bedrooms with four-poster rooms available. Acorn House prides itself on providing its guests with a hearty Lakeland breakfast and a warm welcome.

⊕ Prominently situated on corner of Ambleside Rd & Acorn St opposite St John's Vicarage. See website for more detailed directions.

Room 📠 TV 🖭 ☜  General ☝6 P ⚹ 🍴 ✳  Leisure 🕸

## KESWICK, Cumbria Map ref 5A3

★★★★
**GUEST HOUSE**

B&B per room per night
s £35.00–£37.50
d £56.00–£75.00

# Appletrees

The Heads, Keswick CA12 5ER  **t** (017687) 80400  **e** john@armstrong2001.fsnet.co.uk
**w** appletreeskeswick.com

**open** All year except Christmas
**bedrooms** 5 double, 1 twin, 1 single
**bathrooms** All en suite
**payment** Credit/debit cards, cash/cheques

Strictly non-smoking. Appletrees is a spacious Victorian house with spectacular views over Crow Park, Borrowdale Valley and Derwentwater to the south and Skiddaw and Latrigg to the north. Friendly hosts, full English and vegetarian breakfasts, limited parking. Ideal location close to town centre, lake, park and theatre.

⊕ M6 jct 40, A66 to Keswick. Follow signs to Keswick. Left at mini-roundabout. 4th right turn into The Heads. Appletrees is 200yds on right.

Room 📠 TV 🖭  General ☝3 P ⚹ ✳  Leisure ☍ ♒ 🚲 🕸

## KESWICK, Cumbria Map ref 5A3

★★★★
**GUEST ACCOMMODATION**

B&B per room per night
s £30.00–£34.00
d £60.00–£68.00

# Avondale Guest House

20 Southey Street, Keswick CA12 4EF  **t** (017687) 72735  **e** enquiries@avondaleguesthouse.com
**w** avondaleguesthouse.com

**open** All year
**bedrooms** 4 double, 1 twin, 1 single
**bathrooms** All en suite
**payment** Credit/debit cards, cash/cheques

Comfortable Victorian guesthouse with well-appointed, en suite rooms. Close to town centre, theatre, lake and parks. Excellent English and vegetarian breakfasts. In our guest lounge you can just relax and chat to fellow guests or read from the choice of books and magazines. Non-smokers only please.

⊕ A66 to Keswick, 1st turning onto A591 towards town centre, just before pelican lights, left into Station Street and sharp left into Southey Street. Avondale 100yds on right.

♥ Weekly B&B rate from £196.

Room TV 🖭 ☜  General ☝12 ⚹ 🍴🍴  Leisure 🚲 🕸

## KESWICK, Cumbria Map ref 5A3

★★★★
**GUEST ACCOMMODATION**

B&B per room per night
s Min £31.00
d Min £60.00

# Badgers Wood

30 Stanger Street, Keswick CA12 5JU  t (017687) 72621  e ctb@badgers-wood.co.uk
w badgers-wood.co.uk

**bedrooms** 3 double, 1 twin, 2 single
**bathrooms** All en suite
**payment** Cash/cheques

Charmingly restored Victorian guesthouse situated in a quiet cul-de-sac just a two-minute walk from the heart of the town and the bus station. Our well-appointed rooms are all en suite with colour TVs, tea/coffee facilities and views towards the surrounding fells. Special diets catered for. Maps/guidebooks available. Closed Christmas. Open New Year.

⊕ Exit A66 at junction with A59, head towards Keswick. At T-junction left towards town centre, over mini-roundabout and first left into Stanger Street.

Room 📺 ♿ ⚒  General ✂ ⌱ ❄  Leisure ∪ ⚓ ☂ 🏛

## KESWICK, Cumbria Map ref 5A3

★★★★
**GUEST HOUSE**

B&B per room per night
d £56.00–£58.00

# Brundholme Guest House

The Heads, Keswick CA12 5ER  t (017687) 73305  e barbara@brundholme.co.uk
w brundholme.co.uk

**open** All year
**bedrooms** 2 double, 1 twin
**bathrooms** All en suite
**payment** Cash/cheques

We are a totally non-smoking guesthouse centrally located on a quiet road with wonderful mountain views from all our large rooms. Close to all amenities and a two-minute walk to Theatre by the Lake. Large car park available. A warm welcome awaits you.

Room 📺 ♿ ⚒  General ⌕6 P ✂ ⌱ ❄  Leisure ∪ ☂

## KESWICK, Cumbria Map ref 5A3

★★★★
**GUEST HOUSE**

B&B per room per night
d £60.00–£90.00

# Burleigh Mead

The Heads, Keswick CA12 5ER  t (017687) 75935  e info@burleighmead.co.uk  w burleighmead.co.uk

Conveniently situated between town centre and Derwentwater, our charming Victorian house offers excellent accommodation with outstanding views of surrounding fells.

**open** All year except Christmas and New Year
**bedrooms** 2 double, 2 twin, 2 family
**bathrooms** All en suite
**payment** Cash/cheques

Room 📺 ♿ ⚒  General ⌕ ⌱ ⚑ P ✂ ⌱ ⌱ ❄ 🛐  Leisure ∪ ⚓ ☂ 🏛

# enjoyEngland.com

Get in the know – log on for a wealth of information and inspiration. All the latest news on places to visit, events and quality-assessed accommodation is literally at your fingertips. Explore all that England has to offer.

**KESWICK,** Cumbria Map ref 5A3

★★★★
**GUEST HOUSE
SILVER AWARD**

B&B per room per night
d £58.00–£62.00

# Dunsford Guest House

16 Stanger Street, Keswick CA12 5JU **t** (017687) 75059 **e** enquiries@dunsford.net **w** dunsford.net

**open** All year except Christmas and New Year
**bedrooms** 4 double
**bathrooms** All en suite
**payment** Cash/cheques

A warm welcome is assured at our beautifully restored Victorian house which provides high-quality accommodation and a homely, friendly atmosphere exclusively for couples and non-smokers. All rooms have en suites, double beds, colour televisions, clock/radios, hairdryers and tea-/coffee-making facilities. Vegetarians welcome. Private parking at rear of property.

⊕ Exit M6 jct 40. Take A66 to first Keswick exit. Follow town centre sign. Stanger Street is 1st right after 2nd set of traffic lights.

Room 📺 🖤 🍵 General 16 P ⅌

**KESWICK,** Cumbria Map ref 5A3

★★★
**FARMHOUSE**

B&B per room per night
s £34.00–£40.00
d £68.00–£80.00

# Littletown Farm

Newlands, Keswick CA12 5TU **t** (017687) 78353 **f** (017687) 78437 **e** info@littletownfarm.co.uk **w** littletownfarm.co.uk

**bedrooms** 4 double, 2 twin, 2 family
**bathrooms** 6 en suite, 2 private
**payment** Credit/debit cards, cash/cheques

A 150-acre mixed farm in the beautiful, unspoilt Newlands Valley. The perfect place for hard or leisurely walking, relaxing round lakes Derwent and Buttermere, or strolling around the market towns of Keswick and Cockermouth. Breakfast comprises a selection of fruits and cereals followed by our famous farmhouse grill, to keep you going all day.

⊕ Bypass Keswick on A66 (west), take left into Portinscale, follow signs for Swinside and Stair. Take middle road, straight ahead past phone kiosk. Littletown Farm 1 mile on right.

Room 🖤 🍵 General 🐎 🍴 ♟ P ♜ 🏛 🎿 ☼ 🐾 Leisure ∪ ⤶ ▶ 🚲 🚣

**KESWICK,** Cumbria Map ref 5A3

★★★★
**GUEST HOUSE**

B&B per room per night
s £25.00–£35.00
d £50.00–£70.00

# Sandon Guesthouse

13 Southey Street, Keswick CA12 4EG **t** (017687) 73648 **e** enquiries@sandonguesthouse.com **w** sandonguesthouse.com

Charming Lakeland-stone Victorian guesthouse, conveniently situated for town, theatre or lake. Friendly, comfortable accommodation. Ideal base for walking or cycling holidays. Superb English breakfast.

**open** All year except Christmas
**bedrooms** 3 double, 1 twin, 2 single
**bathrooms** 5 en suite, 1 private
**payment** Cash/cheques

Room 📺 🖤 🍵 General 🐎 4 ⅌ ☼ Leisure ∪ ⤶ ▶ 🚲 🚣

## To your credit

If you book by phone you may be asked for your credit card number. If so, it is advisable to check the proprietor's policy in case you have to cancel your reservation at a later date.

## KESWICK, Cumbria Map ref 5A3

★★★★
**GUEST HOUSE**

B&B per room per night
d £56.00–£70.00

# Thornleigh Guest House

23 Bank Street, Keswick CA12 5JZ  t (017687) 72863  e thornleigh@btinternet.com
w thornleighguesthouse.co.uk

**open** All year except Christmas
**bedrooms** 5 double, 1 twin
**bathrooms** All en suite
**payment** Credit/debit cards, cash/cheques

A quality, elevated, traditional Lakeland stone guesthouse with views of the magnificent surrounding mountains. Within a minute's walk of Keswick centre. Attractive, well-appointed bedrooms with quality furnishings. Expert advice on local walks and climbs. A warm and friendly welcome awaits you.

⊕ *M6 jct 40. A66 to Keswick (17 miles). Left off A66, right onto A591. After 1 mile Thornleigh is opposite Bell Close car park.*

♥ *Single occupancy negotiable. Winter and early spring discounted breaks for 3 nights or more. Please telephone for details.*

Room 📺 ♨ ⏲  General ☞5 P ✂ 🍴  Leisure ♪ ▶ 🚲 🖼

## KIRKBY LONSDALE, Cumbria Map ref 5B3

★★
**GUEST ACCOMMODATION**

B&B per room per night
s  Min £27.00
d  £40.00–£47.00
Evening meal per person
£5.50–£9.00

# Copper Kettle Restaurant & Guest House

3-5 Market Street, Kirkby Lonsdale, Carnforth LA6 2AU  t (015242) 71714  f (015242) 71714

Part of an old manor house, built in 1610, on the border between the Yorkshire Dales and the Lakes.

**open** All year
**bedrooms** 3 double, 1 twin, 1 family
**bathrooms** 3 en suite, 2 private
**payment** Credit/debit cards, cash/cheques, euros

Room 📺 ♨  General ☞ 🎱 🍷 ✕ 🍴 🐾

## KIRKBY LONSDALE, Cumbria Map ref 5B3

★★★★
**GUEST ACCOMMODATION**

B&B per room per night
s  £32.00–£35.00
d  £56.00–£60.00

# High Green Farm

Middleton in Lonsdale, Carnforth, Kirkby Lonsdale LA6 2NA  t (01524) 276256
e nora@highgreenfarm.com  w highgreenfarm.com

A working farm situated in the Lune Valley, an idyllic rural setting and an ideal location for those wanting to escape from life's pressures and enjoy a rural experience away from crowds and pollution, yet only 10 minutes from M6.

**open** All year except Christmas and New Year
**bedrooms** 2 double
**bathrooms** All en suite
**payment** Cash/cheques

Room 🛗 📺 ♨ ⏲  General ☞ ✂ 🏠 ✿  Leisure ∪ ♪ ▶ 🚲

# Take a break

Look out for special promotions and themed breaks. It's a golden opportunity to indulge an interest, find a new one, or just relax and enjoy exceptional value. Offers and promotions are highlighted in colour (and are subject to availability).

## KIRKBY LONSDALE, Cumbria Map ref 5B3

★ ★ ★ ★
**GUEST ACCOMMODATION**

B&B per room per night
s £28.00–£35.00
d £48.00–£54.00

# Ullathorns Farm

Middleton, Kirkby Lonsdale, Carnforth LA6 2LZ  **t** (015242) 76214 & 07800 990689  **f** (015242) 76214
**e** pauline@ullathorns.co.uk  **w** ullathorns.co.uk

**open** All year except Christmas and New Year
**bedrooms** 1 double, 1 family
**bathrooms** All en suite
**payment** Cash/cheques

A warm welcome awaits you at Ullathorns, a working farm situated in the unspoilt Lune Valley midway between Sedbergh and Kirkby Lonsdale. An ideal touring base for lakes and dales. Good overnight stopping-off point, situated between junctions of the M6. Refreshments served upon arrival. Individual breakfast tables.

⊕ Ullathorns is set midway between Sedbergh and Kirkby Lonsdale just off the A683.

♥ Stay 3 nights or more and receive a 10% discount (excl Bank Holidays).

Room 📺 ♿ 🍵   General 🛏 🏛 🔥 P 🚭 🍴 🌳 ♿ 🐕   Leisure ∪ ♪ ▶ 🚣

## KIRKBY STEPHEN, Cumbria Map ref 5B3

★ ★ ★ ★ ★
**GUEST ACCOMMODATION**
**SILVER AWARD**

B&B per room per night
s  £100.00–£140.00
d  £120.00–£140.00
Evening meal per person
£35.00–£40.00

# Augill Castle

Kirkby Stephen CA17 4DE  **t** (017683) 41937  **e** augill@aol.com  **w** stayinacastle.co.uk

**open** All year except Christmas
**bedrooms** 6 double, 4 twin
**bathrooms** All en suite
**payment** Credit/debit cards, cash/cheques, euros

A neo-Gothic Victorian fantasy. Romantic, quirky, laid back and utterly beguiling. The ultimate escape or the ultimate house party. A real family home where children aren't just tolerated, but welcomed. Be part of the family or keep yourself to yourself. Anything goes except hushed tones or a false formality.

⊕ From M6 take jct 38 onto A685 to Brough. Turn right 0.5 miles before village. Exit A66 at Brough then left 0.5 miles outside village.

Room 🖨 📺 ♿ 🍵   General 🛏 🏛 🔥 P 🚭 🍷 ✕ 🍴 🌳 ☀   Leisure ♣ 🔍 ∪ ♪ ▶ 🚲 🚣

## KNUTSFORD, Cheshire Map ref 4A2

★ ★ ★
**INN**

B&B per room per night
s  Max £60.00
d  Max £80.00
Evening meal per person
Max £16.00

# The Dog Inn

Well Bank Lane, Over Peover, Knutsford WA16 8UP  **t** (01625) 861421  **f** (01625) 864800
**e** thedog-inn@paddockinns.fsnet.co.uk  **w** doginn-overpeover.co.uk

Quiet setting deep in the Cheshire countryside, yet only 20 minutes from the M6.

**open** All year
**bedrooms** 4 double, 2 twin
**bathrooms** All en suite
**payment** Credit/debit cards, cash/cheques

Room 📞 📺 ♿ 🍵   General 🛏 🔥 P 🚭 🍷 ✕ ☀   Leisure ♣

# Best foot forward

Walkers feel at home in accommodation participating in our Walkers Welcome scheme. Look out for the symbol. Consider walking all or part of a long-distance route – go online at nationaltrail.co.uk.

## KNUTSFORD, Cheshire Map ref 4A2

★★★

**GUEST ACCOMMODATION**

B&B per room per night
s £30.00–£45.00
d £40.00–£60.00

# Moat Hall Motel

Chelford Road, Marthall, Knutsford WA16 8SU  t (01625) 860367  f (01625) 861136
e val@moathall.fsnet.co.uk  w moat-hall-motel.co.uk

**open** All year
**bedrooms** 2 double, 2 twin, 1 single, 1 family
**bathrooms** All en suite
**payment** Credit/debit cards, cash/cheques

Attractive accommodation on Cheshire farm, six miles from Manchester Airport. Knutsford three miles (M6 junction 19). All rooms en suite with TV, microwave and fridge. Suitable for business and touring guests.

Room ♿ TV ♨ ⚲  General ⟲ ⤋ P ✂ ⊙ ✿

## LANCASTER, Lancashire Map ref 5A3

★★★★

**FARMHOUSE**

B&B per room per night
d £54.00–£60.00

# Low House Farm

Claughton, Lancaster LA2 9LA  t (01524) 221260 & 07870 635854
e shirley@lunevalley.freeserve.co.uk  w lowhousefarm.co.uk

Working mixed dairy farm in beautiful Lune Valley with large garden and within walking distance of country pub. Bedrooms have tea/coffee facilities and TV. Guests' lounge, large garden. Ideal base for Lakes and Yorkshire Dales.

**open** All year except Christmas and New Year
**bedrooms** 1 double, 1 family
**bathrooms** 1 en suite, 1 private
**payment** Cash/cheques

Room TV ♨ ⚲  General ⟲ ⤋ ∦ P ✂ ⊞ 졏 ✿ ⋔  Leisure 🏞

## LANGDALE, Cumbria Map ref 5A3

★★★

**INN**

B&B per room per night
s £45.00–£100.00
d £90.00–£110.00

# Britannia Inn

Elterwater, Ambleside LA22 9HP  t (015394) 37210  f (015396) 78075  e info@britinn.co.uk
w britinn.co.uk

**open** All year
**bedrooms** 7 double, 2 twin
**bathrooms** 8 en suite, 1 private
**payment** Credit/debit cards, cash/cheques

Five-hundred-year-old traditional inn nestled in picturesque Elterwater. Relax in front of our cosy log fires or on the sheltered patio with glorious views. Our broad menu comprises home-cooked dishes, many using local produce, complemented by real ales and fine wines. Refurbished, en suite accommodation. Non-smoking.

⊕ From Ambleside, take A593 (Coniston), turning right at Skelwith Bridge onto B5343. Cross cattle grid then turn left into Elterwater. We're on the village green.

♥ Pets most welcome. Ask for special midweek-break prices, and midweek winter offers.

Room ☎ TV ♨ ⚲  General ⟲ ⤋ ∦ P ⚑ ✕ ⊞ 졏 ✿ ⋔  Leisure ∪ ♫ ⴕ ⚲ 🏞

## Using map references

The map references refer to the colour maps at the front of this guide. The first figure is the map number, the letter and figure that follow indicate the grid reference on the map.

## LITTLE BOLLINGTON, Greater Manchester Map ref 4A2

★★
**BED & BREAKFAST**

B&B per room per night
s £25.00–£30.00
d £45.00–£50.00

# Bollington Hall Farm

Park Lane, Little Bollington, Altrincham WA14 4TJ **t** (0161) 928 1760

18thC Georgian farmhouse, family-run, comfortable rooms with exceptional views overlooking Dunham Hall, superb, quiet location, outstanding hospitality and good food. Pub within five minutes' walk for evening meals.

**open** All year except Christmas and New Year
**bedrooms** 1 single, 2 family
**payment** Cash/cheques, euros

Room TV 🛏 🖤    General P 🥄 🍳 ☼    Leisure 🚲 🏛

## LIVERPOOL, Merseyside Map ref 4A2

★★★
**GUEST ACCOMMODATION**

B&B per room per night
s £35.00–£45.00
d £54.00–£65.00

# Aachen

89-91 Mount Pleasant, Liverpool L3 5TB **t** (0151) 709 3477 **f** (0151) 709 1126
**e** enquiries@aachenhotel.co.uk **w** aachenhotel.co.uk

**open** All year except Christmas
**bedrooms** 5 double, 5 twin, 2 single, 4 family
**bathrooms** 9 en suite
**payment** Credit/debit cards, cash/cheques

Award-winning hotel situated in the heart of the city convenient for all road, rail and air links. Within walking distance of all attractions, and famous for the 'Eat as much as you like' breakfast. Late bar.

⊕ *Follow City Centre signs towards Catholic cathedral. The Aachen is situated 100yds on the left of the main entrance.*

Room 🛏 📞 TV 🛏 🖤    General 🏢 🍽 🍷 ✕ 🍳 🛋 ◉ ☼ 🐾    Leisure 🏛

## LIVERPOOL, Merseyside Map ref 4A2

★★
**BED & BREAKFAST**

B&B per room per night
s Min £30.00
d Min £50.00

# Carey's B&B

89 Walton Breck Road, Anfield, Liverpool L4 0RD **t** (0151) 286 7965

A small family-run B&B. Warm and friendly atmosphere, clean comfortable rooms, with separate TV lounge for additional comfort.

**open** All year
**bedrooms** 2 twin
**payment** Cash/cheques

Room TV 🛏    General 🛋 🍳 🛋

## LIVERPOOL, Merseyside Map ref 4A2

★★★
**GUEST ACCOMMODATION**

B&B per room per night
s £17.00–£25.00
d £38.00–£48.00

# Holme-Leigh Guest House

93 Woodcroft Road, Wavertree, Liverpool L15 2HG **t** (0151) 734 2216 **f** (0151) 222 1400
**e** info@holmeleigh.com **w** holmeleigh.com

Victorian, red-brick, three-storey corner guesthouse, just 2.5 miles from city centre, two miles from M62 and close to Sefton Park.

**open** All year
**bedrooms** 2 double, 8 twin, 2 single, 1 family
**bathrooms** All en suite
**payment** Credit/debit cards, cash/cheques

Room 🛏 TV 🛏    General 🛋 🏢

## If you have access needs...

Look for the National Accessible Scheme symbols if you have special hearing, visual or mobility needs. An index of accommodation participating in the scheme can be found at the back of this guide.

## LONGRIDGE, Lancashire Map ref 4A1

★★★★
**INN**

B&B per room per night
s  Min £47.50
d  Min £65.00
Evening meal per person
£8.00–£25.00

# The Corporation Arms

Lower Road, Longridge, Preston PR3 2YJ  **t** (01772) 782644  **f** (01772) 785126
**w** corporationarms.co.uk

**open** All year except Christmas and New Year
**bedrooms** 4 double, 1 family
**bathrooms** All en suite
**payment** Credit/debit cards, cash/cheques

A traditional, family-run country inn offering good-quality, home-cooked food using fresh, local produce. Three guest ales, continuously changing. A warm, friendly welcome guaranteed.

Room 📺 ⚭ 🍵  General 🛏 ♿ P 🍴 ♨ 🔥 ❄  Leisure ►

## MACCLESFIELD, Cheshire Map ref 4B2

★★
**FARMHOUSE**

B&B per room per night
s  £25.00–£35.00
d  £45.00–£60.00

# Astle Farm East

Chelford, Macclesfield SK10 4TA  **t** (01625) 861270  **f** (01625) 861270  **e** gill.farmhouse@virgin.net

**open** All year
**bedrooms** 1 double, 1 twin, 1 family
**bathrooms** All en suite
**payment** Credit/debit cards, cash/cheques

A warm and friendly welcome awaits you and your family on our picturesque arable farm. Astle Farm East is surrounded by a large garden, down a small rural lane, where we can offer you a quiet stay in an idyllic setting. Farm tours and nature walks available by appointment.

⊕ From Chelford roundabout, take the A537 towards Macclesfield. After 0.5 miles turn right, after lay-by.

Room 📺 ⚭  General 🛏 ▥ P ✂ 🛁 ❄ 🐾  Leisure 🏛

## MACCLESFIELD, Cheshire Map ref 4B2

★★★★
**INN**

B&B per room per night
s  Max £45.00
d  Max £55.00
Evening meal per person
£6.95–£15.95

# Ryles Arms

Hollin Lane, Sutton, Macclesfield SK11 0NN  **t** (01260) 252244  **f** (01260) 253591
**e** info@rylesarms.com  **w** rylesarms.com

**open** All year
**bedrooms** 3 double, 1 twin, 1 family
**bathrooms** All en suite
**payment** Credit/debit cards, cash/cheques, euros

Traditional country inn with award-winning restaurant and en suite accommodation along the Gritstone Trail, amid breathtaking scenery. Quality cuisine using local produce. Rural setting, only three miles from Macclesfield town. Popular with business travellers and walkers. Close to Manchester Airport, Derbyshire and the Peak District. Free wireless broadband access.

⊕ M6 jct 18, follow A54 east to Congleton, then onto A523, follow signs to Sutton and Langley (left turn off A523) through Sutton, continue for 1 mile.

♥ Short-break rates and walking packages; please contact us for current available offers.

Room 🛏 📺 ⚭ 🍵  General 🛏 ▥ ♿ P ✂ ♨ ✕ 🛁 ❄  Leisure ∪ ♪ ► 🏛

## MANCHESTER, Greater Manchester Map ref 4B1

★★★
GUEST ACCOMMODATION

B&B per room per night
s Min £42.50
d Min £49.50

# Luther King House

Brighton Grove, Wilmslow Road, Manchester M14 5JP **t** (0161) 224 6404 **f** (0161) 248 9201
**e** reception@lkh.co.uk **w** lkh.co.uk

**open** All year except Christmas and New Year
**bedrooms** 11 double, 6 twin, 25 single, 3 family
**bathrooms** All en suite
**payment** Credit/debit cards, cash/cheques

Located in a tree-lined suburb just a short way from the city centre in a private two-acre site, Luther King House provides a full range of bed and breakfast and conference/meeting facilities. Noted for its peaceful location and very friendly atmosphere, it is the perfect choice for quality, inexpensive accommodation.

⊕ *From M56 jct 5 (5 miles), follow signs to the universities. Luther King House is opposite Platt Fields Park.*

Room General Leisure

## MANCHESTER, Greater Manchester Map ref 4B1

★★★
GUEST ACCOMMODATION

B&B per room per night
s £52.00–£58.00
d £55.00–£58.00
Evening meal per person
£5.95–£10.00

# Stay Inn Hotel – Manchester

55 Blackfriars Road, Salford, Manchester M3 7DB **t** (0161) 907 2277 **f** (0161) 907 2266
**e** info@stayinn.co.uk **w** stayinn.co.uk

**open** All year
**bedrooms** 41 double, 12 twin, 12 family
**bathrooms** All en suite
**payment** Credit/debit cards, cash/cheques, euros

Modern, purpose-built hotel offering excellent value for money. Free car parking, city-centre location, close to railway station. Five minutes' walk from the MEN Arena, and further five minutes from GMEX and MICC. Residents' bar open until 0100. Breakfast from £5.50 to £6.95 for a full English.

⊕ *Piccadilly and Victoria train stations are both 10 minutes away from the hotel.*

Room General

## MANCHESTER AIRPORT

*See under Alderley Edge, Knutsford, Manchester, Sale*

## MORECAMBE, Lancashire Map ref 5A3

★★★
GUEST HOUSE

B&B per room per night
s £23.00–£25.00
d £46.00–£50.00

# The Wimslow

374 Marine Road East, Morecambe LA4 5AH **t** (01524) 417804 **f** (01524) 417804
**e** morecambewimslow@aol.com

Family-run hotel offering excellent value accommodation, situated on the quiet East Promenade convenient for all amenities.

**open** All year except Christmas
**bedrooms** 8 double, 3 twin, 2 single, 1 family
**bathrooms** All en suite
**payment** Credit/debit cards, cash/cheques

Room General Leisure

## Town, country or coast

The entertainment, shopping and innovative attractions of the big cities, the magnificent vistas of the countryside or the relaxing and refreshing coast – this guide will help you find what you're looking for.

## MUNCASTER, Cumbria Map ref 5A3

★★★★
**GUEST ACCOMMODATION**

B&B per room per night
s  Max £45.00
d  £75.00–£100.00

# Muncaster Coachman's Quarters

Muncaster Castle, Muncaster, Ravenglass CA18 1RQ  **t** (01229) 717614  **f** (01229) 717010
**e** info@muncaster.co.uk  **w** muncaster.co.uk

**open** All year
**bedrooms** 4 double, 4 twin, 2 family
**bathrooms** 9 en suite
**payment** Credit/debit cards, cash/cheques

The Coachman's Quarters are within the stable yard of the magnificent Muncaster Gardens. One room has facilities for people with disabilities. The Granary is a large bedroom with lounge area and kitchenette. Tariff includes admission to the Gardens, World Owl Centre, MeadowVole Maze, Darkest Muncaster when operational, and reduced entry to the Castle.

⊕ 1 mile south Ravenglass on A595. From south: jct 36 of M6 follow brown western Lake District signs. From north: From Carlisle follow A595 Cockermouth – Whitehaven – Ravenglass.

Room 🛏 📺 ♿ 🍴  General 🛎 🏧 ♿ P 🍽 🛗 ◉ ✻ 🐾  Leisure ∪

## MUNGRISDALE, Cumbria Map ref 5A2

★★★★
**GUEST ACCOMMODATION**

B&B per room per night
s  £30.00–£45.00
d  £60.00–£90.00

# Near Howe Cottages

Mungrisdale, Penrith CA11 0SH  **t** (017687) 79678  **f** (017687) 79678  **e** enquiries@nearhowe.co.uk
**w** nearhowe.co.uk

**open** All year
**bedrooms** 2 double, 1 twin, 2 family
**bathrooms** 3 en suite, 2 private
**payment** Cash/cheques, euros

The ideal answer for a stress-free, away-from-it-all holiday. Set amidst 350 acres of open moorland. All bedrooms have spectacular views over the Cumbrian fells. The comfortable residents' lounge and bar both have real coal/log fires. Easily accessible, yet isolated enough to ensure peace and tranquillity.

⊕ From M6 jct 40 travel west towards Keswick (A66). After 9 miles pass Troutbeck. After 1 mile turn right to Mungrisdale/Caldbeck. Drive is 1 mile on right.

Room ♿ 🍴  General 🛎 🏧 ♿ P 🍽 🍽 🛗 ◉ ✻  Leisure ∪ ♉ ⟊ ✓ 🚲 🐎

## OLDHAM, Greater Manchester Map ref 4B1

★★★
**GUEST ACCOMMODATION**

B&B per room per night
s  £28.00–£37.50
d  £53.00–£65.00
Evening meal per person
£5.00–£8.00

# Grains Bar Farm

Ripponden Road, Oldham OL1 4SX  **t** (0161) 624 0303  **f** (0161) 678 2973
**e** info@grainsbarhotel.co.uk

Set in nine acres of land where horses graze. Fabulous views of Saddleworth and the Pennines. Warm, relaxed atmosphere with two comfortable lounges and licensed bar with Sky TV. Ideal for motorway links.

**open** All year
**bedrooms** 8 double, 8 twin, 6 single, 2 family
**bathrooms** 16 en suite
**payment** Credit/debit cards, cash/cheques

Room 🛏 📺 ♿  General 🛎 🏧 ♿ P 🍽 ✕ 🛗 ◉ 🐾  Leisure ⟊

# Friendly help and advice

Tourist Information Centres offer friendly help with accommodation and holiday ideas as well as suggestions of places to visit and things to do. You'll find contact details at the beginning of each regional section.

## PENRITH, Cumbria Map ref 5B2

★★★★
**GUEST ACCOMMODATION**

B&B per room per night
s £32.00–£57.00
d £52.00–£88.00
Evening meal per person
£15.00–£26.50

# Hornby Hall Country Guest House

Brougham, Penrith CA10 2AR **t** (01768) 891114 **f** (01768) 891114 **e** enquire@hornbyhall.co.uk
**w** hornbyhall.co.uk

**open** All year except Christmas and New Year
**bedrooms** 2 double, 4 twin
**bathrooms** 3 en suite, 2 private
**payment** Credit/debit cards, cash/cheques

You will receive a warm welcome to this 16thC farmhouse. It is situated in open farmland yet only four miles from the M6. Fresh flowers, log fires in winter and full of antiques. Home-cooked local produce, generous breakfast. Easy reach of Lakes and Yorkshire. Private fishing available on River Eamont.

⊕ From M6 jct 40, follow A66 east. Left turn after Center Parcs. From A1 two miles beyond Temple Sowerby, right turn after dual carriageway sign.

♥ 3 nights for the price of 2 Oct-Mar.

Room 🖐 ♦    General ➰ 🏠 ♿ P ⬆ ✕ 🍴 🅿 ❄ 🐾    Leisure 🎣

## PENRITH, Cumbria Map ref 5B2

★★★
**FARMHOUSE**

B&B per room per night
s £25.00–£30.00
d £23.00–£27.00
Evening meal per person
£12.00–£16.00

# Little Blencowe Farm

Blencow, Penrith CA11 0DG **t** (017684) 83338 & 07745 460186 **f** (017684) 83054
**e** bef@littleblencowe.wanadoo.co.uk

Friendly, comfortable accommodation in 18thC, Grade III Listed house. Bedrooms have TV and hostess tray. Situated on a working dairy farm. Breakfasts using local produce and homemade bread.

**open** All year except Christmas and New Year
**bedrooms** 1 double, 1 twin
**bathrooms** 1 en suite, 1 private
**payment** Cash/cheques

Room 📺 ♦    General ➰ P ✂ ✕ 🍴 ❄    Leisure 🎣 🚲 ⛵

## PREESALL, Lancashire Map ref 4A1

★★★
**BED & BREAKFAST**

B&B per room per night
s £20.00–£30.00
d £40.00–£60.00

# Grassendale

Green Lane, Preesall, Poulton-le-Fylde FY6 0NS **t** (01253) 812331 **e** rondeyo@aol.com

Family home in a quiet location offering bed and breakfast. Three rooms available, ample parking and pets welcome. Only one hour from Southern Lakes and 30 minutes from Blackpool.

**open** All year
**bedrooms** 1 double, 1 twin, 1 family
**bathrooms** 2 en suite, 1 private
**payment** Cash/cheques

Room 📺 ♦    General ➰ P ✂ ❄ 🐾

## RAINOW, Cheshire Map ref 4B2

★★★★
**BED & BREAKFAST**

B&B per room per night
s £30.00–£35.00
d £56.00

# Common Barn Farm B&B

Smith Lane, Rainow, Macclesfield SK10 5XJ **t** (01625) 574878 **e** g_greengrass@hotmail.com
**w** cottages-with-a-view.co.uk

**open** All year
**bedrooms** 1 double, 3 twin, 1 family
**bathrooms** All en suite
**payment** Credit/debit cards, cash/cheques, euros

Our bed and breakfast accommodation is ideal for groups, families, couples and individuals. It is the perfect base for exploring the Peak District, Lyme Park, and Cheshire. All rooms have wireless broadband and en suite bathrooms. One room with an en suite wet room is particularly suitable for disabled guests.

⊕ For directions please visit our website.

Room 🏠 📺 ♦ ♦    General ➰ 🏠 ♿ P ✂ ✕ 🍴 🅿 ♿ ◉ ❄    Leisure 🎣 🚲 ⛵

**RAINOW,** Cheshire Map ref 4B2

★★★★★
**FARMHOUSE
SILVER AWARD**

# Harrop Fold Farm Bed & Breakfast

Macclesfield Road, Rainow, Macclesfield SK10 5UU  **t** (01625) 560085  **e** stay@harropfoldfarm.co.uk
**w** harropfoldfarm.co.uk

B&B per room per night
**s** £50.00
**d** £75.00–£80.00
Evening meal per person
£15.00–£30.00

**open** All year
**bedrooms** 2 double, 1 twin
**bathrooms** All en suite
**payment** Credit/debit cards, cash/cheques, euros

Somewhere very special … A quintessentially English experience. Award-winning luxury guest farmhouse and self-catering accommodation offering art courses and delicious regional dinners and traditional English high tea. Sumptuous English oak king-size four-poster bed or a delightful antique Louis XV twin bedroom. Breathtaking views over the Cheshire plain to the Welsh mountains.

⊕ *B5470 from Macclesfield for 4 miles to Highwayman pub on right, and we're 0.25 miles on left-hand side (at 'slow' sign) before right-hand bend.*

♥ *Book a short break and enjoy a traditional full English afternoon high tea on the day of your choice.*

Room 🛏 📠 📺 ♿ 🍵  General 🐕 P ⚡ ✕ 🚽 🛗 🔥 ▣ ✿

**RIBBLE VALLEY**

See under Chipping, Clitheroe, Whalley

**ST BEES,** Cumbria Map ref 5A3

★★★★
**FARMHOUSE**

# Stonehouse Farm

133 Main Street, St Bees CA27 0DE  **t** (019468) 22224  **e** csmith.stonehouse@btopenworld.com
**w** stonehousefarm.net

B&B per room per night
**s** £26.00–£30.00
**d** £50.00–£52.00

50-acre livestock farm. Modernised, Georgian, listed farmhouse, conveniently and attractively situated next to station, shops and hotels. Start of coast-to-coast walk. Golf course, long-stay car park.

**open** All year except Christmas
**bedrooms** 2 double, 1 twin, 1 single, 2 family, 1 suite
**bathrooms** All en suite
**payment** Credit/debit cards, cash/cheques, euros

Room 🛏 📺 ♿ 🍵  General 🐕 🚻 ⚹ P ⚡ 🚽 🛗 ▣ ✿ 🐾  Leisure ∪ ▶ 🛶

**SALE,** Greater Manchester Map ref 4A2

★★★
**GUEST ACCOMMODATION**

# The Belforte House

7-9 Broad Road, Sale M33 2AE  **t** (0161) 973 8779  **f** (0161) 973 8779  **e** belfortehotel@aol.com
**w** belfortehousehotel.co.uk

B&B per room per night
**s** £32.00–£42.50
**d** £45.00–£50.00
Evening meal per person
£4.95–£12.95

Privately owned hotel with a personal, friendly approach. Ideally located for Manchester Airport, the Metrolink and the city centre. Situated directly opposite Sale Leisure Centre.

**open** All year except Christmas
**bedrooms** 2 double, 3 twin, 14 single, 2 family
**bathrooms** 17 en suite
**payment** Credit/debit cards, cash/cheques

Room 🛏 ☎ 📺 ♿  General 🐕 🚻 P ⚡ ✕ 🚽 🛗 ▣ ✿ 🐾  Leisure 🛶

**SAWREY,** Cumbria Map ref 5A3

★★★★
**GUEST HOUSE**

# Buckle Yeat Guest House

Nr Sawrey, Ambleside LA22 0LF  **t** (015394) 36446  **e** info@buckle-yeat.co.uk  **w** buckle-yeat.co.uk

B&B per room per night
**s** £33.00–£35.00
**d** £66.00–£70.00

17thC oak-beamed cottage, famous for its connections with Beatrix Potter, provides a warm, friendly and centrally located base, and excellent value for money.

**open** All year except Christmas
**bedrooms** 4 double, 2 twin, 1 single
**bathrooms** 6 en suite, 1 private
**payment** Credit/debit cards, cash/cheques

Room 🛏 📺 ♿ 🍵  General 🐕 🚻 ⚹ P 🚽 🛗 ✿ 🐾  Leisure ∪ 🚣 🚲

## SOUTHPORT, Merseyside Map ref 4A1

★★★
**FARMHOUSE**

B&B per room per night
s Min £28.00
d Max £43.00

# Sandy Brook Farm

52 Wyke Cop Road, Scarisbrick, Southport PR8 5LR  t (01704) 880337 & 07719 468712
e sandybrookfarm@lycos.co.uk  w sandybrookfarm.co.uk

Twenty-seven-acre arable farm. Comfortable accommodation in converted farm buildings in rural area of Scarisbrick, 3.5 miles from Southport. Special facilities for disabled guests.

**open** All year except Christmas
**bedrooms** 1 double, 2 twin, 1 single, 2 family
**bathrooms** All en suite
**payment** Cash/cheques

Room 🛏 📺 ♿  General 🕭 🏬 ♿ P ⅍ 🎱 Ⓜ ❄  Leisure ∪ ⌁ ▶

## TARPORLEY, Cheshire Map ref 4A2

★★★
**INN**

B&B per room per night
s £37.50
d £50.00
Evening meal per person
£3.50–£8.25

# Foresters Arms

92 High Street, Tarporley CW6 0AX  t (01829) 733151  f (01829) 730020
e foresters-arms@btconnect.com  w theforesters.co.uk

A country public house on the edge of Tarporley offering a homely and friendly service. Weekly rates negotiable.

**open** All year
**bedrooms** 2 double, 2 twin, 1 single
**bathrooms** All en suite
**payment** Credit/debit cards, cash/cheques

Room 📺 ♿  General 🕭 10 ♿ P ⅍ 🎱 ✗ Ⓜ ❄  Leisure ♦ ⌁ ▶ 🏡

## THRELKELD, Cumbria Map ref 5A3

★★★★
**INN**

B&B per room per night
s £35.00–£50.00
d £70.00–£100.00
Evening meal per person
£7.00–£16.50

# Horse and Farrier Inn

Threlkeld, Keswick CA12 4SQ  t (017687) 79688  f (017687) 79823  e info@horseandfarrier.com
w horseandfarrier.com

**open** All year
**bedrooms** 4 double, 1 twin, 6 double/twin
**bathrooms** 9 en suite, 2 private
**payment** Credit/debit cards, cash/cheques

The Horse and Farrier Inn is situated beneath Blencathra and is ideally located for walking or touring the Lake District. All bedrooms are en suite, with TV, tea-/coffee-making facilities and hairdryer. Our head chef has recently won the Cumbria Tourist Board's Most Inspiring Chef of the Year 2005/2006.

Room 📺 ♿ 🍵  General 🕭 🏬 ♿ P 🎱 ✗ Ⓜ ❄ 🐾  Leisure ∪ ⌁ ▶ 🚲 🏡

## ULLSWATER, Cumbria Map ref 5A3

★★★
**GUEST HOUSE**

B&B per room per night
s £35.00–£50.00
d £60.00–£70.00

# Knotts Mill Country Lodge

Watermillock, Penrith CA11 0JN  t (017684) 86699  f (017684) 86699  e relax@knottsmill.com
w knottsmill.com

**open** All year
**bedrooms** 4 double, 2 twin, 3 family
**bathrooms** All en suite
**payment** Credit/debit cards, cash/cheques, euros

A country lodge offering quality, serviced accommodation and big breakfasts. In private grounds, set in magnificent scenery around Ullswater with stunning views of the surrounding hills. Ideal for walking, touring, bird-watching and sailing. Relaxed, welcoming atmosphere in a peaceful setting, yet only ten minutes from the M6. Pets by arrangement.

♥ Rheged discount vouchers.

Room 🛏 📺 ♿ 🍵  General 🕭 🏬 ♿ P ⅍ 🎱 ✗ Ⓜ ❄ 🐾  Leisure ∪ ⌁ 🚲 🏡

## ULLSWATER, Cumbria Map ref 5A3

★★★
**GUEST HOUSE**

B&B per room per night
s £40.00
d £70.00–£84.00

### Land Ends Country Lodge

Watermillock, Ullswater CA11 0NB  t (017684) 86438  f (017684) 86903
e infolandends@btinternet.com  w landends.co.uk

**open** All year except Christmas and New Year
**bedrooms** 4 double, 1 twin, 2 single, 2 family
**bathrooms** All en suite
**payment** Cash/cheques

A haven of peace and quiet, set in 25 acres with two pretty lakes, ducks, red squirrels and wonderful birdlife, our traditional farmhouse has been tastefully restored providing en suite bedrooms, one with four-poster. Sandwiches available evenings. Cosy lounge and bar. Close to lake Ullswater and high fells.

⊕ M6 jct 40. Take A66 towards Keswick for 4 miles. Turn left at sign Hutton. Land Ends 2 miles on right. White sign.

♥ Reduced rates for 3 or more nights.

Room ♿ 🖨 📺 🛁 🍵  General 🛇 🛏 ♿ P 🔌 🍽 🍴 🔄 🎱 ☀  Leisure ∪ ⏚ 🚵

## ULLSWATER, Cumbria Map ref 5A3

★★★★
**FARMHOUSE**

B&B per room per night
s £35.00–£40.00
d £60.00–£70.00

### Tymparon Hall

Newbiggin, Penrith CA11 0HS  t (017684) 83236  f (017684) 83236
e margaret@tymparon.freeserve.co.uk  w tymparon.freeserve.co.uk

**open** All year except Christmas and New Year
**bedrooms** 1 double, 1 twin, 1 family
**bathrooms** 2 en suite, 1 private
**payment** Cash/cheques

Spacious and very comfortable 18thC manor house situated on fringe of quiet village, a ten-minute drive to Lake Ullswater and close to M6 junction 40. En suite rooms available and excellent home cooking. Cosy residents' lounge with log fire. Ample private parking.

⊕ M6 jct 40, take A66 towards Keswick, in approx 1.75 miles turn right for Newbiggin. Tymparon Hall is at end of village on the right.

♥ Reductions for 3-night, midweek breaks.

Room 🛁 🍵  General 🛇 🔌 🔄 ☀ 🐾

## ULVERSTON, Cumbria Map ref 5A3

★★★★★
**GUEST ACCOMMODATION**

B&B per room per night
s Min £35.00
d Min £70.00
Evening meal per person
£20.00–£25.00

### St Marys Mount

Belmont, Ulverston LA12 7HD  t (01229) 583372  e gerry.bobbett@virgin.net  w stmarysmount.co.uk

A Victorian house in its own grounds with stunning views of Morecambe Bay. Quiet and peaceful.

**open** All year
**bedrooms** 2 double, 2 twin, 1 single, 1 family
**bathrooms** 5 en suite, 1 private
**payment** Credit/debit cards, cash/cheques

Room ♿ 🖨 📺 🛁 🍵  General 🛇 🔌 P 🔌 ✕ 🎱 🔄 🐾 ☀ 🐾  Leisure ∪ ⏚ ▶ 🚲 🚵

## Check it out

Information on accommodation listed in this guide has been supplied by proprietors. As changes may occur you should remember to check all relevant details at the time of booking.

## WARRINGTON, Cheshire Map ref 4A2

★★★
**BED & BREAKFAST**

B&B per room per night
s £25.00–£35.00
d £45.00–£55.00
Evening meal per person
£4.00–£6.00

# New House Farm Cottages

Hatton Lane, Hatton, Warrington WA4 4BZ  t (01925) 730567

Fully modernised farm-workers' cottages which still retain their original features. Fields surround the cottages. Organic fruit sold from garden. Close to motorways.

**open** All year
**bedrooms** 1 double, 1 twin, 1 single, 1 family
**bathrooms** 2 en suite, 2 private
**payment** Cash/cheques, euros

Room 🛏 General ☎ P ⚡ ✕ 🍴 🗓 ⧖ ⚶ 🐴  Leisure ∪ ♪ ⚲ ⚵ 🏛

## WARRINGTON, Cheshire Map ref 4A2

★★★
**GUEST ACCOMMODATION**

B&B per room per night
s £46.00–£53.00
d £46.00–£53.00

# Tall Trees Lodge

Tarporley Road, Lower Whitley, Warrington WA4 4EZ  t (01928) 790824 & (01928) 715117
f (01928) 791330  e booking@talltreeslodge.co.uk  w talltreeslodge.co.uk

Set in the beautiful Cheshire countryside, a warm welcome awaits you at Tall Trees. The rooms are large, bright and have TV, hairdryer, telephone and coffee-making facilities. All en suite.

**open** All year except Christmas and New Year
**bedrooms** 14 double, 1 twin, 5 family
**bathrooms** All en suite
**payment** Cash/cheques

Room 🛏 ☎ 📺 👜 🍴  General ☜ 🍴 ⚶ P ⚷ 🐴

## WEST KIRBY, Merseyside Map ref 4A2

★★★★
**GUEST HOUSE**

B&B per room per night
s £40.00–£45.00
d £55.00–£65.00

# 21 Park House

21 Park Road, Wirral CH48 4DN  t (0151) 625 4665  e enquiries@21parkhouse.co.uk
w 21parkhouse.co.uk

**open** All year
**bedrooms** 4 double, 4 twin
**bathrooms** 4 en suite, 4 private
**payment** Credit/debit cards, cash/cheques

An elegant privately-owned Edwardian town house in centre of West Kirby offering high quality bed and breakfast. Ideal for leisure breaks and business trips. Special occasions catered for. Five minutes' walk from the promenade, beach and other amenities including cafes, shops and a wealth of restaurants and bars for the evening.

⊕ *Chester and Liverpool both within 30 mins' drive. West Kirby station 2 mins walk. Motorway link approx 10 mins. Airport (Liverpool) approx 40 mins.*

♥ *Golfing breaks to link with Royal Liverpool Golf Club only 5 mins away. Cycling and walking breaks catered for (discounts on stays over 4 nights).*

Room 🛏 ☎ 📺 👜 🍴  General ☜ ⚶ P ⚷ 🍴 ⚶ ⧖  Leisure ∪ ♪ ⚲ 🏛

# A holiday for Fido?

Some proprietors welcome well-behaved pets. Look for the 🐴 symbol in the accommodation listings. You can also buy a copy of our new guide – Welcome Pets! – available from good bookshops and online at visitbritaindirect.com.

## WEST KIRBY, Merseyside Map ref 4A2

★★★★
**GUEST HOUSE
SILVER AWARD**

B&B per room per night
s  Min £59.00
d  Min £79.00

# At Peel Hey

Frankby Road, Frankby, Wirral CH48 1PP  t (0151) 677 9077  e enquiries@peelhey.co.uk
w peelhey.co.uk

**open** All year
**bedrooms** 4 double, 2 twin, 1 single, 2 family
**bathrooms** All en suite
**payment** Credit/debit cards, cash/cheques

Award-winning country house offering luxury, en suite accommodation, a warm welcome and excellent breakfasts and cream teas. Located in picturesque village, yet minutes from Hoylake, British Open Championship venue 2006 and West Kirby for restaurants and bars. Close to M53 for Chester and 15 minutes from Liverpool – European Capital of Culture 2008.

⊕ *M53 jct 2. B5139 to Frankby.*

Room 🛏 TV 🍵 🐾  General 🛗 🛏 P ✂ ♥ ✕ 🏫 🏥 🗲 ☆  Leisure ∪ ᄼ 🏠

## WEST KIRBY, Merseyside Map ref 4A2

★★★★★
**BED & BREAKFAST**

B&B per room per night
s  Min £59.00
d  Min £79.00

# Caldy Warren Cottage

42 Caldy Road, West Kirby, Wirral CH48 2HQ  t (0151) 625 8740  f (0151) 625 4115
e office@warrencott.demon.co.uk  w warrencott.demon.co.uk

**open** All year except Christmas and New Year
**bedrooms** 2 double, 1 twin
**bathrooms** 3 en suite
**payment** Credit/debit cards, cash/cheques

Beautiful, privately-owned guesthouse offering luxury accommodation. Spectacular views across Dee Estuary towards Wales. Close to all local amenities, Marine Lake, restaurants and bars, and conveniently located for Hoylake – Open Championship venue 2006, Liverpool – European Capital of Culture 2008, and Chester, making us an excellent touring base. Non-smoking.

⊕ *M53 jct 2. Follow B5139 to West Kirby. Caldy Road off A540.*

♥ *3 nights for the price of 2 Oct-Mar (excl Christmas and New Year). Special weekly rates.*

Room TV 🍵 🐾  General P ✂ 🏥

## WHALLEY, Lancashire Map ref 4A1

★★★★
**GUEST ACCOMMODATION**

B&B per room per night
s  Min £42.00
d  Min £84.00
Evening meal per person
Min £13.75

# Whalley Abbey

The Sands, Whalley, Clitheroe BB7 9SS  t (01254) 828400  f (01254) 825519
e office@whalleyabbey.org  w whalleyabbey.co.uk

Set amongst beautiful and tranquil grounds, Whalley Abbey offers en suite accommodation, and there is a visitors' centre which is open daily.

**open** All year
**bedrooms** 1 double, 10 twin, 6 single
**bathrooms** 16 en suite, 1 private
**payment** Cash/cheques

Room 🛏 📞 TV 🍵  General 🛗 🛏 ☂ P ♥ ✕ 🏫 🏥 ☆

## Ancient and modern

Experience timeless favourites or discover the latest must-sees. Whatever your choice, be inspired by the places of interest and events highlighted for each region.

## WHITEHAVEN, Cumbria Map ref 5A3

★ ★ ★ ★ ★
**GUEST HOUSE
GOLD AWARD**

B&B per room per night
s  £75.00–£95.00
d  £100.00–£140.00
Evening meal per person
£25.00–£30.00

# Moresby Hall

Moresby, Whitehaven CA28 6PJ  **t** (01946) 696317  **f** (01946) 694385  **e** info@moresbyhall.co.uk
**w** moresbyhall.co.uk

**open** All year
**bedrooms** 1 double, 1 twin, 2 suites
**bathrooms** All en suite
**payment** Credit/debit cards, cash/cheques, euros

A Grade I Listed building (circa 1620) – one of the oldest residences in Cumbria. Delightful four-poster rooms with hydromassage power shower, sauna or jacuzzi bath and TileVision colour TV. Delicious breakfasts and imaginative dinners. Semi-rural location, walled gardens, good parking. Near Whitehaven, a Georgian harbour town.

⊕ *M6 jct 40 onto A66. Then A595 for Whitehaven. After 7 miles go past Howgate Inn. Take 1st right for Lowca/ Panton. Moresby Hall is 50yds on right.*

♥ *Sep-Mar: book dinner on 2 consecutive nights and receive a free bottle of house wine each night (2 or more diners).*

Room 🛏 📺 👜 ♖  General ひ8 P ⚡ ⛏ ✕ 🍴 ♫ ᕱ ✿  Leisure ∪ ♪ ▶ 🚴 🏛

## WINDERMERE, Cumbria Map ref 5A3

★ ★ ★
**BED & BREAKFAST**

B&B per room per night
s  Min £30.00
d  £46.00–£54.00
Evening meal per person
Min £13.00

# Bowfell Cottage

Middle Entrance Drive, Bowness-on-Windermere, Windermere LA23 3JY  **t** (015394) 44835

**open** All year
**bedrooms** 1 double, 1 twin, 1 family
**bathrooms** 1 en suite
**payment** Cash/cheques

Cottage in a delightful setting, about one mile south of Bowness just off the A5074, offering traditional Lakeland hospitality with comfortable accommodation and good home-cooking. Secluded parking in own grounds surrounding the property.

Room 📺 👜 ♖  General ひ P ✕ 🍴 ♫ ▣ ✿ ★  Leisure ∪ ♪ ▶ 🚴

## WINDERMERE, Cumbria Map ref 5A3

★ ★ ★ ★
**GUEST HOUSE**

B&B per room per night
s  £25.00–£36.00
d  £48.00–£66.00

# College House

15 College Road, Windermere LA23 1BU  **t** (015394) 45767  **e** clghse@aol.com  **w** college-house.com

**open** All year
**bedrooms** 2 double, 1 twin
**bathrooms** All en suite
**payment** Credit/debit cards, cash/cheques

Quiet, comfortable, Victorian family house offering a warm and friendly welcome. Close to village centre and bus/railway station. Front rooms have superb mountain views, all are en suite and have colour TV, tea/coffee-making facilities and full central heating. Delicious breakfast choice. Colourful, sunny garden. Non-smoking. Private parking.

⊕ *M6 jct 36, take A591 to Windermere. From A591, left into Elleray Road (100yds north of Windermere Hotel). College Road is the next turn on the right.*

Room 📺 👜  General ひ12 P ⚡ ♫ ✿  Leisure ∪ 🚴 🏛

**WINDERMERE,** Cumbria Map ref 5A3

★★★
GUEST HOUSE

B&B per room per night
s £24.00–£28.00
d £44.00–£74.00

## Elim Lodge

Biskey Howe Road, Bowness, Windermere LA23 2JP **t** (015394) 47299 **e** enquiries@elimlodge.co.uk
**w** elimlodge.co.uk

**open** All year except Christmas
**bedrooms** 2 double, 1 twin, 1 single, 2 family
**bathrooms** 3 en suite, 1 private
**payment** Credit/debit cards, cash/cheques

An attractive, family-run B&B only five minutes' walk from Lake Windermere. Clean, smart, value-for-money accommodation with private parking and garden in a quiet and pretty part of Bowness village. Superb breakfasts with local ingredients and Fairtrade tea/coffee. Gay-friendly. Pets welcome by arrangement.

⊕ *M6 jct 36. A590/591 to Windermere. Down hill to Bowness, 2nd road left after police station.*

♥ *Discounts for stays of 3 or more nights (excl school holidays). Phone for last-minute deals.*

Room General P Leisure

**WINDERMERE,** Cumbria Map ref 5A3

★★★★
GUEST HOUSE

B&B per room per night
s £30.00–£40.00
d £60.00–£98.00

## Fairfield Garden Guesthouse

Brantfell Road, Bowness Bay LA23 3AE **t** (015394) 46565 **e** relax@the-fairfield.co.uk
**w** the-fairfield.co.uk

**open** All year except Christmas
**bedrooms** 5 double, 2 twin, 1 single, 1 family, 2 suites
**bathrooms** 10 en suite, 1 private
**payment** Credit/debit cards, cash/cheques, euros

Secluded Georgian house set in own grounds with beautiful garden and private car park. Informally run B&B with exceptional breakfasts. King-size four-poster bedrooms available. All rooms en suite, some with state-of-the-art, deluxe bathrooms. Guest lounge with Internet access. Located central Bowness – close to Lake Windermere, restaurants, shops and pubs.

⊕ *M6 jct 36. Follow signs Kendal, Windermere. Through Windermere town to Bowness. 1st left after roundabout and left in front of Spinnery restaurant.*

♥ *Reduced prices for 3 nights during weekdays, or extended weekends in low season. DB&B available Nov-Mar.*

Room General 6 P Leisure

**WINDERMERE,** Cumbria Map ref 5A3

★★★★
GUEST HOUSE

B&B per room per night
s £27.00–£35.00
d £52.00–£70.00

## Holly Lodge

6 College Road, Windermere LA23 1BX **t** (015394) 43873 **f** (015394) 43873
**e** enquiries@hollylodge20.co.uk **w** hollylodge20.co.uk

Traditional Lakeland, family-run guesthouse in a quiet location close to shops, restaurants, buses and trains. Friendly atmosphere. Hearty English breakfast. Each bedroom individually furnished.

**open** All year except Christmas
**bedrooms** 4 double, 1 single, 4 family
**bathrooms** All en suite
**payment** Credit/debit cards, cash/cheques

Room General P Leisure

### One to five stars

More stars means higher quality accommodation plus a greater range of facilities and services.

## WINDERMERE, Cumbria Map ref 5A3

★ ★ ★ ★
GUEST ACCOMMODATION

B&B per room per night
s £33.00–£35.00
d £56.00–£64.00

# Holly-Wood Guest House

Holly Road, Windermere LA23 2AF   t (015394) 42219   e info@hollywoodguesthouse.co.uk
w hollywoodguesthouse.co.uk

open All year
bedrooms 3 double, 1 twin, 1 single, 1 family
bathrooms All en suite
payment Credit/debit cards, cash/cheques

Minutes from Windermere village centre and a short stroll from Lake Windermere, Holly-Wood is a family-run guesthouse where you are assured of a warm welcome. Our comfortable bedrooms are equipped with thoughtful extras. Private parking available. Excellent, hearty English breakfast. A perfect base to explore the Lake District.

⊕ M6 jct 36, A590 onto A591 to Windermere. Through Windermere to 1st set of traffic lights, 2nd left into Ellerthwaite Road. Left into Holly Road.

♥ 3- and 7-night breaks (excl Bank Holidays). See website for details of all special offers.

Room TV 🖤 🗓   General 🛏3 P ⚲ 🎮 ✿   Leisure ∪ 🚣 🚴

## WINDERMERE, Cumbria Map ref 5A3

★ ★ ★ ★
GUEST HOUSE

B&B per room per night
s £32.00–£40.00
d £56.00–£80.00

# Kirkwood Guest House

Princes Road, Windermere LA23 2DD   t (015394) 43907   e info@kirkwood51.co.uk
w kirkwood51.co.uk

open All year except Christmas
bedrooms 4 double, 2 twin, 1 family
bathrooms All en suite
payment Credit/debit cards, cash/cheques

Family-run guesthouse offering individual, personal service. Situated within easy walking distance of shops and restaurants. Ideally positioned for exploring the countryside, Lakes and fells. We have a selection of four-poster, twin and family rooms, all en suite. Ask about our special breaks.

⊕ M6 jct 36, A591 into Windermere. Take directions from the Cumbria Tourist Information Centre near the train station, or ring when close to Windermere.

Room 🛗 📺 TV 🖤 🗓   General 🛏2 🎮 ♿ P 🎮 ✿   Leisure ∪ 🚣 🏇 🚴

## WINDERMERE, Cumbria Map ref 5A3

★ ★ ★ ★
GUEST HOUSE

B&B per room per night
d £48.00–£80.00

# Lindisfarne Guest House

Sunny Bank Road, Windermere LA23 2EN   t (015394) 46295   e enquiries@lindisfarne-house.co.uk
w lindisfarne-house.co.uk

open All year except Christmas
bedrooms 2 double, 1 twin, 1 family
bathrooms 3 en suite, 1 private
payment Cash/cheques

A traditional, detached Lakeland-stone house built in 1881. Situated in a quiet area within easy walking distance of Windermere village centre, shops, restaurants, pubs and scenic walks, Bowness and Lake Windermere. Healthy, home-cooked English breakfasts. Non-smoking. Garage storage for bicycles/motorbikes.

⊕ M6 jct 36, A591 into Windermere. Take directions from the Tourist Information Centre near the train station or ring when close to Windermere.

Room TV 🖤 🗓   General 🛏5 P ⚲ 🎮 ✿   Leisure 🚴 🏛

---

**WINDERMERE,** Cumbria Map ref 5A3

★★★★
**GUEST HOUSE**
**SILVER AWARD**

## The Lonsdale

Lake Road, Bowness-on-Windermere, Windermere LA23 2JJ  t (015394) 43348  f (015394) 43247
e info@lonsdale-hotel.co.uk  w lonsdale-hotel.co.uk

B&B per room per night
s £60.00
d £78.00–£110.00

**open** All year except Christmas
**bedrooms** 3 double, 7 family
**bathrooms** All en suite
**payment** Credit/debit cards, cash/cheques

UK Accommodation of the Year 2004. Traditional Victorian house with luxury, spacious, en suite bedrooms either with lake view or four-poster. Comfortable lounge with well-stocked bar. Convenient, central location near to all bars, restaurants, promenade and attractions. Parking. A warm welcome.

⊕ M6 jct 36, A590/A591 to Windermere, turn left into Windermere village, continue for approx 1 mile. Upon entering Bowness, Lonsdale is on the right.

♥ 10% discount on stays over 5 nights.

Room 🖼 📞 📺 👄 🍷  General 🛋 🛏 🚪 P 🍽 🏠 Ⓜ  Leisure ∪ 🎣 🚶 🚲

---

**WINDERMERE,** Cumbria Map ref 5A3

★★★★
**GUEST HOUSE**

B&B per room per night
d £65.00–£90.00

## New Hall Bank

Fallbarrow Road, Windermere LA23 3DJ  t (015394) 43558  e info@newhallbank.co.uk
w newhallbank.com

**open** All year
**bedrooms** 12 double, 3 twin, 3 family
**bathrooms** 10 en suite, 2 private
**payment** Credit/debit cards, cash/cheques

Wonderful Victorian guesthouse standing in one of the most envied positions in Bowness overlooking the lake! Comfortable en suite rooms, many with lake views, contain all you require for a relaxing stay in the heart of the Lake District. English or vegetarian breakfasts provided, on-site car parking, personal attention.

⊕ Leave M6 at jct 36, follow signs to Windermere. Left into Windermere onto mini roundabout, turn right, Rayrigg Road, 200yds sharp left, straight on 200yds – there!

♥ Seasonal specials – please see our website for details. Discounts on stays of 3 nights or longer.

Room 🛏 🖼 📺 👄 🍷  General 🌳5 P ✂ 🏠 Ⓜ 🎵 ✳  Leisure ∪ 🎣 🚶 🚲

---

# Get on the road

Take yourself on a journey through England's historic towns and villages, past stunning coastlines and beautiful countryside with VisitBritain's series of inspirational touring guides. You can purchase the guides from good bookshops and online at visitbritaindirect.com.

**WINDERMERE,** Cumbria Map ref 5A3

★★★
**GUEST HOUSE**

B&B per room per night
s  £20.00–£40.00
d  £40.00–£80.00

# St John's Lodge

Lake Road, Windermere LA23 2EQ  **t** (015394) 43078  **f** (015394) 88054
**e** mail@st-johns-lodge.co.uk  **w** st-johns-lodge.co.uk

**open** All year except Christmas
**bedrooms** 9 double, 1 twin, 2 single, 2 family
**bathrooms** 12 en suite, 2 private
**payment** Credit/debit cards, cash, euros

Pretty guesthouse between Windermere and lake, and close to all amenities including Beatrix Potter attraction. Exclusively for adult non-smokers. Large breakfast menu including traditional English, veggie/vegan, gluten-free, fresh fish and some house speciality dishes. Free internet access via communal PC and 24-hour Wi-Fi. Free use of nearby luxury leisure club.

⊕ *A591 to Windermere, left at Windermere Hotel, follow signs Bowness and lake. New Road/Lake Road. We are 100m after Catholic church on left.*

♥ *3-day breaks (price per person): low season from £60, mid-season from £75, high season from £84.*

Room 📺 ♿ 🐾  General 🕿12 P ✂ 🛏 ♿  Leisure ∪ ⏏ ► ⚙

**WINDERMERE,** Cumbria Map ref 5A3

★★★★
**GUEST HOUSE**

B&B per room per night
s  £35.00–£100.00
d  £50.00–£120.00

# Southview House & Indoor Pool

Cross Street, Windermere LA23 1AE  **t** (015394) 42951  **f** 0870 486 4900
**e** stay@southviewwindermere.co.uk  **w** southviewwindermere.co.uk

**open** All year except Christmas
**bedrooms** 9 double, 1 twin
**bathrooms** All en suite
**payment** Credit/debit cards, cash/cheques

The Southview is a licensed B&B with its own heated indoor swimming pool. A bed and breakfast guesthouse with a 'splash of luxury'. Southview consists of ten en suite bedrooms, three superior with en suite spa baths, one contemporary king-size four-poster room and six classic rooms.

⊕ *From M6 jct 36 follow the A590/591 to Windermere for approx 15 miles. Turn left into Windermere and second left into Cross Street.*

♥ *Stay any 3 nights Sun-Thu and get a short-break discount. Weekend breaks from £100.00.*

Room 🛏 📺 ♿ 🐾  General 🕿6 P ⏏ 🏠 ❄  Leisure ⚲ ∪ ⏏ ⚙ 🏊

## WINDERMERE, Cumbria Map ref 5A3

★★★★
**GUEST HOUSE**

B&B per room per night
s £45.00–£60.00
d £50.00–£80.00

# Tarn Rigg Guest House

Thornbarrow Road, Windermere LA23 2DG  t (015394) 88777  f (015394) 88777
e info@tarnrigg-guesthouse.co.uk  w tarnrigg-guesthouse.co.uk

**open** All year except Christmas
**bedrooms** 3 double, 2 family
**bathrooms** All en suite
**payment** Credit/debit cards, cash/cheques, euros

Welcome to the Lake District. Built in 1903, Tarn Rigg is situated in an ideal position midway between Windermere and Bowness. Panoramic Langdale Pike views. Quiet, convenient location, ample parking, beautiful 0.75-acre grounds. Spacious, en suite rooms with excellent modern facilities. Rooms with lake views available.

⊕ *M6 jct 36. Follow A591 to Windermere. Through Windermere town centre, past the shops. After 0.5 miles, left into Thornbarrow Road. We are 0.7 miles on right.*

♥ *Special off-peak offer: 3 nights for £165. Discount from high-season prices available all year for 3-night stays.*

Room TV 🍴 🍵  General 🛏 🎱 ≜ P ⚡ 🛁 🗑 ✿ 🐾  Leisure ∪ 🚣 🚲 🏊

## WINDERMERE, Cumbria Map ref 5A3

★★★
**GUEST HOUSE**

B&B per room per night
s £27.00–£30.00
d £48.00–£52.00

# Westbury House

27 Broad Street, Windermere LA23 2AB  t (015394) 46839  e stay@windermerebnb.co.uk
w windermerebnb.co.uk

**open** All year
**bedrooms** 3 double, 1 twin, 1 single
**bathrooms** All en suite
**payment** Credit/debit cards, cash/cheques

A charming Victorian residence offering all en suite rooms with hairdryer, radio-alarm clock, tea/coffee facilities and colour TV. Westbury House is a ten-minute walk from the bus/train station and a 15/20-minute walk from Lake Windermere. There are plenty of pubs and restaurants close by.

⊕ *Leave M6 jct 36. A591 to Windermere. Turn left into Windermere. Follow one-way system to traffic lights. Turn left after lights, and Westbury is halfway along.*

♥ *3-night special from £135 (based on 2 sharing and excl Bank Holidays, Christmas and New Year period).*

Room TV 🍴 🍵  General ⚡ 🛁

## WIRRAL

See under West Kirby

## WORKINGTON, Cumbria Map ref 5A2

★★★★
**INN**

B&B per room per night
s £53.00–£58.00
d £65.00–£105.00

# Old Ginn House

Moor Road, Great Clifton, Workington CA14 1TS  t (01900) 64616  f (01900) 873384
e enquiries@oldginnhouse.co.uk  w oldginnhouse.co.uk

The Old Ginn House has been successfully converted from a 17thC farm into a charming village inn offering quality accommodation, great food and a warm welcome. Ideal for exploring the Western Lake District.

**open** All year except Christmas
**bedrooms** 10 double, 4 twin, 4 family, 1 suite
**bathrooms** All en suite
**payment** Credit/debit cards, cash/cheques

Room ♿ 📞 TV 🍴  General 🛏 🎱 ≜ P ⚡ ✕ 🛁 🍴 ✿  Leisure ∪ 🚣 ⛳

## If you have access needs...

Look for the National Accessible Scheme symbols if you have special hearing, visual or mobility needs.

## WRIGHTINGTON, Lancashire Map ref 4A1

★★★★
**BED & BREAKFAST**

B&B per room per night
s £25.00–£30.00
d £50.00–£60.00

### Kings

170 Mossy Lea Road, Wrightington, Wigan WN6 9RD  t (01257) 425053  e kingwrightington@aol.com

Quality accommodation in a pleasant, rural area, two minutes from M6 junction 27. TV and hospitality tray in bedrooms. Lounge with TV and video.

**open** All year except Christmas and New Year
**bedrooms** 1 double, 1 twin
**bathrooms** 1 en suite, 1 private
**payment** Cash/cheques

Room TV 👍 🖐  General 🛏8 P ✂ 🏠  Leisure ∪ 🎵

# Help before you go

**i**

When it comes to your next English break, the first stage of your journey could be closer than you think.

You've probably got a Tourist Information Centre nearby which is there to serve the local community – as well as visitors. Knowledgeable staff will be happy to help you, wherever you're heading.

Many Tourist Information Centres can provide you with maps and guides, and it's often possible to book accommodation and travel tickets too.

You'll find the address of your nearest centre in your local phone book, or look at the beginning of each regional section in this guide for a list of Official Partner Tourist Information Centres.

# North East England

County Durham, NewcastleGateshead,
South Tyneside & North Tyneside,
Sunderland, Tees Valley

# Natural treasures and a rich history

If dramatic coastlines and
wild countryscapes are your
thing, you'll be in your
element in North East
England. Add a turbulent
history and warm welcome,
and this region has it all.

One NorthEast Tourism Team
visitnortheastengland.com
0870 160 1781

Lindisfarne Castle, Northumberland

High Force, Middleton-in-Teesdale

The Alnwick Garden, Northumberland

NewcastleGateshead

Few regions can compare with North East England for its natural attractions. Ramblers will have a field day in the glorious wilds of the North Pennines, whilst the rolling heather-blue Cheviot Hills in the Northumberland National Park are a picnickers' paradise. The Northumberland coast is another must-see, with its miles of clean sandy beaches such as Spittal and St Aidans. You can't miss the magnificent coastal castles like Bamburgh, but make sure you catch historic Durham Castle and the town's epic cathedral. But it's not all magical landscapes and colourful history. NewcastleGateshead is a vital, modern city with cutting-edge architecture like the Baltic Centre for Contemporary Art and The Sage Gateshead, along with some of the most glamorous shopping in England and vibrant culture.

No visit to the region would be complete without a trip to the Holy Island of Lindisfarne to admire the Castle and Priory. Cut off twice a day by racing tides, you can now visit the heritage centre and 'turn the pages' of the priceless Lindisfarne Gospels on computer. Or try seal spotting around the Farne Islands – just hop on a boat at Seahouses and you'll be enchanted by these wonderful creatures.

While you're in the North East, take a walk to see Hadrian's Wall and explore the Housesteads outpost with its evocative remains including a Roman barracks. In complete contrast, the latest attraction is the Middlesbrough Institute of Modern Art (mima), a gallery of national importance housing works by Emin, Hockney, Frink and many others. Or discover the twin Anglo-Saxon monastery of Wearmouth-Jarrow. It's the UK's nomination for World Heritage Site status in 2009 because of its links to celebrated Christian scholar the Venerable Bede.

# Destinations

### Berwick-upon-Tweed

England's northernmost town guards the mouth of the River Tweed. Marvel at some of the finest 16th century city walls in Europe, built by Elizabeth I to protect a town that changed hands between England and Scotland 14 times in the medieval era. Nowadays the town is more than part Scottish. Visit the great edifice of Bamburgh Castle and the beautiful gardens at Alnwick. Roam the magnificent Heritage coastline and see Holy Island and the fairytale Lindisfarne Castle.

### Darlington

Gateway to the North East and pioneering railway town. Darlington's Railway Centre and Museum displays Stephenson's Locomotion, which opened the Stockton and Darlington Railway in 1825. Discover a civilised town with a pedestrian heart, where medieval 'yards and wynds' link the main streets. Explore the designer Imperial Quarter with over 400 shops to choose from. Culture-lovers will find plenty to occupy them at the Arts Centre and the superb facilities at the Forum Music Centre.

### Durham

Described by Bill Bryson as 'a perfect little city.' Its history shows in every cobble. Explore majestic Durham Cathedral, a World Heritage Site, and thought by many to be the finest Norman church architecture in England. Visit the tombs of St Cuthbert and the Venerable Bede. Stroll around a relaxed city centre mainly closed to traffic, take a coffee in the cobbled Market Place and enjoy the stunning floral displays. Take a path to the riverbank and take in the stunning views from the River Wear.

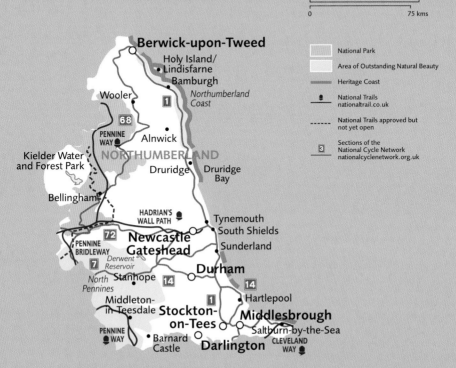

| | 0 | 50 miles |
| | 0 | 75 kms |

National Park

Area of Outstanding Natural Beauty

Heritage Coast

National Trails
nationaltrail.co.uk

National Trails approved but
not yet open

3  Sections of the
National Cycle Network
nationalcyclenetwork.org.uk

Saltburn-by-the-Sea, Cleveland coast

Darlington Railway Centre and Museum

NewcastleGateshead Quayside

Durham Cathedral

Bamburgh Castle, Northumberland

Stockton-on-Tees

## Middlesbrough

Visit the heart of the North East. Middlesbrough was home to Captain Cook whose life is celebrated at the award-winning Captain Cook Birthplace Museum. Learn about the region at The Dorman, the superb museum of local life. Let the historic, floodlit Transporter Bridge convey you across the River Tees. Sports fans can enjoy Premier League football at Middlesbrough, while walkers can explore the North York Moors and the Cleveland coast.

## NewcastleGateshead

In the North East of England, Newcastle and Gateshead face each other across the River Tyne coming together at the dazzling Quayside. Must-see attractions including the award-winning Gateshead Millennium Bridge, the Baltic Centre for Contemporary Art and the magnificent new Sage Gateshead, a stunning Sir Norman Foster building, with billowing curves of glass and steel catering for every genre of music. Rich in culture, architecture and history and with a great reputation for style, shopping and nightlife, the variety of life in NewcastleGateshead surprises even the most well travelled visitor.

## Stockton-on-Tees

Most famous for its associations with the Stockton & Darlington railway. Discover this friendly town, situated in the heart of the Tees Valley, and surrounded by smaller towns and villages including the charming Georgian town of Yarm. For lovers of outdoor activity, Stockton-on-Tees is fast becoming an impressive international watersports destination, from fishing to white water rafting to river cruising. You'll also find an impressive network of town and country parks.

# Places to visit

### Alnwick Castle
Large Visitor Attraction
of the Year - Gold Winner
Northumberland
(01665) 510777
alnwickcastle.com
*Magnificent medieval
castle often used as a
film location*

### The Alnwick Garden
Northumberland
(01665) 511350
alnwickgarden.com
*Exciting contemporary garden*

### BALTIC Centre for
Contemporary Art
Gateshead,
Tyne and Wear
(0191) 478 1810
balticmill.com
*Diverse international art*

### Bamburgh Castle
Northumberland
(01668) 214515
bamburghcastle.com
*Magnificent coastal castle*

### Beamish, The North
of England Open
Air Museum
County Durham
(0191) 370 4000
beamish.org.uk
*Let the past come to life*

### Bede's World
Jarrow, Tyne and Wear
(0191) 489 2106
bedesworld.co.uk
*Discover the extraordinary life of
the Venerable Bede*

### Belsay Hall,
Castle and Gardens
Newcastle upon Tyne,
Northumberland
(01661) 881636
english-heritage.org.uk
*Medieval castle, 17th-century
manor and gardens*

### Blue Reef Aquarium
Tynemouth, Tyne and Wear
(0191) 258 1031
bluereefaquarium.co.uk
*Giant tanks with spectacular
underwater walkthrough tunnels*

### The Bowes Museum
Barnard Castle,
County Durham
(01833) 690606
bowesmuseum.org.uk
*Outstanding fine and decorative
arts*

### Captain Cook
Birthplace Museum
Middlesbrough
(01642) 311211
captcook-ne.co.uk
*Explore Cook's early life and
seafaring career*

### Centre for Life
Newcastle upon Tyne,
Tyne and Wear
(0191) 243 8210
life.org.uk
*Hands-on science for all*

### Cragside House, Gardens and
Estate
Morpeth, Northumberland
(01669) 620333
nationaltrust.org.uk
*Woodland estate and adventure
playground*

### Discovery Museum
Newcastle upon Tyne,
Tyne and Wear
(0191) 232 6789
twmuseums.org.uk/discovery
*Explore world-changing
inventions*

### Dunstanburgh Castle
Craster, Northumberland
(01665) 576231
english-heritage.org.uk
*Dramatic ruins of 14th-century
castle*

### Durham Castle
(0191) 334 4106
durhamcastle.com
*Fine example of motte
and bailey*

### Durham Cathedral
(0191) 386 4266
durhamcathedral.co.uk
*Magnificent Norman architecture*

### Hadrian's Wall Path
National Trail
Hexham, Northumberland
(01434) 322002
nationaltrail.co.uk/hadrianswall
*An unmissable, historic 84-mile trail*

### Hartlepool's Maritime
Experience
County Durham
(01429) 860077
hartlepoolsmaritimeexperience.com
*Authentic reconstruction of an
18th-century seaport*

### Housesteads Roman
Fort (Vercovicium)
Hadrian's Wall
near Haydon Bridge,
Northumberland
(01434) 344363
english-heritage.org.uk
*Best preserved Roman Fort*

### Laing Art Gallery
Newcastle upon Tyne,
Tyne and Wear
(0191) 232 7734
twmuseums.org.uk
*An important collection of
18th- and 19th-century art*

### Locomotion
The National Railway
Museum at Shildon
Shildon, County Durham
(01388) 777999
locomotion.uk.com
*Over 100 locomotives*

# Diary dates 2008

**mima, Middlesbrough Institute of Modern Art**
(01642) 726720
visitmima.com
*Internationally significant fine and applied art*

**National Glass Centre**
Sunderland, Tyne and Wear
(0191) 515 5555
nationalglasscentre.com
*Glass exhibitions and live glass-blowing*

**Nature's World**
Middlesbrough
(01642) 594895
naturesworld.org.uk
*A pioneering eco-experience*

**Raby Castle**
Darlington,
County Durham
(01833) 660202
rabycastle.com
*Medieval castle with deer park and gardens*

**The Sage Gateshead**
Tyne and Wear
(0191) 443 4666
thesagegateshead.org
*Pioneering centre for musical discovery*

**Vindolanda
(Chesterholm)
Hadrian's Wall**
near Haydon Bridge,
Northumberland
(01434) 344277
vindolanda.com
*Remains of a Roman fort and settlement*

**Northern Rocks: The North Pennines Festival of Geology and Landscape**
Weardale
northpennines.org.uk
17 May – 1 Jun*

**South Tyneside Summer Festival**
southtyneside.info
1 Jun – 31 Aug*

**Durham Regatta**
River Wear
durham-regatta.org.uk
Jun*

**Alnwick Fair**
Market Square
northumberland.gov.uk
9 – 13 Jul*

**Sunderland International Friendship Festival featuring the Kite Festival**
Northern Area Playing Fields, Washington
sunderland-kites.co.uk
5 – 6 Jul

**Whitley Bay International Jazz Festival**
whitleybayjazzfest.org
11 – 13 Jul

**Sunderland International Air Show**
The promenade
sunderland-airshow.com
26 – 27 Jul

**Stockton International Riverside Festival**
sirf.co.uk
30 Jul – 3 Aug

**Hexham Abbey Festival**
hexhamabbey.org.uk/festival
25 Sep – 4 Oct

**City of Durham Christmas Festival**
Various locations, Durham
1 – 2 Dec*

* provisional date at time of going to press

# Tourist Information Centres

When you arrive at your destination, visit an Official Partner Tourist Information Centre for quality assured help with accommodation and information about local attractions and events, or email your request before you go. To search for attractions and Tourist Information Centres on the move just text INFO to 62233, and a web link will be sent to your mobile phone.

| | | | |
|---|---|---|---|
| **Alnwick** | 2 The Shambles | (01665) 511333 | alnwicktic@alnwick.gov.uk |
| **Barnard Castle** | Flatts Road | (01833) 690909 | tourism@teesdale.gov.uk |
| **Darlington** | 13 Horsemarket | (01325) 388666 | tic@darlington.gov.uk |
| **Durham** | 2 Millennium Place | (0191) 384 3720 | touristinfo@durhamcity.gov.uk |
| **Hartlepool** | Church Square | (01429) 869706 | hpooltic@hartlepool.gov.uk |
| **Hexham** | Wentworth Car Park | (01434) 652220 | hexham.tic@tynedale.gov.uk |
| **Morpeth** | Bridge Street | (01670) 500700 | tourism@castlemorpeth.gov.uk |
| **Newcastle upon Tyne** | 8-9 Central Arcade | (0191) 277 8000 | tourist.info@newcastle.gov.uk |
| **Once Brewed\*** | Military Road | (01434) 344396 | tic.oncebrewed@nnpa.org.uk |
| **Sunderland** | 50 Fawcett Street | (0191) 553 2000 | tourist.info@sunderland.gov.uk |

\* *seasonal opening*

# Travel info

**By road:**
There is excellent motorway access via the A1(M), and the A69 and A66 connect directly to the M6 from the west. North East England is just two hours from Edinburgh, two-and-a-half hours from Manchester and four-and-a-half hours from London by road.

**By rail:**
Take the train and you're free to unwind all the way, with a tasty meal, your favourite read or just enjoying the view. North East England is easily reached on the East Coast Main Line from the north and south and via many direct connections from the west. Trains between London and Newcastle take just three hours, Birmingham to Darlington in just under three hours and Sheffield to Newcastle in just over three hours.

**By air:**
North East England has two international airports enabling easy access from UK, Europe and worldwide. Low cost flights fly into the region from a number of UK and European locations. Fly into Durham Tees Valley or Newcastle International airports.

Berwick-upon-Tweed

Hadrian's Wall, Northumberland

# Find out more

Log onto the North East England website at **visitnortheastengland.com** for further information on accommodation, attractions, events and special offers throughout the region. A range of free guides are available for you to order online or by calling **0870 160 1781**:

- **Holiday and Short Breaks Guide**
  Information on North East England, including hotels, bed and breakfast, self-catering, caravan and camping parks and accessible accommodation as well as events and attractions throughout the region.

- **Cycling Guide**
  A guide to day rides, traffic-free trails and challenging cycling routes.

- **Gardens Guide**
  A guide to the region's most inspirational gardens.

- **Walking Guide**
  Circular trails and long distance routes through breathtaking countryside.

## where to stay in
# North East England

All place names in the blue bands are shown on the maps at the front of this guide.

A complete listing of all Enjoy England assessed accommodation covered by this guide appears at the back.

**Accommodation symbols**
Symbols give useful information about services and facilities. Inside the back-cover flap you can find a key to these symbols. Keep it open for easy reference.

---

**ALLENDALE,** Northumberland Map ref 5B2

★★★★
FARMHOUSE

B&B per room per night
s £25.00–£30.00
d £50.00–£60.00
Evening meal per person
£13.00

## Struthers Farm
Catton, Hexham NE47 9LP  t (01434) 683580

Working farm in beautiful countryside near Hadrian's Wall. Well-appointed, en suite rooms, double/twin optional. Evening meal. Nine miles from Hexham. Good parking. A69 Newcastle to Hexham, B6305 to Allendale.

**open** All year except Christmas
**bedrooms** 1 double, 1 twin
**bathrooms** All en suite
**payment** Cash/cheques

Room 📺 🕭 🖳  General ➹ P ✕ 🛏 ❀ 🐾

---

**ALNMOUTH,** Northumberland Map ref 5C1

★★★
GUEST ACCOMMODATION

B&B per room per night
s £35.00
d £70.00

## Alnmouth Golf Club
Foxton Hall, Alnwick NE66 3BE  t (01665) 830231  f (01665) 830922
e secretary@alnmouthgolfclub.com  w alnmouthgolfclub.com

Situated on the magnificent Northumberland coast, Foxton Hall provides the perfect base to tour the delights of Northumberland.

**open** All year except Christmas and New Year
**bedrooms** 8 twin, 2 single
**bathrooms** All en suite
**payment** Credit/debit cards, cash/cheques

Room 📺 🕭 🖳  General P ⅍ ☕ ✕ 🕮 🛏

---

**ALNMOUTH,** Northumberland Map ref 5C1

★★★★
BED & BREAKFAST
SILVER AWARD

B&B per room per night
d £64.00–£68.00

## Beech Lodge
8 Alnwood, Alnwick NE66 3NN  t (01665) 830709  e beechlodge@hotmail.com  w alnmouth.com

**bedrooms** 2 double
**bathrooms** 1 en suite, 1 private
**payment** Cash/cheques

A warm and friendly welcome awaits guests at our spacious, detached, modern bungalow in a quiet woodland setting, close to village shops, pubs and restaurants. Our en suite rooms are decorated and furnished to a high and modern standard. An ideal base for exploring all the wonderful coast and countryside. Open April to October.

⊕ Take A1068 from Alnwick, follow via Lesbury to Hipsburn. Take B1338 to Alnmouth, cross bridge, turn right into Alnwood. Last bungalow on left is Beech Lodge.

Room 🛁 📺 🕭 🖳  General P ⅍ 🛏 ☐ ❀  Leisure 🏊

ALNWICK, Northumberland Map ref 5C1

## Alndyke Bed and Breakfast

Alnmouth Road, Alnwick NE66 3PB  **t** (01665) 510252  **e** laura@alndyke.co.uk  **w** alndyke.co.uk

★★★★
**FARMHOUSE
SILVER AWARD**

B&B per room per night
**d** £60.00–£70.00

**open** All year except Christmas and New Year
**bedrooms** 3 double, 1 twin
**bathrooms** All en suite
**payment** Cash/cheques

Listed Georgian farmhouse set in 500 acres of arable farmland with open rural views. All bedrooms are tastefully decorated with en suite, TV and beverages. Guest lounge, with woodburner and TV, to relax in with a good book. South-facing lounge and dining room receive the morning sun. Come along, relax and enjoy Northumbria.

⊕ *From A1 take first sign for Alnwick A1068. Pass 24hr garage on right then fire station on left. Come to roundabout, follow A1068 Alnmouth over flyover, farmhouse on right.*

Room TV 🖊 ⏣  General P ⅍ 🗵 ✲  Leisure ∪ ♪ 🖼

ALNWICK, Northumberland Map ref 5C1

## Castle Gate Guest House

★★★
**BED & BREAKFAST**

B&B per room per night
**s** £25.00–£49.00
**d** £49.00–£59.00

23 Bondgate Without, Alnwick NE66 1PR  **t** (01665) 602657 & 07706 113434  **e** tracy@amfr.co.uk
**w** castlegatealnwick.co.uk

Friendly, family-run guesthouse in the town centre of Alnwick. 300yds from castle, gardens, shops, pubs and restaurants. All rooms have Freeview TV and tea-/coffee-making facilities.

**open** All year
**bedrooms** 2 double, 1 twin
**bathrooms** 2 en suite, 1 private
**payment** Cash/cheques

Room 🖾 TV 🖊 ⏣  General 🕹 🎞 ♠ P ⅍ 🗵 ✝  Leisure ∪ ♪ 🚲 🖼

ALNWICK, Northumberland Map ref 5C1

## Redfoot Lea Bed & Breakfast

★★★★
**BED & BREAKFAST
SILVER AWARD**

B&B per room per night
**s** £45.00–£55.00
**d** £70.00–£80.00

Greensfield Moor Farm, Alnwick NE66 2HH  **t** (01665) 603891  **f** (01665) 606141
**e** info@redfootlea.co.uk  **w** redfootlea.co.uk

Tastefully converted farm steading, situated on outskirts of Alnwick within easy reach of the castle, gardens and coastal route. Ground-floor accommodation.

**open** All year except Christmas
**bedrooms** 1 double, 1 twin
**bathrooms** All en suite
**payment** Credit/debit cards, cash/cheques

Room 🖾 TV 🖊 ⏣  General 🕹 12 P ⅍ 🗵 🗵 ✲  Leisure ∪ ♪ ⮞ 🚲

AMBLE, Northumberland Map ref 5C1

## Amble In

★★★
**GUEST ACCOMMODATION**

B&B per room per night
**s** £25.00–£30.00
**d** £50.00–£55.00

16 Leazes Street, Amble, Morpeth NE65 0AL  **t** (01665) 714661  **e** stephmclaughlin@aol.com
**w** amble-in.co.uk

Bed and breakfast accommodation in the coastal town of Amble. Steph and Eddy's family-run guesthouse provides a friendly haven for guests to relax and enjoy their stay.

**open** All year except Christmas and New Year
**bedrooms** 1 double, 1 twin, 1 single, 1 family
**bathrooms** All en suite
**payment** Credit/debit cards, cash/cheques

Room TV 🖊 ⏣  General 🕹 12 ⅍ 🗵 ✝  Leisure ♪ ⮞ 🚲 🖼

## Place index

If you know where you want to stay, the index at the back of the guide will give you the page number listing accommodation in your chosen town, city or village. Check out the other useful indexes too.

---

**BAMBURGH,** Northumberland Map ref 5C1

★★★★
**BED & BREAKFAST**
**SILVER AWARD**

B&B per room per night
s £30.00–£50.00
d £55.00–£60.00

## Glenander Bed & Breakfast

27 Lucker Road, Bamburgh NE69 7BS  t (01668) 214336  f (01668) 214695
e johntoland@tiscali.co.uk  w glenander.com

Long-established, quality bed and breakfast. All
rooms are individually and tastefully furnished
with hospitality tray, hairdryer, colour TV.
Selected in the top 20 Good Bed and Breakfast
Guide 2004, published by Which? Books.

**open** All year except Christmas
**bedrooms** 2 double, 1 twin
**bathrooms** All en suite
**payment** Cash/cheques

Room 📺 ♿ 🐾   General 👥 ✂

---

**BAMBURGH,** Northumberland Map ref 5C1

★★★★
**BED & BREAKFAST**

B&B per room per night
d £65.00–£75.00

## Squirrel Cottage

1 Friars Court, Bamburgh NE69 7AE  t (01668) 214494  e theturnbulls2k@btinternet.com
w holidaynorthumbria.co.uk

Established quality accommodation. All rooms
with sea or castle view. A short stroll to the
magnificent castle and beaches.

**open** All year except Christmas and New Year
**bedrooms** 2 double, 1 twin
**bathrooms** 2 en suite, 1 private
**payment** Cash/cheques

Room 📺 ♿ 🐾   General 👥 P ✂ 🍽 🏠 ✿

---

**BARDON MILL,** Northumberland Map ref 5B2

★★★★
**BED & BREAKFAST**

B&B per room per night
s £36.00–£45.00
d £60.00–£75.00

## Maple Lodge Bed and Breakfast

Birkshaw, Bardon Mill, Hexham NE47 7JL  t (01434) 344365  e rosearmstrong@tiscali.co.uk
w maplelodge-hadrianswall.co.uk

Maple Lodge is a 16thC bastle house next to
Vindolanda. An ideal base to visit Hadrian's Wall
and Northumberland's many attractions. A warm
welcome with wonderful views.

**open** All year
**bedrooms** 1 double, 1 single, 1 family
**bathrooms** All en suite
**payment** Cash/cheques

Room 🛏 📺 ♿ 🐾   General 👥 ♿ P ✂ 🍽 ✿   Leisure ✈ ▶ 🚲 🏛

---

**BARDON MILL,** Northumberland Map ref 5B2

★★★
**INN**

B&B per room per night
s £25.00–£30.00
d £50.00–£75.00
Evening meal per person
£6.50–£14.75

## Twice Brewed Inn

Bardon Mill, Hexham NE47 7AN  t (01434) 344534  e info@twicebrewedinn.co.uk
w twicebrewedinn.co.uk

**open** All year except Christmas
**bedrooms** 6 double, 6 twin, 2 single
**bathrooms** 6 en suite
**payment** Credit/debit cards, cash/cheques

Family-run inn situated 0.5 miles from Hadrian's Wall
offering accommodation, a warm welcome, good
food, real ales, breathtaking views and wide-open
spaces. Centrally placed for visits to Scotland,
Cumbria and the North East (all within one hour's
drive).

⊕ Situated North of Bardon Mill on B6318 adjacent to youth
  hostel and National Park information centre. 7 miles east of
  Greenhead, 3 miles west of Housesteads.

♥ Biannual bridge weekend held first weekend in Mar and
  first weekend in Nov.

Room ♿   General 👥 🏢 ♿ P ✂ 🍺 ✕ 🍽 🏠 👥 ✿   Leisure ∪ ▶ 🚲 🏛

---

## Key to symbols
Open the back flap for a key to symbols.

---

**BARNARD CASTLE,** County Durham Map ref 5B3

★★★★
**GUEST ACCOMMODATION**
**SILVER AWARD**

B&B per room per night
s £42.00–£46.00
d £65.00–£70.00

# Crich House Bed & Breakfast

94 Galgate, Barnard Castle DL12 8BJ  t (01833) 630357  e info@crich-house.co.uk
w crich-house.co.uk

Beautiful Victorian family house close to centre of town, offering luxurious bedrooms with attention to detail. Wonderful breakfasts using local produce, all making for a warm and friendly stay.

**open** All year except Christmas and New Year
**bedrooms** 1 double, 1 twin
**bathrooms** All en suite
**payment** Cash/cheques

Room TV ♿ ⚲  General ♨6 ⚥ ⌂ ✿

---

**BEAL,** Northumberland Map ref 5B1

★★★
**GUEST ACCOMMODATION**

B&B per room per night
s  Min £30.00
d  Min £56.00

# Brock Mill Farmhouse

Brock Mill, Beal, Berwick-upon-Tweed TD15 2PB  t (01289) 381283 & 07889 099517
f (01289) 381283  e brockmillfarmhouse@btinternet.com  w lindisfarne.org.uk/brock-mill-farmhouse

**open** All year except Christmas
**bedrooms** 1 double, 1 twin, 1 single, 1 family
**payment** Credit/debit cards, cash/cheques

A 220-acre mixed farm. Peaceful, idyllic surroundings, ideal as a base for touring North Northumberland and Scottish Borders. Quality accommodation with spacious, well-furnished rooms. Residents' lounge. Enjoy our superb English breakfasts or our tasty vegetarian alternatives. Golf and fishing nearby. A warm, friendly welcome awaits.

⊕ About 1.5 miles from A1 at Beal on the Holy Island road.

♥ Midweek deals. Christmas and New Year packages on self-catering basis. Discount for 3 or more nights.

Room ⚿ TV ♿ ⚲  General ♨ ♣ P ⚥ ⌂ ✿ ♞  Leisure ∪ ♪ ▶ ⛵

---

**BERWICK-UPON-TWEED,** Northumberland Map ref 5B1

★★★
**BED & BREAKFAST**

B&B per room per night
d £50.00–£60.00

# 6 Parade

Berwick-upon-Tweed TD15 1DF  t (01289) 308454  f (01289) 308454

Two minutes' walk from golf course, five minutes' walk from seaside, on our doorstep are the historic walls of Berwick and museums.

**open** All year except Christmas and New Year
**bedrooms** 1 double, 1 twin
**bathrooms** All en suite
**payment** Cash/cheques

Room TV ♿ ⚲  General ♨ ⌂ ♟  Leisure ♌ ♪ ⚲

---

**BERWICK-UPON-TWEED,** Northumberland Map ref 5B1

★★★★
**BED & BREAKFAST**

B&B per room per night
s £35.00–£45.00
d £56.00–£60.00

# Alannah House

84 Church Street, Berwick-upon-Tweed TD15 1DU  t (01289) 307252
e steven@berwick1234.freeserve.co.uk  w alannahhouse.com

Georgian town house, originally married quarters of historic barracks. Situated in town centre with walled garden and residential parking. Close to all amenities.

**open** All year
**bedrooms** 1 double, 1 twin, 1 family
**bathrooms** All en suite
**payment** Cash/cheques

Room TV ♿ ⚲  General ♨ ▦ ♣ ⚥ ⌂ ▣ ✿  Leisure ⛵

---

## It's all quality-assessed accommodation

Our commitment to quality involves wide-ranging accommodation assessment. Rating and awards were correct at the time of going to press but may change following a new assessment. Please check at time of booking.

## BERWICK-UPON-TWEED, Northumberland Map ref 5B1

★★★
**BACKPACKER**

Per person per night
B&B £14.95-£29.95

### Berwick Backpackers

56 Bridge Street, Berwick-upon-Tweed TD15 1AQ  **t** (01289) 331481
**e** bkbackpacker@aol.com  **w** berwickbackpackers.co.uk

This excellent hostel has a series of rooms around a central courtyard in the outbuildings of a Grade II Listed Georgian town house. Free internet access. Highly recommended.

**open** All year
**bedrooms** 1 single, 2 double, 1 twin, 1 triple, 1 quad, 1 dormitory. Total no of beds 20
**bathrooms** 2 en suite, 3 public
**meals** Breakfast available
**payment** Cash/cheques

Room 🛏 📺 👤  General 🔥 🕮 ♿ 🛗 ◎ 🎱 ✉ ❄  Leisure 🚲 🏡

## BERWICK-UPON-TWEED, Northumberland Map ref 5B1

★★★
**INN**

B&B per room per night
s £31.00
d £52.00

### The Cat Inn

Great North Road, Cheswick, Berwick-upon-Tweed TD15 2RL  **t** (01289) 387251  **f** (01289) 387251

Seven-bedroom inn situated five miles south of Berwick, providing accommodation, good food and range of ales and lagers.

**open** All year except Christmas and New Year
**bedrooms** 1 double, 4 twin, 2 family
**bathrooms** All en suite
**payment** Credit/debit cards, cash/cheques

Room 📺 👤 🍴  General 🔥5 P🍷✕🍴❄  Leisure ♣ ∪ ⟩ 🚲 🏡

## BERWICK-UPON-TWEED, Northumberland Map ref 5B1

★★★★
**BED & BREAKFAST**

B&B per room per night
s £25.00-£40.00
d £46.00-£70.00

### Ladythorne Guest House

Cheswick, Berwick-upon-Tweed TD15 2RW  **t** (01289) 387382  **f** (01289) 387382
**e** valparker@ladythorne.wanadoo.co.uk  **w** ladythorne.wanadoo.co.uk

Grade II Listed Georgian house dated 1721. Magnificent views of the countryside, close to unspoilt beaches. Large garden, families welcome. Meals available within five minutes' drive.

**open** All year
**bedrooms** 1 double, 2 twin, 2 family
**bathrooms** 1 en suite, 1 private
**payment** Cash/cheques

Room 🍴  General 🔥 🕮 ♿ P ⚡ 🍴 ✉ ❄  Leisure ∪ ⟩ 🚲 🏡

## BERWICK-UPON-TWEED, Northumberland Map ref 5B1

★★★★
**GUEST HOUSE**
**SILVER AWARD**

B&B per room per night
s £35.00-£55.00
d £60.00-£72.00
Evening meal per person
£15.00-£22.00

### The Old Vicarage Guest House

Church Road, Berwick-upon-Tweed TD15 2AN  **t** (01289) 306909 & 07730 234236
**e** stay@oldvicarageberwick.co.uk  **w** oldvicarageberwick.co.uk

**open** All year except Christmas and New Year
**bedrooms** 4 double, 1 twin, 1 single, 1 family
**bathrooms** 6 en suite, 1 private
**payment** Credit/debit cards, cash/cheques

Quiet Victorian luxury awaits you at The Old Vicarage. Enjoy home-baked products on arrival, superb breakfasts, evening meals and a warm welcome from proprietors Maurice and Ruth. Our delightful rooms have lots of character with many original features, ensuring a relaxing and very comfortable stay.

⊕ *Easy access from the A1. See map on website.*

♥ *Sole use of vicarage for special occasions. Murder Mystery evenings. Wildlife/birdwatching trips. Contact us for details.*

Room 🛏 📺 👤 🍴  General 🔥 🕮 P ⚡ ✕ 🍴 🎱 ✉ ❄  Leisure ⟩ 🚲

## Using map references

Map references refer to the colour maps at the front of this guide.

## CORBRIDGE, Northumberland Map ref 5B2

### Broxdale

★★★★
**BED & BREAKFAST**

B&B per room per night
s £25.00–£30.00
d £50.00–£60.00

Station Road, Corbridge NE45 5AY  t (01434) 632492  e mike@broxdale.co.uk

Bed and breakfast accommodation within the historic and picturesque village of Corbridge. Close to Hadrian's Wall, Housesteads and other noted Roman sites. The property is tastefully decorated, retaining many original fixtures and fittings.

**open** All year
**bedrooms** 2 double
**bathrooms** All en suite
**payment** Cash/cheques

Room 📺 👜 ৭  General P ⅟ 🏠  Leisure ✈ 🏠

## CORBRIDGE, Northumberland Map ref 5B2

### Fellcroft

★★★★
**BED & BREAKFAST**

B&B per room per night
s Min £30.00
d Min £50.00
Evening meal per person
Min £12.00

Station Road, Corbridge NE45 5AY  t (01434) 632384  f (01434) 633918
e tove.brown@ukonline.co.uk

Well-appointed, stone-built Edwardian house with full, private facilities. Quiet road in country setting, 0.5 miles south of market square. Non-smokers only please.

**open** All year except Christmas and New Year
**bedrooms** 1 twin, 1 family
**bathrooms** 1 en suite, 1 private
**payment** Cash/cheques

Room 📞 📺 👜 ৭  General 🛏 ⅟ ✗ 🏠 ❄ 🐾

## CORBRIDGE, Northumberland Map ref 5B2

### The Hayes

★★★
**GUEST ACCOMMODATION**

B&B per room per night
s £29.00–£32.00
d £58.00–£64.00

Newcastle Road, Corbridge NE45 5LP  t (01434) 632010  e camon@surfree.co.uk
w hayes-corbridge.co.uk

Large, late-19thC country house with splendid views southwards. Set in spacious grounds, in historic village with easy access to Hadrian's Wall, A69 and A68. Family-run.

**open** All year except Christmas and New Year
**bedrooms** 1 twin, 1 single, 2 family
**bathrooms** 2 en suite, 2 private
**payment** Credit/debit cards, cash/cheques

Room 📺 👜 ৭  General 🛏 ▥ ♨ P ⅟ ▥ 🏠 ❄  Leisure ∪ ✈ ▸ 🏠

## CORNHILL-ON-TWEED, Northumberland Map ref 5B1

### The Coach House at Crookham

★★★★
**GUEST ACCOMMODATION**
**SILVER AWARD**

B&B per room per night
d £70.00–£96.00
Evening meal per person
£19.95

Crookham, Cornhill-on-Tweed TD12 4TD  t (01890) 820293  f (01890) 820284
e stay@coachhousecrookham.com  w coachhousecrookham.com

**open** All year except Christmas
**bedrooms** 5 double, 5 twin
**bathrooms** 8 en suite, 2 private
**payment** Credit/debit cards, cash/cheques

17thC dower house with spacious, fully equipped, en suite bedrooms, set in a rustic courtyard. The perfect location to explore the Scottish Borders, Northumberland coast and Alnwick. Offering unsurpassed hospitality in extremely comfortable surroundings. Fine, fresh, home-cooked food with afternoon tea served. Fully licensed. Your home in the country.

⊕ On the A697, 9 miles north of Wooler, 5 miles south of Coldstream. By the turning for Crookham Village.

♥ 3 nights for the price of 2, Nov-Feb.

Room 🛁 📞 📺 👜 ৭  General 🛏 ▥ ♨ P ⅟ 🍷 ▥ 🏠 🎿 ▣ ❄ 🐾  Leisure ∪ ✈ ▸ 🚲

## B&B prices

Rates for bed and breakfast are shown per room per night.
Double room prices are usually based on two people sharing the room.

## CRASTER, Northumberland Map ref 5C1

★★★

**BED & BREAKFAST**

B&B per room per night
d Min £50.00

### Howick Scar Farmhouse

Craster, Alnwick NE66 3SU  t (01665) 576665  f (01665) 576665  e howick.scar@virgin.net
w howickscar.co.uk

Comfortable farmhouse with television lounge.
Sea view from bedrooms. Shared bathroom.
Seven miles from Alnwick between Craster and
Howick on the coast. Lovely scenery and walks.
Open April to October.

**bedrooms** 2 double
**payment** Cash/cheques

Room ♿ ☕  General ☺12 P ⚡ ⏴ 🍴 ✳  Leisure ▶ 🏊

## CROOK, County Durham Map ref 5C2

★★★

**BED & BREAKFAST**

B&B per room per night
s £42.00–£48.00
d £53.00–£66.00

### Dowfold House

Low Jobs Hill, Crook DL15 9AB  t (01388) 762473  e enquiries@dowfoldhouse.co.uk
w dowfoldhouse.co.uk

Dowfold House is in a quiet location overlooking
Crook, with stunning views over Weardale and
the Pennines. We welcome tourers, cyclists,
walkers, dogs and children. People keep coming
back!

**open** All year
**bedrooms** 1 double, 2 twin
**bathrooms** 2 en suite, 1 private
**payment** Cash/cheques, euros

Room 📺 ♿ ☕  General ☺ ⏴ ♣ P ⚡ 🍴 ⟲ ☀ ✳ 🐕  Leisure ∪ ♪ ▶ 🚲 🏊

## DARLINGTON, Tees Valley Map ref 5C3

★★★

**INN**

B&B per room per night
s £30.00–£35.00
d £45.00–£50.00

### Boot & Shoe

Church Row, Darlington DL1 5QD  t (01325) 287501  f (01325) 287501
e enquiries@bootandshoe.com  w bootandshoe.com

A Grade II Listed building situated on Darlington's
busy marketplace, fully refurbished in 2000. Only
minutes away from train and bus station, and A1.

**open** All year except Christmas
**bedrooms** 5 double, 2 twin, 2 family
**bathrooms** 7 en suite
**payment** Credit/debit cards, cash/cheques

Room 📺 ♿  General ☺ 🍽 ⏴ 🐕

## DARLINGTON, Tees Valley Map ref 5C3

★★★

**GUEST HOUSE**

B&B per room per night
s £30.00–£35.00
d £52.00–£58.00

### Harewood Lodge

40 Grange Road, Darlington DL1 5NP  t (01325) 358152  f (01325) 244432
e harewood.lodge@ntlworld.com  w harewood-lodge.co.uk

Harewood Lodge is a friendly, family-run,
Victorian town house five- to ten-minutes' walk to
town. All rooms are en suite and have tea/coffee
facilities and colour TV.

**open** All year except Christmas
**bedrooms** 4 double, 3 twin, 4 single, 3 family
**bathrooms** 10 en suite, 1 private
**payment** Cash/cheques

Room 📺 ♿ ☕  General ☺ ⏴ ♣ ⚡ 🍴 ☀ 🐕

## DURHAM, County Durham Map ref 5C2

★★★

**GUEST HOUSE**

B&B per room per night
s £35.00–£45.00
d £45.00–£55.00

### Burnhope Lodge Guest House

1 Wrights Way, Burnhope, Durham DH7 0DL  t (01207) 529596  f (01207) 529596

Relaxing, family-run guesthouse. TV, tea and
coffee in rooms, en suite facilities, private parking,
non-smoking rooms. Twins can be let as singles,
and family room can be let as double.

**open** All year except Christmas and New Year
**bedrooms** 2 twin, 1 family
**bathrooms** All en suite
**payment** Credit/debit cards, cash/cheques

Room ♿ 📺 ♿ ☕  General ☺ ♣ P  Leisure ∪ ♪ ▶ 🚲

## If you have access needs...

Look for the National Accessible Scheme symbols if you have special hearing,
visual or mobility needs.

**DURHAM,** County Durham Map ref 5C2

★★★★
GUEST ACCOMMODATION

B&B per room per night
s  £50.00–£60.00
d  £75.00–£80.00

## Castle View Guest House

4 Crossgate, Durham DH1 4PS  **t** (0191) 386 8852  **e** castle_view@hotmail.com  **w** castle-view.co.uk

Two-hundred-and-fifty-year-old listed building in the heart of the old city, with woodland and riverside walks and a magnificent view of the cathedral and castle.

**open** All year except Christmas and New Year
**bedrooms** 3 double, 2 twin, 1 single
**bathrooms** All en suite
**payment** Credit/debit cards, cash/cheques

Room 📺 👐 🖎  General ☎2 ⅍ 🄼 ✿

**DURHAM,** County Durham Map ref 5C2

★★★★
GUEST ACCOMMODATION
SILVER AWARD

B&B per room per night
s  £60.00–£85.00
d  £80.00–£90.00

## Cathedral View Town House

212 Gilesgate, Durham DH1 1QN  **t** (0191) 386 9566  **e** cathedralview@hotmail.com  **w** cathedralview.com

Georgian town house in conservation area of city. Close to restaurants, shops and theatre. 10 minutes' walk to castle and cathedral. Elevated position with panoramic views of cathedral and surrounding countryside.

**open** All year
**bedrooms** 4 double, 2 twin
**bathrooms** All en suite
**payment** Credit/debit cards, cash/cheques

Room ⬚ 📺 👐 🖎  General ⅍ 🛏 🄼 ⟲ ✿

**DURHAM,** County Durham Map ref 5C2

★★★
INN

B&B per room per night
s  £45.00
d  £65.00
Evening meal per person
£2.50–£15.00

## Garden House

North Road, Durham DH1 4NQ  **t** (0191) 384 3460  **f** (0191) 384 3460

Family-run business within walking distance of Durham city centre. Traditional bar menu and top quality Four Seasons Conservatory menu. A very warm welcome to all visitors.

**open** All year
**bedrooms** 2 double, 3 family
**bathrooms** All en suite
**payment** Credit/debit cards, cash/cheques

Room 📺 👐 🖎  General ☎ 🛏 🉐 P ♟ ✕ 🛏 🄼 🖵 ✿  Leisure ♠ ↑ 🚲 🏛

**DURHAM,** County Durham Map ref 5C2

★★★
GUEST ACCOMMODATION

B&B per room per night
s  £35.00
d  £60.00–£70.00

## Hillrise Guest House

13 Durham Road West, Bowburn, Durham DH6 5AU  **t** (0191) 377 0302  **f** (0191) 377 0898  **e** enquiries@hill-rise.com  **w** hill-rise.com

Conveniently placed 200yds from junction 61 A1(M). Family, twin and double rooms with en suite facilities. Friendly atmosphere and a high standard of cleanliness.

**open** All year
**bedrooms** 2 double, 2 twin, 1 family
**bathrooms** All en suite
**payment** Credit/debit cards, cash, euros

Room ⬚ 📺 👐 🖎  General ☎12 ⅍ 🛏 🄼 ✿  Leisure 🏛

# Check the maps

Colour maps at the front pinpoint all the cities, towns and villages where you will find accommodation entries in the regional sections. Pick your location and then refer to the place index at the back to find the page number.

**DURHAM,** County Durham Map ref 5C2

★★
GUEST ACCOMMODATION

B&B per room per night
s  £25.00–£32.00
d  £40.00–£50.00

# St Chad's College

18 North Bailey, Durham DH1 3RH  **t** (0191) 334 3358  **f** (0191) 334 3371
**e** St-Chads.www@durham.ac.uk  **w** dur.ac.uk/StChads

**open** All year except Christmas
**bedrooms** 3 double, 40 twin, 66 single
**bathrooms** 23 en suite
**payment** Credit/debit cards, cash/cheques

In the heart of historic Durham, adjacent to the castle and cathedral, designated a World Heritage Site. Comfortable and convenient accommodation, friendly service.

⊕ *Follow the A1(M) until the A690, direct to Durham, through the marketplace towards cathedral. The college lies opposite the rose window of Durham Cathedral.*

Room 🖤 💧  General 👜 🛏 🔥 🍽 ✕ 🎱 ♨ 💻 ✿  Leisure ✦ ▶ 🏊

**DURHAM,** County Durham Map ref 5C2

★★
GUEST ACCOMMODATION

B&B per room per night
s  £24.00–£27.00
d  £24.00–£27.00

# St Johns College

3 South Bailey, Durham DH1 3RJ  **t** (0191) 334 3877  **f** (0191) 334 3501  **e** s.l.hobson@durham.ac.uk
**w** durham.ac.uk/st-johns.college

Located in the heart of Durham City alongside the cathedral, St John's offers accommodation in distinctive, historic buildings with riverside gardens.

**open** All year except Christmas and New Year
**bedrooms** 9 twin, 36 single
**payment** Credit/debit cards, cash/cheques

Room 🖤 💧  General 👜 🛏 🍽 ✕ 🎱 ♨ 🔥 💻 ✿  Leisure 🏊

**DURHAM,** County Durham Map ref 5C2

★★★
INN

B&B per room per night
s  £50.00–£65.00
d  £65.00–£85.00
Evening meal per person
£6.95–£27.50

# Seven Stars Inn

High Street North, Shincliffe, Durham DH1 2NU  **t** (0191) 3848454  **f** (0191) 3741173
**e** info@sevenstarsinn.co.uk  **w** sevenstarsinn.co.uk

**open** All year
**bedrooms** 4 double, 1 twin, 2 single, 1 family
**bathrooms** All en suite
**payment** Credit/debit cards, cash/cheques

Charming old coaching inn, built in 1724, one mile from Durham City. Eight individually decorated rooms, each with en suite shower room, TV and tea-/coffee-making facilities. Excellent reputation for food. Entry in Good Pub Guide 2003.

⊕ *From A1(M) follow A177 signposted Bowburn and Peterlee. Off at Durham service station.*

♥ *See our website for offers.*

Room 📺 💧 🍴  General 👜 🛏 🔥 🍽 ✕ ✿

**GREENHAUGH,** Northumberland Map ref 5B2

★★★
INN

B&B per room per night
s  £37.00
d  £54.00
Evening meal per person
£7.95–£16.95

# Hollybush Inn

Greenhaugh, Hexham NE48 1PW  **t** (01434) 240391  **e** timmorris.hollybush@virgin.net
**w** thehollybushinn.co.uk

A 200-year-old inn with original beamed ceilings, open log fire and cosy atmosphere. Convenient for Kielder Water, Hadrian's Wall and the Borders.

**open** All year except Christmas
**bedrooms** 3 double
**bathrooms** All en suite
**payment** Credit/debit cards, cash/cheques

Room 💧 🍴  General 👜 🛏 🔥 🍽 ✕ 🎱 💻 ✿ 🐾  Leisure ✦ 🚲 🏊

## HALTWHISTLE, Northumberland Map ref 5B2

**★★★★**
BED & BREAKFAST

B&B per room per night
s £26.00–£40.00
d £55.00

# Hall Meadows

Main Street, Haltwhistle NE49 0AZ  t (01434) 321021  f (01434) 321021

Built in 1888, a large family house with pleasant garden in the centre of town. Ideally placed for Hadrian's Wall and close to bus and rail connections.

**open** All year except Christmas and New Year
**bedrooms** 2 double, 1 twin
**bathrooms** 2 en suite
**payment** Cash/cheques

Room 📺 ♿ ⏰  General 👁 P 🛇 🍴 🅿 ❄

## HAMSTERLEY, County Durham Map ref 5B2

**★★★★**
BED & BREAKFAST
SILVER AWARD

B&B per room per night
s Min £35.00
d £50.00–£55.00

# Hamsterley B&B

Fern Lea, Hamsterley, Bishop Auckland DL13 3PT  t (01388) 488056 & 07710 908735
w hamsterleybedandbreakfast.co.uk

Hamsterley B&B is fully equipped and furnished to the highest standards. Situated in a beautiful village near Raby Castle, Durham Cathedral and Hamsterley Forest for walking and mountain biking.

**open** All year except Christmas and New Year
**bedrooms** 1 double, 1 twin
**bathrooms** All en suite
**payment** Cash/cheques

Room 📠 📺 ♿ ⏰  General 👁 ♨ P 🛇 🍴 🔲 ❄  Leisure ∪ ♣ ▶ 🚴 ⛵

## HAMSTERLEY FOREST

*See under Barnard Castle, Crook*

## HARBOTTLE, Northumberland Map ref 5B1

**★★★★**
BED & BREAKFAST

B&B per room per night
s £23.00–£25.00
d £46.00–£50.00

# Parsonside Bed & Breakfast

Newton Farm, Harbottle, Morpeth NE65 7DP  t (01669) 650275  e carolyn.graham@harbottle.net

Parsonside is situated in the Upper Coquet Valley, close to Alwinton village. A peaceful setting with a large garden.

**open** All year except Christmas and New Year
**bedrooms** 1 double, 1 twin
**bathrooms** All en suite
**payment** Cash/cheques

Room 📠 ♿ ⏰  General 👁 🅿 ❄

## HARTLEPOOL, Tees Valley Map ref 5C2

**★★★★**
FARMHOUSE

B&B per room per night
s £30.00
d £50.00–£55.00

# Catlow Hall

Catlow Hall Farm, Hart Bushes, South Wingate TS28 5NJ  t (01429) 836275  f (01429) 836275
e margery.shotton@btinternet.com

17thC country house with panoramic views of open countryside. Extensive gardens, ponds and wildlife. All rooms are en suite with TV and refreshments.

**open** All year except Christmas and New Year
**bedrooms** 2 double, 1 single
**bathrooms** All en suite
**payment** Cash/cheques

Room 📺 ♿ ⏰  General 👁4 P 🛇 🍴 🅿 🔲 ❄

# Get on the road

Take yourself on a journey through England's historic towns and villages, past stunning coastlines and beautiful countryside with VisitBritain's series of inspirational touring guides. You can purchase the guides from good bookshops and online at visitbritaindirect.com.

---

**HAYDON BRIDGE,** Northumberland Map ref 5B2

★★★★
**BED & BREAKFAST**

B&B per room per night
s £30.00–£33.00
d £60.00–£66.00
Evening meal per person
Min £15.00

## Grindon Cartshed

Haydon Bridge, Hexham NE47 6NQ **t** (01434) 684273 **f** (01434) 684273
**e** cartshed@grindon.force9.co.uk **w** grindon-cartshed.co.uk

**open** All year
**bedrooms** 1 double, 2 twin
**bathrooms** All en suite
**payment** Credit/debit cards, cash/cheques

A warm welcome awaits at the beautifully converted cartshed, within walking distance of Hadrian's Wall. Ideal location for touring. Licensed and offering delicious meals prepared from local produce.

⊕ *Four miles north of Haydon Bridge, 3 miles east of Housesteads, 7 miles west of Chollerford.*

♥ *3 or more nights: £27.50 pppn.*

Room 📺 🌡 ⏿ General ⛄ ⚓ P ⚷ 🍽 ✕ 🎱 ✻ Leisure ∪ 🏊

---

**HAYDON BRIDGE,** Northumberland Map ref 5B2

★★★★
**BED & BREAKFAST**

B&B per room per night
s £29.00–£39.00
d £58.00–£70.00

## The Reading Rooms

2 Church Street, Hexham NE47 6JG **t** (01434) 688199 **f** (01434) 688999
**e** thereadingrooms@aol.com **w** thereadingroomshaydonbridge.co.uk

Large en suite rooms furnished to a high standard with TV and drinks. Ideally suited for touring on foot, cycle or by car.

**open** All year
**bedrooms** 2 double, 1 twin
**bathrooms** All en suite
**payment** Credit/debit cards, cash/cheques

Room 🛏 📺 🌡 ⏿ General ⛄ 🏛 🛗 ⚷ ▣ Leisure 🏊

---

**HEXHAM,** Northumberland Map ref 5B2

★★★★
**FARMHOUSE**

B&B per room per night
s £30.00–£40.00
d £60.00–£90.00
Evening meal per person
£12.00–£15.00

## HallBarns B&B

Simonburn, Hexham NE48 3AQ **t** (01434) 681419 & 07788 998959
**e** enquiries@hallbarns-simonburn.co.uk **w** hallbarns-simonburn.co.uk

**open** All year
**bedrooms** 2 twin, 1 family
**bathrooms** 2 en suite, 1 private
**payment** Cash/cheques

A welcoming and friendly stay awaits you in a tranquil and peaceful setting with scenic views near Hadrian's Wall, the National Park and historic Corbridge. Garden in which to relax and enjoy the sunsets or have a barbecue. Comfortable lounge with log fire, quality en suite rooms. Hearty breakfast.

⊕ *A69 to Hexham, A6079 at Acomb. At Low Brunton left B6320. Approx 4 miles left at Nunwick into Simonburn, over bridge left. House up hill.*

♥ *Discounts on 4-day stays or more, excl Sat.*

Room 📺 🌡 ⏿ General ⛄ 🏛 ⚓ P ⚷ ✕ 🎱 ▣ ✻ Leisure ∪ ♪ ⮕ 🚲 🏊

---

## Looking for a little luxury

Gold and Silver Awards are given to establishments achieving the highest levels of quality and service. There's more information at the front of the guide, and an index to all accommodation achieving these awards at the back.

## KIELDER, Northumberland Map ref 5B1

★★
**BED & BREAKFAST**

B&B per room per night
s £28.00–£35.00
d Min £56.00
Evening meal per person
£6.50–£10.00

# Twenty Seven

27 Castle Drive, Hexham NE48 1EQ  t (01434) 250462 & (01434) 250366
e twentyseven@staykielder.co.uk  w staykielder.co.uk

Twenty Seven offers three rooms, bed and breakfast, evening meals on request, TV, tea-/coffee-making facilities. Lounge and snug with wood-burning stove. Cyclists and walkers welcome. Laundry facilities and secure bike storage.

**open** All year
**bedrooms** 1 twin, 1 single, 1 family
**payment** Cash/cheques

Room 📺 ♿ ☎  General ⌂ ▥ ⚥ ✕ 🍴 🅿 ▣ ✿ 🐕  Leisure ♪ ► 🚲 🏊

## KIELDER FOREST

*See under Kielder, Kielder Water*

## KIELDER WATER, Northumberland Map ref 5B2

★★★★

**INN
SILVER AWARD**

B&B per room per night
s £45.00–£50.00
d £80.00–£85.00
Evening meal per person
£8.25–£12.95

# The Pheasant Inn (by Kielder Water)

Stannersburn, Hexham NE48 1DD  t (01434) 240382  f (01434) 240382
e enquiries@thepheasantinn.com  w thepheasantinn.com

**open** All year except Christmas
**bedrooms** 4 double, 3 twin, 1 family
**bathrooms** All en suite
**payment** Credit/debit cards, cash/cheques

Charming 16thC inn, retaining its character while providing comfortable, modern, en suite accommodation. Features include stone walls and low-beamed ceilings in the bars, antique artefacts and open fires. Emphasis on traditional home cooking, using fresh vegetables, served in bar or dining room. Sunday roasts are renowned for their quality.

⊕ *Leave A69 at Acomb junction and travel through Wall, Chollerford, Wark. Turn left over bridge at Bellingham. The establishment is 9 miles up the valley.*

♥ *Reduced rates 1 Nov-30 Apr, DB&B £65pppn.*

Room ♨ 📺 ♿ ☎  General ⌂ ▥ ♟ 🍷 ✕ 🍴 🅿 ▣ ✿ 🐕  Leisure ∪ 🚲

## LONGHORSLEY, Northumberland Map ref 5C1

★★★★★
**FARMHOUSE
GOLD AWARD**

B&B per room per night
s £50.00–£75.00
d £75.00
Evening meal per person
£20.00

# Thistleyhaugh Farm

Thistleyhaugh, Morpeth NE65 8RG  t (01665) 570629  f (01665) 570629  e stay@thistleyhaugh.co.uk
w thistleyhaugh.co.uk

This Georgian farmhouse is set on the picturesque banks of the River Coquet. The organic farm is situated within easy reach of most Northumbrian places of interest.

**open** All year except Christmas and New Year
**bedrooms** 3 double, 1 twin, 1 single
**bathrooms** All en suite
**payment** Credit/debit cards, cash/cheques

Room 🖥 📺 ♿ ☎  General ⌂ ▥ ♟ 🅿 ⚥ 🍷 ✕ 🍴 ✿  Leisure ♪

## LONGHOUGHTON, Northumberland Map ref 5C1

★★★★
**GUEST ACCOMMODATION**

B&B per room per night
s £30.00–£35.00
d £50.00–£60.00
Evening meal per person
£16.00–£20.00

# Chestnut Tree House

7 Crowlea Road, Longhoughton, Alnwick NE66 3AN  t (01665) 577153  f (01665) 577153
e janetholtuk@btinternet.com

Chestnut Tree House provides comfortable bed and breakfast accommodation with twin or double en suite bedrooms and single with private facilities. Situated in a rural location, close to the sea.

**open** All year except Christmas and New Year
**bedrooms** 1 double, 1 twin, 1 single
**bathrooms** 2 en suite, 1 private
**payment** Cash/cheques, euros

Room 📺 ♿ ☎  General 🅿 ⚥ 🍴 ✿  Leisure ♪ ► 🚲 🏊

## MATFEN, Northumberland Map ref 5B2

★★★★
**GUEST ACCOMMODATION**

B&B per room per night
s  Min £35.00
d  Min £70.00

### Matfen High House

Nr Corbridge, Newcastle upon Tyne NE20 0RG  **t** (01661) 886592  **f** (01661) 886847
**e** struan@struan.enterprise-plc.com

Spacious stone-built former farmhouse, dating from 1735, in quiet rural location one mile north of Hadrian's Wall and Trail. Ideal base for local attractions. 18-hole golf course two miles.

**open** All year except Christmas
**bedrooms** 2 double, 2 twin
**bathrooms** 2 en suite, 2 private
**payment** Cash/cheques

Room 📺 ♿ ⌨  General 🛏 📕 ⚓ P ⚡ ❄ 🐾  Leisure ▶ 🏖

## MORPETH, Northumberland Map ref 5C2

★★★
**BED & BREAKFAST**

B&B per room per night
s  £28.00–£45.00
d  £50.00–£58.00
Evening meal per person
£7.50–£9.50

### Cottingburn House B&B

40 Bullers Green, Morpeth NE61 1DE  **t** (01670) 503195  **f** (01670) 503195
**e** veeherbert@hotmail.com  **w** cottingburnhouse.co.uk

5 minutes' walk from the centre of the ancient and historic market town of Morpeth, close to shopping, pubs and restaurants. Excellent food with special dietary arrangements on request, full English and continental breakfasts.

**open** All year
**bedrooms** 1 double, 2 twin, 1 single
**bathrooms** 2 en suite, 2 private
**payment** Credit/debit cards, cash/cheques, euros

Room 🛏 📺 ♿  General 🛏 📕 ⚓ P ⚡ ✗ 🍴 🎿 ☀ ❄ 🐾  Leisure 🚴 🏖

## MORPETH, Northumberland Map ref 5C2

★★★
**BED & BREAKFAST**

B&B per room per night
s  £27.50–£30.00
d  £55.00–£60.00

### Kington

East Linden, Longhorsley, Morpeth NE65 8TH  **t** (01670) 788554  **e** clivetaylor.services@tiscali.co.uk
**w** kington-longhorsley.com

Attractive converted farm building. Rural location six miles north of Morpeth and close to Alnwick Castle and Gardens. Friendly atmosphere, wonderful breakfasts. Suite consists of one double and one twin room, both en suite.

**open** All year
**bedrooms** 1 suite
**bathrooms** 1 private
**payment** Cash/cheques

Room 📺 ♿ ⌨  General 🛏 P 🍴 🎿 ❄ 🐾  Leisure ▶ 🏖

## MORPETH, Northumberland Map ref 5C2

★★★
**BED & BREAKFAST**

B&B per room per night
s  £40.00–£50.00
d  £60.00–£70.00

### Lansdowne House

90 Newgate Street, Morpeth NE61 1BU  **t** (01670) 511129  **e** kitchendiva@gmail.com
**w** lansdownehouse.co.uk

**open** All year
**bedrooms** 2 double, 1 twin
**bathrooms** All en suite
**payment** Cash/cheques

Separate entrance to en suite rooms in Georgian property with walled garden, unique to Morpeth. Quiet rooms at rear of house. Off-road parking. Within walking distance of pubs and restaurants. Organic and locally sourced food used wherever possible.

⊕ Type in postcode to Googlemap for precise directions.

Room 📺 ♿  General 🎿 ❄  Leisure ∪ ♪ ▶ 🏖

**PETS!**
WELCOME
WELCOME
**PETS!**

## Pet-friendly breaks

Want to take your cherished companion with you on holiday? Proprietors participating in our Welcome Pets! scheme go out of their way to make special provision for you and your pet. Look out for the symbol.

## NEWCASTLE UPON TYNE, Tyne and Wear Map ref 5C2

★★★
GUEST ACCOMMODATION

B&B per room per night
s £29.00–£40.00
d £69.00–£72.00
Evening meal per person
£12.50–£20.00

# Clifton House

46 Clifton Road, Off Grainger Park Road, Newcastle upon Tyne NE4 6XH  t (0191) 273 0407
f (0191) 273 0407  e cliftonhousehotel@hotmail.com  w cliftonhousehotel.com

Comfortable, elegant country-style house with private grounds and car park. Close to the city, central for travel, sightseeing and shopping.

open All year except Christmas
bedrooms 2 double, 2 twin, 4 single, 3 family
bathrooms 9 en suite
payment Credit/debit cards, cash/cheques

## NEWCASTLE UPON TYNE, Tyne and Wear Map ref 5C2

★★★★
GUEST ACCOMMODATION

B&B per room per night
s £47.00
d £67.00
Evening meal per person
£5.00–£15.00

# The Keelman's Lodge

Grange Road, Newcastle upon Tyne NE15 8NL  t (0191) 267 1689 & (0191) 414 0156
f (0191) 267 7387  e admin@biglampbrewers.co.uk  w keelmanslodge.co.uk

The Keelman's Lodge is a purpose-built accommodation lodge which stands in its own grounds on the edge of the Tyne Riverside Country Park. Sharing its grounds are the Big Lamp Brewery (listed building) and the very popular Keelman pub, selling good food and real ale on tap.

open All year
bedrooms 8 double, 5 twin, 1 family
bathrooms All en suite
payment Credit/debit cards, cash/cheques

## NEWCASTLE UPON TYNE, Tyne and Wear Map ref 5C2

★★★
CAMPUS

Per person per night
B&B  £24.50–£39.50

# Northumbria University Claude Gibb Hall and Camden Court

University Precinct, Northumberland Road, Newcastle upon Tyne NE1 8ST  t (0191) 227 4027
f (0191) 227 3197  e rc.conferences@northumbria.ac.uk  w northumbria.ac.uk/conferences

Ideally situated just five minutes from the city centre, we offer value-for-money comfortable accommodation. Suitable for individual short stays or social and group bookings.

open mid-June – mid-September
bedrooms 500 single, 15 double/twin
Total no of beds 515
bathrooms 248 en suite
meals Breakfast available
payment Credit/debit cards

## NEWCASTLE UPON TYNE, Tyne and Wear Map ref 5C2

★★★
GUEST HOUSE

B&B per room per night
s £25.00–£30.00
d £50.00–£60.00

# Stonehaven Lodge

Prestwick Road Ends, Ponteland, Newcastle upon Tyne NE20 9BX  t (01661) 872363
e stonehavenlodge@hotmail.co.uk  w stonehavenlodge.co.uk

Stone semi-detached property facing the Cheviots on the Prestwick roundabout, on the A696 to Jedburgh, 200yds past Newcastle Airport.

open All year except Christmas and New Year
bedrooms 1 double, 2 twin, 1 single
bathrooms 2 en suite, 2 private
payment Cash/cheques, euros

## Check the maps

Colour maps at the front pinpoint all the places you will find accommodation entries in the regional sections. Pick your location and then refer to the place index at the back to find the page number.

## OTTERBURN, Northumberland Map ref 5B1

★★★★
**GUEST HOUSE**

B&B per room per night
s £35.00–£40.00
d £60.00–£65.00

# Butterchurn Guest House

Main Street, Otterburn NE19 1NP  t (01830) 520585  e keith@butterchurn.freeserve.co.uk
w butterchurnguesthouse.co.uk

Excellent family-run guesthouse, quiet village location, renowned for its welcome, quality of service and ambience. Situated in Northumberland National Park, route to Scotland, Hadrian's Wall, Kielder Water, coast and castles.

**open** All year
**bedrooms** 4 double, 2 twin, 1 family
**bathrooms** All en suite
**payment** Credit/debit cards, cash/cheques

Room 🛏️📺♨️  General 🅿️⚲🏠  Leisure ∪♪▶🚲

## OVINGTON, County Durham Map ref 5B3

★★★
**INN**

B&B per room per night
s £32.50
d £60.00
Evening meal per person
£7.50–£15.00

# The Four Alls

Ovington, Richmond DL11 7BP  t (01833) 627302

**open** All year
**bedrooms** 1 double, 2 twin, 2 single
**bathrooms** 3 en suite, 2 private
**payment** Credit/debit cards

Privately run establishment offering quality accommodation and food in a quiet and beautiful village setting. Centrally located for exploring local area and places of interest.

⊕ *From A1(M) Scotch Corner, take A66 towards Brough. After 6 miles, turn right to Hutton Magna, through village and on to Ovington.*

♥ *2 nights' B&B £100 – based on 2 people sharing double or twin room. Subject to availability.*

Room 📺♨️  General 8 🅿️⚲🍽️✕♨️  Leisure ✎

## POWBURN, Northumberland Map ref 5B1

★★★★★
**FARMHOUSE**
**SILVER AWARD**

B&B per room per night
s Min £40.00
d £60.00

# Low Hedgeley Farm

Powburn, Alnwick NE66 4JD  t (01665) 578815  f (01665) 578815

Grade II Listed farmhouse with extensive grounds. Situated in the Breamish Valley at the foot of the Cheviot Hills. Ideal base for visiting Cragside, and Alnwick Castle and Garden.

**open** All year except Christmas and New Year
**bedrooms** 1 double, 1 twin
**bathrooms** 1 en suite, 1 private
**payment** Cash/cheques

Room 📺♨️  General 🅿️⚲♨️  Leisure ∪🏠

## REDCAR, Tees Valley Map ref 5C3

**Rating Applied For**
**GUEST ACCOMMODATION**

B&B per room per night
s £20.00–£25.00
d £40.00–£45.00

# Armada Guest House

28-30 Henry Street, Redcar TS10 1BJ  t (01642) 471710  e info@armadaguesthouse.co.uk
w armadaguesthouse.co.uk

Small, friendly, family-run B&B close to all local amenities. Only seconds from seafront, also very close to the town centre.

**open** All year
**bedrooms** 2 double, 5 twin, 5 single, 3 family
**bathrooms** 5 en suite
**payment** Cash/cheques

Room 📺♨️  General ♨️⚲🍽️♨️  Leisure ♪▶🏠

## It's all in the detail

Please remember that all information in this guide has been supplied by the proprietors well in advance of publication. Since changes do sometimes occur it's a good idea to check details at the time of booking.

## REDCAR, Tees Valley Map ref 5C3

★★
**GUEST HOUSE**

B&B per room per night
s £10.00–£15.00
d £20.00–£25.00
Evening meal per person
£5.00–£7.00

# The Kastle View

55 Newcomen Place, Redcar TS10 1DB  t (01642) 489313

Situated on the seafront opposite the leisure centre and golf course, The Kastle Hotel provides good food and inexpensive accommodation.

**open** All year
**bedrooms** 3 double, 5 twin, 5 single, 2 family, 5 suites
**bathrooms** 5 en suite
**payment** Credit/debit cards, cash/cheques, euros

Room 🛏 📻 TV ♿ ⚑   General 👥 🍷 ✕ 🛄 ✿ 🐾

## ROTHBURY, Northumberland Map ref 5B1

★★★
**INN**

B&B per room per night
s £38.00–£45.00
d £65.00–£70.00

# The Queens Head

Townfoot, Rothbury, Morpeth NE65 7SR  t (01669) 620470  e enqs@queensheadrothbury.com
w queensheadrothbury.com

Traditional, friendly pub in the lovely village of Rothbury in the heart of the Coquet Valley. Excellent food, comfortable rooms and great service. Non-smoking bedrooms and restaurant.

**open** All year
**bedrooms** 3 double, 3 twin, 1 family
**bathrooms** All en suite
**payment** Credit/debit cards, cash/cheques, euros

Room TV ♿ ⚑   General 👥 🏬 ♨ P ⚿ 🍷 ✕ 🛄 ✿   Leisure ♣ ✎ ➤ 🚲 🛥

## RYTON, Tyne and Wear Map ref 5C2

★★★
**GUEST ACCOMMODATION**

B&B per room per night
s £25.00–£50.00
d £60.00–£90.00

# A1 Hedgefield House

Stella Road, Blaydon-on-Tyne NE21 4LR  t (0191) 413 7373  f (0191) 413 7373
e david@hedgefieldhouse.co.uk  w hedgefieldhouse.co.uk

**open** All year
**bedrooms** 4 double, 3 twin, 3 single, 2 family, 2 suites
**bathrooms** 5 en suite
**payment** Credit/debit cards, cash/cheques

Georgian residence in three acres of wooded gardens. Sauna and gym facilities. Peaceful, yet only minutes from Newcastle city centre, Gateshead MetroCentre and A1(M). A warm welcome guaranteed.

⊕ From A1(M) take A695 (Blaydon). From Blaydon centre take B6317 (Ryton and Newburn). 1 mile along B6317, on the left.

Room 🛏 📻 TV ♿ ⚑   General 👥 P 🍴 🛄 ✿   Leisure ∪ ✎ ➤ 🛥

## SALTBURN-BY-THE-SEA, Tees Valley Map ref 5C3

★★★★
**GUEST HOUSE**

B&B per room per night
s £35.00–£40.00
d £60.00–£80.00

# The Arches

Low Farm, Ings Lane, Brotton, Saltburn-by-the-Sea TS12 2QX  t (01287) 677512  f (01287) 677150
e hotel@gorallyschool.co.uk  w thearcheshotel.co.uk

**open** All year
**bedrooms** 4 double, 3 twin, 1 family
**bathrooms** All en suite
**payment** Credit/debit cards, cash/cheques

The Arches offers a relaxing environment and overlooks spectacular views of cliffs and golf course. All the rooms are individually furnished with en suite bathrooms.

Room 🛏 TV ♿ ⚑   General 👥 🏬 ♨ P ⚿ 🍷 ✕ 🍴 🛄 ◉ ✿ 🐾   Leisure ∪ ✎ ➤ 🛥

## SKELTON, Tees Valley Map ref 5C3

★★
INN

B&B per room per night
s £25.00
d £45.00

### The Wharton Arms

133 High Street, Saltburn-by-the-Sea TS12 2DY  t (01287) 650618  e p.cummings4@ntlworld.com

Wharton Arms was built in 1878 and is a Grade II Listed building. Village location, two miles from the coast, three miles from North York Moors National Park. About 0.25 miles from Cleveland Way.

**open** All year
**bedrooms** 1 double, 1 twin, 1 single, 2 family
**bathrooms** All en suite
**payment** Cash/cheques

Room 📺 ♿ 🖱  General ⛤ P ‼ ♞  Leisure ♠ ∪ ♪ ⊦

## SPENNYMOOR, County Durham Map ref 5C2

★★★★
GUEST HOUSE

B&B per room per night
s £35.00–£40.00
d £60.00

### Highview Country House

Kirk Merrington, Spennymoor DL16 7JT  t (01388) 811006  f (01388) 811006
e jayne@highviewcountryhouse.co.uk  w highviewcountryhouse.com

Country house in one acre of gardens surrounded by countryside. Peace and tranquillity await. Safe parking. Situated on the edge of delightful village. Good pubs, Saxon church. Ten minutes from motorway/Durham.

**open** All year
**bedrooms** 5 double, 1 twin, 1 single, 1 family
**bathrooms** All en suite
**payment** Credit/debit cards, cash/cheques

Room ♨ 📺 ♿ 🖱  General ⛤ 🎿 ♟ P ❄ ♞  Leisure ∪ ♪

## STANLEY, County Durham Map ref 5C2

★★
INN

B&B per room per night
d £54.00–£60.00

### Oak Tree Inn

Front Street, Tantobie, Stanley DH9 9RF  t (01207) 235445

A beautiful old coach house inn, dating back to the 1700s. Warm and friendly atmosphere and inviting decor. Close to Tanfield Railway and Beamish Museum.

**open** All year
**bedrooms** 2 double, 2 twin, 1 family
**bathrooms** All en suite
**payment** Credit/debit cards, cash/cheques

Room 📼 ☎ 📺 ♿ 🖱  General ⛤ ♟ P ‼ ✕ 🎿 🅜 ❄ ♞  Leisure ♠ ∪ ♪ ⊦ 🏠

## STOCKSFIELD, Northumberland Map ref 5B2

★★★
GUEST ACCOMMODATION

B&B per room per night
s £30.00–£35.00
d £60.00–£70.00

### Old Ridley Hall

Stocksfield NE43 7RU  t (01661) 842816  e josephinealdridge@oldridleyhall.force9.co.uk
w oldridley.co.uk

**open** All year except Christmas
**bedrooms** 2 twin, 1 single, 1 family
**bathrooms** 1 private
**payment** Cash/cheques

Country house with rambling garden, dovecote. Listed buildings. Easy reach of MetroCentre, places to eat, Prudhoe, Corbridge Roman Wall, Newcastle, railway.

⊕ *From A68, south of Tyne at roundabout, east for Stocksfield. B6309 right, signed Hindley. 1st left, then biggest house at end.*

Room 📺  General ⛤ 🎿 ♟ P ✂ 🅜 ❄ ♞

## enjoyEngland.com

Big city buzz or peaceful panoramas? Take a fresh look at England and you may be surprised at what's right on your doorstep. Explore the diversity online at enjoyengland.com

**WALL,** Northumberland Map ref 5B2

★★★
**INN**

B&B per room per night
s £45.00–£50.00
d £58.00–£68.00
Evening meal per person
£6.25–£14.25

### The Hadrian Wall Inn

Wall, Hexham NE46 4EE **t** (01434) 681232 **e** david.lindsay13@btinternet.com **w** hadrianhotel.com

Attractive 18thC former coaching inn. Excellent bar meals, real ales, open fires and tranquil gardens. Situated close to Hadrian's Wall and near Hexham.

**open** All year
**bedrooms** 2 double, 4 twin
**bathrooms** 4 en suite
**payment** Credit/debit cards, cash/cheques

Room 🛏 📺 🕯  General 🛎 🚪 🛗 ♀ ✗ ✿ 🐕

**WHICKHAM,** Tyne and Wear Map ref 5C2

★★★★
**GUEST HOUSE**

B&B per room per night
s £40.00–£50.00
d £65.00–£75.00

### East Byermoor Guest House

Fellside Road, Whickham, Newcastle upon Tyne NE16 5BD **t** (01207) 272687
**e** stay@eastbyermoor.co.uk **w** eastbyermoor.co.uk

17thC stone farmhouse in open countryside. Ideally placed for visiting Hadrian's Wall, Durham Cathedral, Beamish Museum and the Northumberland coastline as well as the MetroCentre and Newcastle city centre.

**open** All year
**bedrooms** 3 double, 2 twin
**bathrooms** All en suite
**payment** Credit/debit cards, cash/cheques

Room 🛁 📺 🕯 🍵  General 🛎 P 🍴 🛗 ✿ 🐕  Leisure ∪ ▸ 🏛

# Walkers and cyclists welcome

Look out for quality-assessed accommodation displaying the Walkers Welcome and Cyclists Welcome signs.

Participants in these schemes actively encourage and support walking and cycling. In addition to special meal arrangements and helpful information, they'll provide a water supply to wash off the mud, an area for drying wet clothing and footwear, maps and books to look up cycling and walking routes and even an emergency puncture-repair kit! Bikes can also be locked up securely undercover.

The standards for these schemes have been developed in partnership with the tourist boards in Northern Ireland, Scotland and Wales, so wherever you're travelling in the UK you'll receive the same welcome.

# Yorkshire

East Yorkshire, North Yorkshire,
South Yorkshire, West Yorkshire

## The land of romantic moors and vibrant cities

Yorkshire is the country's largest region, and it packs plenty in. From its three national parks brimming with breathtaking countryside to its stylish cosmopolitan cities, Yorkshire is big, beautiful and welcoming.

Yorkshire Tourist Board
yorkshire.com
0870 609 0000

Cow and Calf Rock, Ilkley

Boulby Cliffs

Millennium Galleries, Sheffield

York Minster

Yorkshire is blessed with some of England's wildest, most rugged countryside, including the vast expanse of the North York Moors and the dramatic carved valleys of the Peak District. Prefer your landscape a little lusher? Take a relaxing stroll across the rolling Yorkshire Dales or pretty Herriot Country. And you'll fall in love with the Yorkshire seaside whether it's lively resorts or the fossil-filled Heritage Coast. You'll also be in your element if you are into the urban scene. Vibrant cities like Leeds, Bradford, Hull and Sheffield offer designer shopping, Michelin-starred eateries and a buzzing cultural life. And then there's York. It may boast world-famous Viking roots and masses of medieval appeal, but today it also oozes contemporary chic with its continental café bar culture.

One place you won't want to miss is Fountains Abbey and Studley Royal Water Garden. This World Heritage Site features the impressive remains of a Cistercian abbey and elegant ornamental lakes. Or discover the Forbidden Corner, a unique labyrinth of tunnels, chambers and follies in the Dales. It's an unforgettable day out for the whole family. And you can while away a pleasant afternoon exploring the antique shops of historic Harrogate or the Victorian village of Saltaire. Don't miss York Minster, one of Europe's greatest gothic cathedrals, and while you're in York why not stop off at the National Railway Museum?

Yorkshire is a unique mix of influences and inspirational places. It's restful and zestful, forward looking yet founded on a bedrock of traditional values. The people are a friendly, straight-talking lot and take great pride in introducing visitors to Yorkshire's many and varied faces. Plain speaking may be part of Yorkshire's character, but there's nothing plain about this captivating part of Britain. Country or city, trendy or traditional, ancient history or cutting-edge – Yorkshire has it all.

# Destinations

## Barnsley

Barnsley, gateway to Pennine Yorkshire, boasts a rich industrial heritage. You'll also find an exciting mix of entertainment to suit all tastes. Shop for bargains at the 700-year-old indoor/outdoor market, then sample the famous 'Barnsley Chop'. Close by is the RSPB Old Moor, a 250-acre wetlands nature reserve and a superb place to watch wildlife. The surrounding rural villages offer quiet, cosy restaurants and pubs.

## Halifax

If you appreciate outstanding architecture and a thriving cultural life, Halifax is for you. Visit the superb Borough Market, the galleried Piece Hall, and Eureka! the fascinating Museum for Children. Take in a series of exciting galleries including the Henry Moore Studio and the Dean Clough and find a full programme of great acts at the Victoria Theatre.

## Hull

Enjoy the invigorating yet relaxing atmosphere that only a waterfront city can offer. Visit the Museum Quarter linking four of Hull's eight free museums including the interactive Streetlife Museum. Don't miss the £40 million aquarium, 'The Deep', home to 40 sharks and one of the most sea-life attractions in the world. Marvel at the engineering of the Humber Bridge and, after dark, experience Hull's very own café bar culture and take in a show at Hull Truck or Hull New Theatre.

| | |
|---|---|
| 0 | 50 miles |
| 0 | 75 kms |

National Park

Area of Outstanding Natural Beauty

Heritage Coast

National Trails
nationaltrail.co.uk

National Trails approved but
not yet open

3 Sections of the
National Cycle Network
nationalcyclenetwork.org.uk

The Deep, Hull

Leeds

Eureka! Museum for Children, Halifax

Village in the Pennines

The Shambles, York

Whitby Abbey

## Leeds

Experience a combination of fast-paced, buzzing city centre with the serenity of the Yorkshire Dales on the doorstep. Rich local history, world-class sport and diverse year-round entertainment make Leeds a great place for everyone to enjoy. You'll find a shopaholic's dream, from the elegant Corn Exchange to the exquisite Victoria Quarter, not to mention the only Harvey Nichols outside London. See opera and dance at the internationally acclaimed Opera North and Northern Ballet, jousting at the Royal Armouries and outstanding collections in the many museums and galleries.

## Whitby

Visit one of Britain's finest stretches of coastline with cliffs, bays, sandy beaches and attractive villages. Follow Whitby's quaint cobbled streets and climb the steps to the parish church of St Mary, whose churchyard inspired Bram Stocker's 'Dracula'. Then down to the historic quayside of this 1,000-year-old port and celebrate the town's seafaring tradition at the Captain Cook Festival, named in honour of Whitby's most famous son.

## York

The history of York is the history of England. Visit award-winning attractions including the magnificent York Minster, and the world's biggest and best railway museum. Let 21st-century technology transport you back to the Viking age at Jorvik, and wander through the terrifying York Dungeon. Pedestrianised streets make York an ideal city to explore on foot. Follow the city's specialist shopping trails '5 Routes to Shopping Heaven', or browse the specialist antique and book dealers. Then take the weight off your feet in one of the many quaint teashops.

# Places to visit

### Bolton Abbey Estate
Skipton, North Yorkshire
(01756) 718009
boltonabbey.com
*Priory ruins in beautiful setting*

### Brodsworth Hall and Gardens

Doncaster, South Yorkshire
(01302) 722598
english-heritage.org.uk
*Country home of Victorian gentry*

### Brontë Parsonage Museum
Haworth, West Yorkshire
(01535) 642323
bronte.org.uk
*Home of the famous literary sisters*

### Castle Howard
York, North Yorkshire
(01653) 648444
castlehoward.co.uk
*Majestic 18th century house in breathtaking parkland*

### The Deep
Hull, East Yorkshire
(01482) 381000
thedeep.co.uk
*One of the most spectacular aquariums in the world*

### Eureka! The Museum for Children
Halifax, West Yorkshire
(01422) 330069
eureka.org.uk
*Britain's leading interactive museum for children*

### Fountains Abbey and Studley Royal
Ripon, North Yorkshire
(01765) 608888
fountainsabbey.org.uk
*Outstanding 800-acre World Heritage Site*

### Go Ape! High Wire Forest Adventure
near Pickering, North Yorkshire
0870 444 5562
goape.co.uk
*Rope bridges, swings and zip slides*

### Harewood House
West Yorkshire
(0113) 218 1010
harewood.org
*Exquisite Adams interiors and Chippendale furniture*

### The Henry Moore Institute
Leeds, West Yorkshire
(0113) 246 7467
henry-moore-fdn.co.uk
*Beautiful exhibition space housing four sculpture galleries*

### Jorvik - The Viking City
York, North Yorkshire
(01904) 543400
vikingjorvik.com
*Viking history comes to life*

### Magna Science Adventure Centre
Rotherham,
South Yorkshire
(01709) 720002
visitmagna.co.uk
*Extraordinary science adventure*

### National Coal Mining Museum for England
Wakefield, West Yorkshire
(01924) 844560
ncm.org.uk
*Unique museum of coalfields*

### National Media Museum
Bradford, West Yorkshire
0870 701 0200
nmpft.org.uk
*With spectacular 3D IMAX cinema and interactive television gallery*

### National Railway Museum
York, North Yorkshire
0870 421 4001
nrm.org.uk
*See the Flying Scotsman at the world's largest railway museum*

### North Yorkshire Moors Railway

Pickering
(01751) 472508
nymr.co.uk
*Heritage railway steaming through stunning scenery*

### The Norwich Union Yorkshire Wheel
York, North Yorkshire
(01904) 686263
nrm.org.uk
*York's new landmark aerial attraction*

### RHS Garden Harlow Carr
Harrogate,
North Yorkshire
(01423) 565418
rhs.org.uk
*Stunning garden with year-round events*

### Royal Armouries Museum
Leeds, West Yorkshire
(0113) 220 1916
armouries.org.uk
*Jousting tournaments and fabulous exhibitions*

### Sewerby Hall and Gardens
Bridlington,
East Yorkshire
(01262) 673769
eastriding.gov.uk/sewerby
*Country house in dramatic cliff-top location*

### Skipton Castle
North Yorkshire
(01756) 792442
skiptoncastle.co.uk
*Fine preserved medieval castle*

# Diary dates 2008

**Thackray Museum**
Leeds, West Yorkshire
(0113) 244 4343
thackraymuseum.org
*Interactive museum telling the story of medicine*

**Whitby Abbey**
North Yorkshire
(01904) 601974
english-heritage.org.uk
*Moody and magnificent ruins*

**The World of James Herriot**
Thirsk, North Yorkshire
(01845) 524234
worldofjamesherriot.org
*Restored home of the famous vet and author*

**Xscape Castleford**
West Yorkshire
0871 200 3221
xscape.co.uk
*Ice-climbing, assault course and real snow slope*

**York Castle Museum**
North Yorkshire
(01904) 687687
yorkcastlemuseum.org.uk
*England's most popular museum of everyday life*

**York Minster**
North Yorkshire
(01904) 557216
yorkminster.org
*One of the great cathedrals of the world*

**Yorkshire Sculpture Park**
Wakefield, West Yorkshire
(01924) 832631
ysp.co.uk
*Open-air gallery in beautiful grounds*

**Family History Festival**
Kings Hall & Winter Gardens, Ilkley
familyhistoryfestival.co.uk
13 January

**Jorvik Viking Festival**
Various locations, York
jorvik-viking-centre.co.uk
13 – 17 Feb

**Wakefield Festival of Food, Drink and Rhubarb**
Various locations, Wakefield
wakefield.gov.uk
29 Feb – 1 Mar

**Dales Festival of Food and Drink**
Leyburn
dalesfestivaloffood.org
3 – 5 May

**The Great Yorkshire Show**
Harrogate
greatyorkshireshow.com
8 – 10 Jul

**Kettlewell Scarecrow Festival**
kettlewell.info
9 – 17 Aug

**York Festival of Food and Drink**
Various locations, York
yorkfestivaloffoodanddrink.com
19 – 28 Sep

**Hull Fair**
Walton Street, Hull
hullfair.net
10 – 18 Oct

**Dickensian Christmas Fayre**
Various locations, Grassington
grassington.net
First three Saturdays in Dec

# Tourist Information Centres

When you arrive at your destination, visit an Official Partner Tourist Information Centre for quality assured help with accommodation and information about local attractions and events, or email your request before you go. To search for attractions and Tourist Information Centres on the move just text INFO to 62233, and a web link will be sent to your mobile phone.

| | | | |
|---|---|---|---|
| **Aysgarth Falls** | Aysgarth Falls National Park | (01969) 662910 | aysgarth@ytbtic.co.uk |
| **Beverley** | 34 Butcher Row | (01482) 391672 | beverley.tic@eastriding .gov.uk |
| **Bradford** | Centenary Square | (01274) 433678 | tourist.information@bradford.gov.uk |
| **Bridlington** | 25 Prince Street | (01262) 673474 | bridlington.tic@eastriding.gov.uk |
| **Brigg** | Market Place | (01652) 657053 | brigg.tic@northlincs.gov.uk |
| **Cleethorpes** | 42-43 Alexandra Road | (01472) 323111 | cleetic@nelincs.gov.uk |
| **Danby\*** | Lodge Lane | (01439) 772737 | moorscentre@northyorkmoors-npa.gov.uk |
| **Filey\*** | John Street | (01723) 383637 | fileytic@scarborough.gov.uk |
| **Grassington** | Hebden Road | (01756) 751690 | grassington@ytbtic.co.uk |
| **Guisborough** | Church Street | (01287) 633801 | guisborough_tic@redcar-cleveland.gov.uk |
| **Halifax** | Piece Hall | (01422) 368725 | halifax@ytbtic.co.uk |
| **Harrogate** | Crescent Road | (01423) 537300 | tic@harrogate.gov.uk |
| **Haworth** | 2/4 West Lane | (01535) 642329 | haworth@ytbtic.co.uk |
| **Hebden Bridge** | New Road | (01422) 843831 | hebdenbridge@ytbtic.co.uk |
| **Holmfirth** | 49-51 Huddersfield Road | (01484) 222444 | holmfirth.tic@kirklees.gov.uk |
| **Hornsea\*** | 120 Newbegin | (01964) 536404 | hornsea.tic@eastriding.gov.uk |
| **Huddersfield** | 3 Albion Street | (01484) 223200 | huddersfield.tic@kirklees.gov.uk |
| **Hull** | 1 Paragon Street | (01482) 223559 | tourist.information@hullcc.gov.uk |
| **Humber Bridge** | Ferriby Road | (01482) 640852 | humberbridge.tic@eastriding.gov.uk |
| **Ilkley** | Station Rd | (01943) 602319 | ilkley@ytbtic.co.uk |
| **Knaresborough** | Market Place | 0845 389 0177 | kntic@harrogate.gov.uk |
| **Leeds** | The Arcade, City Station | (0113) 242 5242 | touristinfo@leeds.gov.uk |
| **Leyburn** | Railway Street | (01969) 623069 | leyburn@ytbtic.co.uk |
| **Malham** | National Park Centre | (01969) 652380 | malham@ytbtic.co.uk |
| **Malton** | Malton Museum | (01653) 600048 | maltontic@btconnect.com |
| **Pateley Bridge\*** | 18 High Street | 0845 389 0177 | pbtic@harrogate.gov.uk |
| **Pickering** | The Ropery | (01751) 473791 | pickering@ytbtic.co.uk |
| **Redcar** | Esplanade | (01642) 471921 | redcar_tic@redcar-cleveland.gov.uk |
| **Reeth** | The Green | (01748) 884059 | reeth@ytbtic.co.uk |
| **Richmond** | Victoria Road | (01748) 850252 | richmond@ytbtic.co.uk |
| **Ripon** | Minster Road | (01765) 604625 | ripontic@harrogate.gov.uk |
| **Rotherham** | 40 Bridgegate | (01709) 835904 | tic@rotherham.gov.uk |
| **Scarborough** | Brunswick Shopping Centre | (01723) 383636 | tourismbureau@scarborough.gov.uk |
| **Scarborough (Harbourside)** | Sandside | (01723) 383636 | harboursidetic@scarborough.gov.uk |

| | | | |
|---|---|---|---|
| **Selby** | 52 Micklegate | (01757) 212181 | selby@ytbtic.co.uk |
| **Settle** | Cheapside | (01729) 825192 | settle@ytbtic.co.uk |
| **Sheffield** | 14 Norfolk Row | (0114) 221 1900 | visitor@sheffield.gov.uk |
| **Skipton** | 35 Coach Street | (01756) 792809 | skipton@ytbtic.co.uk |
| **Sutton Bank** | Sutton Bank | (01845) 597426 | suttonbank@ytbtic.co.uk |
| **Thirsk** | 49 Market Place | (01845) 522755 | thirsktic@hambleton.gov.uk |
| **Wakefield** | 9 The Bull Ring | 0845 601 8353 | tic@wakefield.gov.uk |
| **Whitby** | Langborne Road | (01723) 383637 | whitbytic@scarborough.gov.uk |
| **Withernsea*** | 131 Queen Street | (01964) 615683 | withernsea.tic@eastriding.gov.uk |
| **York (De Grey Rooms)** | Exhibition Square | (01904) 550099 | tic@visityork.org |
| **York (Railway Station)** | Station Road | (01904) 550099 | kg@visityork.org |

* *seasonal opening*

Semer Water, near Bainbridge

# Find out more

The following publications are available from Yorkshire Tourist Board by logging on to yorkshire.com or calling 0870 609 0000:

- **Yorkshire Accommodation Guide 2008**
  Information on Yorkshire, including hotels, self catering, camping and caravan parks.

- **Make Yorkshire Yours Magazine**
  This entertaining magazine is full of articles and features about what's happening in Yorkshire, including where to go and what to do.

# Travel info

**By road:**
Motorways: M1, M62, M606, M621, M18, M180, M181, A1(M).
Trunk roads: A1, A19, A57, A58, A59, A61, A62, A64, A65, A66.

**By rail:**
InterCity services to Bradford, Doncaster, Harrogate, Kingston upon Hull, Leeds, Sheffield, Wakefield and York. Frequent regional railway services city centre to city centre, including Manchester Airport service to Scarborough, York and Leeds.

**By air:**
Fly into Durham Tees Valley, Humberside, Leeds/Bradford International or Robin Hood, Doncaster, Sheffield.

North York Moors

## where to stay in
# Yorkshire

All place names in the blue bands are shown on the maps at the front of this guide.

A complete listing of all Enjoy England assessed accommodation covered by this guide appears at the back.

### Accommodation symbols
Symbols give useful information about services and facilities. Inside the back-cover flap you can find a key to these symbols. Keep it open for easy reference.

---

**AMPLEFORTH,** North Yorkshire Map ref 5C3

★★★★★
**BED & BREAKFAST
GOLD AWARD**

B&B per room per night
d £64.00–£76.00

## Daleside

East End, Ampleforth, York YO62 4DA  **t** (01439) 788266  **f** (01439) 788266
**e** dalesidepaul@hotmail.com

**open** All year except Christmas and New Year
**bedrooms** 1 double, 1 twin
**bathrooms** All en suite
**payment** Cash/cheques

Listed stone house, cruck beams over 400 years old, in pretty cottage garden in centre of charming village. Private parking. Delicious home baking. Excellent pub/restaurant 80 yards distant. Pleasant walks in surrounding countryside. Abbeys and stately homes nearby including Castle Howard. Pretty market town of Helmsley four miles north; city of York 30 minutes' drive south.

⊕ *From Thirsk take A19 south, following 'caravan route' via Coxwold and Byland Abbey. Drive straight through Ampleforth past White Swan. Daleside is 80 yds further on right.*

Room 📺 🐾 ⏰  General 🛏11 ⚒ ✿  Leisure 🏡

---

**AUSTWICK,** North Yorkshire Map ref 5B3

★★★★
**GUEST HOUSE**

B&B per room per night
s £40.00–£51.00
d £52.00–£74.00

## Wood View

The Green, Austwick LA2 8BB  **t** (01524) 251190  **e** woodview@austwick.org
**w** woodviewbandb.com

**open** All year except Christmas
**bedrooms** 4 double, 2 twin
**bathrooms** All en suite
**payment** Credit/debit cards, cash/cheques

Enjoy the warm, friendly atmosphere of log fires and beamed ceilings in one of Austwick's oldest farmhouses. Wood View is situated in the centre of this typical Dales village and is the ideal base for exploring stunning limestone scenery in the Three Peaks area of the Yorkshire Dales National Park.

⊕ *Off the A65, 5 miles west of Settle. At village green turn past the post office; Wood View is 50yds on the left.*

Room 📺 🐾 ⏰  General 🛏12 P ⚒ 🍴 🗎 ✿ 🐕  Leisure 🏊 🏇 🚴 🏡

## AYSGARTH, North Yorkshire Map ref 5B3

★★★★★
**GUEST ACCOMMODATION**

B&B per room per night
s £35.00–£40.00
d £90.00
Evening meal per person
£15.00

# Thornton Lodge

Thornton Rust, Leyburn DL8 3AP  **t** (01969) 663375  **f** (01969) 663375
**e** enquiries@thorntonlodgenorthyorkshire.co.uk  **w** thorntonlodgenorthyorkshire.co.uk

**open** All year
**bedrooms** 2 double, 2 twin, 2 single, 2 family, 1 suite
**bathrooms** All en suite
**payment** Credit/debit cards, cash/cheques, euros

Thornton Lodge is a beautiful Edwardian mansion with something for everyone. Its setting, within acres of landscaped grounds, woodlands and pasture, offers peace and tranquillity, which visitors find difficult to draw away from. Located in the National Park, there are walks and cycle routes from the doorstep.

⊕ *Located on a spur road off the A684. Thornton Lodge is in open countryside 0.25 miles outside the hamlet of Thornton Rust.*

♥ *Winter breaks available at special rates.*

Room 🛁 📠 TV 🔌  General 🕐 P ✂ 🍴 🎱 ✿  Leisure ∪ ✈ ► 🚲 🛶

## AYSGARTH, North Yorkshire Map ref 5B3

★★★
**INN**

B&B per room per night
s £35.00
d £68.00–£85.00
Evening meal per person
£6.25–£16.95

# Wheatsheaf Inn

Main Street, Carperby, Nr Aygarth DL8 4DF  **t** (01969) 663216  **f** (01969) 663019
**e** wheatsheaf@paulmit.globalnet.uk  **w** wheatsheafinwensleydale.co.uk

Delightful Dales country hotel made famous when the real-life James Herriot spent his honeymoon here. Log fires in winter. Cosy panelled dining room. Some four-poster beds. New luxury rooms added.

**open** All year except Christmas
**bedrooms** 8 double, 2 twin, 1 single, 1 family
**bathrooms** All en suite
**payment** Credit/debit cards, cash/cheques

Room 📠 TV 🔌  General 🕐 🍴 ⅋ P ⬥ ✕ 🎱 �... Leisure ∪ ✈ ► 🚲 🛶

## BEDALE, North Yorkshire Map ref 5C3

★★★★
**INN**

B&B per room per night
s £50.00–£60.00
d £65.00–£75.00

# The Castle Arms Inn

Bedale DL8 2TB  **t** (01677) 470270  **f** (01677) 470837  **e** castlearms@aol.com  **w** thecastlearms.co.uk

**open** All year
**bedrooms** 6 double, 3 twin
**bathrooms** All en suite
**payment** Credit/debit cards, cash/cheques

A family-run, 14thC inn which has been completely refurbished. All twin and double bedrooms are en suite, and have been furnished to an exceptional standard, and include TV and tea-/coffee-making facilities. A warm welcome awaits you, with open fires, traditional ales and real home cooking.

⊕ *From A1 Leeming Bar take A684 to Bedale. Follow B6268 to Masham for 2 miles. Turn left to Arboretum. One mile after Arboretum turn left to Snape.*

♥ *Special seasonal rates available Oct-Mar.*

Room 🛁 TV 🔌  General 🕐 5 P ⬥ ✕ ✿ 🐾

## Place index

If you know where you want to stay, the index at the back of the guide will give you the page number listing accommodation in your chosen town, city or village. Check out the other useful indexes too.

---

**BEDALE,** North Yorkshire Map ref 5C3

★★★★
**GUEST HOUSE
SILVER AWARD**

B&B per room per night
s £50.00–£55.00
d £70.00–£80.00
Evening meal per person
£12.50–£18.50

# Elmfield House

Bedale DL8 1NE  **t** (01677) 450558  **f** (01677) 450557  **e** stay@elmfieldhouse.co.uk
**w** elmfieldhouse.co.uk

**open** All year
**bedrooms** 4 double, 2 twin, 1 family
**bathrooms** All en suite
**payment** Credit/debit cards, cash/cheques

Family-run country house in peaceful, open countryside with long-distance views. Enjoy a drink in the garden or a walk in the grounds with fishing lake and woodland paths. All rooms are spacious and well appointed with en suite facilities. Hearty Yorkshire breakfast using local ingredients. Evening meal by arrangement.

⊕ A684 from Bedale to Leyburn. Turn right at crossroads past church at Patrick Brompton. 1.5 miles on right after turn-off to Hunton.

♥ Seasonal offers and discounts on stays of 7 or more nights – see website. Packages for group bookings – please enquire.

Room 🛗 📻 📺 ⓦ 🍵  General 🛏 🎱 ♿ P 🍴 🍷 ✕ 🎮 🎪 ❀  Leisure ∪ 🚣 🚤

---

**BEVERLEY,** East Riding of Yorkshire Map ref 4C1

★★★★★
**GUEST ACCOMMODATION
GOLD AWARD**

B&B per room per night
s £54.00–£60.00
d £82.50–£89.00
Evening meal per person
£32.50–£36.00

# Burton Mount Country House

Malton Road, Cherry Burton HU17 7RA  **t** (01964) 550541  **f** (01964) 551955
**e** pg@burtonmount.co.uk  **w** burtonmount.co.uk

Burton Mount Country House is a beautiful home, renowned for warm hospitality and delicious home cooking. An excellent location for visiting the East Riding of Yorkshire.

**open** All year
**bedrooms** 1 double, 2 twin
**bathrooms** All en suite
**payment** Credit/debit cards, cash/cheques

Room 📺 ⓦ 🍵  General 🛏 12 ♿ 🍷 ✕ 🎮 🎪 🔍 🖥 ❀  Leisure ∪ 🚣 ▸ 🚴 🚤

---

**BEVERLEY,** East Riding of Yorkshire Map ref 4C1

**GUEST ACCOMMODATION**

B&B per room per night
s £45.00
d £55.00–£65.00

# North Bar Lodge

28 North Bar Without, Beverley HU17 7AB  **t** (01482) 881375  **f** (01482) 861184

The lodge has an outstanding panelled lounge and dining room, where breakfast is served on our 18-place mahogany dining table.

**open** All year except Christmas
**bedrooms** 4 double, 2 twin
**bathrooms** All en suite
**payment** Credit/debit cards, cash/cheques

Room 📺 ⓦ  General 🛏 🎪  Leisure ▸

---

**BINGLEY,** West Yorkshire Map ref 4B1

★★★★
**GUEST ACCOMMODATION**

B&B per room per night
s £50.00–£60.00
d £72.00
Evening meal per person
Min £9.95

# Five Rise Locks Hotel & Restaurant

Beck Lane, Bingley BD16 4DD  **t** (01274) 565296  **f** (01274) 568828  **e** info@five-rise-locks.co.uk
**w** five-rise-locks.co.uk

Named after historic canal locks nearby. Individual and stylish decor, informal atmosphere, an antidote to chain hotels. Victorian stone building in tranquil area, but close to tourist sites, cities, airport.

**open** All year
**bedrooms** 6 double, 2 twin, 1 single
**bathrooms** All en suite
**payment** Credit/debit cards, cash/cheques

Room 🛗 ☎ 📺 ⓦ 🍵  General 🛏 🎱 ♿ P 🍷 ✕ 🎮 🎪 ❀ 🐾

---

## Key to symbols
Open the back flap for a key to symbols.

### BRADFORD, West Yorkshire Map ref 4B1

★★
**GUEST HOUSE**

B&B per room per night
s £25.00
d £38.00

# Ivy Guest House

3 Melbourne Place, Bradford BD5 0HZ  **t** (01274) 727060  **f** (01274) 306347
**e** enquiries@ivyguesthousebradford.com  **w** ivyguesthousebradford.com

Large, detached, listed, Yorkshire-stone house. Close to city centre, National Media Museum, Alhambra Theatre and the University of Bradford.

**open** All year
**bedrooms** 4 double, 4 twin, 2 single
**payment** Credit/debit cards, cash/cheques, euros

Room TV 🌡  General 🛋 ✿  Leisure 🏠

### BRIDLINGTON, East Riding of Yorkshire Map ref 5D3

★★★★
**GUEST ACCOMMODATION**
**SILVER AWARD**

B&B per room per night
s £38.00–£55.00
d £70.00–£80.00
Evening meal per person
£5.99–£23.00

# The Seacourt

76 South Marine Drive, Bridlington YO15 3NS  **t** (01262) 400872  **f** (01262) 400411
**e** seacourt.hotel@tiscali.co.uk  **w** seacourthotel.co.uk

The Seacourt Hotel is located in Bridlington and stands quietly in a prime position overlooking the beautiful south bay with panoramic sea views.

**open** All year
**bedrooms** 5 double, 4 twin, 2 single, 1 family
**bathrooms** All en suite
**payment** Credit/debit cards, cash/cheques

Room 🛁 ☎ TV 🌡 ☕  General 🛋 🏛 🅿 ✂ ♟ ✕ 🛏 ⚷ ✿ 🐕  Leisure ♪ ▶ 🏠

### BRIDLINGTON, East Riding of Yorkshire Map ref 5D3

★★★
**GUEST HOUSE**

B&B per room per night
s £22.00–£23.00
d £44.00–£46.00

# The Waverley

105 Cardigan Road, Bridlington YO15 3LP  **t** (01262) 671040  **e** info@waverley-bridlington.co.uk
**w** waverley-bridlington.co.uk

Small, friendly, family-run bed and breakfast in a quiet residential area close to the South Beach, Spa Theatre and golf course. Parking.

**open** All year except Christmas and New Year
**bedrooms** 2 double, 1 twin, 2 family
**bathrooms** All en suite
**payment** Cash/cheques

Room TV 🌡  General 🛋 🏛 🅿 ✂ 🛏

### CASTLE HOWARD, North Yorkshire Map ref 5C3

★★★
**FARMHOUSE**

B&B per room per night
s £30.00
d £60.00
Evening meal per person
Min £15.00

# Ganthorpe Gate Farm

Ganthorpe, York YO60 6QD  **t** (01653) 648269  **f** (01653) 648269  **e** millgate001@msn.com
**w** ganthorpegatefarm.co.uk

Working dairy farm in quiet hamlet near to Castle Howard, offering friendly, traditional, Yorkshire hospitality. Convenient for the Moors, east coast and York.

**open** All year
**bedrooms** 1 double, 1 twin, 1 family
**bathrooms** 1 en suite
**payment** Cash/cheques, euros

Room TV 🌡 ☕  General 🛋 🏛 🏅 🅿 🍴 🛏 ⚷ ✿ 🐕

### CRAYKE, North Yorkshire Map ref 5C3

★★★
**BED & BREAKFAST**

B&B per room per night
s Min £32.00
d Min £64.00

# The Hermitage

Mill Lane, Crayke YO61 4TD  **t** (01347) 821635

Peaceful location with panoramic views. Overlooking our own farm and the Howardian Hills. Offering a warm and friendly welcome at our comfortable modern farmhouse. Hot tub on patio.

**open** All year except Christmas
**bedrooms** 1 double, 2 twin
**bathrooms** 1 en suite
**payment** Cash/cheques

Room 🌡 ☕  General 🛋 🏛 🏅 🅿 🛏 ▢ ✿  Leisure 🏠

## Using map references

Map references refer to the colour maps at the front of this guide.

## DALBY, North Yorkshire Map ref 5C3

**★★★★**
FARMHOUSE

B&B per room per night
d £54.00–£65.00
Evening meal per person
£10.00–£20.00

# South Moor Farm

Dalby Forest Drive, Scarborough YO13 0LW  t (01751) 460285  e vb@southmoorfarm.co.uk
w southmoorfarm.co.uk

**open** All year
**bedrooms** 1 double, 1 twin, 1 single, 1 family
**bathrooms** 3 en suite, 1 private
**payment** Credit/debit cards, cash/cheques

Quiet rural location on Dalby Forest Drive between Pickering and Scarborough. An excellent base to explore Dalby Forest on foot, bike or horse after a full English breakfast. Packed lunches and evening meals by arrangement. Children's play area, orienteering courses, quad bikes, 4x4 driving and astronomy in Dalby Forest.

⊕ *Follow Dalby Forest Drive (look for brown tourism signs). We are 10 miles from Thornton-le-Dale, 6 miles from Hackness. Grid Ref SE905905.*

♥ *Reduced rates for children under 14 years. Discounts on stays of 5 nights or more.*

Room 📺 ♨ 🍃   General ♨ ▥ ♿ P ✗ 🎱 ♨ 🐾   Leisure ∪ ♨ 🏊

## DANBY, North Yorkshire Map ref 5C3

**★★★★**
INN

B&B per room per night
s £40.00–£55.00
d £68.00–£80.00

# The Fox & Hounds Inn

45 Brook Lane, Ainthorpe, Whitby YO21 2LD  t (01287) 660218  f (01287) 660030
e info@foxandhounds-ainthorpe.com  w foxandhounds-ainthorpe.com

**open** All year except Christmas
**bedrooms** 3 double, 3 twin, 1 family
**bathrooms** All en suite
**payment** Credit/debit cards, cash/cheques

16thC former coaching inn, now a high-quality residential country inn and restaurant. Set amidst the beautiful North York Moors National Park.

⊕ *Turn off A171 Guisborough to Whitby road. Follow signs to Castleton or Danby, then Ainthorpe.*

Room 📺 ♨ 🍃   General ♨ ▥ ♿ P ♟ ✗ 🛏 ✿ 🐾   Leisure ♠ ♨ ∪ ♩ ▸ 🚲 🏊

## DINNINGTON, South Yorkshire Map ref 4C2

**★★★★★**
GUEST ACCOMMODATION
GOLD AWARD

B&B per room per night
d £55.00–£85.00

# Throapham House Bed & Breakfast

Throapham House, Oldcotes Road, Sheffield S25 2QS  t (01909) 562208  f (01909) 567825
e enquiries@throapham-house.co.uk  w throapham-house.co.uk

**open** All year
**bedrooms** 2 double, 1 twin
**bathrooms** All en suite
**payment** Credit/debit cards, cash/cheques

Family-run guest accommodation in a Grade II Listed Georgian property. Three spacious double rooms, all en suite with quality furniture and fittings. Free broadband Internet access. Varied breakfast menu using local produce. Off-road parking. Rural setting within easy reach of Sheffield, Rotherham, Doncaster, Worksop and M1, M18 and A57.

⊕ *From M1 jct 31, take A57 towards Worksop. Left at traffic lights towards Dinnington. At roundabout take Oldcotes exit. We are 1 mile on the left.*

Room 📺 ♨ 🍃   General ♨ P ✗ 🎱 ♨ ✿

## DONCASTER, South Yorkshire Map ref 4C1

★★★
**FARMHOUSE**

B&B per room per night
s £25.00–£32.00
d £46.00–£55.00

# Rock Farm

Hooton Pagnell, Doncaster DN5 7BT  t (01977) 642200 & 07785 916186  f (01977) 642200
e info@rockfarm.info  w rockfarm.info

**open** All year
**bedrooms** 1 double, 1 twin, 1 family
**bathrooms** 1 en suite
**payment** Cash/cheques, euros

A warm welcome and hearty breakfast await you at our Grade II Listed stone farmhouse on a 200-acre mixed farm. Situated in the picturesque stone-built village of Hooton Pagnell, six miles north-west of Doncaster. Five minutes A1 and Brodsworth Hall, ten minutes M62, M1 and M18.

Room 📺 ♨  General ♿ ♟ P ✗ 📓 ✿  Leisure ∪ ⁑ ⌖ ☖

## DUNSWELL, East Riding of Yorkshire Map ref 4C1

★★★
**INN**

B&B per room per night
s £40.00
d £50.00

# The Ship Inn

Beverley High Road, Dunswell, Hull HU6 0AJ  t (01482) 859160  f (01482) 859160
w theshipsquarters.co.uk

**open** All year
**bedrooms** 4 double, 1 twin
**bathrooms** All en suite
**payment** Credit/debit cards, cash/cheques

Ideally situated between Hull and Beverley, this newly opened, all-en suite accommodation nestles in the grounds of a 19thC ale house, with hand-pulled beers, open fires and wholesome food.

⊕ *The Ship's Quarters is located behind the Ship Inn at Dunswell, on the A1174 between Hull and Beverley.*

Room ♨ 📺 ♨ 🍵  General ♿ ▥ P ✂ ♟ ✿  Leisure ∪ ⁑ ☖

## EGTON BRIDGE, North Yorkshire Map ref 5D3

★★★★
**GUEST HOUSE
SILVER AWARD**

B&B per room per night
s £39.00–£40.00
d £67.00–£73.00

# Broom House

Egton Bridge, Whitby YO21 1XD  t (01947) 895279  f (01947) 895657  e mw@broom-house.co.uk
w egton-bridge.co.uk

**open** All year except Christmas and New Year
**bedrooms** 3 double, 1 twin, 1 single, 1 family
**bathrooms** All en suite
**payment** Credit/debit cards, cash/cheques

Broom House is an excellent place to stay. We provide comfortable, en suite rooms and guest lounge. An idyllic setting with views over the Esk Valley. Non-smoking. Visit website for more details.

Room ♨ 📺 ♨ 🍵  General ♿ P ✂ ✗ 🍽 📓 ✿  Leisure ⁑ ⚲ ☖

## B&B prices

Rates for bed and breakfast are shown per room per night.
Double room prices are usually based on two people sharing the room.

## FINGHALL, North Yorkshire Map ref 5C3

★★★★
**INN**

B&B per room per night
s £50.00
d £65.00–£85.00
Evening meal per person
£10.00–£17.00

# Queens Head Bed & Breakfast

West Moor Lane, Finghall, Leyburn DL8 5ND **t** (01677) 450259 **e** info@queenshead-finghall.co.uk
**w** queenshead-finghall.co.uk

A Dales village inn with restaurant and en suite accommodation.

**open** All year
**bedrooms** 2 double, 1 family, 1 suite
**bathrooms** All en suite
**payment** Credit/debit cards, cash/cheques

Room 🛏 📺 👟 ✉ General 👓 🔥 P ⚑ 🎱 🅿 🛋 ☀ Leisure ♠ ♪ ►

## GARFORTH, West Yorkshire Map ref 4B1

★★★
**GUEST HOUSE**

B&B per room per night
s £22.00–£25.00
d £44.00–£48.00

# Myrtle House

31 Wakefield Road, Garforth, Leeds LS25 1AN **t** (0113) 286 6445

Spacious Victorian terraced house between M62 and A1 (M1, junction 47). All rooms have tea-/coffee-making facilities, TV, vanity basin and central heating.

**open** All year except Christmas and New Year
**bedrooms** 1 double, 1 twin, 1 single, 3 family
**payment** Cash/cheques, euros

Room 📺 👟 General 👓 🔥 ✂ 🎱 ☀ 🐕

## GOATHLAND, North Yorkshire Map ref 5D3

★★★★
**GUEST HOUSE**

B&B per room per night
s £36.00–£45.00
d £72.00–£90.00
Evening meal per person
£16.00

# Fairhaven Country Guest House

The Common, Goathland, Whitby YO22 5AN **t** (01947) 896361 **f** (01947) 896099
**e** enquiries@fairhavencountryguesthouse.co.uk **w** fairhavencountryguesthouse.co.uk

**open** All year except Christmas
**bedrooms** 4 double, 1 twin, 2 single, 1 family
**bathrooms** 7 en suite, 1 private
**payment** Credit/debit cards, cash/cheques

Edwardian country guesthouse set in the heart of the North York Moors National Park, in the picturesque village of Goathland. A warm welcome awaits you in comfortable and relaxed surroundings. Excellent breakfasts and traditional, home-cooked evening meals are served in our dining room with panoramic views of the surrounding countryside.

⊕ *Goathland is off the A169 Pickering to Whitby road. Fairhaven Country Guesthouse is situated on The Common between the shops and the church.*

Room 📺 👟 ✉ General 👓 🏠 🔥 P ✂ ⚑ ✕ 🅿 ☀ Leisure 🏛

## GRANTLEY, North Yorkshire Map ref 5C3

★★★★
**FARMHOUSE**

B&B per room per night
s £40.00–£50.00
d £65.00–£75.00

# St Georges Court

Old Home Farm, Ripon HG4 3PJ **t** (01765) 620618 **e** stgeorgescourt@bronco.co.uk
**w** stgeorges-court.co.uk

**open** All year
**bedrooms** 3 double, 1 twin, 1 family
**bathrooms** All en suite
**payment** Credit/debit cards, cash/cheques

Farmhouse B&B with five en suite rooms, all on ground level, situated around a pretty courtyard.

⊕ *Take B6265 from Ripon to Pateley Bridge. Approx 6 miles right turn to Grantley. Kirkby Malzeard and Masham. Up hill approx 1 mile on right.*

Room 🛏 📺 👟 ✉ General 👓 🏠 🔥 P 🎱 ☀ 🐕 Leisure ∪ ♪ 🚲 🏛

## GRASSINGTON, North Yorkshire Map ref 5B3

★★★★
**GUEST ACCOMMODATION**

B&B per room per night
d £58.00–£72.00

# New Laithe House

Wood Lane, Grassington, Skipton BD23 5LU  **t** (01756) 752764  **e** enquiries@newlaithehouse.co.uk
**w** newlaithehouse.co.uk

**bedrooms** 4 double, 1 twin, 1 family
**bathrooms** 4 en suite, 1 private
**payment** Cash/cheques, euros

Family-run guesthouse with spacious rooms. Situated in a quiet location in Grassington with lovely views over open countryside. Ideal base for walking, fishing and visiting the many historic towns in North and West Yorkshire. Large garden with private parking. Closed January to February.

⊕ *Follow the B6265 from Skipton to Grassington. Turn 1st left into Wood Lane. The house is 100yds on the left.*

Room 🛏 📺 ♿ 🍴   General 🐾 P ☼   Leisure ∪ ♪ 🏞

## GREAT AYTON, North Yorkshire Map ref 5C3

★★★★
**GUEST ACCOMMODATION**
**SILVER AWARD**

B&B per room per night
s £55.00–£80.00
d £69.50–£95.00
Evening meal per person
£10.00–£40.00

# The Kings Head at Newton under Roseberry

The Green, Newton under Roseberry, Middlesbrough TS9 6QR  **t** (01642) 722318  **f** (01642) 724750
**e** info@kingsheadhotel.co.uk  **w** kingsheadhotel.co.uk

**open** All year except Christmas and New Year
**bedrooms** 5 double, 1 twin, 1 single, 1 family
**bathrooms** All en suite
**payment** Credit/debit cards, cash/cheques

Tourism NorthEast Bed and Breakfast of the Year 2005. A delightful family-owned hotel and restaurant, situated at the foot of Roseberry Topping. Our individually designed, luxurious en suite bedrooms are developed from two adjoining 18thC cottages oozing character and charm. The guest bedrooms are fitted with the latest facilities, and our restaurant serves a selection of freshly cooked dishes.

⊕ *From A19 exit onto A174. 3rd exit onto A172/171. At roundabout take 2nd exit. Next roundabout take 3rd exit. Follow signs A173 Newton under Roseberry.*

♥ *Business rates available. Winter offers available, from 1 Oct – 31 Mar inclusive.*

Room 🛏 🚪 📞 📺 ♿ 🍴   General 🐾 🏛 ♨ P ⚒ 🍷 ✕ 🎱 🏟 ▣ ☼   Leisure ∪ ♪ ► 🚴

## GUISELEY, West Yorkshire Map ref 4B1

★★★
**BED & BREAKFAST**

B&B per room per night
s £28.00–£30.00
d £55.00–£65.00

# Bowood

Carlton Lane, Leeds LS20 9NL  **t** (01943) 874556

Detached family residence in rural setting. Ideal for walking and within easy reach of Leeds, Bradford, Harrogate and the Yorkshire Dales. A warm welcome awaits at Bowood.

**open** All year except Christmas and New Year
**bedrooms** 1 double, 1 twin, 1 family
**bathrooms** 1 en suite
**payment** Cash/cheques

Room 🛏 📺 ♿ 🍴   General 🐾 10 P ⚒ 🎱 ☼   Leisure 🏞

## It's all quality-assessed accommodation

Our commitment to quality involves wide-ranging accommodation assessment. Rating and awards were correct at the time of going to press but may change following a new assessment. Please check at time of booking.

★★★★
GUEST ACCOMMODATION

B&B per room per night
s £35.00–£50.00
d £70.00–£90.00

## Acorn Lodge

1 Studley Road, Harrogate HG1 5JU  **t** (01423) 525630  **f** (01423) 564413
**e** info@acornlodgehotel.com  **w** acornlodgehotel.co.uk

**open** All year except Christmas and New Year
**bedrooms** 3 double, 2 twin, 2 single
**bathrooms** 6 en suite, 1 private
**payment** Credit/debit cards, cash/cheques, euros

Philip and Ali Standen extend a warm welcome to guests at Acorn Lodge, an elegant Edwardian period property which provides contemporary accommodation to the most discerning of guests. Delightful location in quiet, central, tree-lined street. Private parking. Near conference centre and railway. Four-poster room and whirlpool baths available. Licensed. WiFi Internet. TV/DVD players in all rooms.

♥ *Celebration packs available.*

Room 🛏 📺 ⚲ 🕯  General 🗝 🍴 🅿 ✂ ❗ 🛏 🎮 ☺ ✳  Leisure ♨ ⚓ 🅿 🚲 🖼

★★★★
GUEST HOUSE

B&B per room per night
s £35.00–£40.00
d £65.00–£75.00

## Alamah Guest House

88 Kings Road, Harrogate HG1 5JX  **t** (01423) 502187  **e** alamahguesthouse@btconnect.com
**w** alamah.co.uk

An ideal base to explore North Yorkshire. A short walk to Harrogate's stylish shops, restaurants and Harrogate International Conference Centre. Nidderdale Area of Outstanding Natural Beauty within a short drive.

**open** All year
**bedrooms** 2 double, 2 twin, 2 single, 1 family
**bathrooms** 6 en suite, 1 private
**payment** Credit/debit cards, cash/cheques

Room 📺 ⚲ 🕯  General 🗝5 🅿 🛏 🎮

★★★★★
GUEST ACCOMMODATION
GOLD AWARD

B&B per room per night
d £80.00–£95.00
Evening meal per person
Min £10.00

## Cold Cotes

Cold Cotes Road, Felliscliffe, Harrogate HG3 2LW  **t** (01423) 770937  **e** info@coldcotes.com
**w** coldcotes.com

Situated in a tranquil and beautiful setting on the edge of Nidderdale in the picturesque Yorkshire Dales. Cold Cotes is conveniently located for Harrogate, York and Leeds. Extensive gardens.

**open** All year
**bedrooms** 3 double, 1 twin, 1 suite
**bathrooms** All en suite
**payment** Credit/debit cards, cash/cheques

Room 🛎 📺 ⚲ 🕯  General 🗝12 🅿 🛏 🎮 ✳

★★★★
GUEST ACCOMMODATION

B&B per room per night
s £59.00–£70.00
d £65.00–£75.00

## Lavender House

94 Franklin Road, Harrogate HG1 5EN  **t** (01423) 549949 & 07732 422478
**e** lavenderhouse@ntlworld.com  **w** lavenderhouseharrogate.co.uk

Elegant Victorian residence close to town and five minutes' walk to conference/exhibition centre. Welcoming, friendly service. Non-smoking. Luxury double or twin rooms with brass beds and beautiful en suites.

**open** All year except Christmas
**bedrooms** 1 double, 1 twin
**bathrooms** All en suite
**payment** Cash/cheques

Room 📺 ⚲ 🕯  General 🅿 🛏 🎮  Leisure ♨ 🖼

## Check it out

Please check prices, quality ratings and other details when you book.

## HARTWITH, North Yorkshire Map ref 4B1

★★★
**FARMHOUSE**

B&B per room per night
d Max £60.00

# Brimham Lodge

Brimham Rocks Road, Harrogate HG3 3HE   t (01423) 771770   f (01423) 770370
e neil.clarke@virgin.net   w brimhamlodge.co.uk

Brimham Lodge is a farmhouse located in
Hartwith, close to Brimham Rocks and Harrogate.
On the Nidderdale Way. Features include oak
beams, open fires and friendly surroundings.

**open** All year except Christmas and New Year
**bedrooms** 1 double, 1 twin
**bathrooms** 2 private
**payment** Cash/cheques

Room 📺 ♿ 🍵   General 👥 🏛 🅿 🎱 ✿

## HAWES, North Yorkshire Map ref 5B3

★★★★★
**GUEST ACCOMMODATION
GOLD AWARD**

B&B per room per night
s £55.00–£65.00
d £90.00–£100.00

# Thorney Mire Barn B&B

Appersett, Hawes DL8 3LU   t (01969) 666122   e stay@thorneymirebarn.co.uk
w thorneymirebarn.co.uk

**open** All year except Christmas and New Year
**bedrooms** 2 double, 1 twin
**bathrooms** All en suite
**payment** Credit/debit cards, cash/cheques, euros

Luxurious accommodation in a 250-year-old barn,
two miles from Hawes. Generous rooms with quality
furnishings. Double rooms have full en suite
bathrooms. The disabled-friendly, ground-floor twin/
double has an en suite shower room and private
patio.

⊕ We are at the midpoint of the lane between Appersett, on
the A684, and the B6255, the Hawes to Ingleton road.

Room ♿ 📺 ♿ 🍵   General 🅿 ✂ 🎱 ✿   Leisure 🚣 🚲 🏰

## HAWES, North Yorkshire Map ref 5B3

★★★
**INN**

B&B per room per night
s £25.00–£30.00
d £50.00–£60.00
Evening meal per person
Min £7.50

# White Hart Inn

Main Street, Hawes DL8 3QL   t (01969) 667259   f (01969) 667259   e whiteharthawes@fsmail.net
w whiteharthawes.co.uk

17thC coaching inn with open fires and a friendly
welcome. Superb-quality cuisine and comfortable
rooms. Central for exploring the Dales.

**open** All year except Christmas
**bedrooms** 4 double, 2 twin, 1 single
**payment** Credit/debit cards, cash/cheques

Room ♿   General 👥 🏛 🅿 🍽 ✕ 🎱 🅿 ◉ 🐾   Leisure ♦ 🚣 🏇 🚲 🏰

## HAWORTH, West Yorkshire Map ref 4B1

★★
**GUEST HOUSE**

B&B per room per night
s £25.00–£30.00
d £45.00–£55.00

# The Apothecary Guest House

86 Main Street, Haworth, Keighley BD22 8DP   t (01535) 643642   f (01535) 643642
e Nicholasapt@aol.com   w theapothecaryguesthouse.co.uk

**open** All year
**bedrooms** 3 double, 2 twin, 1 single, 1 family
**bathrooms** All en suite
**payment** Credit/debit cards, cash/cheques

Friendly, family-run guesthouse at the top of
Haworth Main Street, opposite the famous Brontë
church. We are one minutes' walk from the Brontë
Parsonage, and ten minutes' walk from the KWV
Railway. All rooms are en suite, have colour TVs and
tea-making facilities. Enjoy your stay!

⊕ Take the A629 Keighley-Halifax road, turn right at the
village of Cross Roads, follow signs to Haworth (approx
1 mile).

Room ♿ 📺 ♿   General 👥 🏛 🅿 ✂ 🎱 ✿   Leisure ∪ 🏇 🏰

★★★

**GUEST ACCOMMODATION**

B&B per room per night
s £30.00–£40.00
d £50.00–£70.00

## The Bronte

Lees Lane, Haworth, Keighley BD22 8RA  t (01535) 644112  f (01535) 646725
e brontehotel@btinternet.com  w bronte-hotel.co.uk

On the edge of the Moors, five minutes' walk from the station and 15 minutes' walk to the Parsonage, the former home of the Brontës.

**open** All year except Christmas
**bedrooms** 3 double, 1 twin, 4 single, 3 family
**bathrooms** 8 en suite
**payment** Credit/debit cards, cash/cheques

Room  General

★★★★★

**GUEST HOUSE
SILVER AWARD**

B&B per room per night
s £55.00–£75.00
d £65.00–£85.00

## The Manor Guest House

Sutton Drive, Cullingworth, Bradford BD13 5BQ  t (01535) 274374  e michele.cotter@btinternet.com
w cullingworthmanor.co.uk

Large, elegant, Victorian manor house. All rooms are en suite, luxurious and equipped with TV/DVD, hairdryer and tea/coffee facilities.

**open** All year except Christmas and New Year
**bedrooms** 2 double, 1 twin
**bathrooms** All en suite
**payment** Credit/debit cards, cash/cheques, euros

Room  General  Leisure

★★★

**BED & BREAKFAST**

B&B per room per night
d £50.00–£70.00

## Court Croft

Church Lane, Hebden, Skipton BD23 5DX  t (01756) 753406

Five-hundred-acre livestock farm. Farmhouse in village location close to the Dales Way. Ideal for touring the Dales, Nidderdale and Ribblesdale.

**open** All year
**bedrooms** 3 twin
**bathrooms** 2 en suite, 1 private
**payment** Cash/cheques

Room  General  Leisure

★★★★

**INN**

B&B per room per night
s £65.00–£69.00
d £80.00–£89.00
Evening meal per person
£10.00–£25.00

## The Inn at Hawnby

Hilltop, Hawnby, York YO62 5QS  t (01439) 798202  f (01439) 798344  e info@hawnbyhotel.co.uk
w hawnbyhotel.co.uk

**open** All year
**bedrooms** 6 double, 3 twin
**bathrooms** All en suite
**payment** Credit/debit cards

Situated in an unspoilt village in the heart of the North York Moors National Park, offering spectacular views from its hill-top location. Exceptional en suite bedrooms. A peaceful, relaxing break at any time of year. Easy access for hiking, climbing, horse-riding, hang-gliding and stately homes. York 45 miles.

♥ *3-night stay: £80 per room per night at any time.*

Room  General  Leisure

## Looking for a little luxury

Gold and Silver Awards are given to establishments achieving the highest levels of quality and service. There's more information at the front of the guide, and an index to all accommodation achieving these awards at the back.

## HELMSLEY, North Yorkshire Map ref 5C3

★★★★
**FARMHOUSE
SILVER AWARD**

B&B per room per night
s £38.50–£40.00
d £77.00–£80.00

# Laskill Grange

Easterside, Hawnby, Nr Helmsley, York YO62 5NB **t** (01439) 798268
**e** suesmith@laskillfarm.fsnet.co.uk **w** laskillgrange.co.uk

Laskill Grange has earned its reputation from attention to detail and personal service. Peaceful, idyllic setting in North Yorkshire Moors. Luxury accommodation in beautiful grounds, with lake, swans, peacocks and ducks. Recommended on the BBC Holiday Programme. Own spring water.

**open** All year except Christmas
**bedrooms** 1 double, 1 twin, 1 single
**bathrooms** 2 en suite, 1 private
**payment** Credit/debit cards, cash/cheques

Room 📺 ♿ 🎇 General 🛁 🏧 🅿 💟 🛌 ✳ 🐓 Leisure 🎣 ♻ 🚣 🏇

## HOLMFIRTH, West Yorkshire Map ref 4B1

★★
**GUEST ACCOMMODATION**

B&B per room per night
s £25.00–£34.00
d £50.00–£56.00

# Elephant and Castle

Hollowgate, Huddersfield HD9 2DG **t** (01484) 683178

Situated in the heart of the Pennines, a traditional local with a friendly welcoming atmosphere. The rooms are all centrally heated and en suite.

**open** All year
**bedrooms** 2 double, 1 twin, 1 family
**bathrooms** All en suite
**payment** Credit/debit cards, cash/cheques

Room 📺 ♿ General 🏧 ✳ 🐓 Leisure 🎣 ⛳

## HORNSEA, East Riding of Yorkshire Map ref 4D1

★★★★
**GUEST HOUSE**

B&B per room per night
s £35.00–£50.00
d £59.00–£65.00
Evening meal per person
£7.50–£20.00

# Wentworth House

12 Seaside Road, Aldbrough, Hull HU11 4RX **t** (01964) 527246 **f** (01964) 527246
**e** mteale@eduktion.co.uk **w** wentworthhousehotel.com

**open** All year except Christmas
**bedrooms** 4 double, 1 twin, 2 family, 1 suite
**bathrooms** 7 en suite, 1 private
**payment** Credit/debit cards, cash/cheques, euros

A family-run hotel set in spacious gardens, offering delightful accommodation with a friendly and homely atmosphere. It is ideally suited to those who are working and require first-class facilities in a peaceful environment. Close to many amenities, rural and city. Away from the crowd in a safe, secure and pleasant environment.

⊕ Take the A165, then the B1238 from Hull to Hornsea. See website for further details.

❤ Fishing, bird-watching and art-themed breaks. Stately-home tours and Murder Mystery evenings. Licensed for civil ceremonies.

Room 🛏 🖵 📞 📺 ♿ 🎇 General 🛁 🏧 🅿 🛌 💟 ✗ 🍴 🐴 🦽 💻 ✳ 🐓 Leisure 🎣 🚣 🏇 ⛳

## HUDDERSFIELD, West Yorkshire Map ref 4B1

★★★
**GUEST ACCOMMODATION**

B&B per room per night
s £35.00
d £45.00

# Cambridge Lodge

4 Clare Hill, Huddersfield HD1 5BS **t** (01484) 519892 **f** (01484) 534534
**e** cambridge.lodge.hudd@btconnect.com **w** cambridgelodge.co.uk

Thirty-four en suite rooms with tea-/coffee-making facilities, telephones, colour TV. Free parking. Less than 0.5 miles from train and bus station. Easy to find on Clare Hill off St Johns Road.

**open** All year
**bedrooms** 11 double, 7 twin, 12 single, 4 family
**bathrooms** All en suite
**payment** Credit/debit cards, cash/cheques, euros

Room 🛏 📞 📺 ♿ General 🛁 🏧 🅿 ✗ 💻

## Confirm your booking

It's always advisable to confirm your booking in writing.

★★★★
**GUEST ACCOMMODATION
SILVER AWARD**

B&B per room per night
s £47.00–£55.00
d £65.00

## Huddersfield Central Lodge

11-15 Beast Market, Huddersfield HD1 1QF  **t** (01484) 515551  **f** (01484) 432349
**e** enquiries@centrallodge.com  **w** centrallodge.com

**open** All year
**bedrooms** 7 double, 7 twin, 4 single, 4 family
**bathrooms** All en suite
**payment** Credit/debit cards, cash/cheques

The Huddersfield Central Lodge is family owned and managed. All rooms are fully en suite. Free Sky channels, free, secure, on-site, overnight parking. Fully licensed bar in refurbished lounge area. Large, newly constructed conservatory. Within five minutes' walk are the Kingsgate Shopping Centre, theatre, bus and train stations.

⊕ *Huddersfield town centre, signs for Beast Market, travel up Kirkgate to traffic lights. Right and sharp right again into Beast Market, 1st left.*

♥ *Discounts available for long-stay or group bookings. Company accounts can be arranged. Self-catering rooms with kitchenettes available.*

Room 🛏 📺 💇 🍵  General ⌂ 🏬 🔥 P 🍽 ✕ 🎖 🏄 🏖 ♿ 🐾  Leisure 🏖

**Rating Applied For**

**CAMPUS**

Per person per night
Bed only £15.00–£21.00
B&B   £20.00–£24.00
Per person per week
HB    £175.00–£210.00
FB    £210.00–£240.00

## Storthes Hall Park

Storthes Hall Lane, Kirkburton, Huddersfield HD8 0WA  **t** (01484) 488820  **f** (01484) 609061
**w** stortheshall.co.uk

**open** July to September
**bedrooms** 1365 single, 52 double/twin
Total no of beds 1417
**bathrooms** 1417 en suite
**meals** Breakfast, lunch and evening meals available
**payment** Credit/debit cards, cash/cheques

With prices starting from just £15.00 per night, we offer quality accommodation at amazing prices. Purpose-built adult/student accommodation. Lounge, shop, bar, gym, sports and conferencing facilities all on site. A wide variety of packages available from self-catering to full board for any size of group. Available July to September.

⊕ *From Huddersfield town centre take Wakefield road (A642) to Penistone road (A629). After 4 miles turn right onto Storthes Hall Lane.*

♥ *Perfect for holidays, training and team-building courses, away days, and residential conferences. Special discounted rates for large group bookings.*

Room 🛏 📞 💇 ✂  General ⌂ P 🔥 🍽 🎖 🏄 ♿ 🍵 🚌  Leisure 🎯 ⚲

★★★
**BED & BREAKFAST**

B&B per room per night
s £27.00–£30.00
d £35.00–£40.00
Evening meal per person
£5.00

## The Admiral Guest House

234 The Boulevard, Hull HU3 3ED  **t** (01482) 329664  **f** (01482) 329664

The guesthouse is located in a conservation area. The building is a spacious, late-Victorian, former vicarage set in a tree-lined boulevard with a newly-restored working fountain.

**open** All year except Christmas and New Year
**bedrooms** 1 double, 1 twin, 2 single
**bathrooms** 1 en suite, 1 private
**payment** Cash/cheques

Room 💇 🍵  General ⌂ 1 ✄ ✕ 🏄 ♿ 🐾  Leisure 🏖

## INGLETON, North Yorkshire Map ref 5B3

★★★★
**GUEST ACCOMMODATION**

B&B per room per night
s £32.00–£34.00
d £48.00–£52.00

# Springfield Country Guest House

26 Main Street, Ingleton, Carnforth LA6 3HJ  **t** (01524) 241280  **f** (01524) 241280
**w** destination-england.co.uk/springfield.html

**open** All year except Christmas and New Year
**bedrooms** 2 double, 1 twin, 1 single, 1 family
**bathrooms** All en suite
**payment** Credit/debit cards, cash/cheques

Detached Victorian villa, large garden with patio down to River Greta. Home-grown vegetables in season, home cooking. Private fishing. Pets welcome. All credit cards are accepted.

♥ *Special terms for 2 or more days: single £32, double £48. B&B £161pp weekly. Plus evening meal £260.50pp. Weekly single supplement £56.*

Room TV 🖥 🍴  General 🛏 ⏰ 🅿 🌽 ✕ 🛏 🐾 🌸 🐕  Leisure ♪ ♭ 🏛

## INGLETON, North Yorkshire Map ref 5B3

★★★
**INN**

B&B per room per night
s £38.50
d £66.00–£77.00
Evening meal per person
£5.00–£15.95

# Station Inn

Ribblehead, Carnforth LA6 3AS  **t** (01524) 241274  **e** enquiries@thestationinn.net  **w** thestationinn.net

Public house with good beer, food and accommodation and excellent views. Centre of the Yorkshire Three Peaks and next to the impressive Ribblehead viaduct.

**open** All year
**bedrooms** 3 double, 1 twin, 3 single, 1 family, 3 suites
**bathrooms** 3 en suite, 2 private
**payment** Credit/debit cards, cash/cheques

Room 🖼 TV 🖥 🍴  General 🛏 ⏰ 🅿 🍴 ✕ 🛏 🌸 🐕  Leisure ♦ 🏛

## KIRKBYMOORSIDE, North Yorkshire Map ref 5C3

★★★★
**GUEST HOUSE
SILVER AWARD**

B&B per room per night
d £75.00–£110.00
Evening meal per person
Min £30.00

# The Cornmill

Kirby Mills, Kirkbymoorside, York YO62 6NP  **t** (01751) 432000  **e** cornmill@kirbymills.demon.co.uk
**w** kirbymills.demon.co.uk

**open** All year
**bedrooms** 4 double, 1 twin
**bathrooms** All en suite
**payment** Credit/debit cards, cash/cheques

Converted 18thC watermill and Victorian farmhouse providing well-appointed bed and breakfast accommodation on the River Dove. Bedrooms (two with four-posters), lounge, wood-burning stove and bootroom are in the farmhouse. Sumptuous breakfasts and pre-booked group dinners are served in the mill, with viewing panel in the floor.

⊕ *From Thirsk, A170 to Scarborough. 1km after Kirkbymoorside roundabout take left turn into Kirby Mills. Entrance to car park is 20m up on right.*

Room 🛁 🖼 TV 🖥 🍴  General 🛏 ⏰ 🅿 🌽 🍴 ✕ 🛏 ▣ 🌸  Leisure ∪ ♪ ♭ 🚲 🏛

## A holiday on two wheels

For a fabulous freewheeling break, seek out accommodation participating in our Cyclists Welcome scheme. Look out for the symbol and plan your route online at nationalcyclenetwork.org.

## KNARESBOROUGH, North Yorkshire Map ref 4B1

★★★★
**GUEST ACCOMMODATION**
**GOLD AWARD**

B&B per room per night
s  Min £75.00
d  Min £99.00
Evening meal per person
Min £25.00

### Gallon House

47 Kirkgate, Knaresborough HG5 8BZ  **t** (01423) 862102  **e** gallon-house@ntlworld.com
**w** gallon-house.co.uk

**open** All year except Christmas and New Year
**bedrooms** 2 double, 1 twin
**bathrooms** All en suite
**payment** Cash/cheques

Overlooking the beautiful Nidd Gorge, Gallon House offers award-winning accommodation and mouthwatering, locally sourced fresh food. Recognised as a unique, special hotel, Gallon House offers individual service in a breathtaking setting. A recent guest said: 'thank you for making your special place our special place too.'

⊕ *Follow A59 through Knaresborough, turning left into the marketplace. Follow the road, turning right into Kirkgate. Gallon House is at the bottom by the railway station.*

♥ *Discounts are available for stays of 3 or more nights. Special midweek DB&B rates.*

Room 📺 ♨ ⦿  General ⌂ ▦ ♣ ♚ ✕ ▨ ⚙ ☂ ♞  Leisure ♪ ⚑ 🏊

## LEEDS, West Yorkshire Map ref 4B1

★★★
**GUEST HOUSE**

B&B per room per night
s  £30.00–£40.00
d  £45.00–£50.00

### Avalon Guest House

132 Woodsley Road, Leeds LS2 9LZ  **t** (0113) 243 2545  **f** (0113) 242 0649
**e** info@woodsleyroad.com  **w** avalonguesthouseleeds.co.uk

Superbly decorated Victorian establishment close to the university and Leeds General Infirmary. Less than one mile from the city centre.

**open** All year
**bedrooms** 2 double, 3 twin, 4 single, 1 family
**bathrooms** 5 en suite
**payment** Cash/cheques

Room ♨ 📺 ♨ ⦿  General ⌂ P ▨

## LEEDS, West Yorkshire Map ref 4B1

★★
**GUEST ACCOMMODATION**

B&B per room per night
s  £27.00–£37.00
d  £39.00–£49.00

### Broomhurst Guest House

12 Chapel Lane, Headingley LS6 3BW  **t** (0113) 278 6836  **f** (0113) 230 7099

Small, comfortable B&B in a quiet, pleasantly wooded conservation area, 1.5 miles from the city centre. Convenient for university. Private car parking. Warm welcome.

**open** All year except Christmas and New Year
**bedrooms** 3 double, 3 twin, 10 single, 3 family
**bathrooms** 13 en suite
**payment** Credit/debit cards, cash/cheques

Room ♨ ☎ 📺 ♨  General ⌂ P ♚ ✕ ▨ ⚙

## LEEDS, West Yorkshire Map ref 4B1

★★
**GUEST HOUSE**

B&B per room per night
s  £30.00–£45.00
d  £55.00–£59.00

### City Centre Guest House

51a New Briggate, Leeds LS2 8JD  **t** (0113) 242 9019  **f** (0113) 247 1917
**e** info@leedscitycentrehotel.com  **w** citycentrehotelleeds.co.uk

Family-run hotel in the heart of the city opposite Grand Theatre and close to all major shops, restaurants and nightlife.

**open** All year
**bedrooms** 3 double, 2 twin, 4 single, 3 family
**bathrooms** 9 en suite
**payment** Credit/debit cards, cash/cheques

Room 📺 ♨ ⦿  General ⌂ ▨ ⚫ ♞  Leisure 🏊

## Take a break

Look out for special promotions and themed breaks. This could be your chance to indulge an interest, find a new one, or just relax and enjoy exceptional value. Offers (highlighted in colour) are subject to availability.

## LEEDS, West Yorkshire Map ref 4B1

★★★
**GUEST HOUSE**

B&B per room per night
s £30.00–£40.00
d £45.00–£50.00

### Glengarth Inn

162 Woodsley Road, Leeds LS2 9LZ  t (0113) 245 7940  f (0113) 216 8033
e info@woodsleyroad.com  w glengarthhotel.co.uk

Attractive, clean, family-run hotel close to city centre, university and city hospital. Twenty minutes from Leeds City Airport. Easy access to M1 and M62. Most of the rooms have en suite facilities and colour TV.

**open** All year
**bedrooms** 6 double, 3 twin, 2 single, 3 family
**bathrooms** 8 en suite
**payment** Credit/debit cards, cash/cheques, euros

Room 🛁 📺 👤 🕯  General 🛏 P ✕ 🗒 ✤

## LEEDS, West Yorkshire Map ref 4B1

★★★
**GUEST ACCOMMODATION**

B&B per room per night
s £49.75–£52.50
d £59.75–£65.00
Evening meal per person
£16.25–£16.95

### Hinsley Hall

62 Headingley Lane, Leeds LS6 2BX  t (0113) 261 8000  f (0113) 224 2406  e info@hinsley-hall.co.uk
w hinsley-hall.co.uk

Set in landscaped grounds, an attractive listed building built in 1867, with a complete internal refurbishment whilst retaining many of the original features.

**open** All year except Christmas
**bedrooms** 49 twin, 1 family, 2 suites
**bathrooms** 47 en suite, 3 private
**payment** Credit/debit cards, cash/cheques

Room 🛁 👤  General 🛏 P ⅄ 🍷 ✕ 🗒 🔥 ✿ 🐴

## LEEDS, West Yorkshire Map ref 4B1

★★
**GUEST ACCOMMODATION**

B&B per room per night
s £30.00–£45.00
d £40.00–£55.00

### Manxdene Guest House

154 Woodsley Road, Leeds LS2 9LZ  t (0113) 243 2586  f (0113) 243 0512
e manxdenehotel@leedscity.wanadoo.co.uk  w manxdeneguesthouse.com

A friendly, family-run hotel in a Victorian house. Convenient for city centre, universities, hospitals, football and Yorkshire cricket. A warm, comfortable welcome awaits you.

**open** All year
**bedrooms** 3 double, 3 twin, 6 single
**bathrooms** 4 en suite
**payment** Credit/debit cards, cash/cheques

Room 🛁 📺 👤  General 🛏 🍷 🗒 ✤

## LEEDS, West Yorkshire Map ref 4B1

★★★
**GUEST ACCOMMODATION**

B&B per room per night
s Min £45.00
d Min £58.00

### Rosehurst

8 Grosvenor Road, Leeds LS6 2DZ  t (0113) 278 8600  f (0113) 278 7417
e gmspencer@spencer-properties.co.uk

A beautiful Victorian mansion set in gorgeous grounds, located close to Leeds University, offering both short- and long-term bookings.

**open** All year except Christmas
**bedrooms** 6 double, 3 twin, 1 single, 1 family
**bathrooms** All en suite
**payment** Credit/debit cards, cash/cheques

Room 🛁 📺 👤  General 🛏 🛋 P 🗒 💻 ✤

## LEEDS, West Yorkshire Map ref 4B1

★★★
**GUEST HOUSE**

B&B per room per night
s £27.00–£37.00
d £40.00–£50.00

### St Michael's Guest House

5 St Michael's Villas, Cardigan Road, Leeds LS6 3AF  t (0113) 275 5557  f (0113) 230 7491
e stmichaelstowerhotel@hotmail.co.uk  w stmichaelstowerhotel.co.uk

Well-presented, licensed B&B, 1.5 miles from city centre and close to Headingley Cricket Ground and university. Easy access to Headingley and the city centre. Warm welcome from friendly staff.

**open** All year except Christmas and New Year
**bedrooms** 8 double, 6 twin, 8 single, 2 family
**bathrooms** 13 en suite
**payment** Credit/debit cards, cash/cheques

Room 🛁 📺 👤  General 🛏 P 🍷 ✕ 🗒

## LEEDS BRADFORD INTERNATIONAL AIRPORT

*See under Bingley, Bradford, Leeds*

## LEYBURN, North Yorkshire Map ref 5B3

★★★★
**GUEST ACCOMMODATION**

B&B per room per night
s  £27.00–£30.00
d  £48.00–£58.00

### The Old Vicarage

West Witton, Leyburn DL8 4LX  **t** (01969) 622108  **e** info@dalesbreaks.co.uk  **w** dalesbreaks.co.uk

**open** All year except Christmas and New Year
**bedrooms** 1 double, 1 twin, 1 family
**bathrooms** All en suite
**payment** Cash/cheques, euros

Four-poster, family and double en suite rooms with all facilities provided. This charming Grade II Listed former Dales vicarage has wonderful views right across Wensleydale. Spacious private car parking. Centrally placed for visiting the Dales, Lake District, Whitby or York. Friends old and new most welcome.

⊕ *Follow the A684 from Leyburn in direction of Hawes for 3 miles. On entering West Witton the property is the 1st guesthouse on the left-hand side.*

♥ *Stay 4 nights for the price of 3, Sun-Thu, Sep-Mar inclusive (mention 'Where to Stay' guide offer).*

Room 🖾 TV 👌 🍵  General 🛏 🎞 🛋 P ✕ 🏠 ✿ 🐾  Leisure 🥾 🚲

## LIVERSEDGE, West Yorkshire Map ref 4B1

★★
**BED & BREAKFAST**

B&B per room per night
s  £35.00
d  £45.00–£90.00
Evening meal per person
Min £13.50

### Heirloom Carriage Driving B&B

9 Windsor Drive, Norristhorpe WF15 7RA  **t** (01924) 235120  **f** (01924) 235120

B&B specialising in local carriage-driving courses (pony/horse). Quiet location. Full English breakfast. Easy access to M62/M1 for touring West Yorkshire.

**open** All year except Christmas
**bedrooms** 1 double, 1 twin
**payment** Cash/cheques

Room 🛁 TV 👌 🍵  General 🛏 10 P ✕ ✕ 🍴 ✿ 🐾  Leisure ∪ ᛒ 🛶

## MARKET WEIGHTON, East Riding of Yorkshire Map ref 4C1

★★★★
**GUEST ACCOMMODATION**

B&B per room per night
s  £28.00–£34.00
d  £46.00–£56.00
Evening meal per person
£15.00

### Red House

North Cliffe, Market Weighton, York YO43 4XB  **t** (01430) 827652  **e** simon.lyn@virgin.net
**w** redhousenorthcliffe.co.uk

**open** All year except Christmas
**bedrooms** 2 double, 1 twin
**bathrooms** 1 en suite, 1 private
**payment** Cash/cheques

Red House is a listed Georgian country house set in a peaceful rural environment. You will be warmly welcomed to relaxing accommodation with beamed rooms and a spacious guests' sitting room with wood-burning stove. Only minutes from the M62 and conveniently located for visiting historic York, Beverley and the Yorkshire Wolds.

⊕ *Jct 38, M62. B1230 to North Cave. At 30mph limit, left, follow signs to North Cliffe. Red House is 300m beyond village on right.*

Room TV 👌 🍵  General 🛏 P ✕ ✕ 🍴 🥄 ⚲ ✿  Leisure ᛒ 🛶

## To your credit

If you book by phone you may be asked for your credit card number. If so, it is advisable to check the proprietor's policy in case you have to cancel your reservation at a later date.

## PICKERING, North Yorkshire Map ref 5D3

★★★★★
**GUEST HOUSE
GOLD AWARD**

B&B per room per night
**s** £65.00–£75.00
**d** £85.00–£105.00
Evening meal per person
Min £7.50

# 17 Burgate

Pickering YO18 7AU  **t** (01751) 473463  **f** (01751) 473463  **e** info@17burgate.co.uk
**w** 17burgate.co.uk

**open** All year except Christmas
**bedrooms** 2 double, 1 twin, 2 suites
**bathrooms** All en suite
**payment** Credit/debit cards, cash/cheques, euros

Superb, award-winning, renovated town house between town centre and castle. Luxury for the stressed and weary. 17 Burgate is different, 17 Burgate is special – indulge yourselves, and make it part of your North Yorkshire experience. 'The boutique B&B has arrived in North Yorkshire' – The Times.

⊕ *From top of Market Hill, head up Burgate towards the Castle. Pass '17', turn right, then right again (Willowgate) into car park.*

♥ *Midweek Madness deals available in selected periods – see our website for details.*

Room 📞 📺 👤 🍵   General 🐾12 P ⚡ 🍽 🏋 🛠 ✻ 🐕   Leisure ∪ 🎣 ► 🏊 ⛵

## PICKERING, North Yorkshire Map ref 5D3

★★★★
**BED & BREAKFAST
SILVER AWARD**

B&B per room per night
**s** £35.00–£55.00
**d** £55.00–£70.00

# Eleven Westgate

Eden House, Pickering YO18 8BA  **t** (01751) 475111  **e** info@westgatebandb.co.uk
**w** westgatebandb.co.uk

**open** All year except Christmas and New Year
**bedrooms** 2 double, 1 twin
**bathrooms** All en suite
**payment** Cash/cheques

Elegant Victorian town house offering luxury accommodation and hospitality, three minutes' walk from Pickering town centre. Spacious en suite rooms. Home comforts include log fire, Wi-Fi, Sky+, DVD, iPod dock. Lovely garden. Aga-cooked breakfast using fresh local produce. Ideal for North Yorkshire and renowned steam railway. Secure bike storage, bikewash and workshop.

⊕ *We are on Westgate, a tree-lined road into Pickering on the A170 towards Scarborough. You will find us on the right-hand side.*

♥ *Mountain-biking holidays (Dalby Forest and North York Moors) including guiding and instruction from £50pppn. Instructor and mechanic on site.*

Room 📺 👤 🍵   General 🐾 🏯 ♿ ⚡ 🏋 🛠 ✻   Leisure ∪ 🎣 🚲 ⛵

## PICKERING, North Yorkshire Map ref 5D3

★★★★
**BED & BREAKFAST**

B&B per room per night
**s** £35.00–£40.00
**d** £64.00–£70.00
Evening meal per person
£15.00–£20.00

# The Hawthornes

High Back Side, Middleton, Pickering YO18 8PB  **t** (01751) 474755  **e** paulaappleby@btinternet.com
**w** the-hawthornes.com

The Hawthornes offers comfortable accommodation in three generous-sized rooms, two on ground floor. Aga-cooked breakfast, home-baked bread. Tea and fresh baked scones on arrival. Ample parking.

**open** All year except Christmas and New Year
**bedrooms** 2 double, 1 twin
**bathrooms** All en suite
**payment** Cash/cheques

Room 🛗 📺 👤 🍵   General 🐾 🏯 ♿ P ⚡ ✗ 🏋 ● ✻   Leisure ∪ 🎣 ► 🚲 ⛵

## Mention our name
Please mention this guide when making your booking.

---

**REETH,** North Yorkshire Map ref 5B3

★★★★
**GUEST HOUSE
SILVER AWARD**

## Cambridge House

Arkengarthdale Road, Richmond DL11 6QX **t** (01748) 884633 **f** (01748) 884633
**e** scambridge@fsbdial.co.uk **w** cambridge-house-reeth.co.uk

B&B per room per night
**s** £33.00
**d** £66.00
Evening meal per person
£16.50

**open** All year
**bedrooms** 3 double, 1 twin, 1 single
**bathrooms** All en suite
**payment** Cash/cheques

Quality accommodation, recently renovated and refurbished to a high standard. A warm welcome assured. Complementary tea tray on arrival, served in conservatory. All rooms with spectacular views. Peaceful location.

⊕ *Entering Reeth, take the road between the Buck Hotel and the public toilets. The house is 0.25 miles on left-hand side, before cattle grid.*

♥ *Reduced price for three nights or more. Special out-of-season rates. Weekend specials.*

Room 📺 ♿ 🍴  General ☁14 P ⅃ ✕ 🍴 ❧ 🕿 🎱 ❄  Leisure ∪ ♪ 🚲 🎣

---

**RICHMOND,** North Yorkshire Map ref 5C3

★★★★
**GUEST ACCOMMODATION**

## Frenchgate Guest House

66 Frenchgate, Richmond DL10 7AG **t** (01748) 823421 & 07889 768696 **f** (01748) 823421
**e** info@66frenchgate.co.uk

B&B per room per night
**s** £40.00–£70.00
**d** Min £56.00

Panoramic views overlooking the Swale Valley, Richmond Castle, Easby Abbey and rolling countryside over the Dales. The historic marketplace and castle are nearby.

**open** All year
**bedrooms** 4 double, 3 twin
**bathrooms** All en suite
**payment** Credit/debit cards, cash/cheques, euros

Room ⌨ 📺 ♿ 🍴  General ☁8 ⅃ 🍴 ❧ 🕿 🎱 ❄  Leisure ∪ ♪ ► 🚲 🎣

---

**RICHMOND,** North Yorkshire Map ref 5C3

★★★★
**GUEST ACCOMMODATION**

## Nuns Cottage

5 Hurgill Road, Richmond DL10 4AR **t** (01748) 822809 **e** the.flints@ukgateway.net
**w** nunscottage.co.uk

B&B per room per night
**s** £60.00–£70.00
**d** £70.00–£80.00

Nuns Cottage is an 18thC house set in secluded gardens. Comfortable bedrooms. Five minutes from the centre of Richmond. Easy access to the A1 and the beautiful Yorkshire Dales.

**open** All year except Christmas and New Year
**bedrooms** 1 double, 1 twin
**bathrooms** 2 private
**payment** Cash/cheques, euros

Room 📺 ♿ 🍴  General ☁12 ⅃ ❧ ❄  Leisure ∪ ►

---

**RIPON,** North Yorkshire Map ref 5C3

★★★★
**GUEST HOUSE**

## Box Tree Cottages

Coltsgate Hill, Ripon HG4 2AB **t** (01765) 698006 **e** riponbandb@aol.com **w** boxtreecottages.com

B&B per room per night
**s** £40.00–£70.00
**d** £60.00–£80.00

**open** All year except Christmas and New Year
**bedrooms** 3 double, 2 twin, 1 family
**bathrooms** All en suite
**payment** Credit/debit cards, cash/cheques

A pretty row of listed cottages now combined into one property. Very quietly situated but only minutes from the marketplace. Completely refurbished, furnished with antiques. Homely atmosphere, spacious rooms, best-quality food. Ample parking, large gardens.

⊕ *Take road to marketplace, then north into Fishergate and North Street. Coltsgate Hill is about 400m from the marketplace. Box Tree Cottages are 100m from North Street.*

Room 📺 ♿ 🍴  General ☁ 🏵 ☂ P ⅃ ✕ 🍴 ❧ ❄

## RIPON, North Yorkshire Map ref 5C3

★★★
**INN**

B&B per room per night
s £40.00-£50.00
d £60.00-£75.00
Evening meal per person
£8.00-£15.00

# The Royal Oak

36 Kirkgate, Ripon HG4 1PB  **t** (01765) 602284  **f** (01765) 690031  **w** timothy.taylor.co.uk/royaloak

**open** All year
**bedrooms** 3 double, 2 twin, 1 family
**bathrooms** All en suite
**payment** Credit/debit cards, cash/cheques

The recently refurbished Royal Oak is one of Ripon's historic inns and is conveniently located close to the bustling market place and the city's shops and tourist attractions. Time-honoured Yorkshire hospitality with busy, lively bars serving Timothy Taylor's award-winning cask ales and excellent food every day using fresh local produce.

⊕ Centrally situated on Kirkgate, 'twixt market square and Cathedral. Small guest car park at rear accessed via Sainsbury's car park.

♥ Call for details of off-peak special rates.

Room 📺 ♨ 🍵   General 🍳 ♨ 🎿 ✗ 🍴 🐾 🌸   Leisure ♪ ▶ 🏛

## RIPON, North Yorkshire Map ref 5C3

★★★
**INN**

B&B per room per night
s £30.00
d £50.00

# The White Horse

61 North Street, Ripon HG4 1EN  **t** (01765) 603622  **f** (01765) 609040
**e** david.bate13@btopenworld.com  **w** white-horse-ripon.co.uk

A friendly, family-run pub close to Ripon market square. Entertainment at weekends and various midweek activities.

**open** All year
**bedrooms** 3 twin, 4 single, 5 family
**bathrooms** All en suite
**payment** Credit/debit cards, cash/cheques

Room 🛁 📺 ♨   General 🍳 ♨ P 🍷 🌸 🐾   Leisure ♪

## RUNSWICK BAY, North Yorkshire Map ref 5D3

★★★★
**GUEST HOUSE**

B&B per room per night
s £45.00-£55.00
d £70.00-£80.00
Evening meal per person
Min £18.50

# The Firs

26 Hinderwell Lane, Runswick Bay, Nr Whitby TS13 5HR  **t** (01947) 840433  **f** (01947) 841616
**e** mandy.shackleton@talk21.com  **w** the-firs.co.uk

In a coastal village, eight miles north of Whitby. All rooms en suite with colour TV, tea/coffee facilities. Private parking. Children and dogs welcome. Open April to October.

**bedrooms** 3 double, 2 twin, 1 single, 5 family
**bathrooms** All en suite
**payment** Cash/cheques, euros

Room 🛁 🍴 📞 📺 ♨ 🍵   General 🌸 P ✗ 🍴 🍱 🐾   Leisure 🏛

# Get on the road

Take yourself on a journey through England's historic towns and villages, past stunning coastlines and beautiful countryside with VisitBritain's series of inspirational touring guides. You can purchase the guides from good bookshops and online at visitbritaindirect.com.

★★★★
**GUEST HOUSE**

B&B per room per night
s £22.00–£25.00
d £50.00–£60.00

## Howdale

121 Queen's Parade, Scarborough YO12 7HU  **t** (01723) 372696  **f** (01723) 372696
**e** mail@howdalehotel.co.uk  **w** howdalehotel.co.uk

**open** All year except Christmas and New Year
**bedrooms** 10 double, 2 twin, 1 single, 2 family
**bathrooms** 13 en suite
**payment** Credit/debit cards, cash/cheques

Beautifully situated overlooking North Bay and Scarborough Castle, yet close to town. We are renowned for cleanliness and the friendly, efficient service provided in a comfortable atmosphere. Our substantial breakfasts are deservedly famous. Thirteen of our excellent bedrooms are en suite, many have sea views. All have TV, tea/coffee facilities, hairdryer etc.

⊕ *At traffic lights opposite railway station turn left. Next traffic lights turn right. At 1st roundabout turn left. Property is 0.5 miles on the right.*

♥ *Mini-breaks (3 nights min) Mar-early Jul, Sep and Oct, from £23pppn.*

Room 📺 ♨ ⏰  General 🛏 🏊 ♿ P ⚡ ⛳ 🍴 ❄ 🐕

★★★★
**BED & BREAKFAST**
**SILVER AWARD**

B&B per room per night
s £40.00–£50.00
d £60.00–£80.00
Evening meal per person
Min £15.00

## Killerby Cottage Farm

Killerby Lane, Cayton, Scarborough YO11 3TP  **t** (01723) 581236  **f** (01723) 585146
**e** val@stainedglasscentre.co.uk  **w** smoothhound.co.uk/hotels/killerby

Situated between Scarborough and Filey, 1.5 miles from Cayton Bay. Farmhouse of character adjacent to Stained-Glass Centre. Good food, lovely garden, warm welcome.

**open** All year except Christmas
**bedrooms** 2 double, 1 twin
**bathrooms** All en suite
**payment** Credit/debit cards, cash/cheques

Room 📺 ♨ ⏰  General ✗ ♿ ❄  Leisure ⚓

★★★
**GUEST HOUSE**

B&B per room per night
s £30.00–£35.00
d £52.00–£56.00
Evening meal per person
£12.00–£14.00

## Robyn's Guest House

139 Columbus Ravine, Scarborough YO12 7QZ  **t** (01723) 374217  **e** info@robynsguesthouse.co.uk
**w** robynsguesthouse.co.uk

Robyn's Guest House offers you the very best in comfortable, luxury accommodation at affordable rates in the heart of Yorkshire's premier seaside resort.

**open** All year
**bedrooms** 3 double, 3 family
**bathrooms** All en suite
**payment** Credit/debit cards, cash/cheques

Room 📺 ♨ ⏰  General 🛏 🏊 ✗ 🍴 ♿ 🐾 🐕  Leisure ⚓ ⛵ 🚲 🏊

★★★★
**FARMHOUSE**
**SILVER AWARD**

B&B per room per night
s £35.00–£40.00
d £60.00–£70.00

## Sawdon Heights

Scarborough YO13 9EB  **t** (01723) 859321  **f** (01723) 859321  **e** info@sawdonheights.com
**w** sawdonheights.com

A warm welcome awaits on our family farm adjacent to forest. Quiet location, stunning views. Cycle hire and storage, walks and pack-ups available. Ideal location for exploring east coast and moors. Extra bed may be added on request.

**open** All year except Christmas
**bedrooms** 2 double, 1 twin
**bathrooms** All en suite
**payment** Cash/cheques

Room ♿ 📺 ♨ ⏰  General 🛏10 P ⚡ 🍴 ♿ 🖥 ❄  Leisure U ⚓ ⛵ 🚲 🏊

**SCARBOROUGH,** North Yorkshire Map ref 5D3

★★★★
**GUEST HOUSE**

B&B per room per night
s £30.00
d £52.00–£54.00

## Sylvern House

25 New Queen Street, Scarborough YO12 7HJ  **t** (01723) 360952  **e** sylvernhouse@aol.com
**w** smoothhound.co.uk/hotels/sylvern.html

**open** All year
**bedrooms** 3 double, 1 twin, 2 single, 3 family
**bathrooms** All en suite
**payment** Credit/debit cards, cash/cheques

Enjoy a warm welcome, good home cooking and a friendly atmosphere with Vicki and Richard at Sylvern House. We are ideally situated close to both bays and the town centre. All rooms en suite, children and pets welcome. Internet access. Open all year, including Christmas and New Year.

⊕ *Directions to the hotel will be included with your booking acknowledgement.*

Room 📺 👤 🍴  General 🛋 🏛 🏃 🍴 🎨 ☆ 🐾  Leisure ♪ ⚑

**SCARBOROUGH,** North Yorkshire Map ref 5D3

★★★★
**GUEST ACCOMMODATION**

B&B per room per night
s £29.50–£31.00
d £23.50–£29.00

## The Whiteley

99-101 Queens Parade, Scarborough YO12 7HY  **t** (01723) 373514  **f** (01723) 373007
**e** whiteleyhotel@bigfoot.com  **w** yorkshire-coast.co.uk/whiteley

**bedrooms** 7 double, 3 family
**bathrooms** All en suite
**payment** Credit/debit cards, cash/cheques

Small, family-run, non-smoking, licensed guest accommodation located in an elevated position overlooking the North Bay, close to the town centre and ideally situated for all amenities. The bedrooms are well co-ordinated and equipped with useful extras, many with sea views. Good home cooking is served in the traditional dining room. Open February to November inclusive.

⊕ *Left at traffic lights near railway station, right at next lights, continue on Castle Road to roundabout. Left onto North Marine Road. 2nd right, then left onto Queens Parade.*

♥ *Oct-May inclusive (excl Bank Holidays): reduction of £1.50pppn when staying 2 nights or more.*

Room 🛏 📺 👤 🍴  General 🛋3 P 🍴 ♟ 🎨 ☆

**SCOTCH CORNER,** North Yorkshire Map ref 5C3

★★
**INN**

B&B per room per night
s £29.95–£47.45
d £49.50–£65.50
Evening meal per person
£8.95–£28.00

## Vintage Inn

Scotch Corner, Middleton Tyas DL10 6NP  **t** (01748) 824424  **f** (01748) 826272
**e** thevintagescotchcorner@btopenworld.com  **w** thevintagehotel.co.uk

Family-run roadside inn with friendly atmosphere, conveniently situated on A66 (Penrith road) only 200m from A1 Scotch Corner junction. (Richmond three miles). Closed Sunday evenings.

**open** All year except Christmas and New Year
**bedrooms** 3 double, 2 twin, 3 single
**bathrooms** 5 en suite
**payment** Credit/debit cards, cash/cheques, euros

Room 📞 📺 👤  General 🛋 🏃 P ♟ ✕ 🎨 ☆  Leisure ♪ ⚑

**WALKERS WELCOME WELCOME WALKERS**

## Best foot forward

Walkers feel at home in accommodation participating in our Walkers Welcome scheme. Look out for the symbol. Consider walking all or part of a long-distance route – go online at nationaltrail.co.uk.

★★★★
**BED & BREAKFAST
SILVER AWARD**

B&B per room per night
d £70.00–£90.00
Evening meal per person
£18.00–£22.00

# Halsteads Barn

Mewith, Bentham, Lancaster LA2 7AR  **t** (01524) 262641  **e** info@halsteadsbarn.co.uk
**w** halsteadsbarn.co.uk

**open** All year
**bedrooms** 3 double
**bathrooms** All en suite
**payment** Credit/debit cards, cash/cheques

Situated in some of the country's finest scenery. Located within the Forest of Bowland, three miles from the Yorkshire Dales National Park and 30 minutes' drive from the Lake District. Personal attention is always guaranteed along with a fine table and eclectic wine list at Halsteads Barn.

⊕ *Follow A65 follow sign to Clapham station. Under railway bridge, follow road. Turn right at crossroads, follow road, take first track on left after Burnhead.*

Room 📺 ♿ 🍷  General P 🍷 ✕ 🔥 🛏 🌀 💻 ✿  Leisure ∪ ♪ ► 🚲 🏛

★★★★
**GUEST HOUSE**

B&B per room per night
s £45.00–£55.00
d £70.00–£90.00

# King William The Fourth Guest House

King William House, High Street, Settle BD24 9EX  **t** (01729) 825994
**e** info@kingwilliamthefourthguesthouse.co.uk  **w** kingwilliamthefourthguesthouse.co.uk

**open** All year except Christmas and New Year
**bedrooms** 3 double, 1 twin
**bathrooms** All en suite
**payment** Credit/debit cards, cash/cheques

King William The Forth Guest House is a one-minute walk from the Market Square in Settle and a four-minute walk from the train station. This former public house was lovingly restored last year to a very high standard and rooms have beautiful en suite showers or spa bathroom.

♥ *Discounts for stays of more than 3 nights. Spring or autumn breaks available upon request.*

Room 🛁 📺 ♿ 🍷  General 🌀 ♿ P ✕ 🔥 🌀  Leisure 🚲

★★★
**INN**

B&B per room per night
s £34.00–£39.00
d £60.00–£65.00
Evening meal per person
£7.95–£13.95

# Maypole Inn

Maypole Green, Long Preston, Skipton BD23 4PH  **t** (01729) 840219  **f** (01729) 840727
**e** robert@maypole.co.uk  **w** maypole.co.uk

**open** All year
**bedrooms** 2 double, 1 twin, 1 single, 2 family
**bathrooms** All en suite
**payment** Credit/debit cards, cash/cheques, euros

Traditional 17thC village inn on the Maypole Green, situated within the Yorkshire Dales and close to the Trough of Bowland and the Lake District. Restaurant serving home-made food with a good local reputation. Traditional beers – we are four-times winner of the CAMRA Pub of the Season.

⊕ *We are on the main A65 road, between the market towns of Skipton and Settle. 45 mins from the M6 motorway.*

♥ *Midweek and winter breaks available – please telephone for details.*

Room ☎ 📺 ♿  General 🌀 🏳 ♿ P ✕ 🍷 🔥 🛏 💻 ✿ ♟  Leisure ♦ ✧ ∪ ♪ ► 🚲 🏛

## What's in an award?
Further information about awards can be found at the front of this guide.

**SETTLE,** North Yorkshire Map ref 5B3

★★★★
**FARMHOUSE**

B&B per room per night
s £36.00
d £52.00

## Scar Close Farm

Feizor, Austwick, Lancaster LA2 8DF  **t** (01729) 823496  **f** (01729) 823496

**open** All year except Christmas and New Year
**bedrooms** 1 double, 1 twin, 1 family, 1 suite
**bathrooms** All en suite
**payment** Cash/cheques

High-standard, en suite accommodation and food. Farmhouse in picturesque hamlet in Yorkshire Dales. Popular for touring and walking. Double, twin, family rooms. Ground-floor room available.

⊕ *Take A65, Settle bypass towards Kendal. After 3 miles (red markings) sharp right. After 0.25 miles 1st right, 0.5 miles to crossroads. Bed and breakfast on right.*

Room ⚏ TV ⚐ ⚐  General ⚐ ✂ ⚐ ✿  Leisure U

**SHEFFIELD,** South Yorkshire Map ref 4B2

★★★
**GUEST ACCOMMODATION**

B&B per room per night
s £45.00
d £45.00
Evening meal per person
£5.00–£15.00

## Parson House Farm

Longshaw, Sheffield S11 7TZ  **t** (01433) 631017  **f** (01433) 630794  **e** debbel@btconnect.com
**w** parsonhouse.co.uk

Quality comfortable rooms with private bathroom. Set in Peak District, great for families/couples, breakfast, half or full board available. Pets welcome. Outdoor activities available.

**open** All year
**bedrooms** 2 family
**bathrooms** 2 private
**payment** Cash/cheques

Room ⚏ TV ⚐  General ⚐ 🏠 ⚐ P ✗ 🎱 ⚐ ⚐ ✿ 🐾  Leisure ♠ U ♪ ▶ ⚐ ⚐

**SHELLEY,** West Yorkshire Map ref 4B1

★★★★
**RESTAURANT WITH ROOMS**

B&B per room per night
s £65.00–£70.00
d £90.00–£100.00
Evening meal per person
£15.00–£35.00

## Three Acres Inn and Restaurant

Roydhouse, Shelley HD8 8LR  **t** (01484) 602606  **f** (01484) 608411  **e** 3acres@globalnet.co.uk
**w** 3acres.com

An attractive country inn conveniently situated for all of Yorkshire's major conurbations and motorway networks. Restaurant. Traditional beers.

**open** All year except Christmas and New Year
**bedrooms** 10 double, 1 twin, 8 single, 1 suite
**bathrooms** All en suite
**payment** Credit/debit cards, cash/cheques

Room ⚏ ⚐ ✆ TV ⚐ ⚐  General ⚐ 🏠 ⚐ P ⚐ ✗ 🎱 ⚐ ✿

Log on to **enjoyengland.com** to find a break that matches your mood. **experience** scenes that inspire and traditions that baffle. **discover** the world's most inventive cultural entertainment and most stimulating attractions. **explore** vibrant cities and rugged peaks. **relax** in a country pub or on a sandy beach.

## enjoy**England**.com

★ ★ ★ ★ ★
**BED & BREAKFAST**
**SILVER AWARD**

B&B per room per night
s £45.00–£50.00
d £70.00–£80.00

# Cononley Hall Bed & Breakfast

Main Street, Cononley, Skipton BD20 8LJ  **t** (01535) 633923  **f** (01756) 700114
**e** cononleyhall@madasafish.com  **w** cononleyhall.co.uk

**open** All year except Christmas and New Year
**bedrooms** 2 double, 1 twin
**bathrooms** All en suite
**payment** Credit/debit cards, cash/cheques

Grade II Listed Georgian house in unspoilt village, near to Skipton. Cononley Hall is ideally located for those wishing to explore the picturesque Yorkshire Dales or the Brontë countryside and attractions. All rooms are en suite and offer excellent facilities. Breakfast consists of local produce, including our own free-range eggs.

⊕ *From A629, follow sign for Cononley station. Across level crossing, up Main Street. New Inn on right. We are 25yds further up on left.*

♥ *Stays of 3 nights or more only £35pp (based on 2 people sharing). Children aged 3 and under – free.*

Room   General ⌂ ▥ ♠ P ⅍ ▦ ℳ ⚕ ✿   Leisure ▶ 🏛

★ ★ ★
**INN**

B&B per room per night
s £35.00
d £55.00
Evening meal per person
£3.50–£8.95

# The Masons Arms Inn

Barden Road, Skipton BD23 6SN  **t** (01756) 792754  **f** (01756) 792754
**e** info@masonsarmseastby.co.uk  **w** masonsarmseastby.co.uk

Quaint village inn with superb dales views and ample parking. A warm welcome awaits. Open fires, excellent food and service.

**open** All year except Christmas and New Year
**bedrooms** 1 double, 1 twin
**bathrooms** All en suite
**payment** Credit/debit cards, cash/cheques

Room 📺 ♿ ♒   General ⌂ ♠ P ▯ ✕ ▦ ℳ ✿ ♜   Leisure ♦ ∪ ♪ ▶ ⚲ 🏛

★ ★ ★ ★
**BED & BREAKFAST**

B&B per room per night
s £40.00–£50.00
d £80.00

# Newton Grange

Bank Newton, Gargrave, Skipton BD23 3NT  **t** (01756) 748140 & (01756) 796016
**e** bookings@banknewton.fsnet.co.uk  **w** cravencountryconnections.co.uk

A Grade II Listed Georgian farmhouse in rolling countryside, suitable for walking, cycling, horse-riding or touring. Rooms en suite or with private bathroom. Eating places nearby.

**open** All year
**bedrooms** 2 double, 1 twin
**bathrooms** 2 en suite, 1 private
**payment** Cash/cheques

Room 📺 ♿ ♒   General P ⅍ ▦ ▣ ✿   Leisure ∪ ♪ 🏛

# Our quality rating schemes

For a detailed explanation of the quality and facilities represented by the stars, please refer to the information pages at the back of this guide.

## SLINGSBY, North Yorkshire Map ref 5C3

★★★★
**GUEST ACCOMMODATION**

B&B per room per night
d £65.00–£75.00

# Slingsby Hall

Slingsby YO62 4AL  **t** (01653) 628375  **e** info@slingsbyhall.co.uk  **w** slingsbyhall.co.uk

**open** All year except Christmas and New Year
**bedrooms** 3 double, 1 twin
**bathrooms** All en suite
**payment** Cash/cheques

Elegant Georgian family home set in beautiful gardens in the pretty village of Slingsby. Tastefully decorated bedrooms offering very comfortable and spacious accommodation, with a welcoming and relaxed atmosphere. Delicious breakfasts using local produce and home-made preserves. Ideally situated for Castle Howard, York and North York Moors.

⊕ *From York follow A64 Scarborough. Take Castle Howard turning and follow signs to Slingsby. Located in the village just past the pub.*

Room 📺 ♿ 🍽  General 🏠 🔥 P ✂ ❄ 🐕  Leisure ∪ ♪ ► 🚲 🏡

## STAITHES, North Yorkshire Map ref 5C3

★★★
**BED & BREAKFAST**

B&B per room per night
s  Min £27.50
d  Min £50.00

# Brooklyn

Browns Terrace, Staithes TS13 5BG  **t** (01947) 841396  **e** m.heald@tesco.net  **w** brooklynuk.co.uk

**open** All year except Christmas
**bedrooms** 2 double, 1 twin
**payment** Cash/cheques

Sea-captain's house in picturesque, historic fishing village. Comfortable, individually decorated rooms with view of Cowbar cliffs. Pets and children welcome. Generous breakfasts. Vegetarians welcome.

Room 📺 ♿ 🍽  General 🛋 🍽 🅜 🐕

## STAPE, North Yorkshire Map ref 5D3

★★★★
**BED & BREAKFAST**
**SILVER AWARD**

B&B per room per night
s  £35.00–£41.00
d  £58.00–£68.00

# High Muffles

Pickering YO18 8HP  **t** (01751) 417966  **e** candrew840@aol.com  **w** highmuffles.co.uk

Beautifully renovated farmhouse accommodation with en suite bathrooms. Situated within Cropton Forest, North Yorkshire National Park. Perfect for walking and cycling.

**open** All year except Christmas and New Year
**bedrooms** 2 double
**bathrooms** All en suite
**payment** Cash/cheques

Room 🛁 📺 ♿ 🍽  General 🛋 14 P ✂ 🍽 🅜 ❄  Leisure ∪ ♪ ► 🚲 🏡

# Key to symbols

The symbols at the end of each entry help you pick out the services and facilities which are most important to you. A key to the symbols can be found inside the back-cover flap. Keep this open for easy reference.

---

**THIRSK,** North Yorkshire Map ref 5C3

★★★★
**GUEST ACCOMMODATION
SILVER AWARD**

B&B per room per night
s  £37.50–£60.00
d  £66.00–£70.00
Evening meal per person
£20.00–£25.00

# Borrowby Mill, Bed and Breakfast

Borrowby, Nr Thirsk YO7 4AW  **t** (01845) 537717  **e** markandvickipadfield@btinternet.com
**w** borrowbymill.co.uk

**open** All year except Christmas and New Year
**bedrooms** 1 double, 2 twin
**bathrooms** All en suite
**payment** Credit/debit cards, cash/cheques

Tastefully converted 18thC flour mill in a secluded location between Thirsk and Northallerton. Convenient for touring North Yorkshire Moors and Dales. Cosy en suite rooms, excellent breakfasts and dinners prepared by chef/proprietor. Relax in our drawing room with library or explore our woodland gardens.

⊕ From A19 trunk road take turn for Borrowby. The mill is situated just before turning into the village.

♥ In spring and autumn we run courses in all types of embroidery. Please ask for our brochure.

Room 📺 👤 🗢   General 🛏 ⅋ P ✕ 🛗 🅟 ❄ 🐾   Leisure ∪ ♪ ♪ 🚲

---

**THIRSK,** North Yorkshire Map ref 5C3

★★★★
**GUEST ACCOMMODATION**

B&B per room per night
s  £40.00–£55.00
d  £50.00–£65.00
Evening meal per person
£12.95–£15.95

# Manor House Cottage

Hag Lane, South Kilvington, Thirsk YO7 2NY  **t** (01845) 527712  **e** info@manor-house-cottage.co.uk
**w** manor-house-cottage.co.uk

**open** All year
**bedrooms** 2 double, 1 twin
**bathrooms** 2 en suite, 1 private
**payment** Credit/debit cards

Superior accommodation in quiet rural location, three minutes from town centre, close to the dales and the North York Moors.

Room 📺 👤 🗢   General 🛏 P ⅋ ✕ 🅟 ▣ ❄ 🐾   Leisure ∪ ♪ ♪ 🏊

---

**THIRSK,** North Yorkshire Map ref 5C3

★★★
**FARMHOUSE**

B&B per room per night
s  £30.00
d  £24.00–£27.00

# Town Pasture Farm

Thirsk YO7 2DY  **t** (01845) 537298

Comfortable farmhouse in picturesque Boltby village within the North York Moors National Park. Views of the Hambleton Hills. Excellent walks. Horse-riding available in village. Central for east coast, York and the Dales. Colour TV in lounge.

**open** All year except Christmas
**bedrooms** 1 twin, 1 family
**bathrooms** All en suite
**payment** Cash/cheques

Room 👤 🗢   General 🛏 ⅋ 🅟 ❄ 🐾   Leisure ∪ 🏊

---

**THIXENDALE,** North Yorkshire Map ref 4C1

★★★
**INN**

B&B per room per night
s  Max £27.50
d  Max £55.00

# The Cross Keys

Thixendale, Malton YO17 9TG  **t** (01377) 288272

Family-run, award-winning, small village pub nestling in the valleys of the Yorkshire Wolds. Well situated on four major and several short, circular walks. Single occupancy available.

**open** All year except Christmas and New Year
**bedrooms** 1 double, 2 twin
**bathrooms** All en suite
**payment** Credit/debit cards, cash/cheques

Room 👤 🗢   General 🛏 14 ⅋ ♟ ✕ 🛗 ▣ ❄   Leisure 🏊

## THORALBY, North Yorkshire Map ref 5B3

★★★★
**INN**

B&B per room per night
**d** £60.00–£70.00
Evening meal per person
£13.25–£20.50

# The George Inn

Thoralby, Leyburn DL8 3SU  **t** (01969) 663256  **e** visit@thegeorge.tv  **w** thegeorge.tv

**open** All year
**bedrooms** 2 double
**bathrooms** All en suite
**payment** Credit/debit cards, cash/cheques

The George Inn is situated in the picturesque village of Thoralby in Bishopdale, a hidden oasis in the heart of the Dales. This is an ideal location for exploring the Yorkshire Dales National Park. We provide en suite bed and breakfast accommodation, together with excellent meals, real ales and good wines.

⊕ Thoralby is reached from the A684, between Leyburn and Hawes, and is 1.25 miles from Aysgarth village.

♥ Apr to Oct, min 3-night stay, Mon-Thu – 5% discount. Nov to Mar, min 3-night stay, Mon-Thu – 10% discount.

Room 🛇 TV 👆 🍷  General 🏵14 ♿ P ⁇ ✕ 🍽 🐾  Leisure ∪ ♪ ↑ 🚲 🏠

## THORALBY, North Yorkshire Map ref 5B3

★★★★
**GUEST ACCOMMODATION
SILVER AWARD**

B&B per room per night
**d** £59.00–£69.00

# The Old Barn

Thoralby, Leyburn DL8 3SZ  **t** (01969) 663590  **e** holidays@dalesbarn.co.uk  **w** dalesbarn.co.uk

Relax and unwind in the serenity of Bishopdale, a little gem of a dale. Stylish accommodation, superb breakfasts, four excellent dining-out pubs close by. A warm, homely welcome awaits.

**open** All year except Christmas and New Year
**bedrooms** 1 double
**bathrooms** En suite
**payment** Cash/cheques, euros

Room TV 👆 🍷  General P ⁇ 🍽  Leisure ∪ ♪ ↑ 🚲 🏠

## THORNTON DALE, North Yorkshire Map ref 5D3

★★★★
**BED & BREAKFAST**

B&B per room per night
**d** £26.00–£33.00

# Banavie

Roxby Road, Thornton-le-Dale, Pickering YO18 7SX  **t** (01751) 474616  **e** info@banavie.uk.com  **w** banavie.uk.com

Banavie is in a quiet area with splendid views overlooking this famous village with its meandering stream and thatched cottage. Close to moors and coast. Car park.

**open** All year except Christmas
**bedrooms** 2 double, 1 twin
**bathrooms** All en suite
**payment** Cash/cheques

Room TV 👆 🍷  General 🕁 P ⁇ 🛏 ❀ 🐾  Leisure ∪ 🚲 🏠

## THORNTON DALE, North Yorkshire Map ref 5D3

Rating Applied For
**GUEST ACCOMMODATION**

B&B per room per night
**d** £72.00–£80.00
Evening meal per person
£20.00–£25.00

# Cherry Garth

Church Hill, Pickering YO18 7QH  **t** (01751) 473404  **e** claire@cherrygarthholidays.com  **w** cherrygarthholidays.com

**open** All year
**bedrooms** 2 double
**bathrooms** All en suite
**payment** Cash/cheques

Experience two cultures, English and Scandinavian. We have taken the best elements from B&B, hotels and self-catering to create your unique holiday experience. Two separate apartments with en suite shower room and fully equipped kitchen to be serviced accommodation with the opportunity for guests to self-cater for other meals.

♥ Out-of-season discounts from Nov-Mar excl Christmas and New Year. 4 nights for the price of 3.

Room 🛇 TV 👆 🍷  General 🏵 ♿ P ⁇ ✕ 🍽 🖴 ❀  Leisure ∪ ♪ 🚲 🏠

**TODMORDEN,** West Yorkshire Map ref 4B1

★★★★

BED & BREAKFAST

B&B per room per night
s £18.00–£30.00
d £50.00

## Cherry Tree Cottage

Woodhouse Road, Todmorden OL14 5RJ  t (01706) 817492

Sympathetically restored, part-17thC country cottage, nestling amid the beautiful Pennine countryside, with modern amenities and lovely views. Easy access to the Pennine Way and the Calderdale Way. Friendly atmosphere.

**open** All year except Christmas and New Year
**bedrooms** 1 double, 2 twin
**bathrooms** All en suite
**payment** Cash/cheques, euros

Room 📺 ♨ 🖱   General 🛆 🎏 ✂ 🛏 ✿

**WAKEFIELD,** West Yorkshire Map ref 4B1

★★★★

FARMHOUSE

B&B per room per night
s £32.00
d £50.00

## Upper Midgley Farm

Midgley, Wakefield WF4 4JH  t (01924) 830294  f (01924) 830294  e uppermidgleyfarm@tiscali.co.uk

Farmhouse accommodation, beautifully located on working farm, near junction 38 of the M1. Walking distance to Yorkshire Sculpture Park, National Mining Museum and local pubs. Close to Leeds, Bradford, Huddersfield, Wakefield and Barnsley.

**open** All year
**bedrooms** 1 double, 1 single, 1 family
**bathrooms** All en suite
**payment** Cash/cheques, euros

Room 📺 ♨ 🖱   General 🛆 🎏 🔥 P ✂ 🗄 🛏 ▣ ✿   Leisure ∪ ✦ ☇ 🖼

**WELBURN,** North Yorkshire Map ref 5C3

★★★

BED & BREAKFAST

B&B per room per night
d £60.00–£80.00

## The Barley Basket

Main Road, York YO60 7DX  t (01653) 618352  e marianlacey@btinternet.com

A warm welcome awaits you. Situated on the fringe of Castle Howard, York, Scarborough and the Howardian Hills.

**open** All year
**bedrooms** 2 family
**bathrooms** 1 en suite, 1 private
**payment** Cash/cheques

Room 📺 ♨   General 🛆10 P ✂ 🗄

**WEST WITTON,** North Yorkshire Map ref 5B3

★★★

GUEST ACCOMMODATION

B&B per room per night
s £22.00–£40.00
d £42.00–£52.00

## The Old Star

Main Street, West Witton, Leyburn DL8 4LU  t (01969) 622949  e enquiries@theoldstar.com
w theoldstar.com

17thC, stone-built former coaching inn. Set in a farming community with uninterrupted views of Wensleydale from the rear of the property. Oak beams, log fire and a friendly atmosphere.

**open** All year except Christmas
**bedrooms** 4 double, 1 twin, 2 family
**bathrooms** 5 en suite
**payment** Cash/cheques

Room 🛋 📺 ♨ 🖱   General 🛆 🎏 🔥 P 🗄 🛏 ✿ 🐕   Leisure ✦ 🚲 🖼

**WETHERBY,** West Yorkshire Map ref 4B1

★★

GUEST HOUSE

B&B per room per night
s £27.00–£28.00
d £54.00–£56.00

## Prospect House

8 Caxton Street, Wetherby LS22 6RU  t (01937) 582428

Established 45 years. En suite rooms available. Near York, Harrogate, Dales, Herriot Country. Midway London/Edinburgh. Restaurants nearby. Pets welcome.

**open** All year
**bedrooms** 2 double, 2 twin, 2 single
**bathrooms** 4 en suite
**payment** Cash/cheques

Room ♨   General 🛆 🛏 ✿ 🐕

## Using map references

The map references refer to the colour maps at the front of this guide. The first figure is the map number, the letter and figure that follow indicate the grid reference on the map.

**WHITBY,** North Yorkshire Map ref 5D3

★★★
BED & BREAKFAST

B&B per room per night
s £30.00–£36.00
d £60.00–£72.00

## Bruncliffe Guest House

9 North Promenade, Whitby YO21 3JX **t** (01947) 602428 **e** bruncliffewhitby@aol.com
**w** bruncliffewhitby.co.uk

**open** All year except Christmas and New Year
**bedrooms** 2 double, 1 twin
**bathrooms** All en suite
**payment** Cash/cheques

Bruncliffe Guest House is located in Whitby. We are situated on North Promenade seafront with views from Sandsend and Kettleness cliffs to Whitby piers and abbey. Off-street parking. 10-15 minute walk to town and piers and harbour.

Room General P

**WHITBY,** North Yorkshire Map ref 5D3

★★★
HOSTEL

Per person per night
B&B £24.00-£34.00
Per person per week
HB £224.00-£294.00
FB £273.00-£343.00

## Sneaton Castle Centre

Castle Road, Whitby YO21 3QN **t** (01947) 600051
**e** sneaton@globalnet.co.uk **w** sneatoncastle.co.uk

Excellent facilities in beautiful location for bed and breakfast, holidays, conferences, meetings and many other events. Excellent home cooking, ample free and safe parking. Ideal base for touring the North York Moors area.

**open** All year except Christmas and New Year
**bedrooms** 34 single, 16 twin, 7 quad, 1 dormitory. Total no of beds 120
**bathrooms** 12 en suite, 24 public
**meals** Breakfast, lunch and evening meals available
**payment** Credit/debit cards, cash/cheques

Room General P Leisure

**WHITBY,** North Yorkshire Map ref 5D3

★★★★
GUEST ACCOMMODATION

B&B per room per night
s Min £33.50
d Min £67.00
Evening meal per person
Min £8.50

## Sneaton Castle Centre

Sneaton Castle, Whitby YO21 3QN **t** (01947) 600051 **f** (01947) 603490 **e** sneaton@globalnet.co.uk
**w** sneatoncastle.co.uk

St Francis House, set in stunning grounds of Sneaton Castle, on outskirts of Whitby and edge of the North York Moors. High quality en suite accommodation. Excellent breakfast. Ample parking.

**open** All year except Christmas and New Year
**bedrooms** 9 twin, 3 family
**bathrooms** All en suite
**payment** Credit/debit cards, cash/cheques

Room General P Leisure

# Country Code

always follow the Country Code

- Be safe – plan ahead and follow any signs
- Leave gates and property as you find them
- Protect plants and animals, and take your litter home
- Keep dogs under close control
- Consider other people

---

**WORTLEY,** South Yorkshire Map ref 4B1

★★★

**GUEST ACCOMMODATION**

B&B per room per night
s £39.00–£65.00
d £78.00–£90.00
Evening meal per person
£6.50–£19.50

## Wortley Hall Ltd

Wortley, Sheffield S35 7DB  **t** (0114) 288 2100  **f** (0114) 283 0695  **e** info@wortleyhall.org.uk
**w** wortleyhall.org.uk

**open** All year except Christmas
**bedrooms** 22 double, 15 twin, 5 single, 7 family
**bathrooms** All en suite
**payment** Credit/debit cards, cash/cheques, euros

An 18thC, Grade II Listed building, set within 26 acres of formal gardens and woodlands. You can be assured of a warm, friendly welcome. Managed on co-operative principles on a 'not for profit' basis.

⊕ M1 jct 35a. Take A616 to Manchester. After 1.7 miles exit left A629 (Wortley) left at the junction. 1 mile to Wortley.

♥ Two-night short break Jul and Aug £45. DB&B per person per night.

Room 🛏🖂☎📺♿🍴  General 🕐🏢♿🅿♥✕🖾📷🖧🈵  Leisure ♨∪♪🏃🏊

---

**YORK,** North Yorkshire Map ref 4C1

★★★★
**GUEST HOUSE**
**SILVER AWARD**

B&B per room per night
s £45.00–£55.00
d £70.00–£90.00

## 23 St Marys

York YO30 7DD  **t** (01904) 622738  **f** (01904) 628802  **e** stmarys23@hotmail.com  **w** 23stmarys.co.uk

**open** All year
**bedrooms** 6 double, 1 twin, 1 single, 1 family
**bathrooms** All en suite
**payment** Credit/debit cards, cash/cheques, euros

Large Victorian terraced house peacefully set within five minutes' stroll of city centre. Spacious rooms, antique furnishings, en suite bedrooms of different sizes and character. Extensive breakfast menu in elegant surroundings. Julie and Chris will offer you a warm welcome to their home.

♥ 3rd night at 50% reduction (excl peak periods).

Room 🖂☎📺♿🍴  General 🕐🏢🅿✂📷🈵  Leisure ♪🏃

---

**YORK,** North Yorkshire Map ref 4C1

★★★
**GUEST HOUSE**

B&B per room per night
s £50.00–£55.00
d £70.00–£80.00

## Abbey Guest House

13-14 Earlsborough Terrace, Marygate YO30 7BQ  **t** (01904) 627782  **e** info@abbeyghyork.co.uk
**w** abbeyghyork.co.uk

Small, family-run guesthouse on banks of river. Private car park, well-appointed rooms all en suite, no-smoking. Five minutes' walk to city centre. Lovely garden and terrace.

**open** All year except Christmas
**bedrooms** 3 double, 1 twin, 1 family
**bathrooms** All en suite
**payment** Credit/debit cards, cash/cheques

Room 🖂📺♿🍴  General 🕐🏢♿🅿✂🖧📷🈵  Leisure 🏊

---

**YORK,** North Yorkshire Map ref 4C1

★★★★
**GUEST HOUSE**

B&B per room per night
s £55.00
d £75.00–£90.00

## The Acer

52 Scarcroft Hill, York YO24 1DE  **t** (01904) 653839  **f** (01904) 677017  **e** info@acerhotel.co.uk
**w** acerhotel.co.uk

Licensed; parking; high standards of service and housekeeping. Quiet residential location very close to city, racecourse and station. Visit www.tripadvisor.co.uk for independent reviews.

**open** All year except Christmas
**bedrooms** 3 double, 1 twin, 1 family
**bathrooms** 5 en suite
**payment** Credit/debit cards, cash/cheques, euros

Room ♿🖂📺♿🍴  General 🕐4 🅿✂♥🈵

---

**YORK,** North Yorkshire Map ref 4C1

★★★★
**BED & BREAKFAST**

B&B per room per night
d £70.00–£85.00

# Amber House

36 Bootham Crescent, Bootham, York YO30 7AH **t** (01904) 620275 **e** feebutler@btinternet.com
**w** amberhouse-york.co.uk

**open** All year except Christmas
**bedrooms** 2 double
**bathrooms** All en suite
**payment** Credit/debit cards, cash/cheques

Attractive Victorian property with elegant and comfortable rooms. En suite accommodation with half-tester king-sized beds. Exclusively tailored for extreme comfort and a relaxing stay. Within five minutes' walk of the city centre, the Minster, tourist attractions, shops, pubs and restaurants. We look forward to seeing you.

⊕ *Bootham is situated to the north west of the town centre, in from the ringroad on the A19.*

♥ *We have special offers for midweek breaks.*

Room 📺 ♿ ☎ General 🏛 ⏰ P ✂ Leisure ♨

**YORK,** North Yorkshire Map ref 4C1

★★★
**GUEST HOUSE**

B&B per room per night
d £66.00–£90.00

# Ambleside Guest House

62 Bootham Crescent, Bootham YO30 7AH **t** (01904) 637165 **f** (01904) 637165
**e** ambles@globalnet.co.uk **w** ambleside-gh.co.uk

Tastefully furnished Victorian townhouse, a few minutes' walk to the city centre. Cleanliness and hospitality guaranteed at all times. Non-smoking establishment.

**open** All year except Christmas and New Year
**bedrooms** 6 double, 1 twin, 1 family
**bathrooms** 6 en suite
**payment** Credit/debit cards, cash/cheques

Room 📺 ♿ General 🛏10 ✂ 🐾

**YORK,** North Yorkshire Map ref 4C1

★★★★
**GUEST ACCOMMODATION
SILVER AWARD**

B&B per room per night
s £30.00–£65.00
d £60.00–£75.00

# Ascot House

80 East Parade, York YO31 7YH **t** (01904) 426826 **f** (01904) 431077 **e** admin@ascothouseyork.com
**w** ascothouseyork.com

**open** All year except Christmas
**bedrooms** 8 double, 3 twin, 1 single, 3 family
**bathrooms** 12 en suite, 1 private
**payment** Credit/debit cards, cash/cheques

A family-run Victorian villa, built in 1869, with en suite rooms of character and many four-poster or canopy beds. Delicious English, continental and vegetarian breakfasts served. Fifteen minutes' walk to historic walled city centre, castle museum or York Minster. Residential licence and residents' lounge, sauna and private, enclosed car park.

⊕ *From A1/M1 take A64 then A1036 from the east into York. About 100yds past 30mph signs, take 2nd exit off roundabout. Right at traffic lights into East Parade.*

Room 🖥 📠 📺 ♿ ☎ General 🏛 ⏰ P ♟ 🍽 🐾

## If you have access needs...

Look for the National Accessible Scheme symbols if you have special hearing, visual or mobility needs. An index of accommodation participating in the scheme can be found at the back of this guide.

**YORK,** North Yorkshire Map ref 4C1

★★★★

**GUEST ACCOMMODATION**

B&B per room per night
s £30.00–£35.00
d £60.00–£70.00

## Ascot Lodge

112 Acomb Road, York YO24 4EY  **t** (01904) 798234  **f** (01904) 786742  **e** info@ascotlodge.com
**w** ascotlodge.com

**open** All year
**bedrooms** 1 twin, 4 single, 5 family
**bathrooms** 7 en suite
**payment** Cash/cheques

Receive a warm welcome at this beautiful mid-Victorian guesthouse on the west side of York. Peaceful, yet near to the city centre – 25 minutes' walk or 5-10 minutes by regular bus service. Luxurious, en suite double, family and single rooms. Non-smoking throughout. Secure, private car park. Vegetarians catered for.

⊕ *We are situated on the B1224 just to the east of Acomb, a mile from the city centre. Take taxi or Blue Line No 1 bus from station.*

♥ *Single-night price reduction for 2 or more nights' stay.*

Room 🛏 📺 ♨ 🕭  General 🛆 🚪 🔥 P ✂ 🕮 ✿ 🐕  Leisure ▶ 🏠

**YORK,** North Yorkshire Map ref 4C1

★★★

**GUEST ACCOMMODATION**

B&B per room per night
s £35.00–£45.00
d £60.00–£75.00

## The Bar Convent

17 Blossom Street, York YO24 1AQ  **t** (01904) 643238  **f** (01904) 631792  **e** info@bar-convent.org.uk
**w** bar-convent.org.uk

**bedrooms** 3 double, 5 twin, 9 single, 1 family
**bathrooms** 3 en suite, 3 private
**payment** Credit/debit cards, cash/cheques

Grade 1 Listed Georgian convent. We provide self-catering facilities but have a superb licensed in-house cafe providing home-cooked fare. Coin-operated washing facilities for guests, two sitting rooms with TVs. Comfortable bedrooms. There is also a museum in the convent and garden to the rear. Chapel open daily. Closed Christmas and Easter.

⊕ *From station turn right down hill to traffic lights. Convent is opposite. By car enter York via A1036. Turn right at Micklegate Bar.*

♥ *A 10% discount is available for charities and delegates using our conference facilities.*

Room 📞 ♨ 🕭  General 🛆 🔥 ✂ ✕ 🕮 🛏 📼 🖥 ✿  Leisure ◉

# Discover Britain's heritage

Discover the history and beauty of over 250 of Britain's best-known historic houses, castles, gardens and small manor houses. You can purchase Britain's Historic Houses and Gardens – Guide and Map from good bookshops and online at visitbritaindirect.com.

**YORK,** North Yorkshire Map ref 4C1

★★★★
**GUEST ACCOMMODATION
SILVER AWARD**

B&B per room per night
s £66.00–£82.00
d £76.00–£90.00

# Barbican House

20 Barbican Road, York YO10 5AA  t (01904) 627617  f (01904) 647140  e info@barbicanhouse.com
w barbicanhouse.com

**open** All year except Christmas and New Year
**bedrooms** 6 double, 1 twin, 1 family
**bathrooms** All en suite
**payment** Credit/debit cards, cash/cheques

Welcome to our wonderful restored Victorian villa overlooking the medieval city walls. Delightful bedrooms, each individually decorated to complement the charm and character of the period. All rooms are en suite and non-smoking. Full English breakfast using local, free-range produce. Free private parking available.

⊕ *Proceed north on A19 through Fulford then follow sign for Barbican Leisure Centre. This will take you to Barbican Road. Barbican House on right at junction with inner ring road.*

♥ *Discount on stays of 3 or more days (excl Fri and Sat). See website for details.*

Room ♿ TV 🐾 ☕  General ☼ 10 P ✂ 🍴 🦶 ✳  Leisure ✔ 🏊

**YORK,** North Yorkshire Map ref 4C1

★★★★★
**GUEST ACCOMMODATION
SILVER AWARD**

B&B per room per night
s £40.00–£50.00
d £70.00–£120.00

# Bishops

135 Holgate Road, York YO24 4DF  t (01904) 628000  f (01904) 628181
e enquiries@bishopshotel.co.uk  w bishopshotel.co.uk

**open** All year except Christmas
**bedrooms** 2 double, 1 twin, 1 single, 3 family, 6 suites
**bathrooms** 11 en suite
**payment** Credit/debit cards, cash

Elegant Victorian villa, peaceful yet near to the city centre. Spacious, comfortable interior with individually styled suites and bedrooms all en suite. Hearty breakfast using fresh, local produce. Non-smoking, fully licensed establishment with a friendly family atmosphere. Ideal base for exploring our beautiful Roman city and the Yorkshire countryside. 5% surcharge on credit cards.

⊕ *Take the A59 from the A1. This becomes Holgate Road where the establishment is situated. Or a 15-minute walk from the railway station.*

♥ *Celebration Package of flowers, chocolates and champagne. Business-traveller and off-peak, midweek, short-break rates available Sun-Thu.*

Room ♿ 🛏 TV 🐾 ☕  General ☼ 🖿 ♿ P ✂ ❗ ✕ 🍴 🦶 ♿  Leisure ∪ ✔ ➤ 🚲 🏊

# Suit yourself

The symbols at the end of each entry mean you can enjoy virtually made-to-measure accommodation with the services and facilities most important to you. A key to the symbols can be found inside the back-cover flap. Keep this open for easy reference.

★★★
**GUEST HOUSE**

B&B per room per night
s £28.00–£30.00
d £44.00–£60.00

# Bull Lodge Guest House

37 Bull Lane, Lawrence Street, York YO10 3EN  **t** (01904) 415522  **f** (01904) 415522
**e** stay@bulllodge.co.uk  **w** bulllodge.co.uk

**open** All year except Christmas and New Year
**bedrooms** 4 double, 1 twin, 1 single
**bathrooms** 3 en suite
**payment** Credit/debit cards, cash/cheques

Modern, detached property in quiet, tree-lined side-street location off A1079, 0.75 miles to centre. Close to bus route, University of York, business/science park, nature park/cycleway. En suites include ground-floor double ideal for mobility-impaired guests. Dogs welcome by arrangement. Freshly-cooked, full-choice breakfast. Private on-site parking, bicycle/motorbike garaging.

⊕ Bull Lane is off Lawrence Street (A1079 Hull Road), 2 miles A64, 500yds city walls at Walmgate Bar. Local bus (no 10) from rail station.

♥ Quote advert for discount when booking, 5% 3/4 nights, 10% 5 or more nights (excl Bank Holidays and special events).

Room 🛁 TV ♿ 🍵  General ➰5 P ⚡ ♨ 🐾  Leisure 🚲 ⛵

★★★★
**GUEST ACCOMMODATION**

B&B per room per night
s £40.00–£65.00
d £60.00–£80.00

# Carlton House

134 The Mount, York YO24 1AS  **t** (01904) 622265  **f** (01904) 637157  **e** etb@carltonhouse.co.uk
**w** carltonhouse.co.uk

**open** All year except Christmas and New Year
**bedrooms** 9 double, 4 family
**bathrooms** All en suite
**payment** Credit/debit cards, cash/cheques

Charming Georgian townhouse situated on The Mount, gateway to the City of York. Five minutes' walk to city walls, ten minutes to city centre, railway station, racecourse and all major tourist attractions.

⊕ From A64 Leeds road take A1036 (signposted York West). After approx 1 mile, racecourse on right. Go up slight hill, past traffic lights. Hotel is 100m on left.

Room TV ♿  General ➰ P ⚡ 🛏 ♨

★★★
**GUEST HOUSE**

B&B per room per night
s £35.00–£65.00
d £60.00–£85.00

# The Cavalier

39 Monkgate, York YO31 7PB  **t** (01904) 636615  **f** (01904) 636615  **e** julia@cavalierhotel.co.uk
**w** cavalierhotel.co.uk

**open** All year
**bedrooms** 4 double, 2 twin, 1 single, 3 family
**bathrooms** 7 en suite
**payment** Cash/cheques

Georgian, family-run hotel close to the city centre, only yards from the ancient Bar Walls, minster and many of York's famous historic landmarks. High standards, traditional English breakfast, sauna and private parking ensure the comfort of our guests. Please phone for a map and brochure.

Room TV ♿ 🍵  General ➰ 🏛 🔥 P ⚡ ♨

**YORK,** North Yorkshire Map ref 4C1

★★★★
GUEST ACCOMMODATION SILVER AWARD

B&B per room per night
s £37.00–£41.00
d £64.00–£72.00

## City Guest House

68 Monkgate, York YO31 7PF **t** (01904) 622483 **e** info@cityguesthouse.co.uk
**w** cityguesthouse.co.uk

Small, friendly, family-run guesthouse in attractive Victorian town house. Five minutes' walk to York Minster, close to attractions. Private parking. Cosy, en suite rooms. Restaurants nearby. Non-smoking.

**open** All year except Christmas and New Year
**bedrooms** 4 double, 1 twin, 1 single, 1 family
**bathrooms** 6 en suite, 1 private
**payment** Credit/debit cards, cash/cheques, euros

Room General 1 P

**YORK,** North Yorkshire Map ref 4C1

★★★
GUEST HOUSE

B&B per room per night
s £30.00–£40.00
d £60.00–£65.00

## Cook's Guest House

120 Bishopthorpe Road, York YO23 1JX **t** (01904) 652519 **f** (01904) 652519
**e** jennieslcook@hotmail.co.uk **w** cooksguesthouse.co.uk

Featured on TV's 'This Morning' and in Hull Journal. Small, friendly and comfortable guesthouse, ten minutes' walk to city, railway station and racecourse. Suitable for walking disabled guests.

**open** All year
**bedrooms** 1 double, 1 family
**bathrooms** 2 en suite
**payment** Cash/cheques

Room General 7 Leisure

**YORK,** North Yorkshire Map ref 4C1

★★★
GUEST HOUSE

B&B per room per night
s £25.00–£30.00
d £50.00–£60.00

## Cumbria House

2 Vyner Street, York YO31 8HS **t** (01904) 636817 **e** candj@cumbriahouse.freeserve.co.uk
**w** cumbriahouse.com

Family-run guesthouse, warm welcome assured, 12 minutes' walk from York Minster. En suites available. Easily located from ring road. Private car park.

**open** All year except Christmas
**bedrooms** 3 double, 1 single, 2 family
**bathrooms** 2 en suite
**payment** Credit/debit cards, cash/cheques, euros

Room General P

**YORK,** North Yorkshire Map ref 4C1

★★★★
GUEST HOUSE

B&B per room per night
s £49.50–£58.00
d £65.00–£85.00

## Curzon Lodge and Stable Cottages

23 Tadcaster Road, York YO24 1QG **t** (01904) 703157 **f** (01904) 703157
**e** admin@curzonlodge.com **w** smoothhound.co.uk/hotels/curzon.html

**open** All year except Christmas and New Year
**bedrooms** 6 double, 2 twin, 1 single, 1 family
**bathrooms** All en suite
**payment** Credit/debit cards, cash/cheques

Charming 17thC listed house and former stables in a conservation area overlooking York racecourse. Comfortable, en suite rooms, some with four-poster or brass beds. Country antiques, books, prints, fresh flowers and complimentary sherry lend traditional ambience. Delicious breakfasts. Warm, relaxed atmosphere with restaurants a minute's walk. Entirely non-smoking. Parking in grounds.

⊕ *From A64 bypass, take A1036 (York west exit), follow City Centre signs. We are 2 miles on right between York Holiday Inn and Marriott hotels.*

♥ *Midweek and 3-night-stay deals off-peak – please enquire.*

Room General 10 P Leisure

Travel update
Get the latest travel information – just dial RAC on 1740 from your mobile phone.

**YORK,** North Yorkshire Map ref 4C1

★ ★ ★ ★
GUEST ACCOMMODATION

B&B per room per night
s £42.00–£50.00
d £64.00–£74.00

# Feversham Lodge

1 Feversham Crescent, York YO31 8HQ  t (01904) 623882  f (01904) 339280
e bookings@fevershamlodge.co.uk  w fevershamlodge.co.uk

open All year except Christmas and New Year
bedrooms 3 double, 2 twin
bathrooms All en suite
payment Credit/debit cards, cash/cheques

Converted Victorian rectory, voted York Guest House of the Year 2005/6/7. Within easy walking distance of city centre and major attractions. Spacious, individually-themed en suite bedrooms (see website) offering TV/DVD, quality toiletries, courtesy trays. Comprehensive book/DVD library and internet access. Delicious English, continental or vegetarian breakfast. Car park.

⊕ From A1(M) take A64 York then A1237 northern ring road, turn at B1363 towards York city centre. After 2nd traffic lights turn right into Feversham Crescent.

♥ 3 nights for the price of 2, Nov-Mar incl, Sun-Thu.

Room 🖭 📺 👜 ☕  General ♨8 P 🚳 🎪 🛒  Leisure 🚲 🏛

**YORK,** North Yorkshire Map ref 4C1

★ ★ ★
GUEST HOUSE

B&B per room per night
s Min £28.00
d Min £46.00

# Greenside

124 Clifton, York YO30 6BQ  t (01904) 623631  f (01904) 623631  e greenside@surfree.co.uk
w greensideguesthouse.co.uk

open All year except Christmas and New Year
bedrooms 2 double, 2 twin, 1 single, 3 family
bathrooms 3 en suite
payment Cash/cheques, euros

Charming, detached, conservation area, owner-run guesthouse fronting onto Clifton Green. Ideally situated, ten minutes' walk from the city walls and all York's attractions. Offers many facilities, including an enclosed, locked car park. All types of ground-/first-floor bedrooms are available in a warm, homely atmosphere.

⊕ Leave A64 York/Leeds road to the A1237, North York outer ring road. Take A19 to the city centre and follow the signs to Clifton Green.

Room 👜 📺 👜  General ♨ 🍴 ♿ P 🚳 🛒 ❄ 🐾  Leisure 🏛

**YORK,** North Yorkshire Map ref 4C1

★ ★ ★ ★
GUEST ACCOMMODATION
SILVER AWARD

B&B per room per night
s £50.00–£95.00
d £80.00–£125.00

# The Hazelwood

24-25 Portland Street, York YO31 7EH  t (01904) 626548  f (01904) 628032
e reservations@thehazelwoodyork.com  w thehazelwoodyork.com

open All year
bedrooms 7 double, 3 twin, 1 single, 2 family
bathrooms All en suite
payment Credit/debit cards, cash/cheques

Situated in the very heart of York only 400yds from York Minster in an extremely quiet residential area. An elegant Victorian town house with private car park providing high-quality accommodation in individually designed en suite bedrooms. Extensive breakfast menu catering for all tastes including vegetarian. Completely non-smoking.

⊕ Situated in city centre close to York Minster in side street off inner ring road (Gillygate). Best approached from the north on the A19.

♥ 3 nights for the price of 2, Sun-Thu, 1 Nov-Easter (excl school holidays).

Room 👜 🖭 📺 👜 ☕  General ♨8 P 🚳 🍷 🎪 🍴 ⊡ ❄  Leisure 🚲 🏛

**YORK,** North Yorkshire Map ref 4C1

★★★★
GUEST ACCOMMODATION

B&B per room per night
s £58.00–£88.00
d £68.00–£98.00

# Holly Lodge

206 Fulford Road, York YO10 4DD  t (01904) 646005  e geoff@thehollylodge.co.uk
w thehollylodge.co.uk

**open** All year except Christmas
**bedrooms** 3 double, 1 twin, 1 family
**bathrooms** All en suite
**payment** Credit/debit cards, cash/cheques

Award-winning, beautifully appointed, Georgian Grade II Listed building where you are assured of a warm welcome. Ten minutes' riverside stroll to centre, conveniently located for all York's attractions including the university. All rooms individually furnished, each overlooking garden or terrace. On-site parking, easy to find. Booking recommended.

⊕ On the A19 in south York, 1.5 miles towards centre from A19/A64 intersection.

Room   General ⏣7 ⚎ 𝄞 ❋

**YORK,** North Yorkshire Map ref 4C1

★★★★
INN

B&B per room per night
s £25.00–£45.00
d £50.00–£70.00

# The Lighthorseman

124 Fulford Road, Fishergate YO10 4BE  t (01904) 624818  f (01904) 624818
e janinerobinson03@aol.com  w lighthorseman.co.uk

**open** All year
**bedrooms** 5 double, 2 twin, 1 single
**bathrooms** All en suite
**payment** Credit/debit cards, cash/cheques

Local inn with eight letting bedrooms all en suite. Full breakfast, car parking. Short walk along river to town centre and racecourse. For more information visit our website.

Room 📺 ⚎ 🕯  General P ⏣ ✕ 🍴 ▣ ❋  Leisure ♦ ⤚

**YORK,** North Yorkshire Map ref 4C1

★★★★
GUEST ACCOMMODATION

B&B per room per night
s £45.00–£55.00
d £65.00–£80.00
Evening meal per person
£12.50–£25.00

# Manor Guest House

Main Street, Linton-on-Ouse YO30 2AY  t (01347) 848391  f (01347) 848391
e manorguesthouse@tiscali.co.uk  w manorguesthouse.co.uk

**open** All year
**bedrooms** 2 double, 2 twin, 1 single, 2 family, 1 suite
**bathrooms** All en suite
**payment** Credit/debit cards, cash/cheques, euros

Award-winning en suite accommodation in a listed Georgian manor house. Period oak-beamed rooms and ground-floor family suite. Ideal for Yorkshire Dales and Moors and picturesque towns, yet only 10 minutes York 'park and ride'. Lovely village location, river walks, pubs/restaurants. Spacious grounds with ample private parking. Dogs welcome.

⊕ A1 jct 47, A59 towards York. Left at Green Hammerton, follow signs for RAF Linton-on-Ouse. 1st house on left in village.

♥ Book full week and pay for 6 nights. Various seasonal and midweek offers. Excellent dinners available on request from £12.50.

Room ⛺ 📷 📺 ⚎ 🕯  General ⏣ 𝍢 ♿ P ⚎ 🍴 ▣ ⌨ ❋ 🐾  Leisure ♦ ∪ ⤚ ▸ 🚲 🏯

**YORK,** North Yorkshire Map ref 4C1

★★★

**GUEST HOUSE**

B&B per room per night
s £40.00–£50.00
d £60.00–£90.00

# Mont-Clare Guest House

32 Claremont Terrace, Gillygate, York YO31 7EJ  t (01904) 651011  f (01904) 626773
e mont.clare@dsl.pipex.com  w mont-clare.co.uk

**open** All year except Christmas
**bedrooms** 4 double, 2 twin, 1 single
**bathrooms** All en suite
**payment** Credit/debit cards, cash/cheques

Enjoy city-centre accommodation with free parking.
Located in a quiet cul-de-sac close to York Minster,
within easy walking distance of the city centre and all
the historic attractions. The railway station is a
fifteen-minute walk. All rooms are en suite and we
offer a traditional English breakfast including
vegetarian option.

⊕ From A1237 (outer ring road) take A19 into York.

♥ Winter breaks 10% discount for 3 midweek nights or more
(Sun-Thu) Nov 1st 2007 – March 31st 2008.

Room 🗎 📺 📶 ⚲   General ☎8 P ⚲ ⛾ ☕ 🎱 ✿   Leisure ⚲

**YORK,** North Yorkshire Map ref 4C1

★★★

**GUEST ACCOMMODATION**

B&B per room per night
s £28.00–£32.00
d £54.00–£64.00

# Romley House

2 Millfield Road, York YO23 1NQ  t (01904) 652822  e info@romleyhouse.co.uk
w romleyhouse.co.uk

**open** All year
**bedrooms** 2 double, 1 twin, 1 single, 2 family
**bathrooms** 2 en suite
**payment** Credit/debit cards, cash/cheques, euros

A family-run guesthouse, a few minutes' walk from
the city centre and all attractions, offering a
happy atmosphere, hearty breakfast and home comforts. All
rooms are well appointed (en suite available) with
colour TV, radio/alarm clock and tea-/coffee-making
facilities.

Room 📺 ⚲   General ☎ ⛾ ♿ P ♨ ☕ ⛾   Leisure ⚲

**YORK,** North Yorkshire Map ref 4C1

★★★★

**INN**

B&B per room per night
s Min £55.00
d Min £80.00
Evening meal per person
£6.95–£15.75

# The Windmill

Hull Road, Dunnington, York YO19 5LP  t (01904) 481898  f (01904) 488480
e j.saggers@btopenworld.com  w thewindmilldunnington.co.uk

**open** All year
**bedrooms** 5 double, 5 twin
**bathrooms** All en suite
**payment** Credit/debit cards, cash/cheques

Eat – drink – relax – sleep. Home-made food is
available daily; traditional Sunday lunches; a
selection of ales and lagers. A function/meeting
room is also available. Large car park.

Room ♿ 📺 📶 ⚲   General ☎ ⛾ ♿ P ⚲ ♨ ⛾ ✿

## Star ratings

Detailed information about star ratings can be found at the back of this guide.

**YORK,** North Yorkshire Map ref 4C1

★★★★
**GUEST ACCOMMODATION**

B&B per room per night
s £28.00–£33.00
d £57.00–£67.00

# York House

62 Heworth Green, York YO31 7TQ  **t** (01904) 427070  **f** (01904) 427070
**e** yorkhouse.bandb@tiscali.co.uk  **w** yorkhouseyork.com

**open** All year except Christmas and New Year
**bedrooms** 5 double, 1 twin, 1 single, 1 family
**bathrooms** 7 en suite, 1 private
**payment** Credit/debit cards, cash/cheques

Located a short stroll from the heart of one of Europe's most historic cities. York House is the perfect base for a visit to beautiful York or the surrounding area. A Georgian house with later additions, rooms feature all the modern conveniences you could possibly need for a relaxing, enjoyable stay.

⊕ *North east of York, A1036 signed city centre. Straight over roundabout and traffic lights, next mini-roundabout 3rd exit. York House is 300yds on left.*

♥ *Four-poster rooms £34.00–£39.00 pppn.*

Room ♿ 🖨 📺 ♨ 🍴  General 🛎 🏛 ♿ P ✂ 🎮 ✿

# If you have accessible needs...

Guests with hearing, visual or mobility needs can feel confident about booking accommodation that participates in the National Accessible Scheme.

You can also buy a copy of VisitBritain's Easy Access Britain guide, available from Tourism for All (tel 0845 124 9971) and online at **visitbritaindirect.com.**

# Heart of England

Herefordshire, Shropshire, Staffordshire, Warwickshire, West Midlands, Worcestershire

# Wholesome fun and a whole lot more

When it comes to good food and simple pleasures, people make a bee-line for the Heart of England. Whether it's dining out, gliding along a canal or catching a nerve-jangling rollercoaster, there's nowhere better.

visittheheart.com

Wrekin Reservoir, Shropshire

Malvern Hills, Worcestershire

Charlecote Park, Warwickshire

Symonds Yat, Herefordshire

From Vale of Evesham asparagus to Herefordshire Beef, this region's rich soil and lush pastureland produces some of the UK's finest ingredients. Small wonder that from village pubs to Michelin-starred restaurants, your eating experience will be a highlight of your stay. Great family days out are a speciality, too. Whether it's throwing pots at the famous Wedgwood factory, braving the rides at Drayton Manor Theme Park or unwinding on a narrow boat, there are simply attractions galore. And if you like picnics, take a spread along to Symond's Yat RSPB Nature Reserve overlooking the gorgeous Wye Valley.

Want to get the most from your stay? Pick up a Thrill Hopper ticket that gives you great value access to four top theme park attractions – Drayton Manor Theme Park, Alton Towers, SnowDome and Waterworld. And don't miss Trentham's splendid Italian Garden and the Eastern Pleasure Garden restoration at one of the 19th century's most celebrated gardens. Then there's the National Cold War Exhibition at RAF Museum Cosford, an illuminating and exciting look at the tensions that tormented the superpowers during the 20th century (prepare to be amazed by Britain's three V-Bombers – Vulcan, Valiant and Victor). And Walsall Illuminations transform the town's arboretum into an enchanting wonderland of lakeside lights, laser shows and floodlit gardens.

The region is also famous as the cradle of the Industrial Revolution, so make a pilgrimage to Ironbridge Gorge World Heritage Site and catch ten fantastic museums in one truly spectacular setting.

The Heart of England's appeal lies in both its timelessness and modernity. The cultural diversity and vibrancy of Birmingham reflects a very different England to the one of Shakespeare's Stratford-upon-Avon, the sleepy villages of Warwickshire and Herefordshire and beauty of the Cotswolds.

# Destinations

## Birmingham

Birmingham is a dynamic city combining a fascinating history with a world-class cultural scene. Lose yourself in shopping heaven in the stunningly remodelled Bullring, wander through the historic Jewellery Quarter then sit back and enjoy the Symphony Orchestra in the magnificent Symphony Hall. Indulge your sweet tooth at Cadbury World, or take in a major event at the NEC or NIA. You'll also find yourself at the heart of a region full of history and heritage, beautiful quaint villages and access to lush rolling countryside – Birmingham really is a gateway to the heart of England!

## Coventry

Discover the city that is re-inventing itself. Coventry, the setting for myth and legend, famous for Lady Godiva and St George the dragon-slayer, is now an ideal visitor destination building on its rich heritage with up-to-the-minute shopping, bars and restaurants. Browse one of the oldest indoor markets in Europe, gaze at the beauty of St Mary's Guildhall, visit the late 20th century cathedral standing amid the ruins of its predecessor, and don't miss the Transport Museum for the largest collection of British road transport in the world.

## Hereford

Visit this ancient city on the banks of the River Wye. You'll find historic buildings housing modern shops and modern buildings holding historic treasures. Don't miss Hereford Cathedral with its priceless Mappa Mundi and Chained Library. Wander through the spacious High Town and intriguing side streets. The ancient and modern grace the banks of the beautiful River Wye – including the new Left Bank Village, while the Cider Museum tells a fascinating story and bolsters Hereford's claim to be 'The Apple of England's Eye'.

| | 0 | 50 miles |
| --- | --- | --- |
| | 0 | 75 kms |

National Park

Area of Outstanding Natural Beauty

National Trails
nationaltrail.co.uk

Sections of the
National Cycle Network
nationalcyclenetwork.org.uk

Bullring Shopping Centre, Birmingham

Hereford Cider Museum

Coventry Cathedral

Wedgewood Visitor Centre, Stoke-on-Trent

Bancroft Gardens, Stratford-upon-Avon

River Severn, Shrewsbury

Ludlow

## Ludlow

Discover the place Betjemen described as 'the loveliest town in England.' With over 500 listed buildings, Ludlow is a feast for the eyes. Britain's first 'slow' town is also a gastronomic capital and host to the renowned Ludlow Marches Food & Drink Festival. You'll find a host of speciality food shops, and more restaurants and inns than you can shake a cocktail stick at. To walk off lunch, stroll in the enchanting Angel Gardens, or take in a performance at the open-air theatre in the stunning medieval ruin of Ludlow Castle.

## Shrewsbury

This charming county town boasts over 660 listed buildings. Wander the Shuts and Passages – a medieval maze of narrow alleys criss-crossing the town, and admire the Norman abbey, medieval castle, and Shrewsbury Museum and Art Gallery housed in Rowley's House. Interesting, independent shops are plentiful, with food a speciality. Track the evolution of Charles Darwin, Shrewsbury's famous son, and, for a summer treat, breathe the scent of more than three million blooms at the internationally famous Shrewsbury Flower Show in August.

## Stoke-on-Trent

Visit the UK's capital of china, 'The Potteries'. Award-winning museums tell the full story and the opportunity to throw your own pot. Take in a show at the magnificent Regent Theatre and Victoria Hall with their star-studded programmes of West End shows. Given its close proximity to Alton Towers and its excellent shopping and leisure facilities, Stoke-on-Trent is sure to fire your imagination.

## Stratford-upon-Avon

Unearth a magical blend of heritage and drama in and around Shakespeare's home town. Explore five houses with Shakespeare connections including Anne Hathaway's Cottage and Shakespeare's Birthplace. Visit one of England's most beautiful parish churches at Holy Trinity to see Shakespeare's grave and enjoy some of his great works performed by the world's largest classical theatre company, the RSC. Take a boat out on the River Avon, wander the boutiques, specialist stores and gift shops, and discover some of Britain's finest historic houses and gardens.

# Places to visit

**Birmingham Museum
& Art Gallery**
(0121) 303 2834
bmag.org.uk
*Fine and applied art, archaeology
and local history collections*

**Black Country
Living Museum**
Dudley, West Midlands
(0121) 557 9643
bclm.co.uk
*Twenty-six acres of fascinating
living history*

**Brockhampton Estate
National Trust**
near Bromyard, Herefordshire
(01885) 482077
nationaltrust.org.uk
*14th-century moated manor
house*

**Cadbury World**
Bournville, West Midlands
0845 450 3599
cadburyworld.co.uk
*Chocolate-making
demonstrations and samples*

**Cider Museum and
King Offa Distillery**
Hereford
(01432) 354207
cidermuseum.co.uk
*Be sure to sample a free tasting of
distillery products*

**The Commandery**
Worcester
(01905) 361821
worcestercity-
museums.org.uk
*Exciting stories of power, greed,
war, wealth and romance*

**The Complete
Working Historic Estate
of Shugborough**
**(The National Trust)**
Milford, Staffordshire
(01889) 881388
shugborough.org.uk
*Explore 900 acres of historic
parkland with working Georgian
buildings*

**Compton Verney House**
Stratford-upon-Avon,
Warwickshire
(01926) 645500
comptonverney.org.uk
*Art collection in a listed building*

**Coventry Cathedral**
West Midlands
(024) 7652 1200
coventrycathedral.org.uk
*Unique 20th-century architecture
to both inspire and enthral*

**Coventry Transport Museum**
West Midlands
(024) 7623 4270
transport-museum.com
*Fascinating collection of vehicles
spanning all the ages*

**Drayton Manor Theme Park**
near Tamworth, Staffordshire
0870 872 5252
draytonmanor.co.uk
*Great rides and attractions set in
280 acres of parkland*

**Hampton Court Gardens**
Leominster, Herefordshire
(01568) 797777
hamptoncourt.org.uk
*Stunning organic gardens*

**Ironbridge Gorge**
**Museums**
Ironbridge, Shropshire
(01952) 432405
ironbridge.org.uk
*Revolutionary inventions in
inspiring museums*

**Kenilworth Castle**
Warwickshire
(01926) 852078
english-heritage.org.uk
*A vast complex of ruined
fortifications and palatial apartments*

**The Museum of the Jewellery
Quarter**
Hockley, Birmingham
(0121) 554 3598
bmag.org.uk
*The story of jewellery making in
Birmingham*

**National Motorcycle Museum**
Solihull, West Midlands
(01675) 443311
nationalmotorcyclemuseum.co.uk
*Largest of its kind in the world*

**National Sea Life Centre**
Birmingham, West Midlands
(0121) 643 6777
sealifeeurope.com
*Features tubular underwater walk-
though tunnel*

**Royal Air Force Museum**
Cosford, Shropshire
(01902) 376200
rafmuseum.org
*One of the largest aviation
collections in the UK*

**Royal Worcester Visitor Centre**
(01905) 746000
royalworcester.co.uk
*See craftmanship at work*

**Severn Valley Railway**
Bewdley, Worcestershire
(01299) 403816
svr.co.uk
*Steam trains running along the
beautiful Severn Valley*

**Shakespeare's Birthplace**
Stratford-upon-Avon,
Warwickshire
(01789) 204016
shakespeare.org.uk
*The bard's inspiring dwelling place*

**Shakespearience**
Stratford-upon-Avon,
Warwickshire
(01789) 290111
shakespearience.co.uk
*Thrilling show of Shakespeare's
lifestory*

**The Snowdome Leisure Island**
Tamworth, Staffordshire
0870 500 0011
snowdome.co.uk
*UK's premier real snow centre*

**Thinktank – Birmingham Science Museum**
(0121) 202 2222
thinktank.ac
*Hands on exhibits and interactive fun*

**Trentham Leisure Ltd**
Stoke-on-Trent,
Staffordshire
(01782) 657341
trenthamleisure.co.uk
*England's largest garden restoration project*

**The Wedgwood Visitor Centre**
Stoke-on-Trent,
Staffordshire
0870 606 1759
thewedgwoodvisitorcentre.com
*Displays, factory tours and sweeping parkland*

**West Midland Safari & Leisure Park**
Bewdley, Worcestershire
(01299) 402114
wmsp.co.uk
*Observe rare white lions*

**Weston Park**
near Shifnal, Staffordshire
(01952) 852100
weston-park.com
*One thousand acres of natural beauty with three centuries of garden design*

# Diary dates 2008

**The National Boat, Caravan & Outdoor Show**
NEC, Birmingham
boatandcaravan.co.uk
19 – 24 Feb

**Crufts**
NEC, Birmingham
thekennelclub.org.uk
6 – 9 Mar

**The Ordnance Survey Outdoors Show**
NEC, Birmingham
theoutdoorsshow.co.uk
14 – 16 Mar

**The Cosford Air Show**
cosfordairshow.co.uk
1 Jun

**Three Counties Countryside Show**
The Malvern Showground, Worcestershire
threecounties.co.uk
13 – 15 Jun

**Godiva Festival**
Memorial Park, Coventry
godivafestival.co.uk
11 – 13 Jul*

**The Big Chill**
Eastnor Castle, Ledbury
bigchill.net
1 – 3 Aug

**Ludlow Marches Food and Drink Festival**
foodfestival.co.uk
12 – 14 Sep

**Worcester Christmas Fayre**
worcestershire.gov.uk
27 – 30 Nov

**Frankfurt Christmas Market**
Victoria Square/New Street, Birmingham
birmingham.gov.uk
13 Nov – 23 Dec*

* provisional date at time of going to press

# Tourist Information Centres

When you arrive at your destination, visit an Official Partner Tourist Information Centre for quality assured help with accommodation and information about local attractions and events, or email your request before you go.

| | | | |
|---|---|---|---|
| Bewdley | Load Street | (01299) 404740 | bewdleytic@wyreforestdc.gov.uk |
| Birmingham Rotunda | 150 New Street | 0870 225 0127 | callcentre@marketingbirmingham.com |
| Bridgnorth | Listley Street | (01746) 763257 | bridgnorth.tourism@shropshire-cc.gov.uk |
| Burton upon Trent | Coors Visitor Centre | (01283) 508111 | tic@eaststaffsbc.gov.uk |
| Coventry Airport | Coventry Airport South | (024) 7622 7264 | tic@cvone.co.uk |
| Coventry Cathedral | Cathedral Ruins | (024) 7622 7264 | tic@cvone.co.uk |
| Coventry Ricoh Arena | Phoenix Way | 0870 111 6397 | tic@cvone.co.uk |
| Coventry Transport Museum | Hales Street | (024) 7622 7264 | tic@cvone.co.uk |
| Hereford | 1 King Street | (01432) 268430 | tic-hereford@herefordshire.gov.uk |
| Ironbridge | Ironbridge Gorge Museum Trust | (01952) 884391 | tic@ironbridge.org.uk |
| Leamington Spa | The Parade | 0870 160 7930 | info@shakespeare-country.co.uk |
| Leek | 1 Market Place | (01538) 483741 | tourism.services@staffsmoorlands.gov.uk |
| Lichfield | Lichfield Garrick | (01543) 412112 | info@visitlichfield.com |
| Ludlow | Castle Street | (01584) 875053 | ludlow.tourism@shropshire-cc.gov.uk |
| Malvern | 21 Church Street | (01684) 892289 | malvern.tic@malvernhills.gov.uk |
| Oswestry | Mile End | (01691) 662488 | tic@oswestry-bc.gov.uk |
| Ross-on-Wye | Edde Cross Street | (01989) 562768 | tic-ross@herefordshire.gov.uk |
| Rugby | Little Elborow Street | (01788) 534970 | visitor.centre@rugby.gov.uk |
| Shrewsbury | The Square | (01743) 281200 | visitorinfo@shrewsbury.gov.uk |
| Stafford | Market Street | (01785) 619619 | tic@staffordbc.gov.uk |
| Stoke-on-Trent | Victoria Hall | (01782) 236000 | stoke.tic@stoke.gov.uk |
| Stratford-upon-Avon | Bridgefoot | 0870 160 7930 | info@shakespeare-country.co.uk |
| Tamworth | 29 Market Street | (01827) 709581 | tic@tamworth.gov.uk |
| Warwick | Jury Street | (01926) 492212 | touristinfo@warwick-uk.co.uk |
| Worcester | High Street | (01905) 726311 | touristinfo@cityofworcester.gov.uk |

# Travel info

**By road:**
Britain's main motorways (M1/M6/M5) meet in the Heart of England; the M40 links with the M42 south of Birmingham while the M4 provides fast access from London to the south of the region. These road links ensure that the Heart of England is more accessible by road than any other region in the UK.

**By rail:**
The Heart of England is served by an excellent rail network. InterCity rail services are fast and frequent from London and other major cities into the region. Trains run from Euston to Birmingham, Coventry and Rugby; from Paddington to the Cotswolds, Stratford-upon-Avon and Worcester; and from Marylebone to Birmingham and Stourbridge. From the main stations a network of regional routes take you around the Heart of England.

**By air:**
Fly into Birmingham, Coventry or Nottingham East Midlands.

Brindleyplace, Birmingham

# Find out more

Further information is available from the following organisations:

**Marketing Birmingham**
(0121) 202 5115
visitbirmingham.com

**Black Country Tourism**
blackcountrytourism.co.uk

**Visit Coventry & Warwickshire**
(024) 7622 7264
visitcoventryandwarwickshire.co.uk

**Visit Herefordshire**
(01432) 260621
visitherefordshire.co.uk

**Shakespeare Country**
0870 160 7930
shakespeare-country.co.uk

**Shropshire Tourism**
(01743) 462462
shropshiretourism.info

**Destination Staffordshire**
0870 500 4444
enjoystaffordshire.com

**Stoke-on-Trent**
(01782) 236000
visitstoke.co.uk

**Destination Worcestershire**
(01905) 728787
visitworcestershire.org

# Help before you go

To search for attractions and Tourist Information Centres on the move just text INFO to 62233, and a web link will be sent to your mobile phone.

## where to stay in
# Heart of England

All place names in the blue bands are shown on the maps at the front of this guide.

A complete listing of all Enjoy England assessed accommodation covered by this guide appears at the back.

### Accommodation symbols

Symbols give useful information about services and facilities. Inside the back-cover flap you can find a key to these symbols. Keep it open for easy reference.

---

**ALTON,** Staffordshire Map ref 4B2

★ ★ ★
**GUEST ACCOMMODATION**

B&B per room per night
s £35.00–£45.00
d £55.00–£65.00
Evening meal per person
£5.95–£13.95

## Bulls Head Inn

High Street, Alton, Stoke-on-Trent ST10 4AQ  t (01538) 702307  f (01538) 702065
e janet@thebullsheadalton.co.uk  w altontowers-bedandbreakfast.co.uk

**open** All year
**bedrooms** 5 double, 1 twin, 1 family
**bathrooms** All en suite
**payment** Credit/debit cards, cash/cheques

This family-owned business is in the village of Alton, close to Alton Towers. An 18thC inn offering traditional cask ales and home cooking, with a real log fire and a friendly atmosphere. All rooms en suite, separate restaurant.

♥ *Group bookings welcome if over 18 years of age. Birthday celebrations and hen parties accommodated. Small-conference facilities available.*

Room 📺 🐾  General 🗂 🏭 🖐 P ⚡ ✕ ✿  Leisure 🚲

---

**ALTON,** Staffordshire Map ref 4B2

★ ★ ★ ★
**BED & BREAKFAST**

B&B per room per night
s £28.00–£35.00
d £40.00–£46.00
Evening meal per person
£8.00–£15.00

## Fields Farm

Chapel Lane, Threapwood Alton, Stoke-on-Trent ST10 4QZ  t (01538) 752721 & 07850 310381
f (01538) 757404  e pat.massey@fieldsfarmbb.co.uk  w fieldsfarmbb.co.uk

Traditional farmhouse hospitality and comfort in picturesque Churnet Valley, ten minutes from Alton Towers near Peak District National Park, Potteries, stately homes. Stabling available. Ideal walking, cycling, riding, fishing. Family rooms.

**open** All year
**bedrooms** 1 double, 1 twin, 1 family
**bathrooms** 2 en suite, 1 private
**payment** Cash/cheques

Room 📺 🐾 🍵  General 🗂 🏭 🖐 P ✂ ✕ 🧺 🐴 ✿ 🐎  Leisure ∪ 🚲 🏛

---

## Place index

If you know where you want to stay, the index at the back of the guide will give you the page number listing accommodation in your chosen town, city or village. Check out the other useful indexes too.

## ALTON, Staffordshire Map ref 4B2

★★★
**BED & BREAKFAST**

B&B per room per night
s £25.00–£30.00
d £40.00–£60.00

# Hillside Farm

Alton Road, Uttoxeter ST14 5HG  **t** (01889) 590760  **f** (01889) 590760
**w** smoothhound.co.uk/hotels/hillside.html

**open** All year
**bedrooms** 1 double, 3 family
**bathrooms** 1 en suite, 1 private
**payment** Cash/cheques

Victorian farmhouse with extensive views to the
Weaver Hills and Churnet Valley. Situated two miles
south of Alton Towers on B5032.

⊕ From A50 Uttoxeter onto B5030 (signed Ashbourne) for
4.5 miles, at Rocester turn left for Denstone and Alton
Towers, T-junction left onto B5032, 1st farm on left.

Room 📺 ♨ 🛎  General 🐾 🗏 ⅍ P ⛺ 🐾 ☼

## ALTON, Staffordshire Map ref 4B2

★★★★
**GUEST HOUSE**

B&B per room per night
s Min £30.00
d Min £50.00

# Windy Arbour

Hollis Lane, Denstone, Uttoxeter ST14 5HP  **t** (01889) 591013  **f** (01889) 591053
**e** stay@windyarbour.co.uk  **w** windyarbour.co.uk

**open** All year except Christmas and New Year
**bedrooms** 1 twin, 2 family, 2 suites
**bathrooms** 4 en suite, 1 private
**payment** Credit/debit cards, cash/cheques

Windy Arbour is a peaceful haven graced with
superb views and big skies. A warm country
welcome is guaranteed. The farmhouse and
converted outbuildings can accommodate up to 24.
Alton Towers, Peak District and Derbyshire Dales all
within easy reach.

⊕ From A50 follow signs for Alton Towers. Turn left into
Denstone, following signs for college. Ahead is Hollis Lane,
leading to the hilltop farm.

♥ Family rooms: £60 (4 sharing), £80 (5 sharing), £100
(8 sharing). 4 nights for 3; 7 nights for 5.

Room 🛁 📺 ♨ 🛎  General 🐾 🗏 ⅍ P ⛺ 🐾 ◉ ☼ 🐕

## ALVECHURCH, Worcestershire Map ref 4B3

★★★
**FARMHOUSE**

B&B per room per night
s £40.00
d £60.00

# Alcott Farm

Icknield Street, Weatheroak, Alvechurch B48 7EH  **t** (01564) 824051  **f** (01564) 829779
**e** alcottfarm@btinternet.com  **w** alcottfarm.co.uk

**open** All year
**bedrooms** 2 double, 2 twin
**bathrooms** All en suite
**payment** Cash/cheques

Country residence close to M42 junction 3. 20
minutes from Birmingham International Airport and
NEC. Solihull, Stratford and Redditch are close by.
This interesting country home has spacious en suite
bedrooms with one double room located on the
ground floor. Good pubs and restaurants close by.

⊕ Leave M42 at jct 3, take A435 towards Birmingham, past
garage. Take slip road on left signposted Weatheroak, go
left for 1.5 miles to crossroads, turn left down steep hill,
then left immediately opposite Coach and Horses pub.
Alcott farm is 0.5 miles on right-hand side, up long post
and rail drive.

Room 🛁 📺 ♨ 🛎  General 🐾 10 P ⅍ 🐾 🗎 ◉ ☼ 🐕  Leisure ∪ ♩ ⅂

## ASTLEY, Worcestershire Map ref 4A3

★★★★
**BED & BREAKFAST**

B&B per room per night
s £35.00–£40.00
d £55.00–£60.00

# Woodhampton House

Weather Lane, Astley, Stourport-on-Severn DY13 0SF  **t** (01299) 826510  **f** (01299) 827059
**e** pete-a@sally-a.freeserve.co.uk  **w** woodhamptonhouse.co.uk

Delightful coach house set in rural location, yet
close to Stourport and other places of interest.
Always a warm and friendly welcome. Excellent
breakfast. Family room £65.00–£75.00.

**open** All year except Christmas
**bedrooms** 1 twin, 1 family
**bathrooms** All en suite
**payment** Cash/cheques

Room 🛏 📺 🛜 🍵  General 🏅5 🍴 🐾

## ASTON MUNSLOW, Shropshire Map ref 4A3

★★★★★
**BED & BREAKFAST**
**SILVER AWARD**

B&B per room per night
s £30.00–£35.00
d £60.00–£70.00
Evening meal per person
£20.00

# Chadstone

Aston Munslow, Craven Arms SY7 9ER  **t** (01584) 841675  **f** (01584) 841620
**e** chadstone.lee@btinternet.com  **w** chadstonebandb.co.uk

**open** All year
**bedrooms** 1 double, 2 twin
**bathrooms** All en suite
**payment** Cash/cheques, euros

Chadstone offers friendly, personal service and
luxurious en suite accommodation in the renowned
Corvedale. Enjoy panoramic views and the peace
and quiet of the South Shropshire countryside.
Quoting our guests: 'Superb accommodation,
delicious food served by wonderful hosts'. 'Highly
recommended. Will come again soon'. 'Every detail
made it all so perfect.'

⊕ In Craven Arms, turn off A49 onto B4368 towards
Bridgnorth. In Aston Munslow, pass Swan public house on
left. Chadstone is 50m further on, on right.

Room 🛏 📺 🛜 🍵  General 🏅12 P 🍴 ✕ 🅷 ❊  Leisure 🎣 🏊

## ATHERSTONE, Warwickshire Map ref 4B3

★★★
**BED & BREAKFAST**

B&B per room per night
s £25.00
d £35.00

# Manor Farm Bed & Breakfast

Main Road, Ratcliffe Culey, Hinckley CV9 3NY  **t** (01827) 712269  **e** user88024@aol.com

A bed and breakfast at a working dairy farm in a
small village. Within close distance of a public
house and two miles from a town. Four miles from
M42, 25 minutes from NEC.

**open** All year except Christmas
**bedrooms** 1 double, 1 twin
**payment** Cash/cheques

Room 📺 🛜 🍵  General 🏅 🍳 ♨ 🍴 🖼 🅷 ❊ 🐾  Leisure ∪ 🏊

## BARFORD, Warwickshire Map ref 2B1

★★★★
**BED & BREAKFAST**
**SILVER AWARD**

B&B per room per night
s £50.00–£65.00
d £60.00–£75.00

# Westham House B&B

Westham Lane, Warwick CV35 8DP  **t** (01926) 624148  **f** (01926) 624388
**e** westham_house@hotmail.com  **w** westhamhouse.co.uk

**open** All year except Christmas and New Year
**bedrooms** 3 double, 2 twin, 1 single
**bathrooms** 3 en suite, 3 private
**payment** Credit/debit cards, cash/cheques, euros

Westham House is a large country house built in
1877, originally a hunting lodge, now tastefully
modernised but retaining a quiet, relaxed, country
house atmosphere with a friendly welcome to
business and holiday guests. A peaceful setting in
five acres. A perfect location to explore the historic
surrounding area.

⊕ M40 jct 15, A429 towards Stow. 1.2 miles on right is
Westham Lane. Follow brown tourist sign. Westham House
300m on right.

Room 🛏 📺 🛜 🍵  General P 🍴 🅷 🖵 ❊

## BIRMINGHAM, West Midlands Map ref 4B3

★ ★ ★
GUEST ACCOMMODATION

B&B per room per night
s £34.00–£44.00
d £48.00–£58.00

# Elmdon Guest House

2369 Coventry Road, Sheldon, Birmingham B26 3PN  t (0121) 688 1720 & (0121) 742 1626
f (0121) 742 1626  e elmdonhouse@blueyonder.co.uk  w elmdonguesthouse.co.uk

Family-run guesthouse with en suite facilities. TV in all rooms, including Sky. On main A45 close to the NEC, airport, railway and city centre.

**open** All year except Christmas and New Year
**bedrooms** 1 double, 2 twin, 2 single, 1 family, 1 suite
**bathrooms** All en suite
**payment** Credit/debit cards, cash/cheques

Room 🛏 📺 🛜 ♨  General 🛎 🏠 🖩 P 🎱 🛋 🔥 ✿ 🐾  Leisure 🏛

## BIRMINGHAM, West Midlands Map ref 4B3

★ ★
GUEST ACCOMMODATION

B&B per room per night
s £22.00–£41.00
d £39.00–£51.00
Evening meal per person
£5.00–£9.00

# Rollason Wood

130 Wood End Road, Erdington, Birmingham B24 8BJ  t (0121) 373 1230  f (0121) 382 2578
e rollwood@globalnet.co.uk  w rollasonwoodhotel.co.uk

Friendly, family-run hotel, one mile from M6, exit 6. Convenient for city centre, NEC and Convention Centre. A la carte restaurant and bar.

**open** All year except Christmas
**bedrooms** 3 double, 5 twin, 19 single, 8 family
**bathrooms** 10 en suite, 1 private
**payment** Credit/debit cards, cash/cheques

Room 🛏 📺 🛜 ♨  General 🛎 🖩 P 🎱 ✕ 🛋 ▣ ✿ 🐾  Leisure ♣

## BIRMINGHAM INTERNATIONAL AIRPORT

See under Birmingham, Coleshill, Coventry, Meriden, Solihull

## BROADWAY, Worcestershire Map ref 2B1

★ ★ ★ ★
GUEST ACCOMMODATION

B&B per room per night
s £65.00–£70.00
d £75.00–£80.00
Evening meal per person
£10.25–£14.95

# The Bell at Willersey

The Bell Inn, Willersey, Broadway WR12 7PJ  t (01386) 858405  f (01386) 853563
e enq@bellatwillersey.fsnet.co.uk  w the-bell-willersey.com

**open** All year
**bedrooms** 2 double, 1 twin, 2 suites
**bathrooms** All en suite
**payment** Credit/debit cards, cash/cheques

17thC inn overlooking the village green and duck pond. One mile from Broadway, a perfect location for touring. Enjoys a high reputation for home-produced food. Restaurant open lunchtime and evenings. Relax in our superb bedrooms situated in our courtyard.

⊕ From the A44, take the B4632 (signposted Willersey). A full map is on our website.

Room 🛏 📠 📺 🛜 ♨  General 🛎 🏠 P ⚔ 🎱 ✕ 🍳 ✿  Leisure ▶

# Country Code always follow the Country Code

- Be safe – plan ahead and follow any signs
- Leave gates and property as you find them
- Protect plants and animals, and take your litter home
- Keep dogs under close control
- Consider other people

## BROADWAY, Worcestershire Map ref 2B1

★★★★
**GUEST ACCOMMODATION**

B&B per room per night
s £51.50
d £93.00
Evening meal per person
£15.65

# Farncombe Estate Centre

Farncombe House, Broadway WR12 7LJ  **t** (01386) 854100  **e** visit@farncombeestate.co.uk
**w** farncombeestate.co.uk

**open** All year except Christmas and New Year
**bedrooms** 9 double, 5 twin, 39 single
**bathrooms** All en suite
**payment** Credit/debit cards, cash/cheques

Comfortable B&B accommodation set in 300 acres of beautiful grounds in the North Cotswolds near the picturesque village of Broadway. 53 en suite bedrooms and fully equipped meeting rooms are available for hire. Group travel or exclusive-use bookings welcome by arrangement. Weekend leisure course and event programme available.

⊕ *Direct train from London Paddington to Moreton-in-Marsh. By road: located just off the A44 (Fish Hill) outside Broadway. 30 minutes from Cheltenham/Stratford-upon-Avon/Tewkesbury.*

♥ *Weekend leisure-course breaks and 3-night deals throughout the year. Last-minute discounts available.*

Room 🛏 ✆ 📺 🕯 ♨   General 🛎 P ⚡ ✕ 🍴 🏛 🌳 🐾   Leisure ● ⚘ ⚑ 🚲

## BROSELEY, Shropshire Map ref 4A3

★★★★★
**GUEST HOUSE**
**SILVER AWARD**

B&B per room per night
s £59.95
d £79.95–£129.95
Evening meal per person
£9.95–£29.95

# The Old Rectory at Broseley

46 Ironbridge Road, Broseley TF12 5AF  **t** (01952) 883399  **f** (01952) 882857
**e** info@theoldrectoryatbroseley.co.uk  **w** theoldrectoryatbroseley.co.uk

**open** All year except Christmas and New Year
**bedrooms** 8 double, 1 twin, 1 single, 2 family
**bathrooms** 7 en suite, 5 private
**payment** Credit/debit cards, cash/cheques

The Old Rectory at Broseley is located within a mile of the Ironbridge and the other gorge attractions, enjoys a tranquil setting in two acres of established gardens, and has recently been tastefully restored to very high standards. It offers comfort, quality, charm and character second to none.

⊕ *Please go to our website for a full set of directions.*

♥ *Please got to our website where our current and future promotions can be seen.*

Room 🛏 🍳 📺 🕯 ♨   General 🛎 2 🍴 🏛 P ⚡ 🌳 🌸   Leisure 🚣 🚲 🏊

## BURTON UPON TRENT, Staffordshire Map ref 4B3

Rating Applied For
**GUEST ACCOMMODATION**

B&B per room per night
s £30.00–£40.00
d £50.00–£55.00

# A511.co.uk

20 Station Road, Hatton, Derby DE65 5EL  **t** (01283) 815996  **e** rod@invictaindustrial.co.uk
**w** A511.co.uk

Convenient for Burton-on-Trent, Uttoxeter and Derby. National Forest, Tutbury Castle, Peak District, East Midlands Airport, Donington Park, Sudbury Hall and other National Trust properties nearby.

**open** All year
**bedrooms** 1 double, 1 twin, 1 family
**bathrooms** All en suite
**payment** Credit/debit cards

Room 🛏 📺 🕯 ♨   General 🛎 P ⚡ 🌳

# It's all quality-assessed accommodation

Our commitment to quality involves wide-ranging accommodation assessment. Rating and awards were correct at the time of going to press but may change following a new assessment. Please check at time of booking.

## CHEADLE, Staffordshire Map ref 4B2

★★★★
FARMHOUSE

B&B per room per night
s £25.00
d £50.00
Evening meal per person
£7.50–£10.00

# Rakeway House Farm B&B

Rakeway Road, Cheadle, Alton Towers Area ST10 1RA  t (01538) 755295
e enquiries@rakewayhousefarm.co.uk  w rakewayhousefarm.co.uk

Charming farmhouse, beautiful gardens. Fantastic views over Cheadle and surrounding countryside. Alton Towers 15 minutes' drive. Good base for Peak District and Potteries. First-class accommodation, excellent menu, superb hospitality.

open All year
bedrooms 1 double, 1 twin, 1 family
bathrooms All en suite
payment Cash/cheques

Room  General  Leisure

## CLEOBURY MORTIMER, Shropshire Map ref 4A3

★★★
FARMHOUSE

B&B per room per night
s £35.00
d £60.00
Evening meal per person
£10.00–£15.00

# Broome Park Farm

Catherton Road, Cleobury Mortimer, Kidderminster DY14 0LB  t (01299) 270647
e catherine@broomeparkfarm.co.uk  w broomeparkfarm.co.uk

Family-friendly, recently restored farmhouse accommodation. Peaceful location on working farm. Spacious en suite rooms, guest sitting and dining rooms. Evening meals by arrangement. Excellent facilities for families.

open All year
bedrooms 1 double, 1 family
bathrooms All en suite
payment Cash/cheques

Room  General  Leisure

## CLUN, Shropshire Map ref 4A3

★★★
INN

B&B per room per night
s Min £30.00
d Min £50.00
Evening meal per person
£5.25–£12.00

# The White Horse Inn

The Square, Clun SY7 8JA  t (01588) 640305  f (01588) 640460  e jack@whi-clun.co.uk
w whi-clun.co.uk

Small, friendly, Good Beer Guide-listed public house with well-appointed, en suite family bedrooms in a traditional style. Wide-ranging menu available in the dining room.

open All year except Christmas
bedrooms 1 double, 3 family
bathrooms All en suite
payment Credit/debit cards, cash/cheques

Room  General  Leisure

## COLESHILL, Warwickshire Map ref 4B3

★★★★
BED & BREAKFAST

B&B per room per night
s £50.00–£55.00
d £55.00–£65.00

# Merrimoles Bed & Breakfast

Back Lane, Shustoke, Coleshill, Birmingham B46 2AW  t (01675) 481158  e stella@merrimoles.co.uk
w merrimoles.co.uk

open All year except Christmas and New Year
bedrooms 2 double, 1 twin
bathrooms 2 en suite, 1 private
payment Cash/cheques

Merrimoles provides a quiet respite ideal for breaks in North Warwickshire. Just minutes from the M6, M6 Toll and M42, whether you are visiting the area on holiday, visiting the NEC or on a shopping break in Birmingham, take advantage of the modern rooms, relaxed atmosphere and excellent breakfast on offer.

⊕ From Coleshill, B4114 to Shustoke. Pass The Plough on right, first right onto The Green, first right into Back Lane, first house on the right.

Room  General 5  Leisure

## Key to symbols
Open the back flap for a key to symbols.

## COLTON, Staffordshire Map ref 4B3

★ ★ ★ ★ ★
**GUEST HOUSE**

B&B per room per night
s £42.00–£70.00
d £58.00–£90.00
Evening meal per person
£8.00–£11.00

# Colton House

Bellamour Way, Colton, Rugeley WS15 3LL  **t** (01889) 578580  **f** (01889) 578580
**e** mail@coltonhouse.com  **w** coltonhouse.com

**open** All year
**bedrooms** 4 double
**bathrooms** All en suite
**payment** Credit/debit cards, cash/cheques

Set in a pretty, peaceful village this superbly restored luxurious large Georgian home has breathtaking views, individually designed rooms, comfortable guest lounge, four poster bed, 5ft jacuzzi, power showers, Egyptian fluffy towels, large patio and 1.5 acre garden, where you can enjoy dinner with home grown vegetables and a glass of wine.

⊕ From M6 Toll jct 7, take A460 to Rugeley then B5013 towards Uttoxeter. After 2 miles, turn right into Colton. Colton House is 0.25 miles on the right.

♥ Occasional special offers.

Room ▥ TV ♿ 🍳  General P ⚡ ✕ 🍴 ♨ 🛁 ❄  Leisure ∪ ⚓ ⚐

## COTSWOLDS

See under Broadway, Long Compton
See also Cotswolds in the South East England and South West England sections

## COUGHTON, Warwickshire Map ref 2B1

★ ★ ★ ★
**GUEST HOUSE**

B&B per room per night
s £45.00–£55.00
d £60.00–£75.00

# Coughton Lodge

Coughton, Alcester B49 5HU  **t** (01789) 764600  **f** (01789) 400150
**e** enquiries@coughtonlodge.co.uk  **w** coughtonlodge.co.uk

**open** All year except Christmas and New Year
**bedrooms** 9 double, 2 twin, 1 family
**bathrooms** All en suite
**payment** Credit/debit cards, cash/cheques, euros

Attractive half-timbered lodge standing in large garden with ample parking. Newly refurbished. The lodge provides high-quality en suite, ground-floor rooms set around an interior courtyard and water garden. An ideal base for exploring nearby Stratford-on-Avon, Warwick, Broadway and the Cotswolds. A warm welcome and magnificent breakfast guaranteed.

⊕ M42 jct 3. A435 towards Evesham. Continue on A435 through Studley to village of Coughton. Coughton Lodge is on right, opposite entrance to Coughton Court.

♥ Discounts for group bookings or for stays of more than 3 days. Telephone for details.

Room ♿ TV ♿ 🍳  General 🛋 🍴 ♨ P 🛁 ❄  Leisure ∪ ⚓ ⚐ 🚲 🏇

# Discover Britain's heritage

Discover the history and beauty of over 250 of Britain's best-known historic houses, castles, gardens and small manor houses. You can purchase Britain's Historic Houses and Gardens – Guide and Map from good bookshops and online at visitbritaindirect.com.

## COVENTRY, West Midlands Map ref 4B3

★★★
GUEST HOUSE

B&B per room per night
s £30.00–£40.00
d £50.00–£55.00

# Ashdowns Guest House

12 Regent Street, Earlsdon, Coventry CV1 3EP   t (024) 7622 9280

**open** All year except Christmas and New Year
**bedrooms** 3 double, 2 twin, 2 single, 1 family
**bathrooms** 7 en suite
**payment** Cash/cheques

Family-run guesthouse offering quality accommodation convenient for city centre, rail and bus services, NEC, NAC, university and Coventry and Birmingham airports. A warm welcome awaits you in this relaxed, non-smoking family home. Own private car park.

⊕ *From ring road, turn right into Westminster Road and then right into Regent Street.*

Room 🛏 📺 🕪 ☃   General ☃12 P ⅙ 🍴 🎿 ✿   Leisure 🏊

## COVENTRY, West Midlands Map ref 4B3

★★★
GUEST HOUSE

B&B per room per night
s £29.50–£35.00
d £45.00–£52.00
Evening meal per person
£6.00–£8.00

# Ashleigh House

17 Park Road, Coventry CV1 2LH   t (024) 7622 3804   f (024) 7622 3804

Experience a warm welcome from friendly, helpful staff. Well maintained and equipped, en suite accommodation. All city amenities and railway station five minutes' walk. Licensed. Evening meals (varied menu available).

**open** All year except Christmas and New Year
**bedrooms** 2 twin, 5 single, 3 family
**bathrooms** All en suite
**payment** Cheques

Room 📺 🕪 ☃   General ☃ 🍴 P 🍴 ✕ 🍴 🎿 ▣

## COVENTRY, West Midlands Map ref 4B3

★★★
GUEST ACCOMMODATION

B&B per room per night
s £22.00–£35.00
d £36.00–£46.00
Evening meal per person
£3.00–£5.00

# Highcroft Guest House

65 Barras Lane, Coundon, Coventry CV1 4AQ   t (024) 7622 8157   f (024) 7663 1609
e deepakcov@hotmail.com

Large, detached guesthouse close to city centre. A family-run business that endeavours to make guests feel at home. Discounts available. Good transport to airports, train stations and motorways.

**open** All year
**bedrooms** 1 double, 2 single, 2 family
**bathrooms** 2 en suite, 3 private
**payment** Cash/cheques

Room 📺 🕪 ☃   General ☃ P ✕ 🍴 🎿 ✿ 🐾   Leisure ▶ 🏊

## ENDON, Staffordshire Map ref 4B2

★★★
FARMHOUSE

B&B per room per night
s £20.00–£25.00
d £44.00–£50.00

# Hollinhurst Farm

Park Lane, Endon, Stoke-on-Trent ST9 9JB   t (01782) 502633   e joan.hollinhurst@btconnect.com

Dairy farm, 116 acres. 17thC farmhouse within easy reach of The Potteries, Peak District and Alton Towers. Panoramic views, walking and touring.

**open** All year
**bedrooms** 1 double, 1 twin, 1 family
**bathrooms** 2 en suite, 1 private
**payment** Cash/cheques

Room 🛏 📺 🕪 ☃   General ☃ 🍴 P ⅙ ✿ 🐾   Leisure U ♪

## Looking for a little luxury

Gold and Silver Awards are given to establishments achieving the highest levels of quality and service. There's more information at the front of the guide, and an index to all accommodation achieving these awards at the back.

---

**FILLONGLEY,** Warwickshire Map ref 4B3

★★★★
**FARMHOUSE**
**SILVER AWARD**

B&B per room per night
s £30.00–£35.00
d £60.00–£65.00

## Grooms Cottage

Manor House Farm, Green End Road, Fillongley, Coventry CV7 8DS  **t** (01676) 540256

The groom's cottage at Manor House Farm was built in 1874 and has twin-bedded rooms with en suite facilities. Close to National Exhibition Centre.

**open** All year except Christmas
**bedrooms** 1 twin
**bathrooms** En suite
**payment** Cash/cheques

Room 🛏 📺 🌙 🗑  General 🐴

---

**GREAT WOLFORD,** Warwickshire Map ref 2B1

★★★★★
**BED & BREAKFAST**
**SILVER AWARD**

B&B per room per night
s £40.00–£50.00
d £60.00–£80.00

## The Old Coach House

Great Wolford, Shipston-on-Stour CV36 5NQ  **t** (01608) 674152
**e** theoldcoachhouse@thewolfords.net  **w** theoldecoachhouse.co.uk

**open** All year
**bedrooms** 2 double
**bathrooms** All en suite
**payment** Cash/cheques

This delightful old coach house, formerly part of the pub next door, with many original features, is set in a lovely garden, perfect for afternoon tea. A night in our pretty, en suite rooms and a delicious breakfast with local produce will prepare you for a day exploring the Cotswolds.

⊕ We are 2.75 miles off A44 Moreton, Chipping Norton, signposted Great Wolford. The Old Coach House is 1st on the right on entering the village.

♥ Double room, 3 nights for £180. Single room, 3 nights for £120.

Room 📺 🌙 🗑  General 🔔10 P ⚷ 🍴 ⚘, ✿  Leisure 🏊

---

**HEREFORD,** Herefordshire Map ref 2A1

## THE BOWENS COUNTRY HOUSE

Delightful Georgian house set in peaceful Wye Valley village, midway Hereford and Ross-on-Wye (B4224). Well appointed, en suite rooms (including ground floor, single and family rooms). All home-cooked meals using local produce. Vegetarians welcome. Fully licensed bar, good wine list. Large garden, putting green and grass tennis court (summer only).

**Fownhope, Hereford HR1 4PS**
**T: (01432) 860430  F: (01432) 860430**
**E: thebowenshotel@aol.com**
**www.thebowenshotel.co.uk**

● Dinner Bed & Breakfast breaks available all year ●

---

**HEREFORD,** Herefordshire Map ref 2A1

★★★★
**GUEST ACCOMMODATION**

B&B per room per night
s Min £45.00
d Min £75.00
Evening meal per person
Min £10.00

## Hedley Lodge

Belmont Abbey, Abergavenny Road, Hereford HR2 9RZ  **t** (01432) 374747
**e** hedley@belmontabbey.org.uk  **w** hedleylodge.com

Set in lovely grounds of Belmont Abbey, this friendly, modern guesthouse offers comfortably appointed rooms with en suite facilities. Licensed restaurant. 2.5 miles from Hereford. Ideal for visiting the Wye Valley.

**open** All year
**bedrooms** 6 double, 7 twin, 3 single, 1 family
**bathrooms** All en suite
**payment** Credit/debit cards, cash/cheques

Room 📞 📺 🌙  General 🔔 🛏 ♿ P 🍽 ✕ 🎱 🖥 ✿  Leisure ⚐ 🏊

## HEREFORD, Herefordshire Map ref 2A1

★★★
**GUEST HOUSE**

B&B per room per night
s Min £40.00
d Min £55.00

# Hopbine House

The Hopbine, Roman Road, Holmer, Hereford HR1 1LE  **t** (01432) 268722  **f** (01432) 268722
**e** info@hopbine.com  **w** hopbine.com

Twelve ground-floor rooms, comfortable and attractive. All en suite. Tea/coffee, TV, clock/radio, hairdryers. Large car parks. Two-acre grounds. One mile city centre.

**open** All year
**bedrooms** 4 double, 4 twin, 4 family
**bathrooms** All en suite
**payment** Cash/cheques, euros

Room 👤 📺 🛏 ♨  General 🔥 🛍 ♿ P 🍴 🐾 ✿  Leisure ∪ 🚣 🚴 ⛵

## HOCKLEY HEATH, West Midlands Map ref 4B3

★★★★
**GUEST HOUSE**

B&B per room per night
s £35.00–£40.00
d £50.00–£60.00

# Illshaw Heath Farm

Kineton Lane, Hockley Heath, Solihull B94 6RX  **t** (01564) 782214  **e** janetgarner@btinternet.com
**w** illshawheathfarm.com

Working farm in quiet location, minutes away from M42 junction 4, National Exhibition Centre and airport. Conveniently situated for Birmingham, Coventry and Shakespeare Country.

**open** All year except Christmas and New Year
**bedrooms** 1 double, 4 twin
**bathrooms** 4 en suite, 1 private
**payment** Cash/cheques

Room 👤 📺 🛏 ♨  General 🔥 P 🍴 🛍 ♿ 🍽 ✿ 🐴  Leisure ∪ 🚣 ⛵

## IRONBRIDGE, Shropshire Map ref 4A3

★★★★★
**GUEST ACCOMMODATION
SILVER AWARD**

B&B per room per night
s £52.00–£55.00
d £70.00–£75.00

# Bridge House

Buildwas Road, Ironbridge, Telford TF8 7BN  **t** (01952) 432105  **f** (01952) 432105
**w** smoothhound.co.uk

**open** All year except Christmas and New Year
**bedrooms** 2 double, 1 twin, 1 family
**bathrooms** All en suite
**payment** Credit/debit cards, cash/cheques

Charming 17thC country house situated by the River Severn and close to the famous Ironbridge. A house full of character and charm. Beautiful rooms all individually decorated and en suite, with a breakfast to be remembered. In all, the place to stay when visiting the famous Ironbridge Gorge. Family room rates also available.

⊕ *From M54 jct 6, approx 6 miles to Bridge House.*

Room 📺 🛏 ♨  General 🔥 ♿ P 🍴 🐾 ✿  Leisure 🚣

## KENILWORTH, Warwickshire Map ref 4B3

★★★★
**GUEST ACCOMMODATION
SILVER AWARD**

B&B per room per night
s £47.00–£62.00
d £70.00–£80.00

# Victoria Lodge

180 Warwick Road, Kenilworth CV8 1HU  **t** (01926) 512020  **f** (01926) 858703
**e** info@victorialodgehotel.co.uk  **w** victorialodgehotel.co.uk

**open** All year except Christmas
**bedrooms** 7 double, 2 twin, 1 single
**bathrooms** All en suite
**payment** Credit/debit cards, cash/cheques

Small, friendly hotel with individually styled en suite bedrooms, guest lounge, licensed bar, garden and off-street parking. Non-smoking establishment. Ideal for NEC, NAC, university, M40, airports.

Room 👤 📺 📞 📺 🛏 ♨  General 🔥 P 🍴 🍷 ✿

**KIDDERMINSTER,** Worcestershire Map ref 4B3

★★★★
GUEST HOUSE

B&B per room per night
s £35.00
d £55.00

# Bewdley Hill House

8 Bewdley Hill, Kidderminster DY11 6BS  t (01562) 60473  f 0871 236 1608
e info@bewdleyhillhouse.co.uk  w bewdleyhillhouse.co.uk

Attractive, en suite accommodation, colour TVs, tea/coffee facilities. Noted for full English breakfasts. Cosy surroundings, warm welcome and off-road parking. Wi-Fi Internet.

open All year except Christmas
bedrooms 2 double, 2 twin, 2 family
bathrooms All en suite
payment Credit/debit cards, cash/cheques

Room 🛏 TV 🍴 ☕  General 🛏 ♿ P ✂ 🛏  Leisure ✦ 🏠

---

**LEAMINGTON SPA,** Warwickshire Map ref 4B3

★★★★
BED & BREAKFAST

B&B per room per night
d £50.00–£60.00

# Braeside Bed & Breakfast

26 Temple End, Harbury, Nr Royal Leamington Spa CV33 9NE  t (01926) 613402
e rosemary@braesidebb.co.uk  w braesidebb.co.uk

Comfortable accommodation in Warwickshire village, close to historic Warwick. Within reach of Stratford-upon-Avon, the Cotswolds, Kenilworth, Coventry, Oxford, NEC, Stoneleigh Park, Gaydon Heritage Centre and the M40.

open All year except Christmas
bedrooms 1 double, 1 twin
bathrooms 1 en suite, 1 private
payment Cash/cheques

Room TV 🍴 ☕  General 🛏 🖼 ♿ ✂

---

**LEAMINGTON SPA,** Warwickshire Map ref 4B3

★★★
GUEST HOUSE

B&B per room per night
s £25.00–£35.00
d £35.00–£45.00

# Charnwood Guest House

47 Avenue Road, Leamington Spa CV31 3PF  t (01926) 831074  f (01926) 831074
e ray@charnwoodguesthouse.com  w charnwoodguesthouse.com

Semi-detached Victorian guesthouse, established for over 25 years, situated within walking distance of Leamington Spa town centre, railway station and leisure facilities. Parking. Open all year.

open All year
bedrooms 2 double, 2 twin, 1 single, 1 family
bathrooms 4 en suite, 1 private
payment Cash/cheques

Room TV 🍴  General 🛏3 P 🛏  Leisure ✦ ⛳ ♪ ▶ 🚴

---

**LEAMINGTON SPA,** Warwickshire Map ref 4B3

★★★★
FARMHOUSE
SILVER AWARD

B&B per room per night
s £39.00–£41.00
d £49.00–£51.00

# The Coach House

Snowford Hall Farm, Hunningham, Royal Leamington Spa CV33 9ES  t (01926) 632297
f (01926) 633599  e the_coach_house@lineone.net  w http://website.lineone.net/~the_coach_house

A 200-acre arable farm. Converted barn farmhouse off the Fosse Way, on the edge of Hunningham village. On elevated ground overlooking quiet surrounding countryside.

open All year except Christmas
bedrooms 1 double, 2 twin
bathrooms 2 en suite, 1 private
payment Cash/cheques

Room 🛏 🍴 ☕  General 🛏 🖼 ♿ P 🛏 ❄

---

**LEAMINGTON SPA,** Warwickshire Map ref 4B3

★★★★
FARMHOUSE

B&B per room per night
s £25.00–£35.00
d £25.00–£30.00

# Hill Farm

Lewis Road, Radford Semele, Leamington Spa CV31 1UX  t (01926) 337571
e rebecca@hillfarm3000.fsnet.co.uk  w hillfarm.info

Mixed, 350-acre farm. Farmhouse set in large attractive garden, two miles from Leamington town centre and close to Warwick Castle and Stratford-upon-Avon.

open All year except Christmas and New Year
bedrooms 3 double, 1 twin
bathrooms 3 en suite, 1 private
payment Cash/cheques

Room TV 🍴 ☕  General 🛏3 P ✂ 🛏 🖳 🖥 ❄

---

## Using map references

Map references refer to the colour maps at the front of this guide.

## LEAMINGTON SPA, Warwickshire Map ref 4B3

★★★★
**GUEST HOUSE**

B&B per room per night
s Min £49.00
d £54.00–£75.00

# Victoria Park Lodge

12 Adelaide Road, Leamington Spa CV31 3PW  t (01926) 424195  f (01926) 421521
e info@victoriaparkhotelleamingtonspa.co.uk  w victoriaparkhotelleamingtonspa.co.uk

Well-appointed bedrooms, all with en suite facilities and broadband Internet access. We pride ourselves on cleanliness and comfort, offering a home away from home in an excellent location.

open All year except Christmas and New Year
bedrooms 10 double, 2 twin, 8 single, 9 family
bathrooms All en suite
payment Credit/debit cards, cash/cheques

Room 🛏 📞 📺 🖥 🍵  General 👥 P 🍴 🎱 🔥 ☼  Leisure ∪ 🚣 🚴

## LEOMINSTER, Herefordshire Map ref 2A1

★★★★★
**BED & BREAKFAST
GOLD AWARD**

B&B per room per night
s £58.00–£75.00
d £80.00–£100.00

# Ryelands

Ryelands Road, Leominster HR6 8QB  t (01568) 617575  e info@ryelandsbandb.co.uk
w ryelandsbandb.co.uk

open All year except Christmas and New Year
bedrooms 1 double, 1 twin
bathrooms All en suite
payment Cash/cheques

Elegant Grade II Listed Regency house, in grounds of three acres. Well-equipped bedrooms furnished to a high standard with selected antique furniture; guest lounge with comfy sofas and a cosy fire. Ryelands is conveniently located on the outskirts of Leominster, whilst being surrounded by fields with splendid views towards the Black Mountains.

⊕ At Somerfield roundabout take Ryelands road, signposted Ivington. Continue for half mile to the national speed limit signs. Ryelands is 50yds on the left.

Room 🚪 📺 🖥 🍵  General 👥16 P 🔥 🎱 🔥 ☼  Leisure ∪ 🚣 ▸ 🚴 🏛

## LICHFIELD, Staffordshire Map ref 4B3

★★★★
**GUEST HOUSE**

B&B per room per night
s £35.00–£43.00
d £52.00–£64.00

# Coppers End Guest House

Walsall Road, Muckley Corner, Lichfield WS14 0BG  t (01543) 372910  f (01543) 360423
e info@coppersendguesthouse.co.uk  w coppersendguesthouse.co.uk

open All year except Christmas and New Year
bedrooms 3 double, 3 twin
bathrooms 4 en suite
payment Credit/debit cards, cash/cheques

Detached guesthouse of character and charm in its own grounds. Conservatory dining room, large walled garden with patio, guests' lounge. All bedrooms non-smoking. Vegetarians catered for. Off-road parking, safes in rooms, luggage racks. Easy access M6, M42 and M1, Lichfield, Walsall and Birmingham. Sixteen miles to NEC, six miles Whittington Barracks. Motorcyclist, cyclist and walker friendly.

⊕ 100yds from Muckley Corner roundabout off the A5, 3 miles south of Lichfield, Walsall 5 miles. Ordnance survey ref. SK083067. We are not pub/hotel at corner.

Room 🛏 📺 🖥 🍵  General 👥 🍳 P 🎱 🔥 ☼  Leisure ▸ 🏛

## Friendly help and advice

Tourist Information Centres offer friendly help with accommodation and holiday ideas as well as suggestions of places to visit and things to do. You'll find contact details at the beginning of each regional section.

**LONG COMPTON,** Warwickshire Map ref 2B1

★★★
**FARMHOUSE**

B&B per room per night
s Min £30.00
d Min £45.00

## Butlers Road Farm

Long Compton, Shipston-on-Stour CV36 5JZ  t (01608) 684262  f (01608) 684262
e eileen@butlersroad.com  w butlersroadfarm.co.uk

120-acre stock farm. Listed Cotswold-stone farmhouse adjacent to A3400 between Oxford and Stratford-upon-Avon. Home comforts. Local pub nearby. Rooms also function as family rooms.

open All year
bedrooms 1 double, 1 twin
payment Cash/cheques

Room General Leisure

**LOWER LOXLEY,** Staffordshire Map ref 4B2

Rating Applied For
**BED & BREAKFAST**

B&B per room per night
s £30.00–£35.00
d £56.00–£65.00
Evening meal per person
£8.00–£15.00

## The Grange

Uttoxeter ST14 8RZ  t (01889) 502021  e mary.grange@hotmail.co.uk  w bandbthegrangestaffs.co.uk

Unwind and enjoy old-fashioned hospitality and home cooking in our 17thC barn conversion. Log fire. Bridle paths. River fishing.

open All year
bedrooms 2 double, 1 family
bathrooms All en suite
payment Cash/cheques, euros

Room General Leisure

**LUDLOW,** Shropshire Map ref 4A3

★★★
**GUEST ACCOMMODATION**

B&B per room per night
s £45.00–£65.00
d £65.00

## The Bull

14 The Bull Ring, Ludlow SY8 1AD  t (01584) 873611  f (01584) 873666  e info@bull-ludlow.co.uk
w bull-ludlow.co.uk

open All year
bedrooms 2 double, 1 twin, 1 family
bathrooms All en suite
payment Credit/debit cards, cash/cheques

Situated in the town centre. The oldest pub in Ludlow, (earliest mention c1343). It was known as Peter of Proctor's house and probably dates back to c1199.

Room General Leisure

**LUDLOW,** Shropshire Map ref 4A3

★★★
**GUEST HOUSE**

B&B per room per night
s £22.00–£41.00
d £56.00–£62.00
Evening meal per person
£18.00

## Cecil Guest House

Sheet Road, Ludlow SY8 1LR  t (01584) 872442  f (01584) 872442

Attractive guesthouse 15 minutes' walk from town centre and station. Freshly cooked food from local produce. Residents' bar and lounge. Off-street parking.

open All year
bedrooms 2 double, 4 twin, 2 single, 1 family
bathrooms 7 en suite
payment Cash/cheques

Room General Leisure

## Check it out

Information on accommodation listed in this guide has been supplied by proprietors.
As changes may occur you should remember to check all relevant details at the time of booking.

## LUDLOW, Shropshire Map ref 4A3

★★★★★
**RESTAURANT WITH ROOMS**
**SILVER AWARD**

B&B per room per night
s £50.00–£75.00
d £75.00–£97.50
Evening meal per person
£25.00–£30.00

# The Clive Bar and Restaurant With Rooms

Bromfield, Ludlow SY8 2JR  t (01584) 856565 & (01584) 856665  f (01584) 856661
e info@theclive.co.uk  w theclive.co.uk

**open** All year except Christmas
**bedrooms** 8 double, 5 twin, 2 family
**bathrooms** All en suite
**payment** Credit/debit cards, cash/cheques

Set in the heart of South Shropshire's beautiful countryside, The Clive offers en suite bedrooms in period outbuildings that have been tastefully converted to provide contemporary accommodation and complimented by the 2 AA rosette Clive Restaurant, open every day. Located on main A49 road in the village of Bromfield, just two miles north of Ludlow with ample parking.

⊕ Situated in the village of Bromfield approx 2 miles north of Ludlow on main A49, next to Ludlow Food Centre.

♥ 3 nights for the price of 2, Sun-Thu nights (excl Christmas, New Year and Bank Holiday weekends). Oct-May only.

Room 🛏 ✆ 📺 🛁 ☜  General ⬠ 🎱 ♿ P ⚡ ♟ ✕ 🍴 ⚙ ✤  Leisure ∪ ♪ ► 🚲

## MALVERN, Worcestershire Map ref 2B1

★★★★
**GUEST HOUSE**

B&B per room per night
s £35.00–£45.00
d £60.00–£75.00

# Cannara Guest House

147 Barnards Green Road, Malvern WR14 3LT  t (01684) 564418  f (01684) 564418
e info@cannara.co.uk  w cannara.co.uk

Feel at home at Cannara, where style, ambience, attention to detail and guest comfort is of paramount importance to us.

**open** All year
**bedrooms** 2 double, 2 twin, 1 family
**bathrooms** All en suite
**payment** Credit/debit cards, cash/cheques

Room 🛏 📺 🛁 ☜  General ⬠ P ⚡ 🍴 ♟ 🖥 ✤ 🐾  Leisure 🏛

## MALVERN, Worcestershire Map ref 2B1

★★★
**BED & BREAKFAST**

B&B per room per night
s £30.00–£40.00
d £58.00–£65.00

# Harmony House Malvern

184 West Malvern Road, Malvern WR14 4AZ  t (01684) 891650  e catherine@harmonymalvern.com
w harmonyhousemalvern.com

A warm and spacious home set on the western slopes of the Malvern Hills. Close to footpaths and bus route. Wonderful views. Double/twin bed option. Organic/local food.

**open** All year
**bedrooms** 2 double, 1 family
**bathrooms** All en suite
**payment** Cash/cheques

Room 🛁 ☜  General 🍴 ♟ 🖥 🐾

# Accessible needs?

If you have special hearing, visual or mobility needs, there's an index of National Accessible Scheme participants featured in this guide. For more accessible accommodation buy a copy of Easy Access Britain available online at visitbritaindirect.com.

**MALVERN,** Worcestershire Map ref 2B1

★★★★
BED & BREAKFAST
SILVER AWARD

B&B per room per night
s Max £44.95
d Max £73.90

## Hidelow House

Acton Green, Acton Beauchamp, Malvern WR6 5AH **t** (01886) 884547 **f** (01886) 884658
**e** vist@hidelow.co.uk **w** hidelow.co.uk

**open** All year
**bedrooms** 2 double, 1 twin
**bathrooms** All en suite
**payment** Credit/debit cards, cash/cheques, euros

Small country house in peaceful pastureland, central for many places of historical interest, walking and golf. En suite rooms, magnificent residents' lounge with grand piano and sun terrace overlooking extensive, landscaped gardens, fish pool, waterfall and stunning views across unspoilt countryside. Breakfasts using local produce. Disabled accommodation in adjacent bespoke cottages.

⊕ *Leave M5 jct 7, take A4103 from Worcester to Hereford. Turn right at B4220, signposted Bromyard. Hidelow House is 2 miles on the left.*

♥ *For special occasions: champagne, roses and breakfast in bed. Four-poster suite available (3 nights minimum).*

Room General Leisure

**MALVERN,** Worcestershire Map ref 2B1

★★★★
BED & BREAKFAST
SILVER AWARD

B&B per room per night
s £30.00–£35.00
d £55.00–£60.00

## Orchid House

19 St Wulstans Drive, Upper Welland, Malvern WR14 4JA **t** (01684) 568717
**e** sally@oml.demon.co.uk **w** orchidmalvern.co.uk

Modern spacious house. Views to the Malvern Hills. Convenient for the Three Counties Showground. Walkers welcome.

**open** All year except Christmas and New Year
**bedrooms** 1 double, 1 twin
**bathrooms** All en suite
**payment** Cash/cheques

Room General

**MERIDEN,** West Midlands Map ref 4B3

★★★
GUEST HOUSE

B&B per room per night
s Min £25.00
d Min £45.00

## Bonnifinglas Guest House

3 Berkswell Road, Meriden, Coventry CV7 7LB **t** (01676) 523193 **f** (01676) 523193
**e** bookings@bonnifinglas.co.uk **w** bonnifinglas.co.uk

Country house, all rooms en suite with TV. Several pubs and restaurants within walking distance. Fire certificate. Large, off-road car park. Five minutes NEC. Wi-Fi Internet.

**open** All year except Christmas and New Year
**bedrooms** 2 double, 3 twin, 2 single, 1 family
**bathrooms** All en suite
**payment** Credit/debit cards, cash/cheques, euros

Room General Leisure

**MINSTERLEY,** Shropshire Map ref 4A3

★★★
BED & BREAKFAST

B&B per room per night
s £19.00–£30.00
d £44.00–£49.98
Evening meal per person
£5.00–£8.00

## Holly House B&B

Bromlow, Minsterley SY5 0EA **t** (01743) 891435 **e** paul.jaques1@btinternet.com
**w** stmem.com/hollyhouseb&b

A large family house with conservatory and two acres of garden with stunning views and sunsets. Excellent for walking, cycling and birdwatching, with pick-up transport available. Art gallery and facilities.

**open** All year except Christmas
**bedrooms** 1 double, 1 twin, 1 single
**bathrooms** 2 en suite, 1 private
**payment** Cash/cheques, euros

Room General Leisure

## B&B prices

Rates for bed and breakfast are shown per room per night.
Double room prices are usually based on two people sharing the room.

## NEWPORT, Shropshire Map ref 4A3

★★★
**RESTAURANT WITH ROOMS**

B&B per room per night
s Max £45.00
d Max £59.00
Evening meal per person
£10.00–£19.00

### Norwood House Restaurant with Rooms

Pave Lane, Newport TF10 9LQ  t (01952) 825896  f (01952) 825896  e info@norwoodhouse.org.uk
w norwoodhouse.org.uk

Family-run hotel of character, just off the A41 Wolverhampton to Whitchurch road. Close to Lilleshall National Sports Centre, RAF Cosford and Ironbridge Gorge.

**open** All year
**bedrooms** 2 double, 1 twin, 1 single, 1 family
**bathrooms** All en suite
**payment** Credit/debit cards, cash/cheques

Room  TV ♿ ⬚  General ♿ ⊞ ⚼ P ♥ ✕ ▦ ☗

## NEWPORT, Shropshire Map ref 4A3

★★★
**FARMHOUSE**

B&B per room per night
s £32.00–£35.00
d £52.00–£56.00

### Offley Grove Farm

Adbaston, Stafford ST20 0QB  t (01785) 280205  f (01785) 280205
e enquiries@offleygrovefarm.co.uk  w offleygrovefarm.co.uk

You will consider this a good find! Traditional farmhouse offering spacious, comfortable accommodation. Many guests return. Play area for children. Self catering also available. Brochure available on request.

**open** All year except Christmas and New Year
**bedrooms** 1 double, 1 family
**bathrooms** All en suite
**payment** Cash/cheques

Room TV ♿ ⬚  General ♿ ⊞ ⚼ P ✂ ✳

## NEWTON ST MARGARETS, Herefordshire Map ref 2A1

★★★★
**GUEST ACCOMMODATION**

B&B per room per night
s £30.00–£40.00
d £60.00–£80.00
Evening meal per person
£10.00–£18.00

### Marises Barn

Newton St Margarets, Hereford HR2 0QG  t (01981) 510101  f (01981) 510101
e marisesbaanb@aol.com  w marisesbarn.co.uk

Marises Barn offers a very warm welcome and quality bed and breakfast accommodation in Herefordshire's beautiful Golden Valley.

**open** All year
**bedrooms** 2 double, 1 twin, 1 single
**bathrooms** 2 en suite, 2 private
**payment** Cash/cheques

Room ⚲ TV ♿ ⬚  General ♿12 P ✂ ✕ ▦ ◪ ◙ ✳  Leisure ∪ ► 🏠

## PERSHORE, Worcestershire Map ref 2B1

★★★★
**BED & BREAKFAST**

B&B per room per night
s £35.00–£45.00
d £55.00–£65.00

### Arbour House

Main Road, Wyre Piddle, Pershore WR10 2HU  t (01386) 555833  f (01386) 555833
e liz@arbour-house.com  w arbour-house.com

**open** All year
**bedrooms** 2 double, 2 twin
**bathrooms** 3 en suite, 1 private
**payment** Cash/cheques, euros

A fine Grade II Listed character home with oak beams, overlooking Bredon Hill and close to the River Avon. Comfortable accommodation and generous breakfasts in a relaxed, friendly atmosphere. Riverside pub opposite. No smoking. Private car park. An ideal base for visiting the Cotswolds, Stratford, Worcester and Malvern.

⊕ *Follow A44 from M5 jct 6 for 9 miles. Wyre Piddle has been bypassed. Follow signs directly into village. We are on the left behind small village green.*

♥ *Special 3- and 4-night breaks available – see website for details.*

Room TV ♿ ⬚  General ♿ P ✂ ▦ ◪ ◙ ✳  Leisure 🏠

## Star ratings

Detailed information about star ratings can be found at the back of this guide.

## REDDITCH, Worcestershire Map ref 4B3

★★★
INN

B&B per room per night
s £50.00–£55.00
d £50.00–£55.00
Evening meal per person
£5.00–£8.00

### White Hart Inn

157 Evesham Road, Redditch B97 5EJ  t (01527) 545442  e enquiries@whitehartredditch.co.uk

Ten bedrooms. Newly completed free large car park. Specially adapted disabled room. No smoking. Free internet access.

**open** All year
**bedrooms** 2 double, 8 twin, 1 family
**bathrooms** All en suite
**payment** Credit/debit cards, cash/cheques

Room 🛏 ☎ 📺 🖥 ♨  General 🗄 P ✗ 🍽 ✗ ♿ ▣ ❄

## RUGBY, Warwickshire Map ref 4C3

★★★★
FARMHOUSE
SILVER AWARD

B&B per room per night
s £35.00–£40.00
d £55.00–£60.00

### Lawford Hill Farm

Lawford Heath Lane, Lawford Heath, Rugby CV23 9HG  t (01788) 542001  f (01788) 537880
e lawford.hill@talk21.com  w lawfordhill.co.uk

Bed and breakfast all the year round in our spacious Georgian farmhouse and converted stables. Close to Warwick, Stratford, NEC, NAC and Ryton Gardens.

**open** All year except Christmas and New Year
**bedrooms** 2 double, 2 twin, 1 single, 1 family
**bathrooms** All en suite
**payment** Credit/debit cards, cash/cheques

Room 🛏 📺 🖥 ♨  General 🗄 🏢 ♿ P ✗ 🍽 ♿ ▣ ❄ 🐾  Leisure ✎ 🚣

## RUGBY, Warwickshire Map ref 4C3

★★★
INN

B&B per room per night
s £26.00–£36.00
d £46.00–£56.00
Evening meal per person
£5.25–£14.75

### White Lion Inn

Coventry Road, Pailton, Rugby CV23 0QD  t (01788) 832359  f (01788) 832359
w whitelionpailton.co.uk

17thC coaching inn, recently refurbished but retaining all old-world features. Close to Rugby, Coventry and Stratford. Within four miles of motorways. Home-cooked food served daily.

**open** All year
**bedrooms** 7 double, 2 family
**bathrooms** 5 en suite, 3 private
**payment** Credit/debit cards, cash/cheques

Room 🛏 ☎ 📺 🖥  General 🗄 🏢 ♿ P ✗ 🍽 ♿ ▣ ❄ 🐾  Leisure ♨ ✎ ▶ 🚣

## RUGELEY, Staffordshire Map ref 4B3

★★
FARMHOUSE

B&B per room per night
s £24.00–£26.00
d £48.00–£52.00

### Park Farm

Hawkesyard, Armitage Lane, Rugeley WS15 1PS  t (01889) 583477  f (01889) 583477

A 70-acre livestock farm. While convenient for towns and attractions in the area, Park Farm is quietly tucked away in scenic hills.

**open** All year except Christmas
**bedrooms** 2 family
**bathrooms** All en suite
**payment** Cash/cheques

Room 🛏 📺 🖥  General 🗄 P 🍽 ❄ 🐾  Leisure ♒ ✎ ▶ 🚣

# Take a break

Look out for special promotions and themed breaks. It's a golden opportunity to indulge an interest, find a new one, or just relax and enjoy exceptional value. Offers and promotions are highlighted in colour (and are subject to availability).

★★★
INN

B&B per room per night
s Min £42.50
d £52.50–£57.50
Evening meal per person
£10.00–£25.00

# Odfellows – The Wine Bar

Market Place, Shifnal TF11 9AU  **t** (01952) 461517  **e** odfellows@odley.co.uk

**open** All year
**bedrooms** 5 double, 1 twin, 1 family
**bathrooms** All en suite
**payment** Credit/debit cards, cash/cheques

Comfortable, well-appointed bedrooms upstairs, with a lively, friendly bar/restaurant downstairs. Modern British food delights, complemented by an intelligently assembled wine list and draught-beer range. Served caddishly late, the cooked breakfast is well worth the wait, whilst the early birds are amply served the continental.

⊕ *M54 jct 4, follow signs to Shifnal. 1st roundabout take 3rd exit. Follow road past petrol station and under bridge. Odfellows is on the left just after the bridge.*

Room 📞 📺 🏃 ➴   General P 🍷 ✕ 🍽 ❄

Rating Applied For
GUEST HOUSE

B&B per room per night
s £35.00–£40.00
d £55.00–£60.00

# Abbey Court House

134 Abbey Foregate, Shrewsbury SY2 6AU  **t** (01743) 364416  **f** (01743) 358559
**e** info@abbeycourt.biz  **w** abbeycourt.biz

**open** All year
**bedrooms** 3 double, 4 twin, 2 single, 1 family
**bathrooms** All en suite
**payment** Credit/debit cards, cash/cheques, euros

Delightful former coaching house, convenient for town centre. Abbey Court is a designated Grade II Listed building, refurbished to a high standard. Comfortable en suite rooms, each with hospitality tray, TV and telephone. Wonderful breakfasts including vegetarian options. Off-road parking, some ground-floor rooms. A warm welcome is guaranteed.

⊕ *A5 (M54), exit at junction for Shrewsbury (2nd roundabout after M54). Proceed 1 mile to next roundabout (column landmark). Take exit marked Shirehall. 400yds on left.*

❤ *Discounted rates available for longer stays.*

Room 🛁 📞 📺 🏃   General 🥐 🏦 🔒 P 🍽 🔧   Leisure 🏠

★★★★
GUEST HOUSE
SILVER AWARD

B&B per room per night
s Min £25.00
d Min £50.00

# Acorn Guest House

29 Links Drive, Solihull B91 2DJ  **t** (0121) 705 5241  **e** acorn.wood@btinternet.com
**w** acorn-guest-house.com

**open** All year except Christmas and New Year
**bedrooms** 1 double, 2 twin, 2 single
**bathrooms** 1 en suite
**payment** Cash/cheques

Homely service in a comfortable, quiet, superb family home overlooking golf course. All rooms have wash basin, fridge, microwave, hairdryer, hospitality tray. Walk to Solihull centre and Touchwood Shopping Centre. Plentiful choice of local restaurants. Three miles to NEC, Birmingham International Rail and Airport. Car parking.

⊕ *M42, jct 5. A41 Birmingham. After 1.5 miles turn right at 3rd set of lights (Lode Lane). 1st left (Buryfield Road), then 1st right.*

Room 📺 🏃 ➴   General 🥐 P 🔒 ❄

## STAFFORD, Staffordshire Map ref 4B3

★★★
**FARMHOUSE**

B&B per room per night
s Max £35.00
d Max £55.00

### Rooks Nest Farm

Weston Bank, Weston, Stafford ST18 0BA  t (01889) 270624  e info@rooksnest.co.uk
w rooksnest.co.uk

Modern farmhouse on working farm, with far-reaching views over the Trent valley. Close to Weston Hall and County Showground, easy access to all Staffordshire attractions.

**open** All year
**bedrooms** 1 double, 1 twin
**bathrooms** All en suite
**payment** Cash/cheques

Room TV 🖳 🍵  General 🔥 P ⊁ ✿

## STAFFORD, Staffordshire Map ref 4B3

★★
**GUEST HOUSE**

B&B per room per night
s £29.00–£36.00
d £52.00–£60.00
Evening meal per person
£6.00–£14.00

### Wyndale Guest House

199 Corporation Street, Stafford ST16 3LQ  t (01785) 223069

The Wyndale is a comfortable Victorian house conveniently situated 0.25 miles from the town centre and en route to the county showground, hospital, university and technology park.

**open** All year except Christmas
**bedrooms** 2 double, 2 twin, 2 single, 2 family
**bathrooms** 5 en suite
**payment** Credit/debit cards, cash/cheques

Room 🛏 TV 🖳 🍵  General 🔥 ▥ ♨ P ✕ ᄤ 🔥 ✿ 🐾

## STOKE-ON-TRENT, Staffordshire Map ref 4B2

★★★★
**BED & BREAKFAST**
**SILVER AWARD**

B&B per room per night
s £30.00–£35.00
d £50.00–£60.00

### Cedar Tree Cottage

41 Longton Road, Trentham, Stoke-on-Trent ST4 8ND  t (01782) 644751  e n.portas@btinternet.com

A warm welcome is assured with comfortable bedrooms, beamed lounge with seasonal log fire, and hearty Staffordshire breakfasts. 300yds from Trentham Gardens. Wedgewood factory shop one mile.

**open** All year except Christmas and New Year
**bedrooms** 1 double, 1 twin
**bathrooms** 1 en suite, 1 private
**payment** Cash/cheques, euros

Room TV 🖳 🍵  General 🔥 P ⊁ ᄤ 🔥 ● ✿ 🐾  Leisure ▶ ⌂

## STOKE-ON-TRENT, Staffordshire Map ref 4B2

★★
**GUEST HOUSE**

B&B per room per night
s Min £24.00
d £40.00–£44.00

### Verdon Guest House

44 Charles Street, Stoke-on-Trent ST1 3JY  t (01782) 264244  f (01782) 264244
w verdonguesthouse.co.uk

Large, friendly guesthouse in town centre, close to bus station. Convenient for the Potteries and museums. Alton Towers 20 minutes, M6 ten minutes. All rooms with Sky TV. Excellent value.

**open** All year
**bedrooms** 4 double, 3 twin, 1 single, 5 family
**bathrooms** 5 en suite
**payment** Credit/debit cards, cash/cheques

Room 🛏 TV 🖳  General 🔥 P 🐾

## STOURBRIDGE, West Midlands Map ref 4B3

★★★★
**BED & BREAKFAST**

B&B per room per night
s £32.00–£35.00
d £60.00–£65.00

### St Elizabeth's Cottage

Woodman Lane, Clent, Stourbridge DY9 9PX  t (01562) 883883
e st.elizabeth.cottage@btconnect.com

Beautiful country cottage with lovely garden and swimming pool. Many excellent local restaurants. Within easy reach of Symphony Hall, Convention Centre in Birmingham, Black Country Museum, Stourbridge crystal factories, Severn Valley railway.

**open** All year
**bedrooms** 1 double, 1 twin, 1 family
**bathrooms** All en suite
**payment** Cash/cheques, euros

Room ☎ TV 🖳 🍵  General 🔥 P ⊁ ✿ 🐾  Leisure ▶

## Take a break

Look out for special promotions and themed breaks highlighted in colour.
(Offers subject to availability.)

## STOURBRIDGE, West Midlands Map ref 4B3

★★★
**BED & BREAKFAST**

B&B per room per night
s £25.00–£30.00
d £45.00–£55.00

### The Willows B&B

4 Brook Road, Stourbridge DY8 1NH  t (01384) 396964  e trickard@blueyonder.co.uk
w willowguests.com

Comfortable, friendly, family-run. Two bedrooms en suite, one twin, private bathroom. Convenient for town centre, railway station, pubs, restaurants and Merry Hill.

**open** All year except Christmas
**bedrooms** 1 double, 1 twin, 1 family
**bathrooms** 2 en suite, 1 private
**payment** Cash/cheques

Room 📺 👍 ☕   General ♿ 🏭 ♣ P ✂ 🍴 🔥 🖥   Leisure 🏖

## STRATFORD-UPON-AVON, Warwickshire Map ref 2B1

★★★★
**GUEST HOUSE**

B&B per room per night
s £30.00–£45.00
d £54.00–£78.00

### Avonlea

47 Shipston Road, Stratford-upon-Avon CV37 7LN  t (01789) 205940  f (01789) 209115
e avonlea-stratford@lineone.net  w avonlea-stratford.co.uk

**open** All year except Christmas
**bedrooms** 4 double, 2 twin, 1 single, 1 family
**bathrooms** 7 en suite, 1 private
**payment** Credit/debit cards, cash/cheques, euros

Stylish Victorian town house situated only five minutes' walk from the theatre and town centre. All rooms are en suite and furnished to the highest quality. Our guests are assured of a warm welcome and friendly atmosphere.

♥ *3 nights for the price of 2 from Oct-Mar.*

Room ♿ 📺 👍 ☕   General ♿ P ✂ ❀

## STRATFORD-UPON-AVON, Warwickshire Map ref 2B1

★★★★
**GUEST HOUSE**
**SILVER AWARD**

B&B per room per night
s £48.00–£65.00
d £78.00–£90.00

### Broadlands Guest House

23 Evesham Place, Stratford-upon-Avon CV37 6HT  t (01789) 299181  f (01789) 551382
e philandjohn@broadlandsguesthouse.co.uk  w broadlandsguesthouse.co.uk

**open** All year
**bedrooms** 3 double, 1 twin, 2 single
**bathrooms** 5 en suite, 1 private
**payment** Credit/debit cards, cash/cheques, euros

Located just five minutes' walk from the centre of the beautiful and historic market town of Stratford-upon-Avon, Broadlands offers an exemplary standard of accommodation. The atmosphere is relaxed and friendly and each of our bedrooms has either en suite or private facilities, colour TV, hairdryer, and complimentary refreshment tray.

⊕ *From jct 15, A46 then A439 to Stratford. At T-junction (Holiday Inn), right then left (Waterside), continue to T-junction, turn right, continue to T-junction, left into Evesham Place.*

Room 📺 👍 ☕   General ♿ 12 P 🍴   Leisure 🚲 🏖

## Ancient and modern

Experience timeless favourites or discover the latest must-sees. Whatever your choice, be inspired by the places of interest and events highlighted for each region.

---

**STRATFORD-UPON-AVON,** Warwickshire Map ref 2B1

★★★
INN

B&B per room per night
s £30.00–£37.50
d £50.00–£60.00
Evening meal per person
£5.00–£20.00

## Broom Hall Inn

Bidford Road, Alcester, Stratford-upon-Avon B50 4HE  **t** (01789) 773757  **f** (01789) 778741
**w** broomhallinn.co.uk

**open** All year
**bedrooms** 6 double, 6 twin, 1 single
**bathrooms** All en suite
**payment** Credit/debit cards, cash/cheques

Family-owned country inn with carvery restaurant and extensive range of bar meals. Close to Stratford-upon-Avon and Cotswolds. Roaring log fires in the winter and a large garden with rare trees to relax in during the summer months.

⊕ *One mile north of Bidford-on-Avon off the main Stratford to Evesham road.*

Room 📺 ♿  General 🛎 🏠 ♨ P ♟ ✕ 🍽 ❀ 🐾  Leisure ♜ ∪ ♪ ▸

---

**STRATFORD-UPON-AVON,** Warwickshire Map ref 2B1

★★★★
GUEST HOUSE

B&B per room per night
s £60.00–£70.00
d £80.00–£95.00

## Caterham House

58-59 Rother Street, Stratford-upon-Avon CV37 6LT  **t** (01789) 267309  **f** (01789) 414836
**e** caterhamhousehotel@btconnect.com  **w** caterhamhouse.co.uk

**open** All year except Christmas and New Year
**bedrooms** 10 double
**bathrooms** 8 en suite, 2 private
**payment** Credit/debit cards, cash/cheques

Grade II Listed Regency-style building with excellent town centre location, comfortable rooms and ample on-site car park.

Room 📺 ♿ ☕  General 🏠 P ✂ ♟ 🍴 ❀

---

**STRATFORD-UPON-AVON,** Warwickshire Map ref 2B1

★★★★
FARMHOUSE

B&B per room per night
s £50.00–£60.00
d £75.00–£80.00

## Drybank Farm

Fosseway, Ettington, Stratford-upon-Avon CV37 7DP  **t** (01789) 740476  **e** drybank@btinternet.com
**w** drybank.co.uk

**open** All year except Christmas
**bedrooms** 1 double, 1 twin, 1 suite
**bathrooms** All en suite
**payment** Cash/cheques

Set in 17 acres of peaceful farmland with superb views overlooking the open countryside. Recently refurbished bedrooms. Breakfast is prepared from local farm produce. There are many beautiful walks just a step from the front door, whilst Stratford-upon-Avon, Warwick and the Cotswolds are all only a short drive away.

Room 🖕 📺 ♿ ☕  General 🛎 🏠 ♨ P ✂ ✕ 🍽 🎱 🔒 ❀  Leisure ∪ 🏊

---

## Stay focused

Don't forget your camera. Take home shots of the greatest scenery, super seascapes and family fun.

★★★★
INN

B&B per room per night
s £50.00–£125.00
d £75.00–£200.00
Evening meal per person
£10.00–£30.00

## Halford Bridge Inn

Fosse Way, Halford, Shipston-on-Stour CV36 5BN  **t** (01789) 748217  **f** (01789) 748159
**e** sue@thehalfordbridge.co.uk  **w** thehalfordbridge.co.uk

**open** All year
**bedrooms** 8 double, 3 suites
**bathrooms** All en suite
**payment** Credit/debit cards, cash/cheques, euros

A Grade II Listed coaching inn, dating from 1567 and located on the Fosse Way close to Stratford-upon-Avon, the Halford Bridge offers the very best in 'countryside dining, drinking & dozing'. Twelve individually styled en suite bedrooms. Our dining room offers freshly cooked dishes and our bar is the perfect spot to unwind.

⊕ *M40 jct 15, 4th exit (A429 to Cirencester). After 9 miles, right into Halford. Inn on right-hand side, car park opposite.*

Room ♿ ☎ TV ♨ ☕  General ☒ ▥ ♿ P ⚲ ♥ ✗ 🖳 ♨ 🐾 ✿ 🐕  Leisure ∪ ♪ ▶ 🚲

★★★
BED & BREAKFAST

B&B per room per night
s £30.00
d £48.00

## Larkrise Cottage

Upper Billesley, Stratford-upon-Avon CV37 9RA  **t** (01789) 268618  **e** alanbailey17@hotmail.com
**w** larkrisecottage.co.uk

Larkrise Cottage provides quality fare in a tranquil rural location. It is within easy reach of the theatres of Stratford and the charm of the Cotswolds.

**open** All year except Christmas and New Year
**bedrooms** 1 double, 1 twin
**bathrooms** 2 private
**payment** Cash/cheques, euros

Room TV ♨ ☕  General ☒ ♿ P ⚲  Leisure 🖼

★★★★
GUEST ACCOMMODATION

B&B per room per night
s £42.00–£54.00
d £69.00–£89.00

## Melita

37 Shipston Road, Stratford-upon-Avon CV37 7LN  **t** (01789) 292432  **f** (01789) 204867
**e** info@melitaguesthouse.co.uk  **w** melitaguesthouse.co.uk

**open** All year except Christmas and New Year
**bedrooms** 5 double, 2 twin, 3 single, 2 family
**bathrooms** 10 en suite, 2 private
**payment** Credit/debit cards, cash/cheques

Once a Victorian home, the Melita is now a warm, friendly establishment managed by caring proprietors. Accommodation and service are of a high standard. Breakfasts are individually prepared to suit guests' requirements. The Melita is only 400m from the theatres and town centre and has free, private, on-site car parking.

⊕ *We are 200yds from the Clopton Bridge on the A3400 south to Oxford.*

♥ *Discounts available Nov-Mar 2007 (excl Sat and locally important dates).*

Room ♿ ☎ TV ♨ ☕  General ☒ ▥ ♿ P ⚲ ♨ 🐾 ✿ 🐕  Leisure ♪ ▶ 🚲 🖼

## Family-friendly breaks

For accommodation offering additional facilities and services for a range of ages and family units, look out for the Families Welcome symbol. Owners of these properties will go out of their way to welcome families.

# Heart of England

**STRATFORD-UPON-AVON,** Warwickshire Map ref 2B1

★★★
GUEST HOUSE

B&B per room per night
s £26.00–£50.00
d £50.00–£60.00

## Quilt and Croissants

33 Evesham Place, Stratford-upon-Avon CV37 6HT  t (01789) 267629  f (01789) 551651
e rooms@quilt-croissants.demon.co.uk  w quiltcroissants.co.uk

**open** All year except Christmas
**bedrooms** 2 double, 1 twin, 3 single, 1 family
**bathrooms** 5 en suite
**payment** Cash/cheques

Comfortable Victorian guesthouse with modern facilities close to the town centre, theatres and Shakespeare properties. Stratford has much to offer its visitors and Richard and Sue add to it with their local knowledge. No matter whether you are on holiday or business, Quilt and Croissants is ideal for your stay.

⊕ Situated on A4390. From the train station head towards town, turn right at traffic lights. Quilt and Croissants on the left after the pelican crossing.

Room TV 🖎 General 🔥 🗐 ✗ 🍴 Leisure 🚲 🏠

**STRATFORD-UPON-AVON,** Warwickshire Map ref 2B1

★★★★
GUEST HOUSE
SILVER AWARD

B&B per room per night
s Max £55.00
d Max £70.00

## Victoria Spa Lodge

Bishopton Lane, Bishopton, Stratford-upon-Avon CV37 9QY  t (01789) 267985  f (01789) 204728
e ptozer@victoriaspalodge.demon.co.uk  w stratford-upon-avon.co.uk/victoriaspa.htm

Elegant English home, with antique furnishings, in country setting. Beautifully decorated and comfortable en suite bedrooms. Vegetarians catered for. Hosts Paul and Dreen Tozer. Park & Ride close by.

**open** All year except Christmas and New Year
**bedrooms** 3 double, 1 twin, 3 family
**bathrooms** All en suite
**payment** Credit/debit cards, cash/cheques

Room 📞 TV 🖎 General 🔥 🗐 P 🍴 Leisure 🚲 🏠

**STRATFORD-UPON-AVON,** Warwickshire Map ref 2B1

★★★
GUEST ACCOMMODATION

B&B per room per night
s £29.00–£35.00
d £50.00–£70.00

## Virginia Lodge

12 Evesham Place, Stratford-upon-Avon CV37 6HT  t (01789) 292157 & (01789) 266605
f (01789) 292157  e enquiries@virginialodge.co.uk  w virginialodge.co.uk

**open** All year
**bedrooms** 4 double, 1 twin, 1 single, 1 family
**bathrooms** 6 en suite
**payment** Credit/debit cards, cash/cheques, euros

Beautiful Victorian house in the centre of Stratford. Bedrooms beautifully designed with en suite, TV, hairdryer, tea/coffee. Four-poster rooms. Full English breakfast, real coffee. Private car park. Non-smoking. Near the racecourse, theatre and Shakespeare houses. Caters for vegetarians.

⊕ A34 into Stratford, right at traffic lights into Arden Street, over traffic lights into Grove Road which becomes Evesham Place. Virginia Lodge on right after pedestrian crossing.

♥ 3 nights for the price of 2, Nov-Apr, Sun-Thu (excl Bank Holidays).

Room 🛏 TV 🖎 General P 🍴 Leisure 🏠

## Pet-friendly breaks

PETS! WELCOME

Want to take your cherished companion with you on holiday? Proprietors participating in our Welcome Pets! scheme go out of their way to make special provision for you and your pet. Look out for the symbol.

## TANWORTH-IN-ARDEN, Warwickshire Map ref 4B3

★★★★
FARMHOUSE
SILVER AWARD

B&B per room per night
s £40.00–£60.00
d £70.00–£120.00
Evening meal per person
£18.00–£25.00

# Grange Farm

Forde Hall Lane, Tanworth-in-Arden, Solihull B94 5AX  t (01564) 742911
e enquiries@grange-farm.com  w grange-farm.com

Peaceful 17thC farmhouse set in 200 acres of beautiful countryside with footpaths and wildlife pools. Very attractive en suite bedrooms. Three miles from M42, junction three.

**open** All year except Christmas
**bedrooms** 1 double, 1 twin, 1 family
**bathrooms** All en suite
**payment** Cash/cheques

Room ⚄ 📺 👖 ☕  General 📖 ✕ 🏤 ✳  Leisure ♫

## TANWORTH-IN-ARDEN, Warwickshire Map ref 4B3

★★★★
FARMHOUSE
SILVER AWARD

B&B per room per night
s £37.50–£45.00
d £75.00

# Mows Hill Farm

Mows Hill Road, Kemps Green, Tanworth-in-Arden B94 5PP  t (01564) 784312  f (01564) 783378
e mowshill@farmline.com  w b-and-bmowshill.co.uk

**open** All year
**bedrooms** 1 double, 1 family
**bathrooms** 1 en suite, 1 private
**payment** Cash/cheques, euros

Luxury B&B in beautiful farmhouse on working Warwickshire farm. Convenient for visiting NAC (Royal Show, etc), the NEC, Warwick, Stratford and the Cotswolds. Many National Trust properties nearby. Boot room/drying facilities for walkers, cyclists. Children welcome from any age. Fresh farm produce for breakfast. Vegetarian and special diets catered for.

⊕ A3400 towards Stratford/Henley-in-Arden. At Hockley Heath, right onto B4101 (Spring Lane), over bridge, next left (Kemps Green). 2nd right (Mows Hill Road). Farm on right.

Room 📺 👖 ☕  General 📖 🏤 ♿ P ✂ 🍴 🏤 ✳  Leisure ♨ ▶ 🚴 🎣

## TELFORD, Shropshire Map ref 4A3

★★★★
BED & BREAKFAST

B&B per room per night
s £35.00–£40.00
d £48.00–£55.00

# The Mill House

Shrewsbury Road, High Ercall, Telford TF6 6BE  t (01952) 770394  e cjpy@lineone.net
w ercallmill.co.uk

**open** All year
**bedrooms** 2 double/twin, 1 family
**bathrooms** All en suite
**payment** Cash/cheques

Beautiful, Grade II Listed, converted water mill (no machinery) beside River Roden. Peaceful, rural setting. All rooms en suite. Large, timbered guest lounge with colour TV. Working smallholding. Ideal for visiting Ironbridge, Telford, Shrewsbury and mid-Wales.

⊕ From M4 jct 6. One mile south of High Ercall on B5062.

Room 👖 ☕  General 📖 🏤 ♿ P ✂ 🏤 ✳ 🐾  Leisure ♫ 🎣

## Check the maps

Colour maps at the front pinpoint all the places you will find accommodation entries in the regional sections. Pick your location and then refer to the place index at the back to find the page number.

## TELFORD, Shropshire Map ref 4A3

★★★★
**GUEST ACCOMMODATION**

B&B per room per night
s £34.00–£37.00
d £49.00–£52.00

### Stone House

Shifnal Road, Priorslee, Telford TF2 9NN   t (01952) 290119   e stonehousegh@aol.com
w stonehouseguesthouse.co.uk

Comfortable, friendly guesthouse, convenient to M54, station, town centre, Ironbridge and university. Personal attention assured. Good home cooking.

**open** All year
**bedrooms** 2 double, 3 twin
**bathrooms** All en suite
**payment** Cash/cheques

Room 🛏 📺 🖕 🍵   General 🗑 🛗 P 🍴 🎮 ▣ ✿   Leisure 🎣 ► 🚤

## TENBURY WELLS, Worcestershire Map ref 4A3

★★★★
**BED & BREAKFAST**

B&B per room per night
s £40.00–£45.00
d £60.00–£70.00

### Millbrook

Tenbury Wells WR15 8NP   t (01584) 781720   e keithoddy@onetel.com   w millbrook01584.co.uk

Set in beautiful Teme Valley, a centre for retreat and renewal. Ideally situated as a base for exploring. Organic local produce.

**open** All year
**bedrooms** 2 double
**bathrooms** 1 en suite, 1 private
**payment** Credit/debit cards, cash/cheques

Room 📺 🖕 🍵   General P ✕ 🎮 🎭 ✿   Leisure ∪ 🎣 ►

## UPTON UPON SEVERN, Worcestershire Map ref 2B1

★★★★
**BED & BREAKFAST**

B&B per room per night
s £40.00–£60.00
d £65.00–£130.00

### Sunnyside Bed & Breakfast

Station Road, Ripple GL20 6EY   t (01684) 592461   f (01684) 592618
e sunnysideripple@btinternet.com   w sunnysidebandb.co.uk

Charming cottage set in the shadow of the Malverns offering a relaxed friendly atmosphere, real fires. High standard of accommodation. Home-made and locally-sourced produce. Excellent motorway links.

**open** All year except Christmas and New Year
**bedrooms** 2 double
**bathrooms** 1 en suite, 1 private
**payment** Cash/cheques

Room 📺 🖕 🍵   General P 🍴 🎮 🎭 ✿   Leisure ∪ 🚲 🚴

## VOWCHURCH, Herefordshire Map ref 2A1

★★★★
**BED & BREAKFAST**
**SILVER AWARD**

B&B per room per night
s £35.00–£50.00
d £60.00–£69.00
Evening meal per person
£15.00–£25.00

### Yew Tree House

Vowchurch, Hereford HR2 9PF   t (01981) 251195   e enquiries@yewtreehouse-hereford.co.uk
w yewtreehouse-hereford.co.uk

Two hundred-year-old house with magnificent views of the Golden Valley, offering luxurious accommodation in an extremely comfortable family home.

**open** All year
**bedrooms** 1 double, 1 twin, 1 family
**bathrooms** All en suite
**payment** Cash/cheques, euros

Room 📺 🖕 🍵   General 🗑 ▥ 🛗 P 🍴 ✕ 🎮 🎭 🦮 ▣ ✿   Leisure ∪ 🎣 ► 🚲 🚴

## WARWICK, Warwickshire Map ref 2B1

★★★★
**GUEST HOUSE**

B&B per room per night
s Min £40.00
d Max £60.00

### Croft Guesthouse

Haseley Knob, Warwick CV35 7NL   t (01926) 484447   f (01926) 484447
e david@croftguesthouse.co.uk   w croftguesthouse.co.uk

A friendly, non-smoking family guesthouse providing clean, high quality en suite accommodation at reasonable prices. Centrally located for exploring Warwick, Stratford, Coventry and Kenilworth, or for visiting the NEC (15 minutes).

**open** All year except Christmas and New Year
**bedrooms** 3 double, 2 twin, 1 single, 1 family
**bathrooms** 6 en suite, 3 private
**payment** Credit/debit cards, cash/cheques, euros

Room 🛏 📺 🖕 🍵   General 🗑 ▥ 🛗 P 🍴 🎭 🦮 ✿ 🐾   Leisure ►

## WARWICK, Warwickshire Map ref 2B1

★★★★
**BED & BREAKFAST**

B&B per room per night
s £30.00–£35.00
d £50.00–£55.00
Evening meal per person
£10.00–£20.00

### Longbridge Farm

Longbridge, Warwick CV34 6RB **t** (01926) 401857

Charming and comfortable 16thC farmhouse set in 20 acres of meadows located 1.5 miles from Warwick town centre on A429 and convenient for the M40. Evening meal by arrangement.

**open** All year
**bedrooms** 1 double, 1 family
**bathrooms** 1 en suite, 1 private
**payment** Cash/cheques, euros

Room 📺 ♨ ♑  General ♻5 ⚡ ✗ ⛨ ㎡ ❀  Leisure ⚲ ∪ ♩

## WARWICK, Warwickshire Map ref 2B1

★★★
**BED & BREAKFAST**

B&B per room per night
s £42.50–£47.50
d £65.00–£67.50

### Peacock Lodge

97 West Street, Warwick CV34 6AH **t** (01926) 419480

Three-storey, early-Victorian terraced house. Two of the guest rooms are situated in adjoining converted stables, one on the ground floor.

**open** All year except Christmas and New Year
**bedrooms** 4 double
**bathrooms** All en suite
**payment** Credit/debit cards, cash/cheques

Room ♨ 📺 ♨ ♑  General ✗ ㎡

## WARWICK, Warwickshire Map ref 2B1

★★★★
**FARMHOUSE**
**SILVER AWARD**

B&B per room per night
s £40.00–£50.00
d £55.00–£65.00

### Shrewley Pools Farm

Haseley, Warwick CV35 7HB **t** (01926) 484315 **e** cathydodd@hotmail.co.uk
**w** s-h-systems.co.uk/hotels/shrewley.html

**open** All year except Christmas
**bedrooms** 1 twin, 1 family
**bathrooms** All en suite
**payment** Cash/cheques

Glorious 17thC traditional family farmhouse with log fires, oak floors, beams etc, set in an acre of outstanding garden featuring herbaceous borders and unusual trees and shrubs. Two spacious en suite bedrooms and own sitting room with books and games. Perfectly situated for numerous attractions. Surrounded by picturesque farmland. Private fishing.

⊕ A46, take A4177 from Warwick through Hatton, past Falcon Inn. At roundabout take 1st exit. After 0.5 miles we are on left.

♥ Four-acre lake stocked with carp and tench: £7 per day.

Room 📺 ♨ ♑  General ♻ ⛨ ♿ P ✗ ㎡ ▣ ❀  Leisure ∪ ♩ ▶ 🏠

## WATERHOUSES, Staffordshire Map ref 4B2

★★★★
**BED & BREAKFAST**
**SILVER AWARD**

B&B per room per night
s £30.00–£35.00
d £50.00–£60.00

### Leehouse Farm

Leek Road, Waterhouses, Leek ST10 3HW **t** (01538) 308439

Charming, 18thC house in centre of a Staffordshire Moorlands village in Peak District National Park. Ideal for Derbyshire Dales, the Potteries and Alton Towers.

**open** All year except Christmas
**bedrooms** 2 double, 1 twin
**bathrooms** All en suite
**payment** Cash/cheques

Room 📺 ♨ ♑  General ♻8 P ✗ ⛨ ㎡ ❀  Leisure 🚲 🏠

## It's all in the detail

Please remember that all information in this guide has been supplied by the proprietors well in advance of publication. Since changes do sometimes occur it's a good idea to check details at the time of booking.

**WELLAND,** Worcestershire Map ref 2B1

★★★
GUEST ACCOMMODATION

B&B per room per night
s £35.00
d £60.00

## North Farm

Hancocks Lane, Welland, Malvern WR13 6LG  t (01684) 574365

North Farm is a welcoming B&B with comfortable en suite rooms. Set in a beautiful rural location close to Three Counties Showground, Upton upon Severn, The Malvern Hills.

open All year
bedrooms 1 double, 1 twin
bathrooms All en suite
payment Cash/cheques

Room ▦ ● ⊗  General ♿ ⚓ P ⊁ ▦ ❄ ♞

---

**WISHAW,** Warwickshire Map ref 4B3

★★★★
BED & BREAKFAST

B&B per room per night
s £35.00–£40.00
d £50.00–£60.00

## Ash House

The Gravel, Wishaw, Sutton Coldfield B76 9QB  t (01675) 475782  f (01675) 475782
e kate@rectory80.freeserve.co.uk

Former rectory with lovely views. Few minutes' walk from Belfry Golf and Leisure Hotel. Half a mile M42, ten minutes' drive from Birmingham Airport/NEC. Drayton Manor Park and zoo five miles.

open All year
bedrooms 1 double, 1 twin, 1 family
bathrooms All en suite
payment Cash/cheques

Room ▦ ● ⊗  General ♿ P ⊁ ▦  Leisure ∪ ▶

---

**WORCESTER,** Worcestershire Map ref 2B1

★★★
FARMHOUSE

B&B per room per night
s £35.00–£40.00
d £55.00–£60.00

## The Barn House

Broadwas, Worcester WR6 5NS  t (01886) 888733  f (01886) 888733  e info@barnhouseonline.co.uk
w barnhouseonline.co.uk

Period property set in over two acres of mature garden, surrounded by open countryside, 15 minutes from Worcester city centre.

open All year
bedrooms 1 double, 1 twin
bathrooms All en suite
payment Cash/cheques

Room ♨ ▦ ● ⊗  General ♿5 P ⊁ ▦ ⚿ ❄ ♞  Leisure ♪ ♨

---

**WORCESTER,** Worcestershire Map ref 2B1

★★★★
BED & BREAKFAST
SILVER AWARD

B&B per room per night
s £45.00
d £45.00–£75.00

## Hill Farm House

Dormston Lane, Dormston, Worcester WR7 4JS  t (01386) 793159  f (01386) 793239
e jim@hillfarmhouse.co.uk  w hillfarmhouse.co.uk

A traditional former farmhouse and converted buildings in quiet rural location. King-size, en suite rooms with pastoral views. Ideal for Stratford, Cotswolds, Worcester and the Malverns.

open All year except Christmas
bedrooms 1 double, 1 twin, 2 suites
bathrooms All en suite
payment Cash/cheques

Room ♨ ▦ ● ⊗  General ♿ ▥ ⚓ P ⊁ ❄  Leisure ♪

---

**WORCESTER,** Worcestershire Map ref 2B1

★★★
BED & BREAKFAST

B&B per room per night
s £42.00–£52.50
d £52.50–£57.75
Evening meal per person
£7.00–£10.00

## Holland House

210 London Road, Worcester WR5 2JT  t (01905) 353939  f (01905) 353939
e beds@holland-house.me.uk  w holland-house.me.uk

A warm welcome awaits you at this Victorian mid-terrace house, situated within easy walk of the cathedral and shops. It retains many original features and offers fully en suite rooms throughout.

open All year
bedrooms 2 double, 1 family
bathrooms All en suite
payment Credit/debit cards, cash/cheques

Room ▦ ● ⊗  General ♿ ▥ P ⊁ ✕ ▦ ⚿  Leisure ♨

---

**WYE VALLEY**

*See under Hereford*

# Never has a rose meant so much

Everyone has a trusted friend, someone who tells it straight. Well, that's what the Enjoy England Quality Rose does: reassures you before you check into your holiday accommodation that it will be just what you want, because it's been checked out by independent assessors. Which means you can book with confidence and get on with the real business of having a fantastic break.

enjoy**England**.com

★★★

**BED & BREAKFAST**

The **Quality Rose** is the mark of England's *official*, nationwide quality assessment scheme and covers just about every place you might want to stay, using a clear star rating system: from caravan parks to stylish boutique hotels, farmhouse B&Bs to country house retreats, self-catering cottages by the sea to comfy narrowboats perfect for getting away from it all. Think of the Quality Rose as your personal guarantee that your expectations will be met.

## Our ratings made easy

★      Simple, practical, no frills

★★     Well presented and well run

★★★    Good level of quality and comfort

★★★★   Excellent standard throughout

★★★★★ Exceptional with a degree of luxury

## Look no further. Just look out for the Quality Rose. Find out more at enjoy**England**.com/quality

# East Midlands

Leicestershire & Rutland, Lincolnshire, Northamptonshire, Nottinghamshire, Peak District & Derbyshire

# Fresh air, fabulous countryside and festivals galore

If you love getting out into the open air, you'll adore the East Midlands. Whether you're the sporty type or just a fresh air addict, the East Midlands has lots in store for the whole family.

East Midlands Tourism
discovereastmidlands.com

National Space Centre, Leicester

Sherwood Forest Country Park

Chatsworth House, Derbyshire

Walkers be warned: you'll never want to leave. The idyllic River Dove is surrounded by the remains of ancient coral reefs which form Dovedale, and it's reckoned to be the ultimate ramble. Then there's the Pennine Way with its towering mountain plateau of Kinder Scout, not to mention the wild High Peak Trail. Cycling's big in these parts too. Take on the 'Black Death Challenge' and spin into seven medieval plague villages; or tackle the terrifying slalom descent at Sherwood Pines. Feeling adventurous? Try your hand at dragon boat racing at Carsington Water, or water-skiing at the National Watersports Centre. And then there are golf courses galore, the British Grand Prix at Silverstone, the famous Burghley Horse Trials...not forgetting the World Conker Championship in Ashton.

The East Midlands is home to many arts festivals, so be sure to keep an eye out for the Stamford Shakespeare Festival at Tolethorpe Hall and Buxton's Gilbert and Sullivan Festival. With heritage in mind, there are a whole host of dramatic castles such as Bosworth and Peveril to explore. And if you want to be swept off your feet, you won't want to miss the National Space Centre where you can test your ability to survive a perilous voyage into deep space by taking the interactive Human Spaceflight.

Discover Creswell Crags, a limestone gorge honeycombed with caves that were home to Ice Age man. Or lose yourself in the maze at Chatsworth House. And don't miss Snibston Discovery Park in the heart the National Forest, an award-winning family attraction exploring the impact of technology on our everyday lives.

Prefer to live it up? Make for historic Lincoln, Nottingham, Derby or Leicester where fine Asian cuisine is spicily sumptuous. Seek out traditional local fare too – delicious cheeses, gingerbread and the famous Melton Mowbray pork pies.

# Destinations

## Derby

This multi-cultural city bursts with entertainment venues, attractions, shopping experiences and open green spaces. The compact city centre makes exploring easy. Visit the indoor market housed in the wonderful Victorian Market Hall and take advantage of free attractions including the Museum and Art Gallery where you'll find work by famous local artist, Joseph Wright. Don't miss the cathedral, which has the second highest church tower in England, Royal Crown Derby and Pride Park football stadium.

## Leicester

A cosmopolitan and cultured city, Leicester offers unusual shops, fine restaurants, a vibrant nightlife and a strong cultural diversity. Discover designer labels in the Leicester Lanes, and exquisitely embroidered silks along the Golden Mile. Travel to infinity and beyond at the National Space Centre and experience live music at De Montfort Hall. Witness top class action from Leicester's sporting teams and savour a glass of champagne at one of the city's stylish café bars.

## Lincoln

Possessing magnificent architectural heritage, Lincoln is a blend of history, cultural variety, shopping and lively entertainment. Approach the city from any direction and you are drawn to the magnificent outline of the cathedral, one of the finest Gothic buildings in Europe. From the cobbled streets and antiques to the modern art scattered throughout the city, the past and present is all around. Events throughout the year make Lincoln irresistible – the famous Christmas Market, the Brayford Waterfront Festival, and the weekend that most attractions open for free – Lincoln weekend.

| | |
|---|---|
| National Park | |
| Area of Outstanding Natural Beauty | |
| National Trails nationaltrail.co.uk | |
| Sections of the National Cycle Network nationalcyclenetwork.org.uk | |
| Regional Route | |

Lincoln Castle

Gibralter Point, near Skegness

The National Forest, near Derby

Peak District

Rutland Water

Leicester

Nottingham

## Nottingham

Nottingham is the undisputed capital of the East Midlands, boasting a sophisticated urban environment with an enviable reputation for clubs, theatres, cinemas and galleries, not to mention a deserved reputation as one of the top retail centres in the country. History is never far away, though, with reminders of Nottingham's legendary hero Robin Hood and his adversary the Sheriff of Nottingham. Explore the Castle Museum and Art Gallery, and Wollaton Hall, one of the most ornate Tudor buildings in Britain, complete with 500-acre deer park.

## Peak District

The Peak District is Britain's first and most popular National Park. Roam on open moorland to the north and take in the magnificent views over the Derwent Dams. Further south, stroll alongside sparkling rivers in wildlife-rich valleys far from the hustle and bustle of town. The Peak Park Rangers lead regular guided walks – choose from long hikes to village tours. Take in the grandeur of Chatsworth House or Haddon Hall, and sample the local oatcakes with Hartington Stilton, followed by a delicious Bakewell pudding.

## Rutland

Tiny Rutland, less than 20 miles across, may be the smallest county in England, but it's packed with hidden treasures. Explore the castle in the historic county town of Oakham, browse the antiquarian bookshops of Uppingham and choose from more than 50 picturesque villages of thatched stone-built cottages. Rutland Water is a must – a giant reservoir where you can fish, walk, cycle and sail. Enjoy Shakespeare at Rutland Open Air Theatre or ride the locomotives at the Rutland Railway Museum. Discover the natural beauty of Rutland – England's best-kept secret!

## Skegness

Take time to explore some of the UK's finest seaside resorts. The Lincolnshire coastline, stretching from Skegness to Mablethorpe offers you sun, fun, excitement and laughter, but also tranquillity, clean beaches, and glorious fresh air. Skegness, Lincolnshire's premier resort, features an award-winning six-mile-long beach. Enjoy the seafront illuminations from mid-summer, indulge in family fun at the Pleasure Beach, and visit the seals at the Natureland Sanctuary.

# Places to visit

**78 Derngate**
Northampton
(01604) 603407
78derngate.org.uk
*Terraced house transformed by Charles Rennie Mackintosh*

**Alford Manor House**
Alford, Lincolnshire
(01507) 463073
alfordmanorhouse.co.uk
*Large thatched manor house*

**Althorp**
Northampton
(01604) 770107
althorp.com
*Spencer family home since 1508*

**Belton House, Park and Gardens**
Grantham, Lincolnshire
(01476) 566116
nationaltrust.org.uk
*Restoration-period country house*

**Bolsover Castle**
Bolsover, Derbyshire
(01246) 822844
english-heritage.org.uk
*17th-century house on the site of a Norman fortress*

**Burghley House**
Stamford, Lincolnshire
(01780) 752451
burghley.co.uk
*The largest and grandest Elizabethan house*

**Castle Ashby Gardens**
near Northampton
(01604) 696187
castleashby.co.uk
*Capability Brown landscaped gardens and parkland*

**Chatsworth House, Garden, Farmyard & Adventure Playground**
Bakewell, Derbyshire
(01246) 582204
chatsworth.org
*Beautiful house, garden and fountains*

**Clumber Park**
Worksop, Nottinghamshire
(01909) 476592
nationaltrust.org.uk
*Year-round colour and interest*

**Creswell Crags Museum and Education Centre, Picnic site, Caves & Gorge**
Worksop, Derbyshire
(01909) 720378
creswell-crags.org.uk
*Limestone gorge, caves and lake*

**Doddington Hall**
Lincoln
(01522) 694308
doddingtonhall.com
*Superb Elizabethan mansion and gardens*

**Gainsborough Old Hall**
Gainsborough, Lincolnshire
(01427) 612669
lincolnshire.gov.uk
*Medieval manor house*

**Go Ape! High Wire Forest Adventure**
near Edwinstowe, Nottinghamshire
0870 444 5562
goape.co.uk
*Rope bridges, swings and zip slides*

**Grimsthorpe Castle, Park and Gardens**
near Bourne, Lincolnshire
(01778) 591205
grimsthorpe.co.uk
*Castle covering four periods of architecture*

**Haddon Hall**
Bakewell, Derbyshire
(01629) 812855
haddonhall.co.uk
*Medieval and Tudor manor house*

**Hardwick Hall**
Chesterfield, Derbyshire
(01246) 850430
nationaltrust.org.uk
*Elizabethan country house and parkland*

**Kirby Hall**
Corby, Northamptonshire
(01536) 203230
english-heritage.org.uk
*Elizabethan and 17th-century house*

**Lincoln Castle**
(01522) 511068
lincolnshire.gov.uk/lincolncastle
*Historic former court and prison*

**Lincoln Cathedral**
(01522) 561600
lincolncathedral.com
*One of the finest gothic buildings in Europe*

**National Space Centre**
Leicester
0870 607 7223
spacecentre.co.uk
*The UK's largest space attraction*

**Newark Castle and Conflict**
Nottinghamshire
(01636) 655765
newark-sherwood.gov.uk
*Fortress, museum and exhibition*

**Newstead Abbey**
near Nottingham
(01623) 455900
newsteadabbey.org.uk
*800-year-old remains of a priory church*

**Nottingham Castle Museum and Gallery**
(0115) 915 3700
nottinghamcity.gov.uk/museums
*17th-century mansion on medieval-castle site*

**Peveril Castle**
Castleton, Derbyshire
(01433) 620613
english-heritage.org.uk
*Ruined Norman castle*

**Rockingham Castle**
Corby, Northamptonshire
(01536) 770240
rockinghamcastle.com
*Rose gardens and exquisite art*

**Sherwood Forest Country Park**
near Mansfield, Nottinghamshire
(01623) 823202
sherwood-forest.org.uk
*Native woodland packed with adventure*

**Silverstone Circuit**
Northamptonshire
0870 458 8260
silverstone-circuits.co.uk
*The home of British motor racing*

**Tattershall Castle**
Lincoln
(01526) 342543
nationaltrust.org.uk
*Dramatic 15th-century red-brick tower*

# Diary dates 2008

**Peak District Walking Festival**
Various locations, Peak District
visitpeakdistrict.com
Apr – May*

**Lincolnshire Wolds Walking Festival**
Various locations, Lincolnshire
visitlincolnshire.com
17 May – 1 Jun

**Stamford Shakespeare Festival**
Rutland Open Air Theatre, Stamford
stamfordshakespeare.co.uk
Jun – Aug*

**Althorp Literary Festival**
Althorp House, Northamptonshire
althorp.com/literaryfestival
14 – 15 Jun

**Buxton Festival**
Various locations, Buxton
buxtonfestival.co.uk
4 – 20 Jul*

**Robin Hood Festival**
Sherwood Forest Visitor Centre, Edwinstowe
sherwoodforest.org.uk
First week in Aug*

**Festival of History**
Kelmarsh Hall, Northamptonshire
kelmarsh.com
9 – 10 Aug

**DH Lawrence Festival**
Eastwood, Nottinghamshire
broxtowe.gov.uk/festival
Mid-Aug – mid-Sep*

**East Midlands Food Festival**
Melton Mowbray, Leicestershire
eastmidlandsfoodfestival.co.uk
4 – 5 Oct

**Lincoln Christmas Market**
lincoln.gov.uk
4 – 7 Dec

# Tourist Information Centres

When you arrive at your destination, visit an Official Partner Tourist Information Centre for quality assured help with accommodation and information about local attractions and events, or email your request before you go. To search for attractions and Tourist Information Centres on the move just text INFO to 62233, and a web link will be sent to your mobile phone.

| | | | |
|---|---|---|---|
| Ashbourne | 13 Market Place | (01335) 343666 | ashbourneinfo@derbyshiredales.gov.uk |
| Bakewell | Bridge Street | (01629) 816558 | bakewell@peakdistrict-npa.gov.uk |
| Buxton | The Crescent | (01298) 25106 | tourism@highpeak.gov.uk |
| Castleton | Buxton Road | (01433) 620679 | castleton@peakdistrict-npa.gov.uk |
| Chesterfield | Rykneld Square | (01246) 345777 | tourism@chesterfield.gov.uk |
| Derby | Market Place | (01332) 255802 | tourism@derby.gov.uk |
| Leicester | 7/9 Every Street | 0906 294 1113** | info@goleicestershire.com |
| Lincoln Castle Hill | 9 Castle Hill | (01522) 873213 | tourism@lincoln.gov.uk |
| Matlock | Crown Square | (01629) 583388 | matlockinfo@derbyshiredales.gov.uk |
| Matlock Bath | The Pavillion | (01629) 55082 | matlockbathinfo@derbyshiredales.gov.uk |
| Ripley | Market Place | (01773) 841488 | touristinformation@ambervalley.gov.uk |
| Sleaford | Carre Street | (01529) 414294 | tic@n-kesteven.gov.uk |
| Swadlincote | West Street | (01283) 222848 | tic@sharpespotterymuseum.org.uk |

** *calls to this number are charged at premium rate*

# Travel info

The central location of the East Midlands makes it easily accessible from all parts of the UK.

**By road:**
From the north and south, the M1 bisects the East Midlands with access to the region from junctions 14 through to 31. The A1 offers better access to the eastern part of the region, particularly Lincolnshire and Rutland. From the west, the M69, M/A42 and A50 provide easy access.

**By rail:**
The region is well served by InterCity services, offering direct routes from London, the north of England and Scotland to the East Midlands' major cities and towns. East/west links offer not only access to the region but also travel within it.

**By air:**
East Midlands Airport (Nottingham, Leicester, Derby) is located centrally in the region, with scheduled domestic flights from Aberdeen, Belfast, Edinburgh, Glasgow, Isle of Man and the Channel Islands. Manchester, Birmingham, Luton, Stansted and Humberside airports also offer domestic scheduled routes, with easy access to the region by road and rail.

# Find out more

Whinstone Lee Tor, Peak District

Further publications are available from the following organisations:

**East Midlands Tourism**
w discovereastmidlands.com
• Discover East Midlands

**Experience Nottinghamshire**
t (0115) 915 5330
w visitnotts.com
• Nottinghamshire Essential Guide,
  Where to Stay Guide, Stay Somewhere Different,
  City Breaks, Attractions – A Family Day Out
• Robin Hood Breaks
• Pilgrim Fathers

**Peak District and Derbyshire**
t 0870 444 7275
w visitpeakdistrict.com
• Peak District Visitor Guide
• Savour the Flavour of the Peak District
• Derbyshire – the Peak District Visitor Guide
• Derbyshire – the Peak District Attractions Guide
• Camping and Caravanning Guide
• What's on Guide

**Lincolnshire**
t (01522) 873213
w visitlincolnshire.com
• Visit Lincolnshire – Destination Guide,
  Great days out, Gardens & Nurseries,
  Aviation Heritage, Good Taste
• Go with the flow

**Explore Northamptonshire**
t (01604) 838800
w explorenorthamptonshire.co.uk
• Explore Northamptonshire Visitor Guide,
  County Map, Food and Drink

**Leicestershire and Rutland**
t 0906 294 1113
w goleicestershire.com
• Rutland Visitor Guide
• Market Harborough & Lutterworth Guide
• Ashby de la Zouch and The National Forest Guide
• Melton Mowbray and the Vale of Belvoir
• Loughborough and Charnwood Forest
• GoLeicestershire
• Must See 3

Whinstone Lee Tor, Peak District

# enjoyEngland ™

## official tourist board guides

Hotels, including country house and town house hotels, metro and budget hotels in England 2008

**£10.99**

Guest accommodation, B&Bs, guest houses, farmhouses, inns, restaurants with rooms, campus and hostel accommodation in England 2008

**£11.99**

Self-catering holiday homes, including serviced apartments and approved caravan holiday homes, boat accommodation and holiday cottage agencies in England 2008

**£11.99**

Touring parks, camping holidays and holiday parks and villages in Britain 2008

**£8.99**

## informative, easy to use and great value for money

Pet-friendly hotels, B&Bs and self-catering accommodation in England 2008

**£9.99**

Great ideas for places to visit, eat and stay in England

**£10.99**

Places to stay and visit in South West England

**£9.99**

Places to stay and visit in Northern England

**£9.99**

Accessible places to stay in Britain

**£9.99**

Now available in good bookshops.
For special offers on VisitBritain publications,
please visit **enjoyenglanddirect.com**

where to stay in
# East Midlands

All place names in the blue bands are shown on the maps at the front of this guide.

A complete listing of all Enjoy England assessed accommodation covered by this guide appears at the back.

## Accommodation symbols

Symbols give useful information about services and facilities. Inside the back-cover flap you can find a key to these symbols. Keep it open for easy reference.

---

**ASHBOURNE,** Derbyshire Map ref 4B2

★ ★ ★ ★
BED & BREAKFAST

B&B per room per night
s £30.00–£35.00
d £46.00–£52.00

## Mona Villas Bed and Breakfast

1 Mona Villas, Church Lane Mayfield, Ashbourne DE6 2JS  t (01335) 343773  f (01335) 343773
e info@mona-villas.fsnet.co.uk  w mona-villas.fsnet.co.uk

A warm, friendly welcome to our Edwardian home with purpose-built, en suite accommodation. Beautiful views over open countryside. Near Alton Towers and Dovedale.

**open** All year except Christmas and New Year
**bedrooms** 2 double, 1 twin
**bathrooms** All en suite
**payment** Cash/cheques

Room 🛏 TV 🍴 ♨  General 🕭 🕮 ♿ P ⚡ 🍳 ☼  Leisure 🚲 🏛

---

**ATTERBY,** Lincolnshire Map ref 4C2

★ ★ ★ ★
BED & BREAKFAST

B&B per room per night
s Min £30.00
d £55.00–£60.00
Evening meal per person
£7.50–£10.00

## East Farm Farmhouse Bed and Breakfast

East Farm, Atterby LN8 2BJ  t (01673) 818917  f (01673) 818917  e anneastfarm@hotmail.com
w eastfarm.me.uk

Farmhouse bed and breakfast where a warm welcome awaits you in peaceful surroundings. En suite rooms with tea-/coffee-making facilities and hearty farmhouse fare.

**open** All year except Christmas and New Year
**bedrooms** 3 double
**bathrooms** All en suite
**payment** Cash/cheques

Room 🛏 TV 🍴 ♨  General P ⚡ 🍳 🏮 🕮 🖥 ☼  Leisure 🏛

---

**BAKEWELL,** Derbyshire Map ref 4B2

★ ★ ★ ★
GUEST ACCOMMODATION

B&B per room per night
s £45.00–£50.00
d £55.00–£80.00

## Castle Cliffe Guest House

Monsal Head, Bakewell DE45 1NL  t (01629) 640258  f (01629) 640258  e relax@castle-cliffe.com
w castle-cliffe.com

**open** All year except Christmas
**bedrooms** 3 double, 2 twin, 2 family
**bathrooms** All en suite
**payment** Credit/debit cards, cash/cheques

Stunning position overlooking the beautiful Monsal Dale. Noted for its friendly atmosphere, hearty breakfasts and exceptional views. Drinks in the garden or around an open log fire in winter. Centrally situated for Chatsworth, Haddon Hall and other attractions. Choice of dinner venues within an easy stroll. Walks in all directions.

⊕ From the A6 at Ashford-in-the-Water, take the B6465 to Monsal Head.

Room TV 🍴 ♨  General 🕭 🕮 ♿ P ⚡ 🏮 ☼  Leisure ∪ ⚑ 🚲

---

## BAKEWELL, Derbyshire Map ref 4B2

★★★★
**BED & BREAKFAST**

B&B per room per night
s £32.00–£36.00
d £48.00–£53.00

### Housley Cottage

Housley, Nr Foolow, Hope Valley S32 5QB  t (01433) 631505  e kevin@housleycottages.co.uk
w housleycottages.co.uk

**open** All year except Christmas and New Year
**bedrooms** 2 double, 1 twin, 1 family
**bathrooms** All en suite
**payment** Credit/debit cards, cash/cheques, euros

A 16thC farm cottage set in open countryside but within ten minutes' walk of the Bulls Head pub in Foolow village. Public footpaths pass our garden gate to Millers Dale, Chatsworth House, Eyam and Castleton. All rooms en suite with views over open countryside. Full English breakfast or vegetarian.

⊕ Buxton A6, A623, junction to Foolow; we are opposite on right-hand side. Chesterfield A619/A623; 300m past Housley sign on left-hand side.

♥ Family room (sleeps 4): children half price. 10% reduction when booking 3 or more nights. See website for latest offers.

Room TV 👍 🖥️  General 🛅 🏃 P ⚡ 🍽️ ✳️  Leisure 🏖️

## BARROW UPON SOAR, Leicestershire Map ref 4C3

★★★★
**INN**

B&B per room per night
s £90.00–£120.00
d £90.00–£120.00
Evening meal per person
£8.00–£20.00

### Hunting Lodge

38 South Street, Barrow upon Soar, Loughborough LE12 8LZ  t (01509) 412337  f (01509) 410838
w probablythebestpubsintheworld.com

**open** All year
**bedrooms** 3 double, 3 twin
**bathrooms** All en suite
**payment** Credit/debit cards, cash/cheques

This beautiful, spectacular, three-storey granite building boasts open fires, leather sofas, private dining and restaurant areas, all suited perfectly to any type of occasion. The rooms, each individually designed, range from the traditional and ornate 'Fagin' room, the luxurious 'Louis' suite to the quirky 'Dali' room.

⊕ Situated in the village of Barrow upon Soar, only a short distance from the A6 between Loughborough (3 miles) and Leicester (8 miles).

♥ Register with us online to receive all the latest offers and promotions: www.probablythebestpubintheworld.com.

Room 🛏️ 📞 TV 👍 🖥️  General 🛅 🏛️ 🏃 P ⚡ 🍽️ ✕ 🍴 🎿 ✳️  Leisure 🎣 🏇

# A holiday for Fido?

Some proprietors welcome well-behaved pets. Look for the 🐕 symbol in the accommodation listings. You can also buy a copy of our new guide – Welcome Pets! – available from good bookshops and online at visitbritaindirect.com.

## BEELEY, Derbyshire Map ref 4B2

★★★★
**INN**

B&B per room per night
s £145.00–£185.00
d £145.00–£185.00
Evening meal per person
£15.00–£30.00

# The Devonshire Arms at Beeley

Devonshire Square, Beeley, Matlock DE4 2NR  t (01629) 733259  f (01629) 733259
e enquiries@devonshirebeeley.co.uk  w devonshirebeeley.co.uk

**open** All year
**bedrooms** 2 double, 1 twin, 1 suite
**bathrooms** All en suite
**payment** Credit/debit cards, cash/cheques, euros

Tucked away in a picturesque country village is an historic inn full of charm and character with a contemporary twist. A serious wine list and local cask beers complement delicious food, served all day, in the original inn or the brightly coloured brasserie. Stay in one of the four stylish and characterful bedrooms.

⊕ *The Devonshire Arms is 17 miles from the M1 jct 29 via Chesterfield. Past Chatsworth House and Beeley is 1 mile on the left.*

♥ *2 children up to 14 years old stay free including breakfast when sharing with their parents in the family suite.*

Room 📞 📺 🛁 🍳  General 🛏 🎱 🔥 P ♨ ✕ 🛒 🌀 ✿ 🐾  Leisure ∪ ♪ ► 🚲 🏊

## BEESTON, Nottinghamshire Map ref 4C2

★★★
**GUEST HOUSE**

B&B per room per night
s £25.00–£50.00
d £50.00–£60.00
Evening meal per person
£7.95–£15.00

# Hylands

Queens Road, Beeston, Nottingham NG9 1JB  t (0115) 925 5472  f (0115) 922 5574
e hyland.hotel@btconnect.com  w s-h-systems.co.uk/hotels/hylands.html

**open** All year except Christmas
**bedrooms** 6 double, 7 twin, 17 single, 8 family
**bathrooms** 23 en suite
**payment** Credit/debit cards, cash

A family-run hotel offering comfortable, clean accommodation within a warm and friendly atmosphere. Situated close to Nottingham University, the city indoor tennis centre and Attenborough nature reserve. Within easy walking distance of an award-winning pub and several excellent restaurants, and with frequent transport links to the city centre.

⊕ *Leave M1 at jct 25. Follow A52 towards Nottingham. At roundabout take B6003 (Long Eaton). At T-junction follow A6005 (Nottingham). Hylands is 2.5 miles along on right.*

♥ *Discounts available for groups and stays of 4 nights or longer. Extra discounts during winter. Please contact for details.*

Room 🛗 📞 📺 🛁 🍳  General 🛏 🎱 🔥 P ♨ ✕ 🛒 🌀 ✿ 🐾  Leisure 🎣 🏊

## BOURNE, Lincolnshire Map ref 3A1

★★★★
**GUEST ACCOMMODATION**

B&B per room per night
s £24.00–£32.00
d £46.00–£54.00

# Maycroft Cottage Bed and Breakfast

6 Edenham Road, Hanthorpe, Bourne PE10 0RB  t (01778) 571689  f (01778) 571689
e enquiries@maycroftcottage.co.uk  w maycroftcottage.co.uk

Maycroft Cottage is a modern residence with a cottage atmosphere, accommodating the tourist or the business person wishing to relax in this idyllic setting. Walkers and cyclists welcome.

**open** All year except Christmas and New Year
**bedrooms** 1 double, 1 twin
**payment** Credit/debit cards, cash/cheques

Room 🛗 📺 🛁 🍳  General 🛏 8 P ♨ 🌀 ✿  Leisure ∪ ♪ ► 🚲 🏊

## Key to symbols
Open the back flap for a key to symbols.

## BRACKLEY, Northamptonshire Map ref 2C1

**★★★★**
FARMHOUSE

B&B per room per night
s  Min £28.00
d  Min £45.00

# Astwell Mill

Helmdon, Brackley NN13 5QU  t (01295) 760507  f (01295) 768602  e astwell01@aol.com
w astwellmill.co.uk

Converted watermill with sizeable garden overlooking large lake. Excellent views. Convenient for Stowe, Sulgrave, Canons Ashby and Silverstone. Warwick, Blenheim Palace, Oxford and Stratford within an hour.

**open** All year except Christmas
**bedrooms** 2 double
**bathrooms** 1 en suite, 1 private
**payment** Cash/cheques

Room 📺 ♦ 🍴  General 👜 🏬 P ⅟ 🛏 ❄

## BRACKLEY, Northamptonshire Map ref 2C1

**★★★★**
FARMHOUSE

B&B per room per night
s  £35.00–£45.00
d  £40.00–£70.00

# Hill Farm

Halse, Brackley NN13 6DY  t (01280) 703300 & 07860 865146  f (01280) 704999
e j.g.robinson@btconnect.com

A charming Georgian farmhouse set in beautiful countryside. Antique four-poster bed. Close to Silverstone, Stowe, Oxford, Blenheim and the Cotswolds. Peaceful location, warm welcome, delicious breakfasts.

**open** All year except Christmas and New Year
**bedrooms** 2 double, 1 twin, 2 suites
**bathrooms** 2 en suite, 3 private
**payment** Cash/cheques, euros

Room 🔔 🖤 📺 ♦ 🍴  General 👜 P ⅟ 🍽 ⚘ ◉ ❄ 🐾  Leisure 🏊

## BRADWELL, Derbyshire Map ref 4B2

**★★★★**
GUEST ACCOMMODATION

B&B per room per night
s  £40.00–£46.00
d  £68.00–£72.00

# Stoney Ridge

Granby Road, Bradwell, Hope Valley S33 9HU  t (01433) 620538  e toneyridge@aol.com
w stoneyridge.org.uk

**open** All year
**bedrooms** 3 double, 1 twin
**bathrooms** 3 en suite, 1 private
**payment** Credit/debit cards, cash/cheques

Large private bungalow, set in established gardens, enjoying wonderful views over Hope Valley. The friendly village of Bradwell is three miles east of Castleton. Enjoy a swim at no extra charge in our 28ft indoor heated pool. Three double en suite rooms and one twin with private facilities. Plus legendary breakfasts.

⊕ Take directions to Bowling Green Inn. Carry on uphill for 200m. Turn sharp left onto Granby Road, Stoney Ridge is 4th on right.

♥ Winter and midweek offers. See website for details.

Room 📺 ♦ 🍴  General 👜 10 P 🍽 🛏 ⚘ ❄ 🐾  Leisure ⚲ ∪

## BRADWELL, Derbyshire Map ref 4B2

**★★★**
INN

B&B per room per night
s  £30.00–£45.00
d  £55.00–£80.00
Evening meal per person
£6.95–£12.95

# Travellers Rest

Brough Lane End, Brough, Hope Valley S33 9HG  t (01433) 620363  f (01433) 623338
e elliottstephen@btconnect.com  w travellers-rest.net

Country inn set in the picturesque Hope Valley in the Peak District. Friendly, with great food and beer.

**open** All year except Christmas
**bedrooms** 3 double, 2 twin
**bathrooms** All en suite
**payment** Credit/debit cards, cash/cheques

Room 🔔 📺 ♦ 🍴  General 👜 🏛 P ‼ ✗ ❄ 🐾  Leisure ⚫ ✦ 🚴

## Using map references

Map references refer to the colour maps at the front of this guide.

## BRETBY, Derbyshire Map ref 4B3

★ ★ ★
**GUEST ACCOMMODATION**

B&B per room per night
s £50.00
d £60.00
Evening meal per person
£5.95–£17.95

# Bretby Conference Centre

Ashby Road, Bretby, Burton-on-Trent DE15 0YZ  t (01283) 553440  f (01283) 553448
e enquiries@bretbycc.co.uk  w bretbycc.co.uk

A multipurpose venue catering for anything from small meetings up to large exhibitions, with luxury en suite accommodation.

**open** All year except Christmas and New Year
**bedrooms** 24 double, 14 twin, 1 family
**bathrooms** All en suite
**payment** Cash/cheques

Room 🛏 ☎ 📺 🕯  General 🛋 ▥ ⚓ P ⚑ ✕ 🌡 ㎡ 🔥 ✿ 🐾  Leisure ♣

## BRIGG, Lincolnshire Map ref 4C1

★ ★ ★ ★
**GUEST HOUSE**

B&B per room per night
s £20.00–£27.50
d £30.00–£45.00
Evening meal per person
£6.00–£10.00

# Holcombe Guest House

34 Victoria Road, Barnetby DN38 6JR  t 07850 764002  f (01652) 680841
e holcombe.house@virgin.net  w holcombeguesthouse.co.uk

Pleasant, homely accommodation near the railway station and airport. Only 15 minutes from Scunthorpe, Grimsby and Hull. Bedroom for disabled guests.

**open** All year
**bedrooms** 3 twin, 8 single, 2 family
**bathrooms** 7 en suite
**payment** Credit/debit cards, cash/cheques

Room 🛏 📺 🕯 ⍟  General 🛋 P ✕ ㎡ 🔥 ✿ 🐾  Leisure ⛵

## BUXTON, Derbyshire Map ref 4B2

★ ★ ★ ★ ★
**GUEST HOUSE**
**SILVER AWARD**

B&B per room per night
s £50.00–£78.00
d £68.00–£92.00

# Buxton's Victorian Guest House

3a Broad Walk, Buxton SK17 6JE  t (01298) 78759  e buxtonvictorian@btconnect.com
w buxtonvictorian.co.uk

Built in 1860, an elegant, Grade II Listed townhouse, recently refurbished in classical Victorian style. On a quiet, tree-lined promenade, overlooking 40-acre park and Opera House.

**open** All year except Christmas and New Year
**bedrooms** 5 double, 1 twin, 2 family
**bathrooms** All en suite
**payment** Credit/debit cards, cash/cheques

Room 🛏 🖭 📺 🕯 ⍟  General 🛋 5 P ✂ 🌡 ㎡  Leisure ⚐ ⛵

## BUXTON, Derbyshire Map ref 4B2

★ ★ ★
**INN**

B&B per room per night
s Min £45.00
d Min £55.00
Evening meal per person
£7.50–£12.50

# Devonshire Arms

Peak Forest, Buxton SK17 8EJ  t (01298) 23875  f (01298) 23598  e fiona.clough@virgin.net
w devarms.com

**open** All year except Christmas
**bedrooms** 4 double, 2 family
**bathrooms** All en suite
**payment** Credit/debit cards, cash/cheques

Traditional Peak District inn. High-standard, en suite rooms with TV and coffee facilities. Excellent food, traditional ales, coal fire. Dogs and children free. Guaranteed warm welcome.

Room 📺 🕯 ⍟  General 🛋 ⚓ P ⚑ ✕ 🌡 ✿ 🐾  Leisure ∪ ⚲

## Place index

If you know where you want to stay, the index at the back of the guide will give you the page number listing accommodation in your chosen town, city or village. Check out the other useful indexes too.

## BUXTON, Derbyshire Map ref 4B2

★★★★
**FARMHOUSE**
**SILVER AWARD**

B&B per room per night
s £39.00–£45.00
d £58.00–£70.00
Evening meal per person
£14.50–£18.00

# Fernydale Farm

Earl Sterndale, Nr Buxton SK17 0BS  t (01298) 83236  f (01298) 83605  e wjnadin@btconnect.com

**open** All year
**bedrooms** 1 double, 1 twin, 1 family
**bathrooms** All en suite
**payment** Cash/cheques

A friendly, warm welcome awaits you at Fernydale. A working farm nestling in the Peaks with stunning views. Attractive bedrooms with modern bathrooms. Spacious conservatory and garden to relax in. Excellent breakfast to set you up for the day. Buxton, Bakewell, Ashbourne and numerous attractions/walks within easy access.

⊕ From Buxton take A515. When you come to Country Bookstore turn right onto B5053 to Longnor. At small crossroads turn left (Earl Sterndale). Farm 200yds on left.

♥ Discounts on stays of 4 or more nights (excl Bank Holidays).

Room 📺 ♨ 🍴  General ⌕ 🏠 P ✕ 🖾 ♨ 🛏  Leisure 🚲 🏛

## BUXTON, Derbyshire Map ref 4B2

★★★★★
**GUEST HOUSE**
**GOLD AWARD**

B&B per room per night
s £33.00–£50.00
d £65.00–£90.00
Evening meal per person
£15.00

# Grendon Guest House

Bishops Lane, Buxton SK17 6UN  t (01298) 78831  e grendonguesthouse@hotmail.com
w grendonguesthouse.co.uk

Grendon is spacious and elegant, with exquisite bedrooms, scrumptious food and the friendliest hospitality. Set in lovely one-acre gardens. Easy driveway parking. Beautiful location, fifteen minutes' walk to town centre.

**open** All year
**bedrooms** 3 double, 1 twin, 1 single
**bathrooms** All en suite
**payment** Credit/debit cards, cash/cheques

Room 🖾 📺 ♨ 🍴  General ⌕9 P ✕ ✕ 🖾 ♨ 🄵 ◨ ♨ 🛏

## BUXTON, Derbyshire Map ref 4B2

★★★★
**GUEST HOUSE**
**SILVER AWARD**

B&B per room per night
s Min £45.00
d £65.00–£80.00

# Grosvenor House

Broad Walk, Buxton SK17 6JE  t (01298) 72439  e grosvenor.buxton@btopenworld.com
w grosvenorbuxton.co.uk

**open** All year except Christmas
**bedrooms** 6 double, 1 twin, 1 family
**bathrooms** All en suite
**payment** Credit/debit cards, cash/cheques

Quiet, privately run, Grade II Listed Victorian residence situated in the heart of this historic spa town. All en suite rooms have many interesting features. Imaginative, freshly cooked breakfast menu. Non-smoking throughout. Stairlift to first floor.

⊕ From A6 take bypass around town shops and railway station. Straight over roundabout and 2nd left past Opera House. Guest house 100yds on right, facing gardens.

Room 📺 ♨ 🍴  General ⌕ P ✕ ♨ 🄵 ◨  Leisure ∪ 🎵 ♪ 🚲 🏛

# It's all quality-assessed accommodation

Our commitment to quality involves wide-ranging accommodation assessment. Rating and awards were correct at the time of going to press but may change following a new assessment. Please check at time of booking.

## BUXTON, Derbyshire Map ref 4B2

★★★★
**GUEST HOUSE
SILVER AWARD**

B&B per room per night
s £35.00–£40.00
d £60.00–£80.00

# Kingscroft Guest House

10 Green Lane, Buxton SK17 9DP  t (01298) 22757  f (01298) 27858

**open** All year except Christmas
**bedrooms** 6 double, 1 twin, 1 single
**bathrooms** All en suite
**payment** Cash/cheques

Late-Victorian luxury guesthouse, in a central yet quiet position in the heart of the Peak District. Comfortable surroundings with period decor. Enjoy our hearty, delicious, home-cooked full English or continental breakfasts.

♥ *10% discount on stays of 4 nights or more.*

Room ▨ TV ◖ ☌   General P ⬥ ✕ ▦ ⩍ ✿ ⍐   Leisure ♪ ▸ ⊶ 🚲 🏠

## BUXTON, Derbyshire Map ref 4B2

★★★★
**GUEST HOUSE**

B&B per room per night
d £70.00–£80.00

# Lakenham Guest House

11 Burlington Road, Buxton SK17 9AL  t (01298) 79209  e enquiries@lakenhambuxton.co.uk
w lakenhambuxton.co.uk

**open** All year
**bedrooms** 5 double, 4 family
**bathrooms** 7 en suite, 2 private
**payment** Credit/debit cards, cash/cheques

Sample Victorian elegance in one of Buxton's finest guesthouses. Lakenham offers all modern facilities yet retains its Victorian character. Period furniture and antiques. Superb, central location overlooking picturesque Pavilion Gardens. Spacious, tastefully furnished, en suite bedrooms with TV, hospitality tray. First-class, personal service in a friendly, relaxed atmosphere.

⊕ *Lakenham is located opposite the Pavilion Gardens on Burlington Road. Burlington Road is situated between St Johns Road (A54) and Macclesfield Road/ West Road.*

Room ♿ TV ◖   General P

## CASTLETON, Derbyshire Map ref 4B2

★★★
**INN**

B&B per room per night
s £35.00–£40.00
d £65.00–£80.00

# Ye Olde Cheshire Cheese Inn

How Lane, Castleton, Hope Valley S33 8WJ  t (01433) 620330  f (01433) 621847
e info@cheshirecheeseinn.co.uk  w cheshirecheeseinn.co.uk

**open** All year except Christmas
**bedrooms** 8 double, 1 twin, 1 single
**bathrooms** All en suite
**payment** Credit/debit cards, cash/cheques

Situated in the heart of the picturesque Peak District. A family-run, 17thC free house full of character offering good pub food and non-smoking restaurant and a wide selection of draught beers. Renowned bed and breakfast accommodation. Ten en suite, comfortably furnished bedrooms. Large car park adjacent to the premises.

Room ♿ ▨ TV ◖ ☌   General P ⬥ ▦   Leisure ∪ ♪ ▸ 🚲 🏠

# B&B prices

Rates for bed and breakfast are shown per room per night.
Double room prices are usually based on two people sharing the room.

## CHAPEL-EN-LE-FRITH, Derbyshire Map ref 4B2

★ ★ ★ ★ ★
**GUEST HOUSE**
**SILVER AWARD**

### High Croft

Manchester Road, Chapel-en-le-Frith, High Peak SK23 9UH **t** (01298) 814843
**e** elaine@highcroft-guesthouse.co.uk **w** highcroft-guesthouse.co.uk

B&B per room per night
**s** £50.00–£60.00
**d** £70.00–£90.00

**open** All year
**bedrooms** 2 double, 2 family
**bathrooms** All en suite
**payment** Cash/cheques

A luxurious Edwardian country house set in 1.5 acres of peaceful, mature gardens adjoining Chapel-en-le-Frith golf course and Combs Reservoir with magnificent views and superb walks from the door. Beautifully furnished, en suite bedrooms, spacious, comfortable sitting room, log fires, elegant dining room, and an extensive and appetizing breakfast menu.

⊕ M1 jct 29. A617 to Chesterfield, A619 to Baslow, A623 to A6, right at roundabout towards Stockport. Left onto B5470 through Chapel-en-le-Frith for 1 mile, High Croft on left.

♥ Discounts on stays of 4 or more days (excl Sat).

Room 📺 ♿ 🕾  General 🛏 P 🅿 📦 ☼  Leisure ∪ ♪ ▶ 🚴 🛶

## CHESTERFIELD, Derbyshire Map ref 4B2

★ ★ ★
**GUEST HOUSE**

### Abigails Guest House

62 Brockwell Lane, Chesterfield S40 4EE **t** (01246) 279391 **f** (01246) 854468
**e** gail@abigails.fsnet.co.uk **w** abigailsguesthouse.co.uk

B&B per room per night
**s** Min £36.00
**d** Min £48.00

Relax taking breakfast in the conservatory overlooking Chesterfield and surrounding moorlands. Garden with pond and waterfall, private car park. Best B&B winners 2000.

**open** All year
**bedrooms** 3 double, 2 twin, 2 single
**bathrooms** All en suite
**payment** Cash/cheques

Room 📺 ♿ 🕾  General 🛏 ▥ ⚲ P 🅿 ☼ 🍴

## CHESTERFIELD, Derbyshire Map ref 4B2

★ ★ ★
**BED & BREAKFAST**

### Locksley

21 Tennyson Avenue, Chesterfield S40 4SN **t** (01246) 273332

B&B per room per night
**s** Max £24.00
**d** Max £48.00

Comfortable and attractive house. Pretty garden viewed from windows. Walking distance from town centre.

**open** All year except Christmas and New Year
**bedrooms** 1 double, 1 twin
**payment** Cash/cheques

Room 🕾 📺 ♿ 🕾  General 🛏 1 🍴 ☼  Leisure 🛶

**COALVILLE,** Leicestershire Map ref 4B3

Rating Applied For
**INN**

B&B per room per night
s Max £30.00
d Max £55.00
Evening meal per person
Max £5.75

# The New Ellistown

Whitehill Road, Ellistown, Coalville LE67 1EL  t (01530) 260502  e val786@btinternet.com
w thenewellistown.co.uk

**open** All year
**bedrooms** 1 double, 1 twin, 2 single
**bathrooms** All en suite
**payment** Credit/debit cards, cash/cheques

Public house with B&B, all rooms en suite. Live entertainment at weekends. Beer garden and new sheltered seating area to enjoy, surrounded by pot plants. New golf studio for 2008. Car parking for approximately 20 cars.

⊕ We are within 5 miles of the M1 and A42/M42, and 20 minutes' drive from East Midlands Airport and Castle Donington racetrack.

♥ We are a registered charity group and hold a fund-raising quiz on Sunday evenings with proceeds to local charities.

Room 📺 ♨  General 🛗 ▦ ♿ P ⚲ ♛ 🍴 ⌨ 🌣  Leisure 🏠

**CORBY,** Northamptonshire Map ref 3A1

★ ★ ★
**BED & BREAKFAST**

B&B per room per night
s Min £35.00
d £50.00–£60.00

# Home Farm

Main Street, Sudborough, Kettering NN14 3BX  t (01832) 730488  e bandbhomefarmsud@aol.com
w homefarmsudborough.co.uk

**open** All year
**bedrooms** 1 double, 1 twin
**bathrooms** 2 private
**payment** Cash/cheques, euros

Just three miles from the A14, a restored barn to yourself in the picturesque village of Sudborough. The barn has a breakfast room, double bedroom, shower room, lounge with sofa bed and single bed, lockable storage room, private parking, and seating area in the garden, and includes a self-service continental breakfast.

⊕ A14 jct 12, A6116 for Corby. After 3 miles, left into Sudborough and Home Farm is on the right, 500yds past the village hall.

♥ Discount for full occupancy.

Room 🛁 📺 ♨ 🍵  General 🛗 P ⚲ ♿ 🔥 ☐ 🌣  Leisure ⚓ 🏠

**CORBY,** Northamptonshire Map ref 3A1

★ ★ ★ ★
**GUEST ACCOMMODATION**

B&B per room per night
s Min £35.00
d Min £70.00

# Manor Farm Guest House

Station Road, Rushton, Kettering NN14 1RL  t (01536) 710305  w rushtonmanorfarm.co.uk

16thC manor house, family home in small village of Rushton, situated between Kettering, Corby and Desborough. 15 minutes to Rockingham Speedway.

**open** All year
**bedrooms** 6 double
**bathrooms** 5 en suite, 1 private
**payment** Credit/debit cards, cash/cheques

Room 🛁 📺 ♨ 🍵  General 🛗 ▦ ♿ P ✕ ⌨ 🌣 🐾

## Looking for a little luxury

Gold and Silver Awards are given to establishments achieving the highest levels of quality and service. There's more information at the front of the guide, and an index to all accommodation achieving these awards at the back.

## COTTESMORE, Rutland Map ref 3A1

★★★★
**GUEST ACCOMMODATION**

B&B per room per night
s £35.00–£40.00
d £55.00–£70.00

# Tithe Barn

Clatterpot Lane, Cottesmore, Oakham LE15 7DW  **t** (01572) 813591  **f** (01572) 812719
**e** jp@thetithebarn.co.uk  **w** tithebarn-rutland.co.uk

**open** All year
**bedrooms** 3 double, 2 twin, 2 family
**bathrooms** 5 en suite, 2 private
**payment** Credit/debit cards, cash/cheques

An attractive 17thC converted tithe barn. Spacious, comfortable, en suite rooms. Two superior rooms have power showers and king-size beds. Five minutes from Rutland Water, Barnsdale Gardens and A1. A warm and friendly home with a panelled dining room, striking hall and a wealth of original features. All rooms have tea/coffee facilities.

⊕ *B668 from A1 or Oakham into Cottesmore and turn beside the petrol station into Mill Lane. We are on junction of Clatterpot Lane.*

♥ *Discounts on stays of 5 or more days.*

Room 🛁 📺 👤 ♨  General 🛎 🅰 P ✂ 🗒 ☼ 🐕  Leisure ✦ ♣

## CREATON, Northamptonshire Map ref 4C3

★★★★
**GUEST ACCOMMODATION**

B&B per room per night
s £45.00–£123.37
d £58.00–£149.80
Evening meal per person
£20.00–£30.00

# Highgate House – A Sundial Group Venue

Grooms Lane, Creaton NN6 8NN  **t** (01604) 505505  **f** (01604) 505565
**e** claire.fonville@sundialgroup.com  **w** sundialgroup.com

Originally a 17thC coaching inn, Highgate has evolved to become one of the country's top events venues, boasting excellent accommodation and catering for all private events. Some rooms can be used as family rooms.

**open** All year except Christmas
**bedrooms** 50 double, 18 twin, 30 single
**bathrooms** All en suite
**payment** Credit/debit cards, cash/cheques

Room 🛁 📠 📞 📺 👤 ♨  General 🛎 ▥ 🅰 P ▮ ✕ 🗒 🎱 ☼  Leisure ⚑ ♣ ♠ P

## CRESSBROOK, Derbyshire Map ref 4B2

★★★★
**GUEST ACCOMMODATION**

B&B per room per night
d £95.00–£115.00

# Cressbrook Hall

Cressbrook, Buxton SK17 8SY  **t** (01298) 871289  **f** (01298) 871845  **e** stay@cressbrookhall.co.uk
**w** cressbrookhall.co.uk

Accommodation with a difference. Enjoy this magnificent family home built in 1835, set in 23 acres, with spectacular views around the compass.

**open** All year except Christmas
**bedrooms** 2 double, 1 suite
**bathrooms** All en suite
**payment** Credit/debit cards, cash/cheques

Room 🛁 📠 📺 👤 ♨  General 🛎 ▥ 🅰 P ✂ 🗒 ☼ 🐕  Leisure ♣ ✦

## DARLEY ABBEY, Derbyshire Map ref 4B2

★★★
**GUEST ACCOMMODATION**

B&B per room per night
s £26.00–£35.00
d £52.50–£55.00

# The Coach House

185a Duffield Road, Derby DE22 1JB  **t** (01332) 551795  **e** carolcoachhousederby@tiscali.co.uk

A 19thC gentleman's residence situated on the A6, one mile north of the city centre, ideal for touring or business. Residents' lounge, interesting garden and a warm welcome. Rooms available for single occupancy.

**open** All year
**bedrooms** 1 double, 1 twin, 2 single
**bathrooms** 2 en suite
**payment** Cash/cheques, euros

Room 📺 👤 ♨  General 🛎 P ✂ 🗒 ☼ 🐕  Leisure P ⌂

## To your credit

If you book by credit card, it's advisable to check the proprietor's cancellation policy in case you have to change your plans.

### DAVENTRY, Northamptonshire Map ref 2C1

★★
**BED & BREAKFAST**

B&B per room per night
s £30.00–£40.00
d £60.00–£70.00

# The Mill House

West Farndon, Nr Daventry NN11 3TX  t (01327) 261727  f 0870 460 1018
e josephinelincoln53@amserve.com  w millhousebandb.co.uk

Superb former mill set in very peaceful rural south
Northamptonshire countryside.

**open** All year
**bedrooms** 2 double, 1 twin, 1 single
**bathrooms** 1 private
**payment** Cash/cheques

Room 🛏  General 🛋 P 🗡 🍽 🔥  Leisure ⟲ ◎ ∪

### DERBY, Derbyshire Map ref 4B2

★★★
**BED & BREAKFAST**

B&B per room per night
s £25.00–£30.00
d Min £50.00

# Bonehill Farm

Etwall Road, Mickleover, Derby DE3 0DN  t (01332) 513553  e bonehillfarm@hotmail.com
w bonehillfarm.co.uk

**open** All year except Christmas
**bedrooms** 1 double, 1 twin, 1 family
**bathrooms** 2 en suite
**payment** Cash/cheques

A 120-acre mixed farm. Comfortable Georgian
farmhouse in rural setting, three miles from Derby.
Alton Towers, Peak District, historic houses and the
Potteries within easy reach. Peaceful location.

Room 📺 🛏  General 🛋 🗡 🍽 ❀ 🐕

### DERBY, Derbyshire Map ref 4B2

★★★★
**GUEST HOUSE**

B&B per room per night
s Min £45.00
d Min £60.00

# Braeside Guest House

113 Derby Road, Risley, Derby DE72 3SS  t (0115) 939 5885  e bookings@braesideguesthouse.co.uk
w braesideguesthouse.co.uk

**open** All year except Christmas
**bedrooms** 4 double, 2 twin
**bathrooms** All en suite
**payment** Credit/debit cards, cash/cheques

The enthusiastic hosts of this delightful property
offer a very warm welcome to guests. The
bedrooms, located in a characteristic conversion of
barns close to the house, are attractively appointed,
with many extras, and set in extensive gardens.
Breakfast is served in the conservatory with superb
views over open countryside.

⊕ M1 jct 25, take exit signed Risley. At crossroads turn left
into Risley. Continue straight on past Risley Park pub on
left. 2nd cottage on left.

Room 📺 🛏 🍵  General 🛋 P 🗡 🍽 ▣ ❀  Leisure ∪ 🚴 🕯 🏰

### DERBY, Derbyshire Map ref 4B2

★★★
**GUEST ACCOMMODATION**

B&B per room per night
s £25.00–£35.00
d £40.00–£50.00

# Rose and Thistle Guest House

21 Charnwood Street, Derby DE1 2GU  t (01332) 344103

High standard Victorian guesthouse situated just
five minutes from the city centre of Derby. Quality
accommodation, open all year round for
bookings. Situated just 5 minutes from Derby
train station.

**open** All year except Christmas and New Year
**bedrooms** 5 twin, 3 single
**bathrooms** 2 en suite, 2 private
**payment** Cash/cheques

Room 📺 🛏 🍵  General 🛋 🗡 ❀

## EMPINGHAM, Rutland Map ref 3A1

★★★★
**BED & BREAKFAST**

B&B per room per night
s £40.00–£45.00
d £55.00
Evening meal per person
£15.00

### Shacklewell Lodge

Stamford Road, Empingham, Oakham LE15 8QQ  t (01780) 460646  e shacklewell@hotmail.com

Ancaster stone farmhouse set in large gardens close to Rutland Water. Family rooms available £65 – £85.

**open** All year except Christmas and New Year
**bedrooms** 1 double, 1 twin, 1 family
**bathrooms** 2 en suite, 1 private
**payment** Cash/cheques

Room 📺 ⚓ General 🛏 🍽 🅿 ✂ ✕ 🛎 ✿  Leisure ⚓ ∪ ♪ ♟ 🚲 🏛

## EYDON, Northamptonshire Map ref 2C1

★★★★
**FARMHOUSE**
**SILVER AWARD**

B&B per room per night
s £44.00–£49.00
d £78.00–£88.00

### Crockwell Farm

Eydon, Daventry NN11 3QA  t (01327) 361358  f (01327) 361573  e info@crockwellfarm.co.uk
w crockwellfarm.co.uk

Beautiful 17thC ironstone farmhouse and cottages in idyllic rural setting. Both cottages are self-contained. Evening meals available at local pub.

**open** All year
**bedrooms** 3 twin, 4 family
**bathrooms** All en suite
**payment** Credit/debit cards, cash/cheques

Room 🚪 📺 ⚓ ☕ General 🛏 🍽 🅿 🛎 ♨ ✿ 🐕  Leisure ∪ ♪ ♟

## GRANTHAM, Lincolnshire Map ref 3A1

★★★★
**BED & BREAKFAST**

B&B per room per night
s £27.00–£35.00
d £54.00–£65.00
Evening meal per person
£10.00–£15.00

### The Cedars

Low Road, Barrowby, Grantham NG32 1DL  t (01476) 563400  f (01476) 563400
e pbcbennett@mac.com

**open** All year
**bedrooms** 1 double, 1 twin
**bathrooms** 2 private
**payment** Cash/cheques, euros

Enjoy the relaxed atmosphere of this Grade II Listed farmhouse and its gardens. Delicious breakfasts, and evening meals if required, using our own, and local fresh produce. Italian cuisine a speciality. A five-minute drive from A1 motorway, and two miles from Grantham mainline station. French and Italian spoken.

Room 📺 ⚓ ☕ General 🛏 🍽 🅿 ✂ ✕ 🛎 ♨ ✿ 🐕  Leisure 🏛

## HOPE, Derbyshire Map ref 4B2

★★★★★
**GUEST ACCOMMODATION**
**GOLD AWARD**

B&B per room per night
s £55.00
d £75.00–£90.00

### Underleigh House

Off Edale Road, Hope, Hope Valley S33 6RF  t (01433) 621372  f (01433) 621324
e info@underleighhouse.co.uk  w underleighhouse.co.uk

**bedrooms** 4 double, 1 twin, 1 suite
**bathrooms** All en suite
**payment** Credit/debit cards, cash/cheques

Secluded cottage and barn conversion near the village of Hope with magnificent countryside views. Ideal for walking and exploring the Peak District. Delicious breakfasts, featuring local and home-made specialities, served in flagstoned dining hall. Welcoming and relaxing atmosphere with a log fire on chilly evenings in the charming, beamed lounge. Closed Christmas, New Year and January.

⊕ From Hope village, take Edale Road opposite parish church for about 0.6 miles. At house directly facing road, take lane to left for 0.3 miles.

Room 🚪 📞 📺 ⚓ ☕ General 🛏 12 🅿 ✂ 🛎 ♨ ✿  Leisure ♪ ♟ 🚲

## HOPE VALLEY, Derbyshire Map ref 4B2

★★★★
**INN**
**SILVER AWARD**

B&B per room per night
s £70.00–£95.00
d £70.00–£95.00

### The Chequers Inn

Froggatt Edge, Hope Valley S32 3ZJ  t (01433) 630231  f (01433) 631072
e info@chequers-froggatt.com  w chequers-froggatt.com

A traditional coaching inn offering first-class accommodation and exquisite food. Further seating available in our woodland garden. Five beautifully appointed en suite rooms.

**open** All year except Christmas
**bedrooms** 4 double, 1 twin
**bathrooms** All en suite
**payment** Credit/debit cards, cash/cheques

Room 🖵 ☎ 📺 🖐 🍵  General ☼ P ⊬ ♀ 🏠 ✿

## HORSLEY, Derbyshire Map ref 4B2

★★★★
**GUEST ACCOMMODATION**
**SILVER AWARD**

B&B per room per night
s £69.00–£79.00
d £90.00–£106.00
Evening meal per person
£10.00–£15.00

### Horsley Lodge

Smalley Mill Road, Horsley, Derby DE21 5BL  t (01332) 780838  f (01332) 781118
e enquiries@horsleylodge.co.uk  w horsleylodge.co.uk

**open** All year
**bedrooms** 6 double, 4 twin
**bathrooms** All en suite
**payment** Credit/debit cards, cash/cheques, euros

Magnificent stone country-house hotel. This hidden gem specialises in exclusive golf breaks for couples (maximum ten). Great restaurant, lovely views, championship golf course. All rooms individually themed.

⊕ From north, M1 jct 28 go south on A38. From A38 follow tourist signs for Denby Pottery then Horsley Lodge. From south, exit M1 at jct 25.

♥ 'Learn to golf' breaks. Discounts available Sun nights.

Room 🖵 ☎ 📺 🖐 🍵  General ☼1 🏠 ⓐ P ♀ ✕ 🏠 🐴 ✿ 🐓  Leisure ♦ ∪ ✈ ►

## KETTERING, Northamptonshire Map ref 3A2

★★★★
**FARMHOUSE**

B&B per room per night
s £25.00–£38.00
d £50.00–£76.00
Evening meal per person
Max £18.00

### Dairy Farm

Cranford St Andrew, Kettering NN14 4AQ  t (01536) 330273

17thC thatched farmhouse in a lovely Northamptonshire village just off the A14. Large garden containing ancient dovecote and summerhouse. Good food and friendly welcome. Safe off-road parking. Many places of interest nearby.

**open** All year except Christmas and New Year
**bedrooms** 2 double, 1 twin
**bathrooms** 2 en suite, 1 private
**payment** Cash/cheques

Room 🍴 🖵 📺 🖐 🍵  General ☼ 🏠 P ⊬ ✕ 🏠 ✿ 🐴  Leisure ►

## KEXBY, Lincolnshire Map ref 4C2

★★★
**FARMHOUSE**

B&B per room per night
s Min £25.00
d Min £44.00

### The Grange

Kexby, Gainsborough DN21 5PJ  t (01427) 788265

650-acre mixed farm. Victorian farmhouse offering warm welcome. Four miles from Gainsborough. Convenient for Lincoln, Hemswell Antique Centre and Wolds. Double room has private bathroom.

**open** All year except Christmas and New Year
**bedrooms** 1 double, 1 twin
**bathrooms** 1 private
**payment** Cash/cheques

Room 📺 🖐  General P ⊬ 🏠 ✿  Leisure ✈

## enjoyEngland.com

Big city buzz or peaceful panoramas? Take a fresh look at England and you may be surprised at what's right on your doorstep. Explore the diversity online at enjoyengland.com

## KING'S CLIFFE, Northamptonshire Map ref 3A1

**★★★★**
BED & BREAKFAST

B&B per room per night
s £35.00–£40.00
d £50.00–£60.00

# 19 West Street

King's Cliffe, Peterborough PE8 6XB  t (01780) 470365  f (01780) 470623  e kjhl_dixon@hotmail.com
w kingjohnhuntinglodge.co.uk

**open** All year
**bedrooms** 1 double, 1 twin, 1 single
**bathrooms** 3 private
**payment** Cash/cheques

Grade II Listed, 500-year-old stone house, beautiful walled garden, reputedly one of King John's hunting lodges. Situated in centre of unspoilt stone village near Stamford. Rooms have private bathroom and colour TV. Central location for many stately homes and a number of other attractions. Secure parking.

⊕ A1 at Wansford, take A47 Leicester road, shortly turn left signposted King's Cliffe, 500yds turn right, 4 miles to village. Opposite church, turn right.

Room 📞 📺 👪 🔌    General ⚡ ✕ ❖

## KNIPTON, Leicestershire Map ref 4C2

**★★★★**
RESTAURANT WITH ROOMS

B&B per room per night
s £60.00–£70.00
d £90.00–£130.00
Evening meal per person
£35.00–£45.00

# Manners Arms

Croxton Road, Knipton, Grantham NG32 1RH  t (01476) 879222  f (01476) 879228
e info@mannersarms.com  w mannersarms.com

Nestled in the charming village of Knipton, close to Belvoir Castle, this delightful country inn has ten bedrooms, a bar and restaurant, serving fresh, local seasonal food seven days a week.

**open** All year
**bedrooms** 6 double, 2 twin, 2 single
**bathrooms** All en suite
**payment** Credit/debit cards, cash/cheques

Room 📞 📺 👪 🔌   General 🛏 🏛 🏃 P ⚡ 🍷 ✕ 🏨 🏵 ❖ 🐂   Leisure ∪ ♪

## LAXTON, Nottinghamshire Map ref 4C2

INN

B&B per room per night
s Min £38.00
d Min £60.00
Evening meal per person
£7.25–£13.50

# Dovecote Inn

Moorhouse Road, Laxton, Newark NG22 0NU  t (01777) 871586  e lisashepardo@yahoo.com

Situated in a farming village. The rooms, which are set in farm buildings adjacent to the inn, are tastefully decorated in soft colours with exposed wooden floors and original beams.

**open** All year
**bedrooms** 2 double/twin
**bathrooms** All en suite
**payment** Credit/debit cards, cash/cheques

Room 📺 👪 🔌   General 🛏 🏃 P ⚡ 🍷 ✕ 🏨 🏵 ❖ 🐂   Leisure ♣ ⚐ ⛱

## LEICESTER, Leicestershire Map ref 4C3

**★★★**
GUEST HOUSE

B&B per room per night
s £33.00–£39.00
d £45.00–£52.00

# Abinger Guest House

175 Hinckley Road, Leicester LE3 0TF  t (0116) 255 4674  f (0116) 271 9833
e abinger@btinternet.com  w leicesterguest.co.uk

Extensively modernised guesthouse situated 0.8 miles from Leicester city centre. Friendly staff, great breakfasts and extremely comfortable beds. Freeview TV in every room, and free Wi-Fi Internet throughout.

**open** All year except Christmas and New Year
**bedrooms** 2 double, 3 twin, 1 single, 2 family
**payment** Credit/debit cards, cash/cheques, euros

Room 🛁 📺 👪 🔌   General 🛏 P ⚡ 🏨 ⛖ ❖

**CYCLISTS WELCOME**

## A holiday on two wheels

For a fabulous freewheeling break, seek out accommodation participating in our Cyclists Welcome scheme. Look out for the symbol and plan your route online at nationalcyclenetwork.org.

## LEICESTER, Leicestershire Map ref 4C3

### Wondai B&B

★★★
**BED & BREAKFAST**

B&B per room per night
s £35.00
d £50.00

47-49 Main Street, Newtown Linford, Leicester LE6 0AE  t (01530) 242728

Our bed and breakfast is located in the village just a short walk from Bradgate Park which was home to Lady Jane Grey, Queen of England for nine days in 1553.

**open** All year except Christmas
**bedrooms** 1 twin, 1 family
**bathrooms** All en suite
**payment** Cash/cheques

Room 👗   General 🛏 🍳 🕹 P ⚹ 🎰 🐕 📺   Leisure ▶ 🏊

## LINCOLN, Lincolnshire Map ref 4C2

### Damon's Motel

★★★★
**GUEST ACCOMMODATION**

B&B per room per night
s £64.00
d £69.00

997 Doddington Road, Lincoln LN6 3SE  t (01522) 887733  f (01522) 887734

Four miles from the historic city of Lincoln, a superior-grade motel. Relax in our indoor pool, gym and solarium or dine in the adjacent, world-famous Damon's Restaurant.

**open** All year except Christmas
**bedrooms** 27 double, 20 single
**bathrooms** All en suite
**payment** Credit/debit cards, cash/cheques

Room 👗 📞 📺 👗 🍷   General 🛏 🍳 P ⚹ X 🎰 🔊   Leisure 🏊

## LINCOLN, Lincolnshire Map ref 4C2

### Duke William House

★★★
**INN**

B&B per room per night
s £65.00–£80.00
d £75.00–£105.00
Evening meal per person
Min £15.00

44 Bailgate, Lincoln LN1 3AP  t (01522) 533351  f (01522) 531169  e enquiries@dukewilliam.com
w dukewilliam.com

**open** All year
**bedrooms** 6 double, 1 twin, 1 single, 3 family
**bathrooms** 11 en suite, 1 private
**payment** Credit/debit cards, cash/cheques

First registered as an inn in 1791, this establishment combines modern facilities with an old-world atmosphere. Near to historic Newport Arch, Lincoln Cathedral and Lincoln Castle. Boasting 12 newly refurbished en suite bedrooms.

⊕ *Once in Lincoln, follow the signs for Historic Lincoln. Duke William Hotel is the first public house on the right as you enter the Bailgate.*

Room 📺 👗 🍷   General 🛏 🍳 🕹 P 🍷 X 🎰 🔊 ❊ 🐕

## LINCOLN, Lincolnshire Map ref 4C2

### The Old Bakery Restaurant with Rooms

★★★★
**RESTAURANT WITH ROOMS**
**SILVER AWARD**

B&B per room per night
s £40.00–£50.00
d £50.00–£63.00
Evening meal per person
£25.00–£30.00

26/28 Burton Road, Lincoln LN1 3LB  t (01522) 576057  e enquiries@theold-bakery.co.uk
w theold-bakery.co.uk

**open** All year
**bedrooms** 2 double, 1 twin, 1 family
**bathrooms** 2 en suite, 2 private
**payment** Credit/debit cards, cash/cheques

Converted Victorian bakery full of rustic charm, minutes from Lincoln Cathedral and castle. Secluded, walled garden, international restaurant serving full a la carte evening, lunchtime meals and Sunday lunches. All rooms have colour TV with Freeview, central heating and either en suite or private bathrooms. Strictly non-smoking throughout.

⊕ *From A46 enter Lincoln on A15, follow brown tourist signs for Lawns Visitor Centre and the Museum of Lincolnshire Life. The Old Bakery is halfway between the two.*

Room 📺 👗 🍷   General 🛏 ⚹ 🍷 X 🎰 🔊 🔊 ❊   Leisure 🏊

**LINCOLN,** Lincolnshire Map ref 4C2

★★★★
**GUEST ACCOMMODATION**

B&B per room per night
s  Max £40.00
d  Max £55.00

# The Old Vicarage

East Street, Nettleham, Lincoln LN2 2SL  t (01522) 750819  f (01522) 750819  e susan@oldvic.net
w oldvic.net

**open** All year
**bedrooms** 1 double, 1 twin
**bathrooms** 1 en suite, 1 private
**payment** Credit/debit cards, cash/cheques

Welcome to our listed Georgian farmhouse near the centre of an attractive village with traditional village green and beck. A warm welcome, tastefully furnished rooms and excellent location make us an ideal base when visiting historic Lincoln and surrounding counties.

⊕ *Follow A46 from Lincoln towards Grimsby, take 2nd right turn to Nettleham, entrance is on the right-hand side.*

Room TV ♨ ☜   General ☜15 P ⅍ ⅀   Leisure 🏊

**LINCOLN,** Lincolnshire Map ref 4C2

★★★★
**BED & BREAKFAST**

B&B per room per night
s  £30.00
d  £50.00
Evening meal per person
Min £10.00

# Welbeck Cottage B&B

19 Meadow Lane, South Hykeham, Lincoln LN6 9PF  t (01522) 692669  e maggied@hotmail.co.uk

**open** All year except Christmas and New Year
**bedrooms** 2 double, 1 twin
**bathrooms** All en suite
**payment** Cash/cheques

A friendly welcome to our home, set in a quiet, village location on the outskirts of the city of Lincoln. Use as a base to explore many local attractions. Close to Whisby Nature Park and Doddington Hall. Only a short drive to Lincoln's beautiful and historic cathedral area and shopping centre.

⊕ *Map and directions supplied on request.*

Room TV ♨ ☜   General ☜ ▥ ☗ P ⅍ ✕ ▦ ⋒ ✿ ♞   Leisure ⌿ ► 🏊

**LITTLE BYTHAM,** Lincolnshire Map ref 3A1

★★★★
**INN**

B&B per room per night
s  £45.00
d  £55.00–£65.00
Evening meal per person
£4.95–£8.95

# The Willoughby Arms

Station Road, Grantham NG33 4RA  t (01780) 410276  w willoughbyarms.co.uk

Set in beautiful countryside north of Stamford – easy access from A1. A traditional country free house with micro-brewery, open fire and large garden, serving real ales and superb bar meals.

**open** All year
**bedrooms** 1 double, 1 single, 1 family
**bathrooms** 2 en suite, 1 private
**payment** Credit/debit cards, cash/cheques

Room TV ♨   General ☜ ☗ P ♟ ▦ ⅀ ✿   Leisure ⌿ ► ♣

# Accessible needs?

If you have special hearing, visual or mobility needs, there's an index of National Accessible Scheme participants featured in this guide. For more accessible accommodation buy a copy of  Easy Access Britain available online at visitbritaindirect.com.

## LOUGHBOROUGH, Leicestershire Map ref 4C3

★★★
**GUEST HOUSE**

B&B per room per night
s £30.00–£60.00
d £55.00–£80.00
Evening meal per person
£6.50–£16.50

# Forest Rise Hotel

55-57 Forest Road, Loughborough LE11 3NW  t (01509) 215928  f (01509) 210506

**open** All year except Christmas and New Year
**bedrooms** 11 double, 1 twin, 8 single, 3 family
**bathrooms** 11 en suite, 8 private
**payment** Credit/debit cards, cash/cheques

Family-run establishment, friendly, personal service, excellent standards throughout. Short walking distance to the town centre, university. Easy access to M1, M42, airport, Donington Park, Prestwold and Beaumanour Halls. Ample, secure car parking, bar, a la carte menu and night porter. En suite bedrooms including executive, bridal, family and four-poster rooms.

⊕ *M1 jct 23, 1st roundabout straight over, 2nd roundabout right, next roundabout left. Short stretch of dual carriageway. Hotel just after this on left-hand side.*

♥ *Stay 7 consecutive nights and you only pay for 6 nights (not including weekend prices).*

Room 🛁 🖨 📞 📺 👇 🧺   General 👜 🛏 🚿 P 🍽 ✕ 🧺 🎿 ❋ 🐾   Leisure ∪ ♣ ► 🚲

## LOUGHBOROUGH, Leicestershire Map ref 4C3

★★★
**GUEST HOUSE**

B&B per room per night
s £30.00–£45.00
d £48.00–£55.00
Evening meal per person
£7.00–£11.50

# Highbury Guest House

146 Leicester Road, Loughborough LE11 2AQ  t (01509) 230545  f (01509) 233086
**e** cosmo@thehighburyguesthouse.co.uk  **w** thehighburyguesthouse.co.uk

Well-run family guesthouse surrounded by well-kept gardens. Conservatory/dining room, car park for off-road parking.

**open** All year except Christmas and New Year
**bedrooms** 4 double, 3 twin, 3 single, 6 family
**bathrooms** 14 en suite
**payment** Credit/debit cards, cash/cheques

Room 🛁 🖨 📺 👇   General 👜 🛏 🚿 P 🍽 🍽 ✕ 🧺 🎿 🔊 ❋ 🐾

## LOUTH, Lincolnshire Map ref 4D2

★★★★
**BED & BREAKFAST**

B&B per room per night
s £30.00
d £45.00

# The Old Rectory

Muckton LN11 8NU  t (01507) 480608  f (01507) 480608  e francis.warr@ntlworld.com
**w** louth-bedandbreakfast.co.uk

Very comfortable bed and breakfast accommodation offering peace and quiet in a very beautiful area of Lincolnshire. Large sitting room with TV and log fire in winter for the use of our guests.

**open** All year
**bedrooms** 2 double, 1 twin
**bathrooms** 2 en suite, 1 private
**payment** Cash/cheques

Room 👇 🧺   General P 🎿 ❋   Leisure ♣ ► 🏛

# Don't forget www.

Web addresses throughout this guide are shown without the prefix www. Please include www. in the address line of your browser.
If a web address does not follow this style it is shown in full.

**LUTTERWORTH,** Leicestershire Map ref 4C3

★★★★
GUEST ACCOMMODATION

B&B per room per night
s  £43.00–£54.00
d  £54.00–£67.00
Evening meal per person
£9.50–£15.00

# Ashlawn Country Guest House

Ashlawn House, Church Lane, Dunton Bassett, Lutterworth LE17 5JZ  t (01455) 208277
e kate@ashlawnhouse.com  w ashlawnhouse.com

**open** All year
**bedrooms** 1 double, 1 twin, 1 family
**bathrooms** 1 en suite, 1 private
**payment** Cash/cheques

Ashlawn House is set in beautiful surroundings with country views from all our bedrooms. A warm, friendly atmosphere awaits you, making your stay with us enjoyable and relaxing. For the more energetic, there are lovely country walks and a leisure centre. Foxton Locks and various activities including shooting and golf nearby.

⊕ *From M1 jct 20 take Lutterworth signs at roundabout. Through Lutterworth on the A426 towards Leicester approx 2.5 miles. First left after Dunton Bassett sign.*

Room 📺 ♿ ♘  General 🏵 P ⅍ ✕ 🍳 🏛 ▣ ✿  Leisure ✦ 🏠

**MARKET HARBOROUGH,** Leicestershire Map ref 4C3

★★★★
BED & BREAKFAST

B&B per room per night
s  £35.00–£38.00
d  Min £54.00

# Hunters Lodge

By Foxton Locks, Gumley, Market Harborough LE16 7RT  t (0116) 279 3744  f (0116) 279 3855
e info@hunterslodgefoxton.co.uk  w hunterslodgefoxton.co.uk

Attractive bungalow set in open countryside a short walk from Foxton Locks, convenient for many local attractions. Comfortable, en suite rooms, separate dining/sitting room and patio.

**open** All year
**bedrooms** 1 twin, 1 family
**bathrooms** All en suite
**payment** Credit/debit cards, cash/cheques, euros

Room ♿ 📺 ♿ ♘  General 🏵 P ⅍ 🏛 ✿ 🐾  Leisure 🏠

**MATLOCK,** Derbyshire Map ref 4B2

★★★★
GUEST ACCOMMODATION

B&B per room per night
d  £65.00–£85.00

# Yew Tree Cottage

The Knoll, Tansley, Matlock DE4 5FP  t (01629) 583862  e enquiries@yewtreecottagebb.co.uk
w yewtreecottagebb.co.uk

18thC cottage property in secluded grounds offering high class bed and breakfast. Award-winning breakfasts. All produce locally sourced, home-made or home-grown when season permits.

**open** All year
**bedrooms** 2 double, 1 suite
**bathrooms** All en suite
**payment** Cash/cheques

Room 📺 ♿ ♘  General 12 P ⅍ 🍳 🏛 ⑀ ▣ ✿  Leisure ► 🚲 🏠

**MATLOCK BATH,** Derbyshire Map ref 4B2

★★★
GUEST ACCOMMODATION

B&B per room per night
s  £35.00–£40.00
d  £60.00–£65.00

# Ashdale Guest House

92 North Parade, Matlock Bath, Matlock DE4 3NS  t (01629) 57826
e ashdale@matlockbath.fsnet.co.uk  w ashdaleguesthouse.co.uk

A Grade II Listed Victorian villa situated in the centre of Matlock Bath. Large, comfortable rooms, level walking to restaurants, pubs, museums and station. Home-made bread and marmalade.

**open** All year
**bedrooms** 1 double, 1 twin, 2 family
**bathrooms** All en suite
**payment** Credit/debit cards, cash/cheques, euros

Room ♿ 📺 ♿  General 🏵 🏛 ≛ P ⅍ 🍳 ✿ 🐾  Leisure ✦ 🚲

## What's in a quality rating?
Information about ratings can be found at the back of this guide.

## MEDBOURNE, Leicestershire Map ref 4C3

★★★★
**BED & BREAKFAST**
**SILVER AWARD**

B&B per room per night
**s** Min £30.00
**d** Min £50.00

# Homestead House

5 Ashley Road, Medbourne, Market Harborough LE16 8DL **t** (01858) 565724 **f** (01858) 565324
**e** june@homesteadhouse.co.uk **w** homesteadhouse.co.uk

**open** All year
**bedrooms** 1 double, 2 twin
**bathrooms** All en suite
**payment** Credit/debit cards, cash/cheques

In an elevated position overlooking the Welland Valley on the outskirts of Medbourne, a picturesque village dating back to Roman times. Surrounded by open countryside and within easy reach of many places of interest. Tastefully decorated bedrooms with rural views. A warm welcome awaits you.

⊕ *On B664 between Market Harborough and Uppingham.*

Room 📞 📺 ♿ 🏳  General 🛏 P 🏠  Leisure ✈ 🏡

## MONYASH, Derbyshire Map ref 4B2

★★★
**FARMHOUSE**

B&B per room per night
**s** £40.00–£45.00
**d** £60.00–£70.00
Evening meal per person
£10.00–£20.00

# Arbor Low B&B

Arbor Low, Upper Oldhams Farm, Bakewell DE45 1JS **t** (01629) 636337 **e** nicola@arborlow.co.uk
**w** arborlow.co.uk

Absolutely stunning views from the farmhouse adjacent to Arbor Low Stone Circle. Your own lounge any time of day with log fires, books, games. Cycling, riding and walking on the doorstep.

**open** All year
**bedrooms** 1 double, 1 twin
**bathrooms** 1 en suite, 1 private
**payment** Cash/cheques

Room ♿ 🏳  General 🛏 🏬 ♿ P ⚡ ✕ 🍴 🏠 📷 ✿  Leisure ∪ 🚴 🏡

## MUMBY, Lincolnshire Map ref 4D2

★★★
**GUEST ACCOMMODATION**

B&B per room per night
**s** £25.00–£30.00
**d** £50.00–£70.00
Evening meal per person
£5.00–£15.00

# Brambles

Occupation Lane, Alford LN13 9JU **t** (01507) 490174 **e** suescrimshaw@btinternet.com

Newly built rural bungalow, quiet scenic setting, close to the costal resorts. Two en suite double rooms for bed and breakfast.

**open** All year
**bedrooms** 1 double, 1 family
**bathrooms** All en suite
**payment** Cash/cheques

Room 🏬 📺 ♿ 🏳  General 🏬 ♿ P ✕ 🍴 🏠 📷 ✿ 🐾  Leisure ● ∪ ⚓ 🏡

## NORTH KILWORTH, Leicestershire Map ref 4C3

★★★★
**BED & BREAKFAST**
**SILVER AWARD**

B&B per room per night
**s** £35.00–£50.00
**d** £60.00

# The Old Rectory

Church Street, Lutterworth LE17 6EZ **t** (01858) 881130 **f** (01858) 880069
**e** info@oldrectorybandb.co.uk **w** oldrectorybandb.co.uk

Attractive and peaceful village location convenient for M6, M1, A14. Luxury en suite rooms with independent access. Free off-road parking and residents' garden. Kitchenette with microwave and refrigerator.

**open** All year except Christmas and New Year
**bedrooms** 2 double
**bathrooms** All en suite
**payment** Cash/cheques, euros

Room 📺 ♿ 🏳  General 🛏 🏬 P ✿  Leisure ✈ 🏴

## Take a break

Look out for special promotions and themed breaks. This could be your chance to indulge an interest, find a new one, or just relax and enjoy exceptional value. Offers (highlighted in colour) are subject to availability.

## NORTHAMPTON, Northamptonshire Map ref 2C1

★★
**GUEST HOUSE**

B&B per room per night
s £35.00–£47.00
d £49.00–£64.00

### The Aarandale Regent

6-8 Royal Terrace, Barrack Road (A508), Northampton NN1 3RF  **t** (01604) 631096  **f** (01604) 621035
**e** info@aarandale.co.uk  **w** aarandale.co.uk

Small and cosy, family-run hotel/guesthouse within easy walking distance of town centre, bus and train stations.

**open** All year except Christmas
**bedrooms** 4 double, 4 twin, 2 single, 2 family
**bathrooms** 6 en suite
**payment** Credit/debit cards, cash/cheques

Room 📺 ✿  General ⟲ ⚡ ♦ ✕ ▦ ♨ ★  Leisure ♠ ↑

## NORTHAMPTON, Northamptonshire Map ref 2C1

★★★★
**BED & BREAKFAST**

B&B per room per night
s £55.00–£65.00
d £65.00–£80.00

### Lake House Bed and Breakfast

Brixworth Hall Park, Brixworth, Northampton NN6 9DE  **t** (01604) 880280
**e** rosemarytuckley@talktalk.net  **w** brixworthlakehouse.com

**open** All year except Christmas and New Year
**bedrooms** 1 double, 1 family
**bathrooms** All en suite
**payment** Cash/cheques, euros

A deluxe 18thC converted coach house and stables set in 4.5 acres of tranquil gardens and koi lake. The bedrooms, having lake view, are beautifully appointed and are supplied with large fluffy towels and dressing gowns. Breakfast served in grand dining room or conservatory. We use locally grown products where possible.

⊕ A508 (jct 2 off A14) opposite Coach and Horses public house onto private road. 7th property on left.

♥ Grand Prix Silverstone – Jul 3-night special weekend B&B. Champagne, transport to circuit and return. POA. Advance booking essential.

Room 📺 ✿ ♖  General ⟲ ▦ ♣ P ♦ ♨ ⟲ ✿ ★  Leisure ∪ ✦ ⚲ ⌂

## NORTHAMPTON, Northamptonshire Map ref 2C1

★★★★
**GUEST ACCOMMODATION**

B&B per room per night
s Min £34.00
d Min £62.50
Evening meal per person
Min £12.50

### The Poplars

Cross Street, Moulton NN3 7RZ  **t** (01604) 643983  **f** (01604) 790233  **e** info@thepoplarshotel.com
**w** thepoplarshotel.com

**open** All year except Christmas and New Year
**bedrooms** 6 double, 1 twin, 6 single, 4 family
**bathrooms** 13 en suite
**payment** Credit/debit cards, cash/cheques

A small, comfortable, family-run country hotel of character, situated in picturesque village of Moulton. Perfect location for visiting family, friends and local attractions. Special weekend rates. Quality food provided, sourced locally whenever possible.

Room ♨ 📺 ✿ ♖  General ⟲ ▦ ♣ P ♦ ♥ ✕ ▦ ♨ ⟲ ✿ ★  Leisure ∪ ✦ ↑ ⚲ ⌂

## To your credit

If you book by phone you may be asked for your credit card number. If so, it is advisable to check the proprietor's policy in case you have to cancel your reservation at a later date.

**NORTON DISNEY,** Lincolnshire Map ref 4C2

★★★★
FARMHOUSE

B&B per room per night
s £51.00
d £82.00
Evening meal per person
£15.50–£25.00

## Brills Farm

Brills Hill, Norton Disney, Lincoln LN6 9JN **t** (01636) 892311
**e** admin@brillsfarm-bedandbreakfast.co.uk **w** brillsfarm-bedandbreakfast.co.uk

**open** All year except Christmas and New Year
**bedrooms** 2 double, 1 twin/double
**bathrooms** All en suite
**payment** Credit/debit cards, cash/cheques

This beautifully renovated 1720 Georgian farmhouse with fabulous views, provides warm hospitality, luxurious bedrooms, open fireplaces and a lovely drawing room for relaxation. Dine under the crystal chandelier or in the gardens under the stars. Gourmet breakfasts use home-grown and home-made produce. Ideally located for Newark and Swinderby antiques fairs.

⊕ *From A1/A46/A17 junction, take A46 towards Lincoln. Take exit signed Brough, Stapleford and Norton Disney. Right at T-junction. Follow approx 0.75 miles. 1st left, 1 mile, wide gravel entrance on right.*

❤ *15% discount for stays of 3 nights or more between 1 Nov and 28 Feb, excl Christmas and New Year.*

Room General 12 P Leisure

**NOTTINGHAM,** Nottinghamshire Map ref 4C2

★★★★
BED & BREAKFAST

B&B per room per night
s £45.00–£55.00
d £55.00–£70.00

## Orchard Cottage

Moor Cottages, Nottingham Road, Trowell Moor, Nottingham NG9 3PQ **t** (0115) 928 0933
**f** (0115) 928 0933 **e** orchardcottage.bandb@virgin.net **w** orchardcottages.com

**open** All year
**bedrooms** 2 double, 1 twin
**bathrooms** All en suite
**payment** Credit/debit cards, cash/cheques

Pat and Martin Woodland extend a warm welcome to visitors to Orchard Cottage. The cottage is a totally refurbished wing of a workhouse built in 1817 and is situated in a tranquil greenbelt location, surrounded by open farmland. Free private parking for six vehicles is provided on-site.

Room General P Leisure

**OAKHAM,** Rutland Map ref 4C3

★★★★
BED & BREAKFAST

B&B per room per night
s £45.00–£55.00
d £75.00–£85.00

## 17 Northgate

Oakham LE15 6QR **t** (01572) 759271 **f** (01572) 759271 **e** dane@danegould.wanadoo.co.uk
**w** 17northgate.co.uk

**open** All year except Christmas and New Year
**bedrooms** 1 twin, 1 single
**bathrooms** All en suite
**payment** Credit/debit cards, cash/cheques, euros

A recently renovated, 300-year-old thatched farmhouse in the centre of Oakham close to Rutland Water, the church, railway station and the excellent pubs and restaurants. The two en suite rooms are newly built, with their own patios and private entrance from the drive, where off-road parking is available.

⊕ *Northgate is in the centre of Oakham, off Church Street and opposite the church. Number 17 is 250m along on right, away from church.*

❤ *Discounts are available for stays of 3 or more nights.*

Room General P Leisure

## PEAK DISTRICT

See under Ashbourne, Bakewell, Buxton, Castleton, Chapel-En-le-Frith, Cressbrook, Hope, Monyash, Youlgreave

## RUSKINGTON, Lincolnshire Map ref 3A1

★★★

**FARMHOUSE**

B&B per room per night
s  Min £25.00
d  Min £50.00

### Sunnyside Farm

Leasingham Lane, Ruskington, Sleaford NG34 9AH  t (01526) 833010
e sunnyside_farm@btinternet.com  w sunnysidefarm.co.uk

A family-run farmhouse with en suite guest bedrooms. Warm, friendly welcome. Local golf courses. Coast 40 miles. Boston, Grantham, Lincoln, Newark all within easy reach.

**open** All year
**bedrooms** 1 double, 1 twin
**bathrooms** All en suite
**payment** Cash/cheques

Room 📺 ♿ 🕮   General 🛏 🍴 ♿ P ⭐ ⚬ 🐾   Leisure ∪ ♪ ▶ 🏖

## RUTLAND WATER

See under Empingham, Oakham

## SHERWOOD FOREST

See under Laxton

## SKEGNESS, Lincolnshire Map ref 4D2

★★★

**GUEST ACCOMMODATION**

B&B per room per night
s  £35.00–£42.00
d  £60.00–£82.00
Evening meal per person
£12.00–£19.00

### Chatsworth

16 North Parade, Skegness PE25 2UB  t (01754) 764177  f (01754) 761173
e info@chatsworthskegness.co.uk  w chatsworthskegness.co.uk

The Chatsworth is centrally situated on the main Skegness seafront and is just a short walk to most of the attractions. Delicious home-made food, friendly staff, comfortable beds and an outstanding position on the seafront.

**open** All year
**bedrooms** 14 double, 15 twin, 10 single, 1 family
**bathrooms** All en suite
**payment** Credit/debit cards, cash/cheques, euros

Room 📺 ♿   General 🛏 🍴 ♿ P ⭐ ✕ 🍴 🏠 ⚬   Leisure ▶ 🏖

## SKEGNESS, Lincolnshire Map ref 4D2

★★★

**GUEST ACCOMMODATION**

B&B per room per night
s  £32.50–£42.00
d  £65.00–£84.00
Evening meal per person
£11.00–£11.50

### Grosvenor House Hotel

North Parade, Skegness PE25 2TE  t (01754) 763376  f (01754) 764650

A family hotel, well renowned for its friendly atmosphere and service. Situated midway along seafront, near all foreshore attractions, Embassy Centre and bowling greens.

**bedrooms** 10 double, 2 twin, 9 single, 11 family
**bathrooms** All en suite
**payment** Credit/debit cards, cash/cheques

Room 📺 ♿   General 🛏 🍴 ♿ ⭐ ✕ 🍴 🏠 ⚬

## SKEGNESS, Lincolnshire Map ref 4D2

★★★

**GUEST ACCOMMODATION**

B&B per room per night
d  £42.00–£52.00
Evening meal per person
£8.50–£10.50

### Roosevelt Lodge

59 Drummond Road, Skegness PE25 3EQ  t (01754) 766548  e skegnessinfo@e-lindsey.gov.uk

A warm and friendly welcome awaits you at Roosevelt Lodge, a popular family-run hotel, which offers an excellent menu and comfortable accommodation. Situated near the seafront, town centre, bowling green, theatre and all other amenities.

**open** All year
**bedrooms** 3 double, 2 twin, 1 family
**bathrooms** 5 en suite, 1 private
**payment** Credit/debit cards, cash/cheques

Room 🛏 📺 ♿ 🕮   General 🛏 🍴 ♿ P ✕ 🍴 🏠   Leisure ▶ 🏖

🟦 WALKERS 🟦
WELCOME   WELCOME
🟦 WALKERS 🟦

## Best foot forward

Walkers feel at home in accommodation participating in our Walkers Welcome scheme. Look out for the symbol. Consider walking all or part of a long-distance route – go online at nationaltrail.co.uk.

## SKEGNESS, Lincolnshire Map ref 4D2

★★★
**GUEST HOUSE**

B&B per room per night
s £18.00–£30.00
d £36.00–£60.00
Evening meal per person
£12.00

### The Tudor Lodge Guest House

61-63 Drummond Road, Skegness PE25 3EQ  t (01754) 766487  e info@thetudorlodge.co.uk
w thetudorlodge.co.uk

A delightful guesthouse. All rooms en suite, licensed bar, colour TV, tea-/coffee-making facilities. Free parking, close to all amenities, ground-floor rooms available. Open fire in winter months.

**open** All year
**bedrooms** 3 double, 1 twin, 2 family
**bathrooms** All en suite
**payment** Credit/debit cards, cash/cheques

Room 🛏 TV 🕸  General 🪑 P ⚡ ⅋ ✗ 🍽 🎯 ✿

## SOUTH COCKERINGTON, Lincolnshire Map ref 4D2

★★★★
**BED & BREAKFAST**

B&B per room per night
s £35.00–£40.00
d £50.00–£60.00

### West View Bed & Breakfast

South View Lane, South Cockerington, Louth LN11 7ED  t (01507) 327209 & 07855 291185
e enquiries@west-view.co.uk  w west-view.co.uk

Single-storey barn conversion with old-world charm. All bedrooms en suite. beamed ceilings, disabled facilities, newly painted and furnished, broadband Internet access.

**open** All year except Christmas
**bedrooms** 2 double, 1 twin
**bathrooms** All en suite
**payment** Cash/cheques

Room 🛏 TV 🕸 🍴  General P ⚡ 🎯 📶 ✿  Leisure ∪ ♪ 🏊

## STAMFORD, Lincolnshire Map ref 3A1

★★
**GUEST HOUSE**

B&B per room per night
s £27.50–£60.00
d £45.00–£65.00

### Dolphin Guesthouse

12 East Street, Stamford PE9 1QD  t (01780) 757515  e mikdolphin@mikdolphin.demon.co.uk

En suite, hotel-style accommodation. Off-road secure car parking and only 100yds from the town centre.

**open** All year except Christmas and New Year
**bedrooms** 4 double, 3 twin, 1 family
**bathrooms** 6 en suite
**payment** Credit/debit cards, cash/cheques

Room 🛏 TV 🕸 🍴  General 🛋 P 🎯 ✿  Leisure 🏊

## STAMFORD, Lincolnshire Map ref 3A1

★★★★
**BED & BREAKFAST**
**SILVER AWARD**

B&B per room per night
s £45.00–£70.00
d £70.00–£90.00

### Park Farm

Careby, Stamford PE9 4EA  t (01780) 410515  e enquiries@parkfarmcareby.co.uk
w parkfarmcareby.co.uk

**open** All year
**bedrooms** 1 double, 1 twin
**bathrooms** 1 en suite, 1 private
**payment** Cash/cheques

Nestling on the hillside overlooking the peaceful hamlet of Careby, just ten minutes from the centre of Stamford, Park Farm offers spacious bed and breakfast accommodation in a welcoming country home, and home-cooked breakfasts from a varied menu.

♥ *Take advantage of our 10% discount for 3-night midweek breaks.*

Room 🛏 TV 🕸 🍴  General P ⚡ 🍽 📶 ✿  Leisure ♪ 🚲 🏊

## Using map references

The map references refer to the colour maps at the front of this guide. The first figure is the map number, the letter and figure that follow indicate the grid reference on the map.

**STAMFORD,** Lincolnshire Map ref 3A1

★★★★★
**GUEST ACCOMMODATION**
**GOLD AWARD**

## Rock Lodge

Empingham Road, Stamford PE9 2RH **t** (01780) 481758 **f** (01780) 481757
**e** rocklodge@innpro.co.uk **w** rock-lodge.co.uk

B&B per room per night
**s** £60.00–£70.00
**d** £75.00–£95.00

Philip and Jane Sagar have over 30 years' experience of operating luxury hotels. Individually decorated en suite rooms with fridges. Set in walled garden with off-street parking. Five minutes' walk to town centre.

**open** All year except Christmas and New Year
**bedrooms** 3 double, 1 twin, 1 family, 1 suite
**bathrooms** All en suite
**payment** Credit/debit cards, cash/cheques, euros

Room  General ﹖3 P ﹖ ﹖ ﹖ Leisure ﹖

**STANTON-BY-BRIDGE,** Derbyshire Map ref 4B3

★★★★
**GUEST ACCOMMODATION**
**SILVER AWARD**

## Ivy House Farm

Ingleby Road, Stanton-by-Bridge, Derby DE73 7HT **t** (01332) 863152 **f** (01332) 863152
**e** info@ivy-house-farm.com **w** ivy-house-farm.com

B&B per room per night
**s** Min £32.00
**d** £52.00–£60.00

An 18thC farmhouse with some ground-floor chalet bedrooms. The farmhouse is in a quiet, picturesque village. Two bedrooms in a recently built barn conversion.

**open** All year
**bedrooms** 4 double, 2 twin
**bathrooms** All en suite
**payment** Credit/debit cards, cash/cheques

Room ﹖ ﹖ ﹖ ﹖ General ﹖ ﹖ ﹖ P ﹖ ﹖ ﹖ ﹖ ﹖ Leisure ﹖ ﹖ ﹖

**THORNTON CURTIS,** Lincolnshire Map ref 4C1

★★★★
**INN**

## Thornton Hunt Inn

17 Main Street, Thornton Curtis, Nr Ulceby DN39 6XW **t** (01469) 531252 **f** (01469) 531252
**e** peter@thornton-inn.co.uk **w** thornton-inn.co.uk

B&B per room per night
**s** £39.70–£42.70
**d** £65.45–£75.45
Evening meal per person
£7.39–£14.95

Family-run, Grade II Listed building. Traditional home-made bar meals and desserts available lunch and dinner. Extensive garden with children's fun trail and slide. Convenient for airport, Humber Bridge and M180.

**open** All year except Christmas and New Year
**bedrooms** 5 double, 1 single
**bathrooms** All en suite
**payment** Credit/debit cards, cash/cheques

Room ﹖ ﹖ ﹖ ﹖ General ﹖ ﹖ ﹖ P ﹖ ﹖ X ﹖ Leisure ﹖ ﹖

**TOWCESTER,** Northamptonshire Map ref 2C1

★★★★
**FARMHOUSE**
**SILVER AWARD**

## Slapton Manor Accommodation

Slapton Manor, Slapton NN12 8PF **t** (01327) 860344 **f** (01327) 860758
**e** accommodation@slaptonmanor.co.uk

B&B per room per night
**s** £25.00–£45.00
**d** £45.00–£65.00

En suite rooms within stable/hay loft conversion and self-catering studios adjoining village 12thC manor-house on working farm.

**open** All year
**bedrooms** 1 double, 1 twin, 1 family
**bathrooms** All en suite
**payment** Cash/cheques, euros

Room ﹖ ﹖ ﹖ General ﹖ P ﹖ ﹖ ﹖ Leisure ﹖ ﹖ ﹖

# A breath of fresh air

Love the great outdoors? Britain's Camping, Caravan & Holiday Parks 2008 is packed with information on quality sites in some spectacular locations. You can purchase the guide from good bookshops and online at visitbritaindirect.com.

★★★★★
**GUEST ACCOMMODATION
GOLD AWARD**

B&B per room per night
**s** £45.00–£60.00
**d** £70.00–£90.00
Evening meal per person
£12.00–£18.00

# Spanhoe Lodge

Harringworth Road, Laxton, Corby NN17 3AT **t** (01780) 450328 **f** (01780) 450328
**e** jennie.spanhoe@virgin.net **w** spanhoelodge.co.uk

**open** All year
**bedrooms** 8 double, 4 twin, 2 family
**bathrooms** All en suite
**payment** Credit/debit cards, cash/cheques

A warm, friendly welcome awaits you at this gold-awarded establishment in the heart of Rockingham Forest. Luxuriously appointed, en suite accommodation, wide choice of gourmet breakfasts, fine dining, licensed bar, conferencing. Ideally situated for Stamford, Corby, Uppingham, Oundle, Oakham, Rutland Water and Rockingham Motor Speedway. You will not be disappointed!

⊕ From Stamford or Corby take A43. Turn at signpost marked Laxton and Harringworth. Spanhoe Lodge is situated 0.5 miles past Laxton village on right-hand side.

Room 🛏 🖾 📺 👆 🍵  General 🏕 🏠 🛎 P ♨ ♀ ✕ 🍴 🏛 ▣ ✿ 🐾  Leisure ∪ ♪ 🚲 🏯

★★
**BED & BREAKFAST**

B&B per room per night
**s** Min £25.00
**d** Min £40.00

# Wellbeck Farmhouse B&B

Well, Alford LN13 9LT **t** (01507) 462453 **f** (01507) 462453

**open** All year
**bedrooms** 1 single, 2 family
**bathrooms** 3 private
**payment** Cash/cheques

Traditional farmhouse B&B at the foot of the Lincolnshire Wolds. Near the market town of Alford. Short drive to the coast. Large lock-up shed.

⊕ Directions given at time of booking.

Room 📺 👆 🍵  General 🏕 🏠 🛎 P ♨ 🏛 ✿ 🐾  Leisure ∪ ♪ ▷ 🚲 🏯

★★★
**GUEST HOUSE**

B&B per room per night
**s** £25.00–£29.00
**d** £35.00–£45.00

# Firs Guesthouse

96 Radcliffe Road, West Bridgford, Nottingham NG2 5HH **t** (0115) 981 0199 **f** (01582) 767829
**e** firs.hotel@btinternet.com

High-quality Victorian establishment, well maintained with reasonable rates. Guest lounge with pool table and Sky TV. Close to Trent Bridge, Nottingham Forest FC, watersports and all amenities. Good city accessibility.

**open** All year except Christmas
**bedrooms** 3 twin, 6 family
**bathrooms** 2 en suite
**payment** Credit/debit cards, cash/cheques

Room 🛏 📺 👆 🍵  General 🏕 🛎 P 🍴 🏛  Leisure ♠ ♪

★★★★
**INN**

B&B per room per night
**s** £50.00–£60.00
**d** £60.00–£70.00
Evening meal per person
Min £9.95

# The Snooty White Lion

38 Main Street, Oakham LE15 7ET **t** (01664) 474233 **e** snootywhitelion@btconnect.com
**w** snootyinns.com

Accommodation comprises eight comfortable en suite bedrooms with the added extra of a large garden overlooking a willow-hung brook.

**open** All year
**bedrooms** 7 double, 1 twin
**bathrooms** All en suite
**payment** Credit/debit cards, cash/cheques

Room 📺 👆 🍵  General 🏕 🏠 🛎 P ♀ 🍴 ✿ 🐾  Leisure ∪ ♪ ▷ 🏯

## WOODHALL SPA, Lincolnshire Map ref 4D2

**★ ★ ★ ★**
GUEST ACCOMMODATION

B&B per room per night
s £45.00–£60.00
d £60.00
Evening meal per person
£15.00–£17.50

# Chaplin House

92 High Street, Martin LN4 3QT  **t** (01526) 378795  **f** (01526) 378795  **e** m.lockyer@tiscali.co.uk
**w** chaplin-house.co.uk

**open** All year except Christmas and New Year
**bedrooms** 2 double, 1 twin, 1 family
**bathrooms** All en suite
**payment** Cash/cheques

You'll find a warm, friendly welcome at Chaplin House, in the heart of the Lincolnshire countryside. In our barn conversion, we have three spacious en suite rooms, together with a guests' lounge; there is one guest room in the house. Most of our produce is locally sourced, free-range and organic.

⊕ We are in the village of Martin on B1191 between Metheringham and Woodhall Spa. We are next door to the post office.

♥ Indulge in midweek 3-night break (two people sharing a double/twin room) Mon-Thu for £165 (£15 discount).

Room 🛏 📺 🕭 ᐡ    General 🕭 ▥ 🕯 P ⅍ ᪺ 🎔 ☀    Leisure ✈ ► 🏛

## WOODHALL SPA, Lincolnshire Map ref 4D2

**★ ★ ★**
BED & BREAKFAST

B&B per room per night
s £28.00–£30.00
d £44.00–£46.00

# The Vale

50 Tor-O-Moor Road, Woodhall Spa LN10 6SB  **t** (01526) 353022  **f** (01526) 354949
**e** margot.mills@hotmail.co.uk

Accommodation in an Edwardian house in a unique woodlands village. The house is on three floors and stands in one acre of mature gardens with private lake. Ground-floor room available.

**open** All year
**bedrooms** 1 double, 1 twin, 1 family
**bathrooms** All en suite
**payment** Cash/cheques

Room 🛏 📺 🕭    General 🕭2 ▥ 🕯 P ⅍ ᪺ ☀ 🕇    Leisure ✈ ► 🚲 🏛

## WOODHALL SPA, Lincolnshire Map ref 4D2

**★ ★ ★ ★**
GUEST ACCOMMODATION

B&B per room per night
s £42.00–£50.00
d £65.00–£75.00

# Village Limits Motel

Stixwould Road, Woodhall Spa LN10 6UJ  **t** (01526) 353312  **f** (01526) 352203
**e** info@villagelimits.co.uk  **w** villagelimits.co.uk

**open** All year
**bedrooms** 8 twin
**bathrooms** All en suite
**payment** Credit/debit cards, cash/cheques

Award-winning Tastes of Lincolnshire Best Pub 2006. Village Limits Country Pub and Restaurant has a friendly, relaxing welcome. The comfortable ground-floor bedrooms all have en suite bathrooms, one with full facilities for the disabled. Food daily 1200-1400 and 1900-2100. Closed Sunday evening and Mondays. B&B seven days.

⊕ We are located 0.75 miles from the roundabout in Woodhall Spa on Stixwould Road, 500m past Jubilee Park on the right-hand side.

♥ 10% discount for 4 nights or more.

Room 🛏 📺 🕭    General 🕭 P 🍽 ᪺

## If you have access needs...

Look for the National Accessible Scheme symbols if you have special hearing, visual or mobility needs. An index of accommodation participating in the scheme can be found at the back of this guide.

**YOULGREAVE,** Derbyshire Map ref 4B2

★ ★ ★
**BED & BREAKFAST**

B&B per room per night
s Min £28.00
d £21.00–£32.00

## The Old Bakery

Church Street, Youlgrave, Bakewell DE45 1UR  **t** (01629) 636887
**w** cressbrook.co.uk/youlgve/oldbakery

Our accommodation offers you the choice of either: our first-floor self-contained suite (with fridge and microwave) in a tastefully converted barn; or twin/double-bedded accommodation within the guest wing of the main house.

**open** All year
**bedrooms** 1 double, 2 twin
**bathrooms** 1 en suite
**payment** Cash/cheques

Room ⬦   General ⬦ ⬦ ⬦   Leisure U

# Families Welcome

If you are looking for a great family break in quality-assessed accommodation, look out for the Families Welcome sign.

Participants in this scheme offer additional facilities and services catering for a range of ages and family units.
For families with young children, they'll have facilities such as cots and highchairs, storage for push-chairs and somewhere to heat baby food or milk. Where meals are provided, children's choices will be clearly indicated, with healthy options available. They'll also have information on local walks, attractions, activities or events suitable for children, as well as local child-friendly pubs and restaurants.

Of course, not all accommodation is able to cater for all ages or combinations of family units, so do check when you book.

Wherever you're travelling in England, the Families Welcome scheme will help you find just the right place to stay to ensure everyone has a great time.

# East of England

Bedfordshire, Cambridgeshire, Essex, Hertfordshire, Norfolk, Suffolk

# Simple pleasures in a fascinating setting

There's more to the East of England than the Broads and teeming wildlife; explore this fascinating region and you'll discover fairytale castles, ancient cathedrals and exquisite gardens. (Oh, and dinosaurs and ghosts.)

East of England Tourism
visiteastofengland.com
(01284) 727470

Tring, Hertfordshire

Ely Cathedral, Cambridgeshire    Shuttleworth Collection, Bedfordshire

Southwold, Suffolk

The East of England is crammed full of secrets. Wander around the stupendous Ely Cathedral (star of the movie 'The Golden Age') that towers like a ship over the fens. Take a chariot-ride over to historic Colchester with its chilling links with Boudica. Journey to deepest Bedfordshire and feel like royalty at Wrest Park, a French- inspired Chateau with Versailles-like gardens. Explore the Swiss Garden at Old Warden, a charming Victorian folly garden complete with grotto, Monet bridges and peacocks. And discover the gigantic Dinosaur Adventure Park near Norwich for a monster day of family thrills and fact-finding. Finally, delight the ghostbuster in you and enter Castle Rising Castle, a 12th century Norman hall-keep near King's Lynn where the cries of Queen Isabella can still be heard on dark winter afternoons.

This region holds one of the nation's greatest relics – the astonishing treasure of the mystery Saxon King in his burial ship at Sutton Hoo. If contemporary treasures are more you, check out the landmark Firstsite visual arts centre in the heart of Colchester. And be sure to catch some of the colourful local events such as the World Snail Racing Championship in Congham where 300 snails battle for the silver tankard stuffed with lettuce. Time to up the tempo? Tune-in to the high-octane drag racing at Santa Pod, back a winner at Newmarket Races or head back to the coast for a lively fun-filled day at Great Yarmouth. And for a real echo of the past, gallop over to Royston Cave in Hertfordshire where you can see a bell-shaped chamber containing medieval carvings by the Knights Templar.

Whatever your interest, you'll find something to fascinate you in this unspoilt and very special corner of England.

# Destinations

## Cambridge

The name Cambridge instantly summons breathtaking images – the Backs carpeted with spring flowers, King's College Chapel, punting on the river Cam and, of course, the calm of the historic college buildings. Cambridge still has the atmosphere of a bustling market town, notwithstanding its international reputation. Explore its winding streets and splendid architecture, and choose from a range of attractions, museums, hotels, restaurants and pubs. Situated in the heart of East Anglia but less than an hour from London by high-speed rail link.

## Colchester

If variety's the spice of life, Colchester's the place to savour it! Two thousand years of history and everything you need for a day trip, short break or longer stay. Art lovers will find cutting-edge contemporary galleries and there's a shopper's heaven of little specialist shops and big name stores. The range of cuisine makes Colchester a magnet for food lovers – don't miss the annual Colchester Oyster Feast. Find internationally important treasures located in award-winning museums and view lush landscapes in Victorian Castle Park. At night, discover clubs, theatres, music and open-air vibes.

## Great Yarmouth

One of the UK's most popular seaside resorts, with an enviable mix of sandy beaches, attractions, entertainment, heritage and quality accommodation. And beyond the seaside fun is a charming town that is steeped in history. Visit the medieval town walls, stroll the historic South Quay and discover Nelson's 'other' column. When the sun goes down, Great Yarmouth becomes a wonderland of colour as the illuminations light your way to a night on the town. Full of holiday contrasts, the area also boasts 21 villages set in beautiful coastal and rural settings alongside the famous Norfolk Broads.

| | |
| --- | --- |
| 0 | 50 miles |
| 0 | 75 kms |

National Park & The Broads

Area of Outstanding Natural Beauty

Heritage Coast

National Trails
nationaltrail.co.uk

**3** Sections of the National Cycle Network
nationalcyclenetwork.org.uk

River Cam, Cambridge

The Broads, near Great Yarmouth

Peterborough Cathedral

Colchester Castle Museum

Aldeburgh, near Ipswich

Luton Carnival

Ruins in Norwich Cathedral grounds

## Ipswich

In England's oldest continuously settled Anglo-Saxon town, you'll find numerous architectural gems, including twelve medieval churches. Browse important collections of work by Constable and Gainsborough and enjoy the beautifully landscaped gardens and fine Tudor mansion at Christchurch Park. You'll be able to 'shop 'til you drop' in one of the region's best retail centres, and explore the historic waterfront where the Victorian wet dock is currently undergoing an exciting renaissance. Stay longer, and explore the beautiful, unspoilt Suffolk coastline.

## Luton

Discover a friendly and cosmopolitan town. Luton is surprisingly 'green' with over 7% of its area made up of open space, with more than ten sites of importance for wildlife. Shoppers will be spoilt for choice with over 100 shops in the Arndale Centre and a large, thriving market. You'll find a lively and exciting night scene with bars and nightclubs playing music from the UK dance, house and garage scenes. Visit in the spring and catch Luton International Carnival.

## Norwich

Norwich, county town of Norfolk, is an enchanting cathedral city and a thriving modern metropolis. See some of the finest medieval architecture in Britain in the cathedral and castle, and wander an intricate network of winding streets. The city's newest centrepiece, The Forum, represents contemporary architecture at its best. You'll find excellent shopping as well as a vibrant mix of theatres, cinemas, arts festivals, exhibitions, museums, and a vast array of restaurants.

## Peterborough

With 3,000 years of heritage, Peterborough will exceed your expectations. Its magnificent Norman cathedral sits amid peaceful precincts just a few metres from the city's superb shopping and leisure facilities. You'll find a great range of outdoor activities in picturesque countryside – including 2,000 acres of riverside parkland. And there are plenty of attractions, events and festivals to thrill all ages and interests – just 45 minutes from central London by high-speed rail link.

# Places to visit

### Anglesey Abbey, Gardens and Lode Mill

near Cambridge
(01223) 810080
nationaltrust.org.uk
*Abbey, Jacobean-style house and Fairfax collection*

### Audley End House and Gardens

Saffron Walden, Essex
(01799) 522399
english-heritage.org.uk
*Sumptuous splendour of a grand stately home*

### Banham Zoo
Norfolk
(01953) 887771
banhamzoo.co.uk
*Wildlife spectacular with tigers and leopards*

### Blickling Hall
near Norwich, Norfolk
(01263) 738030
nationaltrust.org.uk
*Jacobean mansion with parkland and orangery*

### Bressingham Steam Experience and Gardens
near Diss, Norfolk
(01379) 686900
bressingham.co.uk
*Fun-packed family day out*

### Colchester Castle
Essex
(01206) 282939
colchestermuseums.org.uk
*Spectacular displays of Colchester's early history*

### Colchester Zoo

Essex
(01206) 331292
colchester-zoo.com
*Over 250 species with superb cat and primate collections*

### Ely Cathedral
Cambridgeshire
(01353) 667735
cathedral.ely.anglican.org
*One of England's finest cathedrals*

### Go Ape!
### High Wire Forest Adventure
Thetford Forest, Suffolk
0870 444 5562
goape.co.uk
*Rope bridges, swings and zip slides*

### Hatfield House
Hertfordshire
(01707) 287010
hatfield-house.co.uk
*Magnificent Jacobean house with exquisite gardens*

### Holkham Hall
near Wells-next-the-Sea, Norfolk
(01328) 710227
holkham.co.uk
*Classic 18th-century Palladian-style mansion*

### Imperial War Museum Duxford
near Cambridge
(01223) 835000
duxford.iwm.org.uk
*The sights, sound and power of aircraft*

### Knebworth House, Gardens and Park
near Stevenage, Hertfordshire
(01438) 812661
knebworthhouse.com
*Re-fashioned Tudor manor house in 250-acre grounds*

### National Stud

Newmarket, Cambridgeshire
(01638) 663464
nationalstud.co.uk
*Conducted tour of thoroughbreds*

### Norfolk Lavender Limited

near King's Lynn
(01485) 570384
norfolk-lavender.co.uk
*Lavender farm and fragrant gardens*

### Norwich Cathedral
Norfolk
(01603) 218300
cathedral.org.uk
*Imposing Norman cathedral with 14th-century roof bosses*

### The Royal Air Force Air Defence Radar Museum

Small Visitor Attraction of the Year – Gold Winner

Norwich, Norfolk
(01692) 631485
radarmuseum.co.uk
*History of radar featuring Cold War Operations Room*

### RSPB Minsmere Nature Reserve
Saxmundham, Suffolk
(01728) 648281
rspb.org.uk
*Bird-watching hides and trails plus year-round events*

### Sandringham House
Norfolk
(01553) 612908
sandringhamestate.co.uk
*The country retreat of HM The Queen*

### Shuttleworth Collection
Biggleswade, Bedfordshire
(01767) 627927
shuttleworth.org
*Unique collection of aircraft – see a Spitfire in flying condition*

## Diary dates 2008

**Somerleyton Hall & Gardens**
near Lowestoft, Suffolk
(01502) 734901
somerleyton.co.uk
*Lavish early Victorian mansion*

**Sutton Hoo Burial Site**
Woodbridge, Suffolk
(01394) 389700
nationaltrust.org.uk
*Burial mounds overlooking River Deben*

**Thursford Collection**
Norfolk
(01328) 878477
thursford.com
*Organ collection with daily show*

**Verulamium Museum**
St Albans, Hertfordshire
(01727) 751810
stalbansmuseums.org.uk
*Re-creation of life in Roman Britain*

**Woburn Abbey**
Bedfordshire
(01525) 290333
woburnabbey.co.uk
*Palladian mansion set in 3,000-acre deer park*

**Woburn Safari Park**
Bedfordshire
(01525) 290407
woburnsafari.co.uk
*30 species of animals just a windscreen's width away*

**ZSL Whipsnade Zoo**
Dunstable, Bedfordshire
(01582) 872171
zsl.org/zsl-whipsnade-zoo
*More than 2,500 animals, many endangered in the wild*

**Whittlesea Straw Bear Festival**
strawbear.org.uk
11 – 13 Jan

**St George's Day Festival**
Wrest Park, Bedfordshire
english-heritage.org.uk
19 – 20 Apr

**Stilton Cheese Rolling Competition**
Main Street, Stilton
stilton.org/about_rolling.html
5 May

**Southend Air Show**
The seafront
southendairshow.com
25 – 26 May

**Luton International Carnival**
Various locations, Luton
luton.gov.uk/carnival
26 May

**Aldeburgh Festival**
Snape, Suffolk
aldeburgh.co.uk
13 – 29 Jun

**Royal Norfolk Show**
Norwich
royalnorfolkshow.co.uk
25 – 26 Jun

**Bedford River Festival**
River Great Ouse
bedford.gov.uk
12 – 13 Jul

**World Snail Racing Championships**
The Cricket Field, Congham
snailracing.net
19 Jul

**Annual British Crabbing Championship**
The seafront, Walberswick
explorewalberswick.co.uk
10 Aug

# Tourist Information Centres

When you arrive at your destination, visit an Official Partner Tourist Information Centre for quality assured help with accommodation and information about local attractions and events, or email your request before you go. To search for attractions and Tourist Information Centres on the move just text INFO to 62233, and a web link will be sent to your mobile phone.

| | | | |
|---|---|---|---|
| **Bishop's Stortford** | The Old Monastery | (01279) 655831 | tic@bishopsstortford.org |
| **Bury St Edmunds** | 6 Angel Hill | (01284) 764667 | tic@stedsbc.gov.uk |
| **Flatford** | Flatford Lane | (01206) 299460 | flatfordvic@babergh.gov.uk |
| **Harwich** | Iconfield Park | (01255) 506139 | harwichtic@btconnect.com |
| **Hunstanton** | The Green | (01485) 532610 | hunstanton.tic@west-norfolk.gov.uk |
| **Ipswich** | St Stephens Lane | (01473) 258070 | tourist@ipswich.gov.uk |
| **King's Lynn** | Purfleet Quay | (01553) 763044 | kings-lynn.tic@west-norfolk.gov.uk |
| **Lavenham*** | Lady Street | (01787) 248207 | lavenhamtic@babergh.gov.uk |
| **Lowestoft** | East Point Pavilion | (01502) 533600 | touristinfo@waveney.gov.uk |
| **Maldon** | Coach Lane | (01621) 856503 | tic@maldon.gov.uk |
| **Saffron Walden** | 1 Market Place | (01799) 510444 | tourism@uttlesford.gov.uk |
| **Southwold** | 69 High Street | (01502) 724729 | southwold.tic@waveney.gov.uk |
| **Stowmarket** | The Museum of East Anglian Life | (01449) 676800 | tic@midsuffolk.gov.uk |
| **Sudbury** | Market Hill | (01787) 881320 | sudburytic@babergh.gov.uk |

* seasonal opening

Knebworth House, Hertfordshire

# Find out more

East of England Tourism has a comprehensive website, updated daily. Log on to visiteastofengland.com

Online brochures and information sheets can be downloaded including Major Events; Lights, Camera, Action! (film and television locations); Stars and Stripes (connections with the USA) and a range of Discovery Tours around the region.

For more information, please call (01284) 727470 or email info@eet.org.uk

# Travel info

**By road:**
The region is easily accessible: from London and the South via the A1(M), M11, M25, A10, M1 and A12; from the North via the A1(M), A17, A15, A5, M1 and A6; from the West via the A14, A47, A421, A428, A418, A41, A422 and A427.

**By rail:**
Regular fast and frequent trains run to all major cities and towns. London stations which serve the region are Liverpool Street, King's Cross, Fenchurch Street, Marylebone, St Pancras and Euston. Bedford, Luton and St Albans are on the Thameslink line which runs to King's Cross and on to London Gatwick Airport. There is also a direct link between London Stansted Airport and Liverpool Street. Through the Channel Tunnel, there are trains direct from Paris and Brussels to Waterloo Station, London. A short journey on the Underground will bring passengers to those stations operating services into the East of England. Further information on rail journeys in the East of England can be obtained on 0845 748 4950.

**By air:**
Fly into London Luton, London Stansted or Norwich International.

Holkham Hall Estate, Norfolk

where to stay in

# East of England

All place names in the blue bands are shown on the maps at the front of this guide.

A complete listing of all Enjoy England assessed accommodation covered by this guide appears at the back.

**Accommodation symbols**
Symbols give useful information about services and facilities. Inside the back-cover flap you can find a key to these symbols. Keep it open for easy reference.

**ALDBOROUGH,** Norfolk Map ref 3B1

★★★★
GUEST HOUSE

B&B per room per night
s £28.00–£30.00
d £55.00–£60.00
Evening meal per person
£10.50–£14.95

## Butterfly Cottage

The Green, Aldborough, Norwich NR11 7AA **t** (01263) 768198 & (01263) 761689 **f** (01263) 768198
**e** butterflycottage@btopenworld.com **w** butterflycottage.com

On the Weavers Way. Comfortable, cottage style, well equipped, friendly atmosphere. Rooms overlook large garden or village green. Each has DVD player, fridge and own entrance. Car parking.

**open** All year
**bedrooms** 1 double, 1 twin, 1 single, 1 family
**bathrooms** 3 en suite, 1 private
**payment** Cash/cheques

Room General P Leisure

**ALDEBURGH,** Suffolk Map ref 3C2

★★★★
GUEST HOUSE

B&B per room per night
s Max £55.00
d Max £70.00

## Toll House

50 Victoria Road, Aldeburgh IP15 5EJ **t** (01728) 453239 **f** (01728) 453239 **e** tollhouse@fsmail.net
**w** tollhouse.travelbugged.com

**open** All year
**bedrooms** 5 double, 2 twin
**bathrooms** All en suite
**payment** Credit/debit cards, cash/cheques, euros

The Toll House is a delightful Victorian guesthouse which offers en suite rooms with TV and tea-/coffee-making facilities. Freshly prepared, full English breakfast using local produce is served daily, with vegetarian/continental option provided. Parking available.

*Follow A1094 from A12 all the way to Aldeburgh. We are to the right on the roundabout as you enter town, directly opposite Railway pub.*

Room General 1 P Leisure

## Place index

If you know where you want to stay, the index at the back of the guide will give you the page number listing accommodation in your chosen town, city or village. Check out the other useful indexes too.

## AYLSHAM, Norfolk Map ref 3B1

★★★★
GUEST ACCOMMODATION

B&B per room per night
s £50.00–£60.00
d £65.00–£85.00
Evening meal per person
£20.00–£25.00

# Old Pump House

Holman Road, Aylsham NR11 6BY  t (01263) 733789  f (01263) 733789
e theoldpumphouse@btconnect.com  w smoothhound.co.uk/hotels/oldpumphouse.html

Creature comforts, home cooking. Rambling 1750s house beside the thatched pump, a minute from church and market place. Non-smoking.

**open** All year except Christmas and New Year
**bedrooms** 1 double, 2 twin, 2 family
**bathrooms** All en suite
**payment** Credit/debit cards, cash/cheques

Room 🖼 📞 📺 ♿ ⌨   General ⛱ 🏛 ♿ ⚡ ✕ 🖥 📷 ⚘ 🐾

## BECCLES, Suffolk Map ref 3C1

★★★★
GUEST ACCOMMODATION

B&B per room per night
s £36.00–£42.00
d £52.00–£54.00

# Catherine House

2 Ringsfield Road, Beccles NR34 9PQ  t (01502) 716428  f (01502) 716428

Family home, tastefully decorated to high standard, in quiet position overlooking Waveney Valley. Five minutes' walk to town centre. Private parking. Good breakfast with local produce.

**open** All year except Christmas
**bedrooms** 2 double, 1 family
**bathrooms** 2 en suite, 1 private
**payment** Cash/cheques

Room 🖼 📺 ♿ ⌨   General ⛱ 🏛 ♿ P 🖥 📷 ⚘

## BECCLES, Suffolk Map ref 3C1

★★★★
GUEST ACCOMMODATION

B&B per room per night
s £40.00–£42.00
d £50.00–£52.00

# Pinetrees

Park Drive, Beccles NR34 7DQ  t (01502) 470796  e info@pinetrees.net  w pinetrees.net

Attractive timber-constructed, contemporary-style, eco-friendly B&B set in 5.5 acres of the peaceful Waveney Valley in Beccles, North Suffolk. Organic food served, plus our free-range hens' eggs.

**open** All year except Christmas
**bedrooms** 3 double
**bathrooms** All en suite
**payment** Cash/cheques

Room 📷 ⌨   General P ✂ 🖥 📷 ◉ ⚘   Leisure ⛰

## BEETLEY, Norfolk Map ref 3B1

★★★★
GUEST ACCOMMODATION
SILVER AWARD

B&B per room per night
s £35.00–£40.00
d £53.00–£57.00
Evening meal per person
£7.50–£12.50

# Peacock House

Peacock Lane, Old Beetley, East Dereham NR20 4DG  t (01362) 860371  w peacock-house.co.uk

**open** All year
**bedrooms** 1 double, 1 twin, 1 single, 1 family
**bathrooms** 3 en suite
**payment** Credit/debit cards, cash/cheques

Beautiful old Tudor farmhouse, peacefully situated in lovely garden and grounds. Offering excellent accommodation with all facilities, evening meals, guests' lounge, open fires, lovely dining room, home cooking and a warm welcome. Centrally situated with Norwich, Sandringham, National Trust houses and the coast all within easy reach.

⊕ *From Dereham, take B1146 (becomes B1110), continue for 3.5 miles. Continue on towards North Elmham. Our farmhouse is on right, up a short lane opposite Toad Hall.*

Room 📺 ♿ ⌨   General ⛱ 5 P ✂ ✕ 🖥 📷 ⚘ 🐾   Leisure ∪ ♪ ↑ 🚲

## It's all quality-assessed accommodation

Our commitment to quality involves wide-ranging accommodation assessment. Rating and awards were correct at the time of going to press but may change following a new assessment. Please check at time of booking.

## BIGGLESWADE, Bedfordshire Map ref 2D1

★★★
**BED & BREAKFAST**

B&B per room per night
s Min £30.00
d Min £50.00

### Old Warden Guesthouse

Shop & Post Office, Old Warden SG18 9HQ  t (01767) 627201  e owgh@idnet.co.uk

Listed 19thC building, adjacent to shop and post office. Between Biggleswade and Bedford. One mile from Shuttleworth Collection. All rooms en suite. In the heart of the Bedfordshire countryside.

**open** All year except Christmas and New Year
**bedrooms** 2 double, 1 twin
**bathrooms** All en suite
**payment** Credit/debit cards, cash/cheques

Room TV 👍 ꒜   General 🛏 🎘 ♨ P ✿   Leisure 🕭

## BOCKING, Essex Map ref 3B2

★★★★
**GUEST ACCOMMODATION**

B&B per room per night
s £25.00–£27.50
d £50.00–£56.00

### Fennes View

131 Church Street, Bocking CM7 5LF  t (01376) 326080  w tiscover.co.uk

Grade II Listed Victorian semi-detached family house within walking distance of local amenities. Thirty minutes from Stansted. No smoking.

**open** All year
**bedrooms** 2 double, 1 single
**bathrooms** 2 en suite, 1 private
**payment** Cash/cheques

Room TV 👍 ꒜   General ✂ 🎘 🌳 ▣ ✿   Leisure ⌥

## BRANCASTER, Norfolk Map ref 3B1

★★★
**INN**

B&B per room per night
s £50.00–£60.00
d £60.00–£80.00
Evening meal per person
£8.00–£15.00

### Ship Inn

Main Road, Brancaster PE31 8AP  t (01485) 210333  e mike.ali.ship@btinternet.com
w shipinnbrancaster.co.uk

The Ship Inn at Brancaster is warm and welcoming. Serving home-cooked food in the bars, dining room or beer garden. A traditional, old-fashioned 18thC English pub.

**open** All year
**bedrooms** 3 double, 1 twin
**bathrooms** 3 en suite, 1 private
**payment** Credit/debit cards, cash/cheques

Room TV 👍   General 🛏 ♨ ✿   Leisure ⏏

## BRUNDALL, Norfolk Map ref 3C1

★★★★
**BED & BREAKFAST**

B&B per room per night
s £40.00
d £55.00

### Breckland B&B

12 Strumpshaw Road, Brundall NR13 5PA  t (01603) 712122  e brecklandbandb@hotmail.co.uk
w breckland-bandb.co.uk

At Breckland B&B in Brundall, David and Tina Ward have two superior, self-contained bedrooms both with en suite facilities. Convenient for Strumpshaw RSPB, the Broads and Norwich. Recommended.

**open** All year except Christmas and New Year
**bedrooms** 1 double, 1 twin
**bathrooms** 2 private
**payment** Cash/cheques, euros

Room 🛆 TV 👍 ꒜   General 🛏 🎘 ♨ P ✂ 🕮 ✿   Leisure ⌥ 🕭

## BURNHAM-ON-CROUCH, Essex Map ref 3B3

★★★★
**INN**
**SILVER AWARD**

B&B per room per night
s Min £51.00
d Min £67.00

### The Railway Hotel

Station Road, Burnham-on-Crouch CM0 8BQ  t (01621) 786868  f (01621) 783002
w therailwayhotelburnham.co.uk

Originally built in the late 1800s, and lovingly restored by Jenny and Colin Newcombe to incorporate 21st-century luxuries with Victorian charm.

**open** All year
**bedrooms** 6 double, 1 twin, 1 single
**bathrooms** All en suite
**payment** Credit/debit cards, cash/cheques

Room 📞 TV 👍 ꒜   General 🛏 ♨ P ⏸ ✕

## Key to symbols
Open the back flap for a key to symbols.

## BURNHAM THORPE, Norfolk Map ref 3B1

★★★★
**FARMHOUSE**

B&B per room per night
s £45.00–£80.00
d £70.00

# Whitehall Farm

Burnham Thorpe PE31 8HN **t** (01328) 738416 **f** (01328) 730937 **e** barrysoutherland@aol.com
**w** tiscover.co.uk

Barry and Valerie welcome you for a quiet, relaxed stay in North Norfolk, two miles from the coast. Family rooms with full facilities in 16thC farmhouse.

**open** All year except Christmas
**bedrooms** 1 double, 1 twin, 1 family
**bathrooms** 2 en suite, 1 private
**payment** Credit/debit cards, cash/cheques, euros

Room 📺 🎧 General ⏲ 🎬 🖈 P 🗃 ❄ 🐾 Leisure ∪ ♪ 🚴 🛶

## BURY ST EDMUNDS, Suffolk Map ref 3B2

★★★★
**BED & BREAKFAST**

B&B per room per night
s £35.00–£45.00
d £55.00–£65.00

# Brambles Lodge

Welham Lane, Risby, Bury St Edmunds IP28 6QS **t** (01284) 810701

**open** All year except Christmas
**bedrooms** 1 double, 1 twin, 1 single, 1 family
**bathrooms** 3 en suite
**payment** Cash/cheques

The lodge stands amid attractive landscape gardens in the delightful and peaceful village of Risby, three miles from Bury St Edmunds. The individual rooms, which are beautifully furnished, are equipped with many thoughtful touches. Breakfast is served in a smart conservatory overlooking a large pond and garden which attract wildlife. Two village pubs serve food.

⊕ East along A14, jct 41 turn off sign for Saxham Business Park/Saxham/Risby, turn left into village, past Crown & Castle pub, left into Welham Lane.

Room 🛗 📺 🎧 General ⏲6 P ⚡

## CAMBRIDGE, Cambridgeshire Map ref 2D1

★★★★
**BED & BREAKFAST**

B&B per room per night
s £40.00–£50.00
d £60.00–£75.00

# Allenbell

517a Coldham Lane, Cambridge CB1 3JS **t** (01223) 210353 **e** sandragailturner@hotmail.com
**w** allenbell.co.uk

Warm, friendly bed and breakfast providing newly-furnished, en suite, comfortable accommodation. Quality breakfast served in light, spacious dining room. Easy access from A14/M11, close to city centre.

**open** All year except Christmas
**bedrooms** 3 double, 1 twin
**bathrooms** 3 en suite, 1 private
**payment** Credit/debit cards, cash/cheques

Room 🛗 📺 🎧 General ⏲5 P 🍴 ❄ Leisure 🚴 🛶

## CAMBRIDGE, Cambridgeshire Map ref 2D1

★★★★
**GUEST HOUSE**

B&B per room per night
s £30.00–£55.00
d £50.00–£70.00

# Arbury Lodge Guesthouse

82 Arbury Road, Cambridge CB4 2JE **t** (01223) 364319 **f** (01223) 566988
**e** arbury-lodge@btconnect.com **w** arburylodgeguesthouse.co.uk

Comfortable, family-run guesthouse offering excellent service, good home cooking, cleanliness and friendly atmosphere. 1.5 miles north of city centre and colleges. Easy access from A14/M11. Large car park, garden.

**open** All year except Christmas and New Year
**bedrooms** 2 double, 2 twin, 1 single, 1 family
**bathrooms** 3 en suite
**payment** Credit/debit cards, cash/cheques

Room 🛗 📺 🎧 General ⏲ 🎬 🖈 P ⚡ 🍴 ❄

## Using map references

Map references refer to the colour maps at the front of this guide.

## CAMBRIDGE, Cambridgeshire Map ref 2D1

★★★

**BED & BREAKFAST**

B&B per room per night
s £35.00–£40.00
d £50.00–£60.00

# Avondale

35 Highfields Road, Caldecote CB3 7NX   **t** (01954) 210746   **e** avondalecambs@amserve.com
**w** tiscover.co.uk

Small exclusive bungalow offering friendly accommodation. Situated in peaceful village location. Long country walkways.

**open** All year except Christmas
**bedrooms** 1 twin, 1 family
**bathrooms** All en suite
**payment** Cash/cheques

Room 🛗 📺 ♿ 🍴   General 🛗 🔥 P ✂ ✳ 🐾   Leisure ▶

## CAMBRIDGE, Cambridgeshire Map ref 2D1

★★★

**GUEST HOUSE**

B&B per room per night
s £40.00–£60.00
d £60.00–£75.00

# Bridge Guest House

151 Hills Road, Cambridge CB2 2RJ   **t** (01223) 247942   **f** (01223) 416585   **e** bghouse@gmail.com
**w** bridgeguesthouse.co.uk

Family-run business. Close to Addenbrooks Hospital, Cambridge Leisure Park, Botanic Gardens and city centre. M11 (Stansted) two miles. Easy access to buses and railway.

**open** All year except Christmas and New Year
**bedrooms** 2 double, 2 twin, 2 single, 1 family
**bathrooms** All en suite
**payment** Credit/debit cards, cash/cheques, euros

Room 🛗 📺 ♿   General 🛗 P 🍴 🔥 🛗 ✳

## CAMBRIDGE, Cambridgeshire Map ref 2D1

★★★★

**BED & BREAKFAST**

B&B per room per night
s £30.00
d £60.00

# City Centre North Bed And Breakfast

328a Histon Road, Cambridge CB4 3HT   **t** (01223) 312843   **f** (01223) 366162
**e** gscambs@tiscali.co.uk   **w** citycentrenorth.co.uk

Light and airy contemporary house. Off A14/M11 with parking. Ten minute bus to town centre with market, shops, restaurant and colleges. Closed January – March.

**bedrooms** 1 twin, 1 single
**bathrooms** 1 private
**payment** Cash/cheques

Room 📺 ♿ 🍴   General 3 🔥 P ✂ ✳

## CAMBRIDGE, Cambridgeshire Map ref 2D1

★★★

**BED & BREAKFAST**

B&B per room per night
s £35.00–£40.00
d £55.00

# Granta House

53 Eltisley Avenue, Newnham CB3 9JQ   **t** (01223) 560466   **e** tj.dathan@ntlworld.com
**w** tiscover.co.uk

Edwardian family home in quiet location, within walking distance of city centre, the Backs and library. Delightful walk across meadows to village of Grantchester. Easy access to M11 junction 12.

**open** All year
**bedrooms** 1 double, 1 single
**payment** Cash/cheques

Room 📺 ♿ 🍴   General 🛗 🛗 🔥 ✂ 🛗   Leisure 🚴

## CAMBRIDGE, Cambridgeshire Map ref 2D1

★★★

**GUEST HOUSE**

B&B per room per night
s £30.00–£60.00
d £60.00–£85.00

# Hamilton Lodge

156 Chesterton Road, Cambridge CB4 1DA   **t** (01223) 365664   **f** (01223) 314866
**e** hamiltonhotel@talk21.com   **w** hamiltonhotelcambridge.co.uk

Recently refurbished and less than one mile from centre of city. Easy access from A14 and M11. Most rooms have en suite shower and toilet. All rooms have colour TV, direct-dial telephone and hospitality tray.

**open** All year except Christmas
**bedrooms** 9 double, 7 twin, 4 single, 5 family
**bathrooms** 19 en suite
**payment** Credit/debit cards, cash/cheques

Room 🛗 📠 ☎ 📺 ♿ 🍴   General 🛗 🛗 🔥 P ⚡ ✕ 🛗 🔥

## B&B prices

Rates for bed and breakfast are shown per room per night.
Double room prices are usually based on two people sharing the room.

## CAMBRIDGE, Cambridgeshire Map ref 2D1

★★★★
**GUEST HOUSE**

B&B per room per night
s £40.00–£55.00
d £65.00–£75.00

# Harry's Bed and Breakfast

39 Milton Road, Cambridge CB4 1XA  **t** (01223) 503866  **f** (01223) 503866
**e** cjmadden@ntlworld.com  **w** welcometoharrys.co.uk

Edwardian semi-detached house only ten minutes from centre. Close to science park and all major routes. Excellent local amenities.

**open** All year
**bedrooms** 3 double, 1 twin, 1 family
**bathrooms** All en suite
**payment** Credit/debit cards, cash/cheques

Room 🛏 📺 ♿ ☕  General ⌒ 🍴 ☂ P ⚡ ✂ 🖥 ✿  Leisure ⚓ ♟ 🚲 🏛

## CAMBRIDGE, Cambridgeshire Map ref 2D1

★★★
**GUEST ACCOMMODATION**

B&B per room per night
s £35.00–£45.00
d £48.00–£58.00

# Southampton Guest House

7 Elizabeth Way, Cambridge CB4 1DE  **t** (01223) 357780  **f** (01223) 314297
**e** southamptonhouse@telco4u.net  **w** southamptonguesthouse.com

Victorian property with friendly atmosphere, only 15 minutes' walk along riverside to city centre, colleges and shopping mall.

**open** All year
**bedrooms** 1 double, 1 single, 3 family
**bathrooms** All en suite
**payment** Cash/cheques, euros

Room 🛏 ☎ 📺 ♿ ☕  General ⌒ ☂ ✂

## CAMBRIDGE, Cambridgeshire Map ref 2D1

★★★★
**BED & BREAKFAST**

B&B per room per night
s £25.00–£45.00
d £45.00–£60.00

# Tudor Cottage

292 Histon Road, Cambridge CB4 3HS  **t** (01223) 565212  **f** (01954) 251117
**e** email@tudor-cottage.net  **w** tudorcottageguesthouse.co.uk

**open** All year
**bedrooms** 2 double, 1 twin, 1 single
**bathrooms** 2 en suite
**payment** Cash/cheques

Comfortable, friendly, Tudor-style cottage situated within 30 minutes' walking distance of city centre. En suite or shared facilities, central heating, colour TV, tea-/coffee-making facilities. Excellent food and friendly, personal service. Off-street parking. Easy access to A14/M11.

⊕ *Close to A14 and M11.*

Room 🛏 📺 ♿ ☕  General ⌒ ✂ ✿

## CAMBRIDGE, Cambridgeshire Map ref 2D1

★★★★
**GUEST HOUSE**
**SILVER AWARD**

B&B per room per night
s £40.00–£65.00
d £60.00–£85.00

# Worth House

152 Chesterton Road, Cambridge CB4 1DA  **t** (01223) 316074  **f** (01223) 316074
**e** enquiry@worth-house.co.uk  **w** worth-house.co.uk

Worth House offers quiet, comfortable and spacious accommodation in this Victorian home. Within easy reach of the city centre. 'Which?' recommended.

**open** All year
**bedrooms** 4 suites
**bathrooms** All en suite
**payment** Credit/debit cards, cash/cheques, euros

Room 🛏 📺 ♿ ☕  General ⌒ ✂ ⚡ ✿

## Looking for a little luxury

Gold and Silver Awards are given to establishments achieving the highest levels of quality and service. There's more information at the front of the guide, and an index to all accommodation achieving these awards at the back.

## CAVENDISH, Suffolk Map ref 3B2

★★★★
**GUEST ACCOMMODATION**
**SILVER AWARD**

# Embleton House

Melford Road, Cavendish, Sudbury CO10 8AA  **t** (01787) 280447  **f** (01787) 282396
**e** silverned@aol.com  **w** embletonhouse.co.uk

B&B per room per night
**s** £40.00–£50.00
**d** £58.00–£75.00

**open** All year
**bedrooms** 2 double, 2 twin, 1 family
**bathrooms** All en suite
**payment** Cash/cheques

A large, family-run, 1930s' house set well back from the road within its own secluded, mature gardens at the eastern edge of Cavendish village. Spacious, recently appointed en suite bedrooms. Stour Valley views. Suffolk breakfast. Good pub within eight minutes' walk. Ideal base for exploring Long Melford, Clare, Lavenham and beyond.

⊕ *We are situated at the eastern end of Cavendish village, halfway between Long Melford and Clare on the A1092.*

♥ *Special rates for stays of 3 nights or more. Holistic therapies on site, heated pool (May-Sep) and tennis court.*

Room ⛉ 📺 👌 🕾   General 🏷5 P 🍴 🎱 🔥 🐴   Leisure 🔱 🎣 ⚓ ► 🚲 🏛

## CHELMSFORD, Essex Map ref 3B3

★★★
**INN**

# Compasses Motel

141 Broomfield Road, Chelmsford CM1 1RY  **t** (01245) 292051  **w** tiscover.co.uk

B&B per room per night
**s** £50.00–£55.00
**d** £50.00–£60.00

Public house, two bars. Bed and breakfast chalets available at rear.

**open** All year except Christmas and New Year
**bedrooms** 4 twin, 1 family
**bathrooms** All en suite
**payment** Credit/debit cards, cash/cheques

Room ⛉ 📺 👌   General 🏷1 P 🍴 🔥   Leisure 🔍

## CHEVELEY, Cambridgeshire Map ref 3B2

★★★★
**BED & BREAKFAST**

# Old Farmhouse

165 High Street, Cheveley CB8 9DG  **t** (01638) 730771 & 07909 970047  **e** amrobinson@clara.co.uk
**w** cheveleybandb.co.uk

B&B per room per night
**s** £35.00–£40.00
**d** £40.00–£70.00
Evening meal per person
£18.00–£25.00

Grade II Listed farmhouse offering a warm welcome and good dining. Perfect base to explore East Anglia, and for horse-racing and Icknield Way for walkers. Private parking. French, Spanish and some German spoken. Closed Christmas and Easter.

**bedrooms** 1 double, 1 twin
**bathrooms** 1 en suite, 1 private
**payment** Credit/debit cards, cash/cheques

Room 📺 👌 🕾   General 🏷 P 🍴 🎱 🔥 ▣ 🔥 🐴

# enjoyEngland.com

Get in the know – log on for a wealth of information and inspiration. All the latest news on places to visit, events and quality-assessed accommodation is literally at your fingertips. Explore all that England has to offer.

### CLACTON-ON-SEA, Essex Map ref 3B3

★★★★
**GUEST ACCOMMODATION**

B&B per room per night
s £42.00–£45.00
d £62.00–£65.00

## The Chudleigh

13 Agate Road, Marine Parade West, Clacton-on-Sea CO15 1RA  **t** (01255) 425407  **f** (01255) 470280
**e** reception@chudleighhotel.com  **w** tiscover.co.uk/chudleigh-hotel

**open** All year
**bedrooms** 4 double, 2 twin, 2 single, 2 family
**bathrooms** All en suite
**payment** Credit/debit cards, cash/cheques, euros

An oasis in a town centre location, 200m from seafront gardens, near pier and main shops. Ideal for the business visitor, the tourist and for overnight stays. Free parking. The Chudleigh, owned by the same family since 1963, welcomes you and assures you of every comfort, with friendly atmosphere and attention to detail.

⊕ From A12 follow signs to Clacton, then to seafront and pier. 1st road after pier gap at traffic lights with sea on left. Right into Agate Road.

♥ Reduced terms by negotiation Oct-Mar (excl Christmas and Bank Holidays).

Room 🛏 📞 📺 ♿ 🍴  General 🛋 1 🏊 🛎 P 🍽 🎱 🐾 🔭  Leisure ►

### CLAPHAM, Bedfordshire Map ref 2D1

★★★★
**BED & BREAKFAST**

B&B per room per night
s Min £30.00
d £50.00–£55.00

## Narly Oak Lodge

Narly Oak, The Baulk, Green Lane, Bedford MK41 6AA  **t** (01234) 350353  **f** (01234) 350353
**e** mollie.foster07@btinternet.com  **w** narlyoaklodge.com

Secluded location. Was a wartime officers' mess. Area has military history. Twinwood Airfield 0.25 miles (Glen Miller). Double rooms can be converted to single rooms.

**open** All year
**bedrooms** 1 double, 2 twin
**bathrooms** All en suite
**payment** Cash/cheques

Room 🛏 📺 ♿  General 🛋 P 🍴 🎱 ❄  Leisure ∪ ♪ ►

### COLCHESTER, Essex Map ref 3B2

★★
**GUEST HOUSE**

B&B per room per night
s £31.00–£40.00
d £47.00–£55.00

## Scheregate Hotel

36 Osborne Street, Via St John's Street, Colchester CO2 7DB  **t** (01206) 573034  **f** (01206) 541561

Interesting 15thC building, centrally situated, providing accommodation at moderate prices.

**open** All year except Christmas
**bedrooms** 6 double, 8 twin, 12 single, 2 family
**bathrooms** 10 en suite
**payment** Credit/debit cards, cash/cheques

Room 🛏 📺 ♿  General 🛋 🍽 🎱

# Country Code

always follow the Country Code

- Be safe – plan ahead and follow any signs
- Leave gates and property as you find them
- Protect plants and animals, and take your litter home
- Keep dogs under close control
- Consider other people

**COLTISHALL,** Norfolk Map ref 3C1

★★★★
**GUEST ACCOMMODATION**

B&B per room per night
s  £30.00–£44.00
d  £50.00–£55.00

# Hedges Guesthouse

Tunstead Road, Coltishall NR12 7AL  t (01603) 738361  f (01603) 738983
e info@hedgesbandb.co.uk  w hedgesbandb.co.uk

**open** All year except Christmas
**bedrooms** 1 double, 2 twin, 2 family
**bathrooms** All en suite
**payment** Credit/debit cards, cash/cheques

Hear evening owlsong and the dawn chorus at this friendly, family-run guesthouse. Set in large, peaceful gardens surrounded by open countryside, yet convenient for local amenities. Ideal base for exploring the Norfolk Broads, Norwich and Norfolk coast. Families welcome, lounge, plenty of parking.

⊕ *B1150 North Walsham Road to Coltishall. Continue towards Wroxham. Left at White Lion Road (signposted St James) then right fork onto Tunstead Road. The Hedges is 100m on right.*

♥ *3 nights for the price of 2 Nov-Apr. Quote 342 when booking.*

Room ♿ 📺 ♨ 🍳  General 🔥 ▥ ♟ P ✂ 🗚 ❀  Leisure ∪ ♪ ▶ ৬

**CROMER,** Norfolk Map ref 3C1

★★★★★
**BED & BREAKFAST**

B&B per room per night
d  £140.00–£150.00

# Incleborough House Luxury Bed and Breakfast

East Runton, Cromer NR27 9PG  t (01263) 515939  f (01263) 510022
e enquiries@incleboroughhouse.co.uk  w incleboroughhouse.co.uk

**open** All year
**bedrooms** 3 double
**bathrooms** All en suite
**payment** Credit/debit cards, cash/cheques

Incleborough House, built in 1687, (King James II was on the throne) is a stunning Grade II Listed country house overlooking the Lower Common in the heart of a small unspoilt fishing village just 300 metres from the beach, on the coast at East Runton, near Cromer in Norfolk.

⊕ *Take A149 from Sheringham towards Cromer. At East Runton turn right turn into Felbrigg Road, 200 metres and Incleborough House is on your left.*

♥ *Special offers for midweek breaks, see our website or ring for details. Honeymoon, birthday and anniversary stays.*

Room ♿ 📺 ♨ 🍳  General 🔥 14 P ✂ ✗ ▥ 🗚 🔊 ▣ ❀ 🐾  Leisure ∪ ♪ ▶ ৬ 🛥

**DEREHAM,** Norfolk Map ref 3B1

★★★★
**FARMHOUSE**

B&B per room per night
s  £40.00–£60.00
d  £60.00–£80.00

# Hunters Hall

Park Farm, Swanton Morley, Dereham NR20 4JU  t (01362) 637457  f (01362) 637987
e office@huntershall.com  w huntershall.com

A traditional working farm offering accommodation, function and conference facilities in a conservation area.

**open** All year
**bedrooms** 5 double, 5 twin, 2 family
**bathrooms** 8 en suite
**payment** Credit/debit cards, cash/cheques, euros

Room ♿ 📺 ♨ 🍳  General 🔥 ▥ ♟ P ✗ ▥ 🗚 ▣ ❀ 🐾  Leisure ♪

# Town, country or coast

The entertainment, shopping and innovative attractions of the big cities, the magnificent vistas of the countryside or the relaxing and refreshing coast – this guide will help you find what you're looking for.

## DERSINGHAM, Norfolk Map ref 3B1

★ ★ ★ ★
**GUEST ACCOMMODATION**

B&B per room per night
s £35.00–£50.00
d £50.00–£70.00

# Barn House Bed And Breakfast

14 Station Road, Dersingham, King's Lynn PE31 6PP  **t** (01485) 543086
**e** tom.chapman@eidosnet.co.uk  **w** smoothhound.co.uk/hotels/barnho

**open** All year
**bedrooms** 1 double, 1 twin
**bathrooms** All en suite
**payment** Cash/cheques

Barn conversion offering comfortable, relaxed, character accommodation. Lovely, spacious en suite rooms provide a warm welcome and home comforts for holidaymakers, walkers, bird-watchers and cyclists. Sandringham Estate and Country Park one mile. RSPB reserve 2.5 miles. Peddars Way four miles. Drying room. Cycle facilities. Extensive beach, woodland and countryside walks.

⊕ *A149 north from King's Lynn. After approx 7 miles, B1440 at Dersingham roundabout into village. Left at lights into Station Road. Barn House 100m on right.*

Room 📺 🛇 ♨  General ♨10 P⚲☼🐾  Leisure ∪ ♪ ⏵ 🚲 🏛

## DISS, Norfolk Map ref 3B2

★ ★ ★ ★ ★
**BED & BREAKFAST
GOLD AWARD**

B&B per room per night
s £47.50–£62.50
d £95.00
Evening meal per person
£27.50–£35.00

# Old Rectory Hopton

High Street, Hopton, Diss IP22 2QX  **t** (01953) 688135  **e** llewellyn.hopton@btinternet.com
**w** theoldrectoryhopton.com

**open** All year except Christmas and New Year
**bedrooms** 2 double, 1 twin
**bathrooms** 2 en suite, 1 private
**payment** Cash/cheques

The Old Rectory is a listed building, dating from the 16th century, standing in walled grounds. The house is well situated to explore East Anglia, being on the Norfolk/Suffolk border. The house is beautifully furnished, and many period features add to the charm of this lovely home. A non-smoking house.

⊕ *From Bury take the A143. In Stanton take the B1111 signed to Garboldisham. The Old Rectory is immediately after the church in Hopton.*

♥ *10% discount on B&B rate for 3 nights or more, 1 Nov to 31 Mar.*

Room 🛇 ♨  General ♨8 P⚲♀✕🍴📷☼🐾  Leisure ⏵ 🏛

## DOCKING, Norfolk Map ref 3B1

★ ★ ★ ★
**GUEST ACCOMMODATION**

B&B per room per night
s £30.00
d £50.00

# Jubilee Lodge

Station Road, Docking PE31 8LS  **t** (01485) 518473  **f** (01485) 518473  **e** eghoward62@hotmail.com
**w** jubilee-lodge.com

Bed and breakfast in a Tudor-style, centrally heated, double-glazed house, in a pleasant village setting, only four miles from the beach.

**open** All year
**bedrooms** 2 double, 1 twin
**bathrooms** All en suite
**payment** Cash/cheques

Room 📺 🛇 ♨  General P⚲✕📷☼  Leisure ◌ ∪ ♪ 🚲

## Friendly help and advice

Tourist Information Centres offer friendly help with accommodation and holiday ideas as well as suggestions of places to visit and things to do. You'll find contact details at the beginning of each regional section.

## EARLS COLNE, Essex Map ref 3B2

★★★

**GUEST ACCOMMODATION**

B&B per room per night
s £50.00–£52.00
d £58.00–£62.00

### Riverside Lodge

40 Lower Holt Street, Earls Colne, Colchester CO6 2PH  **t** (01787) 223487  **f** (01787) 223487
**e** bandb@riversidelodge-uk.com  **w** riversidelodge-uk.com

Single, en suite chalets on banks of River Colne.
Restaurants, pubs and village amenities within
walking distance. Fine country walks from Lodge.
All rooms on ground level.

**open** All year
**bedrooms** 2 double, 3 twin
**bathrooms** All en suite
**payment** Credit/debit cards, cash/cheques

Room 🛏 📺 👤 🍳   General 🌳 🛏 P ⚲ �ると

## ELY, Cambridgeshire Map ref 3A2

★★★★

**RESTAURANT WITH ROOMS**

B&B per room per night
s £59.50–£89.50
d £79.50–£155.00
Evening meal per person
£15.00–£35.00

### Anchor Inn

Sutton Gault, Sutton CB6 2BD  **t** (01353) 778537  **f** (01353) 776180  **e** anchorinn@popmail.bta.com
**w** anchorsuttongault.co.uk

**open** All year
**bedrooms** 1 double, 1 twin, 2 suites
**bathrooms** All en suite
**payment** Credit/debit cards, cash/cheques

Tranquil and away from it all, very friendly 17thC
riverside inn. Spotless, well-equipped rooms most
with stunning fen views. Close to Ely Cathedral,
Cambridge, Welney and Newmarket. Ideal for
walking, bird-watching or just relaxing. High quality
award-winning food – Good Food Guide, Michelin,
Sawdays, Good Pub Guide, AA Rosette.

⊕ *Sutton Gault is signposted off the B1381 in Sutton village,
6 miles west of Ely via the A142. From the A14 take B1050
then B1381.*

Room 📞 📺 👤 🍳   General 🌳 🛏 P ⚲ 🍷 🍴 ✳   Leisure ⊿ ►

## ELY, Cambridgeshire Map ref 3A2

★★★★

**FARMHOUSE**

B&B per room per night
d £60.00–£64.00

### Spinney Abbey

Stretham Road, Wicken CB7 5XQ  **t** (01353) 720971  **e** spinney.abbey@tesco.net
**w** spinneyabbey.co.uk

**open** All year except Christmas
**bedrooms** 1 double, 1 twin, 1 family
**bathrooms** 2 en suite, 1 private
**payment** Cash/cheques, euros

This attractive Georgian Grade II Listed farmhouse,
surrounded by pasture fields, stands next to our
livestock farm which borders the National Trust
Nature Reserve, 'Wicken Fen', on the southern edge
of the Fens. Guests are welcome to make full use of
the spacious garden and all-weather tennis court. All
rooms have en suite or private facilities.

⊕ *Just off the A1123, 0.75 miles west of Wicken.*

Room 📺 👤 🍳   General 🌳5 P 🍴 ✳   Leisure ⚲

## FAKENHAM, Norfolk Map ref 3B1

★★★

**FARMHOUSE**

B&B per room per night
s £26.00–£30.00
d £52.00–£60.00

### Abbott Farm

Walsingham Road, Binham NR21 0AW  **t** (01328) 830519  **f** (01328) 830519
**e** abbot.farm@btinternet.com  **w** abbottfarm.co.uk

A 190-acre arable farm. Rural views of North
Norfolk including the historic Binham Priory. Liz
and Alan offer a warm welcome to their
guesthouse.

**open** All year except Christmas
**bedrooms** 1 double, 2 twin
**bathrooms** All en suite
**payment** Cash/cheques, euros

Room 🛏 📺 👤 🍳   General 🌳 🛏 🛏 P ⚲ ✕ 🍴 🐴 ✳ 🐓   Leisure ∪ 🚲 🏛

## FEERING, Essex Map ref 3B2

★★★★
**FARMHOUSE**

B&B per room per night
s £35.00–£40.00
d £55.00–£85.00

# Old Wills Farm

Little Tey Road, Feering, Colchester CO5 9RP  t (01376) 570259  e janecrayston@btconnect.com

**open** All year except Christmas
**bedrooms** 1 double, 1 twin, 1 family
**bathrooms** All en suite
**payment** Cash/cheques

Attractive and comfortable Essex farmhouse on a working, arable farm with large garden offering homely surroundings and atmosphere. Ample, safe parking. We are within reach of the historic town of Colchester and its zoo, Dedham Vale, Constable Country and Colne Valley Railway.

⊕ Take Kelvedon sign off A12, follow sign to Feering village. Turn right at village green, signed The Teys. Farm is approx 0.75 miles on right.

Room 📺 💺 ☎  General 🛏 🏠 🛗 P ⚲ 🍴 🍽 ᕦ ⚘ 🐾  Leisure 🚶 ⚑ 🏛

## FRAMLINGHAM, Suffolk Map ref 3C2

★★★
**FARMHOUSE**

B&B per room per night
s £36.00–£46.00
d £50.00–£60.00

# High House Farm

Cransford, Woodbridge IP13 9PD  t (01728) 663461  f (01728) 663409  e info@highhousefarm.co.uk
w highhousefarm.co.uk

A warm welcome awaits you in our beautifully restored 15thC farmhouse, featuring exposed beams, inglenook fireplaces and attractive gardens. Situated midway between Framlingham and Saxmundham. Open all year.

**open** All year
**bedrooms** 1 double, 1 family
**bathrooms** 1 en suite, 1 private
**payment** Cash/cheques

Room 📺 💺 ☎  General 🛏 🏠 🛗 P 🍽 ⚘ 🐾  Leisure 🚶 🏛

## FRECKENHAM, Suffolk Map ref 3B2

★★★★
**INN**

B&B per room per night
s  Min £40.00
d  Min £80.00
Evening meal per person
£10.00–£30.00

# The Golden Boar Inn

The Street, Freckenham, Bury St. Edmunds IP28 8HZ  t (01638) 723000  f (01638) 721166
e thegoldenboarinn@aol.com

**open** All year
**bedrooms** 4 twin, 2 single
**bathrooms** All en suite
**payment** Credit/debit cards, cash/cheques, euros

16thC, Grade II Listed inn, formerly on quay of most inland port in England. Within easy reach of Newmarket, Ely, Bury St Edmunds and Cambridge. Ideally placed for touring East Anglia. Split-level restaurant and patio dining areas for weddings and functions.

⊕ A11/A14 junction. North on A11. Exit signed for Freckenham and Red Lodge. Left at T-junction to centre of village.

Room 🛋 📺 💺 ☎  General 🛏 🏠 P ⚲ 🍴 ▼ ✕ 🍽 🖥 ⚘  Leisure ⚑ 🏛

## FRINTON-ON-SEA, Essex Map ref 3C2

★★★
**BED & BREAKFAST**

B&B per room per night
s £25.00
d £50.00

# Russell Lodge

47 Hadleigh Road, Frinton-on-Sea CO13 9HQ  t (01255) 675935 & 07891 899824
e stay@russell-lodge.fsnet.co.uk  w russell-lodge.fsnet.co.uk

A friendly, homely bed and breakfast in a quiet seaside town. Situated close to beaches, shops and train station. Approximately 300yds to the Greensward, town centre and Crescent Gardens.

**open** All year
**bedrooms** 1 double, 1 single, 1 family
**bathrooms** 2 en suite
**payment** Cash/cheques

Room 📺 💺 ☎  General 🛏 🏠 🛗 P ⚲ 🍽 ⚘ 🐾  Leisure 🚶 ⚑ 🚲 🏛

## FRITTON, Norfolk Map ref 3C1

★★★★

**BED & BREAKFAST**

B&B per room per night
s £45.00–£55.00
d £60.00–£69.00

# Decoy Barn Bed & Breakfast

Beccles Road, Great Yarmouth NR31 9AB  **t** (01493) 488222  **e** karenwilder9@aol.com
**w** decoybarn.co.uk

**open** All year
**bedrooms** 2 double, 1 twin
**bathrooms** All en suite
**payment** Credit/debit cards, cash

Decoy Barn is a charming 200-year-old converted barn, retaining many original features, which offers our guests a warm, cosy, welcoming atmosphere. The grounds extend to over half an acre with outstanding views across Fritton Lake Country Park. Decoy Barn is situated very close to Caldecott and the local tavern for lunch/evening meals.

⊕ *Decoy Barn is located on the A143 in Fritton (directly opposite the Decoy Tavern). 6 miles from Beccles and 5 miles from Great Yarmouth.*

Room 🛁 📺 🐾 ♨ General ♨10 P ⅓ ⚕ ❀ Leisure ∪ ♪ ► ⚙ ⚓

## GAMLINGAY, Cambridgeshire Map ref 2D1

★★★

**BED & BREAKFAST**

B&B per room per night
s Min £35.00
d Min £70.00
Evening meal per person
£12.50–£20.00

# Emplins

Church Street, Gamlingay SG19 3ER  **t** (01767) 650581  **e** philip.gorton@virgin.net
**w** smoothhound.co.uk

15thC Grade II* Listed hall house with wall paintings. Peaceful location in the village conservation area. Convenient for Cambridge, A1 and M11.

**open** All year except Christmas
**bedrooms** 1 double, 2 twin
**bathrooms** 2 en suite, 1 private
**payment** Cash/cheques, euros

Room 📺 🐾 ♨ General ♨ ⚏ ⚱ P ⅓ ✕ ⚒ ⚜ ⚐ ❀ ⚶ Leisure ♪ ► ⚓

## GREAT EASTON, Essex Map ref 3B2

★★★★

**INN**

B&B per room per night
s £50.00
d £80.00
Evening meal per person
£7.50–£28.00

# The Swan Inn

The Endway, Dunmow CM6 2HG  **t** (01371) 870359  **e** theswangreateaston@tiscali.co.uk
**w** theswangreateaston.co.uk

**open** All year except Christmas and New Year
**bedrooms** 2 double, 2 twin
**bathrooms** All en suite
**payment** Credit/debit cards, cash/cheques

15thC village freehouse inn and restaurant. The accommodation is of a superior standard, and all food is homemade. In the Camra ' Good Beer' and 'Good Pub Food' guides. Set in beautiful countryside just ten minutes from the M11 and Stansted Airport.

⊕ *From the B184, turn into Great Easton village at the Rolls Royce garage. Past the church. The Swan is down the hill on the right.*

♥ *Champagne weekends and others – visit website for current details.*

Room 📺 🐾 ♨ General ♨ ⚱ P ⅓ ♈ ✕ ⚒ ⚜ ❀ Leisure ⚘ ∪ ►

## Check it out

Information on accommodation listed in this guide has been supplied by proprietors. As changes may occur you should remember to check all relevant details at the time of booking.

## GREAT YARMOUTH, Norfolk Map ref 3C1

★★★
**GUEST ACCOMMODATION**

B&B per room per night
s £18.00–£25.00
d £35.00–£50.00
Evening meal per person
£8.00–£13.50

### Cavendish House

19-20 Princes Road, Great Yarmouth NR30 2DG **t** (01493) 843148

In a prominent position, close to all holiday amenities, shopping centre, theatres and beaches. En suite rooms with colour TV available.

**open** All year
**bedrooms** 8 double, 4 twin, 3 single, 4 family
**bathrooms** 17 en suite, 2 private
**payment** Cash/cheques

Room 🛏 📺 ✆  General 🛋 🕮 🛈 🍴 ✕ 🎱 🎿 🛴 🖭 ♘  Leisure ♣

## HALESWORTH, Suffolk Map ref 3C2

★★★
**BED & BREAKFAST**

B&B per room per night
s £24.99–£30.00
d £40.00–£50.00

### Fen-Way Guest House

Fen-Way, School Lane, Halesworth IP19 8BW **t** (01986) 873574

Spacious bungalow in seven acres of peaceful meadowland. Pets include sheep and lambs. Five minutes' walk from town centre. Convenient for many places including Southwold (nine miles).

**open** All year
**bedrooms** 2 double, 1 twin
**bathrooms** 1 en suite
**payment** Cash/cheques

Room 🛏 📺 ✆ ⚲  General 🛋5 P 🚫 🎿 ☼  Leisure ∪ ⊳ 🚵

## HARLESTON, Norfolk Map ref 3C2

★★★★
**FARMHOUSE**

B&B per room per night
s £29.00–£39.50
d £48.00–£65.00

### Weston House Farm

Mendham, Harleston IP20 0PB **t** (01986) 782206 **e** holden@farmline.com **w** westonhousefarm.co.uk

**bedrooms** 2 double, 1 twin
**bathrooms** All en suite
**payment** Cash/cheques

Peacefully located farmhouse set in one-acre garden on a mixed farm. Comfortable, spacious, en suite rooms, well equipped and offering fine views. Ground-floor room available. Guest lounge has TV, piano, books and local magazines. Traditional breakfasts served at separate tables in the dining room. Perfect base for exploring the Suffolk coast and countryside. Open March to November.

⊕ *Turn off A143 Harleston bypass (signposted Mendham) then follow signs from crossroad in centre of village.*

Room 🛏 📺 ✆  General 🛋1 P 🚫 🎿 ☼ ♘  Leisure ∪ 🚣 🚵

## HAUGHLEY, Suffolk Map ref 3B2

★★★★
**FARMHOUSE**

B&B per room per night
s £35.00–£40.00
d £55.00–£60.00

### Red House Farm

Haughley, Stowmarket IP14 3QP **t** (01449) 673323 **f** (01449) 675413
**e** mary@redhousefarmhaughley.co.uk **w** farmstayanglia.co.uk

Attractive farmhouse in rural location on small grassland farm. First-class breakfast. Central heating and large garden.

**open** All year except Christmas and New Year
**bedrooms** 1 double, 1 twin, 2 single
**bathrooms** All en suite
**payment** Credit/debit cards, cash/cheques

Room ✆  General 🛋8 P 🚫 🎿 🖭 ☼  Leisure 🚵

## Ancient and modern

Experience timeless favourites or discover the latest must-sees. Whatever your choice, be inspired by the places of interest and events highlighted for each region.

## HEMEL HEMPSTEAD, Hertfordshire Map ref 2D1

★ ★ ★ ★
**BED & BREAKFAST**

B&B per room per night
s Min £55.00
d Min £65.00

# Marsh Farm

Ledgemore Lane, Great Gaddesden HP2 6HA  t (01442) 252517  f (01442) 232023
e nicky@bennett-baggs.com  w marshfarm.org

**open** All year except Christmas and New Year
**bedrooms** 1 twin
**bathrooms** En suite
**payment** Cash/cheques

Situated on the private Gaddesden estate, Marsh Farm is a beautiful 18thC farmhouse in a stunning rural location, with excellent local pubs and restaurants and wonderful country walks from our front door. You can be assured of a comfortable, well-appointed room with good breakfasts using local produce.

⊕ *From Gt Gaddesden (Berkhamsted – 4 miles, Hemel Hempsted – 4 miles) cross A4146 onto Ledgemore Lane. Take first right onto track, then left at barns.*

Room 🛏 📺 👤 ☕   General P ⅄ ♨ ▣ ✤   Leisure ∪ ♩ ► 🏡

## HEVINGHAM, Norfolk Map ref 3B1

★ ★ ★ ★
**INN**

B&B per room per night
s £54.50–£65.00
d £85.00–£95.00
Evening meal per person
£12.50–£30.00

# Marsham Arms Inn

Holt Road, Hevingham NR10 5NP  t (01603) 754268  f (01603) 754839  e info@marshamarms.co.uk
w marshamarms.co.uk

Set in peaceful Norfolk countryside within reach of Norwich, the Broads and the coast. Comfortable and spacious accommodation, good food and a fine selection of ales.

**open** All year
**bedrooms** 3 double, 8 family
**bathrooms** All en suite
**payment** Credit/debit cards, cash/cheques

Room 🛏 📞 📺 👤 ☕   General ⛺ ▦ ♨ P ▯ ✕ ✤   Leisure ♩ ►

## HICKLING, Norfolk Map ref 3C1

★ ★ ★ ★
**FARMHOUSE
GOLD AWARD**

B&B per room per night
s £45.00
d £60.00–£64.00

# The Dairy Barns

Lound Farm, Hickling, Norwich NR12 0BE  t (01692) 598243  f (01692) 598243
e enquiries@dairybarns.co.uk  w dairybarns.co.uk

The accommodation is in self-contained, converted barns. Breakfast is the best farmhouse cooking using local produce. Spacious en suite rooms. One mile from beaches and Norfolk Broads. Disabled facilities. Children welcome.

**open** All year
**bedrooms** 3 double, 3 twin
**bathrooms** All en suite
**payment** Credit/debit cards, cash/cheques

Room 🛏 📺 👤 ☕   General ⛺ ▦ ♨ P ✕ ⋈ ✤   Leisure ♩ 🚲 🏡

## HINTLESHAM, Suffolk Map ref 3B2

★ ★ ★ ★
**FARMHOUSE
SILVER AWARD**

B&B per room per night
s £35.00–£40.00
d £56.00–£64.00

# College Farm

Hintlesham, Ipswich IP8 3NT  t (01473) 652253  f (01473) 652253  e bandb@collegefarm.plus.com
w collegefarm.net

Peaceful 500-year-old house on 600-acre arable farm near Ipswich (six miles). Convenient for Constable Country, Sutton Hoo (National Trust) and the coast. Well-appointed, comfortable rooms. Good food locally.

**open** All year except Christmas and New Year
**bedrooms** 3 double/twin
**bathrooms** 2 en suite, 1 private
**payment** Cash/cheques

Room 🛏 📺 👤 ☕   General ⛺10 P ⅄ ⋈ ✤   Leisure ∪ ♩ ►

## Look at the maps

Colour maps at the front pinpoint the location of all accommodation found in the regional sections.

**HONINGTON,** Suffolk Map ref 3B2

★★★
GUEST ACCOMMODATION

B&B per room per night
s £20.00–£25.00
d £40.00–£50.00

## North View Guesthouse

North View, Malting Row, Honington IP31 1RE **t** (01359) 269423 **f** (01359) 269423

North View Guesthouse is situated in the village of Honington opposite the church. Close to Thetford and Bury St Edmunds stations.

**open** All year
**bedrooms** 1 double, 1 single, 1 family
**payment** Cash/cheques

Room General P Leisure

**HOUGHTON,** Cambridgeshire Map ref 3A2

★★★★★
GUEST ACCOMMODATION
SILVER AWARD

B&B per room per night
s £65.00–£70.00
d £75.00–£85.00

## Cheriton House

Mill Street, Houghton PE28 2AZ **t** (01480) 464004 **f** (01480) 496960
**e** sales@cheritonhousecambs.co.uk **w** cheritonhousecambs.co.uk

Award-winning bed and breakfast 150yds from river in picturesque village of Houghton, two miles from St Ives and Huntingdon, and just 20/25 minutes from Cambridge/Ely. Great breakfasts, home-made breads, jams and marmalades.

**open** All year except Christmas
**bedrooms** 4 double, 1 twin
**bathrooms** All en suite
**payment** Credit/debit cards, cash/cheques

Room General P Leisure

**HUNSTANTON,** Norfolk Map ref 3B1

★★★★
INN
SILVER AWARD

B&B per room per night
s £50.00–£60.00
d £85.00–£90.00
Evening meal per person
£8.00–£25.00

## The King William IV Country Inn & Restaurant

Heacham Road, Sedgeford, Hunstanton PE36 5LU **t** (01485) 571765 **f** (01485) 571743
**e** info@thekingwilliamsedgeford.co.uk **w** thekingwilliamsedgeford.co.uk

**open** All year
**bedrooms** 4 double/twin
**bathrooms** All en suite
**payment** Credit/debit cards, cash/cheques

Popular and busy traditional country inn, amid Norfolk countryside. Close to North Norfolk's beautiful coastline, Peddars Way, RSPB bird reserves and golf. High-standard, comfortable en suite accommodation with king-size beds. Extensive menu and daily specials served in two non-smoking restaurants, bar and garden. A delightful escape – whatever the season.

⊕ *From King's Lynn, follow A149 Hunstanton, turn right at Norfolk Lavender onto B1454 (signposted Sedgeford) into village. From Fakenham follow B1454 through Docking into Sedgeford.*

♥ *Midweek offer: third night half price (Sun-Thu).*

WALKERS WELCOME · CYCLISTS WELCOME

Room General P Leisure

# Take a break

Look out for special promotions and themed breaks. It's a golden opportunity to indulge an interest, find a new one, or just relax and enjoy exceptional value. Offers and promotions are highlighted in colour (and are subject to availability).

## KETTLEBURGH, Suffolk Map ref 3C2

★★★
**FARMHOUSE**

B&B per room per night
s £28.00–£30.00
d £56.00–£60.00
Evening meal per person
Min £16.00

### Church Farm

Kettleburgh, Woodbridge IP13 7LF  t (01728) 723532  e jbater@suffolkonline.net

**open** All year
**bedrooms** 1 double, 2 twin
**bathrooms** 1 en suite
**payment** Cash/cheques

Oak-beamed, 350-year-old farmhouse on a working farm. Bedrooms with lovely views and every comfort. Excellent food from home-grown produce.

⊕ *From A12, take B1116 through Easton to Kettleburgh. The farm is situated behind the church. From A14 take A1120, through Earl Soham and Brandeston to Kettleburgh.*

Room 🛁 ♿ 🍷  General ᴆ 🎖 ♿ P ✕ 🎮 🎛 ✿ 🐾  Leisure ∪ ♪ ↑ ♿

## LAVENHAM, Suffolk Map ref 3B2

★★★★
**BED & BREAKFAST**

B&B per room per night
s £40.00–£65.00
d £65.00–£70.00

### Brett Farm

The Common, Sudbury, Lavenham CO10 9PG  t (01787) 248533  e brettfarmbandb@aol.com
w brettfarm.com

Riverside bungalow set in rural surroundings within walking distance of Lavenham High Street. Comfortable bedrooms, with either en suite or private bathroom. Stabling available.

**open** All year
**bedrooms** 2 double, 1 twin
**bathrooms** 2 en suite, 1 private
**payment** Cash/cheques

Room 🛁 📺 ♿ 🍷  General ᴆ 🎖 ♿ P ✂ 🎛 ✿  Leisure ∪ ♿ 🏠

## LAVENHAM, Suffolk Map ref 3B2

★★★★
**BED & BREAKFAST**
**SILVER AWARD**

B&B per room per night
s £45.00–£60.00
d £75.00–£90.00

### Guinea House Bed & Breakfast

16 Bolton Street, Lavenham, Sudbury CO10 9RG  t (01787) 249046  e gdelucy@aol.com
w guineahouse.co.uk

Very comfortable, heavily beamed medieval house, tucked away yet close to market square and Guildhall. Excellent Suffolk breakfasts with local or home-grown produce. Excellent base for exploring Suffolk.

**open** All year
**bedrooms** 2 double, 1 twin
**bathrooms** All en suite
**payment** Cash/cheques, euros

Room 📺 ♿ 🍷  General ᴆ 🎖 ♿ P ✂ 🎛 ✿  Leisure ∪ ↑ ♿ 🏠

## LONG MELFORD, Suffolk Map ref 3B2

★★★★
**BED & BREAKFAST**
**SILVER AWARD**

B&B per room per night
s £35.00–£54.00
d £50.00–£70.00

### High Street Farmhouse

High Street, Long Melford, Sudbury CO10 9BD  t (01787) 375765  e mail@gallopingchef.co.uk
w highstreetfarmhouse.co.uk

Charming 16thC farmhouse offers cosy rooms with pretty gardens. Set on the edge of a picturesque Tudor village.

**open** All year
**bedrooms** 2 double, 1 twin
**bathrooms** All en suite
**payment** Cash/cheques

Room 🛁 📻 📺 ♿ 🍷  General ᴆ 🎖 ♿ P ✂ 🎮 🎛 ✿ 🐾  Leisure ∪ ♪ ↑ ♿

## Family-friendly breaks

For accommodation offering additional facilities and services for a range of ages and family units, look out for the Families Welcome symbol. Owners of these properties will go out of their way to welcome families.

---

**LOWESTOFT,** Suffolk Map ref 3C1

★★★★
**BED & BREAKFAST**

B&B per room per night
s £42.50–£60.00
d £65.00–£85.00

# Fairways Bed and Breakfast

288 Normanston Drive, Oulton Broad, Lowestoft NR32 2PS  t (01502) 582756  f (01502) 561021
e info@fairwaysbb.co.uk  w fairwaysbb.co.uk

A warm and friendly welcome awaits you at Fairways, where we offer a very comfortable and relaxing break.

**open** All year
**bedrooms** 1 double, 1 twin
**bathrooms** All en suite
**payment** Credit/debit cards, cash/cheques

Room 👤 📺 🛁 🍷  General 🛏 P ⌖ 🛋 ✿  Leisure ⚓ 🏛

---

**LOWESTOFT,** Suffolk Map ref 3C1

★★★
**GUEST HOUSE**

B&B per room per night
s £28.00–£30.00
d £50.00
Evening meal per person
£8.50

# Homelea Guest House

Marine Parade, Lowestoft NR33 0QN  t (01502) 511640  e info@homeleaguesthouse.co.uk
w homeleaguesthouse.co.uk

Family-run guesthouse on seafront. Homely accommodation for tourists and travellers.

**open** All year except Christmas
**bedrooms** 2 double, 1 single, 2 family
**bathrooms** 4 en suite, 1 private
**payment** Credit/debit cards, cash/cheques, euros

Room 👤 📺 🛁  General 🛏3 ✕ 🛋 🐾 🐕

---

**MALDON,** Essex Map ref 3B3

★★★★
**BED & BREAKFAST**

B&B per room per night
d Max £55.00

# Tatoi Bed & Breakfast

31 Acacia Drive, Maldon CM9 6AW  t (01621) 853841 & 07860 162328
e diana.rogers2@btinternet.com

Detached family house standing on a large plot in a quiet residential area. It is within easy walking distance of the town and historic maritime quay.

**open** All year except Christmas
**bedrooms** 2 double
**payment** Cash/cheques

Room 👤 📺 🛁 🍷  General P ⌖ ✿  Leisure ⚓ ▶ 🏛

---

**MANNINGTREE,** Essex Map ref 3B2

★★★★
**BED & BREAKFAST**

B&B per room per night
s £40.00–£55.00
d £55.00–£65.00

# Emsworth House

Station Road, Ship Hill, Bradfield, Manningtree CO11 2UP  t (01255) 870860
e emsworthhouse@hotmail.com  w emsworthhouse.co.uk

**open** All year
**bedrooms** 1 double, 1 twin, 1 single, 1 family
**bathrooms** 2 en suite
**payment** Cash/cheques

Formerly the vicarage. Spacious rooms with stunning views of the countryside and River Stour. Near Colchester and Harwich. On holiday, business or en route to the continent, it's perfect!

Room 📺 🛁 🍷  General 🛏 ♿ P ⌖ 🛋 🐾 ✿  Leisure ⚓ ∪ ▶ 🚴 🏛

---

**MARCH,** Cambridgeshire Map ref 3A1

★★★
**GUEST HOUSE**

B&B per room per night
s Max £30.00
d Max £48.00

# Causeway Guest House

6 The Causeway, March PE15 9NT  t (01354) 650823  f (01354) 661068

This 19thC house offers en suite accommodation, colour TV and tea/coffee facilities in all rooms. Private car park. Situated five minutes' walk from town centre.

**open** All year
**bedrooms** 13 double, 5 twin, 6 single, 1 family
**bathrooms** All en suite
**payment** Credit/debit cards, cash/cheques

Room 👤 🍳 📺 🛁 🍷  General 🛏 ♿ P ⌖ 🐕

---

## MARCH, Cambridgeshire Map ref 3A1

★★★
GUEST ACCOMMODATION

B&B per room per night
s Min £30.00
d £45.00–£60.00

### Willows Motel

Elm Road, March PE15 8PS  t (01354) 661292  f (01354) 661292  e david.coe4@btinternet.com
w willowsmotel.co.uk

Small, family-run bed and breakfast. Courtyard parking. All rooms en suite. Full English breakfast. Convenient for railway and about one mile from town.

**open** All year
**bedrooms** 2 double, 3 twin, 1 family
**bathrooms** All en suite
**payment** Credit/debit cards, cash/cheques

Room ⛲ 📺 ⚭  General ⌂ P ✗

## MUNDESLEY, Norfolk Map ref 3C1

★★★★
GUEST ACCOMMODATION

B&B per room per night
s £30.00–£55.00
d £50.00–£90.00

### The Durdans

36 Trunch Road, Mundesley NR11 8JX  t (01263) 722225  f (01263) 722225
e info@thedurdans.co.uk  w thedurdans.co.uk

**open** All year except Christmas and New Year
**bedrooms** 3 double, 2 twin, 1 single, 1 family
**bathrooms** 6 en suite, 1 private
**payment** Credit/debit cards, cash/cheques, euros

An imposing Victorian house standing in two acres and reached by tree-lined drive. The property is in a picturesque seaside village in an Area of Outstanding Natural Beauty. All bedrooms and public rooms have been tastefully decorated and stylishly furnished. Breakfasts are a speciality and are both superb and substantial.

⊕ From Norwich take B1150 to North Walsham, then B1145 to Mundesley. From Cromer take B1159 road to Mundesley. Property situated 0.75 miles from village centre.

♥ Sun-Thu, 5 nights' B&B in double room – £125pp. 7 nights' B&B in double room – £175pp.

Room 📺 ⚭ 🍽  General ⌂ ▦ ⏏ P ✗ 🖼 ⛋ ❈  Leisure ∪ ♪ ↑ ⚞

## NAYLAND, Suffolk Map ref 3B2

★★★★
FARMHOUSE

B&B per room per night
s £45.00–£55.00
d £65.00–£75.00

### Gladwins Farm

Harpers Hill, Nayland CO6 4NU  t (01206) 262261  f (01206) 263001  e gladwinsfarm@aol.com
w gladwinsfarm.co.uk

**open** All year except Christmas and New Year
**bedrooms** 2 double
**bathrooms** All en suite
**payment** Credit/debit cards, cash/cheques, euros

Homely farmhouse B&B set in 22 acres of Suffolk's beautiful, rolling Constable Country. Marvellous views, charming heritage villages, birdwatching and NT gardens. Only 25 minutes from the sea. Heated indoor pool, sauna, hot tub, tennis court, fishing, farm animals. Plus nine charming award-winning self-catering cottages sleeping from two to eight.

⊕ Located on the A134 between Colchester and Sudbury, 800m north of Nayland village. Illuminated white gates at the end of the drive.

Room ☎ 📺 ⚭ 🍽  General ⌂8 ✗ ⛋ ❈  Leisure ⚞ ⚲ ∪ ♪ ↑

★ PETS! ★

WELCOME    WELCOME

★ PETS! ★

## Pet-friendly breaks

Want to take your cherished companion with you on holiday? Proprietors participating in our Welcome Pets! scheme go out of their way to make special provision for you and your pet. Look out for the symbol.

## NAYLAND, Suffolk Map ref 3B2

★★★★★
**RESTAURANT WITH ROOMS**
**GOLD AWARD**

B&B per room per night
s £76.00–£109.00
d £96.00–£129.00
Evening meal per person
£23.00–£42.00

# White Hart Inn

High Street, Nayland CO6 4JF  **t** (01206) 263382  **f** (01206) 263638  **e** nayhart@aol.com
**w** whitehart-nayland.co.uk

**open** All year
**bedrooms** 5 double, 1 twin
**bathrooms** All en suite
**payment** Credit/debit cards, cash/cheques, euros

The White Hart, a 15thC coaching inn, is a restaurant with rooms located in the sleepy but pretty Suffolk village of Nayland, on the border with Essex, close to the coast.

⊕ *The village of Nayland is just off the A134 Colchester to Sudbury road.*

Room **☎** TV 🖥 🍵   General 🕭 ▥ ♿ P ⅍ ♟ ✕ 🐾 ❄   Leisure ⅃

## NEWMARKET, Suffolk Map ref 3B2

★★★★
**GUEST ACCOMMODATION**

B&B per room per night
s £25.00–£35.00
d £50.00–£60.00

# Meadow House

2a High Street, Burwell, Cambridge CB25  0HB  **t** (01638) 741926  **f** (01638) 741861
**e** hilary@themeadowhouse.co.uk  **w** themeadowhouse.co.uk

**open** All year
**bedrooms** 1 double, 1 twin, 3 family, 1 suite
**bathrooms** 4 en suite
**payment** Cash/cheques, euros

Large, well-equipped, modern house set in grounds of two acres, close to Newmarket Racecourse, Cambridge and Ely. King-size beds. Family suites available, also coach house available in grounds. Large car park. Generous breakfasts. Two rooms suitable for moderately disabled people. More colour pictures available on our website.

⊕ *Leave A14 at Stow-cum-Quy. Follow B1102 via the Swaffhams to Burwell. Larger house on right as you enter village, before you get to the church.*

Room ♿ TV 🖥 🍵   General 🕭 ▥ ♿ P ⅍ ❄ 🐾

## NORFOLK BROADS

*See under Aylsham, Beccles, Brundall, Coltishall, Great Yarmouth, Hevingham, Hickling, Lowestoft, Norwich, South Walsham, Wroxham.*

## NORWICH, Norfolk Map ref 3C1

★★★★
**GUEST ACCOMMODATION**

B&B per room per night
s £35.00–£40.00
d £55.00–£60.00

# Becklands

105 Holt Road, Norwich NR10 3AB  **t** (01603) 898582  **f** (01603) 755010  **e** becklands@aol.com

Quietly located modern house overlooking open countryside five miles north of Norwich. Central for the Broads and coastal areas.

**open** All year
**bedrooms** 2 double, 2 twin, 4 single, 1 family
**bathrooms** 7 en suite, 1 private
**payment** Credit/debit cards, cash/cheques

Room ♿ TV 🖥   General 🕭 ▥ ♿ P ⅍ 🐾 ❄

## Check the maps

Colour maps at the front pinpoint all the places you will find accommodation entries in the regional sections. Pick your location and then refer to the place index at the back to find the page number.

---

**NORWICH,** Norfolk Map ref 3C1

★★★★
BED & BREAKFAST

B&B per room per night
s Max £29.50
d Max £55.00

## Cavell House

The Common, Swardeston, Norwich NR14 8DZ  t (01508) 578195  f (01508) 578195
e joljean.harris@virgin.net

Birthplace of nurse Edith Cavell. Georgian
farmhouse on edge of Swardeston village. Off
B1113 five miles south of Norwich centre. Near
university, new hospital and showground.

**open** All year except Christmas
**bedrooms** 1 double, 1 twin
**payment** Cash/cheques

Room 📺 ♿ 🍴    General 🛏 🏠 ♿ P ✗ 🖥 ❄ ⛄    Leisure ♦ ♦ 🏛

---

**NORWICH,** Norfolk Map ref 3C1

★★★★
GUEST ACCOMMODATION

B&B per room per night
s £35.00–£45.00
d £50.00–£60.00

## Church Farm Guesthouse

Church Street, Norwich NR10 3DB  t (01603) 898020  f (01603) 891649
e churchfarmguesthouse@btopenworld.com  w tiscover.co.uk

Quiet, modernised, 17thC farmhouse. Separate
entrance, lounge and dining room for guests.
Approximately four miles north of Norwich. All
rooms en suite.

**open** All year
**bedrooms** 8 double, 1 single, 1 family
**bathrooms** All en suite
**payment** Credit/debit cards, cash/cheques

Room 🛏 📺 ♿ 🍴    General 🛏 🖥 ❄

---

**NORWICH,** Norfolk Map ref 3C1

★★★
GUEST ACCOMMODATION

B&B per room per night
s £35.00–£40.00
d £40.00–£48.00

## Edmar Lodge

64 Earlham Road, Norwich NR2 3DF  t (01603) 615599  f (01603) 495599  e mail@edmarlodge.co.uk
w edmarlodge.co.uk

**open** All year
**bedrooms** 3 double, 1 twin, 1 family
**bathrooms** All en suite
**payment** Credit/debit cards, cash/cheques, euros

Edmar Lodge is a family-run guesthouse where you
will receive a warm welcome from Ray and Sue. We
are situated only ten minutes' walk from the city
centre. All rooms have en suite facilities and digital
TV. We are well known for our excellent breakfasts
that set you up for the day.

⊕ *On the B1108. Off the Norwich ring road.*

Room 🛏 📺 ♿ 🍴    General 🛏 🖥 🏠 P ✗ 🖥 ♿ ❄ ⛄

---

**NORWICH,** Norfolk Map ref 3C1

★★★★
GUEST ACCOMMODATION

B&B per room per night
s £30.00–£35.00
d £58.00–£62.00

## Manor Barn House

Back Lane, Rackheath, Norwich NR13 6NN  t (01603) 783543  e jane.roger@manorbarnhouse.co.uk
w manorbarnhouse.co.uk

Traditional Norfolk barn conversion with exposed
beams in quiet setting with pleasant gardens.
Close to the heart of the Broads, five miles from
Norwich.

**open** All year
**bedrooms** 3 double, 2 twin
**bathrooms** 4 en suite, 1 private
**payment** Cash/cheques

Room 🛏 📺 ♿    General 🛏 5 P ✗ 🖥 ❄ ⛄    Leisure ⬤ 🚲

---

**NORWICH,** Norfolk Map ref 3C1

★★★
GUEST HOUSE

B&B per room per night
s £30.00–£40.00
d £54.00–£58.00

## Marlborough House

22 Stracey Road, Norwich NR1 1EZ  t (01603) 628005  f (01603) 628005

Long-established family hotel close to city centre,
new Riverside development, Castle Mall, museum
and cathedral. All double, twin and family rooms
are en suite. Licensed bar, car park.

**open** All year except Christmas
**bedrooms** 3 double, 1 twin, 5 single, 2 family
**bathrooms** 6 en suite
**payment** Cash/cheques, euros

Room 🛏 📺 ♿    General 🛏 🖥 🏠 P ✗ 🍴 🖥

## NORWICH, Norfolk Map ref 3C1

★★★
**GUEST ACCOMMODATION**

B&B per room per night
s £25.00–£40.00
d £38.00–£60.00
Evening meal per person
Min £12.50

# Oakbrook House – South Norfolk's Guest House

Frith Way, Great Moulton, Norwich NR15 2HE  **t** (01379) 677359  **f** (01379) 677359
**e** oakbrookhouse@btinternet.com  **w** oakbrookhouse.co.uk

Between Norwich and Diss. We offer a warm welcome to all. Also available for package holidays. Explore East Anglia from a central location with your friends. Contact us for more information.

**open** All year
**bedrooms** 5 double, 2 twin, 2 family
**bathrooms** 5 en suite, 4 private
**payment** Credit/debit cards, cash/cheques, euros

Room 🛏 📺 🕯 ⚏  General 🛋 🏠 P ✗ ✕ 🍴 🎱 ✿ 🐾  Leisure ✈ ► 🏊

## RIVENHALL, Essex Map ref 3B3

★★★★
**FARMHOUSE**

B&B per room per night
s £36.00–£50.00
d £58.00–£80.00

# Granary B and B Apartments

Clarks Farm, Cranes Lane, Kelvedon CO5 9AY  **t** (01376) 570321  **f** (01376) 570321
**e** enquiries@thegranary.me.uk  **w** tiscover.co.uk

Accommodation consists of superior bridal suite plus four en suite bed and breakfast apartments. Luxuriously equipped. Situated in the heart of rural East Anglia, but a stone's throw from Colchester.

**open** All year
**bedrooms** 3 double, 2 twin
**bathrooms** All en suite
**payment** Credit/debit cards, cash/cheques, euros

Room 📺 🕯 ⚏  General 🛋 🏠 P ✗ ✿ 🐾

## ROYSTON, Hertfordshire Map ref 2D1

★★★★
**GUEST ACCOMMODATION**

B&B per room per night
s £45.00–£55.00
d £65.00–£75.00

# Hall Farm

Hall Lane, Great Chishill Nr Royston SG8 8SH  **t** (01763) 838263  **f** (01763) 838263
**e** wisehall@tiscali.co.uk  **w** hallfarmbb.co.uk

Georgian manor house in secluded garden. Ground-floor room with wheelchair access and flat-floor shower available. Quiet accommodation only 30 minutes from Cambridge or Stansted. London one hour by train.

**open** All year
**bedrooms** 1 double, 1 twin, 1 family
**bathrooms** All en suite
**payment** Credit/debit cards, cash/cheques, euros

Room 🛏 📺 🕯 ⚏  General 🛋 🏠 🏃 P ✗ 🍴 🎱 🔦 ✿  Leisure U ✈ ►

## ROYSTON, Hertfordshire Map ref 2D1

★★★★
**FARMHOUSE**

B&B per room per night
s £35.00–£45.00
d £50.00–£60.00

# New Farm

Hollow Road High Street, Chrishall, Royston SG8 8RJ  **t** (01763) 838282  **e** nfwiseman@waitrose.com
**w** dianabb.co.uk

**open** All year except Christmas and New Year
**bedrooms** 2 double, 1 family
**bathrooms** 1 en suite, 1 private
**payment** Cash/cheques

Victorian farmhouse surrounded by beautiful countryside on Essex/Cambridgeshire border between Saffron Walden and Royston (B1039). Within easy reach of Cambridge, M11 and Imperial War Museum. Rural walks.

⊕ *Set outside Chrishall New Farm. 80yds off the B1039 road running between Saffron Walden and Royston.*

Room 📺 🕯 ⚏  General 12 P ✗ 🍴 ✿  Leisure U ✈ ►

# It's all in the detail

Please remember that all information in this guide has been supplied by the proprietors well in advance of publication. Since changes do sometimes occur it's a good idea to check details at the time of booking.

## SAFFRON WALDEN, Essex Map ref 2D1

★★★★
**INN**
**SILVER AWARD**

# The Cricketers

Wicken Road, Clavering, Saffron Walden CB11 4QT  **t** (01799) 550442  **f** (01799) 550882
**e** cricketers@lineone.net  **w** thecricketers.co.uk

B&B per room per night
**s** £75.00
**d** £110.00
Evening meal per person
£18.00–£27.00

**open** All year except Christmas
**bedrooms** 11 double, 3 twin
**bathrooms** All en suite
**payment** Credit/debit cards, cash/cheques

16thC freehouse near Stansted Airport with beamed interior. Well-established restaurant and bar-meal trade with adjacent accommodation. Jamie Oliver grew up here and cooked here from the age of eight. Although he no longer cooks here, it is still owned and run by his parents, Trevor and Sally Oliver. Wireless Internet access.

⊕ M11, jct 8. A120 west and B1383 to Newport. B1038 to Clavering.

♥ 20% reduction for B&B on any Sun or Fri. Please quote 'English Tourism Council'.

Room ⬛ 🛏 ☎ 📺 🐾 🍵  General 🛎 🖼 🎨 P ⚡ 🍽 ✕ 🎰 🔥 ✿  Leisure ♪

## ST ALBANS, Hertfordshire Map ref 2D1

★★★
**BED & BREAKFAST**

# Tresco

76 Clarence Road, St Albans AL1 4NG  **t** (01727) 864880  **e** pat_leggatt@hotmail.com
**w** geocities.com/patleggatt/index.htm

B&B per room per night
**s** £30.00–£36.00
**d** £50.00–£58.00

Spacious Edwardian house with quiet, comfortable rooms and pleasant conservatory. Park nearby. Easy walk to station for fast trains to London (20 minutes).

**open** All year
**bedrooms** 1 twin, 1 single
**payment** Cash/cheques

Room 📺 🐾 🍵  General P ⚡ 🎰 🖥 ✿ 🐕

## ST NEOTS, Cambridgeshire Map ref 2D1

★★★
**GUEST ACCOMMODATION**

# Nags Head

2 Berkley Street, Eynesbury, St Neots PE19 2NA  **t** (01480) 476812  **e** nags.stneots@btconnect.com
**w** stneots.co.uk/nagshead/main.htm

B&B per room per night
**s** £45.00–£48.00
**d** £58.00–£62.00

Former village inn set in quiet location. Friendly family atmosphere. Nearest pubs two minutes, St Neots town centre five minutes. All rooms en suite, guest lounge, Sky TV, Wi-Fi broadband, off-road parking.

**open** All year except Christmas
**bedrooms** 3 double, 2 twin, 1 single, 2 family
**bathrooms** All en suite
**payment** Credit/debit cards, cash/cheques, euros

Room ⬛ 📺 🐾 🍵  General 🛎 🖼 🎨 P ⚡ 🍽 🔥 ✿ 🐕  Leisure U ♪ ▶ 🚲 🏛

## SANDY, Bedfordshire Map ref 2D1

★★★★
**BED & BREAKFAST**

# Pantiles

6 Swaden, Sandy SG19 2DA  **t** (01767) 680668  **e** pantilesbandb@onetel.com
**w** thepantilesbandb.co.uk

B&B per room per night
**s** £35.00–£40.00
**d** Min £60.00

**open** All year except Christmas and New Year
**bedrooms** 2 double, 1 twin
**bathrooms** All en suite
**payment** Credit/debit cards, cash/cheques

The Pantiles is a converted onion loft in a lovely wooded valley, overlooking large gardens with potager and fruit trees. A warm welcome is assured and we offer home-made jam and cakes. Easy access to A1, mainline railway and local services and attractions. French and some Spanish spoken.

⊕ From A1, drive through Sandy on B1042 direction Potton. After railway bridge take left turn to Everton. We are approximately 300 yds on the left.

Room ⬛ 📺 🐾 🍵  General 🎨 P ⚡ ✿ 🐕  Leisure ▶ 🏛

## SANDY, Bedfordshire Map ref 2D1

★★★★
**BED & BREAKFAST**

B&B per room per night
s £30.00
d £50.00–£60.00

# The Tythe Barn

Drove Road, Gamlingay, Sandy SG19 2HT  t (01767) 650156  f (01767) 650156
e thetythebarn@supanet.com  w tythebb.co.uk

A sympathetically converted listed barn, surrounded by our own paddocks. Rooms are en suite and comfortably furnished. Situated on Bedfordshire/Cambridgeshire border.

**open** All year except Christmas and New Year
**bedrooms** 1 double, 1 twin, 1 single
**bathrooms** All en suite
**payment** Cash/cheques

Room 📺 ✆ 🕯  General 🖥 ⊞ ♨ P ⚡ ✳  Leisure ▶ 🕱

## SHERINGHAM, Norfolk Map ref 3B1

★★★★
**GUEST HOUSE**

B&B per room per night
s £26.00–£28.00
d £52.00–£56.00

# Sheringham Lodge

Cromer Road, Sheringham NR26 8RS  t (01263) 821954  e mikewalker19@hotmail.com
w sheringhamlodge.co.uk

Edwardian detached house. Centrally located. Convenient for beach and town. Off-road parking. Non-smoking. No pets. No children under five years.

**open** All year except Christmas and New Year
**bedrooms** 3 double, 1 twin, 1 single
**bathrooms** 4 en suite, 1 private
**payment** Cash/cheques

Room 📺 ✆  General 🖥 5 P ⚡ 🏠 ✳  Leisure ▶ 🚲 🕱

## SHINGLE STREET, Suffolk Map ref 3C2

Rating Applied For
**BED & BREAKFAST**

B&B per room per night
d Min £50.00
Evening meal per person
£10.50–£12.50

# Lark Cottage

Shingle Street, Nr Woodbridge IP12 3BE  t (01394) 411292

Beachside bungalow, very quiet location. Interesting sea/land birds, plants of special interest. Sutton Hoo four miles, Snape Maltings 14 miles. One double with private shower/wc and lounge with TV.

**open** All year except Christmas and New Year
**bedrooms** 1 double
**bathrooms** 1 private
**payment** Cash/cheques

Room 🛏 ✆ 🕯  General P ⚡ ✕ 🏠 ✳  Leisure ∪ ♪ 🕱

## SIBTON, Suffolk Map ref 3C2

★★★★
**INN**

B&B per room per night
s £50.00–£60.00
d £75.00–£85.00
Evening meal per person
£20.00–£30.00

# Sibton White Horse Inn

Halesworth Road, Sibton, Saxmundham IP17 2JJ  t (01728) 660337  f (01728) 660337
e info@sibtonwhitehorseinn.co.uk  w sibtonwhitehorseinn.co.uk

**open** All year
**bedrooms** 3 double, 1 twin, 2 single, 1 family
**bathrooms** All en suite
**payment** Credit/debit cards, cash/cheques

You probably couldn't find a more quintessential country inn. Grade II Listed, wonderful features and timber frame dating back to 1580. Quiet village 15 minutes from coast. Peaceful attractive en suite bedrooms in separate building within spacious gardens. Good food, all freshly prepared, enchanting dining areas. Special in both summer and winter.

⊕ A12 at Yoxford, turn onto A1120, proceed for 3 miles until reaching Peasenhall. Turn right into Pouy Street opposite Creaseys butchers. White Horse 600m ahead.

♥ Discounts on 4 or more nights. Special winter deals often available. Telephone or see website for further details.

Room 🛏 📺 ✆ 🕯  General 🖥 ⊞ ♨ P ⚡ ✕ 🍴 🗝 ✳  Leisure ♪ 🚲 🕱

## Out and about

For ideas on places to visit, see the beginning of this regional section or go online at enjoyengland.com.

## SOUTH WALSHAM, Norfolk Map ref 3C1

★★★★
**GUEST ACCOMMODATION**

B&B per room per night
s Min £35.00
d £50.00–£55.00

### Old Hall Farm

Newport Road, South Walsham, Norwich NR13 6DS  t (01603) 270271  f (01603) 270017
e veronica@oldhallfarm.co.uk  w oldhallfarm.co.uk

**bedrooms** 2 double, 1 twin
**bathrooms** All en suite
**payment** Cash/cheques

17thC thatched farmhouse with large garden on the edge of Broadland village. Within walking distance of Fairhaven Gardens, Ranworth and St Lawrence Arts Centre, South Walsham. Wide range of cooked breakfasts using our own free-range eggs. Business guests welcome. Wireless broadband available. Non-smoking. Open April to October.

⊕ *Two miles from A47, turning signposted South Walsham. Turn right and then immediately right again.*

Room 📺 ♿ 🍴  General ⌚ 🏠 🔥 P ⚡ 🍳 🛏 💺 ❄  Leisure 🚴 🛶

## SOUTHWOLD, Suffolk Map ref 3C2

★★★★
**BED & BREAKFAST**

B&B per room per night
d £70.00–£90.00

### Avocet House

1 Strickland Place, Southwold IP18 6HN  t (01502) 724720  e barnett@beeb.net
w southwold.ws/avocet-house

A large Edwardian house overlooking common golf course with sea views. Large rooms, en suite or with own bathroom and shower. Family room available, en suite.

**open** All year
**bedrooms** 2 double, 1 family
**bathrooms** 2 en suite
**payment** Cash/cheques, euros

Room ♿ 📺 ♿ 🍴  General ⌚5 🏠 🔥 P ⚡ 🍳 ❄  Leisure 🚣 🏇 🚴 🛶

## SOUTHWOLD, Suffolk Map ref 3C2

★★★★
**GUEST HOUSE**

B&B per room per night
d £80.00–£100.00

### Northcliffe Guesthouse

20 North Parade, Southwold IP18 6LT  t (01502) 724074  e northcliffe.southwold@virgin.net
w northcliffe-southwold.co.uk

Select, en suite accommodation. Individually designed rooms of a high standard. Panoramic sea views. In quiet location next to beach, close to town centre.

**open** All year
**bedrooms** 5 double, 1 twin
**bathrooms** All en suite
**payment** Cash/cheques

Room 📺 ♿ 🍴  General ⚡ ❄  Leisure ♨ 🚣 🏇 🚴

## SOUTHWOLD, Suffolk Map ref 3C2

★★★★
**BED & BREAKFAST**

B&B per room per night
s £38.00–£55.00
d Min £75.00

### Poplar Hall

Frostenden Corner, Frostenden, Southwold NR34 7JA  t (01502) 578549  e poplarhall@tiscali.co.uk
w southwold.ws/poplar-hall

**open** All year except Christmas
**bedrooms** 1 double, 1 single, 1 suite
**bathrooms** 1 en suite, 2 private
**payment** Cash/cheques

Peaceful and quiet, yet only minutes from the lovely seaside town of Southwold, Poplar Hall is a 16thC thatched house in a 1.5-acre garden. Luxury accommodation with TV, tea/coffee facilities and vanity units in all rooms. Enjoy our famed breakfasts of fresh fruit, local fish, sausage, bacon and home-made preserves.

⊕ *A12 past Wangford, Plough Inn on left. Right at Frostenden sign. Left fork. We are just past the green. From north: 3rd left after Wrentham, then as above.*

Room 🚪 📺 ♿ 🍴  General ⌚9 P ⚡ 🍳 ❄  Leisure 🚣 🚴 🛶

**STANSTED,** Essex Map ref 2D1

★★★★
GUEST ACCOMMODATION
SILVER AWARD

# The Cottage

71 Birchanger Lane, Birchanger, Bishop's Stortford CM23 5QA  **t** (01279) 812349  **f** (01279) 815045
**e** bookings@thecottagebirchanger.co.uk  **w** thecottagebirchanger.co.uk

B&B per room per night
**s** £50.00–£60.00
**d** £70.00–£80.00

**open** All year except Christmas and New Year
**bedrooms** 7 double, 5 twin, 2 single
**bathrooms** 13 en suite, 1 private
**payment** Credit/debit cards, cash/cheques

17thC Listed house with panelled rooms and woodburning stove. Conservatory-style breakfast room overlooks mature garden. Quiet, peaceful village setting yet near M11 junction 8, Stansted Airport and Bishop's Stortford. Ample off-road parking. Guest rooms furnished in traditional cottage style, with colour TV, tea/coffee facilities and free Wi-Fi Internet. Award-winning pub in village.

⊕ *From M11 jct 8 take A120 signed to Hertford. After 1 mile turn right onto B1383 signed to Newport. Take next right into Birchanger Lane.*

Room   General   Leisure

**STANSTED,** Essex Map ref 2D1

★★★★
GUEST ACCOMMODATION

B&B per room per night
**s** Max £60.00
**d** Max £65.00

# White House

Smiths Green, Takeley CM22 6NR  **t** (01279) 870257  **f** (01279) 870423
**e** enquiries@whitehousestansted.co.uk  **w** whitehousestansted.co.uk

**open** All year except Christmas and New Year
**bedrooms** 1 double, 1 twin, 1 family
**bathrooms** 2 en suite, 1 private
**payment** Credit/debit cards, cash/cheques, euros

A 15thC manor house set in one acre with ample parking. Two miles from Stansted Airport (but not on flight path). Recently renovated. Modern, en suite facilities in a traditional family environment. Evening meal available at nearby Lion and Lamb pub/restaurant, which is also owned by Mike and Linda.

⊕ *Exit M11 jct 8. On roundabout take B1256 Takeley. The White House is 400yds past the traffic lights on the left, opposite the carpet shop.*

Room   General   Leisure

**STOKE-BY-NAYLAND,** Suffolk Map ref 3B2

★★★★
INN

B&B per room per night
**s** £65.00–£85.00
**d** £65.00–£95.00
Evening meal per person
£8.00–£25.00

# The Angel Inn

Polstead Street, Stoke by Nayland, Colchester CO6 4SA  **t** (01206) 263245  **e** info@theangelinn.net
**w** theangelinn.net

A 16thC inn situated in one of Constable's favourite villages. Offering quality food and a busy ambience. Five miles from the A12 and two miles from the A134.

**open** All year
**bedrooms** 5 double, 1 twin
**bathrooms** All en suite
**payment** Credit/debit cards, cash/cheques

Room   General   Leisure

# enjoyEngland.com

Big city buzz or peaceful panoramas? Take a fresh look at England and you may be surprised at what's right on your doorstep. Explore the diversity online at enjoyengland.com

## STOWMARKET, Suffolk Map ref 3B2

★★★★★
**GUEST ACCOMMODATION**
**GOLD AWARD**

B&B per room per night
**s** Min £50.00
**d** Min £60.00

# Bays Farm

Forward Green, Stowmarket IP14 5HU  **t** (01449) 711286  **e** info@baysfarmsuffolk.co.uk
**w** baysfarmsuffolk.co.uk

**open** All year
**bedrooms** 3 double
**bathrooms** All en suite
**payment** Credit/debit cards, cash/cheques, euros

A 17thC beamed farmhouse in the heart of the Suffolk countryside stands ready to welcome you. Four acres of formal garden and grassland with a wealth of wildlife, including bats, owls and bird life.

Room 📺 ♿ 🍴    General P ⚡ 🛏 ✿ 🐾    Leisure 🏛

## SUDBURY, Suffolk Map ref 3B2

★★★
**GUEST ACCOMMODATION**

B&B per room per night
**s** £44.00–£60.00
**d** £60.00–£95.00
Evening meal per person
£4.00–£15.00

# Hill Lodge

8 Newton Road, Sudbury CO10 2RL  **t** (01787) 377568  **f** (01787) 373636
**e** enquiries@hilllodgehotel.co.uk  **w** hilllodgehotel.co.uk

Hill Lodge Hotel extends a warm welcome and offers a comfortable stay.

**open** All year
**bedrooms** 7 double, 4 twin, 1 single, 2 family
**bathrooms** All en suite
**payment** Credit/debit cards, cash/cheques

Room ⚿ 📞 📺 ♿ 🍴    General 🕰 🎱 ⓖ P ⚡ 🔌 🖥 ✿    Leisure 🏛

## SUDBURY, Suffolk Map ref 3B2

★★★
**BED & BREAKFAST**

B&B per room per night
**s** Min £35.00
**d** Min £45.00

# Hillview Studio

58 Clarence Road, Sudbury CO10 1NJ  **t** (01787) 374221 & 07779 854199  **e** sooteapot@hotmail.com

Friendly, modern, self-contained, en suite room with own access. Five minutes' walk to town centre and water meadows.

**open** All year
**bedrooms** 1 twin
**bathrooms** En suite
**payment** Cash/cheques

Room ⚿ 📺 ♿ 🍴    General P ⚡ 🖥 ✿    Leisure U ♪ 🏛

## TAKELEY, Essex Map ref 2D1

★★
**BED & BREAKFAST**

B&B per room per night
**s** £25.00
**d** £50.00

# Crossroads B and B

2 Hawthorn Close, Takeley CM22 6SD  **t** (01279) 870619  **e** ajcaiger884@aol.com  **w** tiscover.co.uk

Two-bedroom bed and breakfast situated two kilometres from Stansted Airport. Early continental breakfast. All rooms have hairdryer, TV, radio, tea-/coffee-making facilities and internet use.

**open** All year except Christmas and New Year
**bedrooms** 1 double, 1 single
**bathrooms** 1 en suite, 1 private
**payment** Cash/cheques

Room 📺 ♿ 🍴    General 🕰 🎱 ⓖ P ⚡ 🛏 ⓕ ✿

# A holiday on two wheels

For a fabulous freewheeling break, seek out accommodation participating in our Cyclists Welcome scheme. Look out for the symbol and plan your route online at nationalcyclenetwork.org.

## THOMPSON, Norfolk Map ref 3B1

★★★★
**INN**

B&B per room per night
s £40.00
d £60.00
Evening meal per person
£6.00–£25.00

# Chequers Inn

Griston Road, Thompson IP24 1PX  **t** (01953) 483360  **f** (01953) 488092
**e** richard@chequers-inn.wanadoo.co.uk  **w** thompson-chequers.co.uk

**open** All year
**bedrooms** 2 double, 1 twin
**bathrooms** All en suite
**payment** Credit/debit cards, cash/cheques

The Chequers is a 16thC village inn with a thatched roof, still retaining all of its original character. A true country retreat, in the heart of Breckland. Local produce and fresh fish a speciality. Local real ales include Breckland Gold, Wolf, Wherry, Adnams and Greene King IPA to name a few.

⊕ *Twelve miles north east of Thetford, just off the A1075.*

Room 🛏 📞 📺 🕹 🍵  General 🛋 🅿 ⚡ 🍽 ✕ 🗺 ⚷ ☼ 🐕  Leisure ∪ ⚓ ►

## THORNHAM MAGNA, Suffolk Map ref 3B2

★★★★★
**GUEST ACCOMMODATION**
**SILVER AWARD**

B&B per room per night
s £65.00–£95.00
d £100.00
Evening meal per person
£17.50–£25.00

# Thornham Hall and Restaurant

Thornham Hall, Thornham Magna, Eye IP23 8HA  **t** (01379) 783314  **f** (01379) 788347
**e** hallrestaurant@aol.com  **w** thornhamhallandrestaurant.com

**open** All year
**bedrooms** 2 double, 1 suite
**bathrooms** All en suite
**payment** Credit/debit cards, cash

Thornham Hall & Restaurant offer exclusive accommodation in the hall and delightful dining in the restaurant in the converted coach house. Thornham Hall is situated in its own private park at the centre of the Thornham estate, the baronial home of the Henniker family since 1750.

⊕ *From Stoke Ash on A140 turn left towards Thornham Magna. After 300yds turn right and go through village past road to Gislingham and past church. Turn in at drive marked Thornham Hall.*

Room 🖼 🕹 🍵  General 🛋 🅿 ⚡ ✕ 🗄 ⚷ ☼ 🐕  Leisure ♦ ⚲ ∪ ► 🏠

## TOPPESFIELD, Essex Map ref 3B2

★★★
**BED & BREAKFAST**

B&B per room per night
d £44.00–£50.00
Evening meal per person
Max £12.00

# Harrow Hill Cottage

Harrow Hill, Toppesfield CO9 4LX  **t** (01787) 237425  **w** tiscover.co.uk

A 17thC cottage in a quiet location, set in one-acre gardens with outdoor swimming pool, surrounded by pleasant views and farmland.

**open** All year except Christmas
**bedrooms** 1 double, 1 family
**bathrooms** 1 en suite
**payment** Cash/cheques

Room 📺 🕹 🍵  General 🛋 10 🅿 ⚡ ✕ 🗄 ☼  Leisure ⚲ ∪

## WELLS-NEXT-THE-SEA, Norfolk Map ref 3B1

★★★★
**GUEST HOUSE**

B&B per room per night
s £37.50
d £75.00

# The Cobblers

Standard Road, Wells-next-the-Sea NR23 1JU  **t** (01328) 710155  **e** info@cobblers.co.uk
**w** cobblers.co.uk

The Cobblers is situated in the centre of town, close to the harbour and restaurants, in Wells-next-the-Sea. An ideal base for exploring north Norfolk. Pets by arrangement.

**open** All year except Christmas and New Year
**bedrooms** 4 double, 1 twin, 3 single
**bathrooms** 7 en suite, 1 private
**payment** Credit/debit cards, cash/cheques

Room 🛏 📺 🕹  General 🛋 🅿 ⚡ 🗄 ⚷ ☼ 🐕

## WESTLETON, Suffolk Map ref 3C2

**★★★★**
BED & BREAKFAST

B&B per room per night
s £40.00–£42.00
d £56.00–£60.00

### Pond House

The Hill, Westleton IP17 3AN  **t** (01728) 648773  **w** tiscover.co.uk

Seventeenth-century beamed cottage by village green and duck pond. Just two miles from Minsmere and three miles from Dunwich. Off-season single occupancy available from November to March only.

**open** All year except Christmas
**bedrooms** 2 twin
**bathrooms** 1 en suite, 1 private
**payment** Cash/cheques

Room 🛏 ♨  General P ⚡ ♨ ♨ ✿  Leisure ♿ ⌂

## WINGFIELD, Suffolk Map ref 3B2

**★★★★**
BED & BREAKFAST
SILVER AWARD

B&B per room per night
s £38.00–£42.00
d £58.00–£62.00

### Gables Farm

Earsham Street, Wingfield, Diss IP21 5RH  **t** (01379) 586355 & 07824 445464
**e** enquiries@gablesfarm.co.uk  **w** gablesfarm.co.uk

**open** All year except Christmas and New Year
**bedrooms** 2 double, 1 twin
**bathrooms** All en suite
**payment** Cash/cheques

A 16thC timbered farmhouse in moated gardens. Wingfield is a quiet village in the centre of East Anglia, central to everywhere and in the middle of nowhere!

⊕ *See website for details of how to find us.*

Room 📺 ♨ ♨  General ⚭ ▥ ♨ P ⚡ ♨ ♨ ✿ ➤  Leisure ∪

## WIX, Essex Map ref 3B2

**★★★★**
BED & BREAKFAST
SILVER AWARD

B&B per room per night
s Min £38.00
d Min £55.00

### Periwinkle Cottage

Colchester Road, Wix, Nr Harwich CO11 2PD  **t** (01255) 870167  **w** tiscover.co.uk

**open** All year except Christmas and New Year
**bedrooms** 1 double, 1 twin, 1 family
**bathrooms** All en suite
**payment** Cash/cheques, euros

Periwinkle Cottage is set in a semi-rural position, close to the busy passenger port of Harwich, Constable Country and Clacton-on-Sea. Direct access to UK trunk road network, approximately one hour from London. All rooms well furnished, TV/DVD, teasmade, ironing facility, toiletries.

⊕ *Follow A120 London from Harwich. Approx 7 miles turn left signposted Wix, follow through village approx 3 miles. Periwinkle Cottage on right just before rejoining A120.*

Room ♨ 📺 ♨ ♨  General ⚭ 5 P ⚡ ♨ ♨ ♨ ● ✿  Leisure ♪ ⍨ ⌂

## WOODBRIDGE, Suffolk Map ref 3C2

**♦♦♦**
GUEST ACCOMMODATION

B&B per room per night
s Min £40.00
d Min £70.00

### Pettistree House

Main Road, Pettistree, Woodbridge IP13 0HL  **t** (01728) 748008  **f** (01728) 748007
**e** henrikay@aol.com  **w** pettistreereceptions-marquees.co.uk

A large country house built in 1740, set in parkland. Log fires to welcome you and a terrace on which to relax and view the old oaks and grazing horses. Peaceful setting, yet just off A12.

**open** All year except Christmas and New Year
**bedrooms** 2 double
**bathrooms** 1 en suite, 1 private
**payment** Cash/cheques

Room 📺 ♨ ♨  General P ⚡ ♨ ♨ ✿  Leisure ∪ ♪ ⍨ ⌂

## WOODHURST, Cambridgeshire Map ref 3A2

★★★
GUEST ACCOMMODATION

B&B per room per night
s £40.00
d £40.00–£60.00

### The Raptor Foundation

The Heath, St Ives Road, Huntingdon PE28 3BT  t (01487) 741140  f (01487) 841140
e heleowl@aol.com  w raptorfoundation.org.uk

Bed and breakfast within the grounds of a bird of prey centre which is open to the public.

open All year
bedrooms 5 double, 1 twin, 1 family
bathrooms 6 en suite, 1 private
payment Credit/debit cards, cash/cheques

Room 🛏 ☎ TV 🖕  General 🛏 🏧 🌂 P ⚒ ✕ ◉ ✿

## WOOLPIT, Suffolk Map ref 3B2

★★★
INN

B&B per room per night
s £40.00–£45.00
d £75.00–£80.00
Evening meal per person
£4.75–£20.00

### Bull Inn and Restaurant

The Street, Woolpit, Bury St Edmunds IP30 9SA  t (01359) 240393  f (01359) 240393
e info@bullinnwoolpit.co.uk  w bullinnwoolpit.co.uk

Public house and restaurant offering good accommodation in centre of pretty village. Large garden, ample parking. Ideal base for touring Suffolk.

open All year
bedrooms 4 double, 1 twin, 2 single, 1 family
bathrooms All en suite
payment Credit/debit cards, cash/cheques

Room 🛏 TV 🖕  General 🌂2 🏧 P ⚍ 🍴 🕮 ✿  Leisure ♣ ∪ ♪

## WORTHAM, Suffolk Map ref 3B2

★★★★
FARMHOUSE
SILVER AWARD

B&B per room per night
s £30.00–£35.00
d £50.00–£70.00

### Rookery Farm

Old Bury Road, Wortham, Diss IP22 1RB  t (01379) 783236  f (01379) 783236
e russell.ling@ukgateway.net  w tiscover.co.uk

A warm welcome awaits at this comfortable Georgian farmhouse with its spacious tastefully decorated fully en suite rooms. Enjoy a traditional farmhouse breakfast made, wherever possible, from fresh local produce.

open All year except Christmas and New Year
bedrooms 2 double, 1 twin
bathrooms All en suite
payment Cash/cheques

Room 📠 TV 🖕 ☜  General 🌂 🏧 P ⚒ 🕮 ✿  Leisure 🎣

## WRENTHAM, Suffolk Map ref 3C2

★★★
INN

B&B per room per night
s £60.00–£70.00
d £80.00–£90.00

### Five Bells

Southwold Road, Wrentham NR34 7JF  t (01502) 675249  f (01502) 676127  e victoriapub@aol.com
w five-bells.com

Traditional country inn set in a rural location. Close to Southwold.

open All year except Christmas
bedrooms 1 double, 3 twin, 1 family
bathrooms All en suite
payment Credit/debit cards, cash/cheques

Room 🛏 TV 🖕 ☜  General 🌂 P ⚍ ✕ ✿  Leisure 🚲

## WROXHAM, Norfolk Map ref 3C1

★★★★
BED & BREAKFAST

B&B per room per night
s £32.00–£40.00
d £50.00–£58.00

### Wroxham Park Lodge

142 Norwich Road, Wroxham, Norwich NR12 8SA  t (01603) 782991
e parklodge@computer-assist.net  w wroxhamparklodge.com

Warm welcome in comfortable Victorian house. Tastefully furnished en suite rooms all with TV and tea/coffee tray. Hearty breakfast menu, large garden, patio and car park. Situated in Norfolk Broads.

open All year
bedrooms 2 double, 1 twin
bathrooms All en suite
payment Cash/cheques

Room TV 🖕 ☜  General P ⚒ ✿  Leisure ♪ ▶ 🚲 🎣

## Rest assured

All accommodation in this guide has been rated, or is awaiting assessment, by a professional assessor.

# London

# A city of secrets and surprises

So you think you know London? Take a closer look and you'll discover a treasure house of secret attractions just crying out to be explored. Just remember to leave yourself with enough time (a year should do).

Visit London
visitlondon.com
0870 156 6366

The Globe Theatre, Bankside    Hampton Court

South Bank

Marvel (and cringe) at how operations were performed in The Old Operating Theatre Museum in Southwark. This fascinating theatre along with its Herb Garret were built in the roof space of the English Baroque Church of St Thomas's. Get even more surreal and visit Dali Universe on the South Bank, where you can enter the psyche of the genius artist and see mind-bending furniture, film sets and original Dali sculptures. But if there's only one thing you see, make it the Tutankhamun and the Golden Age of the Pharaohs exhibition at The O2 (formerly the Dome). This is the first time in almost 30 years that artefacts of the boy-king's burial chamber have left their home in Egypt. See the fabulous golden canopic cofinette and get a glimpse of the golden age of the Pharaohs.

One of the joys of London is the shopping. From the 83 colourful street markets such as Brick Lane to the most exclusive designer stores on Bond Street, there's retail therapy enough to keep anyone sane. Check out the Mall Antiques Arcade in Islington. Set in a former tram station and packed with over 35 specialist dealers, it's a magnet for interior designers.

And did you know there's a viewing area inside Wellington Arch in Hyde Park Corner where you can see into the gardens of Buckingham Palace? Or that Britain's first botanical garden was at the enigmatic Chelsea Physic Garden? Or that at Firepower – the Royal Artillery Museum in Woolwich – you can trace the story of the Royal Arsenal from Henry VIII and the battle of Crecy to peacekeeping mission in Bosnia?

Another fascinating trip out is to HMS Belfast, the historic World War II battleship that's now a floating naval museum. Explore all nine decks from the Captain's Bridge to the boiler room.

# Destinations

## Greenwich

Stand with one foot in the East and one foot in the West astride the Greenwich Meridian, and set your watch by the red 'Time Ball' that drops each day at 1300hrs precisely and has done so for 170 years. There's a laid-back feel to Greenwich. Take time to browse the market stalls – crafts, antiques, records, bric-a-brac and, most famously, vintage clothing. Then pop into a riverside pub for lunch and some mellow jazz.

## Kew

Stroll the finest botanic gardens in the country – 400 acres and 40,000 plant varieties. The Palm House hosts a tropical jungle of plants including bananas, pawpaws and mangoes. Marvel at the giant Amazonian water lily, aloe vera and several carnivorous plants in the Princess of Wales Conservatory where ten climatic zones are recreated. You'll find activities for children and a full calendar of special events.

## Notting Hill

A colourful district filled with clubs, bars and dance venues, and now trendier than ever. Wander the celebrated Portobello Road market where over 1,500 traders compete for your custom at the Saturday antiques market. Find jewellery, silverware, paintings and more. Summertime is carnival time and the Caribbean influence has ensured the phenomenal growth of the world-famous, multi-cultural Notting Hill Carnival. Join the throng of millions – exotic costume recommended. On a quieter day, visit beautiful Holland Park, a haven of greenery with its own theatre.

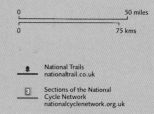

| 0 | | 50 miles |
| 0 | | 75 kms |

National Trails
nationaltrail.co.uk

Sections of the National
Cycle Network
nationalcyclenetwork.org.uk

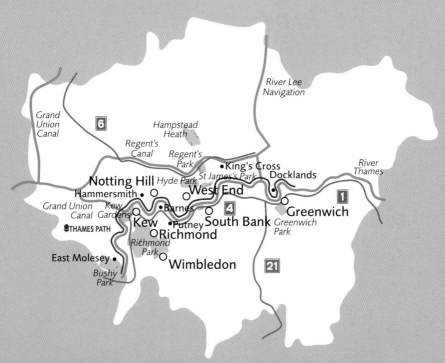

Notting Hill Carnival

Greenwich Park

West End

Tate Modern, South Bank

Wimbledon

Richmond Park

Palm House, Kew

## Richmond

The River Thames runs through the heart of the beautiful borough of Richmond. Arrive by summer riverboat from Westminster Pier and explore the delightful village with its riverside pubs, specialist boutiques, galleries and museums. Glimpse herds of deer in the Royal parks and step into history in Henry VIII's magnificent Hampton Court Palace, the oldest Tudor palace in England. Round off your visit with a world-class rugby match at England's Twickenham Stadium.

## South Bank

One of London's coolest quarters, the South Bank positively teems with must-see attractions and cultural highlights. Tate Modern has gained a reputation as one of the greatest modern art galleries in the world boasting works by Moore, Picasso, Dali, Warhol and Hepworth. Take in a play at the National Theatre or Shakespeare's magnificently restored Globe, and hit the heights on British Airways London Eye, the world's highest observation wheel.

## West End

Shop in the best department stores and international designer boutiques in Oxford Street, Regent Street and Bond Street. Take lunch in a stylish eatery, and then see a major exhibition at the Royal Academy of Arts. At the heart of the West End are the landmarks of Trafalgar Square and Piccadilly Circus, and just a few minutes' stroll will take you into legendary Soho, the entertainment heart of the city, crammed with bars, pubs, clubs and restaurants.

## Wimbledon

Wimbledon village is only ten miles from the centre of London but you could be in the heart of the countryside. Enjoy the open spaces of Wimbledon Common then wander along the charming high street with its unique medieval buildings, boutiques and pavement cafes. Visit the legendary All England Club where the Lawn Tennis Museum is a must-see for fans of the sport, not to mention the chance to tour the legendary Centre Court.

# Places to visit

**BBC Television
Centre Tours**
Shepherd's Bush, W12
0870 603 0304
bbc.co.uk/tours
*Behind the scenes of world-
famous television studios*

**Ben Uri Art Gallery,
London Jewish
Museum of Art**
St John's Wood, NW8
(020) 7604 3991
benuri.org.uk
*Europe's only dedicated Jewish
museum of art*

**British Airways
London Eye**
South Bank, SE1
0870 990 8883
ba-londoneye.com
*The world's largest observation
wheel*

**British Museum**
WC1
(020) 7323 8299
thebritishmuseum.ac.uk
*One of the great museums of the
world*

**Buckingham Palace**
SW1
(020) 7766 7300
royalcollection.org.uk
*HM The Queen's official London
residence*

**Churchill Museum and
Cabinet War Rooms**
SW1
(020) 7930 6961
iwm.org.uk/cabinet
*Churchill's wartime headquarters*

**Hampton Court Palace**
East Molesey, KT8
0870 752 7777
hrp.org.uk
*Outstanding Tudor palace with
famous maze*

**HMS Belfast**
Southwark, SE1
(020) 7940 6300
iwm.org.uk
*World War II cruiser, now a naval
time capsule*

**Imperial War Museum**
Lambeth, SE1
(020) 7416 5320
iwm.org.uk
*History of Britain at war since 1914*

**Kensington Palace
State Apartments**
W8
0870 751 5170
hrp.org.uk
*Home to the Royal Ceremonial
Dress Collection*

**Kew Gardens
(Royal Botanic Gardens)**
Richmond, TW9
(020) 8332 5655
kew.org
*Stunning plant collections and
magnificent glasshouses*

**London Aquarium**
South Bank, SE1
(020) 7967 8000
londonaquarium.co.uk
*Come face-to-face with two-metre
long sharks*

**The London Dungeon**
Southwark, SE1
(020) 7403 7221
thedungeons.com
*So much fun it's frightening!*

**London Wetland Centre**
Barnes, SW16
(020) 8409 4400
wwt.org.uk
*Observe wildlife in recreated
wetland habitats*

**Madame Tussauds and the
London Planetarium**
Marylebone, NW1
0870 999 0046
madame-tussauds.com
*Meet the stars then enter the
Chamber of Horrors*

**National Gallery**
Trafalgar Square, WC2
(020) 7747 2885
nationalgallery.org.uk
*One of the great collections of
European art*

**National Maritime
Museum**
Outstanding
Customer Service
– Silver Winner
Greenwich, SE10
(020) 8858 4422
nmm.ac.uk
*Over 2 million exhibits of
seafaring history*

**Natural History Museum**
Kensington, SW7
(020) 7942 5000
nhm.ac.uk
*World-class collections bringing
the natural world to life*

**Royal Observatory Greenwich**
SE10
(020) 8858 4422
nmm.ac.uk
*Explore the history of time and
astronomy*

**Science Museum**
Kensington, SW7
0870 870 4868
sciencemuseum.org.uk
*State-of-the-art simulators, IMAX
cinema and more*

# Diary dates 2008

**Shakespeare's Globe Exhibition and Tour**
Bankside, SE1
(020) 7902 1400
shakespeares-globe.org
*A fascinating introduction to Shakespeare's London*

**Somerset House**
Strand, WC2
(020) 7845 4600
somerset-house.org.uk
*Magnificent art collections in grand 18th century house*

**Tate Britain**
Millbank, SW1
(020) 7887 8888
tate.org.uk
*The greatest single collection of British art*

**Tate Modern**
Bankside, SE1
(020) 7887 8008
tate.org.uk
*Britain's flagship museum of modern art*

**Tower Bridge Exhibition**
SE1
(020) 7403 3761
towerbridge.org.uk
*Learn all about the world's most famous bridge*

**Tower of London**
EC3
0870 756 6060
hrp.org.uk
*The Crown Jewels and 900 years of history*

**Victoria and Albert Museum**
Kensington, SW7
(020) 7942 2000
vam.ac.uk
*3,000 years of art and design*

**ZSL London Zoo**
Regent's Park, NW1
(020) 7722 3333
londonzoo.co.uk
*The hairiest and scariest animals on the planet*

**London Boat Show**
ExCeL London, E16
londonboatshow.com
11 – 20 Jan

**Oxford and Cambridge Boat Race**
River Thames from Putney, SW15 to Mortlake, SW14
theboatrace.org
29 Mar

**Chelsea Flower Show**
rhs.org.uk
20 – 24 May*

**Trooping the Colour**
Horseguards Parade, SW1
royal.gov.uk
14 Jun

**Wimbledon Lawn Tennis Championships**
wimbledon.org
23 Jun – 6 Jul

**The Proms**
Royal Albert Hall, SW7
bbc.co.uk/proms
18 Jul – 13 Sep

**Notting Hill Carnival**
Streets around Ladbroke Grove, W10 and W11
visitlondon.com
24 – 25 Aug

**The Mayor's Thames Festival**
Westminster Bridge, SW1 to Tower Bridge, SE1,
thamesfestival.org
13 – 14 Sep

**Lord Mayor's Show**
From the Guildhall, EC2 to the Royal Courts of Justice, WC2 and back
lordmayorsshow.org
8 Nov

* provisional date at time of going to press

# Tourist Information Centres

When you arrive at your destination, visit an Official Partner Tourist Information Centre for quality assured help with accommodation and information about local attractions and events, or email your request before you go. To search for attractions and Tourist Information Centres on the move just text INFO to 62233, and a web link will be sent to your mobile phone.

| | | | |
|---|---|---|---|
| **Britain & London Visitor Centre** | 1 Regent Street | 0870 156636 | blvcenquiries@visitlondon.com |
| **Croydon** | Katharine Street | (020) 8253 1009 | tic@croydon.gov.uk |
| **Greenwich** | 2 Cutty Sark Gardens | 0870 608 2000 | tic@greenwich.gov.uk |
| **Lewisham** | 199-201 Lewisham High Street | (020) 8297 8317 | tic@lewisham.gov.uk |
| **Swanley** | London Road | (01322) 614660 | touristinfo@swanley.org.uk |

The London Eye

# Travel info

**By road:**
Major trunk roads into London include: A1, M1, A5, A10, A11, M11, A13, A2, M2, A23, A3, M3, A4, M4, A40, M40, A41, M25 (London orbital).
Transport for London is responsible for running London's bus services, the underground rail network and the DLR (Docklands Light Railway), and river and tram services.
(020) 7222 1234 (24-hour telephone service; calls answered in rotation).

**By rail:**
Main rail terminals: Victoria/Waterloo/ Charing Cross – serving the South/South East; King's Cross – serving the North East; Euston – serving the North West/Midlands; Liverpool Street – serving the East; Paddington – serving the Thames Valley/West.

**By air:**
Fly into London City, London Gatwick, London Heathrow, London Luton and London Stansted.

For more information, go to visitlondon.com/travel or tfl.gov.uk/journeyplanner

# Find out more

By logging on to visitlondon.com
or calling 0870 1 LONDON for the following:

- **A London tourist information pack**
- **Tourist information on London**
  Speak to an expert for information and advice on
  museums, galleries, attractions, riverboat trips,
  sightseeing tours, theatre, shopping, eating out and
  much more! Or simply go to visitlondon.com.
- **Accommodation reservations**

Or visit one of London's tourist information centres
listed opposite.


**Which part of London?**
The majority of tourist accommodation is situated in the
central parts of London and is therefore very convenient
for most of the city's attractions and nightlife.

However, there are many establishments in Outer
London which provide other advantages, such as easier
parking. In the accommodation pages which follow, you
will find establishments listed under INNER LONDON
(covering the E1 to W14 London Postal Area) and
OUTER LONDON (covering the remainder of Greater
London). Colour maps 6 and 7 at the front of the guide
show place names and London postal area codes and will
help you to locate accommodation in your chosen area.

Horse Guards Parade

# where to stay in
# London

All place names in the blue bands are shown on the maps at the front of this guide.

A complete listing of all Enjoy England assessed accommodation covered by this guide appears at the back.

## Accommodation symbols
Symbols give useful information about services and facilities. Inside the back-cover flap you can find a key to these symbols. Keep it open for easy reference.

**INNER LONDON**

**LONDON N1**

★ ★ ★
GUEST ACCOMMODATION

B&B per room per night
s £44.00–£54.00
d £59.00–£71.00

## Kandara Guest House

68 Ockendon Road, Islington, London N1 3NW **t** (020) 7226 5721 **f** (020) 7226 3379
**e** admin@kandara.co.uk **w** kandara.co.uk

**open** All year except Christmas
**bedrooms** 2 double, 1 twin, 4 single, 4 family
**payment** Credit/debit cards, cash/cheques, euros

A family-run guesthouse near the Angel, Islington. Quietly situated in a conservation area. All bedrooms and bathrooms have recently been decorated and fitted to a high standard. Ten bus routes and two underground stations provide excellent public transport services. Free overnight street parking and free cycle storage.

⊕ From A1, Highbury Corner roundabout take St Paul's Road for 0.5 miles. Turn right at junction onto Essex Road. Ockendon Road is 5th on the left.

♥ Book for 3 nights or more and save up to 15%.

Room 🛏 📺 🛁 🍵  General 🛎 🛗 ♿ ✂

**LONDON N7**

★ ★ ★
GUEST ACCOMMODATION

B&B per room per night
s £35.00–£40.00
d £50.00–£55.00

## Europa

62 Anson Road, London N7 0AA **t** (020) 7607 5935 **f** (020) 7607 5909
**e** info@europahotellondon.co.uk **w** europahotellondon.co.uk

We are a listed building, over 100 years old. All rooms en suite with private facilities. We are only 15 minutes from central London.

**open** All year
**bedrooms** 12 double, 8 twin, 6 single, 7 family
**bathrooms** All en suite
**payment** Credit/debit cards, cash/cheques

Room 🛏 📺 🛁 🍵  General 🛎 🛗 ♿ 🚭 ✿

## Place index

If you know where you want to stay, the index at the back of the guide will give you the page number listing accommodation in your chosen town, city or village. Check out the other useful indexes too.

## LONDON N10

★ ★ ★
**GUEST HOUSE**

B&B per room per night
s £48.00–£50.00
d £62.00–£65.00

### The Muswell Hill

73 Muswell Hill Road, London N10 3HT  **t** (020) 8883 6447  **f** (020) 8883 5158
**e** reception@muswellhillhotel.co.uk  **w** muswellhillhotel.co.uk

A comfortable, three-storey, Edwardian corner property, close to Muswell Hill and Alexandra Palace, offering a warm, friendly service.

**open** All year except Christmas
**bedrooms** 3 double, 3 twin, 4 single, 2 family
**bathrooms** 8 en suite
**payment** Credit/debit cards, cash/cheques

Room 🛏 📺 ⛅  General 🛋 🎮 ♿ P ☼

## LONDON N22

★ ★
**BED & BREAKFAST**

B&B per room per night
s £22.00–£24.00
d £34.00–£38.00

### Pane Residence

154 Boundary Road, London N22 6AE  **t** (020) 8889 3735

In a pleasant location six minutes' walk from Turnpike Lane underground station and near Alexandra Palace. Kitchen facilities available.

**open** All year
**bedrooms** 1 double, 1 single
**payment** Cash/cheques, euros

Room ⛅ 🍴  General 🛋 P ✂ ☼

## LONDON NW3

★ ★ ★
**GUEST ACCOMMODATION**

B&B per room per night
s £38.00–£52.00
d £56.00–£70.00

### Dillons

21 Belsize Park, London NW3 4DU  **t** (020) 7794 3360  **f** (020) 7431 7900  **e** desk@dillonshotel.com
**w** dillonshotel.com

**open** All year
**bedrooms** 4 double, 4 twin, 3 single, 4 family
**bathrooms** 9 en suite
**payment** Credit/debit cards, cash/cheques, euros

Located just six minutes' walk from either Swiss Cottage or Belsize Park underground stations, close to the Royal Free Hospital and convenient for Camden Market and central London. Dillons Hotel provides comfortable, reasonably priced bed and breakfast accommodation. All rooms have colour TV and many have private shower/wc.

⊕ From Swiss Cottage intersection on Finchley Road, A41, take College Crescent towards Hampstead, then 1st right. The hotel is 200m along on the left.

♥ Discounts available for stays of 7 nights or more. Ask at the time of booking.

Room 📺 ⛅ 🍴  General 🛋 🎮 ♿ 🔍

## LONDON SE3

★ ★
**BED & BREAKFAST**

B&B per room per night
s £23.00–£25.00
d £46.00–£48.00

### 3 Tilbrook Road

London SE3 9QD  **t** (020) 8319 8843  **e** m.hutson@talktalk.net

Semi-detached house, eight minutes from Eltham High Street station by bus and 20 minutes to Greenwich. Central London is 20 minutes by train. Easy access to major roads.

**open** All year except Christmas and New Year
**bedrooms** 1 twin, 1 single
**payment** Cash/cheques

Room 📺 ⛅ 🍴  General 🛋 14 ✂

## It's all quality-assessed accommodation

Our commitment to quality involves wide-ranging accommodation assessment. Rating and awards were correct at the time of going to press but may change following a new assessment. Please check at time of booking.

## LONDON SE3

★★★
**BED & BREAKFAST**

B&B per room per night
s £45.00
d £60.00

# 59a Lee Road, Blackheath

London SE3 9EN  **t** (020) 8318 7244  **e** ac@blackheath318.freeserve.co.uk

Charming accommodation in leafy location. Minutes from amenities of Blackheath village. Extremely convenient for historic Greenwich, central London and Docklands Light Railway. Free off-road parking.

**open** All year except Christmas and New Year
**bedrooms** 1 double
**payment** Cash/cheques

Room TV 🍵  General ✂ 🔥 ✿

## LONDON SE6

★★★
**GUEST ACCOMMODATION**

B&B per room per night
s £33.00–£35.00
d £45.00–£50.00

# The Heathers

71 Verdant Lane, London SE6 1JD  **t** (020) 8698 8340  **f** (020) 8698 8340  **e** berylheath@yahoo.co.uk
**w** theheathersbb.com

A clean and comfortable, family-run, home from home. Beryl and Ron will do their best to ensure you really enjoy your visit. Nothing too much trouble.

**open** All year
**bedrooms** 2 twin
**payment** Cash/cheques

Room TV 🖐 🍵  General ☸5 ✂ 🍽 🔥

## LONDON SE6

★★
**BED & BREAKFAST**

B&B per room per night
s £30.00–£35.00
d £50.00–£55.00

# Tulip Tree House

41 Minard Road, London SE6 1NP  **t** (020) 8697 2596

English home in quiet residential area off A205 South Circular Road. Ten minutes' walk to Hither Green station for 20-minute journey to central London.

**open** All year except Christmas
**bedrooms** 1 double, 1 twin, 1 single
**payment** Cash/cheques

Room TV 🖐 🍵  General ☸ P 🔥 ✿

## LONDON SE10

★★
**GUEST ACCOMMODATION**

B&B per room per night
s £40.00–£45.00
d £65.00

# The Corner House

28 Royal Hill, London SE10 8RT  **t** (020) 8692 3023  **f** (020) 8692 3023  **e** joannacourtney@aol.com

Period property in prestigious area of West Greenwich. Near all places of interest, museums, park, river and antiques market. Railway station, buses and Docklands Light Railway within five minutes' walk.

**open** All year
**bedrooms** 1 double, 1 twin
**bathrooms** 1 private
**payment** Cash/cheques

Room 🛏 TV 🖐  General ✂ 🔥 ✿  Leisure 🏊

## LONDON SE20

★★★★
**GUEST ACCOMMODATION**

B&B per room per night
s £35.00–£45.00
d £55.00–£65.00
Evening meal per person
£6.50–£17.00

# Melrose House

89 Lennard Road, London SE20 7LY  **t** (020) 8776 8884  **f** (020) 8778 6366
**e** melrosehouse@supanet.com  **w** uk-bedandbreakfast.com

Superb accommodation in Victorian house with spacious, en suite bedrooms. Easy access to West End. Quiet, respectable, friendly and welcoming. Ground-floor rooms opening onto the lovely garden.

**open** All year except Christmas and New Year
**bedrooms** 4 double, 3 twin, 1 single, 1 family
**bathrooms** 8 en suite, 1 private
**payment** Credit/debit cards, cash/cheques, euros

Room 🛏 🖼 📞 TV 🖐 🍵  General ☸8 P ✂ 🔥 ✿

## Key to symbols

Open the back flap for a key to symbols.

## LONDON SW1

★★
GUEST ACCOMMODATION

B&B per room per night
s £45.00–£65.00
d £50.00–£75.00

# The Dover

44 Belgrave Road, London SW1V 1RG  t (020) 7821 9085  f (020) 7834 6425
e reception@dover-hotel.co.uk  w dover-hotel.co.uk

Friendly bed and breakfast hotel within minutes of Victoria station and Gatwick Express. Most rooms with satellite TV, shower/wc, telephone, hairdryer. Walking distance of Buckingham Palace, Big Ben and London Eye.

open All year
bedrooms 13 double, 7 twin, 5 single, 8 family
bathrooms 29 en suite
payment Credit/debit cards, cash/cheques, euros

Room 🛏 ☎ 📺 🍴 General 🕯 ▥ ⅍ ᕟ

## LONDON SW1

★★★
GUEST ACCOMMODATION

B&B per room per night
s £50.00–£75.00
d £70.00–£110.00

# Melita House

35 Charlwood Street, London SW1V 2DU  t (020) 7828 0471  f (020) 7932 0988
e reserve@melitahotel.com  w melitahotel.com

Elegant, family-run hotel in excellent location close to Victoria station. Rooms have extensive modern facilities. Warm, friendly welcome, full English breakfast included.

open All year
bedrooms 10 double, 3 twin, 4 single, 2 family
bathrooms All en suite
payment Credit/debit cards, cash/cheques, euros

Room 🛏 ☎ 📺 🍴 General 🕯 ⅍ ᕟ Leisure 🚲

## LONDON SW1

★★
GUEST ACCOMMODATION

B&B per room per night
s £40.00–£50.00
d £50.00–£60.00

# Stanley House

19-21 Belgrave Road, London SW1V 1RB  t (020) 7834 5042 & (020) 7834 7292  f (020) 7834 8439
e cmahotel@aol.com  w londonbudgethotels.co.uk

In elegant Belgravia, only a few minutes' walk from Victoria station and with easy access to West End. All rooms en suite, with colour TV, direct-dial telephone, hairdryer. Friendly, relaxing atmosphere at affordable rates.

open All year
bedrooms 18 double, 11 twin, 7 single, 8 family
bathrooms 33 en suite
payment Credit/debit cards, cash/cheques, euros

Room 🛏 ☎ 📺 🍴 General 🕯7 ᕟ

## LONDON SW1

★★★
GUEST ACCOMMODATION

B&B per room per night
s Min £44.00

# Vandon House

1 Vandon Street, London SW1H 0AH  t (020) 7799 6780  f (020) 7799 1464
e info@vandonhouse.com  w vandonhouse.com

bedrooms 12 twin, 14 single, 6 family
bathrooms 16 en suite
payment Credit/debit cards, cash/cheques

Excellent-value, friendly guest accommodation in superb location. Buckingham Palace, St James's Park and Westminster Abbey lie only a few minutes away. We pride ourselves on our family atmosphere. A terrific base for exploring London. Open mid-May to end of August and two weeks over New Year.

⊕ Available on request.

♥ 10% discount on stays of 7 nights or more.

Room ☎ 📺 🍴 General 🕯 ▥ ⅍ ᕟ 🛋 ▣

## Looking for a little luxury

Gold and Silver Awards are given to establishments achieving the highest levels of quality and service. There's more information at the front of the guide, and an index to all accommodation achieving these awards at the back.

## LONDON SW5

**★★**
GUEST ACCOMMODATION

B&B per room per night
s £40.00–£60.00
d £60.00–£76.00

# Mowbray Court

28-32 Penywern Road, London SW5 9SU  **t** (020) 7370 2316  **f** (020) 7370 5693
**e** mowbraycrthot@hotmail.com  **w** mowbraycourthotel.co.uk

Close to Earls Court underground and West Brompton station with links to Heathrow and Gatwick airports. Good shopping available in the locality of Kensington and Knightsbridge.

**open** All year
**bedrooms** 10 double, 12 twin, 29 single, 29 family
**bathrooms** 70 en suite
**payment** Credit/debit cards, cash/cheques, euros

Room ⬆ ✆ TV ☏  General ⬧ ♿ ✄ ☕ ♨ ⊡ ♆

## LONDON SW5

**★★**
GUEST ACCOMMODATION

B&B per room per night
s £30.00–£48.00
d £45.00–£70.00

# Rasool Court Hotel

19-21 Penywern Road, London SW5 9TT  **t** (020) 7373 8900  **f** (020) 7244 6835
**e** rasool@rasool.demon.co.uk  **w** rasoolcourthotel.com

**open** All year
**bedrooms** 14 double, 8 twin, 11 single, 6 family
**bathrooms** All en suite
**payment** Credit/debit cards, cash/cheques

Family-run hotel in fashionable Kensington, with easy access to shopping areas and tourist attractions via the Underground.

⊕ *From the M4 take the A4 towards central London. Turn right into Earl's Court Road and then right into Penywern Road.*

Room ⬆ ✆ TV ♨  General ⬧ ♨

## LONDON W1

**★★**
GUEST ACCOMMODATION

B&B per room per night
s £59.00–£79.00
d £69.00–£89.00

# Lincoln House – Central London

33 Gloucester Place, London W1U 8HY  **t** (020) 7486 7630  **f** (020) 7486 0166
**e** reservations@lincoln-house-hotel.co.uk  **w** lincoln-house-hotel.co.uk

**open** All year
**bedrooms** 6 double, 4 twin, 7 single, 7 family
**bathrooms** All en suite
**payment** Credit/debit cards, cash/cheques

A town-house hotel with Georgian character and nautical theme throughout. En suite rooms and free wireless Internet connection. Centrally located in the heart of London, near to Oxford Street shopping, theatres, museums and exhibitions. On coach route to airports. Commended by many travel guidebooks.

⊕ *Enter Euston Road. Upon reaching Baker Street station, left into Baker Street. Fourth set of lights, right into George Street. First set of lights turn into Gloucester Place.*

♥ *Long-stay discounts on request. Most Sundays discounted. For latest long-stay and other special offers visit our website.*

Room ⬆ ✆ TV ♨ ☏  General ⬧ ▦ ☀ ♨ ♿ ♆  Leisure ∪

## Take a break

Look out for special promotions and themed breaks. This could be your chance to indulge an interest, find a new one, or just relax and enjoy exceptional value. Offers (highlighted in colour) are subject to availability.

## LONDON W1

★★
GUEST ACCOMMODATION

B&B per room per night
s £35.00–£75.00
d £35.00–£85.00

# Marble Arch Inn

49-50 Upper Berkeley Street, London W1H 5QR  t (020) 7723 7888  f (020) 7723 6060
e sales@marblearch-inn.co.uk  w marblearch-inn.co.uk

Friendly bed and breakfast hotel within minutes of Hyde Park, Oxford Street, Heathrow Express. Most rooms with satellite TV, shower/wc, telephone, hairdryer. Very competitive prices.

**open** All year
**bedrooms** 11 double, 7 twin, 2 single, 9 family
**bathrooms** 23 en suite
**payment** Credit/debit cards, cash/cheques, euros

Room   General

## LONDON W2

★★★
GUEST ACCOMMODATION

B&B per room per night
s £52.00–£59.00
d £64.00–£74.00

# Abbey Court & Westpoint Hotel

174 Sussex Gardens, London W2 1TP  t (020) 7402 0281  f (020) 7224 9114  e info@abbeycourt.com
w abbeycourthotel.com

Good value accommodation in central London, with easy access to London's tourist attractions and shopping areas. Within walking distance of Hyde Park. Car parking available.

**open** All year
**bedrooms** 60 double, 18 twin, 19 single, 30 family, 15 suites
**bathrooms** All en suite
**payment** Credit/debit cards, cash/cheques

Room   General

## LONDON W2

★★★
GUEST ACCOMMODATION

B&B per room per night
s £39.00–£60.00
d £70.00–£80.00

# Barry House

12 Sussex Place, London W2 2TP  t (020) 7723 7340  f (020) 7723 9775  e hotel@barryhouse.co.uk
w barryhouse.co.uk

**open** All year
**bedrooms** 4 double, 6 twin, 2 single, 6 family
**bathrooms** 14 en suite, 1 private
**payment** Credit/debit cards, cash/cheques

The family-run Barry House offers warm hospitality in a Victorian townhouse. Comfortable en suite rooms with English breakfast served each morning. Located close to the West End. Paddington Station and Hyde Park are just three minutes' walk away.

⊕ From A40 take Paddington exit and follow the road, then turn left into Sussex Gardens, then 1st right into Sussex Place.

♥ Ask for your Visit Britain discount.

Room   General   Leisure U

## LONDON W2

★★
GUEST ACCOMMODATION

B&B per room per night
s £30.00–£45.00
d £48.00–£60.00

# Hyde Park Rooms

137 Sussex Gardens, London W2 2RX  t (020) 7723 0225  e reception@hydeparkrooms.com
w hydeparkrooms.com

Small, centrally located, private hotel with personal service. Clean, comfortable and friendly. Within walking distance of Hyde Park and Kensington Gardens. Car parking available.

**open** All year except Christmas
**bedrooms** 4 double, 4 twin, 4 single, 3 family
**bathrooms** 7 en suite
**payment** Credit/debit cards, cash/cheques

Room   General   Leisure U

## To your credit

If you book by phone you may be asked for your credit card number. If so, it is advisable to check the proprietor's policy in case you have to cancel your reservation at a later date.

## LONDON W2

★ ★ ★
GUEST ACCOMMODATION

B&B per room per night
s £45.00–£60.00
d £50.00–£66.00

# The Oxford

13-14 Craven Terrace, London W2 3QD  **t** (020) 7402 6860  **f** (020) 7262 7574
**e** info@oxfordhotel.freeserve.co.uk  **w** oxfordhotellondon.co.uk

Located in a quiet one-way street, close to underground and bus routes to Oxford Street. Five minutes' walk from Hyde Park.

**open** All year
**bedrooms** 5 double, 4 twin, 1 single, 10 family
**bathrooms** All en suite
**payment** Credit/debit cards, cash/cheques

Room 🛏 ☎ TV 🕯 🍵   General 🖾 🎑

## LONDON W2

★ ★ ★
GUEST ACCOMMODATION

B&B per room per night
s £50.00–£75.00
d £65.00–£95.00

# Rhodes House

195 Sussex Gardens, London W2 2RJ  **t** (020) 7262 5617  **f** (020) 7723 4054
**e** chris@rhodeshotel.com  **w** rhodeshotel.com

**open** All year
**bedrooms** 3 double, 3 twin, 3 single, 9 family
**bathrooms** All en suite
**payment** Credit/debit cards, cash/cheques

All rooms with private facilities, secondary glazing, free internet access, voice mail, air-conditioning, satellite TV and DVD, telephone, refrigerator, hairdryer and tea-/coffee-making facilities. Room with jacuzzi and balcony. Friendly atmosphere. Families especially welcome. Excellent transport for sightseeing and shopping.

⊕ *Follow A40 and signs into Paddington. Follow Westbourne Terrace. At roundabout joining Sussex Gardens, left. Hotel is on other side of the road on 1st block.*

Room 🛏 ☎ TV 🕯 🍵   General 🖾 🎑 🀄 P 🀫 ♿

## LONDON W5

★ ★
GUEST HOUSE

B&B per room per night
s £37.00–£49.00
d £49.00–£61.00

# Grange Lodge

48-50 Grange Road, London W5 5BX  **t** (020) 8567 1049  **f** (020) 8579 5350
**e** enquiries@londonlodgehotels.com  **w** londonlodgehotels.com

Quiet, comfortable hotel, close to three Underground stations. Midway central London and Heathrow. Colour TV, tea-/coffee-making facilities, radio/alarm, most rooms en suite.

**open** All year
**bedrooms** 2 double, 2 twin, 8 single, 2 family
**bathrooms** 9 en suite
**payment** Credit/debit cards, cash/cheques, euros

Room 🛏 TV 🕯   General 🖾 🎑 P 🀫 ♿ 🖵 ✿ 🐾

# Tales of the city

Allow the London Explorer to guide you through the streets of the capital leaving no stone unturned. All you need for the perfect day out is in this handy package – featuring an easy-to-use fold out map and illustrated guide. You can purchase the Explorer series from good bookshops and online at visitbritaindirect.com.

**LONDON W6**

★★★★
HOSTEL

Per person per night
B&B £19.00–£65.00

# The Globetrotter Inn London

Ashlar Court, Ravenscourt Gardens, London W6 0TU  t (020) 8746 3112  f (020) 8748 9912
e london@globetrotterinns.com  w globetrotterinns.com

**open** All year
**bedrooms** 13 double, 26 twin, 29 quad, 33 dormitories. Total no of beds 392
**bathrooms** 44 en suite, 10 public
**max group size** 100
**meals** Evening meals available
**payment** Credit/debit cards, cash/cheques

The Globetrotter Inn London provides high quality, clean, secure and comfortable accommodation for individuals or groups. The extensive facilities include a bar, DVD cinema, mini-market, internet café, gym, TV rooms, meals (self-catered or provided), travel desk, and much more. Voted 'Best Hostel in London 2006' by Visit London.

Room ♿  General 🛏 ▥ ♨ ▥ P ⚡ ♟ ◎ ▨ ♪ ⬛ ✿  Leisure ✗ ♦ 🏛

**OUTER LONDON**
**CROYDON**

★★★
GUEST HOUSE

B&B per room per night
s £40.00–£45.00
d £70.00

# The Woodstock Guest House

30 Woodstock Road, Croydon CR0 1JR  t (020) 8680 1489  f (020) 8667 1229
e woodstockhotel@tiscali.co.uk  w woodstockhotel.co.uk

**open** All year except Christmas
**bedrooms** 1 double, 1 twin, 4 single, 2 family
**bathrooms** 2 en suite, 4 private
**payment** Credit/debit cards, cash/cheques

Located in a quiet residential area, yet only five minutes' walk to town centre and East Croydon railway station. Well-appointed and spacious rooms. High standard of housekeeping.

Room ♿ 📺 ♨ ♟  General 🛏3 P ▨ ✿  Leisure ▶ ⚙

**HAMPTON**

★★★
GUEST ACCOMMODATION

B&B per room per night
s £45.00–£55.00
d £55.00–£75.00

# Houseboat Riverine

Riverine, Taggs Island, Hampton TW12 2HA  t (020) 8979 2266  e malcolm@feedtheducks.com
w feedtheducks.com

A Thames houseboat moored on Taggs Island which is just upstream from Hampton Court Palace. Easy access and private parking. Delightfully different.

**open** All year
**bedrooms** 2 double, 1 twin
**bathrooms** All en suite
**payment** Cash/cheques

Room ♿ 📺 ♨ ♟  General ⚔ ✿

## It's all in the detail

Please remember that all information in this guide has been supplied by the proprietors well in advance of publication. Since changes do sometimes occur it's a good idea to check details at the time of booking.

## RICHMOND

★★★
GUEST ACCOMMODATION

B&B per room per night
s £45.00–£70.00
d £75.00–£95.00

# Hobart Hall Guest House

43-47 Petersham Road, Richmond TW10 6UL  t (020) 8940 0435  f (020) 8332 2996
e hobarthall@aol.com  w smoothhound.co.uk/hotels/hobarthall.html

open All year
bedrooms 8 double, 5 twin, 10 single, 5 family, 1 suite
bathrooms 26 en suite
payment Credit/debit cards, cash/cheques

Built c1690. Past occupants include the Countess of Buckinghamshire and William IV. Historic setting overlooking River Thames, 200yds from Richmond Bridge. Heritage, cultural and business centres in near proximity. Heathrow, M3, M4 15 minutes. Over ground and underground trains: Waterloo 20 minutes, West End 45 minutes.

Room ♿ 🖨 📞 📺 ♨  General 🛗 🏪 ♿ P ✂ ♨ ● ❊  Leisure ♨ ♪ ▸ ⚲

## RICHMOND

★★★
GUEST ACCOMMODATION

B&B per room per night
s £32.50–£39.50
d £55.00–£69.00

# Ivy Cottage

Upper Ham Road, Ham Common, Richmond TW10 5LA  t (020) 8940 8601 & 07742 278247
e taylor@dbta.freeserve.co.uk  w dbta.freeserve.co.uk

Charming, wisteria-clad Georgian home offering exceptional views over Ham Common. Period features dating from 1760. Large garden. Self-catering an option. Good bus route and parking.

open All year
bedrooms 1 double, 1 twin, 1 single, 1 family
bathrooms 2 en suite, 2 private
payment Cash/cheques, euros

Room 📺 ♨ ♛  General 🛗8 ✂ ✕ ❊ 🐾  Leisure 🏛

## RICHMOND

★★★
INN

B&B per room per night
s £60.00–£70.00
d £70.00–£90.00

# The Red Cow

59 Sheen Road, Richmond TW9 1YJ  t (020) 8940 2511  f (020) 8940 2581  e tom@redcowpub.com
w redcowpub.com

open All year
bedrooms 2 double, 1 twin, 1 family
bathrooms All en suite
payment Credit/debit cards, cash/cheques

Traditional Victorian inn retaining some lovely original features. Just a short walk from Richmond town centre, river, royal parks and rail links to London. Other nearby places include Heathrow Airport, Twickenham rugby ground, Hampton Court and Windsor.

⊕ Five-minute walk from Richmond town centre and train station. Easily accessed from M25, M4 and M3.

Room 📺 ♨ ♛  General 🛗 ♈ ✕ ❊  Leisure ♪ ▸ ⚲

## SURBITON

★★
GUEST HOUSE

B&B per room per night
s £35.00–£40.00
d £48.00–£60.00

# The Broadway Lodge

41 The Broadway, Tolworth, Surbiton KT6 7DJ  t (020) 8399 6555  f (020) 8399 6678
e broadway.lodge@tiscali.co.uk  w broadway-stgeorgeslodge.com

Clean and cosy bed and breakfast next to Tolworth Tower. Two miles from Kingston shopping centre and Hampton Court.

open All year
bedrooms 2 double, 3 twin, 4 single
bathrooms 6 en suite, 1 private
payment Credit/debit cards, cash/cheques

Room 📺 ♨  General 🛗5 🏪 ♿ ✂ ♈ ✕ ♨ ❊

## SURBITON

★★
**BED & BREAKFAST**

B&B per room per night
s £20.00
d £36.00–£40.00

# Villiers Lodge Bed and Breakfast

1 Cranes Park, Surbiton KT5 8AB  t (020) 8399 6000

Villiers Lodge is a large, detached house in a quiet residential road very close to excellent bus and train services.

**open** All year
**bedrooms** 2 twin, 1 single
**bathrooms** 1 private
**payment** Cash/cheques

Room ♨ 📺 ✆  General ♿8 P ⚡  Leisure ∪ ⌥

## SUTTON

★★
**GUEST ACCOMMODATION**

B&B per room per night
s £25.00–£35.00
d £45.00–£55.00

# St Margarets Guest House

31 Devon Road, Sutton SM2 7PE  t (020) 8643 0164  f (020) 8643 0717
e margarettrotman@hotmail.com  w stmargaretsbandb.co.uk

Family-run, established 19 years. Detached house in a quiet residential area. Long-term stays welcomed. Washing machines, fridges and microwaves available for own use.

**open** All year
**bedrooms** 1 double, 1 twin, 2 single
**bathrooms** 1 en suite
**payment** Cash/cheques

Room ♨ 📺 ✆ ☕  General ♿ P ⚡ 🅿 ❋ 🐕  Leisure ▶ ⚲

# Gold and Silver Awards

enjoyEngland.com  enjoyEngland.com
*Gold* AWARD  *Silver* AWARD

**Enjoy England's unique Gold and Silver Awards recognise exceptional quality in serviced accommodation.**

Our assessors make recommendations for Gold and Silver Awards during assessments in recognition of levels of quality over and above that expected of a particular rating.

Look for the Gold and Silver Awards in the regional sections, or you can find an index to accommodation with a Gold or Silver Award at the back of this guide.

# South East England

Berkshire, Buckinghamshire, East Sussex,
Hampshire, Isle of Wight, Kent,
Oxfordshire, Surrey, West Sussex

# Family fun in classic England

The South East is your quintessential slice of England. And whilst there's plenty for singles and couples to enjoy, this region is bursting with great family days out that the kids will treasure forever.

Tourism South East
visitsoutheastengland.com
(023) 8062 5400

Deal Beach, Kent Coast

Sheffield Park Garden, East Sussex  Winchester Cathedral, Hampshire

Uffington, Oxfordshire

With 400 miles of glorious coastline including the towering chalk cliff of Beachy Head and kid-friendly beaches galore, the South East has always been a family favourite. Add the gorgeous countryside of the South Downs, evocative castles like Leeds and a wealth of colourful venues such as Woburn Safari Park, and this region has it all. As you'd expect, sailing is big in these parts, and you can simply stroll around one of the many marinas or set sail for a course at Calshot Activities Centre near Southampton. And if you're really brave, try one of the extreme watersports like wakeboarding. Finally, head off to a rural inn where you can unwind, enjoy a pint of real ale and savour a superb bistro-like meal.

Experience life in the Dickens era at Dickens World Kent with its Victorian shopping mall, music hall and an exciting time travel ride. With a new Viking Land and two top-secret new rides, Legoland Windsor is even more of a draw for all the family (time your visit right and catch their flagship firework bonanza). And if you're in battle mood, charge over to the interactive visitor centre at Battle Abbey in East Sussex and experience the Battle of Hastings brought to terrifying life.

Check out the atmospheric Winchester Cathedral where the foundations were laid in 1079 in stone brought from the Isle of Wight. Drop anchor at the Portsmouth Historic Dockyard, too, and marvel at HMS Victory and the Mary Rose. And don't miss Oxford Castle, where boutique stalls, pulsating bars and a feast of visual arts are set against the prison backdrop.

South East England is a region rich in experiences. It has something to offer every age group and every traveller. Whether you are looking at visiting for a weekend or a month this region has everything you could want.

# Destinations

## Brighton

England's favourite seaside city, Brighton is historic, elegant and offbeat. Wander a beachfront packed with cafes and bars, then step into town for fine antiques and designer boutiques. Don't miss the Royal Pavilion, surely the most extravagant royal palace in Europe, and come in springtime for an arts festival second to none. Find the world's cuisine in over 400 restaurants, and then relax with dance, comedy or music in the thriving pub and club culture. Brighton has it all – and just 49 minutes from central London.

## Canterbury

Marvel with fellow 'pilgrims' from the four corners of the world as Canterbury Cathedral dominates your approach to this World Heritage Site. Let Canterbury Tales 'Medieval Misadventures' take you on a journey back to Chaucer's England. Wander traffic-free daytime streets to enjoy historic buildings and modern attractions, and then head further afield to explore the valleys, woods and coastline of this beautiful region of Kent.

## Dover

Discover the rich history of Dover – 'the lock and key of England' - and its celebrated White Cliffs. Tour Dover Castle and relive the epic sieges of 1216-17. Delve into the secrets contained in the Wartime Tunnels, nerve centre for the evacuation of Dunkirk and Command Centre from whose depths Churchill witnessed the Battle of Britain. Enjoy the pier and stroll the stylish marina before heading out of town to tour the scenic beaches of White Cliffs Country.

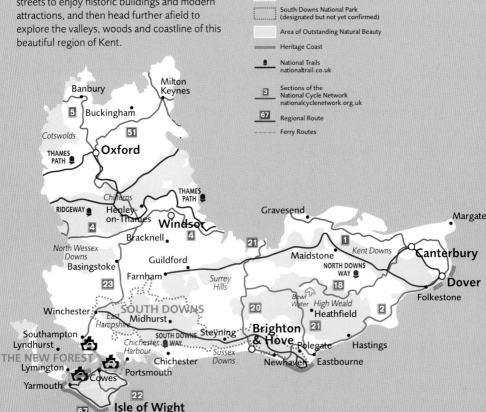

| 0 | 50 miles |
| 0 | 75 kms |

National Park

South Downs National Park (designated but not yet confirmed)

Area of Outstanding Natural Beauty

Heritage Coast

National Trails
nationaltrail.co.uk

**3** Sections of the National Cycle Network
nationalcyclenetwork.org.uk

**67** Regional Route

Ferry Routes

Windsor Castle

Canterbury Cathedral

Freshwater Bay, Isle of Wight

Dover Castle

New Forest

Oxford spires

Brighton seafront

## Isle of Wight

Sixty miles of spectacular coastline, picturesque coves and safe bathing in bays of golden sand. Explore the maritime history of Cowes, the beautiful and historic town of Newport and take the family to the welcoming resorts of Shanklin and Ventnor. Follow the trail of dinosaurs, ancient tribes, Romans and monarchs in this diamond-shaped treasure trove.

## New Forest

Roam a landscape little changed since William the Conqueror gave it his special protection over 900 years ago. You'll meet wild heath and dappled woodland, thatched hamlets, bustling market towns, and tiny streams meandering to the sparkling expanse of the Solent. Watch ponies eating by the roadside, pigs foraging for beechnuts, and donkeys ambling along the streets. As evening falls, hear the humming song of the nightjar, glimpse deer and watch bats flitting across the darkening sky.

## Oxford

This ancient university city is both timeless and modern. Wander among its 'dreaming spires' and tranquil college quadrangles. Find national and international treasures, displayed in a family of museums whose scope and scholarship is second to none. Hire a punt and spend the afternoon drifting along the River Cherwell or seek out bustling shops and fashionable restaurants. Experience candlelit evensong in college chapels or Shakespeare in the park, and after dark enjoy the cosmopolitan buzz of countless cafés, pubs and theatres.

## Windsor

Explore Windsor and the Royal Borough, to the west of London. Gaze at the priceless treasures in the Royal Collection at Windsor Castle, royal home and fortress for over 900 years. Henry VI founded Eton College in 1440. Lose yourself in the history of the cloisters and the chapel. Sail the churning rapids at Legoland's incredible Vikings' River Splash, and find peace and quiet in the rural landscape of Royal Berkshire, traversed by the timeless flow of the Thames.

# Places to visit

**Bedgebury National Pinetum & Forest**
Goudhurst, Kent
(01580) 879820
forestry.gov.uk/bedgebury
*World's finest conifer collection*

**Blenheim Palace**
Woodstock, Oxfordshire
(01993) 811091
blenheimpalace.com
*Baroque palace and beautiful parkland*

**Canterbury Cathedral**
Kent
(01227) 762862
canterbury-cathedral.org
*Seat of the Archbishop of Canterbury*

**Carisbrooke Castle**
Newport, Isle Of Wight
(01983) 522107
english-heritage.org.uk
*Splendid Norman castle*

**Dickens World**
Chatham, Kent
(01634) 890421
dickensworld.co.uk
*Fascinating journey through Dickens' lifetime*

**Dinosaur Isle**
Sandown, Isle Of Wight
(01983) 404344
dinosaurisle.com
*Britain's first purpose-built dinosaur attraction*

**Dover Castle and Secret Wartime Tunnels**
Kent
(01304) 211067
english-heritage.org.uk
*Historic nerve centre for Battle of Britain*

**Exbury Gardens and Steam Railway**
Hampshire
(023) 8089 1203
exbury.co.uk.
*Over 200 acres of woodland garden*

**Explosion! Museum of Naval Firepower**
Gosport, Hampshire
(023) 9250 5600
explosion.org.uk
*Naval firepower from gunpowder to the Exocet*

**Go Ape! High Wire Forest Adventure**
Farnham, Surrey
0870 444 5562
goape.co.uk
*Rope bridges, swings and zip slides*

**Groombridge Place Gardens and Enchanted Forest**
Tunbridge Wells, Kent
(01892) 861444
groombridge.co.uk
*Peaceful gardens and ancient woodland*

**Harbour Park (Family Amusement Park)**
Littlehampton, West Sussex
(01903) 721200
harbourpark.com
*Traditional ride favourites on the seafront*

**Hever Castle and Gardens**
near Edenbridge, Kent
(01732) 865224
hevercastle.co.uk
*Beautiful childhood home of Anne Boleyn*

**Highclere Castle and Gardens**
Newbury, Hampshire
(01635) 253210
highclerecastle.co.uk
*Imposing Victorian castle and parkland*

**The Historic Dockyard Chatham**
Kent
(01634) 823800
thedockyard.co.uk
*Maritime heritage site with stunning architecture*

**Howletts Wild Animal Park**
Canterbury, Kent
0870 750 4647
totallywild.net
*Wild animals in 90 acres of parkland*

**INTECH Science Centre**
Winchester, Hampshire
(01962) 863791
intech-uk.com
*Hands-on science and technology exhibits*

**LEGOLAND Windsor**
Berkshire
0870 504 0404
legoland.co.uk
*More Lego bricks than you ever dreamed possible*

**Loseley Park**
Guildford, Surrey
(01483) 304440
loseley-park.com
*Beautiful Elizabethan mansion and gardens*

**National Motor Museum Beaulieu**
Brockenhurst, Hampshire
(01590) 612345
beaulieu.co.uk
*Vintage cars and stately home in New Forest*

**Osborne House**
East Cowes, Isle Of Wight
(01983) 200022
english-heritage.org.uk
*Queen Victoria's seaside retreat*

**Paultons Park**
Romsey, Hampshire
(023) 8081 4442
paultonspark.co.uk
*Over 50 rides for all the family*

# Diary dates 2008

**Polesden Lacey**
near Dorking, Surrey
(01372) 452048
nationaltrust.org.uk
*Opulent Edwardian interiors in downland setting*

**RHS Garden Wisley**
Woking, Surrey
0845 260 9000
rhs.org.uk
*A working encyclopedia of British gardening*

**Royal Botanic Gardens, Wakehurst Place**
near Haywards Heath, West Sussex
(01444) 894000
rbgkew.org.uk
*Beautiful gardens throughout the seasons*

**Spinnaker Tower**
Portsmouth, Hampshire
(023) 9285 7520
spinnakertower.co.uk
*Breathtaking views from 170-metre landmark*

**Thorpe Park**
Chertsey, Surrey
0870 444 4466
thorpepark.com
*An adrenaline-charged day out for all the family*

**Windsor Castle**
Berkshire
(020) 7766 7304
royalcollection.org.uk
*Official residence of HM The Queen*

**New Year Steamday**
Didcot Railway
didcotrailwaycentre.org.uk
1 Jan

**Brighton Festival**
Various locations, Brighton
brightonfestival.org
3 – 25 May*

**Royal Windsor Horse Show**
Windsor Castle
royal-windsor-horse-show.co.uk
8 – 11 May

**Royal Ascot**
ascot.co.uk
17 – 21 Jun

**Henley Royal Regatta**
River Thames
hrr.co.uk
2 – 6 Jul

**Parham Garden Weekend**
Pulborough, West Sussex
parhaminsussex.co.uk
5 – 6 Jul*

**Farnborough International Air Show**
farnborough.com
14 – 20 Jul

**New Forest Show**
Brockenhurst, Hampshire
newforestshow.co.uk
29 – 31 Jul

**Cowes Week**
The Solent, Isle of Wight
skandiacowesweek.co.uk
2 – 9 Aug

**Ringwood Carnival**
ringwoodcarnival.org
20 Sep

* provisional date at time of going to press

# Tourist Information Centres

When you arrive at your destination, visit an Official Partner Tourist Information Centre for quality assured help with accommodation and information about local attractions and events, or email your request before you go. To search for attractions and Tourist Information Centres on the move just text INFO to 62233, and a web link will be sent to your mobile phone.

| | | | |
|---|---|---|---|
| **Bicester** | Unit 86a, Bicester Village | (01869) 369055 | bicester.vc@cherwell-dc.gov.uk |
| **Brighton** | Pavilion Buildings | 0906 711 2255** | brighton-tourism@brighton-hove.gov.uk |
| **Canterbury** | 12/13 Sun Street | (01227) 378100 | canterburyinformation@canterbury.gov.uk |
| **Chichester** | 29a South Street | (01243) 775888 | chitic@chichester.gov.uk |
| **Cowes** | 9 The Arcade | (01983) 813818 | info@islandbreaks.co.uk |
| **Dover** | The Old Town Gaol | (01304) 205108 | tic@doveruk.com |
| **Hastings** | Queens Square | 0845 274 1001 | hic@hastings.gov.uk |
| **Lyndhurst & New Forest** | Main Car Park | (023) 8028 2269 | information@nfdc.gov.uk |
| **Newport** | High Street | (01983) 813818 | info@islandbreaks.co.uk |
| **Oxford** | 15/16 Broad Street | (01865) 726871 | tic@oxford.gov.uk |
| **Portsmouth** | The Hard | (023) 9282 6722 | vis@portsmouthcc.gov.uk |
| **Rochester** | 95 High Street | (01634) 843666 | visitor.centre@medway.gov.uk |
| **Royal Tunbridge Wells** | The Pantiles | (01892) 515675 | touristinformationcentre@tunbridgewells.gov.uk |
| **Ryde** | 81-83 Union Street | (01983) 813818 | info@islandbreaks.co.uk |
| **Sandown** | 8 High Street | (01983) 813818 | info@islandbreaks.co.uk |
| **Shanklin** | 67 High Street | (01983) 813818 | info@islandbreaks.co.uk |
| **Southampton** | 9 Civic Centre Road | (023) 8083 3333 | tourist.information@southampton.gov.uk |
| **Winchester** | High Street | (01962) 840500 | tourism@winchester.gov.uk |
| **Windsor** | Windsor Royal Shopping | (01753) 743900 | windsor.tic@rbwm.gov.uk |
| **Yarmouth** | The Quay | (01983) 813818 | info@islandbreaks.co.uk |

*** calls to this number are charged at premium rate*

The Lee, Buckinghamshire

Chatham, Kent

# Find out more

The following publications are available from Tourism
South East by logging on to visitsoutheastengland.com
or calling (023) 8062 5400:

**Publications**

- **Escape into the Countryside**
- **Great Days Out in Berkshire, Buckinghamshire
  and Oxfordshire**
- **Distinctive Country Inns**
- **We Know Just the Place**

**E-Brochures**

- **Family Fun**
- **Fine Tradition**
- **Just the Two of Us**
- **Great Days Out**
- **Go Golf**
- **Countryside**
- **Cities**

# Travel info

**By road:**
From the North East – M1 & M25;
the North West – M6, M40 & M25;
the West and Wales – M4 & M25;
the East – M25;
the South West – M5, M4 & M25;
London – M25, M2, M20, M23, M3, M4 or M40.

**By rail:**
Regular services from London's Charing Cross, Victoria,
Waterloo and Waterloo East stations to all parts of the
South East. Further information on rail journeys in the
South East can be obtained on 0845 748 4950.

**By air:**
Fly into London City, London Heathrow, London
Gatwick, London Southend, Luton, Southampton,
Shoreham (Brighton City) or Stanstead.

where to stay in

# South East England

All place names in the blue bands are shown on the maps at the front of this guide.

A complete listing of all Enjoy England assessed accommodation covered by this guide appears at the back.

**Accommodation symbols**
Symbols give useful information about services and facilities. Inside the back-cover flap you can find a key to these symbols. Keep it open for easy reference.

**ABINGDON,** Oxfordshire Map ref 2C1

★★★★
BED & BREAKFAST

B&B per room per night
s £30.00–£35.00
d £50.00–£55.00

## Barrows End

3 The Copse, Abingdon OX14 3YW **t** (01235) 523541 **f** (01235) 523541 **e** dsharm@tesco.net

Modern, architect-designed chalet bungalow in a peaceful setting backing onto a nature reserve. Easy walking distance to Abingdon. Near bus stops to Oxford/Abingdon.

**open** All year except Christmas and New Year
**bedrooms** 3 twin
**bathrooms** 2 en suite, 1 private
**payment** Cash/cheques

Room General P

**ADDERBURY,** Oxfordshire Map ref 2C1

★★★
INN

B&B per room per night
s £45.00–£65.00
d £55.00–£85.00
Evening meal per person
£6.00–£15.00

## The Bell Inn

High Street, Adderbury, Banbury OX17 3LS **t** (01295) 810338 **e** info@the-bell.com **w** the-bell.com

**open** All year
**bedrooms** 1 double, 1 twin
**bathrooms** 1 en suite, 1 private
**payment** Credit/debit cards, cash/cheques

Traditional English inn serving award-winning ales and home-cooked food. With its striking inglenook fireplace, the Bell offers a warm and friendly welcome to customers old and new. Quiet location, pretty village on the edge of the Cotswolds. Regular folk and quiz nights. Traditional pub games including 'Aunt Sally'!

*M40 jct 11 straight through Banbury (A4260). Once in Twyford, turn right after traffic lights, signposted West Adderbury. Bell situated on left down by church.*

Room General Leisure

## Place index

If you know where you want to stay, the index at the back of the guide will give you the page number listing accommodation in your chosen town, city or village. Check out the other useful indexes too.

---

**ALDWORTH,** Berkshire Map ref 2C2

★★★★

**BED & BREAKFAST**

B&B per room per night
s £30.00–£35.00
d £60.00–£70.00

# Fieldview Cottage

Bell Lane, Aldworth, Reading RG8 9SB  **t** (01635) 578964  **e** hunt@fieldvu.freeserve.co.uk

**bedrooms** 1 double, 1 twin, 1 single
**bathrooms** 2 private
**payment** Cash/cheques

Fieldview is a pretty cottage in the centre of Aldworth, situated high on the Downs and adjoining the Ridgeway, an ideal base for walking, cycling and horse-riding. M4/A34 junction 12/13, Oxford, Bath, Windsor and Heathrow within easy reach. Only 2.5 miles from main railway line – Paddington 45 minutes.

⊕ *Please request directions at time of booking.*

Room 🛏 TV ♿ 🍵  General 🐾 🎱 ♿ P ⚲  Leisure ⚓

---

**ALRESFORD,** Hampshire Map ref 2C2

★★★

**BED & BREAKFAST**

B&B per room per night
s £25.00–£30.00
d £50.00–£60.00

# Haygarth

John and Val Ramshaw, 82 Jacklyns Lane, Alresford SO24 9LJ  **t** (01962) 732715 & 07986 372895

**open** All year
**bedrooms** 3 double, 1 single
**bathrooms** 2 en suite, 2 private
**payment** Cash/cheques

A pleasant welcome awaits visitors to Haygarth. Located close to town centre and golf course. Convenient for Winchester, Salisbury, New Forest, Watercress Line and Wayfarers Walk. Relax and unwind in the heart of Hampshire. Guest annexe includes separate entrance, lounge, kitchen, en suite bedrooms. Sky TV.

⊕ *From Winchester take A31 towards Alton. Turn off at B3047 (Alresford), at Running Horse public house next right (B3046 to Cheriton). House 0.5 miles on right.*

Room 🛏 TV ♿ 🍵  General 🐾 P 🍽 🎱 ⊙ ❀  Leisure ⚓ ► ⚓

---

**ALTON,** Hampshire Map ref 2C2

★★★★

**BED & BREAKFAST**

B&B per room per night
s £53.00–£59.00
d £70.00–£78.00

# Neatham Barn

Holybourne, Neatham, Alton GU34 4NP  **t** (01420) 544215  **f** (01420) 541626
**e** neathambarn@f2s.com  **w** neathambarn.com

**open** All year
**bedrooms** 1 double
**bathrooms** En suite
**payment** Cash/cheques

Situated in a tiny hamlet, up a quiet country lane, this detached oak-barn annexe occupies a lovely setting in the grounds of Neatham Cottage. Self-catering an option.

Room TV ♿ 🍵  General P ⚲ ❀  Leisure ⚲

---

## Key to symbols
Open the back flap for a key to symbols.

## ANDOVER, Hampshire Map ref 2C2

★★★★
**BED & BREAKFAST**
**SILVER AWARD**

B&B per room per night
s £40.00–£55.00
d £65.00–£80.00

# May Cottage

Thruxton, Andover SP11 8LZ  t (01264) 771241  f (01264) 771770
e info@maycottage-thruxton.co.uk  w maycottage-thruxton.co.uk

**open** All year
**bedrooms** 2 double, 1 twin
**bathrooms** 2 en suite, 1 private
**payment** Cash/cheques

May Cottage dates back to 1740 and is situated in the heart of this picturesque, tranquil village with two old inns serving food. All rooms have en suite/private bathroom, TV, radio, beverage tray. Guests' own sitting/dining room. Pretty, secluded garden with stream. Many National Trust properties and stately homes/gardens within easy reach. Private parking. Non-smoking establishment.

⊕ *From Andover take A303 towards Exeter, then take turning for Thruxton (village only). Left at T-junction. May Cottage is on right opposite The George Inn.*

Room 🛏 📺 👤 🍷  General 🏖 🛅 P ⚡ 🍴 🎮 ✿  Leisure ∪ ♪ ▶ 🏊

## ARUNDEL, West Sussex Map ref 2D3

★★★
**BED & BREAKFAST**

B&B per room per night
s £35.00–£50.00
d £50.00–£70.00

# Sandfield House

Lyminster Road, Wick, Littlehampton BN17 7PG  t (01903) 724129
e francesfarrerbrown@btconnect.com  w visitsussex.org/sandfieldhouse

**open** All year
**bedrooms** 1 double, 1 twin
**payment** Cash/cheques, euros

Are you looking for comfortable, relaxed surroundings? Do you want to be within easy reach of many of West Sussex's prime attractions? Come and stay at Sandfield House, our spacious Victorian family home, set in two acres of grounds. Locally sourced breakfast wherever possible. Warm welcome guaranteed. Walkers and cyclists welcomed.

⊕ *From A27 turn south on A284 at Crossbush. We are last house on right before level crossing.*

Room 📺 👤  General 🏖 🛏 P ⚡ 🍴 🎮 ✿  Leisure ∪ ♪ 🚲 🏊

## ASHFORD, Kent Map ref 3B4

★★★
**GUEST ACCOMMODATION**

B&B per room per night
s Min £35.00
d Min £60.00
Evening meal per person
£12.00–£15.00

# Dean Court Farm

Challock Lane, Westwell, Ashford TN25 4NH  t (01233) 712924

**open** All year except Christmas
**bedrooms** 1 double, 1 twin, 1 family
**bathrooms** 1 en suite
**payment** Cash/cheques

Period farmhouse on working farm with modern amenities. Magnificent views in quiet valley. Comfortable accommodation with separate sitting room for guests.

⊕ *At The Wheel public house in Westwell take Challock Lane north for 1 mile. Dean Court Farm is in the valley on the left-hand side.*

Room 👤  General 🏖 🛏 🛅 P ⚡ ✕ 🎮 ✿  Leisure 🏊

## Using map references

Map references refer to the colour maps at the front of this guide.

## ASHURST, Hampshire Map ref 2C3

**♦♦♦♦**
GUEST ACCOMMODATION

B&B per room per night
s £25.00–£35.00
d £50.00–£60.00

# Forest Gate Lodge

161 Lyndhurst Road, Ashurst, Southampton SO40 7AW  **t** (023) 8029 3026  **f** (023) 8029 3026
**w** forestgatelodge.co.uk

**open** All year except Christmas
**bedrooms** 3 double, 1 twin, 1 family
**bathrooms** All en suite
**payment** Cash/cheques

Large Victorian house with direct access to New Forest and its attractions – walks, riding, cycling. Pubs and restaurants nearby, Lyndhurst – 'capital of the New Forest' – five minutes' drive. Multi-choice breakfast or vegetarian by prior arrangement. London direct, railway station five minutes' walk, golf course nearby, also local bike hire.

⊕ *From Lyndhurst town centre take main road towards Southampton where the establishment will be found 2 miles along on right in village of Ashurst.*

♥ *Special rates: 3 nights for price of 2, weekdays only; 7 nights – 2 nights free. 1 Oct – 1 Apr inclusive.*

Room 📺 ♨  General ♨5 P ✂  Leisure ∪ ♪ ▶ ♿

## BANBURY, Oxfordshire Map ref 2C1

**★★★**
GUEST ACCOMMODATION

B&B per room per night
s £35.00–£40.00
d £50.00

# Avonlea Guest House

41 Southam Road, Banbury OX16 2EP  **t** (01295) 267837  **f** (01295) 267837
**e** whitforddebbie@hotmail.com  **w** avonleaguesthouse.co.uk

A friendly, family-run guesthouse, always being updated. Five minutes' walk to town centre. All rooms en suite. Off-road parking.

**open** All year
**bedrooms** 3 double, 1 twin, 1 family
**bathrooms** All en suite
**payment** Credit/debit cards, cash/cheques

Room 📺 ♨  General ♨ 🏛 P ✂  Leisure ∪ ♪ ▶

## BANBURY, Oxfordshire Map ref 2C1

**★★★★**
BED & BREAKFAST

B&B per room per night
s £27.50–£30.00
d £55.00–£60.00
Evening meal per person
Min £18.00

# St Martins House

Warkworth, Banbury OX17 2AG  **t** (01295) 712684  **f** (01295) 712838

**open** All year
**bedrooms** 2 double
**bathrooms** 1 en suite, 1 private
**payment** Cash/cheques

600-year-old listed converted barn with galleried dining room. Comfortable en suite rooms with TV. Safe parking, evening meals by arrangement, French and English country cooking.

⊕ *From M40 jct 11, take A422. At roundabout take 4th exit for Warkworth. St Martins House is on the left.*

Room 📺 ♨  General ♨2 ✂ ✕ ❀ 🐾

# It's all quality-assessed accommodation

Our commitment to quality involves wide-ranging accommodation assessment. Rating and awards were correct at the time of going to press but may change following a new assessment. Please check at time of booking.

## BATTLE, East Sussex Map ref 3B4

★★★

GUEST ACCOMMODATION

B&B per room per night
s Max £70.00
d Max £95.00
Evening meal per person
£6.95–£9.95

# Battle Golf Club

Netherfield Hill, Battle TN33 0LH  **t** (01424) 775677  **f** (01424) 777497  **e** clare@battlegolfclub.com
**w** battlegolfclub.com

Challenging golf course situated in scenic location
with excellent on-site accommodation facilities.
Just five minutes' drive from historic Battle. Bed
and breakfast, half board and full board available.
Golf school on site.

**open** All year
**bedrooms** 4 double
**bathrooms** All en suite
**payment** Credit/debit cards, cash/cheques

Room 📺 ♿ ♋  General P ♟ ✕ 🍴 🎿 🔥 ✳  Leisure ∪ ♪ ►

## BEAULIEU, Hampshire Map ref 2C3

★★★★

GUEST ACCOMMODATION

B&B per room per night
s £30.00–£45.00
d £50.00–£75.00

# Dale Farm House

Manor Road, Applemore Hill, Dibden, Southampton SO45 5TJ  **t** (023) 8084 9632  **f** (023) 8084 0285
**w** dalefarmhouse.co.uk

**open** All year
**bedrooms** 3 double, 2 family
**bathrooms** 4 en suite
**payment** Cash/cheques

Beautiful 18thC farmhouse in secluded wooded
setting with direct access for walks or cycling.
Peaceful garden in which to unwind and a bird-
watcher's paradise. Excellent food to satisfy your
appetite. Barbecues on request. Near beaches and
ferry link to Southampton. Spoil yourself at this BBC-
holiday-programme-featured bed and breakfast.

⊕ At Dibden roundabout go across and turn right into Manor
Road, follow lane for 250yds, turn right into drive, left at
bottom of drive before haybarn behind stables.

♥ 10% discount for Christmas breaks on a room-only basis.
3-for-2 weekend breaks Oct-Mar (excl Bank Holidays).

Room 🛁 📺 ♿  General 🔥 🛏 🅰 P ✂ 🍴 🎿 ✳  Leisure ∪ ♪ ► 🚲 🏊

## BEAULIEU, Hampshire Map ref 2C3

★★★★

BED & BREAKFAST

B&B per room per night
s £37.00–£40.00
d Max £65.00

# Leygreen Farm House

Lyndhurst Road, Beaulieu, Brockenhurst SO42 7YP  **t** (01590) 612355  **f** (01590) 612355
**w** newforest.demon.co.uk/leygreen.htm

**open** All year except Christmas
**bedrooms** 2 double, 1 twin
**bathrooms** All en suite
**payment** Cash/cheques

Victorian farmhouse in rural setting, one mile from
Beaulieu village. Ideal for Motor Museum, Bucklers
Hard, New Forest and Exbury Gardens. Mountain
bikes available for guests' use. Off-road parking.
Discounts for three days or more. A warm welcome
assured. Horse-riding, sports centre and golf within
three miles.

⊕ M27 jct 2. Follow brown signs to Motor Museum. We are
on B3056 0.5 miles past museum on the left.

Room 📺 ♿ ♋  General 🔥 14 P ✂ 🍴 ✳  Leisure 🚲

## Looking for a little luxury

Gold and Silver Awards are given to establishments achieving the highest levels of
quality and service. There's more information at the front of the guide, and an index to
all accommodation achieving these awards at the back.

---

**BEXHILL-ON-SEA,** East Sussex Map ref 3B4

★★★
**BED & BREAKFAST**

B&B per room per night
**s** £20.00–£30.00
**d** £40.00–£60.00
Evening meal per person
£5.00–£10.00

# Barkers Bed and Breakfast

16 Magdalen Road, Bexhill-on-Sea TN40 1SB  **t** (01424) 218969

Large friendly family home. Close to station, small town and ten minutes from seafront and sandy beach.

**open** All year except Christmas
**bedrooms** 1 double, 1 twin
**payment** Cash/cheques

Room 📺 ☕ General ☺5 ✕ ♞

---

**BIDDENDEN,** Kent Map ref 3B4

★★★★
**GUEST ACCOMMODATION**

B&B per room per night
**s** £40.00–£50.00
**d** £50.00–£65.00
Evening meal per person
£17.50

# Heron Cottage

Biddenden, Ashford TN27 8HH  **t** (01580) 291358  **w** heroncottage.info

**bedrooms** 3 double, 2 twin, 2 family
**bathrooms** 6 en suite
**payment** Cash/cheques

Situated between historic Biddenden and Sissinghurst Castle, this delightful cottage is set in five acres surrounded completely by farmland. The carefully furnished bedrooms are thoughtfully equipped and have co-ordinated soft furnishings. Breakfast is served in the smart dining room and there is a cosy lounge with an open fire. Open February to December.

⊕ *From Biddenden A262 west. 1st right after 0.25m, sharp left bend, cross bend, through stone pillars opposite, then left along unmade road.*

Room ⚿ 📺 ☕ ☕ General ☺ 🏠 🌣 P ✕ 🛏 ◉ ❄ ♞  Leisure ⌇ 🏊

---

**BLADBEAN,** Kent Map ref 3B4

★★★★
**GUEST ACCOMMODATION**

B&B per room per night
**s** £30.00–£35.00
**d** £50.00–£55.00
Evening meal per person
£8.00–£12.00

# Molehills

Bladbean, Canterbury CT4 6LU  **t** (01303) 840051  **e** molehills84@hotmail.com

**open** All year except Christmas
**bedrooms** 1 double, 1 twin
**bathrooms** All en suite
**payment** Cash/cheques, euros

The house, in large gardens, is in a peaceful hamlet within the beautiful Elham Valley. We are within easy reach of Canterbury and the Channel terminals. We produce home-grown vegetables and excellent home cooking. Our comfortable accommodation includes ground floor bedrooms, sitting room with woodburning stove and conservatory.

⊕ *From A2 take exit for Barham. Beyond Barham (1.5 miles) pass the Palm Tree pub, take right turn at small crossroads. Continue for 0.5 mile over crossroads. Molehills is 3rd house on right.*

Room ⚿ 📺 ☕ ☕ General ☺ P ⚲ ✕ 🛏 ❄ ♞

---

**BOGNOR REGIS,** West Sussex Map ref 2C3

★★★★
**BED & BREAKFAST**
**SILVER AWARD**

B&B per room per night
**s** £40.00–£45.00
**d** £60.00–£80.00

# Alderwasley Cottage

Off West Street, Bognor Regis PO21 1XH  **t** (01243) 821339  **e** alderwasley@btinternet.com
**w** alderwasleycottage.co.uk

Lovely old cottage set in award-winning walled garden on private road close to beach. Adjacent, off-road parking. Comfortable rooms overlooking sea. Ideal base for exploring beautiful West Sussex and Hampshire.

**open** All year
**bedrooms** 2 double, 1 twin
**bathrooms** 1 en suite, 2 private
**payment** Cash/cheques

Room 📺 ☕ ☕ General ☺ 🏠 🌣 P ⚲ 🛏 🛏 ❄  Leisure ⌇ ♟ 🚲

---

---

**BOGNOR REGIS,** West Sussex Map ref 2C3

★ ★ ★
GUEST ACCOMMODATION

B&B per room per night
s £25.00–£40.00
d £50.00–£80.00

## Jubilee Guest House

5 Gloucester Road, Bognor Regis PO21 1NU  t (01243) 863016  f (01243) 868017
e jubileeguesthouse@tiscali.co.uk  w jubileeguesthouse.com

Family-run business, 75yds from seafront and beach. Ideal for visiting Butlins family entertainment resort, Chichester, Goodwood, Fontwell, Arundel, Portsmouth and the Isle of Wight.

**open** All year except Christmas and New Year
**bedrooms** 1 double, 2 single, 3 family
**bathrooms** 2 en suite, 1 private
**payment** Credit/debit cards, cash, euros

Room 📺 ♿ 🍵  General ⎈ ⊞ ♿ P

---

**BOGNOR REGIS,** West Sussex Map ref 2C3

★ ★ ★ ★
BED & BREAKFAST

B&B per room per night
s £40.00–£45.00
d £70.00–£90.00

## White Horses Felpham Bed & Breakfast

Clyde Road, Felpham, Bognor Regis PO22 7AH  t (01243) 824320  e info@whitehorsesfelpham.co.uk
w whitehorsesfelpham.co.uk

**open** All year
**bedrooms** 2 double, 1 twin, 1 family
**bathrooms** 3 en suite, 1 private
**payment** Cash/cheques

White Horses is located in a quiet cul-de-sac 20yds from Felpham beach. It has recently been refurbished and offers high-quality accommodation in a friendly environment. A three-mile promenade close to the entrance provides easy seaside walking with a variety of amenities for all ages.

Room 📺 ♿  General ⎈ ⊞ ♿ P ✂ ❁

---

**BONCHURCH,** Isle of Wight Map ref 2C3

★ ★ ★ ★
GUEST ACCOMMODATION

B&B per room per night
s £35.00–£43.00
d £70.00–£88.00
Evening meal per person
£12.00

## The Lake

Shore Road, Bonchurch, Ventnor PO38 1RF  t (01983) 852613  f (01983) 852613
e enquiries@lakehotel.co.uk  w lakehotel.co.uk

**bedrooms** 10 double, 5 twin, 1 single, 4 family
**bathrooms** All en suite
**payment** Credit/debit cards, cash/cheques, euros

Charming country-house hotel in two acres of beautiful gardens. Located on the seaward side of Bonchurch Pond in the 'olde worlde' village of Bonchurch. Run by the same family for over 40 years, we are confident of offering you the best-value accommodation and food on our beautiful island. Open February to November.

⊕ *Car ferry breaks available. Public transport directions on our website.*

♥ *4-night special break including breakfast, dinner and car ferry from any port from £160.00.*

Room 🛁 🗄 📺 ♿  General ⎈3 P ▯ ☕ 🔥 ❁ 🐕  Leisure ▶ 🚲

---

## Using map references

The map references refer to the colour maps at the front of this guide. The first figure is the map number, the letter and figure that follow indicate the grid reference on the map.

## BONCHURCH, Isle of Wight Map ref 2C3

★★★★★
**GUEST HOUSE
SILVER AWARD**

B&B per room per night
s £60.00–£65.00
d £100.00–£190.00

# Winterbourne Country House

Bonchurch Village Road, Ventnor PO38 1RQ  t (01983) 852535  f (01983) 857529
e info@winterbournehouse.co.uk  w winterbournehouse.co.uk

**open** All year except Christmas and New Year
**bedrooms** 3 double, 1 twin, 1 single, 2 suites
**bathrooms** 6 en suite, 1 private
**payment** Credit/debit cards, cash/cheques

Winterbourne is a country house of great charm and character, located in one of the most beautiful and tranquil settings on the island. Enchanting gardens ablaze with colour in season. You will receive a welcome of genuine warmth in the house where Charles Dickens made his home whilst writing 'David Copperfield'.

Room 🖭 📞 📺 👜 🖵  General P ⚹ 🍽 🎿 ✿ 🐾  Leisure ⌇

## BRASTED, Kent Map ref 2D2

★★★★
**BED & BREAKFAST**

B&B per room per night
s £30.00–£35.00
d £60.00–£70.00

# The Mount House

Brasted, Westerham TN16 1JB  t (01959) 563617  f (01959) 561296  e diana@themounthouse.com
w themounthouse.com

Large, early-Georgian family residence in centre of village. Listed Grade II. Convenient for Knole, Hever, Penshurst and fast trains to London from Sevenoaks.

**open** All year except Christmas and New Year
**bedrooms** 1 double, 1 twin, 1 single
**bathrooms** 1 en suite, 1 private
**payment** Cash/cheques

Room 📺 👜 🖵  General ⌷1 P ⚹ 🎿 ✿  Leisure ⚲

## BREDE, East Sussex Map ref 3B4

★★★
**BED & BREAKFAST**

B&B per room per night
s £25.00–£30.00
d £50.00–£55.00
Evening meal per person
£12.00–£18.00

# 2 Stonelink Cottages

Stubb Lane, Brede, Rye TN31 6BL  t (01424) 882943 & 07802 573612  f (01424) 883052
e stonelinkC@aol.com  w visit-rye.co.uk

Traditional clapboard house overlooking Brede Valley, surrounded on all sides by 134 acres of farming land. Quiet, relaxing. Close to Rye, Hastings and Tunbridge Wells. Evening meals by prior arrangement.

**open** All year except Christmas and New Year
**bedrooms** 1 double, 1 single
**payment** Cash/cheques

Room 📺 👜  General ⌷ P ✕ 🎿 ✿  Leisure 🏠

## BRIGHSTONE, Isle of Wight Map ref 2C3

★★★★
**FARMHOUSE**

B&B per room per night
s £35.00–£45.00
d £60.00–£70.00

# Chilton Farm B&B

Chilton Farm, Chilton Lane, Newport PO30 4DS  t (01983) 740338  f (01983) 741370
e info@chiltonfarm.co.uk  w chiltonfarm.co.uk

A warm welcome assured on our 800-acre working farm. All rooms en suite in separate accommodation behind main farmhouse. Breakfast in farmhouse. Two tennis courts, large garden, close to sea.

**open** All year except Christmas and New Year
**bedrooms** 2 double, 1 twin, 1 suite
**bathrooms** All en suite
**payment** Credit/debit cards, cash/cheques

Room ♿ 📺 👜  General ⌷ P ▣ ✿  Leisure ⚲ ⚓

## If you have access needs...

Look for the National Accessible Scheme symbols if you have special hearing, visual or mobility needs. An index of accommodation participating in the scheme can be found at the back of this guide.

**BRIGHTON & HOVE,** East Sussex Map ref 2D3

★★★
GUEST ACCOMMODATION

B&B per room per night
s £25.00–£40.00
d £60.00–£80.00

## Andorra Guest Accommodation

15-16 Oriental Place, Brighton BN1 2LJ  t (01273) 321787  f (01273) 721418
w andorrahotelbrighton.co.uk

Try our established, comfortable hotel with well-appointed bedrooms. Whether your stay is for a holiday, attending a conference or visiting town overnight, it will be an enjoyable one.

**open** All year
**bedrooms** 7 double, 2 twin, 6 single, 4 family
**bathrooms** 17 en suite, 2 private
**payment** Credit/debit cards

Room ⊟ ⌨ 📞 📺 💧 ⌇   General ⌛16 ⍩

**BRIGHTON & HOVE,** East Sussex Map ref 2D3

★★★
GUEST ACCOMMODATION

B&B per room per night
s £25.00–£50.00
d £50.00–£100.00

## Atlantic Seafront

16 Marine Parade, Brighton BN2 1TL  t (01273) 695944  f (01273) 694944
e majanatlantic@hotmail.com  w atlantichotelbrighton.co.uk

Attractive family-run, sea-facing hotel opposite Brighton Pier and Sea Life centre. The historic Royal Pavilion and famous Lanes are across the road. Brighton Centre nearby. Non-smoking.

**open** All year
**bedrooms** 6 double, 1 twin, 1 single, 2 family
**bathrooms** All en suite
**payment** Credit/debit cards, cash/cheques

Room 📞 📺 💧 ⌇   General ⌛ ♨ ✂ ⍩ ✳

**BRIGHTON & HOVE,** East Sussex Map ref 2D3

★★★
GUEST ACCOMMODATION

B&B per room per night
s £29.00–£45.00
d £55.00–£115.00

## The Dove

18 Regency Square, Brighton BN1 2FG  t (01273) 779222  f (01273) 746912
e enquiries@thedovehotel.co.uk  w thedovehotel.co.uk

Seafront-square hotel with bright, recently refurbished, en suite bedrooms, freshly cooked breakfast and a genuine, warm welcome.

**open** All year
**bedrooms** 3 double, 3 twin, 2 single, 1 family
**bathrooms** All en suite
**payment** Credit/debit cards, cash

Room ⊟ 📞 📺 💧   General ⌛ ▥ ✕ ⍥ ⍩ ✳   Leisure ♪ ⚑ ⚙

**BRIGHTON & HOVE,** East Sussex Map ref 2D3

★★★
GUEST ACCOMMODATION

B&B per room per night
s £15.00–£32.00
d £30.00–£64.00

## Sandpiper Guest House

11 Russell Square, Brighton BN1 2EE  t (01273) 328202  f (01273) 329974
e sandpiper@brighton.co.uk

Recently refurbished guesthouse, two minutes from conference centre, shopping area, leisure centres and seafront. Rooms have central heating, colour TV. Unrestricted access. Non-smoking rooms available.

**open** All year
**bedrooms** 2 double, 1 twin, 3 single, 2 family
**payment** Credit/debit cards, cash/cheques, euros

Room 📺 💧 ⌇   General ⌛

# A holiday for Fido?

Some proprietors welcome well-behaved pets. Look for the 🐾 symbol in the accommodation listings. You can also buy a copy of our new guide – Welcome Pets! – available from good bookshops and online at visitbritaindirect.com.

### BRIGHTON & HOVE, East Sussex Map ref 2D3

★★★★
GUEST ACCOMMODATION

B&B per room per night
d £85.00–£135.00
Evening meal per person
£15.00–£35.00

# The Townhouse Brighton

19 New Steine, Brighton BN2 1PD  t (01273) 607456  f (01273) 677276
e info@thetownhousebrighton.com  w thetownhousebrighton.com

**open** All year
**bedrooms** 7 double, 1 twin
**bathrooms** All en suite
**payment** Credit/debit cards, cash

The Townhouse offers all the amenities of a luxury hotel but in unique interior-designed rooms that transport you away from the mundane. Eight stunning rooms, a new restaurant and cocktail bar and a view of the beach and pier in the heart of the city. Travel the world without ever leaving Brighton.

⊕ *Once at the beach and pier, turn left (east) and 500 yds on left is a grass square called New Steine. Number 19 is at the top on the right.*

Room 🛏 🚪 ☎ 📺 👝 ↻   General 🕮 🏠 🔌 🍴 ⛄   Leisure ∪ ♪ ▶ ☂

### BRIZE NORTON, Oxfordshire Map ref 2C1

★★★
GUEST ACCOMMODATION

B&B per room per night
s £30.00–£45.00
d £55.00–£80.00

# The Priory

Manor Farm, Manor Road, Brize Norton OX18 3NA  t (01993) 843062  f (01993) 843062
e mail@priorymanor.wanadoo.co.uk  w priorymanor.co.uk

Situated in Brize Norton village, a beautiful character house in natural stone, set in 0.75 acres of beautiful gardens. Ample parking, comfortable rooms with tea-/coffee-making facilities and colour TV.

**open** All year
**bedrooms** 2 double, 1 twin, 1 family, 2 suites
**bathrooms** 5 en suite, 1 private
**payment** Cash/cheques, euros

Room 🛏 📺 👝   General 🕮 🛏 P ✂ ✕ ⛄ ✿   Leisure ∪ ♪ ▶ ⛷ ☂

### BROADSTAIRS, Kent Map ref 3C3

★★★★
GUEST ACCOMMODATION

B&B per room per night
s £40.00–£60.00
d £80.00–£90.00
Evening meal per person
£25.00

# The Bay Tree

12 Eastern Esplanade, Broadstairs CT10 1DR  t (01843) 862502  f (01843) 860589

**open** All year except Christmas and New Year
**bedrooms** 9 double, 1 twin, 1 single
**bathrooms** All en suite
**payment** Credit/debit cards, cash/cheques

Situated on the lovely Eastern Esplanade overlooking Stone Bay, the hotel enjoys panoramic sea views across the English Channel. Minutes from the town centre and sandy beaches. A warm welcome awaits you at this family-run hotel.

⊕ *A299 to Broadstairs. Eastern Esplanade is close to High Street.*

Room 🛏 📺 👝 ↻   General 🕮 10 P ✂ ✕ ✿

### BROCKENHURST, Hampshire Map ref 2C3

★★
BED & BREAKFAST

B&B per room per night
s £20.00–£25.00
d £40.00–£50.00

# Goldenhayes

9 Chestnut Road, Brockenhurst SO42 7RF  t (01590) 623743

Single-storey, owner-occupied home, in central but quiet situation. Close to village, station and open forest. Large garden.

**open** All year
**bedrooms** 1 twin, 1 family
**payment** Cash/cheques, euros

Room 🛏 📺 ↻   General 🕮 🏠 P ✂ ⛄ ✿ 🐕   Leisure ∪ ♪ ▶ ⛷ ☂

## BUCKINGHAM, Buckinghamshire Map ref 2C1

★★★★
**FARMHOUSE**

B&B per room per night
s £35.00–£60.00
d £35.00–£60.00

# Radclive Dairy Farm

Radclive Road, Buckingham MK18 4AA  **t** (01280) 813433  **f** (01280) 813433
**e** rosalind.fisher@radclivedairyfarm.co.uk  **w** radclivedairyfarm.co.uk

Quality accommodation. Stunning views across unspoilt countryside. Colour TV, coffee facilities, en suite. Ample parking. Convenient for Stowe Landscaped Gardens and Silverstone Circuit.

**open** All year except Christmas and New Year
**bedrooms** 1 double, 1 twin
**bathrooms** All en suite
**payment** Credit/debit cards, cash/cheques

Room 📺 ♿ ☕  General ⛱ 🏠 P ⚡ 🔥

## BURFORD, Oxfordshire Map ref 2B1

★★★★
**GUEST ACCOMMODATION**

B&B per room per night
s £35.00–£45.00
d £60.00–£80.00

# Cotland House B&B

Fulbrook Hill, Burford OX18 4BH  **t** (01993) 822382  **e** info@cotlandhouse.com  **w** otlandhouse.com

**open** All year except Christmas and New Year
**bedrooms** 1 double, 1 twin, 1 single, 1 family
**bathrooms** All en suite
**payment** Cash/cheques

Cotland House B&B is a charming Cotswold-stone home restored to an exceptional standard with stylish, luxurious en suite rooms. A fabulous breakfast, made from organic/local produce, is served in front of a wood-burning stove or on the sunny terrace depending on the season. A perfect Cotswold base.

⊕ *From Burford head north 300m following signs to Chipping Norton/Banbury. Property is on the right-hand side past Fulbrook sign. 3 minutes' walk to Burford.*

♥ *Midweek special offers available on two nights or more. Discount given on Sunday night when staying the weekend.*

Room 📺 ♿ ☕  General ⛱ 🏠 ⚼ P ⚡ 🏕 🔥 ▣ ✿  Leisure ∪ ⚓ ► 🚲 🏛

## BURLEY, Hampshire Map ref 2B3

★★★★
**BED & BREAKFAST
GOLD AWARD**

B&B per room per night
s £40.00–£45.00
d £75.00–£80.00

# Holmans

Bisterne Close, Burley, Ringwood BH24 4AZ  **t** (01425) 402307  **f** (01425) 402307
**e** holmans@talktalk.net

Charming country house set in four acres overlooking New Forest. All bedrooms en suite and tastefully furnished. Superb walking. Pub within walking distance. Own horses welcome, stabling available.

**open** All year except Christmas
**bedrooms** 2 double, 1 twin
**bathrooms** All en suite
**payment** Cash/cheques

Room 📺 ♿ ☕  General ⛱ 🏠 ⚼ P ⚡ 🐴 ✿ 🐎  Leisure ∪ ⚓ ► 🚲 🏛

# Check the maps

Colour maps at the front pinpoint all the cities, towns and villages where you will find accommodation entries in the regional sections. Pick your location and then refer to the place index at the back to find the page number.

## BURLEY, Hampshire Map ref 2B3

★★★★
**BED & BREAKFAST**

B&B per room per night
s £35.00–£45.00
d £55.00–£65.00
Evening meal per person
£15.00–£25.00

# Wayside Cottage

27 Garden Road, Burley, Ringwood BH24 4EA  t (01425) 403414  e jwest@wayside-cottage.co.uk
w wayside-cottage.co.uk

**open** All year
**bedrooms** 3 double, 2 twin, 1 family
**bathrooms** 5 en suite, 1 private
**payment** Cash/cheques

Enchanting wisteria-covered Edwardian cottage in peaceful location in the heart of the New Forest. A haven of tranquillity, full of antique furniture and china, ideal for walking, cycling or exploring the forest and coast, or just relax in our delightful cottage gardens. Local produce cooked by ex-professional chef. Dinners by arrangement.

⊕ *Leave A31 Picket Post services east of Ringwood. Through Burley Street to Burley. Right onto Garden Road, opposite Burley Manor, 200yds on left.*

Room 🛁 📻 📺 👜 🍴   General 🛏 🎱 🖊 P 🍴 ✕ 🎮 🅟 ✳   Leisure ∪ 🎣 🏂 🚲 🚣

## CADNAM, Hampshire Map ref 2C3

★★★★
**GUEST ACCOMMODATION**

B&B per room per night
s Min £35.00
d Min £58.00

# Kingsbridge House

Southampton Road, Cadnam SO40 2NH  t (023) 8081 1161
e linda@kingsbridgehouse.freeserve.co.uk  w kingsbridgehousebandb.co.uk

A warm, friendly welcome awaits you at this distinctive house. Local amenities/pubs available, easy access to the New Forest and surrounding areas.

**open** All year
**bedrooms** 2 double, 1 family
**bathrooms** All en suite
**payment** Cash/cheques, euros

Room 📺 👜 🍴   General 🛏 🎱 🖊 P 🍴 🎮 🅟 ✳   Leisure ∪ 🎣 🏂 🚲 🚣

## CANTERBURY, Kent Map ref 3B3

★★★★
**GUEST ACCOMMODATION**

B&B per room per night
s £35.00
d £55.00–£65.00

# Alexandra House

1 Roper Road, Canterbury CT2 7EH  t (01227) 786617  e reservations@alexandrahouse.net
w alexandrahouse.net

Family-run guesthouse close to city centre, cathedral, university, Canterbury West station and Marlowe Theatre. Private car parking. Full English breakfast with vegetarian options. All rooms are en suite.

**open** All year
**bedrooms** 2 double, 2 twin, 1 single, 2 family
**bathrooms** All en suite
**payment** Credit/debit cards, cash/cheques

Room 🛁 📺 👜 🍴   General 🛏 🎱 🖊 P 🍴 ✳ 🐕   Leisure 🚲 🚣

## CANTERBURY, Kent Map ref 3B3

★★★
**GUEST HOUSE**

B&B per room per night
s £28.00–£40.00
d £50.00–£65.00
Evening meal per person
Min £15.00

# Anns House

63 London Road, Canterbury CT2 8JZ  t (01227) 768767  f (01227) 768172
e info@annshousecanterbury.co.uk  w annshousecanterbury.co.uk

**open** All year
**bedrooms** 4 double, 3 twin, 2 single, 3 family
**bathrooms** All en suite
**payment** Credit/debit cards, cash/cheques, euros

A beautiful Victorian house restored with love and care to accommodate the modern traveller or holiday guest. Close to the city centre, university and train station. Ample private parking.

Room 🛁 📻 📺 👜 🍴   General 🛏 P 🍴 ✕ 🎮 🐕   Leisure 🚲 🚣

---

**CANTERBURY,** Kent Map ref 3B3

★★★★
**BED & BREAKFAST**
**SILVER AWARD**

## Bower Farm House

Bossingham Road, Stelling Minnis, Canterbury CT4 6BB  **t** (01227) 709430
**e** anne@bowerbb.freeserve.co.uk  **w** bowerfarmhouse.co.uk

B&B per room per night
**s** £42.00
**d** £60.00

**open** All year except Christmas
**bedrooms** 1 double, 1 twin
**bathrooms** All en suite
**payment** Cash/cheques, euros

Delightful, heavily beamed, 17thC farmhouse
between the villages of Stelling Minnis and
Bossingham. Canterbury and Hythe are
approximately seven miles away. Home-laid eggs,
home-made bread … a peaceful countryside
experience.

⊕ *From B2086 turn to Stelling Minnis. Into Curtis Lane, 1st
left past Rose and Crown. Turn left at T-junction towards
Bossingham. Down track on right signed B&B.*

Room ♿ ♨  General ⛱ ▥ ♿ P ⚲ ﹏ ⌨ ❀ 🐾  Leisure ∪ ⏰ ▸ ⚓ 🏊

---

**CANTERBURY,** Kent Map ref 3B3

★★★★
**GUEST ACCOMMODATION**
**SILVER AWARD**

## Castle House

28 Castle Street, Canterbury CT1 2PT  **t** (01227) 761897  **e** enquries@castlehousehotel.co.uk
**w** castlehousehotel.co.uk

B&B per room per night
**s** £45.00–£65.00
**d** £65.00–£75.00

Castle House, located in the heart of the city, was
built in 1720. Castle House takes its name from
the Norman Castle opposite.

**open** All year
**bedrooms** 3 double, 2 twin, 1 single, 1 family
**bathrooms** All en suite
**payment** Cash/cheques

Room ♿ 📺 ♨  General ⛱ ▥ ♿ P ⚲ ﹏ ⌨ ✆ ▣ ❀  Leisure 🚲 ⚓

---

**CANTERBURY,** Kent Map ref 3B3

**Rating Applied For**
**GUEST HOUSE**

## Clare Ellen Guest House

9 Victoria Road, Wincheap, Canterbury CT1 3SG  **t** (01227) 760205  **f** (01227) 784482
**e** enquiry@clareellenguesthouse.co.uk  **w** clareellenguesthouse.co.uk

B&B per room per night
**s** £32.00–£34.00
**d** £58.00–£68.00

**open** All year
**bedrooms** 3 double, 2 twin, 1 single, 1 family
**bathrooms** All en suite
**payment** Credit/debit cards, cash/cheques, euros

A family-run Victorian guesthouse, situated in quiet
area minutes from town centre, benefits from private
parking, garden, swimming pool and free internet
access. Large, elegant en suite bedrooms feature TV,
hairdryer, clock radio, mini-fridge and tea-/coffee-
making facilities. Full English breakfast, vegetarian
and special diets catered for on request.

⊕ *From A2 to Canterbury, A2050 Rheims Way. Turn right at
3rd roundabout, A28, Victoria Road 4th on left.*

♥ *Discounts for 2-/3-night stay Nov-Mar (excl Christmas and
New Year).*

Room 📺 ♿ ♨  General ⛱ ▥ ♿ P ⚲ ✕ ﹏ ✆ ▣ ❀  Leisure ✎

---

## Town, country or coast

The entertainment, shopping and innovative attractions of the big cities, the
magnificent vistas of the countryside or the relaxing and refreshing coast – this guide
will help you find what you're looking for.

**CANTERBURY,** Kent Map ref 3B3

★★★★
**FARMHOUSE**

B&B per room per night
s £35.00–£45.00
d £70.00–£80.00
Evening meal per person
£15.00–£20.00

# Hornbeams

Jesses Hill, Kingston, Canterbury CT4 6JD  **t** (01227) 830119  **f** (01227) 830119
**e** bandb@hornbeams.co.uk  **w** hornbeams.co.uk

**open** All year except Christmas
**bedrooms** 1 double, 1 twin, 1 single
**bathrooms** 1 en suite, 1 private
**payment** Cash/cheques

Rolling hills and woodland, long views over luscious Kent, and a lovely garden. Full English breakfast on patio (weather permitting). Hornbeams is an idyllic place to stay, the ultimate escapism, yet near to local town and historical landmarks. Canterbury seven miles, Dover ten miles, Channel Tunnel 20 minutes. Good private parking.

⊕ *From A2 (Canterbury to Dover), right to Kingston. Right at bottom of hill into The Street. Top of the hill, right fork. 1st left, left into farm.*

Room 🛏 📺 ♿ 🍵  General 🛎 🏕 P ⚹ ✕ 🍽 ❉ 🐾  Leisure ∪ 🏖

**CANTERBURY,** Kent Map ref 3B3

★★★★
**GUEST HOUSE**

B&B per room per night
s £30.00–£60.00
d £50.00–£75.00

# Kingsbridge Villa

15 Best Lane, Canterbury CT1 2JB  **t** (01227) 766415  **f** (01227) 766415
**e** info@canterburyguesthouse.com  **w** canterburyguesthouse.com

Family-run, city-centre Victorian guesthouse. Free car parking. Licensed restaurant. Fire certificate. Close to cathedral and shops.

**open** All year
**bedrooms** 4 double, 2 twin, 1 single, 2 family
**bathrooms** All en suite
**payment** Cash/cheques, euros

Room 🛏 📞 📺 ♿ 🍵  General 🛎 🏕 🏠 P ⚹ 🍽 🍴 ❉ 🐾  Leisure 🚶 🚲

**CANTERBURY,** Kent Map ref 3B3

★★★★★
**GUEST ACCOMMODATION
GOLD AWARD**

B&B per room per night
s £55.00–£65.00
d £95.00–£145.00
Evening meal per person
£30.00–£35.00

# Magnolia House

36 St Dunstans Terrace, Canterbury CT2 8AX  **t** (01227) 765121  **f** (01227) 765121
**e** info@magnoliahousecanterbury.co.uk  **w** magnoliahousecanterbury.co.uk

**open** All year except Christmas
**bedrooms** 5 double, 1 twin, 1 single
**bathrooms** All en suite
**payment** Credit/debit cards, cash/cheques

Charming, late-Georgian house in quiet residential street, a ten-minute stroll from the city centre. Bedrooms have every facility for an enjoyable stay. Varied breakfasts are served overlooking the attractive walled garden.

Room 🛏 🖳 📺 ♿ 🍵  General 🛎 12 P ⚹ ✕ 🍴 ❉

**CANTERBURY,** Kent Map ref 3B3

★★★★
**GUEST ACCOMMODATION**

B&B per room per night
s £35.00–£40.00
d £60.00–£70.00

# Oak Cottage

Elmsted, Ashford TN25 5JT  **t** (01233) 750272  **f** (01233) 750543  **e** oakcottage@invictanet.co.uk
**w** oakcottage-elmsted.co.uk

An attractive 17thC cottage with independent guest wing with own TV, conservatory and beautiful garden set in unspoilt, wooded countryside. Ideally placed for Canterbury, castles, gardens, golf, steam trains, restaurants.

**open** All year except Christmas
**bedrooms** 1 double, 2 single
**bathrooms** 1 en suite
**payment** Cash/cheques, euros

Room 📺 ♿ 🍵  General 🛎 🏕 🏠 P ⚹ 🍴 🔥 ❉ 🐾  Leisure ∪ ⏸ 🏖

## CANTERBURY, Kent Map ref 3B3

★★★★
**GUEST HOUSE**
**SILVER AWARD**

B&B per room per night
s £50.00–£60.00
d £90.00–£115.00

# Yorke Lodge

50 London Road, Canterbury CT2 8LF  **t** (01227) 451243  **f** (01227) 462006
**e** enquiries@yorkelodge.com  **w** yorkelodge.com

**open** All year
**bedrooms** 5 double, 1 twin, 1 single, 1 family
**bathrooms** All en suite
**payment** Credit/debit cards, cash/cheques

Yorke Lodge is the ideal retreat after a long day sightseeing or a busy day at the office. Built in 1887 and fully refurbished over the last two years, this quintessential Victorian town house offers a warm home-from-home atmosphere, with all the modern conveniences now expected by the discerning traveller.

⊕ *From London via M2 and A2, take 1st exit signposted Canterbury. At 1st roundabout turn left into London Road, we are 100m on the left.*

♥ *Special low season deals. See website or ring for details.*

Room 🖼 📺 🛇 🖰  General 🕭 🏃 P 🍴 🗒 🔥 ✿ ⛟  Leisure ∪ ♪ ⊁ ♿

## CASSINGTON, Oxfordshire Map ref 2C1

★★★★
**FARMHOUSE**

B&B per room per night
d £65.00–£70.00

# Burleigh Farm

Bladon Road, Nr Cassington, Oxford OX29 4EA  **t** (01865) 881352  **e** cook_jane@btconnect.com
**w** oxfordcity.co.uk/accom/burleighfarm

Warm and comfortable stone farmhouse in a quiet location near Woodstock, six miles from Oxford, on Blenheim Palace Estate. On the edge of the Cotswolds, yet only an hour's drive from London.

**open** All year
**bedrooms** 1 double, 1 family
**bathrooms** All en suite
**payment** Cash/cheques

Room 📺 🛇 🖰  General 🕭 🗒 🏃 P 🍴 🗒 ✿ ⛟  Leisure 🚴

## CHALFONT ST GILES, Buckinghamshire Map ref 2D2

★★★★
**BED & BREAKFAST**

B&B per room per night
s £30.00
d £60.00

# Gorelands Corner

Gorelands Lane, Chalfont St Giles HP8 4HQ  **t** (01494) 872689  **f** (01494) 872689
**e** bickfordcsg@onetel.com

**open** All year
**bedrooms** 1 double, 1 suite
**bathrooms** 1 en suite, 1 private
**payment** Cash/cheques

Family home, set in large garden, close to picturesque village. Easy access to M25, M40, M4, London underground and London Heathrow Airport.

⊕ *Gorelands Lane is off the B4446. Gorelands Corner is on the junction with Deadmearn Lane.*

Room 📺 🛇 🖰  General 🕭 🍴 ✿  Leisure 🚴

## CHALGROVE, Oxfordshire Map ref 2C2

★★
**BED & BREAKFAST**

B&B per room per night
s Min £25.00
d Min £50.00

# Cornerstones

1 Cromwell Close, Chalgrove, Oxford OX44 7SE  **t** (01865) 890298  **e** corner.stones@virgin.net
**w** http://freespace.virgin.net/corner.stones

Bungalow in pretty village with thatched cottages. The Red Lion (0.5 miles away) serves good and reasonably priced food.

**open** All year except Christmas and New Year
**bedrooms** 2 twin
**payment** Cash/cheques

Room 🖮 📺 🛇 🖰  General 🕭 5 🍴 ✿ ⛟

## CHELWOOD GATE, East Sussex Map ref 2D2

★★★★
**GUEST HOUSE**

B&B per room per night
s £33.00–£45.00
d £66.00–£68.00

# Holly House

Beaconsfield Road, Chelwood Gate RH17 7LF  **t** (01825) 740484
**e** deebirchell@hollyhousebnb.demon.co.uk  **w** hollyhousebnb.demon.co.uk

**open** All year
**bedrooms** 2 double, 2 twin, 1 single
**bathrooms** 3 en suite
**payment** Cash/cheques

Holly House, an early Victorian forest farmhouse, now a comfortable family home, offers a warm welcome with an inviting lounge, comfortable beds and memorable breakfasts.

⊕ *From M25, A22 through East Grinstead to Wych Cross. Left on A275 1 mile, left into Beaconsfield Road. 800yds on right opposite village hall.*

♥ *Discount for 3 nights or more.*

Room 🛁 📺 👤 🍷   General 🛏 🎡 ⚓ P ⚒ 🎮 🐾 ❀ 🐕   Leisure ⚓ ∪ ↗ ⚓ 🚲 🏛

## CHICHESTER, West Sussex Map ref 2C3

★★★
**BED & BREAKFAST**

B&B per room per night
s £30.00
d £60.00

# Kia-ora

Main Road, Nutbourne, Chichester PO18 8RT  **t** (01243) 572858  **f** (01243) 572858
**e** ruthiefp@tiscali.co.uk

Views to Chichester Harbour. Warm welcome in comfortable family house. Large garden. Restaurants and country pubs within walking distance. Closed Christmas.

**open** All year except Christmas
**bedrooms** 1 double
**bathrooms** En suite
**payment** Cash/cheques, euros

Room 🛁 📺 👤 🍷   General 🛏 P ⚒ ❀ 🐕   Leisure 🏛

## CHICHESTER, West Sussex Map ref 2C3

★★★★
**BED & BREAKFAST**

B&B per room per night
s £40.00–£45.00
d £70.00–£95.00

# Spooners

1 Maplehurst Road, Chichester PO19 6QL  **t** (01243) 528467  **e** sue-spooner@tiscali.co.uk

Two spacious en suite rooms with TV in quiet area of northern Chichester. Overlooking countryside, adjacent to walking country, yet city and Chichester Festival Theatre within 1.5 miles. No smoking.

**open** All year except Christmas
**bedrooms** 1 double, 1 twin
**bathrooms** All en suite
**payment** Cash/cheques

Room 📺 👤 🍷   General P ⚒ 🎮 ❀   Leisure 🏛

## CHILGROVE, West Sussex Map ref 2C3

★★★★
**BED & BREAKFAST**

B&B per room per night
s £55.00–£75.00
d £80.00–£120.00

# Chilgrove Farm

Chilgrove Park Road, Chichester PO18 9HU  **t** (01243) 519436  **f** (01243) 519438
**e** simonrenwick@aol.com

**open** All year except Christmas and New Year
**bedrooms** 2 double
**bathrooms** All en suite
**payment** Credit/debit cards, cash/cheques

Rooms in farmhouse and new annexe situated seven miles north of Chichester in the South Downs. One first-floor room in house, two ground-floor rooms in annexe, 15 metres from house. All en suite.

Room 🛁 📺 👤   General P ⚒ ❀

## COLWELL BAY, Isle of Wight Map ref 2C3

★★★★
**GUEST HOUSE**

B&B per room per night
s £36.00–£40.00
d £52.00–£60.00

### Rockstone Cottage

Colwell Chine Road, Colwell Bay, Freshwater PO40 9NR  **t** (01983) 753723
**e** enquiries@rockstonecottage.co.uk  **w** rockstonecottage.co.uk

Charming cottage built in 1790, situated 300
yards from Colwell Bay and its safe, sandy beach.
Surrounded by lovely walks and picturesque
countryside. Riding stables, golf course and
leisure centre nearby.

**open** All year
**bedrooms** 2 double, 2 twin, 1 family
**bathrooms** All en suite
**payment** Cash/cheques

Room 📺 ♨ ⚑  General ➺12 P ⚹ ᕄ 🅟 ✿  Leisure ∪ ⚲ 🏠

## COTSWOLDS

See under Brize Norton, Burford, Cassington, Shipton-under-Wychwood, Woodstock
See also Cotswolds in the Heart of England and South West England sections

## COWES, Isle of Wight Map ref 2C3

★★★★
**GUEST ACCOMMODATION**

B&B per room per night
s Min £35.00
d £60.00–£80.00

### Anchorage Guest House

23 Mill Hill Road, Cowes PO31 7EE  **t** (01983) 247975  **e** peterandjenni@anchoragecowes.co.uk
**w** anchoragecowes.co.uk

Detached guesthouse with parking, recently
refurbished to a high standard, all rooms en suite,
either double, twin or family. Located close to
water, marinas, shops and restaurants.

**open** All year
**bedrooms** 2 double, 1 twin, 1 family
**bathrooms** All en suite
**payment** Credit/debit cards, cash/cheques

Room ♨ 📺 ♨ ⚑  General ➺3 P ⚹ ✕ ᕄ 🅟 ⚮  Leisure ⚲ 🏠

## CUBLINGTON, Buckinghamshire Map ref 2C1

★★★
**BED & BREAKFAST**

B&B per room per night
s Min £35.00
d Min £55.00

### Manor Farm B&B

Whitchurch Road, Cublington, Leighton Buzzard LU7 0LP  **t** (01296) 681107  **f** (01296) 681107
**e** honor.vale@tesco.net

**open** All year except Christmas and New Year
**bedrooms** 2 twin
**bathrooms** All en suite
**payment** Cash/cheques

Our modern farm with countryside around is situated
just out of the village providing a warm and
comfortable stay.

Room 📺 ♨ ⚑  General ➺5 P ⚹ ᕄ 🅟 ✿  Leisure ⤴ ▸ 🏠

**CUCKFIELD,** West Sussex Map ref 2D3

★★★★
**BED & BREAKFAST
SILVER AWARD**

B&B per room per night
**s** Min £45.00
**d** Min £70.00
Evening meal per person
Min £30.00

# Highbridge Mill

Cuckfield Road, Haywards Heath RH17 5AE  **t** (01444) 450881  **w** highbridgemill.com

**open** All year except Christmas and New Year
**bedrooms** 1 double, 1 twin
**bathrooms** 1 en suite, 1 private
**payment** Cash/cheques

A slightly eccentric welcome awaits you at this converted water mill. Highbridge Mill was built in 1810 and was converted into a family home 20 years ago. Nestling in its own hidden valley of some five acres, the garden offers peace and tranquillity with the River Adur flowing through it.

⊕ On the A272 after the Ansty roundabout on the Cuckfield Road; before the roundabout to Cuckfield and Haywards Heath, on the right.

♥ Companies who would like to entertain sponsors or clients for dinner may use our dining room; maximum 16 seated.

Room ♦ ✑   General P ✕ ✿

**DANEHILL,** East Sussex Map ref 2D3

★★★★
**GUEST ACCOMMODATION**

B&B per room per night
**d** £50.00–£70.00

# New Glenmore

Sliders Lane, Furners Green, Uckfield TN22 3RU  **t** (01825) 790783  **e** alan.robinson@bigfoot.com

**open** All year except Christmas and New Year
**bedrooms** 1 twin, 1 family
**bathrooms** 1 en suite, 1 private
**payment** Cash/cheques

Spacious bungalow set in six acres of grounds. Rural location close to Bluebell Steam Railway and Sheffield Park. Breakfast includes our own eggs, honey and home-baked bread.

⊕ A22 through Forest Row, right onto A275 at Wych Cross, through Danehill. One mile after Danehill right into Sliders Lane. New Glenmore is last property on right.

Room ♦ TV ♦ ✑   General ⌂ ▥ ♣ P ✁ ▨ ✿

**DEAL,** Kent Map ref 3C4

★★★★
**GUEST ACCOMMODATION**

B&B per room per night
**s** £45.00–£50.00
**d** £60.00–£70.00

# Ilex Cottage

Temple Way, Worth, Deal CT14 0DA  **t** (01304) 617026  **f** (01304) 620890  **e** info@ilexcottage.com
**w** ilexcottage.com

Renovated 1736 house with lovely conservatory and country views. Secluded yet convenient village location north of Deal. Sandwich five minutes, Canterbury, Dover and Ramsgate 25 minutes.

**open** All year
**bedrooms** 1 double, 2 twin
**bathrooms** All en suite
**payment** Credit/debit cards, cash/cheques

Room ♦ TV ♦ ✑   General ⌂ ▥ ♣ P ✁ ▨ ✿ ✝   Leisure ✎ U ♪ ► ♛ ⚓

# Don't forget www.

Web addresses throughout this guide are shown without the prefix www. Please include www. in the address line of your browser.
If a web address does not follow this style it is shown in full.

---

**DORKING,** Surrey Map ref 2D2

★★★
**BED & BREAKFAST**

B&B per room per night
s £40.00–£45.00
d £60.00–£65.00

# Broomhill

15 Broomfield Park, Dorking RH4 3QQ  t (01306) 885565  f (01306) 881457
e suzanne.willis@virgin.net

**open** All year except Christmas and New Year
**bedrooms** 1 double, 1 family
**payment** Cash/cheques

Spacious house, walking distance of Westcott village. Dorking 1.5 miles. Two double/family rooms, shared bathroom, TV/DVD, coffee/tea. Magnificent views and safe parking. Gatwick 30 mins, M25 15 mins (junctions 8/9), London 40 mins by train. Fabulous walking countryside (North Downs and Greensand Way). Children welcome.

⊕ From centre of Dorking, take A25 towards Guildford into Westcott village, turn left, immediately after Crown Inn, into Broomfield Park.

Room ⊤⊽ 👐  General 🖐 🔥 P ⊠ 🐕  Leisure 🏌 🐾

---

**DORKING,** Surrey Map ref 2D2

★★★★
**FARMHOUSE**

B&B per room per night
s £65.00–£95.00
d £95.00

# Denbies Farmhouse

Denbies Wine Estate, London Road, Dorking RH5 6AA  t (01306) 876777  f (01306) 876777
e bandb@denbiesvineyard.co.uk  w denbiesvineyard.co.uk

Located in heart of England's largest vineyard on beautiful North Downs of Surrey. Tastefully converted, offering double en suite bedrooms with tea/coffee facilities and trouser-press. Spectacular scenery, popular with walkers, wine lovers and artists.

**open** All year
**bedrooms** 5 double, 2 family
**bathrooms** All en suite
**payment** Credit/debit cards, cash/cheques

Room 🛏 ⊤⊽ 👐 🍵  General 🖐6 P 🔥 ⧎ 🐾 ❄

---

**DORKING,** Surrey Map ref 2D2

★★★★
**BED & BREAKFAST**
**SILVER AWARD**

B&B per room per night
s £38.00–£45.00
d £60.00–£70.00

# Stylehurst Farm

Weare Street, Capel, Dorking RH5 5JA  t (01306) 711259  e rosemary.goddard@virgin.net
w stylehurstfarm.com

**open** All year except Christmas and New Year
**bedrooms** 1 double, 2 twin
**bathrooms** All en suite
**payment** Cash/cheques

Stylehurst Farm is a small working farm set in the beautiful Surrey countryside. The house was recently converted from old farm buildings, providing comfortable and welcoming bed and breakfast accommodation. There is an attractive garden and many places of interest nearby. London and the south coast are within easy reach.

⊕ Five miles south of Dorking on A24. At Clarks Green roundabout take 4th exit to Dorking. 100yds left into Coles Lane. 200yds after station, left into Weare Street.

Room 🛏 ⊤⊽ 👐 🍵  General 🖐3 P 🔥 ❄  Leisure 🏊

---

## Friendly help and advice

Tourist Information Centres offer friendly help with accommodation and holiday ideas as well as suggestions of places to visit and things to do. You'll find contact details at the beginning of each regional section.

## DOVER, Kent Map ref 3C4

★★★★
BED & BREAKFAST

B&B per room per night
s £35.00–£40.00
d £60.00–£65.00

# Colret House

The Green, Coldred, Dover CT15 5AP  t (01304) 830388  f (01304) 830348  e jackiecolret@aol.com
w colrethouse.co.uk

open All year
bedrooms 1 double, 1 twin
bathrooms All en suite
payment Cash/cheques, euros

An early-Edwardian property with modern, purpose-built, en suite garden rooms, standing in extensive, well-maintained grounds. Situated beside the village green in a conservation area on downs above Dover. Ideally situated for overnight stays when travelling by ferries or shuttle. Close to Canterbury and Sandwich. Ample, secure parking.

⊕ *Leave A2 at the junction signposted Coldred. Colret House is a large house facing the village green, painted pale yellow, and only 0.25 miles from the A2.*

Room 🛌 📞 📺 ⛽ 🍷   General 🛋 🏛 🚶 P ✂ 🍽 🧺 ◉ ❄ 🐾   Leisure ✦ ▶ 🏊

## DOVER, Kent Map ref 3C4

★★★★
GUEST HOUSE

B&B per room per night
s £28.25–£32.25
d £44.00–£52.50

# Maison Dieu Guest House

89 Maison Dieu Road, Dover CT16 1RU  t (01304) 204033  f (01304) 242816
e info@maisondieu.co.uk  w maisondieu.com

open All year
bedrooms 1 double, 1 twin, 2 single, 3 family
bathrooms 4 en suite, 1 private
payment Credit/debit cards, cash/cheques

Welcoming, convenient and comfortable – open all year (including Christmas and New Year). Maison Dieu Guest House is central, has forecourt parking, and is minutes from Dover Castle, White Cliffs, Dover Museum, Roman Painted House, ferry/cruise terminals, bus/train stations, local restaurants and amenities. For business, stop-over or short break.

⊕ *A20/Townhall Street, turn into York Street, at roundabout take 2nd exit (Priory Road). At lights turn right (Ladywell). At lights turn right (Maison Dieu Road).*

♥ *Special offer for families – free breakfasts for children under 13. Apr/May/Jun/Sep/Oct (excl. school/bank/ public holidays)*

Room 📺 ⛽ 🍷   General 🛋 🏛 🚶 P ✂ 🍽 🔧   Leisure ∪ ✦ 🏊

## DUMMER, Hampshire Map ref 2C2

★★★
FARMHOUSE

B&B per room per night
s £25.00–£30.00
d £40.00–£50.00

# Oakdown Farm Bungalow

Oakdown Farm, Dummer, Basingstoke RG23 7LR  t (01256) 397218  f (01256) 397218

Mixed, 600-acre farm. Comfortable bungalow in a secluded cul-de-sac next to M3, junction 7, overlooking farmland.

open All year
bedrooms 1 double, 2 twin
payment Cash/cheques, euros

Room 🛌 📺 ⛽   General 🛋12 P ✂ 🍽 🔧 ❄   Leisure ▶ 🏊

## Check it out

Information on accommodation listed in this guide has been supplied by proprietors. As changes may occur you should remember to check all relevant details at the time of booking.

**DYMCHURCH,** Kent Map ref 3B4

★★★★

GUEST ACCOMMODATION

B&B per room per night
**s** £37.50–£67.50
**d** £60.00–£67.50
Evening meal per person
£12.50

# Waterside Guest House

15 Hythe Road, Dymchurch, Romney Marsh TN29 0LN  **t** (01303) 872253  **f** (01303) 872253
**e** info@watersideguesthouse.co.uk  **w** watersideguesthouse.co.uk

Cottage-style house offering comfortable rooms and attractive gardens, ideally situated for Channel crossings and historic Romney Marsh. Experience the RH&D railway, visit Port Lympne Wild Animal Park or stroll nearby sandy beaches.

**open** All year
**bedrooms** 2 double, 2 twin, 1 family
**bathrooms** All en suite
**payment** Credit/debit cards, cash/cheques, euros

Room 📺 ♿ ☕  General 🐾 🏚 ♨ P ☎ ✕ 🍴 🎱 ⚷ 🔲 ✿  Leisure 🏊 🚲 🚗

**EAST ASHLING,** West Sussex Map ref 2C3

★★★★

INN

B&B per room per night
**s** Min £40.00
**d** Min £65.00
Evening meal per person
£6.50–£15.95

# Horse & Groom

East Ashling, Chichester PO18 9AX  **t** (01243) 575339  **f** (01243) 575560
**e** info@thehorseandgroomchichester.co.uk  **w** thehorseandgroomchichester.co.uk

**open** All year
**bedrooms** 6 double, 5 twin
**bathrooms** All en suite
**payment** Credit/debit cards, cash/cheques

A traditional 17thC inn with en suite accommodation. Friendly, country-style inn with fine cuisine, real ales and cast-iron range. Plenty of parking. Close to Goodwood. All rooms can function as single/double.

Room 🏚 📺 ♿  General 🐾 P ☒ ☎ ✕ 🍴 ✿ 🐕  Leisure ⛳ 🏊 🏌

**EASTBOURNE,** East Sussex Map ref 3B4

★★★

GUEST ACCOMMODATION

B&B per room per night
**s** £35.00–£65.00
**d** £60.00–£80.00
Evening meal per person
£8.00–£19.00

# The Birling Gap

Birling Gap, Seven Sisters Cliffs, Eastbourne BN20 0AB  **t** (01323) 423197  **f** (01323) 423030
**e** reception@birlinggaphotel.co.uk  **w** birlinggaphotel.co.uk

**open** All year
**bedrooms** 5 double, 2 twin, 1 single, 1 family
**bathrooms** All en suite
**payment** Credit/debit cards, cash/cheques, euros

Magnificent cliff-top position on Seven Sisters cliffs with views of country, sea and beach. Superb downland and beach walks. Old-world Thatched Bar and Oak Room Restaurant. Coffee shop and games room, function and conference suite. Off A259 coast road at East Dean, 1.5 miles west of Beachy Head.

⊕ *One mile south of East Dean off A259 coast road. One mile west of Beachy Head. Eastbourne 4 miles, Seaford 5 miles, Brighton 26 miles.*

♥ *3 nights for the price of 2, Oct–Mar (excl Bank Holidays, Christmas and New Year). Pre-booked only.*

Room 🏚 ☎ 📺 ♿  General 🐾 🏚 ♨ P ☎ ✕ 🍴 ✿  Leisure 🎾 🏊 🚲

## Ancient and modern

Experience timeless favourites or discover the latest must-sees. Whatever your choice, be inspired by the places of interest and events highlighted for each region.

## EASTBOURNE, East Sussex Map ref 3B4

★★★★
**GUEST HOUSE
GOLD AWARD**

B&B per room per night
s £35.00–£36.00
d £70.00–£72.00
Evening meal per person
Min £15.00

# Brayscroft House

13 South Cliff Avenue, Eastbourne BN20 7AH  t (01323) 647005  e brayscroft@hotmail.com
w brayscrofthotel.co.uk

**open** All year except Christmas
**bedrooms** 3 double, 2 twin, 1 single
**bathrooms** All en suite
**payment** Credit/debit cards, cash/cheques

Elegant, award-winning, small hotel, one of only a handful in Eastbourne with coveted rating and award for 'outstanding accommodation and hospitality'. Superb position. Selected by the Which? Hotel Guide. Near to the sea, theatres and tennis.

⊕ *From A22 to town centre. At station roundabout, 2nd exit into Grove Road, leading to Grange Road, continue to T-junction, turn left, next right is South Cliff Avenue.*

Room 📺 ♿ 🍽  General ☕12 ⚒ ⚍ ✕ 🎐 ♨ 🎷

## EASTBOURNE, East Sussex Map ref 3B4

★★★
**GUEST HOUSE**

B&B per room per night
s Min £30.00
d Min £60.00
Evening meal per person
Min £12.00

# Cambridge House

6 Cambridge Road, Eastbourne BN22 7BS  t (01323) 721100  f (01323) 721100

A friendly guesthouse run by resident proprietors, David and Ralph. The warm and friendly atmosphere ensures you have an enjoyable stay. Home-cooked meals, full English breakfast, generous 4-course dinner.

**open** All year except Christmas and New Year
**bedrooms** 1 double, 1 twin, 1 single, 1 family, 3 suites
**bathrooms** 4 en suite
**payment** Cash/cheques

Room 📺 ♿  General ☕ ✕ ♨

## EASTBOURNE, East Sussex Map ref 3B4

★★★★
**GUEST HOUSE**

B&B per room per night
s £30.00–£35.00
d £65.00–£70.00

# The Gladwyn

16 Blackwater Road, Eastbourne BN21 4JD  t (01323) 733142  e gladwynhotel@aol.com
w gladwynhotel.com

Family-run hotel overlooking Devonshire Park. Close to sea, shops and theatres. Residential licence. TV and tea-/coffee-making facilities in recently redecorated and refurbished en suite bedrooms.

**open** All year
**bedrooms** 4 double, 3 twin, 2 single, 1 family
**bathrooms** 8 en suite
**payment** Credit/debit cards, cash/cheques, euros

Room 🛏 📺 ♿ 🍽  General ☕ 🎐 🏃 ✕ ⚍ 🎐 ♨ 🖥 ✿ 🐾

## EASTBOURNE, East Sussex Map ref 3B4

★★★
**BED & BREAKFAST**

B&B per room per night
s £22.00–£28.00
d £44.00–£56.00

# Little Foxes

24 Wannock Road, Eastbourne BN22 7JU  t (01323) 640670 & 07957 565951  f (01323) 640670
e Gunnersmith2001@yahoo.co.uk  w thelittlefoxes.com

Personally run B&B. Close to beach and 1km from town centre. En suite facilities. Guests' lounge with Sky TV. All ages welcome. No smoking.

**open** All year
**bedrooms** 1 twin, 1 single
**bathrooms** All en suite
**payment** Cash/cheques

Room 📺 ♿ 🍽  General ☕ 🎐 ✕ 🎐 ♨ ✿ 🐾

# Family-friendly breaks

For accommodation offering additional facilities and services for a range of ages and family units, look out for the Families Welcome symbol. Owners of these properties will go out of their way to welcome families.

## EASTBOURNE, East Sussex Map ref 3B4

★★★★
**GUEST HOUSE**

B&B per room per night
s £30.00–£36.00
d £60.00–£72.00
Evening meal per person
£10.00–£12.00

# St Omer's

13 Royal Parade, Eastbourne BN22 7AR  **t** (01323) 722152  **f** (01323) 723400
**e** stomerhotel@hotmail.com  **w** st-omer.co.uk

**open** All year
**bedrooms** 6 double, 2 twin, 2 single, 1 family
**bathrooms** All en suite
**payment** Credit/debit cards, cash/cheques

Family-run, friendly, non-smoking hotel situated directly on Eastbourne seafront within five minutes' walk of the pier and carpet gardens. Easy access to town centre and theatres. All rooms have en suite facilities. Home-cooked food served from a varied menu all year round.

⊕ *Situated on main seafront road (A259), 400m east of pier.*

♥ *Midweek specials Oct, Apr & May: 3 nights half board £105pp. Ring for Christmas packages.*

Room 🛏 📺 🚿 🍵  General 🛏 🖥 🔥 ⚡ 🍽 ✗ 🎱 🎵 ✳

## EASTBOURNE, East Sussex Map ref 3B4

★★★★
**GUEST HOUSE**
**SILVER AWARD**

B&B per room per night
s £35.00–£40.00
d £35.00–£40.00
Evening meal per person
£12.00–£14.00

# Southcroft

15 South Cliff Avenue, Eastbourne BN20 7AH  **t** (01323) 729071
**e** southcroft@eastbourne34.freeserve.co.uk  **w** southcrofthotel.co.uk

**open** All year
**bedrooms** 3 double, 2 twin, 1 single
**bathrooms** All en suite
**payment** Credit/debit cards, cash/cheques, euros

Edwardian family house in quiet area, adjacent to sea. Minutes to town centre and theatres. Double/twin-bedded rooms are well appointed, all en suite. Totally non-smoking. Bed and breakfast and half board available. Open all year round.

⊕ *20 minutes' walk from Eastbourne station. Situated in western (Meads) area close to Grand Parade.*

♥ *Perfect for holidays and short breaks. Good home cooking with freshly prepared ingredients, special diets catered for.*

Room 📺 🚿 🍵  General 🛏8 🔥 🎵 ✳

## EDGCOTT, Buckinghamshire Map ref 2C1

★★
**FARMHOUSE**

B&B per room per night
s Min £30.00
d Min £45.00

# Perry Manor Farm

Buckingham Road, Edgcott, Aylesbury HP18 0TR  **t** (01296) 770257

Two-hundred-acre working sheep farm, offering peaceful and comfortable accommodation, with en suite toilet and basin. Extensive views over Aylesbury Vale. Walkers welcome. Non-smokers only, please.

**open** All year
**bedrooms** 2 double, 1 single
**payment** Cash/cheques

Room 📺 🚿  General 🛏 P 🔥 ✳  Leisure 🏛

## EGHAM, Surrey Map ref 2D2

★★★
**GUEST ACCOMMODATION**

B&B per room per night
s £50.00–£55.00
d £65.00

# Bulkeley House

Englefield Green, Egham TW20 0JU  **t** (01784) 431287  **f** (01784) 431287

Bulkeley House is a Grade II Listed building of great historic interest, built c1750. It is situated adjacent to the village green.

**open** All year
**bedrooms** 4 double, 2 twin, 1 single, 2 family
**bathrooms** All en suite
**payment** Cash/cheques, euros

Room 🛏 📺 🚿  General 🛏 🖥 P 🔥 ✳ 🐾

## FAREHAM, Hampshire Map ref 2C3

★★★★
**BED & BREAKFAST**

B&B per room per night
s £40.00–£45.00
d £60.00–£65.00

# Bridge House

1 Waterside Gardens, Wallington, Fareham PO16 8SD  **t** (01329) 287775  **f** (01329) 287775
**e** maryhb8@aol.com

Comfortable Georgian family home, all facilities, Japanese garden. Full English or continental breakfast. Ample parking. Immediate access to M27 junction 11 and town centre.

**open** All year except Christmas
**bedrooms** 2 twin
**bathrooms** 1 en suite, 1 private
**payment** Cash/cheques

Room TV ♦ ⏁   General P ⌸ 💺 ✿

## FARNBOROUGH, Hampshire Map ref 2C2

★★★
**BED & BREAKFAST**

B&B per room per night
s £25.00–£35.00
d £50.00–£70.00
Evening meal per person
£7.00–£20.00

# Langfords Bed & Breakfast

165 Cheyne Way, Farnborough GU14 8SD  **t** (01252) 547311  **e** bookings@langfordsbandb.co.uk
**w** langfordsbandb.co.uk

**open** All year except Christmas
**bedrooms** 2 twin, 1 single
**payment** Cash/cheques

Twin- and single-bedded rooms. Quiet estate approximately two miles from the town centre, buses and trains. Near junction 4 of the M3. Children and domesticated pets accepted, evening meal on request.

Room TV ♦   General ♿ ▥ ♣ P ✂ ✕ ⌸ 💺 ▣ ✿ 🐾   Leisure ∪ ✈ 🏊

## FAVERSHAM, Kent Map ref 3B3

★★★
**GUEST ACCOMMODATION**

B&B per room per night
s £28.00–£48.00
d £42.00–£72.00

# Barnsfield

Fostall, Hernhill, Faversham ME13 9JG  **t** (01227) 750973  **f** (01227) 750973  **e** barnsfield@yahoo.com
**w** barnsfield.co.uk

Grade II Listed country cottage accommodation, just off A299, set in three acres of orchards, six miles from Canterbury. Convenient for ports and touring.

**open** All year
**bedrooms** 1 double, 1 twin, 1 family
**bathrooms** 1 en suite
**payment** Cash/cheques

Room TV ♦   General ♿ ▥ ♣ P ✂ ▣ ✿   Leisure ✈ 🏊

## FINDON, West Sussex Map ref 2D3

★★★★
**INN**

B&B per room per night
s £65.00
d £80.00–£90.00
Evening meal per person
Min £13.00

# John Henry's Inn

The Forge, Nepcote Lane, Findon, Worthing BN14 0SE  **t** (01903) 877277  **f** (01903) 877178
**e** enquiries@john-henrys.com  **w** john-henrys.com

**open** All year
**bedrooms** 3 double, 2 family, 1 suite
**bathrooms** All en suite
**payment** Credit/debit cards, cash/cheques, euros

In the heart of the village, John Henry's Inn has luxury en suite rooms, most with vaulted ceilings, including a suite with washer/dryer, satellite TV/DVD and air-conditioning. Fully licensed bar and restaurant. Open to non-residents. Ideally situated for Goodwood, Arundel, Chichester and Brighton. WiFi Internet.

⊕ *Signposted at roundabout on A24 and A280. Take Findon direction. Downhill to crossroads. Straight for 350yds. Establishment is on left and ahead.*

Room ⛭ TV ♦ ⏁   General ♿ ▥ ♣ P ♉ ⚷ ✿ 🐾   Leisure ♦ ∪ ✈ ↑ 🚲 🏊

## FITTLEWORTH, West Sussex Map ref 2D3

★★★★
INN

B&B per room per night
s £55.00–£85.00
d £85.00–£120.00
Evening meal per person
Min £10.95

### Swan Inn

Lower Street, Fittleworth, Petworth RH20 1EN  t (01798) 865429  f (01798) 865721
e hotel@swaninn.com  w swaninn.com

open All year
bedrooms 10 double, 3 twin, 2 single
bathrooms All en suite
payment Credit/debit cards, cash

Listed 14thC coaching inn, well placed for visiting many of the historic houses and places of interest in the area. Public bar with welcoming log fires in the winter. Large garden. Cosy oak-beamed restaurant serving homemade food with a fine selection of fresh fish, meat and poultry dishes.

⊕ 3 miles from Pulborough station, 3 miles from main A29 Bognor/London road, only 6 miles from the historic castle town of Arundel.

♥ Long-stay discounts available on request.

Room 📺 👍 🍷  General 👜 🎱 ✂ 🍷 ✕ 🛏 ⅙ ✿  Leisure ∪ ⌖

## FLEET, Hampshire Map ref 2C2

★★★
BED & BREAKFAST

B&B per room per night
s £25.00–£32.00
d £50.00–£52.00

### Copperfield

16 Glen Road, Fleet GU51 3QR  t (01252) 616140  e bill@copperfieldbnb.co.uk
w copperfieldbnb.co.uk

A long-established, friendly B&B backing onto the Basingstoke Canal only minutes' walk from the town centre. Good quality accommodation at reasonable prices, TV and wireless broadband in all rooms.

open All year except Christmas and New Year
bedrooms 2 double, 2 single
bathrooms 1 en suite, 2 private
payment Cash/cheques

Room 📺 👍 🍷  General P ⅙ ✿  Leisure ✈

## FLEET, Hampshire Map ref 2C2

★★★★
BED & BREAKFAST

B&B per room per night
s £50.00–£55.00
d Min £65.00

### Tinkers Furze

Gough Road, Fleet GU51 4LL  t (01252) 615995  f (01252) 612527  e judykeep@yahoo.co.uk
w tinkersfurze.co.uk

Tinkers Furze is an original 1920s Pool house, with extensive, well maintained gardens and off-road parking, close to Fleet town centre and station.

open All year except Christmas
bedrooms 1 double, 1 twin, 1 single
payment Credit/debit cards, cash/cheques

Room 📺 👍 🍷  General 👜7 P 🛏 ⅙ 🖥 ✿  Leisure 🛶

# A breath of fresh air

Love the great outdoors? Britain's Camping, Caravan & Holiday Parks 2008 is packed with information on quality sites in some spectacular locations. You can purchase the guide from good bookshops and online at visitbritaindirect.com.

**FOLKESTONE,** Kent Map ref 3B4

★ ★ ★ ★
GUEST ACCOMMODATION

B&B per room per night
s £46.00–£50.00
d £68.00–£90.00
Evening meal per person
Min £18.65

# Garden Lodge

324 Canterbury Road, Densole, Folkestone CT18 7BB  t (01303) 893147  f (01303) 894581
e stay@garden-lodge.com  w garden-lodge.com

**open** All year except Christmas and New Year
**bedrooms** 1 twin, 2 single, 2 family
**bathrooms** 4 en suite, 1 private
**payment** Credit/debit cards, cash/cheques, euros

This award-winning family-run guesthouse and restaurant is the Garden of England's greatest secret. Guaranteed private parking. Beautiful garden. Aviaries. Solar-heated swimming pool (summer). Restaurant open to non-residents. Home cooking. Near Channel Tunnel terminal. Ground-floor rooms available. Alternative therapy holidays with tuition. Motorcycle-friendly. Contractors welcome.

⊕ From M20/A20 go through tunnel in hill. Bear left A260 Canterbury direction. Garden Lodge is situated on right 1.5 miles from roundabout.

♥ Stay minimum of 3 nights and take a foot passenger day trip to France with our compliments with SeaFrance.

Room 🛏 ⊟ TV ⚲ ☜   General ⌛ ▥ ♿ P ⚑ ✕ ﬚ 🍴 ♨ ◉ ✿   Leisure ⇗ ∪ ⤷ ↾ ᪥ 🛶

**FOLKESTONE,** Kent Map ref 3B4

★ ★ ★
GUEST HOUSE

B&B per room per night
s £23.00–£29.00
d £46.00–£55.00

# Kentmere Guest House

76 Cheriton Road, Folkestone CT20 1DG  t (01303) 259661  f (01303) 220208
e enquiries@kentmere-guesthouse.co.uk  w kentmere-guesthouse.co.uk

Family-run B&B, recently refurbished, all rooms en suite. Catering for families and business persons alike.

**open** All year
**bedrooms** 2 double, 1 twin, 2 single, 2 family
**bathrooms** All en suite
**payment** Credit/debit cards, cash/cheques, euros

Room 🛏 TV ⚲ ☜   General ⌛ ▥ ♿ P ✿ ↾   Leisure 🛶

**FOLKESTONE,** Kent Map ref 3B4

★ ★ ★
GUEST HOUSE

B&B per room per night
s £28.00–£29.00
d £42.00–£47.00

# The Rob Roy Guest House

227 Dover Road, Folkestone CT19 6NH  t (01303) 253341  f (01303) 770060
e robroy.folkestone@ntlworld.com  w therobroyguesthouse.co.uk

**open** All year except Christmas
**bedrooms** 3 double, 3 twin, 1 family
**bathrooms** 3 en suite
**payment** Credit/debit cards, cash/cheques, euros

The Rob Roy: friendly service, comfortable accommodation and tasty breakfasts. Ideally situated ten minutes from M20 and Channel Tunnel and 20 minutes from Dover ferries and Eurostar Ashford. Only minutes from Folkestone's famous Leas, cliffs, beaches and promenade and the lovely Folkestone Downs and North Downs Way.

⊕ M20 jct 13. A259 then A260 towards Folkestone harbour until Dover Road. The Rob Roy is halfway down on right.

♥ Weekend and midweek breaks from £80–£106pp, min 2 nights. Also free child off-peak offers.

Room 🛏 TV ⚲   General ⌛ ▥ ♿ P ﬚ ↾   Leisure ⤷ ↾ ᪥

## B&B prices
Rates for bed and breakfast are shown per room per night.
Double room prices are usually based on two people sharing the room.

## FRESHWATER, Isle of Wight Map ref 2C3

★★★★
GUEST ACCOMMODATION

B&B per room per night
s £27.00–£31.00
d £54.00–£62.00

### Seahorses

Victoria Road, Freshwater PO40 9PP  t (01983) 752574  f (01983) 752574
e seahorses-iow@tiscali.co.uk  w seahorsesisleofwight.com

A charming early-19thC rectory, standing in
2.5 acres of lovely gardens with direct footpath
access to Yarmouth and Freshwater Bay. Art
courses available in our studio. Pets welcome.

open All year
bedrooms 1 double, 1 twin, 2 family
bathrooms All en suite
payment Cash/cheques

Room 📺 ♿ 🐕  General ♨ P ✂ ⛬ 🗄 ☉ ❄ 🐾  Leisure ∪ ♪ 🚲 🏊

## GATWICK, West Sussex Map ref 2D2

★★★★
GUEST HOUSE
SILVER AWARD

B&B per room per night
s £45.00–£50.00
d £60.00–£65.00

### The Lawn Guest House

30 Massetts Road, Horley RH6 7DF  t (01293) 775751  f (01293) 821803
e info@lawnguesthouse.co.uk  w lawnguesthouse.co.uk

open All year
bedrooms 3 double, 3 twin, 6 family
bathrooms All en suite
payment Credit/debit cards, cash/cheques, euros

Imposing Victorian house in pretty gardens. Five
minutes Gatwick. Two minutes' walk Horley. Station
300yds. London 40 minutes. Bedrooms all en suite.
Full English breakfast and continental for early
departures. Guests' ice machine. On-line residents'
computer for emails. Overnight/long-term parking.
Airport transfers by arrangement.

⊕ M23 jct 9 (Gatwick). 1st 2 roundabouts A23 (Redhill). 3rd
roundabout, Esso petrol station on left – 3rd exit. 300yds
right, Massetts Road. Property 500yds on left.

Room 📞 📺 ♿ 🐕  General ♨ ⛬ ♿ P ✂ 🗄 ❄ 🐾  Leisure ►

## GATWICK, West Sussex Map ref 2D2

★★★★
GUEST HOUSE

B&B per room per night
s £45.00–£50.00
d £60.00–£65.00

### Southbourne Guest House Gatwick

34 Massetts Road, Horley RH6 7DS  t (01293) 771991  f (01293) 820112
e reservations@southbournegatwick.com  w southbournegatwick.com

open All year
bedrooms 3 double, 3 twin, 2 single, 4 family
bathrooms All en suite
payment Credit/debit cards, cash/cheques

A warm welcome awaits you in our family-run
guesthouse. Ideally located for Gatwick Airport, and
exploring Surrey, Sussex and London. Five minutes'
walk from Horley train station, restaurants, shops and
pubs and 30 minutes by train from London. Five
minutes' drive from Gatwick with free courtesy
transport from 0930-2130.

⊕ M23 jct 9, follow the A23 through 3 roundabouts. At 3rd
roundabout take 3rd exit and continue to the 2nd right-
hand turn into Massetts Road.

Room 🛗 📻 📺 ♿  General ♨ ⛬ ♿ P ✂ ❄

## GATWICK AIRPORT

See under Horley

See under Horley

### Pet-friendly breaks

PETS!
WELCOME

WELCOME
PETS!

Want to take your cherished companion with you on holiday? Proprietors participating
in our Welcome Pets! scheme go out of their way to make special provision for you and
your pet. Look out for the symbol.

## GILLINGHAM, Kent Map ref 3B3

★★★

**GUEST ACCOMMODATION**

B&B per room per night
s £44.00
d £54.00
Evening meal per person
£5.00–£25.00

# King Charles Hotel

Brompton Road, Gillingham ME7 5QT  t (01634) 830303  f (01634) 829430
e enquiries@kingcharleshotel.co.uk  w kingcharleshotel.co.uk

**open** All year
**bedrooms** 30 double, 30 twin, 10 single, 26 family, 2 suites
**bathrooms** All en suite
**payment** Credit/debit cards, cash/cheques, euros

A privately owned, modern hotel with a cosy restaurant and first-class conference and banqueting facilities. All bedrooms have en suite bathroom, tea-/coffee-making facilities, hairdryer, telephone and TV. We are ideal as a base for exploring South East England and London, and we offer extremely competitive group rates.

⊕ M2 jct 4 to Gillingham/Medway Tunnel. Turn left to Brompton before tunnel. We are on left.

Room 🛏 🖭 📞 📺 ♿ 🍵  General 🕰 🏭 🔥 P 🍷 ✕ 🎧 🛏 ⊙ ❄ 🦮  Leisure ♦ ✈ ▶ 🚲 🏛

## GODALMING, Surrey Map ref 2D2

★★★

**BED & BREAKFAST**

B&B per room per night
s £35.00–£40.00
d £70.00–£80.00

# Combe Ridge

Pook Hill, Chiddingfold, Godalming GU8 4XR  t (01428) 682607  f (01428) 682607
e brendaessex@btinternet.com

**open** All year except Christmas and New Year
**bedrooms** 2 double, 1 single
**bathrooms** 1 en suite, 1 private
**payment** Cash/cheques

Combe Ridge is in an Area Of Outstanding Natural Beauty with grazing sheep and views of gently wooded hills. London is an hour away by train, and both Heathrow and Gatwick are less than an hour by car. Combe Ridge is a family-run B&B where there's always a warm welcome.

⊕ M25 exit jct 10. A3 to A283. At Wormley, right to Combe Lane/Witley Station. Right to Haslemere. Left Pook Hill. After 500m left to house.

Room 📺 ♿ 🍵  General 🕰 ⚄

## GODALMING, Surrey Map ref 2D2

★★★

**FARMHOUSE**

B&B per room per night
s £32.00–£37.00
d £62.00–£67.00

# Heath Hall Farm

Bowlhead Green, Godalming GU8 6NW  t (01428) 682808  f (01428) 684025
e heathhallfarm@btinternet.com  w heathhallfarm.co.uk

**open** All year
**bedrooms** 1 double, 1 twin, 1 single, 1 family
**bathrooms** 3 en suite, 1 private
**payment** Credit/debit cards, cash/cheques, euros

Secluded farmhouse, converted stable courtyard, surrounded by own land. Free-range fowl. Tennis court. Relaxed atmosphere. Ground-floor accommodation. Ample parking. Single pet welcome by arrangement. Wonderful walking. Green Sand Way and National Nature Reserve. Easy access to A3.

⊕ A3, 8.5 miles south of Guildford. Bypass Milford, after Milford take 2nd turning on left signed Bowlhead Green. Up lane 400m, drive on left.

Room 🛏 📺 ♿ 🍵  General 🕰 🏭 P ⚄ 🎐 ❄ 🦮  Leisure ♦ ✈ ▶ 🏛

## GREAT MISSENDEN, Buckinghamshire Map ref 2C1

★★★★

**BED & BREAKFAST**

B&B per room per night
s £29.50
d £55.00

# Forge House

10 Church Street, Great Missenden HP16 0AX  t (01494) 867347

**open** All year
**bedrooms** 2 double, 1 twin, 1 single
**bathrooms** 3 en suite
**payment** Cash/cheques

Set in the wooded Chiltern Hills, quiet village location – a charming 18thC beamed house traditionally refurbished with three en suite double bedrooms. English/continental breakfast included. Chiltern Line to Marylebone 35 minutes. Car access to Waddesdon Manor, Hughenden Manor, West Wycombe Park and caves, Milton's Cottage, Bekonscot Model Village. Walking/cycling The Ridgeway, Chiltern Way.

Room TV ♿ 🍴  General 🏠 ✿  Leisure ⚓

## GUILDFORD, Surrey Map ref 2D2

★★★

**FARMHOUSE**

B&B per room per night
s Max £50.00
d Max £70.00

# Littlefield Manor

Littlefield Common, Guildford GU3 3HJ  t (01483) 233068  f (01483) 233686
e john@littlefieldmanor.co.uk  w littlefieldmanor.co.uk

A 17thC listed manor house with Tudor origins set in large walled garden surrounded by farmland.

**open** All year except Christmas
**bedrooms** 2 double, 1 twin
**bathrooms** 1 en suite, 2 private
**payment** Credit/debit cards, cash/cheques

Room TV ♿ 🍴  General ⌂1 ✗ 🏠 ✿  Leisure ▶

## GUILDFORD, Surrey Map ref 2D2

★★★

**GUEST ACCOMMODATION**

B&B per room per night
s Min £27.00
d Min £27.00

# Matchams

35 Boxgrove Avenue, Guildford GU1 1XQ  t (01483) 567643  f (01483) 567643

**open** All year
**bedrooms** 1 twin, 2 single
**payment** Cash/cheques

Detached private residence in quiet road. Close to bus routes and only five minutes' walk from Spectrum Leisure Complex. Equidistant from Heathrow and Gatwick airports. Within easy reach of south coast, London and Windsor.

⊕ From M25 jct 10, take A3 southbound towards Guildford, leave at Burpham/Merrow turning. Continue until 4th roundabout after which Boxgrove Avenue is 2nd left.

Room TV ♿  General ⌂ ✂ ✿

## GUILDFORD, Surrey Map ref 2D2

★★★

**BED & BREAKFAST**

B&B per room per night
s £28.00–£34.00
d £45.00

# The Old Malt House

Bagshot Road, Worplesdon, Guildford GU3 3PT  t (01483) 232152  f (01483) 232152

Old country house in extensive grounds with ancient trees and swimming pool. Easy access to Heathrow, Gatwick and central London.

**open** All year except Christmas
**bedrooms** 1 double, 2 twin, 1 single
**payment** Credit/debit cards, cash/cheques

Room TV ♿  General P ✂ 🏠 ✿ 🐕  Leisure ⚓

## One to five stars

More stars means higher quality accommodation plus a greater range of facilities and services.

## HAILSHAM, East Sussex Map ref 2D3

★★★★★

**GUEST ACCOMMODATION**

B&B per room per night
s £50.00–£60.00
d £75.00–£110.00

# Hailsham Grange

Vicarage Road, Hailsham BN27 1BL  **t** (01323) 844248  **e** noel-hgrange@amserve.com
**w** hailshamgrange.co.uk

**open** All year except Christmas and New Year
**bedrooms** 3 double, 1 twin
**bathrooms** All en suite
**payment** Cash/cheques

Hailsham is conveniently located for the numerous historic houses and gardens in East Sussex/West Kent. Also ideal for those wishing to explore the south coast and the South Downs, while Glyndebourne is close by. The accommodation epitomises the comfort and elegance of classic English style and the garden is a haven of peace and tranquillity.

Room 🛏 📺 🕯 ♨   General P ⅍ 🛏 🗃 ✿

## HAILSHAM, East Sussex Map ref 2D3

★★★★

**BED & BREAKFAST**

B&B per room per night
s £26.00–£28.00
d £42.00–£48.00
Evening meal per person
£6.00–£8.00

# Windesworth

Carters Corner, Hailsham BN27 4HT  **t** (01323) 847178  **f** (01323) 440696
**e** windesworth.bedandbreakfast@virgin.net  **w** visitsussex.org/windesworth

Family home in quiet, rural location with views towards the Pevensey Levels and South Downs. Coast and 1066 Country within easy reach.

**open** All year except Christmas and New Year
**bedrooms** 1 double, 1 twin
**bathrooms** 1 en suite, 1 private
**payment** Cash/cheques

Room 📺 🕯 ♨   General P ⅍ ✕ 🗃   Leisure ▶ 🚴

## HASLEMERE, Surrey Map ref 2C2

★★★★

**BED & BREAKFAST**

B&B per room per night
s Min £38.00
d £56.00–£60.00

# Deerfell

Blackdown, Haslemere GU27 3BU  **t** (01428) 653409  **f** (01428) 656106  **e** deerfell@tesco.net
**w** deerfell.co.uk

**open** All year except Christmas and New Year
**bedrooms** 1 double, 1 twin, 1 single
**bathrooms** 2 en suite, 1 private
**payment** Cash/cheques

Delightful country house only four miles from Haslemere. Spacious, comfortable, en suite rooms with TV and tea-/coffee-making facilities. Good local pubs/restaurants.

⊕ Take A286 Midhurst road from Haslemere. After West Sussex sign, left into Fernden Lane. At 2.6 miles bear right into Blackdaw Park (automatic gate). Deerfell 1st house on left.

Room 📺 🕯 ♨   General ⅍ 🗃 ▣ ✿   Leisure ▶ 🏛

## HASLEMERE, Surrey Map ref 2C2

★★★

**INN**

B&B per room per night
s Min £55.00
d Min £75.00

# The Wheatsheaf Inn

Grayswood Road, Haslemere GU27 2DE  **t** (01428) 644440  **f** (01428) 641285
**e** ken@thewheatsheafgrayswood.co.uk

A delightful building in wooded area. Award-winning menu. Comfortable en suite rooms. Also has a bright and airy non-smoking conservatory.

**open** All year
**bedrooms** 4 double, 1 twin, 2 single
**bathrooms** All en suite
**payment** Credit/debit cards, cash/cheques

Room ♿ 📞 📺 🕯   General 🅰 P 🍽 ✿ 🐕

---

**HASTINGS,** East Sussex Map ref 3B4

★ ★ ★ ★
**BED & BREAKFAST**

B&B per room per night
s £50.00–£60.00
d £60.00–£70.00

# The Laindons

23 High Street, Hastings TN34 3EY  **t** (01424) 437710  **e** janebrumfield@mac.com  **w** laindons.co.uk

**open** All year
**bedrooms** 3 double
**bathrooms** All en suite
**payment** Credit/debit cards, cash/cheques

In the heart of Hastings' Old Town, this elegant Georgian town house has three en suite double rooms, each with its own unique character. It offers a quiet, comfortable retreat, friendly welcome and hearty breakfast. Breakfast includes organic, free-range and local produce, with vegetarian and vegan options.

Room 🖾 📺 🖦 ✇    General ✂ 🍴 🛏    Leisure ▶ 🏛

---

**HASTINGS,** East Sussex Map ref 3B4

Rating Applied For
**GUEST ACCOMMODATION**

B&B per room per night
s £25.00–£40.00
d £50.00–£65.00

# The Old Town Guest House

1a George Street, Hastings TN34 3EG  **t** (01424) 423342 & 07870 163818  **e** sophiejlw@tiscali.co.uk

A guesthouse of character situated in the heart of Hastings Old Town. Relax in our simple, yet comfortable rooms and wake up to a full English breakfast.

**open** All year
**bedrooms** 1 double, 1 twin, 1 single
**bathrooms** 1 en suite
**payment** Cash/cheques

Room 📺 🖦    General 🛏 🐾    Leisure 🎵

---

**HASTINGS,** East Sussex Map ref 3B4

★ ★ ★ ★ ★
**GUEST ACCOMMODATION**
**SILVER AWARD**

B&B per room per night
s £70.00–£95.00
d £90.00–£130.00
Evening meal per person
£9.00–£24.00

# Swan House

1 Hill Street, Old Town, Hastings TN34 3HU  **t** (01424) 430014  **e** res@swanhousehastings.co.uk
**w** swanhousehastings.co.uk

**open** All year except Christmas
**bedrooms** 2 double, 1 twin, 1 suite
**bathrooms** All en suite
**payment** Credit/debit cards, cash/cheques, euros

Swan House continues to receive widespread press recognition for its service and style. More than just a guesthouse, we offer luxury and relaxation unprecedented in Hastings Old Town. Guests enjoy a gourmet, locally-sourced breakfast menu, spacious guest lounge, computer room, wireless broadband internet access and a landscaped patio garden.

Room 🛋 📺 🖦 ✇    General 🛏5 ✂ 🍷 ✕ 🍴 🛏 🔥 🖥 ✿    Leisure 🎵

---

**HAWKINGE,** Kent Map ref 3B4

★ ★ ★ ★
**BED & BREAKFAST**

B&B per room per night
s Min £30.00
d Min £50.00

# Braeheid Bed & Breakfast

2 Westland Way, Hawkinge, Folkestone CT18 7PW  **t** (01303) 893928  **e** bill@forrest68.fsnet.co.uk

Property in quiet cul-de-sac. Near Channel Tunnel and Dover ferries. Westland Way is on the Downs, an Area of Outstanding Natural Beauty.

**open** All year
**bedrooms** 1 double, 1 twin
**bathrooms** All en suite
**payment** Cash/cheques

Room 📺 🖦 ✇    General 🛏14 🚪 P 🍴 🛏 ✿    Leisure 🏛

---

## If you have access needs...

Look for the National Accessible Scheme symbols if you have special hearing, visual or mobility needs.

# South East England

## HENFIELD, West Sussex Map ref 2D3

### 1 The Laurels

★★★★ BED & BREAKFAST

B&B per room per night
s £25.00–£35.00
d Min £60.00

Martyn Close, Henfield BN5 9RQ  t (01273) 493518  e malc.harrington@lineone.net
w no1thelaurels.co.uk

A detached house faced with traditional knapped Sussex flint stones. Comfortable rooms, a warm welcome, easy access to Brighton. Many places of interest nearby.

open All year
bedrooms 2 double, 1 twin, 1 single
bathrooms 3 en suite
payment Cash/cheques

Room TV 🐾 ♨ General ☺ P 🍴 🛏 ✿ Leisure 🚲

## HENLEY-ON-THAMES, Oxfordshire Map ref 2C2

### Abbottsleigh

★★★ GUEST ACCOMMODATION

B&B per room per night
s £38.00–£55.00
d £65.00–£75.00

107 St Marks Road, Henley-on-Thames RG9 1LP  t (01491) 572982  f (01491) 572982
e abbottsleigh@hotmail.com

open All year
bedrooms 1 double, 2 twin
bathrooms 2 en suite, 1 private
payment Cash/cheques

A large, mature, comfortable detached home in quiet location with excellent free parking, some off-road, within walking distance of town centre, river, restaurants, pubs, station and museum. Henley offers river boat trips and walks along the Thames Path and Chiltern countryside. Convenient for Oxford, Windsor and Heathrow. Warm welcome.

⊕ Left at lights on Henley Bridge. Follow road around river to T-junction. Turn left into Reading Road A4155 – then second right into St Marks Road.

Room TV 🐾 ♨ General ☺ 10 P 🍴 🛏 ✿ Leisure ▸ 🚲

## HENLEY-ON-THAMES, Oxfordshire Map ref 2C2

### Avalon

★★★ BED & BREAKFAST

B&B per room per night
s £32.00–£45.00
d £55.00–£60.00

36 Queen Street, Henley-on-Thames RG9 1AP  t (01491) 577829  e avalon@henleybb.fsnet.co.uk
w henleybb.fsnet.co.uk

Spacious Victorian terraced house in a quiet, central location two minutes' walk from river, station and town centre.

open All year
bedrooms 1 double, 1 twin, 1 single
bathrooms All en suite
payment Cash/cheques

Room 🛁 TV 🐾 ♨ General ☺ 10 🍴 Leisure 🚲

## HENLEY-ON-THAMES, Oxfordshire Map ref 2C2

### Brackenhurst

★★★ BED & BREAKFAST

B&B per room per night
s £45.00–£50.00
d £60.00–£75.00

Russells Water, Henley-on-Thames RG9 6EU  t (01491) 642399  e info@foolonthehill.co.uk
w foolonthehill.co.uk

Henley ten minutes, in Area of Outstanding Natural Beauty in Chilterns. Pub food nearby. Rooms with fresh white linen, luxury towels, TV, hairdryer, hospitality trays, complimentary mineral water and chocolates.

open All year
bedrooms 1 double, 1 twin
bathrooms All en suite
payment Credit/debit cards

Room 🛁 TV 🐾 ♨ General ☺ ☆ P 🍴 ⚘ Leisure ∪ ♪ ▸ 🚲

## Check the maps

Colour maps at the front pinpoint all the places you will find accommodation entries in the regional sections. Pick your location and then refer to the place index at the back to find the page number.

## HENLEY-ON-THAMES, Oxfordshire Map ref 2C2

★ ★ ★ ★ ★
**BED & BREAKFAST**

B&B per room per night
s £50.00
d £70.00–£75.00

### Lenwade

3 Western Road, Henley-on-Thames RG9 1JL  **t** (01491) 573468  **f** (01491) 411664
**e** lenwadeuk@aol.com  **w** w3b-ink.com/lenwade

**open** All year except Christmas
**bedrooms** 2 double, 1 twin
**bathrooms** 2 en suite, 1 private
**payment** Cash/cheques, euros

A premier B&B, in a quiet residential road within walking distance of Henley town centre, river, restaurants etc. Superb buffet and individually cooked breakfasts. All rooms have en suite or private facilities with many electrical extras. Free WI-FI Internet. Ample parking. Wonderful walking in Chiltern Hills and Thames Path. Convenient Heathrow, Windsor.

⊕ *Left at lights on Henley bridge. Go past Hobbs Boatyard to T-junction. Left into Reading Road. 3rd right into St Andrews Road, second left into Western Road.*

Room 📺 ⌖ 🥤  General 🛏 🖈 P ⚒ 🍵  Leisure ▸ 🏛

## HENLEY-ON-THAMES, Oxfordshire Map ref 2C2

★ ★ ★ ★
**BED & BREAKFAST**

B&B per room per night
s £30.00–£35.00
d £50.00–£70.00

### Orchard Dene Cottage

Lower Assendon, Henley-on-Thames RG9 6AG  **t** (01491) 575490  **f** (01491) 575490
**e** info@orcharddenecottage.co.uk  **w** orcharddenecottage.co.uk

**open** All year
**bedrooms** 1 double, 1 single
**payment** Cash/cheques, euros

Two miles from Henley in beautiful Chilterns countryside, with all the comfort and friendly relaxation you'd expect in an old family home. Enjoy an interesting garden in summer, log fires in winter and full English breakfast all year. Excellent evening meals in nearby village pub. Ideal for London Heathrow access.

⊕ *Follow A4130 (Wallingford) through Henley; after 1 mile, fork right to Assendons, then after 150yds fork left (narrow lane). Cottage 150yds on left.*

Room 📺 ⌖ 🥤  General 🛏 🍽 P ⚒ 🍵 ⚘ ✿ 🐕  Leisure ∪ ▸ 🚲

## HENLEY-ON-THAMES, Oxfordshire Map ref 2C2

★ ★ ★
**GUEST ACCOMMODATION**

B&B per room per night
s £40.00–£55.00
d £55.00–£85.00

### Riverside Guest House

4 River Terrace, Henley-on-Thames RG9 1BG  **t** (01491) 571133  **f** (01491) 413651
**e** no4.riverside@virgin.net  **w** no4riverside.co.uk

Riverside Guest House is uniquely positioned on the riverfront in the centre of Henley-on-Thames with stunning views over the river from five of the six bedrooms.

**open** All year
**bedrooms** 2 double, 2 twin, 2 single
**bathrooms** 4 en suite, 2 private
**payment** Credit/debit cards, cash

Room 📺 ⌖ 🥤  General 🛏 ⚒ 🍴 🍵 🏵 ✿ 🐕

## HERNE BAY, Kent Map ref 3B3

★ ★ ★ ★
**GUEST ACCOMMODATION**

B&B per room per night
s £45.00–£50.00
d £55.00–£70.00

### Priory B&B

203 Canterbury Road, Herne Bay CT6 5UG  **t** (01227) 366670  **e** stephen@guy200.demon.co.uk
**w** thepriorybandb.co.uk

Six bedroom en suite accommodation. Grade II Listed building. Built in 1750s. Freeview TV in each room. Situated in the conservation area of Herne Bay.

**open** All year
**bedrooms** 3 double, 1 single, 2 family
**bathrooms** All en suite
**payment** Credit/debit cards, cash/cheques

Room 📺 ⌖ 🥤  General 🛏 🍽 🖈 P ⚒ ✿  Leisure ▸

**HERSTMONCEUX,** East Sussex Map ref 3B4

★★★★
GUEST ACCOMMODATION

B&B per room per night
s  £40.00–£60.00
d  £60.00–£80.00

# Sandhurst

Church Road, Herstmonceux, Hailsham BN27 1RG  t (01323) 833088  f (01323) 833088
e junealanruss@aol.com

Large bungalow with plenty of off-road parking. Within walking distance of Herstmonceux village and close to Herstmonceux Castle. Twenty minutes' drive to sea. No smoking.

**open** All year except Christmas
**bedrooms** 2 double, 2 family
**bathrooms** 3 en suite, 1 private
**payment** Cash/cheques

Room 🛁 📺 🕯  General 🐾 P ⅍

**HEVER,** Kent Map ref 2D2

★★★★
BED & BREAKFAST
SILVER AWARD

B&B per room per night
s  £48.00–£65.00
d  £70.00–£85.00

# Becketts

Pylegate Farm, Hartfield Road, Cowden, Edenbridge TN8 7HE  t (01342) 850514  f (01342) 851281
e jacqui@becketts-bandb.co.uk  w becketts-bandb.co.uk

**open** All year except Christmas
**bedrooms** 1 double, 2 twin
**bathrooms** All en suite
**payment** Credit/debit cards, cash/cheques, euros

Beautiful, character 300-year-old barn with vaulted dining room and beams throughout, set in glorious countryside. Antique four-poster bed. All rooms en suite. Hever Castle, Penshurst and Chartwell all within four miles. Many other NT properties. Great walking and cycling. Cosy pubs with good food nearby. Wireless broadband. Online booking.

⊕ *From Edenbridge (B2026) travel south for 3 miles. Pass the Queens Arms on your right, continue for another 500m. Turn off left at the bend.*

❤ *Discount for stays of 4 days or more.*

Room 🛁 🖨 📺 🕯 🍵  General 🐾 🛏 P ⅍ 🎿 🔥 ✿  Leisure ▸ 🏛

**HIGH WYCOMBE,** Buckinghamshire Map ref 2C2

★★★
BED & BREAKFAST

B&B per room per night
s  Min £35.00
d  Min £55.00

# 9 Sandford Gardens

Daws Hill, High Wycombe HP11 1QT  t (01494) 441723 & 07980 439 560

Georgian-style house in quiet residential area with off-street parking. Self-contained annexe. Easy access to motorways and Heathrow.

**open** All year
**bedrooms** 1 twin, 1 single
**payment** Cash/cheques

Room 🛁 📺 🕯 🍵  General ⅍ ✿

**HIGH WYCOMBE,** Buckinghamshire Map ref 2C2

★★★
GUEST HOUSE

B&B per room per night
s  £35.00–£45.00
d  £58.00–£68.00

# Amersham Hill Guest House

52 Amersham Hill, High Wycombe HP13 6PQ  t (01494) 520635

Conveniently located five minutes' walk from High Wycombe station. Easy access to M40 and M4. All rooms have colour TV, radio alarm, tea-/coffee-making facilities. Full English breakfast included. Ample parking.

**open** All year
**bedrooms** 2 double, 1 twin, 4 single
**bathrooms** 2 en suite
**payment** Cash/cheques

Room 🛁 📺 🕯  General 🐾5 P

## It's all in the detail

Please remember that all information in this guide has been supplied by the proprietors well in advance of publication. Since changes do sometimes occur it's a good idea to check details at the time of booking.

## HIGH WYCOMBE, Buckinghamshire Map ref 2C2

**★★★★**
**INN**
**GOLD AWARD**

B&B per room per night
s Min £75.00
d £110.00–£145.00
Evening meal per person
£22.50–£30.00

### The Three Horseshoes Inn

Horseshoe Road, Bennett End, Radnage, High Wycombe HP14 4EB  **t** (01494) 483273
**f** (01494) 483464  **e** threehorseshoe@btconnect.com  **w** thethreehorseshoes.net

Unpretentious old country inn, full of character, set in a beautiful, tranquil village offering real ales and home-cooked food.

**open** All year
**bedrooms** 3 double, 1 twin, 1 single, 1 suite
**bathrooms** 6 private
**payment** Credit/debit cards, cash/cheques

Room ⌂ 📺 ♨ ♋  General 🖙 🏬 ♿ P ⚡ ♟ ✕ 🍷 🖉 ☼  Leisure ∪ ☞ ⛵

## HOLMBURY ST MARY, Surrey Map ref 2D2

**★★★★**
**GUEST ACCOMMODATION**

B&B per room per night
s £35.00–£45.00
d £60.00–£75.00

### Holmbury Farm

Holmbury St Mary, Dorking RH5 6NB  **t** (01306) 621443  **f** (01306) 621498
**e** virginiallloyd@onetel.com  **w** smoothhound.co.uk/hotels/holmbury.html

Working farm, outstanding views, set high in the Surrey hills. Tennis court and fishing lake. Golf, horse-riding and polo nearby. Ideal for walking, cycling and pubs.

**open** All year except Christmas
**bedrooms** 1 double, 1 single, 1 family
**bathrooms** 2 en suite, 1 private
**payment** Cash/cheques, euros

Room 📺 ♨ ♋  General 🖙 🏬 ♿ P ⚡ ♟ ☼ 🐴  Leisure ♣ ♦ ∪ ☞ ⛵

## HORLEY, Surrey Map ref 2D2

**★★★**
**GUEST ACCOMMODATION**

B&B per room per night
s £39.00–£45.00
d £54.00–£57.00

### The Turret Guest House

48 Massetts Road, Horley RH6 7DS  **t** (01293) 782490 & 07970 066471  **f** (01293) 431492
**e** info@theturret.com  **w** theturret.com

**open** All year
**bedrooms** 3 double, 2 twin, 2 single, 3 family
**bathrooms** All en suite
**payment** Credit/debit cards, cash/cheques

Very comfortable, non-smoking Victorian house. All rooms en suite. Five minutes' walk to pubs, restaurants and station. Gatwick Airport 1.5 miles. Broadband internet access.

♥ *Special offers on accommodation plus 8 days parking from £55.*

Room 📺 ♨ ♋  General 🖙 🏬 ♿ P ⚡ 🖉 ☼  Leisure ∪ ☞ ☞ 🚲 ⛵

## HOVE

*See under Brighton & Hove*

## ISLE OF WIGHT

*See under Bonchurch, Brighstone, Colwell Bay, Cowes, Freshwater, Ryde, Sandown, Shanklin, Ventnor, Wroxall, Yarmouth*

## KINGSTON BLOUNT, Oxfordshire Map ref 2C1

**★★★**
**GUEST ACCOMMODATION**

B&B per room per night
s £70.00
d £80.00
Evening meal per person
£15.00–£25.00

### The Cherry Tree

High Street, Kingston Blount, Chinnor OX39 4SJ  **t** (01844) 352273  **e** cherrytreepub@btconnect.com
**w** thecherrytreepub.com

Award-winning South Oxfordshire country pub offering good food, real ales and newly converted accommodation.

**open** All year except Christmas and New Year
**bedrooms** 3 double, 1 twin
**bathrooms** 3 en suite
**payment** Credit/debit cards, cash/cheques

Room ⌂ 📺 ♨ ♋  General P ⚡ ♟ ✕ 🍷 🔲 ☼  Leisure ☞

## KINTBURY, Berkshire Map ref 2C2

★★★
INN

B&B per room per night
s £80.00–£90.00
Evening meal per person
£8.00–£18.00

### The Dundas Arms

Station Road, Kintbury, Hungerford RG17 9UT  t (01488) 658263  f (01488) 658568
e info@dundasarms.co.uk  w dundasarms.co.uk

Canal and riverside pub selling good food, beer and wine in both bar and restaurant, with hotel rooms overlooking the river.

**open** All year except Christmas and New Year
**bedrooms** 3 double, 2 twin
**bathrooms** All en suite
**payment** Credit/debit cards, cash/cheques

Room ♿ ☎ TV 🕭 🍵  General 🐶 P ⊁ 🍷 ✿  Leisure ♪ 🏖

## LAMBERHURST, Kent Map ref 3B4

★★★★★
BED & BREAKFAST
SILVER AWARD

B&B per room per night
s £40.00–£45.00
d £60.00–£75.00
Evening meal per person
£13.00–£23.00

### Woodpecker Barn

Wickhurst Farm, Tunbridge Wells TN3 8BH  t (01892) 891958  e martinloveday@btinternet.com
w woodpeckerbarn.co.uk

Elegantly converted 17thC barn, combining traditional and contemporary styles, set in a tranquil spot on Kent/East Sussex borders.

**open** All year
**bedrooms** 2 suites
**bathrooms** 2 private
**payment** Cash/cheques, euros

Room ♿ TV 🕭 🍵  General 🐶 P ⊁ ✕ 🍴 🅿 🔥 ✿  Leisure ∪ ♪ ↑ 🚲

## LEWES, East Sussex Map ref 2D3

★★★
BED & BREAKFAST

B&B per room per night
s £35.00–£40.00
d £60.00–£65.00

### 13 Hill Road

Lewes BN7 1DB  t (01273) 477723  e kmyles@btclick.com

House with self-contained flat which is the only part to be let. Property positioned on a hill with far-reaching views.

**open** All year
**bedrooms** 1 twin
**bathrooms** En suite
**payment** Cash/cheques

Room TV 🕭 🍵  General 🐶 P ⊁ ✿

## LEWES, East Sussex Map ref 2D3

★★★★
INN
SILVER AWARD

B&B per room per night
s £50.00–£70.00
d £65.00–£80.00
Evening meal per person
£9.00–£18.00

### The Blacksmiths Arms

London Road, Offham, Lewes BN7 3QD  t (01273) 472971  f (01273) 472971
e blacksmithsarms@tiscali.co.uk  w theblacksmithsarms-offham.co.uk

18thC village inn close to South Downs Way on main A275. Close to historic town of Lewes. Convenient for Sussex University and Glyndebourne. Mentioned in Good Pub Guide.

**open** All year
**bedrooms** 4 double
**bathrooms** All en suite
**payment** Credit/debit cards, cash/cheques

Room 🖵 TV 🕭  General 🐶3 P ⊁ 🍷 ✕ 🍴 🔥 ✿  Leisure 🏖

## LEWES, East Sussex Map ref 2D3

★★★
INN

B&B per room per night
s £38.00–£48.00
d £60.00–£70.00

### The Crown Inn

191 High Street, Lewes BN7 2NA  t (01273) 480670  f (01273) 480679
e crowninnlewes@yahoo.co.uk  w crowninn-lewes.co.uk

Family-run inn, at the centre of historic town, offering traditional food. Licensed bar open all day. Most rooms en suite. Meeting room available. Discount for long-stay or parties.

**open** All year
**bedrooms** 4 double, 3 twin, 1 family
**bathrooms** 6 en suite
**payment** Credit/debit cards, cash/cheques

Room 🖵 TV 🕭 🍵  General 🐶 🍺 ♨ ⊁ 🍷 ✕ 🍴 🔥 ✿ 🐕  Leisure 🏖

## Check it out

Please check prices, quality ratings and other details when you book.

## LITTLEHAMPTON, West Sussex Map ref 2D3

★★
**INN**

B&B per room per night
s £27.50–£35.00
d £42.50–£50.00
Evening meal per person
£6.95–£25.00

# Arun View Inn

Wharf Road, Littlehampton BN17 5DD  **t** (01903) 722335  **f** (01903) 722335  **w** thearunview.co.uk

A pleasant riverside pub, offering a good range of home-cooked food and a wide selection of drinks in a friendly atmosphere.

**open** All year except Christmas and New Year
**bedrooms** 1 double, 4 twin
**payment** Credit/debit cards, cash/cheques, euros

Room TV ♿   General ⌕ P ⅍ ⅄ ✗ 🛏 ✿   Leisure ♣ ♪ ► ♿

## LONGFIELD, Kent Map ref 3B3

★★★
**INN**

B&B per room per night
s £45.00–£50.00
d £65.00–£75.00
Evening meal per person
£6.00–£18.00

# The Rising Sun Inn

Fawkham Green, Fawkham, Longfield DA3 8NL  **t** (01474) 872291  **f** (01474) 872779

**open** All year
**bedrooms** 2 double, 3 twin
**bathrooms** All en suite
**payment** Credit/debit cards, cash/cheques

The Rising Sun Inn is a 16thC public house situated close to Brands Hatch. A popular inn with en suite rooms, two with superb four-poster beds. Other facilities include a busy restaurant, main bar with inglenook fireplace and large patio for al fresco dining in warmer weather.

⊕ *From M25 take jct 3. From M20 take jct 3 (signposted M26), then take 1st exit. Follow signs for Brands Hatch then Fawkham Green.*

Room ♿ 🖾 TV ♿   General ⌕2 P ⅄ ✗ 🛏 ✿

## LYMINGTON, Hampshire Map ref 2C3

★★★
**BED & BREAKFAST**

B&B per room per night
s £35.00–£45.00
d £60.00–£70.00
Evening meal per person
£15.00–£45.00

# Bluebird Restaurant

4 - 5 Quay Street, Lymington SO41 3AS  **t** (01590) 676908  **f** (01590) 676908
**w** bluebirdrestaurant.co.uk

Picturesque location on Lymington Quay, just ten minutes from New Forest. Open all year. Beautifully decorated and furnished rooms, all en suite. Quaint and comfortable restaurant with original wooden beams.

**open** All year
**bedrooms** 1 double, 2 twin, 1 family
**bathrooms** All en suite
**payment** Credit/debit cards, cash/cheques

Room 🖾 TV ♿   General ⌕ ♨ P ⅍ ⅄ ✗ 🛏 🅿 ℅   Leisure ♿ 🏊

## LYMINGTON, Hampshire Map ref 2C3

★★★
**GUEST HOUSE**

B&B per room per night
s £45.00–£55.00
d £90.00
Evening meal per person
Min £30.00

# Gorse Meadow Guest House

Sway Road, Pennington, Lymington SO41 8LR  **t** (01590) 673354  **f** (01590) 673336

**open** All year
**bedrooms** 3 double, 1 twin, 2 family
**bathrooms** All en suite
**payment** Credit/debit cards, cash/cheques

Beautiful Edwardian residence in 16 acres, close to New Forest. Period furniture, modern utilities. Splendid galleried hall, impressive dining room (evening dinners) seating 12. Licensed. Residents'/visitors' lounge. Landscaped grounds with fish pond. Cookery courses, bike and boat hire, beaches, riding, golf and good pubs nearby.

⊕ *From M27 west, A337 to Brockenhurst, over level crossing towards Lymington. Before Lymington, go under railway bridge, over mini-roundabout, turn right, then 1.25 miles on right.*

Room ♿ TV ♿   General ⌕ P ⅄ ✗ 🅿 ✿ ♞   Leisure ∪ ♪ ♿

★★★★
GUEST ACCOMMODATION

B&B per room per night
s £35.00–£60.00
d £70.00

# Burwood Lodge

27 Romsey Road, Lyndhurst SO43 7AA  **t** (023) 8028 2445  **f** (023) 8028 4722
**e** burwoodlodge@yahoo.co.uk  **w** burwoodlodge.co.uk

**open** All year
**bedrooms** 2 double, 1 twin, 1 single, 2 family, 1 suite
**bathrooms** All en suite
**payment** Credit/debit cards, cash/cheques

Lovely Edwardian house in half-acre grounds, located two minutes' from village high street, close to open forest. Guest lounge and separate dining room overlooking the gardens, promoting a relaxing environment. Four-poster room available for those special, romantic occasions. Ground-floor bedroom with specially equipped bathroom for the less able.

Room 🛗 📺 👜 🍵  General 👜6 🍴 🛋 🅿 ✿  Leisure ∪ ⊢ 🚲 🏛

★★★
BED & BREAKFAST

B&B per room per night
s £30.00–£35.00
d £60.00–£70.00
Evening meal per person
Max £13.00

# Rosedale Bed & Breakfast

24 Shaggs Meadow, Lyndhurst SO43 7BN  **t** (023) 8028 3793  &  (023) 8013 4253
**e** rosedalebandb@btinternet.com

Family-run bed and breakfast in the centre of Lyndhurst. We cater for all. Colour TV, tea/coffee facilities. New Forest breakfast served up to 0900. Evening meals by arrangement.

**open** All year
**bedrooms** 1 double/twin, 1 family
**bathrooms** 2 en suite
**payment** Cash/cheques

Room 📺 👜 🍵  General 👜 🛋 ★ 🅿 ✂ ✕ 🍳 ✿  Leisure ∪ ⊿ 🚲 🏛

★★★★
RESTAURANT WITH ROOMS
SILVER AWARD

B&B per room per night
d £85.00–£95.00
Evening meal per person
£7.95–£30.00

# The Black Boys Inn

Henley Road, Hurley, Maidenhead SL6 5NQ  **t** (01628) 824212

**open** All year except Christmas and New Year
**bedrooms** 7 double, 1 twin
**bathrooms** All en suite
**payment** Credit/debit cards, cash/cheques

This 16thC inn has en suite bedrooms of style and character and looks onto sweeping views of the Chilterns. Water is supplied by the inn's very own well. The restaurant retains original beams and polished oak floors and has gained many awards over the years.

⊕ *Located on the Henley Road, easily reached from the M4, M40 and M25.*

Room 🛗 📺 👜 🍵  General 👜12 🅿 🍽 🍳 ✿  Leisure ∪ ⊢

★★
BED & BREAKFAST

B&B per room per night
s £35.00–£47.50
d £55.00–£70.00

# Cartlands Cottage

Kings Lane, Cookham Dean, Maidenhead SL6 9AY  **t** (01628) 482196

Family room in self-contained garden studio. Meals in delightful, timbered character cottage with exposed beams. Traditional cottage garden opposite National Trust common land. Very quiet.

**open** All year
**bedrooms** 1 family
**bathrooms** En suite
**payment** Cash/cheques

Room 🛗 📺 👜 🍵  General 👜 🛋 ★ 🅿 🍳 ✿

## Confirm your booking
It's always advisable to confirm your booking in writing.

## MAIDSTONE, Kent Map ref 3B3

★★★
GUEST ACCOMMODATION

B&B per room per night
s £30.00
d £40.00

### 29 Pickering Street

Maidstone ME15 9RS  t (01622) 747453  f (01622) 747453  e ron@camcorder.plus.com

Quiet area two miles south of Maidstone. Pub and restaurants within walking distance. TV/video, films and refreshment tray in rooms.

open All year except Christmas and New Year
bedrooms 1 double, 1 suite
bathrooms 1 en suite
payment Cash/cheques

Room 📺 ♨ ☕  General ☺ P ✂ ❈ 🐾  Leisure ♨

## MAIDSTONE, Kent Map ref 3B3

★★★★
BED & BREAKFAST
SILVER AWARD

B&B per room per night
s £30.00–£35.00
d £40.00–£50.00

### Grove House

Grove Green Road, Maidstone ME14 5JT  t (01622) 738441

open All year except Christmas and New Year
bedrooms 1 double, 1 twin
bathrooms 1 en suite, 1 private
payment Credit/debit cards, cash/cheques

Attractive comfortable detached house in quiet road. Off-street parking. Close to Leeds Castle, pubs, restaurants, M20 and M2 motorways.

✪ Leave M2 jct 7. Follow signs to TV studios, left into Grovewood Drive. Past Tesco, 2nd left at mini-roundabout into Weavering Street. 1st left into Grove Green Road.

Room 📺 ♨ ☕  General P ✂ 🛏  Leisure ▶ ♨

## MAIDSTONE, Kent Map ref 3B3

★★★★
GUEST ACCOMMODATION

B&B per room per night
s £30.00
d £50.00

### The Hazels

13 Yeoman Way, Maidstone ME15 8PQ  t (01622) 737943  e carolbuse@hotmail.com
w the-hazels.co.uk

Family home in quiet location with attractive garden. Close to Leeds Castle, Maidstone and M20. Visitors' lounge with TV. Summer breakfasts in plant-filled conservatory. Twin available for single occupancy.

open All year
bedrooms 1 twin
bathrooms En suite
payment Cash/cheques

Room ♨ ☕  General ☺ P ✂ 🛏 ❈

## MARDEN, Kent Map ref 3B4

★★★★
FARMHOUSE

B&B per room per night
s Min £45.00
d £55.00–£60.00

### Tanner House

Tanner Farm, Goudhurst Road, Tonbridge TN12 9ND  t (01622) 831214  f (01622) 832472
e enquiries@tannerfarmpark.co.uk  w tannerfarmpark.co.uk

Tudor farmhouse in centre of family farm. Good access in secluded, rural position. Shire horses kept on farm. Also, award-winning caravan and camping park.

open All year except Christmas
bedrooms 1 double, 2 twin
bathrooms All en suite
payment Credit/debit cards, cash/cheques, euros

Room 🛏 📺 ♨ ☕  General ☺12 P ✂ 🕮 🛏 🌣 ❈  Leisure ♪

## enjoyEngland.com

Big city buzz or peaceful panoramas? Take a fresh look at England and you may be surprised at what's right on your doorstep. Explore the diversity online at enjoyengland.com

---

**MARLOW,** Buckinghamshire Map ref 2C2

★★★★★
**GUEST ACCOMMODATION**

B&B per room per night
s £85.00–£90.00
d £100.00–£110.00

# Glade End

2 Little Marlow Road, Marlow SL7 1HD  **t** (01628) 471334  **f** (01628) 478154  **e** sue@gladeend.com
**w** gladeend.com

Our guesthouse is a stylish haven with luxury, en suite bedrooms. Many distinctive touches mark Glade End out from the ordinary.

**open** All year
**bedrooms** 6 double, 3 twin
**bathrooms** 8 en suite, 1 private
**payment** Credit/debit cards, cash/cheques

Room 🛏 📺 💆 🍽   General 🖼 P ✂ 🏃 ✳   Leisure ♪ ⚐ 🚴 🎣

---

**MIDHURST,** West Sussex Map ref 2C3

★★★
**BED & BREAKFAST**

B&B per room per night
s £40.00–£50.00
d £70.00–£80.00

# Oakhurst Cottage

Carron Lane, Midhurst GU29 9LF  **t** (01730) 813523

Beautifully converted early Victorian coach house next to Midhurst Common, yet within walking distance of Midhurst town centre.

**open** All year except Christmas and New Year
**bedrooms** 1 double
**bathrooms** En suite
**payment** Cash/cheques

Room 🛏 💆

---

**MIDHURST,** West Sussex Map ref 2C3

★★★
**BED & BREAKFAST**

B&B per room per night
d £70.00–£90.00

# Sunnyside

Cocking Causeway, Midhurst GU29 9QH  **t** (01730) 814370

Sunnyside is close to the South Downs Way, Goodwood for golf, motor-racing and horse-racing, and Cowdray Park for polo. Easy reach of Arundel and the south coast. Always a friendly welcome.

**open** All year except Christmas and New Year
**bedrooms** 2 double, 1 twin
**bathrooms** 2 en suite, 1 private
**payment** Cash/cheques, euros

Room 🛏 📺 💆 🍽   General 🛋 🖼 🛗 P ✂ 🛏 🐾   Leisure ∪ ⚐ 🚴 🎣

---

**MILFORD ON SEA,** Hampshire Map ref 2C3

★★★★
**BED & BREAKFAST**

B&B per room per night
d £60.00–£70.00

# Alma Mater

4 Knowland Drive, Milford on Sea, Lymington SO41 0RH  **t** (01590) 642811  **f** (01590) 642811
**e** bandbalmamater@aol.com  **w** almamater.org.uk

**open** All year
**bedrooms** 2 double, 1 twin
**bathrooms** 2 en suite, 1 private
**payment** Cash/cheques, euros

Detached, quiet, spacious, non-smoking chalet bungalow with en suite bedrooms overlooking lovely garden. In quiet residential area close to village, beaches, New Forest and IOW. Secure, off-road parking.

Room 🛏 📺 💆 🍽   General 🛋15 P ✂ 🛏 🅿 ♿ ✳   Leisure ∪ 🚴

---

## A holiday on two wheels

For a fabulous freewheeling break, seek out accommodation participating in our Cyclists Welcome scheme. Look out for the symbol and plan your route online at nationalcyclenetwork.org.

## MILTON KEYNES, Buckinghamshire Map ref 2C1

★★★
**BED & BREAKFAST**

B&B per room per night
s £25.00–£35.00
d £50.00–£70.00

# Chantry Farm

Pindon End, Hanslope, Milton Keynes MK19 7HL  **t** (01908) 510269  **f** (01908) 510269
**e** chuff.wake@tiscali.co.uk  **w** chantryfarmbandb.com

A 600-acre friendly working farm. Old stone farmhouse (1650) with inglenook fireplace in beautiful countryside overlooking lake. Near Milton Keynes, London train 40 minutes, convenient for Northampton, Silverstone, Woburn Abbey.

**open** All year except Christmas and New Year
**bedrooms** 1 double, 2 twin
**bathrooms** 1 en suite
**payment** Cash/cheques, euros

Room 📺 🛏 🍵  General 🛆 🏥 🛉 P 🅿 ✿ 🐕  Leisure ⬚ ♣ ♪ ►

## MILTON KEYNES, Buckinghamshire Map ref 2C1

★★★★
**BED & BREAKFAST**
**SILVER AWARD**

B&B per room per night
s £40.00–£50.00
d £60.00–£85.00

# Fairview Cottage

1 Newport Road, Woughton on the Green, Milton Keynes MK6 3BS  **t** (01908) 665520
**f** (01908) 246445  **e** info@fairviewmk.co.uk

**open** All year except Christmas and New Year
**bedrooms** 1 double, 2 twin, 1 single, 1 suite
**bathrooms** 1 en suite, 2 private
**payment** Cash/cheques

A beautiful large Georgian cottage, set amidst conservation parkland and village. Guests are amazed at the location within a city! Freshly cooked breakfasts, range of refreshments, complimentary toiletries. Warm, friendly welcome guaranteed, attention to detail and comfort. Ideally situated approximately five minutes from city centre, National Bowl, Xscape, train/bus station, theatre district, M1.

⊕ M1 jct 14, follow A4146 (H6), 3rd roundabout left (V10), next roundabout right (H7), take 2nd left turning, first white house on left-hand side.

Room 📺 🛏 🍵  General P ✂ 🍴 🅿 ◉ ✿  Leisure ∪ ♪ ► 🚲 🎣

## NEW FOREST

See under Ashurst, Beaulieu, Brockenhurst, Burley, Cadnam, Lymington, Lyndhurst, Milford on Sea, New Milton, Ringwood

## NEW MILTON, Hampshire Map ref 2B3

★★★★
**BED & BREAKFAST**
**SILVER AWARD**

B&B per room per night
s £33.00–£44.00
d £56.00–£66.00

# Taverners Cottage

Bashley Cross Road, Bashley, New Milton BH25 5SZ  **t** (01425) 615403  **f** (01425) 632177
**e** judith@tavernerscottage.co.uk  **w** tavernerscottage.co.uk

**open** All year except Christmas and New Year
**bedrooms** 1 double, 1 family
**bathrooms** All en suite
**payment** Cash/cheques, euros

Attractive 300-year-old cob cottage overlooking open farmland. Warm welcome guaranteed. Great breakfasts. Care and attention to detail a priority. Ideal for touring, golf, cycling, walking and riding.

⊕ From A35 Lyndhurst-Christchurch road, take B3055 to Beckley/Sway for 1.75 miles to white cottage on left-hand side (past motorcycle museum).

♥ Winter discounts (excl Bank Holidays). Discount for more than 7 days.

Room 🛁 📺 🛏 🍵  General 🛆 🏥 🛉 P ✂ 🍴 🅿 🐕  Leisure ∪ ♪ 🚲 🎣

## Mention our name
Please mention this guide when making your booking.

**NEW MILTON,** Hampshire Map ref 2B3

★ ★ ★ ★
BED & BREAKFAST

B&B per room per night
s £40.00–£45.00
d £60.00–£70.00

# Willy's Well

Bashley Common Road, Bashley, New Milton BH25 5SF  t (01425) 616834
e moyramac2@hotmail.com

**open** All year
**bedrooms** 1 double, 1 twin
**bathrooms** All en suite
**payment** Cash/cheques, euros

A warm welcome awaits you at our mid-17thC listed thatched cottage standing in one acre of mature gardens, also available for your enjoyment. We have direct forest access through six acres of pasture and are three miles from the sea. Ideal for walking, cycling, horse-riding.

⊕ From A35 Lyndhurst to Christchurch road, travel east on B3058 towards New Milton. Cottage approx 200yds south of Rising Sun public house.

♥ Midweek reduced breaks: 4 nights for the price of 3.

Room 🛁 TV 📶 ♋   General ☎12 P ⛅ ❄ 🐾   Leisure ∪ ♪ ▶ ⛴ 🚴

**NEWBURY,** Berkshire Map ref 2C2

★ ★ ★
GUEST ACCOMMODATION

B&B per room per night
s £50.00–£70.00
d £60.00–£85.00

# The Bell at Boxford

Boxford, Newbury RG20 8DD  t (01488) 608721  f (01488) 608749  e paul@bellatboxford.com
w bellatboxford.com

**open** All year
**bedrooms** 6 double, 2 twin, 2 single
**bathrooms** All en suite
**payment** Credit/debit cards, cash/cheques, euros

Situated in the beautiful Lambourn valley, only four miles from both Newbury and Lambourn. Newbury racecourse is only ten minutes away. Golf, fishing and riding are all local pursuits.

⊕ M4 jct 14, follow signs to A338 Wantage. Turn onto B4000 towards Wickham/Stockcross. Turn left at sign to Boxford. We are at the bottom of this lane.

♥ Please see website for current offers.

Room 🛁 📞 TV 📶 ♋   General ☎ P 🍷 ⛅ ❄ 🐾   Leisure ♠ ♪ ▶

**NEWBURY,** Berkshire Map ref 2C2

★ ★ ★ ★
GUEST ACCOMMODATION

B&B per room per night
s £40.00–£45.00
d £68.00–£80.00

# East End Farm

East End, Newbury RG20 0AB  t (01635) 254895  f (01635) 250664  e mp@eastendfarm.co.uk
w eastendfarm.co.uk

**open** All year
**bedrooms** 1 double, 1 twin
**bathrooms** All en suite
**payment** Cash/cheques, euros

Five miles south of Newbury, in an Area of Outstanding Natural Beauty, this small working farm will give you a warm welcome. Accommodation is in a beautifully converted barn. Choice of breakfasts with home-made and local produce. Ideal base for country lovers or stopover for business or travel.

⊕ M4, jct 13, take A34 southbound to exit for Highclere. Onto A343 towards Highclere. At crossroads, right then 2nd left (Church Road). Through East End, farm on left.

♥ Packages available for riders, walkers and cyclists, including stabling/grazing, meals and luggage drop-off service.

Room 🛁 TV 📶 ♋   General ☎ 🖥 🅿 P 🍴 ✗ ⛅ 🅰 ▣ ❄ 🐾   Leisure ⇗ ⚘ ∪ ♪ ▶ ⛴

**NEWBURY,** Berkshire Map ref 2C2

★★★★
**BED & BREAKFAST**

B&B per room per night
s £40.00–£45.00
d £65.00–£70.00

# Highclere Farm

Highclere, Newbury RG20 9PY  **t** (01635) 255013  **e** walshhighclere@newburyweb.net

An extremely comfortable and peaceful converted coach house close to Highclere Castle in an Area of Outstanding Natural Beauty. Within reach of Stonehenge, Winchester, Salisbury and Oxford.

**open** All year except Christmas
**bedrooms** 1 double, 1 twin
**bathrooms** All en suite
**payment** Cash/cheques

Room 📺 ♿  General ⌂ P ⋈ 🐾  Leisure ∪ ♪ ➤ 🏛

---

**NEWBURY,** Berkshire Map ref 2C2

★★★★
**FARMHOUSE**
**SILVER AWARD**

B&B per room per night
s £44.65–£47.00
d £70.50–£76.37

# Manor Farm House

Church Street, Hampstead Norreys, Newbury RG18 0TD  **t** (01635) 201276  **f** (01635) 201035
**e** bettsbedandbreakfast@hotmail.com  **w** bettsbedandbreakfast.co.uk

**open** All year except Christmas
**bedrooms** 1 double, 1 twin, 1 suite
**bathrooms** All en suite
**payment** Cash/cheques

Welcoming and superbly comfortable accommodation on our working farm in centre of peaceful village. A 17thC farmhouse with 21stC comfort, including splendid en suite with whirlpool bath, and self-contained ground-floor apartment. Pub two minutes' stroll. Labrador dogs available for longer walks on farm or in neighbouring woods.

⊕ From north, south and west: A34/M4 jct 13, to Hermitage, then B4009 to Hampstead Norreys. From east: M4 jct 12, through Bradfield and Yattendon to Hampstead Norreys.

Room ♿ 📺 ♿ 🍴  General ⌂ 10 P ✂ ⋈ ❋

---

**NEWBURY,** Berkshire Map ref 2C2

★★★★
**BED & BREAKFAST**

B&B per room per night
s £45.00–£55.00
d £75.00–£80.00

# The Old Farmhouse

Downend Lane, Chieveley, Newbury RG20 8TN  **t** (01635) 248361  **e** palletts@aol.com
**w** smoothhound.co.uk/hotels/oldfarmhouse

**open** All year
**bedrooms** 1 suite
**bathrooms** En suite
**payment** Cash/cheques

Period farmhouse on edge of village within two miles of M4/A34 (jct13), five miles north of Newbury. Accommodation in ground-floor annexe comprising hall, kitchenette, sitting room (with bed-settee), double bedroom, bathroom. Large gardens overlooking countryside. Oxford, Bath, Windsor and Heathrow Airport within easy reach. London approximately one hour. Family room rates also available.

⊕ A34/M4 jct 13 roundabout, Chieveley exit. At junction, left towards Chieveley then right into Oxford Road towards Beedon. 2nd left into Downend Lane. 1st house on right after 300m.

Room ♿ 📺 ♿ 🍴  General ⌂ ▥ ♨ P ✂ ⋈ ❋ 🐾  Leisure 🏛

## Take a break

Look out for special promotions and themed breaks. This could be your chance to indulge an interest, find a new one, or just relax and enjoy exceptional value. Offers (highlighted in colour) are subject to availability.

**NEWHAVEN,** East Sussex Map ref 2D3

★ ★ ★
**GUEST HOUSE**

B&B per room per night
s £22.50–£30.00
d £45.00–£60.00

# Newhaven Lodge Guest House

12 Brighton Road, Newhaven BN9 9NB  **t** (01273) 513736  **f** (01273) 734619
**e** newhavenlodge@aol.com  **w** newhavenlodge.co.uk

A comfortable, bright, family-run establishment located close to the Newhaven/Dieppe ferry terminal. Brighton, Lewes and South Downs nearby. The establishment motto is 'Arrive as a guest and leave as a friend'.

**open** All year
**bedrooms** 1 double, 2 single, 3 family
**bathrooms** 4 en suite
**payment** Credit/debit cards, cash/cheques, euros

Room 🛏 📺 👜 ♨  General ⛱ ▥ ☂ P ✿ ⛟  Leisure ∪ ♪ ► ♿

**NEWPORT PAGNELL,** Buckinghamshire Map ref 2C1

★ ★ ★ ★
**BED & BREAKFAST**

B&B per room per night
s £33.00–£39.00
d £55.00–£65.00
Evening meal per person
£6.99–£12.99

# Rosemary House

7 Hill View, Newport Pagnell MK16 8BE  **t** (01908) 612198  **f** (01908) 612198
**e** rosemaryhouse@btinternet.com

All rooms have TV and video, tea and coffee facilities and hot and cold water vanity units. Full English breakfast included. Ample parking. Wi-Fi Internet.

**open** All year
**bedrooms** 2 twin, 1 suite
**bathrooms** 1 en suite, 2 private
**payment** Cash/cheques

Room 📺 👜 ♨  General ⛱ ▥ ☂ P ⅙ ✕ 🍴 ✿  Leisure ♪ ♿ ⌂

**OCKLEY,** Surrey Map ref 2D2

★ ★ ★ ★
**INN**

B&B per room per night
s £55.00
d £80.00
Evening meal per person
£10.00–£25.00

# The Kings Arms Inn

Stane Street, Ockley, Dorking RH5 5TS  **t** (01306) 711224  **f** (01306) 711224
**e** enquiries@thekingsarmsockley.co.uk  **w** thekingsarmsockley.co.uk

Charming, beamed 16thC freehouse in the picturesque village of Ockley. Welcoming log fires and an ideal retreat for sampling our candlelit restaurant or delicious bar menu. All bedrooms en suite. Award-winning country garden.

**open** All year
**bedrooms** 5 double, 1 twin
**bathrooms** All en suite
**payment** Credit/debit cards, cash/cheques

Room 🛏 ☎ 📺 👜 ♨  General P ⅃ ✕ 🍴 ✿

**OXFORD,** Oxfordshire Map ref 2C1

★ ★
**GUEST ACCOMMODATION**

B&B per room per night
s £40.00–£60.00
d £50.00–£70.00

# Becket House

5 Becket Street, Oxford OX1 1PP  **t** (01865) 724675  **f** (01865) 724675
**e** becketguesthouse@yahoo.co.uk

Friendly guesthouse convenient for rail and bus station, within walking distance of city centre and colleges. Good, clean accommodation, en suite rooms.

**open** All year
**bedrooms** 4 double, 2 twin, 2 single, 2 family
**bathrooms** 5 en suite
**payment** Credit/debit cards

Room 🛏 📺 👜  General ⛱ ⅙ ▥

# Our quality rating schemes

For a detailed explanation of the quality and facilities represented by the stars, please refer to the information pages at the back of this guide.

---

**OXFORD,** Oxfordshire Map ref 2C1

★ ★ ★ ★

**BED & BREAKFAST**

B&B per room per night
s  £40.00–£50.00
d  £60.00–£80.00

## Broomhill

Lincombe Lane, Boars Hill, Oxford OX1 5DZ  **t** (01865) 735339  **e** sara@broomhill-oxford.co.uk
**w** broomhill-oxford.co.uk

**open** All year
**bedrooms** 2 double, 1 twin, 2 single
**bathrooms** 4 en suite
**payment** Cheques, euros

Broomhill is situated five minutes from Oxford. Heathrow 45 minutes. Large house in family environment in extensive grounds. Large double and single rooms, all en suite. Excellent pub five minutes' walk, serving good, all-day food. See website or email for more information.

⊕ *From North, Leave A34 at Hinksey Hill interchange. Go over A34 and up hill. At top turn right. Continue 1 mile. Lincombe Lane on left. Map available on website.*

Room 📺 ♿  General 🕮 ♨ P ⚡ ✆  Leisure ▶ 🏊

---

**OXFORD,** Oxfordshire Map ref 2C1

★ ★ ★ ★

**GUEST ACCOMMODATION**

B&B per room per night
s  £52.00–£62.00
d  £80.00–£90.00

## Cotswold House

363 Banbury Road, Oxford OX2 7PL  **t** (01865) 310558  **f** (01865) 310558  **e** d.r.walker@talk21.com
**w** cotswoldhouse.co.uk

A well-situated and elegant property, offering good accommodation and service. Cotswold House is in a most desirable part of Oxford.

**open** All year
**bedrooms** 2 double, 1 twin, 2 single, 2 family
**bathrooms** All en suite
**payment** Credit/debit cards, cash/cheques

Room 🖥 📺 ♿ ♨  General 🕮 6 P ⚡ ✆  Leisure 🏊

---

**OXFORD,** Oxfordshire Map ref 2C1

★ ★ ★ ★ ★

**GUEST ACCOMMODATION SILVER AWARD**

B&B per room per night
s  £50.00–£60.00
d  £70.00–£80.00

## Gables Guest House

6 Cumnor Hill, Oxford OX2 9HA  **t** (01865) 862153  **f** (01865) 864054  **e** stay@gables-oxford.co.uk
**w** gables-guesthouse.co.uk

**open** All year
**bedrooms** 2 double, 2 twin, 1 single
**bathrooms** All en suite
**payment** Credit/debit cards, cash/cheques, euros

Award-winning guest house with beautiful large garden. Quiet area yet close to the city centre and university. Most attractive interior design throughout with particularly comfortable beds. Freshly cooked breakfasts and large selection of healthy options. Perfect base for visiting Oxford, Blenheim Palace and Cotswolds.

⊕ *M40 jct 9. Join A34 south. Exit A34, A420 Oxford, Swindon. At roundabout take Oxford/Botley exit. Right at traffic lights. Gables is on right.*

♥ *Special weekend breaks in winter season. Corporate rates available.*

Room 🖥 ☎ 📺 ♿ ♨  General 🕮 10 P ⚡ 🖳 ✆ ❀  Leisure ∪ ▶ 🚲 🏊

---

## To your credit

If you book by phone you may be asked for your credit card number. If so, it is advisable to check the proprietor's policy in case you have to cancel your reservation at a later date.

## OXFORD, Oxfordshire Map ref 2C1

★★★★
**GUEST ACCOMMODATION**
**SILVER AWARD**

B&B per room per night
s £38.00–£45.00
d £54.00–£62.00

# Gorselands Hall

Boddington Lane, North Leigh, Witney OX29 6PU  t (01993) 882292  f (01993) 881895
e hamilton@gorselandshall.com  w gorselandshall.com

Old Cotswold-stone country house in quiet, rural location. Large, secluded garden. Convenient for Oxford, Blenheim Palace and Cotswolds. Wide choice of excellent eating places nearby.

**open** All year except Christmas and New Year
**bedrooms** 4 double, 1 twin, 1 family
**bathrooms** All en suite
**payment** Credit/debit cards, cash/cheques

Room ... General ... Leisure ...

## OXFORD, Oxfordshire Map ref 2C1

★★★
**GUEST ACCOMMODATION**

B&B per room per night
s £45.00–£55.00
d £75.00–£85.00

# Milka's Guest House

379 Iffley Road, Oxford OX4 4DP  t (01865) 778458  f 0845 127 5173  e reservations@milkas.co.uk
w milkas.co.uk

A pleasant, family-run guesthouse on main road, only one mile from city centre.

**open** All year
**bedrooms** 4 double, 1 twin, 1 single
**bathrooms** All en suite
**payment** Credit/debit cards, cash/cheques, euros

Room ... General ...

## OXFORD, Oxfordshire Map ref 2C1

★★★
**BED & BREAKFAST**

B&B per room per night
s £35.00–£40.00
d Min £60.00

# Park House

7 St Bernard's Road, Oxford OX2 6EH  t (01865) 310824  e krynpark@hotmail.com

Traditional Victorian terraced house in north Oxford, five minutes' walk from city centre and within easy reach of all amenities.

**open** All year except Christmas
**bedrooms** 1 double, 1 single
**bathrooms** 1 private
**payment** Cash/cheques

Room ... General ...

## OXFORD, Oxfordshire Map ref 2C1

★★★★
**GUEST HOUSE**

B&B per room per night
s £30.00–£50.00
d £70.00–£80.00

# Pickwicks Guest House

15-17 London Road, Headington, Oxford OX3 7SP  t (01865) 750487  f (01865) 742208
e pickwicks@tiscali.co.uk  w pickwicksguesthouse.co.uk

Comfortable guesthouse within easy reach of Oxford's universities and hospitals. Nearby coach stop for 24-hour service to central London, Heathrow, Gatwick and Stansted Airports. Free car parking and Wi-Fi Internet. Please contact us for family room rates.

**open** All year except Christmas and New Year
**bedrooms** 4 double, 3 twin, 4 single, 4 family
**bathrooms** 13 en suite
**payment** Credit/debit cards, cash/cheques

Room ... General ...

# Key to symbols

The symbols at the end of each entry help you pick out the services and facilities which are most important to you. A key to the symbols can be found inside the back-cover flap. Keep this open for easy reference.

★★★
**GUEST ACCOMMODATION**

B&B per room per night
s £70.00–£75.00
d £80.00–£90.00

## River Hotel

17 Botley Road, Oxford OX2 0AA  **t** (01865) 243475  **f** (01865) 724306  **e** reception@riverhotel.co.uk
**w** riverhotel.co.uk

**open** All year except Christmas and New Year
**bedrooms** 9 double, 2 twin, 4 single, 5 family
**bathrooms** 18 en suite, 2 private
**payment** Credit/debit cards, cash/cheques

Excellent, picturesque location beside Osney Bridge on River Thames Walk. Originally a master builder's home built c1870s, run for many years as an independent small hotel by proprietor and staff. The property is owned by an Oxford College. Well-equipped bedrooms. Family rooms also let as double or twin occupancy. Car park on site. Easy walk to city.

⊕ From A34, hotel is 1 mile from west exit at Seacourt/Botley interchange. Turn left onto Botley road (A420). After Osney Bridge, right and right again for car park.

Room ☎ 📺 ♿ 🍵  General ♨5 🖥 P ✂ 🍽 🛍 🗲 ✳  Leisure 🎵

★★★
**GUEST ACCOMMODATION**

B&B per room per night
s £35.00–£50.00
d £62.00–£72.00

## Sportsview Guest House

106-110 Abingdon Road, Oxford OX1 4PX  **t** (01865) 244268  **f** (01865) 249270
**e** stay@sportsviewguesthouse.co.uk  **w** sportsviewguesthouse.co.uk

Friendly, family-run Victorian guesthouse overlooking Queen's College sports ground, 0.5 miles from city centre. Close to open-air swimming pool. See famous Oxford landmarks. Frequent buses to London and Blenheim Palace.

**open** All year except Christmas and New Year
**bedrooms** 6 double, 4 twin, 5 single, 5 family
**bathrooms** 19 en suite, 1 private
**payment** Credit/debit cards, cash/cheques

Room 🛗 ☎ 📺 ♿  General ♨3 🖥 P ✂ 🛍 🗲 ✳

★★★★
**GUEST ACCOMMODATION**

B&B per room per night
d £80.00–£95.00

## Weir View House

9 Shooters Hill, Pangbourne, Reading RG8 7DZ  **t** (0118) 984 2120  **f** (0118) 984 3777
**e** info@weirview.co.uk  **w** weirview.co.uk

Luxury bed and continental breakfast guest accommodation with views overlooking River Thames and Pangbourne Weir. Adjacent to excellent village shops, restaurants and rail link.

**open** All year except Christmas and New Year
**bedrooms** 3 double, 6 suites
**bathrooms** All en suite
**payment** Credit/debit cards, cash/cheques

Room 🛗 🖨 ☎ 📺 ♿ 🍵  General ♨ 🖥 P ✂ 🗲 ▣  Leisure U 🚲 🏛

★★★★
**BED & BREAKFAST**

B&B per room per night
s £36.00–£45.00
d £58.00–£60.00

## 1 The Spain

Sheep Street, Petersfield GU32 3JZ  **t** (01730) 263261  **f** (01730) 261084  **e** allantarver@ntlworld.com
**w** 1thespain.com

18thC house with charming walled garden, in conservation area of Petersfield. Good eating places nearby, lovely walks, plenty to see and do.

**open** All year
**bedrooms** 2 double, 1 twin
**bathrooms** 2 en suite, 1 private
**payment** Cash/cheques

Room 📺 ♿ 🍵  General ♨ 🖥 🛋 ✂ 🍽 🛍 ✳ 🐾  Leisure ▶ 🏛

**WALKERS WELCOME** **WELCOME WALKERS**

## Best foot forward

Walkers feel at home in accommodation participating in our Walkers Welcome scheme. Look out for the symbol. Consider walking all or part of a long-distance route – go online at nationaltrail.co.uk.

## PETERSFIELD, Hampshire Map ref 2C3

★★★★
**BED & BREAKFAST**

B&B per room per night
s £30.00–£40.00
d £60.00–£70.00

# Quinhay Farmhouse

Alton Road, Froxfield, Petersfield GU32 1BZ  **t** (01730) 827183  **f** (01730) 827184
**e** janerothery@quinhaybandb.co.uk  **w** quinhaybandb.co.uk

We offer three rooms, a double en suite and a single and a twin room, both with private bathrooms. There is a large guest lounge with garden access. Close to Winchester, Chichester and Portsmouth. Access to glorious countryside. Non-smoking.

**open** All year except Christmas and New Year
**bedrooms** 1 double, 1 twin, 1 single
**bathrooms** 1 en suite, 2 private
**payment** Credit/debit cards, cash/cheques

Room 📺 👍 🕾  General 🛇 10 P ⅙ 🛏 ✿  Leisure ∪ 🚲 🏛

## PETWORTH, West Sussex Map ref 2D3

★★★
**FARMHOUSE**

B&B per room per night
s £25.00–£30.00
d £50.00–£60.00

# Burton Park Farm

Burton Park Road, Petworth GU28 0JT  **t** (01798) 342431

Farmhouse with beautiful view of the South Downs. Warm welcome. Good food, vegetarians catered for. Off-road parking. Guide dogs only.

**open** All year except Christmas and New Year
**bedrooms** 1 double, 1 twin
**bathrooms** All en suite
**payment** Cash/cheques

Room 📺 👍 🕾  General 🛇 ⅙ 🛏

## PETWORTH, West Sussex Map ref 2D3

★★★★
**BED & BREAKFAST**

B&B per room per night
s £40.00
d £60.00–£65.00

# Eedes Cottage

Bignor Park Road, Bury Gate, Pulborough RH20 1EZ  **t** (01798) 831438  **f** (01798) 831942
**e** eedes.bandb.hare@amserve.com  **w** visitsussex.org/eedescottage

Quiet country house surrounded by farmland. Convenient for main roads to Arundel, Chichester and Brighton. Dogs and children welcome. All bedrooms large and comfortable.

**open** All year
**bedrooms** 2 double, 2 twin
**bathrooms** 2 en suite
**payment** Cash/cheques, euros

Room 🛁 📞 📺 👍  General 🛇 P ✿ 🛉  Leisure ∪ 🏛

## PETWORTH, West Sussex Map ref 2D3

★★★★
**BED & BREAKFAST**

B&B per room per night
s £60.00
d £80.00–£110.00

# Garden Cottage

Park Road, Petworth GU28 0DS  **t** (01798) 342414  **e** a.wolseley@ukonline.co.uk

This beautiful cottage is set within a secluded garden in the centre of the historic town of Petworth. It has its own entrance and private sitting room, with a small kitchen that can be used for long-stay visitors.

**open** All year
**bedrooms** 1 suite
**bathrooms** 1 private
**payment** Cash/cheques

Room 🛁 📺 👍 🕾  General 🛇 🛎 🍽 🛏 ✿  Leisure ∪ ♪ ➤ 🏛

## PORTSMOUTH & SOUTHSEA, Hampshire Map ref 2C3

★★★★
**GUEST ACCOMMODATION**

B&B per room per night
s £40.00–£55.00
d £58.00–£66.00

# Hamilton House Bed & Breakfast

95 Victoria Road North, Portsmouth PO5 1PS  **t** (023) 9282 3502  **f** (023) 9282 3502
**e** sandra@hamiltonhouse.co.uk  **w** hamiltonhouse.co.uk

Delightful Victorian town house, many original features. Five minutes continental/Isle of Wight ferry ports, stations, University of Portsmouth, The Historic Dockyard, museums, Gunwharf Quays, tourist attractions. Ideal touring base. Breakfast served from 0600.

**open** All year
**bedrooms** 5 double, 2 twin, 2 family
**bathrooms** 5 en suite
**payment** Credit/debit cards, cash/cheques, euros

Room 📺 👍 🕾  General 🛇 ▥ 🛎 ⅙ 🍽 🛏 🎿 ✿

## What's in an award?

Further information about awards can be found at the front of this guide.

## PULBOROUGH, West Sussex Map ref 2D3

★★★★
INN

B&B per room per night
s £50.00–£60.00
d £90.00–£120.00
Evening meal per person
£6.95–£16.95

### The Labouring Man

Old London Road, Pulborough RH20 1LF  t (01798) 872215  e philip.beckett@btconnect.com
w thelabouringman.co.uk

Pub/restaurant with five luxury bed and breakfast rooms. Walkers, car park, home-cooked food, real ales, log fire.

**open** All year
**bedrooms** 4 double, 1 twin
**bathrooms** All en suite
**payment** Credit/debit cards, cash/cheques

Room 🛏 📺 ♿  General 🏃 ♿ P ⅙ ♟ ✗ ⌖ ⌖ ❄ ↟  Leisure ⌁ ⍫ 🏛

## PULBOROUGH, West Sussex Map ref 2D3

★★★★
BED & BREAKFAST
SILVER AWARD

B&B per room per night
s £30.00–£40.00
d £55.00–£60.00

### St Cleather

Rectory Lane, Pulborough RH20 2AD  t (01798) 873038  e enquiries@stcleather.me.uk
w stcleather.me.uk

Located in Pulborough village, the centre of historic West Sussex, with views to the South Downs. Close to Arundel, Chichester, Goodwood, Petworth and a short train ride to Gatwick Airport.

**open** All year except Christmas and New Year
**bedrooms** 1 double, 1 twin
**bathrooms** 1 en suite, 1 private
**payment** Cash/cheques

Room 📺 ♿ ⍩  General 🏃 10 ⅙ ❄  Leisure 🏛

## RAMSGATE, Kent Map ref 3C3

★★★★
GUEST HOUSE

B&B per room per night
s £35.00
d £55.00–£60.00

### Glendevon Guest House

8 Truro Road, Ramsgate CT11 8DB  t (01843) 570909  f (01843) 570909
e rebekah.smith1@btinternet.com  w glendevonguesthouse.co.uk

Delightful Victorian house near beach, harbour and town. Very comfortable rooms, all en suite, and each containing attractive feature of modern kitchen/dining area. TV/VCR, Fairtrade tea and coffee.

**open** All year
**bedrooms** 3 double, 1 twin, 2 family
**bathrooms** All en suite
**payment** Credit/debit cards, cash/cheques

Room 🛏 📺 ♿  General 🏃 ⌖ ⌖ ◻  Leisure ⌁ 🚲 🏛

## READING, Berkshire Map ref 2C2

★★★★
GUEST ACCOMMODATION

B&B per room per night
s £30.00–£65.00
d £65.00–£80.00

### Belle Vue House

2 Tilehurst Road, Reading RG1 7TN  t (0118) 959 4445  f (0118) 959 6090
e bellevuehotel@btconnect.com  w bellevuehousehotel.co.uk

Central location, newly refurbished, ample parking, wireless broadband, walking distance to shops, bars, restaurants. Five minutes to mainline railway station.

**open** All year except Christmas
**bedrooms** 4 double, 1 twin, 10 single, 1 family
**bathrooms** 9 en suite
**payment** Credit/debit cards

Room 🛏 ☎ 📺 ♿  General 🏃 ⌖ ☂ P

## READING, Berkshire Map ref 2C2

★★★
GUEST ACCOMMODATION

B&B per room per night
s £28.50–£37.50
d £40.00–£60.00

### Dittisham Guest House

63 Tilehurst Road, Reading RG30 2JL  t (0118) 956 9483  e dittishamgh@aol.com

Renovated Edwardian property with garden, in a quiet but central location. Good value and quality. On bus routes for centre of town. Car park.

**open** All year
**bedrooms** 1 double, 1 twin, 3 single
**bathrooms** 3 en suite
**payment** Credit/debit cards, cash/cheques, euros

Room 🛏 📺 ♿ ⍩  General 🏃 ❄

## RINGMER, East Sussex Map ref 2D3

**★★★★**
GUEST ACCOMMODATION

B&B per room per night
s £35.00–£50.00
d £55.00–£65.00

# Bryn-Clai

Uckfield Road, Ringmer, Lewes BN8 5RU  t (01273) 814042  w brynclai.co.uk

**open** All year
**bedrooms** 1 double, 1 twin, 1 family
**bathrooms** 1 en suite, 1 private
**payment** Cash/cheques

Large, modern house set in seven acres with beautiful garden and good parking. Spacious, comfortable interior. Large, airy bedrooms (including ground-floor rooms) with views over farmland. Within walking distance of 16thC country pub with excellent food. Nearby attractions include Glyndebourne, East Sussex Golf Course, South Downs and Brighton.

⊕ From A26, 2 miles north of Lewes, 4 miles south of Uckfield.

Room 🛁 📺 👪 🍽  General 🛏 🏚 ⨯ P ⚟ 🛏 ✳  Leisure ⚓ ►

## RINGWOOD, Hampshire Map ref 2B3

**★★★★**
GUEST ACCOMMODATION

B&B per room per night
s Min £67.50
d £84.00–£94.00

# Moortown Lodge

244 Christchurch Road, Ringwood BH24 3AS  t (01425) 471404  f (01425) 476527
e enquiries@moortownlodge.co.uk  w moortownlodge.co.uk

**open** All year
**bedrooms** 3 double, 3 twin, 1 family
**bathrooms** All en suite
**payment** Credit/debit cards, cash/cheques

A charming family-run Georgian guesthouse offering a warm welcome and luxurious B&B accommodation. Seven elegantly furnished and fully equipped en suite rooms, including a four-poster. All rooms with broadband. Moortown Lodge is an ideal stopover for business people and an excellent base for leisure visitors, with many attractions nearby.

⊕ Turn off A31 at Ringwood. Follow B3347 signposted Sopley for 0.5 miles. Moortown Lodge is on right-hand side next to David Lloyd Leisure Club.

♥ 3 nights B&B for the cost of 2. Double/twin occupancy. Sun/Fri incl, Oct-Mar, excl public holidays.

Room 🛁 🖼 ☎ 📺 👪 🍽  General 🛏 🏚 ⨯ P ⚟ 🏞 ✳ 🐾  Leisure ✧ ⤳ ⚲ U ⚓ ► 🚲 🏊

## ROCHESTER, Kent Map ref 3B3

**★★★★**
GUEST ACCOMMODATION

B&B per room per night
s £40.00
d £65.00

# Salisbury House

29 Watts Avenue, Rochester ME1 1RX  t (01634) 400182

Victorian house within easy walking distance of Rochester Castle, Cathedral, historic High Street, the River Medway and railway stations. Large, comfortable, well-appointed rooms.

**open** All year
**bedrooms** 1 double, 1 twin
**bathrooms** All en suite
**payment** Cash/cheques

Room 📺 👪 🍽  General 🛏 🏚 ⚟ 🛏 ✳

## RODMELL, East Sussex Map ref 2D3

**★★★★**
GUEST ACCOMMODATION

B&B per room per night
s £30.00
d £60.00

# Garden Studio

Robin Hill, Mill Lane, Rodmell, Lewes BN7 3HS  t (01273) 476715 & 07775 624235

Self-contained studio flat on South Downs Way. Twin beds, bed-settee, own kitchen, breakfast supplied. Close to Glyndebourne, Brighton, port of Newhaven. Use of garden. Popular village inn.

**open** All year
**bedrooms** 1 family
**bathrooms** En suite
**payment** Cash/cheques

Room 🛁 📺 👪 🍽  General 🛏 🏚 P ⚟ 🛏 ▣ ✳  Leisure ⚓

---

**ROMNEY MARSH,** Kent Map ref 3B4

★★★★
**BED & BREAKFAST**

B&B per room per night
d £60.00–£70.00

## Stable Cottage

The Sheiling, Donkey Street, Burmarsh, Romney Marsh TN29 0JN  t (01303) 872335 & 07870 918387
e eric777@tiscali.co.uk  w stablecottageburmarsh.co.uk

Self-contained cottage, ideal for anyone seeking total peace and quiet. Off-road parking. Breakfast hamper provided.

**open** All year
**bedrooms** 1 double
**bathrooms** En suite
**payment** Credit/debit cards, cash

Room 🛏 📺 👤 🍵   General P 🍴 🎱 ✿

---

**ROMSEY,** Hampshire Map ref 2C3

★★★★
**INN**

B&B per room per night
s £59.95–£89.95
d £74.95–£104.95
Evening meal per person
£6.00–£20.00

## Mortimer Arms

Romsey Road, Ower, Romsey SO51 6AF  t (023) 8081 4379  f (023) 8081 2548

**open** All year
**bedrooms** 11 double, 1 twin, 2 suites
**bathrooms** 14 en suite
**payment** Credit/debit cards, cash/cheques

The Mortimer Arms – an establishment with a difference. This Victorian building has been fully refurbished and combines old-world charm and modern sophistication. Soak into the comfort of one of our unique, en suite rooms, each decorated to a very high standard. Excellent restaurant, modern function room and meeting room for up to 100 people.

⊕ Close to jct 2 of the M27 at the entrance to Paultons Park.
♥ Special breaks available.

Room 🛏 🖼 ☎ 📺 👤 🍵   General 🛎 🎱 ♿ P 🍽 🎱 ♿ ◉ ✿   Leisure ∪ ⏳ ▶

---

**ROMSEY,** Hampshire Map ref 2C3

★★
**BED & BREAKFAST**

B&B per room per night
s £35.00–£45.00
d £45.00–£50.00

## Nursery Cottage

East Tytherley, Nr Romsey, Salisbury SP5 1LF  t (01794) 341060  e nursery-cottage@waitrose.com
w nursery-cottage.com

A delightful, rural Victorian cottage in a small Test Valley hamlet with beautiful views across the surrounding countryside. An excellent location for walking and cycling.

**open** All year except Christmas and New Year
**bedrooms** 2 double, 1 twin
**bathrooms** 1 en suite
**payment** Cash/cheques

Room 📺 👤   General P 🍴 🎱 ✿   Leisure ⏳ 🚲 ⛵

---

**ROMSEY,** Hampshire Map ref 2C3

★★★
**GUEST ACCOMMODATION**

B&B per room per night
s Min £37.00
d Min £74.00

## Wessex Guest House

5 Palmerston Street, Romsey SO51 8GF  t (01794) 512038  f (01794) 528331

A listed Georgian house in historic market town. Comfortable rooms. Near Broadlands, Abbey and restaurants.

**open** All year except Christmas and New Year
**bedrooms** 3 double, 3 twin, 2 single
**bathrooms** All en suite
**payment** Cash/cheques

Room 🛏 ☎ 📺 👤   General 🛎 12 🍴 🎱 ♿   Leisure ⏳ ▶

---

## Place index

If you know where you want to stay, the index at the back of the guide will give you the page number listing accommodation in your chosen town, city or village. Check out the other useful indexes too.

## ROYAL TUNBRIDGE WELLS, Kent Map ref 2D2

**★★★★**
BED & BREAKFAST
SILVER AWARD

B&B per room per night
s £40.00–£60.00
d £60.00–£75.00

### The Brick House

21 Mount Ephraim Road, Tunbridge Wells TN1 1EN  t (01892) 516517
e info@thebrickhousebandb.co.uk  w thebrickhousebandb.co.uk

Elegant Edwardian house in the centre of Tunbridge Wells. Very convenient although quietly located in the conservation area. Spacious rooms full of antiques. Parking, swimming pool. All bedrooms en suite. Warm welcome.

**open** All year except Christmas and New Year
**bedrooms** 1 double, 1 twin
**bathrooms** All en suite
**payment** Cash/cheques

Room TV 👜 ⏛  General 1 ☆ P 💺 🍳 ✿  Leisure ⚓ ⤵ ⟶

## ROYAL TUNBRIDGE WELLS, Kent Map ref 2D2

**★★★★**
BED & BREAKFAST

B&B per room per night
d £50.00–£56.00

### Hawkenbury Farm

Hawkenbury Road, Royal Tunbridge Wells TN3 9AD  t (01892) 536977  f (01892) 536200
e rhwright1@aol.com

Accommodation on small working farm, set in quiet location 1.5 miles south east of Tunbridge Wells. Unlimited parking, views and walks.

**open** All year except Christmas and New Year
**bedrooms** 2 double, 1 twin
**bathrooms** All en suite
**payment** Credit/debit cards, cash/cheques, euros

Room ♿ TV 👜 ⏛  General ⌚ P 💺  Leisure ⤵ ⟶

## ROYAL TUNBRIDGE WELLS, Kent Map ref 2D2

**★★★**
FARMHOUSE

B&B per room per night
s £29.00–£40.00
d £58.00–£66.00

### Manor Court Farm

Ashurst Road, Ashurst, Tunbridge Wells TN3 9TB  t (01892) 740279  f (01892) 740919
e jsoyke@jsoyke.freeserve.co.uk  w manorcourtfarm.co.uk

**open** All year
**bedrooms** 1 double, 2 twin
**payment** Cash/cheques, euros

Georgian farmhouse with friendly atmosphere, spacious rooms and lovely views of Medway Valley. Mixed 350-acre farm, many animals. Good base for walking. Penshurst Place, Hever Castle, Chartwell, Sissinghurst etc all within easy reach by car. Excellent camping facilities. Good train service to London from Ashurst station (two minutes away).

⊕ *Situated on A264, 5 miles west of Tunbridge Wells, 0.5 miles east of Ashurst village. A264 – Tunbridge Wells, East Grinstead road.*

♥ *Reductions for longer stays. Reductions for children.*

Room TV 👜  General ⌚ 🛏 ☆ P 💺 🍳 🔌 ✿ ♞  Leisure U ⤵ ⟶ 🚲 🏛

the
**Gardens**
**Explorer**

visit**Britain**.com®

# The great outdoors

Discover Britain's green heart with this easy-to-use guide. Featuring a selection of the most stunning gardens in the country, The Gardens Explorer is complete with a handy fold-out map and illustrated guide. You can purchase the Explorer series from good bookshops and online at visitbritaindirect.com.

---

**RUDGWICK,** West Sussex Map ref 2D2

★ ★ ★ ★ ★
**BED & BREAKFAST**
**SILVER AWARD**

## Alliblaster House

Hillhouse Lane, Horsham RH12 3BD  **t** (01403) 822860  **f** (01403) 824033
**e** info@alliblasterhouse.com  **w** alliblasterhouse.com

B&B per room per night
**d** Min £90.00

**open** All year except Christmas and New Year
**bedrooms** 3 double, 3 twin
**bathrooms** 5 en suite, 1 private
**payment** Credit/debit cards, cash/cheques, euros

A beautiful 18thC Sussex-style country house set in nine acres of lush West Sussex countryside. On-site award-winning spa and conference facilities. Large, well-appointed rooms with designer touches. Organic cooking and Fairtrade produce. Free internet access. Ideal for work, rest or play.

⊕ *Midway between Guildford and Horsham on the A281. 30 minutes to Epsom, Gatwick and Goodwood. 45 minutes to Ascot, Heathrow and Windsor.*

♥ *Special rates for long stays and single travellers.*

Room 📺 ♿ ♨  General P 🍴 🅼 ⚒ ✿  Leisure ∪ ⚓ ► 🚲

---

**RUSTINGTON,** West Sussex Map ref 2D3

★ ★ ★ ★
**GUEST ACCOMMODATION**
**SILVER AWARD**

## Kenmore

Claigmar Road, Rustington, Littlehampton BN16 2NL  **t** (01903) 784634  **f** (01903) 784634
**e** thekenmore@amserve.net  **w** kenmoreguesthouse.co.uk

B&B per room per night
**s** £30.00–£32.00
**d** £56.00–£60.00

Secluded Edwardian house in a garden setting in the heart of the village and close to the sea. Attractive en suite rooms, individually decorated and comfortably furnished. Private parking.

**open** All year except Christmas and New Year
**bedrooms** 2 double, 2 twin, 2 single, 1 family
**bathrooms** All en suite
**payment** Credit/debit cards, cash/cheques, euros

Room ♿ 📺 ♿ ♨  General ➘ P ✂ 🅼 ✿ 🐾

---

**RYDE,** Isle of Wight Map ref 2C3

★ ★
**GUEST HOUSE**

## Seaward Guest House

14-16 George Street, Ryde PO33 2EW  **t** (01983) 563168  **f** (01983) 563168  **e** seaward@fsbdial.co.uk

B&B per room per night
**s** £22.00–£24.00
**d** £36.00–£52.00

Guesthouse, conveniently located for beach, pier and all amenities. English, continental or vegetarian breakfast served.

**open** All year
**bedrooms** 3 double, 1 twin, 1 single, 2 family
**bathrooms** 2 en suite
**payment** Credit/debit cards, cash/cheques

Room ♿ 📺 ♿ ♨  General ➘ 🏧 🍴  Leisure 🎣

---

**RYE,** East Sussex Map ref 3B4

★ ★ ★
**GUEST HOUSE**

## Aviemore Guest House

28-30 Fishmarket Road, Rye TN31 7LP  **t** (01797) 223052  **f** (01797) 223052
**e** info@aviemorerye.co.uk  **w** aviemorerye.co.uk

B&B per room per night
**s** £30.00–£35.00
**d** £60.00–£65.00

Owner-operated, imposing Victorian guesthouse overlooking green expanse of the Salts. Five minutes' walk town centre. En suite and standard rooms, breakfast room, guests' lounge and bar.

**open** All year except Christmas
**bedrooms** 5 double, 3 twin
**bathrooms** 4 en suite, 4 private
**payment** Cash/cheques

Room 📺 ♿  General ➘ 🍴 ♈ 🅼 ✿ 🐾  Leisure 🚲 🎣

---

## It's all quality-assessed accommodation

Our commitment to quality involves wide-ranging accommodation assessment. Rating and awards were correct at the time of going to press but may change following a new assessment. Please check at time of booking.

**RYE,** East Sussex Map ref 3B4

★★★★★
**GUEST ACCOMMODATION
GOLD AWARD**

B&B per room per night
s  £68.00–£90.00
d  £95.00–£110.00

# Durrant House

2 Market Street, Rye TN31 7LA  **t** (01797) 223182  **f** (01797) 226940  **e** Info@durranthouse.com
**w** durranthouse.com

**bedrooms** 4 double, 1 family
**bathrooms** All en suite
**payment** Credit/debit cards, cash/cheques

A charming and welcoming Georgian town house situated in a quiet street in the centre of medieval Rye. Individually decorated bedrooms, including four-poster, all en suite. Cosy lounge and bar. Delicious breakfasts to suit all tastes. Fabulous views from rear garden where breakfast is served in the summer. Closed January.

⊕ *From M25, A21 to Rye. Town centre, under Landgate Arch, up East Cliff. First left is East Street, house looks down East Street.*

♥ *Nov-Mar, Sun-Thu mini breaks – 15% discount for 2 or more night's stay, based on 2 people sharing a room.*

Room 🛏 📺 ♿ 🍵  General ⏰10 ✂ 🍽 🎱 👶❄  Leisure ∪ ♪ ► 🚲 🏊

---

**RYE,** East Sussex Map ref 3B4

★★★★★
**BED & BREAKFAST**

B&B per room per night
s  £55.00–£65.00
d  £80.00–£100.00
Evening meal per person
£20.00–£30.00

# Hayden's

108 High Street, Rye TN31 7JE  **t** (01797) 224501  **f** (01797) 223813  **e** richard.hayden@mac.com
**w** cheynehouse.co.uk

**open** All year except Christmas
**bedrooms** 2 double
**bathrooms** All en suite
**payment** Credit/debit cards, cash/cheques

Hayden's is a small, family-run, eco-friendly B&B and restaurant in the heart of the ancient town of Rye, set in a beautiful 18thC town house. Visitors can enjoy home cooking using organic local produce while gazing out at panoramic views across the Romney Marsh.

⊕ *M25 jct 5. A21 to Flimwell. Left onto A268. Right onto Wish Street. Follow one-way system. Left onto Cinque Port Street. Right onto High Street.*

♥ *Discounts on stays of 3 days or more (excluding Saturdays).*

Room 📺 ♿ 🍵  General 🚶 ✂ 🍽 🎮❄  Leisure ∪ ♪ ► 🚲 🏊

---

**RYE,** East Sussex Map ref 3B4

★★★★★
**GUEST ACCOMMODATION
GOLD AWARD**

B&B per room per night
s  £70.00–£79.00
d  £90.00–£124.00

# Jeake's House

Mermaid Street, Rye TN31 7ET  **t** (01797) 222828  **f** (01797) 222623  **e** stay@jeakeshouse.com
**w** jeakeshouse.com

**open** All year
**bedrooms** 6 double, 2 twin, 3 suites
**bathrooms** 10 en suite, 1 private
**payment** Credit/debit cards, cash/cheques

Ideally located historic house on winding, cobbled street in the heart of ancient medieval town. Individually restored rooms provide traditional luxury combined with all modern facilities. Book-lined bar, cosy parlours, extensive breakfast menu to suit all tastes. Easy walking distance to restaurants and shops. Private car park.

⊕ *Within the cobbled medieval town centre, approached either from the High Street via West Street or from The Strand Quay, A259.*

♥ *Reductions for a stay of 7 or more nights. Midweek winter breaks.*

Room 🛏 📞 📺 ♿ 🍵  General ⏰8 🍽 🎱 🐕  Leisure ∪ ♪ ► 🚲

---

## RYE, East Sussex Map ref 3B4

★★★★
GUEST ACCOMMODATION

B&B per room per night
s £40.00
d £50.00–£60.00

### The Mill House, Holmdale

Holmdale Farm, Peasmarsh Road, Rye TN31 7UN  t (01797) 280154  e jen@pay7900.freeserve.co.uk

Quality bed and breakfast, one mile from the centre of Rye. Large rooms with sitting area and beautiful views. Delicious breakfasts. Use of garden and play area.

**open** All year
**bedrooms** 1 double, 1 suite
**bathrooms** 1 en suite, 1 private
**payment** Cash/cheques, euros

Room 📺 ♨ 🕯  General 🐾 🏠 P ⚡ 🌙 ▣ ❁  Leisure ♪ 🚲 🛥

## SANDHURST, Berkshire Map ref 2C2

★★★
INN

B&B per room per night
s £55.00–£62.95
d £55.00–£70.90
Evening meal per person
£4.95–£14.95

### The Wellington Arms

203 Yorktown Road, Sandhurst GU47 9BN  t (01252) 872408  f (01252) 861873
w thewellingtonarms.co.uk

En suite rooms in converted stable block next to friendly local pub serving great food and drinks. View our rooms and our menu on our website.

**open** All year except Christmas and New Year
**bedrooms** 3 double, 2 twin, 1 single
**bathrooms** All en suite
**payment** Credit/debit cards, cash/cheques

Room 📶 📺 ♨ 🕯  General P ⚡ 🍷 ✕ 🌙 ❁

## SANDHURST, Kent Map ref 3B4

★★★★
BED & BREAKFAST

B&B per room per night
s £35.00–£40.00
d £55.00–£60.00

### Lamberden Cottage

Rye Road, Cranbrook TN18 5PH  t (01580) 850743  e thewalledgarden@hotmail.co.uk
w lamberdencottage.co.uk

**open** All year except Christmas
**bedrooms** 1 double, 1 twin/family
**bathrooms** All en suite
**payment** Cash/cheques

An 18thC detached cottage with sympathetic additions in approximately 1.75 acres. Friendly and peaceful atmosphere. Many historic places and gardens of interest to visit. Great Dixter, Sissinghurst, Pashley Manor, Bodiam Castle, the Kent and East Sussex Steam Train Railway are a few of the many attractions. Family room from £70 per night.

Room 📺 ♨ 🕯  General 🐾 P ⚡ ✕ 🌙 ❤ ❁  Leisure ♪ ▶ 🛥

## SANDOWN, Isle of Wight Map ref 2C3

★★★
GUEST ACCOMMODATION

B&B per room per night
s £23.00–£29.00
d £46.00–£58.00

### The Montpelier

Pier Street, Sandown PO36 8JR  t (01983) 403964  f 07092 212734  e enquiries@themontpelier.co.uk
w themontpelier.co.uk

The Montpelier is situated opposite the pier and beaches with the high street just around the corner. We offer B&B, room-only and ferry-inclusive packages. Sea views available.

**open** All year
**bedrooms** 3 double, 2 twin, 1 single, 2 family
**bathrooms** All en suite
**payment** Credit/debit cards, cash/cheques

Room 📺 ♨  General 🐾 🛏 ⚡ ❁

## Looking for a little luxury

Gold and Silver Awards are given to establishments achieving the highest levels of quality and service. There's more information at the front of the guide, and an index to all accommodation achieving these awards at the back.

## SANDOWN, Isle of Wight Map ref 2C3

★★★
**GUEST HOUSE**

B&B per room per night
s £19.00–£23.00
d £42.00–£50.00
Evening meal per person
£10.00–£12.00

# The Philomel

21 Carter Street, Sandown PO36 8BL  **t** (01983) 406413  **f** 0870 094 0601
**e** enquiries@philomel-hotel.co.uk  **w** philomel-hotel.co.uk

Centrally, yet quietly located in Sandown, this family-run hotel offers comfortably furnished rooms, some with balcony and sea view, a hearty English breakfast, a colourful garden and a guest lounge with open fire.

**open** All year
**bedrooms** 6 double, 1 twin, 2 single
**bathrooms** 6 en suite, 1 private
**payment** Credit/debit cards, cash/cheques

Room ● ◆  General ◇ ▦ ♦ P ⅟ ♥ ✕ ▦ ▥ ⚄ ✿  Leisure ⌂

## SANDOWN, Isle of Wight Map ref 2C3

★★★★
**GUEST HOUSE**

B&B per room per night
s £29.00–£38.00
d £58.00–£76.00
Evening meal per person
Min £20.00

# Rooftree Guesthouse

26 Broadway, Sandown PO36 9BY  **t** (01983) 403175  **e** rooftree@btconnect.com
**w** rooftree-hotel.co.uk

Rooftree is a friendly, family-run hotel set in its own grounds. Children are welcome (toys available). English and Japanese alternative menu. Free dance lessons. We welcome you to our hotel.

**open** All year except Christmas
**bedrooms** 6 double, 1 twin, 2 family
**bathrooms** All en suite
**payment** Credit/debit cards, cash/cheques

Room ♨ ▥ TV ● ◆  General ◇ ▦ ♦ P ⅟ ♥ ✕ ▦ ▥ ✿

## SEAFORD, East Sussex Map ref 2D3

★★★★
**GUEST HOUSE**

B&B per room per night
s £40.00–£45.00
d £40.00–£70.00
Evening meal per person
£15.00–£20.00

# The Silverdale

21 Sutton Park Road, Seaford BN25 1RH  **t** (01323) 491849  **f** (01323) 890854
**e** silverdale@mistral.co.uk  **w** silverdaleseaford.co.uk

**open** All year
**bedrooms** 3 double, 2 family, 2 suites
**bathrooms** All en suite
**payment** Credit/debit cards, cash/cheques, euros

Small, expertly run house-hotel in the centre of peaceful Edwardian town. Beautiful food, a host of English wines and over 120 single malts. Only a few minutes' walk to the beach, antique shops and the friendly pubs. National dog-friendly prize winner. Green Tourism Business Scheme gold-award winner.

⊕ *On A259 in centre of Seaford.*

♥ *Special winter deals – contact us for more details.*

Room ♨ ▥ ☎ TV ● ◆  General ◇ ▦ ♦ P ♥ ✕ ▦ ⊁  Leisure ∪ ▶ ⚲ ⌂

Log on to **enjoyengland.com** to find a break that matches your mood.
**experience** scenes that inspire and traditions that baffle. **discover** the world's most inventive cultural entertainment and most stimulating attractions. **explore** vibrant cities and rugged peaks. **relax** in a country pub or on a sandy beach.

# enjoyEngland.com

## SELSEY, West Sussex Map ref 2C3

★★★★
GUEST ACCOMMODATION

B&B per room per night
s £36.00–£50.00
d £62.50–£85.00

# St Andrews Lodge Guest Accommodation

Chichester Road, Selsey, Chichester PO20 0LX  t (01243) 606899  f (01243) 607826
e info@standrewslodge.co.uk  w standrewslodge.co.uk

open All year except Christmas and New Year
bedrooms 4 double, 1 twin, 1 single, 4 family
bathrooms All en suite
payment Credit/debit cards, cash/cheques

Situated in the small seaside town of Selsey close to unspoilt beaches and five minutes from Pagham Harbour. Enjoy our delicious breakfast and stay in one of our pretty rooms, five of which are ground floor and open directly onto our large south-facing garden. Dogs welcome, licensed bar, ample parking.

⊕ From the A27 at Chichester take the B2145 and follow signs to Selsey for 7 miles. St Andrews is on the right opposite Church Road.

♥ Special winter offers available Oct-Feb. 25% discount for stay of 3 or more nights. Please telephone for details.

Room 🛏 📞 📺 ♿ 🍵  General 🐾 ♿ P ♨ 🛏 ✿ 🐾  Leisure ∪ ♪ ►

## SEVENOAKS, Kent Map ref 2D2

★★★★
BED & BREAKFAST

B&B per room per night
d £60.00–£70.00

# Hornshaw House

47 Mount Harry Road, Sevenoaks TN13 3JN  t (01732) 465262  e elizabeth.bates4@btinternet.com
w hornshaw-house.co.uk

Attractive family house in quiet garden setting. Warm bedrooms with comfortable beds and en suite baths and showers. Off-road parking. Hornshaw House is a five-minute walk from Sevenoaks station.

open All year except Christmas and New Year
bedrooms 1 double, 1 twin
bathrooms All en suite
payment Cash/cheques, euros

Room 📺 ♿ 🍵  General 🐾 6 P ✂ ✿

## SHANKLIN, Isle of Wight Map ref 2C3

★★★
GUEST ACCOMMODATION

B&B per room per night
s £25.00–£32.50
d £50.00–£65.00

# The Palmerston

16 Palmerston Road, Shanklin PO37 6AS  t (01983) 865547  f (01983) 868008
e info@palmerston-hotel.co.uk  w palmerston-hotel.co.uk

Located in an ideal position in Shanklin just a few minutes' walk to the beach, town centre and Old Village. A family-run hotel offering a friendly and attentive service.

open All year
bedrooms 3 double, 1 twin, 1 single, 2 family, 1 suite
bathrooms All en suite
payment Credit/debit cards, cash/cheques

Room 📺 ♿ 🍵  General 🐾 P ♨ 🔥 ✿ 🐾  Leisure ∪ ♪ ► 🚴

## SHIPTON-UNDER-WYCHWOOD, Oxfordshire Map ref 2B1

★★★
BED & BREAKFAST

B&B per room per night
s £35.00–£40.00
d £50.00–£55.00

# Lodge Cottage

High Street, Shipton-under-Wychwood, Chipping Norton OX7 6DG  t (01993) 830811
e h.a.savill@tiscali.co.uk

Country house in 13 acres with lovely garden, between Burford and Chipping Norton. Quiet location. Ideal for touring the Cotswolds. Golf courses nearby. Open all year except Christmas.

open All year except Christmas
bedrooms 1 double
bathrooms En suite
payment Cash/cheques

Room ♿ 🍵  General P ♨ 💻 ✿  Leisure ९ ♪ ► 🏯

## Star ratings

Detailed information about star ratings can be found at the back of this guide.

## SLOUGH, Berkshire Map ref 2D2

★★★★
**GUEST HOUSE**

B&B per room per night
s £40.00–£52.00
d £60.00–£75.00

### Furnival Lodge

53-55 Furnival Avenue, Slough SL2 1DH  t (01753) 570333  f (01753) 670038
e info@furnival-lodge.co.uk  w furnival-lodge.co.uk

Choose Furnival Lodge, Slough's premier guest accommodation. Located within easy reach of Windsor Castle, Legoland, Savill Gardens and London attractions, we offer an ideal base for family breaks.

**open** All year
**bedrooms** 4 double, 2 twin, 3 single, 1 family
**bathrooms** All en suite
**payment** Credit/debit cards, cash/cheques, euros

Room 👗 TV  General 🐕 P 🗓 ⚬ ✿  Leisure ▶ 🏊

## SOUTHAMPTON, Hampshire Map ref 2C3

★★★★
**GUEST ACCOMMODATION**

B&B per room per night
s £53.00–£67.00
d £66.00–£74.00

### Dormy House Guest Accommodation

21 Barnes Lane, Sarisbury Green, Southampton SO31 7DA  t (01489) 572626  f (01489) 573370
e dormyhousehotel@warsash.globalnet.co.uk  w dormyhousehotel.net

**open** All year except Christmas and New Year
**bedrooms** 5 double, 3 twin, 3 single, 1 family
**bathrooms** All en suite
**payment** Credit/debit cards, cash/cheques, euros

A tranquil Victorian house set in an attractive garden, featuring en suite bedrooms, one of which is a superior, queen-bedded room, all with tea-/coffee-making facilities, direct-dial telephone, hairdryer and remote-control TV. Close to River Hamble, Portsmouth and local business parks. Eight miles from Southampton.

⊕ *M27 jct 9. A27 west towards Southampton. At Sarisbury Green, left into Barnes Lane. Dormy House is 1 mile on the right-hand side.*

Room 👗 📞 TV 👄 🍵  General 🐕 🍴 🛏 P 🍽 🗓 ✿  Leisure 🏊

## SOUTHAMPTON, Hampshire Map ref 2C3

★★★
**GUEST ACCOMMODATION**

B&B per room per night
s £36.00–£46.00
d £52.00–£58.00

### Eaton Court

32 Hill Lane, Southampton SO15 5AY  t (023) 8022 3081  f (023) 8032 2006  e ecourthot@aol.com
w eatoncourtsouthampton.co.uk

Comfortable, small, owner-run hotel for business or leisure stays. Bedrooms have all amenities, and a generous, traditional breakfast is served.

**open** All year except Christmas and New Year
**bedrooms** 3 double, 3 twin, 8 single
**bathrooms** 8 en suite
**payment** Credit/debit cards, cash/cheques

Room 📞 TV 👄  General 🐕 🛏 P 🍽 🗓 🐾

## SOUTHAMPTON, Hampshire Map ref 2C3

★★★
**GUEST ACCOMMODATION**

B&B per room per night
s £25.00
d £50.00–£60.00

### Mayview Guest House

30 The Polygon, Southampton SO15 2BN  t (023) 8022 0907  f 0845 127 4055
e info@mayview.co.uk  w mayview.co.uk

Small, family-run guesthouse in the city centre, providing a comfortable stay in clean and friendly surroundings. Free Wi-Fi Internet access, payphone, hairdryer and iron available on request.

**open** All year except Christmas
**bedrooms** 1 double, 2 twin, 5 single, 1 family
**bathrooms** 1 en suite
**payment** Credit/debit cards, cash/cheques

Room 👗 TV 👄  General 🐕 1 ✂

## SOUTHSEA

*See under Portsmouth & Southsea*

## Take a break

Look out for special promotions and themed breaks highlighted in colour.
(Offers subject to availability.)

**STELLING MINNIS,** Kent Map ref 3B4

★★★★
FARMHOUSE
SILVER AWARD

## Great Field Farm

Misling Lane, Stelling Minnis, Canterbury CT4 6DE  **t** (01227) 709223  **f** (01227) 709223
**e** Greatfieldfarm@aol.com  **w** great-field-farm.co.uk

B&B per room per night
**s** £35.00–£65.00
**d** £50.00–£80.00

Delightful farmhouse set amidst lovely gardens and countryside. Spacious, private suites; B&B or self-catering. Hearty breakfasts with home-grown fruits and eggs. Ten minutes to Canterbury/ Channel Tunnel.

**open** All year
**bedrooms** 2 double, 1 twin
**bathrooms** All en suite
**payment** Credit/debit cards, cash/cheques, euros

Room 📺 ♨ ⏰  General ☍ 🎱 ♿ P ⅍ ⚡ ✿  Leisure ∪ 🏛

**STEYNING,** West Sussex Map ref 2D3

★★★★★
GUEST HOUSE
SILVER AWARD

## Penfold Gallery Guest House

30 High Street, Steyning BN44 3GG  **t** (01903) 815595  **e** johnturner57@aol.com
**w** artyguesthouse.co.uk

B&B per room per night
**s** £76.00
**d** £98.00
Evening meal per person
£18.00–£26.00

Medieval hall house with later extensions. One of the oldest 15thC houses in Steyning, full of architectural interest.

**open** All year
**bedrooms** 2 double
**bathrooms** All en suite
**payment** Credit/debit cards, cash/cheques, euros

Room ☎ 📺 ♨ ⏰  General ☍ 12 ⅍ ♟ ✕ 🎱 ✿  Leisure 🏛

**STOKE ROW,** Oxfordshire Map ref 2C2

★★★★
INN

## The Cherry Tree Inn

Stoke Row, Henley-on-Thames RG9 5QA  **t** (01491) 680430  **e** info@thecherrytreeinn.com
**w** thecherrytreeinn.com

B&B per room per night
**d** £95.00
Evening meal per person
£9.95–£22.50

**open** All year except Christmas
**bedrooms** 4 double
**bathrooms** All en suite
**payment** Credit/debit cards, cash/cheques

The Cherry Tree is situated in an Area of Outstanding Natural Beauty within the Chilterns, and is a perfect blend of classic and contemporary: modern, but with classic original features such as beamed ceilings and flagstone floors. Both the bar and restaurant are non-smoking. Rosette awarded for food – Brakspears Ale – ten wines by the glass.

⊕ *From Henley (A4130) towards Nettlebed, at 1st roundabout left towards Sonning Common (B481). After 2 miles, right (Stoke Row). Follow road into village; pub on right-hand side.*

Room 🛏 📺 ♨  General ☍ ♿ P ♟ ⚡ ✿  Leisure ∪ ⌐

**STONE-IN-OXNEY,** Kent Map ref 3B4

★★★★
FARMHOUSE

## Tighe Farmhouse

Stone-in-Oxney, Tenterden TN30 7JU  **t** (01233) 758251  **f** (01233) 758054
**e** robin.kingsley@ndierct.co.uk  **w** accommodationrye.co.uk

B&B per room per night
**s** £50.00–£85.00
**d** £80.00–£100.00

Attractive, quiet, 16thC farmhouse in unrivalled position. Extensive views over Romney Marsh. En suite bedrooms. Four-poster. Inglenook fireplaces in living room. Close Rye/Great Dixter. Large, sunny terrace and gardens.

**open** All year except Christmas
**bedrooms** 2 double, 1 family
**bathrooms** All en suite
**payment** Cash/cheques, euros

Room 📠 📺 ♨ ⏰  General ☍ ♿ P ⅍ 🎱 ✿ 🐾  Leisure ♣ ⌐ 🏛

## Stay focused

Don't forget your camera. Take home shots of the greatest scenery, super seascapes and family fun.

---

**STROOD,** Kent Map ref 3B3

★★
**GUEST ACCOMMODATION**

B&B per room per night
s Min £23.50
d Min £47.00

## The Sundial

18 Ranscombe Close, Rochester ME2 2PB  **t** (01634) 721831  **e** sean@company8234.freeserve.co.uk

Comfortable accommodation. TV/VCR. Easy access to motorways, ten minutes from restaurants and entertainment centre. Use of attractive courtyard.

**open** All year except Christmas and New Year
**bedrooms** 2 double, 1 single
**bathrooms** 1 en suite, 2 private
**payment** Cash/cheques, euros

Room ⊤⊽ ⓦ  General ♋5 ✿  Leisure ⌂

---

**THURNHAM,** Kent Map ref 3B3

★★★★
**INN**

B&B per room per night
s £60.00–£70.00
d £80.00–£100.00
Evening meal per person
£7.50–£18.00

## Black Horse Inn

Pilgrims Way, Thurnham, Maidstone ME14 3LD  **t** (01622) 737185  **f** (01622) 739170
**e** info@wellieboot.net  **w** wellieboot.net

Kentish country pub with award-winning restaurant in the heart of the North Downs. Beautiful gardens with fountains and ponds. Alfresco terrace dining. Fantastic walking area.

**open** All year
**bedrooms** 8 double, 4 twin, 4 family
**bathrooms** All en suite
**payment** Credit/debit cards, cash/cheques

Room ♨ ⊞ ⊤⊽ ⓦ ℘  General ♋ ▥ ⅋ P ¶ ✗ ⊞ ✿ ★  Leisure ∪ ♪ ▶ ♿ ⌂

---

**TUNBRIDGE WELLS**

*See under Royal Tunbridge Wells*

---

**UCKFIELD,** East Sussex Map ref 2D3

★★★★
**FARMHOUSE**

B&B per room per night
s Min £28.00
d £56.00–£60.00

## Old Mill Farm B&B

Chillies Lane, High Hurstwood, Uckfield TN22 4AD  **t** (01825) 732279  **f** (01825) 732279

Sussex barn and buildings converted to a comfortable home, situated in the quiet village of High Hurstwood, off the A26. Ashdown Forest nearby.

**open** All year
**bedrooms** 1 twin, 1 single, 1 family
**bathrooms** 2 en suite, 1 private
**payment** Cash/cheques

Room ♨ ⊤⊽ ⓦ ℘  General ♋ P ✂ ⊞ ✿ ★

---

**VENTNOR,** Isle of Wight Map ref 2C3

Rating Applied For
**GUEST HOUSE**

B&B per room per night
s £30.00–£38.00
d £60.00–£76.00

## Brunswick House

Victoria Street, Ventnor PO38 1ET  **t** (01983) 852656
**e** brunswick.house.services.ltd@unicombox.co.uk  **w** brunswickhouse-web.co.uk

**open** All year
**bedrooms** 2 double, 2 twin, 2 single
**bathrooms** All en suite
**payment** Credit/debit cards, cash/cheques, euros

A family-run guesthouse, over 150 years old, but retaining it's spacious Victorian character and, with its recent refurbishment, offering warm, comfortable and welcoming accommodation. Located in the heart of Ventnor, ideally situated for walking, cycling and the many places of interest locally and around the island.

⊕ *Car: From East Cowes via Newport and Godshill. Bus: East Cowes-Newport No 5, Cowes-Newport No 1, Newport-Ventnor No 3.*

♥ *Weekend breaks including ferry and parking permits. Minimum 2 nights £85-£120 per person.*

Room ⊤⊽ ⓦ ℘  General ♋ ▥ ⅋ ¶ ⊞ ◉ ✿ ★  Leisure ⌂

---

## To your credit

If you book by credit card, it's advisable to check the proprietor's cancellation policy in case you have to change your plans.

## WALLINGFORD, Oxfordshire Map ref 2C2

★★★
**BED & BREAKFAST**

B&B per room per night
s Min £35.00
d Min £55.00

### Huntington House

18 Wood Street, Wallingford OX10 0AX  t (01491) 839201  f (01491) 579723  e hunting311@aol.com

18thC, Grade II Listed building. Quiet town-centre location, easy parking. Traditional decor and delightful walled garden.

**open** All year except Christmas
**bedrooms** 1 double, 1 twin
**payment** Cash/cheques, euros

Room 📺 ♿ 🍸  General 🛋 ✂ ❀ 🐾  Leisure ∪ ⚓ ►

## WALLINGFORD, Oxfordshire Map ref 2C2

★★★★
**BED & BREAKFAST**

B&B per room per night
s £45.00–£65.00
d £65.00–£85.00

### Little Gables

166 Crowmarsh Hill, Crowmarsh Gifford, Wallingford OX10 8BG  t (01491) 837834 & 07860 148882
f (01491) 834426  e jill@stayingaway.com  w stayingaway.com

Detached house, close to Ridgeway, Wallingford and Thames Path. Includes single and family room (cot), or twin, double or triple, en suite or private. Tea-/coffee-making facilities, colour TV, fridge. Internet access.

**open** All year
**bedrooms** 1 double, 1 twin, 1 family
**bathrooms** 2 en suite, 1 private
**payment** Cash/cheques, euros

Room ♿ 📺 ♿ 🍸  General 🛋 ▥ 🧍 P ✂ ▦ 🔥 ❀  Leisure ∪ ⚓ ► 🚲 🛶

## WALMER, Kent Map ref 3C4

★★★★
**BED & BREAKFAST**

B&B per room per night
s Min £30.00
d £56.00–£60.00

### Hardicot Guest House

Kingsdown Road, Walmer, Deal CT14 8AW  t (01304) 373867  e guestboss@btopenworld.com
w hardicot-guest-house.co.uk

**open** All year except Christmas
**bedrooms** 1 double, 2 twin
**bathrooms** 1 en suite, 2 private
**payment** Cash/cheques, euros

Large, quiet, detached Victorian house with Channel views and secluded garden, situated 100yds from the beach. Guests have unrestricted access to rooms. Close to three championship golf courses, ferries and the Channel Tunnel. Ideal centre for cliff walks and exploring Canterbury and the castles and gardens of East Kent.

⊕ *From A2 Canterbury to Dover, take Deal road A258. At Ringwould turn right onto B2057 to Kingsdown, follow for 1.5 miles.*

♥ *7 nights for the price of 6.*

Room ♿ 🍸  General 🛋5 P ✂ ▦ ❀  Leisure ⚓ 🛶

## WANTAGE, Oxfordshire Map ref 2C2

★★★★
**BED & BREAKFAST**

B&B per room per night
s £26.00–£30.00
d £40.00–£48.00

### B&B in Wantage

50 Foliat Drive, Wantage OX12 7AL  t (01235) 760495  e eleanor@eaturner.freeserve.co.uk
w geocities.com/bandbinwantage

B&B in Wantage is a clean, comfortable and quiet establishment within easy walking distance of the town centre and buses.

**open** All year
**bedrooms** 2 double, 1 twin
**bathrooms** 1 en suite
**payment** Credit/debit cards

Room ♿ 📺 ♿ 🍸  General 🛋 ▥ 🧍 P ✂ ▣ ❀

## Using map references

The map references refer to the colour maps at the front of this guide. The first figure is the map number, the letter and figure that follow indicate the grid reference on the map.

## WATERLOOVILLE, Hampshire Map ref 2C3

★★★
**BED & BREAKFAST**

B&B per room per night
s £35.00–£40.00
d £55.00–£60.00

# New Haven Bed & Breakfast

193 London Road, Waterlooville PO7 7RN **t** (023) 9226 8559 **f** (023) 9226 8559
**e** newhaven@toucansurf.com **w** smoothhound.co.uk/hotels/newhavenbedandbreakfast.html

A warm welcome awaits you in our spacious home. We offer you comfortably equipped en suite rooms with full English and continental breakfast.

**open** All year
**bedrooms** 1 double, 1 twin, 1 single, 1 family
**bathrooms** All en suite
**payment** Cash/cheques

Room 🖫 📺 👶 🥛  General 🛏 P ⅔ 🔥 ❄

## WATERSFIELD, West Sussex Map ref 2D3

★★★★
**BED & BREAKFAST**

B&B per room per night
s Min £35.00
d Min £60.00

# The Willows

London Road, Watersfield, Pulborough RH20 1NB **t** (01798) 831576 **e** mount@ukonline.co.uk
**w** mountbandb.co.uk

**open** All year except Christmas
**bedrooms** 2 double
**bathrooms** 1 en suite, 1 private
**payment** Cash/cheques

Comfortable family house on A29, close to South Downs, Parham House, Petworth, Arundel, Goodwood, RSPB Reserve Pulborough. Ample off-road parking, clock radio, colour TV, tea-/coffee-making facilities, friendly atmosphere.

Room 📺 👶 🥛  General 🛏8 P ⅔ 🛏 ▣ ❄  Leisure 🏞

## WEYBRIDGE, Surrey Map ref 2D2

★★★★★
**GUEST ACCOMMODATION**
**SILVER AWARD**

B&B per room per night
d £75.00–£120.00

# Riverdene Gardens

1 Oatlands Drive, Weybridge KT13 9NA **t** (01932) 223574 **f** (01932) 223574
**e** riverdenegardens@btinternet.com **w** riverdenegardens.co.uk

**open** All year except Christmas and New Year
**bedrooms** 4 double, 1 family
**bathrooms** 4 en suite, 1 private
**payment** Credit/debit cards, cash/cheques

Riverdene Gardens is a Grade II Listed Victorian house offering accommodation of a standard exceeding that of many hotels, with all the comforts of home whilst retaining the original charm and atmosphere of this Norman Shaw-designed property. We pride ourselves on our attention to detail and our courteous service.

⊕ M25 jct 11, A317, Weybridge High Street, Oatlands Drive, Riverdene Gardens close to Walton Bridge, just before the traffic lights, on the right.

Room 📺 👶 🥛  General 🛏 🎢 ⅄ P ⅔ 🛏 🔥 ▣ ❄

## WHITSTABLE, Kent Map ref 3B3

★★★★
**GUEST ACCOMMODATION**
**SILVER AWARD**

B&B per room per night
s £40.00–£75.00
d £75.00–£125.00

# The Pearl Fisher

103 Cromwell Road, Whitstable CT5 1NL **t** (01227) 771000 **f** (01227) 771000
**e** stay@thepearlfisher.co.uk **w** thepearlfisher.com

Close to restaurants, harbour, shops and seafront. Excellent rail and road links to Canterbury and coast. Delightful garden. Themed rooms, high quality beds, extensive breakfast menu. Private parking.

**open** All year
**bedrooms** 3 double, 1 twin, 1 suite
**bathrooms** All en suite
**payment** Credit/debit cards, cash/cheques

Room 🖫 🎢 📺 👶 🥛  General 🛏 🎢 P 🍴 🛏 🔥 ❄  Leisure ▶ 🚲 🏞

**WINCHESTER,** Hampshire Map ref 2C3

★ ★ ★
**BED & BREAKFAST**

B&B per room per night
s £35.00–£40.00
d £45.00–£50.00

# 12 Christchurch Road

Winchester SO23 9SR  **t** (01962) 854272  **e** pjspatton@yahoo.co.uk

Elegant Victorian house furnished with style. Easy, pleasant walk to city centre, cathedral and water meadows. Breakfast in conservatory, overlooking beautiful gardens, features home-made bread, preserves and local produce.

**open** All year except Christmas and New Year
**bedrooms** 1 double, 1 twin
**payment** Cash/cheques

Room ♿ 🍴   General ⌚ 🖥 🅿 ⚡ 🛏 🐾   Leisure ⛵

---

**WINCHESTER,** Hampshire Map ref 2C3

★ ★ ★ ★
**BED & BREAKFAST**
**SILVER AWARD**

B&B per room per night
d £65.00–£75.00

# Acacia

44 Kilham Lane, Winchester SO22 5PT  **t** (01962) 852259  **f** (01962) 852259
**e** eric.buchanan@btinternet.com

Charming house set in beautiful gardens. Quiet country lane, yet only a five-minute drive to city centre. Excellent food and that little extra friendliness that makes for a special break. Open March to end of October.

**bedrooms** 2 double, 1 twin
**bathrooms** 2 en suite, 1 private
**payment** Credit/debit cards

Room ♿ 🍴   General ⌚10 ⚡ 🛏 🅿 ❄   Leisure ▶ ⛵

---

**WINCHESTER,** Hampshire Map ref 2C3

★ ★ ★ ★ ★
**GUEST ACCOMMODATION**
**GOLD AWARD**

B&B per room per night
s £69.00–£109.00
d £85.00–£115.00

# Giffard House

50 Christchurch Road, Winchester SO23 9SU  **t** (01962) 852628  **f** (01962) 856722
**e** giffardhotel@aol.com  **w** giffardhotel.co.uk

**open** All year
**bedrooms** 6 double, 2 twin, 4 single, 1 suite
**bathrooms** All en suite
**payment** Credit/debit cards, cash/cheques, euros

A warm welcome awaits those who visit this stunning Victorian house, recently refurbished to the highest standard. Relax in crisp, white bed linen and in luxurious, en suite bathrooms. Start the day with a traditional breakfast in our elegant dining room. Ten minutes' walk to town centre.

⊕ *From M3 jct 11, follow signs to Winchester travelling St Cross Road. After BP garage, take 1st left (Ranelagh), 2nd right (Christchurch). Hotel opposite Grafton.*

Room ♿ 📞 📺 ♿ 🍴   General ⌚ 🖥 🅿 🛏 ⚡ 🍽 🛏 ❄ 🔲 ❄   Leisure ∪ ♪ ▶ 🚲

---

**WINCHESTER,** Hampshire Map ref 2C3

★ ★ ★
**CAMPUS**

Per person per night
Bed only £19.60–£26.90
B&B    £23.70–£30.80

# The University of Winchester

West Hill, Winchester SO22 4NR  **t** (01962) 827332  **f** (01962) 827264
**e** conferences@winchester.ac.uk

Located on the outskirts of the ancient city of Winchester, the university offers high quality and value for money for groups and tours. Self-catering and full board available.

**open** mid-June – mid-September
**bedrooms** 903 single, 10 double/twin
Total no of beds 913
**Groups only** 923
**bathrooms** 267 en suite
**meals** Breakfast, lunch and evening meal available
**payment** Credit/debit cards, cash/cheques

Room ♿   General ⌚ 🅿 🖥 🍽 ◎ 🛏 📖 ❄ ⚡ 🍴 ❄ 🚌   Leisure 🎯 🏹 🎾 ∪ ♪ ▶ 🚲 ⛵

---

## What's in a quality rating?
Information about ratings can be found at the back of this guide.

## WINDSOR, Berkshire Map ref 2D2

★★★
**BED & BREAKFAST**

B&B per room per night
s £40.00–£50.00
d Min £60.00

# Barbara's Bed & Breakfast

16 Maidenhead Road, Windsor SL4 5EQ  t (01753) 840273  e bbandb@btinternet.com

Welcoming, friendly, Victorian family home, many original features. Situated close to the River Thames and leisure centre. Ten minutes' walk from Windsor Castle and town centre. Heathrow 20 minutes.

**open** All year except Christmas
**bedrooms** 2 double, 1 twin
**bathrooms** 1 en suite, 2 private
**payment** Cash/cheques, euros

Room 📺 👙 ♉  General 12 P ⅍ 🍽

## WINDSOR, Berkshire Map ref 2D2

★★★★
**GUEST ACCOMMODATION**

B&B per room per night
d Min £69.00

# Bluebell House

Lovel Lane, Woodside, Winkfield, Windsor SL4 2DG  t (01344) 886828
e registrations@bluebellhousehotel.co.uk  w bluebellhousehotel.co.uk

Ex-coaching inn dating from 1700. Charming, but with every modern convenience. Large garden, private parking. Ideal base for Windsor, Legoland, Ascot racing. Close to several good pubs.

**open** All year except Christmas
**bedrooms** 3 double, 2 twin
**bathrooms** 3 en suite, 2 private
**payment** Credit/debit cards, cash/cheques

Room ♿ 🖨 📺 👙 ♉  General ⌛ ▥ P ⅍ ❄  Leisure ♪

## WINDSOR, Berkshire Map ref 2D2

★★★
**GUEST HOUSE**

B&B per room per night
s £45.00–£67.00
d £55.00–£78.00

# The Clarence

9 Clarence Road, Windsor SL4 5AE  t (01753) 864436  f (01753) 857060  w clarence-hotel.co.uk

**open** All year except Christmas
**bedrooms** 4 double, 6 twin, 4 single, 6 family
**bathrooms** All en suite
**payment** Credit/debit cards, cash/cheques

Comfortable hotel with licensed bar and steam-sauna. Located near town centre and short walk from Windsor Castle, Eton College and River Thames. All rooms with en suite bathroom, TV, tea-/coffee-making facilities, hairdryer and radio-alarm. Free Wi-Fi Internet. Convenient for Legoland and Heathrow Airport.

⊕ *From M4 jct 6 take the road to Windsor. Stay on dual carriageway and turn left at the roundabout onto Clarence Road.*

Room ♿ 📺 👙 ♉  General ⌛ P 🍴 🗑 ♉ ❄ 🐕

## WOODSTOCK, Oxfordshire Map ref 2C1

★★★★
**BED & BREAKFAST**
**SILVER AWARD**

B&B per room per night
s £50.00–£65.00
d £65.00–£75.00

# The Laurels

40 Hensington Road, Woodstock OX20 1JL  t (01993) 812583  f (01993) 810041
e stay@laurelsguesthouse.co.uk  w laurelsguesthouse.co.uk

Fine Victorian house in Woodstock. Charmingly furnished, with an emphasis on comfort and quality. Just off town centre and a short walk from Blenheim Palace.

**open** All year except Christmas and New Year
**bedrooms** 1 double, 1 twin
**bathrooms** All en suite
**payment** Credit/debit cards, cash/cheques

Room 📺 👙 ♉  General ⌛10 P ⅍ 🍽 🗑

## If you have access needs...

Look for the National Accessible Scheme symbols if you have special hearing, visual or mobility needs. An index of accommodation participating in the scheme can be found at the back of this guide.

## WOODSTOCK, Oxfordshire Map ref 2C1

★★★
**GUEST HOUSE**

B&B per room per night
s £32.50–£38.50
d £60.00–£70.00

### Shepherds Hall

Witney Road, Freeland, Oxford OX29 8HQ  **t** (01993) 881256  **f** (01993) 883455
**w** shepherdshall.co.uk

Well-appointed private hotel offering good food and accommodation. All rooms en suite. Ideally situated for Oxford, Woodstock and the Cotswolds, on the A4095 Woodstock to Witney road.

**open** All year except Christmas and New Year
**bedrooms** 2 double, 2 twin, 1 single
**bathrooms** All en suite
**payment** Credit/debit cards, cash/cheques

Room 📞 📺 🛁 🍷  General 🅿 🍽 ✗ 🛌 🐾  Leisure ♣

## WROXALL, Isle of Wight Map ref 2C3

★★★
**FARMHOUSE**

B&B per room per night
s £25.00–£50.00
d £50.00–£54.00

### Little Span Farm B&B

Rew Lane, Ventnor PO38 3AU  **t** (01983) 852419  **f** (01983) 852419  **e** info@spanfarm.co.uk
**w** spanfarm.co.uk

**open** All year
**bedrooms** 2 double, 1 twin, 1 family
**bathrooms** All en suite
**payment** Cash/cheques

17thC stone farmhouse on working sheep farm in Area of Outstanding Natural Beauty. Short drive to sandy beaches of Shanklin, Sandown and Ventnor. Close to footpaths, cycle route, golf course and tourist attractions. Ideal for family holidays. Kennels available for dogs. English or vegetarian breakfast.

⊕ *B3327 to Wroxall. By post office turn into West Street. Drive out of village up hill around bend, ignore next turning, first farm on right.*

Room 📺 🛁 🍷  General 🛋 🎑 🚪 🅿 ✂ 🍴 🛋 ✳ 🐾  Leisure 🏊

## WYE, Kent Map ref 3B4

★★★★
**BED & BREAKFAST**

B&B per room per night
s £30.00
d £60.00

### Mistral

3 Oxenturn Road, Wye, Ashford TN25 5BH  **t** (01233) 813011  **f** (01233) 813011
**e** geoff@chapman.invictanet.co.uk  **w** chapman.invictanet.co.uk

Small bed and breakfast offering high-quality food and facilities in a central but secluded part of Wye village. Parking is available by arrangement.

**open** All year except Christmas
**bedrooms** 1 twin, 1 single
**bathrooms** 1 private
**payment** Cash/cheques

Room 🛁 🍷  General 🛋 🅿 ✂ 🍴 ✳  Leisure 🏊

## YARMOUTH, Isle of Wight Map ref 2C3

★★★
**BED & BREAKFAST**

B&B per room per night
s Min £35.00
d £25.00–£28.00

### Medlars

Halletts Shute, Norton, Yarmouth PO41 0RH  **t** (01983) 761541  **f** (01983) 761541
**e** greye@tiscali.co.uk  **w** milford.co.uk

**open** All year except Christmas
**bedrooms** 1 double, 1 twin
**bathrooms** 1 en suite, 1 private
**payment** Cash/cheques

Medlars is an attractive, stone-built converted barn in a quiet, rural location but within easy walking distance of Yarmouth. Well positioned for walking the excellent routes in this area. Dogs are welcome by arrangement and good, off-road parking is available.

⊕ *From Yarmouth, cross swing bridge over harbour and continue up Halletts Shute. Leave turning to Fort Victoria on right. Turn left between stone pillars and Medlars is second house.*

Room 📠 📺 🛁 🍷  General 👁5 🅿 ✂ 🐾  Leisure ∪ 🚲 🏊

# Quality
# visitor attractions

## VisitBritain operates a Visitor Attraction Quality Assurance Service.

Participating attractions are visited annually by trained, impartial assessors who look at all aspects of the visit, from initial telephone enquiries to departure, customer service to catering, as well as all facilities and activities.

Only those attractions which have been assessed by Enjoy England and meet the standard receive the quality marque, your sign of a Quality Assured Visitor Attraction.

**Look out for the quality marque and visit with confidence.**

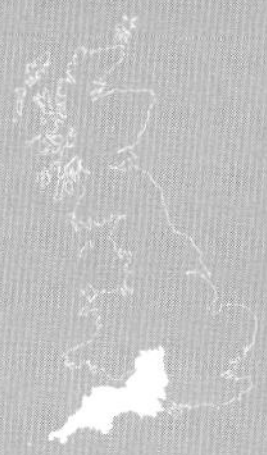

# South West England

Bath, Bristol, Cornwall, Cotswolds and the
Forest of Dean, Devon, Dorset, Gloucestershire,
Isles of Scilly, Somerset, Wiltshire

# Sun, surf, sensational wildlife – and so much more

The South West has always
been a magnet for
holidaymakers. And with a
great climate, masses of
activities, teeming wildlife
and magical landscapes, is it
any wonder?

South West Tourism
visitsouthwest.co.uk
(01392) 360050

Forest of Dean, Gloucestershire

Tarr Steps, Exmoor National Park

Corfe, Dorset

The coastline is one of this region's real gems, from Dorset's spectacular Lulworth Cove and the fossil-rich Jurassic Coast to the elegant English Riviera and Devon's surf-piled north Atlantic coast. Look closely and you may spot whales, dolphins, basking sharks or even a dinosaur tooth or two. And with more Blue Flag beaches than anywhere else in England, you can enjoy high adrenaline watersports or simply build sandcastles to your heart's content. Inland you'll find the romantic wilderness of Dartmoor and Exmoor National Parks along with the scenic Forest of Dean, secret wooded valleys and the Tarka Trail. It's the perfect terrain for mountain biking and horse riding. And from family theme parks to special interest holidays in yoga or glass making, this region has it all.

One of the must-see attractions is 'Breaking the Chains', a major exhibition at Bristol's British Empire and Commonwealth Museum. Marking the bicentenary of the abolition of the slave trade, it's a moving account of one of the darkest episodes in human history. Another great new attraction is the Artificial Surf Reef at Boscombe seafront, set to deliver rollers on the calmest of days. And when you need a little peace and quiet, head off to Gloucester Cathedral. This architectural marvel features massive cylindrical pillars in the Norman nave, glorious fan-vaulted cloisters and the tomb of King Edward II.

Wherever you go you will see spectacular scenery, wonderful countryside and a beautiful coastline. Discover St Nectan's Glen near Tintagel, where a 60ft waterfall cascades into a stone basin before pouring out through an arch in the rock. Another mystical place is Silbury Hill near Marlborough, Wiltshire. Dating back to 2,780 BC and covering 5 acres, it's the largest man made mound in Europe and still shrouded in mystery.

# Destinations

## Bath

Beautiful Bath is not to be missed. Set in rolling countryside, less than two hours from London, this exquisite Georgian spa city was founded by the Romans and is now a World Heritage Site. Explore the compact city centre on foot and discover a series of architectural gems including the Roman baths and Pump Room, the 15th-century Abbey, and stunning Royal Crescent. Follow in the footsteps of Romans and Celts and bathe in the naturally warm waters of the Thermae Bath Spa.

## Bournemouth

Award-winning Bournemouth is the perfect holiday and short-break destination, renowned for its seven miles of family-friendly, golden beaches, beautiful parks and gardens and cosmopolitan ambience. Enjoy the buzz of the town then head out and savour the beauty of the New Forest, the splendour of Dorset's spectacular World Heritage Jurassic Coastline, and the rolling countryside immortalised by Thomas Hardy.

## Bristol

In bygone times, explorers and merchants set off on epic journeys from its harbour. Nowadays, Bristol's spirit of boldness and creativity expresses itself in art, architecture and an enviable quality of life. One of the UK's best short-break destinations – take in Georgian terraces, waterfront arts centres, green spaces, great shopping and acclaimed restaurants. The city's treasure chest of heritage glitters with the work of historic figures such as Isambard Kingdom Brunel, and all set against a truly classic view – the River Avon and its dramatic gorge reaching almost into the heart of the city.

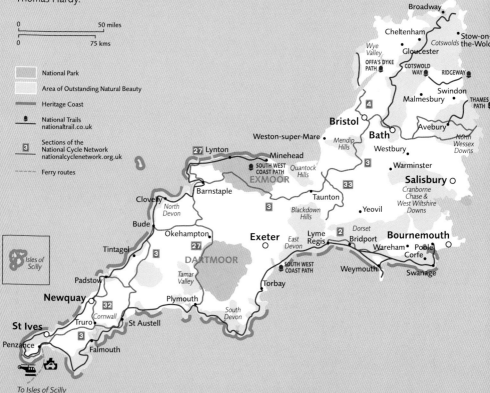

| | |
|---|---|
| 0 | 50 miles |
| 0 | 75 kms |

National Park

Area of Outstanding Natural Beauty

Heritage Coast

National Trails
nationaltrail.co.uk

Sections of the
National Cycle Network
nationalcyclenetwork.org.uk

Ferry routes

Pulteney Bridge, Bath

Russell-Cotes Museum, Bournemouth

SS Great Britain, Bristol

Tate St Ives

Newquay Zoo

Exeter Cathedral

Stonehenge

## Exeter

Devon's regional capital for culture, leisure and shopping is a vibrant city, steeped in ancient history. Don't miss the superb Decorated Gothic cathedral. Stroll along the historic Quayside, once the setting for a thriving wool trade and now a bustling riverside resort. Choose from over 700 shops, join a free Red Coat-guided city tour and dine in any one of numerous acclaimed restaurants. You've also found the perfect base from which to explore the sweeping National Parks of Dartmoor and Exmoor.

## Newquay

A beach paradise, stretching for seven miles, drawing all ages like a magnet and making this one-time fishing village Cornwall's premier resort. Soaring cliffs alternate with sheltered coves, and thundering surf with secluded rock pools, smugglers' caves and soft golden sands. Whatever the weather, make a splash at Waterworld, or visit Newquay Zoo, one of the best wildlife parks in the country. Newquay will offer you an unforgettable holiday memory.

## St Ives

What was once a small, thriving fishing village is now an internationally renowned haven for artists, attracted by the unique light. Explore the narrow streets and passageways and come upon countless galleries, studios and craft shops. Don't miss the Tate Gallery and Barbara Hepworth Museum. Enjoy the natural beauty of the harbour and explore the Blue Flag beaches and coastal walks. Perfectly placed for all of West Cornwall's stunning scenery and famous attractions.

## Salisbury

Nestling in the heart of southern England, Salisbury is every bit the classic English city. The majestic cathedral boasts the tallest spire in England and rises elegantly above sweeping lawns. Wander through this medieval city and you'll find first-class visitor attractions, theatre, shopping, food and drink. And, of course, no trip to Salisbury would be complete without the eight-mile pilgrimage to one of the greatest prehistoric sites in the world – Stonehenge.

# Places to visit

**Babbacombe Model Village**
Torquay, Devon
(01803) 315315
babbacombemodelvillage.co.uk
*England in miniature, in four acres of gardens*

**Bristol City Museum & Art Gallery**
(0117) 922 3571
bristol.gov.uk
*Art and archaeology in a magnificent baroque building*

**Bristol Zoo Gardens**
(0117) 974 7399
bristolzoo.org.uk
*Over 400 exotic and endangered species*

**Buckland Abbey**
Yelverton, Devon
(01822) 853607
nationaltrust.org.uk
*Home of seafarer Sir Francis Drake*

**Cheddar Caves & Gorge**
Somerset
(01934) 742343
cheddarcaves.co.uk
*Britain's finest caves and deepest gorge*

**Eden Project**
St Austell, Cornwall
(01726) 811911
edenproject.com
*A global garden for the 21st century*

**Exmoor Falconry & Animal Farm**
Allerford, Somerset
(01643) 862816
exmoorfalconry.co.uk
*Unique farm with falconry centre and activities*

**Flambards Experience**
Helston, Cornwall
(01326) 573404
flambards.co.uk
*Acclaimed exhibitions and family amusements*

**Kingston Lacy House and Gardens**
Wimborne Minster, Dorset
(01202) 883402
nationaltrust.org.uk
*Elegant country mansion with important collections*

**Living Coasts**
Torquay, Devon
(01803) 202470
livingcoasts.org.uk
*Fascinating coastal creatures in stunning location*

**Longleat**
Warminster, Wiltshire
(01985) 844400
longleat.co.uk
*Lions, tigers and a stately home*

**The Lost Gardens of Heligan**
near St Austell, Cornwall
(01726) 845100
heligan.com
*Beautifully restored gardens*

**Monkey World - Ape Rescue Centre**
Wareham, Dorset
(01929) 462537
monkeyworld.org
*Internationally acclaimed primate rescue centre*

**Morwellham Quay The Morwellham & Tamar Valley Trust**
Tavistock, Devon
(01822) 832766
morwellham-quay.co.uk
*Evocative museum and visitor centre*

**National Marine Aquarium**
Plymouth, Devon
(01752) 600301
national-aquarium.co.uk
*The ocean experience of a lifetime*

**National Maritime Museum Cornwall**
Falmouth, Cornwall
(01326) 313388
nmmc.co.uk
*Award-winning exhibitions and boat collections*

**Newquay Zoo**
Cornwall
(01637) 873342
newquayzoo.org.uk
*Exotic animals in sub-tropical lakeside gardens*

**Oceanarium**
Bournemouth, Dorset
(01202) 311993
oceanarium.co.uk
*Marine life from the furthest reaches of the globe*

**Paignton Zoo Environmental Park**
Devon
(01803) 697500
paigntonzoo.org.uk
*One of England's most beautiful zoos*

**Roman Baths**
Bath, Somerset
(01225) 477785
romanbaths.co.uk
*Magnificent Roman temple and hot spring baths*

**STEAM - Museum of the Great Western Railway**
Swindon, Wiltshire
(01793) 466646
swindon.gov.uk/steam
*Interactive story of pioneering railway network*

**Stonehenge and Avebury World Heritage Site**
near Salisbury, Wiltshire
0870 333 1181
english-heritage.org.uk
*World-famous prehistoric monument*

# Diary dates 2008

**Stourhead House and Garden**
Wiltshire
(01747) 841152
nationaltrust.org.uk
*Celebrated 18th century
landscaped gardens and mansion*

**The Tank Museum**
Wareham, Dorset
(01929) 405096
tankmuseum.co.uk
*The world's finest display of
armoured fighting vehicles*

**Tate St Ives**
St Ives, Cornwall
(01736) 796226
tate.org.uk/stives
*A unique introduction to modern art*

**Thermae Bath Spa**
Bath, Somerset
(01225) 335678
thermaebathspa.com
*Enjoy Britain's only natural thermal
waters*

**Wookey Hole Caves
and Papermill**
near Wells, Somerset
(01749) 672243
wookey.co.uk
*Spectacular caves and family
attractions*

**WWT Slimbridge
Wetlands Centre**
Gloucestershire
(01453) 891900
wwt.org.uk
*Wetland centre with amazing
array of wildlife*

**South West England Food Festival**
Various locations, Exeter
visitsouthwest.co.uk/foodfestival
4 – 6 Apr

**Helston Flora Day**
helstonfloraday.org.uk
8 May

**Bath International Music Festival**
Various locations, Bath
visitbath.co.uk
16 May – 1 Jun

**Salisbury Festival**
Various locations, Salisbury
salisburyfestival.co.uk
23 May – 8 Jun

**Royal Bath and West Show**
Bath & West Showground, Shepton Mallet
bathandwest.com
28 – 31 May

**Golowan Festival Incorporating Mazey Day**
Various locations, Penzance
golowan.org
22 – 29 Jun

**Sidmouth Folk Week**
Various locations, Sidmouth
sidmouthfolkweek.co.uk
1 – 8 Aug

**Great Dorset Steam Fair**
South Down Farm, Tarrant Hinton
gdsf.co.uk
27 – 31 Aug

**Tar Barrels**
Ottery St Mary
otterytourism.org.uk
5 Nov

**Bridgwater Guy Fawkes Carnival Procession**
bridgwaterguyfawkescarnival.co.uk
7 Nov

# Tourist Information Centres

When you arrive at your destination, visit an Official Partner Tourist Information Centre for quality assured help with accommodation and information about local attractions and events, or email your request before you go. To search for attractions and Tourist Information Centres on the move just text INFO to 62233, and a web link will be sent to your mobile phone.

| | | | |
|---|---|---|---|
| Avebury | Green Street | (01672) 539425 | all.atic@kennet.gov.uk |
| Bath | Abbey Church Yard | 0906 711 2000** | tourism@bathnes.gov.uk |
| Bodmin | Mount Folly Square | (01208) 76616 | bodmintic@visit.org.uk |
| Bourton-on-the-Water | Victoria Street | (01451) 820211 | bourtonvic@btconnect.com |
| Bridport | 47 South Street | (01308) 424901 | bridport.tic@westdorset-dc.gov.uk |
| Bristol Harbourside | Harbourside | 0906 711 2191** | ticharbourside@destinationbristol.co.uk |
| Brixham | The Quay | (01803) 211211 | holiday@torbay.gov.uk |
| Bude | The Crescent | (01288) 354240 | budetic@visitbude.info |
| Burnham-on-Sea | South Esplanade | (01278) 787852 | burnham.tic@sedgemoor.gov.uk |
| Camelford* | The Clease | (01840) 212954 | manager@camelfordtic.eclipse.co.uk |
| Cartgate | A303/A3088 Cartgate Picnic Site | (01935) 829333 | cartgate.tic@southsomerset.gov.uk |
| Cheddar | The Gorge | (01934) 744071 | cheddar.tic@sedgemoor.gov.uk |
| Cheltenham | 77 Promenade | (01242) 522878 | info@cheltenham.gov.uk |
| Chippenham | Market Place | (01249) 665970 | tourism@chippenham.gov.uk |
| Chipping Camden | High Street | (01386) 841206 | information@visitchippingcamden.com |
| Christchurch | 49 High Street | (01202) 471780 | enquiries@christchurchtourism.info |
| Cirencester | Market Place | (01285) 654180 | cirencestervic@cotswold.gov.uk |
| Coleford | High Street | (01594) 812388 | tourism@fdean.gov.uk |
| Corsham | 31 High Street | (01249) 714660 | enquiries@corshamheritage.org.uk |
| Devizes | Market Place | (01380) 729408 | all.dtic@kennet.gov.uk |
| Dorchester | 11 Antelope Walk | (01305) 267992 | dorchester.tic@westdorset-dc.gov.uk |
| Falmouth | 11 Market Strand | (01326) 312300 | info@falmouth.co.uk |
| Gloucester | 28 Southgate Street | (01452) 396572 | tourism@gloucester.gov.uk |
| Looe* | Fore Street | (01503) 262072 | looetic@btconnect.com |
| Lyme Regis | Church Street | (01297) 442138 | lymeregis.tic@westdorset-dc.gov.uk |
| Malmesbury | Market Lane | (01666) 823748 | malmesburyip@northwilts.gov.uk |
| Moreton-in-Marsh | High Street | (01608) 650881 | moreton@cotswolds.gov.uk |
| Padstow | North Quay | (01841) 533449 | padstowtic@btconnect.com |
| Paignton | The Esplanade | (01803) 211211 | holiday@torbay.gov.uk |
| Plymouth Mayflower | 3-5 The Barbican | (01752) 306330 | barbicantic@plymouth.gov.uk |
| Salisbury | Fish Row | (01722) 334956 | visitorinfo@salisbury.gov.uk |
| Somerset | Sedgemoor Services | (01934) 750833 | somersetvisitorcentre@ somserset.gov.uk |
| Sherborne | Digby Road | (01935) 815341 | sherborne.tic@westdorset-dc.gov.uk |
| Stow-on-the-Wold | The Square | (01451) 831082 | stowvic@cotswold.gov.uk |
| Stroud | George Street | (01453) 760960 | tic@stroud.gov.uk |

| | | | |
|---|---|---|---|
| Swanage | Shore Road | (01929) 422885 | mail@swanage.gov.uk |
| Swindon | 37 Regent Street | (01793) 530328 | infocentre@swindon.gov.uk |
| Taunton | Paul Street | (01823) 336344 | tauntontic@tauntondeane.gov.uk |
| Tewkesbury | 64 Barton Street | (01684) 295027 | tewkesburytic@tewkesburybc.gov.uk |
| Torquay | Vaughan Parade | (01803) 211211 | holiday@torbay.gov.uk |
| Truro | Boscawen Street | (01872) 274555 | tic@truro.gov.uk |
| Wadebridge | Eddystone Road | (01208) 813725 | wadebridgetic@btconnect.com |
| Wareham | South Street | (01929) 552740 | tic@purbeck-dc.gov.uk |
| Warminster | off Station Rd | (01985) 218548 | visitwarminster@westwiltshire.gov.uk |
| Wells | Market Place | (01749) 672552 | touristinfo@wells.gov.uk |
| Weston-super-Mare | Beach Lawns | (01934) 888800 | westontouristinfo@n-somerset.gov.uk |
| Weymouth | The Esplanade | (01305) 785747 | tic@weymouth.gov.uk |
| Winchcombe | High Street | (01242) 602925 | winchcombetic@tewkesbury.gov.uk |
| Yeovil | Hendford | (01935) 845946 | yeoviltic@southsomerset.gov.uk |

*seasonal opening  ** calls to this number are charged at premium rate*

Avebury, Wiltshire

Lydford, Devon

# Find out more

Visit the following websites for further information on
South West England (or call 01392 360050):

- visitsouthwest.co.uk
- swcp.org.uk
- accessiblesouthwest.co.uk

Also available from South West Tourism:

- The Trencherman's Guide to Top Restaurants in
  South West England
- Adventure South West
  Your ultimate activity and adventure guide.
- World Heritage Map
  Discover our World Heritage.

# Travel info

**By road:**
The region is easily accessible from London, the South
East, the North and the Midlands by the M6/M5 which
extends just beyond Exeter, where it links in with the dual
carriageways of the A38 to Plymouth, the A380 to Torbay
and the A30 into Cornwall. The North Devon Link Road
A361 joins junction 27 with the coast of North Devon
and the A39, which then becomes the Atlantic Highway
into Cornwall.

**By rail:**
The main towns and cities in the South West are served
throughout the year by fast, direct and frequent rail
services from all over the country. Trains operate from
London (Paddington) to Chippenham, Swindon, Bath,
Bristol, Weston-super-Mare, Taunton, Exeter, Plymouth
and Penzance. A service runs from London (Waterloo) to
Exeter, via Salisbury, Yeovil and Crewkerne.

**By air:**
Daily flights into Bristol, Bournemouth, Exeter,
Gloucester, Isles of Scilly, Newquay and Plymouth
operate from airports around the UK and Europe. For
schedules, log on to visitsouthwest.co.uk/flights.

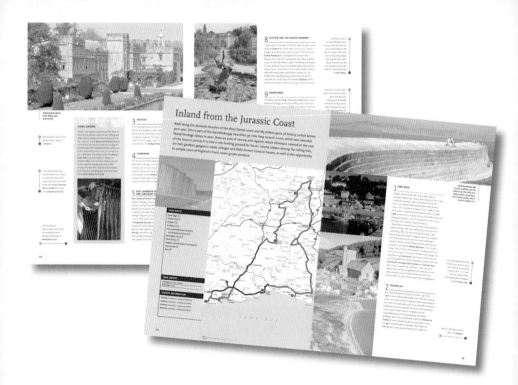

# Take a tour of England

VisitBritain presents a series of **three** inspirational touring guides to the regions of England: South and South West, Northern England and Central England.

Each guide takes you on a fascinating journey through stunning countryside and coastlines, picturesque villages and lively market towns, historic houses and gardens.

- Easy-to-use maps
- Clear directions to follow the route
- Lively descriptions of all the places for you to discover
- Stunning photographs bring each area to life

**Touring Central England** – £14.99
**Touring Northern England** – £14.99
**Touring South and South West England** – £14.99
*plus postage and handling*

Now available in good bookshops.
For special offers on VisitBritain publications,
please visit **enjoyenglanddirect.com**

## where to stay in
# South West England

All place names in the blue bands are shown on the maps at the front of this guide.

A complete listing of all Enjoy England assessed accommodation covered by this guide appears at the back.

**Accommodation symbols**
Symbols give useful information about services and facilities. Inside the back-cover flap you can find a key to these symbols. Keep it open for easy reference.

---

**ABBOTSBURY,** Dorset Map ref 2A3

★★★

GUEST ACCOMMODATION

B&B per room per night
s £50.00–£55.00
d £70.00–£75.00
Evening meal per person
£6.00–£12.00

# Swan Lodge

Rodden Row, Abbotsbury, Weymouth DT3 4JL  t (01305) 871249  f (01305) 871249

Situated on the B3157 coastal road between Weymouth and Bridport. Swan Inn public house opposite, where food is served all day in season, is under the same ownership.

open All year
bedrooms 3 double, 2 twin
bathrooms 4 en suite, 1 private
payment Credit/debit cards, cash/cheques

Room 🛏 📺 🕯 🍵  General 🅿 ♿ 🚫 ✕ 🐾  Leisure ✎ ∪ ♪ 🏕

---

**AMESBURY,** Wiltshire Map ref 2B2

★★★

BED & BREAKFAST

B&B per room per night
s Min £35.00
d Min £48.00

# The Old Bakery

Netton, Salisbury SP4 6AW  t (01722) 782351  e valahen@aol.com  w members.aol.com/valahen

Pleasantly modernised former bakery in small, quiet, picturesque village. Views over fields and water meadows. Ideal base for Stonehenge/Salisbury. Short walk to local inns.

open All year
bedrooms 2 double, 1 twin
bathrooms All en suite
payment Cash/cheques

Room 📺 🕯 🍵  General 🚫5 ❀  Leisure ♪ ▸

---

# A holiday for Fido?

Some proprietors welcome well-behaved pets. Look for the 🐕 symbol in the accommodation listings. You can also buy a copy of our new guide – Welcome Pets! – available from good bookshops and online at visitbritaindirect.com.

### ATHELHAMPTON, Dorset Map ref 2B3

★★★★
**BED & BREAKFAST**
**SILVER AWARD**

**B&B per room per night**
**s** £45.00–£55.00
**d** £70.00–£120.00

# White Cottage

Dorchester DT2 7LG  **t** (01305) 848622  **e** markjamespiper@aol.com
**w** freewebs.com/whitecottagebandb

**open** All year except Christmas
**bedrooms** 1 double, 1 twin, 1 family
**bathrooms** 2 en suite, 1 private
**payment** Cash/cheques

A beautiful 300-year-old cottage, recently refurbished. Double room looks over river and hills, whereas the twin room looks over field and woodland. The new family suite has a large lounge and can sleep up to four. Each room has dressing gowns, fresh fruit and flowers and a mini-fridge. Athelhampton House 200yds.

⊕ *White Cottage is situated in the hamlet of Athelhampton, between the villages of Puddletown and Tolpuddle, just off the A35, 6 miles from Dorchester.*

♥ *3 nights or more: single £35-£40, double £50-£60. Children under 3: free, children under 12: £15 sharing room.*

Room 🖇 ☕ ⚑  General 🛏 ▥ ♨ P ⚹ ✕ ▣ ❈  Leisure ⌇ ⛰

### AVEBURY, Wiltshire Map ref 2B2

★★★
**GUEST ACCOMMODATION**

**B&B per room per night**
**s** £55.00
**d** £60.00

# The New Inn

Winterbourne Monkton, Swindon SN4 9NW  **t** (01672) 539240  **f** (01672) 539150
**e** enquiries@thenewinn.net  **w** thenewinn.net

Bed and breakfast in 200-year-old house. Large garden and car park. Set in outstanding Wiltshire countryside only one mile from Avebury stone circle.

**open** All year except Christmas
**bedrooms** 2 double, 2 twin, 1 family
**bathrooms** All en suite
**payment** Credit/debit cards, cash/cheques

Room 🖇 📺 ☕  General 🛏 ▥ ♨ P ❈

### BARNSTAPLE, Devon Map ref 1C1

★★★★
**GUEST HOUSE**
**SILVER AWARD**

**B&B per room per night**
**s** £26.00–£29.00
**d** £52.00–£58.00
**Evening meal per person**
**Min £16.00**

# The Spinney

Shirwell, Barnstaple EX31 4JR  **t** (01271) 850282  **e** thespinney@shirwell.fsnet.co.uk
**w** thespinneyshirwell.co.uk

**open** All year
**bedrooms** 1 double, 1 twin, 1 single, 2 family
**bathrooms** 3 en suite, 2 private
**payment** Credit/debit cards, cash/cheques

A former rectory, set in over an acre of grounds with views towards Exmoor. Spacious accommodation, en suite available. Centrally heated. Delicious meals cooked by chef/proprietor, served during summer months in our restored Victorian conservatory under the ancient vine. Residential licence. The Spinney is non-smoking.

Room 📺 ☕ ⚑  General 🛏 P ⚹ ♟ ✕ 🍳 🎱 ❈ 🐾

## Place index

If you know where you want to stay, the index at the back of the guide will give you the page number listing accommodation in your chosen town, city or village. Check out the other useful indexes too.

## BARNSTAPLE, Devon Map ref 1C1

★★★★
**GUEST ACCOMMODATION**

B&B per room per night
s Min £50.00
d Min £90.00
Evening meal per person
Min £24.50

### Westcott Barton

Middle Marwood, Barnstaple EX31 4EF  **t** (01271) 812842  **e** westcott_barton@yahoo.co.uk
**w** westcottbarton.co.uk

**open** All year
**bedrooms** 5 double, 2 twin
**bathrooms** 5 en suite
**payment** Cash/cheques

Historic country estate with fine example of a Saxon farmstead; ornamental gardens, streams, ponds and acres of ancient woodland. Perfect for artists, photographers, birdwatchers and naturalists. Beautiful en suite bedrooms in beamed stone cottages and our longhouse. Locally and organically sourced home-cooked breakfasts. Evening meals available on request.

⊕ *Please contact us or see our website for directions.*

Room 🛏 📺 ⓦ ☏  General ☺10 P ⓨ ✗ ▦ 뱎 ✱  Leisure ∪ ♪ 🚲 🏊

## BATH, Somerset Map ref 2B2

★★★★
**GUEST ACCOMMODATION**

B&B per room per night
s £55.00–£79.00
d £65.00–£110.00

### Aquae Sulis

174/176 Newbridge Road, Bath BA1 3LE  **t** (01225) 420061  **f** (01225) 446077
**e** enquiries@aquaesulishotel.co.uk  **w** aquaesulishotel.co.uk

Conveniently situated period bed and breakfast 1.5 miles from Bath centre. Lovely en suite rooms with new bathrooms and lots of extras. Sky, Freeview, Wi-Fi. Bar, patio-garden, car park. Easy access to sights.

**open** All year except Christmas
**bedrooms** 5 double, 2 twin, 3 single, 3 family
**bathrooms** 11 en suite, 2 private
**payment** Credit/debit cards, cash/cheques

Room 🛏 ☏ 📺 ⓦ ☏  General ☺ ▦ 🅿 ✓ ⓨ ▦ 🐾 ✱

## BATH, Somerset Map ref 2B2

★★★★★
**BED & BREAKFAST**
**GOLD AWARD**

B&B per room per night
s £55.00–£65.00
d £75.00–£88.00

### Athole Guest House

33 Upper Oldfield Park, Bath BA2 3JX  **t** (01225) 320000  **f** (01225) 320009
**e** info@atholehouse.co.uk  **w** atholehouse.co.uk

**open** All year
**bedrooms** 4 double, 1 family
**bathrooms** All en suite
**payment** Credit/debit cards, cash/cheques, euros

Large Victorian home restored to give bright, inviting, quiet bedrooms, sleek furniture, sparkling bathrooms, digital TV, Wi-Fi Internet in all bedrooms, safe. Hospitality is old style. Award-winning breakfasts. Relax in our gardens, or let us help you explore the area. Secure parking behind remote-control gates or in garage. Twelve minutes' walk from centre. Free transfer from/to station.

⊕ *M4 jct 18 to Bath. Once in Bath, follow signs for through traffic and Bristol until you see sign for Radstock (Wells Road). Upper Oldfield Park is 1st right.*

♥ *3 nights for 2/50% off second night, Nov-Feb. 4 nights for 3/50% off third night, Mar-May and Sep-Oct.*

Room ☏ 📺 ⓦ ☏  General ☺ ▦ 🅿 ✓ ▦ 🐾 ✱  Leisure 🚲

## It's all quality-assessed accommodation

Our commitment to quality involves wide-ranging accommodation assessment. Rating and awards were correct at the time of going to press but may change following a new assessment. Please check at time of booking.

## BATH, Somerset Map ref 2B2

★★★★★
**GUEST ACCOMMODATION**

B&B per room per night
s £69.00–£79.00
d £96.00–£145.00
Evening meal per person
£9.00–£17.00

# The Carfax

13-15 Great Pulteney Street, Bath BA2 4BS  t (01225) 462089  f (01225) 443257
e reservations@carfaxhotel.co.uk  w carfaxhotel.co.uk

**open** All year
**bedrooms** 13 double, 7 twin, 6 single, 4 family, 1 suite
**bathrooms** All en suite
**payment** Credit/debit cards, cash/cheques

A trio of Georgian houses overlooking Henrietta Park with a view to the surrounding hills. A stroll to the Pump Rooms, Roman baths, canal and river. Recently restored and refurbished, well-appointed rooms. Lift to all floors. Car park for 13 cars. Senior Citizens' rates all year.

⊕ *From M4 jct 18, A4 to London Road. At city traffic lights over Cleveland Bridge, sharp right at Holburne Museum.*

♥ *4 nights for the price of 3, midweek booking Sun to Thu inclusive, quote ETB08.*

Room 🛏 ☎ 📺 ⬧ 🕯  General 🛎 🏛 🕯 P ⚒ ✕ 🍴 📵 ◻  Leisure ∪ ⤴ 🚲 🏛

## BATH, Somerset Map ref 2B2

★★★★
**GUEST ACCOMMODATION**

B&B per room per night
s £65.00–£85.00
d £70.00–£100.00

# Chestnuts House

16 Henrietta Road, Bath BA2 6LY  t (01225) 334279  e reservations@chestnutshouse.co.uk
w chestnutshouse.co.uk

**open** All year except Christmas
**bedrooms** 3 double, 1 twin, 1 family
**bathrooms** All en suite
**payment** Credit/debit cards, cash/cheques, euros

Chestnuts House is a high quality B&B set in the heart of the city with an enclosed garden and private off-street parking. The house is built from natural stone and has five excellent en suite guest rooms and one suite, all of which are tastefully decorated and very well appointed.

Room 🛏 📺 ⬧ 🕯  General 🛎 🏛 🕯 P ⚒ 🍴 📵 🔥 📵 ❈  Leisure ∪

## BATH, Somerset Map ref 2B2

★★★
**FARMHOUSE**

B&B per room per night
s Min £50.00
d Min £60.00

# Church Farm

Monkton Farleigh, Bradford-on-Avon BA15 2QJ  t (01225) 858583  f 08717 145859
e reservations@churchfarmmonktonfarleigh.co.uk  w churchfarmmonktonfarleigh.co.uk

Converted farmhouse barn with exceptional views in peaceful, idyllic setting. Ten minutes from Bath, ideal base for touring/walking South West England. Families/dogs welcome.

**open** All year
**bedrooms** 2 double, 1 twin
**bathrooms** All en suite
**payment** Cash/cheques

Room 📺 ⬧ 🕯  General 🛎 🏛 🕯 P 📵 ❈ 🐎  Leisure ⤴ ↑

## Looking for a little luxury

Gold and Silver Awards are given to establishments achieving the highest levels of quality and service. There's more information at the front of the guide, and an index to all accommodation achieving these awards at the back.

## BATH, Somerset Map ref 2B2

★ ★ ★ ★ ★
**BED & BREAKFAST**

B&B per room per night
s £80.00–£120.00
d £100.00–£150.00

# The Grove

Lyncombe Vale Road, Bath BA2 4LR  **t** (01225) 484282  **f** (01225) 444549  **e** rhstower@aol.com
**w** bathbandb.com

**open** All year except Christmas and New Year
**bedrooms** 2 double
**bathrooms** All en suite
**payment** Credit/debit cards, cash/cheques, euros

An historic Georgian house and Wolsey Lodge, near the city centre – located up a secluded lane where Jane Austen once walked. This delightful relaxed family home has an open fire in the sitting room. Enjoy sumptuous English breakfasts and an optional studio tour of Robert's figurative bronze sculptures. Excellent pubs and restaurants nearby.

⊕ Located 0.5 miles due south of Bath Spa railway station, up a short private road, near to the top of Lyncombe Hill.

♥ 10% discount for stays of 4 nights or more.

Room ♥ ⌇   General ⏃10 P ⌇ ∭ 凪 ⋒ ▢ ✿ 🐎   Leisure ➤ ⚲ 🏊

## BATH, Somerset Map ref 2B2

★ ★ ★
**GUEST HOUSE**

B&B per room per night
s £35.00–£40.00
d £55.00–£60.00

# Hermitage

Bath Road, Box, Corsham SN13 8DT  **t** (01225) 744187  **e** hermitagebb@btconnect.com

16thC house with heated pool in summer. Dining room with vaulted ceiling. Six miles from Bath on A4 to Chippenham, first drive on left by 30mph sign.

**open** All year except Christmas and New Year
**bedrooms** 4 double, 1 family
**bathrooms** All en suite
**payment** Cash/cheques

Room ⛱ TV ♥   General ⏃ P ⌇ 凪 ✿   Leisure ⟋

## BATH, Somerset Map ref 2B2

★ ★ ★ ★
**BED & BREAKFAST**

B&B per room per night
s £39.00–£45.00
d £60.00–£70.00

# Lindisfarne Guest House

41a Warminster Road, Bath BA2 6XJ  **t** (01225) 466342  **e** lindisfarne-bath@talk21.com
**w** bath.org/hotel/lindisfarne.htm

**open** All year except Christmas
**bedrooms** 2 double, 1 twin
**bathrooms** All en suite
**payment** Credit/debit cards, cash/cheques

Comfortable, en suite rooms, good-quality full English breakfast and friendly proprietors. Within walking distance of pub/restaurants. About 1.5 miles from Bath city centre on regular bus route. Near walks along the Kennet & Avon canal. Easy drive to university. Large car park.

⊕ From M4 take A46 to city centre, follow signs for A36 Warminster. Opposite Down Lane, approximately 1.5 miles from centre (1st guesthouse on A36 as you enter Bath from Salisbury).

♥ 10% discount for stays of 4 or more nights.

Room TV ♥ ⌇   General ⏃8 P ⌇ ∭ ✿   Leisure ⚲

## Town, country or coast

The entertainment, shopping and innovative attractions of the big cities, the magnificent vistas of the countryside or the relaxing and refreshing coast – this guide will help you find what you're looking for.

**BATH,** Somerset Map ref 2B2

★★★★
**GUEST HOUSE**

B&B per room per night
s £80.00–£95.00
d £85.00–£130.00

# Marlborough House

1 Marlborough Lane, Bath BA1 2NQ  t (01225) 318175  f (01225) 466127
e mars@manque.dircon.co.uk  w marlborough-house.net

**open** All year except Christmas
**bedrooms** 3 double, 2 twin, 1 single, 2 family
**bathrooms** All en suite
**payment** Credit/debit cards, cash/cheques, euros

Enchanting Victorian town house in Bath's Georgian centre, exquisitely furnished and run in an elegant and friendly style, with beautiful en suite rooms featuring four-poster or antique wood beds. Both vegetarian and organic, our amazing breakfast choices include freshly prepared fruit, organic yoghurts and juices. Also speciality omelettes and Marlborough House potatoes.

⊕ *From the M4 take exit 18 to Bath. Head for Bath city centre and follow the road through Queen Square and Monmouth Street to Marlborough Lane.*

♥ *£5 off each night for stays of 3 nights or more.*

Room ♿ 🍴 📞 📺 🖊 🔌   General 🕐 🏠 🅿 ✂ 🍽 🎱 🐕

---

**BATH,** Somerset Map ref 2B2

★★★
**GUEST HOUSE**

B&B per room per night
s £40.00–£50.00
d £65.00–£110.00

# Pulteney House

14 Pulteney Road, Bath BA2 4HA  t (01225) 460991  f (01225) 460991  e pulteney@tinyworld.co.uk
w pulteneyhotel.co.uk

**open** All year
**bedrooms** 7 double, 3 twin, 2 single, 5 family
**bathrooms** 16 en suite, 1 private
**payment** Credit/debit cards, cash/cheques

Large, elegant, Victorian house in picturesque, south-facing gardens with fine views of Bath Abbey. Large, private car park. Only five to ten minutes' walk from city centre. An ideal base for exploring Bath and surrounding areas. All rooms (except one) en suite with hairdryer, TV, tea/coffee facilities and radio/alarm clocks.

⊕ *Hotel situated on A36, which runs through Bath. From M4 follow signs to Bath on A46. Then follow signs to A36, Exeter and Wells.*

♥ *Reduced rates for stays of 3 nights or more – each booking assessed individually.*

Room ♿ 🍴 📺 🖊 🔌   General 🕐 🏠 🅿 🎱 🔥 ☼   Leisure 🚲 ⛵

---

**BATH,** Somerset Map ref 2B2

★★★★★
**GUEST ACCOMMODATION
GOLD AWARD**

B&B per room per night
s Min £135.00
d Max £300.00
Evening meal per person
£9.50–£40.00

# The Residence

Weston Road, Bath BA1 2XZ  t (01225) 750180  f (01225) 750181  e info@theresidencebath.com
w theresidencebath.com

**open** All year
**bedrooms** 5 double, 1 suite
**bathrooms** 5 en suite, 1 private
**payment** Credit/debit cards, cash/cheques, euros

The Residence is unique in Bath, offering just six rooms. It brings together the exclusivity of a private club and the service of a modern hotel within a large Georgian house near the city centre. Our aim is simple: to be the best home from home you ever had.

Room 📞 📺 🖊 🔌   General 🕐7 🅿 🍽 🎱 🔥 ☼   Leisure 🚲 ⛵

---

## BATH, Somerset Map ref 2B2

★ ★ ★ ★
**GUEST ACCOMMODATION**

B&B per room per night
s £35.00–£45.00
d £55.00–£65.00

### Walton Villa

3 Newbridge Hill, Bath BA1 3PW  **t** (01225) 482792  **f** (01225) 313093  **e** walton.villa@virgin.net
**w** walton.izest.com

Family-run bed and breakfast, offering pretty en suite/private facilities accommodation. One mile from city centre. Off-street parking and bus service nearby.

**open** All year except Christmas and New Year
**bedrooms** 2 double, 1 twin, 1 single
**bathrooms** 3 en suite, 1 private
**payment** Credit/debit cards, cash/cheques

Room 📺 🚿 🍵   General ☎1 ♿ P ⌖ ♨ ❄   Leisure 🚲

## BEAMINSTER, Dorset Map ref 2A3

★ ★ ★ ★
**GUEST ACCOMMODATION**

B&B per room per night
s £45.00–£55.00
d £60.00–£75.00

### The Walnuts

2 Prout Bridge, Beaminster DT8 3AY  **t** (01308) 862211  **f** (01308) 862211
**e** caroline@thewalnuts.co.uk  **w** thewalnuts.co.uk

Tastefully refurbished building with very attractive bedrooms. Friendly, family-run establishment. Very well situated within short walk of local inns and tasteful small shops.

**open** All year
**bedrooms** 2 double, 1 twin
**bathrooms** 2 en suite, 1 private
**payment** Cash/cheques, euros

Room 📺 🚿   General ☎8 P ⌖

## BIBURY, Gloucestershire Map ref 2B1

★ ★ ★ ★
**BED & BREAKFAST**
**GOLD AWARD**

B&B per room per night
s £40.00–£48.00
d £55.00–£65.00

### Cotteswold House

Arlington, Bibury, Cirencester GL7 5ND  **t** (01285) 740609  **f** (01285) 740609
**e** enquiries@cotteswoldhouse.org.uk  **w** cotteswoldhouse.org.uk

**open** All year
**bedrooms** 2 double, 1 twin
**bathrooms** All en suite
**payment** Credit/debit cards, cash/cheques

Situated in this picturesque village, Cotteswold House offers high-quality accommodation in a relaxed, friendly atmosphere. Tastefully furnished bedrooms with en suite facilities, colour TV and tea/coffee. Spacious guest lounge/dining room. Cotteswold House is an ideal centre for touring the Cotswolds and surrounding area. No smoking/pets. Private parking.

⊕ *As you enter the village of Bibury from Cirencester on the B4425, Cotteswold House is on the left before descending the hill.*

Room 📺 🚿 🍵   General ☎ 🖩 ♿ P ⌖ ♨ ❄   Leisure 🚲

## BILBROOK, Somerset Map ref 1D1

★ ★ ★ ★
**GUEST ACCOMMODATION**
**SILVER AWARD**

B&B per room per night
s £37.00–£39.00
d £54.00–£58.00

### The Wayside B&B

Bilbrook, Minehead TA24 6HE  **t** (01984) 641669  **e** thewayside@tiscali.co.uk  **w** thewayside.co.uk

Modern, country accommodation focusing on the highest levels of quality and service. Superb location with easy access to great walking and the coast. Open 1 March to 31 October.

**bedrooms** 2 double
**bathrooms** 1 en suite, 1 private
**payment** Cash/cheques

Room 📺 🚿 🍵   General ☎12 P ⌖ 🍽 ❄   Leisure ∪ ▶ 🚲 ⛵

## Friendly help and advice

Tourist Information Centres offer friendly help with accommodation and holiday ideas as well as suggestions of places to visit and things to do. You'll find contact details at the beginning of each regional section.

---

**BLANDFORD FORUM,** Dorset Map ref 2B3

★★★★★
GUEST ACCOMMODATION
GOLD AWARD

B&B per room per night
s £50.00–£60.00
d £70.00–£80.00

# Farnham Farm House

Blandford Forum DT11 8DG  **t** (01725) 516254  **f** (01725) 516306  **e** info@farnhamfarmhouse.co.uk
**w** farnhamfarmhouse.co.uk

**open** All year except Christmas
**bedrooms** 2 double, 1 twin
**bathrooms** All en suite
**payment** Credit/debit cards, cash/cheques

A private drive leads to this picturesque 19thC farmhouse nestling in the secluded, rolling slopes of Cranborne Chase, having flagstone floors, open fires and an acre of tranquil garden. A comfortable and relaxing base, enhanced by the addition of the Sarpenela Treatment Room offering therapeutic massage and natural therapies.

⊕ *From Thickthorn crossroads on A354, proceed northwards for 1 mile, turn left into village, after 1 mile bear right at signpost to farmhouse.*

Room 📺 🛏 🍵  General 🚭 🎞 ♿ P ⚙ ✿  Leisure ⸚ ▶ 🏊

---

**BLANDFORD FORUM,** Dorset Map ref 2B3

★★★★
BED & BREAKFAST

B&B per room per night
d £60.00

# Lower Bryanston Farm B&B

Lower Bryanston, Blandford Forum DT11 0LS  **t** (01258) 452009  **f** (01258) 452009
**e** andrea@bryanstonfarm.co.uk  **w** brylow.co.uk

**open** All year except Christmas and New Year
**bedrooms** 3 double, 1 twin, 1 family
**bathrooms** 3 en suite, 2 private
**payment** Cash/cheques

Attractive Georgian farmhouse with spacious rooms and beautiful rural views. All rooms equipped with hospitality tray, TV and DVD player. Fantastic full English breakfast. Safe off-road parking. Superb central location to explore the interesting county of Dorset. Within walking distance of Blandford. Blandford Camp and Bryanston school nearby.

⊕ *On A354, from Tesco roundabout, go towards Blandford. 2nd mini-roundabout, left. 2nd right towards Winterborne Stickland. The B&B is 300m on right.*

♥ *B&B for your horse is available.*

Room 📺 🛏 🍵  General 🚭 🎞 ♿ P ⚙ 🍽 🛏 ♿ ✿  Leisure ∪ 🏊

---

**BLANDFORD FORUM,** Dorset Map ref 2B3

★★★★
INN

B&B per room per night
s Min £70.00
d Min £95.00

# The Anvil Inn

Salisbury Road, Pimperne, Blandford Forum DT11 8UQ  **t** (01258) 453431  **f** (01258) 480182
**e** theanvil.inn@btconnect.com  **w** anvilinn.co.uk

**open** All year
**bedrooms** 8 double, 2 twin, 2 single
**bathrooms** All en suite
**payment** Credit/debit cards, cash/cheques

Picturesque, family-run, 16thC thatched hotel. Beamed a la carte restaurant, log fire, mouth-watering menu, delicious desserts. Tasty bar meals and specials cooked from fresh, fine food. Meals available all day.

⊕ *On A354 Salisbury road.*

Room ♿ 🖵 ☎ 📺 🛏 🍵  General 🚭 🎞 ♿ P ⚙ ✕ 🍽 🛏 ✿ 🐕  Leisure ∪ ♪ ▶

### BOSCASTLE, Cornwall Map ref 1B2

Rating Applied For
GUEST ACCOMMODATION

B&B per room per night
s £40.00–£50.00
d £48.00–£60.00

## The Old Coach House

Tintagel Road, Boscastle PL35 0AS  t (01840) 250398  f (01840) 250346
e jackiefarm@btinternet.com  w old-coach.co.uk

Relax in a beautiful 300-year-old former coach house. All rooms en suite with colour TV, tea-making facilities, hairdryer etc. Friendly and helpful owners. Good parking.

**open** All year except Christmas
**bedrooms** 4 double, 2 twin, 2 family
**bathrooms** All en suite
**payment** Credit/debit cards, cash/cheques

Room   General   Leisure

### BOSSINGTON, Somerset Map ref 1D1

★★★★
BED & BREAKFAST

B&B per room per night
s £35.00
d £50.00–£55.00

## Buckley Lodge

Bossington, Minehead TA24 8HQ  t (01643) 862521  e bucklodgeuk@yahoo.co.uk

House is situated in small, picturesque National Trust village. Half a mile from sea and backed by woods. Ideal walking area. Open Easter to end of October.

**bedrooms** 1 twin, 1 family
**bathrooms** 1 en suite, 1 private
**payment** Cash/cheques

Room   General   Leisure

### BOURNEMOUTH, Dorset Map ref 2B3

★★★★
GUEST ACCOMMODATION

B&B per room per night
s £35.00–£42.00
d £60.00–£78.00

## The Blue Palms

26 Tregonwell Road, Bournemouth BH2 5NS  t (01202) 554968  f (01202) 294197
e bluepalmshotel@btopenworld.com  w bluepalmshotel.com

Attractive town-centre hotel with own car park and garden. Good standard of accommodation, service and food. Short walk from beaches, shops, Bournemouth International Centre etc.

**open** All year except Christmas
**bedrooms** 5 double, 2 twin, 1 single, 2 family
**bathrooms** All en suite
**payment** Credit/debit cards, cash

Room   General

### BOURNEMOUTH, Dorset Map ref 2B3

★★★
GUEST ACCOMMODATION

B&B per room per night
s £22.00–£30.00
d £50.00–£60.00

## Denewood

1 Percy Road, Bournemouth BH5 1JE  t (01202) 394493  f (01202) 391155  e info@denewood.co.uk
w denewood.co.uk

Friendly family hotel ideally situated to take advantage of the famous Bournemouth beaches. On-site parking, varied breakfasts served, health and beauty centre.

**open** All year except Christmas and New Year
**bedrooms** 4 double, 2 twin, 2 single, 3 family
**bathrooms** All en suite
**payment** Credit/debit cards, cash/cheques

Room   General   Leisure

### BOURNEMOUTH, Dorset Map ref 2B3

★★★
GUEST ACCOMMODATION

B&B per room per night
s £35.00–£65.00
d £50.00–£76.00
Evening meal per person
£10.00

## The Kings Langley

1 West Cliff Road, Bournemouth BH2 5ES  t (01202) 557349  f (01202) 789739
e john@kingslangleyhotel.com  w kingslangleyhotel.com

**open** All year
**bedrooms** 10 double, 6 twin, 4 family
**bathrooms** All en suite
**payment** Credit/debit cards, cash/cheques

Warm, friendly, family-run hotel providing excellent accommodation and traditional home-cooked food. Located just a few minutes' walk from beach, shops and entertainment. Free parking for all our guests, central heating, tea-making facilities, Sky TV and hairdrying facilities in all bedrooms.

Room   General   Leisure

**BOURNEMOUTH,** Dorset Map ref 2B3

★★★
GUEST ACCOMMODATION

B&B per room per night
s £20.00–£35.00
d £46.00–£60.00

# Southernhay Guest House

42 Alum Chine Road, Westbourne, Bournemouth BH4 8DX  **t** (01202) 761251  **f** (01202) 761251
**e** enquiries@southernhayhotel.co.uk  **w** southernhayhotel.co.uk

High-standard accommodation near beach, restaurants and shops. Full English breakfast, rooms with colour TV, radio-alarm, hairdryer and tea-/coffee-making facilities. Two-for-one golf deals.

**open** All year
**bedrooms** 2 double, 1 twin, 1 single, 2 family
**bathrooms** 4 en suite
**payment** Cash/cheques

Room 👤 TV 👄 🍵  General 🛏 🏠 👤 P ✂ 🍴 🗒 ✿ 🐕  Leisure ∪ ♪ ► 🚲

**BOURNEMOUTH,** Dorset Map ref 2B3

★★★★
GUEST ACCOMMODATION

B&B per room per night
s £25.00–£31.70
d £46.00–£49.00

# Wenrose

23 Drummond Road, Boscombe, Bournemouth BH1 4DP  **t** (01202) 396451 & 07778 800804
**f** (01202) 396451  **e** wenrose@bigfoot.com  **w** bournemouthbedandbreakfast.co.uk

**open** All year except Christmas and New Year
**bedrooms** 2 double, 1 twin, 1 single
**bathrooms** 2 en suite
**payment** Credit/debit cards, cash/cheques, euros

Tranquil guesthouse with garden. Close to shops, sea and public transport. Rooms include desks, tea trays, TVs and wireless broadband. Ideal for business people. Parking. Patio, garden, cooked or continental breakfast, special diets catered for. Non-smoking. No children or pets.

⊕ *M27 to Ringwood, left onto A338 (A35) to Bournemouth, over flyover, first (St Pauls) roundabout turn left (1st exit) – straight over next roundabout (Asda on left). Left at (St Swithins) roundabout. 5th turning on left.*

♥ *10% discount for staying 7 consecutive nights or more. £6 per person extra for one-night stay.*

Room TV 👄 🍵  General P ✂ 🍴 🗒 🔒 ✿  Leisure ► 🚲 🛶

**BOURNEMOUTH,** Dorset Map ref 2B3

★
GUEST ACCOMMODATION

B&B per room per night
s £17.00–£34.00
d £40.00–£80.00

# Whitley Court

West Cliff Gardens, Bournemouth BH2 5HL  **t** (01202) 551302  **f** (01202) 552451

Licensed hotel, close to town and conference centre, with no roads to cross to seafront. Own car park.

**open** All year
**bedrooms** 1 double, 1 twin, 2 single, 9 family
**bathrooms** 11 en suite
**payment** Credit/debit cards, cash/cheques

Room 👤 TV 👄  General 🛏 P 🍽 ✕ 🗒

# Suit yourself

The symbols at the end of each entry mean you can enjoy virtually made-to-measure accommodation with the services and facilities most important to you. A key to the symbols can be found inside the back-cover flap. Keep this open for easy reference.

## BOURNEMOUTH, Dorset Map ref 2B3

★★★★
**GUEST HOUSE**

B&B per room per night
s £30.00–£55.00
d £60.00–£110.00
Evening meal per person
£11.00–£16.00

# Wood Lodge

10 Manor Road, Bournemouth BH1 3EY  t (01202) 290891  f (01202) 290892
e enquiries@woodlodgehotel.co.uk  w woodlodgehotel.co.uk

**open** All year
**bedrooms** 5 double, 4 twin, 2 single, 4 family
**bathrooms** 14 en suite, 1 private
**payment** Credit/debit cards, cash/cheques

A beautiful, lovingly maintained English country house offering superb accommodation in the heart of Bournemouth. Set back from a tranquil, tree-lined road in idyllic, award-winning gardens. Minutes' walk to the town centre, beaches, train and coach stations. Excellent service and delicious, high-quality cooking. Relax, unwind and enjoy.

⊕ *At St Paul's roundabout on the A338 follow the signs for East Cliff. Straight over 2 roundabouts, sharp left into Manor Road. 200yds on left.*

♥ *Please check our website for special offers throughout the year.*

Room 🛏 📺 ♿ ☎  General ♨ 🍴 ♿ P ⚒ ♥ ✕ 🎱 🎿 ♿ ❄ 🐾  Leisure ∪ ♪ ► ⚙

## BOVEY TRACEY, Devon Map ref 1D2

★★★★★
**BED & BREAKFAST**
**GOLD AWARD**

B&B per room per night
s £47.00–£53.00
d £64.00–£76.00

# Brookfield House

Challabrook Lane, Bovey Tracey TQ13 9DF  t (01626) 836181  e enquiries@brookfield-house.com
w brookfield-house.com

**bedrooms** 2 double, 1 twin
**bathrooms** 2 en suite, 1 private
**payment** Credit/debit cards, cash/cheques

Spacious, early-Edwardian residence situated on the edge of Bovey Tracey and Dartmoor and set in two acres with panoramic moor views. Secluded tranquillity yet within easy walking distance of town. Individually decorated bedrooms, all with comfortable seating areas. Gourmet breakfasts, including home-made breads and preserves. Open February to November.

⊕ *From A38 take A382 towards Bovey Tracey. At 1st roundabout, left into Pottery Road. At T-junction, right into Brimley Road, then left into Challabrook Lane. We are on the right.*

♥ *Special rates on application for stays of 4 or more nights.*

Room 📺 ♿ ☎  General ♨ 12 P ⚒ ❄  Leisure ∪ ♪ ► 🏠

## BOX, Wiltshire Map ref 2B2

★★★★
**GUEST HOUSE**

B&B per room per night
s £40.00–£45.00
d £55.00–£65.00

# Lorne House

London Road, Box, Corsham SN13 8NA  t (01225) 742597  e lornehouse2003@yahoo.co.uk
w lornehouse.net

**open** All year except Christmas and New Year
**bedrooms** 2 double, 2 twin
**bathrooms** All en suite
**payment** Credit/debit cards, cash/cheques

A private bed and breakfast located close to the city of Bath. Known locally as the home of Thomas the Tank Engine due to it once having been the home of the Reverend Awdry. Boasting excellent service and accommodation with two twin and two double rooms with en suite facilities. Hot tub.

⊕ *Situated on the A4. Travel from Bath through village, 100yds on left past zebra crossing. From Chippenham, enter village 300yds on the right.*

Room 📺 ♿ ☎  General ♨ P ⚒ 🎿 ❄

## BRADFORD-ON-AVON, Wiltshire Map ref 2B2

★★★★
**BED & BREAKFAST**
**SILVER AWARD**

B&B per room per night
d £50.00–£60.00

# Honeysuckle Cottage

95 The Common, Broughton Gifford, Melksham SN12 8ND  t (01225) 782463
e info@honeysuckle-cottage.org.uk  w honeysuckle-cottage.org.uk

**open** All year except Christmas
**bedrooms** 1 double, 1 twin
**bathrooms** 1 en suite, 1 private
**payment** Cash/cheques

Comfortable country cottage dating back to the 18th century. Tranquil situation facing village common. Ideal base for Bath, Bradford-on-Avon, Lacock and numerous historic locations. Accommodation in double en suite and twin/family with private facilities. Breakfast is freshly prepared using local produce when possible.

⊕ *Information on location will be sent when the booking is confirmed.*

Room 📺 ♿ ❓  General 🛏 🍴 ♿ P ✂ ⚡ ✳  Leisure 🚲 🏛

## BRATTON CLOVELLY, Devon Map ref 1C2

★★★★
**GUEST ACCOMMODATION**

B&B per room per night
s £40.00–£90.00
d £50.00–£120.00
Evening meal per person
£20.00–£35.00

# Eversfield Lodge and Coach House

Ellacott Barton, Bratton Clovelly, Okehampton EX20 4LB  t (01837) 871480
e bookings@eversfieldlodge.co.uk  w eversfieldlodge.co.uk

Beautiful accommodation in Devon longhouse on 850-acre organic farm. En suite rooms with spectacular views. Beamed living room, elegant dining room, bar and gardens. Perfect for relaxation or for exploring Devon and Cornwall.

**open** All year
**bedrooms** 7 double, 1 twin
**bathrooms** All en suite
**payment** Credit/debit cards, cash/cheques

Room 🖥 📺 ♿ ❓  General 🛏12 P ✂ ⚡ 🍷 ✕ 🅿 📶 ✳  Leisure ♨ ∪ ⤵ ▶ 🚲 🏛

## BREAM, Gloucestershire Map ref 2A1

★★★
**INN**

B&B per room per night
s £40.00–£50.00
d £60.00–£70.00
Evening meal per person
£6.00–£15.00

# Rising Sun

High Street, Bream, Lydney GL15 6JF  t (01594) 564555  e jonjo_risingsun@msn.com
w therisingsunbream.co.uk

A village inn dating back to 1729. Ideally situated in the Royal Forest of Dean. Real ales, home-cooked food and hearty breakfasts.

**open** All year
**bedrooms** 4 double, 1 twin
**bathrooms** All en suite
**payment** Credit/debit cards, cash/cheques

Room ♨ 📺 ♿ ❓  General ♿ P 🍷 ✳  Leisure ∪ ⤵ ▶ 🚲 🏛

## BREAN, Somerset Map ref 1D1

★★★★
**GUEST ACCOMMODATION**

B&B per room per night
s £30.00–£35.00
d £53.00–£56.00

WALKERS
WELCOME
CYCLISTS
WELCOME

# The Old Rectory Motel

Church Road, Brean, Burnham-on-Sea TA8 2SF  t (01278) 751447  f (01278) 751800
e helen@old-rectory.fsbusiness.co.uk  w old-rectory.fsbusiness.co.uk

Ground floor, en suite accommodation, within two minutes' walk of the beach and restaurants. Large, walled garden with play area.

**open** All year
**bedrooms** 4 double, 1 twin, 1 single, 2 family
**bathrooms** 7 en suite, 1 private
**payment** Credit/debit cards, cash/cheques

Room ♨ 📺 ♿ ❓  General 🛏 🍴 ♿ P 🍽 📶 ✳ 🐾  Leisure ♨ ∪ ⤵ ▶ 🚲 🏛

## Check it out

Information on accommodation listed in this guide has been supplied by proprietors. As changes may occur you should remember to check all relevant details at the time of booking.

## BREAN, Somerset Map ref 1D1

★★★★
GUEST ACCOMMODATION

B&B per room per night
s £30.00–£37.50
d £50.00–£60.00

# Yew Tree House

Hurn Lane, Berrow, Nr Brean, Burnham-on-Sea TA8 2QT  t (01278) 751382
e yewtree@yewtree-house.co.uk  w yewtree-house.co.uk

**open** All year except Christmas
**bedrooms** 2 double, 2 twin, 1 family, 1 suite
**bathrooms** All en suite
**payment** Credit/debit cards, cash/cheques

We warmly welcome visitors to our charming old house with its spacious rooms, modern facilities, on-site parking and gardens. We are easy to reach from the motorway and in the perfect location for a break. The house is close to the beach and ideally located for Somerset's many attractions.

⊕ *M5 jct 22. B3140 to Burnham and Berrow. Berrow follow signs to Brean. 0.5miles after church turn right, we are 300yds on left.*

♥ *Reduced rates for longer stays and singles out of season (see website for details).*

Room 🛏 📺 💧 🍴  General 🛋 ▥ ⚵ P ⚲ ▥ ⌇ ☀  Leisure ∪ ♪ ⌂ 🕏

## BRIDGWATER, Somerset Map ref 1D1

★★★
INN

B&B per room per night
s £49.50–£75.00
d £65.00–£85.00

# The Boat & Anchor Inn

Meads Crossing, Huntworth, Bridgwater TA7 0AQ  t (01278) 662473  f (01278) 662542
e andrea@theboatandanchor.co.uk  w theboatandanchor.co.uk

Canalside location. Extensive beer garden. Full a la carte menu. En suite accommodation. Function room – all occasions catered for.

**open** All year
**bedrooms** 5 double, 2 twin, 2 single, 2 family
**bathrooms** All en suite
**payment** Credit/debit cards, cash

Room 📺 💧  General 🛋 ⚵ P ⚲ ☀

## BRIDGWATER, Somerset Map ref 1D1

★★★★
RESTAURANT WITH ROOMS

B&B per room per night
s £49.50–£55.00
d £65.00–£75.00

# The Olive Mill

Chilton Polden Hill, Bridgwater TA7 9AH  t (01278) 722202  f (01278) 723327
e enquiries@theolivemill.co.uk  w theolivemill.co.uk

Mediterranean cuisine prepared and served with excellence in the heart of the West Country. Rooms with outstanding views of the Mendips.

**open** All year
**bedrooms** 7 double
**bathrooms** All en suite
**payment** Credit/debit cards, cash

Room 🛏 📺 💧 🍴  General ⚵ P ⚲ ⌇ ☀

## BRIDPORT, Dorset Map ref 2A3

★★★★
GUEST ACCOMMODATION

B&B per room per night
s £40.00–£50.00
d £58.00–£72.00

# Britmead House

West Bay Road, Bridport DT6 4EG  t (01308) 422941  f (01308) 422516  e britmead@talk21.com
w britmeadhouse.co.uk

**open** All year
**bedrooms** 4 double, 2 twin, 2 family
**bathrooms** All en suite
**payment** Credit/debit cards, cash/cheques

Elegant Edwardian house situated just off the A35 between the historic market town of Bridport and the harbour at West Bay, the ideal location for exploring the beautiful Dorset countryside. Family-run, en suite accommodation with many thoughtful extras. Ten minutes' walk to harbour, beaches, golf course and the coastal path.

⊕ *Leave the A35 at roundabout (Crown Inn) due south of Bridport. Take exit signed West Bay, we are 800m on right.*

♥ *Discounts available on stays of 3 or more nights.*

Room 🛏 📺 💧 🍴  General 🛋 ▥ ⚵ P ⚲ ▥ ☀ 🛉  Leisure ∪ ♪ ⌂ 🕏

## BRIDPORT, Dorset Map ref 2A3

★★★★★
**GUEST ACCOMMODATION
GOLD AWARD**

B&B per room per night
s £44.00–£57.00
d £76.00–£98.00

# The Roundham House

Roundham Gardens, West Bay Road, Bridport DT6 4BD  t (01308) 422753
e cyprencom@compuserve.com  w roundhamhouse.co.uk

**bedrooms** 4 double, 2 twin, 1 single, 1 family
**bathrooms** 7 en suite, 1 private
**payment** Credit/debit cards, cash/cheques, euros

An Edwardian country house set in an acre of
gardens on elevated ground overlooking the rolling
West Dorset hills, the majestic World Heritage
Coastline and the sea. Many awards for quality.
Spacious, en suite bedrooms with glorious views.
Ten minutes' walk to the sea. Open March to
November. Licensed bar.

⊕ *From centre of Bridport, take road south to West Bay.
Hotel is 0.25 miles on the left-hand side.*

Room ☎ TV ♿ ☜  General ☜7 P ⚴ ⚑ ⌘ ✿ ☂  Leisure ►

## BRISTOL, City of Bristol Map ref 2A2

★★★★
**BED & BREAKFAST**

B&B per room per night
s £59.00–£79.00
d £75.00–£98.00
Evening meal per person
£10.00–£22.00

# Westfield House

37 Stoke Hill, Sneyd Park, Bristol BS9 1LQ  t (0117) 962 6119  f (0117) 911 8434
e admin@westfieldhouse.net  w westfieldhouse.net

**open** All year
**bedrooms** 1 double, 2 twin
**bathrooms** All en suite
**payment** Credit/debit cards, cash/cheques, euros

Westfield House offers the discerning guest,
whether on business or on holiday, the opportunity
to relax in luxurious, modern accommodation and to
savour extremely high quality and beautifully
prepared food. Westfield House is run solely by
family members therefore you benefit from the
family-run environment and personal attention.

⊕ *Brochure and clear travel instructions from any direction
available on request.*

♥ *3 nights accommodation between Thu-Sun incl breakfast
and supper for 2: £400.00. Feel free to bring your own
wine!*

Room ☎ TV ♿ ☜  General ☜11 P ⚴ ✕ ⌘ ⚑ ☎ ✿  Leisure ∪ ► ⌂

## BRIXHAM, Devon Map ref 1D2

★★★★
**GUEST HOUSE**

B&B per room per night
s £19.00–£27.50
d £38.00–£55.00

# Redlands

136 New Road, Brixham TQ5 8DA  t (01803) 853813  f (01803) 853813  e redlandsbrixham@aol.com
w redlandsbrixham.co.uk

**open** All year
**bedrooms** 3 double, 3 twin, 1 single, 1 family
**bathrooms** All en suite
**payment** Cash/cheques

'Very clean, very welcoming, great breakfast and a
lovely place to stay', say our customers. Just a ten-
minute, easy walk away from picturesque harbour
and restaurants. We have on-site parking. A fresh,
full English breakfast is included in the price.

⊕ *When entering Brixham stay in left-hand filter lane,
signpost harbour/town centre and Redlands is
approximately 400m on the right-hand side.*

Room ⛩ TV ♿ ☜  General ☜ ♿ P ⚴ ⌘  Leisure ♪ ►

## BROAD CHALKE, Wiltshire Map ref 2B3

★★★★
**BED & BREAKFAST**

B&B per room per night
s £25.00–£30.00
d £50.00–£60.00

# Lodge Farmhouse Bed & Breakfast

Lodge Farmhouse, Broad Chalke, Salisbury SP5 5LU  t (01752) 519242  f (01725) 519597
e mj.roe@virgin.net  w lodge-farmhouse.co.uk

**open** All year except Christmas and New Year
**bedrooms** 1 double, 2 twin
**bathrooms** All en suite
**payment** Credit/debit cards, cash/cheques

Peaceful brick and flint farmhouse with Wiltshire's finest views overlooking 1,000 square miles of Southern England. Comfortable and welcoming, the perfect tour base for Wessex. Lying on the Ox Drove 'green lane', a paradise for walkers and byway cyclists. For neighbouring nature reserves and archaeological sites see website.

⊕ A354 from Salisbury (8 miles) or Blandford (14 miles). Turn to Broad Chalke at crossroads on only stretch of dual carriageway on the A354. One mile signposted.

Room 📺 ♿ 🐾  General 🛏12 P ⚡ ❄ 🐕  Leisure ∪ ✈ ⌂

## BUDE, Cornwall Map ref 1C2

★★★
**GUEST ACCOMMODATION**

B&B per room per night
d £56.00–£76.00

# Beach House

Marine Drive, Widemouth Bay, Bude EX23 0AW  t (01288) 361256
e beachhousebookings@tiscali.co.uk  w beachhousewidemouth.co.uk

**bedrooms** 8 double, 1 twin, 2 family
**bathrooms** All en suite
**payment** Credit/debit cards, cash/cheques

The Wilkins family welcome you to their unique site, with private access onto Widemouth Beach. All bedrooms are en suite, the majority with sundeck balconies. Sun lounge, new bar lounge, on-site post office, shop, surf shop and hire. Restaurant serving traditional Cornish and seafood menus. Outside dining on decked patios. Open Easter to end of October.

⊕ Enter Bude from A39. Left at mini-roundabout, proceed over Falcon Bridge. After 2.5 miles Beach House is to the right on the foreshore.

♥ Discounts on bookings of 4 days or more.

Room 📺 ♿  General 🛏 🍴 P ⚡ ✕ 🏠 ❄  Leisure ✈

## BUDE, Cornwall Map ref 1C2

★★★★
**GUEST HOUSE**
**SILVER AWARD**

B&B per room per night
s Min £40.00
d Min £54.00
Evening meal per person
Min £20.00

# Harefield Cottage

Upton, Bude EX23 0LY  t (01288) 352350  f (01288) 352712  e sales@coast-countryside.co.uk
w coast-countryside.co.uk

**open** All year
**bedrooms** 2 double, 1 twin
**bathrooms** All en suite
**payment** Credit/debit cards, cash/cheques

Stone-built cottage with outstanding views. Luxurious and spacious en suite bedrooms, king-size beds and four-poster available. Home cooking our speciality. All diets catered for. Personal attention assured at all times. Only 250yds from the coastal footpath. One mile downhill to the National Cycle network. Hot tub available.

⊕ From A39 follow signs to Bude town centre, turn left at mini-roundabout, over Canal bridge, uphill for 1 mile. Red telephone box on right-hand side, past this there is a left-hand turn to Upton. Harefield Cottage on left.

♥ Special 3-night breaks including DB&B and packed lunch – £130. With walking – £150.

Room 📺 ♿ 🐾  General 🛏 🏠 🍴 P ⚡ ✕ 🏠 ❄ 🐕  Leisure 🚲 ⌂

## BUDE, Cornwall Map ref 1C2

★★★★
**GUEST ACCOMMODATION**

B&B per room per night
s £33.00–£40.00
d £66.00–£80.00
Evening meal per person
£15.00–£25.00

# Stratton Gardens

Cot Hill, Stratton, Bude EX23 9DN  t (01288) 352500  e moira@stratton-gardens.co.uk
w stratton-gardens.co.uk

Our house is 16th century with beautiful terrace gardens, and we invite you to share our home for a time of refreshment. A warm welcome, comfort and delicious food await you.

**open** All year
**bedrooms** 3 double, 3 twin, 1 single
**bathrooms** 6 en suite
**payment** Credit/debit cards, cash/cheques, euros

Room 🗎 📺 🌢 ⏰   General 🕭 🏢 🏋 P ⚡ ❢ ✕ 🎮 🛏 ✳   Leisure ∪ ♪ ↑

## BUDE, Cornwall Map ref 1C2

★★★★
**GUEST HOUSE**

B&B per room per night
s £28.00–£40.00
d £48.00–£60.00
Evening meal per person
£12.00–£15.00

# Surf Haven

31 Downs View, Bude EX23 8RG  t (01288) 353923  e info@surfhaven.co.uk  w surfhaven.co.uk

**open** All year
**bedrooms** 4 double, 2 twin, 3 family
**bathrooms** 7 en suite, 2 private
**payment** Credit/debit cards, cash/cheques

Surf Haven is a warm and friendly guest house. Ideally situated, overlooking the golf course and 200yds from the beach. It is just a short walk to the town with its shops and restaurants. Fresh, locally sourced and organic produce used wherever possible.

⊕ From A3072 follow signs to Bude town centre, bear left at the top of the hill and follow signs for Crooklets Beach.

♥ Special breaks – stay for 3 nights Oct–Apr and get an extra night free (excl Bank Holidays).

Room ♨ 📺 🌢 ⏰   General 🕭 🏢 🏋 P ⚡ ✕ 🎮 🛏 🌢 ✳ 🍴   Leisure ∪ ↑ 🚲 🏡

## BUDLEIGH SALTERTON, Devon Map ref 1D2

★★★★
**GUEST ACCOMMODATION**

B&B per room per night
s £38.00–£42.00
d £79.00–£93.00
Evening meal per person
£18.50–£21.50

# Hansard House

3 Northview Road, Budleigh Salterton EX9 6BY  t (01395) 442773  f (01395) 442475
e enquiries@hansardhotel.co.uk  w hansardhousehotel.co.uk

Adjacent to the World Heritage coastal path and only 400yds from East Devon Golf Club, this small, family-run hotel is ideally situated to enjoy the delights of Budleigh Salterton.

**open** All year
**bedrooms** 3 double, 6 twin, 2 single, 1 family
**bathrooms** All en suite
**payment** Credit/debit cards, cash/cheques, euros

Room ♨ ☎ 📺 🌢 ⏰   General 🕭 🏢 🏋 P ⚡ ❢ ✕ 🎮 ▣ ✳ 🍴   Leisure ∪ ↑ 🏡

## BURTON BRADSTOCK, Dorset Map ref 2A3

★★★★
**GUEST ACCOMMODATION**

B&B per room per night
s £30.00–£32.00
d £60.00–£64.00

# Pebble Beach Lodge

Coast Road, Burton Bradstock, Bridport DT6 4RJ  t (01308) 897428
e pebblebeachlodge@supanet.com  w burtonbradstock.org.uk/pebblebeachlodge

Located on B3157 coast road, affording panoramic views of Heritage Coastline. Direct access to beach. Spacious and attractive accommodation, large conservatory.

**open** All year
**bedrooms** 4 double, 1 twin, 1 single, 2 family
**bathrooms** All en suite
**payment** Cash/cheques

Room ♨ 📺 🌢   General 🕭 🏢 🏋 P ⚡ ❢ 🎮 ✳   Leisure ↑

## Ancient and modern

Experience timeless favourites or discover the latest must-sees. Whatever your choice, be inspired by the places of interest and events highlighted for each region.

**CALLINGTON,** Cornwall Map ref 1C2

★★★★
GUEST HOUSE

B&B per room per night
**s** £44.95–£49.95
**d** £69.90–£79.90
Evening meal per person
£12.95–£15.90

# Hampton Manor

Alston, Callington PL17 8LX **t** (01579) 370494 **f** (01579) 370494 **e** hamptonmanor@supanet.com **w** hamptonmanor.co.uk

**open** All year
**bedrooms** 2 double, 2 twin, 1 family, 1 suite
**bathrooms** All en suite
**payment** Cash/cheques

Small Victorian country-house hotel set in 2.5 acres amidst tranquil countryside bordering Devon. High-quality accommodation (wheelchair access), personal service and home-cooked food (diets catered for). Thirty minutes' drive from north and south coasts, historic Plymouth, Dartmoor and Bodmin Moor. The Eden Project and many well-known gardens are also nearby.

⊕ *A30 to Launceston, then A388 towards Callington. After 7 miles turn left towards Horsebridge. Straight on at 2 crossroads, then left at sign for Alston/Tutwell.*

♥ *Romantic DB&B packages, activity weekends for bridge players, walkers, ornithologists etc. Up to 15% discount for groups and long stays.*

Room 🛏 ♿ 🍵 General 🚭 🎱 🍴 P ⚲ 🍽 ✕ 🗄 🎿 🖵 ❀ Leisure ♨ ∪ ⏐ ⚑ 🏊

**CARBIS BAY,** Cornwall Map ref 1B3

★★★★
GUEST ACCOMMODATION

B&B per room per night
**d** £56.00–£105.00

# Beechwood House

St Ives Road, Carbis Bay, St Ives TR26 2SX **t** (01736) 795170 **f** (01736) 795170 **e** beechwood@carbisbay.wanadoo.co.uk

**open** All year
**bedrooms** 5 double, 1 twin, 2 family
**bathrooms** All en suite
**payment** Credit/debit cards, cash

Five minutes' walk to sandy beach. Looks out over St Ives Bay. All rooms are en suite. Guests' private lounge, garden and parking. We have golf, fishing, St Michael's Mount and trips to the Isles of Scilly all within easy reach. Courtesy lift from local train or bus stations, when available.

⊕ *Exit A30 at St Ives, following A3074 signs. Proceed through Lelant to Carbis Bay. You will pass a convenience store. We are about 50yds further on left.*

Room 🛏 📺 ♿ 🍵 General 🚭 🎱 🍴 P ⚲ 🎿 ❀ Leisure ∪ ⏐ ⚑ 🚲 🏊

**CARBIS BAY,** Cornwall Map ref 1B3

★★★
GUEST ACCOMMODATION

B&B per room per night
**s** £25.00–£36.50
**d** £50.00–£73.00
Evening meal per person
£5.00–£18.00

# Howards Hotel

St Ives Road, Carbis Bay, St Ives TR26 2SB **t** (01736) 795651 **f** (01736) 795535 **e** info@howards-hotel.com **w** howards-hotel.com

Howards is fully licensed with restaurant; rooms are all en-suite with tea-making facilities and TVs; heated outdoor pool. Free car parking.

**open** All year
**bedrooms** 13 double, 6 twin, 3 single, 4 family
**bathrooms** All en suite
**payment** Credit/debit cards, cash/cheques

Room 🛏 🍴 📺 ♿ General 🚭 🎱 🍴 P ⚲ 🗄 🎿 ❀ 🐾 Leisure ⚘ ⏐ ⚑ 🚲 🏊

# Family-friendly breaks

For accommodation offering additional facilities and services for a range of ages and family units, look out for the Families Welcome symbol. Owners of these properties will go out of their way to welcome families.

### CHARD, Somerset Map ref 1D2

★★★★
**GUEST ACCOMMODATION**

B&B per room per night
s £35.00–£37.00
d £60.00–£65.00

# Ammonite Lodge

43 High Street, Chard TA20 1QL  t (01460) 63839  f (01460) 63839  e info@ammonitelodge.co.uk
w ammonitelodge.co.uk

Grade II Listed character house in town centre on main A30. Warm welcome with every comfort, only 20 minutes from M5 motorway. Pretty garden and sumptuous breakfast. Parking at rear.

**open** All year except Christmas
**bedrooms** 3 double, 2 twin, 2 single
**bathrooms** 5 en suite, 2 private
**payment** Credit/debit cards, cash/cheques

Room 📺 ⚡ 🕭   General ⛱ 🏛 🛎 P ✂ 🎱 🍴 🎧 🖥 ❖   Leisure ✈ ▶ 🏖

### CHARMINSTER, Dorset Map ref 2B3

★★★
**INN**

B&B per room per night
s £25.00–£30.00
d £50.00–£55.00
Evening meal per person
£5.00–£10.00

# Three Compasses Inn

The Square, Charminster, Dorchester DT2 9QT  t (01305) 263618

Traditional village inn with skittle alley set in village square. Lunch and evening meals provided.

**open** All year except Christmas
**bedrooms** 1 double, 1 single, 1 family
**bathrooms** 1 en suite
**payment** Cash/cheques

Room 📺 ⚡   General ⛱ P ☕ ✕ 🍴 🐾   Leisure ▶ 🏖

### CHARMOUTH, Dorset Map ref 1D2

★★★★
**GUEST ACCOMMODATION**

B&B per room per night
d £60.00–£65.00

# Cliffend

Higher Sea Lane, Charmouth, Bridport DT6 6BD  t (01297) 561047  f (01297) 561047
w cliffend.org.uk

**open** All year
**bedrooms** 2 double
**bathrooms** All en suite
**payment** Cash/cheques

Chalet bungalow situated in large garden with gate onto coastal path. Two minutes' stroll to beach. Newly refurbished rooms with sitting corner and attractive en suite facilities. Ideal for exploring this beautiful area of Dorset. A warm welcome is guaranteed. Higher price is for one night's stay only.

Room 📺 ⚡ 🕭   General P ✂

### CHEDDAR, Somerset Map ref 1D1

★★
**BED & BREAKFAST**

B&B per room per night
s £25.00–£30.00
d £50.00–£60.00

# Waterside

Cheddar Road, Axbridge BS26 2DP  t (01934) 743182  e gillianaldridge@hotmail.com
w watersidecheddar.co.uk

A warm and friendly welcome awaits you. Surrounded by the Mendip hills, ideal for discovering Glastonbury, Wells, Bream, Weston, Wookey Hole, or Cheddar Gorge and show caves. Children and dogs welcome.

**open** All year
**bedrooms** 1 double, 1 twin, 1 family
**bathrooms** All en suite
**payment** Cash/cheques, euros

Room 🛏 📺 ⚡ 🕭   General ⛱ 🏛 🛎 P ✂ 🎱 🍴 ❖ 🐾   Leisure ∪ 🏖

**PETS!** WELCOME   WELCOME **PETS!**

# Pet-friendly breaks

Want to take your cherished companion with you on holiday? Proprietors participating in our Welcome Pets! scheme go out of their way to make special provision for you and your pet. Look out for the symbol.

**CHEDDAR,** Somerset Map ref 1D1

★★
BED & BREAKFAST

B&B per room per night
s £30.00–£32.00
d £52.00–£58.00
Evening meal per person
£11.50–£15.50

# Yew Tree Farm

Theale, Wedmore BS28 4SN  t (01934) 712475  f (01934) 712475
e enquiries@yewtreefarmbandb.co.uk  w yewtreefarmbandb.co.uk

**open** All year
**bedrooms** 1 double, 1 twin, 1 family
**bathrooms** 2 en suite
**payment** Cash/cheques, euros

17thC farmhouse, ideal for touring being close to Cheddar Gorge, the City of Wells, Glastonbury and Wooky Hole. Idyllic walks, fishing, golf and cycle routes. Family room, en suite facilities and single supplement, as well as lovely two- and three-course home-cooked evening meals.

⊕ *From Wells, take B3139 towards Burnham-on-Sea. Drive through Wookey, Henton, Panborough – welcome to Theale.*

♥ *Special autumn/winter and spring breaks, including 2-course dinner from £65 per couple, per night. Min 2-night stay.*

Room 📺 👜 🕯  General ⚒ ▥ ⚿ P ⛺ ⚄ ☐ ✿ ⚓  Leisure ∪ ⚒ ▶ 🏌

**CHELTENHAM,** Gloucestershire Map ref 2B1

★★★★★
GUEST ACCOMMODATION
SILVER AWARD

B&B per room per night
s £62.00–£178.00
d £89.00–£193.00
Evening meal per person
£12.00–£30.00

# Beaumont House

56 Shurdington Road, Cheltenham GL53 0JE  t (01242) 223311  f (01242) 520044
e reservations@bhhotel.co.uk  w bhhotel.co.uk

**open** All year
**bedrooms** 9 double, 3 twin, 2 single, 1 family, 1 suite
**bathrooms** All en suite
**payment** Credit/debit cards, cash/cheques

Owner-managed, set in a lovely garden with ample parking, Beaumont House offers luxury at affordable rates. The stunning, modern en suite rooms with satellite TV/Sky Sports, free broadband, hairdryer and room safe, ensure a comfortable stay in style. Delicious breakfasts and friendly service. Relax and enjoy our warm hospitality.

⊕ *Situated at the Cheltenham end of the A46 Shurdington Road, which is the extension of the A46 Bath Road, just south of Cheltenham town centre.*

♥ *Champagne, flowers and chocolates can all be arranged in your room for that special day.*

Room ☏ 📺 👜 🕯  General ⚒10 P ✂ ⚟ ⛺ ⚄ ✿ ❋  Leisure 🚲 🏚

# Our quality rating schemes

For a detailed explanation of the quality and facilities represented by the stars, please refer to the information pages at the back of this guide.

---

**CHELTENHAM,** Gloucestershire Map ref 2B1

★ ★ ★ ★
GUEST ACCOMMODATION
SILVER AWARD

# Butlers

Western Road, Cheltenham GL50 3RN  t (01242) 570771  f (01242) 528724
e info@butlers-hotel.co.uk  w butlers-hotel.co.uk

B&B per room per night
s £50.00–£65.00
d £75.00–£120.00

**open** All year
**bedrooms** 4 double, 1 twin, 1 single
**bathrooms** All en suite
**payment** Credit/debit cards, cash/cheques

Welcome to Butlers. Our award-winning guesthouse is situated in a central yet quiet area, and just a short stroll to the promenade and the quaint Montpellier district. The rooms are named after well-known butlers from literature and history. Facilities include free Wi-Fi Internet, guest lounge, garden and parking.

⊕ *GPS REFERENCE GL50 3RN.*
*Follow the A40. Turn into Christchurch Road. At the church, turn left into Malvern Road then 2nd right into Western Road.*

♥ *Self-catering studios within hotel also available for vacation and professional lets.*

Room 📞 📺 🌐 ❄  General 🛏 P ✂ ♨ ⛏ 🍴 ⚓ 🔋 ▣ ✿ 🐾 ⛓  Leisure 🚲

---

**CHELTENHAM,** Gloucestershire Map ref 2B1

★ ★ ★
GUEST ACCOMMODATION

# Cheltenham Guest House

145 Hewlett Road, Cheltenham GL52 6TS  t (01242) 521726  f 0871 661 4405
e info@cheltenhamguesthouse.biz  w cheltenhamguesthouse.biz

B&B per room per night
s £35.00–£45.00
d £55.00–£65.00

Stylish, yet economical, bed and breakfast accommodation; walking distance to town centre. Designer-themed rooms, eg Greek, African, old Scandinavian. Generous breakfasts in grand breakfast room. Free Internet access and car park.

**open** All year
**bedrooms** 3 double, 2 twin, 3 single, 1 family
**bathrooms** 7 en suite, 2 private
**payment** Credit/debit cards, cash/cheques, euros

Room 📺 🌐  General 🛏 ▥ ♿ P ✂ ▣ 🔋 ✿  Leisure ▶

---

**CHELTENHAM,** Gloucestershire Map ref 2B1

★ ★ ★
GUEST HOUSE

# 33 Montpellier

33 Montpellier Terrace, Cheltenham GL50 1UX  t (01242) 526009  f (01242) 579793
e montpellierhotel@btopenworld.com  w montpellier-hotel.co.uk

B&B per room per night
s £28.00–£50.00
d £50.00–£80.00

A Grade II Listed Regency building situated in Montpellier overlooking the park. The area's exclusive shops and restaurants are only a short walk away.

**open** All year
**bedrooms** 5 double, 1 twin, 1 single, 1 family
**bathrooms** 7 en suite, 1 private
**payment** Cash/cheques

Room ♿ 📺 🌐 ❄  General 🛏 ▥ ♿ ✂ ♨ ▣ 🔋

---

**CHEW STOKE,** Somerset Map ref 2A2

★ ★ ★
GUEST ACCOMMODATION

# Orchard House

Bristol Road, Chew Stoke, Bristol BS40 8UB  t (01275) 333143  f (01275) 333754
e orchardhse@ukgateway.net  w orchardhouse-chewstoke.co.uk

B&B per room per night
s £30.00–£35.00
d Min £56.00

Comfortable accommodation in a carefully modernised Georgian house and coach house annexe. Good eating in local pubs. Convenient access to Bristol and Bath.

**open** All year
**bedrooms** 1 double, 2 twin, 1 single, 1 family
**bathrooms** 4 en suite, 1 private
**payment** Credit/debit cards, cash/cheques

Room ♿ 📺 🌐  General 🛏 ▥ ♿ P ✂ ⛏ ▣ ✿  Leisure 🎣 ⛵

---

## Key to symbols

Open the back flap for a key to symbols.

## CHIPPING CAMPDEN, Gloucestershire Map ref 2B1

★★★★
INN

B&B per room per night
s £55.00–£85.00
d £85.00–£125.00
Evening meal per person
£10.00–£25.00

# The Eight Bells

Church Street, Chipping Campden GL55 6JG  t (01386) 840371  f (01386) 841669
e neilhargreaves@bellinn.fsnet.co.uk  w eightbellsinn.co.uk

open All year except Christmas
bedrooms 5 double, 1 single, 1 family
bathrooms All en suite
payment Credit/debit cards, cash/cheques

This unspoilt 14thC Cotswold inn features open fires
in winter and candle-lit tables all year round. There is
a sun-drenched courtyard and terraced beer garden
which overlooks the church. All accommodation has
recently been refurbished to a high standard, and all
bedrooms are en suite. Food is of the very highest
standard, and a friendly welcome awaits you.

⊕ Leave M5 at Evesham/Tewkesbury junction and Chipping
Campden is signposted. The establishment is opposite the
church.

♥ Mid-Jan to mid-Mar '2 for 1' specials board Mon-Thu.

Room General Leisure

## CHIPPING CAMPDEN, Gloucestershire Map ref 2B1

★★★★
BED & BREAKFAST

B&B per room per night
s £40.00–£60.00
d £60.00

# Manor Farm

Weston-Subedge, Chipping Campden GL55 6QH  t (01386) 840390  f 0870 164 0638
e lucy@manorfarmbnb.demon.co.uk  w manorfarmbnb.demon.co.uk

Luxury king-size beds, contemporary bathrooms
with power showers, in a Cotswold-stone, oak-
beamed farmhouse built in 1624. Village pub
serves food.

open All year
bedrooms 2 double, 1 twin
bathrooms All en suite
payment Credit/debit cards, cash/cheques

Room General Leisure

## CHOLDERTON, Wiltshire Map ref 2B2

★★★★
GUEST ACCOMMODATION

B&B per room per night
s Max £62.00
d Max £70.00
Evening meal per person
Max £17.00

# Parkhouse Motel

Cholderton, Salisbury SP4 0EG  t (01980) 629256  f (01980) 629256

Attractive, family-run, 17thC former coaching inn,
five miles east of Stonehenge, ten miles north of
Salisbury and seven miles west of Andover.

open All year
bedrooms 18 double, 6 twin, 6 single, 3 family
bathrooms 23 en suite
payment Credit/debit cards, cash/cheques,
euros

Room General Leisure

## CHRISTCHURCH, Dorset Map ref 2B3

★★★
INN

B&B per room per night
s Min £49.50
d Min £66.00

# Fisherman's Haunt

Salisbury Road, Winkton, Christchurch BH23 7AS  t (01202) 477283  f (01202) 478883
e fishermanshaunt@accommodating-inns.co.uk  w accommodating-inns.co.uk

A lovely hotel which stands in its own grounds,
originally built in 1673. Overlooking the River
Avon and on the edge of the New Forest, only ten
minutes from Bournemouth International Airport.

open All year
bedrooms 8 double, 4 twin
bathrooms All en suite
payment Credit/debit cards, cash/cheques

Room General Leisure

## Check the maps

Colour maps at the front pinpoint all the places you will find accommodation entries
in the regional sections. Pick your location and then refer to the place index at the
back to find the page number.

## CHRISTCHURCH, Dorset Map ref 2B3

★★★
**BED & BREAKFAST**

B&B per room per night
s £30.00–£35.00
d £60.00–£80.00
Evening meal per person
£7.00–£10.00

# Golfers Reach

88 Lymington Road, Highcliffe, Christchurch BH23 4JU  t (01425) 272903  e caoy@amserve.com

**open** All year
**bedrooms** 2 double, 1 twin, 1 single, 1 family
**bathrooms** All en suite
**payment** Credit/debit cards, cash/cheques

Golfers Reach offers non-smoking accommodation. All rooms are en suite with colour TV and tea-/coffee-making facilities. Close to local amenities and Highcliffe Castle.

Room 🛌 📺 👤 🕙  General 🏨 🛄 🍴 ✕ 🎱 🎮 ✿ 🐕

## CHRISTCHURCH, Dorset Map ref 2B3

★★★★★
**BED & BREAKFAST**
**GOLD AWARD**

B&B per room per night
d £25.00–£45.00

# Seawards

13 Avon Run Close, Christchurch BH23 4DT  t (01425) 273188  e seawards13@hotmail.com
w seawards13.plus.com

A 'home from home' bed and breakfast, small, quiet and two minutes from the beautiful Avon beach. Ground floor accommodation. Annexe now available.

**open** All year except Christmas and New Year
**bedrooms** 2 double
**bathrooms** All en suite
**payment** Cash/cheques

Room 🛌 📺 👤 🕙  General P 🍴 🎱 🎮 ✿

## CIRENCESTER, Gloucestershire Map ref 2B1

★★★★
**GUEST ACCOMMODATION**

B&B per room per night
s Min £45.00
d Min £60.00
Evening meal per person
Min £15.00

# Riverside House

Watermoor Road, Cirencester GL7 1LF  t (01285) 647642  f (01285) 647615
e riversidehouse@mitsubishi-cars.co.uk  w riversidehouse.org.uk

**open** All year
**bedrooms** 13 double, 11 twin
**bathrooms** All en suite
**payment** Credit/debit cards, cash/cheques

Located 15 minutes' walk from the centre of the historic market town of Cirencester with easy access to and from M4/M5 and the Cotswolds. Riverside House is fully licensed and provides superb bed and breakfast for private and corporate guests. Built in the grounds of Mitsubishi UK headquarters.

⊕ Located just off A419 opposite the Tesco superstore. Take the turning at roundabout (Kwik-Fit) for Watermoor and turn left after ATS exhausts.

♥ Special group discounts are available at weekends. Ideal for clubs and societies.

Room 📞 📺 👤 🕙  General 🛋 P 🍴 🍷 ✕ 🎱 ✿

## CIRENCESTER, Gloucestershire Map ref 2B1

★★★
**INN**

B&B per room per night
s £45.00–£70.00
d £65.00–£120.00
Evening meal per person
£6.00–£12.00

# The White Lion Inn

8 Gloucester Street, Cirencester GL7 2DG  t (01285) 654053  f (01285) 641316
e mutlow@ashtonkeynes.fsnet.co.uk  w whitelioncirencester.co.uk

A 17thC coaching inn behind a 14thC church in a quiet street. Family-run, with staff who care.

**open** All year
**bedrooms** 2 double, 1 twin, 2 single, 1 family
**bathrooms** All en suite
**payment** Credit/debit cards, cash

Room 🛌 🖥 📺 👤 🕙  General 🛋 🛄 🍷 ✕ ▣ ✿ 🐕  Leisure ♠ ∪ ⤴ ⮞ 🚲 🏛

## CLOVELLY, Devon Map ref 1C1

★★★★
**BED & BREAKFAST**

B&B per room per night
s £22.00
d Min £50.00

### Fuchsia Cottage

Higher Clovelly, Clovelly, Bideford EX39 5RR  t (01237) 431398  e tom@clovelly-holidays.co.uk
w clovelly-holidays.co.uk

Fuchsia Cottage has comfortable, ground- and first-floor, en suite accommodation. Surrounded by beautiful views of sea and country. Good walking area. Ample parking.

**open** All year except Christmas
**bedrooms** 1 double, 1 twin, 2 single
**bathrooms** 2 en suite
**payment** Cash/cheques

Room 🛏 📺 👄 🍳  General 👁 🛏 P 🚭 ✕ ❄  Leisure ∪ ✈ 🚴 🛶

## COLLINGBOURNE KINGSTON, Wiltshire Map ref 2B2

★★★★
**FARMHOUSE**

B&B per room per night
s £40.00–£45.00
d £60.00–£65.00

### Manor Farm B&B

Collingbourne Kingston, Marlborough SN8 3SD  t (01264) 850859  f (01264) 850859
e stay@manorfm.com  w manorfm.com

**open** All year
**bedrooms** 1 double, 1 twin, 1 family
**bathrooms** 2 en suite, 1 private
**payment** Credit/debit cards, cash/cheques, euros

An attractive, Grade II Listed, period village farmhouse with comfortable and spacious rooms (all en suite/private) on a working family farm. Sumptuous traditional, vegetarian, gluten-free and other special-diet breakfasts. Beautiful countryside with superb walking and cycling from the farm. Horses and pets welcome.

⊕ *Opposite the church in the centre of the small village of Collingbourne Kingston, nine miles south of Marlborough.*

♥ *Pleasure flights from our private airstrip over Wiltshire's ancient places, white horses and crop circles by balloon, aeroplane and helicopter.*

Room 📺 👄  General 👁 🛏 P 🚭 🍴 ❄ 🐴  Leisure ∪ ✈ 🏇 🚴 🛶

## CORFE CASTLE, Dorset Map ref 2B3

★★★
**GUEST HOUSE**

B&B per room per night
d £54.00–£72.00

### Norden House

Corfe Castle, Wareham BH20 5DS  t (01929) 480177  f (01929) 480177  e nordenhouse@fsmail.net
w nordenhouse.com

**open** All year except Christmas
**bedrooms** 5 double, 2 twin, 1 family
**bathrooms** All en suite
**payment** Credit/debit cards, cash/cheques

Former Georgian farmhouse in own surroundings, adjacent to working farm. At foot of Purbeck Hills in beautiful countryside, half mile from Corfe Castle – gateway to World Heritage Site. Ideal base for walking, cycling, golf and horse-riding. Six miles from beaches. Licensed restaurant open to non-residents. Separate proprietor accommodation.

⊕ *A351 Wareham to Corfe Castle. Follow Norden Park'n'Ride signs for 2.5 miles and look for us on right-hand side as castle ruins come into view.*

♥ *Off-season special breaks available. Telephone for details or visit our website.*

Room 🛏 📺 👄 🍳  General 👁 🛏 🛏 P 🚭 🍷 🍴 ❄  Leisure ∪ ✈ 🏇 🚴

## It's all in the detail

Please remember that all information in this guide has been supplied by the proprietors well in advance of publication. Since changes do sometimes occur it's a good idea to check details at the time of booking.

## CORFE CASTLE, Dorset Map ref 2B3

★★★★
**BED & BREAKFAST**

B&B per room per night
s Min £45.00
d £65.00

# Westaway

88 West Street, Corfe Castle, Wareham BH20 5HE  t (01929) 480188  e ray_hendes@btinternet.com
w westaway-corfecastle.co.uk

**open** All year except Christmas and New Year
**bedrooms** 2 double, 1 twin
**bathrooms** 2 en suite, 1 private
**payment** Cash/cheques

Luxury accommodation comprising two double en suites and twin with private bathroom, situated in the beautiful village of Corfe Castle, with wonderful views of the Purbeck Hills. First-class Aga breakfast, lovely rear garden, including large wildlife pond. Plenty of local walks including Jurassic Coast – a World Heritage site.

⊕ A351 from Wareham to Corfe Castle. Turn right into village square, bear left into West Street. Westaway is 0.25 miles on right.

♥ All year: book 7 nights and only pay for 6.

Room 📺 ♨ 🍽  General 🛏8 P✂ 🍳 ❄  Leisure ∪ ♪ ▶ 🚲 🎣

## CORSHAM, Wiltshire Map ref 2B2

★★★★
**BED & BREAKFAST
GOLD AWARD**

B&B per room per night
s £42.00–£49.00
d £62.00–£69.00

# Heatherly Cottage

Ladbrook Lane, Gastard, Corsham SN13 9PE  t (01249) 701402  f (01249) 701412
e pandj@heatherly.plus.com  w heatherlycottage.co.uk

**open** All year except Christmas and New Year
**bedrooms** 2 double, 1 twin
**bathrooms** All en suite
**payment** Cash/cheques

Delightful 17thC cottage in a quiet lane with two acres and beautiful views across open countryside. Guests have a separate wing of the house with their own entrance. All rooms en suite, one with king-size bed. Colour TV, clock radio, hospitality tray, hairdryer. Many pubs serving good food nearby. Off-road parking.

⊕ Take the B3353 out of Corsham towards Gastard and Melksham. Ladbrook Lane is 0.8 miles from Corsham.

Room 🛁 📺 ♨ 🍽  General 🛏10 P✂ 🍳 ❄  Leisure ∪ 🚲

## COTSWOLDS

See under Bibury, Cheltenham, Chipping Campden, Cirencester, Fairford, Gloucester, Guiting Power, Lechlade-on-Thames, Moreton-in-Marsh, Slimbridge, Stonehouse, Stow-on-the-Wold, Stroud, Tewkesbury
See also Cotswolds in the Heart of England and South East England sections

## CREWKERNE, Somerset Map ref 1D2

★★★
**GUEST ACCOMMODATION**

B&B per room per night
s £30.00–£100.00
d £65.00–£150.00
Evening meal per person
£6.95–£20.00

# The George & Courtyard Restaurant

Market Square, Crewkerne TA18 7LP  t (01460) 73650  f (01460) 72974
e georgecrewkerne@btconnect.com  w thegeorgehotelcrewkerne.co.uk

Recently refurbished, 17thC, Grade II Listed coaching inn in the market square. Ideally located for touring. Fine food, real ales, warm welcome!

**open** All year
**bedrooms** 7 double, 2 twin, 3 single, 2 family
**bathrooms** 8 en suite, 1 private
**payment** Credit/debit cards, cash/cheques

Room 🖼 ☎ 📺 ♨ 🍽  General 🛏 🍳 ♨ 🍷 ✕ 🍳 🐾 🐴  Leisure ∪ ♪ ▶ 🎣

## Using map references
Map references refer to the colour maps at the front of this guide.

**CREWKERNE,** Somerset Map ref 1D2

★★★
INN

B&B per room per night
s £48.00–£55.00
d £60.00–£80.00
Evening meal per person
£10.00–£25.00

# The Manor Arms

Middle Street, North Perrott, Crewkerne TA18 7SG  t (01460) 72901  f (01460) 74055
e bookings@manorarmshotel.co.uk  w manorarmshotel.co.uk

A 16thC, Grade II Listed coaching inn offering
home-from-home comforts. Ideal base for walks
and touring. Inglenook fireplace, flagstone floors,
beer garden.

**open** All year except Christmas
**bedrooms** 6 double, 2 twin
**bathrooms** All en suite
**payment** Credit/debit cards, cash/cheques

Room ⌂ 🖃 📺 👆 🍴   General 🕭 🏛 🅰 P 🍽 🚬 ⚘   Leisure ∪ ♪ ⊦

**CROYDE,** Devon Map ref 1C1

★★★★
GUEST HOUSE

B&B per room per night
s £35.00–£50.00
d £50.00–£70.00

# Denham House & Cottages

North Buckland, Braunton EX33 1HY  t (01271) 890297  e info@denhamhouse.co.uk
w denhamhouse.co.uk

Country location, three miles to beaches, double
and family rooms all en suite, TV, hot drinks, full
English breakfast, parking.

**open** All year except Christmas
**bedrooms** 4 double, 1 family, 1 suite
**bathrooms** All en suite
**payment** Credit/debit cards, cash/cheques

Room 📺 👆 🍴   General 🕭 🏛 🅰 P 🔆 🍽 🚬 Ⅲ ⚘   Leisure 🎣

**CULLOMPTON,** Devon Map ref 1D2

★★★★
FARMHOUSE

B&B per room per night
s £28.00–£30.00
d £56.00–£60.00

# Langford Court North

Langford, Cullompton EX15 1SQ  t (01884) 277234  f (01884) 277234  e tchattey@yahoo.co.uk

Beautiful thatched medieval farmhouse with large
tastefully furnished rooms. Good home cooking
also excellent country pubs nearby. Central for
touring and walking in Devon.

**open** All year except Christmas and New Year
**bedrooms** 1 double, 1 family
**bathrooms** 1 en suite, 1 private
**payment** Cash/cheques

Room 🖃 📺 👆 🍴   General 🕭 P 🔆 Ⅲ ⚘   Leisure ♪ ⊦

**DARTMOOR**

*See under Bovey Tracey, Moretonhampstead, Okehampton, Tavistock, Yelverton*

**DARTMOUTH,** Devon Map ref 1D3

★★★★
BED & BREAKFAST

B&B per room per night
s £35.00–£45.00
d £60.00–£70.00

# Lower Collaton Farm

Blackawton, Dartmouth TQ9 7DW  t (01803) 712260  e mussen@lower-collaton-farm.co.uk
w lower-collaton-farm.co.uk

**open** All year except Christmas and New Year
**bedrooms** 2 double, 1 twin
**bathrooms** All en suite
**payment** Credit/debit cards, cash/cheques

Three delightful en suite bedrooms in traditional,
comfortable, Devonshire farmhouse overlooking
peaceful valley with views over rolling countryside.
Six miles from Dartmouth and beaches. Friendly
pedigree Shetland sheep, hens and ducks. Price
includes delicious breakfast with finest local produce.
Two self-catering cottages for four and two also
available.

⊕ *Totnes A381 signed Dartmouth. Halwell A3207 signed
Dartmouth. After 1 mile turn right, signed 'Collaton, no
through traffic.' Farm is 350yds on left behind wooden
gate.*

Room ⌂ 📺 👆 🍴   General 🕭 🏛 🅰 P 🔆 Ⅲ ⚘   Leisure 🎿

## B&B prices

Rates for bed and breakfast are shown per room per night.
Double room prices are usually based on two people sharing the room.

## DARTMOUTH, Devon Map ref 1D3

★★★★
**GUEST HOUSE
SILVER AWARD**

B&B per room per night
s £55.00–£75.00
d £65.00–£85.00

# Strete Barton House

Totnes Road, Strete, Dartmouth TQ6 0RN  t (01803) 770364  f (01803) 771182
e info@stretebarton.co.uk  w stretebarton.co.uk

**open** All year
**bedrooms** 3 double, 2 twin, 1 family
**bathrooms** 4 en suite, 2 private
**payment** Credit/debit cards, cash/cheques

16thC manor house with stunning sea views. Exquisitely furnished bedrooms with either en suite or private facilities. All rooms have TV/DVD, Wi-Fi Internet, hairdryer, radio-alarm and extensive beverage tray. Full English or continental breakfast using local produce. Use of residents' lounge. Close to two beautiful beaches.

⊕ A381 from Totnes to Kingsbridge. At Halwell, turn left (A3122) to Dartmouth. After Dartmouth Golf Club turn right to Strete. Strete Barton is near the church.

Room 🖨 📺 👜 🔌  General ⚒3 P ✂ 🍳 🛎 🌿 🌱 🏇  Leisure ⚓ ▶ 🏛

## DARTMOUTH, Devon Map ref 1D3

★★★★
**BED & BREAKFAST**

B&B per room per night
s £60.00–£65.00
d £60.00–£90.00

# Valley House

46 Victoria Road, Dartmouth TQ6 9DZ  t (01803) 834045  e enquiries@valleyhousedartmouth.com
w valleyhousedartmouth.com

**open** All year except Christmas
**bedrooms** 2 double, 1 twin
**bathrooms** All en suite
**payment** Cash/cheques

Receive a warm welcome to Dartmouth from Angela and Martin Cairns-Sharp. Central location, five minutes' walk to River Dart and town centre. Off-road (on-site) parking – a particular advantage in Dartmouth. Well-equipped rooms, lovely breakfasts served in dining room. Britain in Bloom prize winner 2005 and 2006.

⊕ From the end of the M5 at Exeter take A38 (signposted to Plymouth). Leave A38 at Buckfastleigh and follow A384 left to Dartmouth (via Totnes).

♥ Discounts for stays of 4 days or more.

Room 📺 👜 🔌  General ⚒12 P ✂  Leisure ∪ ⚓ ▶ 🏛

## DEVIZES, Wiltshire Map ref 2B2

★★★★
**GUEST ACCOMMODATION**

B&B per room per night
s Min £35.00
d Min £60.00

# Rosemundy Cottage

London Road, Devizes SN10 2DS  t (01380) 727122  f (01380) 720495
e info@rosemundycottage.co.uk  w rosemundycottage.co.uk

**open** All year
**bedrooms** 2 double, 1 twin, 1 family
**bathrooms** All en suite
**payment** Credit/debit cards, cash/cheques

Canal-side cottage, short walk to Market Place. Fully equipped rooms, include a four-poster and a ground floor room. Sitting room with guides provided. Guest office, Wi-Fi Internet. Garden with barbecue and heated pool in summer. Wiltshire Breakfast Award. Off-road parking. Perfect for business or leisure.

⊕ A361 just north of Devizes centre, towards Avebury. Right just past County Police HQ. On Wessex Ridgeway and bridge 137 on canal routes.

♥ Double en suite at single occupancy rate. Discount for 3 or more consecutive nights.

Room 🗝 🖨 📺 👜 🔌  General ⚒ P ✂ 🍳 🛎 🌿 🌱  Leisure ⤴ ∪ ⚓ 🚲 🏛

## DINTON, Wiltshire Map ref 2B3

★★★★
**BED & BREAKFAST**

B&B per room per night
s £40.00–£60.00
d £55.00–£65.00

### Marshwood Farm B&B

Dinton, Salisbury SP3 5ET  t (01722) 716334  e marshwood1@btconnect.com
w marshwoodfarm.co.uk

**open** All year
**bedrooms** 1 double/twin, 1 double/family
**bathrooms** All en suite
**payment** Cash/cheques, euros

Beautiful farmhouse dating from the 17thC on working farm, surrounded by fields and woodland. Ideal location for cycling, walking and exploring the Wiltshire countryside, Salisbury, Stonehenge, Bath and many places of interest. Guests are welcome to relax in our garden and use our tennis court.

⊕ *At A303/A36 intersection turn into Wylye, follow the Dinton signs. Marshwood Farm is approx 4 miles.*

Room 📺 🌢 ➅  General 🜂 🏭 🛆 P ⚅ ✿  Leisure ⚲ 🏞

## DORCHESTER, Dorset Map ref 2B3

★★★★
**BED & BREAKFAST**
**SILVER AWARD**

B&B per room per night
s £30.00–£35.00
d £55.00–£60.00

### Baytree House

4 Athelstan Road, Dorchester DT1 1NR  t (01305) 263696  f (01305) 263696
e info@baytreedorchester.com  w bandbdorchester.co.uk

Three bedrooms, two available for letting at any one time. Ten minutes' walk to Dorchester centre.

**open** All year
**bedrooms** 2 double, 1 twin
**bathrooms** 2 en suite, 1 private
**payment** Cash/cheques

Room 📺 🌢 ➅  General 🜂 🛆 P ⚅ 🍽 🖳 ✿ 🐾  Leisure ⚓ ► 🚲

## DORCHESTER, Dorset Map ref 2B3

★★★★
**GUEST ACCOMMODATION**
**SILVER AWARD**

B&B per room per night
s £45.00–£60.00
d £64.00–£80.00

### Yellowham Farm

Yellowham Wood, Dorchester DT2 8RW  t (01305) 262892  f (01305) 848155
e mail@yellowham.freeserve.co.uk  w yellowham.co.uk

Situated in the heart of Hardy Country on the edge of the idyllic Yellowham Wood in 120 acres of farmland. Excellent base for exploring the Jurassic Coast. Peace and tranquillity guaranteed.

**open** All year
**bedrooms** 2 double, 1 twin, 1 family
**bathrooms** All en suite
**payment** Credit/debit cards, cash/cheques, euros

Room 🛁 📺 🌢 ➅  General 🜂 4 P ⚅ 🍽 🖳 ✿ 🐾  Leisure ⚲ ∪ ⚓ ►  🚲

## DRAKEWALLS, Cornwall Map ref 1C2

★★★
**BED & BREAKFAST**

B&B per room per night
s £30.00–£35.00
d £40.00–£60.00

### Drakewalls House

Gunnislake PL18 9EG  t (01822) 833617  e patsmyth_53@hotmail.com
w drakewallsbedandbreakfast.co.uk

**open** All year
**bedrooms** 2 double, 1 family
**bathrooms** 1 en suite
**payment** Cash/cheques

Large, comfortable Victorian house with attractive gardens and own parking, set in the heart of the Tamar Valley. Ideal for exploring Dartmoor, Tavistock, Plymouth, etc. Within walking distance of the Tamar Valley railway line. Local produce always on the menu. A warm welcome guaranteed. Satellite TV.

Room 📺 🌢  General P ⚅ 🖳 ✿  Leisure ⚓ ► 🏞

**DULVERTON,** Somerset Map ref 1D1

★★★★★
**BED & BREAKFAST**

B&B per room per night
s £50.00–£70.00
d £60.00–£85.00

# Hawkwell Farm House

Dulverton, Somerset TA22 9RU  **t** (01398) 341708  **f** (01398) 341708
**e** jan@hawkwellfarmhouse.co.uk  **w** hawkwellfarmhouse.co.uk

**open** All year
**bedrooms** 1 double, 1 twin, 1 family
**bathrooms** All en suite
**payment** Credit/debit cards, cash/cheques

South-facing, 16thC traditional Devonshire longhouse, on the edge of Exmoor National Park, full of charm and character, dating back to the Domesday era. Secluded, yet easily accessible, standing in 14 acres of mature gardens, paddocks, and woodland. Inglenook fireplaces, exposed beams, four-poster beds, providing luxurious, spacious en suite accommodation. Heated swimming pool. Warm welcome and hearty breakfasts.

⊕ *Easily accessible from jct 27 of M5. Just a few minutes from Dulverton.*

♥ *Discounts on stays of 4 or more days (excl Saturdays) – see website for details.*

Room 🖼 📺 🖐 ♥   General ☎12 P ⅍ 🍳 🏠 ✿ 🐾   Leisure ⚓ ∪ 🎵 🏛

**EAST HARPTREE,** Somerset Map ref 2A2

★★★★★
**GUEST ACCOMMODATION
SILVER AWARD**

B&B per room per night
s £65.00–£75.00
d £80.00–£100.00
Evening meal per person
£17.50–£25.00

# Harptree Court

East Harptree, Bristol BS40 6AA  **t** (01761) 221729  **e** location.harptree@tiscali.co.uk
**w** harptreecourt.co.uk

**open** All year except Christmas and New Year
**bedrooms** 2 double, 1 twin
**bathrooms** 2 en suite, 1 private
**payment** Cash/cheques

Harptree Court is a very special family-run B&B in an elegant Georgian setting in amazing gardens. Enjoy a complimentary tea on the lawn or in front of a roaring log fire. Attention to detail is notable in the bedrooms and guest sitting room, and in the welcome given to guests.

⊕ *From A368 take B3114 for Chewton Mendip. After approx 0.5 miles turn right into drive entrance (straight after crossroad). Turn left at top of drive.*

Room 📺 🖐 ♥   General ☎12 P ⅍ ✕ 🍳 🏠 📶 ◙ ✿   Leisure ⚓ ∪ 🎵 ⮕ 🏛

**EXETER,** Devon Map ref 1D2

★★★
**BED & BREAKFAST**

B&B per room per night
s £30.00–£35.00
d £40.00–£50.00

# Culm Vale Country House

Culm Vale, Stoke Canon, Exeter EX5 4EG  **t** (01392) 841615  **f** (01392) 841615
**e** culmvale@hotmail.com

**open** All year
**bedrooms** 1 double, 1 twin, 1 family
**bathrooms** 1 en suite
**payment** Credit/debit cards, cash/cheques

Family-run bed and breakfast offering spacious, comfortable accommodation. Victorian country house set in one acre of garden, 3.5 miles from Exeter city centre. Free parking. Ideal touring base. Convenient for university, moors and coasts.

⊕ *Travelling down M5, come off at jct 27; go towards Tiverton. Pick up A396 (signed Bickleigh). Stoke Canon is 10 miles from Tiverton on A396.*

Room 📺 🖐 ♥   General ☎ P ⅍ 🍳 ◙ ✿   Leisure ∪ 🎵 🚲 🏛

**EXETER,** Devon Map ref 1D2

★★★★★
**RESTAURANT WITH ROOMS**
**GOLD AWARD**

B&B per room per night
s £87.50–£100.00
d £125.00–£300.00

## The Galley 'Fish and Seafood' Restaurant & Spa with Cabins

41 Fore Street, Topsham, Exeter EX3 0HU  **t** (01392) 876078  **e** fish@galleyrestaurant.co.uk  **w** galleyrestaurant.co.uk

**open** All year except Christmas and New Year
**bedrooms** 2 double, 1 twin, 1 suite
**bathrooms** 4 private
**payment** Credit/debit cards, cash/cheques

What dreams are made of: our accommodation weaves a different kind of magic in Topsham. Discover our nautical cabins, available with panoramic river views. Master Chef of Britain: Paul Da-Costa-Greaves who also happens to be a spiritual healer and alternative therapist. Jacuzzi/spa/hot tub by prior arrangement.

⊕ M5 jct 30, follow signs to Topsham. The Galley Restaurant with Cabins is near the quay.

Room 📞 📺 ♨ 🍴  General 🛏12 P ⚡ 🍴 ✕ 🎱 🅱 🖥 ✿  Leisure ⚡ ∪ ⛳

**EXETER,** Devon Map ref 1D2

★★★★
**GUEST ACCOMMODATION**

B&B per room per night
s £34.00–£38.00
d £52.00–£58.00

## The Grange

Stoke Hill, Exeter EX4 7JH  **t** (01392) 259723  **e** dudleythegrange@aol.com

**open** All year
**bedrooms** 1 double, 1 twin
**bathrooms** All en suite
**payment** Cash/cheques, euros

Country house set in three acres of woodlands, 1.5 miles from the city centre. Ideal for holidays and off-season breaks. All rooms en suite. Off-street parking.

⊕ M5 jct 29 for city centre, first roundabout 4th exit Western Way, next roundabout 2nd exit Old Tiverton Road, over next roundabout – Stoke Hill.

Room 📺 ♨  General P ⚡ 🅱 ✿

**EXETER,** Devon Map ref 1D2

★★★★
**FARMHOUSE**

B&B per room per night
s £35.00–£40.00
d £55.00–£60.00

## Home Farm

Farringdon, Exeter EX5 2HY  **t** (01395) 232293  **f** (01395) 233298

Georgian farmhouse in rural position. Spacious, en suite rooms and yummy breakfasts. Convenient for M5, Exeter University, airport and Westpoint. Woodland walks and warm welcomes.

**open** All year
**bedrooms** 1 double, 2 twin
**bathrooms** 2 en suite, 1 private
**payment** Cash/cheques, euros

Room 📺 ♨ 🍴  General 🛏 P 🎱 🅱 ✿ 🐾  Leisure ⚡ 🥾 ⛳ 🚲

# The great outdoors

Discover Britain's green heart with this easy-to-use guide. Featuring a selection of the most stunning gardens in the country, The Gardens Explorer is complete with a handy fold-out map and illustrated guide. You can purchase the Explorer series from good bookshops and online at visitbritaindirect.com.

★★★★
**FARMHOUSE**

B&B per room per night
s £35.00–£50.00
d £60.00–£70.00

# Rydon Farm

Woodbury, Exeter EX5 1LB  **t** (01395) 232341  **e** sallyglanvill@aol.com  **w** rydonfarmwoodbury.co.uk

**open** All year
**bedrooms** 1 double, 1 twin, 1 family
**bathrooms** 2 en suite, 1 private
**payment** Credit/debit cards, cash/cheques, euros

Guests return time and time again to our delightful, 16thC, Devon longhouse set amidst a 450-acre dairy farm, farmed by my husband's family for many generations. Exposed beams and inglenook fireplace. Romantic four-poster. Delicious farmhouse breakfasts using fresh, local produce. Several local pubs and restaurants. Highly recommended.

⊕ From M5 jct 30 take A376 Exmouth Road. At Clyst St George roundabout take B3179 to Woodbury village, turn right into Rydon Lane just before 30mph signs. Follow signs.

Room 🖼 📺 👜 🍴  General 👫 P 🚲 🛏 ✿ 🐾

★★
**INN**

B&B per room per night
s £40.00–£50.00
d £65.00–£80.00
Evening meal per person
£10.00–£20.00

# Thorverton Arms

Thorverton, Exeter EX5 5NS  **t** (01392) 860205  **e** info@thethorvertonarms.co.uk
**w** thethorvertonarms.co.uk

**open** All year
**bedrooms** 3 double, 1 twin, 1 single, 1 family
**bathrooms** All en suite
**payment** Credit/debit cards, cash/cheques

Traditional English country inn set in the heart of the beautiful village of Thorverton. Situated in the Exe Valley, yet only seven miles from Exeter. Comfortable en suite rooms, bar, award-winning restaurant, large south facing garden and car park. Ideal touring base for Exmoor, Dartmoor and the Devon coasts.

⊕ Just off the A396, seven miles north of Exeter. 11 miles from jct 27 of the M5. Eight miles from Exeter Airport.

♥ DB&B – £50 per person (min 2 people).

Room 📺 👜 🍴  General 👫 ⛪ P 🚲 🍷 ✕ 🎱 🛏 ✿ 🐾  Leisure ∪ 🎣 🏊

See under Bilbrook, Dulverton, Lynton, Porlock

★★★
**BED & BREAKFAST**

B&B per room per night
s Max £30.00
d Max £45.00

# Waiten Hill Farm

Mill Lane, Fairford GL7 4JG  **t** (01285) 712652  **f** (01285) 712652

Imposing 19thC farmhouse overlooking River Coln, old mill and famous church. Short walk to pubs, shops and restaurants. Ideal for touring the Cotswolds and water parks.

**open** All year
**bedrooms** 2 double, 1 twin
**bathrooms** 2 en suite, 1 private
**payment** Cash/cheques

Room 📺 👜  General 👫 🎱 ⛪ P 🛏 ✿  Leisure ♣

# enjoyEngland.com

Big city buzz or peaceful panoramas? Take a fresh look at England and you may be surprised at what's right on your doorstep. Explore the diversity online at enjoyengland.com

## FALMOUTH, Cornwall Map ref 1B3

★★★★
**GUEST ACCOMMODATION**

B&B per room per night
s £40.00
d £70.00–£80.00

### The Beach House

1 Boscawen Road, Falmouth TR11 4EL  **t** (01326) 210407  **e** beachhousefalmouth@hotmail.com
**w** beachhousefalmouth.co.uk

A large detached residence set in its own gardens, The Beach House is in a commanding position overlooking Falmouth Bay with panoramic views towards Pendennis Castle. For those who enjoy a sense of style and calm.

**open** All year
**bedrooms** 3 double
**bathrooms** All en suite
**payment** Cash/cheques

Room 📺 ♿ ☎  General P ✂ 🍴 🍴 ❄  Leisure ⚲

## FALMOUTH, Cornwall Map ref 1B3

★★★★
**GUEST ACCOMMODATION**

B&B per room per night
s £37.00–£44.00
d £46.00–£86.00

### Chelsea House

2 Emslie Road, Falmouth TR11 4BG  **t** (01326) 212230  **e** info@chelseahousehotel.com
**w** chelseahousehotel.com

Beautifully furnished en suite rooms with panoramic sea views over Falmouth Bay, some with own balcony. Parking. Short walk to town and two minutes' walk to lovely sandy, Blue Flag beach. Quiet location. Sumptuous full English breakfast using local award-winning sausages and Cornish produce.

**open** All year
**bedrooms** 6 double, 1 twin, 1 family
**bathrooms** All en suite
**payment** Credit/debit cards, cash/cheques

Room ♿ 🖭 📺 ♿ ☎  General ⌂7 P ✂ ❄

## FALMOUTH, Cornwall Map ref 1B3

★★★★★
**GUEST ACCOMMODATION**
**GOLD AWARD**

B&B per room per night
s £35.00–£45.00
d £70.00–£90.00

### Dolvean House

50 Melvill Road, Falmouth TR11 4DQ  **t** (01326) 313658  **f** (01326) 313995
**e** reservations@dolvean.co.uk  **w** dolvean.co.uk

**open** All year except Christmas
**bedrooms** 6 double, 2 twin, 2 single
**bathrooms** All en suite
**payment** Credit/debit cards, cash/cheques

Award-winning Victorian home in an ideal location for exploring Cornwall. Relaxing ambience, good food and romantic bedrooms to make every stay a special occasion.

⊕ *Situated on A39 to Pendennis Castle.*

♥ *Special breaks available in winter, spring and autumn. Check our website for more details.*

Room ♿ 📺 ♿ ☎  General ⌂12 P ✂ ♟ 🍴 ⚲ ❄

# Suit yourself

The symbols at the end of each entry mean you can enjoy virtually made-to-measure accommodation with the services and facilities most important to you. A key to the symbols can be found inside the back-cover flap. Keep this open for easy reference.

**FALMOUTH,** Cornwall Map ref 1B3

★★★
GUEST ACCOMMODATION

B&B per room per night
s £25.00–£35.00
d £45.00–£55.00

# Engleton House Guest House

67/68 Killigrew Street, Falmouth TR11 3PR  t (01326) 372644 & 07736 684666
e dawnemmerson@aol.com  w falmouth-bandb.co.uk

**open** All year
**bedrooms** 3 double, 3 twin, 2 single, 4 family
**bathrooms** 10 en suite
**payment** Credit/debit cards, cash/cheques

A small, friendly Georgian town house set in the heart of Falmouth close to shops, restaurants and other attractions. We offer comfortable, well-furnished accommodation with en suite rooms. Our breakfasts are legendary for both quality and quantity and include vegetarian options. Our aim is to offer a home from home environment.

⊕ Follow signs for Falmouth and beaches. Past police station and Ryders Jaguar garage. Roundabout turn left into Killigrew Street. We are on left at bottom.

♥ Special promotions vary throughout the year. Please see website for details.

Room 🛏 📺 ♨ ♨  General 🛎 🏛 ⅍ 🛏 🐾  Leisure ∪ ✈ ►

**FALMOUTH,** Cornwall Map ref 1B3

★★★
GUEST ACCOMMODATION

B&B per room per night
s £27.00–£29.00
d £54.00–£62.00

# Wickham Guest House

21 Gyllyngvase Terrace, Falmouth TR11 4DL  t (01326) 311140
e enquiries@wickhamhotel.freeserve.co.uk  w wickham-hotel.co.uk

**bedrooms** 2 double, 1 twin, 2 single, 1 family
**bathrooms** 3 en suite
**payment** Credit/debit cards, cash/cheques

Small, friendly, no-smoking guesthouse. Situated between harbour and beach with views over Falmouth Bay, Wickham is the ideal base for exploring Falmouth and South Cornwall's gardens, castles, harbours, coastal footpath and much more. All rooms have TV and tea/coffee facilities, some have sea views. Open Easter to October.

⊕ Follow A39 to Falmouth. Follow signs for beaches and look for sign for Falmouth Beach Hotel. Take 1st right after this sign, then 1st left.

Room 📺 ♨  General 🛎 ⅍

**FORD,** Gloucestershire Map ref 2B1

★★★★
INN
SILVER AWARD

B&B per room per night
s Min £40.00
d Min £70.00
Evening meal per person
£9.00–£16.00

# The Plough

Ford, Temple Guiting, Cheltenham GL54 5RU  t (01386) 584215  f (01386) 584042
e info@theploughinnatford.co.uk  w theploughinnatford.co.uk

**open** All year
**bedrooms** 1 double, 2 family
**bathrooms** All en suite
**payment** Credit/debit cards, cash/cheques

This quaint cobble-stoned building once used as a hayloft has now been converted to provide separate, comfortable accommodation. The Plough Inn at Ford makes a perfect base for exploring the Cotswolds.

Room 📺 ♨ ♨  General 🛎 ♿ P ⅍ ♈ ✕ 🛏 ✿  Leisure ∪ ✈ ► 🚲 🏊

**FOREST OF DEAN**

*See under Newent*

## FRAMPTON-ON-SEVERN, Gloucestershire Map ref 2B1

**★★★★**
INN

B&B per room per night
s £40.00–£50.00
d £60.00–£90.00
Evening meal per person
£5.95–£15.95

### The Bell

The Green, Frampton-on-Severn, Gloucester GL2 7EP  t (01452) 740346  f (01452) 740544
e hoqben@qotadsl.co.uk

open All year except Christmas
bedrooms 2 double, 2 suites
bathrooms All en suite
payment Credit/debit cards, cash/cheques

Lying at the top of the largest green in England in the centre of the beautiful village of Frampton. The Bell has recently undergone major refurbishment and transformation and is now a contemporary-designed, welcoming pub and restaurant with gastro food. The rooms are large and well equipped, overlooking the village green.

⊕ Exit jct 13 M5 onto A38 towards Bristol. Two miles to Frampton on Severn.

Room 📺 💧 🍵  General 🛆 ㅊ P 🍽 ✕ 🏧 🖳 ❋  Leisure 🎣 ∪ ⌿ 🚲

## FROME, Somerset Map ref 2B2

**★★★**
BED & BREAKFAST

B&B per room per night
s Min £24.00
d Min £44.00

### Granados

Blatchbridge, Frome BA11 5EL  t (01373) 465317  e granadosbandb@aol.com

Welcoming, friendly accommodation in surrounding countryside; one mile from Frome; very close to Longleat, Bath, Stourhead, Bath & West Showground.

open All year
bedrooms 1 double, 1 twin, 1 single
bathrooms 1 en suite, 1 private
payment Cash/cheques

Room 🛁 📺 💧  General 🛆 🎟 ㅊ P ⌿ 🏧 🕮 ❋  Leisure ▸ 🛥

## GLASTONBURY, Somerset Map ref 2A2

**★★★**
INN

B&B per room per night
s £35.00–£55.00
d £69.00–£79.00

### Who'd A Thought It Inn

17 Northload Street, Glastonbury BA6 9JJ  t (01458) 834460  e enquiries@whodathoughtit.co.uk
w whodathoughtit.co.uk

Town-centre located traditional inn; five en suite bedrooms; extensive menus with imaginative flair; restaurant-quality food at pub prices. Excellent real ales. Please phone to reserve rooms.

open All year
bedrooms 3 double, 2 twin
bathrooms All en suite
payment Credit/debit cards, cash/cheques

Room 📺 💧 🍵  General 🛆 ㅊ P 🍽 ❋ 🐕

## GLOUCESTER, Gloucestershire Map ref 2B1

**★★★**
GUEST HOUSE

B&B per room per night
s £30.00–£45.00
d £55.00–£65.00

### Brookthorpe Lodge

Stroud Road, Gloucester GL4 0UQ  t (01452) 812645  f (01452) 812645
e enq@brookthorpelodge.demon.co.uk  w brookthorpelodge.demon.co.uk

open All year except Christmas
bedrooms 3 double, 3 twin, 3 single, 1 family
bathrooms 6 en suite, 4 private
payment Credit/debit cards, cash/cheques

Licensed, family-run, spacious and comfortable Georgian detached house on the outskirts of Gloucester (3.5 miles). Set in lovely countryside at the foot of Cotswold escarpment. Close to ski-slope and golfing facilities. Excellent walking country. Ideal base for visiting the Cotswolds, Cheltenham, Bath and nearby WWT reserve at Slimbridge.

⊕ Situated on main Gloucester to Stroud road (A4173) some 3 miles from Gloucester city centre, 5 miles from Stroud. Four miles from Painswick.

Room 🛁 📺 💧 🍵  General 🛆 🎟 ㅊ P ⌿ 🍽 🏧 🕮 ❋ 🐕  Leisure ∪ ▸

## GUITING POWER, Gloucestershire Map ref 2B1

★ ★ ★ ★
**GUEST HOUSE
SILVER AWARD**

B&B per room per night
s Min £42.50
d Min £85.00
Evening meal per person
Min £32.00

# The Guiting Guest House

Post Office Lane, Guiting Power, Cheltenham GL54 5TZ  t (01451) 850470
e info@guitingguesthouse.com  w guitingguesthouse.com

**open** All year
**bedrooms** 4 double, 1 twin, 1 single, 1 family
**bathrooms** 5 en suite, 2 private
**payment** Credit/debit cards, cash/cheques

Converted 16thC Cotswold-stone farmhouse situated in the centre of a delightful rural village. The dining room features a polished elm floor and large inglenook fireplace. Some rooms have four-poster beds, all have colour TVs, well-stocked hospitality trays, hairdryers, luxury bathrobes, fresh fruit, flowers and bottled water.

⊕ See our website for directions.

Room 🖧 📺 ♨ 🍴  General ⛱ ▥ ♿ P ✗ ⤫ 🎱 ✿ 🐾  Leisure ∪ ♩ ▶ 🚴 🏊

## GUITING POWER, Gloucestershire Map ref 2B1

★ ★ ★ ★
**INN**

B&B per room per night
s £45.00
d £75.00–£90.00
Evening meal per person
£8.00–£16.00

# The Hollow Bottom

Winchcombe Road, Guiting Power, Cheltenham GL54 5UX  t (01451) 850392  f (01451) 850945
e hello@hollowbottom.com  w hollowbottom.com

**open** All year
**bedrooms** 2 double, 1 twin, 1 family
**bathrooms** 3 en suite, 1 private
**payment** Credit/debit cards, cash/cheques

A 17thC Cotswold inn with a horse-racing history and wonderful accommodation. The pub has a wide reputation for superb fresh food and a fine collection of beers, malts and wines. Our head chef Charlie is a former winner of Young Scottish Chef of the Year. A very warm welcome awaits all.

⊕ M5 jct 11, Cheltenham to Stow A436, turn off, 7 miles from Cheltenham signed Guiting Power. Close proximity to Bourton-on-the-Water and Winchcombe.

♥ Discounts available when booking on line. See website for details.

Room 🖧 📺 ♨ 🍴  General ⛱ ▥ ♿ P ⤫ ✗ 🎱 ✿ 🐾  Leisure ℘ ∪ ▶ 🏊

## HALBERTON, Devon Map ref 1D2

**Rating Applied For
GUEST ACCOMMODATION**

B&B per room per night
s £65.00–£75.00
d £130.00–£150.00
Evening meal per person
£20.00–£35.00

# The Priory

11 High Street, Halberton, Tiverton EX16 7AF  t (01884) 821234  e dawnriggs@threads-of-time.co.uk

**open** All year
**bedrooms** 2 double
**bathrooms** All en suite
**payment** Cash/cheques, euros

The Priory dates from c1154 and became a dwelling c1539. Our endeavour is to create a 21stC version of what a 12thC priory would offer – rest and relaxation to the weary traveller. We aim to offer the highest class of comfort and service, and use organic and sustainable produce where possible. Medieval herb garden.

⊕ Take exit 27 from M5. Follow signs for Halberton. The Priory is just past the post office on the left.

♥ Themed breaks include: Historic Foods, Botanical Arts and Crafts, English Folk Music, English Traditional Feasts and Garden History.

Room 🖼 📞 📺 ♨ 🍴  General ⛱ ▥ ♿ P ✗ ⤫ 🎱 ✿  Leisure ∪ ♩ ▶ 🚴 🏊

---

**HELSTON,** Cornwall Map ref 1B3

★★★★
**GUEST HOUSE**

B&B per room per night
s £30.00–£35.00
d £50.00–£55.00

# Lyndale Cottage Guest House

4 Greenbank, Meneage Road, Helston TR13 8JA  t (01326) 561082
e enquiries@lyndalecottage.co.uk  w lyndalecottage.co.uk

**open** All year
**bedrooms** 3 double, 2 twin, 1 single
**bathrooms** All en suite
**payment** Credit/debit cards, cash/cheques

Friendly, delightfully cosy Cornish cottage. Providing modern en suite bedrooms, Freeview TVs, CD/DVD players, hospitality trays, lounge with wood-burning stove, garden with patio, private parking. Completely non-smoking. Breakfast is prepared from local produce, free-range eggs, home-made jams and yoghurt. Ideally situated for exploring West Cornwall's gardens, coastline, beaches and seaside towns.

⊕ *Please contact us for easy-to-follow directions.*

Room 🛏 📞 TV 🕯 ⚅  General P ✂ 🍳 ⛌ 🎐 ✿  Leisure ∪ ⚐ ⊁ 🚲 🚣

---

**HELSTON,** Cornwall Map ref 1B3

★★★
**GUEST HOUSE**

B&B per room per night
s £38.00–£50.00
d £54.00–£58.00

# Mandeley Guesthouse

Clodgey Lane, Helston TR13 8PJ  t (01326) 572550  f (01326) 572550  e mandeley@btconnect.com
w mandeley.co.uk

Mandeley is a family-run guesthouse offering accommodation of the highest quality. Centrally located to explore the south-west peninsula. Secure off-road car parking. Bus stop nearby.

**open** All year except Christmas
**bedrooms** 1 double, 1 twin, 1 family
**bathrooms** 2 en suite, 1 private
**payment** Credit/debit cards, cash/cheques

Room 🛏 TV 🕯 ⚅  General ⏾ P ✂ 🍳 ⛌ 🐾  Leisure ∪ ⚐ 🚲 🚣

---

**HEMYOCK,** Devon Map ref 1D2

★★★★
**FARMHOUSE**

B&B per room per night
d £60.00

# Pounds Farm

Hemyock EX15 3QS  t (01823) 680802  e shillingscottage@yahoo.co.uk  w poundsfarm.co.uk

**open** All year
**bedrooms** 1 double
**bathrooms** En suite
**payment** Cash/cheques

Stone farmhouse set in large gardens. Relax beside the outdoor heated pool or next to a log fire. Gorgeous bedroom, en suite with walk-in shower. Extensive views over the Culm Valley Area of Outstanding Natural Beauty. Delicious farmhouse breakfasts with free-range eggs and home-made marmalade. Half a mile to village pub. Within easy reach of M5/A303.

⊕ *M5 jct 26, A38 to Cullompton (signpost Hemyock on left). Follow through village. After sharp right bend 1st left before ornate pump. 0.5 miles on right.*

♥ *Discounts on stays of 2 or more days. Telephone or see website for details.*

Room TV 🕯 ⚅  General ⏾ P ✂ 🍳 ⛌ ✿  Leisure ⚡ ∪ 🚲 🚣

---

## HEYTESBURY, Wiltshire Map ref 2B2

★★★★
BED & BREAKFAST

B&B per room per night
s £55.00–£65.00
d £60.00–£70.00

### The Resting Post

High Street, Heytesbury, Warminster BA12 0ED  t (01985) 840204  e enquiries@therestingpost.co.uk
w therestingpost.co.uk

Grade II Listed period house offering friendly, comfortable, en suite accommodation in the centre of a delightful village. There are two pubs in the village serving evening meals.

**open** All year except Christmas
**bedrooms** 2 double, 1 twin
**bathrooms** All en suite
**payment** Cash/cheques

Room 📺 🏃 ♨  General ☎ 10 🍴  Leisure ∪ 🚣 ▶ 🏖

## HONITON, Devon Map ref 1D2

★★★★
GUEST ACCOMMODATION

B&B per room per night
s £30.00–£35.00
d £60.00–£70.00

### Claypits Farm

Rawridge, Honiton EX14 9QP  t (01404) 861384  e heather.lockyer@claypitsfarm.co.uk
w claypitsfarm.co.uk

Farmhouse in two acres situated in the picturesque Otter Valley within the Blackdown Hills, offering traditional, welcoming bed and breakfast accommodation. Home-grown and locally sourced produce used.

**open** All year
**bedrooms** 1 double, 1 twin, 1 family
**bathrooms** 2 en suite, 1 private
**payment** Cash/cheques

Room 📺 🏃 ♨  General ☎ 🏕 P 🍴 🛏 ❀ 🐕  Leisure ▶

## ILMINSTER, Somerset Map ref 1D2

★★★
BED & BREAKFAST

B&B per room per night
s £22.00–£24.00
d £42.00–£44.00

### Graden

Peasmarsh, Ilminster TA19 0SG  t (01460) 52371  f (01460) 52371

Everyone welcome, long or short stays. Many local attractions. Nearest beach 20 miles, Taunton 12.5 miles, M5 12 miles, A303 three miles. Television lounge, central heating, fridge and microwave for sole use of guests.

**open** All year
**bedrooms** 2 double, 1 family
**payment** Cash/cheques

Room 🏃 ♨  General ☎ 🏬 🏕 P 🍴 🛏 ❀ 🐕  Leisure ▶ 🏖

## ISLES OF SCILLY, Isles of Scilly Map ref 1A3

Rating Applied For
BED & BREAKFAST

B&B per room per night
d £34.00

### Demelza Bed & Breakfast

Demelza, Jackson's Hill, St Marys TR21 0JZ  t (01720) 422803  e sibleysonscilly@tiscali.co.uk

Self-contained, centrally heated, double en suite bedroom and private use of furnished outside decking area. Open Easter to November.

**bedrooms** 1 double
**bathrooms** En suite
**payment** Cash/cheques

Room 📺 🏃 ♨  General 🍴 ❀  Leisure ∪ 🚣 ▶ 🚲

## KINGSBRIDGE, Devon Map ref 1C3

★★★
GUEST ACCOMMODATION

B&B per room per night
s £31.50–£40.00
d £53.00–£60.00

### Ashleigh House

Ashleigh Road, Kingsbridge TQ7 1HB  t (01548) 852893  e reception@ashleigh-house.co.uk
w ashleigh-house.co.uk

Comfortable, licensed guesthouse. Easy walk to town for quay, tourist information and pubs/restaurants. All rooms en suite with colour TV and beverage tray. Sun lounge. Some off-road parking.

**bedrooms** 5 double, 1 twin, 2 family
**bathrooms** All en suite
**payment** Credit/debit cards, cash/cheques

Room 📺 🏃  General ☎ 🏬 🏕 P 🍴 🍷 🛏 ❀ 🐕  Leisure ∪ 🚣 ▶ 🏖

## Look at the maps
Colour maps at the front pinpoint the location of all accommodation found in the regional sections.

### LACOCK, Wiltshire Map ref 2B2

★★★★
**BED & BREAKFAST**
**SILVER AWARD**

B&B per room per night
s £60.00
d £85.00–£90.00

## King John's Hunting Lodge

21 Church Street, Lacock, Chippenham SN15 2LB  **t** (01249) 730313  **f** (01249) 730725
**e** kingjohns@amserve.com

Romantic Grade II Listed property, built c1200 with tearooms and secluded garden, in National Trust village.

**open** All year except Christmas and New Year
**bedrooms** 1 double, 1 family
**bathrooms** All en suite
**payment** Credit/debit cards, cash/cheques

Room TV ⓦ ⌕   General ⌂ ❋ 🐾

### LANGPORT, Somerset Map ref 1D1

★★★★
**BED & BREAKFAST**

B&B per room per night
s £40.00–£48.00
d £60.00–£68.00
Evening meal per person
£15.00–£20.00

## Orchard Barn

Law Lane, Drayton, Langport TA10 0LS  **t** (01458) 252310  **e** orchardbarn@zoom.co.uk
**w** orchard-barn.com

Comfortable, individual, en suite rooms in beautiful surroundings on the Somerset Levels. Excellent, varied breakfasts, evening meals by arrangement.

**open** All year except Christmas and New Year
**bedrooms** 2 double, 1 twin
**bathrooms** All en suite
**payment** Cash/cheques

Room TV ⓦ ⌕   General ⌂ ▥ ♣ P ♟ ✕ ▨ ❋   Leisure ♪ ▶ 🚴 🏊

### LANREATH-BY-LOOE, Cornwall Map ref 1C2

★★★★
**BED & BREAKFAST**

B&B per room per night
d £60.00–£70.00

## Bocaddon Farm

Looe PL13 2PG  **t** (01503) 220192  **f** (01503) 220245  **e** holidays@bocaddon.com  **w** bocaddon.com

**open** All year except Christmas and New Year
**bedrooms** 1 double, 1 twin
**bathrooms** All en suite
**payment** Credit/debit cards, cash/cheques

Hidden in the centre of our dairy farm, yet within easy reach of beautiful parts of Cornwall. Enjoy the comfort of a lovely old stone farmhouse along with the luxury of recently converted, en suite bedrooms. Swim in our indoor heated pool, then indulge yourself in a really good farmhouse breakfast.

✤ From Plymouth, A38 to Dobwalls. Left at lights to East Taphouse. Left on B3359 towards Looe. After four miles, turn right (signed Bocaddon and Shillamill Lakes).

♥ Discounts for stays of 3 or more nights.

Room TV ⓦ ⌕   General ⌂5 P ⅔ ▨ ❋   Leisure 🏊

### LAUNCESTON, Cornwall Map ref 1C2

★★★★
**BED & BREAKFAST**

B&B per room per night
s £25.00–£27.50
d £50.00–£55.00

## Oakside

South Petherwin, Launceston PL15 7JL  **t** (01566) 86733  **e** janet.crossman@tesco.net

**open** All year
**bedrooms** 2 double, 1 twin
**bathrooms** 2 en suite, 1 private
**payment** Cash/cheques

Panoramic views of Bodmin Moor from farm bungalow, nestling peacefully amongst delightful surroundings, conveniently situated one minute from A30. Ideal base for touring Devon and Cornwall. Twenty-five minutes from Eden Project. English breakfasts a speciality with home-made bread and preserves. Warm welcome awaits. Cosy, well-equipped rooms. Ideal place to relax.

✤ A30 into Cornwall. Three miles west of Launceston, underneath A395, still on A30. Slow down, no slip road. Next left, Oakside 1st bungalow on right.

Room ♿ TV ⓦ ⌕   General ⌂ ▥ ♣ P ⅔ ▨ ❋   Leisure ▶ 🏊

## LAUNCESTON, Cornwall Map ref 1C2

★★★★★
**BED & BREAKFAST
SILVER AWARD**

B&B per room per night
**s** £60.00–£80.00
**d** £70.00–£120.00
Evening meal per person
£10.00–£14.00

### Primrose Cottage

Lawhitton, Launceston PL15 9PE  **t** (01566) 773645  **e** enquiry@primrosecottagesuites.co.uk
**w** primrosecottagesuites.co.uk

**open** All year
**bedrooms** 2 double, 1 twin
**bathrooms** All en suite
**payment** Credit/debit cards, cash/cheques

Primrose Cottage is set in gardens and woodland leading to the River Tamar. Each luxury suite has its own sitting room, entrance and en suite facilities with beautiful views across the Tamar Valley. Five minutes from the A30 with easy access to both north and south coasts and the moors.

⊕ *Leave Launceston on the A388 Plymouth road. After 1 mile turn left on B3362 signposted Tavistock. Primose Cottage is on the left after 2.5 miles.*

♥ *Discounts on stays of 2 or 3 days. Please see website for details.*

Room 🛏 📺 👒 🍵  General 12 P ⅙ ✕ 🍽 🕮 ✿  Leisure 🏊 🏛

## LAUNCESTON, Cornwall Map ref 1C2

★★★★
**BED & BREAKFAST**

B&B per room per night
**s** Max £39.99
**d** Min £60.00
Evening meal per person
£15.00–£25.00

### Trekenner Court

Pipers Pool, Nr Bodmin Moor, Launceston PL15 8QG  **t** (01566) 880118
**e** trekennercourt@hotmail.co.uk  **w** trekennercourt.co.uk

**open** All year except Christmas
**bedrooms** 2 double, 1 twin
**bathrooms** All en suite
**payment** Cash/cheques, euros

Trekenner Court is in a tranquil setting enjoying glorious views over Bodmin Moor. This 200-year-old barn conversion is set in four acres. Ideal for visiting the gardens and houses of Cornwall and Devon and only 20 minutes from the north coast.

⊕ *Leave the A30 at the A395 to Camelford. Drive through Pipers Pool. After approx 1 mile, on the crest of the incline, turn left.*

♥ *Evening meals available by arrangement. Tickets held for the Eden Project.*

Room 🛏 📺 👒 🍵  General P ⅙ 🍽 🕮 ⚲ ✿  Leisure ∪ 🏊 ⌖ 🚲 🏛

## LECHLADE-ON-THAMES, Gloucestershire Map ref 2B1

★★★★
**GUEST ACCOMMODATION**

B&B per room per night
**s** £40.00–£45.00
**d** £50.00–£75.00

### Cambrai Lodge

Oak Street, Lechlade, Lechlade-on-Thames GL7 3AY  **t** (01367) 253173
**e** cambrailodge@btconnect.com  **w** cambrailodgeguesthouse.co.uk

Friendly, family-run guesthouse, recently modernised, close to River Thames. One bedroom contains a king-size bed and corner bath. Ideal base for touring the Cotswolds. Garden and ample parking.

**open** All year
**bedrooms** 2 double, 2 twin, 1 suite
**bathrooms** All en suite
**payment** Cash/cheques, euros

Room 🛏 📺 👒 🍵  General P ⅙ ✿ 🐾  Leisure 🏊 ⌖

## Take a break

Look out for special promotions and themed breaks. This could be your chance to indulge an interest, find a new one, or just relax and enjoy exceptional value. Offers (highlighted in colour) are subject to availability.

## LECHLADE-ON-THAMES, Gloucestershire Map ref 2B1

★★★
**INN**

B&B per room per night
s £40.00–£60.00
d £45.00–£70.00
Evening meal per person
£10.00–£25.00

# New Inn Hotel

Market Square, Lechlade-on-Thames GL7 3AB **t** (01367) 252296 **f** (01367) 252315
**e** info@newinnhotel.co.uk **w** newinnhotel.co.uk

The New Inn Hotel is where a 250-year tradition of hospitality blends with 21st century comfort and Cotswold charm. On the banks of River Thames in the centre of Lechlade.

**open** All year except Christmas
**bedrooms** 10 double, 12 twin, 4 single, 2 family
**bathrooms** All en suite
**payment** Credit/debit cards, cash/cheques, euros

Room 🛏 📺 📶 🍴 🖥️  General P 🍽 🎱 🎰 🪑 💻 ✳️  Leisure 🎣 ⛵ ✈ ► 🚲

## LISKEARD, Cornwall Map ref 1C2

★★★★
**FARMHOUSE**

B&B per room per night
s £36.00–£40.00
d £52.00–£60.00

# Trecorme Barton

Quethiock, Liskeard PL14 3SH **t** (01579) 342646 **f** (01579) 342646
**e** renfree@trecormebarton.fsnet.co.uk **w** trecormebarton.co.uk

Lovely, stone-built farmhouse. Wonderful views, in rolling countryside. En suite room. Near south coast and moors. Close to Eden, Cotehele and Antony House. Relaxing stay assured. Open March to October.

**bedrooms** 1 double
**bathrooms** En suite
**payment** Cash/cheques

Room 📺 🍴 📶  General 🛒2 P ✂ 🛡️ ✳️  Leisure ⛵ ✈

## LIZARD, Cornwall Map ref 1B3

★★★★
**INN**

B&B per room per night
s £50.00–£60.00
d £70.00–£80.00
Evening meal per person
£7.00–£15.00

# The Top House Inn

The Top House, Helston TR12 7NQ **t** (01326) 290974 **w** thetophouselizard.co.uk

Britain's most southerly inn, offering eight beautiful en suite bedrooms. After enjoying the breathtaking scenery, relax and let us provide you with excellent home-cooked food. You won't want to leave!

**open** All year
**bedrooms** 4 double, 2 twin, 2 family
**bathrooms** All en suite
**payment** Credit/debit cards, cash/cheques

Room 🛏 📺 🍴  General 🛒 🛏 📶 P ✂ 🍽 ✳️  Leisure ⛵ ✈ ►

## LOOE, Cornwall Map ref 1C2

★★★★
**FARMHOUSE**
**SILVER AWARD**

B&B per room per night
s £33.00–£45.00
d £57.00–£66.00

# Bucklawren Farm

St Martin, Looe PL13 1NZ **t** (01503) 240738 **f** (01503) 240481 **e** bucklawren@btopenworld.com
**w** bucklawren.com

**bedrooms** 2 double, 2 twin, 2 family
**bathrooms** All en suite
**payment** Credit/debit cards, cash/cheques

Delightful farmhouse set in glorious countryside with spectacular sea views. Quiet location, situated one mile from the beach and three miles from the fishing village of Looe. An award-winning farm with all bedrooms en suite. Granary Restaurant on-site. Open March to November.

✦ *From Looe, B3253 towards Plymouth. After 1.5 miles turn right to Monkey Sanctuary. After 1.5 miles turn right (signposted Bucklawren). Half a mile past 1st house and restaurant.*

Room 🛏 📺 🍴 📶  General 🛒5 P ✂ 🛡️ ✳️  Leisure ✈ ►

## To your credit

If you book by phone you may be asked for your credit card number. If so, it is advisable to check the proprietor's policy in case you have to cancel your reservation at a later date.

**LOOE,** Cornwall Map ref 1C2

★★★★
GUEST HOUSE

B&B per room per night
s £50.00–£70.00
d £68.00–£82.00

## Coombe Farm

Widegates, Looe PL13 1QN **t** (01503) 240223 **e** coombe_farm@hotmail.com
**w** coombefarmhotel.co.uk

**open** All year except Christmas and New Year
**bedrooms** 1 double, 1 twin, 1 family
**bathrooms** All en suite
**payment** Credit/debit cards, cash/cheques

Coombe Farm country house has 11 acres of lawns, woods and paddock. Guests relax in spacious, en suite cottage rooms. Breakfast is served in your room. Heated outdoor pool, ponies, peacocks, small animals and a dog. Nearby are beautiful beaches, gardens, Eden, Heligan and National Trust properties.

⊕ *A38 across Tamar Bridge. Six miles later, at Trerule Foot roundabout, left on A374 to Looe. Follow Looe signs, then Hessenford. Coombe Farm 1 mile after Hessenford on left.*

Room General P Leisure

**LOOE,** Cornwall Map ref 1C2

★★★★
GUEST HOUSE
SILVER AWARD

B&B per room per night
s £45.00–£60.00
d £55.00–£75.00

## Dovers House

St Martins Road, St Martin, Looe PL13 1PB **t** (01503) 265468 **e** twhyte@btconnect.com
**w** dovershouse.co.uk

**open** All year except Christmas
**bedrooms** 2 double, 1 twin, 1 family
**bathrooms** All en suite
**payment** Credit/debit cards, cash/cheques

Just a few minutes drive from Looe harbour, Dovers House is an ideal base for exploring or visiting Cornwall's many attractions and scenic views. Looe is an old fishing port with friendly people and good inns and restaurants. Our accommodation offers twin, double and large family rooms, all with en suite. Comfortably designed to make your stay pleasant and relaxing.

⊕ *Dovers House is located on the B3253 road to Looe. 1.7 miles from the harbour.*

❤ *Call, or visit our website for special promotions.*

Room General 8 P Leisure

**LOOE,** Cornwall Map ref 1C2

★★★★
FARMHOUSE
SILVER AWARD

B&B per room per night
d £55.00–£65.00

## Little Larnick Farm

Pelynt, Looe PL13 2NB **t** (01503) 262837 **f** (01503) 262837 **e** littlelarnick@btclick.com
**w** littlelarnick.co.uk

**open** All year except Christmas
**bedrooms** 4 double, 1 twin, 1 family
**bathrooms** All en suite
**payment** Credit/debit cards, cash/cheques

A 200-acre farm situated in the beautiful West Looe River valley. The farmhouse and recently converted barn offer peaceful and relaxing, character, en suite accommodation, including a barn suite and ground-floor bedroom. Wonderful walks from the door. Drying room available. Special 'Winter Warmer' breaks.

⊕ *From Looe, B3359 to Pelynt. Turn right before Jubilee Inn, 1st farm on left approx 1.25 miles.*

❤ *'Winter Warmer' breaks Nov-Mar.*

Room General 10 P

**LYME REGIS,** Dorset Map ref 1D2

★★★★
GUEST ACCOMMODATION

B&B per room per night
d £50.00–£70.00

## St Andrews House

Uplyme Road, Lyme Regis DT7 3LP  t (01297) 445495

Quality accommodation in large house. Sea and country views. Parking, swimming pool and gardens. Friendly atmosphere and extensive breakfast menu.

**open** All year
**bedrooms** 3 double
**bathrooms** All en suite
**payment** Cash/cheques

Room 📺 👄 🕆  General ☎ P 🏠 ✿  Leisure ⚘

**LYME REGIS,** Dorset Map ref 1D2

★★★★
GUEST ACCOMMODATION

B&B per room per night
s Max £60.00
d Min £64.00

## Springfield

Woodmead Road, Lyme Regis DT7 3LJ  t (01297) 443409  f (01297) 443685
e springfield@lymeregis.com  w lymeregis.com/springfield

Elegantly restored Georgian villa with far-reaching views over the Dorset coastline. A short walk to the shops and seafront.

**open** All year except Christmas and New Year
**bedrooms** 2 double, 2 twin, 2 family
**bathrooms** 5 en suite, 1 private
**payment** Cash/cheques

Room 📺 👄 🕆  General ☎5 P 🏠 ✿  Leisure ▶

**LYNTON,** Devon Map ref 1C1

★★★★
GUEST HOUSE
SILVER AWARD

B&B per room per night
d £46.00–£56.00
Evening meal per person
£12.00–£15.00

## The Denes Guest House

15 Longmead, Lynton EX35 6DQ  t (01598) 753573  e j.e.mcgowan@btinternet.com  w thedenes.com

**open** All year except Christmas
**bedrooms** 3 double, 2 family
**bathrooms** 4 en suite, 1 private
**payment** Credit/debit cards, cash/cheques

Peacefully located close to Valley of Rocks, but a short walk to the heart of the village, The Denes is an ideal base to explore Exmoor, whether walking, cycling or driving. Our bedrooms are spacious, all with en suite or private facilities. Freshly cooked breakfasts and evening meals appeal to discerning appetites.

⊕ *M5 jct 23 signposted Bridgwater. M5 jct 25 onto A358 signposted Minehead. M5 jct 27 onto A361 signposted Tiverton. In Lynton follow signs to Valley of Rocks.*

♥ *Beaujolais Nouveau weekend. New Year specials. Gift vouchers. 3-night DB&B.*

Room 📺 👄 🕆  General ☎ 🏢 🔥 P ✂ 🍽 ✖ 🍴 🏠 ✿  Leisure ⚘

**LYNTON,** Devon Map ref 1C1

★★★★
GUEST ACCOMMODATION
SILVER AWARD

B&B per room per night
s £30.00
d £60.00–£65.00
Evening meal per person
£15.50

## Kingford House

Longmead, Lynton EX35 6DQ  t (01598) 752361  e tricia@kingfordhouse.co.uk
w kingfordhouse.co.uk

Private hotel close to Valley of Rocks. Attractive, comfortable rooms, good home-cooked meals with choice of menu. Individual attention assured.

**open** All year
**bedrooms** 3 double, 1 twin, 2 single
**bathrooms** All en suite
**payment** Cash/cheques

Room 📺 👄 🕆  General ☎8 P ✂ ✖ 🏠 ✿

WALKERS WELCOME

WELCOME WALKERS

## Best foot forward

Walkers feel at home in accommodation participating in our Walkers Welcome scheme. Look out for the symbol. Consider walking all or part of a long-distance route – go online at nationaltrail.co.uk.

## LYNTON, Devon Map ref 1C1

★★★★
**GUEST ACCOMMODATION**

B&B per room per night
s £26.00–£28.00
d £54.00–£60.00

# South View Guest House

23 Lee Road, Lynton EX35 6BP  t (01598) 752289  e maureenroper@hotmail.com
w southview-lynton.co.uk

Comfortable, homely accommodation in the picturesque village of Lynton. Located minutes from South West Coast Path, Valley of Rocks and Cliff Railway. A warm welcome awaits you at South View.

**open** All year except Christmas
**bedrooms** 2 double, 1 twin, 1 single, 1 family
**bathrooms** All en suite
**payment** Credit/debit cards, cash/cheques

Room TV ⬤ ⬤  General ⬤5 P ⬤ ⬤ ⬤

## MARAZION, Cornwall Map ref 1B3

★★★★
**GUEST ACCOMMODATION**

B&B per room per night
s £35.00–£70.00

# Rosario

The Square, Marazion TR17 0BH  t (01736) 711998  w marazion.net

Recently renovated Victorian house keeping most original features. Ideal for Isles of Scilly, St Michael's Mount, birdwatching or beach holidays. One-minute, level walk to pubs and eateries. Well-behaved dogs welcome.

**open** All year
**bedrooms** 2 double, 1 twin, 1 single
**bathrooms** All en suite
**payment** Cash/cheques

Room TV ⬤  General P ⬤ ⬤ ⬤ ⬤ ⬤ ⬤  Leisure U ⬤ ⬤ ⬤

## MARKET LAVINGTON, Wiltshire Map ref 2B2

★★★
**INN**

B&B per room per night
s £25.00–£40.00
d £50.00–£60.00
Evening meal per person
£6.00–£20.00

# The Green Dragon

26-28 High Street, Market Lavington, Devizes SN10 4AG  t (01380) 813235
e greendragonlavington@tiscali.co.uk  w greendragonlavington.co.uk

Family-run public house, situated in the heart of the village; comfortable, non-smoking rooms; good home-cooked food. Ideal for walkers and cyclists.

**open** All year
**bedrooms** 1 double, 1 single, 1 family
**bathrooms** 1 en suite
**payment** Credit/debit cards, cash/cheques

Room TV ⬤ ⬤  General ⬤ ⬤ P ⬤ ⬤ X ⬤ ⬤ ⬤ ⬤  Leisure ⬤ ⬤ ⬤ ⬤

## MARLBOROUGH, Wiltshire Map ref 2B2

★★★★
**BED & BREAKFAST
SILVER AWARD**

B&B per room per night
s £32.50–£37.50
d £65.00–£75.00
Evening meal per person
£15.00–£20.00

# Crofton Lodge

Crofton, Marlborough SN8 3DW  t (01672) 870328  e ali@croftonlodge.co.uk  w croftonlodge.co.uk

**open** All year except Christmas and New Year
**bedrooms** 1 double, 1 twin, 1 single
**bathrooms** 1 en suite, 2 private
**payment** Cash/cheques, euros

Comfortable, welcoming home with large gardens in hamlet next to Kennet and Avon Canal, Crofton Beam Engines and Savernake Forest. Close to Great Bedwyn and good pubs. Easy reach Marlborough and Hungerford. Excellent base for walkers and cyclists. Home grown or local produce.

⊕ *From Great Bedwyn (2 miles south of A4 between Marlborough and Hungerford) follow Crofton Beam Engine signs. Crofton Lodge is 1.5 miles on right.*

♥ *Stay for 3 nights and enjoy a free dinner.*

Room TV ⬤ ⬤  General ⬤12 X ⬤ ⬤ ⬤ ⬤ ⬤  Leisure ⬤ ⬤ ⬤

## Using map references

The map references refer to the colour maps at the front of this guide. The first figure is the map number, the letter and figure that follow indicate the grid reference on the map.

## MARTOCK, Somerset Map ref 2A3

### The White Hart Hotel

★★★★
INN

B&B per room per night
**s** Min £45.00
**d** Min £62.00
Evening meal per person
Min £10.25

East Street, Martock TA12 6JQ  **t** (01935) 822005  **f** (01935) 822056
**e** enquiries@whiteharthotelmartock.co.uk  **w** whiteharthotelmartock.co.uk

Pleasant Hamstone, Grade II Listed coaching inn. Centre of Martock, seven miles from Yeovil and two miles off the A303. Top-class, fresh food served. Real ales, fine wines.

**open** All year except Christmas and New Year
**bedrooms** 5 double, 5 family
**bathrooms** All en suite
**payment** Credit/debit cards, cash/cheques, euros

Room ✆ 📺 🌢 🖳  General 👥 🕮 🎄 P ⚡ ✗ 🖳 🐾

## MEVAGISSEY, Cornwall Map ref 1B3

### Corran Farm B&B

★★★★
FARMHOUSE
SILVER AWARD

B&B per room per night
**s** £31.00–£35.00
**d** £52.00–£56.00

St Ewe, Mevagissey, St Austell PL26 6ER  **t** (01726) 842159  **e** terryandkathy@corranfarm.fsnet.co.uk
**w** corranfarm.co.uk

Quality farmhouse B&B on working farm in open countryside with own farm shop. Farm adjoins Heligan Gardens. Choice of delicious breakfast, beautiful walks, beaches, inns. Ideal for exploring Cornwall. Open February to November.

**bedrooms** 2 double, 1 twin
**bathrooms** All en suite
**payment** Cash/cheques

Room 📺 🌢 🖳  General 👥 P ✂ 🖳 🕮 ✿

## MEVAGISSEY, Cornwall Map ref 1B3

### Tregilgas Farm

★★★★
FARMHOUSE

B&B per room per night
**s** £25.00–£30.00
**d** £50.00–£60.00
Evening meal per person
£15.00–£18.00

Gorran, St Austell PL26 6ND  **t** (01726) 842342  **e** Dclemes88@aol.com
**w** tregilgasfarmbedandbreakfast.co.uk

Tregilgas Farm is central for touring. The spectacular Heligan Gardens and Eden Project are within easy reach. A warm welcome. Local produce used for breakfast.

**open** All year except Christmas and New Year
**bedrooms** 2 double, 1 twin
**bathrooms** 2 en suite, 1 private
**payment** Cash/cheques

Room 📺 🌢 🖳  General 👥3 P ✗ 🖳 🕮 ▣ ✿ 🐾  Leisure ∪ ♪ 🚲 🎣

## MILTON DAMEREL, Devon Map ref 1C2

### Buttermoor Farm

★★★★
FARMHOUSE

B&B per room per night
**s** £25.00–£32.00
**d** £50.00–£64.00
Evening meal per person
£15.00–£20.00

Milton Damerel, Holsworthy EX22 7PB  **t** (01409) 261314  **e** info@buttermoorfarm.co.uk
**w** buttermoorfarm.co.uk

Rediscover tranquillity. With comfortable en suite rooms, real food, gorgeous gardens and a warm welcome.

**open** All year
**bedrooms** 1 double, 1 twin
**bathrooms** All en suite
**payment** Cash/cheques

Room 🛁 📺 🌢  General 👥 🕮 🎄 P ✂ ✗ 🖳 🕮 ▣ ✿  Leisure ♪ 🎣

# Country Code  always follow the Country Code

- Be safe – plan ahead and follow any signs
- Leave gates and property as you find them
- Protect plants and animals, and take your litter home
- Keep dogs under close control
- Consider other people

## MINSTERWORTH, Gloucestershire Map ref 2B1

★★★
**GUEST ACCOMMODATION**

B&B per room per night
s Min £30.00
d Min £60.00

### Severn Bank

Minsterworth, Gloucester GL2 8JH  t (01452) 750146  f (01452) 750357  e info@severnbank.com
w severn-bank.com

**open** All year except Christmas and New Year
**bedrooms** 2 double/twin, 1 family
**bathrooms** All en suite
**payment** Cash/cheques

A fine country house set in large gardens with lovely river walk. All en suite rooms are spacious with beautiful river views, as is the breakfast room in which we serve a healthy buffet breakfast including fruits, yoghurts, cereals and breads. There are good pubs nearby for evening meals.

⊕ *Travel west from Gloucester on A40. Turn left onto A48 towards Chepstow; continue for 2.3 miles. Just past church lane turn left into Severn Bank.*

Room 📺 ♿  General ☺10 P ✗ 🏠 ❄  Leisure 🏛

## MORETON-IN-MARSH, Gloucestershire Map ref 2B1

★★★★
**FARMHOUSE**

B&B per room per night
s £35.00–£45.00
d £55.00–£59.00

### Fosseway Farm B&B

Stow Road, Moreton-in-Marsh GL56 0DS  t (01608) 650503

Fosseway Farm is just a five-minute walk into Moreton-in-Marsh town. All rooms en suite with TV, hairdryer and refreshments. Residents' lounge, conservatory breakfast room. Individual tables.

**open** All year
**bedrooms** 1 double, 2 twin, 1 family
**bathrooms** All en suite
**payment** Credit/debit cards, cash/cheques

Room 📺 ♿ 🕴  General ☺1 ♟ P ✗ 🏠 🖥 ❄ 🐾  Leisure ∪ ♪ ↑ 🚲 🏛

## MORETON-IN-MARSH, Gloucestershire Map ref 2B1

★★★★
**BED & BREAKFAST**

B&B per room per night
d £50.00–£65.00

### Kymalton House

Todenham Road, Moreton-in-Marsh GL56 9NJ  t (01608) 650487  e kymalton@uwclub.net

Family-run, friendly, non-smoking bed and breakfast just three minutes' walk from Moreton High Street. En suite rooms, ample car parking, pleasant gardens.

**open** All year except Christmas and New Year
**bedrooms** 2 double
**bathrooms** All en suite
**payment** Cash/cheques

Room 📺 ♿ 🕴  General P ✗ ❄

## MORETON-IN-MARSH, Gloucestershire Map ref 2B1

★★★
**FARMHOUSE**

B&B per room per night
s £35.00–£40.00
d £55.00–£60.00

### New Farm

Dorn, Moreton-in-Marsh GL56 9NS  t (01608) 650782 & 07811 646320
e catherinerighton@btinternet.com  w newfarmbandb.co.uk

Old Cotswold farmhouse. Lovely large bedrooms, one with four-poster. Breakfast served with hot, crispy bread. Impressive fireplace in dining room. Ideal for touring the Cotswolds.

**open** All year
**bedrooms** 2 double, 1 twin
**bathrooms** All en suite
**payment** Cash/cheques

Room 🖥 📺 ♿ 🕴  General ☺8 ✗ ❄  Leisure 🚲 🏛

## If you have access needs...

Look for the National Accessible Scheme symbols if you have special hearing, visual or mobility needs. An index of accommodation participating in the scheme can be found at the back of this guide.

---

**MORETON-IN-MARSH,** Gloucestershire Map ref 2B1

★★★
FARMHOUSE

B&B per room per night
s £40.00–£60.00
d £60.00–£70.00

## Old Farm

Dorn, Moreton-in-Marsh GL56 9NS  **t** (01608) 650394  **f** (01608) 650394  **e** info@oldfarmdorn.co.uk
**w** oldfarmdorn.co.uk

**open** All year except Christmas
**bedrooms** 2 double, 1 twin
**bathrooms** All en suite
**payment** Credit/debit cards, cash/cheques

'Comfortable beds, friendly hosts and great breakfasts'. A working farm, the house dates back to the 15th century with spacious en suite bedrooms (including four-poster), guest lounge and large gardens. Local breakfast served with home-produced eggs and Old Spot sausages and bacon. Peaceful, rural location but only one mile from Moreton-in-Marsh.

⊕ *1 mile north of Moreton-in-Marsh on A429, turn left for Dorn. Old Farm is 0.25 miles on the left.*

♥ *Discounts available for stays of 3 nights or more.*

Room 🛏 📺 🕯 ⌕  General 🕭 ▥ ♨ P ⅙ 🏕 🍴 👫 ✲  Leisure ∪ ♪ ⚙ 🏛

---

**MORETON-IN-MARSH,** Gloucestershire Map ref 2B1

★★★★
GUEST HOUSE

B&B per room per night
s £40.00
d £55.00–£60.00

## Treetops

London Road, Moreton-in-Marsh GL56 0HE  **t** (01608) 651036  **f** (01608) 651036
**e** treetops1@talk21.com  **w** treetopscotswolds.co.uk

Family guesthouse on the A44, set in 0.5 acres of secluded gardens. Five minutes' walk from the village centre.

**open** All year except Christmas
**bedrooms** 4 double, 2 twin
**bathrooms** All en suite
**payment** Credit/debit cards, cash/cheques

Room 🛏 📺 🕯 ⌕  General 🕭 ▥ ♨ P ⅙ 🍴 ✲  Leisure ♪

---

**MORETONHAMPSTEAD,** Devon Map ref 1C2

★★★★
FARMHOUSE
SILVER AWARD

B&B per room per night
s £30.00–£35.00
d £60.00–£70.00

## Great Sloncombe Farm

Moretonhampstead, Newton Abbot TQ13 8QF  **t** (01647) 440595  **f** (01647) 440595
**e** hmerchant@sloncombe.freeserve.co.uk  **w** greatsloncombefarm.co.uk

13thC farmhouse in a magical Dartmoor valley. Meadows, woodland, wild flowers and animals. Farmhouse breakfast with freshly baked bread. Everything provided for an enjoyable break.

**open** All year
**bedrooms** 2 double, 1 twin
**bathrooms** All en suite
**payment** Cash/cheques

Room 🛏 📺 🕯 ⌕  General 🕭 8 ⅙ 🍴 ✲ 🐾  Leisure ∪ ♪ ▶ ⚙ 🏛

---

**MORETONHAMPSTEAD,** Devon Map ref 1C2

★★★★
FARMHOUSE

B&B per room per night
s £30.00–£40.00
d £60.00–£66.00

## Great Wooston Farm

Moretonhampstead, Newton Abbot TQ13 8QA  **t** (01647) 440367 & 07798 670590  **f** (01647) 440367
**e** info@greatwoostonfarm.com  **w** greatwoostonfarm.com

Great Wooston is a peaceful haven with views across the moor and walks nearby. Two rooms en suite, one with four-poster. Excellent breakfast. Quality accommodation.

**open** All year
**bedrooms** 2 double, 1 twin
**bathrooms** 2 en suite, 1 private
**payment** Credit/debit cards, cash/cheques

Room 🛏 📺 🕯 ⌕  General 🕭 8 P ⅙ 🏕 🍴 ✲  Leisure ∪ ♪

---

## Place index

If you know where you want to stay, the index at the back of the guide will give you the page number listing accommodation in your chosen town, city or village. Check out the other useful indexes too.

## NETHER STOWEY, Somerset Map ref 1D1

★★★★★
**GUEST ACCOMMODATION**
**SILVER AWARD**

B&B per room per night
s £42.00–£92.00
d £104.00–£142.00
Evening meal per person
£16.00–£24.00

# Castle of Comfort Country House

Dodington, Nether Stowey, Bridgwater TA5 1LE  **t** (01278) 741264  **f** (01278) 741144
**e** reception@castle-of-comfort.co.uk  **w** castle-of-comfort.co.uk

16thC country house and restaurant nestling in the Quantock Hills with four acres of grounds. Luxurious accommodation of the highest standard.

**open** All year except Christmas and New Year
**bedrooms** 3 double, 1 twin, 1 single, 1 family
**bathrooms** All en suite
**payment** Credit/debit cards, cash/cheques

Room 🛋🖨📞📺♿🍵  General 🐕🗄🚭♿🅿🍴🍽✕🏊🎱✿🐾  Leisure ⚓♨🎣🚴🐎

## NEWENT, Gloucestershire Map ref 2B1

★★★
**INN**

B&B per room per night
s £30.00–£40.00
d £40.00–£50.00
Evening meal per person
£6.00–£12.00

# The George

Church Street, Newent GL18 1PU  **t** (01531) 820203  **f** (01531) 822392
**e** enquiries@georgehotel.uk.com  **w** georgehotel.uk.com

**open** All year
**bedrooms** 2 double, 5 twin, 2 family
**bathrooms** 6 en suite, 3 private
**payment** Credit/debit cards, cash/cheques

A 17thC coaching house in Newent town centre. Family-run offering bed and breakfast, lunches and evening meal in the bar or restaurant.

Room 📺♿  General 🐕🗄🚭♿🅿🍴✕🏊🎱✿🐾  Leisure ⚓🎣🐎🚴🐎

## NEWQUAY, Cornwall Map ref 1B2

★★
**GUEST ACCOMMODATION**

B&B per room per night
s Min £22.00
d Min £44.00

# Chichester Interest Holidays

14 Bay View Terrace, Newquay TR7 2LR  **t** (01637) 874216  **e** sheila.harper@virgin.net
**w** http://freespace.virgin.net/sheila.harper

Comfortable, licensed, convenient for shops, beaches and gardens. Showers in most bedrooms, many extras. Walking, mineral collecting, archaeology and Cornish Heritage holidays in spring and autumn. Open March to October.

**bedrooms** 3 double, 2 twin, 1 single, 1 family
**payment** Cash/cheques

Room ♿  General 🐕2🅿🍴🏊🎱♿🖥  Leisure 🐎

## NEWQUAY, Cornwall Map ref 1B2

★★★★
**GUEST ACCOMMODATION**

B&B per room per night
s £30.00–£60.00
d £60.00–£85.00

# St Andrews

Island Crescent, Newquay TR7 1DZ  **t** (01637) 873556  **e** enquiries@standrewsnewquay.co.uk
**w** standrewsnewquay.co.uk

St Andrews is a family-run, seafront hotel with magnificent views of Towan Beach, the harbour and Newquay's famous island.

**open** All year except Christmas and New Year
**bedrooms** 6 double, 1 twin, 1 family
**bathrooms** All en suite
**payment** Credit/debit cards, cash/cheques

Room 📺♿🍵  General 🐕🗄🚭🏊✿🐾  Leisure 🎣

## Out and about

For ideas on places to visit, see the beginning of this regional section or go online at enjoyengland.com.

## NEWQUAY, Cornwall Map ref 1B2

★★★
**BED & BREAKFAST**

B&B per room per night
s £35.00–£40.00
d £50.00–£70.00

# Surfside B&B

35 Mount Wise, Newquay TR7 2BH  t (01637) 872707 & 07813 330609
e surfsidehotel@btconnect.com  w surfsidenewquay.co.uk

All en suite accommodation, car park, close to town, beaches, restaurants, clubs and bars. Small groups by prior arrangement only. No stag parties.

**open** All year except Christmas
**bedrooms** 4 double, 4 twin, 1 family
**bathrooms** All en suite
**payment** Credit/debit cards, cash/cheques

Room TV 📞  General ⛱ ♿ P ✂ 🍴 ✿  Leisure ✎ ∪ ▶ 🚲 🛶

## OKEHAMPTON, Devon Map ref 1C2

★★★★
**FARMHOUSE**

B&B per room per night
s £30.00–£32.00
d £52.00–£56.00

# Week Farm Country Holidays

Bridestowe, Okehampton EX20 4HZ  t (01837) 861221  f (01837) 861221
e accom@weekfarmonline.com  w weekfarmonline.com

**open** All year except Christmas
**bedrooms** 3 double, 1 twin, 1 family
**bathrooms** All en suite
**payment** Credit/debit cards, cash/cheques

200-acre beef and sheep farm. A warm welcome awaits at this homely 17thC farmhouse in Devonshire countryside and six miles from Okehampton. Three coarse-fishing lakes. Good home cooking assured and every comfort. Ideal touring base Dartmoor and coasts, walking, cycling, pony-trekking, fishing. Outdoor heated swimming pool. Cream tea on arrival. Come and spoil yourselves.

⊕ *Pass Okehampton. Leave A30 Sourton Cross. Follow sign towards Bridestowe. Tescott Way and Week, turn right. End of three-lane traffic, follow signs to Week.*

♥ *Fishing weekend breaks. 3 well-stocked coarse-fishing lakes, something for the whole family.*

Room 🛏 TV ☕ 📞  General ⛱ 🏞 ♿ P ✂ 🍴 🛍 ✿ 🐴  Leisure ✎ ∪ ▶ 🚲 🛶

## PADSTOW, Cornwall Map ref 1B2

★★★★
**BED & BREAKFAST**

B&B per room per night
d £70.00–£80.00

# Garslade Guest House

52 Church Street, Padstow PL28 8BG  t (01841) 533804  f (01841) 533804
e garsladeguest@btconnect.com  w garslade.com

High standard bed and breakfast accommodation with en suite bedrooms, including one four-poster, in the old part of Padstow.

**open** All year except Christmas and New Year
**bedrooms** 2 double
**bathrooms** All en suite
**payment** Cash/cheques

Room 📺 TV ☕ 📞  General ⛱ 🏞 ✂ 🍴  Leisure ∪ ✎ 🚲

# Discover Britain's heritage

Discover the history and beauty of over 250 of Britain's best-known historic houses, castles, gardens and small manor houses. You can purchase Britain's Historic Houses and Gardens – Guide and Map from good bookshops and online at visitbritaindirect.com.

---

**PADSTOW,** Cornwall Map ref 1B2

★★★★
**BED & BREAKFAST**

B&B per room per night
s £40.00–£50.00
d £60.00–£80.00

# Pendeen House

28 Dennis Road, Padstow PL28 8DE  t (01841) 532 724  e enquire@pendeenhousepadstow.co.uk
w pendeenhousepadstow.co.uk

**open** All year except Christmas
**bedrooms** 3 double, 1 single, 1 family
**bathrooms** All en suite
**payment** Credit/debit cards, cash/cheques

Pendeen House overlooks Padstow's Camel Estuary with beautiful views to Rock and Daymer Bay. Newly refurbished, Pendeen retains its Edwardian character, complemented by stylish, contemporary decor. Quality bed and breakfast with attention to the details that make your stay special. Just three minutes' walk to Padstow centre with private parking.

⊕ Take the A389 to Padstow. Follow the road into town, bear right into Dennis Road, Pendeen is a short distance on the right.

♥ Winter breaks available; 3 nights for the price of 2, Sun-Thu inclusive. Please mention this guide when booking.

Room 🛁 TV 🐾 ♨  General ☏1 🏛 ⚓ P ⚡ 🍳 🍴 ☀  Leisure ∪ 🚲

---

**PADSTOW,** Cornwall Map ref 1B2

★★★★
**BED & BREAKFAST**

B&B per room per night
s £30.00–£35.00
d £60.00

# Tamarisk

13 Grenville Road, Padstow PL28 8EX  t (01841) 532272

Detached house, large rooms. Ample parking. Countryside views, large garden with patio dining room.

**open** All year
**bedrooms** 1 double
**bathrooms** 1 en suite
**payment** Cash/cheques

Room TV 🐾 ♨  General ☏5 P ⚡ 🍳 ☀  Leisure 🚲 ⛵

---

**PADSTOW,** Cornwall Map ref 1B2

★★★★★
**GUEST ACCOMMODATION
SILVER AWARD**

B&B per room per night
s £57.00–£65.00
d £90.00–£132.00

# Woodlands Country House

Treator, Padstow PL28 8RU  t (01841) 532426  f (01841) 533353  e info@woodlands-padstow.co.uk
w woodlands-padstow.co.uk

**bedrooms** 7 double, 1 twin, 1 family
**bathrooms** All en suite
**payment** Credit/debit cards, cash/cheques, euros

Woodlands Country House: an award-winning, family-run guesthouse, with wonderful views of the North Cornish countryside and coastline. Nine stylish rooms, all en suite, designed for comfort and relaxation. In the morning, our famous Cornish breakfasts. Bed and breakfast with a touch of splendour. Closed festive season and January.

⊕ On the B3276 0.5 miles from Padstow to St Merryn.

♥ Nov-Apr: 3 nights for the price of 2, weekday nights only. Excl Easter, Christmas and January.

Room 🛁 📺 TV 🐾 ♨  General ☏ 🏛 ⚓ P ⚡ 🍳 🍴 🐾 ☀ 🐕  Leisure ∪ ⛵ ► 🚲 ⛵

---

# It's all quality-assessed accommodation

Our commitment to quality involves wide-ranging accommodation assessment. Rating and awards were correct at the time of going to press but may change following a new assessment. Please check at time of booking.

## PAIGNTON, Devon Map ref 1D2

★★★
**GUEST HOUSE**

B&B per room per night
s £21.00–£31.00
d £42.00–£62.00
Evening meal per person
£10.50–£12.00

# Benbows

1 Alta Vista Road, Roundham, Paignton TQ4 6DB  t (01803) 558128
e benbowshotel@btinternet.com  w benbowshotel.co.uk

Attractive, licensed family hotel, near tranquil Roundham Gardens, between Paignton and Goodrington beaches, 120 yards from harbour. Free parking. Children welcome. Near town, bus and train station. We speak French.

**open** All year
**bedrooms** 5 double, 2 twin, 1 single, 2 family
**bathrooms** 4 en suite
**payment** Credit/debit cards, cash/cheques, euros

Room 📺 👤 🕾  General 🛋 🏠 🔥 P 🍽 ✕ 🍴 🎿 🔥 ❄ 🐕  Leisure ✒ 🚲 🏊

## PAIGNTON, Devon Map ref 1D2

★★★★
**GUEST ACCOMMODATION**

B&B per room per night
s £20.00–£25.00
d £40.00–£50.00
Evening meal per person
£5.00–£10.00

# Cliveden

27 Garfield Road, Paignton TQ4 6AX  t (01803) 557461  f (01803) 557461
e ros.mager@btconnect.com  w clivedenguesthouse.co.uk

Family-run guest house, close to all amenities, coach/rail stations, town, theatre, own car park, 100 yds level walk seafront.

**open** All year
**bedrooms** 3 double, 1 twin, 1 single, 1 family
**bathrooms** 4 en suite, 2 private
**payment** Credit/debit cards, cash/cheques

Room 📺 👤 🕾  General 🛋 🏠 P ✕ 🍴 🔥 ❄  Leisure ✒

## PAIGNTON, Devon Map ref 1D2

★★★
**GUEST HOUSE**

B&B per room per night
s £20.00–£23.00
d £44.00–£50.00
Evening meal per person
Min £9.00

# Rockview Guest House

13 Queens Road, Paignton TQ4 6AT  t (01803) 556702  e rockview@blueyonder.co.uk
w rockview.co.uk

Rockview is a clean and friendly, family-run guesthouse within a level, short walk to the seafront, shops and stations.

**open** All year except Christmas
**bedrooms** 3 double, 2 twin, 1 single, 1 family
**bathrooms** 6 en suite, 1 private
**payment** Credit/debit cards, cash/cheques

Room 🛏 📺 👤 🕾  General 🛋 2 ✕ 🔥 ❄

## PAIGNTON, Devon Map ref 1D2

★★★★
**GUEST ACCOMMODATION**

B&B per room per night
s £25.00–£30.00
d £50.00–£60.00
Evening meal per person
£15.00

# Sonachan House

35 St Andrews Road, Paignton TQ4 6HA  t (01803) 558021  f (01803) 559233
e info@sonachan.co.uk  w sonachan.co.uk

**open** All year
**bedrooms** 3 double, 2 twin, 2 single, 2 family, 1 suite
**bathrooms** 9 en suite, 1 private
**payment** Credit/debit cards, cash/cheques

Small, friendly, family-run, non-smoking, licensed guesthouse. Ideally situated in the heart of the English Riviera. Close to the many attractions of Paignton including beach, pier, harbour and green. Goodrington beach, Quaywest Water Park and the steam railway are also all within walking distance.

⊕ *From Esplanade Road along the seafront towards harbour, turn right at the roundabout into Sands Road then second left into St Andrews Road.*

Room 🛏 📺 👤 🕾  General 🛋 🏠 🔥 P 🔥 🍽 ✕ 🍴 🔥 ❄

## Rest assured

All accommodation in this guide has been rated, or is awaiting assessment, by a professional assessor.

## PAR, Cornwall Map ref 1B3

★★★★
**BED & BREAKFAST**

B&B per room per night
s £35.00–£45.00
d £50.00–£70.00

# Reynards Rest

The Mount, Par, St Austell PL24 2BZ **t** (01726) 815770 **e** carol@reynardsrest.co.uk
**w** reynardsrest.co.uk

A warm welcome and excellent breakfast await you at this comfortable and very private non-smoking bed and breakfast on the Cornish coast, near South West Coastal Path and Eden Project.

**open** All year
**bedrooms** 1 double, 1 twin
**bathrooms** 1 en suite, 1 private
**payment** Cash/cheques, euros

Room ⚒ TV 🖤 ⏱ General ⌂ 12 P ⅙ ✿ Leisure ∪ ♪

## PAR, Cornwall Map ref 1B3

★★★★
**INN**

B&B per room per night
s £35.00–£40.00
d £60.00–£65.00
Evening meal per person
£8.50–£15.00

# The Royal Inn

66 Eastcliffe Road, Par PL24 2AJ **t** (01726) 815601 **f** (01726) 816415 **e** info@royal-inn.co.uk
**w** royal-inn.co.uk

Completely refurbished in 2003, The Royal offers excellent en suite accommodation at an affordable price. Four miles from Eden, close to bus and rail links, licensed bar and restaurant on site.

**open** All year except Christmas and New Year
**bedrooms** 4 double, 9 twin, 1 family, 3 suites
**bathrooms** All en suite
**payment** Credit/debit cards, cash/cheques

Room ⚒ 🛏 📞 TV 🖤 ⏱ General ⌂ ▥ ⚱ P ⅙ ♟ 📺 ⚗ ✿ Leisure ♪ ▶

## PENSFORD, Somerset Map ref 2A2

★★
**GUEST ACCOMMODATION**

B&B per room per night
s £25.00–£30.00
d £50.00–£60.00

# Green Acres

Stanton Wick, Pensford, Bristol BS39 4BX **t** (01761) 490397 **f** (01761) 490397

A friendly welcome awaits you in a peaceful setting, off the A37/A368. Relax and enjoy panoramic views across Chew Valley to Dundry Hills.

**open** All year
**bedrooms** 1 double, 1 twin, 2 single, 1 family
**bathrooms** 1 en suite
**payment** Cash/cheques, euros

Room ⚒ TV 🖤 ⏱ General ⌂ ▥ P ⅙ 📺 ⚗ ▣ ✿ ⚘ Leisure ♪ 🏛

## PENZANCE, Cornwall Map ref 1A3

★★★★
**FARMHOUSE**

B&B per room per night
d £56.00–£75.00

# Castallack Farm

Castallack, Lamorna, Penzance TR19 6NL **t** (01736) 731969 **e** info@castallackfarm.co.uk
**w** castallackfarm.co.uk

Relax and enjoy our lovely tranquil countryside location between Lamorna Cove and the fishing village of Mousehole. Cosy en suite ground-floor rooms and romantic four-poster suite overlook our lovely courtyard.

**open** All year
**bedrooms** 1 double, 1 twin, 1 suite
**bathrooms** All en suite
**payment** Credit/debit cards, cash/cheques, euros

Room ⚒ 🛏 TV 🖤 ⏱ General ⌂ 7 P ⅙ 📺 ▣ ✿ ⚘ Leisure ∪ ♪ ▶ ⚲ 🏛

## PENZANCE, Cornwall Map ref 1A3

★★★
**GUEST ACCOMMODATION**

B&B per room per night
s £26.00–£29.00
d £52.00–£56.00
Evening meal per person
Min £14.50

# Cornerways Guest House

5 Leskinnick Street, Penzance TR18 2HA **t** (01736) 364645 **f** (01736) 364645
**e** enquiries@cornerways-penzance.co.uk **w** penzance.co.uk/cornerways

Cornerways is an attractively decorated townhouse, four minutes from car parks, bus and railway stations. We offer freshly cooked breakfast to order, and evening meal is optional. Ideal as a base for touring Cornwall.

**open** All year except Christmas
**bedrooms** 1 double, 1 twin, 2 single
**bathrooms** All en suite
**payment** Credit/debit cards, cash/cheques

Room TV 🖤 ⏱ General ⌂ ⅙ ✗ ✿ Leisure ∪ ♪ ⚲ 🏛

## One to five stars

More stars means higher quality accommodation plus a greater range of facilities and services.

## PENZANCE, Cornwall Map ref 1A3

★★★★
GUEST ACCOMMODATION

B&B per room per night
s £20.00–£36.00
d £40.00–£78.00

# Glencree House

2 Mennaye Road, Penzance TR18 4NG  t (01736) 362026  f (01736) 362026
e stay@glencreehouse.co.uk  w glencreehouse.co.uk

Elegant, stylish and friendly Victorian guesthouse.
Sea views and delicious breakfasts. Superb for
exploring Cornwall at any time of year.

**open** All year except Christmas
**bedrooms** 4 double, 1 twin, 2 single, 1 family
**bathrooms** 6 en suite
**payment** Credit/debit cards, cash/cheques

Room 🏠 TV 👤 🍵   General 👜 🏢 ♨ ⅟ 🍽 🛏 🐾   Leisure ♪ 🚲 🏛

## PENZANCE, Cornwall Map ref 1A3

★★★
BED & BREAKFAST

B&B per room per night
s £52.00
d £60.00

# Harbour Heights Bed and Breakfast

Boase Street, Newlyn, Penzance TR18 5JE  t (01736) 350976  e anneofnewlyn@aol.com
w harbour-heights.co.uk

**open** All year except Christmas and New Year
**bedrooms** 2 double, 1 twin
**payment** Credit/debit cards, cash/cheques

In an old and quaint 17thC cobbled street and
situated only 25 metres from Newlyn Harbour, the
property enjoys views over Mount's Bay and down
the Lizard Peninsula. Visit the areas many beautiful
coves and beaches. Locally sourced produce and
extensive breakfast menu. Comfortable rooms and
warm welcome.

⊕ *A30 through Cornwall to Penzance. Follow promenade to
Newlyn. At crossroads turn left signposted Mousehole.
After sharp left bend, take 2nd right – Boase street, (25m
from harbour).*

♥ *Book 3 nights in a row – get 4th free!*

Room TV 👤 🍵   General 👜12 P ♨ ✕ 🍽 🛏 🐾 🖥   Leisure ♪ 🚲 🏛

## PENZANCE, Cornwall Map ref 1A3

★★★
GUEST ACCOMMODATION

B&B per room per night
s £20.00–£27.00
d £40.00–£54.00

# Lynwood Guest House

Morrab Road, Penzance TR18 4EX  t (01736) 365871  f (01736) 365871  e lynwoodpz@aol.com
w lynwood-guesthouse.co.uk

**open** All year
**bedrooms** 2 double, 1 twin, 2 single, 2 family
**bathrooms** 4 en suite, 1 private
**payment** Credit/debit cards, cash/cheques, euros

Lynwood is a family-run, Victorian guesthouse
offering a warm welcome. Recommended for
cleanliness and good food. Ideal base for touring all
the far South West attractions. For getting around
there is a good local bus/train service. Or, for
something different, Harry Safari tours departing
Lynwood or Penzance tourist office.

⊕ *From A30 Penzance. Follow directions for seafront, turn
right into Morrab Road, directly before Queens Hotel,
200yds on the left.*

Room TV 👤 🍵   General 👜5 ✁ 🍽 🛏 🐾   Leisure ♪ 🚲

## Looking for a little luxury

Gold and Silver Awards are given to establishments achieving the highest levels of
quality and service. There's more information at the front of the guide, and an index to
all accommodation achieving these awards at the back.

## PENZANCE, Cornwall Map ref 1A3

★★★
**FARMHOUSE**

B&B per room per night
**s** Min £27.00
**d** Min £54.00
Evening meal per person
Min £12.00

# Menwidden Farm

Ludgvan, Penzance TR20 8BN **t** (01736) 740415 **e** cora@menwidden.freeserve.co.uk

**bedrooms** 4 double, 1 twin
**bathrooms** 3 en suite
**payment** Cash/cheques

Quiet farmhouse set in countryside with views towards St Michael's Mount. Centrally situated in West Cornwall. Land's End, St Ives, Lizard Peninsula and Penzance Heliport all within easy reach. Good home-cooking. Open March to October.

⊕ Turn towards Ludgvan at Crowlas crossroads. 3rd turning right signposted Vellanoweth. Last farm on left, 1 mile up this road.

Room ⚲  General P ⚙ ✕ 🛏 ❄ 🐾  Leisure ∪ ♪

## PENZANCE, Cornwall Map ref 1A3

★★★
**GUEST HOUSE**

B&B per room per night
**s** £29.00–£38.00
**d** £50.00–£56.00

# Penrose Guest House

8 Penrose Terrace, Penzance TR18 2HQ **t** (01736) 362782 **e** enquiries@penrosegsthse.co.uk
**w** penrosegsthse.co.uk

**open** All year except Christmas
**bedrooms** 1 double, 1 twin, 1 family
**bathrooms** 2 en suite, 1 private
**payment** Credit/debit cards, cash/cheques

Marc and Anne offer a warm welcome to their small, friendly, family-run guesthouse. We offer quality en suite accommodation and good food. Situated close to the bus and train stations, town centre, heliport and harbour. The perfect base for exploring the beauty of West Cornwall.

⊕ Follow signs for town centre. Turn right just before train station building, into Penrose Terrace. We are 30m up on the right.

♥ 3 nights for the price of 2 Nov-Feb. Discounts for stays of 7 nights or more.

Room 📺 ⚲ 🍵  General 5 ⚙ 🏓 🔥 ❄  Leisure ∪ ♪ ► 🚴

## PENZANCE, Cornwall Map ref 1A3

★★★★
**FARMHOUSE**

B&B per room per night
**s** £35.00–£40.00
**d** £60.00–£70.00

# Rose Farm

Chyenhal, Buryas Bridge, Penzance TR19 6AN **t** (01736) 731808 **f** (01736) 731808
**e** lally@rosefarmcornwall.co.uk

Twenty-five-acre farm with many animals, including livestock and horses. Near beaches and shops. Land's End seven miles, Mousehole two miles. Lovely walks. Four-poster bed available. Cosy and relaxing.

**open** All year except Christmas
**bedrooms** 2 double, 1 family
**bathrooms** All en suite
**payment** Credit/debit cards, cash/cheques

Room 🛁 📻 📺 ⚲ 🍵  General 🚗 🏓 🅿 🛏 ❄  Leisure ♪ 🚴 ⛰

## Town, country or coast

The entertainment, shopping and innovative attractions of the big cities, the magnificent vistas of the countryside or the relaxing and refreshing coast – this guide will help you find what you're looking for.

## PENZANCE, Cornwall Map ref 1A3

★★★
**GUEST HOUSE**

B&B per room per night
s Min £21.00
d £36.00–£50.00

# Treventon

Alexandra Place, Penzance TR18 4NE  t (01736) 363521  f (01736) 361873

**bedrooms** 3 double, 2 twin, 1 single, 1 family
**bathrooms** 4 en suite
**payment** Credit/debit cards, cash/cheques

This elegant Victorian house, once the home of a very influential gentleman, is situated at the foot of a tree-lined avenue approximately 200m from the sea. The house bears testament to the attention given to it over the past 100 years. Open March to October.

Room 📺 🦽  General ☺5

## PENZANCE, Cornwall Map ref 1A3

Rating Applied For
**GUEST HOUSE**

B&B per room per night
s £26.00–£34.00
d £48.00–£68.00

# Woodstock Guest House

29 Morrab Road, Penzance TR18 4EZ  t (01736) 369049  f (01736) 369049
e info@woodstockguesthouse.co.uk  w woodstockguesthouse.co.uk

**open** All year except Christmas and New Year
**bedrooms** 2 double, 1 twin, 3 single, 1 family
**bathrooms** 5 en suite
**payment** Credit/debit cards, cash/cheques

David and Sandra welcome you to our elegant, family-run Victorian town house offering high standards of comfort, cleanliness and good food. Ideally situated for visiting the quaint harbours, sandy beaches and beautiful gardens nearby. Also close are Penlee Art Gallery and Minack Theatre. Families will enjoy Flambards and Goonhilly.

⊕ *A30 into Penzance. Take left-hand lane past railway station and car park along seafront. Turn right at Queen's Hotel. Woodstock is 200m on right.*

♥ *Bank Holiday breaks from £85-£100pp, 3 nights minimum. Honeymoon and anniversary stays – please ring for details.*

Room 🛏 🖨 📺 🦽 🍽  General ☺5 ⚡ 🍴  Leisure ✏ 🚲 🏊

## PENZANCE, Cornwall Map ref 1A3

★★★
**GUEST ACCOMMODATION**

B&B per room per night
d £46.00–£56.00

# Wymering

Regent Square, Penzance TR18 4BG  t (01736) 362126  e pam@wymering.com  w wymering.com

Small, select guesthouse situated in a peaceful Regency square, just off the beach. Town centre, promenade, bathing pool, bus, coach and train station all nearby.

**open** All year
**bedrooms** 1 double, 1 twin, 1 family, 2 suites
**bathrooms** 2 en suite, 3 private
**payment** Credit/debit cards, cash/cheques

Room 🛏 📺 🦽 🍽  General ☺ ✿

## PERRANPORTH, Cornwall Map ref 1B2

★★★★
**GUEST HOUSE**

B&B per room per night
s £33.00–£35.00
d £33.00–£38.00
Evening meal per person
£10.50–£15.00

# Tides Reach

Ponsmere Road, Perranporth TR6 0BW  t (01872) 572188  f (01872) 572188
e jandf.boyle@virgin.net  w tidesreachhotel.com

Charming, older style, family-run hotel close to shops and one minute from the beach. Dinner, bed and breakfast, and licensed bar. Private garden.

**open** All year except Christmas and New Year
**bedrooms** 5 double, 2 twin, 2 single, 1 family
**bathrooms** 9 en suite, 1 private
**payment** Credit/debit cards, cash/cheques, euros

Room 🛏 📺 🦽 🍽  General ☺5 P ⚡ 🍷 🍴 🖼 ▣ ✿  Leisure ∪ ✏ ⚓ 🏊

## PERRANPORTH, Cornwall Map ref 1B2

★ ★ ★ ★
INN

B&B per room per night
s £48.00–£55.00
d £58.00–£65.00
Evening meal per person
£6.95–£13.95

# The Whitehouse Inn & Luxury Lodge

Penhallow, Nr Truro, St Agnes TR4 9LQ  t (01872) 573306  e whitehouseinn@btconnect.com
w whitehousecornwall.co.uk

Extremely high quality en suite accommodation comprising family, disabled, double, single, twin rooms. Facilities include play areas, bar and restaurant.

**open** All year
**bedrooms** 6 double, 2 twin, 3 family, 1 suite
**bathrooms** All en suite
**payment** Credit/debit cards

Room 🛏 📞 📺 🌡  General 🛋 🏛 🔥 P ⚍ ✕ 🍽 🅿 🈺 ✿  Leisure ● ⚓ ➤

## PIDDLETRENTHIDE, Dorset Map ref 2B3

★ ★ ★ ★
INN

B&B per room per night
s £52.50–£70.00
d £74.00–£120.00
Evening meal per person
£12.00–£22.00

# The Poachers Inn

Piddletrenthide, Dorchester DT2 7QX  t (01300) 348358  f (01300) 348153
e thepoachersinn@piddletrenthide.fsbusiness.co.uk  w thepoachersinn.co.uk

**open** All year
**bedrooms** 8 double, 8 twin, 3 family, 2 suites
**bathrooms** All en suite
**payment** Credit/debit cards, cash/cheques

Set in the heart of the beautiful Piddle Valley, the family-run Poachers Inn has an excellent choice of food in its 17thC restaurant and riverside garden. All bedrooms are en suite and tastefully furnished with the very-best-quality fixtures and fittings. Colour TV, tea- and coffee-making facilities, shaving point, hairdryer, radio and direct-dial telephones.

⊕ *From Dorchester head north on B3143 (Piddletrenthide and Sturminster Newton). The Poachers Inn is approx 7 miles from Dorchester on the north side of Piddletrenthide.*

Room 🛏 🛋 📞 📺 🌡 🍷  General 🛋 🏛 🔥 P ⚍ ✕ 🍽 🅿 🈺 ✿ 🐾  Leisure ⚓ ∪ ⚓ 🏊

## PLYMOUTH, Devon Map ref 1C2

★ ★ ★ ★
GUEST ACCOMMODATION

B&B per room per night
s £30.00–£40.00
d £44.00–£54.00

# Athenaeum Lodge

4 Athenaeum Street, The Hoe, Plymouth PL1 2RQ  t (01752) 665005 & (01752) 670090
f (01752) 665005  e us@athenaeumlodge.com  w athenaeumlodge.com

**open** All year except Christmas and New Year
**bedrooms** 3 double, 2 twin, 1 single, 3 family
**bathrooms** 7 en suite
**payment** Credit/debit cards, cash/cheques

Elegant, Grade II Listed guesthouse, ideally situated on The Hoe. Centrally located for the Barbican, Theatre Royal, Plymouth Pavilions, ferry port and the National Marine Aquarium. The city centre and university are a few minutes' walk. Divers' and sailors' paradise. Excellent, central location for touring Devon and Cornwall. Wi-Fi Internet and free use of computer if required.

⊕ *Follow signs for the city centre, Barbican and Hoe. Pass the Barbican on your left and continue along Notte Street to the Walrus Pub. Turn left.*

Room 🛏 📺 🌡 🍷  General 🛋 5 P ✂ 🍽 🅿  Leisure ⚓ 🏊

# Friendly help and advice

Tourist Information Centres offer friendly help with accommodation and holiday ideas as well as suggestions of places to visit and things to do. You'll find contact details at the beginning of each regional section.

**PLYMOUTH,** Devon Map ref 1C2

★★★★
GUEST ACCOMMODATION

B&B per room per night
s £35.00–£45.00
d £55.00–£70.00

## Berkeleys of St James

4 St James Place East, Plymouth PL1 3AS  **t** (01752) 221654  **f** (01752) 221654
**e** enquiry@onthehoe.co.uk  **w** onthehoe.co.uk

Non-smoking Victorian town house ideally situated for seafront, Barbican, theatre, ferry port and city centre. Flexible accommodation between double/twin/triple. Excellent breakfast serving free-range, organic produce where possible.

**open** All year except Christmas and New Year
**bedrooms** 2 double, 1 twin, 1 single, 1 family
**bathrooms** 4 en suite, 1 private
**payment** Credit/debit cards, cash/cheques

Room 🛏 TV ♿ ⏰  General ☎ ▥ P ⌇ 🍽  Leisure ♨

**PLYMOUTH,** Devon Map ref 1C2

★★★
GUEST HOUSE

B&B per room per night
s £30.00–£40.00
d £45.00–£55.00

## Brittany Guest House

28 Athenaeum Street, The Hoe, Plymouth PL1 2RQ  **t** (01752) 262247
**e** enquiries@brittanyguesthouse.com  **w** brittanyguesthouse.co.uk

Non-smoking, all rooms en suite, some 5ft beds, crisp white linen. Private car park, close to shops, bars, pavilions, seafront. Credit and debit cards taken. Run by resident proprietors.

**open** All year except Christmas and New Year
**bedrooms** 4 double, 2 twin, 2 single, 2 family
**bathrooms** All en suite
**payment** Credit/debit cards, cash/cheques, euros

Room 🛏 TV ♿ ⏰  General ☎3 P ⌇ 🍽

**PLYMOUTH,** Devon Map ref 1C2

★★★★
GUEST HOUSE

B&B per room per night
s £30.00–£45.00
d £45.00–£60.00

## Four Seasons

207 Citadel Road East, Plymouth PL1 2JF  **t** (01752) 223591  **e** bobkatecarter@btconnect.com
**w** fourseasonsguesthouse.co.uk

A non-smoking establishment, the Four Seasons is situated in the centre of an elegant Victorian terrace close to the Hoe and Barbican.

**open** All year
**bedrooms** 5 double, 2 twin
**bathrooms** 5 en suite, 2 private
**payment** Credit/debit cards, cash/cheques

Room 🛏 TV ♿ ⏰  General ☎ ⌇ 🐾 🐕

**PLYMOUTH,** Devon Map ref 1C2

★★★
FARMHOUSE

B&B per room per night
s £22.00–£26.00
d £42.00–£46.00
Evening meal per person
Min £12.00

## Gabber Farm

Gabber Lane, Down Thomas, Plymouth PL9 0AW  **t** (01752) 862269  **f** (01752) 862269
**e** gabberfarm@tiscali.co.uk

A courteous welcome at this farm, near coast and Mount Batten Centre. Lovely walks. Special weekly rates, especially for Senior Citizens and children. Directions provided.

**open** All year
**bedrooms** 1 double, 1 twin, 1 single, 2 family
**bathrooms** 3 en suite
**payment** Credit/debit cards, cash/cheques

Room TV ♿  General ☎ ▥ ⋔ P X 🍽 ▯ ✻  Leisure ⚙

**PLYMOUTH,** Devon Map ref 1C2

★★★
GUEST ACCOMMODATION

B&B per room per night
s £28.00–£40.00
d £40.00–£48.00

## The Moorings Guest House

4 Garden Crescent, West Hoe, Plymouth PL1 3DA  **t** (01752) 250128  **f** (01752) 210219
**e** enquiries@themooringsguesthouseplymouth.com  **w** themooringsguesthouseplymouth.com

Warm and friendly family-run guesthouse with extremely high standards. Situated close to the city centre, Hoe and historic Barbican. Convenient for airport and university.

**open** All year except Christmas
**bedrooms** 2 double, 1 twin, 3 single, 2 family
**bathrooms** 4 en suite
**payment** Credit/debit cards, cash/cheques

Room 🛏 TV ♿ ⏰  General ☎ ▥ ⋔ ⌇ 🍽 ▣ ✻  Leisure ♪

## If you have access needs...

Look for the National Accessible Scheme symbols if you have special hearing, visual or mobility needs.

## PLYMOUTH, Devon Map ref 1C2

**★★**
GUEST HOUSE

B&B per room per night
s £22.50–£30.00
d £40.00–£45.00

# Seymour Guest House

211 Citadel Road East, The Hoe, Plymouth PL1 2JF  t (01752) 667002
e peter@seymourguesthouse.co.uk  w seymourguesthouse.co.uk

A small family-run guest house located opposite Hoe Park and convenient to Barbican, city centre, ferry port and university.

**open** All year except Christmas and New Year
**bedrooms** 2 single, 5 family
**bathrooms** 5 en suite
**payment** Credit/debit cards, cash/cheques

Room   General   Leisure

## POLPERRO, Cornwall Map ref 1C3

**★★★★**
BED & BREAKFAST

B&B per room per night
s £35.00–£50.00
d £55.00–£60.00

# Chyavallon

Landaviddy Lane, Polperro, Looe PL13 2RT  t (01503) 272788  w polperro.org/chyavallon

Born and bred in Polperro, Antony, a local net fisherman, and Petrena, who manages the bed and breakfast, welcome you into their home to enjoy Cornish hospitality at its best.

**open** All year except Christmas
**bedrooms** 1 double, 1 twin
**bathrooms** All en suite
**payment** Cash/cheques, euros

Room   General   Leisure

## POLPERRO, Cornwall Map ref 1C3

**★★★**
INN

B&B per room per night
s £40.00–£45.00
d £60.00–£70.00
Evening meal per person
£6.00–£16.00

# Crumplehorn Inn and Mill

Crumplehorn, Polperro, Looe PL13 2RJ  t (01503) 272348  f (01503) 273148
e host@crumplehorn-inn.co.uk  w crumplehorn-inn.co.uk

**open** All year
**bedrooms** 6 double, 3 twin, 2 family, 8 suites
**bathrooms** All en suite
**payment** Credit/debit cards, cash/cheques

14thC character Cornish inn and mill in quaint, historic fishing village. B&B and self-catering available. En suite, non-smoking rooms with TV, telephone, clock radio and tea and coffee. Local ales and scrumpy. Varied bar menu with daily specials featuring locally caught fish. Pets welcome. Car parking on site.

⊕ *Full directions (via car, train and taxi) available on our website.*

♥ *Winter-break scheme in operation.*

Room   General   Leisure

## POLZEATH, Cornwall Map ref 1B2

**★★★★**
GUEST HOUSE

B&B per room per night
d £58.00–£74.00

# White Heron

Polzeath, Wadebridge PL27 6TJ  t (01208) 863623  e info@whiteheronhotel.co.uk
w whiteheronhotel.co.uk

Family-run, non-smoking, licensed establishment, 500yds from beaches. TV and tea-/coffee-making facilities in bedrooms. All rooms en suite. Open May to October.

**bedrooms** 5 double
**bathrooms** All en suite
**payment** Cash/cheques

Room   General

## Check it out

Information on accommodation listed in this guide has been supplied by proprietors. As changes may occur you should remember to check all relevant details at the time of booking.

**PORLOCK,** Somerset Map ref 1D1

★★★★
**GUEST HOUSE
SILVER AWARD**

B&B per room per night
s  £30.00–£40.00
d  £60.00–£70.00
Evening meal per person
£10.00–£20.00

# Rose Bank Guest House

High Street, Porlock TA24 8PY  **t** (01643) 862728  **f** (01643) 862728
**e** info@rosebankguesthouse.co.uk  **w** rosebankguesthouse.co.uk

Restored Victorian house in the village high
street. Private parking. All rooms en suite. TV,
radio, CD and tea-making facilities. Internet
access. Sea views. Dog friendly. Welcoming
hosts.

**open** All year
**bedrooms** 2 double, 2 twin, 1 single, 1 family
**bathrooms** All en suite
**payment** Credit/debit cards, cash/cheques

Room 📺 ♨ ⓠ   General ♿ 🏚 ♣ P ✕ 🖼 ⟁ ❀ 🕯   Leisure ∪ ⤵ ⟍ 🏠

**PORT ISAAC,** Cornwall Map ref 1B2

★★★★
**INN**

B&B per room per night
s  £75.00–£110.00
d  £95.00–£140.00
Evening meal per person
£12.00–£30.00

# The Slipway

Harbour Front, Port Isaac PL29 3RH  **t** (01208) 880264  **f** (01208) 880408
**e** slipway@portisaachotel.com  **w** portisaachotel.com

**open** All year except Christmas
**bedrooms** 7 double, 1 twin, 2 suites
**bathrooms** All en suite
**payment** Credit/debit cards, cash/cheques, euros

The Slipway Hotel is a small, friendly, family-run
hotel of great character. Bedrooms are stylishly
furnished and many overlook the harbour. Guests
can combine their stay with the delights of one of the
area's finest seafood restaurants. Menus are highly
imaginative, concentrating on the use of the best,
locally sourced fresh fish, meat and produce.

⊕ *In Port Isaac pass Co-op on right. 100m, turn left down
Back Hill and follow road to harbour (narrow streets) where
you will find the Slipway.*

♥ *Special out-of-season breaks available – DB&B and
3 nights' B&B for the price of 2.*

Room ☎ 📺 ♨ ⓠ   General ♿ 🏚 ♣ ✂ 🍷 ✕ 🖼 🛗 ❀   Leisure ∪ ⤵ ⟍ ⚙

**PORTLAND,** Dorset Map ref 2B3

★★
**GUEST ACCOMMODATION**

B&B per room per night
s  £25.00–£45.00
d  £50.00–£70.00

# Alessandria House

71 Wakeham Easton, Portland DT5 1HW  **t** (01305) 822270  **f** (01305) 820561

**open** All year
**bedrooms** 6 double, 2 twin, 3 single, 4 family
**bathrooms** 11 en suite, 1 private
**payment** Credit/debit cards, cash/cheques, euros

Friendly, good old-fashioned personal service and
good value. Under the same management for 17
years, highly commended by our guests. With 15
bedrooms, two on the ground floor, and four
spacious en suite family rooms. Some rooms with sea
view. Quiet, desirable location. Vegetarians catered
for. Free parking.

Room ♿ 📺 ♨   General ♿ 🏚 ♣ P ✂ 🖼 🛗 ⟁ ▣ 🕯   Leisure ∪ ⤵ 🏠

## Ancient and modern

Experience timeless favourites or discover the latest must-sees. Whatever your choice,
be inspired by the places of interest and events highlighted for each region.

---

**PORTLAND,** Dorset Map ref 2B3

★★★

**BED & BREAKFAST**

B&B per room per night
d Min £54.00

## Brackenbury House

Fortuneswell, Portland DT5 1LP  t (01305) 826509  e enquiries@brackenburyhouse.co.uk
w brackenburyhouse.co.uk

Comfortable and friendly, family-run, converted manse, close to shops and eating places. Great area for sailing, diving, fishing, and also for walkers, cyclists and bird/butterfly spotters.

**open** All year except Christmas
**bedrooms** 3 double, 2 twin
**bathrooms** 3 en suite
**payment** Cash/cheques

Room 📺 ⚿  General ⛄ ▥ ☆ ⚲ ⛺ 🐕  Leisure ✈

---

**REDRUTH,** Cornwall Map ref 1B3

★★★★

**GUEST HOUSE**

B&B per room per night
s Min £38.00
d Min £56.00
Evening meal per person
£12.50–£15.00

## Goonearl Cottage

Wheal Rose, Scorrier, Redruth TR16 5DF  t (01209) 891571  f (01209) 891916
e goonearl@onetel.com  w goonearlcottage.com

**open** All year
**bedrooms** 4 double, 1 twin, 1 family, 1 suite
**bathrooms** 5 en suite, 2 private
**payment** Credit/debit cards, cash/cheques, euros

Family-run guesthouse; beaches close by; easy access to the whole of Cornwall; superb English breakfast.

⊕ Leave the A30 at the Scorrier/A3047 sign. Turn right at The Plume of Feathers, first left into Wheal Rose.

Room 🛏 📺 ⚿ ☏  General ⛄ ▥ ☆ P ⚑ ✕ ⛺ ♨ ❀  Leisure ∪ ✈ ► ⛳ 🏛

---

**RUAN HIGH LANES,** Cornwall Map ref 1B3

★★★★

**FARMHOUSE**

B&B per room per night
d £50.00–£60.00

## New Gonitor Farm

Ruan High Lanes, Truro TR2 5LE  t (01872) 501345  f (01872) 501345
e rosemary@newgonitorfarm.wanadoo.co.uk

Farmhouse B&B, rural location. Close to Eden and Heligan. Full English breakfast, tea and coffee, TV in all rooms.

**open** All year except Christmas and New Year
**bedrooms** 1 double, 1 twin
**bathrooms** All en suite
**payment** Cash/cheques

Room 📺 ⚿ ☏  General ⛄ ▥ ☆ P ⚲ ❀  Leisure ∪ ✈ 🏛

---

**RUAN HIGH LANES,** Cornwall Map ref 1B3

★★★

**FARMHOUSE**

B&B per room per night
s £26.00–£38.00
d £52.00–£56.00

## Trenona Farm Holidays

Ruan High Lanes, Truro TR2 5JS  t (01872) 501339  f (01872) 501253
e info@trenonafarmholidays.co.uk  w trenonafarmholidays.co.uk

**bedrooms** 1 double, 3 family
**bathrooms** 3 en suite, 1 private
**payment** Credit/debit cards, cash/cheques

Enjoy a warm welcome in our Victorian farmhouse on a working farm on the beautiful Roseland Peninsula. Our guest bedrooms have en suite or private bathrooms, and we welcome children and pets. Public footpaths lead to Veryan and the south coast (three miles). Open between March and November.

⊕ A390 to Truro. At Hewaswater take B3287 to Tregony then A3078 to St Mawes at Tregony Bridge. After 2 miles, pass Esso garage. 2nd farm on left-hand side.

♥ Discounts for stays of 4 or more nights for children and for family rooms.

Room 📺 ⚿ ☏  General ⛄ ▥ ☆ P ⚲ ♨ ❀ 🐕  Leisure ∪

---

## RUAN MINOR, Cornwall Map ref 1B3

★★★★
**BED & BREAKFAST**

B&B per room per night
d £70.00

# Skyber

Treal, Ruan Minor, Helston TR12 7LS  t (01326) 290684

A beautifully converted barn complex set within a hamlet of similar properties. The property boasts a large farmhouse-style kitchen and diner with Rayburn oven.

**open** All year except Christmas
**bedrooms** 1 double
**bathrooms** 1 private
**payment** Cash/cheques

Room 🛏 📺 ✇ 🔌  General ♿ 🏠 P ☎ ✿  Leisure ∪ 🎣 🏌 🚲 ⛵

## RUDFORD, Gloucestershire Map ref 2B1

★★★★
**GUEST ACCOMMODATION**

B&B per room per night
s Min £35.00
d Min £55.00
Evening meal per person
Min £10.00

# The Dark Barn Cottages

Barbers Bridge, Rudford, Gloucester GL2 8DX  t (01452) 790412  f (01452) 790145
e info@barbersbridge.co.uk  w barbersbridge.co.uk

**open** All year except Christmas and New Year
**bedrooms** 15 double, 1 twin, 1 family
**bathrooms** All en suite
**payment** Credit/debit cards, cash/cheques

Four-hundred-year-old, Grade II Listed buildings with adjacent cottages. In a rural setting, equidistant from Gloucester and Newent. Swimming pool and fitness centre, clay-pigeon shooting every other weekend.

⊕ From M50 jct 2, south on B4215 towards Gloucester, approx 6 miles.

Room 🛏 📺 ✇  General ♿ 🏠 P ✂ ⚑ ✗ 🍴 ♨ ✿ 🐾  Leisure 🎣 ∪ 🎣 🏌 ⛵

## ST AGNES, Cornwall Map ref 1B3

★★
**GUEST HOUSE**

B&B per room per night
s £22.50–£42.50
d £35.00–£55.00
Evening meal per person
Min £15.00

# Penkerris

Penwinnick Road, St Agnes TR5 0PA  t (01872) 552262  f (01872) 552262  e info@penkerris.co.uk
w penkerris.co.uk

**open** All year
**bedrooms** 3 double, 1 twin, 3 family
**bathrooms** 3 en suite
**payment** Credit/debit cards, cash/cheques, euros

Penkerris is a creeper-clad Edwardian residence with a lawned garden and parking. A 'home from home' offering real food, comfortable bedrooms with all facilities (three en suite) and cosy lounge (log fires in winter). Licensed. Dramatic cliff walks and three really beautiful beaches one kilometre away. Excellent surfing, riding and gliding nearby.

⊕ Easy to find on B3277 road from Chiverton roundabout on A30, just by the village sign.

Room 📺 ✇  General ♿ 🏠 P ⚑ ✗ 🍴 ♨ ⚲ ✿ 🐾  Leisure ∪ 🏌 🚲 ⛵

# Accessible needs?

If you have special hearing, visual or mobility needs, there's an index of National Accessible Scheme participants featured in this guide. For more accessible accommodation buy a copy of Easy Access Britain available online at visitbritaindirect.com.

**ST AUSTELL,** Cornwall Map ref 1B3

★★★★★
**GUEST ACCOMMODATION
GOLD AWARD**

# Anchorage House

Nettles Corner, Boscundle, St Austell PL25 3RH  **t** (01726) 814071  **e** info@anchoragehouse.co.uk
**w** anchoragehouse.co.uk

B&B per room per night
**s** £85.00–£125.00
**d** £110.00–£150.00
Evening meal per person
£29.00–£35.00

**bedrooms** 1 double, 2 suites
**bathrooms** All en suite
**payment** Credit/debit cards, cash/cheques

A luxury, national-award-winning, Georgian-style lodge with indoor swimming complex located in the centre of Cornwall and only five minutes from the Eden Project and Carlyon Bay beach. Open March to December.

⊕ *2 miles east of St Austell off the A390. Across from the St. Austell Garden Centre, turn left and then immediately left again into the drive leading to the courtyard.*

Room 📺 ♿ 🍽  General 👁16 P ✂ ✕ 🍴 🏬 ⊡ ✿  Leisure ☂ ♣ ▶ 🏊

**ST AUSTELL,** Cornwall Map ref 1B3

★★★★
**BED & BREAKFAST**

# Greenbank

39 Southbourne Road, St Austell PL25 4RT  **t** (01726) 73326  **f** (01726) 73326
**e** greenbank@cornish-riviera.co.uk  **w** cornish-riviera.co.uk/greenbank.htm

B&B per room per night
**s** £30.00–£35.00
**d** £45.00–£55.00

Southerly aspect character bungalow with country views, offering comfortable rooms, a hearty breakfast and local hospitality. Close to rail/coach, town centre, beaches. Central for Eden, Heligan, touring.

**open** All year except Christmas and New Year
**bedrooms** 1 double, 1 twin
**bathrooms** 1 en suite, 1 private
**payment** Cash/cheques, euros

Room 🔑 📺 ♿ 🍽  General 👁10 P ✂ 🍴 🏬 ✿  Leisure ∪ ⌐ ▶ 🚲 🏊

**ST AUSTELL,** Cornwall Map ref 1B3

★★★★★
**GUEST ACCOMMODATION
SILVER AWARD**

# Highland Court Lodge

Biscovey Road, Biscovey PL24 2HW  **t** (01726) 813320  **f** (01726) 813320
**e** enquiries@highlandcourt.co.uk  **w** highlandcourt.co.uk

B&B per room per night
**s** £95.00–£145.00
**d** £110.00–£190.00
Evening meal per person
£45.00

**open** All year
**bedrooms** 1 double, 2 twin, 1 family, 1 suite
**bathrooms** All en suite
**payment** Credit/debit cards, cash/cheques, euros

Cornwall Tourism Awards 2006 – Guesthouse/B&B of the Year, Bronze Award. An idyllic, luxurious, family-run country house with stunning views over St Austell Bay, and within walking distance of the Eden Project. Standing in two acres of beautifully landscaped grounds, the lodge has impressively equipped en suite bedrooms, a lounge with deep sofas and a terrace with fine views.

⊕ *From the A30 take the A391 to St Austell. Turn left onto the A390 through St Blazey Gate. Turn right into Biscovey Road. The lodge is 400yds down on the right.*

Room 🔑 🖨 📺 ♿ 🍽  General 👁 🛏 ⚓ P ✂ ▼ ✕ 🍴 🏬 ⅙ ⊡ ✿  Leisure ∪ ⌐ ▶ 🚲 🏊

**FAMILIES** **WELCOME** **WELCOME** **FAMILIES**

## Family-friendly breaks

For accommodation offering additional facilities and services for a range of ages and family units, look out for the Families Welcome symbol. Owners of these properties will go out of their way to welcome families.

## ST AUSTELL, Cornwall Map ref 1B3

★★★★
**BED & BREAKFAST**

B&B per room per night
s £45.00
d £50.00–£70.00

### Little Grey Cottage

Trethurgy, St Austell PL26 8YD  t (01726) 850486  f (01726) 850486
e info@littlegreycottagebb.co.uk  w littlegreycottagebb.co.uk

In one-acre grounds of secluded, mature gardens offering peace and tranquillity, yet only one mile from Eden Project. Tastefully renovated period cottage with cosy en suite bedrooms. Ideal touring base.

**open** All year except Christmas and New Year
**bedrooms** 2 double, 1 twin
**bathrooms** 2 en suite, 1 private
**payment** Credit/debit cards

Room 📺 ♨ ☏   General 🛏 ♿ P ⚡ 🍽 Å 🐾 ◧ ✿   Leisure ∪ ♪ ▶ 🚲 🏊

## ST COLUMB MAJOR, Cornwall Map ref 1B2

★★★★★
**FARMHOUSE**
**SILVER AWARD**

B&B per room per night
s £30.00–£32.00
d £60.00–£64.00
Evening meal per person
£15.00–£20.00

### Pennatillie Farm

Talskiddy, St Columb Major TR9 6EF  t (01637) 880280  f (01637) 880280
e angela@pennatillie.fsnet.co.uk  w cornish-riviera.co.uk/pennatilliefarm.htm

**bedrooms** 2 double, 1 twin
**bathrooms** All en suite
**payment** Credit/debit cards, cash/cheques

Family dairy farm set in 450 acres of beautiful countryside. Spacious, well-appointed, en suite guest bedrooms, including a stunning four-poster (super-king-size) bedroom. Eden, the Lost Gardens of Heligan and National Trust properties are all nearby. Excellent choice on breakfast menu. Warm welcome guaranteed. Open March to October.

⊕ *From A39 follow signs into Talskiddy. Drive down past telephone box and continue for 1 mile to end of road.*

Room 🖼 📺 ♨ ☏   General 🛏 ♿ P ⚡ ✗ 🍽 Å ✿   Leisure ∪ ♪ 🏊

## ST IVES, Cornwall Map ref 1B3

★★★
**BED & BREAKFAST**

B&B per room per night
s £25.00–£30.00
d £44.00–£52.00

### Byways

22 Steamers Hill, Angarrack, Hayle TR27 5JB  t (01736) 753463  e bywaysbb@lineone.net
w bywaysbb.co.uk

A friendly, informal family home situated in the picturesque village of Angarrack, two miles from the nearest beach. All rooms comfortably furnished and en suite. Open March to October.

**bedrooms** 2 double, 1 single
**bathrooms** All en suite
**payment** Cash/cheques

Room ♿ 📺 ♨ ☏   General P ⚡ 🍽 Å ✿   Leisure ∪ ♪ ▶ 🚲 🏊

## ST IVES, Cornwall Map ref 1B3

★★★★
**GUEST ACCOMMODATION**

B&B per room per night
s £30.00–£55.00
d £60.00–£80.00

### Chy An Gwedhen

St Ives Road, Carbis Bay, St Ives TR26 2JN  t (01736) 798684  e info@chyangwedhen.com
w chyangwedhen.com

**open** All year except Christmas
**bedrooms** 3 double, 1 twin, 1 family
**bathrooms** All en suite
**payment** Credit/debit cards, cash/cheques

A warm welcome awaits you at Chy An Gwedhen, a haven for non-smokers. Award-winning B&B, comfortable, en suite rooms, delicious choice of breakfasts. Private car park, adjacent to coastal footpath leading to Carbis Bay and St Ives' gorgeous beaches. Tate, Barbara Hepworth, wonderful restaurants within walking distance. Relaxing holiday destination.

⊕ *Leave A30 at roundabout signposted St Ives, follow A3074 through Lelant village to Carbis Bay. Drive to small traffic island. 100yds ahead see our sign.*

Room ♿ 📺 ♨ ☏   General 🛏 🖼 ♿ P ⚡ 🍽 🐾 ◧   Leisure ∪ ♪ ▶ 🚲 🏊

**ST IVES,** Cornwall Map ref 1B3

# The Grey Mullet
## GUEST HOUSE

One of the best known and friendliest guest houses in the old fishing and artists' quarter of St Ives. Situated only 20 yards from the harbour, beaches, car parks, restaurants, pubs, shops and art galleries including the Tate Gallery and Barbara Hepworth Museum. The house though modernised to a high standard retains its "olde worlde" charm. Some private parking available. All major credit cards accepted.

**For brochure please write to:**
**Ken Weston, 2 Bunkers Hill, St Ives TR26 1LJ**
**or telephone: (01736) 796635 Email: greymulletguesthouse@lineone.net**
**www.touristnetuk.com/sw/greymullet**

**ST JUST-IN-PENWITH,** Cornwall Map ref 1A3

★★★
**GUEST ACCOMMODATION**

B&B per room per night
**s** £35.00–£45.00
**d** £60.00–£75.00
Evening meal per person
£7.50–£15.00

# The Commercial

Market Square, St Just, Penzance TR19 7HE **t** (01736) 788455 **f** (01736) 788131
**e** enquiries@commercial-hotel.co.uk **w** commercial-hotel.co.uk

A former coaching inn, well-known locally for its great food and friendly atmosphere. Ideal for exploring nearby World Heritage sites and Land's End coastline. Free Wi-Fi broadband connection available.

**open** All year
**bedrooms** 5 double, 1 twin, 4 family
**bathrooms** 7 en suite, 3 private
**payment** Credit/debit cards, cash/cheques

Room 📺 ♿ 🍵   General ☎11 ⚁ P ⚑ 🍴 ⚄ ⚅ 🔆 ✲ 🕏   Leisure ♦ ∪ ► ⚲ 🏠

**ST JUST IN ROSELAND,** Cornwall Map ref 1B3

★★★★
**BED & BREAKFAST**

B&B per room per night
**d** £75.00–£85.00

# Roundhouse Barns

Truro TR2 5JJ **t** (01872) 580038 **f** (01872) 580067 **e** info@roundhousebarns.co.uk
**w** roundhousebarns.co.uk

**open** All year except Christmas and New Year
**bedrooms** 2 double
**bathrooms** All en suite
**payment** Cash/cheques

Beautifully converted 17thC barn set in peaceful surroundings on the Roseland. Instant access to walks by the Fal river. St Just in Roseland church with its subtropical gardens and the picturesque harbour of St Mawes are both nearby. Delightful, comfortable rooms with luxury bedding. Locally sourced breakfasts.

⊕ *A3078 to St Just in Roseland. Right turn, B3289, signposted King Henry Ferry. After 1.5 miles take left turn, signposted Messack. Follow signs to Roundhouse Barns.*

Room 🛏 📺 ♿ 🍵   General ☎16 P ⚄ 🍴 ⚅ ✲   Leisure ∂ ► 🏠

# Don't forget www.

Web addresses throughout this guide are shown without the prefix www. Please include www. in the address line of your browser. If a web address does not follow this style it is shown in full.

## ST MARY'S, Isles of Scilly Map ref 1A3

★★★
**GUEST HOUSE**

B&B per room per night
**s** Max £48.00
**d** Max £76.00
Evening meal per person
Max £15.00

# Shearwater Guest House

The Parade, St Mary's TR21 0LP **t** (01720) 422402 **e** griswalds00@hotmail.com
**w** shearwater-guest-house.co.uk

**open** All year except Christmas
**bedrooms** 2 double, 2 twin, 2 family
**bathrooms** 5 en suite, 1 private
**payment** Cash/cheques

Shearwater is a family-run guesthouse on the Isles of Scilly, offering bed and full English breakfast. A three-course, candle-lit evening meal is served four nights a week from April to October. We are centrally located close to shops, restaurants and harbour to catch boats to the off islands.

⊕ Ten minutes' walk from St Mary's quay where Scillonian III docks. Transport from airport, located just outside terminal building, will drop you right to Shearwater.

♥ Open all year with winter rates from October to April.

Room 🛏 📺 👜 🍴   General 🕐12 ✂ 🎣 ✳   Leisure ∪ 🎣 🏌 🚴

## ST MAWES, Cornwall Map ref 1B3

★★★
**FARMHOUSE**

B&B per room per night
**s** £26.00
**d** £52.00

# Trenestral Farm

Ruan High Lanes, Truro TR2 5LX **t** (01872) 501259

A 200-year-old, tastefully converted barn on a mixed, family-run working farm situated on the peaceful Roseland Peninsula. All rooms en suite. Children and pets welcome. Open March to October.

**bedrooms** 2 double, 1 twin
**bathrooms** All en suite
**payment** Cash/cheques

Room 🛏 👜   General 🐾 🏛 🎣 P ✂ 🎣 🐕

## ST MAWGAN, Cornwall Map ref 1B2

★★★★
**GUEST ACCOMMODATION**

B&B per room per night
**s** £51.00–£54.00
**d** £72.00–£78.00
Evening meal per person
£18.00

# Dalswinton House

St Mawgan-in-Pydar, Nr Padstow TR8 4EZ **t** (01637) 860385 **e** dalswintonhouse@tiscali.co.uk
**w** dalswinton.com

A former farmhouse standing in eight acres of grounds, specialising in holidays for dogs and their owners. Dog-friendly beach and coastal path 1.5 miles. Good food cooked with local ingredients. Open March to October inclusive.

**bedrooms** 5 double, 3 twin
**bathrooms** All en suite
**payment** Credit/debit cards, cash/cheques, euros

Room 🛏 📺 👜 🍴   General P ✂ ♟ ✗ 🏛 🎣 ♿ ✳ 🐕   Leisure ⚲ ∪ 🎣 🏌 🚴

## ST MINVER, Cornwall Map ref 1B2

★★★
**BED & BREAKFAST**

B&B per room per night
**s** Max £25.00
**d** £50.00–£65.00

# Tredower Barton

St Minver, Wadebridge PL27 6RG **t** (01208) 813501 **f** (01208) 813501

Tredower Barton is a farm bed and breakfast set in beautiful countryside near the North Cornish coast. Good food assured. Open Easter to October.

**bedrooms** 1 twin, 1 family
**bathrooms** All en suite
**payment** Cash/cheques

Room 👜 🍴   General 🐾 🏛 🎣 P ✂ 🎣 ✳

## Pet-friendly breaks

**PETS! WELCOME** · **WELCOME PETS!**

Want to take your cherished companion with you on holiday? Proprietors participating in our Welcome Pets! scheme go out of their way to make special provision for you and your pet. Look out for the symbol.

## ST WENN, Cornwall Map ref 1B2

**Rating Applied For**
**BED & BREAKFAST**

B&B per room per night
s £30.00
d £50.00–£60.00

# Trewithian Farm

St Wenn, Bodmin PL30 5PH  t (01208) 895181  e trewithian@hotmail.co.uk
w cornwall-online.co.uk/trewithianfarm

Large farmhouse set in very rural area. Picturesque location in rolling farmland. En suite double bedroom with colour TV. Tea-/coffee-making facilities. Use of sitting room downstairs.

**open** All year
**bedrooms** 1 double
**bathrooms** En suite
**payment** Cash/cheques

Room 🛏 ♿ ☕  General ✂

## SALISBURY, Wiltshire Map ref 2B3

★★
**GUEST HOUSE**

B&B per room per night
s £35.00–£50.00
d £55.00–£75.00

# Alabare House

15 Tollgate Road, Salisbury SP1 2JA  t (01722) 340206  f (01722) 501586  e bookings@alabare.org
w alabare.org

**open** All year except Christmas
**bedrooms** 2 double, 4 twin, 3 single, 1 family
**bathrooms** 5 en suite, 1 private
**payment** Credit/debit cards, cash/cheques

This is a small oasis in the heart of Salisbury with ample off-road parking. Established as a small retreat centre, the venue is a good choice for a holiday break. There are many local places of interest, and Salisbury offers a wide variety of restaurants and shops. Online booking available.

⊕ From the A338 Salisbury ring road take the A36 Southampton Road. Tollgate Road is 1st on left. Alabare House is on the right behind Hi Q Tyre Service.

♥ Special rates for extended stays of 3 weeks or more out of season. Also 4 nights for the price of 3 Oct-Apr.

Room 🛏 📺 ♿  General ⛁ 🖵 P ✂ ✗ 🎱 ✿  Leisure ∪ ⚲ 🏠

## SALISBURY, Wiltshire Map ref 2B3

★★
**BED & BREAKFAST**

B&B per room per night
s £40.00–£45.00
d £55.00–£60.00

# Burcombe Manor

Burcombe Lane, Burcombe, Salisbury SP2 0EJ  t (01722) 744288
e nickatburcombemanor@btinternet.com  w burcombemanor.co.uk

**open** All year
**bedrooms** 2 double, 1 twin
**bathrooms** 2 en suite, 1 private
**payment** Credit/debit cards, cash/cheques

Burcombe Manor is set in the Nadder Valley four miles west of Salisbury. The house, built in 1865, has large, oak-floor hall, oak banisters, centrally heated bedrooms, most en suite. Guests have their own sitting room in which to plan their day. Local base to visit Wilton, Salisbury and the surrounding area.

⊕ Come out of Wilton 1 mile on A30. Left to Burcombe. Down over river to a T-junction, turn right. Burcombe Manor drive is on the left.

♥ Reduction for stays of 3 or more nights.

Room 📺 ♿ ☕  General ⛁ 🖵 P ✂ 🍴 🎱 ✿  Leisure ∪ ▸ 🏠

## Check the maps

Colour maps at the front pinpoint all the places you will find accommodation entries in the regional sections. Pick your location and then refer to the place index at the back to find the page number.

## SALISBURY, Wiltshire Map ref 2B3

★★★
**GUEST HOUSE**

B&B per room per night
s £38.00–£60.00
d £50.00–£75.00

# Byways House

31 Fowlers Road, Salisbury SP1 2QP  t (01722) 328364  f (01722) 322146
e info@bywayshouse.co.uk  w bywayshouse.co.uk

**open** All year except Christmas and New Year
**bedrooms** 8 double, 7 twin, 4 single, 4 family
**bathrooms** 19 en suite
**payment** Credit/debit cards, cash/cheques

Attractive, large, Victorian guesthouse in quiet location alongside the city centre/restaurants. Free car parking on site. Licensed drinks lounge. Clean and comfortable en suite rooms. Special rates for long stays. Wi-Fi Internet access.

⊕ *Arriving in Salisbury follow A36, then follow Youth Hostel signs until outside hostel. Fowlers Road is opposite. Byways is a large Victorian house on the left.*

Room 🛁 🖨 📺 ♨ 🍵  General 🛏 ▦ ♿ P ☂ ♨ ✿ 🐾  Leisure ▶ 🚲 🏊

## SALISBURY, Wiltshire Map ref 2B3

★★★★
**FARMHOUSE**

B&B per room per night
d £55.00–£60.00

# Manor Farm

Burcombe Lane, Burcombe, Salisbury SP2 0EJ  t (01722) 742177  f (01722) 744600
e suecombes@manorfarmburcombe.fsnet.co.uk  w manorfarmburcombebandb.com

**bedrooms** 1 double, 1 twin
**bathrooms** All en suite
**payment** Credit/debit cards, cash/cheques

A comfortable farmhouse, warm and attractively furnished, on 1,400-acre mixed farm in a quiet, pretty village 0.25 miles off A30, west of Salisbury. Ideal base for touring this lovely area. Nearby attractions include Wilton House, Salisbury and Stonehenge. Wonderful walks, good riding. Pub with good food nearby. Open 1 March to 1 December.

⊕ *From Salisbury A36/30 west to Wilton, left at roundabout, A30 for 2 miles, left for 0.25 miles then turn right. 1st house on left.*

♥ *Reduction for stays of 3 or more nights.*

Room 📺 ♨ 🍵  General 🛏 ♿ P ✂ ♨ ✿  Leisure ∪ ▶ 🏊

## SALISBURY, Wiltshire Map ref 2B3

★★★★
**BED & BREAKFAST**

B&B per room per night
s £40.00–£55.00
d £55.00–£80.00

# The Old Rectory Bed & Breakfast

75 Belle Vue Road, Salisbury SP1 3YE  t (01722) 502702  e stay@theoldrectory-bb.co.uk
w theoldrectory-bb.co.uk

Victorian rectory in quiet street, a short walk from the heart of Salisbury and convenient for all attractions. Warm, welcoming atmosphere and well-appointed rooms. A relaxing bolthole. Wi-Fi Internet.

**open** All year except Christmas and New Year
**bedrooms** 1 double, 1 twin, 1 single
**bathrooms** 2 en suite, 1 private
**payment** Cash/cheques

Room 📺 ♨ 🍵  General 🛏 10 P ✂ 🍴 ♨ ⚲ ✿  Leisure 🚲 🏊

## It's all in the detail

Please remember that all information in this guide has been supplied by the proprietors well in advance of publication. Since changes do sometimes occur it's a good idea to check details at the time of booking.

★★★★
GUEST HOUSE
SILVER AWARD

# The Rokeby Guest House

3 Wain-A-Long Road, Salisbury SP1 1LJ  **t** (01722) 329800  **f** (01722) 329800
**e** karenrogers@rokebyguesthouse.co.uk  **w** rokebyguesthouse.co.uk

B&B per room per night
**s** £45.00–£55.00
**d** £45.00–£80.00

**open** All year
**bedrooms** 3 double, 2 twin, 3 family
**bathrooms** 7 en suite, 1 private
**payment** Cash/cheques

2007 Salisbury Tourism Award and Recognition Scheme winner in the B&B category. Beautiful, nostalgic, Victorian guesthouse, quietly situated, ten minutes' stroll city centre/cathedral. Large landscaped gardens, summer house, elegant two-storey conservatory, gymnasium. Free internet access available. Brochure available. Come and see for yourself.

⊕ *Take Laverstock exit off St Mark's Church roundabout on A30 London road into Wain-a-Long Road. The Rokeby is 2nd house on left.*

Room 📺 ♿ ☎  General ⚒ 🏛 ⚓ P ⚡ ✗ 🅿 ✿

SALISBURY PLAIN

*See under Amesbury, Market Lavington, Salisbury, Warminster*

★★★★★
BED & BREAKFAST
SILVER AWARD

# Glebe Farm

High Street, Ashmore, Salisbury SP5 5AE  **t** (01747) 811974  **f** (01747) 811104
**e** tmillard@glebe.f9.co.uk

B&B per room per night
**s** £35.00–£40.00
**d** £70.00–£80.00
Evening meal per person
£15.00–£20.00

**open** All year except Christmas and New Year
**bedrooms** 1 double, 1 twin
**bathrooms** All en suite
**payment** Cash/cheques

Beautiful, unique, contemporary farmhouse in Dorset's highest village, set in a tranquil location away from traffic noise. Enjoy an evening meal with your bottle of wine and literally soak up the views then retire to bed with open doors and drift off to sleep listening to our resident owls!

Room ♿ 📺 ♿ ☎  General 14 P ✗  Leisure ▶

★★★★
GUEST HOUSE
SILVER AWARD

# The Retreat

47 Bell Street, Shaftesbury SP7 8AE  **t** (01747) 850372  **f** (01747) 850372  **e** info@the-retreat.org.uk
**w** the-retreat.org.uk

B&B per room per night
**s** Min £37.50
**d** £70.00–£75.00

Perfectly positioned in a quiet street, this Georgian townhouse has light and airy, individually furnished, en suite bedrooms with TV and complimentary tray. Off-road parking. 2005 winner of 'Best B&B in North Dorset'.

**open** All year
**bedrooms** 4 double, 1 twin, 1 single, 4 family
**bathrooms** All en suite
**payment** Credit/debit cards, cash/cheques

Room ♿ 📺 ♿  General ⚒ 🏛 ⚓ P ⚡

## enjoyEngland.com

Big city buzz or peaceful panoramas? Take a fresh look at England and you may be surprised at what's right on your doorstep. Explore the diversity online at enjoyengland.com

**SHEPTON MALLET,** Somerset Map ref 2A2

★★★★
RESTAURANT WITH ROOMS

B&B per room per night
s £65.00–£80.00
d £80.00–£110.00
Evening meal per person
£15.00–£27.50

# Bowlish House

Wells Road, Bowlish, Shepton Mallet BA4 5JD  t (01749) 342022  f (01749) 345311
e info@bowlishhouse.com  w bowlishhouse.com

**open** All year
**bedrooms** 4 double, 2 twin
**bathrooms** All en suite
**payment** Credit/debit cards, cash/cheques

Grade II* Listed Georgian Palladian house with character and period charm close to the cathedral city of Wells and other major attractions. Continental breakfast included in price of room.

Room 📞 TV 🌿  General ▦ ♯ P ⚒ ♟ 🍴 ⚔ 👜 ✻  Leisure ▶

**SHERBORNE,** Dorset Map ref 2B3

★★★★
BED & BREAKFAST

B&B per room per night
d £50.00–£65.00

# The Alders

Sandford Orcas, Sherborne DT9 4SB  t (01963) 220666  f (01963) 220106
e jonsue@thealdersbb.com  w thealdersbb.com

**open** All year
**bedrooms** 1 double, 1 twin, 1 family
**bathrooms** All en suite
**payment** Cash/cheques, euros

Secluded stone house set in old walled garden, in picturesque conservation village near Sherborne. The house is tastefully furnished, with original watercolour paintings and hand-made pottery. There is a wood-burning fire in lounge inglenook fireplace. Good breakfasts served around large farmhouse table. Excellent food available in traditional, friendly village pub.

⊕ Take Marston Magna road from Sherborne. After 2 miles turn right and follow signs to Sandford Orcas. In village turn left – house last on left before church and manor-house.

Room TV 🌿 🍴  General ⚔ ⚒ 👜 ✻  Leisure ▶

**SHERBORNE,** Dorset Map ref 2B3

★★★
BED & BREAKFAST

B&B per room per night
s Min £30.00
d £50.00–£60.00

# Honeycombe View

Lower Clatcombe, Sherborne DT9 4RH  t (01935) 814644  e honeycombower@talktalk.net

Delightful rural location within walking distance of Sherborne. Two comfortable en suite rooms, one in new annexe with views. Covered parking. Walkers welcome, drying facilities available.

**open** All year except Christmas and New Year
**bedrooms** 2 twin
**bathrooms** All en suite
**payment** Cash/cheques

Room 🛏 TV 🌿 🍴  General ⚔6 P ⚒ ✻  Leisure 🚲

**SHERBORNE,** Dorset Map ref 2B3

★★★★
BED & BREAKFAST

B&B per room per night
s £50.00–£57.00
d £65.00–£82.00

# The Pheasants B&B

24 Greenhill, Sherborne DT9 4EW  t (01935) 815252  f (01935) 812938  e info@thepheasants.com
w thepheasants.com

A 300-year-old town house in the heart of historic Sherborne, a short walk from the abbey and castles. Elegant guests' lounge. Fine wines by the glass. All rooms en suite.

**open** All year except Christmas and New Year
**bedrooms** 1 double, 1 twin, 1 family
**bathrooms** All en suite
**payment** Cash/cheques

Room TV 🌿 🍴  General ⚔ ⚒ ♟ 👜 ✻  Leisure ▶ 🚲

## SIDBURY, Devon Map ref 1D2

★ ★ ★ ★
**GUEST ACCOMMODATION**
**SILVER AWARD**

B&B per room per night
s £32.50
d £55.00
Evening meal per person
Max £15.00

# Rose Cottage Sidbury

Greenhead, Sidbury, Sidmouth EX10 0RH  **t** (01395) 597357 & 07891 197218
**e** roz.kendall@btinternet.com  **w** rosecottagesidbury.co.uk

Comfortable, family-run guesthouse in Sidbury. A warm welcome and delicious home cooking await you, making this the perfect place to relax and unwind.

**open** All year except Christmas
**bedrooms** 2 double, 1 family
**bathrooms** All en suite
**payment** Credit/debit cards, cash/cheques

Room 📺 ♿ ⏰  General 🕐5 P ✂ 🍳 🍴 🔥 ❄  Leisure ∪ ► 🚲

## SIDMOUTH, Devon Map ref 1D2

★ ★ ★ ★
**GUEST HOUSE**

B&B per room per night
s £29.00–£35.00
d £58.00–£70.00

# Cheriton Guest House

Vicarage Road, Sidmouth EX10 8UQ  **t** (01395) 513810  **e** sara.land1@virgin.net
**w** smoothhound.co.uk/hotels/cheritong.html

Cheriton is a large Victorian townhouse with comfortable, en suite guest rooms, drink-making facilities and colour TV. All non-smoking.

**open** All year
**bedrooms** 2 double, 1 twin, 3 single, 3 family
**bathrooms** All en suite
**payment** Cash/cheques

Room ♿ 📺 ⏰  General 🕐 🍳 🔥 P ✂ 🍴 🔥 ❄  Leisure ∪ ► 🚲

## SIDMOUTH, Devon Map ref 1D2

★ ★ ★ ★
**GUEST HOUSE**

B&B per room per night
d £60.00–£70.00

# Lavenders Blue

33 Sidford High Street, Sidford, Sidmouth EX10 9SN  **t** (01395) 576656
**e** lavendersbluesidmouth@fsmail.net

A warm welcome awaits you at Lavenders Blue. Deluxe en suite rooms with double-size showers. Ideal location for Sidmouth and the World Heritage Site of the Jurassic Coast.

**open** All year except Christmas
**bedrooms** 4 double
**bathrooms** All en suite
**payment** Credit/debit cards, cash/cheques

Room ♿ 📺 ⏰ ⏰  General P ✂ ❄

## SIDMOUTH, Devon Map ref 1D2

★ ★ ★
**GUEST HOUSE**

B&B per room per night
s £25.00–£35.00
d £50.00–£70.00

# Ryton Guest House

52-54 Winslade Road, Sidmouth EX10 9EX  **t** (01395) 513981  **f** (01395) 519210
**e** info@ryton-guest-house.co.uk  **w** ryton-guest-house.co.uk

Ryton is a friendly, established guesthouse, offering spacious, comfortable en suite rooms, private parking and hospitality second to none. River walks and coastal path close by.

**open** All year except Christmas and New Year
**bedrooms** 3 double, 1 twin, 3 single, 2 family
**bathrooms** 6 en suite, 3 private
**payment** Cash/cheques

Room 📺 ♿  General 🕐5 P ✂ 🍳 🍴 🔲 ❄ 🐾  Leisure ∪ ♪ ► 🚲 🚣

# A breath of fresh air

Love the great outdoors? Britain's Camping, Caravan & Holiday Parks 2008 is packed with information on quality sites in some spectacular locations. You can purchase the guide from good bookshops and online at visitbritaindirect.com.

## SIDMOUTH, Devon Map ref 1D2

★★★★★
**RESTAURANT WITH ROOMS**
**GOLD AWARD**

# The Salty Monk

Church Street, Sidford, Sidmouth EX10 9QP  **t** (01395) 513174  **e** saltymonk@btconnect.com
**w** saltymonk.co.uk

B&B per room per night
**s** £70.00–£85.00
**d** £100.00–£180.00
Evening meal per person
£30.00–£35.00

**open** All year
**bedrooms** 2 double, 1 twin, 2 suites
**bathrooms** All en suite
**payment** Credit/debit cards, cash/cheques

A haven of luxury outside the Regency town of Sidmouth, a 16thC restaurant ideally located for exploring Dartmoor and the Heritage Coast. Individual, superbly appointed bedrooms, spa baths and two stunning suites. Award-winning, elegant restaurant overlooking beautiful gardens. Imaginative, fresh food using Devon's finest ingredients, all made on the premises by resident chef proprietors.

⊕ From M5 take exit 30 onto A3052 to Sidmouth. Travelling south on A303, exit Honiton. Follow A375, left at lights in Sidford, 200yds on right.

♥ 3 nights for 2 low season.

Room 🛏 📞 📺 🖤 🍴  General 🛅 🏛 🕏 P ⚡ 🍽 ✕ 🖼 🏄 🌀 ✿ 🐾  Leisure ∪ ⊦ 🚲 🏊

## SLIMBRIDGE, Gloucestershire Map ref 2B1

★★★
**INN**

# Tudor Arms

Shepherds Patch, Slimbridge, Gloucester GL2 7BP  **t** (01453) 890306  **f** (01453) 890103
**e** ritatudorarms@aol.com

B&B per room per night
**s** £50.00–£55.00
**d** £60.00–£70.00
Evening meal per person
£5.00–£15.00

Free house offering real ales, home-cooked food and modern, purpose-built, en suite accommodation. Close to Slimbridge Wildfowl and Wetland Centre. Families and dogs welcome.

**open** All year
**bedrooms** 2 double, 5 twin, 5 family
**bathrooms** All en suite
**payment** Credit/debit cards, cash/cheques

Room 🛏 📞 📺 🖤 🍴  General 🛅 🏛 🕏 P ⚡ 🍽 ✕ 🖼 ✿ 🐾  Leisure ⚓ ∪ ⊅ ⊦ 🚲 🏊

## SPREYTON, Devon Map ref 1C2

★★★
**INN**

# The Tom Cobley Tavern

Spreyton, Crediton EX17 5AL  **t** (01647) 231314  **f** (01647) 231506

B&B per room per night
**s** £24.50
Evening meal per person
Min £11.00

Tom Cobley and friends set out from the Tavern c1802, on their famous journey to Widecombe Fair. CAMRA South West Regional Pub of the Year 2006 and CAMRA National Pub of the Year 2006.

**open** All year
**bedrooms** 1 double, 1 twin, 2 single
**payment** Credit/debit cards, cash/cheques

Room 📺 🖤  General 🛅 🏛 🕏 P ⚡ ✕ ✿ 🐾  Leisure ⊅ ⊦ 🚲

# enjoyEngland.com

Get in the know – log on for a wealth of information and inspiration. All the latest news on places to visit, events and quality-assessed accommodation is literally at your fingertips. Explore all that England has to offer.

**STOGUMBER,** Somerset Map ref 1D1

★★★
INN

B&B per room per night
s £35.00–£40.00
d £64.00–£70.00
Evening meal per person
£5.95–£15.95

## The White Horse Inn

High Street, Stogumber, Taunton TA4 3TA **t** (01984) 656277 **f** (01984) 656873
**w** whitehorsestogumber.co.uk

**open** All year except Christmas
**bedrooms** 2 double, 1 twin
**bathrooms** All en suite
**payment** Credit/debit cards, cash/cheques

The White Horse is a Grade II Listed, traditional freehouse in the picturesque village of Stogumber, hidden away from the rat race on the slopes of the Quantock Hills. The extensive menu uses fresh, local produce, and award-winning, locally brewed real ales are a speciality.

⊕ *A358 Taunton to Minehead; approx 14 miles from Taunton, village signposted on left. In centre of village turn right at T-junction, and right again (White Horse signposted).*

Room General Leisure

**STOGUMBER,** Somerset Map ref 1D1

★★★★
GUEST HOUSE

B&B per room per night
s £30.00–£44.00
d £60.00–£68.00
Evening meal per person
£9.00–£25.00

## Wick House

2 Brook Street, Stogumber, Taunton TA4 3SZ **t** (01984) 656422
**e** sheila@wickhouse.fsbusiness.co.uk **w** wickhouse.fsbusiness.co.uk

**open** All year
**bedrooms** 2 double, 3 twin
**bathrooms** All en suite
**payment** Credit/debit cards, cash/cheques

Listed family home in the picturesque village of Stogumber, situated in a designated Area of Outstanding Natural Beauty. The village nestles between the Quantock and Brendon Hills of Exmoor National Park. Offering a friendly, informal atmosphere and high standard of accommodation – perfect for escaping the stresses of the modern world.

⊕ *From Taunton, A358 to Minehead. After approx 11 miles, left to Stogumber. At crossroads turn left. Wick House 20yds on left. Please park in bay opposite.*

❤ *Special rates for full-week and midweek breaks of 2-5 nights. Residential upholstery and art courses. Honeymoon room available.*

Room General Leisure

**STONEHOUSE,** Gloucestershire Map ref 2B1

★★★
INN

B&B per room per night
s £40.00–£50.00
d £50.00–£70.00
Evening meal per person
£5.00–£25.00

## Beacon Inn

Haresfield, Stonehouse GL10 3DX **t** (01452) 728884 **f** (01452) 721627 **e** terry@thebeaconinn.co.uk
**w** thebeaconinn.co.uk

Family-run inn offering quality food with friendly atmosphere. Situated close to M5 junction 12, just off the Cotswold Way.

**open** All year
**bedrooms** 2 double, 2 twin, 1 single
**bathrooms** All en suite
**payment** Credit/debit cards, cash/cheques

Room General Leisure

CYCLISTS WELCOME WELCOME CYCLISTS

## A holiday on two wheels

For a fabulous freewheeling break, seek out accommodation participating in our Cyclists Welcome scheme. Look out for the symbol and plan your route online at nationalcyclenetwork.org.

---

**STONEHOUSE,** Gloucestershire Map ref 2B1

★★
**BED & BREAKFAST**

B&B per room per night
s £23.00–£25.00
d £46.00–£50.00

## Merton Lodge

8 Ebley Road, Stonehouse GL10 2LQ  t (01453) 822018

Former gentleman's residence offering a warm welcome. Non-smoking. Three miles from M5 junction 13, over four roundabouts. Along Ebley Road, under footbridge.

**open** All year
**bedrooms** 2 double, 1 suite
**bathrooms** 1 private
**payment** Cash/cheques

General ☺ P ⅍ 凵 ✿

---

**STOW-ON-THE-WOLD,** Gloucestershire Map ref 2B1

★★★
**FARMHOUSE**

B&B per room per night
s £35.00–£45.00
d £48.00–£60.00

## Corsham Field Farmhouse

Bledington Road, Stow-on-the-Wold, Cheltenham GL54 1JH  t (01451) 831750  f (01451) 832247
e farmhouse@corshamfield.co.uk  w corshamfield.co.uk

**open** All year except Christmas
**bedrooms** 2 double, 2 twin, 4 family
**bathrooms** 6 en suite, 2 private
**payment** Cash/cheques, euros

Traditional farmhouse with spectacular views of Cotswold countryside. Peaceful location one mile from Stow-on-the-Wold. Ideally situated for exploring all Cotswold villages, Cheltenham, Stratford-upon-Avon, Blenheim and Warwick. All rooms centrally heated with TV, tea tray and hairdryer. Relaxing guest lounge/dining room. Excellent pub food five minutes' walk.

⊕ A436 out of Stow-on-the-Wold, after 1 mile fork right onto B4450 Bledington Road. We are 1st farm on right-hand side opposite the Oddington turn.

Room ⌂ TV ♨ ⚲  General ☺ ⌖ P ⅍ 凵 ✿  Leisure ∪ ♪ ► ♣

---

**STOW-ON-THE-WOLD,** Gloucestershire Map ref 2B1

★★★★
**INN**

B&B per room per night
s Min £85.00
d £85.00–£110.00
Evening meal per person
£8.95–£35.00

## Westcote Inn

Nether Westcote, Chipping Norton OX7 6SD  t (01993) 830888  f (01993) 831657
e info@westcoteinn.co.uk  w westcoteinn.co.uk

**open** All year
**bedrooms** 3 double, 1 family
**bathrooms** All en suite
**payment** Credit/debit cards, cash/cheques

Traditional Cotswold inn situated in glorious countryside with views as far as the eye can see, complete with all modern facilities. Westcote serves traditional British food from our fine dining restaurant, or if you are looking for something simpler the Tack Room menu serves fabulous pub grub in front of open fireplaces. Situated between Burford and Stow-on-the-Wold, and three miles from Kingham Station with direct trains from Paddington.

Room ☎ TV ♨ ⚲  General ☺ ▥ ⌖ P ☕ ✗ ⛱ 凵 ⚘ ◉ ✿ ⚮  Leisure ∪ ♪ ► ♣ ⌂

---

## Take a break

Look out for special promotions and themed breaks. This could be your chance to indulge an interest, find a new one, or just relax and enjoy exceptional value. Offers (highlighted in colour) are subject to availability.

**STROUD,** Gloucestershire Map ref 2B1

★★★★
**BED & BREAKFAST**

B&B per room per night
**s** £32.00–£38.00
**d** £50.00–£60.00
Evening meal per person
£10.00

## 1 Woodchester Lodge

Southfield Road, North Woodchester, Stroud GL5 5PA **t** (01453) 872586
**e** anne@woodchesterlodge.co.uk **w** woodchesterlodge.co.uk

**open** All year except Christmas and New Year
**bedrooms** 1 double, 1 twin
**bathrooms** 1 en suite, 1 private
**payment** Cash/cheques

Historic, Victorian timber merchant's property; peaceful village setting near Cotswold Way. Attractive gardens, parking, spacious and comfortable rooms, separate TV lounge/dining room. Meals cooked by qualified chef using our own produce and eggs. Outdoor activities, scenic villages, local attractions, links to main cities: Bristol, Bath, Gloucester, Cheltenham and London.

⊕ *From Stroud/M5, take A46 towards Bath. Pass the Old Fleece pub. Right into Selsley Road. 2nd left, Southfield Road. 200yds on left-hand side.*

♥ *Weekly rates on request.*

Room 📺 ♨ 🍵 General ➷ P ⚒ ✕ 🍽 ⨒ 🔥 ▣ ✿ Leisure ∪ ▶

---

**STROUD,** Gloucestershire Map ref 2B1

★★★★
**BED & BREAKFAST**
**SILVER AWARD**

B&B per room per night
**s** Min £28.00
**d** Min £56.00

## Pretoria Villa

Wells Road, Eastcombe, Stroud GL6 7EE **t** (01452) 770435 **f** (01452) 770435
**e** glynis@gsolomon.freeserve.co.uk **w** bedandbreakfast-cotswold.co.uk

**open** All year except Christmas
**bedrooms** 1 double, 2 twin
**bathrooms** All en suite
**payment** Cash/cheques

Enjoy luxurious bed and breakfast in a relaxed family country house, set in peaceful secluded gardens. Spacious bedrooms with many home comforts. Guest lounge with TV. Superb breakfast served at your leisure. An excellent base from which to explore the Cotswolds. Personal service and your comfort guaranteed.

⊕ *At bottom of village green in Eastcombe take the lane with the red telephone box, at first crossroad very sharp right. 400yds on right.*

♥ *Discounted rates for 4+ nights.*

Room ♨ 🍵 General ➷ P ⚒ 🍽 ⨒ ✿

---

**SWANAGE,** Dorset Map ref 2B3

★★★★
**GUEST ACCOMMODATION**
**SILVER AWARD**

B&B per room per night
**s** £30.00–£50.00
**d** £60.00–£100.00

## The Castleton

1 Highcliffe Road, Swanage BH19 1LW **t** (01929) 423972 **e** stay@castletonhotel-swanage.co.uk
**w** castletonhotel-swanage.co.uk

**open** All year except Christmas
**bedrooms** 5 double, 2 twin, 1 single, 2 family
**bathrooms** All en suite
**payment** Cash/cheques

You are invited to our family-run B&B situated 100m from the beach. All rooms are en suite, and furnished to ensure that you have a relaxing and comfortable stay. Be it for one week or two, or one night or two, you will be made just as welcome. Please see virtual tour on our website.

⊕ *From town centre follow signs to Studland. We are 100m from where the road veers away from the beach, on the right.*

Room ♿ 📺 ♨ 🍵 General ➷6 P ⚒ 🍽 ⨒ ✿ Leisure ✦ ▶ 🚲 🏡

---

## SWANAGE, Dorset Map ref 2B3

★ ★ ★ ★
**BED & BREAKFAST**

B&B per room per night
d £56.00–£64.00

# Goodwyns

2 Walrond Road, Swanage BH19 1PB  t (01929) 421088 & 07952 991129
e knapman104@btinternet.com

**open** All year except Christmas and New Year
**bedrooms** 3 double
**bathrooms** All en suite
**payment** Credit/debit cards, cash/cheques

A welcoming family home 150m from the seafront and a short, level walk into town. Goodwyns offers three light, airy en suite double bedrooms – two with balcony and sea view. Centrally heated, tea/coffee facilities, radios, colour TVs. Private off-street parking for all guests.

⊕ *From Shore Road turn into Victoria Avenue, first right into De Moulham Road then second left into Walrond Road. Goodwyns is first house on right.*

♥ *10% discount for 7-night stay.*

Room 📺 👍 🍳   General P ⅙ 🚾 ✳

## SWINDON, Wiltshire Map ref 2B2

★ ★ ★
**GUEST ACCOMMODATION**

B&B per room per night
s £33.00–£55.00
d £60.00–£75.00

# The Swandown

36/37 Victoria Road, Swindon SN1 3AS  t (01793) 536695  f (01793) 432551
e swandownhotel@gmail.com  w s-h-systems.co.uk/hotels/swandown

**open** All year except Christmas and New Year
**bedrooms** 2 double, 4 twin, 6 single, 5 family
**bathrooms** 13 en suite
**payment** Credit/debit cards, cash

The Swandown is a friendly, well-maintained, family-run guest accommodation located in Swindon town centre and convenient to most amenities. Offering 17 rooms, mostly en suite, comfortably equipped with colour TV, tea-/coffee-making facilities and hairdryer. Separate TV lounge with a licensed bar and on-site parking facilities.

⊕ *Exit M4 jct15 for town centre. Straight over Magic Roundabout, turn left at second roundabout towards old town. Swandown is 250m up the hill.*

Room 🛏 📺 👍 🍳   General 🗘3 P ♟ 🍴

## SYDLING ST NICHOLAS, Dorset Map ref 2B3

★ ★
**FARMHOUSE**

B&B per room per night
s £20.00
d £40.00
Evening meal per person
£12.00

# Magiston Farm

Sydling St Nicholas, Dorchester DT2 9NR  t (01300) 320295

Four-hundred-acre working farm. 16thC farmhouse with large garden. Very peaceful, in the heart of Dorset, five miles north of Dorchester.

**open** All year
**bedrooms** 1 double, 2 twin, 1 single
**bathrooms** 1 private
**payment** Cash/cheques

Room 🛏 👍   General 🗘10 P ✕ ✳ 🐾   Leisure ⚲ U ▶

# To your credit

If you book by phone you may be asked for your credit card number. If so, it is advisable to check the proprietor's policy in case you have to cancel your reservation at a later date.

## TAVISTOCK, Devon Map ref 1C2

★★★★
**GUEST ACCOMMODATION**

B&B per room per night
s £48.00–£80.00
d £65.00–£95.00
Evening meal per person
Min £18.50

## Harrabeer Country House

Harrowbeer Lane, Yelverton PL20 6EA **t** (01822) 853302 **e** reception@harrabeer.co.uk
**w** harrabeer.co.uk

Delightful, small, quiet country house close to Dartmoor. Finalist for a prestigious Landlady of the Year award. Specialising in food, comfort and service. Two self-catering suites available.

**open** All year except Christmas and New Year
**bedrooms** 3 double, 3 twin, 2 suites
**bathrooms** 7 en suite, 1 private
**payment** Credit/debit cards, cash/cheques

Room 🛏 ✆ 📺 ♿ 🍵 General 🖥 🅿 ⚐ ✕ 🎮 📻 🌸 🐾 Leisure ∪ ✈ ► 🚴 🏛

## TEIGNMOUTH, Devon Map ref 1D2

★★★★★
**BED & BREAKFAST**
**SILVER AWARD**

B&B per room per night
s £40.00–£60.00
d £60.00–£80.00

## Britannia House B&B

26 Teign Street, Teignmouth TQ14 8EG **t** (01626) 770051 **f** (01626) 879903
**e** gillettbritannia@aol.com **w** britanniahouse.org

**open** All year except Christmas and New Year
**bedrooms** 2 double, 1 twin
**bathrooms** All en suite
**payment** Credit/debit cards, cash/cheques, euros

This 17thC listed house is situated in a conservation area of old Teignmouth. Recently refurbished to a high standard, bedrooms are luxuriously equipped, en suite, and have high-pressure, thermostatically-controlled showers. A sumptuous breakfast can be taken in the beautiful dining room or peaceful, walled garden. Closed January.

⊕ Take A380 (to Torquay) and continue until B3192 forks left. Keep on this road until T-junction at traffic lights in town. Left at lights, next right, 1st left.

♥ Prices reduce by £5 per night up to 3 nights for a double room.

Room 📺 ♿ 🍵 General 🎮 📻 🌸 Leisure ∪ ✈ ►

## TEWKESBURY, Gloucestershire Map ref 2B1

★★★★
**BED & BREAKFAST**
**SILVER AWARD**

B&B per room per night
s Min £30.00
d £60.00–£70.00

## Gantier

Church Road, Alderton, Tewkesbury GL20 8NR **t** (01242) 620343 & 07787 504872
**e** johnandsueparry@yahoo.co.uk **w** gantier.co.uk

Traditional stone house, quiet village setting, lovely views. Friendly, relaxed atmosphere with choice of good food locally. Ideal for holidays or business.

**open** All year except Christmas and New Year
**bedrooms** 2 double, 1 single
**bathrooms** 1 en suite, 2 private
**payment** Cash/cheques, euros

Room 📺 ♿ 🍵 General 14 🅿 ✂ 🎮 📻 🌸 Leisure ∪ ✈ ► 🏛

## TINTAGEL, Cornwall Map ref 1B2

★★★
**INN**

B&B per room per night
s £50.00–£90.00
d £90.00–£120.00
Evening meal per person
£12.00–£30.00

## The Mill House

Trebarwith Strand, Tintagel PL34 0HD **t** (01840) 770200 **f** (01840) 770647
**e** management@themillhouseinn.co.uk **w** themillhouseinn.co.uk

An 18thC mill, now a stylish hotel with traditional bar and restaurant, using local fish and produce, half a mile from beach.

**open** All year except Christmas
**bedrooms** 7 double, 1 twin, 1 single
**bathrooms** All en suite
**payment** Credit/debit cards, cash/cheques, euros

Room ✆ 📺 ♿ 🍵 General 🏠 🖥 🅿 ⚐ ✂ 🍸 ✕ 🎮 📻 🌸 🐾 Leisure ∪ ✈ ► 🚴

## Check it out

Please check prices, quality ratings and other details when you book.

**TIVERTON,** Devon Map ref 1D2

★★★
**GUEST HOUSE**

B&B per room per night
s £25.00–£31.00
d £60.00–£62.00
Evening meal per person
£16.00

# Bridge Guest House

23 Angel Hill, Tiverton EX16 6PE  t (01884) 252804  f (01884) 252804
w smoothhound.co.uk/hotels/bridgegh.html

Attractive Victorian town house situated on the banks of the River Exe, with pretty riverside tea garden. Ideal for touring the heart of Devon.

**open** All year
**bedrooms** 2 double, 1 twin, 5 single, 2 family
**bathrooms** 6 en suite
**payment** Cash/cheques, euros

Room ♠ TV ♨  General ♨ ▥ ♣ P ⅙ ♧ ✕ ▨ ♨ ● ❋  Leisure ✦ ♣ ☎

---

**TIVERTON,** Devon Map ref 1D2

★★★
**BED & BREAKFAST**

B&B per room per night
s £25.00–£27.50
d £27.50–£30.00

# Exe-Tor

Ashley, Tiverton EX16 5PA  t (01884) 253197  f (01884) 253197

A two-bedroom bungalow set in 0.33-acre garden, one mile outside Tiverton. Rural outlook. The double room is a king-size room with a king-size bed.

**open** All year
**bedrooms** 1 double, 1 twin
**bathrooms** 1 en suite, 1 private
**payment** Cash/cheques

Room ♠ TV ♨ ♖  General ♨7 P ⅙ ▨ ❋  Leisure ☎

---

**TORQUAY,** Devon Map ref 1D2

★★★★
**GUEST ACCOMMODATION**

B&B per room per night
s £25.00–£30.00
d £50.00–£60.00
Evening meal per person
Min £10.00

# Abingdon House

104 Avenue Road, Torquay TQ2 5LF  t (01803) 201832  e abingdon-house@zen.co.uk
w abingdon-house.co.uk

Informal, friendly bed and breakfast. Comfortable lounge and cheerful breakfast room. Small patio. Parking. Short walk to sea and all attractions. Family rooms are for triple occupancy. Ground-floor room suitable for the mobility-impaired and wheelchair-users.

**open** All year except Christmas
**bedrooms** 2 double, 1 twin, 2 family
**bathrooms** 4 en suite, 1 private
**payment** Credit/debit cards, cash/cheques

Room ♠ TV ♨ ♖  General P ⅙ ✕ ▨ ❋ ✟  Leisure ▶ ♣

---

**TORQUAY,** Devon Map ref 1D2

★★★★
**GUEST ACCOMMODATION**

B&B per room per night
s £24.00–£30.00
d £48.00–£60.00

# Avron House

70 Windsor Road, Ellacombe, Torquay TQ1 1SZ  t (01803) 294182  e avronhouse@blueyonder.co.uk
w avronhouse.co.uk

An eight-bedroom guesthouse with single, twin, double and family rooms. Situated between Babbacombe and Torquay centre in quiet area overlooking wooded green. Ten minute walk from harbour.

**open** All year except Christmas
**bedrooms** 3 double, 2 twin, 2 single, 1 family
**bathrooms** All en suite
**payment** Credit/debit cards, cash/cheques

Room ♠ TV ♨ ♖  General ♨3 ♣ ⅙ ♧ ▨ ❋  Leisure ▶

# Take a break

Look out for special promotions and themed breaks. It's a golden opportunity to indulge an interest, find a new one, or just relax and enjoy exceptional value. Offers and promotions are highlighted in colour (and are subject to availability).

## TORQUAY, Devon Map ref 1D2

★★★

**GUEST HOUSE**

B&B per room per night
d £50.00–£60.00

# Brocklehurst

Rathmore Road, Torquay TQ2 6NZ  **t** (01803) 390883  **e** enquiries@brocklehursthotel.co.uk
**w** brocklehursthotel.co.uk

**open** All year except Christmas and New Year
**bedrooms** 1 double, 3 twin, 1 family
**bathrooms** All en suite
**payment** Credit/debit cards, cash/cheques

A small, family-run guesthouse with a friendly atmosphere. We are set on the level, in a quiet area of Torquay, but within easy walking distance of Torquay station, the Riviera Conference Centre, the main seafront and local shops. We are conveniently placed for buses to local attractions.

⊕ *Approaching Torquay from the north (A380/3022). Turn right at the second traffic lights after Torre Station into Walnut Road. Rathmore Road is first right turn.*

Room 🛏 📺 👜 🍵   General 🛋 P ⅓ 📖 🎿 ❄

## TORQUAY, Devon Map ref 1D2

★★★★★

**GUEST ACCOMMODATION**

B&B per room per night
s £55.00–£88.00
d £70.00–£136.00

# Haldon Priors

Meadfoot Sea Road, Torquay TQ1 2LQ  **t** (01803) 213365  **f** (01803) 215577
**e** travelstyle.ltd@talk21.com  **w** haldonpriors.co.uk

**bedrooms** 4 double, 1 twin, 1 family
**bathrooms** All en suite
**payment** Credit/debit cards, cash/cheques

Haldon Priors is a beautiful Victorian villa adjacent to Meadfoot Bay, set in exquisite subtropical gardens with heated outdoor pool and sauna. All rooms have everything needed to make your stay memorable, with complimentary refreshments on arrival and all the beauty of Devon on the doorstep. Open Easter to end of September. No smoking in hotel.

⊕ *Pass Torquay Harbour on your right. Turn left at the clock tower, right at the 1st lights, to Meadfoot Road. On the left just before the beach.*

Room 📺 👜 🍵   General 🛋 📖 🔥 P ✕ 🎿 ❄   Leisure ⚡ 🔵 ♪ 🔰 🏊

## TORQUAY, Devon Map ref 1D2

★★★★

**GUEST ACCOMMODATION**
**SILVER AWARD**

B&B per room per night
s £50.00
d £60.00–£100.00

# Lanscombe House

Cockington Village, Torquay TQ2 6XA  **t** (01803) 606938  **f** (01803) 607656
**e** enquiries@lanscombehouse.co.uk  **w** lanscombehouse.co.uk

**bedrooms** 6 double, 1 twin, 1 family
**bathrooms** All en suite
**payment** Credit/debit cards, cash/cheques, euros

Relax and unwind, this country-house B&B is tucked away in the picturesque thatched village of Cockington, surrounded by Cockington Country Park – a peaceful haven just a short stroll to the sea. The luxury accommodation is fully refurbished, and includes a four-poster room. Open Easter to October.

⊕ *Follow signs for Torbay and head for seafront. Turn right to Paignton. At Livermead turn right (Cockington). As you enter village we are on left.*

Room 🛏 🖨 📺 👜 🍵   General 📖 🔥 P ⅓ 🍷 🎿 ❄   Leisure ♪ 🏊

## Confirm your booking

It's always advisable to confirm your booking in writing.

---

**TORQUAY,** Devon Map ref 1D2

★★★★
GUEST ACCOMMODATION

B&B per room per night
s £35.00–£60.00
d £52.00–£60.00

# Trafalgar House B&B

30 Bridge Road, Torquay TQ2 5BA  t (01803) 292486  f (01803) 292486
e trafalgar@hotelstorquayuk.com  w hotelstorquayuk.com

**open** All year except Christmas
**bedrooms** 6 double, 2 twin, 2 family
**bathrooms** All en suite
**payment** Credit/debit cards, cash/cheques

A truly English experience: a delightful, comfortable Victorian villa set in lovely gardens, offering an old world welcome and plenty of charm. Quiet location, just 600m from seafront and town. Scandinavian/Australian hosts. Exceptional breakfasts. Car parking. Non-smoking. Children over eight welcome. Holiday planning advice. Open March to end of October. Website tells it all.

⊕ *From Exeter, follow A380 to Torquay. At Torre station take the right traffic light filter into Avenue Road. Turn left into Cleveland Road. Hotel 300m on right.*

Room 🛁 📺 ⋯ 🖐 🕮 💻   General ☺8 P ⋯ 🕮 ⋯ ⋯ 🐾   Leisure ⋯ ► ⚲

---

**TOTNES,** Devon Map ref 1D2

★★★★
GUEST HOUSE

B&B per room per night
s £54.00–£72.00
d £64.00–£88.00

# The Old Forge at Totnes

Seymour Place, Totnes TQ9 5AY  t (01803) 862174  e enq@oldforgetotnes.com
w oldforgetotnes.com

**open** All year
**bedrooms** 6 double, 2 twin, 1 family, 1 suite
**bathrooms** 9 en suite, 1 private
**payment** Credit/debit cards, cash/cheques

A warm welcome assured at this delightful 600-year-old stone building with walled garden and car parking. Whirlpool spa. Extensive breakfast menu. Quiet, yet close to town and river. Coast and Dartmoor nearby, Eden Project 1.5 hours. Two-bedroomed cottage suite and family room with roof terrace available.

⊕ *From A38 Devon Expressway, between Exeter and Plymouth, A384 to Totnes. From monument at town centre, left, then cross Totnes Bridge, then 2nd right by Bridgetown Stores.*

♥ *3-day breaks (Nov-Mar): £4 off price of room per night.*

Room 🛁 📺 ⋯ 🖐   General ☺ 🕮 ⋯ P ⋯ 🍽 🕮 ⋯   Leisure ∪ ⋯ ► ⚲

---

**TROWBRIDGE,** Wiltshire Map ref 2B2

★★★
GUEST HOUSE

B&B per room per night
s £40.00–£45.00
d £65.00–£70.00

# Ring O' Bells

321 Marsh Road, Hilperton Marsh, Trowbridge BA14 7PL  t (01225) 754404  f (01225) 340325
e ringobells@blueyonder.co.uk  w ringobells.biz

**open** All year
**bedrooms** 1 double, 1 twin, 2 single, 2 family
**bathrooms** All en suite
**payment** Credit/debit cards, cash/cheques

Two miles north of Trowbridge. Formerly a pub, we now offer non-smoking, comfortable en suite rooms on the ground and first floors. Rooms have TV, tea/coffee facilities, radio/alarm, hairdryer and room safes. Private car park, disabled access, Wi-Fi internet via BT Openzone, friendly atmosphere. Child- and pet-friendly. CCTV operating.

⊕ *From the A361 follow B3105 into Hilperton, Staverton & Holt. Ring O' Bells is a mile down on your left. Car park in Horse Road.*

Room 🛁 📺 ⋯ 🖐   General ☺ 🕮 ⋯ P ⋯ 🕮 ⋯ ⋯ 🐾   Leisure ∪ ⋯ ► ⚲ 🛶

## TRURO, Cornwall Map ref 1B3

★★★★
**GUEST HOUSE**

B&B per room per night
s £50.00–£57.50
d £70.00–£85.00

# Bissick Old Mill

Ladock, Truro TR2 4PG  **t** (01726) 882557  **e** enquiries@bissickoldmill.plus.com  **w** bissickoldmill.co.uk

**open** All year
**bedrooms** 1 double, 1 twin, 2 suites
**bathrooms** All en suite
**payment** Credit/debit cards, cash/cheques

17thC watermill sympathetically converted to provide well-appointed accommodation with exceptional standards throughout and a relaxing, friendly atmosphere. Top quality breakfasts prepared with fresh, local, quality ingredients. Ideal base for visiting the Eden Project, Heligan, and all of Cornwall's beautiful attractions.

⊕ *Take B3275 signed from A30 Indian Queens/Fraddon bypass. Bissick Old Mill is in Ladock village. Take the 1st left on entering the village.*

Room 🛏 📞 📺 🍵 🍲   General 🛋 🍴 🅿 ⚹ 🐾 ✿

## TRURO, Cornwall Map ref 1B3

★★
**BED & BREAKFAST**

B&B per room per night
s £25.00–£35.00
d £40.00–£50.00

# Stanton House

11 Ferris Town, Truro TR1 3JG  **t** (01872) 223666  **e** iris@stantons.eclipse.co.uk

Late Georgian Grade II Listed town house. Comfortable accommodation, personal service, short level walk to city centre and close to railway station.

**open** All year
**bedrooms** 1 double, 1 single
**payment** Cash/cheques, euros

Room 📺 🍵 🍲   General 🛋 🍴 ⚹ 🐾 🐕

## TRURO, Cornwall Map ref 1B3

★★★★
**BED & BREAKFAST**

B&B per room per night
d £50.00–£60.00

# Treswithian Barn

Ruan High Lanes, Truro TR2 5JT  **t** (01872) 501274

A warm welcome awaits you at our newly converted barn on a small farm. Situated on the beautiful Roseland Peninsula, close to sandy beaches, cliff walks and the Eden Project. Open April to September.

**bedrooms** 1 double, 1 twin
**bathrooms** All en suite
**payment** Cash/cheques

Room 🛏 📺 🍵 🍲   General 🅿 ⚹ ✿

## VERYAN, Cornwall Map ref 1B3

★★★★
**BED & BREAKFAST**

B&B per room per night
s £28.00–£30.00
d £56.00–£60.00

# Treverbyn House

Pendower Road, Veryan, Truro TR2 5QL  **t** (01872) 501201  **e** holiday@treverbyn.fsbusiness.co.uk
**w** cornwall-online.co.uk/treverbyn/ctb.htm

Treverbyn House occupies a commanding position in the picturesque village of Veryan, renowned for its round houses. Treverbyn House is family-run and owned by Alison and Michael Rawling and offers bed and breakfast accommodation.

**open** All year
**bedrooms** 1 double, 1 twin, 1 single
**bathrooms** All en suite
**payment** Cash/cheques

Room 📺 🍵 🍲   General 🛋 ⚹ ✿

WALKERS WELCOME / WELCOME WALKERS

# Best foot forward

Walkers feel at home in accommodation participating in our Walkers Welcome scheme. Look out for the symbol. Consider walking all or part of a long-distance route – go online at nationaltrail.co.uk.

---

**WADEBRIDGE,** Cornwall Map ref 1B2

★ ★ ★ ★
**FARMHOUSE**

B&B per room per night
d £45.00–£50.00

# Polstags Farmhouse Bed & Breakfast

Polstags, Amble, Wadebridge PL27 6EW  t (01208) 895134  e l.dally@btinternet.com
w polstagsfarmhouse.co.uk

**open** All year
**bedrooms** 1 double, 1 family
**bathrooms** All en suite
**payment** Cash/cheques

Polstags is a new farmhouse full of traditional character, situated along a quiet country lane on the edge of our working farm. The newly furnished, en suite rooms have fantastic views overlooking the Camel Estuary. If you are a family and would love to stay near Rock and Polzeath beaches, come to Polstags.

⊕ A39 to Camelford, continue to Wadebridge, B3314 towards Rock Polzeath. After 2 miles take Chapel Amble turning on right. Polstags is 0.5 miles on left.

Room 📺 ♿ 🕯  General 🛏 🏴 🅿 ✂ 🐾 ✳  Leisure ∪ ► 🚲 🏛

---

**WADEBRIDGE,** Cornwall Map ref 1B2

★ ★ ★ ★
**GUEST ACCOMMODATION**

B&B per room per night
d £52.00–£59.00
Evening meal per person
Min £12.50

# Tregolls Farm

St Wenn, Bodmin PL30 5PG  t (01208) 812154  f (01208) 812154  w tregollsfarm.co.uk

**open** All year except Christmas
**bedrooms** 1 double, 1 twin
**bathrooms** All en suite
**payment** Credit/debit cards, cash/cheques

Set in a picturesque valley overlooking fields of cows and sheep. Grade II Listed farmhouse with beautiful countryside views from all windows. En suite bedrooms. Farm trail links up to Saints Way footpath. Pets' corner. Eden, Helligan, Fowey and Padstow all within 25 minutes' drive.

⊕ Four miles south of Wadebridge. O.S. Map 200, ref. 983661 or phone for directions.

♥ 3-night break available at a special price.

Room 📺 ♿  General 🛏 🏴 🅿 ✂ ✕ 🐾 ✳  Leisure ✦ 🎣 🚲 🏛

---

**WARMINSTER,** Wiltshire Map ref 2B2

★ ★ ★ ★
**INN**

B&B per room per night
s £55.00
d £75.00
Evening meal per person
£7.95–£14.95

# The George Inn

Longbridge Deverill, Warminster BA12 7DG  t (01985) 840396  f (01985) 841333
w thegeorgeinnlongbridgedeverill.co.uk

Country inn, set on the edge of River Wylye. Luxury accommodation, home-cooked food, large beer garden, warm welcome.

**open** All year
**bedrooms** 5 double, 4 twin, 1 family, 1 suite
**bathrooms** All en suite
**payment** Credit/debit cards, cash/cheques

Room 🛏 ☎ 📺 ♿ 🕯  General 🛏 🏴 🅿 ✂ ❗ ✕ 🐾 ✳  Leisure ► 🏛

---

**WELLS,** Somerset Map ref 2A2

★ ★ ★
**GUEST ACCOMMODATION**

B&B per room per night
s £25.00
d £50.00

# 30 Mary Road

Mary Road, Wells BA5 2NF  t (01749) 674031  f (01749) 674031  e triciabailey30@hotmail.com

Comfortable, friendly, family home. Easy walking distance from city centre. Choice of breakfasts. TV in rooms. Tea/coffee. Central heating. One double has en suite toilet. Parking. Open February to November.

**bedrooms** 2 double, 2 single
**payment** Cash/cheques, euros

Room 📺 ♿  General 🛏3 🅿 ✂ 🍳 ✳  Leisure ∪ 🎣 ► 🚲 🏛

**WELLS,** Somerset Map ref 2A2

★★★★
**BED & BREAKFAST**

B&B per room per night
s £50.00–£65.00
d £65.00

# Islington Farm

Wells BA5 1US  t (01749) 673445  f (01749) 673445  e islingtonfarm2004@yahoo.co.uk
w islingtonfarmatwells.co.uk

**open** All year except Christmas and New Year
**bedrooms** 1 double, 1 twin
**bathrooms** All en suite
**payment** Credit/debit cards, cash/cheques

Uniquely situated adjacent to the Bishop's Palace, a 300-year-old farmhouse surrounded by fields and parkland, just a three-minute walk from the city centre. Private parking. Quiet riverside location with choice of excellent restaurants and pubs nearby. Home-cooked breakfast with own free-range eggs.

⊕ At roundabout on A371 take 3rd exit. Right by Sherston Hotel. Right opposite Full Moon Inn. Enter Silver Street. 200yds on right with 6ft-high white gates.

Room 📺 👜 🖳  General ⛄ 🎠 🏓 P ⚡ 🍳  Leisure ♪ 🏕 🏊

---

**WELLS,** Somerset Map ref 2A2

★★★
**GUEST ACCOMMODATION**

B&B per room per night
s £30.00
d £55.00

# Worth House

Worth, Wookey, Wells BA5 1LW  t (01749) 672041  e margaret@wookey.eclipse.co.uk

Small country hotel, part dating back to the 16thC. Exposed beams and log fires. Two miles from Wells on the B3139.

**open** All year
**bedrooms** 3 double, 2 twin, 1 single
**bathrooms** All en suite
**payment** Credit/debit cards, cash/cheques

Room 📺 👜 🖳  General P ⚡ ✕ ♨ ❄  Leisure 🏕 🏊

---

**WEMBWORTHY,** Devon Map ref 1C2

★★★★
**GUEST ACCOMMODATION**

B&B per room per night
s £30.00–£35.00
d £50.00–£60.00

# Lymington Arms

Lama Cross, Wembworthy, Chulmleigh EX18 7SA  t (01837) 83572  f (01837) 680074
e lymingtonarms@btconnect.com  w lymingtonarms.co.uk

**open** All year
**bedrooms** 1 double, 1 twin
**bathrooms** 1 en suite, 1 private
**payment** Credit/debit cards, cash/cheques

This busy, good-value gastropub with rooms is in a quiet rural location, and offers a changing selection of dishes made from good-quality local produce. The culinary skills and experience of our chef, Steve Kinsey, are now appreciated by a clientele who travel from far and wide.

⊕ Cross railway at Eggesford station, follow signs for Wembworthy and Winkleigh. Lymington Arms on crossroads before the village.

Room 📺 👜 🖳  General ⛄ 🎠 P ⚡ ✕ ♨ ❄ 🐕  Leisure ∪ ♪ 🏕 🚵

---

# A holiday for Fido?

Some proprietors welcome well-behaved pets. Look for the 🐕 symbol in the accommodation listings. You can also buy a copy of our new guide – Welcome Pets! – available from good bookshops and online at visitbritaindirect.com.

## WEST LOOE, Cornwall Map ref 1C3

★★
**GUEST HOUSE**

B&B per room per night
s £20.00–£28.00
d £46.00–£50.00

# Tidal Court

Church Street, West Looe, Looe PL13 2EX  t (01503) 263695

**open** All year except Christmas
**bedrooms** 1 double, 1 twin, 1 single, 2 family
**bathrooms** 4 en suite, 1 private
**payment** Cash/cheques, euros

Small, family-run guesthouse where a warm welcome is assured. Tidal is situated in the centre of West Looe, less than one minutes' walk from the harbour, quayside and ferry to East Looe. Enjoy the seaside amenities of beaches, coves, boat trips and fishing, or a stunning cliff walk to Polperro.

Room 🛏 📺 ♿  General 🕿 ⚒ 🍴 🐕  Leisure ♪ ▶ 🚲 🏊

## WEST MOORS, Dorset Map ref 2B3

★★★★
**BED & BREAKFAST**

B&B per room per night
s £25.00–£30.00
d £50.00

# Carey

11 Southern Avenue, West Moors, Ferndown BH22 0BJ  t (01202) 861159
e russell@lesmor.fsnet.co.uk

Your comfort is our priority in this quiet neighbourhood. Ample parking. Within easy reach of New Forest, Bournemouth and Poole. Full breakfast menu.

**open** All year except Christmas and New Year
**bedrooms** 1 double, 1 twin
**bathrooms** 1 en suite, 1 private
**payment** Cash/cheques

Room 🛏 📺 ♿  General P ⚒ ✿

## WEST PORLOCK, Somerset Map ref 1D1

★★★★
**GUEST ACCOMMODATION**

B&B per room per night
s Min £35.00
d £64.00–£69.00

# West Porlock House

West Porlock, Minehead TA24 8NX  t (01643) 862880  e westporlockhouse@amserve.com

A small country house overlooking the sea and countryside on the road from Porlock to Porlock Weir. Lovely woodland garden set in five acres with exceptional sea views. Open March to November.

**bedrooms** 2 double, 2 twin, 1 family
**bathrooms** 2 en suite, 3 private
**payment** Credit/debit cards, cash/cheques

Room 📺 ♿  General 🕿6 P ⚒ 🐴 ✿

## WESTON-SUPER-MARE, Somerset Map ref 1D1

★★★
**BED & BREAKFAST**

B&B per room per night
s £23.00–£33.00
d £44.00–£56.00

# Moorlands Country House

30 Main Road, Hutton, Weston-super-Mare BS24 9QH  t (01934) 812283  f (01934) 812283
e margaret-holt@hotmail.co.uk  w guestaccom.co.uk/035.htm

**open** All year
**bedrooms** 1 double, 2 twin, 1 single, 2 family
**bathrooms** 5 en suite
**payment** Credit/debit cards, cash/cheques

Family-run 18thC house in mature, landscaped grounds. The Holts have been at Moorlands for the past 40 years. Hutton is a pretty village with a pub serving meals. Close to hill and country walks and many places of interest easily reached by car. Riding can be arranged for children free.

⊕ *Weston-super-Mare to Taunton (A370), turn left at roundabout near hospital. Proceed 1.5 miles to Hutton, where Moorlands is on main road, on right, opposite garage.*

Room 🛏 📺 ♿  General 🕿 🛏 🅿 P 🍴 ✿ 🐕  Leisure ∪

## WEYMOUTH, Dorset Map ref 2B3

★ ★ ★
GUEST ACCOMMODATION

B&B per room per night
s £49.00–£59.00
d £68.00–£88.00
Evening meal per person
£11.75–£14.75

### The Kinley

98 The Esplanade, Weymouth DT4 7AT  **t** (01305) 782264  **f** (01305) 786676
**e** hotelkinley@hotmail.com  **w** hotelkinley.co.uk

Hotel situated along the seafront, within easy reach of the town centre. Garage for six cars. No supplement for sea view. Evening meals.

**open** All year
**bedrooms** 7 double, 1 twin, 1 family
**bathrooms** All en suite
**payment** Credit/debit cards, cash/cheques, euros

Room 🛏 📺 ⬇ ♨  General 🕭 ▥ ⅋ P ⅍ ♥ 🍴 ₪

## WEYMOUTH, Dorset Map ref 2B3

★ ★ ★ ★
BED & BREAKFAST

B&B per room per night
s £54.00–£60.00
d £75.00–£85.00

### Old Harbour View

12 Trinity Road, Weymouth DT4 8TJ  **t** (01305) 774633 & 07974 422241  **f** (01305) 750828
**e** pv_1st_ind@yahoo.co.uk

Idyllic Georgian harbourside town house, offering two charming double bedrooms. Restaurants, pubs, sandy beach and ferries to the Channel Islands on its doorstep.

**open** All year except Christmas and New Year
**bedrooms** 1 double, 1 twin
**bathrooms** All en suite
**payment** Credit/debit cards, cash/cheques

Room 📺 ⬇  General P ⅍ 🍴 ₪ 🖧 ▣  Leisure ♪ ◁ 🚲

## WEYMOUTH, Dorset Map ref 2B3

★ ★ ★
GUEST ACCOMMODATION

B&B per room per night
d £50.00–£70.00

### St John's Guest House

7 Dorchester Road, Weymouth DT4 7JR  **t** (01305) 775523  **f** (01305) 775815
**e** stayat@stjohnsguesthouse.fsnet.co.uk  **w** stjohnsguesthouse.co.uk

A friendly, family guesthouse ideally situated adjoining the Esplanade, 50yds from the beach. Large, free car park. All rooms en suite, family suite available.

**open** All year except Christmas and New Year
**bedrooms** 4 double, 2 twin, 1 family, 1 suite
**bathrooms** All en suite
**payment** Credit/debit cards, cash/cheques

Room 🛏 📺 ⬇ ♨  General 🕭3 P 🍴 ₪

## WIMBORNE MINSTER, Dorset Map ref 2B3

★ ★
INN

B&B per room per night
s £35.00–£45.00
d £50.00–£70.00

### The Albion

High Street, Wimborne Minster BH21 1HR  **t** (01202) 882492  **f** (01202) 639333
**e** albioninn-wimborne@tiscali.co.uk  **w** albioninn-wimborne.co.uk

The oldest-surviving coaching house in Wimborne, situated just off the town square opposite the minster. All rooms with modern facilities. Large bathroom with WC, shower and bath.

**open** All year except Christmas
**bedrooms** 1 double, 1 twin, 1 family
**payment** Credit/debit cards, cash/cheques, euros

Room 📺 ⬇ ♨  General 🕭 ♥ ✕ ✿  Leisure ♪ ◁

# Check the maps

Colour maps at the front pinpoint all the cities, towns and villages where you will find accommodation entries in the regional sections. Pick your location and then refer to the place index at the back to find the page number.

**WINKLEIGH,** Devon Map ref 1C2

★★★★
GUEST ACCOMMODATION

B&B per room per night
s £35.00
d £60.00

## The Old Parsonage

Court Walk, Winkleigh EX19 8JA **t** (01837) 83772 **f** (01837) 680074 **e** tony@lymingtonarms.co.uk

**open** All year
**bedrooms** 4 double
**bathrooms** All en suite
**payment** Cash/cheques

Typical Devon thatched and cob-walled house. Park-like gardens have many magnificent trees, rhododendrons and azaleas. Comfortable, en suite bedrooms with lots of old-world charm. Garden gate leads to village square. Five minutes away at Wembworthy we recommend the Lymington Arms for its excellent restaurant and blackboard menus.

⊕ *From M5 jct 27, follow signs to Tiverton (A361). Follow signs to Witheridge, Eggesford, Wembworthy, Winkleigh.*

Room General 5 P

**WOOLACOMBE,** Devon Map ref 1C1

★★★★
GUEST HOUSE
SILVER AWARD

B&B per room per night
s £25.00–£30.00
d £60.00–£85.00

## Sandunes Guest House

Beach Road, Woolacombe EX34 7BT **t** (01271) 870661 **e** info@sandwool.fsnet.co.uk
**w** sandwool.fsnet.co.uk

**open** All year except Christmas and New Year
**bedrooms** 4 double, 1 single
**bathrooms** 4 en suite
**payment** Cash/cheques

Small, friendly guesthouse overlooking National Trust land and three miles of golden beach. An ideal base for exploring the beautiful area of North Devon. All rooms tastefully decorated and furnished to a high standard. Balcony rooms available to sit and enjoy the spectacular scenery.

⊕ *From M5 exit jct 27 onto A361. Follow road through Barnstaple towards Ilfracombe. At Mullacott Cross take signposted road to Woolacombe (B3343).*

Room General P Leisure

**WOOLACOMBE,** Devon Map ref 1C1

★★★★
GUEST ACCOMMODATION
SILVER AWARD

B&B per room per night
s £40.00–£50.00
d £60.00–£80.00
Evening meal per person
£18.00

## Sunny Nook

Beach Road, Woolacombe EX34 7AA **t** (01271) 870964 **e** kate@sunnynook.co.uk
**w** sunnynook.co.uk

**open** All year except Christmas and New Year
**bedrooms** 3 double, 1 twin
**bathrooms** All en suite
**payment** Credit/debit cards, cash/cheques, euros

A small, welcoming and friendly B&B for the more discerning guest. A real home from home. Close to Woolacombe's sandy beach, and South West Coastal Path. Open all year except Christmas and New Year.

Room General 12 P Leisure

### Mention our name

Please mention this guide when making your booking.

### YATTON KEYNELL, Wiltshire Map ref 2B2

★★★★
**BED & BREAKFAST**

B&B per room per night
s  Min £65.00
d  Min £75.00

## Combehead Barn

Giddeahall, Yatton Keynell, Chippenham SN14 7ES  **t** (01249) 783487  **e** combe2005@aol.com
**w** thebarncombehead.co.uk

Self-contained stone barn; central heating; twin
bed; en-suite bathroom; sitting room/dining area;
downstairs cloakroom; kitchen; patio area;
garden.

**open** All year
**bedrooms** 1 twin
**bathrooms** En suite
**payment** Cash/cheques

Room TV 🍵  General P 🍴 🛏 ❄

### YELVERTON, Devon Map ref 1C2

★★★★
**GUEST ACCOMMODATION**

B&B per room per night
s  £37.50–£42.50
d  £65.00–£70.00

## Overcombe House

Old Station Road, Yelverton PL20 7RA  **t** (01822) 853501  **f** (01822) 853602
**e** enquiries@overcombehotel.co.uk  **w** overcombehotel.co.uk

**open** All year except Christmas
**bedrooms** 4 double, 3 twin, 1 single
**bathrooms** All en suite
**payment** Credit/debit cards, cash/cheques

Offering a warm, friendly welcome in relaxed,
comfortable surroundings with a substantial
breakfast using local and home-made produce.
Enjoying beautiful views over the village and
Dartmoor. Conveniently located for exploring the
varied attractions of both Devon and Cornwall, in
particular Dartmoor National Park and the adjacent
Tamar Valley.

⊕ *Situated between Plymouth and Tavistock. Located on the
edge of the village of Horrabridge and just over a mile
north-west of Yelverton heading towards Tavistock.*

Room 🛋 TV ♿ 🍵  General ☌5 P 🍴 🍽 🛏 ❄  Leisure ∪ ♪ ▶ 🚲 🚶

# Country ways

The Countryside Rights of Way Act gives
people new rights to walk on areas of open
countryside and registered common land.

To find out where you can go and what you can do, as
well as information about taking your dog to the
countryside, go online at countrysideaccess.gov.uk.

And when you're out and about...

**Always follow the Country Code**

• Be safe – plan ahead and follow any signs
• Leave gates and property as you find them
• Protect plants and animals, and take your litter home
• Keep dogs under close control
• Consider other people

# Enjoy England assessed accommodation

On the following pages you will find an exclusive listing of all bed and breakfast accommodation in England that has been assessed for quality by Enjoy England.

The information includes brief contact details for each place to stay, together with its star rating, classification and quality award if appropriate. The listing also shows if an establishment has a National Accessible rating or participates in the Welcome schemes: Cyclists Welcome, Walkers Welcome, Welcome Pets! and Families Welcome (see the front of the guide for further information).

Accommodation is listed by region and then alphabetically by place name. Establishments may be located in, or a short distance from, the places in the blue bands.

More detailed information on all the properties shown in bold can be found in the regional sections (where establishments have paid to have their details included). To find these entries please refer to the property index at the back of this guide.

The list which follows was compiled slightly later than the regional sections. For this reason you may find that, in a few instances, a rating and quality award may differ between the two sections. This list contains the most up-to-date information and was correct at the time of going to press.

## ENGLAND'S NORTHWEST

### ABBEYSTEAD
Lancashire

**Greenbank Farmhouse**
★★★ *Bed & Breakfast*
Abbeystead, Lancaster
LA2 9BA
t (01524) 792063
e tait@greenbankfarmhouse.
freeserve.co.uk
w greenbankfarmhouse.co.uk

### ACCRINGTON
Lancashire

**Norwood Guest House**
★★★★ *Guest House*
SILVER AWARD
349 Whalley Road, Accrington
BB5 5DF
t (01254) 398132
e stuart@norwoodguesthouse.
co.uk
w norwoodguesthouse.co.uk

### AINTREE
Merseyside

**A Church View Guest House**
★★ *Bed & Breakfast*
7 Church Avenue, Liverpool
L9 4SG
t (0151) 525 8166

### ALDERLEY EDGE
Cheshire

**Mayfield Bed & Breakfast @ Sheila's** ★★★
*Bed & Breakfast*
Wilmslow Road, Alderley Edge
SK9 7QW
t (01625) 583991 &
07703 289663

### ALSTON
Cumbria

**Greycroft** ★★★★
*Bed & Breakfast*
SILVER AWARD
Middle Park, The Raise, Alston
CA9 3AR
t (01434) 381383
e pat@greycroftalston.co.uk
w greycroftalston.co.uk

**Rosemount Cottage** ★★★★
*Guest Accommodation*
Rosemount, Burgh-by-Sands,
Carlisle CA5 6AN
t (01228) 576440
e tweentown@aol.com
w rosemountcottage.co.uk

### AMBLESIDE
Cumbria

**2 Cambridge Villas** ★★★★
*Guest House*
Church Street, Ambleside
LA22 9DL
t (015394) 32142
e charles@black475.fsnet.co.
uk
w 2cambridgevillas.co.uk

**3 Cambridge Villas** ★★★★
*Guest House*
Church Street, Ambleside
LA22 9DL
t (015394) 32307
e cambridgevillas3@aol.com
w 3cambridgevillas.co.uk

**Ambleside Backpackers** ★
*Backpacker*
Old Lake Road, Ambleside
LA22 0DJ
t (015394) 32340
e enquiries@
englishlakesbackpackers.co.uk
w englishlakesbackpackers.co.
uk

**Amboseli Lodge** ★★★★
*Bed & Breakfast*
SILVER AWARD
Rothay Road, Ambleside
LA22 0EE
t (015394) 31110
e enquiries@amboselilodge.
co.uk
w amboselilodge.co.uk

**Barnes Fell Guest House**
★★★★ *Guest House*
SILVER AWARD
Low Gale, Ambleside
LA22 0BB
t (015394) 33311
e ethna@barnesfell.co.uk
w barnesfellguesthouse.co.uk

**Brantfell House** ★★★★
*Guest House*
Rothay Road, Ambleside
LA22 0EE
t (015394) 32239
e brantfell@kencomp.net
w brantfell.co.uk

**Chapel House** ★★★
*Guest House*
Kirkstone Road, Ambleside
LA22 9DZ
t (015394) 33143
e info@chapelhouse-
ambleside.co.uk
w chapelhouse-ambleside.co.
uk

**Claremont House**
Rating Applied For
*Guest House*
Compston Road, Ambleside
LA22 9DJ
t (015394) 33448
e enquiries@
claremontambleside.co.uk
w claremontambleside.co.uk

**Compston House American-Style B&B** ★★★★
*Guest House*
Compston Road, Ambleside
LA22 9DJ
t (015394) 32305
e stay@compstonhouse.co.uk
w compstonhouse.co.uk

**Crow How Country House**
★★★★
*Guest Accommodation*
Rydal Road, Ambleside
LA22 9PN
t (015394) 32193
e stay@crowhow.co.uk
w crowhow.co.uk

**Dower House** ★★★★
*Bed & Breakfast*
Wray Castle, Low Wray,
Ambleside LA22 0JA
t (015394) 33211

**Easedale Lodge Guest House**
★★★★ *Guest House*
SILVER AWARD
Compston Road, Ambleside
LA22 9DJ
t (015394) 32112
e enquiries@
easedaleambleside.co.uk
w easedaleambleside.co.uk

**Elder Grove** ★★★★
*Guest Accommodation*
SILVER AWARD
Lake Road, Ambleside
LA22 0DB
t (015394) 32504
e info@eldergrove.co.uk
w eldergrove.co.uk

**Far Nook** ★★★★★
*Guest Accommodation*
SILVER AWARD
Rydal Road, Ambleside
LA22 9BA
t (015394) 31605
e mary@farnook.co.uk
w farnook.co.uk

**Fern Cottage** ★★★★
*Bed & Breakfast*
6 Waterhead Terrace,
Ambleside LA22 0HA
t (015394) 33007
e hibbertsally@hotmail.com
w ferncottageguesthouse.co.
uk

**Ferndale Lodge** ★★★
*Guest House*
Lake Road, Ambleside
LA22 0DB
t (015394) 32207
e stay@ferndalelodge.co.uk
w ferndalelodge.co.uk

**Fisherbeck** ★★★★
*Guest Accommodation*
SILVER AWARD
Lake Road, Ambleside
LA22 0DH
t (015394) 33215
e email@fisherbeckhotel.co.uk
w fisherbeckhotel.co.uk

**Foxghyll** ★★★★
*Bed & Breakfast*
Under Loughrigg, Ambleside
LA22 9LL
t (015394) 33292
e foxghyll@hotmail.com
w foxghyll.co.uk

**Freshfields Guest House**
★★★★ *Guest House*
SILVER AWARD
Wansfell Road, Ambleside
LA22 0EG
t (015394) 34469
e info@freshfieldsguesthouse.
co.uk
w freshfieldsguesthouse.co.uk

**The Gables** ★★★★
*Guest Accommodation*
Church Walk, Ambleside
LA22 9DJ
t (015394) 33272
e info@thegables-ambleside.
co.uk
w thegables-ambleside.co.uk

**High Wray Farm B&B**
★★★★ *Farmhouse*
High Wray, Ambleside
LA22 0JE
t (015394) 32280
e sheila@highwrayfarm.co.uk
w highwrayfarm.co.uk

**Highfield** ★★★★
*Bed & Breakfast*
Lake Road, Ambleside
LA22 0DB
t (015394) 32671
e info@highfield-ambleside.
co.uk
w highfield-ambleside.co.uk

**Hillsdale in Ambleside**
★★★★
*Guest Accommodation*
Church Street, Ambleside
LA22 0BT
t (015394) 33174
e stay@hillsdaleambleside.co.
uk
w hillsdaleambleside.co.uk

**Holme Lea Guest House**
★★★ *Guest House*
Church Street, Ambleside
LA22 0BT
t (015394) 32114
e enquiries@
holmeleaguesthouse.co.uk
w holmeleaguesthouse.co.uk

**Holmeshead Farm** ★★★★
*Farmhouse*
Skelwith Fold, Ambleside
LA22 0HU
t (015394) 33048
e info@holmesheadfarm.co.uk
w holmesheadfarm.co.uk

**Kingswood 'Bee & Bee'**
★★★★ *Guest House*
SILVER AWARD
Old Lake Road, Ambleside
LA22 0AE
t (015394) 34081
e info@kingswood-
guesthouse.co.uk
w kingswood-guesthouse.co.
uk

**Lacet House** ★★★★
*Guest House*
Kelsick Road, Ambleside
LA22 0EA
t (015394) 34342
e lacethouse@aol.com
w lacethouse.co.uk

**Lancrigg Vegetarian Country House Hotel** ★★★
*Guest Accommodation*
Easedale, Grasmere LA22 9QN
t (015394) 35317
e info@lancrigg.co.uk
w lancrigg.co.uk

**Lattendales Guest House**
★★★★ *Guest House*
Compston Road, Ambleside
LA22 9DJ
t (015394) 32368
e info@lattendales.co.uk
w lattendales.co.uk

**Lyndale Guest House ★★★**
*Guest Accommodation*
Low Fold, Lake Road,
Ambleside LA22 0DN
t (015394) 34244
e alison@lyndale-guesthouse.
co.uk
w lyndale-guesthouse.co.uk

**Meadowbank ★★★**
*Guest Accommodation*
Rydal Road, Ambleside
LA22 9BA
t (015394) 32710
e enquiries@meadowbank.
org.uk

**Melrose Guest House
★★★★**
*Guest Accommodation*
Church Street, Ambleside
LA22 0BT
t (015394) 32500
e info@melrose-guesthouse.
co.uk
w melrose-guesthouse.co.uk

**Norwood House ★★★★**
*Guest Accommodation*
Church Street, Ambleside
LA22 0BT
t (015394) 33349
e mail@norwoodhouse.net
w norwoodhouse.net

**The Old Vicarage ★★★★**
*Guest Accommodation*
Vicarage Road, Ambleside
LA22 9DH
t (015394) 33364
e info@oldvicarageambleside.
co.uk
w oldvicarageambleside.co.uk

**Park House Guest House In
Ambleside ★★★**
*Guest House*
Compston Road, Ambleside
LA22 9DJ
t (015394) 31107
e mail@loughrigg.plus.com
w parkhouseguesthouse.com

**Red Bank ★★★★★**
*Bed & Breakfast*
SILVER AWARD
Wansfell Road, Ambleside
LA22 0EG
t (015394) 34637
e info@red-bank.co.uk
w red-bank.co.uk

**Riverside ★★★★**
*Guest Accommodation*
SILVER AWARD
Under Loughrigg, Rothay
Bridge, Ambleside LA22 9LJ
t (015394) 32395
e info@riverside-at-ambleside.
co.uk
w riverside-at-ambleside.co.uk

**Rothay Garth ★★★★**
*Guest Accommodation*
Rothay Road, Ambleside
LA22 0EE
t (015394) 32217
e book@rothay-garth.co.uk
w rothay-garth.co.uk

**Rothay House ★★★**
*Guest Accommodation*
Rothay Road, Ambleside
LA22 0EE
t (015394) 32434
e email@rothay-house.com
w rothay-house.com

**The Rysdale Hotel ★★★★**
*Guest Accommodation*
Rothay Road, Ambleside
LA22 0EE
t (015394) 32140
e info@rysdalehotel.co.uk
w rysdalehotel.co.uk

**Smallwood House ★★★★**
*Guest Accommodation*
Compston Road, Ambleside
LA22 9DJ
t (015394) 32330
e enq@smallwoodhotel.co.uk
w smallwoodhotel.co.uk

**Stepping Stones ★★★★**
*Bed & Breakfast*
SILVER AWARD
Under Loughrigg, Ambleside
LA22 9LN
t (015394) 33552
e info@
steppingstonesambleside.co.uk
w steppingstonesambleside.
co.uk

**Thorneyfield Guest House
★★★★ *Guest House***
Compston Road, Ambleside
LA22 9DJ
t (015394) 32464
e info@thorneyfield.co.uk
w thorneyfield.co.uk

**Tock How Farm ★★★★**
*Farmhouse*
High Wray, Ambleside
LA22 0JF
t (015394) 36106
e info@tock-how-farm.com
w tock-how-farm.com

**Walmar ★★★ *Guest House***
Lake Road, Ambleside
LA22 0DB
t (015394) 32454
e walmar.ambleside@tiscali.
co.uk
w walmar-ambleside.co.uk

**Wateredge Inn ★★★★ *Inn***
Waterhead Bay, Ambleside
LA22 0EP
t (015394) 32332
e stay@wateredgeinn.co.uk
w wateredgeinn.co.uk

**Waterwheel Guesthouse
★★★★ *Bed & Breakfast***
SILVER AWARD
3 Bridge Street, Ambleside
LA22 9DU
t (015394) 33286
e info@waterwheelambleside.
co.uk
w waterwheelambleside.co.uk

APPLEBY-IN-WESTMORLAND
Cumbria

**Broom House ★★★★**
*Guest Accommodation*
Long Marton, Appleby-in-
Westmorland CA16 6JP
t (01768) 361318
e sandra@bland01.freeserve.
co.uk
w broomhouseappleby.co.uk

**Royal Oak Inn ★★★★ *Inn***
45 Bongate, Appleby-in-
Westmorland CA16 6UN
t (01768) 351463

ARNSIDE
Cumbria

**Arnside YHA ★★★ *Hostel***
Oakfield Lodge, Redhills Road,
Arnside LA5 0AT
t (01524) 761781
e arnside@yha.org.uk
w yha.org.uk

**The Willowfield ★★★★**
*Guest Accommodation*
53 The Promenade, Arnside
LA5 0AD
t (01524) 761354
e info@willowfield.uk.com
w willowfield.uk.com

ASHTON-UNDER-LYNE
Greater Manchester

**Lynwood Hotel ★★★★**
*Guest Accommodation*
3 Richmond Street, Ashton-
under-Lyne OL6 7TX
t (0161) 330 5358

BACUP
Lancashire

**Rossbrook House ★★★★**
*Guest Accommodation*
New Line, Bacup OL13 0BY
t (01706) 878187
e rossbkhouse@aol.com
w a1touristguide.com/
rossbrookhouse

BAMPTON
Cumbria

**Mardale Inn @ St Patricks
Well**
Rating Applied For
*Guest Accommodation*
Bampton, Penrith CA10 2RQ
t (01931) 713244
e info@mardaleinn.co.uk
w mardaleinn.co.uk

BARDSEA
Cumbria

**The Ship Inn ★★★ *Inn***
Main Street, Bardsea,
Ulverston LA12 9QT
t (01229) 869329
e shipinnbardsea@yahoo.co.
uk

BARLEY
Lancashire

**The Pendle Inn ★★★★**
*Guest Accommodation*
Barley, Burnley BB12 9JX
t (01282) 614808
e john@pendleinn.freeserve.
co.uk
w pendleinn.freeserve.co.uk

BARROWFORD
Lancashire

**Holmefield Bed & Breakfast
★★★★ *Bed & Breakfast***
57 Holmefield Gardens,
Barrowford, Nelson BB9 8NW
t (01282) 606984
e jayjay2@supanet.com

**Merok Bed & Breakfast
★★★★ *Bed & Breakfast***
124 Wheatley Lane Road,
Barrowford, Nelson BB9 6QW
t (01282) 612888
e pat@duxbury124.freeserve.
co.uk

BASHALL EAVES
Lancashire

**The Red Pump Inn ★★★★**
*Guest Accommodation*
Clitheroe Road, Bashall Eaves,
Clitheroe BB7 3DA
t (01254) 826227
e info@theredpumpinn.co.uk
w theredpumpinn.co.uk

BASSENTHWAITE
Cumbria

**Herdwick Croft Guest House
★★★★**
*Guest Accommodation*
SILVER AWARD
Bassenthwaite, Keswick
CA12 4RD
t (01768) 776241
e info@herdwick-croft.co.uk
w herdwick-croft.co.uk

**Highside Farm ★★★★**
*Farmhouse* SILVER AWARD
Bassenthwaite, Keswick
CA12 4QG
t (01768) 776952
e info@highside.co.uk
w highside.co.uk

**Link House by
Bassenthwaite Lake ★★★★**
*Guest House*
Bassenthwaite Lake, Keswick
CA13 9YD
t (01768) 776291
e info@link-house.co.uk
w link-house.co.uk

**Ouse Bridge House ★★★★**
*Guest House*
Dubwath, Bassenthwaite Lake,
Bassenthwaite CA13 9YD
t (01768) 776322
e enquiries@ousebridge.com
w ousebridge.com

**Ravenstone Lodge ★★★★**
*Guest House* SILVER AWARD
Bassenthwaite, Keswick
CA12 4QG
t (01768) 776629
e ravenstone.lodge@talk21.
com
w ravenstonelodge.co.uk

BEETHAM
Cumbria

**Barn Close/North West
Birds ★★★ *Bed & Breakfast***
Beetham, Milnthorpe LA7 7AL
t (015395) 63191
e anne@nwbirds.co.uk
w nwbirds.co.uk

BETCHTON
Cheshire

**Yew Tree Farm ★★★★**
*Bed & Breakfast*
Newcastle Road, Betchton,
Sandbach CW11 4TD
t (01477) 500626
e jshollinshead@btinternet.
com

BIRKENHEAD
Merseyside

**Shrewsbury Lodge Hotel
★★★ *Guest Accommodation***
31 Shrewsbury Road, Oxton
CH43 2JB
t (0151) 652 4029
e info@shrewsbury-hotel.com
w shrewsbury-hotel.com

**Villa Venezia** ★★★
*Guest Accommodation*
14-16 Prenton Road West,
Birkenhead CH42 9PN
t (0151) 608 9212
e veneziapizzeria1@aol.com

**The Windmill Hotel and Restaurant**
Rating Applied For
*Guest Accommodation*
Preston New Road, Blackburn
BB2 7NS
t (01254) 812189
e info@windmillatmellor.co.uk
w windmillatmellor.co.uk

**Aberford Hotel** ★★
*Guest Accommodation*
12-14 Yorkshire Street,
Blackpool FY1 5BG
t (01253) 625026
e info@aberfordhotel.co.uk
w aberfordhotel.co.uk

**Adelaide House** ★★★
*Guest Accommodation*
66-68 Adelaide Street,
Blackpool FY1 4LA
t (01253) 625172
e info@adelaidehotelhouse.
com
w adelaidehouse.com

**Alanco** ★★★ *Guest House*
2-4 General Street, Blackpool
FY1 1RW
t (01253) 622416

**Allendale Hotel** ★★★
*Guest House*
104 Albert Road, Blackpool
FY1 4PR
t (01253) 623268
e info@allendale-hotel.co.uk
w allendale-hotel.co.uk

**Almeria Hotel** ★★★
*Guest Accommodation*
61 Hornby Road, Blackpool
FY1 4QJ
t (01253) 294757
e almeria61@hotmail.co.uk

**Ardsley Guest Accommodation** ★★★
*Guest Accommodation*
20 Woodfield Road, Blackpool
FY1 6AX
t (01253) 345419

**Arendale Hotel** ★★★
*Guest Accommodation*
23 Gynn Avenue, Blackpool
FY1 2LD
t (01253) 351044
e arendale@zetnet.co.uk
w arendalehotel.co.uk

**Arncliffe Hotel** ★★★
*Guest House*
24 Osborne Road, Blackpool
FY4 1HJ
t (01253) 345209
e arncliffehotel@talk21.com
w blackpool-internet.co.uk/
homearncliffe.html

**Ascot Hotel** ★★★
*Guest Accommodation*
7 Alexandra Road, Blackpool
FY1 6BU
t (01253) 346439
e info@ascothotel.co.uk
w ascothotel.co.uk

**Ash Lodge** ★★★
*Guest House*
131 Hornby Road, Blackpool
FY1 4JG
t (01253) 627637
e admin@ashlodgehotel.co.uk
w ashlodgehotel.co.uk

**Astoria Hotel** ★★★
*Guest Accommodation*
118-120 Albert Road,
Blackpool FY1 4PN
t (01253) 621321
e enquiries@astoria-hotel.co.
uk
w astoria-hotel.co.uk

**The Avenue** ★★★
*Guest House*
56 Reads Avenue, Blackpool
FY1 4DE
t (01253) 626146
e info@blackpooluk.co.uk
w blackpooluk.co.uk

**The Bambi** ★★★
*Guest Accommodation*
27 Bright Street, Blackpool
FY4 1BS
t (01253) 343756
e bambihotel@hotmail.co.uk

**Bamford House Hotel** ★★★
*Guest House*
28 York Street, Blackpool
FY1 5AQ
t (01253) 622433
e info@
bamfordhotelblackpool.co.
uk
w bamfordhotelblackpool.co.
uk

**Baron Hotel** ★★★★
*Guest Accommodation*
296 North Promenade,
Blackpool FY1 2EY
t (01253) 622729

**Beachwood Guest House**
★★★ *Guest Accommodation*
30 Moore Street, Blackpool
FY4 1DA
t (01253) 401951
e m.coles@tesco.net
w beachwoodhotel.co.uk

**The Beauchief** ★★★
*Guest Accommodation*
48 King Edward Avenue,
Blackpool FY2 9TA
t (01253) 353314
e beauchief2hotel@amserve.
com
w smoothhound.co.uk/hotels/
beauchief.html

**The Beaucliffe** ★★★
*Guest Accommodation*
20-22 Holmfield Road,
Blackpool FY2 9TB
t (01253) 351663

**Belgrave 21** ★★★
*Guest House*
21 Barton Avenue, Blackpool
FY1 6AP
t (01253) 346792
e belgrave21@fsmail.net
w belgrave21.co.uk

**The Berwick** ★★★★
*Guest Accommodation*
23 King Edward Avenue,
Blackpool FY1 2LP
t (01253) 351496
e theberwickhotel@btconnect.
com
w theberwickhotel.co.uk

**Berwyn Guest House** ★★★
*Guest Accommodation*
1-2 Finchley Road, Blackpool
FY1 2LP
t (01253) 352896
e stay@berwynhotel.co.uk
w berwynhotel.co.uk

**The Beverley** ★★★
*Guest Accommodation*
25 Dean Street, Blackpool
FY4 1AU
t (01253) 344426
e holiday@beverleyhotel-
blackpool.co.uk
w beverleyhotel-blackpool.co.
uk

**Boltonia Hotel** ★★★
*Guest Accommodation*
124-126 Albert Road,
Blackpool FY1 4PN
t (01253) 620248
e info@boltoniahotel.co.uk
w boltoniahotel.co.uk

**Bracondale Guest House**
★★★★ *Guest House*
14 Warley Road, Blackpool
FY1 2JU
t (01253) 351650
e bracondale-hotel@
btconnect.com
w nosmokingblackpool.co.uk

**The Brayton** ★★★
*Guest Accommodation*
7-8 Finchley Road, Blackpool
FY1 2LP
t (01253) 351645
e blackpool@the-brayton-
hotel.com
w the-brayton-hotel.com

**Brincliffe Hotel** ★★★
*Guest Accommodation*
168-170 Queens Promenade,
Blackpool FY2 9JN
t (01253) 351654
e susan@brincliffehotel.co.uk
w brincliffehotel.co.uk

**Briny View** ★★
*Guest Accommodation*
2 Woodfield Road, Blackpool
FY1 6AX
t (01253) 346584
e brinyviewhotel@aol.com
w brinyviewhotel.co.uk

**The Brioni** ★★★
*Guest Accommodation*
324 Queens Promenade,
Blackpool FY2 9AB
t (01253) 351988
e hamlinheros@aol.com
w brionihotelblackpool.co.uk

**Broadway Hotel** ★★★
*Guest Accommodation*
4 Burlington Road West,
Blackpool FY1 4NL
t (01253) 341060
e broadwayhotel@btconect.
com
w broadwayhotel-blackpool.
co.uk

**Brooklands Hotel** ★★★
*Guest Accommodation*
28-30 King Edward Avenue,
Blackpool FY2 9TA
t (01253) 351479
e brooklandhotel@btinternet.
com
w brooklands-hotel.com

**Cardoh Lodge** ★★★
*Guest House*
21 Hull Road, Blackpool
FY1 4QB
t (01253) 627755

**Caroldene Hotel** ★★
*Guest Accommodation*
12 Woodfield Road, Blackpool
FY1 6AX
t (01253) 346963
e caroldenehotel2003@yahoo.
co.uk
w http://caroldenehotel.
mysite.wanadoo-members.co.
uk

**Chequers Plaza Hotel**
Rating Applied For
*Guest Accommodation*
24 Queens Promenade,
Blackpool FY2 9RN
t 0800 027 3107
e enquiries@chequersplaza.
com
w chequersplaza.com

**The Cheslyn** ★★★
*Guest Accommodation*
21 Moore Street, Blackpool
FY4 1DA
t (01253) 349672
e june_gerryburgess@hotmail.
co.uk
w cheslynguesthouse.co.uk

**Cliff Head Seafront Guest House** ★★★ *Guest House*
174 Queens Promenade,
Blackpool FY2 9JN
t (01253) 591086
e cliffheadhotelblackpool@
yahoo.co.uk
w cliffheadhotelblackpool.co.uk

**Clovelly** ★★★★
*Guest Accommodation*
22 St Chads Road, Blackpool
FY1 6BP
t (01253) 346087
e kamess2557@aol.com
w clovellyhotel.com

**Collingwood Hotel** ★★★★
*Guest Accommodation*
8-10 Holmfield Road, Blackpool
FY2 9SL
t (01253) 352929
e enquiries@
collingwoodhotel.co.uk

**Colyndene Hotel** ★★★
*Guest Accommodation*
53 Reads Avenue, Blackpool
FY1 4DG
t (01253) 295282

**Corona** ★★★
*Guest Accommodation*
18 Clifton Drive, Blackpool
FY4 1NX
t (01253) 342586
e coronablackpool@aol.com
w thecoronahotel.com

---

**Courtney's of Gynn Square ★★★★**
*Guest Accommodation*
1 Warbreck Hill Road,
Blackpool FY2 9SP
t (01253) 352179
e courtneyshotel@aol.com
w courtneysofgynnsquare.co.
uk

**The Craimar ★★★**
*Guest Accommodation*
32 Hull Road, Blackpool
FY1 4QB
t (01253) 622185
e janetmiveld135@msn.com
w craimarhotel.co.uk

**The Cumbrian Hotel ★★★**
*Guest House*
81 Hornby Road, Blackpool
FY1 4QP
t (01253) 623677
e john@johnbuchanan04.
wanadoo.co.uk

**Denely Private Hotel ★★★**
*Guest House*
15 King Edward Avenue,
Blackpool FY2 9TA
t (01253) 352757
e denely@tesco.net
w denelyhotel.co.uk

**Derwent Private Hotel ★★★**
*Guest House*
42 Palatine Road, Blackpool
FY1 4BY
t (01253) 620004
e chris@
derwenthotelblackpool.co.uk
w derwenthotelblackpool.co.
uk

**The Dudley Hotel ★★★**
*Guest Accommodation*
3 Alexandra Road, South
Shore, Blackpool FY1 6BU
t (01253) 346827

**Dudley Hotel ★★★**
*Guest Accommodation*
67 Dickson Road, Blackpool
FY1 2BX
t (01253) 620281
e dudley.hotel@btconnect.
com
w dudley-hotel.co.uk

**Edenfield Guest House**
Rating Applied For
*Guest House*
17 Cocker Street, Blackpool
FY1 2BY
t (01253) 624009
e info@edenfieldguesthouse.
com
w edenfieldguesthouse.com

**Elgin Hotel ★★★**
*Guest Accommodation*
36-42 Queens Promenade,
Blackpool FY2 9RW
t (01253) 351433
e info@elginhotel.com
w elginhotel.com

**Everglades Hotel ★★★**
*Guest House*
14 Barton Avenue, Blackpool
FY1 6AP
t (01253) 343093
e info@evergladesblackpool.
co.uk
w evergladesblackpool.co.uk

**The Fame ★★★**
*Guest Accommodation*
363 Promenade, Blackpool
FY1 6BJ
t (01253) 346615
e hotelfame@hotmail.co.uk
w hotelfame.com

**Feng Shui Hotel ★★★**
*Guest Accommodation*
661 New South Promenade,
Blackpool FY4 1RN
t (01253) 342266
e kate_burns@btconnect.com
w classic-feng-shui.com

**The Fern Royd ★★★**
*Guest Accommodation*
35 Holmfield Road, Blackpool
FY2 9TE
t (01253) 351066
e fernroyd@btconnect.com
w fern-royd-hotel-blackpool.
co.uk

**Gleneagles Hotel ★★★★**
*Guest Accommodation*
75 Albert Road, Blackpool
FY1 4PW
t (01253) 295266
e gleneaglesblackpool@tiscali.
co.uk
w gleneagles-hotel.com

**Gleneagles Hotel ★★**
*Guest Accommodation*
9 Bairstow Street, Blackpool
FY1 5BN
t (01253) 623771
e gleneagles99@hotmail.com

**The Glenholme Hotel ★★★**
*Guest Accommodation*
44 Alexandra Road, Blackpool
FY1 6BU
t (01253) 345823
e glenholme44@yahoo.co.uk
w glenholmehotel.co.uk

**The Glenmere ★★★**
*Guest Accommodation*
7 Gynn Avenue, Blackpool
FY1 2LD
t (01253) 351259
e glenmerebandb@aol.com
w glenmereguesthouse.co.uk

**The Golden Sands ★★★★**
*Guest Accommodation*
Gynn Avenue, Blackpool
FY1 2LD
t (01253) 352285

**Granville Hotel ★★★**
*Guest Accommodation*
12 Station Road, South Shore,
Blackpool FY4 1BE
t (01253) 343012
e wilft@granvillehotel.s.net.
co.uk
w thegranvillehotel.co.uk

**The Happy Return ★★★**
*Guest Accommodation*
17-19 Hull Road, Blackpool
FY1 4QB
t (01253) 622596
e happyreturn@yahoo.co.uk
w happyreturnhotel.co.uk

**Hartshead ★★★**
*Guest Accommodation*
17 King Edward Avenue, North
Shore, Blackpool FY2 9TA
t (01253) 353133 &
(01253) 357111
e info@hartshead-hotel.co.uk
w hartshead-hotel.co.uk

**Hatton Hotel ★★★**
*Guest Accommodation*
10 Banks Street, Blackpool
FY1 1RN
t (01253) 624944
w hattonhotel.gbr.cc

**Holmsdale Hotel ★★★**
*Guest Accommodation*
6-8 Pleasant Street, Blackpool
FY1 2JA
t (01253) 621008
e office@holmsdalehotel-
blackpool.com
w holmsdalehotel-blackpool.
com

**Holmside House ★★★**
*Guest House*
24 Barton Avenue, Blackpool
FY1 6AP
t (01253) 346045
e holmsidehotel@fsnet.co.uk
w holmsidehotel.fsnet.co.uk

**Hornby Villa Hotel ★★★**
*Guest Accommodation*
130 Hornby Road, Blackpool
FY1 4QS
t (01253) 624959
e hornbyvblackpool@aol.com
w hornbyvillahotel.com

**The Hurstmere ★★★**
*Guest Accommodation*
5 Alexandra Road, Blackpool
FY1 6BU
t (01253) 345843
e stay@thehurstmerehotel.
com
w thehurstmerehotel.com

**Inglewood ★★★**
*Guest House*
18 Holmfield Road, Blackpool
FY2 9TB
t (01253) 351668
e enquiries@
theinglewoodhotel.com
w theinglewoodhotel.com

**Karen Annes Guest House
★★★** *Guest House*
4 Barton Avenue, Blackpool
FY1 6AP
t (01253) 346719
e karen@karen-annes.
freeserve.co.uk
w karenanneshotel.com

**Kendal Private Guest
Accommodation ★★**
*Guest Accommodation*
76 Withnell Road, Blackpool
FY4 1HE
t (01253) 348209
e doberman4@icliffe1.
wanadoo.co.uk

**The Kimberley ★★★★**
*Guest House*
25 Gynn Avenue, Blackpool
FY1 2LD
t (01253) 352264
e thekimberleygynnavenue@
hotmail.com
w kimberleyguesthouse.com

**The King Edward ★★★**
*Guest Accommodation*
44 King Edward Avenue,
Blackpool FY2 9TA
t (01253) 352932
e enquiries@kingedwardhotel.
co.uk
w kingedwardhotel.co.uk

**Kings Court ★★★**
*Guest Accommodation*
34 King Edward Avenue,
Blackpool FY2 9TA
t (01253) 593312
e chris@kingscourthotel.
freeserve.co.uk
w blackpoolkingscourthotel.co.
uk

**Kingscliff Hotel ★★★**
*Guest Accommodation*
78 Hornby Road, Blackpool
FY1 4QJ
t (01253) 620200
e kingscliff.blackpool@virgin.
net
w kingscliffhotel.co.uk

**Kirkstall House ★★★**
*Guest Accommodation*
25 Hull Road, Blackpool
FY1 4QB
t (01253) 623077
e rooms@kirkstallhotel.co.uk
w kirkstallhotel.co.uk

**Llanryan Guest House ★★★**
*Guest Accommodation*
37 Reads Avenue, Blackpool
FY1 4DD
t (01253) 628446
e keith@llanryan.co.uk
w llanryan.co.uk

**Lynbar Guesthouse ★★★**
*Guest House*
32 Vance Road, Blackpool
FY1 4QD
t (01253) 294504
e enquiries@lynbarhotel.co.uk
w lynbarhotel.co.uk

**Lynmoore Guest House
★★★** *Guest Accommodation*
25 Moore Street, Blackpool
FY4 1DA
t (01253) 349888
e stay@lynmooreblackpool.
freeserve.co.uk
w lynmooreblackpool.co.uk

**Mackintosh Hotel ★★★**
*Guest Accommodation*
5 Gynn Avenue, Blackpool
FY1 2LD
t (01253) 352296

**The Manor Grove ★★**
*Guest House*
24 Leopold Grove, Blackpool
FY1 4LD
t (01253) 625577
e themanorgrove@
blueyonder.co.uk
w themanorgrove.co.uk

**The Marina ★★★**
*Guest House*
30 Gynn Avenue, Blackpool
FY1 2LD
t (01253) 352833
e robinglockhart@hotmail.com
w blackpoolmarina.com

**Marlow Lodge Hotel ★★★**
*Guest Accommodation*
76 Station Road, Blackpool
FY4 1EU
t (01253) 341580
e hotelreception@yahoo.co.uk
w blackpoolmarlowhotel.com

**The Middleton** ★★★
*Guest Accommodation*
55 Holmfield Road, Blackpool
FY2 9RU
**t** (01253) 354559
**e** info@middleton-hotel.co.uk
**w** middleton-hotel.co.uk

**Newholme Private Hotel**
★★★ *Guest House*
2 Wilton Parade, Blackpool
FY1 2HE
**t** (01253) 624010
**e** newholmehotel@aol.com
**w** newholme.biz

**North Crest Hotel** ★★★
*Guest House*
22 King Edward Avenue,
Blackpool FY2 9TD
**t** (01253) 355937
**e** info@northcrestblackpool.
co.uk
**w** northcrestblackpool.co.uk

**The Northdene** ★★★
*Guest House*
19 Gynn Avenue, Blackpool
FY1 2LD
**t** (01253) 353005
**e** phil@tackler.org.uk
**w** northdene.co.uk

**Norville House** ★★★
*Guest Accommodation*
44 Warbreck Hill Road,
Blackpool FY2 9SU
**t** (01253) 352714
**e** norvillehouse@btconnect.
com
**w** norvillehousehotel.co.uk

**The Norwood** ★★★
*Guest Accommodation*
35 Hull Road, Blackpool
FY1 4QB
**t** (01253) 621118
**e** norwood35@msn.com
**w** thenorwood.co.uk

**Number One** ★★★★★
*Bed & Breakfast*
**GOLD AWARD**
1 St Lukes Road, Blackpool
FY4 2EL
**t** (01253) 343901
**e** info@numberoneblackpool.
com
**w** numberoneblackpool.com

**Oban House Hotel** ★★★
*Guest Accommodation*
63 Holmfield Road, Blackpool
FY2 9RU
**t** (01253) 352413
**e** obanhousehotel@aol.com
**w** obanhousehotel.co.uk

**Osprey Hotel** ★★★
*Guest House*
27 Charnley Road, Blackpool
FY1 4PE
**t** (01253) 621684
**e** dinesh@theospreyhotel.com
**w** theospreyhotel.com

**The Pembroke** ★★★★
*Guest Accommodation*
11 King Edward Avenue,
Blackpool FY2 9TD
**t** (01253) 351306
**e** info@neartheprom.com
**w** neartheprom.com

**Penrhyn Hotel** ★★★
*Guest Accommodation*
38 King Edward Avenue,
Blackpool FY2 9TA
**t** (01253) 352762
**e** annettepenrhyn@orange.net
**w** thepenrhynhotel.co.uk

**Hotel Pilatus** ★★★
*Guest Accommodation*
10 Willshaw Road, Blackpool
FY2 9SH
**t** (01253) 352470
**e** enquiries@hotelpilatus.co.uk
**w** pilatushotel.co.uk

**The Poldhu** ★★★
*Guest Accommodation*
330 Queens Promenade,
Blackpool FY2 9AB
**t** (01253) 356918
**e** info@poldhu-hotel.co.uk
**w** poldhu-hotel.co.uk

**The Raffles Guest
Accommodation** ★★★★
*Guest Accommodation*
73-77 Hornby Road, Blackpool
FY1 4QJ
**t** (01253) 294713
**e** enquiries@
raffleshotelblackpool.fsworld.
co.uk
**w** raffleshotelblackpool.co.uk

**Rio Rita** ★★★
*Guest Accommodation*
49 Withnell Road, Blackpool
FY4 1HE
**t** (01253) 345203
**e** riorita@btconnect.com
**w** rioritahotel.co.uk

**Rockcliffe Hotel** ★★★
*Guest Accommodation*
248 Promenade, Blackpool
FY1 1RZ
**t** (01253) 623476
**e** rockcliffehotelblackpool@
blueyonder.co.uk
**w** rockcliffehotel.co.uk

**Rossdene Hotel** ★★★★
*Guest Accommodation*
12 Gynn Avenue, Blackpool
FY1 2LD
**t** (01253) 351714
**e** scott@rossdenehotel.
wanadoo.co.uk
**w** rossdenehotel.com

**Royal Seabank Hotel The**
★★★ *Guest Accommodation*
219-221 Promenade, Blackpool
FY1 5DL
**t** (01253) 622717

**Rutland Hotel** ★★★
*Guest Accommodation*
330 Promenade, Blackpool
FY1 2JG
**t** (01253) 622791
**e** enquiries@rutland-hotel.co.
uk
**w** rutland-hotel.co.uk

**The Rutlands** ★★★
*Guest Accommodation*
13 Hornby Road, Blackpool
FY1 4QG
**t** (01253) 623067
**w** rutlandshotel.co.uk

**St Ives Blackpool** ★★★
*Guest Accommodation*
10 King George Avenue,
Blackpool FY2 9SN
**t** (01253) 352122
**e** enquiries@stiveshotel-
blackpool.co.uk
**w** stiveshotel-blackpool.co.uk

**Sea View Guest House** ★★★
*Guest House*
10 Nelson Road, Blackpool
FY1 6AS
**t** (01253) 402316
**e** nelson@seaview.fsnet.co.uk
**w** seaview-blackpool.co.uk

**Seabreeze Guest House**
★★★★
*Guest Accommodation*
1 Gynn Avenue, Blackpool
FY1 2LD
**t** (01253) 351427
**e** info@vbreezey.co.uk
**w** vbreezy.co.uk

**Sheron House** ★★★★
*Guest House*
21 Gynn Avenue, Blackpool
FY1 2LD
**t** (01253) 354614
**e** enquiries@sheronhouse.co.
uk
**w** the-sheron.co.uk

**The South Beach Hotel**
★★★ *Guest Accommodation*
367 Promenade, Blackpool
FY1 6BJ
**t** (01253) 342250
**e** info@southbeachhotel.co.uk
**w** southbeachhotel.co.uk

**Sparkles Hotel** ◆◆◆◆
*Guest Accommodation*
37 Station Road, Blackpool
FY4 1EU
**t** (01253) 343200
**e** mrssparkle@sparkle.co.uk
**w** sparkles.co.uk

**Strathdon Hotel** ★★★★
*Guest Accommodation*
St Chads Road, Blackpool
FY1 6BP
**t** (01253) 343549
**e** stay@strathdonhotel.com
**w** strathdonhotel.com

**Sunny Cliff Hotel** ★★★★
*Guest Accommodation*
98 Queens Promenade,
Blackpool FY2 9NS
**t** (01253) 351155

**Sunnymede Hotel** ★★★
*Guest Accommodation*
50 King Edward Avenue,
Blackpool FY2 9TA
**t** (01253) 352877
**e** enquiries@hotelsunnymede.
fsnet.co.uk
**w** sunnymedehotel.co.uk

**Sunnyside Hotel** ★★★
*Guest Accommodation*
36 King Edward Avenue,
Blackpool FY2 9TA
**t** (01253) 352031
**e** david@sunnysidehotel.com
**w** sunnysidehotel.com

**The Sunset** ★★★★
*Guest Accommodation*
5 Banks Street, Blackpool
FY1 1RN
**t** (01253) 624949
**e** thesunsethotel@msn.com
**w** thesunsethotelblackpool.
com

**Tamarind Cove Hotel** ★★★
*Guest Accommodation*
56 Hornby Road, Blackpool
FY1 4QJ
**t** (01253) 624319

**Tower View Private Hotel**
★★★ *Guest Accommodation*
31 Bethesda Road, Blackpool
FY1 5DT
**t** (01253) 620391

**The Trafalgar** ★★★
*Guest House*
106 Albert Road, Blackpool
FY1 4PR
**t** (01253) 625000
**e** enquiries@trafalgarhotel.co.
uk
**w** trafalgarhotel.co.uk

**Tudor Rose Original** ★★★★
*Guest House*
5 Withnell Road, Blackpool
FY4 1HF
**t** (01253) 343485
**e** tudor_rose@onetel.com
**w** tudorroseoriginal.co.uk

**The Victoria Guest House**
★★★ *Guest House*
24 Park Road, Blackpool
FY1 4HT
**t** (01253) 628564
**e** james@jzd.uklinux.net
**w** guesthouseatblackpool.co.
uk

**The Vidella** ★★★
*Guest Accommodation*
80-82 Dickson Road, North
Shore, Blackpool FY1 2BU
**t** (01253) 621201
**e** info@videllahotel.com
**w** videllahotel.com

**Waverley Hotel** ★★★
*Guest Accommodation*
95 Reads Avenue, Blackpool
FY1 4DG
**t** (01253) 621633
**e** waverleyrooms@aol.com
**w** thewaverleyhotel.net

**Wescoe Private Hotel** ★★★
*Guest Accommodation*
14 Dean Street, Blackpool
FY4 1AU
**t** (01253) 342772

**The Westcliffe** ★★★
*Guest Accommodation*
46 King Edward Avenue, North
Shore, Blackpool FY2 9TA
**t** (01253) 352943
**e** westcliffehotel@aol.com
**w** westcliffehotel.com

**Westdean Hotel** ★★★
*Guest Accommodation*
59 Dean Street, Blackpool
FY4 1BP
**t** (01253) 342904
**e** westdeanhotel@aol.com
**w** westdeanhotel.com

**Westfield Lodge** ★★★
Guest Accommodation
14 Station Road, Blackpool
FY4 1BE
t (01253) 342468
e info@westfieldhotel.co.uk
w westfieldhotel.co.uk

**Wilford Guest House** ★★★
Guest Accommodation
55 Station Road, Blackpool
FY4 1EU
t (01253) 344329
e enquiries@wilfordhotel.co.
uk
w wilfordhotel.co.uk

**Wilton Hotel** ★★★
Guest Accommodation
108-112 Dickson Road,
Blackpool FY1 2HF
t (01253) 627763
e wiltonhotel@supanet.com
w wiltonhotel.co.uk

**The Windsor** ★★★★
Guest Accommodation
21 King Edward Avenue,
Blackpool FY2 9TA
t (01253) 353735
e enquiries@
windsorblackpool.co.uk
w windsorblackpool.co.uk

**Windsor Carlton Guest
Accommodation** ★★★★
Guest Accommodation
6 Warley Road, Blackpool
FY1 2JU
t (01253) 354924
e info@windsorcarlton.com
w windsorcarlton.com

**Woodfield Hotel** ★★★
Guest Accommodation
31-33 Woodfield Road,
Blackpool FY1 6AX
t (01253) 346304
e thewoodfield@hotmail.co.uk
w thewoodfieldhotel.co.uk

### BLEASDALE
Lancashire

**Bleasdale Cottages (B&B)**
★★★★
Guest Accommodation
Lower Fairsnape Farm,
Bleasdale, Nr Preston PR3 1UY
t (01995) 61343
e robert.gardner1@virgin.net
w bleasdalecottages.co.uk

### BLENCARN
Cumbria

**Midtown Farm B&B** ★★★★★
Bed & Breakfast
Midtown Farm, Penrith
CA10 1TX
t (01768) 879091
e info@lakesanddales.co.uk
w lakesanddales.co.uk
▨◪

### BLUNDELLSANDS
Merseyside

**Blundellsands Guesthouse**
★★★★
Guest Accommodation
SILVER AWARD
9 Elton Avenue, Liverpool
L23 8UN
t (0151) 924 6947
e bsbb@blueyonder.co.uk
w blundellsands.info

### BOLTON
Cumbria

**Tarka House** ★★★★
Guest Accommodation
Bolton, Appleby-in-
Westmorland CA16 6AW
t (01768) 361422

### BOLTON
Greater Manchester

**Archangelos** ★★★
Guest Accommodation
82 Pennine Road, Horwich,
Bolton BL6 7HW
t (01204) 692303
e enquiries@archangelos.co.
uk
w archangelos.co.uk

**Highgrove Guest House**
★★★ Guest House
63 Manchester Road, Bolton
BL2 1ES
t (01204) 384928
e thehighgrove@btconnect.
com
w highgroveguesthouse.co.uk

### BOLTON-BY-BOWLAND
Lancashire

**Middle Flass Lodge** ★★★★
Guest House
Forest Becks Brow, Clitheroe
BB7 4NY
t (01200) 447259
e middleflasslodge@
btconnect.com
w middleflasslodge.co.uk

### BOLTONGATE
Cumbria

**Boltongate Old Rectory**
★★★★★
Guest Accommodation
SILVER AWARD
The Old Rectory, Boltongate,
Wigton CA7 1DA
t (01697) 371647
e boltongate@talk21.com
w boltongateoldrectory.com

### BOOT
Cumbria

**Eskdale YHA** ★★★ Hostel
Holmrook CA19 1TH
t (01946) 723219
▨◪

### BOOTLE
Merseyside

**Regent Maritime Hotel** ★★
Guest Accommodation
58-68 Regent Road, Liverpool
L20 8DB
t (0151) 922 4090
e info@regentmaritimehotel.
com
w regentmaritimehotel.com

### BORROWDALE
Cumbria

**Derwentwater YHA** ★★★
Hostel
Barrow House, Keswick
CA12 5UR
t (01768) 777246
▨◪

**Hazel Bank Country House**
★★★★★ Guest House
GOLD AWARD
Rosthwaite, Borrowdale,
Keswick CA12 5XB
t (017687) 77248
e enquiries@hazelbankhotel.
co.uk
w hazelbankhotel.co.uk

**Seatoller Farm** ★★★★
Farmhouse
Borrowdale, Keswick
CA12 5XN
t (01768) 777232

### BOWNESS-ON-SOLWAY
Cumbria

**The Old Chapel** ★★
Bed & Breakfast
Meadow View, Bowness-on-
Solway CA7 5BL
t (01697) 351126
e oldchapelbowness@hotmail.
com
w oldchapelbownessonsolway.
com
▨◪◪

**Wallsend House, The Old
Rectory** ★★★★
Guest Accommodation
Church Lane, Bowness-on-
Solway CA7 5AF
t (01697) 351055
e bill@wallsend.net
w wallsend.net

### BRAITHWAITE
Cumbria

**Coledale Inn** ★★★ Inn
Braithwaite, Keswick
CA12 5TN
t (017687) 78272
e info@coledale-inn.com
w coledale-inn.co.uk

**Middle Ruddings** ★★★ Inn
Braithwaite, Keswick
CA12 5RY
t (01768) 778436
e info@middle-ruddings.co.uk
w middle-ruddings.co.uk

### BRAMPTON
Cumbria

**Bankshead Camping Barn**
Camping Barn
Bankshead Farm, Banks,
Brampton CA8 2BX
t (01697) 73198

**Blacksmiths Arms** ★★★★
Inn
Talkin, Brampton CA8 1LE
t (01697) 73452
e blacksmithsarmstalkin@
yahoo.co.uk
w blacksmithstalkin.co.uk

**Low Rigg Farm** ★★★
Farmhouse
Walton, Brampton CA8 2DX
t (01697) 73233
e lowrigg@toucansurf.com
w lowrigg.com

**Nags Head** ★★★ Inn
Market Place, Brampton
CA8 1RW
t (01697) 72284

**New Mills House** ★★★
Bed & Breakfast
Brampton CA8 2QS
t (01697) 73376
e newmills@btinternet.com
w newmillshouse.co.uk

**Quarry Side** ★★★★
Bed & Breakfast
Banks, Brampton CA8 2JH
t (01697) 72538
e elizabeth.harding@
btinternet.com

**South View** ★★★★
Guest Accommodation
Banks, Brampton CA8 2JH
t (01697) 72309

**Vallum Barn** ★★★★
Bed & Breakfast
SILVER AWARD
Irthington, Carlisle CA6 4NN
t (01697) 742478
e vallumbarn@tinyworld.co.uk
w vallumbarn.co.uk

**Walton High Rigg** ★★★
Farmhouse
Walton, Brampton CA8 2AZ
t (01697) 72117
e mounsey_highrigg@hotmail.
com
w waltonhighrigg.co.uk
▨◪

### BRISCO
Cumbria

**Crossroads House** ★★★★
Bed & Breakfast
SILVER AWARD
Brisco, Carlisle CA4 0QZ
t (01228) 528994
e viv@crossroadshouse.co.uk
w crossroadshouse.co.uk

### BROUGH
Cumbria

**River View** ★★★★
Bed & Breakfast
Brough CA17 4BZ
t (01768) 341894
e riverviewbb@btinternet.com
w riverviewbb.co.uk

### BROUGHTON IN FURNESS
Cumbria

**Dower House** ★★★
Guest Accommodation
High Duddon, Duddon Bridge,
Broughton-in-Furness
LA20 6ET
t (01229) 716279
e rozanne.nichols@
ukgateway.net
w dowerhouse.biz

**Low Hall Farm** ★★★★
Farmhouse
Kirkby-in-Furness, Broughton
in Furness LA17 7TR
t (01229) 889220
e enquiries@low-hall.co.uk
w low-hall.co.uk

**Oakbank** ★★★
Bed & Breakfast
Ulpha, Duddon Valley
LA20 6DZ
t (01229) 716393
e susanbatten@btinternet.com
w duddonvalley.co.uk

### BRUERA
Cheshire

**Churton Heath Farm Bed &
Breakfast** ★★★★ Farmhouse
SILVER AWARD
Churton Heath Farm, Chapel
Lane, Chester CH3 6EW
t (01244) 620420
e info@churtonheathfarm.co.
uk
w churtonheathfarm.co.uk

## BURGH-BY-SANDS
### Cumbria

**Highfield Farm ★★★★**
*Farmhouse*
Boustead Hill, Burgh-by-Sands,
Carlisle CA5 6AA
t (01228) 576060
e info@highfield-holidays.co.
uk
w highfield-holidays.co.uk

**Hillside Farm ★★★**
*Bed & Breakfast*
Boustead Hill, Burgh-by-Sands,
Carlisle CA5 6AA
t (01228) 576398
e ruddshillside1@btinternet.
com
w hadrianswalkbnb.co.uk

## BURNLEY
### Lancashire

**Higher Cockden Barn
★★★★**
*Guest Accommodation*
Todmorden Road, Briercliffe,
Burnley BB10 3QQ
t (01282) 831324
e j.hodkinson_bb@tiscali.co.
uk
w highercockdenfarm.com

**Ormerod Hotel ★★★**
*Guest Accommodation*
123 Ormerod Road, Burnley
BB11 3QW
t (01282) 423255

**Thorneyholme Farm Cottage
★★★★**
*Guest Accommodation*
Barley New Road, Roughlee,
Nelson BB12 9LH
t (01282) 612452

## BURY
### Greater Manchester

**Ashbury Guest House ★★★**
*Guest Accommodation*
235 Rochdale Road, Bury
BL9 7BX
t (0161) 762 9623
e glyniswoodall@btinternet.
com

**Castle Guest House ★★★**
*Guest Accommodation*
Wellington Street, Bury
BL8 2AL
t (0161) 797 3396

**Pennine View Guest House
★★★** *Guest Accommodation*
8 Hunstanton Drive,
Brandlesholme, Bury BL8 1EG
t (0161) 763 1249
e j.mckeon@tinyworld.co.uk

**Victoria Hotel ★★★** *Inn*
12-14 Hall Street, Walshaw,
Bury BL8 3BD
t (0161) 761 5801
e thevictoriahotel@aol.com

## BUTTERMERE
### Cumbria

**Buttermere YHA ★★★**
*Hostel*
King George Vi Memorial
Hostel, Cockermouth
CA13 9XA
t (01768) 770245

## CALDBECK
### Cumbria

**Swaledale Watch ★★★★**
*Guest House* **SILVER AWARD**
Whelpo, Caldbeck CA7 8HQ
t (01697) 478409
e nan.savage@talk21.com
w swaledale-watch.co.uk

## CALDY
### Merseyside

**Cheriton Guest House
★★★★** *Bed & Breakfast*
151 Caldy Road, Caldy, West
Kirby CH48 1LP
t (0151) 625 5271
e cheriton151@hotmail.com
w cheritonguesthouse.co.uk

## CARLETON
### Cumbria

**Birklands House ★★★★**
*Bed & Breakfast*
**SILVER AWARD**
Carleton, Carlisle CA4 0BU
t (01228) 511837
e info@birklandshouse.co.uk
w birklandshouse.co.uk

**River Forge Bed & Breakfast
★★★★** *Bed & Breakfast*
**SILVER AWARD**
River Forge, Carleton, Carlisle
CA4 8LE
t (01228) 523569
e riverforgebandb@aol.com
w river-forge.co.uk

## CARLISLE
### Cumbria

**Abberley House ★★★★**
*Bed & Breakfast*
33 Victoria Place, Carlisle
CA1 1HP
t (01228) 521645
e info@abberleyhouse.co.uk
w abberleyhouse.co.uk

**Abbey Court ★★★★**
*Guest Accommodation*
24 London Road, Carlisle
CA1 2EL
t (01228) 528696
e abbeycourt@virgin.net
w abbeycourtguesthouse.co.
uk

**Ashleigh House ★★★★**
*Guest House*
46 Victoria Place, Carlisle
CA1 1EX
t (01228) 521631

**Bessiestown Farm Country
Guesthouse ★★★★★**
*Guest House* **GOLD AWARD**
Catlowdy, Longtown, Carlisle
CA6 5QP
t (01228) 577219
e info@bessiestown.co.uk
w bessiestown.co.uk

**Carlisle YHA (Old Brewery)
★★★** *Hostel*
Bridge Lane, Caldewgate,
Carlisle CA2 5SR
t 0870 770 5752

**Cartref Guest House ★★★★**
*Guest House* **SILVER AWARD**
44 Victoria Place, Carlisle
CA1 1EX
t (01228) 522077

**Cherry Grove ★★★★**
*Guest Accommodation*
87 Petteril Street, Carlisle
CA1 2AW
t (01228) 541942
w cherrygroveguesthouse.co.
uk

**Cornerways Guest House
★★★★**
*Guest Accommodation*
107 Warwick Road, Carlisle
CA1 1EA
t (01228) 521733
e info@cornerwaysbandb.co.
uk
w cornerwaysbandb.co.uk

**Courtfield House ★★★★**
*Guest House* **SILVER AWARD**
169 Warwick Road, Carlisle
CA1 1LP
t (01228) 522767

**East View Guest House
★★★★**
*Guest Accommodation*
110 Warwick Road, Carlisle
CA1 1JU
t (01228) 522112
e eastviewgh@hotmail.co.uk

**Fernlee Guest House
★★★★** *Guest House*
9 St Aidans Road, Carlisle
CA1 1LT
t (01228) 511930

**Hazeldean Guest House
★★★** *Guest House*
Orton Grange, Wigton Road,
Carlisle CA5 6LA
t (01228) 711953
e hazeldean1@btopenworld.
com
w smoothhound.co.uk/hotels/
hazeldean.html

**Howard Lodge Guest House
★★★★**
*Guest Accommodation*
90 Warwick Road, Carlisle
CA1 1JU
t (01228) 529842
e chrltdavi@aol.com
w howard-lodge.co.uk

**Ivy House ★★★**
*Bed & Breakfast*
101 Warwick Road, Carlisle
CA1 1EA
t (01228) 530432

**Langleigh House ★★★★**
*Guest House*
6 Howard Place, Carlisle
CA1 1HR
t (01228) 530440
e langleighhouse@aol.com
w langleighhouse.co.uk

**Number Thirty One
★★★★★** *Guest House*
**GOLD AWARD**
31 Howard Place, Carlisle
CA1 1HR
t (01228) 597080
e pruirving@aol.com
w number31.co.uk

**St Martins College**
Rating Applied For
*Campus*
Fusehill Street, Carlisle
CA1 2HH
t (01228) 616317
e n.mchachti@ucsm.ac.uk
w ucsm.ac.uk

**Townhouse B&B ★★★★**
*Guest Accommodation*
153 Warwick Road, Carlisle
CA1 1LU
t (01228) 598782
e townhouse@christine60.
freesereve.co.uk
w townhouse-bandb.com

**Vallum House ★★★**
*Guest House*
73-75 Burgh Road, Carlisle
CA2 7NB
t (01228) 521860

**White Lea Guest House
★★★★** *Bed & Breakfast*
191 Warwick Road, Carlisle
CA1 1LP
t (01228) 533139

## CARNFORTH
### Lancashire

**Blue Anchor ★★★** *Inn*
68 Main Road, Bolton le Sands,
Carnforth LA5 8DN
t (01524) 823241

**Capernwray House ★★★★**
*Guest Accommodation*
**SILVER AWARD**
Borrans Lane, Capernwray,
Carnforth LA6 1AE
t (01524) 732363
e thesmiths@
capernwrayhouse.com
w capernwrayhouse.com

**Dale Grove ★★★★**
*Bed & Breakfast*
162 Lancaster Road, Carnforth
LA5 9EF
t (01524) 733382
e stevenage3@btinternet.com

**Galley Hall Farm ★★★★**
*Farmhouse*
Shore Road, Carnforth
LA5 9HZ
t (01524) 732544

**Grisedale Farm ★★★★**
*Farmhouse*
Leighton Hall, Carnforth
LA5 9ST
t (01524) 734360
e ailsarobinson@btconnect.
com
w grisedalefarm.co.uk

**High Bank ♦♦♦♦**
*Guest Accommodation*
Hawk Street, Carnforth
LA5 9LA
t (01524) 733827

**Longlands ★★★★** *Inn*
Tewitfield, Carnforth LA6 1JH
t (01524) 781256
e info@longlandshotel.co.uk
w longlandshotel.co.uk

## CARTMEL
### Cumbria

**Bank Court Cottage ★★★**
*Bed & Breakfast*
The Square, Cartmel, Grange-
over-Sands LA11 6QB
t (015395) 36593

**Cavendish Arms ★★★** *Inn*
Cavendish Street, Cartmel
LA11 6QA
t (015395) 36240
e book@thecavendisharms.co.
uk
w thecavendisharms.co.uk

**Hill Farm B&B For Country Lovers ★★★★★**
*Bed & Breakfast*
**GOLD AWARD**
Cartmel, Grange-over-Sands
LA11 7SS
t (015395) 36477
e hillfarmbb@btinternet.com
w hillfarmbb.co.uk

**Priors Yeat ★★★★**
*Bed & Breakfast*
Aynsome Road, Cartmel,
Grange-over-Sands LA11 6PR
t (015395) 35178
e priorsyeat@hotmail.com
w priorsyeat.co.uk

### CASTLE CARROCK
### Cumbria

**The Weary at Castle Carrock ★★★★**
*Restaurant with Rooms*
**SILVER AWARD**
Castle Carrock, Brampton
CA8 9LU
t (01228) 670230
e relax@theweary.com
w theweary.com

### CHAIGLEY
### Lancashire

**Moorhead House Farm**
**★★★** *Guest Accommodation*
Thornley Road, Chaigley,
Clitheroe BB7 3LY
t (01995) 61108

### CHEADLE
### Greater Manchester

**Curzon House ★★**
*Bed & Breakfast*
3 Curzon Road, Heald Green,
Cheadle, Stockport SK8 3LN
t (0161) 436 2804
e curzonhouse@aol.com
w smoothhound.co.uk

### CHEADLE HULME
### Greater Manchester

**Spring Cottage Guest House**
**★★★** *Guest House*
60 Hulme Hall Road, Cheadle
Hulme, Stockport SK8 6JZ
t (0161) 485 1037

### CHESTER
### Cheshire

**Ba Ba Guest House ★★★★**
*Guest Accommodation*
65 Hoole Road, Hoole, Chester
CH2 3NJ
t (01244) 315047
e reservations@
babaguesthouse.co.uk
w babaguesthouse.co.uk

**Bowman Lodge ★★★**
*Guest Accommodation*
52 Hoole Road, Chester
CH2 3NL
t (01244) 342208

**Chester Backpackers ★★**
*Hostel*
67 Boughton, Chester
CH3 5AF
t (01244) 400185

**Chester Brooklands ★★★**
*Guest Accommodation*
8 Newton Lane, Chester
CH2 3RB
t (01244) 348856
e enquiries@chester-bandb.
co.uk
w chester-bandb.co.uk

**Chester Youth Hostel ★★**
*Hostel*
40 Hough Green, Chester
CH4 8JD
t (015395) 680056
e chester@yha.org.uk
w yha.org.uk

**Chippings ★★★★**
*Bed & Breakfast*
10 Cranford Court, Chester
CH4 7LN
t (01244) 679728
e chippingsbnb@yahoo.co.uk
w visitchester.com

**The Commercial ★★**
*Guest Accommodation*
St Peters Church Yard, Chester
CH1 2HG
t (01244) 320749

**Craigleith Lodge ★★★★**
*Guest Accommodation*
56 Hoole Road, Chester
CH2 3NL
t (01244) 318740
e welcome@craigleithlodge.
co.uk
w craigleithlodge.co.uk

**Derry Raghan Lodge ★★★★**
*Guest Accommodation*
54 Hoole Road, Chester
CH2 3NL
t (01244) 318740
e welcome@
derryraghanlodge.co.uk
w derryraghanlodge.co.uk

**Eastern Guest House ★★**
*Bed & Breakfast*
Eastern Pathway, Chester
CH4 7AQ
t (01244) 680104

**Golborne Manor ★★★★**
*Bed & Breakfast*
Platts Lane, Hatton Heath,
Chester CH3 9AN
t (01829) 770310 &
07774 695268
e annikin@golbornemanor.co.
uk
w golbornemanor.co.uk

**The Golden Eagle ★★★** *Inn*
Castle Street, Chester
CH1 2DS
t (01244) 321098
e dianephil1977@yahoo.co.uk

**Grove Villa ★★★★**
*Bed & Breakfast*
18 The Groves, Chester
CH1 1SD
t (01244) 349713
e grovevilla18@btinternet.com
w visitchester.com/site/where-
to-stay/grove-villa-p611

**Halcyon Guest House ★★★**
*Guest House*
18 Eaton Road, Handbridge,
Chester CH4 7EN
t (01244) 676159
e eric.owen@tiscil.co.uk

**Hameldaeus ★★★**
*Bed & Breakfast*
9 Lorne Street, Chester
CH1 4AE
t (01244) 374913
e joyce_brunton@tiscali.co.uk

**Holly House ★★★**
*Bed & Breakfast*
41 Liverpool Road, Chester
CH2 1AB
t (01244) 383484
e maureenbrady@yahoo.com

**Homeleigh ★★★**
*Guest Accommodation*
14 Hough Green, Chester
CH4 8JG
t (01244) 676761
e colin-judy@tiscali.co.uk
w homeleighchester.co.uk

**Kilmorey Lodge ★★★**
*Guest Accommodation*
50 Hoole Road, Chester
CH2 3NL
t (01244) 324306
e kilmoreylodge@aol.com
w smoothhound.co.uk/hotels/
kilmorey.html

**Kings Guesthouse ★★★★**
*Guest House*
14 Eaton Road, Handbridge,
Chester CH4 7EN
t (01244) 671249
e king@kings.plus.com
w kingsguesthouse.co.uk/

**Laburnum House ★★★**
*Guest House*
2 St Anne Street, Chester
CH1 3HS
t (01244) 380313
e info@
laburnumhousechester.co.uk
w laburnumhousechester.co.
uk

**Latymer House ★★★**
*Guest Accommodation*
82 Hough Green, Chester
CH4 8JW
t (01244) 675074
e info@latymerhotel.com
w latymerhotel.com

**Laurels ★★★★**
*Bed & Breakfast*
14 Selkirk Road, Curzon Park,
Chester CH4 8AH
t (01244) 679682
e howell@ellisroberts.
freeserve.co.uk

**Lavender Lodge ★★★★**
*Guest House*
46 Hoole Road, Chester
CH2 3NL
t (01244) 323204
e bookings@lavenderlodge.
co.uk
w lavenderlodge.co.uk

**The Limes ★★★★**
*Guest Accommodation*
12 Hoole Road, Chester
CH2 3NJ
t (01244) 328239
e limes@chester.co.uk
w limes-chester.co.uk

**Lloyd's of Chester ★**
*Guest Accommodation*
108 Brook Street, Chester
CH1 3DU
t (01244) 325838
e lloydsofchesterhotel@
hotmail.co.uk

**Mitchell's of Chester Guest House ★★★★★**
*Guest House* **SILVER AWARD**
28 Hough Green, Chester
CH4 8JQ
t (01244) 679004
e mitches@dialstart.net
w mitchellsofchester.com

**Newton Hall Farm Bed & Breakfast ★★★★** *Farmhouse*
Tattenhall, Chester CH3 9NE
t (01829) 770153
e newton.hall@farming.co.uk
w newtonhallfarm.co.uk

**Pennies Chester City Centre Guest House**
Rating Applied For
*Guest Accommodation*
18 Queen Street, Chester
CH1 3LG
t 07753 731931
e info@pennieschester.co.uk
w pennieschester.co.uk

**Recorder House ★★★★**
*Guest Accommodation*
19 City Walls, Chester
CH1 1SB
t (01244) 326580
e reservations@recorderhotel.
co.uk
w recorderhotel.co.uk

**Sycamore House Bed & Breakfast ★★★★**
*Bed & Breakfast*
8 Queens Park Road, Chester
CH4 7AD
t (01244) 675417
e helen.speke@btinternet.com
w visitchester.com/site/where-
to-stay/sycamore-house-bed-
and-breakfast-p1951

**Tentry Heys ★★★**
*Bed & Breakfast*
Queens Park Road, Chester
CH4 7AD
t (01244) 677857

**Walpole House ★★★★**
*Bed & Breakfast*
26 Walpole Street, Chester
CH1 4HG
t (01244) 373373
e walphse@aol.com
w walpolehouse.co.uk

**Willow Run Bed & Breakfast ★★★★** *Bed & Breakfast*
**SILVER AWARD**
Barrow Lane, Tarvin Sands,
Chester CH3 8JF
t (01829) 749142
e willowrun@btconnect.com
w willowrun.co.uk

### CHIPPING
### Lancashire

**Chipping Camping Barn**
*Camping Barn*
Forest of Bowland, Chipping,
Preston PR3 2GQ
t (01995) 61209

**Clark House Farm ★★★★**
*Farmhouse*
Chipping, Preston PR3 2GQ
t (01995) 61209
e fpr@agriplus.net
w clarkhousefarm.com

## CHOLMONDELEY
### Cheshire

**Manor Farm Bed & Breakfast** ★★★★ *Farmhouse*
Egerton, Cholmondeley, Malpas SY14 8AW
t (01829) 720261
e manorfarmbandb@btconnect.com
w egertonmanorfarm.co.uk

## CHORLEY
### Lancashire

**Inglewood**
Rating Applied For
*Guest Accommodation*
19 Southport Road, Chorley PR7 1LB
t 07721 764205
e gorsesam@aol.com

**Parr Hall Farm** ★★★★
*Guest Accommodation*
Parr Lane, Eccleston, Chorley PR7 5SL
t (01257) 451917
e enquiries@parrhallfarm.com
w parrhallfarm.com

## CLIFTON
### Cumbria

**The White House Experience Guest House** ★★★★
*Guest Accommodation*
Clifton, Penrith CA10 2EL
t (01768) 865115
e info@thewhitehouseexperience.co.uk
w thewhitehouseexperience.co.uk

## CLITHEROE
### Lancashire

**Bayley Arms** ★★★★ *Inn*
Avenue Road, Hurst Green, Clitheroe BB7 9QB
t (01254) 826478
e sales@bayleyarms.co.uk
w bayleyarms.co.uk

**Rakefoot Farm** ★★★★
*Farmhouse*
Thornley Road, Chaigley, Clitheroe BB7 3LY
t (01995) 61332
e info@rakefootfarm.co.uk
w rakefootfarm.co.uk

**York House Bed & Breakfast** ★★★★ *Bed & Breakfast*
York House, York Street, Clitheroe BB7 2DL
t (01200) 429519
e brindle_susan@hotmail.com
w yorkhousebandb.co.uk

## COCKERMOUTH
### Cumbria

**Cockermouth YHA** ★★
*Hostel*
Double Mills, Fern Bank Road, Cockermouth CA13 0DS
t (01900) 822561
e cockermouth@yha.org.uk

**Croft Guesthouse** ★★★★
*Guest House*
6-8 Challoner Street, Cockermouth CA13 9QS
t (01900) 827533
e info@croft-guesthouse.com
w croft-guesthouse.com

**Graysonside** ★★★★
*Guest Accommodation*
Lorton Road, Cockermouth CA13 9TQ
t (01900) 822351
e stay@graysonside.co.uk
w graysonside.co.uk

**The Melbreak** ★★★★
*Guest Accommodation*
Winscales Road, Little Clifton, Workington CA14 1XS
t (01900) 61443
e themelbreak@tiscali.co.uk
w melbreakhotel.co.uk

**The Old Homestead** ★★★★
*Farmhouse*
Byresteads Farm, Cockermouth CA13 9TW
t (01900) 822223
e info@byresteads.co.uk
w byresteads.co.uk

**Rose Cottage** ★★★★
*Guest House*
Lorton Road, Cockermouth CA13 9DX
t (01900) 822189
e bookings@rosecottageguest.co.uk
w rosecottageguest.co.uk

## COLNE
### Lancashire

**Blakey Hall Farm** ◆◆◆◆
*Guest Accommodation*
SILVER AWARD
Red Lane, Colne BB8 9TD
t (01282) 863121
e blakeyhall@hotmail.com
w blakeyhallfarm.co.uk

**Higher Wanless Farm** ★★★★ *Farmhouse*
Red Lane, Colne BB8 7JP
t (01282) 865301
e info@stayinlancs.co.uk
w stayinlancs.co.uk

**Middle Beardshaw Head Farm** ★★★
*Guest Accommodation*
Burnley Road, Trawden, Colne BB8 8PP
t (01282) 865257
e ursula@mann1940.freeserve.co.uk
w smoothhound.co.uk/a11504.html

**Rowan House B&B** ★★★
*Guest Accommodation*
Harrison Drive, Colne BB8 9SJ
t (01282) 870937
e antony.hartley1@ntlworld.com
w rowanhousebandb.com

## CONGLETON
### Cheshire

**Cloud House Farm** ★★★★
*Farmhouse*
Toft Green, Congleton CW12 3QF
t (01260) 226272

**Coppice Edge Bed & Breakfast** ★★★★
*Bed & Breakfast*
Blackfirs Lane, Somerford, Congleton CW12 4QQ
t (01260) 270605
e nicole@somerford24.freeserve.co.uk
w coppice-edge.co.uk

**HP Bed & Breakfast** ★★★
*Bed & Breakfast*
Norfolk Road, Congleton CW12 1NY
t (01260) 277873
e hpbedandbreakfast@hotmail.com

**Sandhole Farm** ★★★★
*Guest Accommodation*
Hulme Walfield, Congleton CW12 2JH
t (01260) 224419
e veronica@sandholefarm.co.uk
w sandholefarm.co.uk

**The Woodlands** ◆◆◆◆
*Guest Accommodation*
Quarry Wood Farm, Wood Street, Mow Cop ST7 3PF
t (01782) 518877

**Yew Tree Farm B&B** ★★★★
*Farmhouse*
North Rode, Congleton CW12 2PF
t (01260) 223569
e yewtreebb@hotmail.com
w yewtreebb.co.uk

## CONISTON
### Cumbria

**Beech Tree House** ★★★★
*Guest House*
Yewdale Road, Coniston LA21 8DX
t (015394) 41717

**Coniston Coppermines YHA** ★★★ *Hostel*
Coniston Coppermines, Coppermines House, Coniston LA21 8HP
t (015394) 41261
e coppermines@yha.org.uk
w yha.org.uk

**Coniston Lodge** ★★★★★
*Guest Accommodation*
GOLD AWARD
Station Road, Coniston LA21 8HH
t (015394) 41201
e info@coniston-lodge.com
w coniston-lodge.com

**Coniston YHA** ★★★ *Hostel*
Holly How, Far End, Coniston LA21 8DD
t (015394) 41323

**Crown Inn** ★★★★ *Inn*
Tilberthwaite Avenue, Coniston LA21 8ED
t (015394) 41243
e info@crown-hotel-coniston.com
w crown-hotel-coniston.com

**How Head Cottage** ★★★
*Bed & Breakfast*
East of Lake, Coniston LA21 8AA
t (015394) 41594
e howhead@lineone.net
w howheadcottages.co.uk

**Lakeland House** ★★★
*Guest Accommodation*
Tilberthwaite Avenue, Coniston LA21 8ED
t (015394) 41303
e info@lakelandhouse.com
w lakelandhouse.com

**Oaklands** ★★★★
*Guest Accommodation*
Yewdale Road, Coniston LA21 8DX
t (015394) 41245
e judithzeke@oaklandsguesthouse.fsnet.co.uk
w oaklandsconiston.co.uk

**The Old Rectory** ★★★★
*Guest House* SILVER AWARD
Torver, Coniston LA21 8AX
t (015394) 41353
e enquiries@theoldrectoryhotel.com
w theoldrectoryhotel.com

**Orchard Cottage** ★★★★
*Bed & Breakfast*
18 Yewdale Road, Coniston LA21 8DU
t (015394) 41319
e enquiries@conistonholidays.co.uk
w conistonholidays.co.uk

**Thwaite Cottage** ★★★★
*Bed & Breakfast*
Waterhead, Coniston LA21 8AJ
t (015394) 41367
e m@thwaitcot.freeserve.co.uk
w thwaitcot.freeserve.co.uk

**Wilson Arms** ★★★ *Inn*
Torver, Coniston LA21 8BB
t (015394) 41237
e wilsonarms@tesco.net

**Yew Tree Farm**
Rating Applied For
*Farmhouse*
Coniston LA21 8DP
t (015394) 41433
e info@yewtree-farm.com
w yewtree-farm.com

**Yewdale Inn** ★★★ *Inn*
Yewdale Road, Coniston LA21 8DU
t (015394) 41280
e mail@yewdalehotel.com
w yewdalehotel.com

## CROSTHWAITE
### Cumbria

**Crosthwaite House** ★★★★
*Guest House*
Crosthwaite, Kendal LA8 8BP
t (015395) 68264
e bookings@crosthwaitehouse.co.uk
w crosthwaitehouse.co.uk

## CUDDINGTON
### Cheshire

**Acorn House Bed and Breakfast** ★★
*Bed & Breakfast*
34 Forest Close, Cuddington, Northwich CW8 2EE
t (01606) 881714
e alanbridge02@aol.com

## DALTON-IN-FURNESS
### Cumbria

**Park Cottage** ★★★★
*Bed & Breakfast*
SILVER AWARD
Park, Dalton-in-Furness LA15 8JZ
t (01229) 462850
e joan@parkcottagedalton.co.uk
w parkcottagedalton.co.uk

## DENSHAW
### Greater Manchester

**Cherry Clough Farm** ★★★★
*Farmhouse*
Rochdale Road, Oldham
OL3 5UE
t  (01457) 874369
e  info@cherryclough.co.uk
w  cherryclough.co.uk

## DENT
### Cumbria

**The George and Dragon**
★★★ *Inn*
Main Street, Dent, Sedbergh
LA10 5QL
t  (015396) 25256
e  mail@
thegeorgeanddragondent.co.
uk
w  thegeorgeanddragondent.
co.uk

**Smithy Fold Bed & Breakfast**
★★★ *Bed & Breakfast*
Dent, Sedbergh LA10 5RE
t  (015396) 25368
e  cheetham@smithyfold.co.uk
w  smithyfold.co.uk

**Stone Close Tea Room &
Guest House** ★★★
*Bed & Breakfast*
Main Street, Dent, Sedbergh
LA10 5QL
t  (015396) 25231
e  stoneclose@btinternet.com
w  dentdale.com

## DISLEY
### Cheshire

**The Grey Cottage** ★★★
*Bed & Breakfast*
20 Jackson's Edge Road,
Disley, Stockport SK12 2JE
t  (01663) 763286
e  carol.greycottage@talk21.
com

## DOWNHAM
### Lancashire

**New Hey** *Camping Barn*
Twiston Lane, Downham,
Clitheroe BB7 4DF

## DUFTON
### Cumbria

**Brow Farm Bed & Breakfast**
★★★★ *Farmhouse*
SILVER AWARD
Dufton, Appleby-in-
Westmorland CA16 6DF
t  (017683) 52865
e  stay@browfarm.com
w  browfarm.com

**Dufton YHA** ★★★★ *Hostel*
Redstones, Dufton, Appleby-
in-Westmorland CA16 6DB
t  (01768) 351236
e  dufton@yha.org.uk

## DUKINFIELD
### Greater Manchester

**Barton Villa Guest House**
★★★ *Guest House*
Crescent Road, Dukinfield,
Stockport SK16 4EY
t  (0161) 330 3952
e  harrott4@aol.com
w  bartonvilla.co.uk

## DUNSOP BRIDGE
### Lancashire

**Wood End Farm** ★★★★
*Farmhouse*
Dunsop Bridge, Clitheroe
BB7 3BE
t  (01200) 448223

## EARBY
### Lancashire

**Earby Youth Hostel** ★★★
*Hostel*
9-11 Birch Hall Lane,
Barnoldswick BB18 6JX
t  (01282) 842349
e  earby@yha.org.uk
w  yha.org.uk

## ELTERWATER
### Cumbria

**Elterwater Park Country
Guest House** ★★★★
*Guest House*
Skelwith Bridge, Ambleside,
Langdale LA22 9NP
t  (015394) 32227
e  enquiries@elterwater.com
w  elterwater.com

**Elterwater YHA** ★★★ *Hostel*
Elterwater, Ambleside
LA22 9HX
t  (015394) 37245
e  elterwater@yha.org.uk
w  yha.org.uk

## ENNERDALE
### Cumbria

**Black Sail YHA** ★ *Hostel*
Black Sail Hut, Cleator
CA23 3AY
t  07711 108450

**Ennerdale YHA** ★ *Hostel*
Cat Crag, Ennerdale,
Cockermouth CA23 3AX
t  (01946) 861237
e  ennerdale@yha.org.uk
w  yha.org.uk

**High Gillerthwaite**
*Bunkhouse*
Ennerdale, Cleator CA23 3AX
t  (01768) 772645

## FAR SAWREY
### Cumbria

**Fair Rigg at Far Sawrey**
★★★★★ *Bed & Breakfast*
SILVER AWARD
Far Sawrey, Hawkshead,
Sawrey LA22 0LW
t  (015394) 42532
e  enquiries@fair-rigg.com
w  fair-rigg.com

## FARNWORTH
### Greater Manchester

**Fernbank Guest House**
★★★★ *Bed & Breakfast*
61 Rawson Street, Farnworth,
Bolton BL4 7RJ
t  (01204) 708832

## FENCE
### Lancashire

**Grains Barn Farm** ★★★★★
*Bed & Breakfast*
SILVER AWARD
Barrowford Road, Fence,
Burnley BB12 9QQ
t  (01282) 601320
e  stay@grainsbarnfarm.com
w  grainsbarnfarm.com

## FORTON
### Lancashire

**New Holly** ★★★★ *Inn*
A6 Lancaster Road, Forton,
Preston PR3 0BL
t  (01524) 793500
e  stay@newholly.co.uk
w  newholly.co.uk

## FOULRIDGE
### Lancashire

**Bankfield Guest House**
★★★ *Guest Accommodation*
Skipton Road, Foulridge, Colne
BB8 7PY
t  (01282) 863870

**Hare & Hounds Foulridge**
★★★ *Inn*
Skipton Old Road, Foulridge,
Colne BB8 7PD
t  (01282) 864235
e  cherylcrabtree@btconnect.
com
w  hare&houndsfoulridge.co.uk

## GARSTANG
### Lancashire

**Ashdene** ★★★
*Guest Accommodation*
Parkside Lane, Nateby,
Garstang PR3 0JA
t  (01995) 602676
e  ashdene@supanet.com
w  ashdenebedandbreakfast.
gbr.cc

**Guys Thatched Hamlet**
★★★★
*Guest Accommodation*
Canalside, St Michael's Road,
Bilsborrow, Preston PR3 0RS
t  (01995) 640010
e  info@guysthatchedhamlet.
com
w  guysthatchedhamlet.com

## GARSTON
### Merseyside

**Aplin House** ★
*Guest Accommodation*
35 Clarendon Road, Garston,
Liverpool L19 6PJ
t  (0151) 427 5047

## GILSLAND
### Cumbria

**Birdoswald YHA**
Rating Applied For
*Hostel*
Birdoswald Roman Fort,
Brampton CA8 7DD
t  0870 770 8868

**Brookside Villa** ★★★★
*Guest House*
Gilsland, Brampton CA8 7DA
t  (01697) 747300
e  brooksidevilla@hotmail.co.
uk
w  brooksidevilla.com

**Bush Nook** ★★★★
*Guest Accommodation*
SILVER AWARD
Gilsland, Upper Denton,
Brampton CA8 7AF
t  (01697) 747194
e  info@bushnook.co.uk
w  bushnook.co.uk

**Gilsland Spa** ★★★★
*Guest Accommodation*
Gilsland, Brampton CA8 7AR
t  (016977) 47203
w  gilslandspa.co.uk

**Hadrian's Wall Residential
Study Centre** ★★★★
*Group Hostel*
Birdoswald Roman Fort,
Gilsland, Brampton CA8 7DD
t  (01697) 747602
e  birdoswald.romanfort@
english-heritage.org.uk
w  english.heritage.org.uk

**The Hill on the Wall**
★★★★★
*Guest Accommodation*
SILVER AWARD
Gilsland, Brampton CA8 7DA
t  (01697) 747214
e  info@hadrians-
wallbedandbreakfast.com
w  hadrians-
wallbedandbreakfast.com

**Slack House Farm** ★★★★
*Farmhouse*
Gilsland, Brampton CA8 7DB
t  (01697) 747351
e  slackhousefarm@lineone.net
w  slackhousefarm.co.uk

**Willowford Farm B&B** ★★★
*Farmhouse*
Willowford, Gilsland, Brampton
CA8 7AA
t  (01697) 747962
e  stay@willowford.co.uk
w  willowford.co.uk

## GISBURN
### Lancashire

**Foxhill Barn** ★★★★
*Bed & Breakfast*
Great Todber Farm, Howgill
Lane, Gisburn, Clitheroe
BB7 4JL
t  (01200) 415906
e  janet@foxhillbarn.co.uk
w  foxhillbarn.co.uk

## GLENRIDDING
### Cumbria

**Helvellyn YHA** ★★ *Hostel*
Greenside, Glenridding,
Ullswater CA11 0QR
t  (01768) 482269
e  helvellyn@yha.org.uk
w  yha.org.uk

## GOODSHAW
### Lancashire

**The Old White Horse**
★★★★
*Guest Accommodation*
SILVER AWARD
211 Goodshaw Lane,
Goodshaw, Rossendale
BB4 8DD
t  (01706) 215474
e  johnandmaggie54@hotmail.
com
w  theoldwhitehorse.co.uk

## GOOSNARGH
Lancashire

**White Moss Gate** ★★★★
*Bed & Breakfast*
Horns Lane, Goosnargh,
Preston PR3 2NE
t (01772) 782262
e frandewhurst@fsmail.net
w whitemossgate.com

## GRANGE-OVER-SANDS
Cumbria

**The Elton Hotel** ★★★★
*Guest House*
Windermere Road, Grange-
over-Sands LA11 6EQ
t (015395) 32838
e info@eltonprivatehotel.co.uk
w eltonprivatehotel.co.uk

**Greenacres Country
Guesthouse** ★★★★
*Guest House*
Lindale, Grange-over-Sands
LA11 6LP
t (015395) 34578
e greenacres_lindale@hotmail.
com
w greenacres-lindale.co.uk

**The Lymehurst** ★★★★
*Guest House*
Kents Bank Road, Grange-
over-Sands LA11 7EY
t (015395) 33076
e enquiries@lymehurst.co.uk
w lymehurst.co.uk

**Mayfields** ★★★★
*Bed & Breakfast*
30 Mayfield Road, Whitby
YO21 1LX
t (01947) 603228
e mayfield30@btconnect.com
w bandbwhitby.co.uk

## GRASMERE
Cumbria

**Beck Allans Guest House**
★★★★ *Guest House*
**SILVER AWARD**
College Street, Grasmere
LA22 9SZ
t (015394) 35563
e mail@beckallans.com
w beckallans.com

**Chestnut Villa** ★★★
*Guest Accommodation*
Keswick Road, Grasmere,
Ambleside LA22 9RE
t (015394) 35218

**Dunmail House** ★★★★★
*Bed & Breakfast*
Keswick Road, Grasmere
LA22 9RE
t (015394) 35256
e info@dunmailhouse.com
w dunmailhouse.com

**Grasmere Butharlyp Howe
YHA** ★★★★ *Hostel*
Easdale Road, Grasmere
LA22 9QG
t 0870 770 5836
w yha.org.uk

**Grasmere Independent
Hostel** ★★★★ *Hostel*
Broadrayne Farm, Ambleside
LA22 9RU
t (015394) 35055

**The Harwood** ★★★★
*Guest House*
Red Lion Square, Grasmere
LA22 9SP
t (015394) 35248
e enquiries@harwoodhotel.co.
uk
w harwoodhotel.co.uk

**How Foot Lodge** ★★★
*Guest House*
Town End, Grasmere,
Ambleside LA22 9SQ
t (015394) 35366
e enquiries@howfoot.co.uk
w howfoot.co.uk

**Lake View Country House**
★★★★ *Guest House*
**GOLD AWARD**
Lake View Drive, Grasmere
LA22 9TD
t (015394) 35384
e info@lakeview-grasmere.
com
w lakeview-grasmere.com

**Riversdale** ★★★★
*Guest House* **SILVER AWARD**
White Bridge, Grasmere
LA22 9RH
t (015394) 35619
e info@riversdalegrasmere.co.
uk
w riversdalegrasmere.co.uk

**The Travellers Rest Inn**
★★★ *Inn*
Grasmere LA22 9RR
t 05006 00725
e stay@lakedistrictinns.co.uk
w lakedistrictinns.co.uk

**YHA Grasmere (Thorney
How)** ★ *Hostel*
Easedale Road, Ambleside
LA22 9QG
t (015394) 35316

## GREAT CORBY
Cumbria

**The Corby Bridge Inn**
★★★★ *Inn*
Great Corby, Carlisle CA4 8LL
t (01228) 560221
e corbybridgeinn@hotmail.co.
uk
w corbybridge.co.uk

## GREAT ECCLESTON
Lancashire

**The Cartford Inn**
Rating Applied For
*Inn*
Cartford Lane, Little Eccleston,
Nr Great Eccleston PR3 0YP
t (01995) 670166
e info@thecartfordinn.co.uk
w thecartfordinn.co.uk

## GUILDEN SUTTON
Cheshire

**Roseville** ★★★★★
*Bed & Breakfast*
**SILVER AWARD**
Belle Vue Lane, Chester
CH3 7EJ
t (01244) 300602
e traceyandjerry@tiscali.co.uk

## HALE
Greater Manchester

**Clovelly Court** ◆◆◆◆
*Guest Accommodation*
224 Ashley Rd, Hale,
Altrincham WA15 9SR
t (0161) 927 7027
e peter.hale@tiscali.co.uk

## HALEBARNS
Greater Manchester

**Oaklands Farm**
Rating Applied For
*Guest Accommodation*
Shay Lane, Hale Barns
WA15 8SN
t (0161) 980 4111

## HALLBANKGATE
Cumbria

**Belted Will Inn** ★★★ *Inn*
Hallbankgate, Brampton
CA8 2NJ
t (01697) 746236
e stephenbeltedwill@yahoo.
co.uk
w beltedwill.co.uk

## HARRAS MOOR
Cumbria

**The Georgian House** ★★★★
*Guest Accommodation*
9-11 Church Street,
Whitehaven CA28 7AY
t (01946) 696611
e stephanie@
thegeorgianhousehotel.net
w thegeorgianhousehotel.net

## HASLINGTON
Cheshire

**Ferndale House** ★★
*Guest Accommodation*
Gutterscroft, Haslington,
Crewe CW1 5RJ
t (01270) 584048
e lorrdchbowen@yahoo.co.uk

## HAWKSHAW
Greater Manchester

**Loe Lodge** ★★★★★
*Guest Accommodation*
Redisher Lane, Hawkshaw,
Bury BL8 4HX
t (01204) 888860
e loelodge@btinternet.com
w loelodge.co.uk

## HAWKSHEAD
Cumbria

**Borwick Lodge** ★★★★
*Guest House* **SILVER AWARD**
Outgate, Ambleside,
Hawkshead LA22 0PU
t (015394) 36332
e info@borwicklodge.com
w borwicklodge.com

**The Drunken Duck Inn**
★★★★★ *Inn*
Barngates, Ambleside
LA22 0NG
t (015394) 36347
w drunkenduckinn.co.uk

**Hawkshead YHA** ★★★
*Hostel*
Esthwaite Lodge, Ambleside
LA22 0QD
t (015394) 36293

**Ivy House & Restaurant**
★★★★ *Guest House*
Main Street, Hawkshead
LA22 0NS
t (015394) 36204
e ivyhousehotel@btinternet.
com
w ivyhousehotel.com

**Red Lion Inn** ★★★ *Inn*
Main Street, Hawkshead
LA22 0NS
t (015394) 36213
e enquiries@
redlionhawkshead.co.uk
w redlionhawkshead.co.uk

**Walker Ground Manor**
★★★★★ *Bed & Breakfast*
**SILVER AWARD**
Vicarage Lane, Hawkshead
LA22 0PD
t (015394) 36219
e info@walkerground.co.uk
w walkerground.co.uk

**Yewfield** ★★★★
*Guest Accommodation*
Hawkshead Hill, Ambleside
LA22 0PR
t (015394) 36765
e derek.yewfield@btinternet.
com
w yewfield.co.uk

## HAZEL GROVE
Greater Manchester

**Bramdene** ★★
*Bed & Breakfast*
1 Delamere Close, Hazel
Grove, Stockport SK7 4NP
t (0161) 483 4066

## HEADS NOOK
Cumbria

**Croft House** ★★★★
*Farmhouse* **SILVER AWARD**
Newbiggin, Brampton, Carlisle
CA8 9DH
t (01768) 896695
e info@crofthousecumbria.co.
uk
w crofthousecumbria.co.uk

## HELSINGTON
Cumbria

**Helsington Laithes Manor**
★★★★ *Bed & Breakfast*
Helsington, Kendal LA9 5RJ
t (01539) 741253
e themanor@helsington.uk.
com
w helsington.uk.com

## HESKET NEWMARKET
Cumbria

**Denton House** ★★★★
*Guest House*
Hesket Newmarket, Wigton,
Caldbeck CA7 8JG
t (01697) 478415
e dentonhnm@aol.com
w dentonhouseguesthouse.co.
uk

## HESKIN
Lancashire

**Farmers Arms** ★★★ *Inn*
85 Wood Lane, Heskin,
Chorley PR7 5NP
t (01257) 451276
e andy@farmersarms.co.uk
w farmersarms.co.uk

## HIGH LORTON
### Cumbria

**Swinside End Farm ★★★★**
*Farmhouse* **SILVER AWARD**
Scales, High Lorton,
Cockermouth CA13 9UA
t (01900) 85136

**Terrace Farm ★★★★**
*Farmhouse*
High Lorton, Cockermouth
CA13 9TX
t (01900) 85278
w terracefarm.co.uk

## HIGHER BEBINGTON
### Merseyside

**The Bebington Hotel ★★★**
*Guest Accommodation*
24 Town Lane, Wirral
CH63 5JG
t (0151) 645 0608
e vaghena@aol.com
w thebebingtonhotel.co.uk

## HOLMES CHAPEL
### Cheshire

**Bridge Farm Bed &
Breakfast ★★★★** *Farmhouse*
Blackden, Holmes Chapel
CW4 8BX
t (01477) 571202

**Padgate Guest House
★★★★** *Bed & Breakfast*
**SILVER AWARD**
Twemlow Lane, Cranage,
Holmes Chapel CW4 8EX
t (01477) 534291
e lynda@padgate.freeserve.
co.uk
w padgateguesthouse.co.uk/

## HOOLE
### Cheshire

**Chester Stone Villa
★★★★★**
*Guest Accommodation*
3 Stone Place, Hoole, Chester
CH2 3NR
t (01244) 345014
e enquiries@stonevillahotel.
co.uk
w stonevillahotel.co.uk

**Hamilton Court ★★★★**
*Guest Accommodation*
5/7 Hamilton Street, Hoole,
Chester CH2 3JG
t (01244) 345387
e hamiltoncourth@aol.com
w smoothhound.co.uk/hotels/
hamilton.html

**Holly House Guest House
★★★★** *Guest House*
1 Stone Place, Hoole, Chester
CH2 3NR
t (01244) 328967
e marinacassidy@yahoo.com
w hollyhouseguesthouse.co.uk

## HOUGHTON
### Cumbria

**The Steadings ★★★**
*Bed & Breakfast*
Townhead Farm, Houghton,
Carlisle CA6 4JB
t (01228) 523019
w thesteadings.co.uk

## HURST GREEN
### Lancashire

**The Fold ★★★★**
*Bed & Breakfast*
15 Smithy Row, Hurst Green,
Clitheroe BB7 9QA
t (01254) 826252
e derek.harwood1@virgin.net

## HUXLEY
### Cheshire

**Higher Huxley Hall
★★★★★**
*Guest Accommodation*
**SILVER AWARD**
Red Lane, Huxley, Chester
CH3 9BZ
t (01829) 781484
e vcc@huxleyhall.co.uk
w huxleyhall.co.uk

## INGS
### Cumbria

**The Hill ★★★★**
*Guest Accommodation*
Ings, Windermere LA8 9QQ
t (01539) 822217
e thehill@ktdinternet.com
w thehillonline.co.uk

## INSKIP
### Lancashire

**Chelsham Hill B&B ★★★**
*Farmhouse*
Inskip, Preston PR4 0UA
t (01995) 679424

## IREBY
### Cumbria

**Woodlands Country House
★★★★** *Guest House*
Ireby, Wigton, Bassenthwaite
CA7 1EX
t (01697) 371791
e stay@woodlandsatireby.co.
uk
w woodlandsatireby.co.uk

## IRTHINGTON
### Cumbria

**Corbett House ★★★★**
*Bed & Breakfast*
**SILVER AWARD**
Irthington, Carlisle, Brampton
CA6 4NN
t (01697) 741533
e corbetthouse@tiscali.co.uk
w corbetthouse.co.uk

**Newtown Farm ★★★**
*Farmhouse*
Newtown, Irthington, Carlisle
CA6 4NX
t (01697) 72768
e susangrice@tiscali.co.uk

## KENDAL
### Cumbria

**Beech House Hotel
★★★★★**
*Guest Accommodation*
**SILVER AWARD**
40 Greenside, Kendal LA9 4LD
t (01539) 720385
e stay@beechhouse-kendal.
co.uk
w beechhouse-kendal.co.uk

**Burrow Hall ★★★★**
*Bed & Breakfast*
Plantation Bridge, Kendal
LA8 9JR
t (015398) 21711
e burrow.hall@virgin.net
w burrowhall.co.uk

**Cragg Farm ★★★** *Farmhouse*
New Hutton, Kendal LA9 0BA
t (01539) 721760
e olive@craggfarm.com
w craggfarm.com

**The Glen ★★★★**
*Guest House*
Oxenholme, Kendal LA9 7RF
t (01539) 726386 &
07743 604599
e greeninatheglen@btinternet.
com
w glen-kendal.co.uk

**Hillside Bed & Breakfast
★★★★**
*Guest Accommodation*
4 Beast Banks, Kendal LA9 4JW
t (01539) 722836
e info@hillside-kendal.co.uk
w hillside-kendal.co.uk

**Kendal Arms and Hotel ★★**
*Inn*
72 Milnthorpe Road, Kendal
LA9 5HG
t (01539) 720956

**Riversleigh Guest House
★★★** *Guest Accommodation*
49 Milnthorpe Road, Kendal
LA9 5QG
t (01539) 726392

**Sonata Guest House ★★★★**
*Guest Accommodation*
19 Burneside Road, Kendal
LA9 4RL
t (01539) 732290
e chris@sonataguesthouse.
freeserve.co.uk
w sonataguesthouse.co.uk

**Sundial Guest House ★★★**
*Guest Accommodation*
51 Milnthorpe Road, Kendal
LA9 5QG
t (01539) 724468
e info@
sundialguesthousekendal.co.uk
w sundialguesthousekendal.
co.uk

**YHA Kendal ★★★** *Hostel*
118 Highgate, Kendal LA9 4HE
t 0870 770 5892
e kendal@yha.org.uk
w yha.org.uk

## KERMINCHAM
### Cheshire

**The Fields Farm ★★★★**
*Farmhouse*
Forty Acre Lane, Crewe
CW4 8DY
t (01477) 571224

## KESWICK
### Cumbria

**Abacourt House ★★★★**
*Guest Accommodation*
**SILVER AWARD**
Stanger Street, Keswick
CA12 5JU
t (017687) 72967
e abacourt@btinternet.com
w abacourt.co.uk

**Acorn House ★★★★**
*Guest House* **SILVER AWARD**
Ambleside Road, Keswick
CA12 4DL
t (01768) 72553
e info@acornhousehotel.co.uk
w acornhousehotel.co.uk

**Allerdale House ★★★★**
*Guest House*
1 Eskin Street, Keswick
CA12 4DH
t (01768) 773891
e allerdalehouse@btinternet.
com
w allerdale-house.co.uk

**Amble House Guest House
★★★★**
*Guest Accommodation*
**SILVER AWARD**
23 Eskin Street, Keswick
CA12 4DQ
t (01768) 773288
e info@amblehouse.co.uk
w amblehouse.co.uk

**Appletrees ★★★★**
*Guest House*
The Heads, Keswick CA12 5ER
t (017687) 80400
e john@armstrong2001.fsnet.
co.uk
w appletreeskeswick.com

**Avondale Guest House
★★★★**
*Guest Accommodation*
20 Southey Street, Keswick
CA12 4EF
t (017687) 72735
e enquiries@
avondaleguesthouse.com
w avondaleguesthouse.com

**Badgers Wood ★★★★**
*Guest Accommodation*
30 Stanger Street, Keswick
CA12 5JU
t (017687) 72621
e ctb@badgers-wood.co.uk
w badgers-wood.co.uk

**Beckside**
Rating Applied For
*Bed & Breakfast*
5 Wordsworth Street, Keswick
CA12 4HU
t (01768) 773093
e info@beckside-keswick.co.
uk
w beckside-keswick.co.uk

**Beckstones Farm Guest
House ★★★** *Guest House*
Thornthwaite, Keswick
CA12 5SQ
t (01768) 778510
e beckstones@lineone.net
w lineone.net/~beckstones

**Berkeley Guest House
★★★★** *Guest House*
The Heads, Keswick CA12 5ER
t (01768) 774222
e berkeley@tesco.net
w berkeley-keswick.com

**Bowfell House ★★★**
*Bed & Breakfast*
Chestnut Hill, Keswick
CA12 4LR
t (01768) 774859
e bowfell.keswick@virgin.net
w stayinkeswick.co.uk

**Braemar Guest House**
★★★★ *Guest House*
**SILVER AWARD**
21 Eskin Street, Keswick
CA12 4DQ
t (01768) 773743
e enquiries@braemar-
guesthouse.co.uk
w braemar-guesthouse.co.uk

**Bramblewood Cottage
Guest House** ★★★
*Bed & Breakfast*
2 Greta Street, Keswick
CA12 4HS
t (01768) 775918
e dorothy@dorothybell.
wanadoo.co.uk
w bramblewoodkeswick.com
▣

**Brookfield** ★★★★
*Guest House*
Penrith Road, Keswick
CA12 4LJ
t (01768) 772867
e brookfieldgh@supanet.com
w brookfield-keswick.co.uk
▣▨

**Brundholme Guest House**
★★★★ *Guest House*
The Heads, Keswick CA12 5ER
t (017687) 73305
e barbara@brundholme.co.uk
w brundholme.co.uk

**Burleigh Mead** ★★★★
*Guest House*
The Heads, Keswick CA12 5ER
t (017687) 75935
e info@burleighmead.co.uk
w burleighmead.co.uk

**Burnside B&B** ★★★★
*Bed & Breakfast*
Penrith Road, Keswick
CA12 4LJ
t (01768) 772639
e stay@burnside-keswick.co.
uk
w burnside-keswick.co.uk

**The Cartwheel Guest House**
Rating Applied For
*Guest House*
5 Blencathra Street, Keswick
CA12 4HW
t (01768) 773182
e info@thecartwheel.co.uk
w thecartwheel.co.uk

**Castlefell** ★★★
*Bed & Breakfast*
31 The Headlands, Keswick
CA12 5EQ
t (01768) 772849
e castlefell31@tiscali.co.uk
w castlefell.co.uk

**Charnwood Guest House**
★★★★ *Guest House*
6 Eskin Street, Keswick
CA12 4DH
t (01768) 774111

**Cherry Trees Guest House**
★★★★ *Guest House*
16 Eskin Street, Keswick
CA12 4DQ
t (01768) 771048
e info@cherrytrees-keswick.
co.uk
w cherrytrees-keswick.co.uk

**Cumbria House**
Rating Applied For
*Guest House*
1 Derwentwater Place,
Ambleside Road, Keswick
CA12 4DR
t (01768) 773171
e mavisandpatrick@
cumbriahouse.co.uk
w cumbriahouse.co.uk

**Damson Lodge** ★★★★
*Bed & Breakfast*
Eskin Street, Keswick
CA12 4DQ
t (01768) 775547
e damsonlodge@yahoo.co.uk
w damsonlodge.co.uk

**Dolly Waggon** ★★★
*Guest Accommodation*
17 Helvellyn Street, Keswick
CA12 4EN
t (01768) 773593
e info@dollywaggon.co.uk
w dollywaggon.co.uk

**Dunsford Guest House**
★★★★ *Guest House*
**SILVER AWARD**
16 Stanger Street, Keswick
CA12 5JU
t (01768) 75059
e enquiries@dunsford.net
w dunsford.net

**Easedale House** ★★★★
*Guest House*
1 Southey Street, Keswick
CA12 4HL
t (01768) 772710
e info@easedalehouse.com
w easedalehouse.com

**Eden Green Guest House**
★★★★ *Guest House*
20 Blencathra Street, Keswick
CA12 4HP
t (01768) 772077
e enquiries@
edengreenguesthouse.com
w edengreenguesthouse.com

**Edwardene Hotel** ★★★★
*Guest Accommodation*
**SILVER AWARD**
26 Southey Street, Keswick
CA12 4EF
t (01768) 773586
e info@edwardenehotel.com
w edwardenehotel.com

**Ellas Crag** ★★★★
*Guest House*
Newlands Valley, Keswick
CA12 5TS
t (01768) 778217
e ellascrag@talk21.com
w ellascrag.co.uk
▣▨

**Ellergill Guest House**
★★★★ *Guest House*
22 Stanger Street, Keswick
CA12 5JU
t (01768) 773347
e stay@ellergill.co.uk
w ellergill.co.uk

**Fell House** ★★★★
*Guest House*
28 Stanger Street, Keswick
CA12 5JU
t (01768) 772669

**Gill Brow Farm** ★★★
*Farmhouse*
Newlands Valley, Keswick
CA12 5TS
t (01768) 778270
e wilson_gillbrow@hotmail.
com

**Glencoe Guest House**
★★★★ *Guest House*
21 Helvellyn Street, Keswick
CA12 4EN
t (01768) 771016
e enquiries@
glencoeguesthouse.co.uk
w glencoeguesthouse.co.uk

**Glendale Guest House**
★★★★ *Guest House*
7 Eskin Street, Keswick
CA12 4DH
t (01768) 773562
e info@glendalekeswick.co.uk
w glendalekeswick.co.uk

**The Grange Country House**
Rating Applied For
*Guest House*
Manor Brow, Ambleside Road,
Keswick CA12 4BA
t (01768) 772500
e info@grangekeswick.com
w grangekeswick.com

**Grassmoor Guest House**
★★★★ *Guest House*
10 Blencathra Street, Keswick
CA12 4HP
t (01768) 774008
e info@grassmoor-keswick.co.
uk
w grassmoor-keswick.co.uk

**Hawcliffe House** ★★★★
*Guest House*
30 Eskin Street, Keswick
CA12 4DG
t (01768) 773250
e enquiries@hawcliffehouse.
co.uk
w hawcliffehouse.co.uk

**Hazeldene** ★★★★
*Guest Accommodation*
The Heads, Keswick CA12 5ER
t (01768) 772106
e info@hazeldene-hotel.co.uk
w hazeldene-hotel.co.uk

**Hedgehog Hill Guesthouse**
Rating Applied For
*Guest House*
18 Blencathra Street, Keswick
CA12 4HP
t (01768) 780654
e kta@hedgehoghill.co.uk
w hedgehoghill.co.uk

**Howe Keld Lakeland Hotel**
★★★★
*Guest Accommodation*
5-7 The Heads, Keswick
CA12 5ES
t (01768) 772417
e david@howekeld.co.uk
w howekeld.co.uk

**Hunters Way Guest House**
★★★★ *Guest House*
4 Eskin Street, Keswick
CA12 4DH
t (01768) 772324
e liz@huntersway.freeserve.
co.uk
w huntersway.keswick.co.uk

**Keswick Park Hotel** ★★★★
*Guest Accommodation*
33 Station Road, Keswick
CA12 4NA
t (01768) 772072
e enquiries@
keswickparkhotel.com
w keswickparkhotel.com

**Keswick YHA** ★★★★ *Hostel*
Station Road, Keswick
CA12 5LH
t (01768) 772484
▣▨

**Larry's Lodge** ★★★★
*Guest House*
39 Eskin Street, Keswick
CA12 4DG
t (01768) 773965
e suendave@larryslodge.co.uk
w larryslodge.co.uk
▨

**Laurel Bank** ★★★★
*Bed & Breakfast*
Penrith Road, Keswick
CA12 4LJ
t (01768) 773006
e info@laurelbankkeswick.co.
uk
w laurelbankkeswick.co.uk

**Leonard's Field House**
★★★★ *Guest House*
3 Leonard Street, Keswick
CA12 4EJ
t (01768) 774170
e enquiries@
leonardsfieldhouse.com
w leonardsfieldhouse.com

**Lincoln Guest House** ★★★
*Guest House*
23 Stanger Street, Keswick
CA12 5JX
t (01768) 772597
e info@lincolnguesthouse.com
w lincolnguesthouse.com

**Lindisfarne House** ★★★★
*Guest House*
21 Church Street, Keswick
CA12 4DX
t (01768) 773218
e alison230@btinternet.com
w lindisfarnehouse.com

**Linnett Hill** ★★★★
*Guest House*
4 Penrith Road, Keswick
CA12 4HF
t (01768) 773109
e info@linnetthillhotel.com
w linnetthillhotel.com

**Littletown Farm** ★★★
*Farmhouse*
Newlands, Keswick CA12 5TU
t (017687) 78353
e info@littletownfarm.co.uk
w littletownfarm.co.uk

**Lyndhurst** ★★★★
*Guest House*
22 Southey Street, Keswick
CA12 4EF
t (01768) 772303
e stay@lyndhurstkeswick.co.
uk
w lyndhurstkeswick.co.uk

**Lynwood Guest House**
★★★★ *Guest House*
12 Ambleside Road, Keswick
CA12 4DL
t (01768) 772081
e info@lynwood-keswick.co.uk
w lynwood-keswick.co.uk

**The Paddock** ★★★★
*Guest House*
Wordsworth Street, Keswick
CA12 4HU
t (01768) 772510
e val@thepaddock.info
w thepaddock.info

**Parkfield Guest House**
★★★★
*Guest Accommodation*
SILVER AWARD
The Heads, Keswick CA12 5ES
t (01768) 772328
e enquiries@parkfieldkeswick.co.uk
w parkfieldkeswick.co.uk

**Ravensworth Hotel** ★★★★
*Guest Accommodation*
SILVER AWARD
29 Station Street, Keswick
CA12 5HH
t (01768) 772476
e info@ravensworth-hotel.co.uk
w ravensworth-hotel.co.uk

**Rickerby Grange Country
House Hotel** ★★★★
*Guest House*
Portinscale, Nr. Keswick,
Keswick CA12 5RH
t (01768) 772344
e stay@rickerbygrange.co.uk
w rickerbygrange.co.uk

**Rivendell Guest House**
★★★★ *Guest House*
Helvellyn Street, Keswick
CA12 4EN
t (01768) 773822
e info@rivendellguesthouse.com
w rivendellguesthouse.com

**Sandon Guesthouse** ★★★★
*Guest House*
13 Southey Street, Keswick
CA12 4EG
t (017687) 73648
e enquiries@sandonguesthouse.com
w sandonguesthouse.com

**Seven Oaks** ★★★★
*Guest House*
7 Acorn Street, Keswick
CA12 4EA
t (01768) 772088
e info@sevenoaks-keswick.co.uk
w sevenoaks-keswick.co.uk

**Shemara Guest House**
★★★★ *Guest House*
27 Bank Street, Keswick
CA12 5JZ
t (01768) 773936
e info@shemara.uk.com
w shemara.uk.com

**Skiddaw Grove Country
Guest House** ★★★★
*Guest House*
Vicarage Hill, Keswick
CA12 5QB
t (01768) 773324
e info@skiddawgrove.co.uk
w skiddawgrove.co.uk

**Springs Farm Guesthouse**
★★★ *Guest House*
Springs Farm, Springs Road,
Keswick CA12 4AN
t (01768) 772144
e info@springsfarmcumbria.co.uk
w springsfarmcumbria.co.uk

**Squirrel Lodge** ★★★★
*Guest House*
43 Eskin Street, Keswick
CA12 4DG
t (01768) 771189
e squirrel.lodge@btconnect.com
w squirrellodge.co.uk

**Stonegarth Guest House**
★★★★ *Guest House*
2 Eskin Street, Keswick
CA12 4DH
t (01768) 772436
e info@stonegarth.com
w stonegarth.com

**Sweeneys Bar, Restaurant
and Rooms** ★★★★
*Restaurant with Rooms*
20 Lake Road, Keswick
CA12 5BX
t 05006 00725
e stay@lakedistrictinns.co.uk
w lakedistrictinns.co.uk

**The Swinside Inn** ★★★ *Inn*
Newlands, Keswick CA12 5UE
t (01768) 778253
e info@theswinsideinn.com
w theswinsideinn.com

**Swiss Court Guest House**
★★★ *Guest House*
25 Bank Street, Keswick
CA12 5JZ
t (01768) 772637
e enquiries@swisscourt.co.uk
w swisscourt.co.uk

**Tarn Hows** ★★★★
*Guest House* SILVER AWARD
3-5 Eskin Street, Keswick
CA12 4DH
t (01768) 773217
e info@tarnhows.co.uk
w tarnhows.co.uk

**Thornleigh Guest House**
★★★★ *Guest House*
23 Bank Street, Keswick
CA12 5JZ
t (017687) 72863
e thornleigh@btinternet.com
w thornleighguesthouse.co.uk

**Watendlath Guest House**
★★★★ *Guest House*
15 Acorn Street, Keswick
CA12 4EA
t (01768) 774165
e info@watendlathguesthouse.co.uk
w watendlathguesthouse.co.uk

**West View Guest House**
★★★★ *Guest House*
The Heads, Keswick CA12 5ES
t (01768) 773638
e info@westviewkeswick.co.uk
w westviewkeswick.co.uk

**Whitehouse** ★★★★
*Guest Accommodation*
SILVER AWARD
15 Ambleside Road, Keswick
CA12 4DL
t (01768) 773176
e whitehousekeswick@hotmail.com
w whitehouse.co.uk

KIRKBY
Merseyside

**Greenbank Guest House** ★★
*Bed & Breakfast*
193 Rowan Drive, Liverpool
L32 0SG
t (0151) 546 9971

KIRKBY LONSDALE
Cumbria

**Copper Kettle Restaurant &
Guest House** ★★
*Guest Accommodation*
3-5 Market Street, Kirkby
Lonsdale, Carnforth LA6 2AU
t (015242) 71714

**High Green Farm** ★★★★
*Guest Accommodation*
Middleton in Lonsdale,
Carnforth, Kirkby Lonsdale
LA6 2NA
t (01524) 276256
e nora@highgreenfarm.com
w highgreenfarm.com

**The Pheasant Inn** ★★★ *Inn*
Casterton, Kirkby Lonsdale
LA6 2RX
t (01524) 271230
e pheasantinn@fsbdial.co.uk
w pheasantinn.co.uk

**Ullathorns Farm** ★★★★
*Guest Accommodation*
Middleton, Kirkby Lonsdale,
Carnforth LA6 2LZ
t (015242) 76214 &
07800 990689
e pauline@ullathorns.co.uk
w ullathorns.co.uk

KIRKBY STEPHEN
Cumbria

**Augill Castle** ★★★★★
*Guest Accommodation*
SILVER AWARD
Kirkby Stephen CA17 4DE
t (017683) 41937
e augill@aol.com
w stayinacastle.co.uk

**Ing Hill Lodge** ★★★★
*Bed & Breakfast*
Mallerstang Dale, Kirkby
Stephen CA17 4JT
t (01768) 371153
e inghill@fsbdial.co.uk
w ing-hill-lodge.co.uk

**Riddlesay Farm** ★★★★
*Farmhouse*
Soulby, Kirkby Stephen
CA17 4PX
t (01768) 371474
e mrarmstrong@btinternet.com

**Westview** ★★★★
*Bed & Breakfast*
Ravenstonedale, Kirkby
Stephen CA17 4NG
t (015396) 23415

KNUTSFORD
Cheshire

**The Dog Inn** ★★★ *Inn*
Well Bank Lane, Over Peover,
Knutsford WA16 8UP
t (01625) 861421
e thedog-inn@paddockinns.fsnet.co.uk
w doginn-overpeover.co.uk

**Moat Hall Motel** ★★★
*Guest Accommodation*
Chelford Road, Marthall,
Knutsford WA16 8SU
t (01625) 860367
e val@moathall.fsnet.co.uk
w moat-hall-motel.co.uk

LACH DENNIS
Cheshire

**Melvin Holme Farm** ★★★
*Bed & Breakfast*
Pennys Lane, Lach Dennis,
Northwich CW9 7SJ
t (01606) 330008

LAKESIDE
Cumbria

**The Knoll Country House**
★★★★★
*Guest Accommodation*
SILVER AWARD
Lakeside, Newby Bridge,
Ulverston LA12 8AU
t (015395) 31347

LANCASTER
Lancashire

**Crows Nest Hotel**
Rating Applied For
*Restaurant with Rooms*
10 King Street, Lancaster
LA1 1JN
t (01524) 382888
w crows.uk.com

**Edenbreck House** ★★★★
*Bed & Breakfast*
Sunnyside Lane, Lancaster
LA1 5ED
t (01524) 32464
e edenbreckhouse@aol.com
w edenbreckhouse.com

**Lancaster Town House**
★★★ *Guest Accommodation*
11-12 Newton Terrace, Caton
Road, Lancaster LA1 3PB
t (01524) 65527
e hedge-holmes@talk21.com
w lancastertownhouse.com

**Low House Farm** ★★★★
*Farmhouse*
Claughton, Lancaster LA2 9LA
t (01524) 221260 &
07870 635854
e shirley@lunevalley.freeserve.co.uk
w lowhousefarm.co.uk

**Middle Holly Cottage**
Rating Applied For
*Guest House*
Middle Holly, Forton PR3 1AH
t (01524) 792399

**St Martin's College** ★★
*Campus*
Bowerham Road, Lancaster
LA1 3JD
t (01524) 384460
e conferences.lancaster@ucsm.ac.uk
w ucsm.ac.uk

**The Shakespeare (Bed & Breakfast)** ★★★★
*Guest House*
96 St Leonardgate, Lancaster
LA1 1NN
t (01524) 841041
e theshakespearelancaster@
talktalk.net

**The Sun Inn and Bar** ★★★★
*Guest Accommodation*
63 Church Street, Lancaster
LA1 1ET
t (01524) 66006
w thewaterwitch.co.uk/sun/
index.htm

**Britannia Inn** ★★★ *Inn*
Elterwater, Ambleside
LA22 9HP
t (015394) 37210
e info@britinn.co.uk
w britinn.co.uk

**Three Shires Inn** ★★★★
*Guest Accommodation*
Little Langdale, Langdale
LA22 9NZ
t (015394) 37215
e enquiry@threeshiresinn.co.
uk
w threeshiresinn.co.uk

**Larbreck House Farm** ★★★★
*Guest Accommodation*
Well Lane, Larbreck, Preston
PR3 0XR
t (01995) 670416
e harrypatknowles@aol.com
w larbreckhousefarm.co.uk

**Smithy Lodge Guest House** ★★★★
*Guest Accommodation*
310 Dunkirk Lane, Leyland
PR26 7SN
t (01772) 457650
e enquiries@smithy-lodge.co.
uk
w smithy-lodge.co.uk

**Litherland Park Bed and Breakfast** ★★★★
*Bed & Breakfast*
34 Litherland Park, Bootle
L21 9HP
t (0151) 928 1085

**Bollington Hall Farm** ★★
*Bed & Breakfast*
Park Lane, Little Bollington,
Altrincham WA14 4TJ
t (0161) 928 1760

**Elm Cottage Bed & Breakfast** ★★★
*Guest Accommodation*
Chester Lane, Winsford
CW7 2QJ
t (01829) 760544
e chris@elmcottagecp.co.uk
w elmcottagecp.co.uk

**Hollingworth Lake B&B** ★★★★★
*Guest Accommodation*
SILVER AWARD
164 Smithy Bridge Road,
Littleborough, Rochdale
OL15 0DB
t (01706) 376583
w b-visible.co.uk

**Leighton House B&B** ★★★★ *Guest House*
1 Leighton Avenue,
Littleborough, Rochdale
OL15 0BW
t (01706) 378113

**Swing Cottage** ★★★
*Guest House*
31 Lakebank, Hollingworth
Lake, Littleborough OL15 0DQ
t (01706) 379094
e swingcottage@aol.com
w hollingworthlake.com

**Aachen** ★★★
*Guest Accommodation*
89-91 Mount Pleasant,
Liverpool L3 5TB
t (0151) 709 3477
e enquiries@aachenhotel.co.
uk
w aachenhotel.co.uk

**Blenheim Lakeside Hotel** ★★ *Guest Accommodation*
37 Aigburth Drive, Sefton Park,
Liverpool L17 4JE
t (0151) 727 7380
e enquiries@
blenheimlakesidehotel.co.uk
w blenheimlakesidehotel.co.uk

**Carey's B&B** ★★
*Bed & Breakfast*
89 Walton Breck Road, Anfield,
Liverpool L4 0RD
t (0151) 286 7965

**Feathers Hotel** ★★★★
*Guest Accommodation*
117-125 Mount Pleasant,
Liverpool L3 5TF
t (0151) 709 9655

**Holme-Leigh Guest House** ★★★ *Guest Accommodation*
93 Woodcroft Road,
Wavertree, Liverpool L15 2HG
t (0151) 734 2216
e info@holmeleigh.com
w holmeleigh.com

**The International Inn** ★★★
*Hostel*
4 South Hunter Street, Off
Hardman Street, Liverpool
L1 9JG
t (0151) 709 8135

**Lord Nelson Hotel** ★★
*Guest Accommodation*
Hotham Street, Liverpool
L3 5PD
t (0151) 709 5161
e reservations@
lordnelsonliverpool.com
w lordnelsonliverpool.com

**Mulberry Court** ★★ *Campus*
Liverpool University Mulberry
Court, Liverpool L7 7EZ
t (0151) 794 3298

**The Racquet Club** ★★★★
*Restaurant with Rooms*
5 Chapel Street, Liverpool
L3 9AG
t (0151) 236 6676
e info@racquetclub.org.uk
w racquetclub.org.uk

**Real McCoy Guest House** ★★ *Bed & Breakfast*
126 Childwall Park Avenue,
Childwall, Liverpool L16 0JH
t (0151) 722 7116
e ann557@btinternet.com

**Throstles Nest** ★★★★
*Guest Accommodation*
Scotland Road, Liverpool
L5 5AQ
t (0151) 207 9797
e info@throstlesnesthotel.co.
uk
w throstlesnesthotel.co.uk

**Victoria Hall**
Rating Applied For
*Campus*
29 Hatton Garden, Liverpool
L3 2EZ
t (0151) 907 7000
e liverpool@victoriahall.com
w victoriahall.com

**YHA Liverpool International** ★★★★ *Hostel*
25 Tabley Street, Off Wapping,
Liverpool L1 8EE
t 0870 770 5924
e liverpool@yha.org.uk
w yha.org.uk

**The Corporation Arms** ★★★★ *Inn*
Lower Road, Longridge,
Preston PR3 2YJ
t (01772) 782644
w corporationarms.co.uk

**Oak Lea** ★★★★
*Guest Accommodation*
Clitheroe Road, Knowle Green,
Preston PR3 2YS
t (01254) 878486
e tandm.mellor@tiscali.co.uk

**Borrowdale YHA** ★★★★
*Hostel*
Longthwaite, Keswick
CA12 5XE
t (01768) 777257

**Willow Cottage** ★★★★
*Bed & Breakfast*
SILVER AWARD
Longton by Pass, Longton,
Preston PR4 4RA
t (01772) 617570
e info@
lancashirebedandbreakfast.co.
uk

**Briar Lea Guest House** ★★★★
*Guest Accommodation*
Brampton Road, Longtown
CA6 5TN
t (01228) 791538
e info@briarleahouse.co.uk
w briarleahouse.co.uk

**Craigburn Farmhouse** ★★★★ *Farmhouse*
Penton, Longtown CA6 5QP
t (01228) 577214
e louiselawson@hotmail.com
w criagburnfarmhouse.co.uk

**Langdale YHA** ★★ *Hostel*
High Close, Loughrigg,
Langdale LA22 9HJ
t 0870 770 5672
e langdale@yha.org.uk
w yha.org.uk

**Crow Tree Villa** ★★
*Guest House*
Bartle Lane, Bartle, Preston
PR4 0RU
t (01772) 690101
e crowtreevilla@talktalk.net

**Chapel Cottage** ★★★
*Bed & Breakfast*
Dicklow Cob, Lower
Withington, Macclesfield
SK11 9EA
t (01477) 571489
e barbara.hides2@virgin.net

**Askhill Farm** ★★★★
*Farmhouse*
Loweswater, Cockermouth
CA13 0SU
t (01946) 861640
e askhillfarm@aol.com
w countrycaravans.co.uk/
askhillfarm

**Pomona Bed & Breakfast** ★★★★ *Bed & Breakfast*
Lowick Green, Ulverston,
Coniston LA12 8DX
t (01229) 885399
e steve@pomonalakedistrict.
co.uk
w pomonalakedistrict.co.uk

**The Plough Inn** ★★★ *Inn*
Cow Brow, Lupton, Kirkby
Lonsdale LA6 1PJ
t (015395) 67227
e ploughhotel@totalise.co.uk
w theplough-lupton.co.uk

**The Breverton** ★★★
*Guest Accommodation*
64 Orchard Road, Lytham-St-
Annes FY8 1PJ
t (01253) 726179

**Cornubia** ★★★★
Bed & Breakfast
**SILVER AWARD**
13 Derbe Road, St Annes-On
Sea, Lytham-St-Annes FY8 1NJ
**t** (01253) 640834
**e** cornubia@lycos.co.uk

**Endsleigh** ★★★
Guest Accommodation
315 Clifton Drive South, St
Annes-On Sea, Lytham-St-
Annes FY8 1HN
**t** (01253) 725622
**e** endsleighhotel@hotmail.
com

**Fairmile** ★★★
Guest Accommodation
9 St Annes Road East, St Annes
FY8 1TA
**t** (01253) 728375
**w** hotellink.co.uk/lytham/
fairmile.html

**The Queens Inn** ★★★ Inn
Central Beach, Lytham FY8 5LB
**t** (01253) 737316
**e** enquiries@the-queens-
lytham.co.uk
**w** the-queens-lytham.co.uk

**Strathmore Hotel** ★★★
Guest Accommodation
305 Clifton Drive South, St
Annes-On Sea, Lytham-St-
Annes FY8 1HN
**t** (01253) 725478

**Tudor House** ★★★
Guest House
32 St Davids Road South, St
Annes FY8 1TJ
**t** (01253) 722444
**e** stay@tudorhouse.uk.com
**w** tudorhouse.uk.com

MACCLESFIELD
Cheshire

**13 Sherwood Road** ★★
Bed & Breakfast
Macclesfield SK11 7RR
**t** (01625) 420208

**Astle Farm East** ★★
Farmhouse
Chelford, Macclesfield
SK10 4TA
**t** (01625) 861270
**e** gill.farmhouse@virgin.net

**Carr House Farm Bed &**
**Breakfast** ★★ Farmhouse
Mill Lane, Macclesfield
SK10 4LG
**t** (01625) 828337
**e** isobel@carrhousefarm.fsnet.
co.uk
**w** carrhousefarm.com

**Moorhayes House** ★★★
Guest Accommodation
27 Manchester Road,
Tytherington, Macclesfield
SK10 2JJ
**t** (01625) 433228
**e** helen@moorhayes.co.uk
**w** smoothhound.co.uk/hotels/
moorhaye

**Red Oaks Farm B&B** ★★★★
Farmhouse **SILVER AWARD**
Charter Road, Macclesfield
SK10 5NU
**t** (01625) 574280
**e** bb@redoaksfarm.co.uk
**w** redoaksfarm.co.uk

**Ryles Arms** ★★★★ Inn
Hollin Lane, Sutton,
Macclesfield SK11 0NN
**t** (01260) 252244
**e** info@rylesarms.com
**w** rylesarms.com

MACCLESFIELD FOREST
Cheshire

**The Stanley Arms Bed &**
**Breakfast** ★★★★ Inn
Macclesfield Forest,
Wildboarclough SK11 0AR
**t** (01260) 252414
**e** thestanleyarms@btconnet.
com
**w** stanleyarms.com

MANCHESTER
Greater Manchester

**Abbey Lodge** ★★★
Bed & Breakfast
501 Wilbraham Road,
Chorlton, Manchester M21 0UJ
**t** (0161) 862 9266
**e** info@abbey-lodge.co.uk
**w** abbey-lodge.co.uk

**The Hatters** ★★★ Hostel
50 Newton Street, Manchester
M1 2EA
**t** (0161) 236 9500
**e** manchester@hattersgroup.
com
**w** hattersgroup.com

**The Ivy Mount Guest House**
★ Guest Accommodation
35 Half Edge Lane, Manchester
M30 9AY
**t** (0161) 789 1756

**Luther King House** ★★★
Guest Accommodation
Brighton Grove, Wilmslow
Road, Manchester M14 5JP
**t** (0161) 224 6404
**e** reception@lkh.co.uk
**w** lkh.co.uk

**Manchester YHA** ★★★★
Hostel
Potato Wharf, Castlefield,
Manchester M3 4NB
**t** 0870 770 5950

**Monroes Hotel** ★★ Inn
38 London Road, Manchester
M1 2PF
**t** (0161) 236 0564

**Seasons Guest House** ★★★
Guest House
803 Altrincham Road,
Manchester M23 9AH
**t** (0161) 945 3232

**Stay Inn Hotel – Manchester**
★★★ Guest Accommodation
55 Blackfriars Road, Salford,
Manchester M3 7DB
**t** (0161) 907 2277
**e** info@stayinn.co.uk
**w** stayinn.co.uk

**Victoria Hall** ★★★ Campus
28 Higher Cambridge Street,
Manchester M15 6AA
**t** (0161) 908 7000
**e** manchester.hcs@
victoriahall.com
**w** victoriahall.com

MARPLE BRIDGE
Greater Manchester

**Forge Bank Mill**
Rating Applied For
Bed & Breakfast
1 Longhurst Lane, Stockport
SK6 5AE
**t** (0161) 427 9345

MAULDS MEABURN
Cumbria

**Trainlands B&B** ★★★
Farmhouse
Maulds Meaburn, Penrith
CA10 3HX
**t** (01768) 351249
**e** carol@trainlands.co.uk
**w** trainlands.co.uk

MIDDLETON
Greater Manchester

**Three Gates Farm** ★★★★
Bed & Breakfast
Stakehill Lane, Middleton,
Manchester M24 2RT
**t** (0161) 653 8314

MIDDLEWICH
Cheshire

**Hopley House** ★★★
Guest Accommodation
Wimboldsley, Middlewich
CW10 0LN
**t** (01270) 526292
**e** margery@hopleyhouse.co.
uk
**w** hopleyhouse.co.uk

MILBURN
Cumbria

**Low Howgill Farm** ★★★★
Bed & Breakfast
Low Howgill, Milburn,
Appleby-in-Westmorland
CA10 1TL
**t** (01768) 361595
**e** holidays@low-howgill.co.uk
**w** lowhowgill.f9.co.uk

**Slakes Farm** ★★★
Farmhouse
Milburn, Appleby-in-
Westmorland CA16 6DP
**t** (01768) 361385
**e** oakleaves@slakesfarm.
wanadoo.co.uk
**w** slakesfarm.co.uk

MILNTHORPE
Cumbria

**The Cross Keys Hotel**
★★★★ Inn
1 Park Road, Milnthorpe
LA7 7AB
**t** (015395) 62115
**e** stay@thecrosskeyshotel.co.
uk
**w** thecrosskeyshotel.co.uk

MINSHULL VERNON
Cheshire

**Higher Elms Farm** ★★★
Farmhouse
Cross Lane, Minshull Vernon,
Crewe CW1 4RG
**t** (01270) 522252

MORECAMBE
Lancashire

**Ashley Guest House** ★★★
Guest House
371 Marine Road East,
Morecambe LA4 5AH
**t** (01524) 412034
**e** info@ashleyhotel.co.uk
**w** ashleyhotel.co.uk

**Balmoral Hotel** ★★★
Guest House
34 Marine Road West,
Morecambe LA3 1BZ
**t** (01524) 418526
**e** info@
balmoralhotelmorecambe.co.uk
**w** balmoralhotelmorecambe.
co.uk

**Berkeley Guest House** ★★★
Guest House
39 Promenade West,
Morecambe LA3 1BZ
**t** (01524) 418201
**e** donval4144@hotmail.com
**w** hotelmorecambe.co.uk

**The Broadwater** ★★★
Guest Accommodation
356 Marine Road East,
Morecambe LA4 5AQ
**t** (01524) 411333
**e** broadwaterhotel@aol.com

**Crown Morecambe** ★★★★
Guest Accommodation
239 Marine Road Central,
Morecambe LA4 4BJ
**t** (01524) 831841
**e** enquiries@
thecrownhotelmorecambe.co.
uk
**w** thecrownhotelmorecambe.
co.uk

**Highview** ★★★★
Guest Accommodation
235 Heysham Road, Heysham,
Morecambe LA3 1NN
**t** (01524) 424991

**Seacrest** ★★★
Guest Accommodation
9-13 West End Road,
Morecambe LA4 4DJ
**t** (01524) 411006

**Silverwell** ★★★ Guest House
20 West End Road,
Morecambe LA4 4DL
**t** (01524) 410532
**e** svlerwll@aol.com
**w** silverwellhotel.co.uk

**The Wimslow** ★★★
Guest House
374 Marine Road East,
Morecambe LA4 5AH
**t** (01524) 417804
**e** morecambewimslow@aol.
com

**Yacht Bay View Hotel** ★★★
Guest Accommodation
359 Marine Road East,
Morecambe LA4 5AQ
**t** (01524) 414481
**e** yachtbayview@hotmail.com
**w** yachtbay.co.uk

MOSSER
Cumbria

**Mosser Heights** ★★★★
Farmhouse
Mosser, Cockermouth
CA13 0SS
**t** (01900) 822644
**e** amandavickers1@aol.com

## MOTTRAM ST ANDREW
### Cheshire

**Goose Green Farm Bed & Breakfast ★★★** *Farmhouse*
Oak Road, Macclesfield
SK10 4RA
t (01625) 828814
e info@goosegreenfarm.com
w goosegreenfarm.com

## MUNCASTER
### Cumbria

**Muncaster Coachman's Quarters ★★★★**
*Guest Accommodation*
Muncaster Castle, Muncaster,
Ravenglass CA18 1RQ
t (01229) 717614
e info@muncaster.co.uk
w muncaster.co.uk

**Muncaster Country Guest House ★★★★** *Guest House*
Muncaster, Ravenglass
CA18 1RD
t (01229) 717693
e ronandjan@
muncastercountryguesthouse.
com
w muncastercountryguest
house.com

## MUNGRISDALE
### Cumbria

**Near Howe Cottages ★★★★**
*Guest Accommodation*
Mungrisdale, Penrith
CA11 0SH
t (017687) 79678
e enquiries@nearhowe.co.uk
w nearhowe.co.uk

## NANTWICH
### Cheshire

**Coole Hall Farm Bed and Breakfast ★★★★** *Farmhouse*
**SILVER AWARD**
Hankelow, Crewe CW3 0JD
t (01270) 811232
e goodwin200@hotmail.com

**Hamilton House Bed and Breakfast ★★★**
*Bed & Breakfast*
Station Road, Hampton Heath,
Malpas SY14 8JF
t (01948) 820421
e hamiltonhouse5@hotmail.
com
w hamiltonhousecheshire.co.uk

**Outlanes Farmhouse Bed & Breakfast ★★**
*Guest Accommodation*
The Outlanes, Church
Minshull, Nantwich CW5 6DX
t (01270) 522284
e robert.parton@theoutlanes.
com
w theoutlanes.com

## NATEBY
### Cumbria

**The Black Bull ★★★★** *Inn*
Nateby, Kirkby Stephen
CA17 4JP
t (01768) 371588
e enquiries@blackbullnateby.
co.uk

## NELSON
### Lancashire

**Lovett House Guest House ★★★** *Guest House*
6 Howard Street, Nelson
BB9 7SZ
t (01282) 697352
e lovetthouse@ntlworld.com
w lovetthouse.co.uk

## NEW BRIGHTON
### Merseyside

**Sherwood Guest House ★★★** *Guest House*
55 Wellington Road, New
Brighton, Wirral CH45 2ND
t (0151) 639 5198
e info@sherwoodguesthouse.
com
w sherwoodguesthouse.com

## NEW HUTTON
### Cumbria

**1 Ashes Barn ★★★★**
*Guest Accommodation*
New Hutton, Kendal LA8 0AS
t (01539) 729215
e gillian@ashesbarn.co.uk
w ashesbarn.co.uk

## NEWBIGGIN-ON-LUNE
### Cumbria

**Tranna Hill ★★★★**
*Guest Accommodation*
Newbiggin-on-Lune, Kirkby
Stephen CA17 4NY
t (015396) 23227
e enquiries@trannahill.co.uk
w trannahill.co.uk

## NEWBY BRIDGE
### Cumbria

**Old Barn Farm ★★★★**
*Guest House*
Fiddler Hall, Newby Bridge
LA12 8NQ
t (015395) 31842
e peter@oldbarnfarm.com
w oldbarnfarm.com

## NEWCHURCH
### Lancashire

**Old Earth House ★★★★**
*Bed & Breakfast*
33 Newchurch in Pendle,
Newchurch Village, Burnley
BB12 9JR
t (01282) 698812
e isolde@healey7809.fsnet.co.
uk

## NEWLANDS
### Cumbria

**Newlands Fell Guesthouse**
Rating Applied For
*Guest House*
Keswick CA12 5TS
t (01768) 778417
e collin.wood@btinternet.com

## NIBTHWAITE
### Cumbria

**Lakeside YMCA National Centre ★★★** *Hostel*
Lakeside, Newby Bridge
LA12 8BD
t (015395) 39012
e sales@lakesideymca.co.uk
w lakesideymca.co.uk

## NORTHWICH
### Cheshire

**Ash House Farm ★★★★**
*Farmhouse*
Chapel Lane, Northwich
CW8 3QS
t (01606) 852717
e sue_schofield40@hotmail.
com

**Parkdale Guest House ★★★**
*Guest Accommodation*
140 Middlewich Road,
Rudheath, Northwich
CW9 7DS
t (01606) 45228
e srb7@btinternet.com

**The Poplars ★★★★**
*Farmhouse*
Norley Lane, Crowton,
Northwich CW8 2RR
t (01928) 788083

## OAKENCLOUGH
### Lancashire

**Calderbank Country Lodge ★★★★**
*Guest Accommodation*
**SILVER AWARD**
Oakenclough, Preston PR3 1UL
t (01995) 604384
e info@
calderbankcountrylodge.co.uk
w calderbankcountrylodge.
com

## OLD TRAFFORD
### Greater Manchester

**Lancashire County Cricket Club & Old Trafford Lodge ★★★** *Guest Accommodation*
Talbot Road, Old Trafford,
Manchester M16 0PX
t (0161) 874 3333
e lodge@lccc.co.uk
w lccc.co.uk

## OLDHAM
### Greater Manchester

**Boothstead Farm ★★★★**
*Guest Accommodation*
Rochdale Road, Denshaw,
Oldham OL3 5UE
t (01457) 878622
e boothsteadfarm@tiscali.co.
uk

**Grains Bar Farm ★★★**
*Guest Accommodation*
Ripponden Road, Oldham
OL1 4SX
t (0161) 624 0303
e info@grainsbarhotel.co.uk

## OULTON
### Cheshire

**New Farm Bed and Breakfast**
Rating Applied For
*Guest Accommodation*
Long Lane, Wettenhall, Nr
Nantwich CW7 4DW
t (01270) 528213
e info@
newfarmbbandcaravanpark.co.
uk
w newfarmbbandcaravanpark.
co.uk/index.htm

## OVER ALDERLEY
### Cheshire

**Lower Harebarrow Farm ★★**
*Bed & Breakfast*
Alderley Road, Over Alderley,
Macclesfield SK10 4SW
t (01625) 829882
w lowerharebarrowfarm.co.uk/

## PARBOLD
### Lancashire

**The Red Lion Inn ★★★** *Inn*
9 Ash Brow, Newburgh,
Parbold WN8 7NF
t (01257) 462336

## PATTERDALE
### Cumbria

**Deepdale Hall Farmhouse ★★★★** *Farmhouse*
Deepdale Hall, Patterdale,
Ullswater CA11 0NR
t (01768) 482369
e brown@deepdalehall.
freeserve.co.uk
w deepdalehall.co.uk

**Patterdale YHA ★★** *Hostel*
Goldrill House, Penrith
CA11 0NW
t (01768) 482394

## PENRITH
### Cumbria

**Bracken Bank Lodge ★★★★**
*Guest Accommodation*
Lazonby, Penrith CA10 1AX
t (01768) 898241
e info@brackenbank.co.uk
w brackenbank.co.uk

**Brandelhow Guest House ★★★★** *Guest House*
**SILVER AWARD**
1 Portland Place, Penrith
CA11 7QN
t (01768) 864470
e enquiries@
brandelhowguesthouse.co.uk
w brandelhowguesthouse.co.
uk

**Caledonia Guest House ★★★★**
*Guest Accommodation*
8 Victoria Road, Penrith
CA11 8HR
t (01768) 864482
e ian.rhind1@virgin.net
w caledoniaguesthouse.co.uk

**Glendale Guest House ★★★★** *Guest House*
4 Portland Place, Penrith
CA11 7QN
t (01768) 862579
e glendaleguesthouse@yahoo.
co.uk
w glendaleguesthouse.com

**Hornby Hall Country Guest House ★★★★**
*Guest Accommodation*
Brougham, Penrith CA10 2AR
t (01768) 891114
e enquire@hornbyhall.co.uk
w hornbyhall.co.uk

**The Limes Country Guest House ★★★** *Guest House*
Redhills, Penrith CA11 0DT
t (01768) 863343
e jdhanton@aol.com
w members.aol.com/jdhanton/
index.htm

**Little Blencowe Farm** ★★★
*Farmhouse*
Blencow, Penrith CA11 0DG
t (017684) 83338 &
07745 460186
e bef@littleblencowe.
wanadoo.co.uk

**Norcroft Guest House**
★★★★ *Guest House*
Graham Street, Penrith
CA11 9LQ
t (01768) 862365
e info@norcroft-guesthouse.
co.uk
w norcroft-guesthouse.co.uk

**The Old School** ★★★★★
*Guest House* **SILVER AWARD**
Newbiggin, Stainton, Penrith
CA11 0HT
t (01768) 483709
e info@theold-school.com
w theold-school.com

**Roundthorn Country House**
★★★★★
*Guest Accommodation*
Beacon Edge, Roundthorn,
Penrith CA11 8SJ
t (01768) 863952
e info@roundthorn.co.uk
w roundthorn.co.uk

**The Pooley Bridge Inn** ★★★
*Inn*
Pooley Bridge, Lake Ullswater,
Penrith CA10 2NN
t (01768) 486215
e stay@pooleybridgeinn.co.uk
w pooleybridgeinn.co.uk

**Hesket House** ★★★★
*Guest Accommodation*
Port Carlisle, Wigton CA7 5BU
t (01697) 351876
e stay@heskethouse.com
w heskethouse.com

**Lakeview** ★★★★
*Guest House*
Portinscale, Keswick
CA12 5RD
t (01768) 771122
e sandkmuir@aol.com
w lakeviewkeswick.co.uk

**Powe House**
Rating Applied For
*Guest House*
Portinscale, Keswick
CA12 5RW
t (01768) 773611
e a.carey.powehouse@
hotmail.co.uk
w powehouse.com

**The Shard Riverside Inn**
★★★★ *Inn*
Old Bridge Lane, Hambleton,
Poulton-le-Fylde FY6 9BT
t (01253) 700208
e info@shardriversideinn.co.
uk
w shardriversideinn.co.uk

**Grassendale** ★★★
*Bed & Breakfast*
Green Lane, Preesall, Poulton-
le-Fylde FY6 0NS
t (01253) 812331
e rondeyo@aol.com

**Artizana Suite** ★★★★★
*Bed & Breakfast*
The Village, Prestbury,
Macclesfield SK10 4DG
t (01625) 827582
e suite@artizana.co.uk
w artizana.co.uk/suite

**Little Stubbins Bed &
Breakfast** ★★★★
*Bed & Breakfast*
Stubbins Lane, Claughton on
Brock, Preston PR3 0PL
t (01995) 640376
e littlestubbins@aol.com
w littlestubbins.co.uk

**Ye Horns Inn** ★★★★
*Guest Accommodation*
Horns Lane, Goosnargh,
Preston PR3 2FJ
t (01772) 865230
e enquiries@yehornsinn.co.uk
w yehornsinn.co.uk

**The Church Inn – Bury** ★★★
*Inn*
Church Lane, Prestwich,
Manchester M25 1AJ
t (0161) 798 6727
e tom.gribben@virgin.net

**Common Barn Farm B&B**
★★★★ *Bed & Breakfast*
Smith Lane, Rainow,
Macclesfield SK10 5XJ
t (01625) 574878
e g_greengrass@hotmail.com
w cottages-with-a-view.co.uk

**Harrop Fold Farm Bed &
Breakfast** ★★★★★
*Farmhouse* **SILVER AWARD**
Macclesfield Road, Rainow,
Macclesfield SK10 5UU
t (01625) 560085
e stay@harropfoldfarm.co.uk
w harropfoldfarm.co.uk

**A Corner of Eden** ★★★★
*Guest Accommodation*
Low Stennerskeugh,
Ravenstonedale, Kirkby
Stephen CA17 4LL
t (015396) 23370
e enquiries@acornerofeden.
co.uk
w acornerofeden.co.uk

**Coldbeck House** ★★★★★
*Bed & Breakfast*
**GOLD AWARD**
Ravenstonedale, Kirkby
Stephen CA17 4LW
t (015396) 23407
e belle@coldbeckhouse.co.uk
w coldbeckhouse.co.uk

**Lindau Private Guest House**
◆◆ *Guest Accommodation*
131 Haslingden Old Road,
Rawtenstall, Rossendale
BB4 8RR
t (01706) 214592
e enquiries@lindau-guest-
house.co.uk
w lindau-guest-house.co.uk

**Riverside Barn** ★★★★★
*Guest Accommodation*
Riverside, Ribchester, Nr
Preston PR3 3XS
t (01254) 878095
e relax@riversidebarn.co.uk
w riversidebarn.co.uk

**Fernhill Barn B&B** ★★★★
*Guest Accommodation*
Fernhill Lane, Lanehead,
Rochdale OL12 6BW
t (01706) 355671
e info@fernhillbarn.com
w fernhillbarn.com

**Horncliffe Mount Farm**
★★★★ *Bed & Breakfast*
Lomas Lane, Rawtenstall,
Rossendale BB4 6HU
t (01706) 220227
e info@horncliffemountfarm.
co.uk
w horncliffemountfarm.co.uk

**Peers Clough Farm** ★★★
*Guest Accommodation*
Peers Clough Road, Lumb,
Rossendale BB4 9NG
t (01706) 210552
e peerscloughfarm@hotmail.
com
w peerscloughfarm.com

**Low Luckens Organic
Resource Centre** ★★★
*Hostel*
Low Luckens, Carlisle CA6 6LJ
t (01697) 748186
e lowluckensfarm@co.uk
w lowluckensfarm.co.uk

**Crosslands Farm** ★★★★
*Farmhouse*
Rusland, Hawkshead LA22 8JU
t (01229) 860242
e enquiries@crosslandsfarm.
co.uk
w crosslandsfarm.co.uk

**Nab Cottage** ★★★
*Guest House*
Rydal, Grasmere, Ambleside
LA22 9SD
t (015394) 35311
e tim@nabcottage.com
w rydalwater.com

**Cobden Farm** ★★★★
*Farmhouse*
Watt Street, Sabden, Clitheroe
BB7 9ED
t (01282) 776285

**The Shippon at Wiswell
Moor Farm** ★★★★
*Bed & Breakfast*
1 The Barn, Clerk Hill Road,
Clitheroe BB7 9FR
t (01254) 822389

**Fleatham House** ★★★★★
*Guest Accommodation*
High House Road, St Bees
CA27 0BX
t (01946) 822341

**Stonehouse Farm** ★★★★
*Farmhouse*
133 Main Street, St Bees
CA27 0DE
t (019468) 22224
e csmith.stonehouse@
btopenworld.com
w stonehousefarm.net

**The Belforte House** ★★★
*Guest Accommodation*
7-9 Broad Road, Sale M33 2AE
t (0161) 973 8779
e belfortehotel@aol.com
w belfortehousehotel.co.uk

**Garden Gate Guest House**
★★ *Guest Accommodation*
8 Chester Street, Nr Saltney,
Chester CH4 8BJ
t (01244) 682306
e dollywal@msn.com

**Bagmere Bank Farm** ★★★★
*Bed & Breakfast*
**SILVER AWARD**
Brereton Park, Brereton,
Sandbach CW11 1RX
t (01477) 537503

**Plantation Cottage** ★★★★
*Bed & Breakfast*
Arnside Road, Sandside,
Milnthorpe LA7 7JU
t (01524) 762069

Look out for establishments participating in the National Accessible Scheme

## SAWREY
### Cumbria

**Beechmount Country House**
★★★★★ *Bed & Breakfast*
**SILVER AWARD**
Hawkshead, Sawrey LA22 0JZ
t (015394) 36356
e beechmount@btinternet.
com
w beechmountcountryhouse.
co.uk

**Buckle Yeat Guest House**
★★★★ *Guest House*
Nr Sawrey, Ambleside
LA22 0LF
t (015394) 36446
e info@buckle-yeat.co.uk
w buckle-yeat.co.uk

**West Vale Country House & Restaurant** ★★★★★
*Guest Accommodation*
**GOLD AWARD**
Far Sawrey, Hawkshead,
Sawrey LA22 0LQ
t (015394) 42817
e enquiries@
westvalecountryhouse.co.uk
w westvalecountryhouse.co.uk

## SCARROW HILL
### Cumbria

**Scarrowhill House**
Rating Applied For
*Bed & Breakfast*
Scarrow Hill House, Brampton
CA8 2QU
t (01697) 746759
e lanmac2949@aol.com
w scarrowhillhouse.co.uk

## SCORTON
### Lancashire

**The Priory Inn** ★★★★
*Guest Accommodation*
The Square, Scorton, Preston
PR3 1AU
t (01524) 791255
e collinsonjulie@aol.com
w theprioryscorton.co.uk

## SCOTBY
### Cumbria

**Willowbeck Lodge** ★★★★★
*Guest Accommodation*
**GOLD AWARD**
Lambley Bank, Scotby, Carlisle
CA4 8BX
t (01228) 513607
e info@willowbeck-lodge.com
w willowbeck-lodge.com

## SEASCALE
### Cumbria

**Cumbrian Lodge** ★★★★
*Restaurant with Rooms*
58 Gosforth Road, Seascale
CA20 1JG
t (01946) 727309
w cumbrianlodge.com

## SEATOLLER
### Cumbria

**Honister Hause YHA** ★★
*Hostel*
Seatoller, Keswick CA12 5XN
t (01768) 777267

## SEDBERGH
### Cumbria

**Dalesman Country Inn**
★★★★ *Inn*
Main Street, Sedbergh
LA10 5BN
t (015396) 21183
e info@thedalesman.co.uk
w thedalesman.co.uk

**Howgills Bunk Barn** ★★★
*Hostel*
Castlehaw Farm, Castlehaw
Lane, Sedbergh LA10 5BA
t (015396) 21000
e cobblesedbergh@yahoo.co.
uk
w howgillsbunkbarn.co.uk

**St Mark's** ★★★★
*Guest Accommodation*
Cautley, Sedbergh LA10 5LZ
t (015396) 20287
e saint.marks@btinternet.com
w saintmarks.uk.com

## SIDDINGTON
### Cheshire

**Golden Cross Farm** ★★★
*Farmhouse*
Siddington, Macclesfield
SK11 9PJ
t (01260) 224358

## SILLOTH
### Cumbria

**Nith View Guest House**
★★★★
*Guest Accommodation*
1 Pine Terrace, Skinburness
Road, Silloth CA7 4DT
t (01697) 332860
e enquiries@nithview-
guesthouse.co.uk
w nithview-guesthouse.co.uk

## SILVERDALE
### Lancashire

**Silverdale Inn** ★★★
*Guest Accommodation*
Shore Road, Silverdale,
Carnforth LA5 0TP
t (01524) 701206

## SLAIDBURN
### Lancashire

**Slaidburn YHA** ★★★ *Hostel*
Church Street, Slaidburn,
Clitheroe BB7 3ER
t (01282) 842349
e slaidburn@yha.org.uk
w yha.org.uk

## SLYNE
### Lancashire

**Slyne Lodge** ★★★★ *Inn*
92 Main Road, Slyne, Lancaster
LA2 6AZ
t (01524) 825035
e slynelodge@btconnect.com
w slynelodge.co.uk

## SOUTHPORT
### Merseyside

**Aaron Hotel** ★★★
*Guest House*
18 Bath Street, Southport
PR9 0DA
t (01704) 530283
e info@theaaron.co.uk
w theaaron.co.uk

**Adelphi Hotel** ★★★
*Guest Accommodation*
39 Bold Street, Southport
PR9 0ED
t (01704) 544947
e gromad@aol.com
w adelphihotelsouthport.co.uk

**Alexandra & Victoria Hotel**
★★★★
*Guest Accommodation*
38 The Promenade, Southport
PR8 1QU
t (01704) 530072
e info@
alexandraandvictoriahotel.com
w alexandraandvictoriahotel.
com

**Allenby** ★★★
*Guest Accommodation*
56 Bath Street, Southport
PR9 0DH
t (01704) 532953

**Ambassador Hotel** ★★★★
*Guest Accommodation*
13 Bath Street, Southport
PR9 0DP
t (01704) 543998
e info@ambassadorsouthport.
com
w ambassadorsouthport.co.uk

**Andora Hotel** ★★★
*Guest Accommodation*
25 Bath Street, Southport
PR9 0DP
t (01704) 530214
e enquiries@andorahotel.co.uk
w andorahotel.co.uk

**Atlantic Lodge Hotel** ★★
*Guest House*
17 Bath Street, Southport
PR9 0DP
t (01704) 530344

**Bayona Guest House** ★★★
*Guest Accommodation*
71 Bath Street, Southport
PR9 0DN
t (01704) 543166
e johnandlyn@bayona.
freeserve.co.uk
w bayonasouthport.com

**Brae Mar Hotel** ★★★★
*Guest Accommodation*
4 Bath Street, Southport
PR9 0DA
t (01704) 535838
e jackiewilbraham@aol.com
w braemarhotelsouthport.com

**Carleton House** ★★★★
*Guest House*
17 Alexandra Road, Southport
PR9 0NB
t (01704) 538035
e enquiries@thecarleton.co.uk
w thecarleton.co.uk

**Carlton Lodge Hotel** ★★★★
*Guest Accommodation*
43 Bath Street, Southport
PR9 0DP
t (01704) 542290
e christinecoppack@xln.co.uk
w carltonlodgesouthport.co.uk

**Clifton Villa Hotel** ★★★
*Guest Accommodation*
6 Bath Street, Southport
PR9 0DA
t (01704) 535780

**Crescent House Hotel** ★★★
*Guest Accommodation*
27 Bath Street, Southport
PR9 0DP
t (01704) 530339
e enquiries@
crescenthousehotel.co.uk
w crescenthousehotel.co.uk

**Fairfield Private Hotel** ★★★
*Guest Accommodation*
83 The Promenade, Southport
PR9 0JN
t (01704) 530137
e jclulee@toucansurf.com

**Gables Private Hotel** ★★★
*Guest Accommodation*
110 Leyland Road, Southport
PR9 0JG
t (01704) 535554
e info@gableshotel.co.uk
w gableshotel.co.uk

**Heidi Hotel** ★★★
*Guest House*
43 Bold Street, Southport
PR9 0ED
t (01704) 531273
e claudia@heidihotel.co.uk
w heidihotel.co.uk

**Ivydene** ★★★★ *Guest House*
46 Talbot Street, Southport
PR8 1HS
t (01704) 544760
e book@ivydene-southport.
com
w ivydene-southport.com

**Lynwood Private Hotel**
★★★★
*Guest Accommodation*
11a Leicester Street, Southport
PR9 0ER
t (01704) 540794
e info@lynwoodhotel.com
w lynwoodhotel.com

**Le Maitre Hotel** ★★★★
*Guest House*
69 Bath Street, Southport
PR9 0DN
t (01704) 530394
e enquiries@hotel-lemaitre.co.
uk
w hotel-lemaitre.co.uk

**Miway** ★★★★
*Bed & Breakfast*
20 Seabank Road, Southport
PR9 0EL
t (01704) 501495
e irene@inflightsports.net

**The New England** ★★★★
*Guest Accommodation*
67 Bath Street, Southport
PR9 0DN
t (01704) 532988
e info@thenewenglandgh.co.
uk
w thenewenglandgh.co.uk

**Norland Private Hotel** ★★★
*Guest Accommodation*
11 Bath Street, Southport
PR9 0DP
t (01704) 530890

**The Norwood Guest House**
★★★ *Guest Accommodation*
62 Bath Street, Southport
PR9 0DH
t (01704) 500536
e thenorwood@aol.com
w thenorwood.com

**Penkelie Hotel ★★★**
Guest Accommodation
34 Bold Street, Southport
PR9 0ED
t (01704) 538510
e info@penkeliehotel.co.uk
w penkeliehotel.co.uk

**Sandown Private Hotel**
★★★ Guest Accommodation
21 Bath Street, Southport
PR9 0DP
t (01704) 530416
e sandownhotel@rapid.co.uk
w sandownhotel-southport.co.uk

**Sandy Brook Farm ★★★**
Farmhouse
52 Wyke Cop Road,
Scarisbrick, Southport PR8 5LR
t (01704) 880337 &
07719 468712
e sandybrookfarm@lycos.co.uk
w sandybrookfarm.co.uk

**Seaview Hotel ★★★★**
Guest Accommodation
28 Bath Street, Southport
PR9 0DA
t (01704) 530874
e seaview-hotel@hotmail.co.uk
w freewebs.com/seaview-hotel

**Sunnybank Hotel ★★**
Guest Accommodation
19 Bath Street, Southport
PR9 0DP
t (01704) 530209
e sunnybankhotel@tiscali.co.uk
w 4hotels.co.uk/uk/hotels/sunnybankhotel.html

**Sunnyside ★★**
Guest Accommodation
47 Bath Street, Southport
PR9 0DP
t (01704) 536521
e lisahoughton@btconnect.com
w sunny-lisa.co.uk

**Victorian Hotel ★★★**
Guest Accommodation
52 Avondale Road North,
Southport PR9 0NE
t (01704) 530755
e reception@victorianhotel.co.uk
w victorianhotel.co.uk

**Warwick Hotel ★★★**
Guest Accommodation
39 Bath Street, Southport
PR9 0DP
t (01704) 530707
e thewarwickhotel@aol.com
w thewarwickhotel.co.uk

**Waterford Hotel ★★★★**
Guest Accommodation
SILVER AWARD
37 Leicester Street, Southport
PR9 0EX
t (01704) 530559
e reception@waterford-hotel.co.uk
w waterford-hotel.co.uk

**Windsor Lodge Hotel ★★★**
Guest Accommodation
37 Saunders Street, Southport
PR9 0HJ
t (01704) 530070

**Gateway Lodge ★★★**
Guest Accommodation
Speke Church Road, Speke,
Liverpool L24 3TA
t (0151) 284 4801

**Falconwood ★★★★★**
Bed & Breakfast
GOLD AWARD
Moor Road, Stainburn,
Workington CA14 1XW
t (01900) 602563
e info@lakedistrict-bedandbreakfast.co.uk
w lakedistrict-bedandbreakfast.co.uk

**The Eagle and Child Inn**
★★★ Inn
Kendal Road, Staveley LA8 9LP
t (01539) 821320
e info@eaglechildinn.co.uk
w eaglechildinn.co.uk

**Oakfield Lodge Guest House**
★★★ Guest House
38 Arkwright Road, Marple,
Stockport SK6 7DB
t (0161) 427 1633

**Alden Cottage ★★★★**
Guest Accommodation
GOLD AWARD
Kemple End, Birdy Brow,
Clitheroe BB7 9QY
t (01254) 826468
e carpenter@aldencottage.f9.co.uk
w fp.aldencottage.f9.co.uk

**Hullerbank ★★★★**
Farmhouse
Talkin, Brampton CA8 1LB
t (01697) 746668
e info@hullerbank.freeserve.co.uk
w hullerbankbnb.co.uk

**Foresters Arms ★★★** Inn
92 High Street, Tarporley
CW6 0AX
t (01829) 733151
e foresters-arms@btconnect.com
w theforesters.co.uk

**Hill House Farm Bed &
Breakfast ★★★★** Farmhouse
SILVER AWARD
Rushton, Tarporley CW6 9AU
t (01829) 732238
e rayner@hillhousefarm.fsnet.co.uk
w hillhousefarm.info

**Carriages ★★★**
Guest Accommodation
New Russia Hall, Chester Road,
Gatesheath, Chester CH3 9AH
t (01829) 770958

**Fernlea Cottage ★★★★**
Bed & Breakfast
Chester Road, Hatton Heath,
Chester CH3 9AQ
t (01829) 770807
e stevegb@talktalk.net
w visitchester.com/site/where-to-stay/fernlea-cottage-p49311

**Ford Farm ★★★** Farmhouse
Newton Lane, Tattenhall,
Chester CH3 9NE
t (01829) 770307

**Primrose Cottage ★★★★**
Guest Accommodation
Orton Road, Tebay CA10 3TL
t (015396) 24791
e info@primrosecottagecumbria.co.uk
w primrosecottagecumbria.co.uk

**Fisher-Gill Camping Barn**
Camping Barn
Stybeck Farm, Thirlmere,
Keswick CA12 4TN
t (01768) 773232
e stybeckfarm@farming.co.uk
w members.farmline.com/stybeckfarm

**Jenkin Hill Cottage ★★★★**
Guest Accommodation
SILVER AWARD
Thornthwaite, Keswick
CA12 5SG
t (01768) 778443
e bookings@jenkinhill.co.uk
w jenkinhill.co.uk

**The Bungalow Country
Guest House ★★★★**
Bed & Breakfast
The Bungalows, Sunnyside,
Keswick CA12 4SD
t (01768) 779679
e paulsunley@msn.com
w thebungalows.co.uk

**Horse and Farrier Inn**
★★★★ Inn
Threlkeld, Keswick CA12 4SQ
t (017687) 79688
e info@horseandfarrier.com
w horseandfarrier.com

**Scales Farm Country Guest
House ★★★★** Guest House
SILVER AWARD
Scales, Threlkeld, Penrith
CA12 4SY
t (01768) 779660
e scales@scalesfarm.com
w scalesfarm.com

**Heughscar ★★★★**
Bed & Breakfast
Tirril, Penrith, Ullswater
CA10 2JF
t (01768) 840459
e nigelgardham@aol.com
w heughscar.co.uk

**Trawden** Bunkhouse
Middle Beardshaw Head Farm,
Burnley Road, Colne BB8 8PP
t (01282) 865257

**Fellside Studios ◆◆◆◆**
Guest Accommodation
SILVER AWARD
Fellside House, Troutbeck,
Windermere LA23 1PE
t (015394) 34000
e fellside@bestofthelakes.com
w bestofthelakes.com

**Gill Head Farm ★★★★**
Farmhouse
Troutbeck, Penrith CA11 0ST
t (01768) 779652
e enquiries@gillheadfarm.co.uk
w gillheadfarm.co.uk

**High Fold Guest House**
★★★★ Guest House
Troutbeck, Windermere
LA23 1PG
t (015394) 32200
e info@highfoldbedandbreakfast.co.uk
w highfoldbedandbreakfast.co.uk

**Troutbeck Inn ★★★** Inn
Troutbeck, Penrith CA11 0SJ
t (01768) 483635

**YHA Windermere ★★★**
Hostel
Bridge Lane, Troutbeck,
Windermere LA23 1LA
t (015394) 43543
e windermere@yha.org.uk
w yha.org.uk

**Clough Head Farm**
Rating Applied For
Farmhouse
Broadhead Road, Turton,
Bolton BL7 0JN
t (01254) 704758
e ethelhoughton@hotmail.co.uk

**Bank House Farm ★★★★**
Bed & Breakfast
Matterdale End, Ullswater
CA11 0LF
t (01768) 482040
e info@bankhousefarmullswater.co.uk
w bankhousefarmullswater.co.uk

**Elm House ★★★★**
Guest House SILVER AWARD
High Street, Pooley Bridge,
Ullswater CA10 2NH
t (01768) 486334
e enquiries@stayullswater.co.uk
w stayullswater.co.uk

**Knotts Mill Country Lodge**
★★★ *Guest House*
Watermillock, Penrith
CA11 0JN
t (017684) 86699
e relax@knottsmill.com
w knottsmill.com

**Land Ends Country Lodge**
★★★ *Guest House*
Watermillock, Ullswater
CA11 0NB
t (017684) 86438
e infolandends@btinternet.com
w landends.co.uk

**Mosscrag Guest House**
★★★ *Guest House*
Glenridding, Penrith, Ullswater
CA11 0PA
t (01768) 482500
e info@mosscrag.co.uk
w mosscrag.co.uk

**Tymparon Hall** ★★★★
*Farmhouse*
Newbiggin, Penrith CA11 0HS
t (017684) 83236
e margaret@tymparon.freeserve.co.uk
w tymparon.freeserve.co.uk

**Whitbarrow Farm** ★★★★
*Farmhouse* SILVER AWARD
Berrier, Penrith CA11 0XB
t (01768) 483366
e mary@whitbarrowfarm.co.uk
w whitbarrowfarm.co.uk

**St Marys Mount** ★★★★★
*Guest Accommodation*
Belmont, Ulverston LA12 7HD
t (01229) 583372
e gerry.bobbett@virgin.net
w stmarysmount.co.uk

**Virginia House** ★★★★
*Guest House*
24 Queen Street, Ulverston
LA12 7AF
t (01229) 584844
e virginia@ulverstonhotels.wanadoo.co.uk
w ulverstonhotels.com

**Tranthwaite Hall** ★★★★
*Farmhouse*
Underbarrow, Kendal LA8 8HG
t (015395) 68285
e tranthwaitehall@aol.com
w tranthwaitehall.co.uk

**Yew Tree Farm Bed & Breakfast** ★★
*Guest Accommodation*
Fishers Green, Utkinton,
Tarporley CW6 0JG
t (01829) 732441

**Peter Barn Country House**
★★★★
*Guest Accommodation*
Cross Lane, Waddington,
Clitheroe BB7 3JH
t (01200) 428585
e jean@peterbarn.co.uk

**The Waddington Arms**
★★★★
*Guest Accommodation*
Clitheroe Road, Waddington,
Clitheroe BB7 3HP
t (01200) 423262
e info@waddingtonarms.co.uk
w waddingtonarms.co.uk

**Sandysike** *Bunkhouse*
Brampton CA8 2DU
t (01697) 72330

**New House Farm Cottages**
★★★ *Bed & Breakfast*
Hatton Lane, Hatton,
Warrington WA4 4BZ
t (01925) 730567

**Tall Trees Lodge** ★★★
*Guest Accommodation*
Tarporley Road, Lower
Whitley, Warrington WA4 4EZ
t (01928) 790824 &
(01928) 715117
e booking@talltreeslodge.co.uk
w talltreeslodge.co.uk
♿

**Wastwater YHA** ★★★
*Hostel*
Wasdale Hall, Wasdale
CA20 1ET
t 0870 770 6082
e wastwater@yha.org.uk
w yha.org.uk
♿♿

**Ambleside YHA** ★★★ *Hostel*
Waterhead, Ambleside
LA22 0EU
t 0870 770 5672
e ambleside@yha.org.uk
w yha.org.uk
♿♿

**Marlborough Hotel** ★★★
*Guest House*
21 Crosby Road South,
Liverpool L22 1RG
t (0151) 928 7709

**Mellfell House Farm** ★★★★
*Farmhouse*
Watermillock, Penrith,
Ullswater CA11 0LS
t (017684) 486295
e ben@mellfell.co.uk
w mellfell.co.uk

**Blackmoor Bed & Breakfast**
★★★ *Bed & Breakfast*
160 Blackmoor Drive, West
Derby, Liverpool L12 9EF
t (0151) 291 1407

**21 Park House** ★★★★
*Guest House*
21 Park Road, Wirral
CH48 4DN
t (0151) 625 4665
e enquiries@21parkhouse.co.uk
w 21parkhouse.co.uk

**At Peel Hey** ★★★★
*Guest House* SILVER AWARD
Frankby Road, Frankby, Wirral
CH48 1PP
t (0151) 677 9077
e enquiries@peelhey.co.uk
w peelhey.co.uk

**Caldy Warren Cottage**
★★★★★ *Bed & Breakfast*
42 Caldy Road, West Kirby,
Wirral CH48 2HQ
t (0151) 625 8740
e office@warrencott.demon.co.uk
w warrencott.demon.co.uk

**Whalley Abbey** ★★★★
*Guest Accommodation*
The Sands, Whalley, Clitheroe
BB7 9SS
t (01254) 828400
e office@whalleyabbey.org
w whalleyabbey.org

**Moresby Hall** ★★★★★
*Guest House* GOLD AWARD
Moresby, Whitehaven
CA28 6PJ
t (01946) 696317
e info@moresbyhall.co.uk
w moresbyhall.co.uk

**Whitestake Farm**
Rating Applied For
*Bed & Breakfast*
Pope Lane, Whitestake,
Preston PR4 4JR
t (01772) 613005
e marylou@j-maxair.co.uk

**The Inn at Whitewell**
★★★★★ *Inn*
GOLD AWARD
Dunsop Road, Whitewell,
Clitheroe BB7 3AT
t (01200) 448222
e reception@innatwhitewell.com
w innatwhitewell.com

**Hindle Pastures** ★★★★
*Guest Accommodation*
SILVER AWARD
Highgate Lane, Whitworth,
Rochdale OL12 0TS
t (01706) 643310
e hindlepastures@tiscali.co.uk
w hindlepastures.co.uk

**Underbank Camping Barn**
*Camping Barn*
Wildboarclough, Macclesfield
SK11 0BL
t 0870 770 6113

**Heatherlea Guest House**
★★★★
*Guest Accommodation*
106 Lacey Green, Wilmslow
SK9 4BN
t (01625) 522872
e marjorie.n@ntlworld.com
w heatherleaguesthouse.com

**Hill Top Farm** ★★★★
*Farmhouse*
Wincle, Macclesfield
SK11 0QH
t (01260) 227257
e c_brock_22@hotmail.com

**1 Park Road** ★★★★
*Guest House*
Windermere LA23 2AW
t (015394) 42107
e enquiries@1parkroad.com
w 1parkroad.com

**The Applegarth Hotel & JR's Restaurant** ★★★★
*Guest Accommodation*
College Road, Windermere
LA23 1BU
t (015394) 43206
e info@lakesapplegarth.co.uk
w lakesapplegarth.co.uk

**Archway Guesthouse**
★★★★ *Guest House*
13 College Road, Windermere
LA23 1BU
t (015394) 45613
e stay@archwaywindermere.co.uk
w archwaywindermere.co.uk

**Ashleigh Guest House**
★★★★ *Guest House*
11 College Road, Windermere
LA23 1BU
t (015394) 42292
e enquiries@ashleighhouse.com
w ashleighhouse.com

**Autumn Leaves Guest House**
★★★ *Guest Accommodation*
29 Broad Street, Windermere
LA23 2AB
t (015394) 48410
e info@autumnleavesguesthouse.co.uk
w autumnleavesguesthouse.co.uk

**Beaumont B&B** ♦♦♦♦
*Guest Accommodation*
Thornbarrow Road,
Windermere LA23 2DG
t (015394) 45521
e beaumontcottages@aol.com
w beaumont-cottages.co.uk

**Beaumont House** ★★★★★
*Guest House*
Holly Road, Windermere
LA23 2AF
**t** (015394) 47075
**e** thebeaumonthotel@
btinternet.com
**w** lakesbeaumont.co.uk

**Beckmead House** ★★★★
*Guest Accommodation*
5 Park Avenue, Windermere
LA23 2AR
**t** (015394) 42757
**e** beckmead_house@yahoo.
com
**w** beckmead.co.uk

**Beechwood** ★★★★
*Guest Accommodation*
**GOLD AWARD**
South Craig, Beresford Road,
Bowness-on-Windermere
LA23 2JG
**t** (015394) 43403
**e** enquiries@beechwoodlakes.
co.uk
**w** beechwoodlakes.co.uk

**Belsfield House** ★★★★
*Guest House*
Kendal Road, Bowness-on-
Windermere, Bowness
LA23 3EQ
**t** (015394) 45823
**e** enquiries@belsfieldhouse.
co.uk
**w** belsfieldhouse.co.uk

**Boston House** ★★★★
*Guest House* **SILVER AWARD**
4 The Terrace, Windermere
LA23 1AJ
**t** (015394) 43654
**e** stay@bostonhouse.co.uk
**w** bostonhouse.co.uk

**Bowfell Cottage** ★★★
*Bed & Breakfast*
Middle Entrance Drive,
Bowness-on-Windermere,
Windermere LA23 3JY
**t** (015394) 44835

**Briscoe Lodge Guest House**
★★★ *Guest House*
26 Ellerthwaite Road,
Windermere LA23 2AH
**t** (015394) 42928
**e** stay@briscoelodge.co.uk
**w** briscoelodge.co.uk

**Brook House** ★★★
*Guest House*
30 Ellerthwaite Road,
Windermere LA23 2AH
**t** (015394) 44932
**e** stay@brookhouselakes.co.
uk
**w** brookhouselakes.co.uk

**Brooklands** ★★★
*Guest Accommodation*
Ferry View, Bowness-on-
Windermere, Windermere
LA23 3JB
**t** (015394) 42344
**e** enquiries@
brooklandsguesthouse.net
**w** brooklandsguesthouse.net

**Cambridge House** ★★★★
*Guest House*
9 Oak Street, Windermere
LA23 1EN
**t** (015394) 43846
**e** oak.lakes@btinternet.com
**w** cambridge-house.net

**Clifton House** ★★★
*Guest House*
28 Ellerthwaite Road,
Windermere LA23 2AH
**t** (015394) 44968
**e** info@cliftonhse.co.uk
**w** cliftonhse.co.uk

**College House** ★★★★
*Guest House*
15 College Road, Windermere
LA23 1BU
**t** (015394) 45767
**e** clghse@aol.com
**w** college-house.com

**Crompton House** ★★★
*Guest House*
Lake Road, Windermere
LA23 2EQ
**t** (015394) 43020

**Dunvegan Guest House**
★★★★
*Guest Accommodation*
Broad Street, Windermere
LA23 2AB
**t** (015394) 43502
**e** bryan.twaddle@btinternet.
com
**w** dunveganguesthouse.co.uk

**Eastbourne Guest House**
★★★★★ *Guest House*
Biskey Howe Road, Bowness-
on-Windermere, Windermere
LA23 2JR
**t** (015394) 88657
**e** eastbournela23@btconnect.
com
**w** eastbourne-windermere.co.uk

**Elim Lodge** ★★★
*Guest House*
Biskey Howe Road, Bowness,
Windermere LA23 2JP
**t** (015394) 47299
**e** enquiries@elimlodge.co.uk
**w** elimlodge.co.uk

**Ellerthwaite Lodge** ★★★★
*Guest Accommodation*
New Road, Windermere
LA23 2LA
**t** (015394) 45115
**e** al@theknoll.co.uk
**w** ellerthwaitelodge.com

**Fair Rigg** ★★★★
*Guest House* **SILVER AWARD**
Ferry View, Bowness-on-
Windermere, Windermere
LA23 3JB
**t** (015394) 43941
**e** stay@fairrigg.co.uk
**w** fairrigg.co.uk

**Fairfield Garden Guesthouse**
★★★★ *Guest House*
Brantfell Road, Bowness Bay
LA23 3AE
**t** (015394) 46565
**e** relax@the-fairfield.co.uk
**w** the-fairfield.co.uk

**Fir Trees** ★★★★
*Guest House*
Lake Road, Windermere
LA23 2EQ
**t** (015394) 42272
**e** enquiries@fir-trees.com
**w** fir-trees.com

**Firgarth** ★★★ *Guest House*
Ambleside Road, Windermere
LA23 1EU
**t** (015394) 46974
**e** enquiries@firgarth.com
**w** firgarth.com

**Greenriggs Guest House**
★★★ *Guest House*
8 Upper Oak Street,
Windermere LA23 2LB
**t** (015394) 42265
**e** greenriggs@tiscali.co.uk
**w** greenriggs.com

**The Grey Walls** ★★ *Inn*
Elleray Road, Windermere
LA23 1AG
**t** (015394) 43741
**e** info@greywalls-hotel.co.uk
**w** greywalls-hotel.co.uk

**Heatherbank** ★★★
*Guest Accommodation*
13 Birch Street, Windermere
LA23 1EG
**t** (015394) 46503
**e** heatherbank@btinternet.
com
**w** heatherbank.com

**High View** ★★★★★
*Bed & Breakfast*
**SILVER AWARD**
Sun Hill Lane, Troutbeck
Bridge, Windermere LA23 1HJ
**t** (015394) 44618
**e** info@
accommodationlakedistrict.com
**w** accommodationlakedistrict.
com

**Hilton House** ★★★★
*Guest House*
New Road, Windermere
LA23 2EE
**t** (015394) 43934
**e** enquiries@hiltonhouse-
guesthouse.co.uk
**w** hiltonhouse-guesthouse.co.
uk

**Holly Lodge** ★★★★
*Guest House*
6 College Road, Windermere
LA23 1BX
**t** (015394) 43873
**e** enquiries@hollylodge20.co.
uk
**w** hollylodge20.co.uk

**Holly-Wood Guest House**
★★★★
*Guest Accommodation*
Holly Road, Windermere
LA23 2AF
**t** (015394) 42219
**e** info@hollywoodguesthouse.
co.uk
**w** hollywoodguesthouse.co.uk

**Holmlea Guest House** ★★★
*Guest House*
Kendal Road, Bowness-on-
Windermere, Bowness
LA23 3EW
**t** (015394) 42597
**e** info@holmleaguesthouse.co.
uk
**w** holmleaguesthouse.co.uk

**Ivy Bank** ★★★★
*Guest House* **SILVER AWARD**
Holly Road, Windermere
LA23 2AF
**t** (015394) 42601
**e** ivybank@clara.co.uk
**w** ivy-bank.co.uk

**Kays Cottage** ★★★★
*Guest House*
7 Broad Street, Windermere
LA23 2AB
**t** (015394) 44146
**e** rooms@kayscottage.co.uk
**w** kayscottage.co.uk

**Kenilworth Guest House**
★★★★
*Guest Accommodation*
Holly Road, Windermere
LA23 2AF
**t** (015394) 44004
**e** busby@kenilworth-lake-
district.co.uk
**w** kenilworth-lake-district.co.uk

**Kirkwood Guest House**
★★★★ *Guest House*
Princes Road, Windermere
LA23 2DD
**t** (015394) 43907
**e** info@kirkwood51.co.uk
**w** kirkwood51.co.uk

**Lakes Hotel** ★★★
*Guest Accommodation*
1 High Street, Windermere
LA23 1AF
**t** (015394) 42751
**e** admin@lakes-hotel.com
**w** lakes-hotel.com

**Lakeview Guesthouse** ★★★
*Guest Accommodation*
2 Belsfield Terrace, Bowness-
on-Windermere LA23 3EQ
**t** (015394) 47098
**e** lakeview@dsl.pipex.com
**w** lakeview-guesthouse.co.uk

**Langdale View Guest House**
★★★ *Guest House*
114 Craig Walk, Off Helm
Road, Bowness LA23 3AX
**t** (015394) 44076
**e** enquiries@langdaleview.co.uk
**w** langdaleview.co.uk

**Latimer House** ★★★★
*Guest House*
Lake Road, Bowness-on-
Windermere, Windermere
LA23 2JJ
**t** (015394) 46888
**e** enquiries@latimerhouse.
uk
**w** latimerhouse.co.uk

**Laurel Cottage** ★★★★
*Guest House*
Park Road, Windermere
LA23 2BJ
**t** (015394) 43053
**e** info@
laurelcottagewindermere.co.uk
**w** laurelcottagewindermere.co.
uk

**Laurel Cottage Bowness**
★★★★ *Guest House*
Kendal Road, Bowness-on-
Windermere, Bowness
LA23 3EF
**t** (015394) 45594
**e** enquiries@laurelcottage-
bnb.co.uk
**w** laurelcottage-bnb.co.uk

**Lindisfarne Guest House**
★★★★ *Guest House*
Sunny Bank Road, Windermere
LA23 2EN
**t** (015394) 46295
**e** enquiries@lindisfarne-
house.co.uk
**w** lindisfarne-house.co.uk

**Lingmoor Guesthouse** ★★★
*Guest House*
7 High Street, Windermere
LA23 1AF
**t** (015394) 44947
**e** info@lingmoor-guesthouse.
co.uk
**w** lingmoor-guesthouse.co.uk

**The Lonsdale** ★★★★
*Guest House* **SILVER AWARD**
Lake Road, Bowness-on-
Windermere, Windermere
LA23 2JJ
t (015394) 43348
e info@lonsdale-hotel.co.uk
w lonsdale-hotel.co.uk

**Lynwood** ★★★★
*Guest House*
Broad Street, Windermere
LA23 2AB
t (015394) 42550
e enquiries@lynwood-guest-
house.co.uk
w lynwood-guest-house.co.uk

**Meadfoot Guest House**
★★★★
*Guest Accommodation*
New Road, Windermere
LA23 2LA
t (015394) 42610
e queries@meadfoot-
guesthouse.co.uk
w meadfoot-guesthouse.co.uk

**Melbourne Guest House**
★★★ *Guest Accommodation*
2-3 Biskey Howe Road,
Bowness-on-Windermere,
Windermere LA23 2JP
t (015394) 43475
e info@melbournecottage.co.
uk
w melbournecottage.co.uk

**Millbeck Guest House**
★★★★ *Bed & Breakfast*
44 Ellerthwaite Road,
Windermere LA23 2BS
t (015394) 45392
e info@themillbeck.co.uk

**Mount View** ★★★
*Guest House*
New Road, Windermere
LA23 2LA
t (015394) 45548

**Mylne Bridge House** ★★★★
*Guest House*
Brookside, Lake Road,
Windermere LA23 2BX
t (015394) 43314
e mylnebridgehouse@aol.com
w mylnebridgehouse.co.uk

**New Hall Bank** ★★★★
*Guest House*
Fallbarrow Road, Windermere
LA23 3DJ
t (015394) 43558
e info@newhallbank.co.uk
w newhallbank.com

**Newstead** ★★★★★
*Guest House*
New Road, Windermere
LA23 2EE
t (015394) 44485
e info@newstead-guesthouse.
co.uk
w newstead-guesthouse.co.uk

**Oakfold House** ★★★★
*Guest House* **SILVER AWARD**
Beresford Road, Bowness
LA23 2JG
t (015394) 43239
e oakfoldhouse@fsmail.net
w oakfoldhouse.co.uk

**Oldfield House** ★★★★
*Guest House* **SILVER AWARD**
Oldfield Road, Windermere
LA23 2BY
t (015394) 88445
e info@oldfieldhouse.co.uk
w oldfieldhouse.co.uk

**Park Beck** ★★★ *Guest House*
3 Park Road, Windermere
LA23 2AW
t (01539) 444025

**Ravenscroft** ★★★★
*Bed & Breakfast*
**SILVER AWARD**
Lake Road, Windermere
LA23 2EQ
t (015394) 47046
e book@lakesguesthouse.co.
uk
w lakesguesthouse.co.uk

**The Ravensworth** ★★★★
*Guest House*
Ambleside Road, Windermere
LA23 1BA
t (015394) 43747
e info@theravensworth.com
w theravensworth.co.uk

**Rayrigg Villa Guest House**
★★★★ *Guest House*
Ellerthwaite Square,
Windermere LA23 1DP
t (015394) 88342
e rayriggvilla@etherway.net
w rayriggvilla.co.uk

**Rocklea** ★★★★ *Guest House*
Brookside, Lake Road,
Windermere LA23 2BX
t (015394) 45326
e info@rocklea.co.uk
w rocklea.co.uk

**Rockside Guest House**
★★★★ *Guest House*
25 Church Street, Windermere
LA23 1AQ
t (015394) 45343
e info@rockside-guesthouse.
co.uk
w rockside-guesthouse.co.uk

**Rosemount** ★★★
*Guest House*
Lake Road, Windermere
LA23 2EQ
t (015394) 43739
e rosemt@gotadsl.co.uk
w lakedistrictguesthouse.com

**St John's Lodge** ★★★
*Guest House*
Lake Road, Windermere
LA23 2EQ
t (015394) 43078
e mail@st-johns-lodge.co.uk
w st-johns-lodge.co.uk

**Southview House & Indoor
Pool** ★★★★ *Guest House*
Cross Street, Windermere
LA23 1AE
t (015394) 42951
e stay@
southviewwindermere.co.uk
w southviewwindermere.co.uk

**Squirrel Bank** ★★★★
*Bed & Breakfast*
**SILVER AWARD**
Ferry View, Crook Road,
Bowness-on-Windermere
LA23 3JB
t (015394) 43329
e soar@squirrelbank.co.uk
w squirrelbank.co.uk

**Stockghyll Cottage** ★★★★
*Guest Accommodation*
Rayrigg Road, Windermere
LA23 1BN
t (015394) 43246
e stay@stockghyllcottage.co.
uk
w stockghyllcottage.co.uk

**Storrs Gate House** ★★★★
*Guest House*
Longtail Hill, Bowness-on-
Windermere, Windermere
LA23 3JD
t (015394) 43272
e enquiries@storrsgatehouse.
co.uk
w storrsgatehouse.co.uk

**Tarn Rigg Guest House**
★★★★ *Guest House*
Thornbarrow Road,
Windermere LA23 2DG
t (015394) 88777
e info@tarnrigg-guesthouse.
co.uk
w tarnrigg-guesthouse.co.uk

**Thornbank House** ★★★★
*Guest House*
4 Thornbarrow Road,
Windermere LA23 2EW
t (015394) 43724
e enquiries@
thornbankwindermere.co.uk
w thornbankwindermere.co.uk

**Thorncliffe** ★★★
*Bed & Breakfast*
Princes Road, Windermere
LA23 2DD
t (015394) 44338
e thorncliffeis@tiscali.co.uk
w thorncliffe-guesthouse.co.uk

**Watermill Inn** ★★★★ *Inn*
Ings, Kendal, Windermere
LA8 9PY
t (01539) 821309
e watermillinn@tiscali.co.uk
w watermillinn.co.uk

**The Waverley** ★★★
*Guest House*
College Road, Windermere
LA23 1BX
t (015394) 45026
e info@waverleyhotel.com
w waverleyhotel.co.uk

**The Westbourne** ★★★★
*Guest House* **SILVER AWARD**
Biskey Howe Road, Bowness-
on-Windermere, Windermere
LA23 2JR
t (015394) 43625
e westbourne@btinternet.com
w westbourne-lakes.co.uk

**Westbury House** ★★★
*Guest House*
27 Broad Street, Windermere
LA23 2AB
t (015394) 46839
e stay@windermerebnb.co.uk
w windermerebnb.co.uk

**White Lodge** ★★★★
*Guest House*
Lake Road, Bowness-on-
Windermere, Windermere
LA23 2JJ
t (015394) 43624
e enquiries@whitelodgehotel.
com
w whitelodgehotel.com

WINSFORD
Cheshire

**Clivehall Farm** ★★★★
*Farmhouse*
Clive Lane, Wimsford
CW7 3PA
t (01606) 592505
e mail@clivehallfarm.co.uk
w clivehallfarm.co.uk

**The Winsford Lodge** ★★★
*Guest House*
85-87 Station Road, Winsford
CW7 3DE
t (01606) 862008

WIRRAL
Merseyside

**Pendragon House** ★★★★
*Guest House* **SILVER AWARD**
1 Bertram Drive, Wirral
CH47 0LG
t (0151) 632 5344
e pendragonhousehoylake@
uwclub.net
w pendragonhouseuk.com

WISWELL
Lancashire

**Pepper Hill B&B** ★★★★★
*Guest Accommodation*
**SILVER AWARD**
Pendleton Road, Wiswell,
Clitheroe BB7 9BZ
t (01254) 825098

WORKINGTON
Cumbria

**Morven Guest House** ★★★
*Guest House*
Siddick Road, Siddick,
Workington CA14 1LE
t (01900) 602118 &
07718 864 7196
e cnelsonmorven@aol.com
w morvenguesthouse.gbr.cc

**Old Ginn House** ★★★★ *Inn*
Moor Road, Great Clifton,
Workington CA14 1TS
t (01900) 64616
e enquiries@oldginnhouse.co.
uk
w oldginnhouse.co.uk

WORSTON
Lancashire

**The Calf's Head** ★★★★
*Guest Accommodation*
Worston, Clitheroe BB7 1QA
t (01200) 441218
e info@calfshead.co.uk
w calfshead.co.uk

WRIGHTINGTON
Lancashire

**Kings** ★★★★
*Bed & Breakfast*
170 Mossy Lea Road,
Wrightington, Wigan
WN6 9RD
t (01257) 425053
e kingwrightington@aol.com

WYCOLLER
Lancashire

**Parson Lee Farm** ★★★
*Farmhouse*
Trawden, Wycoller, Colne
BB8 8SU
t (01282) 864747
e bookings@parsonleefarm.
co.uk
w parsonleefarm.co.uk

## NORTH EAST ENGLAND

### ACOMB
Northumberland

**The Sun Inn** ★★★ *Inn*
Main Street, Hexham
NE46 4PW
t  (01434) 602934
e  lindsey@inthenorth.
freeserve.co.uk

### ALLENDALE
Northumberland

**High Keenley Fell Farm**
★★★★ *Farmhouse*
Allendale NE47 9NU
t  (01434) 618344
e  camaclean@btinternet.com
w  highkeenleyfarm.co.uk

**Keenley Thorn Farmhouse**
★★★★ *Bed & Breakfast*
**SILVER AWARD**
Keenley Thorn, Allendale
NE47 9NU
t  (01434) 683248
e  keithfairless@aol.com
w  keenleythornfarmhouse.co.
uk

**Struthers Farm** ★★★★
*Farmhouse*
Catton, Hexham NE47 9LP
t  (01434) 683580

**Thornley House** ★★★★
*Bed & Breakfast*
Thornley Gate, Hexham
NE47 9NH
t  (01434) 683255
e  e.finn@ukonline.co.uk
w  http://web.ukonline.co.uk/
e.finn

### ALNMOUTH
Northumberland

**Alnmouth Golf Club** ★★★
*Guest Accommodation*
Foxton Hall, Alnmouth NE66 3BE
t  (01665) 830231
e  secretary@
alnmouthgolfclub.com
w  alnmouthgolfclub.com

**Alnmouth-Westlea** ◆◆◆◆
*Guest Accommodation*
**SILVER AWARD**
29 Riverside Road, Alnmouth
NE66 2SD
t  (01665) 830730
e  ritaandray77@btinternet.
com

**Beaches B&B** ◆◆◆
*Guest Accommodation*
57 Northumberland Street,
Alnmouth NE66 2RS
t  (01665) 830006
e  susaninalnmouth@aol.com
w  beachesbyo.co.uk

**Beech Lodge** ★★★★
*Bed & Breakfast*
**SILVER AWARD**
8 Alnwood, Alnwick NE66 3NN
t  (01665) 830709
e  beechlodge@hotmail.com
w  alnmouth.com

**Bilton Barns Farmhouse**
★★★★ *Farmhouse*
**SILVER AWARD**
Bilton, Alnmouth, Alnwick
NE66 2TB
t  (01665) 830427
e  dorothy@biltonbarns.com
w  biltonbarns.com

**Hope and Anchor** ★★★ *Inn*
44 Northumberland Street,
Alnwick NE66 2RA
t  (01665) 830363
e  debbiephilipson@
hopeandanchorholidays.fsnet.
co.uk
w  hopeandanchorholidays.co.
uk

**Sefton House** ★★★★
*Guest House*
15 Argyle Street, Alnmouth,
Alnwick NE66 2SB
t  (01665) 833174
e  simoneneri@aol.com

### ALNWICK
Northumberland

**Aln House** ★★★★
*Guest Accommodation*
**SILVER AWARD**
South Road, Alnwick NE66 2NZ
t  (01665) 602265
e  enquiries@alnhouse.co.uk
w  alnhouse.co.uk

**Alndyke Bed and Breakfast**
★★★★ *Farmhouse*
**SILVER AWARD**
Alnmouth Road, Alnwick
NE66 3PB
t  (01665) 510252
e  laura@alndyke.co.uk
w  alndyke.co.uk

**Alnwick Lodge**
Rating Applied For
*Guest Accommodation*
West Cawledge Park, Alnwick
NE66 2HJ
t  (01665) 604363
e  alnwicklodge@yahoo.co.uk
w  alnwicklodge.com

**Aydon House** ★★★
*Guest Accommodation*
South Road, Alnwick
NE66 2NT
t  (01665) 602218
w  smoothhound.co.uk/hotels/
aydon.html

**Bailiffgate** ★★★
*Guest Accommodation*
1 Bailiffgate, Alnwick NE66 1LZ
t  (01665) 602078
e  will@wakefield.onyxnet.co.
uk
w  alnwickaccommodation.com

**Boulmer Village B&B**
★★★★ *Bed & Breakfast*
21 Boulmer Village, Alnwick
NE66 3BS
t  (01665) 577262
e  hazel_campbell@
btopenworld.com

**Brunton House** ★★★
*Bed & Breakfast*
Brunton, Alnwick NE66 3HQ
t  (01665) 589198
e  victoriajolliffe@tiscali.co.uk
w  bruntonhouse.co.uk

**Castle Gate Guest House**
★★★ *Bed & Breakfast*
23 Bondgate Without, Alnwick
NE66 1PR
t  (01665) 602657 &
07706 113434
e  tracy@amfr.co.uk
w  castlegatealnwick.co.uk

**Castleview B&B** ★★★★
*Guest Accommodation*
1b Bailiffgate, Alnwick
NE66 1LZ
t  (01665) 606227
e  enquiries@
castleviewalnwick.co.uk
w  castleviewalnwick.co.uk

**Charlton House** ★★★★
*Guest Accommodation*
2 Aydon Gardens, South Road,
Alnwick NE66 2NT
t  (01665) 605185
s  s-h-systems.co.uk/hotels/
charlt2.html

**Crosshills House** ★★★★
*Guest House*
40 Blakelaw Road, Alnwick
NE66 1BA
t  (01665) 602518
e  crosshillshouse@hotmail.
com
w  crosshillshouse.ntb.org.uk/

**The Georgian Guest House**
★★★ *Guest House*
3 Hotspur Street, Alnwick
NE66 1QE
t  (01665) 602398
e  enquiries@
georgianguesthouse.co.uk
w  georgianguesthouse.co.uk

**Hawkhill Farmhouse** ★★★★
*Farmhouse*
Lesbury, Alnwick NE66 3PG
t  (01665) 830380
e  stay@hawkhillfarmhouse.
com
w  hawkhillfarmhouse.com

**Limetree Cottage** ★★★★
*Bed & Breakfast*
38 Eglingham Village,
Eglingham NE66 2TX
t  (01665) 578322
e  viwhillis@aol.com

**The Masons Arms Country
Inn** ★★★★ *Inn*
Stamford Cott, Rennington
NE66 3RX
t  (01665) 577275
e  bookings@masonsarms.net
w  masonsarms.net

**Norfolk** ★★★★
*Bed & Breakfast*
**SILVER AWARD**
41 Blakelaw Road, Alnwick
NE66 1BA
t  (01665) 602892
w  norfolkhouse-alnwick.co.uk

**Percy Terrace Bed and
Breakfast** ★★★
*Bed & Breakfast*
3 Percy Terrace, Alnwick
NE66 1AF
t  (01665) 606867
e  bookings@alnwick-
bedandbreakfast.co.uk
w  alnwick-bedandbreakfast.co.
uk/

**Prudhoe Croft** ★★★★
*Bed & Breakfast*
**SILVER AWARD**
11 Prudhoe Street, Alnwick
NE66 1UW
t  (01665) 606197
e  prudhoecroft@supanet.com
w  prudhoecroft.co.uk

**The Queens Head** ★★★★
*Guest Accommodation*
25 Market Street, Alnwick
NE66 1SS
t  (01665) 604691
e  stay@
alnwickqueensheadhotel.co.uk
w  alnwickqueensheadhotel.co.
uk

**Redfoot Lea Bed & Breakfast**
★★★★ *Bed & Breakfast*
**SILVER AWARD**
Greensfield Moor Farm,
Alnwick NE66 2HH
t  (01665) 603891
e  info@redfootlea.co.uk
w  redfootlea.co.uk
▣◪

**Reighamsyde** ★★★★
*Bed & Breakfast*
The Moor, Alnwick NE66 2AJ
t  (01665) 602535
e  reighamsyde@aol.com

**Rooftops** ★★★★
*Guest Accommodation*
**SILVER AWARD**
14 Blakelaw Road, Alnwick
NE66 1AZ
t  (01665) 604201
e  rooftops.alnwick@tiscali.co.
uk
w  rooftops.ntb.org.uk

**Ros View** ★★★★
*Bed & Breakfast*
14 Mill Hill, Chatton, Alnwick
NE66 5PA
t  (01668) 215289
e  info@coastal-
accommodation.co.uk
w  coastal-accommodation.co.
uk

**Roseworth** ★★★★
*Bed & Breakfast*
Alnmouth Road, Alnwick
NE66 2PR
t  (01665) 603911
e  roseworth@tiscali.co.uk
w  roseworthalnwick.co.uk
▣◪

**St Valery** ★★ *Bed & Breakfast*
27 Northumberland Street,
Alnmouth NE66 2RA
t  (01665) 833221
▣◪

**Sherborne House B&B**
★★★★ *Bed & Breakfast*
9 Percy Street, Alnwick
NE66 1AE
t  (01665) 605626
e  helen@awod.co.uk
w  awod.co.uk

**Tate House Bed & Breakfast**
★★★ *Bed & Breakfast*
11 Bondgate Without, Alnwick
NE66 1PR
t  (01665) 604661
e  bookings@stayinalnwick.co.
uk
w  stayinalnwick.co.uk

**Tower Restaurant and Accommodation** ★★★★
*Restaurant with Rooms*
10 Bondgate Within, Alnwick
NE66 1TD
t (01665) 603888
e roylhardy@o2.co.uk
w tower-alnwick.co.uk

**West Acre House** ★★★★★
*Guest Accommodation*
GOLD AWARD
West Acres, Alnwick
NE66 2QA
t (01665) 510374
e info@westacrehouse.co.uk
w westacrehouse.co.uk

### ALWINTON
Northumberland

**Rose and Thistle Inn** ★★★★
*Inn*
Alwinton NE65 7BQ
t (01669) 650226
e enqs@
roseandthistlealwinton.com
w roseandthistlealwinton.com
▨◪

### AMBLE
Northumberland

**Amble In** ★★★
*Guest Accommodation*
16 Leazes Street, Amble,
Morpeth NE65 0AL
t (01665) 714661
e stephmclaughlin@aol.com
w amble-in.co.uk

**Harbour Guest House** ★★★
*Guest House*
24 Lezers Street, Amble,
Morpeth NE65 0AA
t (01665) 710381
▨◪

**No. 20** ★★★ *Bed & Breakfast*
Marine House, Marine Road,
Amble NE65 0BB
t (01665) 711965
e moe2@hotmail.co.uk
▨◪

### AMBLE-BY-THE-SEA
Northumberland

**Coquetside** ★★★★
*Bed & Breakfast*
16 Broomhill Street, Amble-by-
the-Sea NE65 0AN
t (01665) 710352

**Togston Hall Farmhouse**
★★★ *Guest Accommodation*
North Togston, Morpeth
NE65 0HR
t (01665) 712699
e togstonhallfarmhouse@
yahoo.co.uk

### BAMBURGH
Northumberland

**Glenander Bed & Breakfast**
★★★★ *Bed & Breakfast*
SILVER AWARD
27 Lucker Road, Bamburgh
NE69 7BS
t (01668) 214336
e johntoland@tiscali.co.uk
w glenander.com

**Squirrel Cottage** ★★★★
*Bed & Breakfast*
1 Friars Court, Bamburgh
NE69 7AE
t (01668) 214494
e theturnbulls2k@btinternet.
com
w holidaynorthumbria.co.uk

**The Sunningdale** ★★★
*Guest Accommodation*
21-23 Lucker Road, Bamburgh
NE69 7BS
t (01668) 214334
e enquiries@sunningdale-
hotel.com
w sunningdale-hotel.com

### BARDON MILL
Northumberland

**Gibbs Hill Farm** ★★★★
*Farmhouse*
Once Brewed, Bardon Mill
NE47 7AP
t (01434) 344030
e val@gibbshillfarm.co.uk
w gibbshillfarm.co.uk
▨◪

**Gibbs Hill Farm Hostel** ★★★
*Hostel*
Gibbs Hill Farm, Hexham
NE47 7AP
t (01434) 344030
e val@gibbshillfarm.co.uk
w gibbshillfarm.co.uk
▨◪

**Maple Lodge Bed and Breakfast** ★★★★
*Bed & Breakfast*
Birkshaw, Bardon Mill, Hexham
NE47 7JL
t (01434) 344365
e rosearmstrong@tiscali.co.uk
w maplelodge-hadrianswall.co.
uk
▨◪

**Montcoffer** ◆◆◆◆◆
*Guest Accommodation*
GOLD AWARD
Bardon Mill, Hexham
NE47 7HZ
t (01434) 344138
e john-dehlia@talk21.com
w montcoffer.co.uk
◪

**Once Brewed YHA** ★★★
*Hostel*
Once Brewed, Military Road,
Hexham NE47 7AN
t (01434) 344360
e oncebrewed@yha.org.uk
w yha.org.uk
▨◪

**Strand Cottage Bed and Breakfast** ★★★★
*Bed & Breakfast*
The Strand, 2 Main Road
(A69), Hexham NE47 7BH
t (01434) 344643
e stay@strand-cottage.co.uk
w strand-cottage.co.uk

**Twice Brewed Inn** ★★★ *Inn*
Bardon Mill, Hexham
NE47 7AN
t (01434) 344534
e info@twicebrewedinn.co.uk
w twicebrewedinn.co.uk

**Vallum Lodge** ★★★★
*Guest House*
Military Road, Bardon Mill
NE47 7AN
t (01434) 344248
e stay@vallum-lodge.co.uk
w vallum-lodge.co.uk

### BARNARD CASTLE
County Durham

**33 Newgate** ★★★
*Guest Accommodation*
Barnard Castle DL12 8NJ
t (01833) 690208
e peter.whittaker@tinyworld.
co.uk
w barnard-castle.co.uk

**Crich House Bed & Breakfast** ★★★★
*Guest Accommodation*
SILVER AWARD
94 Galgate, Barnard Castle
DL12 8BJ
t (01833) 630357
e info@crich-house.co.uk
w crich-house.co.uk

**Greta House** ★★★★
*Bed & Breakfast*
GOLD AWARD
89 Galgate, Barnard Castle
DL12 8ES
t (01833) 631193
e kathchesman@btinternet.
com
w gretahouse.co.uk

**The Homelands** ★★★★
*Guest Accommodation*
GOLD AWARD
85 Galgate, Barnard Castle
DL12 8ES
t (01833) 638757
e enquiries@
homelandsguesthouse.co.uk
w homelandsguesthouse.co.uk

**Kirkstone** ★★★★
*Bed & Breakfast*
Marwood, Barnard Castle
DL12 8QS
t (01833) 690497
e dstonekirk@aol.com

**Marwood House** ★★★★
*Bed & Breakfast*
98 Galgate, Barnard Castle
DL12 8BJ
t (01833) 637493
e john@kilgarriff.demon.co.uk
w kilgarriff.demon.co.uk

**Strathmore Lawn East**
★★★★
*Guest Accommodation*
81 Galgate, Barnard Castle
DL12 8ES
t (01833) 637061
e strathmorelawn@aol.com

### BARRASFORD
Northumberland

**Barrasford Arms Camping Barn** *Bunkhouse*
Barrasford NE48 4AA
t (01434) 681237
e barrasfordarmshotel@yahoo.
co.uk
w barrasfordarms.com
▨

### BEADNELL
Northumberland

**Beach Court** ★★★★★
*Guest Accommodation*
SILVER AWARD
Harbour Road, Beadnell
NE67 5BJ
t (01665) 720225
e info@beachcourt.com
w beachcourt.com
▨◪

**Low Dover Beadnell Bay**
★★★★★
*Guest Accommodation*
SILVER AWARD
Harbour Road, Beadnell
NE67 5BJ
t (01665) 720291
e enquiries@lowdover.co.uk
w lowdover.co.uk

**Shepherds Cottage** ★★★★
*Guest Accommodation*
Beadnell NE67 5AD
t (01665) 720497
w shepherdscottage.ntb.org.
uk

### BEAL
Northumberland

**Brock Mill Farmhouse** ★★★
*Guest Accommodation*
Brock Mill, Beal, Berwick-upon-
Tweed TD15 2PB
t (01289) 381283 &
07889 099517
e brockmillfarmhouse@
btinternet.com
w lindisfarne.org.uk/brock-
mill-farmhouse
▨◪

### BEAMISH
County Durham

**The Coach House** ◆◆◆◆
*Guest Accommodation*
High Urpeth, Beamish, Stanley
DH9 0SE
t (0191) 370 0309
e coachhouse@foreman25.
freeserve.co.uk
w coachhousebeamish.ntb.
org.uk

**Malling House** ★★★
*Guest House*
1 Oakdale Terrace, Newfield,
Chester le Street DH2 2SU
t (0191) 370 2571
e heather@
mallingguesthouse.freeserve.
co.uk
w mallingguesthouse.
freeserve.co.uk

### BELFORD
Northumberland

**Detchant Farm** ★★★
*Farmhouse*
Detchant, Belford NE70 7PF
t (01668) 213261
e stay@detchantfarm.co.uk
w detchantfarm.co.uk

**Easington Farm** ★★★★
*Farmhouse* SILVER AWARD
Easington, Belford NE70 7EG
t (01668) 213298

**The Farmhouse Guest House**
★★★★
*Guest Accommodation*
SILVER AWARD
24 West Street, Belford
NE70 7QE
t (01668) 213083
e farmhouseguesthouse@
hotmail.com
w thefarmhouseguesthouse
belford.co.uk

**Seafields** ★★★★
*Guest Accommodation*
7 Cragside Avenue, Belford
NE70 7NA
t (01668) 213502
e seafields.bryden@tiscali.co.
uk
w seafieldsbelford.co.uk

### BELLINGHAM
Northumberland

**Bridgeford Farm** ★★★★
*Farmhouse*
Bellingham NE48 2HU
t (01434) 220940
e info@bridgefordfarmbandb.
co.uk
w bridgefordfarmbandb.co.uk

**Lyndale Guest House**
★★★★ *Guest House*
Riverside Walk, Bellingham
NE48 2AW
t (01434) 220361
e ken&joy@lyndalegh.fsnet.
co.uk
w lyndaleguesthouse.co.uk

### BELMONT
County Durham

**Moor End House Bed and
Breakfast** ★★★★
*Bed & Breakfast*
7-8 Moor End Terrace,
Belmont, Durham DH1 1BJ
t (01913) 842796
e marybnb@hotmail.com
w moorenddurham.co.uk

### BERWICK-UPON-TWEED
Northumberland

**20 Castle Terrace** ★★★★★
*Bed & Breakfast*
GOLD AWARD
Berwick-upon-Tweed
TD15 1NP
t (01289) 302800
e stay@20castleterrace.co.uk
w 20castleterrace.co.uk

**40 Ravensdowne Guest
House** ★★★★
*Guest Accommodation*
40 Ravensdowne, Berwick-
upon-Tweed TD15 1DQ
t (01289) 306992
e bookings@40ravensdowne.
co.uk
w 40ravensdowne.co.uk

**6 Parade** ★★★
*Bed & Breakfast*
Berwick-upon-Tweed
TD15 1DF
t (01289) 308454

**Alannah House** ★★★★
*Bed & Breakfast*
84 Church Street, Berwick-
upon-Tweed TD15 1DU
t (01289) 307252
e steven@berwick1234.
freeserve.co.uk
w alannahhouse.com

**Berwick Backpackers** ★★★
*Backpacker*
56 Bridge Street, Berwick-
upon-Tweed TD15 1AQ
t (01289) 331481
e bkbackpacker@aol.com
w berwickbackpackers.co.uk

**Bridge View** ★★★★
*Guest Accommodation*
14 Tweed Street, Berwick-
upon-Tweed TD15 1NG
t (01289) 308098
e lyndda@tiscali.co.uk
w bridgeviewberwick.co.uk

**Canty's Brig Riverside Bed &
Breakfast** ★★★
*Bed & Breakfast*
Canty's Brig Riverside Bed and
Breakfast, Berwick-upon-
Tweed TD15 1SY
t (01289) 386451
e paulbrooke@hotmail.com
w cantysbrig.co.uk

**Cara House** ◆◆◆
*Guest Accommodation*
44 Castlegate, Berwick-upon-
Tweed TD15 1JT
t (01289) 302749
e pam@carahouse.co.uk
w carahouse.co.uk

**The Cat Inn** ★★★ *Inn*
Great North Road, Cheswick,
Berwick-upon-Tweed
TD15 2RL
t (01289) 387251

**Clovelly House** ★★★★
*Bed & Breakfast*
SILVER AWARD
58 West Street, Berwick-upon-
Tweed TD15 1AS
t (01289) 302337
e vivroc@clovelly53.freeserve.
co.uk
w clovelly53.freeserve.co.uk

**Dervaig Guest House**
★★★★ *Guest House*
1 North Road, Berwick-
Tweed TD15 1PW
t (01289) 307378
e dervaig@talk21.com
w dervaigguesthouse.co.uk

**Eastfield House** ★★★
*Bed & Breakfast*
6 North Road, Berwick-
Tweed TD15 1PL
t (01289) 308949
e info@eastfieldhouse-
berwick.co.uk
w eastfieldhouse-berwick.co.
uk

**Elizabethan Townhouse**
★★★ *Guest Accommodation*
8 Sidey Court, Marygate,
Berwick-upon-Tweed
TD15 1DR
t (01289) 304580
e eliztownhouse@aol.com

**Fairholm** ★★★★
*Guest Accommodation*
East Ord TD15 2NS
t (01289) 305370
e bethiawelsh@ukonline.com
w welcometofairholm.com

**Four North Road** ★★★★
*Guest Accommodation*
SILVER AWARD
4 North Road, Berwick-upon-
Tweed TD15 1PL
t (01289) 306146
e sandra@thorntonfour.
freeserve.co.uk
w fournorthroad.co.uk

**Friendly Hound Cottage**
★★★★ *Bed & Breakfast*
Ford Common, Berwick-upon-
Tweed TD15 2QD
t (01289) 388554
e friendlyhound@aol.com
w friendlyhoundcottage.co.uk

**Ladythorne Guest House**
★★★★ *Bed & Breakfast*
Cheswick, Berwick-upon-
Tweed TD15 2RW
t (01289) 387382
e valparker@ladythorne.
wanadoo.co.uk
w ladythorne.wanadoo.co.uk

**Meadow Hill Guest House**
★★★★ *Guest House*
Duns Road, Berwick-upon-
Tweed TD15 1UB
t (01289) 306325
e pammewing@onetel.com
w meadow-hill.co.uk

**Miranda's Guest House** ★★
*Guest House*
43 Church Street, Berwick-
upon-Tweed TD15 1EE
t (01289) 306483
e mirandasberwick@aol.com

**No. 1 Sallyport** ★★★★★
*Guest House* GOLD AWARD
Off Bridge Street, Berwick-
upon-Tweed TD15 1EZ
t (01289) 308827
e info@sallyport.co.uk
w sallyport.co.uk

**No. 4 Ravensdowne** ★★★★
*Guest Accommodation*
4 Ravensdowne, Berwick-
upon-Tweed TD15 1HX
t (01289) 308082
e fourravensdowne@hotmail.
co.uk
w berwick-accomodation.co.uk

**The Old Vicarage Guest
House** ★★★★ *Guest House*
SILVER AWARD
Church Road, Berwick-upon-
Tweed TD15 2AN
t (01289) 306909 &
07730 234236
e stay@oldvicarageberwick.
co.uk
w oldvicarageberwick.co.uk

**Tweed View House** ★★★★
*Bed & Breakfast*
16 Railway Street, Berwick-
upon-Tweed TD15 1NF
t (01289) 302864

**The Walls** ★★★★
*Bed & Breakfast*
5 Quay Walls, Berwick-upon-
Tweed TD15 1HB
t (01289) 330233
e eric.d_1953@tiscali.co.uk

**West Coates** ★★★★★
*Bed & Breakfast*
GOLD AWARD
30 Castle Terrace, Berwick-
upon-Tweed TD15 1NZ
t (01289) 309666
e karenbrownwestcoates@
yahoo.com
w westcoates.co.uk

**Whyteside House** ★★★★
*Guest Accommodation*
SILVER AWARD
46 Castlegate, Berwick-upon-
Tweed TD15 1JT
t (01289) 331019
e albert.whyte@onetel.net
w secretkingdom.com/whyte/
side.htm

### BILTON
Northumberland

**Toscaig** ★★★
*Bed & Breakfast*
East View, Bilton, Alnwick
NE66 2SU
t (01665) 833139
e bookings@toscaighouse.co.
uk
w toscaighouse.co.uk

### BIRTLEY
Tyne and Wear

**The Bowes Incline Hotel**
★★★★ *Inn*
Northside, Eighton Banks,
Chester le Street DH3 1RF
t (0191) 410 2233
e info@bowesinclinehotel.co.
uk
w bowesinclinehotel.co.uk

### BISHOP AUCKLAND
County Durham

**Parkhead Station** ★★★
*Guest Accommodation*
Stanhope Moor, Bishop
Auckland DL13 2ES
t (01388) 526434
e parkheadstation@aol.com
w parkheadstation.co.uk

### BOWBURN
County Durham

**Prince Bishop Guest House**
★★★ *Guest House*
1 Oxford Terrace, Bowburn,
Durham DH6 5AX
t (0191) 377 8703
e enquiries@
durhamguesthouse.co.uk
w durhamguesthouse.co.uk

### BRANCEPETH
County Durham

**Nafferton Farm** ★★★★
*Farmhouse*
Brancepeth, Durham DH7 8EF
t (0191) 378 0538
e sndfell@aol.com
w nafferton-farm.co.uk

### BRIGNALL
County Durham

**Lily Hill Farm** ★★★★
*Farmhouse*
Brignall, Barnard Castle
DL12 9SF
t (01833) 627254
e karenerrington@yahoo.co.
uk

Look out for establishments participating in the National Accessible Scheme

## BROOMPARK
### County Durham

**My Way Guest House** ★★★
*Guest House*
West Farm, Broompark,
Durham DH7 7RW
t (0191) 375 0874
e info@mywayguesthouse.co.uk

## CASTLESIDE
### County Durham

**Dene View** ★★★★
*Guest Accommodation*
15 Front Street, Castleside,
Consett DH8 9AR
t (01207) 502925
e catherine@deneview.co.uk
w deneview.co.uk

## CHATTON
### Northumberland

**The Old Sycamores** ★★★★
*Bed & Breakfast*
**SILVER AWARD**
13 Mill Hill, Chatton NE66 5PA
t (01668) 215564
e enquiries@theoldsycamores.co.uk
w theoldsycamores.co.uk

**South Hazelrigg Farmhouse**
★★★★ *Farmhouse*
**SILVER AWARD**
Chatton, Alnwick NE66 5RZ
t (01668) 215216
e sed@hazelrigg.fsnet.co.uk
w farmhousebandb.co.uk

## CHESTER-LE-STREET
### County Durham

**Hollycroft** ★★★★
*Bed & Breakfast*
11 The Parade, Chester-le-Street DH3 3LR
t (0191) 388 7088
e staydurham@talktalk.net
w staydurham.co.uk

**Low Urpeth Farm House**
★★★★ *Farmhouse*
**SILVER AWARD**
Ouston, Chester le Street DH2 1BD
t (0191) 410 2901
e stay@lowurpeth.co.uk
w lowurpeth.co.uk

## CONSETT
### County Durham

**Bee Cottage Guesthouse**
★★★★ *Guest House*
Bee Cottage Farm, Consett DH8 9HW
t (01207) 508224
e beecottage68@aol.com
w beecottage.co.uk
▨▧

**Hownsgill Bunkhouse** ★★★
*Hostel*
Consett DH8 9AA
t (01207) 503597
e hownsgill_bunkhouse@hotmail.co.uk
w c2cstopoff.co.uk
▨▧

**St Ives Bed & Breakfast** ★★
*Bed & Breakfast*
22 St Ives Road, Leadgate,
Consett DH8 7PY
t (01207) 580173

## Wharnley Burn Farm ★★★
*Bed & Breakfast*
Castleside, Consett DH8 9AY
t (01207) 508374

## CORBRIDGE
### Northumberland

**Broxdale** ★★★★
*Bed & Breakfast*
Station Road, Corbridge
NE45 5AY
t (01434) 632492
e mike@broxdale.co.uk

**Dilston Mill** ★★★★
*Bed & Breakfast*
Corbridge NE45 5QZ
t (01434) 633493
e susan@dilstonmill.com
w dilstonmill.com

**Fellcroft** ★★★★
*Bed & Breakfast*
Station Road, Corbridge
NE45 5AY
t (01434) 632384
e tove.brown@ukonline.co.uk

**The Hayes** ★★★
*Guest Accommodation*
Newcastle Road, Corbridge
NE45 5LP
t (01434) 632010
e camon@surfree.co.uk
w hayes-corbridge.co.uk

**Low Fotherley Farmhouse
Bed and Breakfast** ★★★★
*Farmhouse*
Low Fotherley Farm, Riding Mill
NE44 6BB
t (01434) 682277
e hugh@lowfotherley.fsnet.co.uk
w westfarm.freeserve.co.uk

**Norgate** ★★★★
*Bed & Breakfast*
7 Leazes Terrace, Corbridge
NE45 5HS
t (01434) 633736
e norgatecorbridge@btinternet.com
w norgatecorbridge.co.uk

**Priorfield** ★★★★
*Bed & Breakfast*
**SILVER AWARD**
Hippingstones Lane, Corbridge
NE45 5JP
t (01434) 633179
e nsteenberg@btinternet.com
w priorfieldbedandbreakfast.co.uk

**Riggsacre** ★★★★★
*Bed & Breakfast*
**GOLD AWARD**
Appletree Lane, Corbridge
NE45 5DN
t (01434) 632617
e atclive@supanet.com
w riggsacrebandb.co.uk

**Town Barns** ★★★★
*Bed & Breakfast*
**SILVER AWARD**
Off Trinity Terrace, Corbridge
NE45 5HP
t (01434) 633345

## CORNHILL-ON-TWEED
### Northumberland

**The Coach House at
Crookham** ★★★★
*Guest Accommodation*
**SILVER AWARD**
Crookham, Cornhill-on-Tweed
TD12 4TD
t (01890) 820293
e stay@coachhousecrookham.com
w coachhousecrookham.com

**Old School House B&B**
★★★★★ *Bed & Breakfast*
**SILVER AWARD**
Tillmouth Park, Tillmouth,
Cornhill-on-Tweed TD12 4UT
t (01890) 882463
e noelhodgson@btinternet.com
w tillmouthschoolhouse.co.uk

## COTHERSTONE
### County Durham

**Glendale** ★★★
*Bed & Breakfast*
Cotherstone, Barnard Castle
DL12 9UH
t (01833) 650384
w barnard-castle.co.uk

## CRASTER
### Northumberland

**Cottage Inn** ★★★
*Guest Accommodation*
Dunstan Village, Craster
NE66 3SZ
t (01665) 576658
e enquiries@cottageinnhotel.co.uk
w cottageinnhotel.co.uk

**Howick Scar Farmhouse**
★★★ *Bed & Breakfast*
Craster, Alnwick NE66 3SU
t (01665) 576665
e howick.scar@virgin.net
w howickscar.co.uk

**Stonecroft** ★★★★
*Bed & Breakfast*
**SILVER AWARD**
Dunstan, Craster, Alnwick
NE66 3SZ
t (01665) 576433
e sally@stonestaff.freeserve.co.uk
w stonecroft-craster.co.uk
▨▧

## CROOK
### County Durham

**Dowfold House** ★★★
*Bed & Breakfast*
Low Jobs Hill, Crook DL15 9AB
t (01388) 762473
e enquiries@dowfoldhouse.co.uk
w dowfoldhouse.co.uk

## DALTON-LE-DALE
### County Durham

**The Chapel House B&B** ★★
*Bed & Breakfast*
Stockton Road, Dalton le Dale,
Seaham SR7 8RG
t (0191) 581 2626
e ryder571@btinternet.com

## DARLINGTON
### Tees Valley

**Boot & Shoe** ★★★ *Inn*
Church Row, Darlington
DL1 5QD
t (01325) 287501
e enquiries@bootandshoe.com
w bootandshoe.com

**Clow-Beck House** ★★★★★
*Guest Accommodation*
**GOLD AWARD**
Monk End, Croft on Tees,
Darlington DL2 2SW
t (01325) 721075
e heather@clowbeckhouse.co.uk
w clowbeckhouse.co.uk

**The Greenbank** ★★★
*Guest Accommodation*
90 Greenbank Road,
Darlington DL3 6EL
t (01325) 462624
e info@greenbankhotel.co.uk

**Harewood Lodge** ★★★
*Guest House*
40 Grange Road, Darlington
DL1 5NP
t (01325) 358152
e harewood.lodge@ntlworld.com
w harewood-lodge.co.uk

**Seafield House Bed and
Breakfast** ★★★★
*Guest Accommodation*
18 Northumberland Street,
Alnmouth, Alnwick NE66 2RJ
t (01665) 833256
e trapps@tiscali.co.uk
w seafieldhouse.co.uk
▨▧

## DURHAM
### County Durham

**12 The Avenue** ★★★
*Bed & Breakfast*
Durham DH1 4ED
t (0191) 384 1020
e janhanim@aol.com

**60 Albert Street** ★★★★
*Bed & Breakfast*
Western Hill, Durham DH1 4RJ
t (0191) 386 0608
e laura@sixtyalbertstreet.co.uk
w sixtyalbertstreet.co.uk

**66 Claypath** ★★
*Bed & Breakfast*
Durham DH1 1QT
t (0191) 384 3193
e richard@66claypath.co.uk
w 66claypath.co.uk
▨

**The Avenue Inn** ★★ *Inn*
Avenue Street, High Shincliffe,
Durham DH1 2PT
t (0191) 386 5954
e info@theavenue.biz

**Broom Farm Guest House**
★★★★ *Guest House*
Front Street, Broompark,
Durham DH7 7QX
t (0191) 386 4755
e liz.welsh@tiscali.co.uk

**Burnhope Lodge Guest
House** ★★★ *Guest House*
1 Wrights Way, Burnhope,
Durham DH7 0DL
t (01207) 529596

**Castle View Guest House ★★★★**
*Guest Accommodation*
4 Crossgate, Durham DH1 4PS
t (0191) 386 8852
e castle_view@hotmail.com
w castle-view.co.uk

**Cathedral View Town House ★★★★**
*Guest Accommodation*
SILVER AWARD
212 Gilesgate, Durham
DH1 1QN
t (0191) 386 9566
e cathedralview@hotmail.com
w cathedralview.com

**College of St Hild & St Bede ★★**
*Guest Accommodation*
St Hild's Lane, Durham
DH1 1SZ
t (0191) 334 8552
e susan.dale@durham.ac.uk
w dur.ac.uk/hild-bede/

**Collingwood College ★★★**
*Guest Accommodation*
South Road, Durham DH1 3LT
t (0191) 334 5000
e event@durham.ac.uk
w dur.ac.uk/collingwood/
conferences/

**The Court Inn ★★★** *Inn*
Court Lane, Durham DH1 3AW
t (0191) 384 7350
w courtinn.co.uk

**Cuthberts Rest ★★★**
*Bed & Breakfast*
42 Oswald Court, Durham
DH1 3DJ
t (0191) 384 0405

**Durham YHA ★★** *Hostel*
St Chads College, University of
Durham, 18 North Bailey,
Durham DH1 3RH
t 0870 770 8868

**Farnley Tower ★★★★**
*Guest Accommodation*
The Avenue, Durham
DH1 4DX
t (0191) 375 0011
e enquiries@farnley-tower.co.
uk
w farnley-tower.co.uk

**Fir Trees**
Rating Applied For
*Bed & Breakfast*
Rosemount, Durham DH1 5GA
t (0191) 374 1815
e violetmorrison@hotmail.com

**Gables Hotel ★★★**
*Guest Accommodation*
Front Street, Haswell Plough
DH6 2EW
t (0191) 526 2982
e jmgables@aol.com
w the-gables-durham.co.uk

**Garden House ★★★** *Inn*
North Road, Durham DH1 4NQ
t (0191) 384 3460

**The Gilesgate Moor Hotel
★★★** *Inn*
Teasdale Terrace, Gilesgate,
Durham DH1 2RN
t (0191) 386 6453
e gilesgatemoorhotel@
hotmail.com
w smoothhound.co.uk

**Hatfield College ★★**
*Guest Accommodation*
North Bailey, Durham
DH1 3RQ
t (0191) 334 2633
e hatfield.reception@dur.ac.
uk
w dur.ac.uk/hatfield.college

**Hatfield College, Melville
Building ★★★★**
*Guest Accommodation*
North Bailey, Durham
DH1 3RQ
t (0191) 334 2615
e a.m.ankers@durham.ac.uk
w dur.ac.uk/hatfield/tourism

**Hillrise Guest House ★★★**
*Guest Accommodation*
13 Durham Road West,
Bowburn, Durham DH6 5AU
t (0191) 377 0302
e enquiries@hill-rise.com
w hill-rise.com

**Moorcroft Bed and
Breakfast ★★★**
*Bed & Breakfast*
Moor End, Belmont, Durham
DH1 1BJ
t (0191) 386 7677
e moorcroft.dur@hotmail.co.
uk

**St Aidan's College ★★★**
*Guest Accommodation*
Durham University, Windmill
Hill, Durham DH1 3LJ
t (0191) 334 5769
e aidans.reception@dur.ac.uk
w dur.ac.uk/st-aidans.college/
conferences

**St Chad's College ★★**
*Guest Accommodation*
18 North Bailey, Durham
DH1 3RH
t (0191) 334 3358
e St-Chads.www@durham.ac.
uk
w dur.ac.uk/StChads

**St Johns College ★★**
*Guest Accommodation*
3 South Bailey, Durham
DH1 3RJ
t (0191) 334 3877
e s.l.hobson@durham.ac.uk
w durham.ac.uk/st-johns.
college

**Seven Stars Inn ★★★** *Inn*
High Street North, Shincliffe,
Durham DH1 2NU
t (0191) 3848454
e info@sevenstarsinn.co.uk
w sevenstarsinn.co.uk

**Trevelyan College, Durham
University ★★★**
*Guest Accommodation*
Elvet Hill Road, Durham
DH1 3LN
t (0191) 334 7000
e trev.coll@durham.ac.uk
w dur.ac.uk/trevelyan.college/
conferences

**Triermayne ★★★★**
*Bed & Breakfast*
SILVER AWARD
Nevilles Cross Bank, Durham
DH1 4JP
t (0191) 384 6036
e annjamesdh1@yahoo.co.uk

**Van Mildert College ★★★**
*Guest Accommodation*
Mill Hill Lane, Durham
DH1 3LH
t (0191) 334 7100
e van-mildert.college@
durham.ac.uk
w dur.ac.uk/van-mildert.
college/conference.tourism

**Victoria Inn ★★★** *Inn*
86 Hallgarth Street, Durham
DH1 3AS
t (0191) 386 5269
w victoriainn-durhamcity.co.uk

EASINGTON
Tees Valley

**Boulby Grange ★★★★**
*Bed & Breakfast*
Easington, Saltburn-by-the-Sea
TS13 4UW
t (01287) 640769
e jonjg526@hotmail.com
w boulbygrange.co.uk

**The Grapes Inn ★★★** *Inn*
Easington, Saltburn-by-the-Sea
TS13 4TP
t (01287) 640461
e thegrapesinn@supanet.com

**Townend Farm B&B ★★★★**
*Bed & Breakfast*
Whitby Road, Easington,
Saltburn-by-the-Sea TS13 4NE
t (01287) 640444
e info@townendfarm.co.uk
w townendfarm.co.uk

EASTGATE-IN-WEARDALE
County Durham

**Rose Hill Farm ★★★★**
*Farmhouse* SILVER AWARD
Rose Hill, Eastgate, Bishop
Auckland DL13 2LB
t (01388) 517209
e info@rosehillfarmbb.co.uk
w rosehillfarmbb.co.uk

EDMUNDBYERS
County Durham

**Edmundbyers YHA. ★★★**
*Hostel*
Edmundbyers, Consett
DH8 9NL
t (01207) 255651
e edmundbyers@yha.org.uk
w yha.org.uk

**Punchbowl Inn ★★★** *Inn*
Edmundbyers, Consett
DH8 9NL
t (01207) 255555

EMBLETON
Northumberland

**Blue Bell Inn ★★★** *Inn*
W T Stead Road, Embleton
NE66 3UP
t (01665) 576573

ESHOTT
Northumberland

**Eshott Hall ★★★★★**
*Guest Accommodation*
SILVER AWARD
Morpeth NE65 9EN
t (01670) 787777
e thehall@eshott.co.uk
w eshott.com

FEATHERSTONE
Northumberland

**The Wallace Arms ★★★★**
*Inn*
Featherstone, Haltwhistle
NE49 0JF
t (01434) 321872
e thewallacearms@aol.com

FENHAM
Tyne and Wear

**The Brighton ★★**
*Guest Accommodation*
47-49 Brighton Grove,
Newcastle-upon-Tyne
NE4 5NS
t (0191) 273 3600
e wendyhaldane@aol.com

FENWICK
Northumberland

**The Manor House ★★★★**
*Bed & Breakfast*
7 The Village, Fenwick
TD15 2PQ
t (01289) 381016
e katemoore@homecall.co.uk
w manorhousefenwick.co.uk

FIR TREE
County Durham

**Greenhead Country House
Hotel**
Rating Applied For
*Guest Accommodation*
Fir Tree, Crook DL15 8BL
t (01388) 763143
e info@thegreenheadhotel.co.
uk
w thegreenheadhotel.co.uk

FORD
Northumberland

**Hay Farm House ★★★★**
*Guest Accommodation*
SILVER AWARD
Ford and Etal Estate, Cornhill-
on-Tweed TD12 4TR
t (01890) 820647
e tinahayfarm@tiscali.co.uk
w hayfarm.co.uk

FOREST-IN-TEESDALE
County Durham

**Langdon Beck YHA ★★★★**
*Hostel*
Forest in Teesdale, Barnard
Castle DL12 0XN
t (01833) 622228
e langdonbeck@yha.org.uk
w yha.org.uk

FROSTERLEY
County Durham

**Newlands Hall ★★★★**
*Guest Accommodation*
Frosterley, Bishop Auckland
DL13 2SH
t (01388) 529233
e carol@newlandshall.co.uk
w newlandshall.co.uk

GATESHEAD
Tyne and Wear

**Alexandra Guest House
★★★** *Guest House*
377 Alexandra Road,
Gateshead NE8 4HY
t (0191) 478 1105

**The Bewick Hotel** ★★★
*Guest House*
145 Prince Consort Road,
Gateshead NE8 4DS
t (0191) 477 1809
e bewickhotel@hotmail.com
w bewickhotel.co.uk

**The Riding Farm House**
★★★★ *Farmhouse*
SILVER AWARD
Riding Lane, Gateshead
NE11 0JA
t (0191) 370 1868
e ridingfarm@btconnect.com
w lowurpeth.co.uk

**Shaftesbury Guest House**
★★★ *Guest House*
245 Prince Consort Road,
Gateshead NE8 4DT
t (0191) 478 2544
e shaftesbury.hotel@hotmail.
com

GILSLAND
Northumberland

**Samson Inn** ★★★
*Guest Accommodation*
Gilsland, Brampton CA8 7DR
t (01697) 747220
e samsoninn@hotmail.co.uk

GREENHAUGH
Northumberland

**Hollybush Inn** ★★★ *Inn*
Greenhaugh, Hexham
NE48 1PW
t (01434) 240391
e timmorris.hollybush@virgin.
net
w thehollybushinn.co.uk

GREENHEAD
Northumberland

**Holmhead Guest House**
★★★★ *Guest House*
On Thirlwall Castle Farm,
Hadrian's Wall, Greenhead
CA8 7HY
t (01697) 747402
w holmhead.com

GUISBOROUGH
Tees Valley

**The Fox and Hounds** ★★★
*Inn*
Slapewath, Guisborough
TS14 6PX
t (01287) 632964
e info@thefoxandhound.co.uk
w thefoxandhound.co.uk

**Fox Inn** ★★★ *Inn*
Bow Street, Guisborough
TS14 6BP
t (01287) 632958

**Three Fiddles** ★★ *Inn*
34 Westgate, Guisborough
TS14 6BA
t (01287) 632417
e jill@hendersoncampbell.co.
uk

HALTWHISTLE
Northumberland

**Ashcroft** ★★★★
*Guest House* GOLD AWARD
Lanty's Lonnen, Ashcroft,
Haltwhistle NE49 0DA
t (01434) 320213
e ashcroft.1@btconnect.com
w ashcroftguesthouse.co.uk

**Burnhead Bed and Breakfast**
★★★★ *Bed & Breakfast*
Cawfields, Haltwhistle
NE49 9PJ
t (01434) 320841
e enquiries@
burnheadbedandbreakfast.co.
uk
w burnheadbedandbreakfast.
co.uk
🅿️🖨️

**The Grey Bull** ★★★★
*Guest Accommodation*
Main Street, Haltwhistle
NE49 0DL
t (01434) 321991
e reception@greybullhotel.co.
uk
w greybullhotel.co.uk

**Hall Meadows** ★★★★
*Bed & Breakfast*
Main Street, Haltwhistle
NE49 0AZ
t (01434) 321021

**The Mount** ★★★
*Bed & Breakfast*
Comb Hill, Haltwhistle
NE49 9NS
t (01434) 321075
e the-mount@talk21.com
w themountbb.com

**Oaky Knowe Farm** ★★★
*Farmhouse*
Oakey Knowe, Haltwhistle
NE49 0NB
t (01434) 320648
e garlinegoldens@aol.com

**Saughy Rigg Farm** ★★★★
*Guest House*
Twice Brewed, Haltwhistle
NE49 9PT
t (01434) 344120
e info@saughyrigg.co.uk
w saughyrigg.co.uk

**Wydon Farm Bed and
Breakfast** ★★★★ *Farmhouse*
Wydon Farm, Haltwhistle
NE49 0LG
t (01434) 321702
e stay@wydon-haltwhistle.co.
uk
w wydon-haltwhistle.co.uk
🅿️🖨️

HAMSTERLEY
County Durham

**Dale End** ★★★★
*Bed & Breakfast*
SILVER AWARD
Hamsterley DL13 3PT
t (01388) 488091
e info@dale-
endhamsterleybandb.co.uk
w dale-endhamsterleybandb.
co.uk
🅿️🖨️

**Hamsterley B&B** ★★★★
*Bed & Breakfast*
SILVER AWARD
Fern Lea, Hamsterley, Bishop
Auckland DL13 3PT
t (01388) 488056 &
07710 908735
w hamsterleybedandbreakfast.
co.uk
🅿️🖨️

**Hamsterley Forest B and B**
Rating Applied For
*Bed & Breakfast*
Redford, Hamsterley, Bishop
Auckland DL13 3NL
t (01388) 488420
e jst_ayhope@yahoo.co.uk

HARBOTTLE
Northumberland

**Bonny Barn** *Camping Barn*
Harbottle, Rothbury NE65 7DG
t (01669) 650476
e rosemary@bonnybarn.co.uk
w bonnybarn.co.uk

**The Byre Vegetarian B&B**
★★★★ *Bed & Breakfast*
SILVER AWARD
Harbottle, Rothbury NE65 7DG
t (01669) 650476
e rosemary@the-byre.co.uk
w the-byre.co.uk
🅿️🖨️

**Parsonside Bed & Breakfast**
★★★★ *Bed & Breakfast*
Newton Hall, Harbottle,
Morpeth NE65 7DP
t (01669) 650275
e carolyn.graham@harbottle.
net

HARTFORD BRIDGE
Northumberland

**Woodside** ★★★★
*Bed & Breakfast*
Hartford Bridge Farm,
Bedlington NE22 6AL
t (01670) 822035

HARTLEPOOL
Tees Valley

**Brafferton Guest House** ★★
*Guest House*
161 Stockton Road, Hartlepool
TS25 1SL
t (01429) 273875
e sales@
braffertonguesthouse.co.uk
w braffertonguesthouse.co.uk

**Catlow Hall** ★★★★
*Farmhouse*
Catlow Hall Farm, Hart Bushes,
South Wingate TS28 5NJ
t (01429) 836275
e margery.shotton@
btinternet.com

**Douglas Hotel** ★★★
*Guest House*
2 Grange Road, Hartlepool
TS26 8JA
t (01429) 272038
e info@douglashotel.demon.
co.uk

**The Oakroyd** ★★★
*Guest Accommodation*
133 Park Road, Hartlepool
TS26 9HT
t (01429) 864361
e mandyoakroydhotel@
hotmail.com

**Ocean View Guest House**
★★★ *Guest House*
2 The Cliff, Seaton Carew,
Hartlepool TS25 1AB
t (01429) 271983
e 2thecliff@tiscali.co.uk
w oceanviewguesthouse.co.uk

**The York House** ★★★★
*Guest Accommodation*
185 York Road, Hartlepool
TS26 9EE
t (01429) 867373
e info@theyorkhotel.co.uk
w theyorkhotel.co.uk

HAYDON BRIDGE
Northumberland

**Grindon Cartshed** ★★★★
*Bed & Breakfast*
Haydon Bridge, Hexham
NE47 6NQ
t (01434) 684273
e cartshed@grindon.force9.
co.uk
w grindon-cartshed.co.uk
🅿️🖨️

**Hadrian Lodge Hotel** ★★★
*Guest Accommodation*
Hindshield Moss, North Road,
Haydon Bridge NE47 6NF
t (01434) 684867
e hadrian-lodge@btconnect.
com
w hadrianlodge.co.uk

**Old Repeater Station** ★★★
*Hostel*
Military Road, Grindon,
Haydon Bridge NE47 6NQ
t (01434) 688668
e les.gibson@tiscali.co.uk
w hadrians-wall-
bedandbreakfast.co.uk
🅿️🖨️

**The Reading Rooms** ★★★★
*Bed & Breakfast*
2 Church Street, Hexham
NE47 6JG
t (01434) 688199
e thereadingrooms@aol.com
w thereadingroomshaydon
bridge.co.uk
🅿️🖨️

HEDDON-ON-THE-WALL
Northumberland

**Heddon Lodge** ★★★★
*Bed & Breakfast*
SILVER AWARD
38 Heddon Banks, Newcastle-
upon-Tyne NE15 0BU
t (01661) 854042

**Houghton North Farm
Visitor Accommodation**
★★★★ *Hostel*
Heddon on the Wall,
Newcastle-upon-Tyne
NE15 0EZ
t (01661) 854364
e wjlaws@btconnect.com
w hadrianswall
accommodation.com
🅿️🖨️

**Ironsign Farm B&B** ★★★★
*Farmhouse*
Military Road, Heddon-on-the-
Wall NE15 0JB
t (01661) 853802
e lowen532@aol.com
w ironsign.co.uk

HESLEDEN
County Durham

**The Ship Inn** ★★★★ *Inn*
SILVER AWARD
Hartlepool TS27 4QD
t (01429) 836453
e sheila@theshipinn.net
🍴🅿️

## HEXHAM
### Northumberland

**Anick Grange ★★★★**
*Farmhouse*
Anick, Hexham NE46 4LP
t (01434) 603807
e julie@anickgrange.fsnet.co.uk
w anickgrange.com

**The Beeches ★★★★**
*Bed & Breakfast*
40 Leazes Park, Hexham
NE46 3AY
t (01434) 605900
e peter@beeches1.demon.co.uk
w bandbhexham.com

**Dukesfield Hall Farm**
**★★★★ Bed & Breakfast**
Hexham NE46 1SH
t (01434) 673634
e cath@dukesfield.supanet.com
w dukesfieldhall.co.uk

**Fairshaw Rigg ★★★★**
*Bed & Breakfast*
SILVER AWARD
Lowgate, Hexham NE46 2NW
t (01434) 602630
e shrimpoathome@aol.com
w fairshawrigg.co.uk

**Hallbank Guest House**
**★★★★★ Guest House**
Hallbank House, Hallgate,
Hexham NE46 1XA
t (01434) 605567
e hallbank@freenetname.co.uk
w hallbankguesthouse.com

**HallBarns B&B ★★★★**
*Farmhouse*
Simonburn, Hexham
NE48 3AQ
t (01434) 681419 &
07788 998959
e enquiries@hallbarns-simonburn.co.uk
w hallbarns-simonburn.co.uk

**High Reins ★★★★**
*Bed & Breakfast*
Leazes Lane, Hexham
NE46 3AT
t (01434) 603590
e walton45@hotmail.com
w highreins.co.uk

**Kitty Frisk House ★★★★**
*Bed & Breakfast*
SILVER AWARD
Corbridge Road, Hexham
NE46 1UN
t (01434) 601533
e alan@kittyfriskhouse.co.uk
w kittyfriskhouse.co.uk

**Loughbrow House ★★★★**
*Guest Accommodation*
Dipton Mill Road, Hexham
NE46 1RS
t (01434) 603351
e patricia@loughbrow.fsnet.co.uk
w loughbrow.fsnet.co.uk

**Rye Hill Farm ★★★★**
*Farmhouse*
Slaley, Hexham NE47 0AH
t (01434) 673259
e info@ryehillfarm.co.uk
w ryehillfarm.co.uk

**Thistlerigg Farm ★★★**
*Farmhouse*
High Warden, Hexham
NE46 4SR
t (01434) 602041
e mitchellthislerigs@virginnet.com

**West Wharmley Farm**
**★★★★ Farmhouse**
West Wharmley, Hexham
NE46 2PL
t (01434) 674227
e info@westwharmley.co.uk
w westwharmley.co.uk

**Woodley Field ★★★★**
*Bed & Breakfast*
Allendale Road, Hexham
NE46 2NB
t (01434) 601600
e woodleyfield@btinternet.com
w woodleyfield.co.uk

## HOLY ISLAND
### Northumberland

**The Bungalow ★★★★**
*Guest Accommodation*
Chare Ends, Holy Island
TD15 2SE
t (01289) 389308
e bungalow@lindisfarne.org.uk
w lindisfarne.org.uk/bungalow

**The Lindisfarne on Holy Island ★★★**
*Guest Accommodation*
Holy Island TD15 2SQ
t (01289) 389273
e lindisfarnehotel@btconnect.com
w lindisfarne.org.uk/lindisfarne.htm

**The Ship ★★★ Inn**
Marygate, Berwick-upon-Tweed TD15 2SJ
t (01289) 389311
e the_ship_inn@btconnect.com
w lindisfarneaccommodate.com

## HOUSESTEADS
### Northumberland

**Beggar Bog ★★★★**
*Bed & Breakfast*
Housesteads, Haydon Bridge
NE47 6NN
t (01434) 344652
e stay@beggarbog.com
w beggarbog.com

## HOWICK
### Northumberland

**The Old Rectory ★★★★**
*Guest Accommodation*
Howick, Craster NE66 3LE
t (01665) 577590
e david@bbi-ltd.co.uk
w oldrectoryhowick.co.uk

## HUMSHAUGH
### Northumberland

**Carraw Bed and Breakfast**
**★★★★ Guest House**
SILVER AWARD
Carraw Farm, Humshaugh,
Hexham NE46 4DB
t (01434) 689857
e relax@carraw.co.uk
w carraw.co.uk

**Greencarts ★★★ Farmhouse**
Humshaugh, Hexham
NE46 4BW
t (01434) 681320
e sandra@greencarts.co.uk
w greencarts.co.uk

## INGRAM
### Northumberland

**Reaveley Farmhouse B&B**
**★★★★ Bed & Breakfast**
Ingram Valley, Alnwick
NE66 4LS
t (01665) 578268 &
07766 834504
e reaveleyfarm@aol.com
w reaveleyfarmhouse.co.uk

## IRESHOPEBURN
### County Durham

**Slack House Farm**
Rating Applied For
*Guest Accommodation*
Ireshopeburn, Bishop Auckland
DL13 1HL
t (01388) 537292
w fleecewithaltitude.co.uk

## JARROW
### Tyne and Wear

**Bedeswell Guest House**
**★★★ Guest House**
146 Bede Burn Road, Jarrow
NE32 5AU
t (0191) 428 4794
w bedeswellguesthouse.com

## KELLAH
### Northumberland

**Kellah Farm B&B ★★★★**
*Farmhouse*
Kellah, Haltwhistle NE49 0JL
t (01434) 320816
e teasdale@ukonline.co.uk
w kellah.co.uk

## KIELDER
### Northumberland

**Kielder YHA ★★★★ Hostel**
Butteryhaugh, Kielder
NE48 1HQ
t 0870 770 5898
e kielder@yha.org.uk
w yha.org.uk

**Twenty Seven ★★**
*Bed & Breakfast*
27 Castle Drive, Hexham
NE48 1EQ
t (01434) 250462 &
(01434) 250366
e twentyseven@staykielder.co.uk
w staykielder.co.uk

## KIELDER WATER
### Northumberland

**The Pheasant Inn (by Kielder Water) ★★★★ Inn**
SILVER AWARD
Stannersburn, Hexham
NE48 1DD
t (01434) 240382
e enquiries@thepheasantinn.com
w thepheasantinn.com

## KIRKNEWTON
### Northumberland

**Hethpool Bed and Breakfast**
**★★★ Bed & Breakfast**
Hethpool, Kirknewton
NE71 6TW
t (01668) 216232
e eildon@hethpoolhouse.co.uk
w hethpoolhouse.co.uk

## KIRKWHELPINGTON
### Northumberland

**Cornhills Farmhouse**
**★★★★ Bed & Breakfast**
SILVER AWARD
Kirkwhelpington NE19 2RE
t (01830) 540232
e cornhills@northumberlandfarmhouse.co.uk
w northumberlandfarmhouse.co.uk

## LESBURY
### Northumberland

**Swallowdale Cottage**
**★★★★ Bed & Breakfast**
Longhoughton Road, Lesbury
NE66 3AT
t (01665) 830389
e swallowdale@fsmail.net
w swallowdale.co.uk

## LONGFRAMLINGTON
### Northumberland

**The Angler's Arms ★★★★**
*Inn*
Weldon Bridge,
Longframlington NE65 8AX
t (01665) 570655
e johnyoung@anglersarms.fsnet.co.uk
w anglersarms.com

**Coquet Bed & Breakfast**
**★★★★ Farmhouse**
SILVER AWARD
Elyhaugh Farm,
Longframlington NE65 8BE
t (01665) 570305
e stay@coquetbb.co.uk
w coquetbb.co.uk

**Dene House Farm ★★★★**
*Farmhouse*
Longframlington, Morpeth
NE65 8EE
t (01665) 570665
w denehousefarm.com

**Lee Farm ★★★★★**
*Farmhouse* GOLD AWARD
Nr Rothbury, Longframlington,
Morpeth NE65 8JQ
t (01665) 570257
e enqs@leefarm.co.uk
w leefarm.co.uk

**The Red Barn ★★★★**
*Guest Accommodation*
SILVER AWARD
Low Hall, Longframlington
NE65 8ED
t (01665) 578223
e jane@theredbarn.uk.com
w theredbarn.uk.com

## LONGHORSLEY
### Northumberland

**The Baronial**
Rating Applied For
*Guest Accommodation*
Longhorsley NE65 8TD
t (01670) 788378
w thebaronial.co.uk

**Thistleyhaugh Farm** ★★★★ *Farmhouse*
**GOLD AWARD**
Thistleyhaugh, Morpeth
NE65 8RG
t (01665) 570629
e stay@thistleyhaugh.co.uk
w thistleyhaugh.co.uk

## LONGHOUGHTON
Northumberland

**Chestnut Tree House** ★★★★
*Guest Accommodation*
7 Crowlea Road,
Longhoughton, Alnwick
NE66 3AN
t (01665) 577153
e janetholtuk@btinternet.com
⊟✐

**Swallows' Rest** ★★★★
*Bed & Breakfast*
**SILVER AWARD**
8 The Croft, Longhoughton
NE66 3DD
t (01665) 577425
e stay@swallows-rest.co.uk
w swallows-rest.co.uk
⊟✐

## LOWICK
Northumberland

**Black Bull Inn** ★★★ *Inn*
Main Street, Lowick, Berwick-
upon-Tweed TD15 2UA
t (01289) 388228

**Burnhouse Bed & Breakfast**
★★★★ *Bed & Breakfast*
Lowick Common, Lowick
TD15 2UG
t (01289) 388457
e margaretsoutter@btinternet.
com
w burn-house.co.uk

**The Old Drapery** ★★★
*Bed & Breakfast*
50 Main Street, Lowick,
Berwick-upon-Tweed
TD15 2UA
t (01289) 388592
e davidlaidle@onetel.com

**Primrose Cottage** ★★★★
*Bed & Breakfast*
Main Street, Berwick-upon-
Tweed TD15 2UA
t (01289) 388900

## MARSKE-BY-THE-SEA
Tees Valley

**Ship Inn** ★★★ *Inn*
High Street, Marske-by-the-
Sea, Redcar TS11 7LL
t (01642) 482640
e shipmates@supanet.com

## MATFEN
Northumberland

**Matfen High House** ★★★★
*Guest Accommodation*
Nr Corbridge, Newcastle upon
Tyne NE20 0RG
t (01661) 886592
e struan@struan.enterprise-
plc.com
⊟✐

## MIDDLESBROUGH
Tees Valley

**Chadwicks Guest House** ★★
*Guest House*
Clairville Road, Middlesbrough
TS4 2HN
t (01642) 287235
e chadwickguesthouse@
hotmail.com
w chadwickguesthouse.com

## MIDDLETON-IN-TEESDALE
County Durham

**Belvedere House** ★★★★
*Bed & Breakfast*
54 Market Place, Middleton-in-
Teesdale DL12 0QH
t (01833) 640884
e belvedere@thecoachhouse.
net
w thecoachhouse.net

**Brunswick House** ★★★★
*Guest House* **SILVER AWARD**
55 Market Place, Middleton-in-
Teesdale DL12 0QH
t (01833) 640393
e enquiries@brunswickhouse.
net
w brunswickhouse.net
⊟✐

**Grove Lodge** ★★★★
*Guest Accommodation*
**GOLD AWARD**
Hude, Middleton in Teesdale,
Barnard Castle DL12 0QW
t (01833) 640798
w grovelodgeteesdale.co.uk

**Lonton South Farm** ★★★
*Farmhouse*
Lonton, Middleton-in-Teesdale
DL12 0PL
t (01833) 640409

**Wemmergill Hall Farm**
★★★★ *Farmhouse*
Lunedale, Middleton in
Teesdale, Barnard Castle
DL12 0PA
t (01833) 640379
e enquiries@wemmergill-farm.
co.uk
w wemmergill-farm.co.uk

## MOHOPE
Northumberland

**YHA Ninebanks** ★★★ *Hostel*
Orchard House, Mohope,
Hexham NE47 8DQ
t (01434) 345288
e ninebanks@yha.org.uk
w yha.ninebanks.org.uk
⊟✐

## MOORSHOLM
Tees Valley

**Green Ghyl** ★★★★
*Bed & Breakfast*
10 Recreation View,
Moorsholm TS12 3HZ
t (01287) 669050
e info@greenghyl.co.uk
w greenghyl.co.uk

## MORPETH
Northumberland

**Castle View B&B** ★★★★
*Guest House*
6 Dacre Street, Morpeth
NE61 1HW
t (01670) 514140
e info@
castleviewbedandbreakfast.co.
uk
w castleviewbedandbreakfast.
co.uk

**Chestnut House** ★★★
*Guest House*
2 Dacre Street, Morpeth
NE61 1HW
t (01670) 518777
e enquiries@chestnuthouse.
net
w chestnuthouse.net

**Cottage View Guesthouse**
★★ *Guest House*
6 Staithes Lane, Morpeth
NE61 1TD
t (01670) 518550
e bookings@cottageview.co.
uk
w cottageview.co.uk

**Cottingburn House B&B**
★★★ *Bed & Breakfast*
40 Bullers Green, Morpeth
NE61 1DE
t (01670) 503195
e veeherbert@hotmail.com
w cottingburnhouse.co.uk
⊟✐

**Kington** ★★★
*Bed & Breakfast*
East Linden, Longhorsley,
Morpeth NE65 8TH
t (01670) 788554
e clivetaylor.services@tiscali.
co.uk
w kington-longhorsley.com

**Lansdowne House** ★★★
*Bed & Breakfast*
90 Newgate Street, Morpeth
NE61 1BU
t (01670) 511129
e kitchendiva@gmail.com
w lansdownhouse.co.uk

**Morpeth Court** ★★★★
*Guest Accommodation*
Castle Bank, Morpeth
NE61 1YJ
t (01670) 517217
e carol_edmundson@hotmail.
com
w morpethcourt.com

**Newminster Cottage** ★★★
*Bed & Breakfast*
High Stanners, Morpeth
NE61 1QL
t (01670) 503124
e enquiries@newminster-
cottage.co.uk
w newminster-cottage.co.uk
⊟✐

**Northumberland Cottage**
★★★★ *Guest House*
Chevington Moor, Morpeth
NE61 3BA
t (01670) 783339
e info@northumberland-
cottage.co.uk
w northumberland-cottage.co.
uk

**Queens Head Hotel** ★★★
*Guest Accommodation*
Bridge Street, Morpeth
NE61 1NB
t (01670) 512083
w queensheadmorpeth.co.uk

**River Cottage** ★★★★
*Guest Accommodation*
Mouldhaugh Farm, Felton
NE65 9NP
t (01670) 787081
e easells@clara.co.uk
w river-cottage-bandb.co.uk

**Riverside Guest House**
★★★ *Guest House*
77 Newgate Street, Morpeth
NE61 1BX
t (01670) 515026
e elaine.riverside@virgin.net
w riverside-guesthouse.co.uk

**Stepping Stones B&B** ★★★
*Guest Accommodation*
75 Newgate Street, Morpeth
NE61 1BX
t (01670) 517869
e steppingstonesbb@aol.com
w steppingstonesbedand
breakfast.co.uk

## NEW BRANCEPETH
County Durham

**Alum Waters Guest House**
★★★★ *Bed & Breakfast*
Unthank Farmhouse, Alum
Waters, New Brancepeth
DH7 7JJ
t (0191) 373 0628
e tony@alumwaters.freeserve.
co.uk

## NEWBIGGIN-BY-THE-SEA
Northumberland

**Seaton House** ★★★
*Bed & Breakfast*
20 Seaton Avenue, Newbiggin-
by-the-Sea NE64 6UX
t (01670) 816057
⊟✐

## NEWBROUGH
Northumberland

**Allerwash Farmhouse**
★★★★★ *Bed & Breakfast*
**GOLD AWARD**
Allerwash, Hexham NE47 5AB
t (01434) 674574

**Carr Edge Farm** ★★★★
*Farmhouse*
Newbrough, Hexham
NE47 5EA
t (01434) 674788
e stay@carredge.co.uk
w carredge.co.uk
⊟✐

**Westfield Bed and Breakfast**
★★★★ *Bed & Breakfast*
Newbrough, Hexham
NE47 5AR
t (01434) 674241
e byhexham@aol.com
w westfieldbandb.co.uk
⊟✐

## NEWCASTLE UPON TYNE
Tyne and Wear

**Albatross** ★★ *Hostel*
51 Grainger Street, Newcastle-
upon-Tyne NE1 5JE
t (0191) 2331330
e info@albatrossnewcastle.co.
uk
w albatrossnewcastle.com

**Avenue Hotel ★★★**
*Guest House*
2 Manor House Road,
Newcastle-upon-Tyne NE2 2LU
**t** (0191) 281 1396
**e** avenue.hotel@amserve.com

**Brandling Guest House**
★★★ *Guest House*
4 Brandling Park, Newcastle-
upon-Tyne NE2 4QA
**t** (0191) 281 3175
**e** johncatto@btconnect.com
**w** brandlingguesthouse.co.uk

**Clifton House ★★★**
*Guest Accommodation*
46 Clifton Road, Off Grainger
Park Road, Newcastle upon
Tyne NE4 6XH
**t** (0191) 273 0407
**e** cliftonhousehotel@hotmail.
com
**w** cliftonhousehotel.com

**Dene Hotel ★★★**
*Guest Accommodation*
38-42 Grosvenor Road,
Newcastle-upon-Tyne NE2 2RP
**t** (0191) 281 1502
**e** denehotel@ukonline.co.uk

**Greenholme ★★★**
*Bed & Breakfast*
40 South View, Newcastle-
upon-Tyne NE5 2BP
**t** (0191) 267 4828 &
07910 529089
**e** info@
greenholmeguesthouse.co.uk
**w** greenholmeguesthouse.co.
uk

**Jesmond Park Hotel ★★★**
*Guest House*
74-76 Queens Road,
Newcastle-upon-Tyne NE2 2PR
**t** (0191) 281 2821
**e** vh@jespark.fsnet.co.uk
**w** jesmondpark.com

**The Keelman's Lodge
★★★★**
*Guest Accommodation*
Grange Road, Newcastle upon
Tyne NE15 8NL
**t** (0191) 267 1689 &
(0191) 414 0156
**e** admin@biglampbrewers.co.
uk
**w** keelmanslodge.co.uk

**The Lynnwood ★★**
*Guest House*
1 Lynnwood Terrace,
Newcastle-upon-Tyne NE4 6UL
**t** (0191) 273 3497
**e** davidreynolds07@aol.com
**w** thelynnwood.co.uk

**Newcastle YHA ★★** *Hostel*
107 Jesmond Road, Newcastle-
upon-Tyne NE2 1NJ
**t** (0191) 2812570
**e** newcastle@yha.org.uk
**w** yha.org.uk

**Northumbria University
Claude Gibb Hall and
Camden Court ★★★**
*Campus*
University Precinct,
Northumberland Road,
Newcastle upon Tyne NE1 8ST
**t** (0191) 227 4027
**e** rc.conferences@
northumbria.ac.uk
**w** northumbria.ac.uk/
conferences

**Stonehaven Lodge ★★★**
*Guest House*
Prestwick Road Ends,
Ponteland, Newcastle upon
Tyne NE20 9BX
**t** (01661) 872363
**e** stonehavenlodge@hotmail.
co.uk
**w** stonehavenlodge.co.uk

**The Waterside ★★★**
*Guest Accommodation*
48-52 Sandhill, Newcastle-
upon-Tyne NE1 3JF
**t** (01912) 300111
**e** enquiries@watersidehotel.
com
**w** watersidehotel.com

**Westland Hotel ★★★**
*Guest Accommodation*
27 Osborne Avenue,
Newcastle-upon-Tyne NE2 1JR
**t** (0191) 281 0412
**e** westland-hotel.co.uk

NEWTON-ON-THE-MOOR
Northumberland

**The Old School ★★★★★**
*Bed & Breakfast*
**GOLD AWARD**
Newton on the Moor, Alnwick
NE65 9JY
**t** (01665) 575767
**e** info@
northumberlandbedand
breakfast.co.uk
**w** theoldschool.biz

NORTH SHIELDS
Tyne and Wear

**No. 61 ★★★★** *Guest House*
Front Street, North Shields
NE30 4BT
**t** (0191) 257 3687
**e** no.61@btconnect.com
**w** no61.co.uk

NORTH SUNDERLAND
Northumberland

**The Old Manse ★★★★**
*Bed & Breakfast*
9 North Lane, North
Sunderland, Seahouses
NE68 7UQ
**t** (01665) 720521
**e** info@theoldemanse.com
**w** theoldemanse.com

**The Old School House ★★★**
*Guest House*
17 North Lane, North
Sunderland, Seahouses
NE68 7UQ
**t** (01665) 720760
**e** theoldeschoolhouse@
hotmail.co.uk
**w** theoldeschoolhouse.com

NORTON
Tees Valley

**Grange Guest House ★★★**
*Guest Accommodation*
33 Grange Road, Norton,
Stockton-on-Tees TS20 2NS
**t** (01642) 552541
**e** grangeguesthouse@tiscali.
co.uk

OAKWOOD
Northumberland

**Oakwood Cottage ★★★★**
*Bed & Breakfast*
Oakwood, Hexham NE46 4LE
**t** (01434) 602013
**e** sturner@oakwoodcottage.
com
**w** oakwoodcottage.com

OLD BEWICK
Northumberland

**Old Bewick Farmhouse
★★★★** *Bed & Breakfast*
Old Bewick, Alnwick NE66 4DZ
**t** (01668) 217372
**e** oldbewickfarmhse@aol.com
**w** oldbewick.co.uk

OTTERBURN
Northumberland

**Butterchurn Guest House
★★★★** *Guest House*
Main Street, Otterburn
NE19 1NP
**t** (01830) 520585
**e** keith@butterchurn.
freeserve.co.uk
**w** butterchurnguesthouse.co.
uk

**Dunns Houses Farmhouse
Bed and Breakfast ★★★★**
*Farmhouse*
Dunns Houses Farm, Otterburn
NE19 1LB
**t** (01830) 520677
**e** dunnshouses@hotmail.com
**w** northumberlandfarm
holidays.co.uk

OVINGHAM
Northumberland

**Dukes Cottages Bed and
Breakfast ★★★★**
*Guest House*
2 Dukes Cottages, Main Road,
Ovingham NE42 6AD
**t** (01661) 832566
**e** info@dukescottages.co.uk
**w** dukescottages.co.uk

OVINGTON
County Durham

**The Four Alls ★★★** *Inn*
Ovington, Richmond DL11 7BP
**t** (01833) 627302

OVINGTON
Northumberland

**Evenwood Cottage ★★★★**
*Bed & Breakfast*
Ovington NE42 6DN
**t** (01661) 832259
**e** stuartoram@btinternet.com
**w** evenwoodcottage.co.uk

**Ovington House Bed and
Breakfast ★★★★**
*Bed & Breakfast*
Ovington House, Ovington
NE42 6DH
**t** (01661) 832442
**e** stay@ovingtonhouse.co.uk
**w** ovingtonhouse.co.uk

PETERLEE
County Durham

**Manor House**
Rating Applied For
*Bed & Breakfast*
Manor House Cottages, South
Side, Peterlee SR8 3AX
**t** (0191) 527 2141
**e** danmullaney3009@hotmail.
com

PIERCEBRIDGE
Tees Valley

**Holme House ★★★**
*Farmhouse*
Piercebridge, Darlington
DL2 3SY
**t** (01325) 374280
**e** graham.holmehouse@gmail.
com

POWBURN
Northumberland

**Cheviot View ★★★★**
*Bed & Breakfast*
Powburn NE66 4HL
**t** (01665) 578306

**Crawley Farmhouse ★★★**
*Farmhouse*
Powburn, Alnwick NE66 4JA
**t** (01665) 578413
**e** crawleyfarmhouse@hotmail.
co.uk

**Low Hedgeley Farm
★★★★★** *Farmhouse*
**SILVER AWARD**
Powburn, Alnwick NE66 4JD
**t** (01665) 578815

QUEBEC
County Durham

**Hamsteels Hall ★★★★**
*Farmhouse*
Hamsteels Lane, Quebec,
Durham DH7 9RS
**t** (01207) 520388
**e** june@hamsteelshall.co.uk
**w** hamsteelshall.co.uk

RAMSHAW
Northumberland

**The Bridge Inn ★★★** *Inn*
1 Gordon Lane, Ramshaw
DL14 0NS
**t** (01388) 832509
**e** thebridgeinnramshaw@
hotmail.com
**w** bridgeinn.ntb.org.uk

REDCAR
Tees Valley

**All Welcome In ★★**
*Guest Accommodation*
81 Queen Street, Redcar
TS10 1BG
**t** (01642) 484790
**e** patredcar2004@yahoo.co.uk
**w** allwelcomein.co.uk

**Armada Guest House**
Rating Applied For
*Guest Accommodation*
28-30 Henry Street, Redcar
TS10 1BJ
**t** (01642) 471710
**e** info@armadaguesthouse.co.
uk
**w** armadaguesthouse.co.uk

**The Kastle View ★★**
*Guest House*
55 Newcomen Place, Redcar
TS10 1DB
**t** (01642) 489313

**Springdale House ★★★★**
*Bed & Breakfast*
3 Nelson Terrace, Redcar
TS10 1RX
**t** (01642) 297169
**e** reservations@
springdalehouse.co.uk
**w** springdalehouse.co.uk

### ROMALDKIRK
County Durham

**Hollin Croft** ★★★★
*Bed & Breakfast*
**SILVER AWARD**
Romaldkirk, Teesdale, Barnard
Castle DL12 9EL
t  (01833) 650192
e  enquiries@hollincroft.co.uk
w  hollincroft.co.uk

**Mill Riggs Cottage** ★★★
*Bed & Breakfast*
Romaldkirk, Barnard Castle
DL12 9EW
t  (01833) 650392

### ROTHBURY
Northumberland

**Burnfoot Guest House**
★★★★
*Guest Accommodation*
Netherton, Morpeth NE65 7EY
t  (01669) 631061
e  burnfootghouse@aol.com
w  burnfoothouse.co.uk

**The Chirnells** ★★★★
*Farmhouse*
Thropton NE65 7JE
t  (01669) 621507
e  thechirnells@aol.com

**Farm Cottage Guest House**
★★★★★ *Guest House*
**GOLD AWARD**
Thropton, Rothbury NE65 7NA
t  (01669) 620831
e  joan@
farmcottageguesthouse.co.uk
w  farmcottageguesthouse.co.
uk

**The Haven** ★★★★
*Guest Accommodation*
Back Crofts, Rothbury
NE65 7YA
t  (01669) 620577
e  the.haven.rothbury@talk21.
com
w  thehavenrothbury.co.uk

**Katerina's Guest House**
★★★★ *Guest House*
**SILVER AWARD**
Sun Buildings, Rothbury
NE65 7TQ
t  (01669) 620691
e  cath@katerinasguesthouse.
co.uk
w  katerinasguesthouse.co.uk

**Lorbottle West Steads**
★★★★ *Farmhouse*
Thropton NE65 7JT
t  (01665) 574672
e  info@lorbottle.com
w  lorbottle.com

**The Queens Head** ★★★ *Inn*
Townfoot, Rothbury, Morpeth
NE65 7SR
t  (01669) 620470
e  enqs@queensheadrothbury.
com
w  queensheadrothbury.com

**Silverton House** ★★★★
*Bed & Breakfast*
**SILVER AWARD**
Silverton Lane, Rothbury
NE65 7RJ
t  (01669) 621395
e  maggie@silvertonhouse.
wanadoo.co.uk
w  silvertonhouse.co.uk

**Springfield House** ★★★★
*Guest House*
Townfoot, Rothbury NE65 7SP
t  (01669) 621277
e  enquiries@
springfeildhousebb.co.uk
w  springfieldguesthouse.co.uk

**Tosson Tower Farm**
★★★★★ *Farmhouse*
**GOLD AWARD**
Great Tosson, Rothbury
NE65 7NW
t  (01669) 620228
e  stay@tossontowerfarm.co.uk
w  tossontowerfarm.com

**Wagtail Farm** ★★★★
*Farmhouse*
Morpeth NE65 7PL
t  (01669) 620367
e  wagtail@tinyworld.co.uk
w  wagtailfarm.info

### RUSHYFORD
County Durham

**Garden House** ★★★★
*Bed & Breakfast*
Windlestone Park,
Windlestone, Ferryhill
DL17 0LZ
t  (01388) 720217
e  info@gardenhousedurham.
co.uk
w  gardenhousedurham.co.uk

### RYTON
Tyne and Wear

**A1 Hedgefield House** ★★★
*Guest Accommodation*
Stella Road, Blaydon-on-Tyne
NE21 4LR
t  (0191) 413 7373
e  david@hedgefieldhouse.co.
uk
w  hedgefieldhouse.co.uk

### SALTBURN-BY-THE-SEA
Tees Valley

**The Arches** ★★★★
*Guest House*
Low Farm, Ings Lane, Brotton,
Saltburn-by-the-Sea TS12 2QX
t  (01287) 677512
e  hotel@gorallyschool.co.uk
w  thearcheshotel.co.uk

**Diamond Guest House**
★★★★ *Guest House*
9 Diamond Street, Saltburn-by-
the-Sea TS12 1EB
t  (01287) 207049
e  diamondhouse9@ntlworld.
com
w  diamondguesthouse.co.uk

**The Rose Garden** ★★★★
*Bed & Breakfast*
20 Hilda Place, Saltburn-by-
the-Sea TS12 1BP
t  (01287) 622947
e  enquiries@therosegarden.
co.uk
w  therosegarden.co.uk

**Victorian Guest House**
★★★★ *Bed & Breakfast*
1 Oxford Street, Saltburn-by-
the-Sea TS12 1LG
t  (01287) 625237
e  sueandstew@saltburn-
accommodation.co.uk
w  saltbrun-accommodation.co.
uk

### SCREMERSTON
Northumberland

**Northumbrian Wigwam
Village** *Camping Barn*
Borewell Farm, Berwick-upon-
Tweed TD15 2RJ
t  (01289) 307107
e  info@
northumbrianwigwams.com
w  northumbrianwigwams.com

### SEAHOUSES
Northumberland

**Fairfield** ★★★
*Bed & Breakfast*
102 Main Street, Seahouses
NE68 7TP
t  (01665) 721736
e  jen2col@fairfield1.fsnet.co.
uk

**Gun Rock** ★★★
*Bed & Breakfast*
15 St Aidans, Seahouses
NE68 7SS
t  (01665) 721980
e  judy.oxley@unn.ac.uk

**Leeholme** ★★★
*Bed & Breakfast*
93 Main Street, Seahouses
NE68 7TS
t  (01665) 720230
e  lisaevans67@tiscali.co.uk

**Railston House** ★★★★
*Guest Accommodation*
**SILVER AWARD**
133 Main Street, North
Sunderland, Seahouses
NE68 7TS
t  (01665) 720912
e  twgrundy@btinternet.com
w  railstonhouse.com

**Rowena** ★★★
*Guest Accommodation*
99 Main Street, North
Sunderland, Seahouses
NE68 7TS
t  (01665) 721309

**Sharrow** ★★★★
*Guest Accommodation*
**SILVER AWARD**
98 Main Street, Seahouses
NE68 7TP
t  (01665) 721794
e  enquiry@sharrow-
seahouses.co.uk
w  sharrow-seahouses.co.uk

**Springwood** ★★★★
*Bed & Breakfast*
**SILVER AWARD**
South Lane, North Sunderland,
Seahouses NE68 7UL
t  (01665) 720320
e  marian@slatehall.freeserve.
co.uk
w  slatehallridingcentre.com

### SEATON CAREW
Tees Valley

**Altonlea Lodge Guest House**
★★★ *Guest House*
The Green, Hartlepool
TS25 1AT
t  (01429) 271289
e  enquiries@altonlea.co.uk
w  altonlea.co.uk

**Norton Hotel** ★★★
*Guest Accommodation*
1a The Green, Seaton Carew,
Hartlepool TS25 1AR
t  (01429) 268317
e  susanrusson@hotmail.com
w  nortonhotel.co.uk

**The Rothbury** ★★★
*Guest Accommodation*
9 The Cliff, Hartlepool
TS25 1AP
t  (01429) 288419
w  rothburyguesthouse.co.uk

### SEDGEFIELD
County Durham

**Todds House Farm** ★★★
*Farmhouse*
Sedgefield, Stockton-on-Tees
TS21 3EL
t  (01740) 620244
e  mail@toddshousefarm.co.uk
w  toddshousefarm.co.uk

### SHOTLEY BRIDGE
County Durham

**The Manor House Inn**
★★★★ *Inn* **SILVER AWARD**
Carterway Heads DH8 9LX
t  (01207) 255268
w  manorhouse-a68.co.uk/

### SIMONBURN
Northumberland

**Simonburn Guest House**
★★★ *Guest Accommodation*
1 The Mains, Simonburn,
Hexham NE48 3AW
t  (01434) 681321

### SKELTON
Tees Valley

**Westerland's Guest House**
★★ *Bed & Breakfast*
27 East Parade, Skelton-in-
Cleveland TS12 2BJ
t  (01287) 650690

**The Wharton Arms** ★★ *Inn*
133 High Street, Saltburn-by-
the-Sea TS12 2DY
t  (01287) 650618
e  p.cummings4@ntlworld.com

### SLAGGYFORD
Northumberland

**Yew Tree Chapel** ★★★★
*Guest Accommodation*
Slaggyford CA8 7NH
t  (01434) 382525
e  info@yewtreechapel.co.uk
w  yewtreechapel.co.uk

### SLALEY
Northumberland

**Flothers Farm** ★★★
*Bed & Breakfast*
Slaley, Hexham NE47 0BJ
t  (01434) 673240
e  flothers@ecosse.net
w  flothers.co.uk

**The Travellers Rest** ★★★★
*Inn* **SILVER AWARD**
Hexham NE46 1TT
t  (01434) 673231
e  info@1travellersrest.com
w  1travellersrest.com

## SOUTH CHARLTON
### Northumberland

**Middle Croft** ★★★★
*Bed & Breakfast*
4 Ditchburn Road, South
Charlton NE66 2JU
t (01665) 579212
e lorna@middlecroft.co.uk
w middlecroft.co.uk

## SOUTH SHIELDS
### Tyne and Wear

**Atlantis Guest House** ★★★
*Guest House*
55 Ocean Road, South Shields
NE33 2JJ
t (0191) 455 6070
e hani.gazia@btinternet.com
w atlantisguesthouse.com

**Beaches Guest House** ★★★
*Guest House*
81 Ocean Road, South Shields
NE33 2JJ
t (0191) 456 3262
e jdocchar@yahoo.co.uk
w smoothhound.co.uk

**Britannia Guesthouse**
★★★★ *Guest House*
54/56 Julian Avenue, South
Shields NE33 2EW
t (0191) 456 0896
e cbgh56@hotmail.com
w britanniaguesthouse.com

**Clifton Guest House** ★★★
*Guest House*
101 Ocean Road, South Shields
NE33 2JL
t (0191) 455 1965
e info@thecliftonguesthouse.
com
w thecliftonguesthouse.co.uk

**Forest Guest House** ★★★★
*Guest House*
117 Ocean Road, South Shields
NE33 2JL
t (0191) 454 8160
e enquiries@
forestguesthouse.com
w forestguesthouse.com

**The Magpies Nest** ★★★
*Guest House*
75 Ocean Road, South Shields
NE33 2JJ
t (0191) 455 2361
e christine.taylor3@btinternet.
com
w magpies-nest.co.uk

**Marina Guest House** ★★★
*Guest Accommodation*
32 Sea View Terrace, South
Shields NE33 2NW
t (0191) 456 1998
e austin@marina32.fsnet.co.uk

**Once Upon a Tyne** ★★
*Guest House*
55 Beach Road, South Shields
NE33 2QU
t (0191) 454 3119
e liveonce@once-tyne.co.uk
w once-tyne.co.uk

**Saraville Guest House** ★★★
*Guest House*
103 Ocean Road, South Shields
NE33 2JL
t (0191) 454 1169
e emma@saraville.freeserve.
co.uk
w geocities.com/saravillehouse

## SPENNYMOOR
### County Durham

**Highview Country House**
★★★★ *Guest House*
Kirk Merrington, Spennymoor
DL16 7JT
t (01388) 811006
e jayne@
highviewcountryhouse.co.uk
w highviewcountryhouse.com

## SPITTAL
### Northumberland

**Caroline House** ★★★
*Bed & Breakfast*
Main Street, Spittal TD15 1RD
t (01289) 307595
e carolinehouse@hotmail.com

**Marlborough House** ★★★★
*Bed & Breakfast*
133 Main Street, Spittal
TD15 1RP
t (01289) 305293
e seaside133@onetel.com

**The Roxburgh** ★★
*Guest House*
117 Main Street, Spittal,
Berwick-upon-Tweed
TD15 1RP
t (01289) 306266
e roxburghhotel@aol.com
w roxburghguesthouse.co.uk

## STANHOPE
### County Durham

**Horsley Hall** ★★★★★
*Guest Accommodation*
**SILVER AWARD**
Eastgate, Bishop Auckland
DL13 2LJ
t (01388) 517239
e hotel@horsleyhall.co.uk
w horsleyhall.co.uk

## STANLEY
### County Durham

**Bushblades Farm** ★★★
*Farmhouse*
Harperley, Stanley DH9 9UA
t (01207) 232722

**Oak Tree Inn** ★★ *Inn*
Front Street, Tantobie, Stanley
DH9 9RF
t (01207) 235445

**South Causey Inn** ★★★ *Inn*
Beamish Burn Road, Stanley
DH9 0LS
t (01207) 235555
e southcauseyhotel@
btconnect.com
w southcauseyhotel.co.uk

## STANNINGTON
### Northumberland

**Cheviot View Farmhouse
Bed & Breakfast** ★★★★
*Farmhouse* **SILVER AWARD**
North Shotton Farm, Morpeth
NE61 6EU
t (01670) 789231
e julie.phili@btconnect.com
w cheviotviewfarmhouse.co.uk

## STARTFORTH
### County Durham

**Startforth House Bed &
Breakfast** ★★★★
*Bed & Breakfast*
**SILVER AWARD**
Church Bank, Startforth,
Barnard Castle DL12 9AE
t (01833) 631126
e joan@startforthhouse.co.uk
w startforthhouse.co.uk

## STOCKSFIELD
### Northumberland

**Locksley, Bed & Breakfast**
★★★★ *Bed & Breakfast*
**SILVER AWARD**
45 Meadowfield Road,
Stocksfield NE43 7PY
t (01661) 844778
e josie@
locksleybedandbreakfast.co.uk
w locksleybedandbreakfast.co.
uk

**Old Ridley Hall** ★★★
*Guest Accommodation*
Stocksfield NE43 7RU
t (01661) 842816
e josephinealdridge@
oldridleyhall.force9.co.uk
w oldridley.co.uk

## STOCKTON-ON-TEES
### Tees Valley

**The Parkwood Hotel** ★★★
*Inn*
64-66 Darlington Road,
Stockton-on-Tees TS18 5ER
t (01642) 587933
e theparkwoodhotel@aol.co.
uk
w theparkwoodhotel.com

## SUNDERLAND
### Tyne and Wear

**Abingdon Guest House**
★★★ *Guest House*
5 St Georges Terrace,
Sunderland SR6 9LX
t (0191) 514 0689
e karen@
abingdonguesthouse.co.uk
w abingdonguesthouse.co.uk

**Acorn Guest House** ★★★
*Guest House*
10 Mowbray Road, Sunderland
SR2 8EN
t (0191) 514 2170
e theacornguesthouse@
hotmail.com

**April Guest House** ★★★★
*Guest House*
12 St Georges Terrace,
Sunderland SR6 9LX
t (0191) 565 9550
e hilda@dickinson2772.fslife.
co.uk
w aprilguesthouse.com

**Areldee Guest House** ★★★
*Guest House*
18 Roker Terrace, Sunderland
SR6 9NB
t (0191) 514 1971
e peter@areldeeguesthouse.
freeserve.co.uk
w abbeyandareldeeguest
houses.co.uk

**The Ashborne** ★★★
*Guest House*
7 St Georges Terrace,
Sunderland SR6 9LX
t (0191) 565 3997
e ashborneguesthouse@
btinternet.com
w ashborne-guesthouse.co.uk

**Balmoral Guest House** ★★★
*Guest House*
3 Roker Terrace, Sunderland
SR6 9NB
t (0191) 565 9217
e thebalmoral@supanet.com
w thebalmoral.supanet.com

**Braeside Holiday Guest
House** ★★★ *Guest House*
26 Western Hill, Sunderland
SR2 7PH
t (0191) 565 4801
e george@the20thhole.co.uk
w the20thhole.co.uk

**Brookside Bed and
Breakfast** ★★★ *Guest House*
6 Brookside Terrace,
Sunderland SR2 7RN
t (0191) 565 6739
e p.edgeworth@btopenworld.
com
w brooksideinsunderland.co.
uk

**The Chaise Guest House**
★★★ *Guest House*
5 Roker Terrace, Sunderland
SR6 9NB
t (0191) 565 9218
e thechaise@aol.com
w activereservations.com/
hotel/en/hotels-in-sunderland/
ah-116306.html

**Felicitations** ★★★
*Bed & Breakfast*
94 Ewesley Road, Sunderland
SR4 7RJ
t (0191) 522 0960
e felicitations_uk@talk21.com
w felicitations.biz

**Lemonfield Guesthouse**
★★★★ *Guest House*
Sea Lane, Sunderland SR6 8EE
t (0191) 529 3018
e gary@lemonfieldhotel.com
w lemonfieldhotel.com

**Mayfield Guesthouse** ★★★
*Guest House*
Sea Lane, Sunderland SR6 8EE
t (0191) 529 3345
e enquiries@
themayfieldguesthouse.co.uk
w themayfieldguesthouse.co.
uk

**St George's Guest House**
★★★ *Guest House*
6 St Georges Terrace,
Sunderland SR6 9LX
t (0191) 514 0689
e karen@
abingdonguesthouse.co.uk
w abingdonguesthouse.co.uk

**Terrace Guest House** ★★★
*Guest House*
2 Roker Terrace, Sunderland
SR6 9NB
t (0191) 565 0132
e thebalmoral@supanet.com
w thebalmoral.supanet.com

### SWARLAND
Northumberland

**East House** ★★★★
*Farmhouse*
East House Farm, Guyzance,
Morpeth NE65 9AH
t (01665) 513022
e easthousebandb@tesco.net

**Swarland Old Hall** ★★★★★
*Farmhouse* **GOLD AWARD**
Alnwick NE65 9HU
t (01670) 787642
e proctor@swarlandoldhall.
fsnet.co.uk
w swarlandoldhall.co.uk

### TARSET
Northumberland

**Snabdough Farm** ★★★★
*Farmhouse*
Tarset, Hexham NE48 1LB
t (01434) 240239

### THORNABY
Tees Valley

**Sporting Lodge Inn
Middlesbrough** ★★★★ *Inn*
Low Lane, Stainton Village,
Middlesbrough TS17 9LW
t (01642) 578100
e reservationsmiddlesbrough
@sportinglodgeinns.co.uk
w sportinglodgeinns.co.uk

### THROPTON
Northumberland

**Rockwood House** ★★★★
*Bed & Breakfast*
Morpeth NE65 7NA
t (01669) 620989
e chris@howey7618.
freeserve.co.uk

**Thropton Demesne
Farmhouse B&B** ★★★★★
*Guest House*
Thropton NE65 7LT
t (01669) 620196
e thropton_demesne@yahoo.
co.uk
w throptondemesne.co.uk

### TRIMDON GRANGE
County Durham

**Polemonium Plantery**
★★★★ *Bed & Breakfast*
28 Sunnyside Terrace, Trimdon
Grange, Trimdon Station
TS29 6HF
t (01429) 881529
e bandb@polemonium.co.uk
w polemonium.co.uk

### TWEEDMOUTH
Northumberland

**Ford Castle** ★★★
*Group Hostel*
Ford Village TD15 2PX
t (01890) 820257
e fordcastle@northumberland.
gov.uk

**Maggies** ★★★
*Bed & Breakfast*
41 Main Street, Tweedmouth
TD15 2AD
t (01289) 307215
e maggie@hefford41.
wanadoo.co.uk
w maggiesguesthouse.co.uk

**West Sunnyside House**
★★★★ *Bed & Breakfast*
**SILVER AWARD**
Tweedmouth, Berwick-upon-
Tweed TD15 2QH
t (01289) 305387
e kjamieson58@aol.com
w westsunnysidehouse.co.uk

### TYNEMOUTH
Tyne and Wear

**Martineau Guest House**
★★★★ *Guest House*
**SILVER AWARD**
57 Front Street, North Shields
NE30 4BX
t (0191) 296 0746
e martineau.house@
ukgateway.net
w martineau-house.co.uk

### WALL
Northumberland

**The Hadrian Wall Inn** ★★★
*Inn*
Wall, Hexham NE46 4EE
t (01434) 681232
e david.lindsay13@btinternet.
com
w hadrianhotel.com

**St Oswalds Farm** ★★
*Bed & Breakfast*
Wall, Hexham NE46 4HB
t (01434) 681307
e ereay@fish.co.uk

### WALLSEND
Tyne and Wear

**The Dorset Arms Hotel** ★★
*Inn*
Dorset Avenue, Wallsend
NE28 8DX
t (0191) 209 9754
e info@dorsetarmshotel.co.uk
w dorsetarmshotel.co.uk

### WARK
Northumberland

**The Black Bull** ★★★ *Inn*
Wark NE48 3LG
t (01434) 230239
w blackbullwark.co.uk

### WARKWORTH
Northumberland

**Beck 'N' Call** ★★★★
*Bed & Breakfast*
Birling West Cottage,
Warkworth NE65 0XS
t (01665) 711653
e beck-n-call@lineone.net
w beck-n-call.co.uk

**Fairfield House** ★★★★★
*Guest House* **SILVER AWARD**
16 Station Road, Warkworth
NE65 0XP
t (01665) 714455
e mandy@fairfield-
guesthouse.co.uk

**Magdalene House** ★★★★
*Bed & Breakfast*
Maudlin Farm, Morpeth
NE65 0TL
t (01665) 711539

**Morwick House Bed and
Breakfast** ★★★★
*Guest Accommodation*
Beal Bank, Warkworth
NE65 0TB
t (01665) 712101
e morwickhouse@tiscali.co.uk

**Number 28** ★★★★
*Bed & Breakfast*
28 Castle Street, Warkworth
NE65 0UL
t (01665) 712869
e johnross57@aol.com

**The Old Manse** ★★★★
*Bed & Breakfast*
20 The Butts, Morpeth
NE65 0SS
t (01665) 710850
e a.coulter1@btinternet.com
w oldmanse.info

**The Old Post Office Bed and
Breakfast** ★★★
*Bed & Breakfast*
32 Castle Street, Warkworth
NE65 0UL
t (01665) 711341
e warkwortholdpostoffice@
hotmail.com

**Roxbro House** ★★★★
*Bed & Breakfast*
**GOLD AWARD**
5 Castle Terrace, Warkworth
NE65 0UP
t (01665) 711416
e roxbrohouse@aol.com
w roxbrohouse.co.uk

**Tower House B&B** ★★★★
*Bed & Breakfast*
47 Castle Street, Warkworth
NE65 0UN
t (01665) 714375
e tower.1@tiscali.co.uk

**West View Lodge** ★★★★
*Bed & Breakfast*
35 Watershaugh Road,
Warkworth NE65 0TX
t (01665) 711532
e smgunn@aol.com

### WASHINGTON
Tyne and Wear

**Ye Olde Cop Shop** ★★★★
*Guest House*
6 The Green, Washington
NE38 7AB
t (0191) 416 5333
e yeoldecopshop@
btopenworld.com

### WATERHOUSES
County Durham

**Ivesley** ★★★★ *Farmhouse*
Waterhouses, Durham
DH7 9HB
t (0191) 373 4324
e ivesley@msn.com
w ridingholidays-ivesley.co.uk

### WEST WOODBURN
Northumberland

**Bay Horse Inn**
Rating Applied For
*Inn*
West Woodburn NE48 2RX
t (01434) 270218
e bayhorseinn@hotmail.co.uk

**Brandy Bank House** ★★★★
*Guest House*
West Woodburn NE48 2RA
t (01434) 270210
e brandybankhse@btinternet.
com
w brandybankhse.com

### WESTGATE-IN-WEARDALE
County Durham

**Lands Farm** ★★★★
*Farmhouse* **SILVER AWARD**
Westgate, Bishop Auckland
DL13 1SN
t (01388) 517210
e barbara@landsfarm.fsnet.co.
uk

### WHICKHAM
Tyne and Wear

**A1 Summerville Guest
House**
Rating Applied For
*Bed & Breakfast*
33 Orchard Road, Whickham
NE16 4TG
t (0191) 488 3388
e info@a1summerville.com
w a1summerville.com

**East Byermoor Guest House**
★★★★ *Guest House*
Fellside Road, Whickham,
Newcastle upon Tyne
NE16 5BD
t (01207) 272687
e stay@eastbyermoor.co.uk
w eastbyermoor.co.uk

### WHITFIELD
Northumberland

**The Elk's Head** ★★★★ *Inn*
Whitfield, Hexham NE47 8HD
t (01434) 345282
e elkshead@amserve.com
w elkshead.co.uk

### WHITLEY BAY
Tyne and Wear

**Avalon Hotel** ★★★
*Guest Accommodation*
26-28 South Parade, Whitley
Bay NE26 2RG
t (0191) 251 0080
e info@theavalon.co.uk
w theavalon.co.uk

**The Cara** ★★★ *Guest House*
9 The Links, Whitley Bay
NE26 1PS
t (0191) 253 0172
w thecara.co.uk

**Chedburgh Hotel** ★★★
*Guest Accommodation*
12 Esplanade, Whitley Bay
NE26 2AH
t (0191) 253 0415
e chedburghhotel@aol.com
w chedburgh-hotel.co.uk

**Lindsay Guest House**
★★★★ *Guest House*
50 Victoria Avenue, Whitley
Bay NE26 2BA
t (0191) 252 7341
e info@lindsayguesthouse.co.
uk
w lindsayguesthouse.co.uk

**Marlborough Hotel** ★★★★
*Guest Accommodation*
20-21 East Parade, Whitley Bay
NE26 1AP
t (0191) 251 3628
e reception@marlborough-
hotel.com
w marlborough-hotel.com

---

**York House** ★★★★
*Guest Accommodation*
106-110 Park Avenue, Whitley
Bay NE26 1DN
t (0191) 252 8313
e reservations@
yorkhousehotel.com
w yorkhousehotel.com

### WHITTINGHAM
Northumberland

**Callaly Cottage Bed and
Breakfast** ★★★★
*Bed & Breakfast*
Alnwick NE66 4TA
t (01665) 574684
e callaly@alnwick.org.uk
w callaly.alnwick.org.uk

### WITTON GILBERT
County Durham

**The Coach House** ★★★★
*Guest Accommodation*
Stobbilee House, Witton
Gilbert, Durham DH7 6TW
t (0191) 373 6132
e suzanne@cronin.org.uk
w stobbilee.com

### WITTON-LE-WEAR
County Durham

**Witton Camping Barn**
*Bunkhouse*
Witton Castle Estate, Witton-le-
Wear, Bishop Auckland
DL14 0DE
t (01388) 488230
w wittoncastle.co.uk

### WOOLER
Northumberland

**Firwood** ★★★★★
*Bed & Breakfast*
**GOLD AWARD**
Middleton Hall, Wooler
NE71 6RD
t (01668) 283699
e welcome@firwoodhouse.co.
uk
w firwoodhouse.co.uk

**The Old Manse** ★★★★★
*Guest Accommodation*
**GOLD AWARD**
New Road, Chatton NE66 5PU
t (01668) 215343
e chattonbb@aol.com
w oldmansechatton.co.uk

**Tallet Country Bed &
Breakfast** ★★★★★
*Bed & Breakfast*
**GOLD AWARD**
Tallet, Wooler NE71 6QN
t (01668) 283488
e stay@coldmartin.co.uk
w coldmartin.co.uk

**Tilldale House** ★★★★
*Guest Accommodation*
**SILVER AWARD**
34/40 High Street, Wooler
NE71 6BG
t (01668) 281450
e tilldalehouse@freezone.co.
uk
w tilldalehouse.co.uk

### WYLAM
Northumberland

**Wormald House** ★★★★
*Bed & Breakfast*
Main Road, Wylam NE41 8DN
t (01661) 852529
e jr.craven@tiscali.co.uk
w wormaldhouse.co.uk

## YORKSHIRE

### ACKLAM
North Yorkshire

**Trout Pond Barn** ★★★★
*Farmhouse*
Acklam Malton, Malton
YO17 9RG
t (01653) 658468
e troutpondbarn@aol.com
w troutpondbarn.co.uk

### ADDINGHAM
West Yorkshire

**The Crown Inn** ★★★★ *Inn*
136 Main Street, Addingham,
Ilkley LS29 0NS
t (01943) 830278
e mariawells350@tiscali.co.uk
w thecrowninnaddingham.co.
uk

**Lumb Beck Farmhouse Bed
and Breakfast** ★★★★
*Bed & Breakfast*
**SILVER AWARD**
Moorside Lane, Addingham
Moorside, Ilkley LS29 9JX
t (01943) 830400
e croft-lumbbeck@tiscali.co.uk

### AIRTON
North Yorkshire

**Lindon House** ★★★
*Bed & Breakfast*
Airton, Skipton BD23 4BE
t (01729) 830418

### AISLABY
North Yorkshire

**Blacksmiths Arms
Restaurant** ★★★
*Restaurant with Rooms*
Aislaby Nr Pickering, Pickering
YO18 8PE
t (01751) 472182
e blacksmiths@mail.com

### ALDBROUGH
East Riding of Yorkshire

**West Carlton Country Guest
House** ★★★★ *Guest House*
**GOLD AWARD**
Carlton Road, Aldbrough,
Hornsea HU11 4RB
t (01964) 527724
e caroline_maltas@hotmail.
com
w west-carlton.co.uk

### ALDFIELD
North Yorkshire

**Bay Tree Farm** ★★★★
*Farmhouse* **GOLD AWARD**
Aldfield, Ripon HG4 3BE
t (01765) 620394
e val@btfarm.entadsl.com
w baytreefarm.co.uk

### AMOTHERBY
North Yorkshire

**Cherry Tree B&B**
Rating Applied For
*Bed & Breakfast*
4 Cherry Tree Walk,
Amotherby, Malton YO17 6TR
t (01653) 690825
e cherrytreeamotherby@
googlemail.com
w 4cherrytree.googlepages.
com

### AMPLEFORTH
North Yorkshire

**Carr House Farm** ★★★
*Farmhouse*
Ampleforth, Helmsley
YO62 4ED
t (01347) 868526
e enquiries@carrhousefarm.
co.uk
w carrhousefarm.co.uk

**Daleside** ★★★★★
*Bed & Breakfast*
**GOLD AWARD**
East End, Ampleforth, York
YO62 4DA
t (01439) 788266
e dalesidepaul@hotmail.com

**Shallowdale House**
★★★★★
*Guest Accommodation*
**GOLD AWARD**
West End, Ampleforth,
Helmsley YO62 4DY
t (01439) 788325
e phillip@shallowdalehouse.
co.uk
w shallowdalehouse.co.uk

### APPLETON-LE-STREET
North Yorkshire

**Cresswell Arms** ★★★★ *Inn*
Malton YO17 6PG
t (01653) 693647

### ARKENGARTHDALE
North Yorkshire

**Chapel Farmhouse** ★★★★
*Bed & Breakfast*
Whaw, Arkengarthdale, Reeth
DL11 6RT
t (01748) 884062
e chapelfarmbb@aol.com

**The Charles Bathurst Inn**
★★★★ *Inn*
Arkengarthdale, Reeth
DL11 6EN
t (01748) 884567
e info@cbinn.co.uk
w cbinn.co.uk

### ARTHINGTON
West Yorkshire

**The Wharfedale Inn &
Restaurant** ★★★★ *Inn*
Arthington Lane, Otley
LS21 1NL
t (0113) 284 2921
e david@thewharfedale.co.uk
w thewharfedale.co.uk

### ASKRIGG
North Yorkshire

**Apothecary's House** ★★★★
*Guest Accommodation*
**SILVER AWARD**
Main Street, Askrigg, Leyburn
DL8 3HT
t (01969) 650626
e bookings@
apothecaryhouse.co.uk
w apothecaryhouse.co.uk

**Helm** ★★★★★
*Guest Accommodation*
**GOLD AWARD**
Askrigg, Leyburn DL8 3JF
t (01969) 650443
e holiday@helmyorkshire.com
w helmyorkshire.com

**Home Farm** ★★★ *Farmhouse*
Stalling Busk, Askrigg, Leyburn
DL8 3DH
t (01969) 650360

**Milton House** ★★★★
*Guest Accommodation*
Leyburn Road, Askrigg,
Leyburn DL8 3HJ
t (01969) 650217

**Stoney End** ★★★★★
*Guest Accommodation*
**SILVER AWARD**
Worton, Nr Askrigg, Leyburn
DL8 3ET
t (01969) 650652
e pmh@stoneyend.co.uk
w stoneyend.co.uk

**Thornsgill House** ★★★★
*Guest Accommodation*
Moor Road, Askrigg, Leyburn
DL8 3HH
t (01969) 650617
e stay@thornsgill.co.uk
w thornsgill.co.uk

## AUSTWICK
### North Yorkshire

**Pengarth** ★★★★
*Bed & Breakfast*
Austwick, Settle LA2 8BD
t (01524) 251073
e jishreid@austwick.org
w pengarthaustwick.co.uk

**Wood View** ★★★★
*Guest House*
The Green, Austwick LA2 8BB
t (01524) 251190
e woodview@austwick.org
w woodviewbandb.com

## AYSGARTH
### North Yorkshire

**Cornlee**
Rating Applied For
*Bed & Breakfast*
Aysgarth, Leyburn DL8 3AE
t (01969) 663779
e cornlee.aysgarth@
btinternet.com
w cornlee.co.uk

**Field House** ★★★★
*Bed & Breakfast*
Aysgarth, Aysgarth Falls
DL8 3AB
t (01969) 663556
e ros@fieldhouseaysgarth.co.
uk
w wensleydale.org

**Heather Cottage
Guesthouse** ★★★★
*Bed & Breakfast*
SILVER AWARD
Heather Cottage, Aysgarth,
Leyburn DL8 3AH
t (01969) 663229
e hcind@btinternet.com
w heathercottage.co.uk

**Stow House Hotel** ★★★★
*Guest Accommodation*
SILVER AWARD
Aysgarth Falls, Aysgarth
DL8 3SR
t (01969) 663635
e info@stowhouse.co.uk
w stowhouse.co.uk

**Thornton Lodge** ★★★★★
*Guest Accommodation*
Thornton Rust, Leyburn
DL8 3AP
t (01969) 663375
e enquiries@
thorntonlodgenorth yorkshire.
co.uk
w thorntonlodgenorth
yorkshire.co.uk

**Wensleydale Farmhouse**
★★★★
*Guest Accommodation*
Aysgarth, Aysgarth Falls
DL8 3SR
t (01969) 663534
e stay@wensleydale-
farmhouse.co.uk
w wensleydale-farmhouse.co.
uk

**Wheatsheaf Inn** ★★★ *Inn*
Main Street, Carperby, Nr
Aygarth DL8 4DF
t (01969) 663216
e wheatsheaf@paulmit.
globalnet.uk
w wheatsheafinwensleydale.
co.uk

**Yoredale House** ★★★★
*Guest House*
Aysgarth, Leyburn DL8 3AE
t (01969) 663423
e info@yoredalehouse.com
w yoredalehouse.com

## BAILDON
### West Yorkshire

**Ford House Farm Bed and
Breakfast** ★★★★
*Guest Accommodation*
Ford House, Buck Lane,
Bradford BD17 7RW
t (01274) 584489
e fordhousefarm@hotmail.
com
w fordhousefarmbedand
breakfast.co.uk

**Langbar House** ★★★★
*Bed & Breakfast*
8 Temple Rhydding Drive,
Bradford BD17 5PU
t (01274) 599900
e enquiry@langbarhouse.co.
uk
w langbarhouse.co.uk

## BAINBRIDGE
### North Yorkshire

**Hazel's Roost** ★★★
*Bed & Breakfast*
Bainbridge, Leyburn DL8 3EH
t (01969) 650400
e hazel@hazelsroost.co.uk

## BAINTON
### East Riding of Yorkshire

**Wolds Village Hotel** ★★★★
*Guest Accommodation*
SILVER AWARD
Manor Park, Driffield
YO25 9EF
t (01377) 217698
e sally@woldsvillage.co.uk
w woldsvillage.co.uk

## BARLOW
### North Yorkshire

**Berewick House** ★★★★
*Guest House* SILVER AWARD
Park Lane, Barlow YO8 8EW
t (01757) 617051
e wilson.guesthouse@
berewick.co.uk
w berewick.co.uk

## BARTON-LE-STREET
### North Yorkshire

**Barn Owl Cottage** ★★★
*Bed & Breakfast*
Barton-le-Street, Malton
YO17 6QB
t (01653) 628329

## BAWTRY
### South Yorkshire

**Granby Inn**
Rating Applied For
*Guest Accommodation*
52 High Street, Bawtry,
Doncaster DN10 6JA
t (01302) 710219
e info@granbyinn.co.uk
w granbyinn.co.uk

## BEDALE
### North Yorkshire

**The Castle Arms Inn** ★★★★
*Inn*
Bedale DL8 2TB
t (01677) 470270
e castlearms@aol.com
w thecastlearms.co.uk

**Elmfield House** ★★★★
*Guest House* SILVER AWARD
Bedale DL8 1NE
t (01677) 450558
e stay@elmfieldhouse.co.uk
w elmfieldhouse.co.uk

**Mill Close Farm** ★★★★★
*Farmhouse* GOLD AWARD
Patrick Brompton, Bedale
DL8 1JY
t (01677) 450257
e pat@millclose.co.uk
w millclose.co.uk

## BEEFORD
### East Riding of Yorkshire

**Pinderhill Farm Bed &
Breakfast** ★★★★ *Farmhouse*
Beverley Road, Beeford,
Driffield YO25 8AE
t (01262) 488645

## BELL BUSK
### North Yorkshire

**Barndale House** ★★★★
*Bed & Breakfast*
Otterburn, Skipton BD23 4DX
t (01729) 830906
e info@r-rugs.co.uk

**Tudor House** ★★★★
*Guest House*
Bell Busk, Skipton BD23 4DT
t (01729) 830301
e bellbusk.hitch@virgin.net
w tudorbellbusk.co.uk

## BEN RHYDDING
### West Yorkshire

**Denton View** ★★★
*Bed & Breakfast*
10 Manley Road, Ilkley
LS29 8QS
t (01943) 430373
e dentonview@blueyonder.
co.uk
w dentonview.co.uk

**Farmhouse at Wharfedale
Grange** ★★★★
*Bed & Breakfast*
Ben Rhydding Drive, Ben
Rhydding, Ilkley LS29 8BG
t (01943) 604204
e sandrine@pickard.co.uk
w pickard.co.uk

## BEVERLEY
### East Riding of Yorkshire

**6 St Mary's Close** ★★
*Bed & Breakfast*
St Mary's Close, Beverley
HU17 7AY
t (01482) 868837

**Beck View Guest House**
★★★★
*Guest Accommodation*
1a Blucher Lane, Beverley
HU17 0PT
t (01482) 882332
e beckviewhouse@aol.com
w beckviewguesthouse.co.uk

**Beverley Friary YHA** ★★★
*Hostel*
Friar's Lane, Beverley
HU17 0DF
t 0870 770 5696
e beverleyfriary@yha.org.uk
w yha.org.uk

**Burton Mount Country
House** ★★★★★
*Guest Accommodation*
GOLD AWARD
Malton Road, Cherry Burton
HU17 7RA
t (01964) 550541
e pg@burtonmount.co.uk
w burtonmount.co.uk

**Eastgate Guest House**
★★★★
*Guest Accommodation*
7 Eastgate, Beverley HU17 0DR
t (01482) 868464
e dodd@dodd.karoo.co.uk

**The Inn on the Bar** ★★★
*Guest House*
8 North Bar Without, Beverley
HU17 7AA
t (01482) 868137

**Market Cross Hotel** ★★★
*Guest Accommodation*
14 Lairgate, Beverley
HU17 8EE
t (01482) 882573

**Minster Garth Guest House**
★★★★ *Guest House*
2 Keldgate, Beverley
HU17 8HY
t (01482) 882402
e bawilson@aol.com
w beverleybedandbreakfast.
com/

**North Bar Lodge**
*Guest Accommodation*
28 North Bar Without, Beverley
HU17 7AB
t (01482) 881375

**Number One** ★★★
*Bed & Breakfast*
1 Woodlands, Beverley
HU17 8BT
t (01482) 862752
e neilandsarah@mansle.karoo.
co.uk
w beverley.net/
accommodation/numberone

**Potts of Flemingate Guest
Accommodation** ★★★
*Bed & Breakfast*
18 Flemingate, Beverley
HU17 0NR
t (01482) 862586
e pottsofflemingate@hotmail.
com
w pottsofflemingate.co.uk

**Rudstone Walk Country
B&B** ★★★★
*Guest Accommodation*
South Cave, Beverley
HU15 2AH
t (01430) 422230
e sylvia@rudstone-walk.co.uk
w rudstone-walk.co.uk

**St Mary's Terrace** ★★★
*Bed & Breakfast*
16 St Mary's Terrace, Beverley
HU17 8EH
t (01482) 860608

**Trinity Guest House** ★★★
*Guest House*
Trinity Lane, Beverley
HU17 0AR
t (01482) 869537
e info@trinity-house.net
w trinity-house.net

---

**Westfield Bed and Breakfast**
★★ *Bed & Breakfast*
13 Westfield Avenue, Beverley
HU17 7HA
t (01482) 860212

## BINGLEY
### West Yorkshire

**Five Rise Locks Hotel & Restaurant** ★★★★
*Guest Accommodation*
Beck Lane, Bingley BD16 4DD
t (01274) 565296
e info@five-rise-locks.co.uk
w five-rise-locks.co.uk

## BISHOP THORNTON
### North Yorkshire

**Dukes Place** ★★★★
*Guest Accommodation*
Harrogate HG3 3JY
t (01765) 620229
e enquiries@dukesplace-
courtyard.co.uk

## BISHOP WILTON
### East Riding of Yorkshire

**High Belthorpe** ★★★
*Farmhouse*
Thorny Lane, Bishop Wilton
YO42 1SB
t (01759) 368238
e meg@holidayswithdogs.com
w holidayswithdogs.com

## BLAXTON
### South Yorkshire

**Barnside Cottage** ★★★
*Bed & Breakfast*
Mosham Road, Blaxton,
Doncaster DN9 3AZ
t (01302) 770315
e info@barnside.net
w barnside.net

**Beech Grove Lodge** ★★★★
*Guest Accommodation*
SILVER AWARD
Station Road, Blaxton,
Doncaster DN9 3AF
t (01302) 771771
e enquiries@
beechgrovelodge.co.uk
w beechgrovelodge.co.uk

## BOLTBY
### North Yorkshire

**Willow Tree Cottage Bed and Breakfast** ★★★★
*Guest Accommodation*
Willow Tree Cottage Bed and
Breakfast, Boltby YO7 2DY
t (01845) 537406
e townsend.sce@virgin.net

## BOROUGHBRIDGE
### North Yorkshire

**Burton Grange** ★★★
*Farmhouse*
Helperby, Harrogate YO61 2RY
t (01423) 360825
e burton_grange@hotmail.
com

## BOSTON SPA
### West Yorkshire

**Crown Hotel** ★★★ *Inn*
128 High Street, Boston Spa,
Wetherby LS23 6BW
t (01937) 842608

**Four Gables** ★★★★★
*Guest Accommodation*
SILVER AWARD
Oaks Lane, Boston Spa,
Wetherby LS23 6DS
t (01937) 845592
e info@fourgables.co.uk
w fourgables.co.uk

## BRADFORD
### West Yorkshire

**Ivy Guest House** ★★
*Guest House*
3 Melbourne Place, Bradford
BD5 0HZ
t (01274) 727060
e enquiries@
ivyguesthousebradford.com
w ivyguesthousebradford.com

**New Beehive Inn** ★★
*Guest Accommodation*
171 Westgate, Bradford
BD1 3AA
t (01274) 721784
e newbeehiveinn.t21@
btinternet.com
w newbeehiveinn.co.uk

**Norland Guest House** ★★★
*Guest Accommodation*
695 Great Horton Road,
Bradford BD7 4DU
t (01274) 571698
e norlandhouse@hotmail.co.
uk
w norlandguesthouse.gbr.cc

**Woodlands Guest House**
★★★★
*Guest Accommodation*
2 The Grove, Shelf, Halifax
HX3 7PD
t (01274) 677533
e suewood45@hotmail.com
w woodlands-yorkshire.com

## BRIDGE HEWICK
### North Yorkshire

**The Black A Moor Hotel**
★★★★ *Inn*
Boroughbridge Road, Bridge
Hewick, Ripon HG4 5AA
t (01765) 603511

## BRIDLINGTON
### East Riding of Yorkshire

**Ashford House** ★★★
*Guest House*
94 Trinity Road, Bridlington
YO15 2HF
t (01262) 675849
e ashfordhousebrid@tiscali.co.
uk

**Balmoral House** ★★★★
*Guest Accommodation*
21 Marshall Avenue,
Bridlington YO15 2DT
t (01262) 676678
e brian@balmoral-house.com
w balmoral-house.com

**Bay Court Hotel** ★★★★
*Guest Accommodation*
35a Sands Lane, Bridlington
YO15 2JG
t (01262) 676288
e bay.court@virgin.net
w baycourt.co.uk

**The Bay Ridge Hotel** ★★★
*Guest Accommodation*
11-13 Summerfield Road,
Bridlington YO15 3LF
t (01262) 673425
e bayridgehotel@aol.com
w bayridgehotel.co.uk

**Blantyre House** ★★★
*Guest Accommodation*
21 Pembroke Terrace,
Bridlington YO15 3BX
t (01262) 400660
e info@blantyre-hotel-
bridlington.co.uk

**Bluebell Guest House**
Rating Applied For
*Guest Accommodation*
3 St Annes Road, Bridlington
YO15 2JB
t (01262) 675163
e pam@mybluebell.net
w mybluebell.co.uk

**Bosville Arms Country Inn & Restaurant** ★★★ *Inn*
Main Street, Rudston
YO25 4UB
t (01262) 420259
e bosvillearms@aol.com

**Brentwood House Hotel**
★★★ *Guest House*
42 Princess Street, Bridlington
YO15 2RB
t (01262) 608739
e info@brentwoodhouse.co.
uk
w brentwoodhouse.co.uk

**Broadfield Hotel** ★★★
*Guest Accommodation*
18 Shaftesbury Road,
Bridlington YO15 3NW
t (01262) 677379
e broadfieldhotel@talktalk.net
w broadfieldbridlington.co.uk

**Charleston Guest House**
★★★ *Guest House*
12 Vernon Road, Bridlington
YO15 2HQ
t (01262) 676228
e charlestongh@aol.com

**Chatley Court Hotel** ★★★
*Guest Accommodation*
54-56 Windsor Crescent,
Bridlington YO15 3JA
t (01262) 674666
e chatlycourt@aol.com
w chatleycourt.co.uk

**The Crescent Hotel** ★★★
*Guest House*
12 The Crescent, Bridlington
YO15 2NX
t (01262) 401015

**Doriam Hotel** ★★★
*Guest Accommodation*
35 Windsor Crescent,
Bridlington YO15 3HX
t (01262) 672513

**Dulverton Court Hotel** ★★★
*Guest Accommodation*
17 Victoria Road, Bridlington
YO15 2BW
t (01262) 672600
e joangbrid@aol.com

**Edelweiss**
Rating Applied For
*Guest Accommodation*
86/88 Windsor Crescent,
Bridlington YO15 3JA
t (01262) 673822
e edelweiss1st@aol.com
w edelweiss-bridlington.co.uk

**The Glen Alan Hotel** ★★★★
*Guest House*
21 Flamborough Road,
Bridlington YO15 2HU
t (01262) 674650
e tonymaddison@aol.com

**The Grantlea Guest House**
★★★ *Guest House*
2 South Street, Bridlington
YO15 3BY
t (01262) 400190
e modey@toucansurf.com
w grantlea-guest-house.co.uk

**Harmony Guesthouse** ★★★
*Guest House*
38 Marshall Avenue,
Bridlington YO15 2DS
t (01262) 603867
e enquiries@
harmonyguesthouse.co.uk
w harmonyguesthouse.co.uk

**Heathfield Guest House** ◆◆◆
*Guest Accommodation*
34 Tennyson Avenue,
Bridlington YO15 2EP
t (01262) 672594
e chris.jacky@tiscali.co.uk

**Ivanhoe Guest House** ★★★
*Guest House*
63 Cardigan Road, Bridlington
YO15 3JS
t (01262) 675983 &
(01262) 675983
w bridlington-hotels.co.uk

**The Jasmine Guest House**
★★★ *Guest House*
27-29 Richmond Street,
Bridlington YO15 3DL
t (01262) 676608
e jasmineguesthouse@
btinternet.com
w jasmineguesthouse.com

**Lincoln House**
Rating Applied For
*Guest Accommodation*
Wellington Road, Bridlington
YO15 2AX
t (01262) 679595
e lincolnhousebrid@fsmail.net
w lincolnhousebridlington.co.
uk

**The London** ★★★★
*Guest Accommodation*
1 Royal Crescent, York Road,
Bridlington YO15 2PF
t (01262) 675377
e londonhotelbrid@yahoo.co.
uk

**Longcroft Hotel** ★★★★
*Guest House*
100 Trinity Road, Bridlington
YO15 2HF
t (01262) 672180
e longcroft_hotel@hotmail.
com

**The Marina** ★★★★
*Guest House*
8 Summerfield Road,
Bridlington YO15 3LF
t (01262) 677138
e themarina8@hotmail.com
w themarina-bridlington.co.uk

**Maryland Bed & Breakfast
★★★★**
*Guest Accommodation*
66 Wellington Road,
Bridlington YO15 2AZ
t (01262) 671088
e ann@maryland.me.uk
w maryland.me.uk

**The Mayville Guest House**
★★★ *Guest Accommodation*
74 Marshall Avenue,
Bridlington YO15 2DS
t (01262) 674420
e mayville@fedaye.fsnet.co.uk
w mayvilleguesthouse.co.uk

**Mont Millais ★★★**
*Guest Accommodation*
64 Trinity Road, Bridlington
YO15 2HF
t (01262) 601890

**The Mount Hotel ★★★★**
*Guest Accommodation*
2 Roundhay Road, Bridlington
YO15 3JY
t (01262) 672306

**Number 7 Guest House**
★★★★ *Bed & Breakfast*
7 South Street, Bridlington
YO15 3BY
t (01262) 601249
e number7.whitbytown@
btinternet.com.
w numbersevenguesthouse.
com

**Park View Licensed Family
Hotel ★★★★**
*Guest Accommodation*
9-11 Tennyson Avenue,
Bridlington YO15 2EU
t (01262) 672140

**Promenade Hotel ★★★**
*Guest Accommodation*
121 Promenade, Bridlington
YO15 2QN
t (01262) 602949
e m-abbott_@tiscali.co.uk
w thepromenadehotel.co.uk

**Providence Place ★★★★**
*Guest Accommodation*
11 North View Terrace,
Bridlington YO15 2QP
t (01262) 603840

**Rags Restaurant & Hotel
★★★★**
*Restaurant with Rooms*
South Pier, Bridlington
YO15 3AN
t (01262) 400355
e ragshotel@tesco.net
w ragshotel.co.uk

**Ransdale Hotel ★★★**
*Guest Accommodation*
30 Flamborough Road,
Bridlington YO15 2JQ
t (01262) 674334
e ransdalehotel@fsmail.net
w ransdalehotel.co.uk

**Ridings Guest House ★★★**
*Guest House*
100 Windsor Crescent,
Bridlington YO15 3JA
t (01262) 671744
e susan.potter7@tesco.net
w ridingsguesthouse.co.uk

**Rivendell Hotel ★★★★**
*Guest Accommodation*
19 Sands Lane, Bridlington
YO15 2JG
t (01262) 679189
e rivendellhoteld@hotmail.co.
uk
w rivendellhotel.net

**Rosebery House ★★★★**
*Guest Accommodation*
1 Belle Vue, Tennsyon Ave,
Bridlington YO15 2ET
t (01262) 670336
e zexuc@btinternet.com

**Sandringham House Hotel**
★★★ *Guest House*
11 The Crescent, Bridlington
YO15 2NX
t (01262) 672064
e sandringham-hotel@talk21.
com

**Sandsend Hotel ★★★**
*Guest House*
8 Sands Lane, Bridlington
YO15 2JE
t (01262) 673265

**Sea View House ★★★★**
*Guest House*
54 South Marine Drive,
Bridlington YO15 3JN
t (01262) 677775
e judybebber@hotmail.com

**The Seacourt ★★★★**
*Guest Accommodation*
**SILVER AWARD**
76 South Marine Drive,
Bridlington YO15 3NS
t (01262) 400872
e seacourt.hotel@tiscali.co.uk
w seacourthotel.co.uk

**Southdowne Hotel ★★★★**
*Guest House*
78 South Marine Drive,
Bridlington YO15 3NS
t (01262) 673270

**Spinnaker House Hotel
★★★★**
*Guest Accommodation*
19 Pembroke Terrace,
Bridlington YO15 3BX
t (01262) 678440

**Stonmar Guest House ★★★**
*Guest House*
15 Flamborough Road,
Bridlington YO15 2HU
t (01262) 674580
e info@stonmar.co.uk
w stonmar.co.uk

**Trinity Hotel ★★★**
*Guest Accommodation*
9 Trinity Road, Bridlington
YO15 2EZ
t (01262) 670444
e davcazz@aol.com
w trinityhotel.co.uk

**Vernon Villa ★★★★**
*Guest Accommodation*
2 Vernon Road, Bridlington
YO15 2HQ
t (01262) 670661
e vernonvillaguesthouse@
yahoo.co.uk

**Victoria Hotel ★★★**
*Guest Accommodation*
25/27 Victoria Road,
Bridlington YO15 2AT
t (01262) 673871
e contact@
victoriahotelbridlington.co.uk
w victoriahotelbridlington.co.
uk

**The Waverley ★★★**
*Guest House*
105 Cardigan Road, Bridlington
YO15 3LP
t (01262) 671040
e info@waverley-bridlington.
co.uk
w waverley-bridlington.co.uk

**White Lodge Guest House**
★★★ *Guest Accommodation*
9 Neptune Terrace, Neptune
Street, Bridlington YO15 3DE
t (01262) 670903
e caitlyn.greene@btinternet.
com
w whitelodgeguesthouse.co.uk

**Winston House Hotel ★★★**
*Guest Accommodation*
5/6 South Street, Bridlington
YO15 3BY
t (01262) 670216
e saraandray@tiscali.co.uk

BROMPTON-ON-SWALE
North Yorkshire

**Brompton-on-Swale
Camping Barn** *Bunkhouse*
Village Farm, 24 Richmond
Road, Richmond DL10 7HE
t (01748) 818326
w yha.org.uk

BUCKDEN
North Yorkshire

**Low Raisgill ★★★★**
*Bed & Breakfast*
Buckden, Skipton BD23 5JQ
t (01756) 760351

**Nethergill Farm**
Rating Applied For
*Bed & Breakfast*
Skipton BD23 5JS
t (01756) 761126
e fiona.clark@nethergill.co.uk
w nethergill.co.uk

**Redmire Farm ★★★★**
*Farmhouse* **SILVER AWARD**
Upper Wharfedale, Buckden,
Settle BD23 5JD
t (01756) 760253
e visit@redmirefarm.co.uk
w redmirefarm.co.uk

**The White Lion Inn ★★★**
*Inn*
Cray, Skipton BD23 5JB
t (01756) 760262
e admin@whitelioncray.com
w whitelioncray.com

BULMER
North Yorkshire

**Grange Farm ★★★★**
*Farmhouse*
Castle Howard, Bulmer, York
YO60 7BN
t (01653) 618376
e grangefarm3@yahoo.co.uk
w grangefarmbulmer.co.uk

BURNT YATES
North Yorkshire

**High Winsley Farm ★★★★**
*Farmhouse*
Brimham Rocks Road, Burnt
Yates, Pateley Bridge HG3 3EP
t (01423) 770376
e highwinsley@aol.com

BURTON-IN-LONSDALE
North Yorkshire

**River Cottage ★★★★**
*Bed & Breakfast*
(2) Brookland, Settle LA6 3ND
t (01524) 264988
e francati@btinternet.com
w rivercottagebandb.tripod.
com

BURYTHORPE
North Yorkshire

**Low Penhowe ★★★★★**
*Guest Accommodation*
**GOLD AWARD**
Burythorpe, Malton YO17 9LU
t (01653) 658336
e lowpenhowe@btinternet.
com
w bedandbreakfastyorkshire.
co.uk

CARLTON
North Yorkshire

**Abbots Thorn ★★★★**
*Guest Accommodation*
Carlton in Coverdale, Leyburn
DL8 4AY
t (01969) 640620
e patricia.lashmar@virgin.net
w abbotsthorn.co.uk

**Middleham House ★★★★**
*Bed & Breakfast*
Carlton, Leyburn DL8 4BB
t (01969) 640645
e info@middlehamhouse.co.
uk
w middlehamhouse.co.uk

CARLTON
West Yorkshire

**Foxwood ★★★★**
*Guest Accommodation*
Carr Lane, Carlton, Wakefield
WF3 3RT
t (0113) 282 4786

CARLTON HUSTHWAITE
North Yorkshire

**Thatched Cottage, Guest
Suite ★★★★**
*Guest Accommodation*
**SILVER AWARD**
Carlton Husthwaite, Thirsk
YO7 2BJ
t (01845) 501022
e john@pheasant1.wanadoo.
co.uk

CASTLE HOWARD
North Yorkshire

**Ganthorpe Gate Farm ★★★**
*Farmhouse*
Ganthorpe, York YO60 6QD
t (01653) 648269
e millgate001@msn.com
w ganthorpegatefarm.co.uk

**Lowry's Restaurant and Bed
& Breakfast ★★★**
*Guest House*
Malton Road, Slingsby, Malton
YO62 4AF
t (01653) 628417
e dgwilliams@onetel.com

## CASTLETON
### North Yorkshire

**The Eskdale Inn ★★★**
*Guest Accommodation*
Castleton, Whitby YO21 2EU
t (01287) 660234
e esk_dale6-9@tiscali.co.uk
w eskdaleinn.co.uk

**Greystones ★★★**
*Guest Accommodation*
High Street, Castleton, Whitby
YO21 2DA
t (01287) 660744
e thewedgwoods@aol.com

## CATTERICK
### North Yorkshire

**Rose Cottage Guest House**
**★★★ Guest Accommodation**
26 High Street, Catterick,
Richmond DL10 7LJ
t (01748) 811164

## CATTERICK BRIDGE
### North Yorkshire

**St Giles Farm ★★★★**
*Farmhouse*
Catterick Bridge, Richmond
DL10 7PH
t (01748) 811372
e janethor@aol.co.uk

## CHAPEL ALLERTON
### West Yorkshire

**Green House ★★★**
*Bed & Breakfast*
5 Bank View Terrace, Leeds
LS7 2EX
t (0113) 268 1380

## CHAPEL LE DALE
### North Yorkshire

**Old School Bunkhouse**
*Bunkhouse*
Carnforth LA6 3AR
t (01524) 242327
w oldschoolbunkhouse.co.uk

## CLIFTON
### North Yorkshire

**Avenue Guest House ★★**
*Guest Accommodation*
6 The Avenue, York YO30 6AS
t (01904) 620575
e allen@avenuegh.fsnet.co.uk
w avenuegh.fsnet.co.uk

## CLOUGHTON
### North Yorkshire

**Blacksmiths Arms ★★★ Inn**
High Street, Cloughton,
Scarborough YO13 0AE
t (01723) 870244

**Cober Hill ★★★**
*Guest Accommodation*
Newlands Road, Cloughton,
Scarborough YO13 0AR
t (01723) 870310
e enquiries@coberhill.co.uk
w coberhill.co.uk

## COLLINGHAM
### West Yorkshire

**Tilworth**
Rating Applied For
*Guest Accommodation*
2 Green Lane, Collingham,
Wetherby LS22 5DE
t (01937) 572254
e joan@tilworth.fsnet.co.uk

## COTTINGHAM
### East Riding of Yorkshire

**Newholme Guest House**
**★★★ Guest House**
47 Thwaite Street, Cottingham,
Hull HU16 4QX
t (01482) 849879
e lorraine.headley@hotmail.
com

## COXWOLD
### North Yorkshire

**Newburgh House ★★★★★★**
*Bed & Breakfast*
Newburgh, Coxwold
YO61 4AS
t (01347) 868177
e info@newburghhouse.com
w newburghhouse.com

## CRAYKE
### North Yorkshire

**The Durham Ox ★★★★**
*Restaurant with Rooms*
West Way, Crayke YO61 4TE
t (01347) 821506
e enquiries@thedurhamox.
com
w thedurhamox.com

**Hazelwood Farm Bed &**
**Breakfast ★★★★ Farmhouse**
**SILVER AWARD**
Hazelwood Farm, York
YO61 4TQ
t (01347) 824654

**The Hermitage ★★★**
*Bed & Breakfast*
Mill Lane, Crayke YO61 4TD
t (01347) 821635

## CROFTON
### West Yorkshire

**Redbeck Motel Ltd ★★**
*Guest Accommodation*
Doncaster Road, Crofton,
Wakefield WF4 1RR
t (01924) 862427
e inquiry@redbeckmotel.co.uk
w redbeckmotel.co.uk

## CROPTON
### North Yorkshire

**High Farm Bed & Breakfast**
**★★★★ Farmhouse**
**SILVER AWARD**
High Farm, Cropton, Pickering
YO18 8HL
t (01751) 417461
e highfarmcropton@aol.com
w hhml.com/bb/
highfarmcropton.htm

**New Inn and Cropton**
**Brewery ★★★ Inn**
Cropton, Pickering YO18 8HH
t (01751) 417330
e info@croptonbrewery.co.uk
w croptonbrewery.com

## CUNDALL
### North Yorkshire

**Cundall Lodge Farm**
**★★★★★ Farmhouse**
**SILVER AWARD**
Cundall YO61 2RN
t (01423) 360203
e info@lodgefarmbb.co.uk
w lodgefarmbb.co.uk

## DACRE BANKS
### North Yorkshire

**Dalriada ★★★**
*Bed & Breakfast*
Cabin Lane, Dacre Banks,
Pateley Bridge HG3 4EE
t (01423) 780512

**Gate Eel Farm ★★★★**
*Guest House*
Dacre Banks, Pateley Bridge
HG3 4ED
t (01423) 781707
e diandpeterdriver@aol.co

**The Royal Oak Inn ★★★★**
*Inn*
Oak Lane, Dacre Banks,
Harrogate HG3 4EN
t (01423) 780200
e steve@the-royaloak-dacre.
co.uk
w the-royaloak-dacre.co.uk

## DALBY
### North Yorkshire

**South Moor Farm ★★★★**
*Farmhouse*
Dalby Forest Drive,
Scarborough YO13 0LW
t (01751) 460285
e vb@southmoorfarm.co.uk
w southmoorfarm.co.uk

## DALTON
### North Yorkshire

**Dunsa Manor ★★★★**
*Guest Accommodation*
Dalton, Richmond DL11 7HE
t 07817 028237
e shaheenburnett@btinternet.
com
w dunsamanor.com

## DANBY
### North Yorkshire

**Botton Grove Farm ★★★**
*Farmhouse*
Danby Head, Danby
YO21 2NH
t (01287) 660284
e judytait@bottongrove.
freeserve.co.uk
w http://mysite.wanadoo-
members.co.uk/botton_grove_
farm/

**Crossley Gate Farm House**
**★★★★ Bed & Breakfast**
**SILVER AWARD**
Fryup, Danby, Whitby
YO21 2NR
t (01287) 660165
e bottomley@
crossleygatefarm.fsnet.co.uk
w http://crossley-gate-farm.
mysite.wanadoo-members.co.
uk

**Duke of Wellington Inn**
**★★★★ Inn**
West Lane, Danby YO21 2LY
t (01287) 660351
e landlord@dukeofwellington.
freeserve.co.uk
w danby-dukeofwellington.co.
uk

## The Fox & Hounds Inn
**★★★★ Inn**
45 Brook Lane, Ainthorpe,
Whitby YO21 2LD
t (01287) 660218
e info@foxandhounds-
ainthorpe.com
w foxandhounds-ainthorpe.
com

**Great Fryupdale**
**Outdoorcentre**
Rating Applied For
*Hostel*
Danby, Whitby YO21 2NP
t (01947) 893333
e enquiries@eastbarnby.co.uk
w eastbarnby.co.uk

**Rowantree Farm ★★★★**
*Farmhouse*
Fryup Road, Ainthorpe, Whitby
YO21 2LE
t (01287) 660396
e krbsatindall@aol.com
w rowantreefarm.co.uk

**Sycamore House ★★★★**
*Bed & Breakfast*
Danby Head, Danby
YO21 2NN
t (01287) 660125
e sycamore.danby@
btinternet.com
w smoothhound.co.uk/hotels/
sycamore1.html

## DEIGHTON
### North Yorkshire

**Grimston House ★★★★**
*Guest Accommodation*
Deighton, York YO19 6HB
t (01904) 728328
e pat_wright@btinternet.com
w grimstonhouse.com

**Rush Farm ★★★**
*Guest Accommodation*
York Road, York YO19 6HQ
t (01904) 728459
e david@rushfarm.co.uk
w rushfarm.fsnet.co.uk

## DINNINGTON
### South Yorkshire

**Throapham House Bed &**
**Breakfast ★★★★★**
*Guest Accommodation*
**GOLD AWARD**
Throapham House, Oldcotes
Road, Sheffield S25 2QS
t (01909) 562208
e enquiries@throapham-
house.co.uk
w throapham-house.co.uk

## DONCASTER
### South Yorkshire

**The Angel Inn & Lodge**
**★★★ Inn**
Dame Lane, Misson, Doncaster
DN10 6EB
t (01302) 710886
e stevedaytime@aol.com

**Caribbean Hotel**
Rating Applied For
*Guest Accommodation*
Thorne Road, Doncaster
DN1 2ES
t (01302) 364605
e dene@caribbean-hotel.co.uk
w caribbean-hotel.co.uk

**Rock Farm ★★★** *Farmhouse*
Hooton Pagnell, Doncaster
DN5 7BT
**t** (01977) 642200 &
07785 916186
**e** info@rockfarm.info
**w** rockfarm.info

**Wheatley Hotel**
Rating Applied For
*Guest Accommodation*
Thorne Road, Doncaster
DN2 5DR
**t** (01302) 364092

**Windsor House ★★★★**
*Guest Accommodation*
7 Windsor Road, Town Moor,
Doncaster DN2 5BS
**t** (01302) 768768
**e** ianmgell@aol.com
**w** ianmgell.tripod.com

**Woodborough Hotel**
Rating Applied For
*Guest Accommodation*
2 Belle-Vue Avenue, Belle-Vue,
Doncaster DN4 5DX
**t** (01302) 361381
**e** mail@woodboroughhotel.co.
uk
**w** woodboroughhotel.co.uk

DOWNHOLME
North Yorkshire

**Walburn Hall ★★★★**
*Farmhouse* **SILVER AWARD**
Richmond DL11 6AF
**t** (01748) 822152
**e** walburnhall@farmersweekly.
net

DRIFFIELD
East Riding of Yorkshire

**Blacksmiths Cottage
Country Guest House ★★★**
*Guest House*
Driffield Road, Kilham, Driffield
YO25 4SN
**t** (01262) 420624
**e** maxatblacksmiths@ukonline.
co.uk
**w** smoothhound.co.uk/hotels/
blacksmithscottage.html

**Kelleythorpe Farm ★★★**
*Farmhouse*
Kelleythorpe, Driffield
YO25 9DW
**t** (01377) 252297
**e** hoppertiffy@hotmail.com

DRINGHOUSES
North Yorkshire

**The Racecourse Centre
★★★★** *Group Hostel*
Tadcaster Road, Dringhouses
YO24 1QG
**t** (01904) 636553
**e** info@racecoursecentre.co.
uk
**w** racecoursecentre.co.uk

DUNGWORTH
South Yorkshire

**Rickett Field Guest
Accommodation ★★★★**
*Guest Accommodation*
Dungworth, Sidling Hollow,
Sheffield S6 6HA
**t** (0114) 285 1218
**w** rickettfieldfarm.co.uk

**The Royal Hotel ★★★★** *Inn*
Main Road, Dungworth,
Bradfield, Sheffield S6 6HF
**t** (0114) 285 1213
**e** reception@royalhotel-
dungworth.co.uk
**w** royalhotel-dungworth.co.uk

DUNSWELL
East Riding of Yorkshire

**The Ship Inn ★★★** *Inn*
Beverley High Road, Dunswell,
Hull HU6 0AJ
**t** (01482) 859160
**w** theshipsquarters.co.uk

EASINGWOLD
North Yorkshire

**Garth Hotel ★★★**
*Restaurant with Rooms*
York Road, York YO61 3PG
**t** (01347) 822988

**Thornton Lodge Farm
★★★★** *Farmhouse*
Thornton Hill, Easingwold
YO61 3QA
**t** (01347) 821306
**e** sue.raper@btopenworld.
com
**w** thorntonlodgefarm.co.uk

EBBERSTON
North Yorkshire

**The Foxholm ★★★** *Inn*
Main Street, Ebberston
YO13 9NJ
**t** (01723) 859550
**e** kay@foxholm.co.uk
**w** foxholm.freeserve.co.uk

**Studley House ★★★★**
*Bed & Breakfast*
**SILVER AWARD**
67 Main Street, Ebberston,
Pickering YO13 9NR
**t** (01723) 859285
**e** brenda@yorkshireancestors.
com
**w** studley-house.co.uk

EDENTHORPE
South Yorkshire

**Beverley Inn ★★★**
*Guest Accommodation*
117 Thorne Road, Edenthorpe,
Doncaster DN3 2JE
**t** (01302) 882724

EGTON BRIDGE
North Yorkshire

**Broom House ★★★★**
*Guest House* **SILVER AWARD**
Egton Bridge, Whitby
YO21 1XD
**t** (01947) 895279
**e** mw@broom-house.co.uk
**w** egton-bridge.co.uk

ELLINGSTRING
North Yorkshire

**Hollybreen ★★★**
*Guest Accommodation*
Holybreen, Ellingstring, Ripon
HG4 4PW
**t** (01677) 460216
**e** dales.accommodation@
virgin.net
**w** dalesaccommodation.org.uk

EMBSAY
North Yorkshire

**Bondcroft Farm ★★★★**
*Farmhouse*
Skipton BD23 6SF
**t** (01756) 793371
**e** bondcroftfarm@
bondcroftfarm.yorks.net
**w** bondcroft.yorks.net

FACEBY
North Yorkshire

**Four Wynds Bed and
Breakfast ★★★**
*Bed & Breakfast*
Faceby, Middlesbrough
TS9 7BZ
**t** (01642) 701315

FILEY
North Yorkshire

**Athol House ★★★★**
*Guest Accommodation*
67 West Avenue, Filey
YO14 9AX
**t** (01723) 515189
**e** atholhouse@tiscali.co.uk
**w** athol-guesthouse.co.uk

**Binton Guest House ★★★★**
*Guest House*
25 West Avenue, Filey
YO14 9AX
**t** (01723) 513753
**e** info@thislldo.co.uk

**Cherries ★★★★**
*Guest House*
59 West Avenue, Filey
YO14 9AX
**t** (01723) 513299
**e** cherriesfiley@talktalk.net

**The Edwardian Guest House
★★★★**
*Guest Accommodation*
2 Brooklands, Filey YO14 9BA
**t** (01723) 514557

**The Forge ★★★★**
*Guest Accommodation*
23 Rutland Street, Filey
YO14 9JA
**t** (01723) 512379
**e** theforge2@btinternet.com
**w** theforgefiley.com

**Gables Guest House ★★★★**
*Guest House*
Rutland Street, Filey YO14 9JB
**t** (01723) 514755
**e** thegablesfiley@aol.com
**w** thegablesfiley.co.uk

**Sea Brink Hotel ◆◆◆**
*Guest Accommodation*
3 The Beach, Filey YO14 9LA
**t** (01723) 513257
**e** anntindall@aol.com
**w** seabrinkhotel.co.uk

**The Seafield ★★★★**
*Guest Accommodation*
Rutland Street, Filey YO14 9JA
**t** (01723) 513715
**e** seafieldhotel@btopenworld.
com
**w** seafieldguesthouse.co.uk

FINGHALL
North Yorkshire

**Queens Head Bed &
Breakfast ★★★★** *Inn*
West Moor Lane, Finghall,
Leyburn DL8 5ND
**t** (01677) 450259
**e** info@queenshead-finghall.
co.uk
**w** queenshead-finghall.co.uk

FLAXBY
North Yorkshire

**Herons Keep B&B ★★**
*Bed & Breakfast*
Shortsill Lane, Flaxby,
Knaresborough HG5 0RT
**t** (01423) 860353

FRYUP
North Yorkshire

**Crossley Side Farm ★★★★**
*Farmhouse*
Whitby YO21 2NR
**t** (01287) 660313

**Furnace Farm ★★★★**
*Farmhouse*
Fryup, Whitby YO21 2AP
**t** (01947) 897271
**e** furnacefarm@hotmail.com

FULFORD
North Yorkshire

**Pinfold Cottage ★★★★**
*Guest House*
145-147 Main Street, York
YO10 4PR
**t** (01904) 634683
**e** pinfoldcottage@aol.com
**w** pinfoldcottageyork.co.uk

FYLINGDALES
North Yorkshire

**The Flask Cafe & Travel
Lodge ★★★★**
*Guest Accommodation*
Fylingdales, Whitby YO22 4QH
**t** (01947) 880692

FYLINGTHORPE
North Yorkshire

**Boggle Hole YHA ★★★**
*Hostel*
Mill Beck, Fylingthorpe, Whitby
YO22 4UQ
**t** 0870 770 5704
**e** bogglehole@yha.org.uk
**w** yha.org.uk

**Croft Farm ★★★★**
*Farmhouse*
Fylingthorpe, Whitby
YO22 4PW
**t** (01947) 880231
**e** croftfarmbb@aol.com

GARFORTH
West Yorkshire

**Myrtle House ★★★**
*Guest House*
31 Wakefield Road, Garforth,
Leeds LS25 1AN
**t** (0113) 286 6445

GARGRAVE
North Yorkshire

**The Masons Arms ★★★** *Inn*
Marton Road, Gargrave,
Skipton BD23 3NL
**t** (01756) 749304

## GIGGLESWICK
### North Yorkshire

**Black Horse Hotel ★★★★**
*Inn*
Church Street, Giggleswick,
Settle BD24 0BE
t (01729) 822506

**The Harts Head Hotel ★★★★** *Inn*
Belle Hill, Giggleswick, Settle
BD24 0BA
t (01729) 822086
e info@hartsheadhotel.fsnet.
co.uk
w hartsheadhotel.co.uk

**Tipperthwaite Barn ★★★★**
*Bed & Breakfast*
Giggleswick, Settle BD24 0DZ
t (01729) 823146
e stephen.craven@tiscali.co.
uk

## GILDERSOME
### West Yorkshire

**End Lea ★★★★** *Guest House*
39 Town Street, Gildersome,
Leeds LS27 7AX
t (0113) 252 1661
e pat_mcbride@talktalk.net

## GILLAMOOR
### North Yorkshire

**Manor Farm ★★★**
*Farmhouse*
Main Street, Gillamoor,
Kirkbymoorside YO62 7HX
t (01751) 432695
e gibson.manorfarm@
btopenworld.com
w manorfarmgillamoor.co.uk

**Royal Oak Inn ★★★★** *Inn*
Main Street, Gillamoor,
Kirkbymoorside YO62 7HX
t (01751) 431414

## GILLING EAST
### North Yorkshire

**The Fairfax Arms ★★★★**
*Restaurant with Rooms*
Main Street, Gilling East,
Helmsley YO62 4JH
t (01439) 788212
e rjfhomes@btinternet.com
w fairfaxarms.co.uk

## GLAISDALE
### North Yorkshire

**Beggars Bridge ★★★★**
*Bed & Breakfast*
Station House, Whitby
YO21 2QL
t (01947) 897409
e info@beggarsbridge.co.uk
w beggarsbridge.co.uk

**Egton Banks Farm ★★★★**
*Farmhouse*
Glaisdale, Whitby YO21 2QP
t (01947) 897289
w egtonbanksfarm.agriplus.net

## GOATHLAND
### North Yorkshire

**Fairhaven Country Guest
House ★★★★** *Guest House*
The Common, Goathland,
Whitby YO22 5AN
t (01947) 896361
e enquiries@
fairhavencountryguesthouse.
co.uk
w fairhavencountryguest
house.co.uk

**Heatherdene Hotel ★★★★**
*Guest House* **SILVER AWARD**
Goathland, Whitby YO22 5AN
t (01947) 896334
e tony.sanchez@diageo.com
w heatherdenehotel.co.uk

## GOLDSBOROUGH
### North Yorkshire

**Bay Horse Inn ★★★★** *Inn*
Main Street, Goldsborough,
Harrogate HG5 8NW
t (01423) 862212
e bayhorseinn@btinternet.
com
w edirectory.co.uk/
bayhorseinn/

## GOOLE
### East Riding of Yorkshire

**The Briarcroft Hotel ★★★**
*Guest Accommodation*
49-51 Clifton Gardens, Goole
DN14 6AR
t (01405) 763024
e briarcrofthotel@aol.com
w briarcrofthotel.co.uk

## GRANTLEY
### North Yorkshire

**St Georges Court ★★★★**
*Farmhouse*
Old Home Farm, Ripon
HG4 3PJ
t (01765) 620618
e stgeorgescourt@bronco.co.
uk
w stgeorges-court.co.uk

## GRASSINGTON
### North Yorkshire

**Craiglands Guest House
★★★★** *Bed & Breakfast*
Brooklyn, Threshfield, Skipton
BD23 5ER
t (01756) 752093
e craiglands@talk21.com
w craiglandsguesthouse.co.uk

**The Devonshire Hotel ★★★**
*Inn*
Main Street, Skipton BD23 3LA
t (01756) 752525
e info@thedevonshirehotel.co.
uk
w devonshirehotelgrassington.
co.uk

**Foresters Arms Hotel ★★★**
*Inn*
20 Main Street, Grassington,
Skipton BD23 5AA
t (01756) 752349
e theforesters@totalise.co.uk

**Grassington Lodge**
★★★★★
*Guest Accommodation*
**GOLD AWARD**
8 Wood Lane, Grassington,
Skipton BD23 5LU
t (01756) 752518
e relax@grassingtonlodge.co.
uk
w grassingtonlodge.co.uk

**Grove House ★★★★**
*Bed & Breakfast*
1 Moor Lane, Grassington,
Skipton BD23 5BD
t (01756) 753364
e fraser.turner@btinternet.
com
w grovehousegrassington.net

**New Laithe House ★★★★**
*Guest Accommodation*
Wood Lane, Grassington,
Skipton BD23 5LU
t (01756) 752764
e enquiries@newlaithehouse.
co.uk
w newlaithehouse.co.uk

**Raines Close Guest House
★★★★** *Guest House*
13 Station Road, Grassington,
Skipton BD23 5LS
t (01756) 752678
e raines.close@btinternet.com
w rainesclose.co.uk

**Scar Croft ★★★**
*Bed & Breakfast*
Chapel Street, Grassington,
Skipton BD23 5BE
t (01756) 752455
e diane@mackridge.com
w scarcroft.net

**Springroyd House ★★★**
*Guest Accommodation*
8a Station Road, Grassington,
Skipton BD23 5NQ
t (01756) 752473
e springroydhouse@hotmail.
com
w springroydhouse.co.uk

**Station House ★★★**
*Bed & Breakfast*
Station Road, Threshfield,
Skipton BD23 5ES
t (01756) 752667
e peter@station-house.
freeserve.co.uk
w yorkshirenet.co.uk

**Yew Tree House ★★★★**
*Bed & Breakfast*
**SILVER AWARD**
Scar Street, Grassington,
Skipton BD23 5AS
t (01756) 753075
e julie@badgergate.com
w yewtreehouse.org

## GREAT AYTON
### North Yorkshire

**Food For Thought ★★**
*Guest House*
Bridge Street, Great Ayton
TS9 6NP
t (01642) 725236
e john@walton2505.freeserve.
co.uk
w greataytonaccommodation.
co.uk

**The Kings Head at Newton
under Roseberry ★★★★**
*Guest Accommodation*
**SILVER AWARD**
The Green, Newton under
Roseberry, Middlesbrough
TS9 6QR
t (01642) 722318
e info@kingsheadhotel.co.uk
w kingsheadhotel.co.uk

**Royal Oak Hotel ★★★** *Inn*
High Street, Great Ayton
TS9 6BW
t (01642) 722361

**Susie D's B&B ★★★**
*Guest Accommodation*
Crossways, 116 Newton Road,
Middlesborough TS9 6DL
t (01642) 724351
e susied's@crossways26.fsnet.
co.uk
w susieds.com

**Travellers Rest ★★★★**
*Bed & Breakfast*
97 High Street, Middlesbrough
TS9 6NF
t (01642) 723409

## GRINTON
### North Yorkshire

**The Bridge Inn ★★★** *Inn*
Grinton, Reeth DL11 6HH
t (01748) 884224
e atkinbridge@btinternet.com
w bridgeinngrinton.co.uk

**Grinton Lodge YHA ★★★★**
*Hostel*
Richmond DL11 6HS
t (01748) 884206
e grinton@yha.org.uk
w yha.org.uk

## GUISELEY
### West Yorkshire

**Bowood ★★★**
*Bed & Breakfast*
Carlton Lane, Leeds LS20 9NL
t (01943) 874556

**Lyndhurst ★★★**
*Bed & Breakfast*
Oxford Road, Guiseley, Leeds
LS20 9AB
t (01943) 879985
w guisley.co.uk/lyndhurst

## HACKFORTH
### North Yorkshire

**Ainderby Myers Farm ★★★**
*Farmhouse*
Ainderby Myers, Bedale
DL8 1PF
t (01609) 748668

## HALIFAX
### West Yorkshire

**Field House ★★★★**
*Guest Accommodation*
Staups Lane, Stump Cross,
Halifax HX3 6XW
t (01422) 355457
e stayatfieldhouse@yahoo.co.
uk
w fieldhouse-bb.co.uk

**Lane Ends Farm ★★★★**
*Farmhouse*
Lane Ends, Halifax HX2 8TW
t (01422) 348351 &
07974 764545
e enquiries@laneendsfarm.co.
uk
w laneendsfarm.co.uk

**Rose Cottage ★★★★★**
*Guest Accommodation*
SILVER AWARD
Shibden Fold, Halifax HX3 6XP
t (01422) 365437
e reservations@shibden-fold.
co.uk
w shibden-fold.co.uk

**Travis Guest House ★★★**
*Guest Accommodation*
8 West Parade, Halifax
HX1 2TA
t (01422) 365727

HARROGATE
North Yorkshire

**17 Peckfield Close ★★★**
*Guest Accommodation*
Hampsthwaite, Pateley Bridge
HG3 2ES
t (01423) 770765

**18 Park Parade ★★★★★**
*Bed & Breakfast*
Harrogate HG1 5AF
t (01423) 563800
e why@globalnet.co.uk

**Acacia ★★★★**
*Bed & Breakfast*
GOLD AWARD
3 Springfield Avenue,
Harrogate HG1 2HR
t (01423) 560752
e dee@acaciaharrogate.co.uk
w acaciaharrogate.co.uk

**Acomb Lodge ★★★**
*Guest House*
6 Franklin Road, Harrogate
HG1 5EE
t (01423) 563599

**Acorn Lodge ★★★★**
*Guest Accommodation*
1 Studley Road, Harrogate
HG1 5JU
t (01423) 525630
e info@acornlodgehotel.com
w acornlodgehotel.co.uk

**Alamah Guest House**
★★★★ *Guest House*
88 Kings Road, Harrogate
HG1 5JX
t (01423) 502187
e alamahguesthouse@
btconnect.com
w alamah.co.uk

**Alderside Guest House**
★★★ *Bed & Breakfast*
11 Belmont Road, Harrogate
HG2 0LR
t (01423) 529400

**Alexandra Court Hotel**
★★★★
*Guest Accommodation*
SILVER AWARD
8 Alexandra Road, Harrogate
HG1 5JS
t (01423) 502764
e office@alexandracourt.co.uk
w alexandracourt.co.uk

**Alvera Court ★★★★**
*Guest Accommodation*
76 Kings Road, Harrogate
HG1 5JX
t (01423) 505735
e reception@alvera.co.uk
w alvera.co.uk

**Applewood House ★★★★**
*Guest Accommodation*
GOLD AWARD
55 St Georges Road, Harrogate
HG2 9BP
t (01423) 544549
e applewood@teamknight.
com
w applewoodhouse.co.uk

**Argyll House ★**
*Guest Accommodation*
80 Kings Road, Harrogate
HG1 5JX
t (01423) 567166
e argyll.harrogate@
btopenworld.com

**Ash Grove Guesthouse**
★★★★ *Guest House*
72 Kings Road, Harrogate
HG1 5JR
t (01423) 569970
e admin@ash-grove.co.uk
w ash-grove.co.uk

**Ashbrooke House Hotel**
★★★★
*Guest Accommodation*
140 Valley Drive, Harrogate
HG2 0JS
t (01423) 564478
e ashbrooke@harrogate.com
w harrogate.com/ashbrooke

**Ashley House Hotel ★★★★**
*Guest House*
36-40 Franklin Road, Harrogate
HG1 5EE
t (01423) 507474
e keith@ashleyhousehotel.
com
w ashleyhousehotel.com

**Askern Guest House ★★★**
*Guest House*
3 Dragon Parade, Harrogate
HG1 5BZ
t (01423) 523057
e info@askernhouse.co.uk
w askernhouse.co.uk

**Azalea Court Hotel ★★★**
*Guest Accommodation*
56-58 Kings Road, Harrogate
HG1 5JR
t (01423) 560424

**Barkers Guest House ★★★**
*Guest Accommodation*
204 Kings Road, Harrogate
HG1 5JG
t (01423) 568494
e eebarkeruk@yahoo.co.uk

**Baytree House ★★★★**
*Guest House*
98 Franklin Road, Harrogate
HG1 5EN
t (01423) 564493
e info@baytreeharrogate.co.
uk

**Belmont Guest House**
★★★★ *Guest House*
86 Kings Road, Harrogate
HG1 5JX
t (01423) 528086
e belmontharrogate@
btinternet.com
w belmont-harrogate.co.uk

**Bowes Green Farm ★★★★**
*Farmhouse* SILVER AWARD
Colber Lane, Bishop Thornton,
Harrogate HG3 3JX
t (01423) 770114

**Brookfield House ★★★★**
*Guest House* SILVER AWARD
5 Alexandra Road, Harrogate
HG1 5JS
t (01423) 506646
e office@
brookfieldhousehotel.co.uk
w brookfieldhousehotel.co.uk

**Brooklands ★★★★**
*Guest House*
5 Valley Drive, Harrogate
HG2 0JJ
t (01423) 564609
e brooklandsbb@supanet.com

**Central House Farm ★★★★**
*Farmhouse* SILVER AWARD
Haverah Park, Beckwithshaw,
Pateley Bridge HG3 1SQ
t (01423) 566050
e jayne@centralhousefarm.
freeserve.co.uk
w centralhousefarm.co.uk

**Cold Cotes ★★★★★**
*Guest Accommodation*
GOLD AWARD
Cold Cotes Road, Felliscliffe,
Harrogate HG3 2LW
t (01423) 770937
e info@coldcotes.com
w coldcotes.com

**Conference View Guest
House ♦♦♦♦**
*Guest Accommodation*
74 Kings Road, Harrogate
HG1 5JR
t (01423) 563075
e admin@conferenceview.co.
uk
w conferenceview.co.uk

**Coppice Guest House**
★★★★ *Guest House*
9 Studley Road, Harrogate
HG1 5JU
t (01423) 569626
e coppice@harrogate.com
w harrogate.com/coppice

**Dragon House ★★★**
*Guest House*
6 Dragon Parade, Harrogate
HG1 5DA
t (01423) 569888
e mariem113@hotmail.com
w dragonhousehotel.com

**Franklin View ★★★★**
*Guest Accommodation*
SILVER AWARD
19 Grove Road, Harrogate
HG1 5EW
t (01423) 541388
e jennifer@franklinview.com
w franklinview.com

**The Gables Hotel ★★★**
*Guest Accommodation*
2 West Grove Road, Harrogate
HG1 2AD
t (01423) 505625
e monicaybanks@hotmail.com
w harrogategables.co.uk

**Garden House ★★★★**
*Guest Accommodation*
14 Harlow Moor Drive,
Harrogate HG2 0JX
t (01423) 503059
e gardenhouse@harrogate.
com
w harrogate.com/gardenhouse

**Geminian Guest House**
★★★★ *Guest House*
11-13 Franklin Road, Harrogate
HG1 5ED
t (01423) 523347
e enquiries@geminian.org.uk
w geminian.org.uk

**Glenayr Hotel ★★★**
*Guest Accommodation*
19 Franklin Mount, Harrogate
HG1 5EJ
t (01423) 504259
e liz-glenayr@boltblue.com
w glenayr.co.uk

**Hollins House ★★★**
*Guest House*
17 Hollins Road, Harrogate
HG1 2JF
t (01423) 503646
e hollinshouse@tiscali.co.uk
w hollinshouse.co.uk

**Kingsway Hotel ★★★**
*Guest Accommodation*
36 Kings Road, Harrogate
HG1 5JW
t (01423) 562179
e tanya@kingswayhotel.com
w kingswayhotel.com

**Knabbs Ash ★★★★**
*Farmhouse* GOLD AWARD
Skipton Road, Kettlesing,
Pateley Bridge HG3 2LT
t (01423) 771040
e sheila@knabbsash.co.uk
w knabbsash.co.uk

**Lamont House ★★★★**
*Guest Accommodation*
12 St Lamont House Marys
Walk, Harrogate HG2 0LW
t (01423) 567143
e lamonthouse@btinternet.
com

**Lavender House ★★★★**
*Guest Accommodation*
94 Franklin Road, Harrogate
HG1 5EN
t (01423) 549949 &
07732 422478
e lavenderhouse@ntlworld.
com
w lavenderhouseharrogate.co.
uk

**Murray House ★★★**
*Guest Accommodation*
67 Franklin Road, Harrogate
HG1 5EH
t (01423) 505857
e enquiries@murray-house.
com
w murray-house.co.uk

**Scotia House Hotel ★★**
*Guest House*
66-68 Kings Road, Harrogate
HG1 5JR
t (01423) 504361
e info@scotiahotel.harrogate.
net
w scotiahotel.harrogate.net

**Sherwood** ★★★★
*Guest Accommodation*
7 Studley Road, Harrogate
HG1 5JU
t (01423) 503033
e sherwood@harrogate.com
w sherwood-hotel.com

**Spring Lodge** ★★★
*Guest House*
22 Spring Mount, Harrogate
HG1 2HX
t (01423) 506036
e dv22harrogate@aol.com
w spring-lodge.co.uk

**The Welford** ★★★
*Guest House*
27 Franklin Road, Harrogate
HG1 5ED
t (01423) 566041
e judith.mudd@btopenworld.
com
w the-welford.co.uk

**Ye Olde Coach House**
★★★★
*Guest Accommodation*
2 Strawberry Dale Terrace,
Harrogate HG1 5EQ
t (01423) 500302
e yeoldecoachhouse@
btinternet.com

### HARTWITH
North Yorkshire

**Brimham Lodge** ★★★
*Farmhouse*
Brimham Rocks Road,
Harrogate HG3 3HE
t (01423) 771770
e neil.clarke@virgin.net
w brimhamlodge.co.uk

### HARWOOD DALE
North Yorkshire

**The Grainary** ★★★★
*Farmhouse*
Harwood Dale, Scarborough
YO13 0DT
t (01723) 870026
e grainary@btopenworld.com
w grainary.co.uk

**Thirley Banks Cottage**
★★★★ *Farmhouse*
Harwood Dale, Scarborough
YO13 0DR
t (01723) 871404
e info@thirleybanks.co.uk
w thirleybanks.co.uk

### HAWES
North Yorkshire

**Cocketts Hotel and
Restaurant** ★★★★
*Guest Accommodation*
Market Place, Hawes DL8 3RD
t (01969) 667312
e enquiries@cocketts.co.uk
w cocketts.co.uk

**East House** ★★★★
*Guest Accommodation*
Gayle, Leyburn DL8 3RZ
t (01969) 667405
e lornaward@lineone.net
w easthouse-hawes.com

**Ebor House** ★★★★
*Guest Accommodation*
Burtersett Road, Hawes
DL8 3NT
t (01969) 667337
e eborhousehawes@yahoo.co.
uk
w eborhouse.co.uk

**FairView House** ★★★★
*Guest House*
Burtersett Road, Hawes
DL8 3NP
t (01969) 667348
e info@fairview-hawes.co.uk
w fairview-hawes.co.uk

**Hawes YHA** ★★★ *Hostel*
Lancaster Terrace, Hawes
DL8 3LQ
t (01969) 667368
e hawes@yha.org.uk
w yha.org.uk

**Herriots Hotel & Restaurant**
★★★★
*Guest Accommodation*
Main Street, Hawes DL8 3QW
t (01969) 667536
e info@herriotsinhawes.co.uk
w herriotsinhawes.co.uk

**Laburnum House** ★★★
*Guest House*
The Holme, Hawes DL8 3QR
t (01969) 667717
e info@stayatlaburnumhouse.
co.uk
w stayatlaburnumhouse.co.uk

**The Old Dairy Farm**
★★★★★
*Guest Accommodation*
Widdale, Hawes DL8 3LX
t (01969) 667070
w olddairyfarm.co.uk

**Pry House** ★★★★
*Bed & Breakfast*
Hawes DL8 3LP
t (01969) 667241
e pryhousefarm@hotmail.com
w pryhousefarm.co.uk

**Rookhurst Country House**
★★★★★ *Guest House*
**GOLD AWARD**
West End, Gayle, Hawes
DL8 3RT
t (01969) 667454
e enquiries@rookhurst.co.uk
w rookhurst.co.uk

**South View** ★★★
*Bed & Breakfast*
Gayle Lane, Hawes DL8 3RW
t (01969) 667447
e carol@bell3630.freeserve.
co.uk

**Springbank House** ★★★
*Guest Accommodation*
Spring Bank, Hawes DL8 3NW
t (01969) 667376

**Thorney Mire Barn B&B**
★★★★★
*Guest Accommodation*
**GOLD AWARD**
Appersett, Hawes DL8 3LU
t (01969) 666122
e stay@thorneymirebarn.co.uk
w thorneymirebarn.co.uk

**Thorney Mire House** ★★★★
*Bed & Breakfast*
Hawes DL8 3LU
t (01969) 667159
e sylvia.turner2@virgin.net
w thorneymire.yorks.net

**White Hart Inn** ★★★ *Inn*
Main Street, Hawes DL8 3QL
t (01969) 667259
e whiteharthawes@fsmail.net
w whiteharthawes.co.uk

### HAWKSWICK
North Yorkshire

**Warren House B&B** ★★★★
*Bed & Breakfast*
Warren House, Skipton
BD23 5PU
t (01756) 770375
e info@warren-house.net
w warren-house.net

### HAWNBY
North Yorkshire

**Easterside Farm** ★★★★
*Farmhouse*
Hawnby, Helmsley YO62 5QT
t (01439) 798277
e sarah@eastersidefarm.co.uk
w eastersidefarm.co.uk

### HAWORTH
West Yorkshire

**Aitches Guest House**
★★★★ *Guest House*
11 West Lane, Haworth
BD22 8DU
t (01535) 642501
e aitches@talk21.com
w aitches.co.uk

**The Apothecary Guest
House** ★★ *Guest House*
86 Main Street, Haworth,
Keighley BD22 8DP
t (01535) 643642
e Nicholasapt@aol.com
w theapothecaryguesthouse.
co.uk

**Ashmount Guest House**
★★★★★ *Guest House*
**SILVER AWARD**
Mytholmes Lane, Haworth
BD22 8EZ
t (01535) 645726
e info@ashmounthaworth.co.
uk
w ashmounthaworth.co.uk

**Bridge House B&B** ★★★
*Bed & Breakfast*
Bridge House, Bridgehouse
Lane, Haworth BD22 8PA
t (01535) 642372
e claire@bridgehouselane.co.
uk
w bridgehouselane.co.uk

**The Bronte** ★★★
*Guest Accommodation*
Lees Lane, Haworth, Keighley
BD22 8RA
t (01535) 644112
e brontehotel@btinternet.com
w bronte-hotel.co.uk

**Haworth Tea Rooms and
Guest House** ★★★
*Guest House*
68 Main Street, Haworth
BD22 8DP
t (01535) 644278
w haworthtearooms.co.uk

**Haworth YHA** ★★★ *Hostel*
Longlands Drive, Lees Lane,
Haworth BD22 8RT
t (01535) 642234
e haworth@yha.org.uk
w yha.org.uk

**Heathfield Bed & Breakfast**
Rating Applied For
*Bed & Breakfast*
1 Bronte Street, Keighley
BD22 8EE
t (01535) 640606

**The Manor Guest House**
★★★★★ *Guest House*
**SILVER AWARD**
Sutton Drive, Cullingworth,
Bradford BD13 5BQ
t (01535) 274374
e michele.cotter@btinternet.
com
w cullingworthmanor.co.uk

**The Old Registry** ★★★★
*Guest Accommodation*
**SILVER AWARD**
2-4 Main Street, Haworth
BD22 8DA
t (01535) 646503
e enquiries@
theoldregistryhaworth.co.uk
w theoldregistryhaworth.co.uk

**Rosebud Cottage** ★★★★
*Guest Accommodation*
1 Belle Isle Road, Haworth
BD22 8QQ
t (01535) 640321
e info@rosebudcottage.co.uk
w rosebudcottage.co.uk

**Woodlands Grange Private
Hotel** ★★★ *Guest House*
Belle Isle, Haworth BD22 8PB
t (01535) 646814
e woodlandsgrange@hotmail.
com
w woodlandsgrange.com

### HEADINGLEY
West Yorkshire

**Oak Villa Hotel** ★★★
*Guest Accommodation*
55-57 Cardigan Road, Leeds
LS6 1DW
t (0113) 275 8439
e oakvillahotel@msn.com
w oakvillahotel.co.uk

### HEALAUGH
North Yorkshire

**Riddings Farm** ★★★★
*Farmhouse*
Reeth DL11 6UR
t (01748) 884267

### HEBDEN
North Yorkshire

**Court Croft** ★★★
*Bed & Breakfast*
Church Lane, Hebden, Skipton
BD23 5DX
t (01756) 753406

### HEBDEN BRIDGE
West Yorkshire

**B@r Place** ★★★★
*Guest Accommodation*
10 Crown Street, Hebden
Bridge HX7 8EH
t (01422) 842814
e intouch@barplace.co.uk
w barplace.co.uk

**Holme House** ★★★★★
*Bed & Breakfast*
**SILVER AWARD**
New Road, Hebden Bridge
HX7 8AD
t (01422) 847588
e mail@
holmehousehebdenbridge.co.
uk
w holmehousehebdenbridge.
co.uk

**Mount Skip Bed & Breakfast**
★★★★ *Bed & Breakfast*
1 Mount Road, Wadsworth,
Hebden Bridge HX7 8PH
t (01422) 842903
e mountskipbandb@hotmail.
com

**Mytholm House** ★★
*Bed & Breakfast*
Mytholm Bank, Hebden Bridge
HX7 6DL
t (01422) 847493
e culvert@care4free.net
w mytholmhouse.co.uk

**The White Lion Hotel**
★★★★ *Inn*
Bridge Gate, Hebden Bridge
HX7 8EX
t (01422) 842197
e enquiries@whitelionhotel.
net
w whitelionhotel.net

### HELMSLEY
### North Yorkshire

**Carlton Lodge** ★★★★
*Guest House* **SILVER AWARD**
Bondgate, Helmsley YO62 5EY
t (01439) 770557
e enquiries@carlton-lodge.
com
w carlton-lodge.com

**Feathers Hotel** ★★★ *Inn*
Market Place, Helmsley
YO62 5BH
t (01439) 770275
e info@feathers.wanadoo.co.
uk
w feathershotelhelmsley.co.uk

**Griff Farm Bed & Breakfast**
★★★★ *Farmhouse*
Griff Farm, York YO62 5EN
t (01439) 771600
e j.fairburn@farmline.com

**Helmsley YHA** ★★★ *Hostel*
Carlton Lane, Helmsley
YO62 5HB
t (01439) 770433
e helmsley@yha.org.uk
w yha.org.uk

**The Inn at Hawnby** ★★★★
*Inn*
Hilltop, Hawnby, York
YO62 5QS
t (01439) 798202
e info@hawnbyhotel.co.uk
w hawnbyhotel.co.uk

**Laskill Grange** ★★★★
*Farmhouse* **SILVER AWARD**
Easterside, Hawnby, Nr
Helmsley, York YO62 5NB
t (01439) 798268
e suesmith@laskillfarm.fsnet.
co.uk
w laskillgrange.co.uk

**No. 54** ★★★★★
*Guest House*
54 Bondgate, Helmsley
YO62 5EZ
t (01439) 771533
e lizzie@no54.co.uk
w no54.co.uk

**Oldstead Grange** ★★★★★
*Guest Accommodation*
**GOLD AWARD**
Oldstead, Coxwold, Helmsley
YO61 4BJ
t (01347) 868634
e anne@yorkshireuk.com
w yorkshireuk.com

**Redroofs** ★★★★
*Bed & Breakfast*
3 Carlton Road, Helmsley
YO62 5HD
t (01439) 770175
e babenm@globalnet.co.uk
w redroofs-helmsley.co.uk

**Stilworth House** ★★★★
*Bed & Breakfast*
1 Church Street, Helmsley
YO62 5AD
t (01439) 771072
e carol@stilworth.co.uk
w stilworth.co.uk

**West View Cottage** ★★★★
*Guest Accommodation*
**GOLD AWARD**
Pockley, Helmsley YO62 7TE
t (01439) 770526
e westviewcottage@
bedbreakfast.freeserve.co.uk
w s-h-systems.co.uk/hotels/
westviewcottage

### HEPTONSTALL
### West Yorkshire

**Poppyfields House** ★★★
*Bed & Breakfast*
29 Slack Top, Heptonstall,
Hebden Bridge HX7 7HA
t (01422) 843636
e poppyfieldshouse29@
yahoo.com

### HETTON
### North Yorkshire

**Angel Inn** ★★★★★
*Restaurant with Rooms*
Hetton, Skipton BD23 6LT
t (01756) 730263
e info@angelhetton.co.uk
w angelhetton.co.uk

### HIGH BENTHAM
### North Yorkshire

**The Coach House** ★★★★
*Inn*
16 Main Street, High Bentham,
Ingleton LA2 7HE
t (01524) 262305
e info@coachhousebentham.
co.uk
w coachhousebentham.co.uk

**Fowgill Park** ◆◆◆◆
*Guest Accommodation*
Bentham, Lancaster, Ingleton
LA2 7AH
t (01524) 261630
e info@fowgillpark.co.uk
w fowgillpark.co.uk

### HIGH STITTENHAM
### North Yorkshire

**Hall Farm** ★★★★ *Farmhouse*
High Stittenham, Sheriff
Hutton, Malton YO60 7TW
t (01347) 878461
e hallfarm@btinternet.com
w hallfarm.btinternet.co.uk

### HIRST COURTNEY
### North Yorkshire

**Royal Oak Inn Hotel** ★★★
*Inn*
Main Street, Selby YO8 8QT
t (01757) 270633
e theroyaloakinnhotel@
hotmail.com
w royaloakinn-hotel.co.uk

### HOLLYM
### East Riding of Yorkshire

**Plough Inn** ★★ *Inn*
Northside Road, Hollym,
Withernsea HU19 2RS
t (01964) 612049
e the.plough.inn@btconnect.
com
w theploughinnhollym.co.uk

### HOLMBRIDGE
### West Yorkshire

**Corn Loft House** ★★★
*Guest Accommodation*
146 Woodhead Road,
Holmbridge, Holmfirth
HD9 2NL
t (01484) 883147

### HOLMFIRTH
### West Yorkshire

**Ash House B&B** ★★★
*Bed & Breakfast*
240 Dunford Road, Holmfirth
HD9 2SJ
t (01484) 688244
e accommodation@swcch.co.
uk
w summerwineclassics.co.uk

**Elephant and Castle** ★★
*Guest Accommodation*
Hollowgate, Huddersfield
HD9 2DG
t (01484) 683178

**The Huntsman** ★★★★
*Guest Accommodation*
Greenfield Road, Holmfirth
HD9 3XF
t (01484) 850705
e kempsterpk@aol.com
w the-huntsman-inn.com

**The Old Bridge Bakery** ★★
*Guest Accommodation*
15 Victoria Street, Holmfirth
HD9 7DF
t (01484) 685807
e oldbridgebakery@tiscali.co.
uk

**Sunnybank Guesthouse**
★★★★★
*Guest Accommodation*
**SILVER AWARD**
78 Upperthong Lane, Holmfirth
HD9 3BQ
t (01484) 684857
e info@
sunnybankguesthouse.co.uk
w sunnybankguesthouse.co.uk

**Uppergate Farm B&B**
★★★★
*Guest Accommodation*
Uppergate, Hepworth,
Holmfirth HD9 1TG
t (01484) 681369
e info@uppergatefarm.co.uk
w uppergatefarm.co.uk

### HOLMPTON
### East Riding of Yorkshire

**Elmtree Farm** ★★★
*Bed & Breakfast*
Holmpton, Withernsea
HU19 2QR
t (01964) 630957
e cft-mcox@supanet.com

**Rysome Garth** ◆◆◆◆
*Guest Accommodation*
Withernsea HU19 2QR
t (01964) 631248
e amandapannett@neoeon.
com

### HORNSEA
### East Riding of Yorkshire

**Earlham House Guest House**
★★★★ *Bed & Breakfast*
**SILVER AWARD**
59a Eastgate, Hornsea
HU18 1NB
t (01964) 537809
e info@earlhamhouse.com
w earlhamhouse.com

**Sandhurst Guest House**
★★★ *Guest House*
3 Victoria Avenue, Hornsea
HU18 1NH
t (01964) 534653
e rhodes@hornsea15.fsnet.co.
uk
w sandhurstguesthouse.co.uk

**Wentworth House** ★★★★
*Guest House*
12 Seaside Road, Aldbrough,
Hull HU11 4RX
t (01964) 527246
e mteale@eduktion.co.uk
w wentworthhousehotel.com

### HUBBERHOLME
### North Yorkshire

**Church Farm** ★★★★
*Farmhouse*
Hubberholme, Skipton
BD23 5JE
t (01756) 760240
e gwhuck@hubberholme.
fsnet.co.uk

### HUDDERSFIELD
### West Yorkshire

**Cambridge Lodge** ★★★
*Guest Accommodation*
4 Clare Hill, Huddersfield
HD1 5BS
t (01484) 519892
e cambridge.lodge.hudd@
btconnect.com
w cambridgelodge.co.uk

**Castle View Guest House**
★★★★★
*Guest Accommodation*
**SILVER AWARD**
148 Ashes Lane, Castle Hill,
Huddersfield HD4 6TE
t (01484) 307460
e info@castleviewyorkshire.
co.uk
w castleviewyorkshire.co.uk

**Croppers Arms** ★★★★
*Guest Accommodation*
136 Westbourne Road,
Huddersfield HD1 4LF
t (01484) 421522

**Elm Crest** ★★★★
*Guest House* **SILVER AWARD**
2 Queens Road, Huddersfield
HD2 2AG
t (01484) 530990
e ginette@elmcrest.biz
w elmcrest.biz

**Holmcliffe Guest House**
★★★★ *Guest House*
16 Mountjoy Road, Edgerton,
Huddersfield HD1 5PZ
t (01484) 429598
e j.wilcockson1@ntlworld.com

**Huddersfield Central Lodge**
★★★★
*Guest Accommodation*
**SILVER AWARD**
11-15 Beast Market,
Huddersfield HD1 1QF
t (01484) 515551
e enquiries@centrallodge.com
w centrallodge.com

**Manor Mill Cottage** ★★★★
*Bed & Breakfast*
21 Linfit Lane, Kirkburton,
Huddersfield HD8 0TY
t (01484) 604109
e d.askham@btinternet.com

**The Old Co-op** ★★★★★
*Bed & Breakfast*
**SILVER AWARD**
96 The Village, Thurstonland,
Huddersfield HD4 6XF
t (01484) 663621
e chris@theoldco-op.com
w theoldco-op.com

**Storthes Hall Park**
Rating Applied For
*Campus*
Storthes Hall Lane, Kirkburton,
Huddersfield HD8 0WA
t (01484) 488820
w stortheshall.co.uk

**Woods End Bed & Breakfast**
★★★★
*Guest Accommodation*
46 Inglewood Avenue,
Huddersfield HD2 2DS
t (01484) 513580 &
07730 030993
e jmsm2306@hotmail.com
w pennineyorkshire.com

HULL
East Riding of Yorkshire

**Acorn Guest House** ★★★
*Guest House*
719 Beverley Road, Hull
HU6 7JN
t (01482) 853248
e janet_the_acorn@yahoo.co.
uk
w smoothhound.co.uk/hotels/
acornhull

**The Admiral Guest House**
★★★ *Bed & Breakfast*
234 The Boulevard, Hull
HU3 3ED
t (01482) 329664

**Allandra Hotel** ★★
*Guest Accommodation*
5 Park Avenue, Princes
Avenue, Hull HU5 3EN
t (01482) 493349
e macklin2003@macklin2003.
karoo.co.uk
w allandrahotel.co.uk

**The Arches** ★★★
*Bed & Breakfast*
38 Saner Street, Hull HU3 2TR
t (01482) 211558

**Clyde House Hotel** ★★★
*Guest Accommodation*
13 John Street, Hull HU2 8DH
t (01482) 214981
e chris@hotel1.karoo.co.uk
w clydehousehotel.co.uk

**Cornerbrook Guest House**
★★★★ *Guest House*
1 Desmond Avenue, Beverley
Road, Hull HU6 7JY
t (01482) 474272
e cornerbrookhouse@
cornerbrookhouse.karoo.co.uk

**The Earlsmere Hotel** ★★★
*Guest House*
76-78 Sunny Bank, Hull
HU3 1LQ
t (01482) 341977
e su@earlsmerehotel.karoo.
co.uk
w earlsmerehotel.karoo.net

**The Hornbeams** ★★★★★
*Bed & Breakfast*
373 Saltshouse Road, Hull
HU8 9HS
t (01482) 718630
e hornbeams@dwestwood.
karoo.co.uk

HUTTON-LE-HOLE
North Yorkshire

**The Barn Hotel and Tea
Rooms** ★★★
*Guest Accommodation*
Hutton-le-Hole, York
YO62 6UA
t (01751) 417311

**Burnley House** ★★★★
*Guest House* **SILVER AWARD**
Hutton-le-Hole,
Kirkbymoorside YO62 6UA
t (01751) 417548
e info@burnleyhouse.co.uk
w burnleyhouse.co.uk

HUTTON SESSAY
North Yorkshire

**Burtree Country Guest
House** ★★★★
*Guest Accommodation*
York Road, Thirsk YO7 3AY
t (01845) 501333
e info@burtreecountryhouse.
co.uk
w burtreecountryhouse.co.uk

ILKLEY
West Yorkshire

**The Coach House**
Rating Applied For
*Guest Accommodation*
Parish Ghyll Road, Ilkley
LS29 9NE
t (01943) 605091
w 28parishghyll.co.uk

**Ilkley Riverside Hotel** ★★★
*Guest Accommodation*
Riverside Gardens, Bridge
Lane, Ilkley LS29 9EU
t (01943) 607338
e enquiries@ilkley-
riversidehotel.com
w ilkley-riversidehotel.com

**One Tivoli Place** ★★★★
*Guest Accommodation*
1 Tivoli Place, Ilkley LS29 8SU
t (01943) 600328
e enquiries@tivoliplace.co.uk
w tivoliplace.co.uk

**Roberts Family Bed and
Breakfast** ★★
*Bed & Breakfast*
63 Skipton Road, Ilkley
LS29 9HF
t (01943) 817542
e ilkleybb@blueyonder.co.uk

INGLEBY CROSS
North Yorkshire

**Blue Bell Inn** ★★ *Inn*
Ingleby Cross DL6 3NF
t (01609) 882272
e bluebell@inglebycross.
wanadoo.co.uk

INGLETON
North Yorkshire

**The Dales Guest House**
★★★ *Guest House*
Main Street, Ingleton LA6 3HH
t (01524) 241401
e dalesgh@hotmail.com

**Gatehouse Farm** ★★★★
*Farmhouse*
Westhouse, Ingleton LA6 3NR
t (01524) 241458
e gatehousefarm@ktdinternet.
com

**Ingleborough View Guest
House** ★★★★ *Guest House*
Main Street, Ingleton LA6 3HH
t (01524) 241523
e stay@ingleboroughview.
com
w ingleboroughview.com

**Inglenook Guest House**
★★★★
*Guest Accommodation*
20 Main Street, Ingleton
LA6 3HJ
t (01524) 241270
e inglenook20@hotmail.com
w inglenookguesthouse.com

**Ingleton YHA** ★★★★ *Hostel*
Greta Tower, Sammy Lane,
Ingleton LA6 3EG
t (01524) 241444
w yha.org.uk

**New Butts Farm** ★★★
*Guest House*
High Bentham, Ingleton
LA2 7AN
t (01524) 241238

**The Pines Country House**
Rating Applied For
*Guest House*
New Road, Ingleton LA6 3HN
t (01524) 241252
e pinesingleton@aol.com
w pinesingleton.com

**Riverside Lodge** ★★★★
*Guest Accommodation*
24 Main Street, Ingleton
LA6 3HJ
t (01524) 241359
e info@riversideingleton.co.uk
w riversideingleton.co.uk

**Springfield Country Guest
House** ★★★★
*Guest Accommodation*
26 Main Street, Ingleton,
Carnforth LA6 3HJ
t (01524) 241280
w destination-england.co.uk/
springfield.html

**Station Inn** ★★★ *Inn*
Ribblehead, Carnforth LA6 3AS
t (01524) 241274
e enquiries@thestationinn.net
w thestationinn.net

**Thorngarth Country Guest
House** ★★★★ *Guest House*
New Road, Ingleton LA6 3HN
t (01524) 241295
e davidegregory@
btopenworld.com
w thorngarth.co.uk

**Wheatsheaf Inn & Hotel**
★★★★ *Inn*
22 High Street, Ingleton
LA6 3AD
t (01524) 241275
e info@wheatsheaf-ingleton.
co.uk

KETTLESING
North Yorkshire

**Green Acres** ★★★★
*Bed & Breakfast*
**GOLD AWARD**
Sleights Lane, Kettlesing,
Pateley Bridge HG3 2LE
t (01423) 771524
e christine@yorkshiredalesbb.
com
w yorkshiredalesbb.com

KETTLEWELL
North Yorkshire

**Kettlewell YHA** ★★★ *Hostel*
Whernside House, Westgate,
Skipton BD23 5QU
t (01756) 760232
e kettlewell@yha.org.uk
w yha.org.uk

**Lynburn** ★★★
*Bed & Breakfast*
Langcliffe Garth, Kettlewell,
Skipton BD23 5RF
t (01756) 760803
e www.lorna@lthornborrow.
fsnet.co.uk

KILBURN
North Yorkshire

**Church Farm** ★★★
*Farmhouse*
Kilburn, Thirsk YO61 4AH
t (01347) 868318
e churchfarmkilburn@yahoo.
co.uk

KILNWICK PERCY
East Riding of Yorkshire

**Paws-A-While** ★★★★
*Farmhouse*
Kilnwick Percy, Pocklington,
Driffield YO42 1UF
t (01759) 301168
e paws.a.while@lineone.net
w pawsawhile.net

## KIRBY HILL
### North Yorkshire

**Shoulder of Mutton** ★★★
*Inn*
Kirby Hill, Reeth DL11 7JH
t (01748) 822772
e info@shoulderofmutton.net
w shoulderofmutton.net

## KIRBY MISPERTON
### North Yorkshire

**Beansheaf Hotel** ★★★★ *Inn*
Malton Road, Kirby Misperton,
Malton YO17 6UE
t (01653) 668614
e enquiries@beansheafhotel.
com
w beansheafhotel.com

## KIRKBURTON
### West Yorkshire

**The Woodman Inn** ★★★★
*Inn*
Thunderbridge Lane,
Kirkburton, Huddersfield
HD8 0PX
t (01484) 603703
e thewoodman@connectfree.
co.uk
w woodman-inn.co.uk

## KIRKBY
### North Yorkshire

**Dromonby Hall Farm** ★★★
*Bed & Breakfast*
Busby Lane, Kirkby-in-
Cleveland, Middlesbrough
TS9 7AP
t (01642) 712312
e pat@dromonby.co.uk
w dromonby.co.uk

## KIRKBY-IN-CLEVELAND
### North Yorkshire

**Dromonby Grange Farm**
★★★★ *Farmhouse*
Busby Lane, Kirkby-in-
Cleveland, Middlesbrough
TS9 7AR
t (01642) 712227
e jehugill@aol.com

## KIRKBYMOORSIDE
### North Yorkshire

**Brickfields Farm** ★★★★
*Farmhouse* **SILVER AWARD**
Kirkby Mills, Kirkbymoorside
YO62 6NS
t (01751) 433074
e janet@brickfieldsfarm.co.uk
w brickfieldsfarm.co.uk

**The Cornmill** ★★★★
*Guest House* **SILVER AWARD**
Kirby Mills, Kirkbymoorside,
York YO62 6NP
t (01751) 432000
e cornmill@kirbymills.demon.
co.uk
w kirbymills.demon.co.uk

**Farndale** *Camping Barn*
Oak House, High Farndale,
York YO62 7LH
t (01751) 433053
e pipmead@aol.com
w yha.org.uk

---

**Feversham Arms Inn** ★★★★
*Inn*
Church Houses, Pickering
YO62 7LF
t (01751) 433206
e fevershamfarndale@hotmail.
com

**The Lion Inn** ★★★ *Inn*
Blakey Ridge, Kirkbymoorside
YO62 7LQ
t (01751) 417320
e lion.blakey@virgin.net
w lionblakey.co.uk

## KNARESBOROUGH
### North Yorkshire

**Ebor Mount** ★★★
*Guest House*
18 York Place, Knaresborough
HG5 0AA
t (01423) 863315

**Gallon House** ★★★★
*Guest Accommodation*
**GOLD AWARD**
47 Kirkgate, Knaresborough
HG5 8BZ
t (01423) 862102
e gallon-house@ntlworld.com
w gallon-house.co.uk

**General Tarleton Inn** ★★★★
*Restaurant with Rooms*
Boroughbridge Road,
Ferrensby HG5 0PZ
t (01423) 340284
e gti@generaltarleton.co.uk
w generaltarleton.co.uk

**Holly Corner Bed &
Breakfast** ★★★★
*Guest Accommodation*
3 Coverdale Drive, High Bond
End, Knaresborough HG5 9BW
t (01423) 864204
e hollycorner3@aol.com
w holly-corner.co.uk

**Watergate Lodge** ★★★★
*Guest Accommodation*
Watergate Haven, Ripley Road,
Knaresborough HG5 9BU
t (01423) 864627
e info@watergatehaven.com
w watergatehaven.com

## KNOTTINGLEY
### West Yorkshire

**Wentvale Court** ★★★★
*Guest House*
Great North Road, Knottingley,
Pontefract WF11 8PF
t (01977) 676714
e wentvale1@btconnect.com
w wentvalecourt.com

## LASTINGHAM
### North Yorkshire

**April Cottage** ★★★★
*Guest Accommodation*
**SILVER AWARD**
Low Street, Lastingham,
Kirkbymoorside YO62 6TJ
t (01751) 417436
e heather-white@tiscali.co.uk

## LEALHOLM
### North Yorkshire

**High Park Farm** ★★★★
*Farmhouse*
Lealholm, Whitby YO21 2AQ
t (01947) 897416
e highparkfarm@btinternet.
com

---

## LEEDS
### West Yorkshire

**Adriatic Hotel** ★★★
*Guest Accommodation*
87 Harehills Avenue, Leeds
LS8 4ET
t (0113) 262 0115
e adriatichotel@btconnect.
com
w theadriatichotel.co.uk

**Avalon Guest House** ★★★
*Guest House*
132 Woodsley Road, Leeds
LS2 9LZ
t (0113) 243 2545
e info@woodsleyroad.com
w avalonguesthouseleeds.co.
uk

**Broomhurst Guest House**
★★ *Guest Accommodation*
12 Chapel Lane, Headingley
LS6 3BW
t (0113) 278 6836

**City Centre Guest House**
★★ *Guest House*
51a New Briggate, Leeds
LS2 8JD
t (0113) 242 9019
e info@leedscityentrehotel.
com
w citycentrehotelleeds.co.uk

**Glengarth Inn** ★★★
*Guest House*
162 Woodsley Road, Leeds
LS2 9LZ
t (0113) 245 7940
e info@woodsleyroad.com
w glengarthhotel.co.uk

**Headingley Lodge Hotel**
★★★ *Guest Accommodation*
Headingley Stadium, St
Michael's Lane, Leeds LS6 3BR
t (0113) 278 5323
e tamsin_lee@talk21.com
w headingleylodge.com

**Hinsley Hall** ★★★
*Guest Accommodation*
62 Headingley Lane, Leeds
LS6 2BX
t (0113) 261 8000
e info@hinsley-hall.co.uk
w hinsley-hall.co.uk

**Manxdene Guest House** ★★
*Guest Accommodation*
154 Woodsley Road, Leeds
LS2 9LZ
t (0113) 243 2586
e manxdenehotel@leedscity.
wanadoo.co.uk
w manxdeneguesthouse.com

**The Moorlea Hotel** ★★
*Guest Accommodation*
146 Woodsley Road, Leeds
LS2 9LZ
t (0113) 243 2653
e themoorleahotel@aol.com

**Number 23** ★★
*Bed & Breakfast*
Number 23 St Chads Rise, Far
Headingly, Leeds LS6 3QE
t (0113) 275 7825

**Rosehurst** ★★★
*Guest Accommodation*
8 Grosvenor Road, Leeds
LS6 2DZ
t (0113) 278 8600
e gmspencer@spencer-
properties.co.uk

---

**St Michael's Guest House**
★★★ *Guest House*
5 St Michael's Villas, Cardigan
Road, Leeds LS6 3AF
t (0113) 275 5557
e stmichaelstowerhotel@
hotmail.co.uk
w stmichaelstowerhotel.co.uk

**University of Leeds** ★★
*Campus*
Conference Office, University
House, University of Leeds,
Leeds LS2 9JT
t (0113) 233 6100
e david@universallyleeds.co.
uk
w leeds.ac.uk/conference

**Wheelgate Guest House**
★★★ *Guest House*
7 Kirkgate, Sherburn in Elmet,
Leeds LS25 6BH
t (01977) 682231
w smoothhound.co.uk/hotels/
wheelgate

## LEEMING BAR
### North Yorkshire

**Little Holtby** ★★★★
*Guest Accommodation*
**SILVER AWARD**
Northallerton DL7 9LH
t (01609) 748762
e littleholtby@yahoo.co.uk
w littleholtby.co.uk

## LEVEN
### East Riding of Yorkshire

**Eastfield House Bed &
Breakfast** ★★★★
*Bed & Breakfast*
Hornsea Road, Leven, Beverley
HU17 5NJ
t (01964) 503959

## LEVISHAM
### North Yorkshire

**The Moorlands Country
House** ★★★★★
*Guest House* **GOLD AWARD**
Main Street, Levisham,
Pickering YO18 7NL
t (01751) 460229
e ronaldoleonardo@aol.com
w moorlandslevisham.co.uk

## LEYBURN
### North Yorkshire

**Clyde House** ★★★★
*Guest Accommodation*
5 Railway Street, Leyburn
DL8 5AY
t (01969) 623941
e lucia.fisher1@btinternet.com
w clydehouseleyburn.co.uk

**Dales Haven Guest House**
★★★★ *Guest House*
Market Place, Leyburn DL8 5BJ
t (01969) 623814
e info@daleshaven.co.uk
w daleshaven.co.uk

**Eastfield Lodge Private
Hotel** ★★★★
*Guest Accommodation*
1 St Matthews Terrace,
Leyburn DL8 5EL
t (01969) 623196
e janetanderson@aol.com
w eastfieldlodge.co.uk

---

**Grove Hotel ★★★**
*Guest House*
8 Grove Square, Leyburn
DL8 5AE
t (01969) 622569
e info@grove-hotel.com
w grove-hotel.com

**Leyburn Bunk Barn**
*Camping Barn*
Craken House Farm,
Middleham Road, Leyburn
DL8 5HF
t (01969) 622204
e campbarnsyha@enterprise.
net

**The Old Vicarage ★★★★**
*Guest Accommodation*
West Witton, Leyburn DL8 4LX
t (01969) 622108
e info@dalesbreaks.co.uk
w dalesbreaks.co.uk

**Street Head Inn ★★★★** *Inn*
Newbiggin-in-Bishopdale,
Leyburn DL8 3TE
t (01969) 663282
e joanne.fawcett@virgin.net
w streetheadinn.co.uk

**Sunnyridge, Argill Farm**
**★★★** *Farmhouse*
Harmby, Leyburn DL8 5HQ
t (01969) 622478
e richah@freenet.co.uk

**Waterford House ★★★★★**
*Guest Accommodation*
GOLD AWARD
19 Kirkgate, Leyburn DL8 4PG
t (01969) 622090
e info@waterfordhousehotel.
co.uk
w waterfordhousehotel.co.uk
▨▧

**West Close Farmhouse**
**★★★★**
*Guest Accommodation*
SILVER AWARD
Melmerby in Coverdale,
Leyburn DL8 4TW
t (01969) 640275
e thompson@westclose.
wanadoo.co.uk
w westclosefarmhouse.co.uk

### LITTLE CRAKEHALL
### North Yorkshire

**Watermill House ★★★**
*Guest Accommodation*
Crakehall Watermill, Little
Crakehall, Bedale DL8 1HU
t (01677) 423240
e crakehallwatermill@tiscali.
co.uk
w crakehallwatermill.co.uk

### LIVERSEDGE
### West Yorkshire

**Geordie Pride Lodge Hotel**
**★★★★**
*Guest Accommodation*
112 Roberttown Lane, Batley
WF15 7LY
t (01924) 412044
e geordiehotel@aol.com

**Heirloom Carriage Driving**
**B&B ★★** *Bed & Breakfast*
9 Windsor Drive, Norristhorpe
WF15 7RA
t (01924) 235120

### LOCKTON
### North Yorkshire

**Farfields Farmhouse ★★★★**
*Farmhouse*
Lockton, Pickering YO18 7NQ
t (01751) 460239
e stay@farfieldsfarm.co.uk
w farfieldsfarm.co.uk

**YHA Lockton ★★★★** *Hostel*
The Old School, Lockton
YO18 7PY
t (01751) 460376
e lockton@yha.org.uk
w yha.org.uk
▨▧▨

### LOFTHOUSE
### North Yorkshire

**Studfold Farm Activity**
**Centre ★★★** *Group Hostel*
Studfold Farm, Lofthouse,
Pateley Bridge HG3 5SG
t (01729) 755399
e ianwalker@studfold.fsnet.
co.uk
w studfoldfarm.co.uk

### LONDESBOROUGH
### East Riding of Yorkshire

**Towthorpe Grange ★★**
*Bed & Breakfast*
Towthorpe Lane,
Londesborough, Driffield
YO43 3LB
t (01430) 873814
e towthorpegrange@hotmail.
com
▨▧

### LONDONDERRY
### North Yorkshire

**Tatton Lodge ★★★**
*Guest House*
Londonderry DL7 9NF
t (01677) 422222
e enquiries@tattonlodge.co.uk
w tattonlodge.co.uk

### LOW ROW
### North Yorkshire

**Low Row Camping Barn/**
**Bunkhouse** *Bunkhouse*
Low Whita Farm, Richmond
DL11 6NT
t (01748) 884601
e rwcclarkson@aol.com

**Summer Lodge Farm ★★★**
*Farmhouse*
Low Row, Reeth DL11 6NP
t (01748) 886504

### LOXLEY
### South Yorkshire

**Barnfield House ★★★★**
*Guest Accommodation*
SILVER AWARD
Loxley Road, Loxley, Sheffield
S6 6RW
t (0114) 233 6365
e enquiries@barnfieldhouse.
com
w barnfieldhouse.com

### LUDDENDENFOOT
### West Yorkshire

**Rockcliffe West ★★★★**
*Bed & Breakfast*
Burnley Road, Luddendenfoot,
Halifax HX2 6HL
t (01422) 882151
e rockcliffe.b.b@virgin.net
w rockcliffewest.co.uk

### MALHAM
### North Yorkshire

**Malham YHA ★★★** *Hostel*
Skipton BD23 4DE
t (01729) 830321
e malham@yha.org.uk
w yha.org.uk
▨▧

**Miresfield Farm ★★★**
*Guest House*
Malham, Skipton BD23 4DA
t (01729) 830414
e chris@miresfield.freeserve.
co.uk
w miresfield-farm.com

### MALHAM MOOR
### North Yorkshire

**High Trenhouse ★★★★**
*Guest Accommodation*
Malham Moor, Settle
BD24 9PR
t (01729) 830322
e bernadette@
changeandinnovation.com
w high-trenhouse.co.uk

### MALTBY
### South Yorkshire

**The Cottages Guest House**
**★★** *Guest House*
1, 3 & 5 Bligh Road, Maltby,
Rotherham S66 8HX
t (01709) 813382

### MALTON
### North Yorkshire

**Barugh House ★★★★**
*Bed & Breakfast*
GOLD AWARD
Great Barugh, Malton
YO17 6UZ
t (01653) 668615
e barughhouse@aol.com

**The George Hotel ★★★** *Inn*
19 Yorkersgate, Malton
YO17 7AA
t (01653) 692884

**Manor Farm ★★★**
*Farmhouse*
Malton YO17 8RN
t (01944) 728268
e info@manorfarmonline.co.
uk
w manorfarmonline.co.uk

**Mill House Bed & Breakfast**
**★★★** *Farmhouse*
East Knapton, Malton
YO17 8JA
t (01944) 728026
e carol@millhouse822.
freeserve.co.uk

**Red House ★★★★**
*Bed & Breakfast*
SILVER AWARD
Wharram, Malton YO17 9TL
t (01944) 768185
e elaineatredhouse@hotmail.
com

### MAPPLEWELL
### South Yorkshire

**The Grange ★★★**
*Guest House*
29 Spark Lane, Mapplewell,
Barnsley S75 6AA
t (01226) 380078
e hwje454@aol.com

### MARKET WEIGHTON
### East Riding of Yorkshire

**Arras Farmhouse ★★★**
*Farmhouse*
Arras, Market Weighton
YO43 4RN
t (01430) 872404

**Red House ★★★★**
*Guest Accommodation*
North Cliffe, Market Weighton,
York YO43 4XB
t (01430) 827652
e simon.lyn@virgin.net
w redhousenorthcliffe.co.uk
▧

### MASHAM
### North Yorkshire

**Garden House ★★★★**
*Guest Accommodation*
1 Park Street, Masham, Ripon
HG4 4HN
t (01765) 689989
e suefurbymasham@gmail.
com

**Glasshouse B&B (Uredale**
**Glass) ★★★★**
*Guest Accommodation*
42 Market Place, Masham,
Ripon HG4 4EF
t (01765) 689780
e info@uredale.co.uk
w uredale.co.uk

**Park House ★★★★★**
*Guest Accommodation*
Jervaulx, Ripon HG4 4PH
t (01677) 460226
e ba123@btopenworld.com

**Warren House Farm ★★★★**
*Farmhouse*
High Ellington, Masham, Ripon
HG4 4PP
t (01677) 460244
e cathebroadley@msn.com

### MENSTON
### West Yorkshire

**Chevin End Guest House**
**★★★** *Guest House*
West Chevin Road, Menston,
Ilkley LS29 6BE
t (01943) 876845
e enquiries@
chevinendguesthouse.co.uk
w chevinendguesthouse.co.uk

### MIDDLEHAM
### North Yorkshire

**The Priory ★★★★**
*Guest House*
West End, Middleham,
Leyburn DL8 4QG
t (01969) 623279
e priory.guesthouse@virgin.
net

### MIDGLEY
### West Yorkshire

**Midgley Lodge Motel**
**★★★★**
*Guest Accommodation*
Bar Lane, Midgley, Wakefield
WF4 4JJ
t (01924) 830069
e midgleylodgemotel@tiscali.
co.uk
w midgleylodgemotel.co.uk

**MIDHOPESTONES**
South Yorkshire

**Ye Olde Mustard Pot**
★★★★ *Inn*
Mortimer Road, Sheffield
S36 4GW
t  (01226) 761155
e  reservations@mustardpot.
co.uk
w  yeoldemustardpot.co.uk

**MILLINGTON**
East Riding of Yorkshire

**Laburnum Cottage** ★★★
*Guest Accommodation*
Millington, Driffield YO42 1TX
t  (01759) 303055
e  roger&maureen@labcott.
fslife.co.uk

**MUKER**
North Yorkshire

**Muker Village Stores & Tea
Shop** ★★★★ *Bed & Breakfast*
The Village Stores, Muker,
Richmond DL11 6QG
t  (01748) 886409
e  mukerteashop@btinternet.
com
w  mukervillage.co.uk

**NAWTON**
North Yorkshire

**Little Manor Farm** ★★★★
*Farmhouse*
Highfield Lane, Nawton, York
YO62 7TH
t  (01439) 771672
e  penny-avison@tiscali.co.uk

**NEWBY WISKE**
North Yorkshire

**Well House** ★★★★
*Guest Accommodation*
Newby Wiske, Northallerton
DL7 9EX
t  (01609) 772253
e  info@wellhouse-
newbywiske.co.uk
w  wellhouse-newbywiske.co.
uk

**NEWTON-ON-RAWCLIFFE**
North Yorkshire

**Elm House Farm** ★★★★
*Farmhouse*
Newton-on-Rawcliffe, Pickering
YO18 8QA
t  (01751) 473223
w  elmhousefarm.co.uk

**The Old Vicarage** ★★★★★
*Guest Accommodation*
SILVER AWARD
Toftly View, Pickering
YO18 8QD
t  (01751) 476126
e  oldvic@toftlyview.co.uk
w  toftlyview.co.uk

**Swan Cottage** ★★★★
*Bed & Breakfast*
Newton-on-Rawcliffe, Pickering
YO18 8QA
t  (01751) 472502
e  swancottagenewton@
yahoo.co.uk

**NORTH CAVE**
East Riding of Yorkshire

**Albion House** ★★
*Bed & Breakfast*
18 Westgate, North Cave
HU15 2NJ
t  (01430) 422958
e  info@hawleys.info
w  hawleys.info

**NORTH FERRIBY**
East Riding of Yorkshire

**B & B @103** ★★★
*Bed & Breakfast*
103 Ferriby High Road, North
Ferriby, Hull HU14 3LA
t  (01482) 633637
e  info@bnb103.co.uk
w  bnb103.co.uk

**NORTHALLERTON**
North Yorkshire

**Elmscott** ★★★★
*Bed & Breakfast*
SILVER AWARD
10 Hatfield Road, Northallerton
DL7 8QX
t  (01609) 760575
e  elmscott@freenet.co.uk
w  elmscottbedandbreakfast.
co.uk

**Lovesome Hill Farm** ★★★★
*Farmhouse*
Lovesome Hill DL6 2PB
t  (01609) 772311
e  pearsonlhf@care4free.net

**Lovesome Hill Farm**
*Camping Barn*
Lovesome Hill, Northallerton
DL6 2PB
t  (01609) 772311

**Victoria House** ★★★★
*Bed & Breakfast*
36 South Parade, Northallerton
DL7 8SG
t  (01609) 776367
e  heslopgill@btinternet.com

**NORTON**
North Yorkshire

**Brambling Fields B&B**
★★★★ *Bed & Breakfast*
Brambling Fields, Scarborough
Road, Malton YO17 8EE
t  (01653) 698510

**The Union Inn** ★★★ *Inn*
46 Commercial Street, Norton,
Malton YO17 9ES
t  (01653) 692945

**NUNNINGTON**
North Yorkshire

**Sunley Court** ★★★
*Farmhouse*
Muscoates, Nunnington,
Helmsley YO62 5XQ
t  (01439) 748233
e  sunleycourt@tiscali.co.uk

**OSMOTHERLEY**
North Yorkshire

**Osmotherley YHA** ★★★
*Hostel*
Cote Ghyll, Osmotherley
DL6 3AH
t  (01609) 883575
e  osmotherley@yha.org.uk
w  yha.org.uk

**Vane House** ★★★★
*Guest Accommodation*
11a North End, Osmotherley
DL6 3BA
t  (01609) 883448
e  allan@vanehouse.co.uk
w  coast2coast.co.uk/
vanehouse

**OTLEY**
West Yorkshire

**Scaife Hall Farm** ★★★★
*Farmhouse* GOLD AWARD
Hardisty Hill, Blubberhouses,
Harrogate LS21 2PL
t  (01943) 880354
e  christine.a.ryder@btinternet.
com
w  scaifehallfarm.co.uk

**Wood Top Farm** ★★★★
*Farmhouse*
Off Norwood Edge, Lindley,
Otley LS21 2QS
t  (01943) 464010
e  mailwoodtop@aol.com

**OVER SILTON**
North Yorkshire

**Greystone Farm** ★★★★
*Farmhouse*
Over Silton, Thirsk YO7 2LH
t  (01609) 883468
e  greystone@freenet.co.uk

**OXENHOPE**
West Yorkshire

**Springfield Guest House**
★★★★ *Guest House*
Springfield, Shaw Lane,
Haworth BD22 9QL
t  (01535) 643951
e  best_bb_uk@msn.com
w  s-h-systems.co.uk/hotels/
springfl.html

**PATELEY BRIDGE**
North Yorkshire

**Bewerley Hall Farm** ★★★
*Farmhouse*
Bewerley, Pateley Bridge
HG3 5JA
t  (01423) 711636
e  chris@farmhouseholidays.
freeserve.co.uk
w  bewerleyhallfarm.co.uk

**Nidderdale Lodge Farm**
★★★ *Farmhouse*
Fellbeck, Harrogate HG3 5DR
t  (01423) 711677

**Talbot House** ★★★
*Guest House*
27 High Street, Pateley Bridge
HG3 5AL
t  (01423) 711597
e  reservations@talbothouse.
co.uk
w  talbothouse.co.uk

**PATRICK BROMPTON**
North Yorkshire

**Neesham Cottage** ★★★★
*Bed & Breakfast*
Patrick Brompton, Leyburn
DL8 1LN
t  (01677) 450271
e  info@neeshamcottage.co.uk
w  neeshamcottage.co.uk

**PATRINGTON**
East Riding of Yorkshire

**Mill Lodge** ★★★
*Guest Accommodation*
Station Road, Patrington
HU12 0NG
t  (01964) 630782
e  milllodge@mail.com
w  milllodge.com

**PENISTONE**
South Yorkshire

**Cubley Hall Inn** ★★★★ *Inn*
Mortimer Road, Penistone,
Sheffield S36 9DF
t  (01226) 766086
e  cubley.hall@ukonline.co.uk
w  cubleyhall.co.uk

**PICKERING**
North Yorkshire

**17 Burgate** ★★★★★
*Guest House* GOLD AWARD
Pickering YO18 7AU
t  (01751) 473463
e  info@17burgate.co.uk
w  17burgate.co.uk

**Apricot Lodge** ★★★★★
*Guest Accommodation*
SILVER AWARD
25 Crossgate Lane, Pickering
YO18 7EX
t  (01751) 477744
e  apricotlodge@beeb.net
w  apricotlodge.com

**Ashfield House** ★★★★
*Bed & Breakfast*
Ruffa Lane, Pickering
YO18 7HN
t  (01751) 477429
e  twotonethomas@hotmail.
com

**August Guest House** ★★★★
*Guest House*
3 Plane Trees, Rosedale,
Pickering YO18 8RF
t  (01751) 417328
e  mary@augustguesthouse.co.
uk
w  augustguesthouse.co.uk

**Barker Stakes Farm** ★★★★
*Farmhouse*
Lendals Lane, Pickering
YO18 8EE
t  (01751) 476759
e  info@barkerstakesfarm.com
w  barkerstakesfarm.co.uk

**Beech Cottage** ★★★
*Bed & Breakfast*
Newton-on-Rawcliffe, Pickering
YO18 8QQ
t  (01751) 417625

**Bramwood Guest House**
★★★★ *Guest House*
SILVER AWARD
19 Hallgarth, Pickering
YO18 7AW
t  (01751) 474066
e  bramwood@fsbdial.co.uk
w  bramwoodguesthouse.co.uk

**Bridge House** ★★★★
*Bed & Breakfast*
**SILVER AWARD**
8 Bridge Street, Pickering
YO18 8DT
t (01751) 477234
e kgbridgehouse@tiscali.co.uk
w pickeringuk.net/
bridgehouse

**Cawthorne House** ★★★★
*Guest House* **SILVER AWARD**
42 Eastgate, Pickering
YO18 7DU
t (01751) 477364
w cawthornehouse.co.uk

**Costa House** ★★★★
*Bed & Breakfast*
**SILVER AWARD**
12 Westgate, Pickering
YO18 8BA
t (01751) 474291
e ruth.leeming@ntlworld.com

**Eleven Westgate** ★★★★
*Bed & Breakfast*
**SILVER AWARD**
Eden House, Pickering
YO18 8BA
t (01751) 475111
e info@westgatebandb.co.uk
w westgatebandb.co.uk
▣☑

**Five Acre View** ★★★★
*Farmhouse*
Rosedale Abbey, Pickering
YO18 8RE
t (01751) 417830
e fiveacreview@aol.com
w 5acreview.co.uk

**Givendale Head Farm**
★★★★ *Farmhouse*
Ebberston, Snainton, Pickering
YO13 9PU
t (01723) 859383
e sue.gwilliam@talk21.com
w givendaleheadfarm.co.uk

**The Hawthornes** ★★★★
*Bed & Breakfast*
High Back Side, Middleton,
Pickering YO18 8PB
t (01751) 474755
e paulaappleby@btinternet.
com
w the-hawthornes.com

**Keld Farm Bed and
Breakfast** ★★★
*Bed & Breakfast*
Newton-on-Rawcliffe, Pickering
YO18 8QA
t (01751) 474039

**Kirkham Garth Bed and
Breakfast** ★★★
*Bed & Breakfast*
Kirkham Garth, Whitby Road,
Pickering YO18 7AT
t (01751) 474931
e kirkhamgarth@hotmail.co.uk
w kirkhamgarth.co.uk

**No. 9 B&B** ★★★★
*Bed & Breakfast*
**SILVER AWARD**
9 Thornton Road, Pickering
YO18 7HZ
t (01751) 476533
e enquiries@no9guesthouse.
co.uk
w no9guesthouse.co.uk

**Rains Farm** ★★★★
*Farmhouse* **SILVER AWARD**
Allerston, Pickering YO18 7PQ
t (01723) 859333
e allan@rainsfarm.freeserve.
co.uk
w rains-farm-holidays.co.uk

**Rectory Farm House** ★★★★
*Guest Accommodation*
Main Street, Levisham,
Pickering YO18 7NL
t (01751) 460491
e michael@levisham.com
w levisham.com

**Tangalwood** ★★★★
*Bed & Breakfast*
Roxby Road, Thornton Dale,
Pickering YO18 7SX
t (01751) 474688

**Vivers Mill** ★★★★
*Guest House*
Mill Lane, Pickering YO18 8DJ
t (01751) 473640
e viversmill@talk21.com
w viversmill.com

**Wildsmith House** ★★★★
*Bed & Breakfast*
**SILVER AWARD**
Marton, Sinnington,
Kirkbymoorside YO62 6RD
t (01751) 432702
e wildsmithhouse@btinternet.
com

**Tower House Executive
Guest House** ★★★★★
*Guest House* **SILVER AWARD**
21 Bondgate, Pontefract
WF8 2JP
t (01977) 699988
e towerhouse.guesthouse@
virgin.net
w towerhouseguesthouse.com

**Little Weghill Farm** ★★★★
*Farmhouse* **SILVER AWARD**
Weghill Road, Preston, Hull
HU12 8SX
t (01482) 897650
e info@littleweghillfarm.co.uk
w littleweghillfarm.co.uk
▣▣☑

**Hawthorn Cottage** ★★★★
*Bed & Breakfast*
Preston-under-Scar, Leyburn
DL8 4AQ
t (01969) 624492
e helen@ricduffield.com
w hawthorn-wensleydale.com

**Lynnwood House** ★★★
*Guest House*
18 Alexandra Road,
Uppermoor, Leeds LS28 8BY
t (0113) 257 1117
w lynnwoodhouse.co.uk

**Old Black Bull Inn** ★★★ *Inn*
Raskelf, Easingwold YO61 3LF
t (01347) 821431
e info@northyorkshotel.co.uk

**Elder Lea House** ★★★★★
*Guest Accommodation*
**GOLD AWARD**
Clough Lane, Rastrick, Halifax
HD6 3QH
t (01484) 717832
e elderleahouse@blueyonder.
co.uk

**Smugglers Rock Country
House** ★★★★
*Guest Accommodation*
Staintondale Road, Ravenscar,
Scarborough YO13 0ER
t (01723) 870044
e info@smugglersrock.co.uk
w smugglersrock.co.uk

**Cambridge House** ★★★★
*Guest House* **SILVER AWARD**
Arkengarthdale Road,
Richmond DL11 6QX
t (01748) 884633
e scambridge@fsbdial.co.uk
w cambridge-house-reeth.co.
uk
▣☑

**Hackney House** ★★★
*Guest Accommodation*
Reeth DL11 6TW
t (01748) 884302
e hackneyhse@tinyworld.co.
uk

**Springfield House** ★★★★
*Guest Accommodation*
Quaker Close, Reeth DL11 6UY
t (01748) 884634
e denise@guy426.fsnet.co.uk

**Dairyman's of Riccall**
★★★★
*Guest Accommodation*
14 Kelfield Road, York
YO19 6PG
t (01757) 248532
e bookings@dairymansriccall.
co.uk
w dairymansriccall.co.uk

**South Newlands Farm** ★★★
*Guest Accommodation*
Selby Road, York YO19 6QR
t (01757) 248203
e southnewlandsfarm@yahoo.
co.uk

**White Rose Villa** ★★★★
*Bed & Breakfast*
33 York Road, York YO19 6QG
t (01757) 248115
e whhiterosevilla@btinternet.
com

**27 Hurgill Road** ★★★
*Guest Accommodation*
Hurgill Road, Richmond
DL10 4AR
t (01748) 824092

**Beechfield** ★★★★
*Bed & Breakfast*
16 Beechfield Road, Richmond
DL10 4PN
t (01748) 824060
e thelmaj@tiscali.co.uk
w beechfieldrichmond.co.uk

**The Buck Inn** ★★★ *Inn*
27-29 Newbiggin, Richmond
DL10 4DX
t (01748) 822259
e info@thebuck-richmond.co.
uk
w thebuck-richmond.co.uk

**Emmanuel Guest House**
★★★ *Guest Accommodation*
41 Maison Dieu, Richmond
DL10 7AU
t (01748) 823584

**Frenchgate Guest House**
★★★★
*Guest Accommodation*
66 Frenchgate, Richmond
DL10 7AG
t (01748) 823421 &
07889 768696
e info@66frenchgate.co.uk
▣☑

**Mount Pleasant Farm**
★★★★ *Farmhouse*
**SILVER AWARD**
Whashton, Reeth DL11 7JP
t (01748) 822784
e info@
mountpleasantfarmhouse.co.uk
w mountpleasantfarmhouse.
co.uk

**Nuns Cottage** ★★★★
*Guest Accommodation*
5 Hurgill Road, Richmond
DL10 4AR
t (01748) 822809
e the.flints@ukgateway.net
w nunscottage.co.uk

**The Old Brewery Guest
House** ★★★ *Guest House*
29 The Green, Richmond
DL10 4RG
t (01748) 822460
e info@
oldbreweryguesthouse.com
w oldbreweryguesthhouse.
com
▣☑

**The Old Dairy** ★★★★
*Guest Accommodation*
Low Row, Reeth DL11 6PE
t (01748) 886215
e theolddairy@swaledale.org

**Pottergate Guest House**
★★★ *Guest House*
4 Pottergate, Richmond
DL10 4AB
t (01748) 823826

**The Restaurant on the Green**
★★★ *Guest Accommodation*
5-7 Bridge Street, Richmond
DL10 4RW
t (01748) 826229
e accom.bennett@talk21.com
w coast2coast.co.uk/
restaurantonthegreen
▣☑

**Richmond Camping Barn**
*Camping Barn*
East Applegarth Farm,
Westfields, Richmond
DL10 4SD
t (01748) 822940

**Rosedale Bed & Breakfast**
★★★★ *Guest House*
2 Pottergate, Richmond
DL10 4AB
t (01748) 823926
e gary53uk@hotmail.com
w richmondbedandbreakfast.
co.uk

**Strawberry House B&B**
★★★★ *Bed & Breakfast*
49 Maison Dieu, Richmond
DL10 7AU
t (01748) 829741
e wfohalloran@yahoo.co.uk

**Victoria House** ★★★★
*Guest Accommodation*
3 Terrace Gardens, Linden
Close, Richmond DL10 7AL
t (01748) 824830

**West End Guest House &
Cottages** ★★★★
*Guest Accommodation*
45 Reeth Road, Richmond
DL10 4EX
t (01748) 824783
e westend@richmond.org
w stayatwestend.com

**Whashton Springs Farm**
★★★★ *Farmhouse*
**SILVER AWARD**
Whashton, Reeth DL11 7JS
t (01748) 822884
e whashtonsprings@
btconnect.com
w whashtonsprings.co.uk

**The White House** ★★★★
*Bed & Breakfast*
Gilling Road, Richmond
DL10 5AA
t (01748) 825491

**Willance House** ★★★★
*Guest House*
24 Frenchgate, Richmond
DL10 7AG
t (01748) 824467
e willancehouse@hotmail.co.
uk
w willancehouse.com

**Barn Close Farm** ★★★★
*Farmhouse*
Old Byland, Helmsley
YO62 5LH
t (01439) 798321

**Slate Rigg Farm** ★★★★
*Farmhouse*
Birthwaite Lane, Ripley
HG3 3JQ
t (01423) 770135
e slateriggfarm@hotmail.com
w slate-rigg-farm.co.uk

**Bishopton Grove House**
★★★ *Guest Accommodation*
Bishopton, Ripon HG4 2QL
t (01765) 600888

**Box Tree Cottages** ★★★★
*Guest House*
Coltsgate Hill, Ripon HG4 2AB
t (01765) 698006
e riponbandb@aol.com
w boxtreecottages.com

**Crescent Lodge** ★★★★
*Guest Accommodation*
42 North Street, Ripon
HG4 1EN
t (01765) 609589
e simpgry@aol.com
w crescent-lodge.com

**Fountain Guest House**
★★★★
*Guest Accommodation*
25 North Road, Ripon HG4 1JP
t (01765) 606012
e reservations@
fountainhouseripon.co.uk
w fountainhouseripon.co.uk

**Fremantle House** ★★★
*Bed & Breakfast*
35 North Road, Ripon HG4 1JR
t (01765) 605819
e jcar105462@aol.com
w riponforward.homestead.
com/freemantle.html

**Mallard Grange** ★★★★★
*Farmhouse* **SILVER AWARD**
Fountains Abbey, Aldfield,
Ripon HG4 3BE
t (01765) 620242
e maggie@mallardgrange.co.
uk
w mallardgrange.co.uk

**Park Street B&B** ★★★★
*Guest Accommodation*
9 Park Street, Ripon HG4 2AX
t (01765) 606102
e maureen@grandison.co.uk
w 9parkstreet.com

**Ravencroft B&B** ★★★★
*Bed & Breakfast*
Moorside Avenue, Ripon
HG4 1TA
t (01765) 602543
e guestmail@btopenworld.
com
w ravencroftbandb.com

**River Side Guest House**
★★★ *Guest Accommodation*
20-21 Iddesleigh Terrace,
Ripon HG4 1QW
t (01765) 603864
e christopher.pearson3@
virgin.net

**The Royal Oak** ★★★ *Inn*
36 Kirkgate, Ripon HG4 1PB
t (01765) 602284
w timothy.taylor.co.uk/
royaloak

**Sharow Cross House**
★★★★★ *Guest House*
**SILVER AWARD**
Dishforth Road, Sharow, Ripon
HG4 5BQ
t (01765) 609866
e sharowcrosshouse@
btinternet.com
w sharowcrosshouse.com

**The White Horse** ★★★ *Inn*
61 North Street, Ripon
HG4 1EN
t (01765) 603622
e david.bate13@btopenworld.
com
w white-horse-ripon.co.uk

**Over The Bridge** ★★★★
*Guest House* **SILVER AWARD**
Bridge End, Ripponden, Halifax
HX6 4DF
t (01422) 820226
e tcgp2@hotmail.com
w over-the-bridge.co.uk

**Thurst House Farm** ★★★★
*Guest Accommodation*
Ripponden, Sowerby Bridge
HX6 4NN
t (01422) 822820
e thursthousefarm@
bushinternet.com

**Cliff Farm** *Camping Barn*
Cliff Farm Holidays, Camping
Barn, Kirkbymoorside
YO62 6SS
t (01751) 473792
e jean.scaling@btinternet.com
w clifffarmholidays.com

**Lee-Side** ★★★★
*Guest Accommodation*
**SILVER AWARD**
Mount Pleasant South, Robin
Hood's Bay, Whitby YO22 4RQ
t (01947) 881143
e lee-side@rhbay.co.uk
w lee-side.rhbay.co.uk

**Marnardale Cottage** ★★★★
*Bed & Breakfast*
8 Sunny Side, Robin Hood's
Bay YO22 4SR
t (01947) 880677
e terry@manardale.co.uk
w marnardalecottage.co.uk

**North Ings** ★★★★
*Guest Accommodation*
Station Road, Robin Hood's
Bay YO22 4RA
t (01947) 880064
e wendy@northings.co.uk
w northings.co.uk

**Bridge End** ★★★
*Bed & Breakfast*
159 Chantry Road,
Northallerton DL7 8JJ
t (01609) 772655

**Sevenford House** ★★★★
*Bed & Breakfast*
**SILVER AWARD**
Rosedale Abbey, Pickering
YO18 8SE
t (01751) 417283
e sevenford@aol.com
w sevenford.com

**Ann's Cottage** ★★★★
*Guest Accommodation*
**SILVER AWARD**
Hill Yard Cottage, Rosedale
East, Pickering YO18 8RH
t (01751) 417646
e ann@annscottage.inuk.com
w annscottage.inuk.com

**Fitzwilliam Arms Hotel**
★★★ *Guest Accommodation*
Taylors Lane, Parkgate,
Rotherham S62 6EE
t (01709) 522744
w fitzwilliam-arms-hotel.co.uk

**Ellerby Hotel** ★★★★ *Inn*
**SILVER AWARD**
Ryeland Lane, Ellerby,
Saltburn-by-the-Sea TS13 5LP
t (01947) 840342
e david@ellerbyhotel.co.uk
w ellerbyhotel.co.uk

**The Firs** ★★★ *Guest House*
26 Hinderwell Lane, Runswick
Bay, Nr Whitby TS13 5HR
t (01947) 840433
e mandy.shackleton@talk21.
com
w the-firs.co.uk

**Esk View Cottage** ★★★★
*Bed & Breakfast*
The Carrs, Whitby YO21 1RL
t (01947) 605658

**Ruswarp Hall** ★★★
*Guest Accommodation*
4-6 High Street, Ruswarp,
Whitby YO21 1NH
t (01947) 602801
e colinscarth@aol.com
w ruswarphallhotel.co.uk

**Aaron House** ★★
*Bed & Breakfast*
20 Lightfoots Avenue,
Scarborough YO12 5NS
t (01723) 354225

**Aartswood Guest House** ★★
*Guest House*
27-29 Trafalgar Square,
Scarborough YO12 7PZ
t (01723) 360689
e william@aartswood.
wanadoo.co.uk
w yorkshirecoast.co.uk/
aartswood

**Acacia Private Hotel** ★★★
*Guest House*
37 Esplanade Road,
Scarborough YO11 2AT
t (01723) 373270
w acaciahotel.co.uk

**Adene Hotel** ★★★
*Guest Accommodation*
39 Esplanade Road,
Scarborough YO11 2AT
t (01723) 373658
e harvey@adenehotel.fsnet.
co.uk

---

**Admiral** ★★★
*Guest Accommodation*
13 West Square, Scarborough
YO11 1TW
t (01723) 375084
e sandy.theadmiral@
btinternet.com
w theadmiralhotel.co.uk

**Ainsley** ★★★
*Guest Accommodation*
4 Rutland Terrace, Queens
Parade, Scarborough YO12 7JB
t (01723) 364832
e info@theainsleyhotel.co.uk
w theainsleyhotel.co.uk

**Ainsley Court Guest House**
★★★★ *Guest House*
112 North Marine Road,
Scarborough YO12 7JA
t (01723) 500352
e lynn@ainsleycourt.co.uk
w ainsleycourt.co.uk

**Airedale Guest House**
★★★★ *Guest House*
23 Trafalgar Square,
Scarborough YO12 7PZ
t (01723) 366809
e shaunatairedale@aol.com
w airedaleguesthouse
scarborough.co.uk

**The Alexander Hotel**
★★★★
*Guest Accommodation*
SILVER AWARD
33 Burniston Road,
Scarborough YO12 6PG
t (01723) 363178
e alex@atesto.freeserve.co.uk
w alexanderhotelscarborough.
co.uk

**Alexandra House** ★★★★
*Guest House*
21 West Street, Scarborough
YO11 2QR
t (01723) 503205
e info@scarborough-
alexandra.co.uk
w scarborough-alexandra.co.
uk

**The Almar** ★★★
*Guest Accommodation*
116 Columbus Ravine,
Scarborough YO12 7QZ
t (01723) 372887
e bevandphill@rendellp.fsnet.
co.uk

**Ashburton Hotel** ★★★★
*Guest Accommodation*
43 Valley Road, Scarborough
YO11 2LX
t (01723) 374382
e stay@ashburtonhotel.co.uk
w ashburtonhotel.co.uk

**Atlanta Hotel** ★★★★
*Guest Accommodation*
60-62 Columbus Ravine,
Scarborough YO12 7QU
t (01723) 360996
e info@atlanta-hotel.co.uk
w atlanta-hotel.co.uk

**Blands Cliff Lodge** ★★★
*Guest Accommodation*
Scarborough YO11 1NR
t (01723) 363653 &
(01723) 363653
e tonight@yorkshire-coast.co.
uk

**Brambles Lodge** ★★★
*Guest Accommodation*
156-158 Filey Road,
Scarborough YO11 3AA
t (01723) 374613
e nightingales22@aol.com
w accommodation.uk.net/
brambleslodge.htm

**Hotel Catania** ★★★★
*Guest House*
141 Queens Parade,
Scarborough YO12 7HU
t (01723) 364516
e catania@yorkshire.net
w hotelcatania.co.uk

**Cavendish Hotel** ★★★★
*Guest Accommodation*
53 Esplanade Road,
Scarborough YO11 2AT
t (01723) 362108
e anne@
cavendishscarborough.co.uk
w cavendishscarborough.co.uk

**Clarence Gardens Hotel**
★★★ *Guest Accommodation*
Blenheim Terrace, Scarborough
YO12 7HF
t (01723) 374884
e enquiries@clarencegardens.
force9.co.uk
w clarencegardenshotel.net

**Cliffside Hotel** ★★★
*Guest House*
79-81 Queens Parade,
Scarborough YO12 7HH
t (01723) 361087
e cliffside@fsmail.net
w yorkshirecoast.co.uk/
cliffside

**Cordelia Hotel** ★★★★
*Guest Accommodation*
51 Esplanade Road,
Scarborough YO11 2AT .
t (01723) 363393
e kathie@cordeliahotel.fsnet.
co.uk
w cordeliahotel.co.uk

**The Croft** ★★★
*Guest Accommodation*
87 Queens Parade,
Scarborough YO12 7HY
t (01723) 373904
e information@crofthotel.co.
uk
w crofthotel.co.uk/

**Derwent House** ★★★
*Guest House*
6 Rutland Terrace, Queens
Parade, Scarborough YO12 7JB
t (01723) 373880
e info@derwenthousehotel.
co.uk
w derwenthousehotel.co.uk

**Dolphin Guest House** ★★★
*Guest House*
151 Columbus Ravine,
Scarborough YO12 7QZ
t (01723) 341914
e dolphinguesthouse@
btinternet.com
w thedolphin.info

**Donnington Hotel** ★★★
*Guest House*
13 Givendale Road,
Scarborough YO12 6LE
t (01723) 374394
e bookings@donningtonhotel.
co.uk
w donningtonhotel.co.uk

**Douglas Guest House** ★★★
*Guest House*
153 Columbus Ravine,
Scarborough YO12 7QZ
t (01723) 371311

**Hotel Ellenby** ★★★★
*Guest House*
95-97 Queens Parade,
Scarborough YO12 7HY
t (01723) 372916
e johnfail@aol.com
w ellenbyhotel.com

**Empire Hotel** ★★★
*Guest House*
39 Albemarle Crescent,
Scarborough YO11 1XX
t (01723) 373564
e gillian@empire1939.
wanadoo.co.uk

**Esplanade Gardens Guest
House** ★★★
*Guest Accommodation*
24 Esplanade Gardens,
Scarborough YO11 2AP
t (01723) 360728
e kerry@khubbard.fsnet.co.uk
w esplanadegardens
scarborough.co.uk

**Gordon Hotel** ★★★★
*Guest House*
Ryndleside, Scarborough
YO12 6AD
t (01723) 362177
e sales@gordonhotel.co.uk
w gordonhotel.co.uk

**Green Gables Private Hotel**
★★★ *Guest House*
West Bank, Scarborough
YO12 4DX
t (01723) 361005

**Greno Seafront Hotel** ★★★
*Guest Accommodation*
25 Blenheim Terrace, Queens
Parade, Scarborough
YO12 7HD
t (01723) 375705

**Harmony Country Lodge**
★★★★ *Guest House*
80 Limestone Road, Burniston,
Scarborough YO13 0DG
t 0800 298 5840
e tony@harmonylodge.net
w harmonylodge.net

**Headlands Hotel** ★★★
*Guest House*
16 Weydale Avenue,
Scarborough YO12 6AX
t (01723) 373717
e info@theheadlandshotel.co.
uk
w theheadlandshotel.co.uk

**Hotel Helaina** ★★★★
*Guest Accommodation*
SILVER AWARD
14 Blenheim Terrace,
Scarborough YO12 7HF
t (01723) 375191
e info@hotelhelaina.co.uk

**Howdale** ★★★★
*Guest House*
121 Queen's Parade,
Scarborough YO12 7HU
t (01723) 372696
e mail@howdalehotel.co.uk
w howdalehotel.co.uk

**Kenways Guest House** ★★★
*Guest House*
9 Victoria Park Avenue,
Scarborough YO12 7TR
t (01723) 365757
e info@kenwaysguesthouse.
co.uk
w kenwaysguesthouse.co.uk

**Killerby Cottage Farm**
★★★★ *Bed & Breakfast*
SILVER AWARD
Killerby Lane, Cayton,
Scarborough YO11 3TP
t (01723) 581236
e val@stainedglasscentre.co.
uk
w smoothhound.co.uk/hotels/
killerby

**Kimberley Hotel** ★★★★
*Guest House*
131 North Marine Road,
Scarborough YO12 7HU
t (01723) 372734
e kimberleyhotel@hotmail.
com
w kimberleyseafronthotel.co.
uk

**The Kingsway** ★★★★
*Guest House*
58 Columbus Ravine,
Scarborough YO12 7QU
t (01723) 372948
e info@
kingswayhotelscarborough.co.
uk
w kingswayhotelscarborough.
co.uk

**Hotel Levante** ★★★
*Guest House*
118 Columbus Ravine,
Scarborough YO12 7QZ
t (01723) 372366

**Lincoln Hotel** ★★★
*Guest House*
112 Columbus Ravine,
Scarborough YO12 7QZ
t (01723) 500897
e enquiries@lincolnhotel.net
w lincolnhotel.net

**The Lonsdale Villa** ★★★★
*Guest Accommodation*
Lonsdale Road, Scarborough
YO11 2QY
t (01723) 363383
e enquiries@lonsdalevilla.com
w lonsdalevilla.com

**Lyncris Manor Hotel** ★★★★
*Guest Accommodation*
45 Northstead Manor Drive,
Scarborough YO12 6AF
t (01723) 361052
e lyncris@manorhotel.fsnet.
co.uk
w manorhotel.fsnet.co.uk

**The Lynton** ★★★
*Guest House*
104 Columbus Ravine,
Scarborough YO12 7QZ
t (01723) 374240
e paul.watson6@btconnect.
com
w thelyntonscarborough.co.uk

**Lysander Hotel** ★★★★
*Guest House*
22 Weydale Avenue,
Scarborough YO12 6AX
t (01723) 373369
w lysanderhotel.co.uk

**Marine View Guest House**
★★★ *Guest House*
34 Blenheim Terrace,
Scarborough YO12 7HD
t (01723) 361864
e info@marineview.co.uk
w marineview.co.uk

**Moseley Lodge Hotel**
★★★★ *Guest House*
26 Avenue Victoria, South Cliff,
Scarborough YO11 2QT
t (01723) 360564
e holidays@moseleylodge.co.
uk
w moseleylodge.co.uk

**Mount House Hotel** ★★★★
*Guest Accommodation*
33 Trinity Road, South Cliff,
Scarborough YO11 2TD
t (01723) 362967
e bookings@mounthouse-
hotel.co.uk
w mounthouse-hotel.co.uk

**Mountview Private Hotel
(Non-Smoking)** ★★★★
*Guest House*
32 West Street, Scarborough
YO11 2QP
t (01723) 500608
e info@mountview-hotel.co.uk
w mountview-hotel.co.uk

**The Newlands** ★★★
*Guest House*
80 Columbus Ravine,
Scarborough YO12 7QU
t (01723) 367261
e newlandshotel@btconnect.
com
w thenewlandshotel.co.uk

**Norlands Hotel** ★★★★
*Guest Accommodation*
10 Weydale Avenue,
Scarborough YO12 6BA
t (01723) 362606
e info@norlandshotel.co.uk
w norlandshotel.co.uk

**Outlook Hotel** ★★★
*Guest Accommodation*
18 Ryndleside, Scarborough
YO12 6AD
t (01723) 364900
e info@outlookhotel.co.uk
w outlookhotel.co.uk

**Parmelia Hotel** ★★★
*Guest Accommodation*
17 West Street, Scarborough
YO11 2QN
t (01723) 361914
e parmeliahotel@btinternet.
com
w parmeliahotel.co.uk

**Philmore** ★★★★
*Guest House*
126 Columbus Ravine,
Scarborough YO12 7QZ
t (01723) 361516
e info@philmorehotel.co.uk
w philmore.co.uk

**Phoenix Court** ★★★★
*Guest House*
8-9 Rutland Terrace, Queens
Parade, Scarborough YO12 7JB
t (01723) 501150
e info@hotel-phoenix.co.uk
w hotel-phoenix.co.uk

**The Phoenix Guest House**
★★★ *Guest House*
157 Columbus Ravine,
Scarborough YO12 7QZ
t (01723) 368319

**Powys Lodge Hotel** ★★★★
*Guest House*
2 Westbourne Road, South
Cliff, Scarborough YO11 2SP
t (01723) 374019
e info@powyslodge.co.uk
w powyslodge.co.uk

**Princess Court Guest House**
★★★★
*Guest Accommodation*
11 Princess Royal Terrace,
Scarborough YO11 2RP
t (01723) 501922
e iruin@princesscourt.co.uk
w princesscourt.co.uk

**Redcliffe Hotel** ★★★★
*Guest Accommodation*
18 Prince of Wales Terrace,
South Bay, Scarborough
YO11 2AL
t (01723) 372310
e b.m.bean@daisybroadband.
co.uk
w theredcliffehotel.com

**Riviera Town House** ★★★★
*Guest Accommodation*
St Nicholas Cliff, Scarborough
YO11 2ES
t (01723) 372277
e rivierahotel@scarborough.
co.uk
w rivierahotel.scarborough.co.
uk

**Robyn's Guest House** ★★★
*Guest House*
139 Columbus Ravine,
Scarborough YO12 7QZ
t (01723) 374217
e info@robynsguesthouse.co.
uk
w robynsguesthouse.co.uk

**Rose Dene** ★★★
*Guest Accommodation*
106 Columbus Ravine,
Scarborough YO12 7QZ
t (01723) 374252
e sandra@rose-denehotel.co.
uk
w rosedenehotel.co.uk

**The Russell Hotel** ★★★★
*Guest House*
22 Ryndleside, Scarborough
YO12 6AD
t (01723) 365453
w russellhotel.net

**Sawdon Heights** ★★★★
*Farmhouse* **SILVER AWARD**
Scarborough YO13 9EB
t (01723) 859321
e info@sawdonheights.com
w sawdonheights.com

**Scarborough Travel and
Holiday Lodge** ★★★
*Guest Accommodation*
33 Valley Road, Scarborough
YO11 2LX
t (01723) 363537
e enquiries@scarborough-
lodge.co.uk
w scarborough-lodge.co.uk

**Scarborough YHA** ★★★
*Hostel*
The White House, Burniston
Road, Scarborough YO13 0DA
t 0870 770 6022
e scarborough@yha.org.uk
w yha.org.uk

**Selomar Hotel** ★★★★
*Guest House*
23 Blenheim Terrace,
Scarborough YO12 7HD
t (01723) 364964
e info@selomarhotel.co.uk
w selomarhotel.co.uk

**The Sheridan** ★★★
*Guest Accommodation*
108 Columbus Ravine,
Scarborough YO12 7QZ
t (01723) 372094
e kimarfhoteljp@aol.com
w thesheridanhotel.co.uk

**Stuart House** ★★★★
*Guest House*
1 & 2 Rutland Terrace, Queens
Parade, Scarborough YO12 7JB
t (01723) 373768
e h.graham@btconnect.com
w thestuarthousehotel.com

**Sunningdale** ★★★★
*Guest House*
105 Peasholm Drive,
Scarborough YO12 7NB
t (01723) 372041
e sunningdale@yorkshire.net
w sunningdale-scarborough.
co.uk

**Sylvern House** ★★★★
*Guest House*
25 New Queen Street,
Scarborough YO12 7HJ
t (01723) 360952
e sylvernhouse@aol.com
w smoothhound.co.uk/hotels/
sylvern.html

**Tall Storeys** ★★★★
*Guest Accommodation*
Old Town, 131 Longwestgate,
Scarborough YO11 1RQ
t (01723) 373696
e gordon@gordonking.
demon.co.uk
w tallstoreyshotel.co.uk

**The Terrace Hotel** ★★
*Guest House*
69 Westborough, Scarborough
YO11 1TS
t (01723) 374937
e theterracehotel@btinternet.
com
w smoothhound.co.uk/
a13751.html

**Toulson Court** ★★★★
*Guest Accommodation*
100 Columbus Ravine,
Scarborough YO12 7QZ
t (01723) 503218
e toulsoncourt@scarborough.
co.uk
w toulsoncourt.scarborough.
co.uk

**Tudor House** ★★★
*Guest House*
164-166 North Marine Road,
Scarborough YO12 7HZ
t (01723) 361270

**Victoria Seaview Hotel**
★★★★
*Guest Accommodation*
125 Queens Parade,
Scarborough YO12 7HY
t (01723) 362164
e info@victoriaseaviewhotel.
co.uk
w victoriaseaviewhotel.co.uk

**Villa Marina** ★★★★
*Guest House*
59 Northstead Manor Drive,
Scarborough YO12 6AF
t (01723) 361088

**West Lodge Private Hotel**
★★ *Guest House*
38 West Street, Scarborough
YO11 2QP
t (01723) 500754

**Weston Hotel** ★★★
*Guest Accommodation*
33-34 Esplanade, Scarborough
YO11 2AR
t (01723) 373423
e info@westonhotel.co.uk
w westonhotel.co.uk

**The Wharncliffe** ★★★★
*Guest Accommodation*
26 Blenheim Terrace,
Scarborough YO12 7HD
t (01723) 374635
e info@
thewharncliffescarborough.co.
uk
w thewharncliffescarborough.
co.uk

**White Rails Hotel** ★★★★
*Guest House*
128 Columbus Ravine,
Scarborough YO12 7QZ
t (01723) 362800
e info@whiterailshotel.co.uk
w whiterailshotel.co.uk

**The Whiteley** ★★★★
*Guest Accommodation*
99-101 Queens Parade,
Scarborough YO12 7HY
t (01723) 373514
e whiteleyhotel@bigfoot.com
w yorkshire-coast.co.uk/
whiteley

**Willow Dene Hotel** ★★★
*Guest House*
110 Columbus Ravine,
Scarborough YO12 7QZ
t (01723) 365173
e andy@willowdenehotel.com
w willowdenehotel.co.uk

**SCOTCH CORNER**
North Yorkshire

**Vintage Inn** ★★ *Inn*
Scotch Corner, Middleton Tyas
DL10 6NP
t (01748) 824424
e thevintagescotchcorner@
btopenworld.com
w thevintagehotel.co.uk

**SELBY**
North Yorkshire

**Hazeldene Guest House**
★★★ *Guest House*
34 Brook Street, Selby
YO8 4AR
t (01757) 704809
e selbystay@breathe.com
w hazeldene-selby.co.uk

**The Old Vicarage ★★★★**
*Guest Accommodation*
Main Street, Kellington, Goole
DN14 0NE
t (01977) 661119
e keloldvic@aol.com
w theoldvicarageyorkshire.co.
uk

**The Willows ★★★**
*Guest House*
White Street, Cockret Close,
Selby YO8 4BS
t (01757) 701271
e thewillowsguesthouse@
hotmail.co.uk
w thewillowsselby.f9.co.uk

### SETTLE
North Yorkshire

**Halsteads Barn ★★★★**
*Bed & Breakfast*
SILVER AWARD
Mewith, Bentham, Lancaster
LA2 7AR
t (01524) 262641
e info@halsteadsbarn.co.uk
w halsteadsbarn.co.uk

**King William The Fourth
Guest House ★★★★**
*Guest House*
King William House, High
Street, Settle BD24 9EX
t (01729) 825994
e info@kingwilliamthefourth
guesthouse.co.uk
w kingwilliamthefourth
guesthouse.co.uk

**Mainsfield ★★★★**
*Bed & Breakfast*
SILVER AWARD
Stackhouse Lane, Giggleswick,
Settle BD24 0DL
t (01729) 823549
e mainsfield_bb@
btopenworld.com
w mainsfieldguesthouse.co.uk

**Maypole Inn ★★★** *Inn*
Maypole Green, Long Preston,
Skipton BD23 4PH
t (01729) 840219
e robert@maypole.co.uk
w maypole.co.uk

**Oast Guest House**
Rating Applied For
*Guest House*
5 Penyghent View, Settle
BD24 9JJ
t (01729) 822989
w oastguesthouse.co.uk

**The Plough Inn at
Wigglesworth ★★★** *Inn*
The Plough Inn, Wigglesworth,
Settle BD23 4RJ
t (01729) 840243
e sue@ploughinn.info
w ploughinn.info

**Royal Oak Hotel ★★★** *Inn*
Market Place, Settle BD24 9ED
t (01729) 822561
e royaloaksettle@hotmail.co.
uk

**Scar Close Farm ★★★★**
*Farmhouse*
Feizor, Austwick, Lancaster
LA2 8DF
t (01729) 823496

**Whitefriars Country Guest
House ★★★★**
*Guest Accommodation*
Church Street, Settle BD24 9JD
t (01729) 823753
e info@whitefriars-settle.co.uk
w whitefriars-settle.co.uk

### SEWERBY
East Riding of Yorkshire

**The Poplars Motel ★★★**
*Guest Accommodation*
45 Jewison Lane, Sewerby
YO15 1DX
t (01262) 677251
w the-poplars.co.uk

### SHAROW
North Yorkshire

**Half Moon Inn ★★★** *Inn*
Sharow Lane, Sharow, Ripon
HG4 5BP
t (01765) 600291
e info@halfmoonsharow.co.uk
w halfmoonsharow.co.uk

### SHEFFIELD
South Yorkshire

**Beighton Bed & Breakfast
★★★** *Bed & Breakfast*
48-50 High Street, Beighton,
Sheffield S20 1EA
t (0114) 269 2004
e beightonbandb@aol.com

**Coniston Guest House ★★★**
*Guest House*
90 Beechwood Road,
Hillsborough, Sheffield S6 4LQ
t (0114) 233 9680
e conistonguest@freeuk.com

**Etruria House Hotel ★★★**
*Guest House*
91 Crookes Road, Sheffield
S10 5BD
t (0114) 266 2241
e etruria@waitrose.com

**Gulliver's Bed And Breakfast
★★★** *Guest Accommodation*
167 Ecclesall Road South,
Sheffield S11 9PN
t (0114) 262 0729

**Ivory House Hotel ★★★**
*Guest Accommodation*
34 Wostenholm Road,
Sheffield S7 1LJ
t (0114) 255 1853
e ivoryhousehotel@amserve.
com

**Loadbrook Cottages ★★★★**
*Bed & Breakfast*
Game Lane, Loadbrook,
Sheffield S6 6GT
t (0114) 233 1619
e alisoncolver@hotmail.com
w smoothhound.co.uk/hotels/
load.html

**The Noose and Gibbet ★** *Inn*
97 Broughton Lane, Attercliffe,
Sheffield S9 2DE
t (0114) 261 7182

**Parson House Farm ★★★**
*Guest Accommodation*
Longshaw, Sheffield S11 7TZ
t (01433) 631017
e debbel@btconnect.com
w parsonhouse.co.uk

**Psalter House ★★★★**
*Bed & Breakfast*
17 Clifford Road, Sheffield
S11 9AQ
t (0114) 255 7758
w smoothhound.co.uk/hotels/
psalter.html

**Riverside Court Hotel ♦♦**
*Guest Accommodation*
4 Nursery Street, Sheffield
S3 8GG
t (0114) 273 1962
e enquire@riversidecourt.co.
uk
w riversidecourt.co.uk

**Tyndale ★★★**
*Guest Accommodation*
164 Millhouses Lane, Sheffield
S7 2HE
t (0114) 236 1660

### SHELLEY
West Yorkshire

**Three Acres Inn and
Restaurant ★★★★**
*Restaurant with Rooms*
Roydhouse, Shelley HD8 8LR
t (01484) 602606
e 3acres@globalnet.co.uk
w 3acres.com

### SHIBDEN
West Yorkshire

**Ploughcroft Cottage ★★★**
*Guest Accommodation*
53 Ploughcroft Lane, Halifax
HX3 6TX
t (01422) 341205
e ploughcroft.cottage@
care4free.net
w ploughcroftcottage.com

### SHIPLEY
West Yorkshire

**Clifton Lodge Guest House
★★★** *Guest House*
75 Kirkgate, Shipley BD18 3LU
t (01274) 580509
e cliftonlodge75@hotmail.com

### SILSDEN
West Yorkshire

**Pickersgill Manor Farm
★★★★** *Farmhouse*
Low Lane, Silsden, Bradford
BD20 9JH
t (01535) 655228
e pickersgillmanorfarm@
tiscali.co.uk
w dalesfarmhouse.co.uk

### SINNINGTON
North Yorkshire

**Green Lea ★★★★**
*Bed & Breakfast*
Main Street, Sinnington,
Pickering YO62 6SH
t (01751) 432008

### SKEEBY
North Yorkshire

**Ewden House ★★★★**
*Guest Accommodation*
Sedbury Lane, Richmond
DL10 5ED
t (01748) 824473

**New Skeeby Grange**
**★★★★★** *Bed & Breakfast*
SILVER AWARD
Sedbury Lane, Richmond
DL10 5ED
t (01748) 822276
e gandmf@tiscali.co.uk
w newskeebygrange.co.uk

**The Old Chapel ★★★★**
*Bed & Breakfast*
Richmond Road, Skeeby,
Richmond DL10 5DR
t (01748) 824170
e hazel@theoldchapel.fsnet.
co.uk

### SKIPSEA
East Riding of Yorkshire

**Village Farm ★★★★**
*Guest Accommodation*
SILVER AWARD
Back Street, Skipsea, Driffield
YO25 8SW
t (01262) 468479
e info@villagefarmskipsea.co.
uk
w villagefarmskipsea.co.uk

### SKIPTON
North Yorkshire

**Carlton House ★★★★**
*Guest Accommodation*
46 Keighley Road, Skipton
BD23 2NB
t (01756) 700921
e carltonhouse@rapidial.co.uk
w carltonhouse.rapidial.co.uk

**Chinthurst ★★★★★**
*Guest House*
Otley Road, Skipton BD23 1EX
t (01756) 799264
e info@chinthurst.co.uk
w chinthurst.co.uk

**Cononley Hall Bed &
Breakfast ★★★★★**
*Bed & Breakfast*
SILVER AWARD
Main Street, Cononley, Skipton
BD20 8LJ
t (01535) 633923
e cononleyhall@madasafish.
com
w cononleyhall.co.uk

**Craven Heifer Inn ★★★** *Inn*
Grassington Road, Skipton
BD23 3LA
t (01756) 792521
e john@cravenheifer.co.uk
w cravenheifer.co.uk

**Cravendale Guest House
★★★** *Guest House*
57 Keighley Road, Skipton
BD23 2LX
t (01756) 795129

**Dalesgate Lodge ★★★★**
*Guest Accommodation*
69 Gargrave Road, Skipton
BD23 1QN
t (01756) 790672
e dalesgatelodge@hotmail.
com

**The Masons Arms Inn ★★★**
*Inn*
Barden Road, Skipton
BD23 6SN
t (01756) 792754
e info@masonsarmseastby.co.
uk
w masonsarmseastby.co.uk

**Napier's Restaurant & Accommodation** ★★★★
*Restaurant with Rooms*
Chapel Hill, Skipton BD23 1NL
t (01756) 799688
e info@accommodation-skipton.co.uk
w restaurant-skipton.co.uk

**Newton Grange** ★★★★
*Bed & Breakfast*
Bank Newton, Gargrave, Skipton BD23 3NT
t (01756) 748140 & (01756) 796016
e bookings@banknewton. fsnet.co.uk
w cravencountryconnections. co.uk

**Red Lion Hotel** ★★★ *Inn*
High Street, Skipton BD23 1DT
t (01756) 790718

**Skipton Park Guest'otel Ltd** ★★★★ *Guest House*
2 Salisbury Street, Skipton BD23 1NQ
t (01756) 700640
e derekchurch@skiptonpark. freeserve.co.uk
w skiptonpark.co.uk

**The Woolly Sheep** ★★★ *Inn*
38 Sheep Street, Skipton BD23 1HY
t (01756) 700966
w timothytaylor.co.uk/ woollysheep

SLAITHWAITE
West Yorkshire

**The Mistal** ★★★★★
*Guest Accommodation*
**SILVER AWARD**
Cop Hill Side, Huddersfield HD7 5XA
t (01484) 845404
e carolineandphil@tiscali.co.uk
w themistal.co.uk

**Weirside Bed & Breakfast** ★★★★
*Guest Accommodation*
Weirside Bungalow, Weirside Marsden, Huddersfield HD7 6BU
t (01484) 842214
e david.elder3@btinternet. com
w marsdenbedandbreakfast. com

SLEDMERE
East Riding of Yorkshire

**Life Hill Farm B&B** ★★★★
*Farmhouse* **GOLD AWARD**
Sledmere, Driffield YO25 3EY
t (01377) 236224
e info@lifehillfarm.co.uk
w lifehillfarm.co.uk

SLEIGHTS
North Yorkshire

**Gramarye Suites B&B** ★★★★ *Bed & Breakfast*
**SILVER AWARD**
15 Coach Road, Sleights, Whitby YO22 5AA
t (01947) 811656
e gramaryesuites@btinternet. com
w gramaryesuites.co.uk

**Hedgefield** ★★★★
*Guest House*
47 Coach Road, Sleights, Whitby YO22 5AA
t (01947) 810647
e hedgefieldguesthouse@ tiscali.co.uk
w hedgefieldguesthouse.co.uk

**The Lawns** ★★★★★
*Guest Accommodation*
**GOLD AWARD**
73 Carr Hill Lane, Briggswath, Whitby YO21 1RS
t (01947) 810310
e lorton@onetel.com

**The Salmon Leap Hotel** ★★
*Inn*
Coach Road, Sleights, Whitby YO22 5AA
t (01947) 810233
w salmonleaphotel.co.uk

SLINGSBY
North Yorkshire

**Slingsby Hall** ★★★★
*Guest Accommodation*
Slingsby YO62 4AL
t (01653) 628375
e info@slingsbyhall.co.uk
w slingsbyhall.co.uk

SOWERBY
North Yorkshire

**Long Acre Bed and Breakfast** ★★★★
*Bed & Breakfast*
86a Topcliffe Road, Sowerby, Thirsk YO7 1RY
t (01845) 522360
e dawsonlongacre@aol.com
w longacrethirsk.co.uk

SPROTBROUGH
South Yorkshire

**The Old Rectory** ★★★★
*Guest House* **SILVER AWARD**
Boat Lane, Sprotbrough, Doncaster DN5 7LU
t (01302) 858561
w theoldrectorydoncaster.co. uk

STAINTONDALE
North Yorkshire

**Island House** ★★★★
*Farmhouse*
Staintondale, Scarborough YO13 0EB
t (01723) 870249
e roryc@tinyworld.co.uk
w islandhousefarm.co.uk

STAIRFOOT
South Yorkshire

**The Old Coach House Guest House** ★★★ *Guest House*
255 Doncaster Road, Barnsley S70 3RH
t (01226) 290612

STAITHES
North Yorkshire

**Brooklyn** ★★★
*Bed & Breakfast*
Browns Terrace, Staithes TS13 5BG
t (01947) 841396
e m.heald@tesco.net
w brooklynuk.co.uk

**Grinkle Lodge** ★★★★★
*Guest Accommodation*
**GOLD AWARD**
Snipe Lane, Easington, Saltburn TS13 4UD
t (01287) 644701
e grinklelodge@yahoo.co.uk
w grinklelodge.co.uk

STAMFORD BRIDGE
East Riding of Yorkshire

**High Catton Grange** ★★★★
*Farmhouse* **SILVER AWARD**
High Catton, Stamford Bridge, York YO41 1EP
t (01759) 371374
e foster-s@sky.com
w highcattongrange.co.uk

STANBURY
West Yorkshire

**Old Silent Inn**
Rating Applied For
*Inn*
Hob Lane, Haworth BD22 0HW
t (01535) 647437
e info@old-silent-inn.co.uk
w old-silent-inn.co.uk

**Ponden House** ★★★★
*Guest House*
Stanbury (Nr Haworth), Haworth BD22 0HR
t (01535) 644154
e brenda.taylor@ pondenhouse.co.uk
w pondenhouse.co.uk

STANNINGTON
South Yorkshire

**The Robin Hood Inn** ★★★★
*Inn* **SILVER AWARD**
Greaves Lane, Sheffield S6 6BG
t (0114) 234 4565
e robinhood.loxley@virgin.net

STAPE
North Yorkshire

**Cropton Forest Lodge** ★★★★
*Guest Accommodation*
**SILVER AWARD**
Stape, Pickering YO18 8HY
t (01751) 471540
e croptonforestlodge@ btopenworld.com
w croptonforestlodge.co.uk

**High Muffles** ★★★★
*Bed & Breakfast*
**SILVER AWARD**
Pickering YO18 8HP
t (01751) 417966
e candrew840@aol.com
w highmuffles.co.uk

**Rawcliffe House Farm** ★★★★ *Farmhouse*
**SILVER AWARD**
Stape, Pickering YO18 8JA
t (01751) 473292
e stay@rawcliffehousefarm.co. uk
w rawcliffehousefarm.co.uk

**Seavy Slack** ★★★★
*Farmhouse* **SILVER AWARD**
Stape, Pickering YO18 8HZ
t (01751) 473131

STARBOTTON
North Yorkshire

**Fox and Hounds** ★★★★ *Inn*
Starbotton, Skipton BD23 5HY
t (01756) 760269
w foxandhounds-starbotton. com

STAVELEY
North Yorkshire

**Staveley Grange** ★★★★★
*Guest Accommodation*
**SILVER AWARD**
Main Street, Staveley HG5 9LD
t (01423) 340265
e staveleygrange@onetel.com

STILLINGFLEET
North Yorkshire

**Harmony House** ★★★★
*Guest Accommodation*
The Green, York YO19 6SH
t (01904) 720933
e hilary.finney@virgin.net
w harmonyhouseyork.com

STIRTON
North Yorkshire

**Tarn House Country Inn** ★★★★
*Guest Accommodation*
Skipton BD23 3LQ
t (01756) 794891
e tarnhse@aol.co.uk
w tarnhouse.co.uk

STOKESLEY
North Yorkshire

**Willow Cottage** ★★★★
*Bed & Breakfast*
**SILVER AWARD**
67 Levenside, Stokesley TS9 5BH
t (01642) 710795
e sue.robinson2@virgin.net

STONEGRAVE
North Yorkshire

**Manor Cottage Bed and Breakfast** ★★★★
*Bed & Breakfast*
Stonegrave, Helmsley YO62 4LJ
t (01653) 628599
e gideon.v@virgin.net
w http://business.virgin.net/ gideon.v/index.html

SUTTON BANK
North Yorkshire

**Cote Faw** ★★
*Bed & Breakfast*
Sutton Bank YO7 2EZ
t (01845) 597363

SWINITHWAITE
North Yorkshire

**Temple Farmhouse B& B** ★★★★
*Guest Accommodation*
Temple Farm, Aysgarth, Aysgarth Falls DL8 4UJ
t (01969) 663246
e stay@templefarmhouse.co. uk
w templefarmhouse.co.uk

THIMBLEBY
North Yorkshire

**Stonehaven** ★★★
*Bed & Breakfast*
Thimbleby DL6 3PY
t (01609) 883689

---

Establishments in bold have a detailed entry in this guide – use the property index to find the page numbers

# Yorkshire

## THIRSK
### North Yorkshire

**Borrowby Mill, Bed and Breakfast ★★★★**
*Guest Accommodation*
**SILVER AWARD**
Borrowby, Nr Thirsk YO7 4AW
t (01845) 537717
e markandvickipadfield@
btinternet.com
w borrowbymill.co.uk

**The Gallery ★★★★**
*Bed & Breakfast*
18 Kirkgate, Thirsk YO7 1PQ
t (01845) 523767
e kathryn@
gallerybedandbreakfast.co.uk
w gallerybedandbreakfast.co.
uk

**Laburnum House ★★★★**
*Bed & Breakfast*
**SILVER AWARD**
31 Topcliffe Road, Sowerby,
Thirsk YO7 1RX
t (01845) 524120
w smoothhound.co.uk/hotels/
laburnumhse.html

**Manor House Cottage
★★★★**
*Guest Accommodation*
Hag Lane, South Kilvington,
Thirsk YO7 2NY
t (01845) 527712
e info@manor-house-cottage.
co.uk
w manor-house-cottage.co.uk

**The Old Rectory ★★★★**
*Bed & Breakfast*
South Kilvington YO7 2NL
t (01845) 526153
e ocfenton@freenet.co.uk

**Oswalds Restaurant with
Rooms ★★★★**
*Restaurant with Rooms*
**SILVER AWARD**
Oswalds Church Farm, Front
Street, Sowerby YO7 1JF
t (01845) 523655
e bookings@
oswaldsrestaurantwithrooms.
co.uk
w oswaldsrestaurantwith
rooms.co.uk

**St James House ★★★**
*Guest Accommodation*
36 St James Green, Thirsk
YO7 1AQ
t (01845) 526565

**Station House ★★★**
*Guest Accommodation*
Station Road, Thirsk YO7 4LS
t (01845) 522063

**Town Pasture Farm ★★★**
*Farmhouse*
Thirsk YO7 2DY
t (01845) 537298

## THIXENDALE
### North Yorkshire

**The Cross Keys ★★★ Inn**
Thixendale, Malton YO17 9TG
t (01377) 288272

## THORALBY
### North Yorkshire

**Bishopdale** *Bunkhouse*
The Old School Bunkhouse,
Leyburn DL8 3TB
t (01969) 663856

**The George Inn ★★★★ Inn**
Thoralby, Leyburn DL8 3SU
t (01969) 663256
e visit@thegeorge.tv
w thegeorge.tv

**The Old Barn ★★★★**
*Guest Accommodation*
**SILVER AWARD**
Thoralby, Leyburn DL8 3SZ
t (01969) 663590
e holidays@dalesbarn.co.uk
w dalesbarn.co.uk

**Pen View ★★★**
*Guest Accommodation*
Thoralby, Leyburn DL8 3SU
t (01969) 663319
e audrey@penview.yorks.net
w penview.yorks.net

## THORNE
### South Yorkshire

**Thorne Central Guest House**
**★★★ Guest House**
11a Queen Street, Doncaster
DN8 5AA
t (01405) 818358
e panksy63@aol.com
w thornecentralguesthouse.co.
uk

## THORNTON
### West Yorkshire

**Ann's Farmhouse ★★★**
*Farmhouse*
New Farm, Thornton Road,
Bradford BD13 3QE
t (01274) 833214
e yorkshirefarmer@hotmail.co.
uk

## THORNTON DALE
### North Yorkshire

**Banavie ★★★★**
*Bed & Breakfast*
Roxby Road, Thornton-le-Dale,
Pickering YO18 7SX
t (01751) 474616
e info@banavie.uk.com
w banavie.uk.com

**Cherry Garth**
Rating Applied For
*Guest Accommodation*
Church Hill, Pickering
YO18 7QH
t (01751) 473404
e claire@cherrygarthholidays.
com
w cherrygarthholidays.com

## THORNTON WATLASS
### North Yorkshire

**The Buck Inn ★★★ Inn**
Thornton Watlass HG4 4AH
t (01677) 422461
e innwatlass1@btconnect.com

## THRUSCROSS
### North Yorkshire

**West End Outdoor Centre**
**★★★ Hostel**
Wagtails, Thruscross,
Harrogate HG3 4AH
t (01943) 880207
e j.verity@virgin.net
w westendoutdoorcentre.co.
uk

## THWAITES BROW
### West Yorkshire

**Golden View Guest House**
**★★★ Guest Accommodation**
21 Golden View Drive,
Thwaites Brow, Haworth
BD21 4SN
t (01535) 662138
e info@goldenview.supanet.
com
w goldenview.supanet.com

## TICKHILL
### South Yorkshire

**Hannah's Guest House**
**★★★ Guest House**
72 Sunderland Street, Tickhill
Doncaster, Doncaster
DN11 9EG
t (01302) 752233
e barry@polarpumps.co.uk

## TODMORDEN
### West Yorkshire

**Cherry Tree Cottage ★★★★**
*Bed & Breakfast*
Woodhouse Road, Todmorden
OL14 5RJ
t (01706) 817492

**Kilnhurst Old Hall ★★★★★**
*Guest Accommodation*
**SILVER AWARD**
Kilnhurst Lane, Todmorden
OL14 6AX
t (01706) 814289
e kilnhurst@aol.com

**Mankinholes YHA ★★★★**
*Hostel*
Mankinholes, Todmorden
OL14 6HR
t (01706) 812340
e mankinholes@yha.org.uk
w yha.org.uk

## TRIANGLE
### West Yorkshire

**The Dene ★★★★**
*Guest Accommodation*
Triangle, Halifax HX6 3EA
t (01422) 823562
e knoble@uk2.net

## WADSWORTH
### West Yorkshire

**Hare & Hounds ★★★★ Inn**
Billy Lane, Hebden Bridge
HX7 8TN
t (01422) 842671
e info@hareandhounds.me.uk
w hareandhounds.me.uk

## WAKEFIELD
### West Yorkshire

**Upper Midgley Farm ★★★★**
*Farmhouse*
Midgley, Wakefield WF4 4JH
t (01924) 830294
e uppermidgleyfarm@tiscali.
co.uk

## WALKINGTON
### East Riding of Yorkshire

**The Barn House ★★★★★**
*Guest Accommodation*
18a East End, Walkington,
Beverley HU17 8RY
t (01482) 881268
e info@barnhouse-walkington.
co.uk
w barnhouse-walkington.co.uk

## WALSDEN
### West Yorkshire

**Birks Clough ★★★**
*Guest House*
Hollingworth Lane, Todmorden
OL14 6QX
t (01706) 814438
e mstorah@mwfree.net

**Highstones Guest House**
**★★★ Bed & Breakfast**
Rochdale Road, Todmorden
OL14 6TY
t (01706) 816534

## WARTHILL
### North Yorkshire

**York Scout Activity Centre**
**★★ Group Hostel**
Snowball Plantation, Stockton-
Forest, York YO19 5XS
t (01904) 410084
w snowballplantation.org.uk

## WASSAND
### East Riding of Yorkshire

**Melstead Hotel ★★★**
*Restaurant with Rooms*
59 Eastgate, Hornsea
HU18 1NB
t (01964) 533068

## WEAVERTHORPE
### North Yorkshire

**Blue Bell Inn ★★★★**
*Restaurant with Rooms*
Main Street, Weaverthorpe,
Malton YO17 8EX
t (01944) 738204

## WEETON
### North Yorkshire

**Arthington Lodge ★★★★**
*Farmhouse*
Wescoe Hill, Weeton,
Harrogate LS17 0EZ
t (01423) 734102
e arthingtonlodge@btinternet.
com

## WELBURN
### North Yorkshire

**The Barley Basket ★★★**
*Bed & Breakfast*
Main Road, York YO60 7DX
t (01653) 618352
e marianlacey@btinternet.com

**Welburn Lodge ★★★★**
*Bed & Breakfast*
Castle Howard Station Road,
Welburn, Malton YO60 7EW
t (01653) 618885
e stay@welburnlodge.com

## WELTON
### East Riding of Yorkshire

**Green Dragon Hotel ★★★★**
*Inn*
Cowgate, Welton, Beverley
HU15 1NB
t (01482) 666700

## WENSLEY
### North Yorkshire

**Wensley House ★★★★**
*Guest House*
Wensley, Leyburn DL8 4HL
t (01969) 624866

## WENSLEYDALE
### North Yorkshire

**Ivy Dene Guesthouse** ★★★
*Guest House*
Main Street, West Witton,
Leyburn DL8 4LP
**t** (01969) 622785
**e** info@ivydeneguesthouse.
co.uk
**w** yorkshirenet.co.uk

## WEST WITTON
### North Yorkshire

**The Old Star** ★★★
*Guest Accommodation*
Main Street, West Witton,
Leyburn DL8 4LU
**t** (01969) 622949
**e** enquiries@theoldstar.com
**w** theoldstar.com

## WESTERDALE
### North Yorkshire

**Westerdale** *Bunkhouse*
Broadgate Farm, Westerdale,
Whitby YO21 2DE
**t** (01287) 660259

## WETHERBY
### West Yorkshire

**Broadleys** ★★★★
*Bed & Breakfast*
39 North Street, Wetherby
LS22 6NU
**t** (01937) 585866

**Linton Close** ★★★★
*Bed & Breakfast*
SILVER AWARD
2 Wharfe Grove, Wetherby
LS22 6HA
**t** (01937) 582711

**Prospect House** ★★
*Guest House*
8 Caxton Street, Wetherby
LS22 6RU
**t** (01937) 582428

**The Royal Oak** ★★★★
*Bed & Breakfast*
60 North Street, Wetherby
LS22 6NR
**t** (01937) 580508
**e** a.johnston11@btconnect.
com

**Swan Guest House** ★★★★
*Guest House*
38 North Street, Wetherby
LS22 6NN
**t** (01937) 582381
**e** info@swanguesthouse.co.uk
**w** swanguesthouse.co.uk

## WHITBY
### North Yorkshire

**Abbotsleigh** ★★★★
*Guest Accommodation*
5 Argyle Road, Whitby
YO21 3HS
**t** (01947) 601142
**e** info@abbotsleigh-whitby.co.
uk
**w** abbotsleigh-whitby.co.uk

**Arches Guesthouse** ★★★★
*Guest House*
The Arches, 8 Havelock Place,
Whitby YO21 3ER
**t** 0800 915 4256 &
0800 915 4256
**e** archeswhitby@freeola.com
**w** whitbyguesthouses.co.uk

**Argyle House** ★★★★
*Guest Accommodation*
18 Hudson Street, Whitby
YO21 3EP
**t** (01947) 602733
**e** argyle-house@fsmail.net
**w** argyle-house.co.uk

**Ashford Guest House** ★★★
*Guest House*
8 Royal Crescent, Whitby
YO21 3EJ
**t** (01947) 602138
**e** info@ashfordguesthouse.co.
uk
**w** ashfordguesthouse.co.uk

**Avalon Hotel** ★★
*Guest Accommodation*
13-14 Royal Crescent, Whitby
YO21 3EJ
**t** (01947) 820313
**e** info@avalonhotelwhitby.co.
uk
**w** avalonhotelwhitby.co.uk

**Boulmer** ★★★ *Guest House*
23 Crescent Avenue, Whitby
YO21 3ED
**t** (01947) 604284
**e** boulmerguesthouse@tiscali.
co.uk

**Bramblewick Guest House**
★★★★ *Guest House*
3 Havelock Place, Whitby
YO21 3ER
**t** (01947) 604504
**e** bramblewick@
havelockplace.wanadoo.co.uk
**w** bramblewick.co.uk

**Bruncliffe Guest House**
★★★ *Bed & Breakfast*
9 North Promenade, Whitby
YO21 3JX
**t** (01947) 602428
**e** bruncliffewhitby@aol.com
**w** bruncliffewhitby.co.uk

**The Captain's Lodge** ★★★★
*Guest House*
3 Crescent Avenue, Whitby
YO21 3EF
**t** (01947) 601178
**e** enquiries@thecaptainslodge.
co.uk
**w** thecaptainslodge.co.uk

**Corner Guest House** ★★★★
*Guest House*
3-4 Crescent Place, Whitby
YO21 3HE
**t** (01947) 602444
**w** thecornerguesthouse.co.uk

**Crescent Lodge** ★★★★
*Guest Accommodation*
27 Crescent Avenue, Whitby
YO21 3EW
**t** (01947) 820073
**e** arthurcrescentlodge@
telco4u.net

**Cross Butts Farm Country
Hotel** ★★★★
*Restaurant with Rooms*
SILVER AWARD
Guisborough Road, Whitby
YO21 1TL
**t** (01947) 820986

**Ellie's Guest House** ★★★★
*Guest Accommodation*
4 Langdale Terrace, Whitby
YO21 3EE
**t** (01947) 600022
**e** info@elliesguesthouse.co.uk
**w** elliesguesthouse.co.uk

**Esklet Guest House** ★★★★
*Guest Accommodation*
22 Crescent Avenue, Whitby
YO21 3ED
**t** (01947) 605663
**e** esklet@axis-connnect.com
**w** esklet.com

**The Esplanade Hotel** ♦♦♦
*Guest Accommodation*
2 Esplanade, Whitby
YO21 3HH
**t** (01947) 605053
**e** esplanadehotel@dsl.pipex.
com

**Glendale Guest House**
★★★★ *Guest House*
16 Crescent Avenue, Whitby
YO21 3ED
**t** (01947) 604242

**Glenora** ★★★★ *Guest House*
8 Upgang Lane, Whitby
YO21 3EA
**t** (01947) 605363
**w** glenora.users.btopenworld.
com

**Grantley House** ★★★★
*Guest House*
26 Hudson Street, Whitby
YO21 3EP
**t** (01947) 600895
**e** andrew.blake10@
btopenworld.com
**w** grantleyhouse.com

**Grove Hotel** ★★★★
*Guest House*
36 Bagdale, Whitby YO21 1QL
**t** (01947) 603551
**e** angelaswales@btconnect.
com
**w** smoothhound.co.uk/hotels/
grove2.html

**Hailwood House** ★★★★
*Bed & Breakfast*
25a Crescent Avenue, Whitby
YO21 3ED
**t** (01947) 602704
**e** carol@carolyates.wanadoo.
co.uk

**Havelock Guest House**
★★★ *Guest House*
30 Hudson Street, Whitby
YO21 3EP
**t** (01947) 602295

**Haven Crest** ★★★★
*Guest Accommodation*
SILVER AWARD
137 Upgang Lane, Whitby
YO21 3JW
**t** (01947) 605187
**e** enquiries@havencrest.co.uk
**w** havencrest.co.uk

**The Haven Guest House**
★★★★ *Guest House*
4 East Crescent, Whitby
YO21 3HD
**t** (01947) 603842
**e** info@thehavenwhitby.co.uk
**w** thehavenwhitby.co.uk

**High Tor** ★★★★
*Guest House*
7 Normanby Terrace, Whitby
YO21 3ES
**t** (01947) 602507
**e** hightorguesthouse@hotmail.
com
**w** hightorguesthousewhitby.
co.uk

**Hillcrest Guest House**
★★★★ *Guest House*
9 Prospect Hill, Whitby
YO21 1QE
**t** (01947) 606604
**e** hillcrestgh@btinternet.com
**w** hillcrestguesthouse.org.uk

**The Langley Hotel** ★★★★★
*Guest Accommodation*
SILVER AWARD
Royal Crescent, West Cliff,
Whitby YO21 3EJ
**t** (01947) 604250
**e** langleyhotel@hotmail.co.uk
**w** langleyhotel.com

**Lavinia House** ★★★★
*Guest Accommodation*
3 East Crescent, Whitby
YO21 3HD
**t** (01947) 602945
**e** info@laviniahouse.co.uk
**w** laviniahouse.co.uk

**The Leeway** ★★★★
*Guest Accommodation*
1 Havelock Place, Whitby
YO21 3ER
**t** (01947) 602604
**e** enquiries@theleeway.co.uk
**w** theleeway.co.uk

**Netherby House** ★★★★
*Guest Accommodation*
SILVER AWARD
Coach Road, Sleights, Whitby
YO22 5EQ
**t** (01947) 810211
**e** info@netherby-house.co.uk
**w** netherby-house.co.uk

**Number Five** ★★★★
*Guest House*
5 Havelock Place, Whitby
YO21 3ER
**t** (01947) 606361

**Number Seven Guest House**
★★★★
*Guest Accommodation*
7 East Crescent, Whitby
YO21 3HD
**t** (01947) 606019
**e** numberseven@whitbytown.
freeserve.co.uk
**w** numbersevenwhitby.co.uk

**The Olde Ford** ★★★★
*Guest Accommodation*
SILVER AWARD
1 Briggswath, Whitby
YO21 1RU
**t** (01947) 810704
**e** gray.theoldeford@
btinternet.com
**w** theoldeford.com/contact.
htm

**Pannett House** ★★★★
*Guest Accommodation*
14 Normanby Terrace, Whitby
YO21 3ES
**t** (01947) 603261
**e** info@pannetthouse.co.uk
**w** pannetthouse.co.uk

**Partridge Nest Farm** ★★★
*Farmhouse*
Eskdaleside, Sleights, Whitby
YO22 5ES
**t** (01947) 810450
**e** barbara@partridgenestfarm.
com
**w** partridgenestfarm.com

**Prospect Villa** ★★★
*Guest House*
13 Prospect Hill, Whitby
YO21 1QE
t (01947) 603118
e janicejancee@aol.co.uk
w prospectvillahotel.co.uk

**Riviera Hotel** ★★★★
*Guest House*
4 Crescent Terrace, West Cliff,
Whitby YO21 3EL
t (01947) 602533
e info@rivierawhitby.com
w rivierawhitby.com

**Rosslyn House** ★★★★
*Guest House*
11 Abbey Terrace, Whitby
YO21 3HQ
t (01947) 604086
e rosslyn_gh@btconnect.com
w guesthousewhitby.co.uk

**Rothbury** ★★★★
*Bed & Breakfast*
2 Ocean Road, Whitby
YO21 3HY
t (01947) 606282
e therothbury@f2s.com
w therothbury.co.uk

**Ryedale House** ★★★★
*Guest Accommodation*
Coach Road, Sleights, Whitby
YO22 5EQ
t (01947) 810534
w ryedalehouse.co.uk

**Sandpiper Guest House**
★★★★ *Guest House*
4 Belle Vue Terrace, Whitby
YO21 3EY
t (01947) 600246
e enquiries@sandpiperhouse.
co.uk
w sandpiperhouse.co.uk

**Seacliffe Hotel** ★★★★
*Guest Accommodation*
12 North Promenade, Whitby
YO21 3JX
t (01947) 603139
e info@seacliffe.fsnet.co.uk
w seacliffe.co.uk

**Sneaton Castle Centre**
★★★★
*Guest Accommodation*
Sneaton Castle, Whitby
YO21 3QN
t (01947) 600051
e sneaton@globalnet.co.uk
w sneatoncastle.co.uk

**Sneaton Castle Centre** ★★★
*Hostel*
Castle Road, Whitby
YO21 3QN
t (01947) 600051
e sneaton@globalnet.co.uk
w sneatoncastle.co.uk

**Storrbeck Guest House**
★★★★ *Bed & Breakfast*
SILVER AWARD
9 Crescent Avenue, Whitby
YO21 3ED
t (01947) 605468
e storrbeck@bigfoot.com
w storrbeck.fsnet.co.uk

**Sunnyvale House** ★★★★
*Guest House*
12 Normanby Terrace, Whitby
YO21 3ES
t (01947) 820389
e sunnyvalehouse@hotmail.
co.uk
w sunnyvalehouse.co.uk

**Wentworth House** ★★★
*Guest House*
27 Hudson Street, Whitby
YO21 3EP
t (01947) 602433
e info@whitbywentworth.co.
uk
w whitbywentworth.co.uk

**Wheeldale Hotel** ★★★★
*Guest House*
11 North Promenade, Whitby
YO21 3JX
t (01947) 602365
w wheeldale-hotel.co.uk
▨◪

**Whitby YHA** ★★★★ *Hostel*
East Cliff, Whitby YO22 4JT
t (01947) 602878
◈♨▥◪◪

**White Linen Guest House**
★★★★
*Guest Accommodation*
24 Bagdale, Whitby YO21 1QS
t (01947) 603635
e info@whitelinenguesthouse.
co.uk
w whitelinenguesthouse.co.uk

**The Willows** ★★★
*Guest House*
35 Bagdale, Whitby YO21 1QL
t (01947) 600288
e martindyer74@hotmail.com
w thewillowsguesthouse.co.uk

**York House Hotel** ★★★★
*Guest Accommodation*
3 Back Lane, Whitby
YO22 4LW
t (01947) 880314
e yorkhtl@aol.com

**Little Orchard** ★★★
*Guest Accommodation*
High Street, Whixley, York
YO26 8AW
t (01423) 330615
▨

**Cowper Cottage** ★★★★
*Bed & Breakfast*
SILVER AWARD
Cowper Terrace,
Wigglesworth, Settle
BD23 4RP
t (01729) 840598

**Wike Ridge Farm** ★★★★
*Guest Accommodation*
Wike Ridge Lane, Leeds
LS17 9JF
t (0113) 266 1190

**Cuckoo Nest Farm** ★★★
*Farmhouse*
York Road, Wilberfoss, York
YO41 5NL
t (01759) 380365

**The Old Forge** ★★★★
*Guest Accommodation*
Wilton, Pickering YO18 7JY
t (01751) 477399
e theoldforge1@aol.com
w forgecottages.co.uk

**The Wold Cottage** ★★★★★★
*Farmhouse* GOLD AWARD
Wold Newton YO25 3HL
t (01262) 470696
e katrina@woldcottage.com
w woldcottage.com

**Rockery Cottage** ★★★★
*Bed & Breakfast*
SILVER AWARD
Main Street, Wombleton,
Kirkbymoorside YO62 7RX
t (01751) 432257
e enquiries@rockerycottage.
co.uk
w rockerycottage.co.uk

**Wortley Hall Ltd** ★★★
*Guest Accommodation*
Wortley, Sheffield S35 7DB
t (0114) 288 2100
e info@wortleyhall.org.uk
w wortleyhall.org.uk

**Willow Cottage B&B** ★★★★
*Guest Accommodation*
Willow Cottage, Ivegate, Leeds
LS19 7RE
t (0113) 250 1189
e info@willowcottage.org.uk
w willowcottage.org.uk

**23 St Marys** ★★★★
*Guest House* SILVER AWARD
York YO30 7DD
t (01904) 622738
e stmarys23@hotmail.com
w 23stmarys.co.uk

**Aaron Guest House** ★★★
*Guest House*
42 Bootham Crescent,
Bootham, York YO30 7AH
t (01904) 625927
w aaronyork.co.uk

**Abbey Guest House** ★★★
*Guest House*
13-14 Earlsborough Terrace,
Marygate YO30 7BQ
t (01904) 627782
e info@abbeyghyork.co.uk
w abbeyghyork.co.uk

**Abbeyfields** ★★★★
*Guest Accommodation*
19 Bootham Terrace, York
YO30 7DH
t (01904) 636471
e enquire@abbeyfields.co.uk
w abbeyfields.co.uk

**Acres Dene Guesthouse**
★★★ *Guest House*
87 Fulford Road, York
YO10 4BD
t (01904) 647482
e acresdene@tesco.net
w acresdene.co.uk

**Airden House** ★★★
*Guest House*
1 St Marys, Bootham, York
YO30 7DD
t (01904) 638915
e info@airdenhouse.co.uk
w airdenhouse.co.uk

**Alcuin Lodge** ★★★★
*Guest House*
15 Sycamore Place, Bootham,
York YO30 7DW
t (01904) 632222
e info@alcuinlodge.com
w alcuinlodge.com
▨

**Alexander House** ★★★★★
*Bed & Breakfast*
GOLD AWARD
94 Bishopthorpe Road, York
YO23 1JS
t (01904) 625016
e info@alexanderhouseyork.
co.uk
w alexanderhouseyork.co.uk

**Amber House** ★★★★
*Bed & Breakfast*
36 Bootham Crescent,
Bootham, York YO30 7AH
t (01904) 620275
e feebutler@btinternet.com
w amberhouse-york.co.uk

**Ambleside Guest House**
★★★ *Guest House*
62 Bootham Crescent,
Bootham YO30 7AH
t (01904) 637165
e ambles@globalnet.co.uk
w ambleside-gh.co.uk

**The Apple House** ★★★★
*Guest House*
74-76 Holgate Road, York
YO24 4AB
t (01904) 625081
e pamelageorge1@yahoo.co.
uk
w applehouseyork.co.uk

**Arnot House** ★★★★★
*Bed & Breakfast*
GOLD AWARD
17 Grosvenor Terrace, York
YO30 7AG
t (01904) 641966
e kim.robbins@virgin.net
w arnothouseyork.co.uk

**Ascot House** ★★★★
*Guest Accommodation*
SILVER AWARD
80 East Parade, York
YO31 7YH
t (01904) 426826
e admin@ascothouseyork.com
w ascothouseyork.com

**Ascot Lodge ★★★★**
*Guest Accommodation*
112 Acomb Road, York
YO24 4EY
t (01904) 798234
e info@ascotlodge.com
w ascotlodge.com

**Ashbury Hotel ★★★★**
*Guest Accommodation*
103 The Mount, York
YO24 1AX
t (01904) 647339
e ashbury@talk21.com
w ashburyhotel.co.uk

**Ashtofts ★★★**
*Bed & Breakfast*
46 Bishopthorpe Road, York
YO23 1JL
t (01904) 635018
e ashtofts@btinternet.com
w ashtofts.co.uk

**Avondale Guest House**
★★★ *Guest Accommodation*
61 Bishopthorpe Road, York
YO23 1NX
t (01904) 633989
e kaleda@
avondaleguesthouse.co.uk
w avondaleguesthouse.co.uk

**The Bar Convent ★★★**
*Guest Accommodation*
17 Blossom Street, York
YO24 1AQ
t (01904) 643238
e info@bar-convent.org.uk
w bar-convent.org.uk

**Barbican House ★★★★**
*Guest Accommodation*
SILVER AWARD
20 Barbican Road, York
YO10 5AA
t (01904) 627617
e info@barbicanhouse.com
w barbicanhouse.com

**Barclay Lodge ★★★**
*Guest Accommodation*
19/21 Gillygate, York
YO31 7EA
t (01904) 633274
w barclaylodge.co.uk

**Barrington House ★★★★**
*Guest Accommodation*
15 Nunthorpe Avenue, York
YO23 1PF
t (01904) 634539
e alan.bell@btinternet.com
w barringtonhouse.net

**Bay Tree Guest House**
★★★★ *Guest House*
92 Bishopthorpe Road, York
YO1 6HQ
t (01904) 659462
e info@baytree-york.co.uk
w baytree-york.co.uk

**Beckett Guest House ★★★**
*Guest Accommodation*
58 Bootham Crescent,
Bootham, York YO30 7AH
t (01904) 644728
e info@becketthotel.co.uk
w becketthotel.co.uk

**Beech House Hotel ★★★★**
*Guest Accommodation*
SILVER AWARD
6-7 Longfield Terrace,
Bootham, York YO30 7DJ
t (01904) 634581
e beechhouse@beeb.net
w beech-house-york.co.uk

**The Bentley Guest House**
★★★★
*Guest Accommodation*
25 Grosvenor Terrace,
Bootham, York YO30 7AG
t (01904) 644313
e a.neighbour@btopenworld.
com
w bentleyofyork.co.uk

**Bishopgarth Guest House**
★★★ *Guest House*
3 Southlands Road, York
YO23 1NP
t (01904) 635220
e bishopgarth@btconnect.com
w bishopgarth.co.uk

**Bishops ★★★★★**
*Guest Accommodation*
SILVER AWARD
135 Holgate Road, York
YO24 4DF
t (01904) 628000
e enquiries@bishopshotel.co.
uk
w bishopshotel.co.uk

**The Bloomsbury ★★★★**
*Guest House*
127 Clifton, York YO30 6BL
t (01904) 634031
e info@bloomsburyhotel.co.uk
w bloomsburyhotel.co.uk

**Blossoms York ★★★**
*Guest Accommodation*
28 Clifton, York YO30 6AE
t (01904) 652391
e nexus@blossomsyork.co.uk
w blossomsyork.co.uk

**Bootham Gardens Guest
House ★★★★** *Guest House*
47 Bootham Crescent, York
YO30 7AJ
t (01904) 625911
e guesthouse@hotmail.com
w bootham-gardens-
guesthouse.co.uk

**Bootham Guest House**
★★★★
*Guest Accommodation*
56 Bootham Crescent, York
YO30 7AH
t (01904) 672123
e boothamguesthouse1@
hotmail.com
w boothamguesthouse.co.uk

**Bootham Park Hotel ★★★★**
*Guest Accommodation*
9 Grosvenor Terrace, York
YO30 7AG
t (01904) 644262
e boothampark@aol.com
w boothamparkhotel.co.uk

**Bowen House ★★★★**
*Guest House*
4 Gladstone Street, Huntington
Road, York YO31 8RF
t (01904) 636881
e info@bowenhouseyork.com
w bowenhouseyork.com

**Bowman's ★★★★**
*Guest House*
33 Grosvenor Terrace, York
YO30 7AG
t (01904) 622204

**Brentwood Guest House**
★★★★
*Guest Accommodation*
54 Bootham Crescent,
Bootham, York YO30 7AH
t (01904) 636419
e brentwoodps@aol.com
w thebrentwood.co.uk

**Briar Lea House ★★★**
*Guest Accommodation*
8 Longfield Terrace, Bootham,
York YO30 7DJ
t (01904) 635061
e briarleahouse@msn.com
w briarlea.co.uk

**Bronte Guesthouse ★★★★**
*Guest Accommodation*
SILVER AWARD
22 Grosvenor Terrace, York
YO30 7AG
t (01904) 621066
e enquiries@bronte-
guesthouse.com
w bronte-guesthouse.com/

**Bull Lodge Guest House**
★★★ *Guest House*
37 Bull Lane, Lawrence Street,
York YO10 3EN
t (01904) 415522
e stay@bulllodge.co.uk
w bulllodge.co.uk

**Burton Villa Guest House**
★★★ *Guest House*
24 Haxby Road, York YO31 8JX
t (01904) 626364
e burtonvilla@hotmail.com
w burtonvilla.com

**Carlton House ★★★★**
*Guest Accommodation*
134 The Mount, York
YO24 1AS
t (01904) 622265
e etb@carltonhouse.co.uk
w carltonhouse.co.uk

**Carousel Guest House**
Rating Applied For
*Guest House*
83 Eldon Street, York
YO31 7NH
t (01904) 646709
e zhuangqi_cn@hotmail.com
w yorkcarousel.co.uk

**The Cavalier ★★★**
*Guest House*
39 Monkgate, York YO31 7PB
t (01904) 636615
e julia@cavalierhotel.co.uk
w cavalierhotel.co.uk

**Chelmsford Place Guest
House ★★★** *Guest House*
85 Fulford Road, York
YO10 4BD
t (01904) 624491
e chelmsfordplace@
btinternet.com
w chelmsfordplace.co.uk

**City Guest House ★★★★**
*Guest Accommodation*
SILVER AWARD
68 Monkgate, York YO31 7PF
t (01904) 622483
e info@cityguesthouse.co.uk
w cityguesthouse.co.uk

**Claxton Hall Cottage Guest
House ★★★★**
*Bed & Breakfast*
Malton Road, York YO60 7RE
t (01904) 468697
e claxcott@aol.com
w claxtonhallcottage.com

**Coach House Hotel ★★★★**
*Guest Accommodation*
20-22 Marygate, York
YO30 7BH
t (01904) 652780
e info@coachhousehotel-york.
com
w coachhousehotel-york.com

**Cook's Guest House ★★★**
*Guest House*
120 Bishopthorpe Road, York
YO23 1JX
t (01904) 652519
e jennieslcook@hotmail.co.uk
w cooksguesthouse.co.uk

**Cottage Hotel ★★★**
*Guest Accommodation*
1 Clifton Green, York
YO30 6LH
t (01904) 643711
e thecottage@hotel1834.fsnet.
co.uk

**Crescent Guest House ★★**
*Guest House*
77 Bootham, York YO30 7DQ
t (01904) 623216
e jason.lowrey@btconnect.
com
w crescentguesthouseyork.co.
uk

**Crook Lodge ★★★★**
*Guest Accommodation*
SILVER AWARD
26 St Marys, Bootham, York
YO30 7DD
t (01904) 655614
e crooklodge@hotmail.com
w crooklodge.co.uk

**Crossways Guest House**
★★★★ *Guest House*
23 Wigginton Road, York
YO31 8HJ
t (01904) 637250
e enquiries@crossways-york.
co.uk
w crossways-york.co.uk/

**Cumbria House ★★★**
*Guest House*
2 Vyner Street, York YO31 8HS
t (01904) 636817
e candj@cumbriahouse.
freeserve.co.uk
w cumbriahouse.com

**Curzon Lodge and Stable
Cottages ★★★★**
*Guest House*
23 Tadcaster Road, York
YO24 1QG
t (01904) 703157
e admin@curzonlodge.com
w smoothhound.co.uk/hotels/
curzon.html

**Dairy Guest House**
Rating Applied For
*Guest Accommodation*
3 Scarcroft Road, York
YO23 1ND
t (01904) 639367
e ian.knibbs@
dairyguesthouse.co.uk
w dairyguesthouse.co.uk

**Dalescroft Guest House**
★★★ *Guest House*
10 Southlands Road, York
YO23 1NP
t (01904) 626801
e info@dalescroft-york.co.uk
w dalescroft-york.co.uk

**Elliotts** ★★★★ *Guest House*
Sycamore Place, Bootham,
York YO30 7DW
t (01904) 623333
e elliottshotel@aol.com
w elliottshotel.co.uk

**Farthings Guest House**
★★★★ *Guest House*
5 Nunthorpe Avenue, York
YO23 1PF
t (01904) 653545
e stay@farthingsyork.co.uk
w farthingsyork.co.uk

**Feversham Lodge** ★★★★
*Guest Accommodation*
1 Feversham Crescent, York
YO31 8HQ
t (01904) 623882
e bookings@fevershamlodge.
co.uk
w fevershamlodge.co.uk

**Foss Bank Guest House**
★★★★ *Guest House*
16 Huntington Road, York
YO31 8RB
t (01904) 635548
w fossbank.co.uk

**Four High Petergate Hotel
and Bistro** ★★★★
*Guest Accommodation*
2-4 High Petergate, York
YO1 7EH
t (01904) 658516
e enquiries@
fourhighpetergate.co.uk

**Four Seasons** ★★★★
*Guest Accommodation*
SILVER AWARD
7 St Peters Grove, York
YO30 6AQ
t (01904) 622621
e roe@fourseasons.supanet.
com
w fourseasons-hotel.co.uk

**Fourposter Lodge** ★★★
*Guest House*
68-70 Heslington Road, York
YO10 5AU
t (01904) 651170
e fourposter.lodge@virgin.net
w fourposterlodge.co.uk

**Friars Rest Guest House**
★★★ *Guest House*
81 Fulford Road, York
YO10 4BD
t (01904) 629823
e friarsrest@btinternet.com
w friarsrest.co.uk

**Galtres Lodge Hotel** ★★
*Guest Accommodation*
54 Low Petergate, York
YO1 7HZ
t (01904) 622478
w galtreslodgehotel.co.uk

**Georgian House Hotel** ★★
*Guest Accommodation*
35 Bootham, York YO30 7BT
t (01904) 622874
e georgian.house@virgin.net
w georgianhouse.co.uk

**Glade Farm** ★★★★
*Bed & Breakfast*
Riccall Road, Escrick YO19 6ED
t (01904) 728098
e victorialeaf@hotmail.com

**Goldsmiths Guest House**
★★★★
*Guest Accommodation*
18 Longfield Terrace, York
YO30 7DJ
t (01904) 655738
e susan@goldsmith18.
freeserve.co.uk
w goldsmithsguesthouse.co.uk

**Grange Lodge** ★★★
*Guest Accommodation*
52 Bootham Crescent, York
YO30 7AH
t (01904) 621137
e nicholasboyle@btinternet.
com
w grange-lodge.com

**Greenside** ★★★
*Guest House*
124 Clifton, York YO30 6BQ
t (01904) 623631
e greenside@surfree.co.uk
w greensideguesthouse.co.uk

**Gregory's** ★★★★
*Guest Accommodation*
SILVER AWARD
160 Bishopthorpe, York
YO23 1LF
t (01904) 627521
e gregorys.york@ntlworld.
com
w gregorysofyork.co.uk

**Groves Hotel** ★★★
*Guest Accommodation*
St Groves Hotel Peters Grove,
Clifton YO30 6AQ
t (01904) 559777
e admin@ecsyork.co.uk
w ecsyork.co.uk

**The Guy Fawkes Hotel**
★★★★
*Guest Accommodation*
25 High Petergate, York
YO1 7HP
t (01904) 671001
e info@theguyfawkeshotel.
com
w theguyfawkeshotel.com

**The Hazelwood** ★★★★
*Guest Accommodation*
SILVER AWARD
24-25 Portland Street, York
YO31 7EH
t (01904) 626548
e reservations@
thehazelwoodyork.com
w thehazelwoodyork.com

**Heworth Guest House** ★★★
*Guest House*
126 East Parade, York
YO31 7YG
t (01904) 426384
e chris@yorkcity.co.uk
w yorkcity.co.uk

**Holgate Bridge Hotel** ★★★
*Guest Accommodation*
106-108 Holgate Road, York
YO24 4BB
t (01904) 635971
e info@holgatebridge.co.uk
w holgatebridge.co.uk

**The Hollies Guest House**
Rating Applied For
*Guest House*
141 Fulford Road, York
YO10 4HG
t (01904) 634279
e stay@hollies-guesthouse.
com
w hollies-guesthouse.co.uk

**Holly Lodge** ★★★★
*Guest Accommodation*
206 Fulford Road, York
YO10 4DD
t (01904) 646005
e geoff@thehollylodge.co.uk
w thehollylodge.co.uk

**Holme Lea Manor Guest
House** ★★★★ *Guest House*
18 St Peters Grove, York
YO30 6AQ
t (01904) 623529
e holmelea@btclick.com
w holmelea.co.uk

**Huntington House** ★★★
*Group Hostel*
18 Huntington Road, York
YO31 8RB
t (01904) 622755
e pp@huntingtonhouse.
demon.co.uk
w huntingtonhouse.demon.co.
uk

**The Lighthorseman** ★★★★
*Inn*
124 Fulford Road, Fishergate
YO10 4BE
t (01904) 624818
e janinerobinson03@aol.com
w lighthorseman.co.uk

**The Limes** ★★★★
*Guest House* SILVER AWARD
135 Fulford Road, York
YO10 4HE
t (01904) 624548
e queries@limeshotel.co.uk
w limeshotel.co.uk

**Linden Lodge** ★★★★
*Guest Accommodation*
6 Nunthorpe Avenue, Scarcroft
Road, York YO23 1PF
t (01904) 620107
w yorkshirenet.co.uk

**Manor Guest House** ★★★★
*Guest Accommodation*
Main Street, Linton-on-Ouse
YO30 2AY
t (01347) 848391
e manorguesthouse@tiscali.
co.uk
w manorguesthouse.co.uk

**Midway House Hotel**
★★★★
*Guest Accommodation*
145 Fulford Road, York
YO10 4HG
t (01904) 659272
e midway.house@virgin.net
w midwayhouseyork.co.uk

**Minster View Guest House**
★★★ *Guest House*
2 Grosvenor Terrace, York
YO30 7AJ
t (01904) 655034
e minsterview@amserve.com

**Monkgate Guest House**
★★★ *Guest House*
65 Monkgate, York YO31 7PA
t (01904) 655947
e 65monkgate@btconnect.
com
w monkgateguesthouse.com

**Mont-Clare Guest House**
★★★ *Guest House*
32 Claremont Terrace,
Gillygate, York YO31 7EJ
t (01904) 651011
e mont.clare@dsl.pipex.com
w mont-clare.co.uk

**Moorgarth Guest House**
★★★ *Guest House*
158 Fulford Road, York
YO10 4DA
t (01904) 636768
e moorgarth@fsbdial.co.uk
w moorgarth-york.co.uk

**Moorland House** ★★★
*Guest Accommodation*
1a Moorland Road, York
YO10 4HF
t (01904) 629354
e g.metcalfe@tesco.net

**Mowbray House** ★★★
*Bed & Breakfast*
34 Haxby Road, York YO31 8JX
t (01904) 637710
e carol@mowbrayhouse.co.uk
w mowbrayhouse.co.uk

**No. 40** ★★★★
*Bed & Breakfast*
40 Queen Annes Road, York
YO30 7AA
t (01904) 655509
e dilys.no40bbyork@
btinternet.com
w no40bbyork.co.uk

**Northolme Guest House**
★★★ *Guest House*
114 Shipton Road, York
YO30 5RN
t (01904) 639132
e g.liddle@tesco.net
w northolmeguesthouse.co.uk

**Oaklands Guest House**
★★★★
*Guest Accommodation*
351 Strensall Road, Earswick
YO32 9SW
t (01904) 768443
e mavmo@oaklands5.fsnet.co.
uk
w holidayguides.com

**Orillia House** ★★★★
*Guest Accommodation*
89 The Village, Stockton-on-
the-Forest YO32 9UP
t (01904) 400600
e info@orilliahouse.co.uk
w orilliahouse.co.uk

**Palm Court Hotel** ★★★★
*Guest Accommodation*
17 Huntington Road, York
YO31 8RB
t (01904) 639387
w thepalmcourt.freeserve.co.
uk

**Papillon Hotel** ★
*Guest House*
43 Gillygate, York YO31 7EA
t (01904) 636505
e papillonhotel@btinternet.
com
w btinternet.com/
~papillonhotel

**Priory Hotel ★★★★**
*Guest House*
126-128 Fulford Road, York
YO10 4BE
t (01904) 625280
e reservations@priory-
hotelyork.co.uk
w priory-hotelyork.co.uk

**Queen Anne's Guest House**
★★★ *Guest Accommodation*
24 Queen Annes Road,
Bootham, York YO30 7AA
t (01904) 629389
e queen.annes@btopenworld.
com
w queen-annes-guesthouse.
co.uk

**Romley House ★★★**
*Guest Accommodation*
2 Millfield Road, York
YO23 1NQ
t (01904) 652822
e info@romleyhouse.co.uk
w romleyhouse.co.uk

**St Deny's Hotel ★★★**
*Guest House*
51 St Deny's Hotel, Denys
Road, York YO1 9QD
t (01904) 622207
e book@stdenyshotel.co.uk
w stdenyshotel.co.uk

**St George's ★★★**
*Guest Accommodation*
6 St Georges Place, Off
Tadcaster Road, York
YO24 1DR
t (01904) 625056
e sixstgeorg@aol.com
w members.aol.com/
sixstgeorg/

**St Mary's Guest House**
★★★★
*Guest Accommodation*
17 Longfield Terrace, Bootham,
York YO30 7DJ
t (01904) 626972
e stmaryshotel@talk21.com
w stmaryshotel.co.uk

**St Paul's Hotel ★★★**
*Guest House*
120 Holgate Road, York
YO24 4BB
t (01904) 611514
e normfran@supanet.com

**St Raphael Guest House**
★★★★
*Guest Accommodation*
44 Queen Annes Road, York
YO30 7AF
t (01904) 645028
e info@straphaelguesthouse.
co.uk
w straphaelguesthouse.co.uk

**Skelton Grange Farmhouse**
★★★★
*Guest Accommodation*
Orchard View, York YO30 1YQ
t (01904) 470780
e info@skelton-farm.co.uk
w skelton-farm.co.uk

**Southland's Guest House**
Rating Applied For
*Guest Accommodation*
69 Nunmill Street, York
YO23 1NT
t (01904) 675966
e enquiries@southlands-
guesthouse.co.uk
w southlands-guesthouse.co.
uk

**Stanley House ★★★**
*Guest House*
Stanley Street, York
YO31 8NW
t (01904) 637111
e stanleyhouseyork@hotmail.
com
w stanleyhouseyork.co.uk

**Staymor Guest House**
★★★★ *Guest House*
2 Southlands Road, York
YO23 1NP
t (01904) 626935
e kathwilson@lineone.net
w staymorguesthouse.com

**The Steer Inn ★★★** *Inn*
Hull Road, Wilberfoss
YO41 5PF
t (01759) 380600
e reception@thesteerinn.co.uk
w steerinn.co.uk

**Sycamore Guest House**
★★★ *Guest House*
19 Sycamore Place, York
YO30 7DW
t (01904) 624712
e mail@thesycamore.co.uk
w thesycamore.co.uk

**The Acer ★★★★**
*Guest House*
52 Scarcroft Hill, York
YO24 1DE
t (01904) 653839
e info@acerhotel.co.uk
w acerhotel.co.uk

**Tower Guest House ★★★★**
*Guest Accommodation*
**SILVER AWARD**
2 Feversham Crescent, York
YO31 8HQ
t (01904) 655571
e enquiries@
towerguesthouseyork.com
w towerguesthouseyork.com

**Tree Tops ★★★** *Guest House*
21 St Marys, York YO30 7DD
t (01904) 658053
e treetops.guesthouse@virgin.
net
w treetopsguesthouse.co.uk

**Turnberry House ★★★★**
*Guest House*
143 Fulford Road, York
YO10 4HG
t (01904) 658435
e turnberry.house@virgin.net
w turnberryhouse.com

**Tyburn House Hotel ★★★**
*Guest Accommodation*
11 Albemarle Road, York
YO23 1EN
t (01904) 655069
e york@tyburnhotel.freeserve.
co.uk

**Warrens ★★★★**
*Guest Accommodation*
30-32 Scarcroft Road, York
YO23 1NF
t (01904) 643139
e info@warrenshotel.co.uk
w warrenshotel.co.uk

**Wellgarth House ★★★**
*Guest Accommodation*
Wetherby Road, York
YO23 3QB
t (01904) 738592 &
07711 252577

**The Windmill ★★★★** *Inn*
Hull Road, Dunnington, York
YO19 5LP
t (01904) 481898
e j.saggers@btopenworld.com
w thewindmilldunnington.co.
uk

**Wood Farm ★★★★**
*Farmhouse*
York YO30 1BU
t (01904) 470333
e email@
woodfarmbedandbreakfast.co.
uk
w woodfarmbedandbreakfast.
co.uk

**YHA York International**
★★★ *Hostel*
Water End, York YO30 6LP
t (01904) 653147
e york@yha.org.uk
w yha.org.uk

**York Backpackers ★** *Hostel*
88-90 Micklegate, York
YO1 6JX
t (01904) 627720
e mail@yorkbackpackers.co.
uk
w yorkbackpackers.co.uk

**York House ★★★★**
*Guest Accommodation*
62 Heworth Green, York
YO31 7TQ
t (01904) 427070
e yorkhouse.bandb@tiscali.co.
uk
w yorkhouseyork.com

**York Lodge Guest House**
★★★ *Guest Accommodation*
64 Bootham Crescent, York
YO30 7AH
t (01904) 654289
e yorkldg@aol.com
w york-lodge.com

## HEART OF ENGLAND

### ALBRIGHTON
### Shropshire

**Boningale Manor ★★★★**
*Bed & Breakfast*
Holyhead Road, Boningale,
Albrighton, Wolverhampton
WV7 3AT
t (01902) 373376
e boningalemanor@aol.com
w boningalemanor.com

**Parkside Farm ★★★★**
*Farmhouse* **SILVER AWARD**
Holyhead Road, Albrighton
WV7 3DA
t (01902) 372310
e margaret@parksidefarm.com
w parksidefarm.com

### ALCESTER
### Warwickshire

**The Globe ★★★★**
*Guest Accommodation*
54 Birmingham Road, Alcester
B49 5EG
t (01789) 763287
e globe_hotel@btconnect.com
w theglobehotel.com

**Sambourne Hall Farm**
★★★★ *Farmhouse*
Wike Lane, Sambourne,
Studley B96 6NZ
t (01527) 852151

### ALL STRETTON
### Shropshire

**All Stretton Bunk House**
*Bunkhouse*
Batch Valley, All Stretton
SY6 6JW
t (01694) 722593
e frankiegoode@zoom.co.uk

### ALSTONEFIELD
### Staffordshire

**Alstonefield YHA ★★★**
*Hostel*
Overdale, Lode Lane,
Ashbourne DE6 2FZ
t (01335) 310206
w yha.org.uk

**Gateham Cottage and the
Coach House** *Camping Barn*
Gateham Grange, Alstonefield,
Ashbourne DE6 2FT
t (01335) 310349
e gateham.grange@btinternet.
com
w cressbrook.co.uk/hartingt/
gateham/

### ALTON
### Staffordshire

**Alton Bridge Inn ★★★★** *Inn*
Red Road, Alton ST10 4BX
t (01538) 702338
e info@altonhotel.co.uk
w altonhotel.co.uk

**Alverton Motel ★★★★**
*Guest Accommodation*
Denstone Lane, Alton
ST10 4AX
t (01538) 702265
e enquiries@alvertonmotel.co.
uk

**Bank House ★★★★**
*Guest Accommodation*
Smithy Bank, Alton ST10 4AD
t (01538) 702524
e gemma@alton-bandb.co.uk
w alton-bandb.co.uk

**Bulls Head Inn ★★★**
*Guest Accommodation*
High Street, Alton, Stoke-on-
Trent ST10 4AQ
t (01538) 702307
e janet@thebullsheadalton.co.
uk
w altontowers-
bedandbreakfast.co.uk

**Fields Farm ★★★★**
*Bed & Breakfast*
Chapel Lane, Threapwood
Alton, Stoke-on-Trent
ST10 4QZ
t (01538) 752721 &
07850 310381
e pat.massey@fieldsfarmbb.
co.uk
w fieldsfarmbb.co.uk

**Hillside Farm ★★★**
*Bed & Breakfast*
Alton Road, Uttoxeter
ST14 5HG
t (01889) 590760
w smoothhound.co.uk/hotels/
hillside.html

**The Malthouse ★★★★**
*Guest Accommodation*
Malthouse Road, Alton
ST10 4AG
t (01538) 703273
e enquiries@the-malthouse.
com

**The Mousehole ★★★★**
*Bed & Breakfast*
Cotton Lane, Cotton ST10 3DS
t (01538) 703351
e themouseholebb@ukf.net

**Peakstones Inn ★★★** *Inn*
Cheadle Road, Alton
ST10 4DH
t (01538) 755776
e info@peakstones.co.uk
w peakstones-inn.co.uk

**Royal Oak ★★★** *Inn*
Cheadle Road, Alton, Stoke-
on-Trent ST10 4BH
t (01538) 702625
e enq@royaloak-alton.co.uk
w royaloak-alton.co.uk

**Trough Ivy House ★★★★**
*Bed & Breakfast*
Farley ST10 3BQ
t (01538) 702683
e info@troughivyhouse.co.uk
w troughivyhouse.co.uk

**Tythe Barn House ★★★**
*Guest Accommodation*
Denstone Lane, Alton
ST10 4AX
t (01538) 702852
w tythebarnhouse.co.uk

**The Warren ★★★★**
*Guest Accommodation*
**SILVER AWARD**
Battlesteads ST10 4BG
t (01538) 702493
e annettebas@tinyworld.co.uk
w thewarren-bb.com

**Windy Arbour ★★★★**
*Guest House*
Hollis Lane, Denstone,
Uttoxeter ST14 5HP
t (01889) 591013
e stay@windyarbour.co.uk
w windyarbour.co.uk

### ALVECHURCH
### Worcestershire

**Alcott Farm ★★★** *Farmhouse*
Icknield Street, Weatheroak,
Alvechurch B48 7EH
t (01564) 824051
e alcottfarm@btinternet.com
w alcottfarm.co.uk

**Woodlands Bed and
Breakfast ★★★★**
*Bed & Breakfast*
Coopers Hill, Alvechurch, Nr
Bromsgrove B48 7BX
t (0121) 445 6772
e john.impey@gmail.com
w woodlandsbedandbreakfast.
com

### ALVELEY
### Shropshire

**Arnside ★★★★**
*Bed & Breakfast*
**SILVER AWARD**
Kidderminster Rd, Alveley,
Bridgnorth WV15 6LL
t (01746) 780007
e terry@recessantiques.
freeserve.co.uk
w virtual-shropshire.co.uk/
arnside

### ALVESTON
### Warwickshire

**YHA Hemmingford House
★★★★** *Hostel*
Alveston, Stratford-upon-Avon
CV37 7RG
t 0870 770 6052
e stratford@yha.org.uk
w yha.org.uk

### ARLEY
### Worcestershire

**Tudor Barn ★★★★**
*Bed & Breakfast*
**GOLD AWARD**
Nib Green, Arley, Bewdley
DY12 3LY
t (01299) 400129
e tudorbarn@aol.com
w tudor-barn.co.uk

### ARMSCOTE
### Warwickshire

**Willow Corner ★★★★**
*Bed & Breakfast*
**SILVER AWARD**
Armscote, Stratford-upon-
Avon CV37 8DE
t (01608) 682391
e trishandalan@willowcorner.
co.uk
w willowcorner.co.uk

### ASH MAGNA
### Shropshire

**Ash Hall Bed and Breakfast
★★** *Bed & Breakfast*
Ash Magna, Whitchurch
SY13 4DL
t (01948) 663151
w stmem.com/ashhall/

### ASHPERTON
### Herefordshire

**Pridewood ★★★**
*Guest Accommodation*
Ashperton, Ledbury HR8 2SF
t (01531) 670416
e julia@pridewoodbandb.co.
uk
w pridewoodbandb.co.uk

### ASTLEY
### Worcestershire

**Woodhampton House
★★★★** *Bed & Breakfast*
Weather Lane, Astley,
Stourport-on-Severn DY13 0SF
t (01299) 826510
e pete-a@sally-a.freeserve.co.
uk
w woodhamptonhouse.co.uk

### ASTON CANTLOW
### Warwickshire

**Tudor Rose Cottage ★★★**
*Bed & Breakfast*
29 Chapel Lane, Aston
Cantlow, Stratford-upon-Avon
B95 6HU
t (01789) 488315
e wendywithspaniels@tiscali.
co.uk

### ASTON MUNSLOW
### Shropshire

**Chadstone ★★★★★**
*Bed & Breakfast*
**SILVER AWARD**
Aston Munslow, Craven Arms
SY7 9ER
t (01584) 841675
e chadstone.lee@btinternet.
com
w chadstonebandb.co.uk

### ATHERSTONE
### Warwickshire

**Manor Farm Bed & Breakfast
★★★** *Bed & Breakfast*
Main Road, Ratcliffe Culey,
Hinckley CV9 3NY
t (01827) 712269
e user88024@aol.com

### BADSEY
### Worcestershire

**Orchard House ★★**
*Guest Accommodation*
99 Bretforton Road, Badsey,
Evesham WR11 7XQ
t (01386) 831245

### BALSALL COMMON
### West Midlands

**Camp Farm ★★★**
*Bed & Breakfast*
Hob Lane, Balsall Common,
Coventry CV7 7GX
t (01676) 533804

**G & G B&B ★★★★**
*Bed & Breakfast*
68 Needlers End Lane, Balsall
Common, Coventry CV7 7AB
t (01676) 532847
e gillymatthew68@hotmail.
com
w gillyandgrant.co.uk

**Willow House ★★★★**
*Bed & Breakfast*
64 Needlers End Lane, Balsall
Common, Coventry CV7 7AB
t (01676) 533901
e christine@glowbox.demon.
co.uk
w glowbox.demon.co.uk/
willowhouse.htm

### BARFORD
### Warwickshire

**Westham House B&B
★★★★** *Bed & Breakfast*
**SILVER AWARD**
Westham Lane, Warwick
CV35 8DP
t (01926) 624148
e westham_house@hotmail.
com
w westhamhouse.co.uk

### BARONS CROSS
### Herefordshire

**Lavender House ★★★★**
*Bed & Breakfast*
**SILVER AWARD**
1 Richmond Villas, Barons
Cross Road, Leominster
HR6 8RS
t (01568) 617559
e lavenderhouse@fsmail.net
w lavenderhouse.
012webpages.com

### BAYSTON HILL
### Shropshire

**Chatford House**
Rating Applied For
*Farmhouse*
Chatford, Bayston Hill,
Shrewsbury SY3 0AY
t (01743) 718301
e b&b@chatfordhouse.co.uk

### BENTHALL
### Shropshire

**Hilltop House ★★★★**
*Guest House*
Bridge Road, Benthall,
Ironbridge TF12 5RB
t (01952) 884441
e info@hilltop-house.co.uk
w hilltop-house.co.uk

### BEWDLEY
### Worcestershire

**Kateshill House ★★★★★**
*Bed & Breakfast*
**GOLD AWARD**
Red Hill, Bewdley DY12 2DR
t (01299) 401563
e info@kateshillhouse.co.uk
w kateshillhouse.co.uk

**Woodcolliers Arms ★★★**
*Inn*
76 Welch Gate, Bewdley
DY12 2AU
t (01299) 400589
e roger.coleman@fsmail.net

### BIDDULPH
### Staffordshire

**Chapel Croft Guest House
★★★★** *Guest House*
Newtown Road, Biddulph Park,
Stoke-on-Trent ST8 7SW
t (01782) 511013
e enquiries@chapelcroft.com
w chapelcroft.com

**Garden Cottage ★★★★**
*Bed & Breakfast*
Halls Road, Biddulph, Stoke-
on-Trent ST8 6DB
t (01782) 510835
e pchood@talktalk.net
w gardencottagebiddulph.co.
uk

BIDFORD-ON-AVON
Warwickshire

**Brookleys Bed & Breakfast**
★★★★ *Bed & Breakfast*
Honeybourne Road, Bidford-
on-Avon, Stratford-upon-Avon
B50 4PD
t (01789) 772785
e brookleyschris@aol.com
w brookleys.co.uk

**Fosbroke House ★★★★**
*Guest House*
4 High Street, Bidford-on-
Avon, Stratford-upon-Avon
B50 4BU
t (01789) 772327
e mark@swiftvilla.fsnet.co.uk
w smoothhound.co.uk/hotels/
fosbroke.html

**The Harbour ★★★★**
*Bed & Breakfast*
20 Salford Road, Bidford-on-
Avon, Stratford-upon-Avon
B50 4EN
t (01789) 772975
e peter@theharbour-gh.com
w theharbour-gh.com

BIRMINGHAM
West Midlands

**Alden Bed & Breakfast**
★★★ *Bed & Breakfast*
7 Elmdon Road, Marston
Green, Birmingham B37 7BS
t (0121) 684 2851
e powellalden@aol.com

**Central Guest House ★★★**
*Guest House*
1637 Coventry Road, Yardley,
Birmingham B26 1DD
t (0121) 706 7757
e stay@centralguesthouse.
com
w centralguesthouse.com

**Clay Towers ★★★★**
*Bed & Breakfast*
51 Frankley Beeches Road,
Northfield, Birmingham
B31 5AB
t (0121) 628 0053
e john@claytowers.co.uk

**Elmdon Guest House ★★★**
*Guest Accommodation*
2369 Coventry Road, Sheldon,
Birmingham B26 3PN
t (0121) 688 1720 &
(0121) 742 1626
e elmdonhouse@blueyonder.
co.uk
w elmdonguesthouse.co.uk

**Rollason Wood ★★**
*Guest Accommodation*
130 Wood End Road,
Erdington, Birmingham B24 8BJ
t (0121) 373 1230
e rollwood@globalnet.co.uk
w rollasonwoodhotel.co.uk

**Springfield Guest House**
★★★★ *Guest House*
69 Coventry Road, Coleshill,
Birmingham B46 3EA
t (01675) 465695

BISHOP'S CASTLE
Shropshire

**Broughton Farm B&B ★★★**
*Farmhouse*
Broughton Farm, Bishop's
Castle SY15 6SZ
t (01588) 638393
e broughtonfarm@micro-plus-
web.net
w virtualshropshire.co.uk/
lower-broughton-farm

**Magnolia ★★★★**
*Bed & Breakfast*
**GOLD AWARD**
3 Montgomery Road, Bishop's
Castle SY9 5EZ
t (01588) 638098
e magnoliabishopscastle@
yahoo.co.uk
w magnoliabishopscastle.co.uk

BOBBINGTON
Staffordshire

**Red Lion Inn ★★★★** *Inn*
Six Ashes Road, Bobbington,
Stourbridge DY7 5DU
t (01384) 221237
e bookings@redlioninn.co.uk
w redlioninn.co.uk

BRADNOP
Staffordshire

**Middle Farm ★★★**
*Guest Accommodation*
Apesford, Bradnop, Leek
ST13 7EX
t (01538) 382839
e susan@middlefarmbandb.
co.uk
w middlefarmbandb.co.uk

BRAMPTON ABBOTTS
Herefordshire

**Brampton Cottage ★★★**
*Bed & Breakfast*
Brampton Abbotts, Ross-on-
Wye HR9 7JD
t (01989) 562459
e caroline-keen@btconnect.
co.uk

BRAMSHALL
Staffordshire

**Bowmore House ★★★★**
*Farmhouse*
Stone Road, Bramshall,
Uttoxeter ST14 8SH
t (01889) 564452
e glovatt@furoris.com

BREDON'S NORTON
Worcestershire

**Sheepfold ★★★**
*Bed & Breakfast*
Manor Lane, Bredon's Norton,
Nr Tewkesbury GL20 7HB
t (01684) 772398

BRIDGNORTH
Shropshire

**Bulls Head Inn ★★★★** *Inn*
Chelmarsh, Bridgnorth
WV16 6BA
t (01746) 861469
e bull_chelmarsh@btconnect.
com
w bullsheadchelmarsh.co.uk

**Churchdown House ★★★★**
*Bed & Breakfast*
**SILVER AWARD**
14 East Castle Street,
Bridgnorth WV16 4AL
t (01746) 761236
e churchdownhouse@tiscali.
co.uk
w churchdownhouse.co.uk

**The Croft ★★★★**
*Guest House*
10/11 St Mary's Street,
Bridgnorth WV16 4DW
t (01746) 762416
e crofthotel@aol.com
w crofthotelbridgnorth.co.uk

**Dinney Farm ★★★★**
*Farmhouse*
Chelmarsh, Bridgnorth
WV16 6AU
t (01746) 861070
e info@thedinney.co.uk
w thedinney.co.uk

**The Golden Lion Inn ★★★**
*Guest Accommodation*
83 High Street, Bridgnorth
WV16 4DS
t (01746) 762016
e jeff@goldenlionbridgnorth.
co.uk
w goldenlionbridgnorth.co.uk

**The Old House ★★★★**
*Bed & Breakfast*
Hilton, Bridgnorth WV15 5PJ
t (01746) 716560
e enquiries@oldhousehilton.
co.uk
w oldhousehilton.co.uk

BROADWAY
Worcestershire

**The Bell at Willersey ★★★★**
*Guest Accommodation*
The Bell Inn, Willersey,
Broadway WR12 7PJ
t (01386) 858405
e enq@bellatwillersey.fsnet.
co.uk
w the-bell-willersey.com

**Burhill Farm ★★★★★**
*Farmhouse* **SILVER AWARD**
Buckland, Broadway
WR12 7LY
t (01386) 858171
e burhillfarm@yahoo.co.uk
w burhillfarm.co.uk

**Dove Cottage ★★★★**
*Bed & Breakfast*
**SILVER AWARD**
Colletts Fields, Broadway
WR12 7AT
t (01386) 859085
e delia.dovecottage@
ukonline.co.uk
w broadway-cotswolds.co.uk

**Farncombe Estate Centre**
★★★★
*Guest Accommodation*
Farncombe House, Broadway
WR12 1LJ
t (01386) 854100
e visit@farncombeestate.co.uk
w farncombeestate.co.uk

**The Old Stationhouse**
★★★★ *Guest House*
**SILVER AWARD**
Station Drive, Broadway
WR12 7DF
t (01386) 852659
e oldstationhouse@
eastbankbroadway.fsnet.co.uk
w broadway-cotswolds.co.uk/
oldstationhouse.html

**The Olive Branch Guest
House ★★★★**
*Guest Accommodation*
**SILVER AWARD**
78 High Street, Broadway
WR12 7AJ
t (01386) 853440
e davidpam@theolivebranch-
broadway.com
w theolivebranch-broadway.
com

**Sheepscombe House**
★★★★ *Bed & Breakfast*
**GOLD AWARD**
Snowshill, Broadway
WR12 7JU
t (01386) 853769
e reservations@snowshill-
broadway.co.uk
w broadway-cotswolds.co.uk/
sheepscombe.html

**Small Talk Lodge ★★★★**
*Guest House*
32 High Street, Broadway
WR12 7DP
t (01386) 858953
e bookings@smalltalklodge.
co.uk
w smalltalklodge.co.uk

**Whiteacres ★★★★**
*Guest Accommodation*
**SILVER AWARD**
Station Road, Broadway
WR12 7DE
t (01386) 852320
e whiteacres@btinternet.com
w whiteacres-cotswolds.co.uk

**Windrush House ★★★★**
*Guest House* **SILVER AWARD**
Station Road, Broadway
WR12 7DE
t (01386) 853577
e evan@broadway-windrush.
co.uk
w broadway-windrush.co.uk

BROBURY
Herefordshire

**Brobury House & Gardens**
★★★★ *Bed & Breakfast*
Brobury, By Bredwardine,
Hereford HR3 6BS
t (01981) 500229
e enquiries@broburyhouse.co.
uk

BROMSGROVE
Worcestershire

**The Durrance ★★★★**
*Farmhouse* **SILVER AWARD**
Berry Lane, Upton Warren,
Bromsgrove B61 9EL
t (01562) 777533
e helenhirons@thedurrance.
co.uk
w thedurrance.co.uk

**Merrivale ★★★★**
*Bed & Breakfast*
309 Old Birmingham Road,
Lickey, Bromsgrove B60 1HQ
t (0121) 445 1694
e anthonysmith309@aol.com

**Overwood** ★★★★
*Bed & Breakfast*
Woodcote Lane, Woodcote
Green, Bromsgrove B61 9EE
t (01562) 777193
e info@overwood.net
w overwood.net

**Woodgate Manor Farm**
★★★★
*Guest Accommodation*
Woodgate Road, Woodgate,
Bromsgrove B60 4HG
t (01527) 821275
e info@woodgatemanorfarm.
co.uk
w woodgatemanorfarm.co.uk
🚶‍♂️ 🚲

### BROMYARD
Herefordshire

**The Old Cowshed** ★★★★
*Bed & Breakfast*
**SILVER AWARD**
Avenbury, Bromyard HR7 4LA
t (01885) 482384
e combes@theoldcowshed.co.
uk
w theoldcowshed.co.uk
🚶‍♂️ 🚲

### BROSELEY
Shropshire

**Broseley House** ★★★★
*Guest House* **SILVER AWARD**
1 The Square, Broseley, Nr
Ironbridge TF12 5EW
t (01952) 882043
e info@broseleyhouse.co.uk
w broseleyhouse.co.uk

**Coalport YHA** ★★★ *Hostel*
c/o John Rose Building, High
Street, Telford TF8 7HT
t 0870 770 5882
e ironbridge@yha.org.uk
w yha.org.uk
🚶‍♂️ 🚲

**The Lion Hotel** ★★★★
*Guest Accommodation*
High Street, Broseley, Telford
TF12 5EZ
t (01952) 881128
e lionhotelshrops@aol.com
w lionhotelshropshire.co.uk

**The Old Rectory at Broseley**
★★★★★ *Guest House*
**SILVER AWARD**
46 Ironbridge Road, Broseley
TF12 5AF
t (01952) 883399
e info@
theoldrectoryatbroseley.co.uk
w theoldrectoryatbroseley.co.
uk
🚶‍♂️ 🚲

**Rock Dell** ★★★★
*Bed & Breakfast*
**SILVER AWARD**
30 Ironbridge Road, Broseley
TF12 5AJ
t (01952) 883054
e rockdell@ukgateway.net
w http://www28.brinkster.
com/rockdell

### BUCKNELL
Shropshire

**The Hall** ★★★★
*Guest Accommodation*
Bucknell, Craven Arms
SY7 0AA
t (01547) 530249
e thehallbucknell@hotmail.
com
w smoothhound.co.uk/hotels/
thehall

**The Willows** ★★★★
*Bed & Breakfast*
Bucknell, Craven Arms
SY7 0AA
t (01547) 530201
e the_willows@btinternet.com
w willows-bucknell.co.uk
🚶‍♂️ 🚲

### BURGHILL
Herefordshire

**Burghill Grange** ★★★★
*Bed & Breakfast*
Burghill, Hereford HR4 7SE
t (01432) 761016
e info@burghillgrange.com
w burghillgrange.com

### BURLTON
Shropshire

**Petton Hall Farm** ★★★★
*Farmhouse* **SILVER AWARD**
Petton, Burlton, Shrewsbury
SY4 5TH
t (01939) 270601
e marypettonhallfarm@
amserve.com
w stmem.com/pettonhallfarm

### BURTON DASSETT
Warwickshire

**Caudle Hill Farm** ★★★★
*Farmhouse* **SILVER AWARD**
Burton Dassett, Southam,
Leamington Spa CV47 2AB
t (01295) 770255
e janeperry@another.com
w caudlehillfarm.co.uk

### BURTON UPON TRENT
Staffordshire

**A511.co.uk**
Rating Applied For
*Guest Accommodation*
20 Station Road, Hatton, Derby
DE65 5EL
t (01283) 815996
e rod@invictaindustrial.co.uk
w A511.co.uk

**Meadowview** ♦♦♦
*Guest Accommodation*
203 Newton Road, Winshill,
Burton-on-Trent DE15 0TU
t (01283) 564046
e cllr-pat-hancox@freeola.com

**New Inn Farm** ★★★
*Bed & Breakfast*
Burton Road, Needwood,
Burton-on-Trent DE13 9PB
t (01283) 575435

**Redmoor Accommodation**
★★ *Bed & Breakfast*
6 Redmoor Close, Winshill,
Burton-on-Trent DE15 0HZ
t (01283) 531977
e petervyze@btinternet.com

### BUTTERTON
Staffordshire

**Butterton A** *Camping Barn*
Feens Farm, Wetton Road,
Leek ST13 7ST
t (01538) 304185

**Butterton B** *Camping Barn*
Fenns Farm, Wetton Road,
Leek ST13 7ST
t (01538) 304185

**Coxon Green Farm** ★★★★
*Farmhouse* **SILVER AWARD**
Butterton, Leek ST13 7TA
t (01538) 304221
e coxongreen@butterton.
fsnet.co.uk

**New Hayes Farm** ★★★★
*Farmhouse*
Trentham Road, Butterton,
Newcastle ST5 4DX
t (01782) 680889
e info@newhayesfarm.co.uk
w newhayesfarm.co.uk

### CALDECOTE
Warwickshire

**Hill House Country Guest
House** ★★★★ *Guest House*
Off Mancetter Road, Nuneaton
CV10 0RS
t (024) 7639 6685

### CANNOCK
Staffordshire

**Hillside Bed & Breakfast**
★★★★ *Bed & Breakfast*
29 Littleworth Hill, Cannock
WS12 1NS
t (01543) 425886
e hillsidebandb@hotmail.co.uk

### CARDINGTON
Shropshire

**Upper Shadymoor Farm**
★★★★ *Farmhouse*
Stapleton, Dorrington,
Shrewsbury SY5 7LB
t (01743) 718670
e kevan@shadymoor.co.uk
w shadymoor.co.uk

**Woodside Farm** ★★★★
*Farmhouse*
Cardington, Church Stretton
SY6 7LB
t (01694) 771314
w virtual-shropshire.co.uk/
woodside-farm

### CHEADLE
Staffordshire

**Ley Fields Farm** ★★★★
*Farmhouse* **SILVER AWARD**
Leek Road, Cheadle ST10 2EF
t (01538) 752875
e leyfieldsfarm@aol.com
w leyfieldsfarm.co.uk

**The Manor** ★★★
*Guest Accommodation*
Watt Place, Cheadle, Stoke-on-
Trent ST10 1NZ
t (01538) 753450
e stay@themanor-cheadle.
com
w themanor-cheadle.com

**Park View Guest House**
★★★ *Guest House*
15 Mill Road, Cheadle
ST10 1NG
t (01538) 755412
e stewart@
parkviewguesthouse.fsworld.
co.uk
w theparkviewguesthouse.co.
uk

**Rakeway House Farm B&B**
★★★★ *Farmhouse*
Rakeway Road, Cheadle, Alton
Towers Area ST10 1RA
t (01538) 755295
e enquiries@
rakewayhousefarm.co.uk
w rakewayhousefarm.co.uk

### CHEDDLETON
Staffordshire

**Brook House Farm** ★★★
*Farmhouse*
Brookhouse Lane, Cheddleton,
Leek ST13 7DF
t (01538) 360296

**The Garden House**
Rating Applied For
*Bed & Breakfast*
150 Cheadle Road, Leek
ST13 7BD
t (01538) 361449
e pearl@garden-house.org
w garden-house.org

**Mosslee Grange Bed and
Breakfast** ★★★
*Bed & Breakfast*
Basford Green, Cheddleton,
Leek ST13 7ES
t 07969 463685
e mossleegrange@supanet.
com
w freewebs.com/
mossleegrangebedand
breakfast

### CHELMARSH
Shropshire

**Hampton House** ★★★★
*Guest Accommodation*
Hampton Loade, Chelmarsh,
Nr Bridgnorth WV16 6BN
t (01746) 861436
w stmem.com/hampton-house

**The Unicorn Inn** ★★ *Inn*
Hampton Loade, Chelmarsh,
Bridgnorth WV16 6BN
t (01746) 861515
e kenunicorninn@aol.com
w http://freespace.virginnet.
co.uk/unicorninn.bridgnorth

### CHETWYND ASTON
Shropshire

**Woodcroft** ★★
*Bed & Breakfast*
Pitchcroft Lane, Chetwynd
Aston, Newport TF10 9AU
t (01952) 812406

### CHURCH STRETTON
Shropshire

**Acton Scott Farm B&B** ★★★
*Farmhouse*
Acton Scott, Church Stretton
SY6 6QN
t (01694) 781260
e shrops@actonscottfarm.co.
uk
w actonscottfarm.co.uk

**Brookfields Guest House**
★★★★★ *Guest House*
SILVER AWARD
Watling Street North, Church
Stretton SY6 7AR
t (01694) 722314
e paulangie@brookfields51.
fsnet.co.uk
w churchstretton-guesthouse.
co.uk

**Highcliffe** ★★★
*Bed & Breakfast*
Madeira Walk, Church Stretton
SY6 6JQ
t (01694) 722908
w stmem.com/highcliffe

**Highlands Bed and
Breakfast** ★★★★
*Bed & Breakfast*
Hazler Road, Church Stretton
SY6 7AF
t (01694) 723737
e info@highlandsbandb.co.uk
w highlandsbandb.co.uk

**Jinlye Guest House**
★★★★★ *Guest House*
GOLD AWARD
Castle Hill, All Stretton, Church
Stretton SY6 6JP
t (01694) 723243
e info@jinlye.co.uk
w jinlye.co.uk

**Juniper Cottage** ★★★★
*Bed & Breakfast*
All Stretton, Church Stretton
SY6 6HG
t (01694) 723427
e colinmcintyre@ukonline.co.
uk

**Mynd House** ★★★★
*Guest House* SILVER AWARD
Little Stretton, Church Stretton
SY6 6RB
t (01694) 722212
e info@myndhouse.co.uk
w myndhouse.co.uk

**Old Rectory House** ★★★
*Bed & Breakfast*
Burway Rd, Church Stretton
SY6 6DW
t (01694) 724462
e smamos@btinternet.com
w oldrectoryhouse.co.uk

**Ragdon Manor** ★★★★
*Bed & Breakfast*
Ragdon, Church Stretton
SY6 7EZ
t (01694) 781389
e ragdon@toucansurf.com
w stmem.com/ragdonmanor

**Rheingold** ★★★★
*Guest Accommodation*
9 The Bridleways, Church
Stretton SY6 7AN
t (01694) 723969
w rheingold-b-and-b.co.uk

**Sayang House** ★★★★
*Bed & Breakfast*
Hope Bowdler, Church
Stretton SY6 7DD
t (01694) 723981
e madegan@aol.com
w sayanghouse.com

**Victoria House** ★★★★
*Guest Accommodation*
48 High Street, Church
Stretton SY6 6BX
t (01694) 723823
e victoriahouse@fsmail.net
w bedandbreakfast-shropshire.
co.uk

**Broome Park Farm** ★★★★
*Farmhouse*
Catherton Road, Cleobury
Mortimer, Kidderminster
DY14 0LB
t (01299) 270647
e catherine@broomeparkfarm.
co.uk
w broomeparkfarm.co.uk

**Clod Hall** ★★
*Guest Accommodation*
Milson, Cleobury Mortimer
DY14 0BJ
t (01584) 781421
w stmem.com/clod-hall

**Cox's Barn** ★★★★
*Farmhouse*
Bagginswood, Cleobury
Mortimer DY14 8LS
t (01746) 718415
e iain.thompson12@
btopenworld.com
w stmem.com/coxs-barn

**Woodview B&B** ★★★★
*Guest Accommodation*
GOLD AWARD
Mawley Oak, Cleobury
Mortimer DY14 9BA
t (01299) 271422
w woodviewcountryvilla.co.uk

CLEVELODE
Worcestershire

**Severnside Bed & Breakfast**
★★★★ *Bed & Breakfast*
SILVER AWARD
Clevelode, Nr Malvern
WR13 6PD
t (01684) 311894
e info@severn-side.co.uk
w severn-side.co.uk

CLIFFORD
Herefordshire

**Cottage Farm** ★★★
*Bed & Breakfast*
Middlewood, Dorstone,
Golden Valley HR3 5SX
t (01497) 831496

CLIFTON UPON TEME
Worcestershire

**Pitlands Farm** ★★★★
*Farmhouse*
Clifton upon Teme, Worcester
WR6 6DX
t (01886) 812220
e pitlandsfarmholidays@
btopenworld.com
w pitlandsfarm.co.uk

CLOWS TOP
Worcestershire

**Colliers Hill Guest House &
Conference Centre** ★★★★
*Bed & Breakfast*
Colliers Hill, Bayton DY14 9NZ
t (01299) 832247
e info@colliershill.co.uk
w colliershill.co.uk

CLUN
Shropshire

**Clun Mill Youth Hostel** ★★
*Hostel*
The Mill, Clun, Craven Arms
SY7 8NY
t (01588) 640582
e reservations@yha.org.uk
w yha.org.uk

**Crown House (Old Stables
and Saddlery)** ★★★★
*Bed & Breakfast*
Crown House, Clun, Craven
Arms SY7 8JW
t (01588) 640780
e crownhouseclun@talk21.
com
w the-wendy-house.com

**Llanhedric Farm** ★★★★
*Farmhouse*
Clun, Craven Arms SY7 8NG
t (01588) 640203
e maryandhugh@btconnect.
com
w stmem.com/llanhedric

**New House Farm** ★★★★★
*Guest Accommodation*
GOLD AWARD
Clun, Craven Arms SY7 8NJ
t (01588) 638314
e sarah@bishopscastle.co.uk
w new-house-clun.co.uk

**The Old Farmhouse** ★★★★
*Bed & Breakfast*
Woodside, Clun SY7 0JB
t (01588) 640695
e helen@vuan1.freeserve.co.
uk
w theoldfarmhousebandb.co.
uk

**Springhill Farm** ★★★
*Farmhouse*
Clun, Craven Arms SY7 8PE
t (01588) 640337
e enquiries@springhill-farm.
com
w springhill-farm.com

**Thomas Cottage** ★★★★
*Bed & Breakfast*
Church Bank, Clun SY7 8LP
t (01588) 640029
e dctucker@btinternet.com
w thomascottageclun.co.uk

**The White Horse Inn** ★★★
*Inn*
The Square, Clun SY7 8JA
t (01588) 640305
e jack@whi-clun.co.uk
w whi-clun.co.uk

COALPORT
Shropshire

**Ironbridge Youth Hostel
(YHA)** ★★ *Hostel*
John Rose Building, High
Street, Telford TF8 7HT
t (01952) 588755
e ironbridge@yha.org.uk
w yha.org.uk

**The Shakespeare Inn**
★★★★ *Inn*
High Street, Coalport, Telford
TF8 7HT
t (01952) 580675
w shakespeare-inn.co.uk

COLESHILL
Warwickshire

**Merrimoles Bed & Breakfast**
★★★★ *Bed & Breakfast*
Back Lane, Shustoke, Coleshill,
Birmingham B46 2AW
t (01675) 481158
e stella@merrimoles.co.uk
w merrimoles.co.uk

**Ye Olde Station Guest
House** ★★★ *Guest House*
Church Road, Shustoke,
Coleshill, Birmingham B46 2AX
t (01675) 481736
e patr@freeuk.com

COLTON
Staffordshire

**Colton House** ★★★★★
*Guest House*
Bellamour Way, Colton,
Rugeley WS15 3LL
t (01889) 578580
e mail@coltonhouse.com
w coltonhouse.com

COLWALL
Herefordshire

**Old Library Lodge** ★★★
*Guest Accommodation*
Stone Drive, Colwall, Malvern
WR13 6QJ
t (01684) 540077

COUGHTON
Warwickshire

**Coughton Lodge** ★★★★
*Guest House*
Coughton, Alcester B49 5HU
t (01789) 764600
e enquiries@coughtonlodge.
co.uk
w coughtonlodge.co.uk

COVENTRY
West Midlands

**Acacia Guest House** ★★★★
*Guest House*
11 Park Road, Coventry
CV1 2LE
t (024) 7663 3622
e acaciaguesthouse@hotmail.
com

**Ashdowns Guest House**
★★★ *Guest House*
12 Regent Street, Earlsdon,
Coventry CV1 3EP
t (024) 7622 9280

**Ashleigh House** ★★★
*Guest House*
17 Park Road, Coventry
CV1 2LH
t (024) 7622 3804

**Barnacle Hall** ★★★★★
*Bed & Breakfast*
GOLD AWARD
Shilton Lane, Shilton, Coventry
CV7 9LH
t (024) 7661 2629
e rose@barnaclehall.co.uk
w barnaclehall.co.uk

**Bede Guest House** ★★★
*Bed & Breakfast*
250 Radford Road, Radford,
Coventry CV6 3BV
t (024) 7659 7837
e bedehouse@aol.com

**Bourne Brook Lodge** ★★★★
*Bed & Breakfast*
Mill Lane, Fillongley, Coventry
CV7 8EE
t (01676) 541898
w bournebrooklodge.co.uk

**Highcroft Guest House**
★★★ *Guest Accommodation*
65 Barras Lane, Coundon,
Coventry CV1 4AQ
t (024) 7622 8157
e deepakcov@hotmail.com

**Merlyn Guest House** ★★★
*Guest House*
105 Holyhead Road, Coundon,
Coventry CV1 3AD
t (024) 7622 2800
e info@merlynguesthouse.co.
uk
w merlynguesthouse.co.uk

**Mount Guest House** ★★★
*Guest House*
9 Coundon Road, Coventry
CV1 4AR
t (024) 7622 5998
e enquiries@
guesthousecoventry.com
w guesthousecoventry.com

**Spire View Guest House**
★★★ *Guest House*
36 Park Road, Coventry
CV1 2LD
t (024) 7625 1602
e bookings@
spireviewguesthouse.co.uk
w spireviewguesthouse.co.uk

### CRACKLEY BANK
Shropshire

**Courtyard Apartments**
★★★ *Inn*
Crackley Bank TF11 8QT
t (01952) 460597
e hareandhoundsinn@
btconnect.com
w hareandhoundsinn.co.uk

### CROPTHORNE
Worcestershire

**Cropvale Farm Bed and
Breakfast** ★★★★ *Farmhouse*
**GOLD AWARD**
Smokey Lane, Cropthorne,
Pershore WR10 3NF
t (01386) 861925
e cropvale@hotmail.com
w smoothhound.co.uk/hotels/
cropvale.html

**Oaklands Farmhouse**
★★★★★ *Bed & Breakfast*
**GOLD AWARD**
Bricklehampton, Pershore
WR10 3JT
t (01386) 861716
e barbara-stewart@lineone.
net
w oaklandsfarmhouse.co.uk

### CROSS HOUSES
Shropshire

**Upper Brompton Farm**
★★★★ *Bed & Breakfast*
**SILVER AWARD**
Cross Houses, Shrewsbury
SY5 6LE
t (01743) 761629
e philippa@upperbrompton.
orangehome.co.uk
w upperbromptonfarm.co.uk

### CUBBINGTON
Warwickshire

**Bakers Cottage** ★★★★
*Bed & Breakfast*
52-54 Queen Street,
Cubbington, Leamington Spa
CV32 7NA
t (01926) 772146

### CULMINGTON
Shropshire

**Seifton Court** ★★★★
*Farmhouse*
Seifton, Ludlow SY8 2DG
t (01584) 861214
e seiftoncourt@aol.com
w seiftoncourt.co.uk

### CURDWORTH
West Midlands

**The Old School House Hotel**
★★★★ *Guest House*
Kingsbury Road, Sutton
Coldfield B76 9DR
t (01675) 470177
e vicki@oldschoolhousehotel.
co.uk
w oldschoolhousehotel.co.uk

### DENSTONE
Staffordshire

**Heywood Hall** ★★★★
*Guest Accommodation*
College Road, Denstone,
Burton-on-Trent ST14 5HR
t (01889) 591747
w heywoodhall.co.uk

**Manor House Farm** ★★★★
*Farmhouse* **SILVER AWARD**
Quixhill Lane, Prestwood,
Uttoxeter ST14 5DD
t (01889) 590415
e cm_ball@yahoo.co.uk
w 4posteraccom.com

**Rowan Cottage** ★★★★
*Guest Accommodation*
Stubwood Lane, Denstone,
Uttoxeter ST14 5HU
t (01889) 590913
e rowanlodge@hotmail.com
w smoothhound.co.uk/hotels/
rowanlodge.html

### DIDDLEBURY
Shropshire

**Larkfield Farm** ★★
*Bed & Breakfast*
Diddlebury, Craven Arms
SY7 9DH
t (01584) 841575
e larkfieldfarm@hotmail.co.uk

### DILWYN
Herefordshire

**Sollars Barn** ★★★★
*Bed & Breakfast*
Dilwyn, Leominster HR4 8JJ
t (01544) 388260

### DORRINGTON
Shropshire

**Meadowlands** ★★★
*Bed & Breakfast*
Lodge Lane, Frodesley,
Shrewsbury SY5 7HD
t (01694) 731350
e meadowlands@talk21.com
w meadowlands.co.uk

### DORSTONE
Herefordshire

**Highfield** ★★★★ *Farmhouse*
**SILVER AWARD**
The Bage, Dorstone, Golden
Valley HR3 5SU
t (01497) 831431
e book@highfieldbandb.com
w highfieldbandb.com

### DOWNTON ON THE ROCK
Shropshire

**Old Downton Lodge** ★★★★
*Restaurant with Rooms*
Ludlow SY8 2HU
t (01568) 770820
e jayne@olddowntonlodge.co.
uk
w olddowntonlodge.co.uk

### DROITWICH
Worcestershire

**Middleton Grange** ★★★★
*Guest Accommodation*
**SILVER AWARD**
Ladywood Road, Salwarpe,
Droitwich Spa WR9 0AH
t (01905) 451678
e salli@middletongrange.com
w middletongrange.com

**The Old Farmhouse**
★★★★★
*Guest Accommodation*
**SILVER AWARD**
Hadley Heath, Ombersley, Nr
Droitwich Spa WR9 0AR
t (01905) 620837
e judylambe@
theoldfarmhouse.uk.com
w theoldfarmhouse.uk.com

### DUNCHURCH
Warwickshire

**Old Thatched Cottage Hotel
& Restaurant** ★★★★
*Guest Accommodation*
Southam Road, Dunchurch,
Rugby CV22 6NG
t (01788) 810417

### EARDISLAND
Herefordshire

**Moat Edge** ★★★★
*Bed & Breakfast*
6 St Marys Walk, Leominster
HR6 9BB
t (01544) 388097
e moatedge@btinternet.com
w moatedge.co.uk

### EARLSWOOD
West Midlands

**The Limes Country Lodge**
★★★ *Guest House*
Forshaw Heath Road, Solihull
B94 5JZ
t (0121) 744 4800
e info@thelimes.biz
w thelimes.biz

### EASTNOR
Herefordshire

**Hill Farmhouse Bed and
Breakfast** ★★★ *Farmhouse*
Eastnor, Ledbury HR8 1EF
t (01531) 632827

### ECCLESHALL
Staffordshire

**Cobblers Cottage** ★★★★
*Guest Accommodation*
Kerry Lane, Eccleshall, Stafford
ST21 6EJ
t (01785) 850116
e cobblerscottage@tinyonline.
co.uk

**George Hotel (The)** ★★★
*Inn*
Castle Street, Eccleshall,
Stafford ST21 6DF
t (01785) 850300
e information@thegeorgeinn.
freeserve.co.uk
w thegeorgeinn.freeserve.co.
uk

### ECKINGTON
Worcestershire

**Anchor Inn & Restaurant**
★★★ *Inn*
Cotheridge Lane, Eckington, Nr
Pershore WR10 3BA
t (01386) 750356
e anchoreck@aol.com
w anchoreckington.co.uk

**Harrowfields Bed and
Breakfast** ★★★★
*Bed & Breakfast*
**SILVER AWARD**
Harrowfields, Cotheridge Lane,
Eckington WR10 3BA
t (01386) 751053
e susie@harrowfields.co.uk
w harrowfields.co.uk

**Myrtle Cottage** ★★★★
*Bed & Breakfast*
Jarvis Street, Eckington,
Pershore WR10 3AS
t (01386) 750893
e veronica@myrtle-cottage.
com
w myrtle-cottage.com

### ELLESMERE
Shropshire

**Oak Hill Farm** ★★★★
*Bed & Breakfast*
Dudleston, Ellesmere SY12 9LL
t (01691) 690548

### ENDON
Staffordshire

**Hollinhurst Farm** ★★★
*Farmhouse*
Park Lane, Endon, Stoke-on-
Trent ST9 9JB
t (01782) 502633
e joan.hollinhurst@btconnect.
com

### EWYAS HAROLD
Herefordshire

**The Old Rectory – Ewyas
Harold** ★★★★
*Bed & Breakfast*
**SILVER AWARD**
Ewyas Harold, Hereford,
Golden Valley HR2 0EY
t (01981) 240498
e jenny.juckes@btopenworld.
com
w theoldrectory.org.uk

## FECKENHAM
### Worcestershire

**Orchard House ★★★★**
*Bed & Breakfast*
**SILVER AWARD**
Berrow Hill Lane, Feckenham,
Nr Redditch B96 6QJ
t (01527) 821497
w orchardhouse-bb.co.uk

**The Steps ★★★★**
*Bed & Breakfast*
6 High Street, Feckenham,
Redditch B96 6HS
t (01527) 892678
e jenny@thesteps.co.uk
w thesteps.co.uk

## FENNY COMPTON
### Warwickshire

**The Grange ★★★** *Farmhouse*
The Slade, Fenny Compton,
Southam CV47 2YB
t (01295) 770590

## FERNHILL HEATH
### Worcestershire

**Dilmore House ★★★★**
*Bed & Breakfast*
**SILVER AWARD**
254 Droitwich Road, Fernhill
Heath, Worcester WR3 7UL
t (01905) 451543
e dilmorehouse@tiscali.co.uk
w dilmorehouse.co.uk

**Heathside ★★★★**
*Guest House*
172 Droitwich Road, Fernhill
Heath, Worcester WR3 7UA
t (01905) 458245
e info@heathsideguesthouse.
co.uk
w heathsideguesthouse.co.uk

## FILLONGLEY
### Warwickshire

**Grooms Cottage ★★★★**
*Farmhouse* **SILVER AWARD**
Manor House Farm, Green End
Road, Fillongley, Coventry
CV7 8DS
t (01676) 540256

## FISHMORE
### Shropshire

**Acorn Place**
Rating Applied For
*Bed & Breakfast*
Fishmore, Ludlow SY8 3DP
t (01584) 875295
w stmem.com/acorn-place

## FOWNHOPE
### Herefordshire

**Bark Cottage ★★★★**
*Bed & Breakfast*
Fownhope, Hereford HR1 4PE
t (01432) 860344
e arthur@wyeleisure.com

## GNOSALL
### Staffordshire

**Leys House ★★★★**
*Bed & Breakfast*
Quarry Lane, Gnosall, Stafford
ST20 0BZ
t (01785) 822532
e proffitt.gnosall@virgin.net

## GREAT WOLFORD
### Warwickshire

**The Old Coach House
★★★★★ Bed & Breakfast**
**SILVER AWARD**
Great Wolford, Shipston-on-
Stour CV36 5NQ
t (01608) 674152
e theoldcoachhouse@
thewolfords.net
w theoldecoachhouse.co.uk

## GRINDON
### Staffordshire

**Summerhill Farm Bed and
Breakfast ★★★** *Farmhouse*
Grindon, Leek ST13 7TT
t (01538) 304264
e info@summerhillfarm.co.uk
w summerhillfarm.co.uk

## HANDSACRE
### Staffordshire

**Olde Peculiar (The) ★★★★**
*Inn*
The Green, Handsacre,
Lichfield WS15 4DP
t (01543) 491891
e corinne.odonnell@ntlworld.
com

## HANLEY
### Staffordshire

**Northwood Hotel ♦♦♦**
*Guest Accommodation*
146 Keelings Road,
Northwood, Stoke-on-Trent
ST1 6QA
t (01782) 279729
e northwoodhotel@ntlworld.
com
w city-hotels.org.uk

## HANLEY CASTLE
### Worcestershire

**The Chestnuts ★★★★**
*Bed & Breakfast*
**SILVER AWARD**
Gilberts End, Hanley Castle
WR8 0AS
t (01684) 311219
e heather@chestnutshp.co.uk
w chestnutshp.co.uk

**Gilberts End Farm B&B
★★★★ Bed & Breakfast**
Gilberts End, Hanley Castle, Nr
Upton-upon-Severn WR8 0AR
t (01684) 311392
e chrissy.bacon@onetel.net
w gilbertsendfarm.co.uk

## HANLEY SWAN
### Worcestershire

**Blackmore Gardens ★★★★**
*Guest Accommodation*
Blackmore Park, Hanley Swan
WR8 0EF
t (01684) 311931

**Meadowbank ★★★★**
*Bed & Breakfast*
**SILVER AWARD**
Picken End, Hanley Swan
WR8 0DQ
t (01684) 310917
e dave@meadowbankhs.
freeserve.co.uk
w http://mysite.freeserve.
com/meadowbank

## HARDWICK, HAY ON WYE
### Herefordshire

**Hardwicke Green ★★★★**
*Bed & Breakfast*
Hardwicke, Hay-on-Wye
HR3 5HA
t (01497) 831051
e info@hardwickegreen.co.uk

## HARLEY
### Shropshire

**Rowley Farm ★★** *Farmhouse*
Harley, Shrewsbury SY5 6LX
t (01952) 727348
e bedandbreakfast@
rowleyfarm.fsnet.co.uk
w stmem.com/rowley-farm

## HEREFORD
### Herefordshire

**Alberta Guest House ★★★**
*Guest House*
7-13 Newtown Road, Hereford
HR4 9LH
t (01432) 270313
e albertaguesthouse@
amserve.com
w thealbertaguesthouse.co.uk

**The Bowens Country House
Hotel ★★★★**
*Guest Accommodation*
Fownhope, Hereford HR1 4PS
t (01432) 860430
e thebowenshotel@aol.com
w thebowenshotel.co.uk

**Brandon Lodge ★★★★**
*Guest House* **SILVER AWARD**
Ross Road, Grafton, Hereford
HR2 8BH
t (01432) 355621
e info@brandonlodge.co.uk
w brandonlodge.co.uk

**Charades ★★★**
*Guest Accommodation*
34 Southbank Road, Hereford
HR1 2TJ
t (01432) 269444
e stay@charadeshereford.co.
uk
w charadeshereford.co.uk

**Graiseley House ★★★**
*Bed & Breakfast*
180 Whitecross Road, Hereford
HR4 0DJ
t (01432) 358289
e mrsjspearpoint@aol.com
w graiseleyhouse.co.uk

**Hedley Lodge ★★★★**
*Guest Accommodation*
Belmont Abbey, Abergavenny
Road, Hereford HR2 9RZ
t (01432) 374747
e hedley@belmontabbey.org.
uk
w hedleylodge.com

**Heron House ★★★**
*Bed & Breakfast*
Canon Pyon Road, Portway,
Hereford HR4 8NG
t (01432) 761111
e info@theheronhouse.com
w theheronhouse.com

**Hopbine House ★★★**
*Guest House*
The Hopbine, Roman Road,
Holmer, Hereford HR1 1LE
t (01432) 268722
e info@hopbine.com
w hopbine.com

## Old Rectory ★★★★
*Guest Accommodation*
**SILVER AWARD**
Byford, Hereford HR4 7LD
t (01981) 590218
e info@cm-ltd.com
w smoothhound.co.uk/hotels/
oldrectory2.html

## HIGHAM ON THE HILL
### Warwickshire

**Bed & Breakfast at Vale
Farm ★★★★** *Farmhouse*
Stoke Golding Lane, Higham-
on-the-Hill, Hinckley CV13 6ES
t 07977 915272
e prestons@valefarm.eleven.
com
w valefarm-bed-and-breakfast.
co.uk

## HIMBLETON
### Worcestershire

**Court Farm**
Rating Applied For
*Farmhouse*
Himbleton, Droitwich
WR9 7JG
t (01905) 391254
e penelopewesner@
courtfarm.info
w courtfarm.info

**Phepson Farm ★★★★**
*Guest Accommodation*
Himbleton, Nr Droitwich Spa
WR9 7JZ
t (01905) 391205
e havard@globalnet.co.uk
w phepsonfarm.co.uk

## HINTON ON THE GREEN
### Worcestershire

**Haselor Farm Bed &
Breakfast ★★** *Farmhouse*
Pershore Road, Hinton-on-the-
Green, Evesham WR11 2RB
t (01386) 860591
e haselorfarm@btinternet.com
w haselorfarm.co.uk

## HOARWITHY
### Herefordshire

**The Old Mill ★★★★**
*Bed & Breakfast*
Hoarwithy, Hereford HR2 6QH
t (01432) 840602
e carol.probert@virgin.net

## HOCKLEY HEATH
### West Midlands

**Eden End Bed & Breakfast
★★★** *Guest House*
Eden End, Stratford Road,
Solihull B94 6NN
t (01564) 783372
e bedandbreakfast@edenend.
com
w edenend.com

**Illshaw Heath Farm ★★★★**
*Guest House*
Kineton Lane, Hockley Heath,
Solihull B94 6RX
t (01564) 782214
e janetgarner@btinternet.com
w illshawheathfarm.com

## HOLLINGTON
### Staffordshire

**The Raddle Inn ★★★** *Inn*
Quarry Bank ST10 4HQ
t (01889) 507278
e peter@logcabin.co.uk
w logcabin.co.uk

---

## HOLLYBUSH
### Worcestershire

**Bank Cottage** ★★★
*Bed & Breakfast*
The Common, Hollybush,
Ledbury HR8 1ET
t (01531) 650683
e hpwhite@bloomberg.net
w bankcottage.net

## HOPE BAGOT
### Shropshire

**Croft Cottage B&B** ★★★★
*Bed & Breakfast*
Cumberley Lane, Knowbury,
Ludlow SY8 3LJ
t (01584) 890664
e info@croftcottagebedand
breakfast.co.uk
w croftcottagebedand
breakfast.co.uk

## HOPTON HEATH
### Shropshire

**Hopton House** ★★★★
*Bed & Breakfast*
**GOLD AWARD**
Hopton Heath, Craven Arms
SY7 0QD
t (01547) 530885
e info@shropshirebreakfast.
co.uk
w shropshirebreakfast.co.uk

## HOW CAPLE
### Herefordshire

**The Falcon House** ★★★★
*Guest Accommodation*
How Caple, Hereford, Ross-on-
Wye HR1 4TF
t (01989) 740223
e falcon.house@gmail.com
w thefalconhouse.co.uk
🖼🖼

**How Caple Grange** ♦♦
*Guest Accommodation*
How Caple, Ross-on-Wye
HR1 4TF
t (01989) 740208

## HULME END
### Staffordshire

**The Manifold Inn** ★★★★
*Inn*
Hulme End, Buxton SK17 0EX
t (01298) 84537
e info@themanifoldinn.co.uk
w themanifoldinn.co.uk

**Raikes Farm** ★★★★
*Farmhouse*
Hulme End, Nr Hartington,
Buxton SK17 0HJ
t (01298) 84344

## ILAM
### Staffordshire

**Beechenhill Farm B&B** ★★★★
★★★★ *Farmhouse*
**SILVER AWARD**
Beechenhill Farm, Ilam,
Ashbourne DE6 2BD
t (01335) 310274
e beechenhill@btinternet.com
w beechenhill.co.uk

**Ilam Hall YHA** ★★★ *Hostel*
Ilam Hall, Ashbourne DE6 2AZ
t 0870 770 5879
e ilam@yha.org.uk
w yha.org.uk
🖼🖼🖼

**Throwley Hall Farm B&B** ★★★★
★★★★ *Farmhouse*
Throwley Hall Farm, Ilam,
Ashbourne DE6 2BB
t (01538) 308202
e throwleyhall@btinternet.
com
w throwleyhallfarm.co.uk
🖼🖼

## IRONBRIDGE
### Shropshire

**Bird In Hand Inn** ★★★ *Inn*
Waterloo Street, Ironbridge,
Telford TF8 7HG
t (01952) 432226
e bird1774@aol.com

**Bridge House** ★★★★★
*Guest Accommodation*
**SILVER AWARD**
Buildwas Road, Ironbridge,
Telford TF8 7BN
t (01952) 432105
w smoothhound.co.uk

**Bridge View Bed & Breakfast**
★★★ *Guest House*
10 Tontine Hill, Ironbridge,
Telford TF8 7AL
t (01952) 684249
e jayne@eleys-ironbridge.co.
uk
w eleys-ironbridge.co.uk

**The Calcutts House** ★★★★
*Guest Accommodation*
Calcutts Road, Jackfield,
Ironbridge, Telford TF8 7LH
t (01952) 882631
e info@calcuttshouse.co.uk
w calcuttshouse.co.uk

**Coalbrookdale Villa Guest
House** ★★★★
*Guest Accommodation*
**SILVER AWARD**
Paradise, Coalbrookdale,
Telford TF8 7NR
t (01952) 433450
e coalbrookdalevilla@
currantbun.com
w coalbrookdale.f9.co.uk

**Golden Ball Inn** ★★★★ *Inn*
1 Newbridge Road, Ironbridge,
Telford TF8 7BA
t (01952) 432179
e info@goldenballinn.com
w goldenballinn.co.uk

**The Library House** ★★★★★
*Guest Accommodation*
**GOLD AWARD**
11 Severn Bank, Ironbridge
TF8 7AN
t (01952) 432299
e info@libraryhouse.com
w libraryhouse.com

**Lord Hill Guest House** ★★
*Guest House*
Duke Street, Broseley
TF12 5LU
t (01952) 884270

**The Malthouse** ★★★★ *Inn*
The Wharfage, Ironbridge,
Telford TF8 7NH
t (01952) 433712

**Post Office House** ★★★
*Guest Accommodation*
6 The Square, Ironbridge,
Telford TF8 7AQ
t (01952) 433201

**Severn Lodge** ★★★★★
*Guest Accommodation*
**GOLD AWARD**
New Road, Ironbridge, Telford
TF8 7AU
t (01952) 432148

**The Swan** ★★★★ *Inn*
The Wharfage, Ironbridge
TF8 7NH
t (01952) 432306
e enquiries@malthousepubs.
co.uk
w malthousepubs.co.uk

**Tontine** ★★★ *Inn*
The Square, Ironbridge,
Telford TF8 7AL
t (01952) 432127
e tontinehotel@tiscali.co.uk
w tontine-ironbridge.com

**Wharfage Cottage** ★★★
*Bed & Breakfast*
17 The Wharfage, Ironbridge,
Telford TF8 7AW
t (01952) 432721
e info@wharfagecottage.co.uk
w wharfagecottage.co.uk

**Woodville B&B** ★★★
*Bed & Breakfast*
4a The Woodlands, Ironbridge
TF8 7PA
t (01952) 433343
e enquiries@enjoywoodville.
com
w enjoywoodville.com
🖼🖼

## KENILWORTH
### Warwickshire

**Abbey Guest House** ★★★★
*Guest House*
41 Station Road, Kenilworth
CV8 1JD
t (01926) 512707
e the-abbey@virgin.net
w abbeyguesthouse.com

**Avondale B&B** ★★★★
*Bed & Breakfast*
18 Moseley Road, Kenilworth
CV8 2AQ
t (01926) 859072

**Castle Laurels Guest House**
★★★★ *Guest House*
22 Castle Road, Kenilworth
CV8 1NG
t (01926) 856179
e mat.belson@btinternet.com
w castlelaurelshotel.co.uk

**Enderley Guest House**
★★★★ *Guest House*
20 Queens Road, Kenilworth
CV8 1JQ
t (01926) 855388
e enderleyguesthouse@
supanet.com
w enderleyguesthouse.co.uk

**Ferndale House** ★★★★
*Guest House*
45 Priory Road, Kenilworth
CV8 1LL
t (01926) 853214
e ferndalehouse@tiscali.co.uk
w kenilworth-guesthouse-
accommodation.com

**Grounds Farm** ★★★★
*Bed & Breakfast*
Kenilworth CV8 1PP
t (01926) 864542
e zoe@groundsfarm.com
w groundsfarm.co.uk

**Quince House** ★★★★
*Guest Accommodation*
29 Moseley Road, Kenilworth
CV8 2AR
t (01926) 858652
w quincehouse.co.uk

**Victoria Lodge** ★★★★
*Guest Accommodation*
**SILVER AWARD**
180 Warwick Road, Kenilworth
CV8 1HU
t (01926) 512020
e info@victorialodgehotel.co.
uk
w victorialodgehotel.co.uk

## KIDDERMINSTER
### Worcestershire

**Bewdley Hill House** ★★★★
*Guest House*
8 Bewdley Hill, Kidderminster
DY11 6BS
t (01562) 60473
e info@bewdleyhillhouse.co.
uk
w bewdleyhillhouse.co.uk

**The Brook House** ★★★★
*Bed & Breakfast*
Hemming Way, Chaddesley
Corbett, Nr Kidderminster
DY10 4SF
t (01562) 777453
e enquiries@thebrookhouse.
co.uk
w thebrookhouse.co.uk

**Collingdale** ★★★
*Guest Accommodation*
197 Comberton Road,
Kidderminster DY10 1UE
t (01562) 515460
e collingdale@sharvell.fsnet.
co.uk

**Garden Cottages** ★★★★
*Guest House* **GOLD AWARD**
Crossway Green, Hartlebury,
Stourport-on-Severn DY13 9SL
t (01299) 250626
e accommodation@
gardencottages.co.uk
w gardencottages.co.uk

**Hollies Farm Cottage B&B**
★★★★ *Farmhouse*
Hollies Lane, Franche,
Kidderminster DY11 5RW
t (01562) 745677
e info@holliesfarmcottage.co.
uk
w holliesfarmcottage.co.uk

## KILPECK
### Herefordshire

**Dippersmoor Manor** ★★★★
*Bed & Breakfast*
Kilpeck, Hereford HR2 9DW
t (01981) 570209
e info@dippersmoor.com
w dippersmoor.com

## KIMBOLTON
### Herefordshire

**Grove Farm** ★★★ *Farmhouse*
Kinbolton, Hereford HR6 0HE
t (01568) 613425
e grove-farm@loneone.net
w grovefarmdirect.co.uk
🖼🖼

**Lower Bache House** ★★★★
*Bed & Breakfast*
Kimbolton, Leominster
HR6 0ER
t (01568) 750304
e leslie.wiles@care4free.net
w smoothhound.co.uk/hotels/
lowerbache

**Ruxton Farm** ★★★★
*Farmhouse*
Kings Caple, Hereford
HR1 4TX
t (01432) 840493

**The Corners Inn** ★★★★ *Inn*
Kingsland, Leominster
HR6 9RY
t (01568) 708385
e enq@cornersinn.co.uk
w cornersinn.co.uk

**Kington Youth Hostel**
★★★★ *Hostel*
Victoria Road, Kington
HR5 3BX
t 0870 770 6128
e kington@yha.org.uk
w yha.org.uk

**Meadowbank Lodge** ★★★★
*Bed & Breakfast*
SILVER AWARD
Dovaston, Nr Kinnerley,
Oswestry SY10 8DP
t (01691) 682023
e meadowbanklodge@
hotmail.com
w meadowbanklodge.co.uk

**Ivy House Guest House**
★★★ *Guest House*
Warwick Road, Heronfield,
Knowle B93 0EB
t (01564) 770247
e john@ivy-guest-house.
freeserve.co.uk

**4 Lillington Road** ★★
*Bed & Breakfast*
Royal Leamington Spa,
Leamington Spa CV32 5YR
t (01926) 429244
e squireburton@aol.com

**8 Clarendon Crescent**
★★★★ *Bed & Breakfast*
SILVER AWARD
Leamington Spa CV32 5NR
t (01926) 429840
e lawson@lawson71.fsnet.co.
uk
w shakespeare-country.co.uk

**Avenue Lodge Guest House**
★★★ *Guest House*
61 Avenue Road, Leamington
Spa CV31 3PF
t (01926) 338555
e avenue_lodge@yahoo.co.uk
w avenue-lodge.co.uk

**Braeside Bed & Breakfast**
★★★★ *Bed & Breakfast*
26 Temple End, Harbury, Nr
Royal Leamington Spa
CV33 9NE
t (01926) 613402
e rosemary@braesidebb.co.uk
w braesidebb.co.uk

**Buckland Lodge** ★★★
*Guest House*
35 Avenue Road, Leamington
Spa CV31 3PG
t (01926) 423843
e john@buckland-lodge.co.uk
w buckland-lodge.co.uk

**Bungalow Farm** ★★★★
*Bed & Breakfast*
Windmill Hill, Cubbington,
Leamington Spa CV32 7LW
t (01926) 423276
e sheila@bungalowfarm.co.uk
w bungalowfarm.co.uk

**Charnwood Guest House**
★★★ *Guest House*
47 Avenue Road, Leamington
Spa CV31 3PF
t (01926) 831074
e ray@charnwoodguesthouse.
com
w charnwoodguesthouse.com

**The Coach House** ★★★★
*Farmhouse* SILVER AWARD
Snowford Hall Farm,
Hunningham, Royal
Leamington Spa CV33 9ES
t (01926) 632297
e the_coach_house@lineone.
net
w http://website.lineone.net/
~the_coach_house

**Corkill B&B** ★★★
*Bed & Breakfast*
27 Newbold Street,
Leamington Spa CV32 4HN
t (01926) 336303
e mrscorkill@aol.com

**Hedley Villa Guest House**
★★★ *Guest House*
31 Russell Terrace, Leamington
Spa CV31 1EZ
t (01926) 424504
e hedley_villa@hotmail.com
w hedleyvillaguesthouse.co.uk

**Hill Farm** ★★★★ *Farmhouse*
Lewis Road, Radford Semele,
Leamington Spa CV31 1UX
t (01926) 337571
e rebecca@hillfarm3000.fsnet.
co.uk
w hillfarm.info

**Thomas James Hotel** ★★★
*Inn*
45-47 Bath Street, Leamington
Spa CV31 3AG
t (01926) 312568
e tourist@thomasjameshotel.
com
w thomasjameshotel.co.uk

**Trendway Guest House**
★★★ *Guest House*
45 Avenue Road, Leamington
Spa CV31 3PF
t (01926) 316644
e avenue_lodge@yahoo.co.uk
w avenue-lodge.co.uk

**Victoria Park Lodge** ★★★★
*Guest House*
12 Adelaide Road, Leamington
Spa CV31 3PW
t (01926) 424195
e info@
victoriaparkhotelleamington
spa.co.uk
w victoriaparkhotelleamington
spa.co.uk

**York House Guest House**
★★★★ *Guest House*
9 York Road, Leamington Spa
CV31 3PR
t (01926) 424671
e reservations@
yorkhousehotel.biz
w yorkhousehotel.biz

**Orchard Cottage** ★★★
*Bed & Breakfast*
Bromyard Road, Ledbury
HR8 1LG
t (01531) 635107

**Russet House** ★★★★
*Guest Accommodation*
Belle Orchard, Ledbury
HR8 1DD
t (01531) 630060
e info@russethousebnb.co.uk
w russethouse.bnb.co.uk

**The Talbot – Ledbury** ★★★
*Inn*
New Street, Ledbury HR8 2DX
t (01531) 632963
e talbot.ledbury@wadworth.
co.uk

**The Green Man** ★★★
*Guest Accommodation*
38 Compton, Leek ST13 5NH
t (01538) 388084
e diannemoir@btconnect.com
w greenman-guesthouse.co.uk

**The Hatcheries** ★★★
*Bed & Breakfast*
Church Lane, Leek ST13 5EX
t (01538) 399552
e jan@l33k.wanadoo.co.uk
w thehatcheries.co.uk

**Little Brookhouse Farm**
★★★★ *Farmhouse*
Brookhouse Lane, Cheddleton,
Leek ST13 7DF
t (01538) 360350

**Peak Weavers Hotel** ♦♦♦♦
*Guest Accommodation*
21 King Street, Leek
ST13 5NW
t (01538) 383729
e info@peakweavershotel.co.
uk
w peakweavershotel.co.uk

**White Hart**
Rating Applied For
*Guest Accommodation*
Stockwell Street, Leek
ST13 6DH
t (01538) 372122
e info@whiteharttearooms.
com
w whiteharttearooms.co.uk

**Chirkenhill Farm** ★★★★
*Farmhouse*
Sherridge Road, Leigh Sinton,
Malvern WR13 5DE
t (01886) 832205
e chirkenhillbandb@tiscali.co.
uk
w chirkenhill.co.uk

**Caradoc** ★★★★
*Bed & Breakfast*
49 Watley Street, Leintwardine,
Nr Craven Arms SY7 0LL
t (01547) 540238
e robinandsue@amserve.com

**Kinton Thatch** ★★★★
*Bed & Breakfast*
Kinton, Leintwardine, Mortimer
Country SY7 0LT
t (01547) 540611
w tuckedup.com/stayat/795/
kinton_thatch.php

**Lower Buckton Country
House** ★★★★
*Bed & Breakfast*
SILVER AWARD
Buckton, Leintwardine,
Wigmore & Lingen, Mortimer
Country SY7 0JU
t (01547) 540532
e carolyn@lowerbuckton.co.
uk
w lowerbuckton.co.uk

**Lower House** ★★★★
*Guest Accommodation*
Adforton, Leintwardine,
Mortimer Country SY7 0NF
t (01568) 770223
e reservations@sy7.com
w sy7.com

**Upper Buckton** ★★★★★
*Farmhouse*
Leintwardine, Ludlow SY7 0JU
t (01547) 540634

**Walford Court** ★★★★
*Farmhouse*
Walford, Leintwardine, Ludlow
SY7 0JT
t (01547) 540570
e enquiries@romanticbreak.
com
w romanticbreak.com

**Copper Hall** ★★★★
*Bed & Breakfast*
134 South Street, Leominster
HR6 8JN
t (01568) 611622
e sccrick@copperhall.
freeserve.co.uk
w smoothhound.co.uk/hotels/
copper

**The Farmhouse** ★★★★
*Bed & Breakfast*
Aymestrey, Mortimer Country
HR6 9ST
t (01568) 708075
e farmbreakfasts@tesco.net

---

**Ford Abbey** ★★★★★
*Guest Accommodation*
**GOLD AWARD**
Pudleston, Leominster
HR6 0RZ
**t** (01568) 760700
**w** fordabbey.co.uk

**Highfield** ★★★★
*Bed & Breakfast*
Newtown, Ivington Road,
Leominster HR6 8QD
**t** (01568) 613216
**e** info@stay-at-highfield.co.uk
**w** stay-at-highfield.co.uk

**Highgate House** ★★★★
*Guest Accommodation*
29 Hereford Road, Leominster
HR6 8JS
**t** (01568) 614562
**e** info@highgate-house.co.uk
**w** highgate-house.co.uk

**Home Farm – Bircher**
★★★★ *Bed & Breakfast*
Bircher, Leominster HR6 0AX
**t** (01568) 780525
**e** dawnhomefarmbb@aol.com
**w** homefarmaccommodation.
co.uk

**The Paddock** ★★★★
*Bed & Breakfast*
**GOLD AWARD**
Shobdon, Leominster
HR6 9NQ
**t** (01568) 708176
**e** thepaddock@talk21.com

**Rossendale Guest House**
★★★★
*Guest Accommodation*
46 Broad Street, Leominster
HR6 8BS
**t** (01568) 612464

**Ryelands** ★★★★★
*Bed & Breakfast*
**GOLD AWARD**
Ryelands Road, Leominster
HR6 8QB
**t** (01568) 617575
**e** info@ryelandsbandb.co.uk
**w** ryelandsbandb.co.uk

**YHA Leominster** ★★★★
*Hostel*
The Priory, Leominster
HR6 8EQ
**t** (01568) 620517
**e** leominster@yha.org.uk
**w** yha.org.uk

**32 Beacon Street** ★★★★
*Bed & Breakfast*
Lichfield WS13 7AJ
**t** (01543) 262378

**Altair House** ★★
*Bed & Breakfast*
21 Shakespeare Avenue,
Lichfield WS14 9BE
**t** (01543) 252900

**Bogey Hole (The)** ★★★
*Guest House*
21-23 Dam Street, Lichfield
WS13 6AE
**t** (01543) 264303

**Coppers End Guest House**
★★★★ *Guest House*
Walsall Road, Muckley Corner,
Lichfield WS14 0BG
**t** (01543) 372910
**e** info@
coppersendguesthouse.co.uk
**w** coppersendguesthouse.co.
uk

**Davolls Cottage** ★★★★
*Bed & Breakfast*
156 Woodhouses Road,
Burntwood WS7 9EL
**t** (01543) 671250

**Old Rectory** ★★★★
*Bed & Breakfast*
**GOLD AWARD**
Mavesyn Ridware, Lichfield
WS15 3QE
**t** (01543) 490792
**e** sandra@oldrectory-
mavesyn.co.uk
**w** oldrectory-mavesyn.co.uk

**Poppies** ★★★★
*Bed & Breakfast*
6 Millbrook Drive, Lichfield
WS14 0JL
**t** (01543) 480652
**e** bill.whitney@btinternet.com

**Spires View** ★★★
*Bed & Breakfast*
4 Friary Road, Lichfield
WS13 6QL
**t** (01543) 306424
**e** tarra.roper-hall@ntlworld.
com

**Church Hill Farm B&B**
★★★★ *Farmhouse*
Lighthorne, Warwick
CV35 0AR
**t** (01926) 651251
**e** sue@churchhillfarm.co.uk
**w** churchhillfarm.co.uk

**Willey Lane Farm** ★★★★
*Farmhouse*
Lower Willey, Presteigne,
Mortimer Country LD8 2LU
**t** (01544) 267148
**e** juliamurray@willeylane.co.
uk
**w** willeylane.co.uk

**The Three Horseshoes Inn**
★★★ *Inn*
Little Cowarne, Bromyard
HR7 4RQ
**t** (01885) 400276

**Perrymill Farm** ★★★
*Bed & Breakfast*
Inkberrow, Worcester
WR7 4JQ
**t** (01386) 792177
**e** alexander@perrymill.com

**Hollies Farm** ★★★
*Bed & Breakfast*
Valeswood, Little Ness,
Shrewsbury SY4 2LH
**t** (01939) 261046
**e** janetwakefield@btinternet.
com

**Butlers Road Farm** ★★★
*Farmhouse*
Long Compton, Shipston-on-
Stour CV36 5JZ
**t** (01608) 684262
**e** eileen@butlersroad.com
**w** butlersroadfarm.co.uk

**Grand Lodge** ★★★★
*Bed & Breakfast*
Horsey Lane, Rugeley
WS15 4LW
**t** (01543) 686103
**e** grandlodge@edbroemt.
demon.co.uk

**Red Gables B&B**
Rating Applied For
*Bed & Breakfast*
Longford TF10 8LN
**t** (01952) 811118
**e** sandracorbett@red-gables.
com
**w** red-gables.com

**Nab End Camping Barn**
*Camping Barn*
Nab End Farm, Hollinsclough,
Buxton SK17 0RJ
**t** (01298) 83225
**e** david@nabendfarm.co.uk
**w** nabendfarm.co.uk

**Spring Cottage B&B** ★★★★
*Guest Accommodation*
Leek Road, Longnor, Buxton
SK17 0PA
**t** (01298) 83101
**e** garry.roe1@btopenworld.
com

**Olchon Cottage Farm** ★★★
*Farmhouse*
Mountain Road, Longtown,
Golden Valley HR2 0NS
**t** (01873) 860233
**e** ivy@olchon.wanadoo.co.uk

**Wilderhope Manor YHA** ★★
*Hostel*
The John Cadbury Memorial
Hostel, Much Wenlock
TF13 6EG
**t** 0870 770 6090
**e** wilderhope@yha.org.uk
**w** yha.org.uk

**The Grange**
Rating Applied For
*Bed & Breakfast*
Uttoxeter ST14 8RZ
**t** (01889) 502021
**e** mary.grange@hotmail.co.uk
**w** bandbthegrangestaffs.co.uk

**Elm Cottage** ★★★
*Bed & Breakfast*
Stratford Road, Loxley,
Stratford-upon-Avon
CV35 9JW
**t** (01789) 840609

**The Bull** ★★★
*Guest Accommodation*
14 The Bull Ring, Ludlow
SY8 1AD
**t** (01584) 873611
**e** info@bull-ludlow.co.uk
**w** bull-ludlow.co.uk

**Cecil Guest House** ★★★
*Guest House*
Sheet Road, Ludlow SY8 1LR
**t** (01584) 872442

**The Church Inn** ★★★★
*Guest Accommodation*
Buttercross, Ludlow SY8 1AW
**t** (01584) 872174
**e** reception@thechurchinn.
com
**w** stmem.com/thechurchinn

**The Clive Bar and
Restaurant With Rooms**
★★★★★
*Restaurant with Rooms*
**SILVER AWARD**
Bromfield, Ludlow SY8 2JR
**t** (01584) 856565 &
(01584) 856665
**e** info@theclive.co.uk
**w** theclive.co.uk

**DeGreys** ★★★★★
*Guest Accommodation*
5-6 Broad Street, Ludlow
SY8 1NG
**t** (01584) 872764
**e** degreys@btopenworld.com
**w** degreys.co.uk

**Elm Lodge B&B** ★★★★
*Bed & Breakfast*
Elm Lodge, Fishmore, Ludlow
SY8 3DP
**t** (01584) 872308
**e** info@elm-lodge.org.uk
**w** elm-lodge.org.uk

**Henwick House** ★★★
*Bed & Breakfast*
Gravel Hill, Ludlow SY8 1QU
**t** (01584) 873338
**w** henwickhouse.co.uk

**Longlands** ★★★★
*Farmhouse*
Woodhouse Lane, Richards
Castle, Ludlow SY8 4EU
**t** (01584) 831636
**e** iankemsley@aol.com

**Mill House** ★★★★
Bed & Breakfast
Squirrel Lane, Lower
Ledwyche, Ludlow SY8 4JX
t  (01584) 872837
e  millhousebnb@
btopenworld.com
w  virtual-shropshire.co.uk/mill

**The Mount Guest House**
★★★★ Guest House
61 Gravel Hill, Ludlow SY8 1QS
t  (01584) 874084
e  rooms@themountludlow.co.
uk
w  themountludlow.co.uk
▣ ✦

**Mr Underhill's** ★★★★★
Restaurant with Rooms
GOLD AWARD
Dinham Weir, Ludlow SY8 1EH
t  (01584) 874431
w  mr-underhills.co.uk

**Mulberry House** ★★★★
Guest Accommodation
10 Corve Street, Ludlow
SY8 1DA
t  (01584) 876765
e  bookings@tencorvestreet.
co.uk
w  tencorvestreet.co.uk

**Nelson Cottage** ★★★★
Bed & Breakfast
Rocks Green, Ludlow SY8 2DS
t  (01584) 878108
e  info@ludlow.uk.com
w  ludlow.uk.com

**Ravenscourt Manor**
★★★★★ Bed & Breakfast
GOLD AWARD
Woofferton, Ludlow SY8 4AL
t  (01584) 711905
e  elizabeth@
ravenscourtmanor.plus.com
w  smoothhound.co.uk/
ravenscourt

**The White House** ✦✦✦
Guest Accommodation
No. 4 Brand Lane, Ludlow
SY8 1NN
t  (01584) 875592
e  enquiries@4brandlane.co.uk
w  4brandlane.co.uk

**Penrhos Farm** ★★★★
Guest Accommodation
Lyonshall, Kington HR5 3LH
t  (01544) 231467

**Shenmore Cottage** ★★★★
Guest Accommodation
Upper Shenmore, Madley,
Hereford HR2 9NX
t  (01981) 250507
▣ ✦

**White House Vegetarian
Bed & Breakfast** ★★★★
Bed & Breakfast
Maesbury Marsh, Oswestry
SY10 8JA
t  (01691) 658524
e  whitehouse@
maesburymarsh.co.uk
w  maesburymarsh.co.uk

**The Brambles** ★★★★
Guest Accommodation
SILVER AWARD
173 Wells Road, Malvern Wells
WR14 4HE
t  (01684) 572994
e  bren.lawler@talk21.com
w  thebramblesmalvern.com

**Cannara Guest House**
★★★★ Guest House
147 Barnards Green Road,
Malvern WR14 3LT
t  (01684) 564418
e  info@cannara.co.uk
w  cannara.co.uk

**Clevelands** ★★★
Bed & Breakfast
SILVER AWARD
41 Alexandra Road, Malvern
WR14 1HE
t  (01684) 572164
e  jonmargstocks@aol.com
w  malvernbandbconsortium.
co.uk

**Como House** ★★★
Guest Accommodation
Como Road, Malvern
WR14 2TH
t  (01684) 561486
e  kevin@comohouse.co.uk
w  comohouse.co.uk

**Copper Beech House**
★★★★ Guest House
32 Avenue Road, Malvern
WR14 3BJ
t  (01684) 565013
e  enquiries@
copperbeechhouse.co.uk
w  copperbeechhouse.co.uk

**Cowleigh Park Farm** ★★★★
Guest Accommodation
Cowleigh Road, Malvern
WR13 5HJ
t  (01684) 566750
e  cowleighpark@ukonline.co.
uk
w  cowleighparkfarm.co.uk

**Edgeworth** ★★★★
Bed & Breakfast
4 Carlton Road, Malvern
WR14 1HH
t  (01684) 572565
e  garlandsidney@yahoo.com

**The Elms** ★★★★
Bed & Breakfast
52 Guarlford Road, Malvern
WR14 3QP
t  (01684) 573466
e  jili_holland@yahoo.co.uk

**Grassendale House** ★★★
Guest Accommodation
3 Victoria Road, Malvern
WR14 2TD
t  (01684) 893348
e  hilary@grassendale.com
w  grassendale.com

**Guarlford Grange** ★★★
Bed & Breakfast
SILVER AWARD
11 Guarlford Road, Malvern
WR14 3QW
t  (01684) 575996
e  guarlfordgrange@msn.com

**Harmony House Malvern**
★★★ Bed & Breakfast
184 West Malvern Road,
Malvern WR14 4AZ
t  (01684) 891650
e  catherine@harmonymalvern.
com
w  harmonyhousemalvern.com

**Hidelow House** ★★★★
Bed & Breakfast
SILVER AWARD
Acton Green, Acton
Beauchamp, Malvern
WR6 5AH
t  (01886) 884547
e  vist@hidelow.co.uk
w  hidelow.co.uk

**Kingfisher Bed & Breakfast**
★★★★ Bed & Breakfast
Kingfisher Barn, Merebrook
Farm, Hanley Swan WR8 0DX
t  (01684) 311922
e  info@kingfisher-barn.co.uk
w  kingfisher-barn.co.uk

**Montrose House** ★★★
Guest Accommodation
23 Graham Road, Malvern
WR14 2HU
t  (01684) 572335
e  info@themontrosehotel.co.
uk
w  themontrosehotel.co.uk

**The Old Coach House**
★★★★ Bed & Breakfast
208 Wells Road, Malvern
Wells, Malvern WR14 4HD
t  (01684) 564382
w  coachhousemalvern.co.uk

**Orchid House** ★★★★
Bed & Breakfast
SILVER AWARD
19 St Wulstans Drive, Upper
Welland, Malvern WR14 4JA
t  (01684) 568717
e  sally@oml.demon.co.uk
w  orchidmalvern.co.uk
▣ ✦

**Priory Holme** ★★★★
Bed & Breakfast
18 Avenue Road, Malvern
WR14 3AR
t  (01684) 568455

**Rosendale Bed & Breakfast**
★★★★ Bed & Breakfast
66 Worcester Road, Malvern
WR14 1NU
t  (01684) 566159

**Thornbury House Hotel**
★★★★ Guest House
16 Avenue Road, Great
Malvern WR14 3AR
t  (01684) 572278
e  thornburyhousehotel@
compuserve.com

**Forest Hills Guest House**
★★★★
Guest Accommodation
Moisty Lane, Marchington,
Uttoxeter ST14 8JY
t  (01283) 820447

**Brooklands B&B** ★★★★
Bed & Breakfast
Adderley Road, Market
Drayton TF9 3SW
t  (01630) 695988
e  brooklandsdirect@
btinternet.com

**Crofton** ★★★★
Bed & Breakfast
80 Rowan Road, Market
Drayton TF9 1RR
t  (01630) 655484
e  ericrussell@f2s.com
w  stmem.com/crofton

**The Hermitage** ★★★
Guest House
44 Stafford Street, Market
Drayton TF9 1JB
t  (01630) 658508
e  info@thehermitagebb.co.uk
w  thehermitagebb.co.uk
▣ ✦

**Red House Cottage**
Rating Applied For
Guest Accommodation
31 Shropshire Street, Market
Drayton TF9 3DA
t  (01630) 655206
w  stmem.com/red-house-
cottage

**Knoll Farm Bed and
Breakfast** ★★★★ Farmhouse
Ladywood Rd, Martin
Hussingtree, Worcester
WR3 7SX
t  (01905) 455565
e  knollfarmwr3@hotmail.com
w  knollfarm.co.uk

**Meole Brace Hall** ★★★★★
Guest Accommodation
SILVER AWARD
Meole Brace, Shrewsbury
SY3 9HF
t  (01743) 235566
e  hathaway@meolebracehall.
co.uk
w  meolebracehall.co.uk

**Barnacle Farm** ★★★★
Farmhouse
Back Lane, Meriden, Coventry
CV7 7LD
t  (024) 7646 8875

**Bonnifinglas Guest House**
★★★ Guest House
3 Berkswell Road, Meriden,
Coventry CV7 7LB
t  (01676) 523193
e  bookings@bonnifinglas.co.
uk
w  bonnifinglas.co.uk

**The Grove Farm** ★★★★
Farmhouse
Michaelchurch Escley, Golden
Valley HR2 0PT
t  (01981) 510229
e  lyn229@hotmail.com

## MILE BANK
### Shropshire

**Mile Bank Farm B&B ★★★**
*Guest Accommodation*
Mile Bank, Whitchurch
SY13 4JY
**t** (01948) 662042
**e** milebankfarmbandb@
hotmail.co.uk
**w** milebankfarmbandb.co.uk

## MILSON
### Shropshire

**Woodlands Barn ★★★★**
*Bed & Breakfast*
Church Court, Milson, Nr
Cledbury, Kidderminster
DY14 0AV
**t** (01299) 272983
**e** rjw261@btopenworld.com

## MINSTERLEY
### Shropshire

**Holly House B&B ★★★**
*Bed & Breakfast*
Bromlow, Minsterley SY5 0EA
**t** (01743) 891435
**e** paul.jaques1@btinternet.
com
**w** stmem.com/hollyhouseb&b

## MONNINGTON-ON-WYE
### Herefordshire

**Dairy House Farm ★★★★**
*Farmhouse*
Monnington-on-Wye, Golden
Valley HR4 7NL
**t** (01981) 500143
**e** pearson-greg@clara.co.uk
**w** dairyhousefarm.org

## MORVILLE
### Shropshire

**Hannigans Farm ★★★★**
*Farmhouse*
Morville, Bridgnorth
WV16 4RN
**t** (01746) 714332
**e** hannigansfarm@btinternet.
com
**w** hannigans-farm.co.uk

**Hurst Farm ★★★★**
*Farmhouse*
Morville, Bridgnorth WV16 4TF
**t** (01746) 714375
**e** info@cottagefishingholidays.
co.uk
**w** cottagefishingholidays.co.uk

## MUCH BIRCH
### Herefordshire

**The Old School ★★★**
*Bed & Breakfast*
Much Birch, Hereford HR2 8HJ
**t** (01981) 541317

## MUCH WENLOCK
### Shropshire

**Bastard Hall ★★★★**
*Guest Accommodation*
56-57 Shineton Street, Much
Wenlock TF13 6HU
**t** (01952) 728775
**e** lynn@adamou.freeserve.co.
uk
**w** bastardhall.co.uk

**Carnewydd ★★★**
*Bed & Breakfast*
Farley Road, Much Wenlock
TF13 6NB
**t** (01952) 728418
**e** clive.ship@sca.com

**Danywenallt ★★★**
*Bed & Breakfast*
Farley Road, Much Wenlock
TF13 6NB
**t** 07974 081618
**e** merlibobs@tiscali.co.uk
**w** stmem.com/danywenallt

**Old Quarry Cottage ★★★★**
*Bed & Breakfast*
**SILVER AWARD**
Brockton, Much Wenlock
TF13 6JR
**t** (01746) 785596
**e** triciawebb@
oldquarrycottage.co.uk
**w** oldquarrycottage.co.uk

**Talbot Inn ★★★** *Inn*
High Street, Much Wenlock
TF13 6AA
**t** (01952) 727077
**e** the_talbot_inn@hotmail.com
**w** the-talbot-inn.com

**Wenlock Pottery & Craft
Centre ★★★** *Bed & Breakfast*
Shineton Street, Much
Wenlock TF13 6HT
**t** (01952) 727600
**e** wenlockpots@btopenworld.
com
**w** wenlockpottery.co.uk

## MUNSTONE
### Herefordshire

**Munstone House Country
Hotel ★★★★** *Guest House*
Munstone, Hereford HR1 3AH
**t** (01432) 267122
**w** munstonehouse.co.uk

## MUXTON
### Shropshire

**The Old Vicarage ★★★**
*Bed & Breakfast*
Wellington Road, Muxton,
Telford TF2 8NN
**t** (01952) 670431
**e** huelin@smartone.co.uk

## MYDDLE
### Shropshire

**Oakfields ★★★**
*Bed & Breakfast*
Baschurch Road, Myddle,
Shrewsbury SY4 3RX
**t** (01939) 290823
**w** stmem.com/oakfields

## NEWCASTLE
### Shropshire

**The Quarry House Bed &
Breakfast ★★★★**
*Bed & Breakfast*
Church Road, Newcastle-upon-
Clun SY7 8QJ
**t** (01588) 640774
**e** info@quarry-house.com
**w** quarry-house.com

## NEWCASTLE-UNDER-LYME
### Staffordshire

**Graythwaite Guest House
★★★★**
*Guest Accommodation*
106 Lancaster Road,
Newcastle-under-Lyme,
Newcastle ST5 1DS
**t** (01782) 612875
**e** cooke.graythwaite@
ntlworld.com
**w** smoothhound.co.uk/
a45962.html

## NEWPORT
### Shropshire

**Lane End Farm ★★★★**
*Bed & Breakfast*
**SILVER AWARD**
Chetwynd, Newport TF10 8BN
**t** (01952) 550337
**e** janicepark854@aol.com
**w** stmem.com/laneendfarm

**Norwood House Restaurant
with Rooms ★★★**
*Restaurant with Rooms*
Pave Lane, Newport TF10 9LQ
**t** (01952) 825896
**e** info@norwoodhouse.org.uk
**w** norwoodhouse.org.uk

**Offley Grove Farm ★★★**
*Farmhouse*
Adbaston, Stafford ST20 0QB
**t** (01785) 280205
**e** enquiries@offleygrovefarm.
co.uk
**w** offleygrovefarm.co.uk

**Pear Tree Farmhouse ◆◆◆◆**
*Guest Accommodation*
Farm Grove, Newport
TF10 7PX
**t** (01952) 811193
**e** philgreen@peartreefarm.co.
uk
**w** peartreefarmhouse.co.uk

**Sambrook Manor ★★★★**
*Farmhouse*
Sambrook, Newport, Telford
TF10 8AL
**t** (01952) 550256
**w** sambrookmanor.com

## NEWTON ST MARGARETS
### Herefordshire

**Marises Barn ★★★★**
*Guest Accommodation*
Newton St Margarets,
Hereford HR2 0QG
**t** (01981) 510101
**e** marisesbaanb@aol.com
**w** marisesbarn.co.uk

## NORTON CANON
### Herefordshire

**Highbury House ★★★★**
*Bed & Breakfast*
**SILVER AWARD**
Hereford HR4 7BH
**t** (01544) 318556
**w** highburyguesthouse.com

## NORTON LINDSEY
### Warwickshire

**Saddlebow Cottage ★★★★**
*Bed & Breakfast*
Norton Lindsey, Warwick
CV35 8JN
**t** (01926) 842083
**e** info@saddlebowcottage.co.
uk
**w** saddlebowcottage.co.uk

## OAKAMOOR
### Staffordshire

**The Beehive Guest House
★★★★** *Guest House*
Churnet View Road, Oakamoor
ST10 3AE
**t** (01538) 702420
**e** thebeehiveoakamoor@
btinternet.com
**w** thebeehiveguesthouse.co.
uk

**Dimmingsdale YHA ★★**
*Hostel*
Little Ranger, Dimmingsdale,
Stoke-on-Trent ST10 3AS
**t** 0870 770 5794
**e** dimmingsdale@yha.org.uk
**w** yha.org.uk

**Ribden Farm ★★★★**
*Farmhouse*
Three Lows, Oakamoor
ST10 3BW
**t** (01538) 702830
**w** ribden.fsnet.co.uk

**Tenement Farm Guest
House ★★★★** *Farmhouse*
Ribden, Oakamoor ST10 3BW
**t** (01538) 702333
**e** stanleese@aol.com
**w** tenementfarm.co.uk

## OAKENGATES
### Shropshire

**Chellow Dene ★★**
*Bed & Breakfast*
Park Road, Malinslee, Telford
TF3 2AY
**t** (01952) 505917

## OFFCHURCH
### Warwickshire

**Mill House ★★★★**
*Bed & Breakfast*
Offchurch Lane, Offchurch,
Leamington Spa CV33 9AP
**t** (01926) 427296
**e** info@millhouse-offchurch.
co.uk
**w** millhouse-offchurch.co.uk

## OMBERSLEY
### Worcestershire

**Uphampton Cottage ◆◆◆◆**
*Guest Accommodation*
**SILVER AWARD**
Uphampton, Ombersley, Nr
Droitwich Spa WR9 0JS
**t** (01905) 621094
**e** eileen@uphampton094.
freeserve.co.uk
**w** smoothhound.co.uk/hotels/
uphampton.html

## ORLETON
### Worcestershire

**Rosecroft ★★★★★**
*Bed & Breakfast*
**SILVER AWARD**
Orleton, Ludlow SY8 4HN
**t** (01568) 780565
**e** gailanddavid@
rosecroftorleton.freeserve.co.
uk

## OSWESTRY
### Shropshire

**BJ's ★★** *Bed & Breakfast*
87 Llwyn Road, Oswestry
SY11 1EW
**t** (01691) 650205
**e** barbara@williams87.fsnet.
co.uk

**Harthill ★★★**
*Bed & Breakfast*
80 Welsh Walls, Oswestry
SY11 1RW
**t** (01691) 679024
**e** thecatmurs@lineone.net

**Llwyn Guest House ★★**
*Bed & Breakfast*
5 Llwyn Terrace, Beatrice
Street, Oswestry SY11 1HR
**t** (01691) 670746

**The Old Rectory Selattyn** ★★★ *Guest Accommodation*
Glyn Road, Selattyn, Oswestry
SY10 7DH
t (01691) 659708
e maggie.barnes.b@
btinternet.com

**Railway Cottage** ★★
*Bed & Breakfast*
51 Gobowen Road, Oswestry
SY11 1HU
t (01691) 654851

OULTON
Staffordshire

**Ye Olde Post Office** ★★★
*Bed & Breakfast*
32 Church Lane, Oulton, Stone
ST15 8UE
t (01785) 813215

OXHILL
Warwickshire

**Stable Croft** ★★★★
*Bed & Breakfast*
Green Lane, Oxhill, Warwick
CV35 0RB
t (01295) 680055
e pam@stablecroft.co.uk
w stablecroft.co.uk

PEMBRIDGE
Herefordshire

**Lowe Farm B&B** ★★★★
*Farmhouse* GOLD AWARD
Lowe Farm, Pembridge,
Leominster HR6 9JD
t (01544) 388395
e williams_family@lineone.net
w bedandbreakfastlowefarm.
co.uk

PERSHORE
Worcestershire

**Aldbury House** ★★★★
*Guest Accommodation*
SILVER AWARD
George Lane, Wyre Piddle,
Pershore WR10 2HX
t (01386) 553754
e stay@aldburyhouse.com
w a1tourism.com/uk/
aldburyhouse.html

**Arbour House** ★★★★
*Bed & Breakfast*
Main Road, Wyre Piddle,
Pershore WR10 2HU
t (01386) 555833
e liz@arbour-house.com
w arbour-house.com

**The Star Inn** ★★★ *Inn*
23 Bridge Street, Pershore
WR10 1AJ
t (01386) 552704
e info@thestarinnpershore.
com
w thestarinnpershore.com

**Tibbitts Farm** ★★★★
*Farmhouse*
Russell Street, Great
Comberton, Nr Pershore
WR10 3DT
t (01386) 710210
w farmstayuk.co.uk

PONTRILAS
Herefordshire

**Station House** ★★★
*Bed & Breakfast*
Station Approach, Pontrilas,
Golden Valley HR2 0EH
t (01981) 240564
e gwrstation04@tesco.net

PRIORS HARDWICK
Warwickshire

**Hill Farm** ★★★ *Farmhouse*
Lower End, Priors Hardwick,
Southam CV47 7SP
t (01327) 260338
e simon.darbishire@farming.
co.uk
w stayathillfarm.co.uk

PULVERBATCH
Shropshire

**Lane Farmhouse B&B** ★★★
*Farmhouse*
Wilderley, Pulverbatch,
Shrewsbury SY5 8DF
t (01743) 718935
e sarahgreig2002@yahoo.com
w lanefarmhouse.co.uk

QUARNFORD
Staffordshire

**Gradbach Mill YHA** ★★★
*Hostel*
Gradbach, Buxton SK17 0SU
t (01260) 227625
e gradbachmill@yha.org.uk
w yha.org.uk

RADFORD SEMELE
Warwickshire

**Hill Cottage** ★★★
*Guest Accommodation*
78 Southam Road, Radford
Semele, Leamington Spa
CV31 1UA
t (01926) 427636
e hillcott78@aol.com

RATLINGHOPE
Shropshire

**Bridges Youth Hostel (Long
Mynd)** ★★ *Hostel*
Ratlinghope, Shrewsbury
SY5 0SP
t (01588) 650656
w yha.org.uk

REDDITCH
Worcestershire

**White Hart Inn** ★★★ *Inn*
157 Evesham Road, Redditch
B97 5EJ
t (01527) 545442
e enquiries@
whitehartredditch.co.uk

ROSS-ON-WYE
Herefordshire

**The Arches** ★★★
*Bed & Breakfast*
Walford Road, Ross-on-Wye
HR9 5PT
t (01989) 563348
e the.arches@which.net

**Broome Farm** ★★★★
*Bed & Breakfast*
Peterstow, Ross-on-Wye
HR9 6QG
t (01989) 562824
e broomefarm@tesco.net
w broomefarmhouse.co.uk

**Lavender Cottage** ★★★
*Bed & Breakfast*
Bridstow, Ross-on-Wye
HR9 6QB
t (01989) 562836
e babsnsh@yahoo.co.uk

**Lumleys B&B** ★★★★
*Bed & Breakfast*
Kerne Bridge, Bishop Wood,
Ross-on-Wye HR9 5TQ
t (01600) 890040
e helen@lumleys.force9.co.uk
w lumleys.force9.co.uk

**Norton House** ★★★★
*Guest Accommodation*
GOLD AWARD
Whitchurch, Ross-on-Wye
HR9 6DJ
t (01600) 890046
e su@norton.wyenet.co.uk
w norton-house.com

**Sunnymount** ★★★★
*Guest House*
Ryefield Road, Ross-on-Wye
HR9 5LU
t (01989) 563880
e sunnymount@tinyworld.co.
uk

**Walnut Tree Cottage**
★★★★
*Guest Accommodation*
SILVER AWARD
Symonds Yat West, Ross-on-
Wye HR9 6BN
t (01600) 890828
e enquiries@walnuttreehotel.
co.uk
w walnuttreehotel.co.uk

**The White House Guest
House** ★★★ *Guest House*
Wye Street, Ross-on-Wye
HR9 7BX
t (01989) 763572
e whitehouseross@aol.com
w whitehouseross.com

ROUGH CLOSE
Staffordshire

**Chestnut Grange** ★★★★
*Guest House*
Windmill Hill, Rough Close,
Stoke-on-Trent ST3 7PJ
t (01782) 396084

RUGBY
Warwickshire

**The Carlton** ★★★★
*Guest Accommodation*
130 Railway Terrace, Rugby
CV21 3HE
t (01788) 560211
e carlton-hotel@btconnect.
com
w thecarltonrugby.com

**Courtyard** ★★★★
*Guest House*
Toft House, Toft, Rugby
CV22 6NR
t (01788) 810540

**Diamond House** ★★★
*Guest House*
28-30 Hillmorton Road, Rugby
CV22 5AA
t (01788) 572701

**Lawford Hill Farm** ★★★★
*Farmhouse* SILVER AWARD
Lawford Heath Lane, Lawford
Heath, Rugby CV23 9HG
t (01788) 542001
e lawford.hill@talk21.com
w lawfordhill.co.uk

**Village Green** ★★★★
*Guest Accommodation*
SILVER AWARD
The Green, Dunchurch, Rugby
CV22 6NX
t (01788) 813434
e info@villagegreenhotel.co.
uk
w villagegreenhotel.co.uk

**White Lion Inn** ★★★ *Inn*
Coventry Road, Pailton, Rugby
CV23 0QD
t (01788) 832359
w whitelionpailton.co.uk

RUGELEY
Staffordshire

**Park Farm** ★★ *Farmhouse*
Hawkesyard, Armitage Lane,
Rugeley WS15 1PS
t (01889) 583477

RUSHTON SPENCER
Staffordshire

**Heaton House Farm** ★★★★
*Farmhouse*
Rushton Spencer, Macclesfield
SK11 0RD
t (01260) 226203
e mick@heatonhouse.fsnet.co.
uk
w heatonhousefarm.co.uk

ST OWENS CROSS
Herefordshire

**The New Inn**
Rating Applied For
*Inn*
Hereford HR2 8LQ
t (01989) 730274
e info@newinn.co.uk

SEVERN STOKE
Worcestershire

**Roseland Bed & Breakfast**
★★★★ *Bed & Breakfast*
Clifton, Severn Stoke WR8 9JF
t (01905) 371463
e guy@roselandworcs.demon.
co.uk
w roselandworcs.demon.co.uk

SHIFNAL
Shropshire

**Odfellows – The Wine Bar**
★★★ *Inn*
Market Place, Shifnal
TF11 9AU
t (01952) 461517
e odfellows@odley.co.uk

SHIRLEY
West Midlands

**Baltimore House** ★★
*Bed & Breakfast*
12 Brampton Crescent, Shirley,
Solihull B90 3SY
t (0121) 744 9100
e egeeborall@aol.com

## SHREWSBURY
### Shropshire

**Abbey Court House**
Rating Applied For
*Guest House*
134 Abbey Foregate,
Shrewsbury SY2 6AU
t (01743) 364416
e info@abbeycourt.biz
w abbeycourt.biz

**Anton Guest House ★★★★**
*Bed & Breakfast*
1 Canon Street, Monkmoor,
Shrewsbury SY2 5HG
t (01743) 359275
e antonguesthouse@
btconnect.com
w stmem.com/
antonguesthouse

**Ashton Lees ★★★★**
*Bed & Breakfast*
Dorrington, Shrewsbury
SY5 7JW
t (01743) 718378
w stmem.com/ashtonlees

**Avonlea ★★** *Bed & Breakfast*
33 Coton Crescent, Coton Hill,
Shrewsbury SY1 2NZ
t (01743) 359398
w stmem.com/avonlea

**The Bell Inn ★★★** *Inn*
Old Wenlock Road, Cross
Houses, Shrewsbury SY5 6JJ
t (01743) 761264
w stmem.com/thebellinn

**Castle Gates House**
Rating Applied For
*Bed & Breakfast*
Castle Gates, Shrewsbury
SY1 2AT
t (01743) 362395

**Castlecote Guest House**
Rating Applied For
*Guest Accommodation*
77 Monkmoor Road,
Shrewsbury SY2 5AT
t (01743) 245473
e soniataplin@yahoo.co.uk
w stmem.com/
castlecoteguesthouse

**Charnwood ★★★★**
*Bed & Breakfast*
110 London Road, Shrewsbury
SY2 6PP
t (01743) 359196
e charnwoodguesthouse@
tiscali.co.uk
w charnwoodguesthouse.co.
uk

**College Hill Guest House**
**★★★** *Guest Accommodation*
11 College Hill, Shrewsbury
SY1 1LZ
t (01743) 365744
w stmem.com/collegehillhouse

**The Golden Cross ★★** *Inn*
Princess Street, Shrewsbury
SY1 1LP
t (01743) 362507
e info@goldencrosshotel.co.
uk
w goldencrosshotel.co.uk

**Kingsland Bed & Breakfast**
**★★★** *Bed & Breakfast*
47 Kennedy Road, Shrewsbury
SY3 7AA
t (01743) 355990
e kate@kingslandbandb.com
w kingslandbandb.com

**Lyth Hill House ★★★★**
*Bed & Breakfast*
**GOLD AWARD**
28 Old Coppice, Lyth Hill,
Shrewsbury SY3 0BP
t (01743) 874660
e bnb@lythhillhouse.com
w lythhillhouse.com

**North Farm ★★★★**
*Farmhouse*
Eaton Mascot, Shrewsbury
SY5 6HF
t (01743) 761031
e northfarm@btinternet.com
w northfarm.co.uk

**The Old Post Office Inn**
**★★★** *Inn*
1 Milk Street, Shrewsbury
SY1 1SZ
t (01743) 236019
e rflukes@hotmail.co.uk
w oldpostofficepub.co.uk

**The Old Station ★★★★**
*Guest House*
Leaton, Bomere Heath,
Shrewsbury SY4 3AP
t (01939) 290905
w stmem.com/oldstation

**The Old Vicarage ◆◆◆◆**
*Guest Accommodation*
**GOLD AWARD**
Leaton, Shrewsbury SY4 3AP
t (01939) 290989
e m-j@oldvicleaton.com
w oldvicleaton.com

**Prynces Villa Guest House**
**★★** *Guest Accommodation*
15 Monkmoor Rd, Shrewsbury
SY2 5AG
t (01743) 356217
e lawrence.wyatt@virgin.net
w stmem.com/pryncesvilla

**Rest-a-while Guest House**
**★★★** *Bed & Breakfast*
36 Coton Crescent, Coton Hill,
Shrewsbury SY1 2NZ
t (01743) 240969
e restawhilebb@yahoo.co.uk
w virtual-shropshire.co.uk/
restawhile

**Sandford House Hotel**
**★★★★**
*Guest Accommodation*
St Julians Friars, Shrewsbury
SY1 1XL
t (01743) 343829
e sandfordhouse@lineone.net
w sandfordhouse.co.uk

**The Stiperstones Guest**
**House ★★★**
*Guest Accommodation*
18 Coton Crescent, Coton Hill,
Shrewsbury SY1 2NZ
t (01743) 246720
e thestiperstones@aol.com
w thestiperstones.com

**Sydney House Hotel ★★★**
*Guest Accommodation*
Coton Crescent, Shrewsbury
SY1 2LJ
t (01743) 354681
e sydneyhouse@
sydneyhousehotel.co.uk
w sydneyhousehotel.co.uk

**Trevellion House Bed &**
**Breakfast ★★★★**
*Bed & Breakfast*
1 Bradford Street, Monkmoor,
Shrewsbury SY2 5DP
t (01743) 249582
e soniataplin@yahoo.co.uk
w stmem.com/1-bradford-
street

**Ye Olde Bucks Head Inn**
**★★★** *Inn*
Frankwell, Shrewsbury SY3 8JR
t (01743) 369392
e adminbucksheadinn@tesco.
net
w bucksheadinn.co.uk

## SOLIHULL
### West Midlands

**Acorn Guest House ★★★★**
*Guest House* **SILVER AWARD**
29 Links Drive, Solihull B91 2DJ
t (0121) 705 5241
e acorn.wood@btinternet.com
w acorn-guest-house.com

**Anthony's Bed and**
**Breakfast ★★★**
*Bed & Breakfast*
1 Radford Rise, Solihull
B91 2QH
t (0121) 705 7666
e judyban@amserve.com
w anthonysbandb.co.uk

**Chelsea Lodge ★★★★**
*Guest Accommodation*
**SILVER AWARD**
48 Meriden Road, Hampton-in-
Arden B92 0BT
t (01675) 442408
e chelsealodgebnb@aol.com

**Ravenhurst Guest House**
**★★★** *Guest House*
56 Lode Lane, Solihull
B91 2AW
t (0121) 705 5754
e ravenhurstaccom@aol.com

## SOUTHAM
### Warwickshire

**Wormleighton Hall ★★★★**
*Farmhouse* **GOLD AWARD**
Wormleighton, Southam,
Leamington Spa CV47 2XQ
t (01295) 770234
e wormleightonbb-bookings@
yahoo.co.uk
w wormleightonhall.com

## STAFFORD
### Staffordshire

**Amerton Farm ★★★**
*Farmhouse*
Amerton, Stowe-by-Chartley,
Stafford ST18 0LA
t (01889) 272777
w amertonfarm.co.uk

**Cedarwood ★★★★**
*Bed & Breakfast*
**SILVER AWARD**
46 Weeping Cross, Stafford
ST17 0DS
t (01785) 662981

**Littywood House ★★★★**
*Bed & Breakfast*
Bradley, Stafford ST18 9DW
t (01785) 780234
e suebusby@amserve.com
w littywood.co.uk

**Park Farm ★★★** *Farmhouse*
Weston Road, Stafford
ST18 0BD
t (01785) 240257
e parkfarm12@hotmail.com

**Rooks Nest Farm ★★★**
*Farmhouse*
Weston Bank, Weston,
Stafford ST18 0BA
t (01889) 270624
e info@rooksnest.co.uk
w rooksnest.co.uk

**Wyndale Guest House ★★**
*Guest House*
199 Corporation Street,
Stafford ST16 3LQ
t (01785) 223069

## STOKE HEATH
### Worcestershire

**Avoncroft Guest House**
**★★★★** *Guest House*
77 Redditch Road, Bromsgrove
B60 4JP
t (01527) 832819
e reservations@
avoncroftguesthouse.co.uk
w avoncroftguesthouse.co.uk

## STOKE-ON-TRENT
### Staffordshire

**Cedar Tree Cottage ★★★★**
*Bed & Breakfast*
**SILVER AWARD**
41 Longton Road, Trentham,
Stoke-on-Trent ST4 8ND
t (01782) 644751
e n.portas@btinternet.com

**The Corrie Guesthouse**
**★★★★** *Guest House*
13 Newton Street, Basford,
Stoke-on-Trent ST4 6JN
t (01782) 614838
e info@thecorrie.co.uk
w thecorrie.co.uk

**The Hollies ★★★**
*Bed & Breakfast*
Clay Lake, Stoke-on-Trent
ST9 9DD
t (01782) 503252

**The Limes B&B ★★★**
*Bed & Breakfast*
The Limes, Cheadle Road,
Stoke-on-Trent ST11 9PW
t (01782) 393278

**Reynolds Hey Farm ★★★★**
*Guest Accommodation*
Park Lane, Endon, Stoke-on-
Trent ST9 9JB
t (01782) 502717
e reynoldshey@hotmail.com
w reynoldshey.co.uk

**Shawgate Farm Guest House**
**★★★★** *Guest House*
Shay Lane, Foxt ST10 2HN
t (01538) 266590
e ken@shawgatefarm.co.uk
w shawgatefarm.co.uk

**Sneyd Arms Hotel ★★★** *Inn*
Tower Square, Stoke-on-Trent
ST6 5AA
t (01782) 826722
w thesneydarms.co.uk

**Verdon Guest House** ★★
*Guest House*
44 Charles Street, Stoke-on-Trent ST1 3JY
t (01782) 264244
w verdonguesthouse.co.uk

### STOKE ST MILBOROUGH
Shropshire

**Stoke Court Bed & Breakfast** ★★★★ *Farmhouse*
Stoke St Milborough, Nr Ludlow SY8 2EQ
t (01584) 823203
e margaret@stokecourtfarm.co.uk
w stokecourtfarm.co.uk

### STONE
Staffordshire

**Mayfield House** ★★★
*Bed & Breakfast*
112 Newcastle Road, Stone ST15 8LG
t (01785) 811446

### STOTTESDON
Worcestershire

**Hardwicke Farm** ★★★★
*Farmhouse* SILVER AWARD
Stottesdon, Bridgnorth DY14 8TN
t (01746) 718220
e althea@hardwickefarm.plus.com
w smoothhound.co.uk/hotels/hardwicke.html

### STOURBRIDGE
West Midlands

**St Elizabeth's Cottage**
★★★★ *Bed & Breakfast*
Woodman Lane, Clent, Stourbridge DY9 9PX
t (01562) 883883
e st.elizabeth.cottage@btconnect.com

**The Willows B&B** ★★★
*Bed & Breakfast*
4 Brook Road, Stourbridge DY8 1NH
t (01384) 396964
e trickard@blueyonder.co.uk
w willowguests.com

### STOURPORT-ON-SEVERN
Worcestershire

**Baldwin House** ★★★★
*Guest House*
8 Lichfield Street, Stourport-on-Severn DY13 9EU
t (01299) 877221
e philpam@dialstart.net
w smoothhound.co.uk

**Victoria Villa Bed & Breakfast** ★★★★
*Guest House*
4 Lion Hill, Stourport-on-Severn DY13 9HD
t (01299) 824017
e jo@victoriavilla.co.uk
w victoriavilla.co.uk

### STRATFORD-UPON-AVON
Warwickshire

**Aidan Guest House** ★★★★
*Guest House*
11 Evesham Place, Stratford-upon-Avon CV37 6HT
t (01789) 292824
e enquiries@aidanhouse.com
w aidanhouse.com

**Ambleside Guest House**
★★★★ *Guest House*
41 Grove Road, Stratford-upon-Avon CV37 6PB
t (01789) 297239
e ruth@amblesideguesthouse.com
w amblesideguesthouse.com

**Arden Park 'non-smoking' Guest House** ★★★★
*Guest House*
6 Arden Street, Stratford-upon-Avon CV37 6PA
t (01789) 262126
e mark@ardenparkhotel.co.uk
w stratford-upon-avon.co.uk/ardenpark.htm

**Arrandale Guest House**
★★★ *Bed & Breakfast*
208 Evesham Road, Stratford-upon-Avon CV37 9AS
t (01789) 267112
w arrandale.netfirms.com

**Avonlea** ★★★★
*Guest House*
47 Shipston Road, Stratford-upon-Avon CV37 7LN
t (01789) 205940
e avonlea-stratford@lineone.net
w avonlea-stratford.co.uk

**Avonpark House** ★★★★
*Guest House*
123 Shipston Road, Stratford-upon-Avon CV37 7LW
t (01789) 417722
e avonparkhouse@sky.com
w avonparkhouse.com

**Blue Boar Inn** ★★★ *Inn*
Temple Grafton, Alcester B49 6NR
t (01789) 750010
e blueboar@covlink.co.uk
w blueboarinn.co.uk

**Bradbourne House** ★★★★
*Guest House*
44 Shipston Road, Stratford-upon-Avon CV37 7LP
t (01789) 204178
e ian@bradbourne-house.co.uk
w bradbourne-house.co.uk

**Broadlands Guest House**
★★★★ *Guest House*
SILVER AWARD
23 Evesham Place, Stratford-upon-Avon CV37 6HT
t (01789) 299181
e philandjohn@broadlandsguesthouse.co.uk
w broadlandsguesthouse.co.uk

**Brook Lodge Guest House**
★★★★ *Guest House*
SILVER AWARD
192 Alcester Road, Stratford-upon-Avon CV37 9DR
t (01789) 295988
e brooklodgeguesthouse@btinternet.com
w brook-lodge.co.uk

**Broom Hall Inn** ★★★ *Inn*
Bidford Road, Alcester, Stratford-upon-Avon B50 4HE
t (01789) 773757
w broomhallinn.co.uk

**Carlton Guest House** ★★★
*Guest House*
22 Evesham Place, Stratford-upon-Avon CV37 6HT
t (01789) 293548

**Caterham House** ★★★★
*Guest House*
58-59 Rother Street, Stratford-upon-Avon CV37 6LT
t (01789) 267309
e caterhamhousehotel@btconnect.com
w caterhamhouse.co.uk

**Church Farm** ★★★
*Farmhouse*
Dorsington, Stratford-upon-Avon CV37 8AX
t (01789) 720471
e chfarmdorsington@aol.com
w churchfarmstratford.co.uk

**Church Farmhouse** ★★★★
*Bed & Breakfast*
Welford Road, Long Marston, Stratford-upon-Avon CV37 8RH
t (01789) 720275
e wiggychurchfarm@hotmail.com
w churchfarmhouse.co.uk

**Courtland House** ★★★★
*Guest House*
12 Guild Street, Stratford-upon-Avon CV37 6RE
t (01789) 292401
e info@courtlandhotel.co.uk
w courtlandhotel.co.uk

**Craig Cleeve House** ★★★★
*Guest House*
67-69 Shipston Road, Stratford-upon-Avon CV37 7LW
t (01789) 296573
e craigcleeve@aol.com
w craigcleeve.com

**Curtain Call** ★★★
*Guest House*
142 Alcester Road, Stratford-upon-Avon CV37 9DR
t (01789) 267734
e curtaincall@onetel.com
w curtaincallguesthouse.co.uk

**Cymbeline House** ★★★
*Guest House*
24 Evesham Place, Stratford-upon-Avon CV37 6HT
t (01789) 292958
e linda@cymbelineguesthouse.co.uk
w cymbelinehouse.co.uk

**Drybank Farm** ★★★★
*Farmhouse*
Fosseway, Ettington, Stratford-upon-Avon CV37 7DP
t (01789) 740476
e drybank@btinternet.com
w drybank.co.uk

**The Emsley Guest House**
★★★★ *Guest House*
4 Arden Street, Stratford-upon-Avon CV37 6PA
t (01789) 299557
e val@theemsley.co.uk
w theemsley.co.uk

**Eversley Bears Guest House**
★★★★ *Guest House*
37 Grove Road, Stratford-upon-Avon CV37 6PB
t (01789) 292334
e eversleybears@btinternet.com

**Faviere Guest House**
★★★★ *Guest House*
127 Shipston Road, Stratford-upon-Avon CV37 7LW
t (01789) 293764
e reservations@faviere.com
w faviere.com

**Green Gables** ★★★
*Bed & Breakfast*
47 Banbury Road, Stratford-upon-Avon CV37 7HW
t (01789) 205 5570
e jke985@aol.com
w stratford-upon-avon.co.uk/greengables.htm

**Green Haven Guest House**
Rating Applied For
*Guest House*
217 Evesham Road, Stratford-upon-Avon CV37 9AS
t (01789) 297874
e info@green-haven.co.uk
w green-haven.co.uk

**Grosvenor Villa** ★★★
*Guest House*
9 Evesham Place, Stratford-upon-Avon CV37 6HT
t (01789) 266192
e contactus@grosvenorvilla.com
w grosvenorvilla.com

**Halford Bridge Inn** ★★★★
*Inn*
Fosse Way, Halford, Shipston-on-Stour CV36 5BN
t (01789) 748217
e sue@thehalfordbridge.co.uk
w thehalfordbridge.co.uk

**Hampton Lodge Guest House** ★★★
*Guest Accommodation*
38 Shipston Road, Stratford-upon-Avon CV37 7LP
t (01789) 299374
e hamptonlodge.info@btopenworld.com
w hamptonlodge.co.uk

**Heron Lodge** ★★★★
*Guest House*
260 Alcester Road, Stratford-upon-Avon CV37 9JQ
t (01789) 299169
e chrisandbob@heronlodge.com
w heronlodge.com

**The Houndshill** ★★★ *Inn*
Banbury Road, Nr Ettington, Stratford-upon-Avon CV37 7NS
t (01789) 740267

**The Howard Arms** ★★★★★
*Inn* SILVER AWARD
Lower Green, Ilmington, Shipston-on-Stour CV36 4LT
t (01608) 682226
e info@howardarms.com
w howardarms.com

**The Hunters Moon Guest House** ★★★ *Guest House*
150 Alcester Road, Stratford-upon-Avon CV37 9DR
t (01789) 292888
e thehuntersmoon@ntlworld.com
w huntersmoonguesthouse.com

**Ingon Bank Farm ★★★**
*Bed & Breakfast*
Warwick Road, Stratford-upon-Avon CV37 0NY
t (01789) 292642
w ingonbankfarmbandb.co.uk

**Larkrise Cottage ★★★**
*Bed & Breakfast*
Upper Billesley, Stratford-upon-Avon CV37 9RA
t (01789) 268618
e alanbailey17@hotmail.com
w larkrisecottage.co.uk

**Linhill Guest House ★★★**
*Guest Accommodation*
35 Evesham Place, Stratford-upon-Avon CV37 6HT
t (01789) 292879
e linhill@bigwig.net
w linhillguesthouse.co.uk

**Melita ★★★★**
*Guest Accommodation*
37 Shipston Road, Stratford-upon-Avon CV37 7LN
t (01789) 292432
e info@melitaguesthouse.co.uk
w melitaguesthouse.co.uk

**Midway Guest House ★★★**
*Guest House*
182 Evesham Road, Stratford-upon-Avon CV37 9BS
t (01789) 204154
e mealing@midway182.fsnet.co.uk
w stratford-upon-avon.co.uk/midway.htm

**Mil-Mar ★★★★** *Guest House*
96 Alcester Road, Stratford-upon-Avon CV37 9DP
t (01789) 267095
e milmar@btinternet.com
w mil-mar.co.uk

**Minola Guest House ★★★**
*Guest House*
25 Evesham Place, Stratford-upon-Avon CV37 6HT
t (01789) 293573

**Penryn Guest House ★★★★**
*Guest Accommodation*
SILVER AWARD
126 Alcester Road, Stratford-upon-Avon CV37 9DP
t (01789) 293718
e penrynhouse@btinternet.com
w penrynguesthouse.co.uk

**The Poplars ★★★** *Farmhouse*
Mansell Farm, Newbold-on-Stour, Stratford-upon-Avon CV37 8BZ
t (01789) 450540
e judith@poplars-farmhouse.co.uk
w warks.co.uk/poplars

**The Queens Head ★★** *Inn*
54 Ely Street, Stratford-upon-Avon CV37 6LN
t (01789) 204914

**Quilt and Croissants ★★★**
*Guest House*
33 Evesham Place, Stratford-upon-Avon CV37 6HT
t (01789) 267629
e rooms@quilt-croissants.demon.co.uk
w quiltcroissants.co.uk

**Salamander Guest House ★★★** *Guest House*
40 Grove Road, Stratford-upon-Avon CV37 6PB
t (01789) 205728
e p.delin@btinternet.com
w salamanderguesthouse.co.uk

**Shakespeare's View ★★★★★** *Bed & Breakfast*
GOLD AWARD
Kings Lane, Snitterfield, Stratford-upon-Avon CV37 0QB
t (01789) 731824
e shakespeares.view@btinternet.com
w shakespeares.view.btinternet.co.uk

**Sunnydale Guest House ★★★** *Guest House*
64 Shipston Road, Stratford-upon-Avon CV37 7LP
t (01789) 295166
e helena.kim@ntlworld.com
w sunny-dale.co.uk

**Victoria Spa Lodge ★★★★**
*Guest House* SILVER AWARD
Bishopton Lane, Bishopton, Stratford-upon-Avon CV37 9QY
t (01789) 267985
e ptozer@victoriaspalodge.demon.co.uk
w stratford-upon-avon.co.uk/victoriaspa.htm

**Virginia Lodge ★★★**
*Guest Accommodation*
12 Evesham Place, Stratford-upon-Avon CV37 6HT
t (01789) 292157 & (01789) 266605
e enquiries@virginialodge.co.uk
w virginialodge.co.uk

**White-Sails ★★★★★**
*Guest House* GOLD AWARD
85 Evesham Road, Stratford-upon-Avon CV37 9BE
t (01789) 264326
e contact@white-sails.co.uk
w white-sails.co.uk

**Woodstock Guest House ★★★★** *Guest House*
30 Grove Road, Stratford-upon-Avon CV37 6PB
t (01789) 299881
e jackie@woodstock-house.co.uk
w woodstock-house.co.uk

**STRETTON ON DUNSMORE**
**Warwickshire**

**Home Farm (A45) ★★★★**
*Bed & Breakfast*
SILVER AWARD
152 London Road (A45), Stretton-on-Dunsmore, Rugby CV23 9HZ
t (024) 7654 1211
e homefarma45@hotmail.com
w homefarma45.co.uk

**SUTTON ST NICHOLAS**
**Herefordshire**

**Pool House ★★★★**
*Guest Accommodation*
Sutton St Nicholas, Hereford HR1 3AY
t (01432) 880494
e mansie@talktalk.net
w poolhouse.org.uk

**SYMONDS YAT EAST**
**Herefordshire**

**Garth Cottage ★★★★**
*Guest Accommodation*
SILVER AWARD
Symonds Yat East, Ross-on-Wye HR9 6JL
t (01600) 890364

**TACHBROOK MALLORY**
**Warwickshire**

**Tachbrook Mallory House ★★★★** *Bed & Breakfast*
Oakley Wood Road, Leamington Spa CV33 9QE
t (01926) 451450
e tmhouse@btinternet.com
w tachbrookmalloryhouse.co.uk

**TAMWORTH**
**Staffordshire**

**Chestnuts Country Guest House ★★★★** *Guest House*
SILVER AWARD
Watling Street, Grendon, Atherstone CV9 2PZ
t (01827) 331355
e ccltd@aol.com
w thechestnutshotel.com

**Middleton House Farm ★★★★**
*Guest Accommodation*
SILVER AWARD
Tamworth Road, Middleton, Tamworth B78 2BD
t (01827) 873474

**The Peel Hotel ★★★★**
*Guest Accommodation*
13-14 Aldergate, Tamworth B79 7DL
t (01827) 67676
w thepeelhotel.com

**TANWORTH-IN-ARDEN**
**Warwickshire**

**Grange Farm ★★★★**
*Farmhouse* SILVER AWARD
Forde Hall Lane, Tanworth-in-Arden, Solihull B94 5AX
t (01564) 742911
e enquiries@grange-farm.com
w grange-farm.com

**Mows Hill Farm ★★★★**
*Farmhouse* SILVER AWARD
Mows Hill Road, Kemps Green, Tanworth-in-Arden B94 5PP
t (01564) 784312
e mowshill@farmline.com
w b-and-bmowshill.co.uk

**TARRINGTON**
**Herefordshire**

**Swan House ★★★★**
*Guest Accommodation*
Tarrington, Ledbury HR1 4EU
t (01432) 890203
e parrylizzy@aol.com
w swanhousetarrington.co.uk

**TELFORD**
**Shropshire**

**Albion Inn ★★★**
*Guest Accommodation*
West Street, St Georges, Telford TF2 9AD
t (01952) 614193
e ian@thealbioninn.freeserve.co.uk

**Coppice Heights ♦♦♦**
*Guest Accommodation*
Spout Lane, Little Wenlock, Telford TF6 5BL
t (01952) 505655

**Grove House Bed and Breakfast ★★★★**
*Guest Accommodation*
1 Stafford Street, St Georges, Telford TF2 9JW
t (01952) 616140
w virtual-shropshire.co.uk/birchesmill

**The Mill House ★★★★**
*Bed & Breakfast*
Shrewsbury Road, High Ercall, Telford TF6 6BE
t (01952) 770394
e cjpy@lineone.net
w ercallmill.co.uk

**The Mount ★★★★**
*Guest Accommodation*
SILVER AWARD
Dawley Road, Arleston Hill, Lawley, Telford TF1 2LZ
t (01952) 503102
e pam@mountguesthouse.co.uk
w mountguesthouse.co.uk

**The Old Orleton Inn**
**★★★★★** *Inn*
SILVER AWARD
Holyhead Road, Wellington TF1 2HA
t (01952) 255011
e info@theoldorleton.com
w theoldorleton.com

**Old Rectory ★★★★**
*Guest Accommodation*
SILVER AWARD
Stirchley Village, Telford TF3 1DY
t (01952) 596308
e hazelmiller@waitrose.com
w stmem.com/theoldrectory

**The Stanage ★★★★**
*Bed & Breakfast*
Dawley, Lawley Village, Telford TF4 2PG
t (01952) 507742
e hazelbexon@yahoo.com
w bedandbreakfastintelford.co.uk

**Stone House ★★★★**
*Guest Accommodation*
Shifnal Road, Priorslee, Telford TF2 9NN
t (01952) 290119
e stonehousegh@aol.com
w stonehouseguesthouse.co.uk

**West Ridge B&B ★★★★**
*Bed & Breakfast*
SILVER AWARD
Kemberton, Shifnal, Telford TF11 9LB
t (01952) 580992
e westridgebb@tiscali.co.uk
w westridgebb.com

**Willow House ★★★**
*Guest Accommodation*
137 Holyhead Road, Wellington, Telford TF1 2DH
t (01952) 223817
e info@telfordguesthouse.co.uk
w telfordguesthouse.co.uk

## TENBURY WELLS
### Worcestershire

**Fountain ★★★★** *Inn*
Oldwood, St Michaels,
Tenbury Wells WR15 8TB
t (01584) 810701
e enquiries@fountain-hotel.co.uk
w fountain-hotel.co.uk

**Millbrook ★★★★**
*Bed & Breakfast*
Tenbury Wells WR15 8NP
t (01584) 781720
e keithoddy@onetel.com
w millbrook01584.co.uk

## TUGFORD
### Shropshire

**Tugford Farm B&B ★★★★**
*Guest Accommodation*
Tugford Farm, Craven Arms
SY7 9HS
t (01584) 841259
e williamstugford@supanet.com
w tugford.com

## TUNSTALL
### Staffordshire

**Victoria Hotel ◆◆◆**
*Guest Accommodation*
4 Roundwell Street, Tunstall,
Stoke-on-Trent ST6 5JJ
t (01782) 835964
e victoria-hotel@tunstall51.fsnet.co.uk

## TUTBURY
### Staffordshire

**Woodhouse Farm Bed and
Breakfast ★★★** *Farmhouse*
Fauld, Tutbury, Burton-on-Trent DE13 9HR
t (01283) 812185
e woodhousetutbury@aol.com
w woodhousebandb.co.uk

## UCKINGHALL
### Worcestershire

**Ivydene House Bed and
Breakfast ★★★★★**
*Bed & Breakfast*
SILVER AWARD
Ivydene House, Uckinghall
GL20 6ES
t (01684) 592453
e rosemaryg@fsmail.net
w ivydenehouse.net

## UFFINGTON
### Shropshire

**Vine Cottage ★★★★**
*Bed & Breakfast*
Uffington SY4 4SN
t (01743) 709009
e l.henrich@msn.com

## UPPER COLWALL
### Worcestershire

**Little Kings Hill ★★★★**
*Bed & Breakfast*
Walwyn Road, Upper Colwall,
Malvern WR13 6PL
t (01684) 540589
e littlekingshill@btinternet.com

## UPPER SAPEY
### Herefordshire

**Tippins Farm ★★★★**
*Farmhouse*
Worcester WR6 6XT
t (01886) 853801
e tippinsfarm@btinternet.com
w tippinsfarm.co.uk

## UPTON
### Warwickshire

**Uplands House ★★★★★**
*Bed & Breakfast*
Upton, Banbury OX15 6HJ
t (01295) 678663
e poppy@cotswolds-uplands.co.uk
w cotswolds-uplands.co.uk

## UPTON SNODSBURY
### Worcestershire

**Bants ★★★★** *Inn*
Worcester Road, Upton
Snodsbury WR7 4NN
t (01905) 381282
e info@bants.co.uk
w bants.co.uk

## UPTON UPON SEVERN
### Worcestershire

**Ryall House Farm ★★★★**
*Farmhouse*
Ryall, Upton-upon-Severn
WR8 0PL
t (01684) 592013
e sevans@ryallhouse.co.uk
w farmstayworcs.co.uk

**Sunnyside Bed & Breakfast
★★★★** *Bed & Breakfast*
Station Road, Ripple GL20 6EY
t (01684) 592461
e sunnysideripple@btinternet.com
w sunnysidebandb.co.uk

**Tiltridge Farm & Vineyard
★★★★** *Farmhouse*
SILVER AWARD
Upper Hook Road, Upton-upon-Severn WR8 0SA
t (01684) 592906
e sandy@tiltridge.com
w tiltridge.com

## VOWCHURCH
### Herefordshire

**New Barns Farm ★★★★**
*Farmhouse*
Vowchurch, Hereford, Golden
Valley HR2 0QA
t (01981) 250250
e lloydnewbarn@tesco.net
w holden-valley.co.uk/newbarns

**The Old Vicarage ★★★★**
*Guest Accommodation*
SILVER AWARD
Vowchurch, Hereford, Golden
Valley HR2 0QD
t (01981) 550357
w golden-valley.co.uk/vicarage

**Upper Gilvach Farm ★★★★**
*Farmhouse* SILVER AWARD
Newton St Margarets,
Vowchurch, Golden Valley
HR2 0QY
t (01981) 510618
e ruth@uppergilvach.freeserve.co.uk
w golden-valley.co.uk/gilvach

**Yew Tree House ★★★★**
*Bed & Breakfast*
SILVER AWARD
Vowchurch, Hereford HR2 9PF
t (01981) 251195
e enquiries@yewtreehouse-hereford.co.uk
w yewtreehouse-hereford.co.uk

## WALSALL
### West Midlands

**Lyndon House Hotel ★★★**
*Inn*
Upper Rushall Street, Walsall
WS1 2HA
t (01922) 612511
e bookings@lyndonhousehotel.co.uk
w lyndonhousehotel.co.uk

## WARWICK
### Warwickshire

**Agincourt Lodge ★★★★**
*Guest House*
36 Coten End, Warwick
CV34 4NP
t (01926) 499399
e enquiries@agincourtlodge.co.uk
w agincourtlodge.co.uk

**Apothecary's Bed and
Breakfast ★★★★**
*Bed & Breakfast*
The Old Dispensary, Stratford
Road, Stratford-upon-Avon
CV35 9RN
t (01789) 470060
e bandbapothecary@aol.com
w stratford-upon-avon.co.uk/apothecarys.htm

**Ashburton Guest House**
★★★ *Guest House*
74 Emscote Road, Warwick
CV34 5QG
t (01926) 499133
e lordnelson@btconnect.com
w ashburtongh.com

**Austons Down ★★★★**
*Bed & Breakfast*
Saddle Bow Lane, Claverdon,
Stratford-upon-Avon
CV35 8PQ
t (01926) 842068
e lmh@austonsdown.com
w austonsdown.com

**Avon Guest House ★★★★**
*Guest House*
7 Emscote Road, Warwick
CV34 4PH
t (01926) 491367
e info@avonguesthouse.co.uk
w avonguesthouse.co.uk

**Cambridge Villa ★★★**
*Guest House*
20a/B Emscote Road, Warwick
CV34 4PP
t (01926) 491169
e cambridgevilla_warwick@yahoo.co.uk

**Chesterfields Guest House**
★★★ *Guest House*
84 Emscote Road, Warwick
CV34 5QT
t (01926) 774864
e jchapman@chesterfields.freeserve.co.uk
w smoothhound.co.uk

**Croft Guesthouse ★★★★**
*Guest House*
Haseley Knob, Warwick
CV35 7NL
t (01926) 484447
e david@croftguesthouse.co.uk
w croftguesthouse.co.uk

**Longbridge Farm ★★★★**
*Bed & Breakfast*
Longbridge, Warwick
CV34 6RB
t (01926) 401857

**Park Cottage ★★★★**
*Guest Accommodation*
SILVER AWARD
113 West Street, Warwick
CV34 6AH
t (01926) 410319
e janet@parkcottagewarwick.co.uk
w parkcottagewarwick.co.uk

**Park House Guest House**
★★★ *Guest House*
17 Emscote Road, Warwick
CV34 4PH
t (01926) 494359
e reservations@warwickparkhouse.co.uk
w parkhousewarwick.co.uk

**Peacock Lodge ★★★**
*Bed & Breakfast*
97 West Street, Warwick
CV34 6AH
t (01926) 419480

**The Seven Stars Guest
Accommodation ★★★★**
*Bed & Breakfast*
SILVER AWARD
Friars Street, Warwick
CV34 6HD
t (01926) 492658
e thesevenstars@btinternet.com

**Shrewley Pools Farm**
★★★★ *Farmhouse*
SILVER AWARD
Haseley, Warwick CV35 7HB
t (01926) 484315
e cathydodd@hotmail.co.uk
w s-h-systems.co.uk/hotels/shrewley.html

**Warwick Lodge ★★★**
*Guest House*
82 Emscote Road, Warwick
CV34 5QJ
t (01926) 492927

**Westham Guest House**
★★★ *Guest House*
76 Emscote Road, Warwick
CV34 5QG
t (01926) 491756
e westham.house@ntlworld.com
w smoothhound.co.uk/hotels/westham.html

## WATERHOUSES
### Staffordshire

**Leehouse Farm ★★★★**
*Bed & Breakfast*
SILVER AWARD
Leek Road, Waterhouses, Leek
ST10 3HW
t (01538) 308439

## WATERS UPTON
### Shropshire

**Groom's Cottage ★★★★**
*Bed & Breakfast*
Waters Upton, Telford
TF6 6NP
t (01952) 541869
e kevin.bright@virgin.net
w grooms-cottage.co.uk

## WEETHLEY
### Warwickshire

**Ridgeway Farm ★★★★**
*Bed & Breakfast*
Evesham Road, Alcester
B49 5LZ
t (01789) 765442
e diane@
ridgewaybedandbreakfast.co.
uk
w ridgewaybedandvreakfast.
co.uk

## WELFORD-ON-AVON
### Warwickshire

**Bridgend Guest House**
**★★★★** *Bed & Breakfast*
Binton Road, Welford-on-
Avon, Stratford-upon-Avon
CV37 8PW
t (01789) 750900
e bridgendhouse@aol.com
w stratford-upon-avon.co.uk/
bridgend.htm

## WELLAND
### Worcestershire

**North Farm ★★★**
*Guest Accommodation*
Hancocks Lane, Welland,
Malvern WR13 6LG
t (01684) 574365

## WELLESBOURNE
### Warwickshire

**Meadow Cottage ★★★**
*Bed & Breakfast*
36 Church Walk,
Wellesbourne, Warwick
CV35 9QT
t (01789) 840220
e thomas.harland@virgin.net
w meadowcottagebandb.co.uk

## WELLINGTON
### Shropshire

**Clairmont ★★★★**
*Guest Accommodation*
54 Haygate Road, Wellington
TF1 1QN
t (01952) 414214
e info@clairmontguesthouse.
co.uk
w clairmontguesthouse.co.uk

**Potford House ♦♦♦**
*Guest Accommodation*
Little Bolas, Nr Wellington,
Telford TF6 6PS
t (01952) 541362
e dsadler@potford.fsnet.co.uk
w shropshirebedandbreakfast.
com

## WELLINGTON HEATH
### Herefordshire

**Hope End House ★★★★★**
*Guest Accommodation*
**GOLD AWARD**
Hope End, Ledbury HR8 1JQ
t (01531) 635890
e info@hopeendhouse.com
w hopeendhouse.com

## WENTNOR
### Shropshire

**Inn on the Green ★★★★** *Inn*
Wentnor, Bishop's Castle
SY9 5EF
t (01588) 650105
e sempleaj@aol.com
w theinnonthegreen.net

## WEOBLEY
### Herefordshire

**Garnstone House ★★★**
*Bed & Breakfast*
Weobley, Hereford HR4 8QP
t (01544) 318943
e macleod@garnstonehouse.
co.uk
w garnstonehouse.co.uk

## WESTHOPE
### Shropshire

**Ward Farm Bed & Breakfast**
**★★★★** *Farmhouse*
Ward Farm, Westhope, Craven
Arms SY7 9JL
t (01584) 861601
e contact@wardfarm.co.uk
w wardfarm.co.uk

## WESTON UNDER WETHERLEY
### Warwickshire

**Wethele Manor Farm**
**★★★★★** *Guest House*
Rugby Road, Weston under
Wetherley, Leamington Spa
CV33 9BZ
t (01926) 831772
e simonmoreton@
wethelemanor.com
w wethelemanor.com

## WETTON
### Staffordshire

**The Old Chapel ★★★★**
*Guest Accommodation*
**SILVER AWARD**
Wetton, Ashbourne DE6 2AF
t (01335) 310450
e lynne.imeson@tiscali.co.uk

## WHISTON
### Staffordshire

**Whiston Hall Mansion Court
Hotel ★★★★**
*Guest Accommodation*
Whiston Hall Golf Club, Black
Lane, Whiston ST10 2HZ
t (01538) 266260
e enquiries@whistonhall.com
w whistonhall.com

## WHITCHURCH
### Shropshire

**Sedgeford House ★★★★**
*Bed & Breakfast*
Sedgeford, Whitchurch
SY13 1EX
t (01948) 665598
e enquiries@sedgefordhouse.
com
w sedgefordhouse.com

## WHITNEY-ON-WYE
### Herefordshire

**Rhydspence Inn ★★★★** *Inn*
Whitney-on-Wye, Hay-on-Wye
HR3 6EU
t (01497) 831262
e info@rhydspence-inn.co.uk

## WHITTINGTON
### Shropshire

**Fitzwarine House ★★★**
*Bed & Breakfast*
Castle Street, Whittington
SY11 4DF
t (01691) 680882
e fitzwarinehouse@supanet.
com
w fitzwarinehouse.co.uk

## WHITTINGTON
### Staffordshire

**Peel Farm Bed & Breakfast**
**★★★★** *Farmhouse*
Fisherwick Road, Whittington,
Lichfield WS14 9LJ
t (01543) 433461
e accommodation@peelfarm.
co.uk
w peelfarm.co.uk

## WICKHAMFORD
### Worcestershire

**Longacres Bed & Breakfast**
**★★★** *Bed & Breakfast*
Longdon Hill, Wickhamford,
Evesham WR11 7RP
t (01386) 442575
e eveshambandb@tiscali.co.uk

## WIGMORE
### Herefordshire

**Gotherment House ★★★**
*Bed & Breakfast*
Wigmore, Leominster HR6 9UR
t (01568) 770547

**Pear Tree Farm ★★★★**
*Guest Accommodation*
**GOLD AWARD**
Wigmore, Mortimer Country
HR6 9UR
t (01568) 770140

## WILTON
### Herefordshire

**Benhall Farmhouse ★★★★**
*Farmhouse* **SILVER AWARD**
Wilton, Ross-on-Wye HR9 6AG
t (01989) 563900
e info@benhallfarm.co.uk

## WINKHILL
### Staffordshire

**Country Cottage ★★★★**
*Guest House*
Back Lane Farm, Winkhill, Leek
ST13 7XZ
t (01538) 308273
e mjb6435@bentleym.plus.
com
w geocities.com/mengli_
55427

## WISHAW
### Warwickshire

**Ash House ★★★★**
*Bed & Breakfast*
The Gravel, Wishaw, Sutton
Coldfield B76 9QB
t (01675) 475782
e kate@rectory80.freeserve.
co.uk

## WISTANSWICK
### Shropshire

**Marsh Farm Bed & Breakfast**
**★★★★** *Bed & Breakfast*
Marsh Farm, Wistanswick,
Market Drayton TF9 2BB
t (01630) 638520
e wiz.light@talk21.com
w marshfarmbandb.co.uk

## WITHERLEY
### Warwickshire

**Old House B&B ★★★★**
*Guest House*
Watling Street, Witherley,
Hinckley CV9 1RD
t (01827) 715634
e enquiries@
theoldhousebandb.co.uk
w theoldhousebandb.co.uk

## WOLSTON
### Warwickshire

**Lords Hill Farm, Farmhouse
B&B ★★★★** *Farmhouse*
Coal Pit Lane, Coventry
CV8 3GB
t (024) 7654 4430
e jane@lordshillfarm.co.uk
w lordshillfarm.co.uk

## WOODBATCH
### Shropshire

**Middle Wood Batch Farm**
Rating Applied For
*Farmhouse*
Woodbatch Road, Woodbatch
SY9 5JS
t (01588) 630141
e info@
middlewoodbatchfarm.co.uk
w middlewoodbatchfarm.co.uk

## WOOFFERTON
### Shropshire

**Orchard House ★★★★**
*Bed & Breakfast*
**SILVER AWARD**
Ashford Bowdler, Ludlow
SY8 4DJ
t (01584) 831270
e judith@orchard-barn.co.uk
w orchard-barn.co.uk

## WOONTON
### Herefordshire

**Rose Cottage ★★★★**
*Guest Accommodation*
**SILVER AWARD**
Woonton, Hereford, Kington
HR3 6QW
t (01544) 340459
e tessa.plummer@ukonline.co.
uk
w rosecottagewoonton.co.uk

## WORCESTER
### Worcestershire

**Barbourne Guest House**
**★★★★** *Guest House*
42-44 Barbourne Road,
Worcester WR1 1HU
t (01905) 27507
w stayinworcester.co.uk

**The Barn House ★★★**
*Farmhouse*
Broadwas, Worcester
WR6 5NS
t (01886) 888733
e info@barnhouseonline.co.uk
w barnhouseonline.co.uk

**City Guest House** ★★★
*Guest House*
36 Barbourne Road, Worcester
WR1 1HU
t  (01905) 24695

**The Croft** ★★★★
*Bed & Breakfast*
25 Station Road, Fernhill Heath,
Worcester WR3 7UJ
t  (01905) 453482
e  thecroft@janetandbrian.
wanadoo.co.uk

**De-Bury House** ★★★
*Bed & Breakfast*
3 The Bullring, St Johns,
Worcester WR2 5AA
t  (01905) 425532
w  de-bury.co.uk

**Green Farm** ★★★★
*Guest Accommodation*
Crowle Green, Nr Worcester
WR7 4AB
t  (01905) 381807
e  thegreenfarm@btinternet.
com
w  thegreenfarm.co.uk

**Hill Farm House** ★★★★
*Bed & Breakfast*
**SILVER AWARD**
Dormston Lane, Dormston,
Worcester WR7 4JS
t  (01386) 793159
e  jim@hillfarmhouse.co.uk
w  hillfarmhouse.co.uk

**Holland House** ★★★
*Bed & Breakfast*
210 London Road, Worcester
WR5 2JT
t  (01905) 353939
e  beds@holland-house.me.uk
w  holland-house.me.uk

**Laburnum Villa** ★★★★
*Bed & Breakfast*
243 Ombersley Road,
Worcester WR3 7BY
t  (01905) 755572
e  laburnumvilla@tiscali.co.uk
w  laburnumvilla.com

**Oldbury Farm** ★★★★
*Farmhouse* **SILVER AWARD**
Lower Broadheath, Worcester
WR2 6RQ
t  (01905) 421357
e  janejordan@oldburyfarm.
freeserve.co.uk
w  smoothhound.co.uk/hotels/
oldburyfarm.html

**Osborne House** ★★★
*Guest Accommodation*
17 Chestnut Walk, Worcester
WR1 1PR
t  (01905) 22296
e  enquiries@osborne-house.
co.uk
w  osborne-house.co.uk

**Shrubbery Guest House** ♦♦♦
*Guest Accommodation*
38 Barbourne Road, Worcester
WR1 1HU
t  (01905) 24871

WORMELOW
Herefordshire

**Lyston Villa** ★★★ *Farmhouse*
Wormelow, Hereford HR2 8EL
t  (01981) 540130
e  sayce@lyston.fsnet.co.uk
w  lystonvilla.co.uk

YORTON HEATH
Shropshire

**Country B&B** ♦♦♦♦♦
*Guest Accommodation*
**SILVER AWARD**
Mayfield, Yorton Heath,
Shrewsbury SY4 3EZ
t  (01939) 210860
e  sue@stayatmayfield.co.uk
w  stayatmayfield.co.uk

YOXALL
Staffordshire

**The Golden Cup** ★★★★ *Inn*
Main Street, Burton-on-Trent
DE13 8NQ
t  (01543) 472295
e  rchltrnr@aol.com
w  thegoldencup.co.uk

## EAST MIDLANDS

AB KETTLEBY
Leicestershire

**White Lodge Farm Bed &
Breakfast** ★★★★ *Farmhouse*
Nottingham Road, Ab Kettleby,
Melton Mowbray LE14 3JB
t  (01664) 822286

ABTHORPE
Northamptonshire

**Rignall Farm Barns** ★★★
*Farmhouse*
Handley Park, Abthorpe Road,
Towcester NN12 8PA
t  (01327) 350766

ALDERTON
Northamptonshire

**Magnolia** ★★★★
*Bed & Breakfast*
Church Lane, Alderton
NN12 7LP
t  (01327) 811479
e  bandb@magnolia.me.uk
w  magnolia.me.uk

ALDWARK
Derbyshire

**Lydgate Farm**
Rating Applied For
*Farmhouse*
Aldwark DE4 4HW
t  (01629) 540250

ALDWINCLE
Northamptonshire

**Pear Tree Farm** ★★★★
*Farmhouse*
Main Street, Aldwincle,
Kettering NN14 3EL
t  (01832) 720614
e  beverley@peartreefarm.net
w  peartreefarm.net

ALFORD
Lincolnshire

**27 Chauntry Road** ★★★
*Bed & Breakfast*
Chauntry Road, Alford
LN13 9HH
t  (01507) 462751
e  nick.ofarrell@virgin.net
w  lincolnshire-isntboring.co.uk

**Windmill Family &
Commercial Hotel** ★★★
*Guest Accommodation*
Market Place, Alford LN13 9EB
t  (01507) 463377
e  keithwindmill@aol.com
w  alfordwindmillhotel.com

ALVASTON
Derbyshire

**Grace Guest House** ★
*Guest House*
1063 London Road, Alvaston,
Derby DE24 8PZ
t  (01332) 571051

**The Maryland B&B**
Rating Applied For
*Guest Accommodation*
1083 London Road, Derby
DE24 8PZ
t  (01332) 754892
e  themaryland7@yahoo.co.uk

AMBERGATE
Derbyshire

**The Lord Nelson Inn** ★★★
*Inn*
Bullbridge, Ambergate, Ripley
DE56 2EW
t  (01773) 852037
w  thelordnelson.fsworld.co.uk

**YHA Shining Cliff** *Bunkhouse*
Shining Cliff Woods, Jackass
Lane, Belper DE56 2RE
t  0870 770 8868
e  reservations@yha.org.uk
w  yha.org.uk

ARTHINGWORTH
Northamptonshire

**The Bull's Head** ★★★ *Inn*
Kelmarsh Road, Arthingworth
LE16 8JZ
t  (01858) 525637
e  thebullshead@btconnect.
com
w  thebullsheadonline.co.uk

ASHBOURNE
Derbyshire

**Bentley Brook Inn** ★★★ *Inn*
Fenny Bentley, Ashbourne
DE6 1LF
t  (01335) 350278
e  all@bentleybrookinn.co.uk
w  bentleybrookinn.co.uk

**Cross Farm** ★★★★
*Bed & Breakfast*
Main Road, Ellastone,
Ashbourne DE6 2GZ
t  (01335) 324668
e  jane@cross-farm.co.uk
w  cross-farm.co.uk

**Holly Meadow Farm** ★★★★
*Farmhouse* **SILVER AWARD**
Pinfold Lane, Bradley,
Ashbourne DE6 1PN
t  (01335) 370261 &
07970 922856
e  babette_lawton@yahoo.com
w  hollymeadowfarm.co.uk

**The Lilacs** ★★★★
*Guest Accommodation*
Mayfield Road, Ashbourne
DE6 2BJ
t  (01335) 343749

**Mona Villas Bed and
Breakfast** ★★★★
*Bed & Breakfast*
1 Mona Villas, Church Lane
Mayfield, Ashbourne DE6 2JS
t  (01335) 343773
e  info@mona-villas.fsnet.co.uk
w  mona-villas.fsnet.co.uk

**Omnia Somnia** ★★★★★
*Guest Accommodation*
**GOLD AWARD**
The Coach House, The Firs,
Ashbourne DE6 1HF
t  (01335) 300145
e  alan@omniasomnia.co.uk
w  omniasomnia.co.uk

**Overfield Farm** ★★★★
*Farmhouse*
Tissington, Ashbourne
DE6 1RA
t  (01335) 390285
e  info@overfieldfarm.co.uk
w  overfieldfarm.co.uk

**Shirley Hall Farm** ★★★★
*Farmhouse* **SILVER AWARD**
Shirley, Ashbourne DE6 3AS
t  (01335) 360346

**Stanshope Hall** ★★★★
*Guest Accommodation*
Stanshope, Ashbourne
DE6 2AD
t  (01335) 310278
e  naomi@stanshope.demon.
co.uk
w  stanshope.net

**Tan Mill Farm** ★★★★
*Farmhouse*
Mappleton Road, Ashbourne
DE6 2AA
t  (01335) 342387
e  tanmill@ashbourne-town.
com

**White Cottage** ★★★★
*Bed & Breakfast*
Ashbourne DE6 2DR
t  (01335) 345503
e  jackie@previll.fsnet.co.uk
w  whitecottage-bandb.co.uk

ASHBY-DE-LA-ZOUCH
Leicestershire

**The Cedars** ★★ *Guest House*
60 Burton Road, Ashby-de-la-
Zouch LE65 2LN
t  (01530) 412017
e  sjsedge@hotmail.co.uk

**Clockmakers House B&B**
★★★★
*Guest Accommodation*
8 Lower Church Street, Ashby-de-la-Zouch LE65 1AB
t (01530) 417974
e mike@clockmakershouse.com
w clockmakershouse.com

**Holywell Guest House** ★★
*Guest House*
58 Burton Road, Ashby-de-la-Zouch LE65 2LN
t (01530) 412005

**Measham House Farm**
★★★★ *Bed & Breakfast*
Gallows Lane, Measham, Ashby-de-la-Zouch DE12 7HD
t (01530) 270465
e dilovett@meashamhouse.freeserve.co.uk
w meashamhouse.co.uk

### ASHFORD IN THE WATER
Derbyshire

**A Woodland View** ★★★★
*Bed & Breakfast*
John Bank Lane, Ashford-in-the-Water, Bakewell DE45 1PY
t (01629) 813008
e woodview@neilellis.free-online.co.uk
w woodlandviewbandb.co.uk

**The Ashford Arms** ★★★★
*Inn*
Church Street, Bakewell DE45 1QB
t (01629) 812725
e enquiries@ashford-arms.co.uk
w ashford-arms.co.uk

**Chy-an-Dour** ★★★★
*Guest Accommodation*
SILVER AWARD
Vicarage Lane, Ashford-in-the-Water, Bakewell DE45 1QN
t (01629) 813162
w stilwell.co.uk

### ASHOVER
Derbyshire

**Old School Farm** ★★★★
*Farmhouse*
Uppertown, Ashover, Chesterfield S45 0JF
t (01246) 590813

**Twitch Nook** ★★★★
*Bed & Breakfast*
Hardwick Lane, Ashover, Matlock S45 0DE
t (01246) 590153
e stay@twitchnook.demon.co.uk
w twitchnook.co.uk

### ATTERBY
Lincolnshire

**East Farm Farmhouse Bed and Breakfast** ★★★★
*Bed & Breakfast*
East Farm, Atterby LN8 2BJ
t (01673) 818917
e anneastfarm@hotmail.com
w eastfarm.me.uk

### BADBY
Northamptonshire

**Meadows Farm** ★★★★★
*Farmhouse*
Newnham Lane, Badby NN11 3AA
t (01327) 703302

### BAKEWELL
Derbyshire

**1 Glebe Croft** ★★★★
*Guest Accommodation*
SILVER AWARD
Monyash Road, Bakewell DE45 1FG
t (01629) 810013
e pat@glebecroft.co.uk
w glebecroft-bakewell.co.uk

**2 Lumford Cottages** ★★★
*Bed & Breakfast*
Off Holme Lane, Bakewell DE45 1GG
t (01629) 813273
w cressbrook.co.uk/bakewell/lumford/

**Bolehill Farm** ★★★★
*Bed & Breakfast*
SILVER AWARD
Monyash Road, Bakewell DE45 1QW
t (01629) 812359
e infobb8@bolehillfarm.co.uk
w bolehillfarm.co.uk/bbi.htm

**Castle Cliffe Guest House**
★★★★
*Guest Accommodation*
Monsal Head, Bakewell DE45 1NL
t (01629) 640258
e relax@castle-cliffe.com
w castle-cliffe.com

**Castle Hill Farm House**
★★★★ *Bed & Breakfast*
SILVER AWARD
Castle Mount Crescent, Baslow Road, Bakewell DE45 1AA
t (01629) 813168
e christine@castlehillfarmhouse.co.uk
w castlehillfarmhouse.co.uk

**Dale View** ★★★★
*Guest Accommodation*
Ashford Road, Bakewell DE45 1GL
t (01629) 813832
e enquiries@dale-view.com
w dale-view.com

**The Garden Room** ♦♦♦♦
*Guest Accommodation*
SILVER AWARD
1 Park Road, Bakewell DE45 1AX
t (01629) 814299
e the.garden.room@talk21.com
w smoothhound.co.uk/hotels/thegarden

**The Haven** ★★★★
*Guest Accommodation*
Haddon Road, Bakewell DE45 1AW
t (01629) 812113
e contact@visitbakewell.com
w visitbakewell.com

**Housley Cottage** ★★★★
*Bed & Breakfast*
Housley, Nr Foolow, Hope Valley S32 5QB
t (01433) 631505
e kevin@housleycottages.co.uk
w housleycottages.co.uk

**Mandale House** ★★★★
*Farmhouse*
Haddon Grove, Over Haddon, Bakewell DE45 1JF
t (01629) 812416
e julia.finney@virgin.net
w mandalehouse.co.uk

**Meadow View** ★★★★
*Bed & Breakfast*
Coombs Road, Bakewell DE45 1AQ
t (01629) 812961

**Melbourne House** ★★★★
*Guest Accommodation*
Buxton Road, Bakewell DE45 1DA
t (01629) 815357
e melbournehouse@supanet.com
w bakewell-accommodation.co.uk

**River Walk Bed & Breakfast**
★★★★ *Bed & Breakfast*
3 New Lumford, Bakewell DE45 1GH
t (01629) 812459
w riverwalkbedandbreakfast.co.uk

**Westmorland House** ★★★★
*Guest Accommodation*
Park Road, Bakewell DE45 1AX
t (01629) 812932
e lesley@westmorlandhouse.co.uk
w westmorlandhouse.co.uk

**Willow Croft** ★★★★
*Guest Accommodation*
Station Road, Great Longstone, Bakewell DE45 1TS
t (01629) 640576
w smoothhound.co.uk

**Wilmadah** ★★★★
*Bed & Breakfast*
The Square, Middleton-by-Youlgreave, Bakewell DE45 1LS
t (01629) 636303

### BALDERTON
Nottinghamshire

**Newark Lodge Guest House**
★★★★★ *Guest House*
SILVER AWARD
5 Bullpit Road, Balderton, Newark NG24 3PT
t (01636) 703999
e coolspratt@aol.com

### BARDNEY
Lincolnshire

**The Black Horse** ★★★
*Guest House*
16 Wragby Road, Bardney LN3 5XL
t (01526) 398900
e black-horse@lineone.net
w blackhorsebardney.co.uk

### BARKSTON
Lincolnshire

**Kelling House** ★★★★
*Bed & Breakfast*
17 West Street, Barkston NG32 2NL
t (01400) 251440
e sue.evans7@btopenworld.com
w kellinghouse.co.uk

### BARLBOROUGH
Derbyshire

**Stone Croft** ★★★★
*Bed & Breakfast*
15 Church Street, Barlborough, Chesterfield S43 4ER
t (01246) 810974
w stone-croft.co.uk

### BARLEYTHORPE
Rutland

**Barleythorpe Training & ConferenceCentre** ★★★
*Guest Accommodation*
Barleythorpe, Oakham LE15 7ED
t (01572) 723711
e info@eef-eastmids.org.uk
w barleythorpe.com

### BARLOW
Derbyshire

**Woodview Cottage** ★★★★
*Bed & Breakfast*
Millcross Lane, Barlow, Dronfield S18 7TA
t (0114) 289 0724
e richard.collis@virgin.net

### BARNSDALE
Rutland

**Lakeside Guest House**
★★★★
*Guest Accommodation*
The Lodge, Barnsdale, North Shore, Rutland Water LE15 8AB
t (01572) 722422

### BARROW-ON-TRENT
Derbyshire

**5 Nook Cottages** ★★★★
*Bed & Breakfast*
SILVER AWARD
The Nook, Barrow-upon-Trent, Derby DE73 7NA
t (01332) 702050
e nookcottage@nookcottage.com
w nookcottage.com

### BARROW UPON SOAR
Leicestershire

**Hunting Lodge** ★★★★ *Inn*
38 South Street, Barrow upon Soar, Loughborough LE12 8LZ
t (01509) 412337
w probablythebestpubsintheworld.com

### BASLOW
Derbyshire

**Bubnell Cliff Farm** ★★★
*Farmhouse*
Wheatlands Lane, Baslow, Bakewell DE45 1RF
t (01246) 582454
e c.k.mills@btinternet.com

### BEELEY
Derbyshire

**The Devonshire Arms at Beeley** ★★★★ *Inn*
Devonshire Square, Beeley, Matlock DE4 2NR
t (01629) 733259
e enquiries@devonshirebeeley.co.uk
w devonshirebeeley.co.uk

## BEESTON
### Nottinghamshire

**Hylands ★★★** *Guest House*
Queens Road, Beeston,
Nottingham NG9 1JB
**t** (0115) 925 5472
**e** hyland.hotel@btconnect.
com
**w** s-h-systems.co.uk/hotels/
hylands.html

## BELPER
### Derbyshire

**Amber Hills ★★★★**
*Guest Accommodation*
Whitehouse Farm, Belper Lane,
Belper DE56 2UJ
**t** (01773) 824080
**e** amberhills@v21.me.uk
**w** amberhills.co.uk

**Hill Top Farm Bed &
Breakfast ★★★★**
*Bed & Breakfast*
Hill Top Farm, 80 Ashbourne
Road, Belper DE56 2LF
**t** (01773) 550338

## BELTON IN RUTLAND
### Rutland

**Old Rectory ★★★**
*Farmhouse*
4 New Road, Belton in Rutland,
Oakham LE15 9LE
**t** (01572) 717279
**e** bb@iepuk.com
**w** theoldrectorybelton.co.uk

## BESTHORPE
### Nottinghamshire

**Lord Nelson Inn ★★★★** *Inn*
Main Road, Besthorpe, Newark
NG23 7HR
**t** (01636) 892265
**e** enquiries@thelordnelsoninn.
plus.com

## BIGGIN-BY-HARTINGTON
### Derbyshire

**The Kings at Ivy House
★★★★★**
*Guest Accommodation*
**GOLD AWARD**
Biggin-by-Hartington,
Newhaven, Buxton SK17 0DT
**t** (01298) 84709
**e** kings.ivyhouse@lineone.net
**w** thekingsativyhouse.co.uk

## BILLINGHAY
### Lincolnshire

**Old Mill Crafts ★★★**
*Bed & Breakfast*
8 Mill Lane, Billinghay, Lincoln
LN4 4ES
**t** (01526) 861996

## BLYTON
### Lincolnshire

**Blyton (Sunnyside) Ponds
★★★** *Bed & Breakfast*
Sunnyside Farm, Station Road,
Blyton, Gainsborough
DN21 3LE
**t** (01427) 628240
**e** blytonponds@msn.com
**w** blytonponds.co.uk

## BONSALL
### Derbyshire

**The Old Schoolhouse ★★★**
*Bed & Breakfast*
The Dale, Bonsall, Matlock
DE4 2AY
**t** (01629) 826017
**e** lydia.art@btinternet.com
**w** oldschoolhousebonsall.co.uk

## BOSTON
### Lincolnshire

**Bramley House ★★★**
*Guest House*
267 Sleaford Road, Boston
PE21 7PQ
**t** (01205) 354538

**Fairfield Guest House ★★★**
*Guest House*
101 London Road, Boston
PE21 7EN
**t** (01205) 362869

**Haven Guest House ★★★**
*Bed & Breakfast*
49 Robin Hoods Walk, Boston
PE21 9EX
**t** (01205) 364076

**Park Lea Guest House ★★★**
*Guest Accommodation*
85 Norfolk Street, Boston
PE21 6PE
**t** (01205) 356309
**e** park.lea@btopenworld.com
**w** park-lea.co.uk/

**Plummer's Place Guest
House ★★★★**
*Guest Accommodation*
Plummers Mews, Freiston
Shore, Boston PE22 0LY
**t** (01205) 761490
**e** frei24@btopenworld.com

**Y-Not Guesthouse ★★★**
*Guest Accommodation*
10 Langrick Road, Boston
PE21 8HT
**t** (01205) 367422
**e** peter.mcgarry@btinternet.
com

## BOTTESFORD
### Leicestershire

**The Thatch Hotel ★★★★**
*Restaurant with Rooms*
**SILVER AWARD**
26 High Street, Bottesford,
Melton Mowbray NG13 0AA
**t** (01949) 842330
**e** the.thatch@btconnect.com
**w** thethatchbottesford.co.uk

## BOURNE
### Lincolnshire

**Maycroft Cottage Bed and
Breakfast ★★★★**
*Guest Accommodation*
6 Edenham Road, Hanthorpe,
Bourne PE10 0RB
**t** (01778) 571689
**e** enquiries@maycroftcottage.
co.uk
**w** maycroftcottage.co.uk

**Mill House ★★★★**
*Bed & Breakfast*
64 North Road, Bourne
PE10 9BU
**t** (01778) 422278
**e** patricia.stratford12@
ntlworld.com
**w** millhouse.healerwoman.
com/

## BRACKLEY
### Northamptonshire

**Astwell Mill ★★★★**
*Farmhouse*
Helmdon, Brackley NN13 5QU
**t** (01295) 760507
**e** astwell01@aol.com
**w** astwellmill.co.uk

**The Cottage B&B ★★★★**
*Bed & Breakfast*
127 Fox Lane, Brackley
NN13 6AY
**t** (01280) 703107
**e** cderekcrane@aol.com

**Floral Hall Guest House
★★★** *Bed & Breakfast*
50 Valley Road, Brackley
NN13 7DQ
**t** (01280) 702950
**e** floralhallguesthouse@talk21.
com

**Hill Farm ★★★★** *Farmhouse*
Halse, Brackley NN13 6DY
**t** (01280) 703300 &
07860 865146
**e** j.g.robinson@btconnect.com

**Manor Grange ★★★★**
*Bed & Breakfast*
Cottisford, Brackley NN13 5SW
**t** (01280) 847770
**e** triciahazan@manor-grange.
com
**w** manor-grange.com

**The Old Surgery ★★★★**
*Bed & Breakfast*
**SILVER AWARD**
Pebble Lane, Brackley
NN13 7DA
**t** (01280) 705090
**e** jaymaddison@aol.com

**The Thatches ★★★**
*Bed & Breakfast*
Whitfield, Brackley NN13 5TQ
**t** (01280) 850358

**Yew Tree House ★★★★**
*Bed & Breakfast*
The Green, Hinton-in-the-
Hedges, Brackley NN13 5NG
**t** (01280) 700547

## BRADLEY
### Derbyshire

**Yeldersley Old Hall Farm
★★★★** *Farmhouse*
**SILVER AWARD**
Yeldersley Lane, Bradley,
Ashbourne DE6 1PH
**t** (01335) 344504
**e** janethindsfarm@yahoo.co.
uk
**w** yeldersleyoldhallfarm.co.uk

## BRADWELL
### Derbyshire

**Stoney Ridge ★★★★**
*Guest Accommodation*
Granby Road, Bradwell, Hope
Valley S33 9HU
**t** (01433) 620538
**e** toneyridge@aol.com
**w** stoneyridge.org.uk

**Travellers Rest ★★★** *Inn*
Brough Lane End, Brough,
Hope Valley S33 9HG
**t** (01433) 620363
**e** elliottstephen@btconnect.
com
**w** travellers-rest.net

## BRACKLEY
### Northamptonshire

## BRAMPTON
### Derbyshire

**Brampton Guest House
★★★** *Guest House*
75 Old Road, Off Chatsworth
Road, Chesterfield S40 2QU
**t** (01246) 276533
**e** enquiries@brampton-
guesthouse.co.uk
**w** brampton-guesthouse.co.uk

## BRATTLEBY
### Lincolnshire

**Robindale ★★★★**
*Bed & Breakfast*
Back Lane, Brattleby, Lincoln
LN1 2SQ
**t** (01522) 730712

## BRAUNSTON
### Northamptonshire

**The Old Workshop ★★★★**
*Bed & Breakfast*
The Wharf, Daventry
NN11 7JQ
**t** (01788) 891421
**e** info@the-old-workshop.com
**w** the-old-workshop.com

## BREEDON ON THE HILL
### Leicestershire

**The Hollybush Inn ★★★★**
*Inn*
1 Melbourne Lane, Breedon-
on-the-Hill DE73 8AT
**t** (01332) 862359

**Underhill Cottage ★★**
*Bed & Breakfast*
9-11 Main Street, Breedon-on-
the-Hill, Castle Donington
DE73 8AN
**t** (01332) 865630
**e** beniceberg@aol.com
**w** t-multimedia.net/
underhillcottage

## BRETBY
### Derbyshire

**Bretby Conference Centre
★★★** *Guest Accommodation*
Ashby Road, Bretby, Burton-
on-Trent DE15 0YZ
**t** (01283) 553440
**e** enquiries@bretbycc.co.uk
**w** bretbycc.co.uk

## BRIGG
### Lincolnshire

**Albert House**
Rating Applied For
*Guest Accommodation*
23 Bigby Street, Brigg
DN20 8ED
**t** (01652) 658081

**Beldon House ★★★★**
*Guest Accommodation*
Wrawby Road, Brigg
DN20 8DL
**t** (01652) 653517
**e** info@beldonhouse.co.uk

**Holcombe Guest House
★★★★** *Guest House*
34 Victoria Road, Barnetby
DN38 6JR
**t** 07850 764002
**e** holcombe.house@virgin.net
**w** holcombeguesthouse.co.uk

### BROOKE
Rutland

**Old Rectory** ★★★
*Bed & Breakfast*
Main Street, Brooke, Oakham
LE15 8DE
t (01572) 770558

### BURTON UPON STATHER
Lincolnshire

**Sheffield Arms Hotel** ★★★
*Inn*
High Street, Scunthorpe
DN15 9BP
t (01724) 720269
e bruce@jbmck.co.uk

### BUXTON
Derbyshire

**9 Green Lane B&B** ★★★★
*Guest Accommodation*
**SILVER AWARD**
Green Lane, Buxton SK17 9DP
t (01298) 73731
e book@9greenlane.co.uk
w 9greenlane.co.uk

**Abbey Guest House** ★★★
*Guest Accommodation*
43 South Avenue, Buxton
SK17 6NQ
t (01298) 26419
e aghbuxton@aol.com

**Braemar** ★★★★
*Guest Accommodation*
10 Compton Road, Buxton
SK17 9DN
t (01298) 78050
e buxtonbraemar@supanet.
com
w cressbrook.co.uk/buxton/
braemar

**Buxton Hilbre** ★★★
*Bed & Breakfast*
8 White Knowle Road, Buxton
SK17 9NH
t (01298) 22358
e min.hilbre@virgin.net

**Buxton's Victorian Guest
House** ★★★★★
*Guest House* **SILVER AWARD**
3a Broad Walk, Buxton
SK17 6JE
t (01298) 78759
e buxtonvictorian@btconnect.
com
w buxtonvictorian.co.uk

**Compton House Guest
House** ★★ *Guest House*
4 Compton Road, Buxton
SK17 9DN
t (01298) 26926
e comptonhousesk17@aol.
com
w cressbrook.co.uk/buxton/
compton

**Cotesfield Farm** ★★
*Farmhouse*
Parsley Hay, Buxton SK17 0BD
t (01298) 83256

**Devonshire Arms** ★★★ *Inn*
Peak Forest, Buxton SK17 8EJ
t (01298) 23875
e fiona.clough@virgin.net
w devarms.com

**Devonshire Lodge Guest
House** ★★★★
*Guest Accommodation*
**SILVER AWARD**
2 Manchester Road, Buxton
SK17 6SB
t (01298) 71487
e enquiries@
devonshirelodgeguesthouse.
co.uk
w devonshirelodgeguest
house.co.uk

**Fairhaven Guest House**
★★★ *Guest Accommodation*
1 Dale Terrace, Buxton
SK17 6LU
t (01298) 24481
e paul@fairhavenguesthouse.
freeserve.co.uk

**Fernydale Farm** ★★★★
*Farmhouse* **SILVER AWARD**
Earl Sterndale, Nr Buxton
SK17 0BS
t (01298) 83236
e wjnadin@btconnect.com

**Grendon Guest House**
★★★★★ *Guest House*
**GOLD AWARD**
Bishops Lane, Buxton
SK17 6UN
t (01298) 78831
e grendonguesthouse@
hotmail.com
w grendonguesthouse.co.uk

**Grosvenor House** ★★★★
*Guest House* **SILVER AWARD**
Broad Walk, Buxton SK17 6JE
t (01298) 72439
e grosvenor.buxton@
btopenworld.com
w grosvenorbuxton.co.uk

**Hawthorn Farm Guest
House** ★★★ *Guest House*
Fairfield Road, Buxton
SK17 7ED
t (01298) 23230
e alan.pimblett@virgin.net

**Kingscroft Guest House**
★★★★ *Guest House*
**SILVER AWARD**
10 Green Lane, Buxton
SK17 9DP
t (01298) 22757

**Lakenham Guest House**
★★★★ *Guest House*
11 Burlington Road, Buxton
SK17 9AL
t (01298) 79209
e enquiries@lakenhambuxton.
co.uk
w lakenhambuxton.co.uk

**Linden Lodge** ★★★★
*Bed & Breakfast*
31 Temple Road, Buxton
SK17 9BA
t (01298) 27591
w lindentreelodge.co.uk

**Lowther Guest House**
★★★★
*Guest Accommodation*
7 Hardwick Square West,
Buxton SK17 6PX
t (01298) 71479
e b&b@pritchardbuxton.fslife.
co.uk
w lowtherguesthouse.co.uk

**Netherdale Guest House**
★★★★ *Guest House*
16 Green Lane, Buxton
SK17 9DP
t (01298) 23896
w smoothhound.co.uk/hotels/
netherdale

**The Old Manse Private Hotel**
★★★★ *Guest House*
6 Clifton Road, Buxton
SK17 6QL
t (01298) 25638
e old_manse@yahoo.co.uk
w oldmanse.co.uk

**Roseleigh Hotel** ★★★★
*Guest House* **SILVER AWARD**
19 Broad Walk, Buxton
SK17 6JR
t (01298) 24904
e enquiries@roseleighhotel.
co.uk
w roseleighhotel.co.uk

**The Royal Oak** *Camping Barn*
Hurdlow, Buxton SK17 9QJ
t (01298) 83288
e info@royaloakpub.org
w royaloakpub.org

**Stoneridge** ★★★★
*Guest Accommodation*
**SILVER AWARD**
9 Park Road, Buxton SK17 6SG
t (01298) 26120
e duncan@stoneridge.co.uk
w stoneridge.co.uk

**Westlands** ★★★★
*Guest Accommodation*
**SILVER AWARD**
Bishops Lane, Burbage, Buxton
SK17 6UN
t (01298) 71122
e enquiries@westlandshouse.
co.uk
w westlandshouse.co.uk

### BYFIELD
Northamptonshire

**Glebe Farm Bed and
Breakfast** ★★★
*Bed & Breakfast*
61 Church Street, Byfield,
Daventry NN11 6XN
t (01327) 260512

### CADEBY
Leicestershire

**Bosworth Accommodation**
★★★★ *Guest House*
Cadeby Lane, Cadeby, Market
Bosworth CV13 0BA
t (01455) 292259
e info@
bosworthaccommodation.co.uk
w bosworthaccommodation.
co.uk

### CAENBY CORNER
Lincolnshire

**Ermine Lodge B&B** ★★★★
*Bed & Breakfast*
**SILVER AWARD**
Ermine Lodge, Market Rasen
LN8 2AR
t (01673) 878152
e info@erminelodgebandb.
com
w erminelodgebanb.com

### CAISTOR
Lincolnshire

**Little Hen Bed & Breakfast**
★★★★ *Bed & Breakfast*
Brocklesby Hilltop Cottage,
Brigg Road, Grasby DN38 6AQ
t (01652) 629005
e polly@littlehen.co.uk
w littlehen.co.uk

**The Queens Head Hotel**
★★★ *Inn*
Station Road, North Kelsey
Moor, Market Rasen LN7 6HD
t (01652) 678055
e info@queens-head.biz
w queens-head.biz

### CALDECOTT
Rutland

**Old Plough – Caldecott**
★★★★
*Guest Accommodation*
41 Main Street, Caldecott,
Uppingham LE16 8RS
t (01536) 772031
e comfort@oldplough-rutland.
co.uk
w oldplough-rutland.co.uk

### CALVER
Derbyshire

**Valley View Guest House
Ltd** ★★★★ *Guest House*
**SILVER AWARD**
Smithy Knoll Road, Calver,
Hope Valley S32 3XW
t (01433) 631407
e sue@a-place-2-stay.co.uk
w a-place-2-stay.co.uk

### CAMMERINGHAM
Lincolnshire

**Field View B&B** ★★★★
*Bed & Breakfast*
Field View, Back Lane,
Cammeringham LN1 2SH
t (01522) 730193
e info@fieldviewbandb.com
w fieldviewbandb.com

### CARLTON IN LINDRICK
Nottinghamshire

**Lindrick Lodge Hotel**
★★★★
*Restaurant with Rooms*
The Green, Carlton in Lindrick
S81 9AB
t (01909) 731649
e info@lindricklodgehotel.co.
uk
w lindricklodgehotel.co.uk

### CARSINGTON
Derbyshire

**Breach Farm** ★★★★
*Farmhouse*
Carsington, Nr Matlock,
Wirksworth DE4 4DD
t (01629) 540265
w breachfarm.co.uk

### CASEWICK
Lincolnshire

**Lindsey Cottage** ★★★★
*Bed & Breakfast*
Greatford Road, Uffington,
Stamford PE9 4ST
t (01780) 752975
e smb@lindseycottage01.
fsbusiness.co.uk

## CASTLE DONINGTON
### Leicestershire

**Castletown House ★★★★**
*Guest House* SILVER AWARD
4 High Street, Castle
Donington DE74 2PP
t (01332) 812018
e enq@castletownhouse.fsnet.
co.uk
w castletownhouse.com

**Churchview Hotel ★★★**
*Guest Accommodation*
73 Clapgun Street, Castle
Donington DE74 2LF
t (01332) 853440
w churchviewhotel.com

**Scot's Corner Guest House**
★★★ *Bed & Breakfast*
82 Park Lane, Castle Donington
DE74 2JG
t (01332) 811226
e linda.deary@ntlworld.com
w scots-corner.com

## CASTLETHORPE
### Lincolnshire

**Arties Mill & Lodge ★★★**
*Inn*
Wressle Road, Brigg DN20 9LF
t (01652) 652094
e arties.mill@elizabethhotels.
co.uk
w elizabethhotels.co.uk

## CASTLETON
### Derbyshire

**Bargate Cottage ★★★★**
*Bed & Breakfast*
Bargate Street, Bargate, Hope
Valley S33 8WG
t (01433) 620201

**Cryer House ★★★**
*Guest Accommodation*
Castle Street, Castleton, Hope
Valley S33 8WG
t (01433) 620244
e fleeskel@aol.com

**Dunscar Farm Bed &
Breakfast ★★★★**
*Guest Accommodation*
Castleton, Hope Valley
S33 8WA
t (01433) 620483
e janet@dunscarfarm.co.uk
w dunscarfarm.co.uk

**Hillside House ★★★★**
*Bed & Breakfast*
Pindale Road, Hope Valley
S33 8WU
t (01433) 620312
w peakdistrictnationalpark.com

**Ramblers Rest ★★★**
*Guest Accommodation*
Back Street, Mill Bridge, Hope
Valley S33 8WR
t (01433) 620125
e mary@ramblersrest.
wanadoo.co.uk
w ramblersrest-castleton.co.uk

**Swiss House ★★★**
*Guest Accommodation*
How Lane, Hope Valley
S33 8WJ
t (01433) 621098
e info@swisshousehotel.co.uk
w swisshousehotel.co.uk

**Trickett Gate House B&B**
★★★★ *Bed & Breakfast*
Trickett Gate House, Mill
Bridge, Hope Valley S33 8WR
t (01433) 621590
w trickettgate.co.uk

**Ye Olde Cheshire Cheese
Inn ★★★** *Inn*
How Lane, Castleton, Hope
Valley S33 8WJ
t (01433) 620330
e info@cheshirecheeseinn.co.
uk
w cheshirecheeseinn.co.uk

**Ye Olde Nag's Head ★★★**
*Inn*
Cross Street, Castleton, Hope
Valley S33 8WH
t (01433) 620248
e nigel@yeoldenagshead.com

**YHA Castleton Hall ★★★**
*Hostel*
Castle Street, Castleton, Hope
Valley S33 8WG
t (01433) 620235
e castleton@yha.org.uk
w yha.org.uk

## CATESBY
### Northamptonshire

**Long Furlong Farm ★★★**
*Farmhouse*
Catesby, Daventry NN11 6LW
t (01327) 264770
e haighfamily@waitrose.com

## CHADDESDEN
### Derbyshire

**Green Gables ★★★**
*Guest House*
19 Highfield Lane,
Chaddesden, Derby DE21 6PG
t (01332) 672298
e enquiries@greengablesuk.
co.uk
w greengablesuk.co.uk

## CHAPEL-EN-LE-FRITH
### Derbyshire

**Forest Lodge ★★★★**
*Bed & Breakfast*
58 Manchester Road, Chapel-
en-le-Frith, High Peak
SK23 9TH
t (01298) 812854
e noreen@forestlodge.org.uk
w forestlodge.org.uk

**High Croft ★★★★★**
*Guest House* SILVER AWARD
Manchester Road, Chapel-en-
le-Frith, High Peak SK23 9UH
t (01298) 814843
e elaine@highcroft-
guesthouse.co.uk
w highcroft-guesthouse.co.uk

**The Potting Shed ◆◆◆◆**
*Guest Accommodation*
Bankhall, Chapel-en-le-Frith,
High Peak SK23 9UB
t (0161) 338 8134
w thepottingshedhighpeak.
com

**Rushop Hall B&B ★★★★**
*Farmhouse*
Rushup Lane, Rushup, High
Peak SK23 0QT
t (01298) 813323
e neil@rushophall.com
w rushophall.com

**Slack Hall Farm ★★★★**
*Farmhouse*
Castleton Road, Chapel-en-le-
Frith, High Peak SK23 0QS
t (01298) 812845

## CHAPEL ST LEONARDS
### Lincolnshire

**South Sands Guesthouse**
★★★ *Guest House*
35 South Road, South Road,
Skegness PE24 5TL
t (01754) 873066
w south-sands.co.uk

## CHARLTON
### Northamptonshire

**Home Farmhouse ★★★★**
*Farmhouse*
Main Street, Charlton, Banbury
OX17 3DR
t (01295) 811683
e grovewhite@lineone.net
w homefarmhouse.co.uk

## CHELLASTON
### Derbyshire

**The Lawns Hotel ★★★** *Inn*
High Street, Chellaston, Derby
DE73 1TB
t (01332) 701553

## CHELMORTON
### Derbyshire

**Church Inn ★★★★** *Inn*
Buxton SK17 9SL
t (01298) 85319

## CHELVESTON
### Northamptonshire

**Middle Farm Villa B&B**
★★★★ *Bed & Breakfast*
The Green, Chelveston,
Wellingborough NN9 6AJ
t (01933) 625541
e middlefarmvilla@aol.com

## CHESTERFIELD
### Derbyshire

**4 The Dell ★★★★**
*Bed & Breakfast*
Ashgate, Chesterfield S40 4DL
t (01246) 237170

**Abigails Guest House ★★★**
*Guest House*
62 Brockwell Lane, Chesterfield
S40 4EE
t (01246) 279391
e gail@abigails.fsnet.co.uk
w abigailsguesthouse.co.uk

**Anis Louise Guest House**
★★★★ *Guest House*
34 Clarence Road, Chesterfield
S40 1LN
t (01246) 235412
e anislouise@gmail.com
w anislouiseguesthouse.co.uk

**Applewood Accommodation**
◆◆◆ *Guest Accommodation*
32 Spring Bank Road,
Chesterfield S40 1NL
t (01246) 550542

**Batemans Mill Country Inn &
Restaurant ★★★★** *Inn*
Mill Lane, Old Tupton,
Chesterfield S42 6AE
t (01246) 862296
e info@batemansmill.co.uk
w batemansmill.co.uk

**Clarendon Guest House**
★★★ *Guest Accommodation*
32 Clarence Road, Chesterfield
S40 1LN
t (01246) 235004

**Locksley ★★★**
*Bed & Breakfast*
21 Tennyson Avenue,
Chesterfield S40 4SN
t (01246) 273332

**Maylands Guest House**
Rating Applied For
*Guest House*
56 Sheffield Road, Chesterfield
S41 7LS
t (01246) 233602

## CHINLEY
### Derbyshire

**Moseley House Farm ★★★**
*Farmhouse*
Maynestone Road, Chinley,
High Peak SK23 6AH
t (01663) 750240
e moseleyhouse@supanet.
com
w smoothhound.co.uk/hotels/
moseleyhouse.html

**The Old Hall Inn ★★★★** *Inn*
Whitehough, Chinley,
Stockport SK23 6EJ
t (01663) 750529
e info@old-hall-inn.co.uk
w old-hall-inn.co.uk

## CLAXBY
### Lincolnshire

**Swallows Barn Bed and
Breakfast ★★★★**
*Bed & Breakfast*
The Barn, St Marys Lane,
Claxby, Market Rasen LN8 3YX
t (01673) 828626
e griffin@thebarn2000.fsnet.
co.uk
w swallowsbarn.co.uk

## CLEETHORPES
### North East Lincolnshire

**Acer House ★★★**
*Bed & Breakfast*
14 Queens Parade,
Cleethorpes DN35 0DF
t (01472) 200289

**Arlana Guest House ★★★**
*Guest House*
53 Princes Road, Cleethorpes
DN35 8AW
t (01472) 699689
e colleen.waters@ntlworld.
com
w arlanaguesthouse.co.uk

**Ginnies ★★★** *Guest House*
27 Queen's Parade,
Cleethorpes DN35 0DF
t (01472) 694997
e enquiries@ginnies.co.uk
w ginnies.co.uk

**Gladson Guest House ★★★**
*Guest Accommodation*
43 Isaacs Hill, Cleethorpes
DN35 8JT
t (01472) 694858
e enquiries@
gladsonguesthouse.co.uk
w gladsonguesthouse.co.uk

**Tudor Terrace Guest House**
★★★★ *Guest House*
11 Bradford Avenue,
Cleethorpes DN35 0BB
t (01472) 600800
e enquiries.tudorterrace@
ntlworld.com
w tudorterrace.co.uk

**The Vines Guest House**
★★★ *Guest Accommodation*
15 Isaacs Hill, Cleethorpes
DN35 8JU
t (01472) 690524
e stevhw3@aol.com
w vinesbandb.co.uk

### CLIFTON
### Derbyshire

**Stone Cottage** ★★★
*Guest Accommodation*
Green Lane, Clifton,
Ashbourne DE6 2BL
t (01335) 343377
e info@stone-cottage.fsnet.co.
uk
w stone-cottage.fsnet.co.uk

### COALVILLE
### Leicestershire

**The New Ellistown**
Rating Applied For
*Inn*
Whitehill Road, Ellistown,
Coalville LE67 1EL
t (01530) 260502
e val786@btinternet.com
w thenewellistown.co.uk

### COLSTERWORTH
### Lincolnshire

**The Stables** ★★★★
*Guest House*
Stainby Rd, Colsterworth
NG33 5JB
t (01476) 861057
e kathleen@btopenworld.com
w stablesbandb.co.uk

### CONINGSBY
### Lincolnshire

**The Leagate Inn** ★★★★ *Inn*
Leagate Road, Coningsby
LN4 4RS
t (01526) 342370
e theleagateinn@hotmail.com
w the-leagate-inn.co.uk/

### CONISHOLME
### Lincolnshire

**Wickham House** ★★★★★
*Guest Accommodation*
SILVER AWARD
Church Lane, Conisholme
LN11 7LX
t (01507) 358465
e cizekann@hotmail.com
w wickham-house.co.uk

### CORBY
### Northamptonshire

**Home Farm** ★★★
*Bed & Breakfast*
Main Street, Sudborough,
Kettering NN14 3BX
t (01832) 730488
e bandbhomefarmsud@aol.
com
w homefarmsudborough.co.uk

**Manor Farm Guest House**
★★★★
*Guest Accommodation*
Station Road, Rushton,
Kettering NN14 1RL
t (01536) 710305
w rushtonmanorfarm.co.uk

### COTTESMORE
### Rutland

**Tithe Barn** ★★★★
*Guest Accommodation*
Clatterpot Lane, Cottesmore,
Oakham LE15 7DW
t (01572) 813591
e jp@thetithebarn.co.uk
w tithebarn-rutland.co.uk

### CRANWELL
### Lincolnshire

**Byards Leap Bed &
Breakfast** ★★★★
*Guest Accommodation*
SILVER AWARD
Byards Leap Cottage, Cranwell
NG34 8EY
t (01400) 261537
e info@byardsleapcottage.co.
uk
w byardsleapcottage.co.uk

**Byards Leap Cottage** ★★★
*Bed & Breakfast*
Byards Leap, Cranwell,
Sleaford NG34 8EY
t (01400) 261537

### CRANWELL VILLAGE
### Lincolnshire

**Oxenford Farm** ★★★★
*Bed & Breakfast*
Cranwell NG34 8DE
t (01400) 261369
e oldblackie50@hotmail.com
w oxenfordfarm.co.uk

### CREATON
### Northamptonshire

**Highgate House – A Sundial
Group Venue** ★★★★
*Guest Accommodation*
Grooms Lane, Creaton
NN6 8NN
t (01604) 505505
e claire.fonville@sundialgroup.
com
w sundialgroup.com

### CRESSBROOK
### Derbyshire

**1 The Old Hay Barn**
★★★★★
*Guest Accommodation*
The Barns, Cressbrook, Buxton
SK17 8SY
t (01298) 873503
e dcmacb@aol.com

**Cressbrook Hall** ★★★★
*Guest Accommodation*
Cressbrook, Buxton SK17 8SY
t (01298) 871289
e stay@cressbrookhall.co.uk
w cressbrookhall.co.uk

### CROPSTON
### Leicestershire

**Horseshoe Cottage Farm**
★★★★★ *Bed & Breakfast*
SILVER AWARD
Hallgates Reservoir Road,
Cropston, Leicester LE7 7GQ
t (0116) 235 0038
e lindajee@ljee.freeserve.co.
uk
w horseshoecottagefarm.com

### CROWDEN
### Derbyshire

**Crowden Youth Hostel**
★★★ *Hostel*
Crowden, Glossop SK13 1HZ
t (01457) 852135

### CROWLAND
### Lincolnshire

**The Abbey Hotel** ★★★ *Inn*
21 East Street, Crowland
PE6 0EN
t (01733) 210200
e bruce.upson@btopenworld.
com

### CROXTON
### Lincolnshire

**Croxton House** ★★★
*Guest Accommodation*
Ulceby DN39 6YD
t (01652) 688306
e juliegallimore@yahoo.co.uk

### DARLEY ABBEY
### Derbyshire

**The Coach House** ★★★
*Guest Accommodation*
185a Duffield Road, Derby
DE22 1JB
t (01332) 551795
e carolcoachhousederby@
tiscali.co.uk

### DARLEY BRIDGE
### Derbyshire

**Square and Compass**
★★★★ *Inn*
Station Road, Darley Dale,
Matlock DE4 2EQ
t (01629) 733255
e info@thesquareandcompass.
co.uk
w thesquareandcompass.co.uk

### DAVENTRY
### Northamptonshire

**Drayton Lodge** ★★★★
*Farmhouse*
Staverton Road, Daventry
NN11 4NL
t (01327) 702449
e ann.spicer@farming.co.uk
w draytonlodge.co.uk

**The Mill House** ★★
*Bed & Breakfast*
West Farndon, Nr Daventry
NN11 3TX
t (01327) 261727
e josephinelincoln53@
amserve.com
w millhousebandb.co.uk

### DEEPDALE
### Lincolnshire

**West Wold Farmhouse**
★★★★ *Guest House*
Barton-upon-Humber
DN18 6ED
t (01652) 633293
e westwoldfarm@aol.com

### DEEPING ST NICHOLAS
### Lincolnshire

**St Nicholas House** ★★★★
*Guest Accommodation*
Main Road, Deeping St
Nicholas PE11 3HA
t (01775) 630484
e stnicholashouse@aol.com
w stnicholashouse.co.uk

### DENTON
### Lincolnshire

**The Byre House** ★★★★
*Guest Accommodation*
Glebe Farm, Casthorpe Road,
Grantham NG32 1JT
t (01476) 870529

### DERBY
### Derbyshire

**Bonehill Farm** ★★★
*Bed & Breakfast*
Etwall Road, Mickleover, Derby
DE3 0DN
t (01332) 513553
e bonehillfarm@hotmail.com
w bonehillfarm.co.uk

**Braeside Guest House**
★★★★ *Guest House*
113 Derby Road, Risley, Derby
DE72 3SS
t (0115) 939 5885
e bookings@
braesideguesthouse.co.uk
w braesideguesthouse.co.uk

**Crompton Coach House**
★★★ *Guest Accommodation*
45 Crompton Street, Derby
DE1 1NX
t (01332) 365735
e enquiries@
coachhousederby.co.uk
w coachhousederby.co.uk

**Red Setters Guest House**
♦♦♦ *Guest Accommodation*
85 Curzon Street, Derby
DE1 1LN
t (01332) 362770
e yvonne.swann3@ntlworld.
com
w derbycity.com/michael/
redset.html

**Rose and Thistle Guest
House** ★★★
*Guest Accommodation*
21 Charnwood Street, Derby
DE1 2GU
t (01332) 344103

**Thornhill Lodge Guest
House** ★★★★ *Guest House*
SILVER AWARD
Thornhill Road, Derby
DE22 3LX
t (01332) 345318
e info@thornhill-lodge.com
w thornhill-lodge.com

### DIGBY
### Lincolnshire

**Digby Manor** ★★★★
*Bed & Breakfast*
SILVER AWARD
North Street, Digby, Lincoln
LN4 3LY
t (01526) 322064
e gill@digbymanor.com
w digbymanor.com

**Woodend Farm Bed and Breakfast ★★★**
*Bed & Breakfast*
Woodend Farm, Digby, Lincoln
LN4 3NG
t (01526) 860347

### DISEWORTH
Leicestershire

**Lady Gate Guest House**
**★★★★** *Guest House*
SILVER AWARD
47 The Green, Diseworth,
Castle Donington DE74 2QN
t (01332) 811565
e ladygateguesthouse@tiscali.
co.uk
w ladygateguesthouse.co.uk

### DONINGTON
Lincolnshire

**Browntoft House ★★★★**
*Guest Accommodation*
Browntoft Lane, Donington
PE11 4TQ
t (01775) 822091
e finchedward@hotmail.com
w browntofthouse.co.uk

### DOVERIDGE
Derbyshire

**Ashmore Bed & Breakfast
★★★★**
*Guest Accommodation*
Derby Road, Ashbourne
DE6 5JU
t (01889) 569620
e ashmorecottage@btinternet.
com
w ashmorecottage.co.uk

### EAST BARKWITH
Lincolnshire

**The Grange ★★★★**
*Farmhouse* SILVER AWARD
Torrington Lane, East Barkwith,
Market Rasen LN8 5RY
t (01673) 858670
e sarahstamp@farmersweekly.
net
w thegrange-lincolnshire.co.uk

### EAST HADDON
Northamptonshire

**East Haddon Lodge ★★★**
*Farmhouse*
Main Street, East Haddon,
Northampton NN6 8BU
t (01604) 770240

### EAST LANGTON
Leicestershire

**West Langton Lodge ★★★**
*Guest Accommodation*
Melton Road, Market
Harborough LE16 7TG
t (01858) 545450
e lindsay@westlangtonlosdge.
co.uk
w westlangtonlodge.co.uk

### EDALE
Derbyshire

**Edale YHA ★★** *Hostel*
Rowland Cote, Nether Booth,
Hope Valley S33 7ZH
t 0870 770 5808

**Stonecroft Country Guest House ★★★★**
*Bed & Breakfast*
GOLD AWARD
Stonecroft, Grindsbrook, Hope
Valley S33 7ZA
t (01433) 670262
e stonecroftdale@aol.com
w stonecroftguesthouse.co.uk

### EDWINSTOWE
Nottinghamshire

**Sherwood Forest YHA
★★★★** *Hostel*
Forest Corner, Mansfield
NG21 9RN
t (01623) 825794

### ELMESTHORPE
Leicestershire

**Badgers Mount ★★★★**
*Guest House* SILVER AWARD
6 Station Road, Elmesthorpe,
Hinckley LE9 7SG
t (01455) 848161
e info@badgersmount.com
w badgersmount.com

### ELTON
Derbyshire

**Hawthorn Cottage ★★★★★**
*Guest Accommodation*
SILVER AWARD
Well Street, Elton, Matlock
DE4 2BY
t (01629) 650372
w hawthorncottage-elton.co.
uk

**Homestead Farm ★★★★**
*Farmhouse*
Main Street, Elton, Matlock
DE4 2BW
t (01629) 650359
w homesteadfarm.co.uk

### EMPINGHAM
Rutland

**Shacklewell Lodge ★★★★**
*Bed & Breakfast*
Stamford Road, Empingham,
Oakham LE15 8QQ
t (01780) 460646
e shacklewell@hotmail.com

**The Wilderness B&B
★★★★★**
*Guest Accommodation*
SILVER AWARD
Main Street, Empingham,
Oakham LE15 8PS
t (01780) 460180
e dearden@empingham.fsnet.
co.uk
w rutnet.co.uk/wilderness

### EPWORTH
Lincolnshire

**Albion House Bed and Breakfast ★★★**
*Bed & Breakfast*
Albion Hill, Doncaster
DN9 1HD
t (01427) 872451
e albionhousebandb@aol.com

**Red Lion Coaching Inn ★★★**
*Inn*
Market Place, Epworth,
Doncaster DN9 1EU
t (01427) 872208
e redlionepworth@tiscali.co.
uk
w redlionepworth.co.uk

**Wisteria Cottage ★★★★**
*Bed & Breakfast*
10 Belton Road, Doncaster
DN9 1JL
t (01427) 873988
e wisteriacottage@hotmail.
com
w wisteriacottage.org.uk

### ETWALL
Derbyshire

**The Barn Retreat ★★★**
*Guest Accommodation*
Tara Centre, Ashe Hall, Derby
DE65 6HT
t 07875 250716
e relax@thebarnretreat.co.uk
w thebarnretreat.co.uk

### EYAM
Derbyshire

**Crown Cottage ★★★★**
*Guest Accommodation*
Main Road, Eyam, Hope Valley
S32 5QW
t (01433) 630858
e janet@eatonfold.demon.co.
uk
w crown-cottage.co.uk

**YHA Bretton ★★** *Hostel*
Bretton, Eyam, Hope Valley
S32 5QD
t 0870 770 5720
e bretton@yha.org.uk
w yha.org.uk

**YHA Eyam ★★★** *Hostel*
Hawkhill Road, Eyam, Hope
Valley S32 5QP
t (01433) 630335
e eyam@yha.org.uk
w yha.org.uk

### EYDON
Northamptonshire

**Crockwell Farm ★★★★**
*Farmhouse* SILVER AWARD
Eydon, Daventry NN11 3QA
t (01327) 361358
e info@crockwellfarm.co.uk
w crockwellfarm.co.uk

### FAIRFIELD
Derbyshire

**Barms Farm ★★★★★**
*Bed & Breakfast*
SILVER AWARD
Fairfield Common, Buxton
SK17 7HW
t (01298) 77723
e barmsfarm@aol.com
w barmsfarm.co.uk

### FENNY BENTLEY
Derbyshire

**Cairn Grove ★★★★**
*Guest Accommodation*
Ashes Lane, Fenny Bentley,
Ashbourne DE6 1LD
t (01335) 350538
e cairngrove@supanet.com
w cairngrove.co.uk

**Millfields ★★★**
*Bed & Breakfast*
Fenny Bentley, Ashbourne
DE6 1LA
t (01335) 350454
w millfieldsbandb.co.uk

### FISKERTON
Lincolnshire

**The Old Tannery ★★★★**
*Bed & Breakfast*
Diamond House, Ferry Road,
Fiskerton, Lincoln LN3 4HU
t (01522) 595956

### GAINSBOROUGH
Lincolnshire

**The Beckett Arms ★★★** *Inn*
25 High Street, Corringham
DN21 5QP
t (01427) 838201

### GAYTON LE MARSH
Lincolnshire

**Westbrook House ★★★★**
*Bed & Breakfast*
Main Street, Gayton le Marsh,
Alford LN13 0NW
t (01507) 450624
e westbrook_house@hotmail.
com
w bestbookwestbrook.co.uk

### GLOSSOP
Derbyshire

**Avondale**
Rating Applied For
*Guest House*
28 Woodhead Road, Glossop
SK13 7RH
t (01457) 853132
e margaret@avondale28.plus.
com
w avondale-guesthouse.co.uk

### GOADBY
Leicestershire

**The Hollies ★★★**
*Guest Accommodation*
Goadby, Leicester LE7 9EE
t (0116) 259 8301

### GRANGEMILL
Derbyshire

**Middlehills Farm ★★★**
*Guest Accommodation*
Grange Mill, Matlock DE4 4HY
t (01629) 650368
e l.lomas@btinternet.com

### GRANTHAM
Lincolnshire

**Albany Guest House ★★★★**
*Bed & Breakfast*
84 North Parade, Grantham
NG31 8AU
t (01476) 561119
e enquiry@albany-
guesthouse.co.uk
w albany-guesthouse.co.uk

**The Cedars ★★★★**
*Bed & Breakfast*
Low Road, Barrowby,
Grantham NG32 1DL
t (01476) 563400
e pbcbennett@mac.com

**The Red House ★★★★**
*Guest House*
74 North Parade, Grantham
NG31 8AN
t (01476) 579869
e enquiry@red-house.com
w red-house.com/

---

**York House** ★★★★
*Bed & Breakfast*
Bourne Road, Colsterworth
NG33 5JE
t (01476) 861955
e rkyorkhouse@dsl.pipex.com
w yorkhousebnb.co.uk/
🖼️🖊️

### GREAT BOWDEN
### Leicestershire

**Langton Brook Farm** ★★★★
*Farmhouse*
Langton Road, Great Bowden,
Market Harborough LE16 7EZ
t (01858) 545730
e mervyn@langtonbrook.
freeserve.co.uk
w langtonbrookfarm.com

### GREAT CASTERTON
### Rutland

**Sandon Barn** ★★★★
*Guest House*
Casterton Road, Stamford
PE9 4BP
t (01780) 757784
e jane.woodhouse@virgin.net

### GREAT DALBY
### Leicestershire

**Dairy Farm** ★★★ *Farmhouse*
8 Burrough End, Great Dalby,
Melton Mowbray LE14 2EW
t (01664) 562783

### GREAT LONGSTONE
### Derbyshire

**The Forge House** ★★★★
*Bed & Breakfast*
SILVER AWARD
Main Street, Great Longstone
DE45 1TF
t (01629) 640735
e emma@theforgehouse.co.uk
w theforgehouse.co.uk

### GRINGLEY ON THE HILL
### Nottinghamshire

**Gringley Hall** ★★★★
*Guest Accommodation*
Mill Road, Gringley-on-the-Hill
DN10 4QT
t (01777) 817262
e dulce@gringleyhall.fsnet.co.
uk

### GUILSBOROUGH
### Northamptonshire

**Lodge Farm** ◆◆◆◆
*Guest Accommodation*
GOLD AWARD
West Haddon Road,
Guilsborough, Northampton
NN6 8QE
t (01604) 740392
w lodgefarmbedandbreakfast.
co.uk

### HABROUGH
### North East Lincolnshire

**Church Farm** ★★★★
*Guest Accommodation*
SILVER AWARD
Immingham Road, Immingham
DN40 3BD
t (01469) 576190

### HACKTHORN
### Lincolnshire

**Honeyholes** ★★★
*Farmhouse*
South Farm, Hackthorn
LN2 3PW
t (01673) 861868
e dgreen8234@aol.com

### HARRINGTON
### Northamptonshire

**Church Farm Lodge** ★★★★
*Guest Accommodation*
Harrington NN6 9NU
t (01536) 713320
e info@churchfarmlodge.com
w churchfarmlodge.com

### HARTINGTON
### Derbyshire

**Bank Top Farm** ★★★★
*Farmhouse*
Pilsbury Lane, Hartington,
Buxton SK17 0AD
t (01298) 84205
e jane@banktophartington.
freeserve.co.uk

**The Hayloft** ★★★★
*Guest Accommodation*
Sennilow Farm, Church Street,
Buxton SK17 0AW
t (01298) 84358
e hartington.hayloft@ii2.com
w hartingtonhayloft.co.uk

**Wolfscote Grange Farm**
★★★★ *Farmhouse*
Hartington, Buxton SK17 0AX
t (01298) 84342
e wolfscote@btinternet.com
w wolfscotegrangecottages.co.
uk

**YHA Hartington Hall**
★★★★ *Hostel*
Hartington, Buxton SK17 0AT
t 0870 770 5848
w yha.org.uk
🖼️🖊️

### HATHERSAGE
### Derbyshire

**Cannon Croft** ★★★★
*Bed & Breakfast*
GOLD AWARD
Cannonfields, Hathersage,
Hope Valley S32 1AG
t (01433) 650005
e soates@cannoncroft.
fsbusiness.co.uk
w cannoncroft.fsbusiness.co.
uk

**The Plough Inn** ★★★★ *Inn*
SILVER AWARD
Leadmill Bridge, Hathersage,
Hope Valley S32 1BA
t (01433) 650319

**Polly's B&B** ★★★★
*Bed & Breakfast*
Cannonfields, Hope Valley
S32 1AG
t (01433) 650110

**YHA Hathersage** ★★ *Hostel*
The Hollies, Castleton Road,
Hope Valley S32 1EH
t 0870 770 5852
w yha.org.uk
🖼️🖊️

### HAXEY
### Lincolnshire

**The Loco** ★★★★ *Inn*
31-33 Church Street,
Doncaster DN9 2HY
t (01427) 752879
e info@thelocohaxey.co.uk
w thelocohaxey.co.uk

### HEATH
### Derbyshire

**Stainsby Mill Farm** ★★★
*Farmhouse*
Stainsby, Heath, Chesterfield
S44 5RW
t (01246) 850288

### HINTON IN THE HEDGES
### Northamptonshire

**The Old Rectory** ★★★
*Bed & Breakfast*
Hinton-in-the-Hedges, Brackley
NN13 5NG
t (01280) 706807
e lavinia@lavinia.demon.co.uk
w northamptonshire.co.uk/
hotels/oldrectory.htm

**Two Hoots** ★★★★
*Bed & Breakfast*
The Green, Hinton-in-the-
Hedges, Brackley NN13 5NG
t (01280) 701220
e louiewithers@aol.com
w northamptonshire.co.uk/
hotels/twohoots.htm

### HOLBEACH
### Lincolnshire

**Cackle Hill House** ★★★★
*Bed & Breakfast*
SILVER AWARD
Cackle Hill Lane, Holbeach
PE12 8BS
t (01406) 426721
e cacklehillhouse@farming.co.
uk

**Ecklinville B&B** ★★★★
*Bed & Breakfast*
34 Fen Road, Holbeach,
Spalding PE12 8QA
t (01406) 423625
e info@poachersden.com
w poachersden.com
🖼️🖊️🖊️

### HOLBECK
### Nottinghamshire

**Browns** ★★★★★
*Bed & Breakfast*
GOLD AWARD
The Old Orchard Cottage,
Holbeck, Worksop S80 3NF
t (01909) 720659
e browns@holbeck.fsnet.co.
uk
w brownsholbeck.co.uk
🖼️

### HOLLINGTON
### Derbyshire

**Reevsmoor** ★★★★
*Bed & Breakfast*
Hoargate Lane, Hollington,
Ashbourne DE6 3AG
t (01335) 330318
w smoothhound.co.uk

### HOLMESFIELD
### Derbyshire

**Carpenter House** ★★★★
*Bed & Breakfast*
Cordwell Lane, Millthorpe,
Chesterfield S18 7WH
t (0114) 289 0307

### HOLYMOORSIDE
### Derbyshire

**Mardon House** ★★★★★
*Guest Accommodation*
SILVER AWARD
Holymoor Road, Holymoorside,
Chesterfield S42 7DS
t (01246) 568708
e linda@xpti.co.uk
w mardonhouse.co.uk

### HOPE
### Derbyshire

**Causeway House B&B** ★★★
*Bed & Breakfast*
Back Street, Castleton, Hope
Valley S33 8WE
t (01433) 623291
e steynberg@btinternet.com
w causewayhouse.co.uk
🖼️🖊️

**Underleigh House** ★★★★★
*Guest Accommodation*
GOLD AWARD
Off Edale Road, Hope, Hope
Valley S33 6RF
t (01433) 621372
e info@underleighhouse.co.uk
w underleighhouse.co.uk
🖼️

**Woodbine B&B** ★★★
*Guest House*
18 Castleton Road, Hope
Valley S33 6RD
t 07778 113882
🖼️🖊️

### HOPE VALLEY
### Derbyshire

**The Chequers Inn** ★★★★
*Inn* SILVER AWARD
Froggatt Edge, Hope Valley
S32 3ZJ
t (01433) 630231
e info@chequers-froggatt.com
w chequers-froggatt.com

**The Rambler Country House
Hotel** ★★★ *Inn*
Edale, Hope Valley S33 7ZA
t (01433) 670268

### HORNCASTLE
### Lincolnshire

**Bank Cottage B&B and Self
Catering** ★★★★
*Guest House*
16 Bank House, Horncastle
LN9 5BW
t (01507) 526666
e horncastleinfo@e-lindsey.
gov.uk
w bankcottage-guesthouse.
com

### HORSLEY
### Derbyshire

**Horsley Lodge** ★★★★
*Guest Accommodation*
SILVER AWARD
Smalley Mill Road, Horsley,
Derby DE21 5BL
t (01332) 780838
e enquiries@horsleylodge.co.
uk
w horsleylodge.co.uk

## HUSBANDS BOSWORTH
Leicestershire

**Mrs Armitage's B&B ★★**
*Bed & Breakfast*
31-33 High Street, Husbands
Bosworth, Lutterworth
LE17 6LJ
t   (01858) 880066

## IDRIDGEHAY
Derbyshire

**Millbank House ★★★**
*Guest Accommodation*
Idridgehay, Nr Wirksworth,
Matlock DE56 2SH
t   (01629) 823161
e   riverdale@clara.co.uk

## KETTERING
Northamptonshire

**2 Wilkie Close ★★★★**
*Bed & Breakfast*
SILVER AWARD
Kettering NN15 7RD
t   (01536) 310270
e   roxmere@aol.com

**Dairy Farm ★★★★**
*Farmhouse*
Cranford St Andrew, Kettering
NN14 4AQ
t   (01536) 330273

## KEXBY
Lincolnshire

**The Grange ★★★** *Farmhouse*
Kexby, Gainsborough
DN21 5PJ
t   (01427) 788265

## KEYWORTH
Nottinghamshire

**Vine Lodge ★★★★**
*Bed & Breakfast*
8 Highbury Road, Keyworth,
Nottingham NG12 5JB
t   (0115) 937 3944
e   enquiries@vine-lodge.co.uk
w   vine-lodge.co.uk

## KING'S CLIFFE
Northamptonshire

**19 West Street ★★★★**
*Bed & Breakfast*
King's Cliffe, Peterborough
PE8 6XB
t   (01780) 470365
e   kjhl_dixon@hotmail.com
w   kingjohnhuntinglodge.co.uk

## KIRKBY-ON-BAIN
Lincolnshire

**Rose Cottage B&B ★★★★**
*Guest Accommodation*
Wharf Lane, Woodhall Spa
LN10 6YW
t   (01526) 354932
e   info@rosecottagebandb.net
w   rosecottagebandb.net

## KIRMINGTON
Lincolnshire

**Blink Bonny Bed and
Breakfast ★★★** *Guest House*
Grimsby Road, Kirmington
DN39 6YJ
t   (01652) 680610
e   terry.watson1@btinternet.
com
w   blinkbonnybedandbreakfast.
co.uk

## KNAPTOFT
Leicestershire

**Bruntingthorpe Farmhouse
B&B ★★★★** *Farmhouse*
Knaptoft House Farm & The
Greenway, Bruntingthorpe
Road, Lutterworth LE17 6PR
t   (0116) 247 8388
e   info@knaptofthousefarm.
com
w   knaptoft.com

## KNIPTON
Leicestershire

**Manners Arms ★★★★**
*Restaurant with Rooms*
Croxton Road, Knipton,
Grantham NG32 1RH
t   (01476) 879222
e   info@mannersarms.com
w   mannersarms.com

## LANGWORTH
Lincolnshire

**The Blackbirds ★★★**
*Guest House*
Wragby Road, Langworth
LN3 5DH
t   (01522) 754404
e   matthew.nellist@
theblackbirds.co.uk
w   theblackbirds.co.uk

**Ferry House Farm ★★★**
*Bed & Breakfast*
Low Barlings, Langworth
LN3 5DG
t   (01522) 751939
e   ifleet@barlings.demon.co.uk
w   barlings.demon.co.uk

## LAXTON
Nottinghamshire

**Dovecote Inn** *Inn*
Moorhouse Road, Laxton,
Newark NG22 0NU
t   (01777) 871586
e   lisashepardo@yahoo.com

**Lilac Farm ★★★**
*Guest House*
Laxton, Newark NG22 0NX
t   (01777) 870376

**Manor Farm ★★★**
*Farmhouse*
Moorhouse Road, Laxton,
Newark NG22 0NU
t   (01777) 870417

## LEADENHAM
Lincolnshire

**George Hotel ★★★** *Inn*
20 High Street, Leadenham
LN5 0PN
t   (01400) 272251
e   the-george-hotel@willgoose.
freeserve.co.uk

## LEICESTER
Leicestershire

**Abinger Guest House ★★★**
*Guest House*
175 Hinckley Road, Leicester
LE3 0TF
t   (0116) 255 4674
e   abinger@btinternet.com
w   leicesterguest.co.uk

**Castle Park ★★★**
*Guest Accommodation*
12 Millstone Lane, Leicester
LE1 5JN
t   (0116) 251 1000
e   castleparkhotel@tiscali.co.uk
w   castleparkhotel.com

**Croft Hotel ★★★**
*Guest House*
3 Stanley Road, Leicester
LE2 1RF
t   (0116) 270 3220
e   crofthotel@hotmail.com
w   crofthotel-web.co.uk

**Glenfield Lodge ★**
*Guest Accommodation*
4 Glenfield Road, Leicester
LE3 6AP
t   (0116) 262 7554
e   glenleic@aol.com
w   glenfieldlodge.co.uk

**The Haynes ★★★★**
*Guest House*
185 Uppingham Road,
Leicester LE5 4BQ
t   (0116) 276 8973
e   hayneshotel@yahoo.co.uk

**Spindle Lodge Hotel ★★★**
*Guest House*
2 West Walk, Leicester
LE1 7NA
t   (0116) 233 8801

**Wondai B&B ★★★**
*Bed & Breakfast*
47-49 Main Street, Newtown
Linford, Leicester LE6 0AE
t   (01530) 242728

## LINCOLN
Lincolnshire

**Aaron Whisby Guest House
★★★** *Guest House*
262 West Parade, Lincoln
LN1 1LY
t   (01522) 526930
e   aaron-whisby@hotmail.co.uk

**Creston Villa Guest House
★★★★** *Guest House*
SILVER AWARD
27 St Catherines, Lincoln
LN5 8LW
t   (01522) 872511
e   info@crestonvilla.co.uk
w   crestonvilla.co.uk

**Damon's Motel ★★★★**
*Guest Accommodation*
997 Doddington Road, Lincoln
LN6 3SE
t   (01522) 887733

**Duke William House ★★★**
*Inn*
44 Bailgate, Lincoln LN1 3AP
t   (01522) 533351
e   enquiries@dukewilliam.com
w   dukewilliam.com

**Good Lane Bed & Breakfast
★★★** *Bed & Breakfast*
31 Good Lane, Lincoln
LN1 3EH
t   (01522) 542994
e   sue@goodlane.co.uk
w   goodlane.co.uk

**Hamilton Hotel ★★**
*Guest Accommodation*
2 Hamilton Road, Lincoln
LN5 8ED
t   (01522) 528243
w   hamiltonhotel.co.uk

**Lincoln YHA ★** *Hostel*
77 South Park, Lincoln LN5 8ES
t   (01522) 522076
e   lincoln@yha.org.uk
w   yha.org.uk

**Manor Farm Stables ★★★★**
*Bed & Breakfast*
Broxholme, Lincoln LN1 2NG
t   (01522) 704220
e   pfieldson@lineone.net
w   manorfarmstables.co.uk

**The Old Bakery Restaurant
with Rooms ★★★★**
*Restaurant with Rooms*
SILVER AWARD
26/28 Burton Road, Lincoln
LN1 3LB
t   (01522) 576057
e   enquiries@theold-bakery.co.
uk
w   theold-bakery.co.uk

**Old Rectory Guest House
★★★** *Guest House*
19 Newport, Lincoln LN1 3DQ
t   (01522) 514774

**The Old Vicarage ★★★★**
*Guest Accommodation*
East Street, Nettleham, Lincoln
LN2 2SL
t   (01522) 750819
e   susan@oldvic.net
w   oldvic.net

**Savill Guest House ★★★★**
*Guest Accommodation*
203 Yarborough Road, Lincoln
LN1 3NQ
t   (01522) 523261
e   info@savillguesthouse.co.uk
w   savillguesthouse.co.uk

**Welbeck Cottage B&B
★★★★** *Bed & Breakfast*
19 Meadow Lane, South
Hykeham, Lincoln LN6 9PF
t   (01522) 692669
e   maggied@hotmail.com

**Wheelwrights Cottage
★★★★** *Bed & Breakfast*
Haddington, Lincoln LN5 9EF
t   (01522) 788154
e   dawn.dunning2@
btopenworld.com

**The Wren Guesthouse ★★★**
*Guest House*
22 St Catherines, Lincoln
LN5 8LY
t   (01522) 537949
e   kateatthewren@aol.com
w   wrenguesthouse.co.uk

## LINTON
Derbyshire

**The Manor ★★★★**
*Guest Accommodation*
SILVER AWARD
Hillside Road, Linton,
Swadlincote DE12 6RA
t   (01283) 761177
e   themanor@ukonline.co.uk

## LITTLE BYTHAM
Lincolnshire

**The Willoughby Arms
★★★★** *Inn*
Station Road, Grantham
NG33 4RA
t   (01780) 410276
w   willoughbyarms.co.uk

## LITTLE CAWTHORPE
Lincolnshire

**The Royal Oak Inn – The Splash** ★★★★ *Inn*
Watery Lane, Little Cawthorpe, Louth LN11 8LZ
t (01507) 600750
e info@royaloaksplash.co.uk
w royaloaksplash.co.uk

## LITTON
Derbyshire

**Beacon House** ★★★★
*Farmhouse*
Litton, Nr Tideswell, Buxton SK17 8QP
t (01298) 871752
e laurj117@gmail.com
w beaconhse.co.uk

**Hall Farm House** ★★★★
*Bed & Breakfast*
SILVER AWARD
Litton, Buxton SK17 8QP
t (01298) 872172
e jfscott@waitrose.com
w users.waitrose.com/~jfscott

## LONG BUCKBY
Northamptonshire

**Murcott Mill** ★★★
*Farmhouse*
Murcott, Long Buckby, Northampton NN6 7QR
t (01327) 842236
e carrie.murcottmill@virgin.net
w murcottmill.com

## LONG CLAWSON
Leicestershire

**Elms Farm** ★★★★
*Bed & Breakfast*
52 East End, Long Clawson, Melton Mowbray LE14 4NG
t (01664) 822395
e elmsfarm@whittard.net
w whittard.net

## LOUGHBOROUGH
Leicestershire

**Charnwood Lodge** ★★★★
*Guest House*
136 Leicester Road, Loughborough LE11 2AQ
t (01509) 211120
e charnwoodlodge@charwat.freeserve.co.uk
w charnwoodlodge.com

**The De Montfort** ★★
*Guest House*
88 Leicester Road, Loughborough LE11 2AQ
t (01509) 216061
e thedemontforthotel@amserve.com
w smoothhound.co.uk/hotels/demont

**Forest Rise Hotel** ★★★
*Guest House*
55-57 Forest Road, Loughborough LE11 3NW
t (01509) 215928

**Garendon Park Hotel** ★★★
*Guest House*
92 Leicester Road, Loughborough LE11 2AQ
t (01509) 236557
e info@garendonparkhotel.co.uk
w morningtonweb.com/garendon

**Highbury Guest House**
★★★ *Guest House*
146 Leicester Road, Loughborough LE11 2AQ
t (01509) 230545
e cosmo@thehighburyguesthouse.co.uk
w thehighburyguesthouse.co.uk

**Holywell House** ★★
*Guest House*
Leicester Road, Loughborough LE11 2AG
t (01509) 267891
e lezanddez@holywell.here.co.uk
w holywell.here.co.uk

**Lane End Cottage** ★★★★
*Bed & Breakfast*
SILVER AWARD
45 School Lane, Old Woodhouse, Loughborough LE12 8UJ
t (01509) 890706

**The Mountsorrel** ★★★★
*Guest House*
217 Loughborough Road, Mountsorrel, Loughborough LE12 7AR
t (01509) 412627
e info@mountsorrelhotel.co.uk
w mountsorrelhotel.co.uk

**New Life Guest House** ★★★
*Guest House*
121 Ashby Road, Loughborough LE11 3AB
t (01509) 216699
e jean-of-newlife@ntlworld.com
w smoothhound.co.uk/hotels/newlife

**Peachnook Guest House** ★★
*Guest Accommodation*
154 Ashby Road, Loughborough LE11 3AG
t (01509) 264390

## LOUTH
Lincolnshire

**Masons Arms** ★★★ *Inn*
Cornmarket, Louth LN11 9PY
t (01507) 609525
e info@themasons.co.uk
w themasons.co.uk

**Nutty Cottage Guest House**
★★★★ *Bed & Breakfast*
Nutty Cottage, Legbourne Road, Louth LN11 8LQ
t (01507) 601766
e janeandmike23@tiscali.co.uk

**The Old Rectory** ★★★★
*Bed & Breakfast*
Muckton LN11 8NU
t (01507) 480608
e francis.warr@ntlworld.com
w louth-bedandbreakfast.co.uk

**The Travellers B&B** ★★★
*Guest House*
104-106 Upgate, Louth LN11 9HG
t (01507) 602765

## LUTTERWORTH
Leicestershire

**Ashlawn Country Guest House** ★★★★
*Guest Accommodation*
Ashlawn House, Church Lane, Dunton Bassett, Lutterworth LE17 5JZ
t (01455) 208277
e kate@ashlawnhouse.com
w ashlawnhouse.com

## LYDDINGTON
Rutland

**Marquess of Exeter** ★★★★
*Inn*
52 Main Street, Lyddington, Uppingham LE15 9LT
t (01572) 822477
e lynne@mulberrypubco.com

## MABLETHORPE
Lincolnshire

**Aura Lee Guest House** ★★★
*Guest House*
22 The Boulevard, Mablethorpe LN12 2AD
t (01507) 477660
e mccarthy@auralee.fsnet.co.uk
w auralee.co.uk

**Colours Guest House**
★★★★ *Guest House*
Queens Park Close, Mablethorpe LN12 2AS
t (01507) 473427
e info@coloursguesthouse.co.uk

**May House Bed & Breakfast**
★★★★ *Bed & Breakfast*
40 Long Acre, Mablethorpe LN12 1JF
t (01507) 473664
e mablethorpe@btinternet.com

**Myrtle Lodge** ★★★
*Guest House*
60 Victoria Road, Mablethorpe LN12 2AJ
t (01507) 472228
e myrtlelodge@aol.com
w myrtlelodge.co.uk

## MALTBY LE MARSH
Lincolnshire

**Farmhouse Bed and Breakfast** ★★★ *Farmhouse*
10 Watermill Lane, Toynton All Saints, Spilsby PE23 5AG
t (01790) 753416
e tojenwills@farmhouse10.fsnet.co.uk

## MANSFIELD
Nottinghamshire

**Blue Barn Farm** ★★★
*Farmhouse*
Langwith, Mansfield NG20 9JD
t (01623) 742248
e bluebarnfarm@supanet.com
w bluebarnfarm-notts.co.uk

## MANTON
Rutland

**Broccoli Bottom** ★★★★
*Bed & Breakfast*
SILVER AWARD
Wing Road, Manton, Oakham LE15 8SZ
t 07702 437102
e sally@udale.wanadoo.co.uk
w http://broccolibottom.mysite.wanadoo-members.co.uk

## MARKET HARBOROUGH
Leicestershire

**Honeypot Lane Bed & Breakfast** ★★★★
*Bed & Breakfast*
32 Honeypot Lane, Husbands Bosworth, Lutterworth LE17 6LY
t (01858) 880836
e bandb@honeypotlane.co.uk
w honeypotlane.co.uk

**Hunters Lodge** ★★★★
*Bed & Breakfast*
By Foxton Locks, Gumley, Market Harborough LE16 7RT
t (0116) 279 3744
e info@hunterslodgefoxton.co.uk
w hunterslodgefoxton.co.uk

**The White Horse Inn**
★★★★ *Inn*
1 Harborough Road, Market Harborough LE16 8PY
t (01858) 535268
e jane.difazio@btconnect.com

## MARKET RASEN
Lincolnshire

**Beechwood Guest House**
★★★★ *Guest House*
54 Willingham Road, Market Rasen LN8 3DX
t (01673) 844043
e beechwoodgh@aol.com
w beechwoodguesthouse.co.uk

**Little Owls** ★★★★
*Farmhouse*
North End Farm, Thornton Road, North Owersby LN8 3PP
t (01673) 828116
e littleowlsuk@yahoo.co.uk
w littleowls.com

**Redhurst B&B** ★★★
*Bed & Breakfast*
Redhurst, Holton cum Beckering, Market Rasen LN8 5NG
t (01673) 857927

**Waveney Cottage Guesthouse** ★★★★
*Bed & Breakfast*
Willingham Road, Market Rasen LN8 3DN
t (01673) 843236
e vacancies@waveneycottage.co.uk
w waveneycottage.co.uk

## MARSTON
Lincolnshire

**Gelston Grange Farm**
★★★★ *Farmhouse*
SILVER AWARD
Nr Marston, Grantham NG32 2AQ
t (01400) 250281

## MARTIN
Lincolnshire

**The Stables Studio ★★★★**
*Bed & Breakfast*
94 High Street, Martin
LN4 3QT
t  (01526) 378528
e  stablesstudio@homecall.co.
uk
w  stablesstudio.co.uk

## MATLOCK
Derbyshire

**Bank House ★★★★**
*Bed & Breakfast*
**SILVER AWARD**
12 Snitterton Road, Matlock
DE4 3LZ
t  (01629) 56101
e  jennyderbydales@hotmail.
com

**Cascades Gardens ★★★★★**
*Guest Accommodation*
Clatterway Hill, Bonsall,
Matlock DE4 2AH
t  (01629) 822464
e  nirvana@gotadsl.co.uk
w  cascadesgardens.com

**Riverbank House ★★★★**
*Guest House* **SILVER AWARD**
Derwent Avenue, Off Olde
English Road, Matlock DE4 3LX
t  (01629) 582593
e  bookings@riverbankhouse.
co.uk
w  riverbankhouse.co.uk

**Robertswood Country
House ★★★★★**
*Guest Accommodation*
**GOLD AWARD**
Farley Hill, Matlock DE4 3LL
t  (01629) 55642
e  robertswoodhouse@aol.com
w  robertswood.co.uk

**Rosegarth ★★★★**
*Bed & Breakfast*
57 Dimple Road, Matlock
DE4 3JX
t  (01629) 56294
e  john@crich.ndo.co.uk
w  rosegarthmatlock.co.uk
▨ ▨

**Sheriff Lodge ★★★★**
*Guest House* **GOLD AWARD**
Dimple Road, Matlock DE4 3JX
t  (01629) 760760
e  info@sherifflodge.co.uk
w  sherifflodge.co.uk

**Town Head Farmhouse
★★★★** *Guest House*
**SILVER AWARD**
70 High Street, Bonsall,
Matlock DE4 2AR
t  (01629) 823762
w  townheadfarmhouse.co.uk

**Yew Tree Cottage ★★★★**
*Guest Accommodation*
The Knoll, Tansley, Matlock
DE4 5FP
t  (01629) 583862
e  enquiries@
yewtreecottagebb.co.uk
w  yewtreecottagebb.co.uk

## MATLOCK BATH
Derbyshire

**Ashdale Guest House ★★★**
*Guest Accommodation*
92 North Parade, Matlock Bath,
Matlock DE4 3NS
t  (01629) 57826
e  ashdale@matlockbath.fsnet.
co.uk
w  ashdaleguesthouse.co.uk

**The Firs ★★★**
*Guest Accommodation*
180 Dale Road, Matlock
DE4 3PS
t  (01629) 582426
e  bernhard@thefirs180.
demon.co.uk

**Fountain Villa ★★★★**
*Guest Accommodation*
86 North Parade, Matlock Bath,
Matlock DE4 3NS
t  (01629) 56195
e  enquiries@fountainvilla.co.
uk
w  fountainvilla.co.uk

**Sunnybank Guest House Ltd
★★★★**
*Guest Accommodation*
**SILVER AWARD**
37 Clifton Road, Matlock Bath,
Matlock DE4 3PW
t  (01629) 584621
e  sunnybank.matlock@
btinternet.com
w  matlockbedandbreakfast.co.
uk

## MEDBOURNE
Leicestershire

**Homestead House ★★★★**
*Bed & Breakfast*
**SILVER AWARD**
5 Ashley Road, Medbourne,
Market Harborough LE16 8DL
t  (01858) 565724
e  june@homesteadhouse.co.
uk
w  homesteadhouse.co.uk

## MELTON MOWBRAY
Leicestershire

**Hall Farm ★★★★** *Farmhouse*
1 Main Street, Holwell, Melton
Mowbray LE14 4SZ
t  (01664) 444275
e  hall_farm1@yahoo.co.uk
w  hallfarmholwell.co.uk

**Hillside House ★★★★**
*Bed & Breakfast*
27 Melton Road, Burton Lazars,
Melton Mowbray LE14 2UR
t  (01664) 566312
e  hillhs27@aol.com
w  hillside-house.co.uk

**The Lodge ★★★★**
*Bed & Breakfast*
Melton Road, Scalford, Melton
Mowbray LE14 4UB
t  (01664) 444205
e  rchfel@aol.com
w  geocities.com/
thelodgebandb

## MIDDLETON
Northamptonshire

**Valley View ★★★**
*Bed & Breakfast*
3 Camsdale Walk, Middleton,
Market Harborough LE16 8YR
t  (01536) 770874

## MIDDLETON-BY-
YOULGREAVE
Derbyshire

**Castle Farm ★★★★**
*Farmhouse*
Middleton-by-Youlgreave,
Bakewell DE45 1LS
t  (01629) 636746

**Castle Farm Camping Barn**
*Bunkhouse*
Middleton-by-Youlgreave,
Bakewell DE45 1LS
t  (01629) 636746

**Smerrill Grange Farm ★★★**
*Farmhouse*
Middleton-by-Youlgreave,
Bakewell DE45 1LQ
t  (01629) 636232

## MILLER'S DALE
Derbyshire

**YHA Ravenstor ★★★** *Hostel*
Millers Dale, Buxton SK17 8SS
t  0870 770 6008
e  ravenstor@yha.org.uk
w  yha.org.uk
▨ ▨

## MILLTHORPE, HOLMESFIELD
Derbyshire

**Cordwell House ★★★★**
*Bed & Breakfast*
Cordwell Lane, Millthorpe,
Dronfield S18 7WH
t  (0114) 289 0271

## MONSAL HEAD
Derbyshire

**Ruskins ★★★★**
*Guest Accommodation*
Monsal Head, Bakewell
DE45 1NL
t  (01629) 640125
e  ruskins@btinternet.co.uk

## MONYASH
Derbyshire

**Arbor Low B&B ★★★**
*Farmhouse*
Arbor Low, Upper Oldhams
Farm, Bakewell DE45 1JS
t  (01629) 636337
e  nicola@arborlow.co.uk
w  arborlow.co.uk

## MUCKTON
Lincolnshire

**The Old Rectory ★★★★**
*Bed & Breakfast*
South Willingham LN8 6NG
t  (01507) 313584
e  paul&maureen@the-old-
rectory.info
w  uniquevenues.org.uk

## MUMBY
Lincolnshire

**Brambles ★★★**
*Guest Accommodation*
Occupation Lane, Alford
LN13 9JU
t  (01507) 490174
e  suescrimshaw@btinternet.
com
▨ ▨

## NASSINGTON
Northamptonshire

**Fairlands ★★★★**
*Bed & Breakfast*
35 Church Street, Nassington,
Peterborough PE8 6QG
t  (01780) 783603
e  marriottann@hotmail.com

**Sunnyside ★★★**
*Bed & Breakfast*
62 Church Street, Nassington,
Peterborough PE8 6QG
t  (01780) 782864

## NETHER HEYFORD
Northamptonshire

**Heyford Bed and Breakfast
★★** *Bed & Breakfast*
27 Church Street, Nether
Heyford NN7 3LH
t  (01327) 340872
e  info@heyfordguesthouse.co.
uk
w  heyfordguesthouse.co.uk

## NETTLETON
Lincolnshire

**Nettleton Lodge Inn ★★★**
*Guest Accommodation*
Off Moortown Road (B1205),
Nettleton LN7 6HX
t  (01472) 851829
e  pubinthewood@btinternet.
com
w  visitlincolnshire.com

## NEVILL HOLT
Leicestershire

**Medbourne Grange ★★★★**
*Farmhouse*
Drayton Road, Nevill Holt,
Market Harborough LE16 8EF
t  (01858) 565249

## NEW MILLS
Derbyshire

**Pack Horse Inn ★★★★** *Inn*
Mellor Road, New Mills, High
Peak SK22 4QQ
t  (01663) 742365
e  info@packhorseinn.co.uk
w  packhorseinn.co.uk

## NEW WALTHAM
North East Lincolnshire

**Peaks Top Farm ★★★★**
*Farmhouse*
Hewitts Avenue, Grimsby
DN36 4RS
t  (01472) 812941
e  lmclayton@tinyworld.co.uk

## NEWARK
Nottinghamshire

**Brecks Cottage Bed and
Breakfast ★★★★**
*Guest Accommodation*
Green Lane, Newark NG23 6LZ
t  (01636) 822445

**Crosshill House Bed and
Breakfast ★★★★**
*Guest Accommodation*
**SILVER AWARD**
Crosshill House, Laxton,
Newark NG22 0NT
t  (01777) 871953

**Ivy Farm B&B ★★★**
*Farmhouse*
Newark Road, Barnby-in-the-
Willows, Newark NG24 2SL
t  (01636) 672568
e  clare@ivyfarm.f9.co.uk
w  ivyfarm.f9.co.uk
▨

## NEWTON SOLNEY
### Derbyshire

**The Unicorn Inn** ★★★ *Inn*
Repton Road, Burton-on-Trent
DE15 0SG
t (01283) 703324
e unicorn.newtonsolney@
barbox.net
w unicorn-inn.co.uk

## NORTH COTES
### Lincolnshire

**The Fleece Inn** ★★★ *Inn*
Lock Road, North Cotes,
Grimsby DN36 5UP
t (01472) 388233

## NORTH HYKEHAM
### Lincolnshire

**The Gables Guest House**
★★★★ *Guest House*
546 Newark Road, North
Hykeham, Lincoln LN6 9NG
t (01522) 829102
e info@gablesguesthouse.com
w gablesguesthouse.com

## NORTH KILWORTH
### Leicestershire

**The Old Rectory** ★★★★
*Bed & Breakfast*
**SILVER AWARD**
Church Street, Lutterworth
LE17 6EZ
t (01858) 881130
e info@oldrectorybandb.co.uk
w oldrectorybandb.co.uk

## NORTH KYME
### Lincolnshire

**Old Coach House Motel &
Cafe** ★★★★
*Guest Accommodation*
Church Lane, North Kyme,
Lincoln LN4 4DJ
t (01526) 861465
e barbara@motel-plus.co.uk
w motel-plus.co.uk

## NORTH SOMERCOTES
### Lincolnshire

**Leslie Cottage Bed and
Breakfast** ★★★★
*Bed & Breakfast*
Jubilee Road, North
Somercotes LN11 7LH
t (01507) 358734
e lesliecottage@msn.com
w lesliecottage.co.uk

## NORTH WINGFIELD
### Derbyshire

**South View** ★★★
*Bed & Breakfast*
95 Church Lane, North
Wingfield, Chesterfield
S42 5HR
t (01246) 850091
e jackie.hopkinson@virgin.net

## NORTHAMPTON
### Northamptonshire

**The Aarandale Regent** ★★
*Guest House*
6-8 Royal Terrace, Barrack
Road (A508), Northampton
NN1 3RF
t (01604) 631096
e info@aarandale.co.uk
w aarandale.co.uk

**Chapel Farmhouse** ♦♦♦
*Guest Accommodation*
Hanslope Road, Hartwell,
Northampton NN7 2EU
t (01908) 510220
e judysmith.asp@virgin.net

**Coton Lodge
Accommodation** ★★★★★
*Bed & Breakfast*
West Haddon Road,
Guilsborough, Northampton
NN6 8QE
t (01604) 740215
e jo@cotonlodge.co.uk
w cotonlodge.co.uk

**Lake House Bed and
Breakfast** ★★★★
*Bed & Breakfast*
Brixworth Hall Park, Brixworth,
Northampton NN6 9DE
t (01604) 880280
e rosemarytuckley@talktalk.
net
w brixworthlakehouse.com

**The Poplars** ★★★★
*Guest Accommodation*
Cross Street, Moulton
NN3 7RZ
t (01604) 643983
e info@thepoplarshotel.com
w thepoplarshotel.com

**Roade House Restaurant
and Hotel** ★★★★
*Restaurant with Rooms*
**SILVER AWARD**
16 High Street, Roade,
Northampton NN7 2NW
t (01604) 863372

## NORTON DISNEY
### Lincolnshire

**Brills Farm** ★★★★
*Farmhouse*
Brills Hill, Norton Disney,
Lincoln LN6 9JN
t (01636) 892311
e admin@brillsfarm-
bedandbreakfast.co.uk
w brillsfarm-bedandbreakfast.
co.uk

**River Farm house B&B**
★★★★ *Bed & Breakfast*
River Farm House, Clay Lane,
Lincoln LN6 9JS
t (01522) 788600
e amandajane500@aol.com

## NOTTINGHAM
### Nottinghamshire

**Acorn Hotel** ★★★
*Guest House*
4 Radcliffe Road, West Brigford
NG2 5FW
t (0115) 981 1297
e reservations@acorn-hotel.
co.uk
w acorn-hotel.co.uk

**Andrews Private Hotel**
★★★ *Guest Accommodation*
310 Queens Road, Beeston,
Nottingham NG9 1JA
t (0115) 925 4902
e andrews.hotel@ntlworld.
com
w s-h-systems.co.uk/hotels/
standrews.html

**Elm Bank Lodge** ★★★
*Bed & Breakfast*
9 Elm Bank, Mapperley Park,
Nottingham NG3 5AJ
t (0115) 962 5493
e elmbanklodge@aol.com

**Greenwood Lodge City
Guesthouse** ★★★★★
*Guest House* **GOLD AWARD**
5 Third Avenue, Sherwood
Rise, Nottingham NG7 6JH
t (0115) 962 1206

**Nelson and Railway Inn** ★★
*Inn*
Station Road, Kimberley,
Nottingham NG16 2NR
t (0115) 938 2177

**Orchard Cottage** ★★★★
*Bed & Breakfast*
Moor Cottages, Nottingham
Road, Trowell Moor,
Nottingham NG9 3PQ
t (0115) 928 0933
e orchardcottage.bandb@
virgin.net
w orchardcottages.com

**Yew Tree Grange** ★★★★
*Guest House*
2 Nethergate, Clifton Village,
Nottingham NG11 8NL
t (0115) 984 7562

## OAKHAM
### Rutland

**17 Northgate** ★★★★
*Bed & Breakfast*
Oakham LE15 6QR
t (01572) 759271
e dane@danegould.wanadoo.
co.uk
w 17northgate.co.uk

**Mayfield B&B** ★★★
*Bed & Breakfast*
19 Ashwell Road, Oakham
LE15 6QG
t (01572) 756656
e sgbruce@onetel.com

## OASBY
### Lincolnshire

**The Pinomar** ★★★★
*Bed & Breakfast*
Mill Lane, Oasby NG32 3ND
t (01529) 455400
e joturner@pinomar.fsnet.co.
uk

## OLD
### Northamptonshire

**Wold Farm** ★★★★
*Farmhouse* **SILVER AWARD**
Harrington Road, Old NN6 9RJ
t (01604) 781258
w woldfarm.co.uk/

## OSBOURNBY
### Lincolnshire

**Barn Gallery** ★★★★
*Bed & Breakfast*
**SILVER AWARD**
18 West Street, Osbournby
NG34 0DS
t (01529) 455631
e enquiries@barngallery.co.uk
w barngallery.co.uk

## OSGATHORPE
### Leicestershire

**Royal Oak House** ★★★
*Guest House*
20 Main Street, Osgathorpe,
Coalville LE12 9TA
t (01530) 222443

## OUNDLE
### Northamptonshire

**2 Benefield Road** ★★★★
*Bed & Breakfast*
Peterborough PE8 4ET
t (01832) 273953

**Ashworth House** ★★★★
*Bed & Breakfast*
75 West Street, Oundle
PE8 4EJ
t (01832) 275312
e sue@ashworthhouse.co.uk
w ashworthhouse.co.uk

**Castle Farm Guesthouse**
★★★★ *Guest House*
Fotheringhay, Peterborough
PE8 5HZ
t (01832) 226200

**Lilford Lodge Farm** ★★★★
*Farmhouse*
Barnwell, Oundle,
Peterborough PE8 5SA
t (01832) 272230
e trudy@lilford-lodge.demon.
co.uk
w lilford-lodge.demon.co.uk

**The Rowan House** ★★★★
*Bed & Breakfast*
45 Hillfield Road, Oundle,
Peterborough PE8 4QR
t (01832) 273252

## PAPPLEWICK
### Nottinghamshire

**Forest Farm** ★★ *Farmhouse*
Mansfield Road, Papplewick
NG15 8FL
t (0115) 963 2310

## PENTRICH
### Derbyshire

**Coney Grey Farm** ★★★
*Farmhouse*
Chesterfield Road, Pentrich,
Ripley DE5 3RF
t (01773) 833179

## QUENIBOROUGH
### Leicestershire

**Three Ways Farm** ★★★
*Farmhouse*
Melton Road, Queniborough,
Leicester LE7 3FN
t (0116) 260 0472

## REARSBY
### Leicestershire

**Manor Farm** ★★★
*Farmhouse*
Brookside, Rearsby, Melton
Mowbray LE7 4YB
t (01664) 424239
e manorfarmb.b@hotmail.co.
uk
w farmstayuk.co.uk

## REPTON
### Derbyshire

**Swallows Rest** ★★★★
*Bed & Breakfast*
29 High Street, Repton, Derby
DE65 6GD
t (01283) 702389

## RETFORD
### Nottinghamshire

**The Barns Country
Guesthouse** ★★★★
*Guest House*
Morton Farm, Babworth,
Retford DN22 8HA
t (01777) 706336
e enquiries@thebarns.co.uk

# East Midlands

**Bolham Manor** ★★★★
*Bed & Breakfast*
**SILVER AWARD**
Off Tiln Lane, Retford
DN22 9JG
t (01777) 703528
e pamandbutch@bolham-manor.com
w bolham-manor.com/

### RIPLEY
### Derbyshire

**Bowling Green Bed & Breakfast** ★★
*Bed & Breakfast*
Blacksmiths Croft, Ripley
DE5 8JL
t (01773) 742921

**Hellinside** ★★
*Bed & Breakfast*
1/3 Whitegates, Codnor,
Ripley DE5 9QD
t (01773) 742750
e hellinside@aol.com

**The Latte Lounge** ★★
*Guest Accommodation*
15 + 15a Church Street, Ripley
DE5 3BU
t (01773) 512000
e misscagarner@hotmail.com

### ROWSLEY
### Derbyshire

**The Old Station House**
★★★★ *Bed & Breakfast*
4 Chatsworth Road, Rowsley,
Matlock DE4 2EJ
t (01629) 732987

### RUCKLAND
### Lincolnshire

**Woodys Top Youth Hostel**
★★★ *Hostel*
Ruckland, Louth LN11 8RQ
t (01507) 533323
e woodystop@yha.org.uk
w yha.org.uk

### RUSKINGTON
### Lincolnshire

**Sunnyside Farm** ★★★
*Farmhouse*
Leasingham Lane, Ruskington,
Sleaford NG34 9AH
t (01526) 833010
e sunnyside_farm@btinternet.com
w sunnysidefarm.co.uk

### SAXILBY
### Lincolnshire

**Orchard Cottage** ★★★★
*Bed & Breakfast*
3 Orchard Lane, Saxilby
LN1 2HT
t (01522) 703192
e margaretallen@orchardcottage.org.uk
w smoothhound.co.uk/hotels/orchardcot.html

### SCALDWELL
### Northamptonshire

**The Old House Bed and Breakfast** ★★★★
*Bed & Breakfast*
East End, Scaldwell NN6 9LB
t (01604) 880359
e mrsv@scaldwell43.fsnet.co.uk
w the-oldhouse.co.uk

### SCALFORD
### Leicestershire

**Roberts Farm B&B** ★★★★★
*Bed & Breakfast*
**SILVER AWARD**
Church Street, Melton
Mowbray LE14 4DL
t (01664) 444730
e info@robertsfarm.co.uk
w robertsfarm.co.uk

### SCAMBLESBY
### Lincolnshire

**The Paddock at Scamblesby**
★★★★ *Bed & Breakfast*
**SILVER AWARD**
Old Main Road, Scamblesby,
Louth LN11 9XG
t 07787 998906
e steve@thepaddockatscamblesby.co.uk
w thepaddockatscamblesby.co.uk

### SCAWBY
### Lincolnshire

**The Old School** ◆◆◆◆
*Guest Accommodation*
Church Street, Brigg
DN20 9AH
t (01652) 654239
e phillips.scawby@amserve.net

**Olivers** ★★★ *Bed & Breakfast*
Church Street, Brigg
DN20 9AH
t (01652) 650446
e eileen_harrison@lineone.net

### SCOTTER
### Lincolnshire

**Ivy Lodge** ★★★★
*Guest Accommodation*
4 Messingham Road, Scotter
DN21 3UQ
t (01724) 763723
e bandb@ivylodgehotel.co.uk
w ivylodgehotel.co.uk

### SCUNTHORPE
### Lincolnshire

**Cocked Hat Hotel** ★★★ *Inn*
Ferry Road, Scunthorpe
DN15 8LQ
t (01724) 841538

**Cosgrove Guest House**
★★★ *Guest House*
33-35 Wells Street, Scunthorpe
DN15 6HL
t (01724) 279405

**The Downs Guest House**
★★★ *Guest Accommodation*
33 Deyne Avenue, Scunthorpe
DN15 7PZ
t (01724) 850710
e thedownsguesthouse@ntlworld.com
w thedownsguesthouse.co.uk

**Elm Field** ★★
*Guest Accommodation*
22 Deyne Avenue, Scunthorpe
DN15 7PZ
t (01724) 869306

**Kirks Korner** ★★
*Guest Accommodation*
12 Scotter Road, Scunthorpe
DN15 8DR
t (01724) 855344
e paul.kirk1@ntlworld.com

**Normanby Hotel** ★★★
*Guest House*
9-11 Normanby Road,
Scunthorpe DN15 6AR
t (01724) 289982
e jonormanby@yahoo.co.uk

### SHENTON
### Leicestershire

**Top House Farm** ★★★
*Farmhouse*
Shenton, Hinckley CV13 6DP
t (01455) 212200
e er.clarke@ukonline.co.uk

### SHEPSHED
### Leicestershire

**Croft Guest House** ★★★
*Guest House*
21 Hall Croft, Shepshed,
Loughborough LE12 9AN
t (01509) 505657
e ray@croftguesthouse.demon.co.uk
w croftguesthouse.demon.co.uk

**Grange Courtyard** ★★★★★
*Guest Accommodation*
**GOLD AWARD**
Forest Street, Shepshed,
Loughborough LE12 9DA
t (01509) 600189
e linda.lawrence@thegrangecourtyard.co.uk
w thegrangecourtyard.co.uk

### SHOBY
### Leicestershire

**Shoby Lodge Farmhouse**
★★★★ *Farmhouse*
**SILVER AWARD**
Shoby, Nr Asfordby, Melton
Mowbray LE14 3PF
t (01664) 812156

### SILVERSTONE
### Northamptonshire

**Pembury House** ★★★★
*Guest Accommodation*
6 Brackley Road, Silverstone
NN12 8UA
t (01327) 858743
e joyce@pembury.f2s.com
w pembury.f2s.com

### SKEGNESS
### Lincolnshire

**Amber Hotel** ★★★
*Guest House*
19 Scarborough Avenue,
Skegness PE25 2SZ
t (01754) 766503

**Beachlands Quality Guest Accommodation** ★★★
*Guest Accommodation*
58 Scarborough Avenue,
Skegness PE25 2TB
t (01754) 764106

**Belmont Guest House** ★★
*Guest House*
30 Grosvenor Road, Skegness
PE25 2DB
t (01754) 765439
e skegnessinfo@e-lindsey.gov.uk
w belmontguesthouse.co.uk

**Chalfonts Hotel** ★★★
*Guest Accommodation*
41 Beresford Avenue,
Skegness PE25 3JF
t (01754) 766374
e info@chalfontshotel.com
w chalfontshotel.com

**Chatsworth** ★★★
*Guest Accommodation*
16 North Parade, Skegness
PE25 2UB
t (01754) 764177
e info@chatsworthskegness.co.uk
w chatsworthskegness.co.uk

**Clarence House** ★★★★
*Guest House*
32 South Parade, Skegness
PE25 3HW
t (01754) 765588
e colin-rita@lineone.net
w clarence-house-hotel.co.uk

**Crawford Hotel** ★★★
*Guest Accommodation*
104 South Parade, Skegness
PE25 3HR
t (01754) 764215
e info@thecrawfordhotel.com
w thecrawfordhotel.com

**Fountaindale Hotel** ★★★★
*Guest Accommodation*
69 Sandbeck Avenue,
Skegness PE25 3JS
t (01754) 762731
e info@fountaindale-hotel.co.uk
w fountaindale-hotel.co.uk

**The Grafton Hotel** ★★★
*Guest Accommodation*
15 Seaview Road, Skegness
PE25 1BW
t (01574) 766158
e thegraftonhotelskegness@fsmail.net
w grafton-skegness.co.uk

**Grosvenor House Hotel**
★★★ *Guest Accommodation*
North Parade, Skegness
PE25 2TE
t (01754) 763376

**Hoylake Guest House** ★★★
*Guest House*
23 Hoylake Drive, Skegness
PE25 1AB
t (01754) 765695
e chazsmith@supanet.com
w hoylakeguesthouse.co.uk

**The Karema** ★★★
*Guest House*
17 Sunningdale Drive,
Skegness PE25 1BB
t (01754) 764440
e info@karema.co.uk
w karema.co.uk

**Kildare Hotel**
Rating Applied For
*Guest Accommodation*
80 Sandbeck Avenue,
Skegness PE25 3JS
t (01754) 762935
e info@kildare-hotel.co.uk
w kildare-hotel.co.uk

**Knighton Lodge** ★★★
*Guest House*
9 Trafalgar Avenue, Skegness
PE25 3EU
t (01754) 764354
e info@knighton-lodge.co.uk
w knighton-lodge.co.uk

**Linroy Guesthouse**
Rating Applied For
*Bed & Breakfast*
26 Lumley Avenue, Skegness
PE25 2AT
t (01754) 763924
e linroy@btopenworld.com

**Mayfair Hotel ★★★**
*Guest Accommodation*
10 Saxby Avenue, Skegness
PE25 3JZ
t (01754) 764687
e info@mayfair-skegness.co.
uk
w mayfair-skegness.co.uk

**Mickleton Guest House**
★★★ *Guest House*
6 North Parade Extension,
Skegness PE25 1BX
t (01754) 763862
e skegnessinfo@e-lindsey.
gov.uk
w mickleton-guesthouse.co.uk

**The Monsell ★★★**
*Guest Accommodation*
2 Firbeck Avenue, Skegness
PE25 3JY
t (01754) 898374
e monsell_hotel@btinternet.
com
w monsell-hotel.co.uk

**North Parade Seafront
Accommodation ★★★**
*Guest Accommodation*
20 North Parade, Skegness
PE25 2UB
t (01754) 762309
e juleebunce@aol.com
w north-parade-hotel.co.uk

**Northdale Hotel ★★★**
*Guest Accommodation*
12 Firbeck Avenue, Skegness
PE25 3JY
t (01754) 610554
e skegnessinfo@e-lindsey.
gov.uk
w northdale-hotel.co.uk

**The Queens Hotel ★★★**
*Guest Accommodation*
49 Scarborough Avenue,
Skegness PE25 2TD
t (01754) 762073

**The Quorn ★★★**
*Guest Accommodation*
11 North Parade, Skegness
PE25 2UB
t (01754) 763508
e reservations@quornhotel.
net
w quornhotel.net

**Roosevelt Lodge ★★★**
*Guest Accommodation*
59 Drummond Road, Skegness
PE25 3EQ
t (01754) 766548
e skegnessinfo@e-lindsey.
gov.uk

**Rufford Hotel ★★★**
*Guest Accommodation*
5 Saxby Avenue, Skegness
PE25 3JZ
t (01754) 763428
e steve@srain.wanadoo.co.uk
w ruffordhotel-skegness.com

**The Sandgate ★★★**
*Guest House*
44 Drummond Road, Skegness
PE25 3EB
t (01754) 762667
e info@sandgate-hotel.co.uk
w sandgate-hotel.co.uk

**The Savoy ★★★**
*Guest Accommodation*
12 North Parade, Skegness
PE25 2UB
t (01754) 763371
e info@savoy-skegness.co.uk
w savoy-skegness.co.uk

**Sherwood Lodge ★★★**
*Guest House*
100 Drummond Road,
Skegness PE25 3EH
t (01754) 762548
e info@sherwood-skegness.
co.uk
w sherwood-skegness.co.uk

**Stoneleigh ★★★★**
*Guest House*
67 Sandbeck Avenue,
Skegness PE25 3JS
t (01754) 769138
e info@stoneleigh-hotel.com
w stoneleighskegness.com

**Thisledome Guest House**
★★★ *Guest House*
5 Glentworth Crescent,
Skegness PE25 2TG
t (01754) 612212
e info@thisledome.com
w thisledome.com

**The Tudor Lodge Guest
House ★★★** *Guest House*
61-63 Drummond Road,
Skegness PE25 3EQ
t (01754) 766487
e info@thetudorlodge.co.uk
w thetudorlodge.co.uk

**Westdene ★★★**
*Guest House*
1 Trafalgar Avenue, Skegness
PE25 3EU
t (01754) 765168
e westdenehotel@aol.com
w westdenehotel.co.uk

**The White Lodge ★★★**
*Guest Accommodation*
129 Drummond Road,
Skegness PE25 3DW
t (01754) 764120
e info@white-lodge.co.uk
w white-lodge.co.uk

**The Barn ★★★★**
*Bed & Breakfast*
Spring Lane, Folkingham
NG34 0SJ
t (01529) 497199
e sjwright@farming.co.uk
w thebarnspringlane.co.uk

**Farthings Guest House**
★★★★ *Bed & Breakfast*
35 Northgate, Sleaford
NG34 7BS
t (01529) 302354
e farthingsguesthouse@
btopenworld.com

**Forest Court
Accommodation ★★**
*Guest Accommodation*
Anwell Lane, Smisby LE65 2TA
t (01530) 411711

**Hillside Lodge Bed &
Breakfast ★★★★**
*Bed & Breakfast*
Derby Road, Smisby, Ashby-
de-la-Zouch LE65 2RG
t (01530) 416411
e barbaraball2000@yahoo.co.
uk
w hillsidelodge.co.uk

**Oldfield House ★★★★★**
*Guest Accommodation*
**SILVER AWARD**
Snelston, Ashbourne DE6 2EP
t (01335) 324510
e s-jarvis@tiscali.co.uk

**West View Bed & Breakfast**
★★★★ *Bed & Breakfast*
South View Lane, South
Cockerington, Louth LN11 7ED
t (01507) 327209 &
07855 291185
e enquiries@west-view.co.uk
w west-view.co.uk

**Hall Farm House ★★★★**
*Farmhouse*
Meadow Lane, South Hykeham
LN6 9PF
t (01522) 686432
e carol@hallfarmhouse.
fsworld.co.uk
w hallfarmhouselincoln.co.uk

**Coach House Inn ★★★★** *Inn*
Stamford Road, South
Luffenham, Oakham LE15 8NT
t (01780) 720166
e lord345@aol.com

**The Old Chapel Bed &
Breakfast ★★★★**
*Bed & Breakfast*
The Old Chapel, Barkwith
Road, South Willingham
LN8 6NN
t (01507) 313395
e oldch03@yahoo.co.uk
w theoldchapelbnb.co.uk

**The Blue Cow Inn and
Brewery ★★** *Inn*
29 High Street, South Witham,
Grantham NG33 5QB
t (01572) 768432
e richard@thirlwell.fslife.co.uk
w thebluecowinn.co.uk

**Lavender Lodge ★★★**
*Bed & Breakfast*
81 Pinchbeck Road, Spalding
PE11 1QF
t (01775) 712800
e teresaegleton@googlemail.
com

**Saville Lodge Guesthouse**
★★★★ *Bed & Breakfast*
11 Kings Road, Spalding
PE11 1QB
t (01775) 722244
e patriciabarnes@fsmail.net

**White Lodge Guest House**
Rating Applied For
*Guest Accommodation*
10 Halmer Gate, Spalding
PE11 2DR
t (01775) 719002
e willie.wood@fresh-link.co.uk
w whitelodge-guesthouse.com

**4 Camphill Cottages ★★★★**
*Bed & Breakfast*
Little Casterton, Stamford
PE9 4BE
t (01780) 763661

**5 Rock Terrace ★★★★**
*Bed & Breakfast*
Scotgate, Stamford PE9 2YJ
t (01780) 755475
e averdieckguest@talk21.com

**Candlesticks Hotel &
Restaurant ★★★**
*Restaurant with Rooms*
1 Church Lane, Stamford
PE9 2JU
t (01780) 764033
e pinto@breathemail.net
w candlestickshotel.co.uk

**Dolphin Guesthouse ★★**
*Guest House*
12 East Street, Stamford
PE9 1QD
t (01780) 757515
e mikdolphin@mikdolphin.
demon.co.uk

**Gwynne House ★★★**
*Bed & Breakfast*
Kings Road, Stamford PE9 1HD
t (01780) 762210
e john@johng.demon.co.uk
w gwynnehouse.co.uk

**Latona ★★★★**
*Bed & Breakfast*
40 Casterton Road, Stamford
PE9 2YL
t (01787) 62765
e carolandbillniehorster@
btopenworld.com

**The Oak Inn ★★★** *Inn*
48 Stamford Road, Easton on
the Hill, Stamford PE9 3PA
t (01780) 752286
e graham@theoakinn.co.uk
w sgmcatering.co.uk

**Park Farm ★★★★**
*Bed & Breakfast*
**SILVER AWARD**
Careby, Stamford PE9 4EA
t (01780) 410515
e enquiries@parkfarmcareby.
co.uk
w parkfarmcareby.co.uk

**Rock Lodge ★★★★★**
Guest Accommodation
**GOLD AWARD**
Empingham Road, Stamford
PE9 2RH
t (01780) 481758
e rocklodge@innpro.co.uk
w rock-lodge.co.uk

**The Royal Oak ★★★★** Inn
High Street, Duddington,
Stamford PE9 3QE
t (01780) 444267
e royaloak@pe93qe.freeserve.
co.uk
w theroyaloakduddington.co.
uk

**The Stamford Lodge
Guesthouse ★★★★**
Guest House
66 Scotgate, Stamford PE9 2YB
t (01780) 482932
e mail@stamfordlodge.co.uk
w stamfordlodge.co.uk

**Ufford Farm ★★★**
Farmhouse
Main Street, Ufford PE9 3BH
t (01780) 740220
e vergette@ufford1.freeserve.
co.uk

STANTON-BY-BRIDGE
Derbyshire

**Ivy House Farm ★★★★**
Guest Accommodation
**SILVER AWARD**
Ingleby Road, Stanton-by-
Bridge, Derby DE73 7HT
t (01332) 863152
e info@ivy-house-farm.com
w ivy-house-farm.com

STANTON IN PEAK
Derbyshire

**Congreave Farm ★★★★**
Farmhouse **GOLD AWARD**
Congreave, Bakewell DE4 2NF
t (01629) 732063
e deborah@matsam16.
freeserve.co.uk
w matsam16.freeserve.co.uk

STOW
Lincolnshire

**Belle Vue Farm ★★★★**
Bed & Breakfast
21 Church Road, Stow
LN1 2DE
t (01427) 788981
e claxtons@bellevuefarm21.
fsnet.co.uk

SUTTON-ON-SEA
Lincolnshire

**The Bacchus Hotel ★★★★**
Inn
17 High Street, Sutton-on-Sea
LN12 2EY
t (01507) 441204
e info@bacchushotel.co.uk
w bacchushotel.co.uk

SUTTON-ON-TRENT
Nottinghamshire

**Fiveways ★★★★**
Bed & Breakfast
Barrel Hill Road, Sutton-on-
Trent, Newark NG23 6PT
t (01636) 822086

**Woodbine Farmhouse ★★★**
Farmhouse
Ingram Lane, Sutton-on-Trent,
Newark NG23 6PD
t (01636) 822549
e woodbinefmhouse@aol.com

SWADLINCOTE
Derbyshire

**Ferne Cottage ★★★**
Bed & Breakfast
5 Black Horse Hill, Appleby
Magna, Ashby-de-la-Zouch
DE12 7AQ
t (01530) 271772
e gbirdapplebymag@aol.com

**Manor Farm ★★★★**
Farmhouse
Coton in the Elms, Swadlincote
DE12 8EP
t (01283) 760340
e cath@manorfarmbb.co.uk
w manorfarmbb.co.uk

SWANNINGTON
Leicestershire

**Hillfield House ★★★★**
Bed & Breakfast
52 Station Hill, Swannington,
Coalville LE67 8RH
t (01530) 837414
e molly@hillfieldhouse.co.uk
w hillfieldhouse.co.uk

SWINESHEAD
Lincolnshire

**Boston Lodge B&B ★★★**
Guest Accommodation
Browns Drove, Boston
PE20 3PX
t (01205) 820983
e info@bostonlodge.co.uk
w bostonlodge.co.uk

**The Wheatsheaf ★★★** Inn
Market Place, Swineshead
PE20 3LJ
t (01205) 821010
e carl@smoke-screen.co.uk
w wheatsheafhotel.co.uk

SWINFORD
Leicestershire

**Ravendale House ★★★★**
Bed & Breakfast
Firtree Lane, Swinford,
Lutterworth LE17 6BH
t (01788) 860442

SWINHOPE
Lincolnshire

**Hoe Hill House Bed &
Breakfast ★★★★**
Bed & Breakfast
Hoe Hill House, Market Rasen
LN8 6HX
t (01472) 399366
e hoehill@hotmail.co.uk
w hoehill.co.uk

TADDINGTON
Derbyshire

**The Old Bake & Brewhouse,
Blackwell Hall ★★★★**
Farmhouse
Blackwell in the Peak,
Taddington, Buxton SK17 9TQ
t (01298) 85271
e christine.gregory@
btinternet.com
w peakdistrictfarmhols.co.uk

**Taddington Camping Barn**
Camping Barn
The Woodlands, Taddington,
Buxton SK17 9UD
t (01298) 85730

TANSLEY
Derbyshire

**Packhorse Farm Bungalow
★★★★** Bed & Breakfast
Foxholes Lane, Tansley,
Matlock DE4 5LF
t (01629) 582781

TEIGH
Rutland

**Teigh Old Rectory ★★★★**
Bed & Breakfast
Main Street, Oakham LE15 7RT
t (01572) 787681
e torowen@btinternet.com

THORNTON CURTIS
Lincolnshire

**Pine Lodge Bed & Breakfast
★★★★** Bed & Breakfast
Laurel Lane, Ulceby DN39 6XJ
t 07880 601476
e carolecouch@hotmail.com

**Thornton Hunt Inn ★★★★**
Inn
17 Main Street, Thornton
Curtis, Nr Ulceby DN39 6XW
t (01469) 531252
e peter@thornton-inn.co.uk
w thornton-inn.co.uk

THORPE
Derbyshire

**Hillcrest House ★★★★**
Guest House
Dovedale, Thorpe, Ashbourne
DE6 2AW
t (01335) 350436
e hillcresthouse@freenet.co.
uk
w hillcresthousedovedale.co.
uk

**The Old Orchard ★★★**
Bed & Breakfast
Thorpe, Ashbourne DE6 2AW
t (01335) 350410
w theoldorchardguesthouse.
co.uk

THURLBY
Lincolnshire

**6 The Pingles ★★★★**
Guest Accommodation
**SILVER AWARD**
Thurlby PE10 0EX
t (01778) 394517

THURMASTON
Leicestershire

**Aaron Lodge ★★★**
Guest Accommodation
3 Coppice Court, Thurmaston,
Leicester LE4 8PJ
t (0116) 269 4494
e info@thelodgeguesthouse.
co.uk
w aaronlodgeguesthouse.co.
uk

TIBSHELF
Derbyshire

**Rosvern House ★★★**
Bed & Breakfast
High Street, Tibshelf, Alfreton
DE55 5NY
t (01773) 874800
e sara.byard@orange.net

TICKNALL
Derbyshire

**The Staff of Life ★★★★**
Guest Accommodation
7 High Street, Ticknall, Derby
DE73 7JH
t (01332) 862479
e info@thestaffoflife.co.uk
w thestaffoflife.co.uk

TIMBERLAND
Lincolnshire

**Clifton Coach House ★★★★**
Guest Accommodation
Clifton House, Church Lane,
Timberland LN4 3SB
t (01526) 378810
e paul.j.hutson@btopenworld.
com

TINWELL
Rutland

**Old Village Hall ★★★★**
Bed & Breakfast
Main Road, Tinwell, Stamford
PE9 3UD
t (01780) 763900
e theoldvillagehall@hotmail.
com

TISSINGTON
Derbyshire

**Bassett Wood Farm ★★★★**
Farmhouse
Tissington, Ashbourne
DE6 1RD
t (01335) 350254
e janet@bassettwood.
freeserve.co.uk

TOWCESTER
Northamptonshire

**Home Farm ★★★★**
Bed & Breakfast
Caldecote, Towcester
NN12 8AG
t (01327) 352651
e gisela@
giselasbedandbreakfast.com
w giselasbedandbreakfast.com

**Seawell Grounds ★★★★★**
Farmhouse
Blakesley, Towcester
NN12 8HW
t (01327) 860226
e seawellcharolais@bt.com
w seawellgrounds.co.uk

**Slapton Manor
Accommodation ★★★★**
Farmhouse **SILVER AWARD**
Slapton Manor, Slapton
NN12 8PF
t (01327) 860344
e accommodation@
slaptonmanor.co.uk

TRUSTHORPE
Lincolnshire

**The Ramblers ★★★★**
Guest House
Sutton Road, Trusthorpe
LN12 2PY
t (01507) 441171
e mablethorpeinfo@e-lindsey.
gov.uk

## UFFINGTON
### Lincolnshire

**Grange Farm** ★★★★
*Bed & Breakfast*
Grange Farm Cottage,
Greatford Road, Stamford
PE9 4ST
t  (01780) 763126
w  stayatgrangefarm.co.uk

## ULLESTHORPE
### Leicestershire

**The Chequers Country Inn**
Rating Applied For
*Inn*
Main Street, Lutterworth
LE17 5BT
t  (01455) 209214
w  chequerscountryinn.com

## UPPER BENEFIELD
### Northamptonshire

**Benefield Wheatsheaf Hotel**
★★★★ *Inn*
Main Street, Upper Benefield,
Oundle PE8 5AN
t  (01832) 205400

## UPPINGHAM
### Rutland

**The Crown Hotel** ★★★ *Inn*
19 High Street East, Oakham
LE15 9PY
t  (01572) 822302
e  thecrownrutland@aol.com

**Grange Farm B&B** ★★★★
*Farmhouse*
Seaton, Rutland, Uppingham
LE15 9HT
t  (01572) 747664
e  david.reading@farmline.com

**Spanhoe Lodge** ★★★★★
*Guest Accommodation*
**GOLD AWARD**
Harringworth Road, Laxton,
Corby NN17 3AT
t  (01780) 450328
e  jennie.spanhoe@virgin.net
w  spanhoelodge.co.uk

## UPTON
### Leicestershire

**Upton Barn Restaurant &
Accommodation** ★★
*Guest Accommodation*
Manor Farm, Upton, Nuneaton
CV13 6JX
t  (01455) 212374
w  uptonbarn.co.uk

## WADSHELF
### Derbyshire

**Temperance House Farm**
★★★★ *Bed & Breakfast*
**SILVER AWARD**
Bradshaw Lane, Wadshelf,
Chesterfield S42 7BT
t  (01246) 566416
w  temperancehousefarm.co.uk

## WELFORD
### Northamptonshire

**West End Farm** ★★★
*Farmhouse*
5 West End, Welford NN6 6HJ
t  (01858) 575226
e  sbevin@fsmail.net

## WELL
### Lincolnshire

**Wellbeck Farmhouse B&B**
★★ *Bed & Breakfast*
Well, Alford LN13 9LT
t  (01507) 462453

## WESSINGTON
### Derbyshire

**Crich Lane Farm** ★★★★
*Farmhouse*
Moorwood Moor Lane,
Wessington, Alfreton
DE55 6DU
t  (01773) 835186
e  crichlanefarm@w3z.co.uk

## WEST BRIDGFORD
### Nottinghamshire

**Firs Guesthouse** ★★★
*Guest House*
96 Radcliffe Road, West
Bridgford, Nottingham
NG2 5HH
t  (0115) 981 0199
e  firs.hotel@btinternet.com

## WESTON HILLS
### Lincolnshire

**The Beeches Bed &
Breakfast** ★★★★
*Guest Accommodation*
Austendyke Road, Weston
Hills, Spalding PE12 6BZ
t  (01406) 370345
e  marierawlings@compuserve.com

## WESTON-ON-TRENT
### Derbyshire

**The Willows** ★★★★
*Guest Accommodation*
**SILVER AWARD**
Trent Lane, Weston-on-Trent,
Derby DE72 2BT
t  (01332) 702525
e  enquiries@willowsinweston.co.uk
w  willowsinweston.co.uk

## WHALEY BRIDGE
### Derbyshire

**Springbank Guest House**
★★★★ *Guest House*
3 Reservoir Road, Whaley
Bridge, High Peak SK23 7BL
t  (01663) 732819
e  margot@whaleyspringbank.co.uk
w  whaleyspringbank.co.uk

## WHATSTANDWELL
### Derbyshire

**Riverdale Guest House**
★★★★ *Bed & Breakfast*
Middle Lane, Crich Carr,
Matlock DE4 5EG
t  (01773) 853905
e  riverdale@clara.co.uk
w  riverdaleguesthouse.co.uk

## WHISSENDINE
### Rutland

**Conifers Bed & Breakfast**
★★★★ *Bed & Breakfast*
37 Main Street, Whissendine,
Oakham LE15 7ES
t  (01664) 474141
e  karentaylor@ukgo.com
w  conifers.ukgo.com

**The Snooty White Lion**
★★★★ *Inn*
38 Main Street, Oakham
LE15 7ET
t  (01664) 474233
e  snootywhitelion@btconnect.com
w  snootyinns.com

## WHITFIELD
### Northamptonshire

**Chestnut View** ★★
*Bed & Breakfast*
Mill Lane, Whitfield, Brackley
NN13 5TQ
t  (01280) 850246

## WHITWELL
### Rutland

**The Noel @ Whitwell** ★★★
*Inn*
Main Road, Oakham LE15 8BW
t  (01780) 460347

## WILBARSTON
### Northamptonshire

**The Fox Inn** ★★★★ *Inn*
Church Street, Market
Harborough LE16 8QG
t  (01536) 77127
e  jane.difazio@btconnect.com

## WINSTER
### Derbyshire

**Brae Cottage** ★★★★
*Guest Accommodation*
**SILVER AWARD**
East Bank, Winster, Matlock
DE4 2DT
t  (01629) 650375

## WIRKSWORTH
### Derbyshire

**Avondale Farm** ★★★★
*Guest Accommodation*
**SILVER AWARD**
Grangemill, Matlock DE4 4HT
t  (01629) 650820
e  avondale@tinyworld.co.uk

**The Glenorchy Centre** ★★
*Group Hostel*
West Derbyshire United
Reformed Church, Coldwell
Street, Wirksworth DE4 4FB
t  (01629) 824323
w  glenorchycentre.org.uk

**Manor Barn** ★★★★
*Guest Accommodation*
**SILVER AWARD**
Hopton, Carsington,
Wirksworth DE4 4DF
t  (01629) 540686
e  yvonneevans55@hotmail.co.uk
w  manor-barn.co.uk

**The Old Lock-Up** ★★★★★
*Guest Accommodation*
**GOLD AWARD**
North End, Wirksworth
DE4 4FG
t  (01629) 826272
e  wheeler@theoldlockup.co.uk
w  theoldlockup.co.uk

## WOLLASTON
### Northamptonshire

**Duckmire** ★★★
*Guest Accommodation*
Duck End, Wollaston,
Wellingborough NN29 7SH
t  (01933) 664249
e  kerry@foreverengland.freeserve.co.uk

## WOODHALL SPA
### Lincolnshire

**Chaplin House** ★★★★
*Guest Accommodation*
92 High Street, Martin
LN4 3QT
t  (01526) 378795
e  m.lockyer@tiscali.co.uk
w  chaplin-house.co.uk

**The Limes** ★★★
*Bed & Breakfast*
Tattershall Road, Woodhall Spa
LN10 6TW
t  (01526) 352219

**Newlands** ★★★★
*Bed & Breakfast*
56 Woodland Drive, Woodhall
Spa LN10 6YG
t  (01526) 352881

**Oglee Guest House** ★★★★
*Guest Accommodation*
16 Stanthorpe Avenue,
Woodhall Spa LN10 6SP
t  (01526) 353512
e  ogleeguesthouse@gmail.com

**Pitchaway** ★★★★
*Guest House*
The Broadway, Woodhall Spa
LN10 6SQ
t  (01526) 352969
e  info@pitchaway.co.uk
w  pitchaway.co.uk

**The Vale** ★★★
*Bed & Breakfast*
50 Tor-O-Moor Road,
Woodhall Spa LN10 6SB
t  (01526) 353022
e  margot.mills@hotmail.co.uk

**Village Limits Motel** ★★★★
*Guest Accommodation*
Stixwould Road, Woodhall Spa
LN10 6UJ
t  (01526) 353312
e  info@villagelimits.co.uk
w  villagelimits.co.uk

## WOODNEWTON
### Northamptonshire

**Bridge Cottage** ★★★★
*Bed & Breakfast*
Oundle Road, Woodnewton
PE8 5EG
t  (01780) 470779
e  enquiries@bridgecottage.net
w  bridgecottage.net

## WRAWBY
### Lincolnshire

**Mowden House** ★★★★
*Guest Accommodation*
Barton Road, Brigg DN20 8SQ
t  (01652) 652145
e  dr@prabhakaran.fsnet.co.uk

## WYMONDHAM
### Leicestershire

**Old Rectory** ★★★★
*Bed & Breakfast*
Spring Lane, Wymondham,
Melton Mowbray LE14 2AZ
t  (01572) 787583
e  oldrectory@rutnet.co.uk
w  rutnet.co.uk/customers/oldrectory

Look out for establishments participating in the National Accessible Scheme

## YOULGREAVE
### Derbyshire

**The Farmyard Inn** ★★★
*Guest Accommodation*
Main Street, Youlgrave,
Bakewell DE45 1UW
t  (01629) 636221

**Lathkill House** ★★★★
*Guest Accommodation*
**SILVER AWARD**
Church Street, Youlgrave
(Youlgreave), Bakewell
DE45 1WL
t  (01629) 636604
e  enquiries@lathkill-house.co.
uk
w  lathkill-house.co.uk

**The Old Bakery** ★★★
*Bed & Breakfast*
Church Street, Youlgrave,
Bakewell DE45 1UR
t  (01629) 636887
w  cressbrook.co.uk/youlgve/
oldbakery

**YHA Youlgreave** ★★★
*Hostel*
Fountain Square, Youlgrave,
Bakewell DE45 1UR
t  (01629) 636518
w  yha.org.uk

---

## EAST OF ENGLAND

## ACLE
### Norfolk

**The Kings Head Inn** ★★★
*Inn*
The Street, Acle, Norwich
NR13 3DY
t  (01493) 750204
e  info@kingsheadinnacle.co.
uk
w  kingsheadinnacle.co.uk

**St Margarets Mill Retreat**
★★★ *Guest Accommodation*
Caister Road, Acle NR13 3AX
t  (01493) 752288
e  mail@stmargaretsmill.co.uk
w  stmargaretsmill.co.uk

## ACTON
### Suffolk

**Barbies** ★★
*Guest Accommodation*
Clay Hall Place, Acton
CO10 0BT
t  (01787) 373702
w  tiscover.co.uk

## ALBURGH
### Norfolk

**Dove Restaurant** ★★★★
*Restaurant with Rooms*
Holbrook Hill, Alburgh,
Harleston IP20 0EP
t  (01986) 788315

## ALDBOROUGH
### Norfolk

**Butterfly Cottage** ★★★★
*Guest House*
The Green, Aldborough,
Norwich NR11 7AA
t  (01263) 768198 &
(01263) 761689
e  butterflycottage@
btopenworld.com
w  butterflycottage.com

## ALDEBURGH
### Suffolk

**Lime Tree House** ★★★
*Bed & Breakfast*
Benhall Green, Saxmundham
IP17 1HU
t  (01728) 602149
e  enquiries@limetreehouse-
suffolk.co.uk
w  limetreehouse-suffolk.co.uk/

**Marygold** ★★★★
*Guest Accommodation*
Beaconsfield Road, Aldeburgh
IP15 5HF
t  (01728) 453323
e  info@marygoldaldeburgh.
co.uk
w  tiscover.co.uk

**Oak** ★★★★ *Bed & Breakfast*
111 Saxmundham Road,
Aldeburgh IP15 5JF
t  (01728) 453503
e  ppask18371@aol.com
w  ppaskletting.co.uk

**Sanviv** ★★★ *Bed & Breakfast*
59 Fairfield Road, Aldeburgh
IP15 5JN
t  (01728) 453107
w  tiscover.co.uk

**Toll House** ★★★★
*Guest House*
50 Victoria Road, Aldeburgh
IP15 5EJ
t  (01728) 453239
e  tollhouse@fsmail.net
w  tollhouse.travelbugged.com

## ALDEBY
### Norfolk

**Old Vicarage** ★★★
*Bed & Breakfast*
Rectory Road, Aldeby
NR34 0BJ
t  (01502) 678229
e  butler@beccles33.freeserve.
co.uk
w  tiscover.co.uk

## ALDHAM
### Essex

**Caterpillar Cottage** ★★★★
*Bed & Breakfast*
Ford Street, Aldham,
Colchester CO6 3PH
t  (01206) 240456
w  tiscover.co.uk

## ALPHETON
### Suffolk

**Amicus** ★★★★
*Bed & Breakfast*
Old Bury Road, Alpheton
CO10 9BT
t  (01284) 828579
e  stanleyburcham@aol.com
w  tiscover.co.uk

## ANSTEY
### Hertfordshire

**Anstey Grove Barn** ★★★★
*Farmhouse*
The Grove, Anstey,
Buntingford SG9 0BJ
t  (01763) 848828
e  enquiries@ansteygrovebarn.
co.uk
w  ansteygrovebarn.co.uk

## ANTINGHAM
### Norfolk

**Wilds Cottage B&B** ★★★★
*Bed & Breakfast*
Cromer Road, North Walsham
NR28 0NJ
t  (01692) 500321
e  info@wildscottage.co.uk
w  wildscottage.co.uk

## ARDLEIGH
### Essex

**Malting Farm** ★★★★
*Bed & Breakfast*
Bromley Road, Ardleigh
CO7 7QG
t  (01206) 230207
e  gallaherhouse@wanadoo.co.
uk
w  tiscover.co.uk

**Old Shields Farm** ★★★★
*Bed & Breakfast*
Waterhouse Lane, Ardleigh
CO7 7NE
t  (01206) 230251
e  ruthmarshall@btinternet.
com
w  tiscover.co.uk

**Park Cottage** ★★★★
*Bed & Breakfast*
**SILVER AWARD**
Bromley Road, Ardleigh
CO7 7SJ
t  (01206) 230170
e  www.parkcottage@talktalk.
net
w  parkcottage.org

**Salix Nursery** ♦♦♦
*Guest Accommodation*
7 Coggeshall Road, Ardleigh
CO7 7LP
t  (01206) 230124

## ARKESDEN
### Essex

**Parsonage Farm** ★★★★
*Guest Accommodation*
Arkesden, Saffron Walden
CB11 4HB
t  (01799) 550306
e  danijaud@aol.com
w  tiscover.co.uk

## ASSINGTON
### Suffolk

**The Case Restaurant with
Rooms** ★★★★
*Restaurant with Rooms*
**SILVER AWARD**
Further Street, Assington
CO10 5LD
t  (01787) 210483
e  rooms@
thecaserestaurantwithrooms.
co.uk
w  thecaserestaurantwith
rooms.co.uk

## ATTLEBOROUGH
### Norfolk

**Home Farm Bed and
Breakfast** ★★★★ *Farmhouse*
Stow Bedon, Attleborough
NR17 1BZ
t  (01953) 483592
e  valerie.dove@virgin.net
w  homefarm-bandb.co.uk

## AYLMERTON
### Norfolk

**Driftway Guest House**
★★★★ *Bed & Breakfast*
**SILVER AWARD**
The Close, Norwich NR11 8PX
t  (01263) 838589
e  dawn@sparrowsnorfolk
holidaycottages.co.uk
w  sparrowsnorfolkholiday
cottages.co.uk

## AYLSHAM
### Norfolk

**Birchdale** ★★★★
*Bed & Breakfast*
Aylsham NR11 6ND
t  (01263) 734531
e  birchdalehouse@hotmail.
com
w  smoothhound.co.uk/hotels/
birchdale.html

**Bure Valley Farm Stays**
★★★★ *Farmhouse*
Bure Valley Farm, Burgh Road,
Norwich NR11 6TZ
t  (01263) 732177
e  burevalleyfarmstays@
btinternet.com
w  burevalleyfarmstays.co.uk

**Old Pump House** ★★★★
*Guest Accommodation*
Holman Road, Aylsham
NR11 6BY
t  (01263) 733789
e  theoldpumphouse@
btconnect.com
w  smoothhound.co.uk/hotels/
oldpumphouse.html

**Pink House Bed & Breakfast**
★★★★ *Bed & Breakfast*
Wickmere NR11 7AL
t  (01263) 577678
e  dee.jupp@btinternet.com
w  pinkhousebb.co.uk

## BADINGHAM
### Suffolk

**Colston Hall** ★★★★
*Farmhouse* **SILVER AWARD**
Badingham, Woodbridge
IP13 8LB
t  (01728) 638375
e  lizjohn@colstonhall.com
w  colstonhall.com

## BARTLOW
### Cambridgeshire

**Westoe Farm** ★★★★★
*Bed & Breakfast*
Bartlow CB21 4PR
t  (01223) 892731
e  enquire@bartlow.u-net.com
w  westoefarm.co.uk

---

## BASILDON
### Essex

**Kelly Road 38 ★★★★**
*Guest Accommodation*
Bowers Gifford, Basildon
SS13 2HL
t (01268) 726701
e patricia.jenkinson@tesco.net
w uk-visit.co.uk

## BATTLESBRIDGE
### Essex

**Frasers ★★★★**
*Guest Accommodation*
5 Maltings Road, Battlesbridge
SS11 7RF
t (01268) 561700
e accommodation@
battlesbridge.com
w battlesbridge.com/
guesthouse.php

## BAWDSEY
### Suffolk

**Bawdsey Manor ★★**
*Guest Accommodation*
Bawdsey IP12 3AZ
t (01394) 411633
e info@bawdseymanor.co.uk
w tiscover.co.uk

## BECCLES
### Suffolk

**Catherine House ★★★★**
*Guest Accommodation*
2 Ringsfield Road, Beccles
NR34 9PQ
t (01502) 716428

**Eveleigh House ★★★★**
*Bed & Breakfast*
49 London Road, Beccles
NR34 9YR
t (01502) 715214

**Pinetrees ★★★★**
*Guest Accommodation*
Park Drive, Beccles NR34 7DQ
t (01502) 470796
e info@pinetrees.net
w pinetrees.net
▣▨

**Saltgate House ★★★★**
*Guest Accommodation*
5 Saltgate, Beccles NR34 9AN
t (01502) 710889
e cazjohns@aol.com
w saltgatehouse.co.uk

## BEDFORD
### Bedfordshire

**Church Farm ★★★★**
*Bed & Breakfast*
SILVER AWARD
High Street, Roxton MK44 3EB
t (01234) 870234
e churchfarm@amserve.net
w tiscover.co.uk

**Cornfields ★★★★**
*Restaurant with Rooms*
SILVER AWARD
Wilden Road, Roothams
Greeb, Colmworth MK44 2NJ
t (01234) 378990
e reservations@
cornfieldsrestaurant.co.uk
w cornfieldsrestaurant.co.uk

## BEESTON
### Norfolk

**Holmdene Farm ★★★**
*Farmhouse*
Syers Lane, Beeston PE32 2NJ
t (01328) 701284
e holmdenefarm@
farmersweekly.net
w northnorfolk.co.uk/
holmdenefarm

## BEESTON REGIS
### Norfolk

**Sheringham View Cottage**
**★★★★ Bed & Breakfast**
SILVER AWARD
Cromer Road, Sheringham
NR26 8RX
t (01263) 820300
e sheringhamview@
btopenworld.com
w sheringhamview.co.uk

## BEETLEY
### Norfolk

**Peacock House ★★★★**
*Guest Accommodation*
SILVER AWARD
Peacock Lane, Old Beetley,
East Dereham NR20 4DG
t (01362) 860371
w peacock-house.co.uk

## BEYTON
### Suffolk

**Bear Inn ★★★★**
*Guest Accommodation*
Tostock Road, Beyton
IP30 9AG
t (01359) 270249
w thebearinn.net

## BIGGLESWADE
### Bedfordshire

**Old Warden Guesthouse**
**★★★ Bed & Breakfast**
Shop & Post Office, Old
Warden SG18 9HQ
t (01767) 627201
e owgh@idnet.co.uk

## BILDESTON
### Suffolk

**Silwood Barns ◆◆◆**
*Guest Accommodation*
Consent Lane, Bildeston
IP7 7SB
t (01449) 741370
e neilashwell@aol.com
w lalaproducts.com

## BILLERICAY
### Essex

**Badgers Rest ★★★★**
*Bed & Breakfast*
GOLD AWARD
2 Mount View, Billericay
CM11 1HB
t (01277) 625384
w tiscover.co.uk

## BINHAM
### Norfolk

**Field House ◆◆◆◆**
*Guest Accommodation*
GOLD AWARD
Walsingham Road, Binham
NR21 0BU
t (01328) 830639
w tiscover.co.uk

## BIRCH
### Essex

**Woodview B&B ★★★**
*Bed & Breakfast*
Mill Lane, Birch, Colchester
CO2 0NH
t (01206) 331956
e lynchcottage@fsmail.net
w tiscover.co.uk

## BISHOP'S STORTFORD
### Hertfordshire

**33 Harrisons**
Rating Applied For
*Bed & Breakfast*
Harrisons, Birchanger Place,
Bishop's Stortford CM23 5QT
t (01279) 815012

**Abacus House ★★**
*Bed & Breakfast*
24 Elm Road, Bishop's
Stortford CM23 2SS
t (01279) 658884
e davehilary@tiscali.co.uk
w tiscover.co.uk

**Acer Cottage ★★★**
*Bed & Breakfast*
17 Windhill, Bishop's Stortford
CM23 2NE
t (01279) 834797
e admill@ntlworld.com
w acercottage.co.uk

**AJ Bed and Breakfast ★★**
*Bed & Breakfast*
5 Ascot Close, Bishop's
Stortford CM23 5BP
t (01279) 652228
e aandjbnb@tesco.net
w aandjbandb.co.uk

**Aldburys Farm ★★★★**
*Bed & Breakfast*
Boxley Lane, Hatfield Broad
Oak CM22 7JX
t (01279) 718282
e aldbury@supanet.com
w tiscover.co.uk

**Ascot B&B ★★**
*Bed & Breakfast*
6 Ascot Close, Bishop's
Stortford CM23 5BP
t (01279) 651027
e derek@derekfox1.wanadoo.
co.uk

**Avery House ★★★★**
*Bed & Breakfast*
52 Thorley Hill, Bishop's
Stortford CM23 3NA
t (01279) 658311
e jacki-ross.accommodation@
virgin.net
w averyhouse.co.uk

**Coral's B&B ★★★★**
*Bed & Breakfast*
Shire House, 14 Cannons Mill
Lane, Bishop's Stortford
CM23 2BN
t (01279) 508544
e shirehouse@coralsbnb.co.uk
w coralsbnb.co.uk

**Lancasters ★★★★**
*Guest Accommodation*
Market Square, Bishop's
Stortford CM23 3UU
t (01279) 501307
e linda@lancasterguesthouse.
com
w lancastersguesthouse.com

**Marie's Bed and Breakfast**
**★★★★ Bed & Breakfast**
26 Heath Row, Bishop's
Stortford CM23 5DE
t (01279) 833870
e mariesbandb@hotmail.com
w mariesbedandbreakfast.co.
uk

**Oakfields ◆◆◆◆**
*Guest Accommodation*
26 Kestral Gardens, Bishop's
Stortford CM23 4LU
t (01279) 506014
e nicola@
oakfieldsbedandbreakfast.co.
uk
w oakfieldsbedandbreakfast.
co.uk

**Park Lane Bed And
Breakfast ★★★★**
*Guest Accommodation*
30 Park Lane, Bishop's
Stortford CM23 3NH
t (01279) 501920
e gillcordell@hotmail.com
w parklanerooms.co.uk

**Phoenix Lodge ★★★**
*Guest House*
No. 91 Dunmow Road,
Bishop's Stortford CM23 5HF
t (01279) 659780
e phoenixlodge@ntlworld.com
w phoenixlodge.co.uk

## BLACKMORE
### Essex

**Little Lampetts ★★★**
*Guest Accommodation*
Hay Green Lane, Blackmore
CM4 0QE
t (01277) 822030
e shelagh.porter@btinternet.
com
w tiscover.co.uk

## BLAKENEY
### Norfolk

**Navestock Bed and
Breakfast ★★★★**
*Bed & Breakfast*
Cley Road, Blakeney NR25 7NL
t (01263) 740998
w tiscover.co.uk

## BLAXHALL
### Suffolk

**Blaxhall YHA ★★★ *Hostel***
Heath Walk, Blaxhall,
Woodbridge IP12 2EA
t 0870 770 5702
e blaxhall@yha.org.uk
w yha.org.uk
⬧

## BLETSOE
### Bedfordshire

**North End Barns ★★★★**
*Farmhouse*
Risley Road, Bletsoe, Bedford
MK44 1QT
t (01234) 781320
w northendbarns.co.uk

## BOCKING
### Essex

**Fennes View ★★★★**
*Guest Accommodation*
131 Church Street, Bocking
CM7 5LF
t (01376) 326080
w tiscover.co.uk

## BOLNHURST
### Bedfordshire

**Old School House ★★★★**
*Bed & Breakfast*
SILVER AWARD
School Lane, Bolnhurst,
Bedford MK44 2EN
t (01234) 376754
e enquiries@breakfastinbeds.
co.uk
w breakfastinbeds.co.uk

## BRADFIELD
### Essex

**Curlews ★★★★**
*Bed & Breakfast*
SILVER AWARD
Bradfield, Manningtree
CO11 2UP
t (01255) 870890
e margherita@
curlewsaccommodation.co.uk
w curlewsacccommodation.co.
uk

## BRADFIELD COMBUST
### Suffolk

**Church Farm Bed and
Breakfast ★★★★** *Farmhouse*
Bradfield Combust, Bury St
Edmunds IP30 0LW
t (01284) 386333
e ruth@churchfarm-bandb.co.
uk
w churchfarm-bandb.co.uk

## BRAINTREE
### Essex

**Brook Farm ★★★★**
*Farmhouse*
Wethersfield, Braintree
CM7 4BX
t (01371) 850284
e abutlerbrookfarm@aol.com
w tiscover.co.uk

**The Old House ★★★**
*Guest House*
Braintree CM7 9AS
t (01376) 550457
e old_house@talk21.com
w theoldhousebraintree.co.uk

## BRANCASTER
### Norfolk

**Ship Inn ★★★** *Inn*
Main Road, Brancaster
PE31 8AP
t (01485) 210333
e mike.ali.ship@btinternet.
com
w shipinnbrancaster.co.uk

## BRENTWOOD
### Essex

**Brentwood Guesthouse
★★★** *Guest Accommodation*
Rose Valley, Brentwood
CM14 4HJ
t (01277) 262713
e info@
brentwoodguesthouse.com
w brentwoodguesthouse.com

## BRIGHTLINGSEA
### Essex

**Paxton Dene ◆◆◆◆**
*Guest Accommodation*
Church Road, Brightlingsea
CO7 0QT
t (01206) 304560
e holben@btinternet.com
w brightlingsea-town.co.uk/
business

## BROCKDISH
### Norfolk

**Grove Thorpe ★★★★★**
*Bed & Breakfast*
GOLD AWARD
Grove Road, Brockdish
IP21 4JR
t (01379) 668305
e grovethorpe@btinternet.
com
w grovethorpe.co.uk

## BROOKE
### Norfolk

**Hillside Farm ★★★★**
*Farmhouse*
Welbeck Road, Brooke,
Norwich NR15 1AU
t (01508) 550260
e carrieholl@tinyworld.co.uk
w hillside-farm.com

**Old Vicarage ★★★★**
*Guest Accommodation*
SILVER AWARD
48 The Street, Brooke
NR15 1JU
t (01508) 558329
w tiscover.co.uk

## BROOKMANS PARK
### Hertfordshire

**Stewards Cottage ★★★★**
*Bed & Breakfast*
60 Bell Lane, Bell Bar, Hatfield
AL9 7AY
t 07076 42091
e info@stewardcottagebandb.
co.uk
w stewardscottagebandb.co.
uk

## BRUNDALL
### Norfolk

**Braydeston House ★★★★**
*Bed & Breakfast*
9 The Street, Brundall
NR13 5AY
t (01603) 713123
e ann@braydeston.freeserve.
co.uk
w tiscover.co.uk

**Breckland B&B ★★★★**
*Bed & Breakfast*
12 Strumpshaw Road, Brundall
NR13 5PA
t (01603) 712122
e brecklandbandb@hotmail.
co.uk
w breckland-bandb.co.uk

## BUNGAY
### Suffolk

**Earsham Park Farm ★★★★**
*Farmhouse* GOLD AWARD
Old Railway Road, Bungay
NR35 2AQ
t (01986) 892180
e eetb@earsham-parkfarm.co.
uk
w earsham-parkfarm.co.uk

## BUNTINGFORD
### Hertfordshire

**Buckland Bury Farm ★★**
*Guest Accommodation*
Buckland Bury, Buntingford
SG9 0PY
t (01763) 272958
e bucklandbury@
shrubbsfarm.deman.co.uk
w tiscover.co.uk

**Chipping Hall Farm ★★★★**
*Bed & Breakfast*
Chipping Hall, Buntingford
SG9 0PH
t (01763) 271514
e jacquelinenoy@aol.com
w chippinghall.co.uk

## BURES
### Suffolk

**Queens House ★★★★**
*Guest Accommodation*
Church Square, Bures
CO8 5AB
t (01787) 227760
e queens-house@btconnect.
com
w queens-house.com

## BURNHAM DEEPDALE
### Norfolk

**Deepdale Granary ★★★**
*Group Hostel*
Deepdale Farms, Burnham
Deepdale PE31 8DD
t (01485) 210256
e info@deepdalefarm.co.uk
w deepdalefarm.co.uk

**Deepdale Stables ★★★★**
*Hostel*
Deepdale Farms, Burnham
Deepdale PE31 8DD
t (01485) 210256
e info@deepdalefarm.co.uk
w deepdalefarm.co.uk

## BURNHAM MARKET
### Norfolk

**Holmesdale ★★★**
*Bed & Breakfast*
Church Walk, Burnham Market
PE31 8DH
t (01328) 738699
e veronica@holmesdale.
eclipse.co.uk
w burnhammarket.co.uk

**Wood Lodge ★★★★**
*Bed & Breakfast*
Millwood, Herring's Lane,
Burnham Market PE31 8DP
t (01328) 730152
e philip.roll@btinternet.com
w tiscover.co.uk

## BURNHAM-ON-CROUCH
### Essex

**The Oyster Smack Motel
★★★** *Guest Accommodation*
Station Road, Burnham-on-
Crouch CM0 8HR
t (01621) 782141

**The Railway Hotel ★★★★**
*Inn* SILVER AWARD
Station Road, Burnham-on-
Crouch CM0 8BQ
t (01621) 786868
w therailwayhotelburnham.co.
uk

## BURNHAM THORPE
### Norfolk

**Whitehall Farm ★★★★**
*Farmhouse*
Burnham Thorpe PE31 8HN
t (01328) 738416
e barrysoutherland@aol.com
w tiscover.co.uk

## BURWELL
### Cambridgeshire

**Chestnut House ★★★★**
*Bed & Breakfast*
14a High Street, Cambridge
CB5 0HB
t (01638) 742996
w tiscover.co.uk

## BURY ST EDMUNDS
### Suffolk

**Brambles Lodge ★★★★**
*Bed & Breakfast*
Welham Lane, Risby, Bury St
Edmunds IP28 6QS
t (01284) 810701

**Brighthouse Farm ★★★★**
*Farmhouse*
Melford Road, Lawshall
IP29 4PX
t (01284) 830385
e info@brighthousefarm.fsnet.
co.uk
w brighthousefarm.fsnet.co.uk

**Dunston Guesthouse ★★★**
*Guest House*
8 Springfield Road, Bury St
Edmunds IP33 3AN
t (01284) 767981
w tiscover.co.uk

**Glen ★★★★** *Guest House*
Eastgate Street, Bury St
Edmunds IP33 1YR
t (01284) 755490
e rallov@aol.com
w smoothhound.co.uk

**Hilltop ★★** *Bed & Breakfast*
Bury St Edmunds IP33 3XB
t (01284) 767066
e bandb@hilltop22br.
freeserve.co.uk
w hilltop22br.freeserve.co.uk

**Manorhouse ★★★★★**
*Bed & Breakfast*
GOLD AWARD
The Green, Beyton IP30 9AF
t (01359) 270960
e manorhouse@beyton.com
w beyton.com

**Ounce House ★★★★★**
*Guest Accommodation*
SILVER AWARD
Northgate Street, Bury St
Edmunds IP33 1HP
t (01284) 761779

**Regency House ★★★★**
*Guest Accommodation*
3 Looms Lane, Bury St
Edmunds IP33 1HE
t (01284) 764676
w regencyhousehotel.co.uk

**Sanctuary B&B ★★★★**
*Bed & Breakfast*
1 Kings Road, Bury St
Edmunds IP33 3DE
t (01284) 706698
e allison814@btinternet.com

**Sycamore House ★★★★**
*Guest Accommodation*
23 Northgate Street, Bury St
Edmunds IP33 1HP
t (01284) 755828
e me.chalkley@btinternet.com
w tiscover.co.uk

**The Wallow** ★★★★
*Bed & Breakfast*
Mount Road, Bury St Edmunds
IP31 2QU
**t** (01284) 788055
**e** info@thewallow.co.uk
**w** thewallow.co.uk

**Westbank House Bandb** ★★
*Guest Accommodation*
Westbank Place, 116a Westley
Road, Bury St Edmunds
IP33 3SD
**t** (01284) 753874
**e** grahampaske@tiscali.co.uk
**w** tiscover.co.uk

### CAMBRIDGE
### Cambridgeshire

**77 Grantchester Meadows**
★★★★ *Bed & Breakfast*
Grantchester Meadows,
Cambridge CB3 9JL
**t** (01223) 316363

**A And B Guesthouse** ★★★
*Guest House*
124 Tenison Road, Cambridge
CB1 2DP
**t** (01223) 315702
**e** abguest@hotmail.com
**w** tiscover.co.uk

**Acorn Guesthouse** ★★★
*Guest House*
154 Chesterton Road,
Cambridge CB4 1DA
**t** (01223) 353888
**e** info@acornguesthouse.co.
uk
**w** acornguesthouse.co.uk

**Alexander Bed And
Breakfast** ★★★★
*Bed & Breakfast*
56 St Barnabas Road,
Cambridge CB1 2DE
**t** (01223) 525725
**e** enquiries@beesley-schuster.
co.uk
**w** beesley-schuster.co.uk

**Allenbell** ★★★★
*Bed & Breakfast*
517a Coldham Lane,
Cambridge CB1 3JS
**t** (01223) 210353
**e** sandragailturner@hotmail.
com
**w** allenbell.co.uk

**Alpha Milton Guesthouse**
★★★ *Bed & Breakfast*
61-63 Milton Road, Cambridge
CB4 1XA
**t** (01223) 311625
**e** welcome@
alphamiltonguesthouse.co.uk
**w** tiscover.co.uk

**Antonys Bed And Breakfast
(town centre)** ★★
*Guest Accommodation*
4 Huntingdon Road,
Cambridge CB3 0HH
**t** (01223) 357444
**w** tiscover.co.uk

**Arbury Lodge Guesthouse**
★★★★ *Guest House*
82 Arbury Road, Cambridge
CB4 2JE
**t** (01223) 364319
**e** arbury-lodge@btconnect.
com
**w** arburylodgeguesthouse.co.
uk

**Archway House** ★★★★
*Bed & Breakfast*
52 Gilbert Road, Cambridge
CB4 3PE
**t** (01223) 575314
**w** tiscover.co.uk

**Ashley** ★★★★
*Guest Accommodation*
74 Chesterton Road,
Cambridge CB4 1ER
**t** (01223) 350059
**e** info@arundelhousehotels.
co.uk
**w** arundelhousehotels.co.uk

**Avalon** ★★★★
*Bed & Breakfast*
62 Gilbert Road, Cambridge
CB4 3PD
**t** (01223) 353071
**e** avalonbandb@btinternet.
com
**w** tiscover.co.uk

**Avondale** ★★★
*Bed & Breakfast*
35 Highfields Road, Caldecote
CB3 7NX
**t** (01954) 210746
**e** avondalecambs@amserve.
com
**w** tiscover.co.uk

**Aylesbray Lodge
Guesthouse** ★★★★
*Guest House*
5 Mowbray Road, Cambridge
CB1 7SR
**t** (01223) 240089

**Brambles** ★★★★
*Bed & Breakfast*
Green End, Landbeach
CB4 8ED
**t** (01223) 861443
**e** info@thebramblesbandb.co.
uk
**w** thebramblesbandb.co.uk

**Bridge Guest House** ★★★
*Guest House*
151 Hills Road, Cambridge
CB2 2RJ
**t** (01223) 247942
**e** bghouse@gmail.com
**w** bridgeguesthouse.co.uk

**Cam Guesthouse** ★★★★
*Guest House*
17 Elizabeth Way, Cambridge
CB4 1DD
**t** (01223) 354512
**e** camguesthouse@btinternet.
com
**w** camguesthouse.co.uk

**Cambridge City Tenison
Towers Bed and Breakfast**
★★★★
*Guest Accommodation*
Cambridge CB1 2DP
**t** (01223) 363924
**e** jpfchance@aol.com
**w** cambridgecitytenisontowers.
com

**Cambridge Guesthouse**
★★★★ *Guest House*
201a Milton Road, Cambridge
CB4 1XG
**t** (01223) 423239
**w** thecambridgeguesthouse.
co.uk

**Cambridge Lodge** ★★★★
*Guest Accommodation*
139 Huntingdon Road,
Cambridge CB3 0DQ
**t** (01223) 352833
**e** cambridge.lodge@
btconnect.com
**w** smoothhound.co.uk/hotels/
cambridge.html

**Cambridge YHA** ★★★
*Hostel*
97 Tenison Road,
Cambridgeshire CB1 2DN
**t** (01223) 354601

**Canterbury House** ★★★★
*Bed & Breakfast*
69 Canterbury Street,
Cambridge CB4 3QG
**t** (01223) 300053
**w** canterburyhouse.co.uk

**Carlton Lodge** ★★★
*Guest House*
245 Chesterton Road,
Cambridge CB4 1AS
**t** (01223) 367792
**e** info@carltonlodge.co.uk
**w** carltonlodge.co.uk

**Carolina** ★★★★
*Bed & Breakfast*
138 Perne Road, Cambridge
CB1 3NX
**t** (01223) 247015
**e** carolina.amabile@tesco.net
**w** carolinaguesthouse.co.uk

**City Centre North Bed And
Breakfast** ★★★★
*Bed & Breakfast*
328a Histon Road, Cambridge
CB4 3HT
**t** (01223) 312843
**e** gscambs@tiscali.co.uk
**w** citycentrenorth.co.uk

**Conifers** ★★★★
*Bed & Breakfast*
SILVER AWARD
213 Histon Road, Cambridge
CB4 3HL
**t** (01223) 311784
**e** maureen.kent@
btopenworld.com
**w** the-conifers.net

**Dresden Villa Guesthouse**
♦♦♦ *Guest Accommodation*
34 Cherry Hinton Road,
Cambridge CB1 7AA
**t** (01223) 247539
**e** raf.ruggiero@btopenworld.
com
**w** dresdenvilla.com

**Fenners Hotel** ★★
*Guest Accommodation*
142-146 Tenison Road,
Cambridge CB1 2DP
**t** (01229) 360246

**Finches** ★★★★
*Bed & Breakfast*
SILVER AWARD
144 Thornton Road, Girton
CB3 0ND
**t** (01223) 276653
**e** enquiry@finches-bnb.co.uk
**w** finches-bnb.com

**Granta House** ★★★
*Bed & Breakfast*
53 Eltisley Avenue, Newnham
CB3 9JQ
**t** (01223) 560466
**e** tj.dathan@ntlworld.com
**w** tiscover.co.uk

**Hamilton Lodge** ★★★
*Guest House*
156 Chesterton Road,
Cambridge CB4 1DA
**t** (01223) 365664
**e** hamiltonhotel@talk21.com
**w** hamiltonhotelcambridge.co.
uk

**Harry's Bed and Breakfast**
★★★★ *Guest House*
39 Milton Road, Cambridge
CB4 1XA
**t** (01223) 503866
**e** cjmadden@ntlworld.com
**w** welcometoharrys.co.uk

**Hawthorn House** ★★★
*Bed & Breakfast*
10 Hawthorn Way, Cambridge
CB4 1AX
**t** (01223) 364483
**e** hawthornhouse@hotmail.co.
uk

**Hobsons House** ★★★
*Bed & Breakfast*
96 Barton Road, Cambridge
CB3 9LH
**t** (01223) 304906
**e** hill-tout@ntlworld.com
**w** tiscover.co.uk

**Home From Home** ★★★★
*Bed & Breakfast*
Milton Road, Cambridge
CB4 1LA
**t** (01223) 323555
**e** homrfromhome2@
btconnect.com
**w** accommodationin
cambridge.com

**Iceni House Bed And Breakf**
Rating Applied For
*Bed & Breakfast*
171 Coleridge Road,
Cambridge CB1 3PN
**t** (01223) 708967
**e** paragon.holdings@ntlworld.
com
**w** icenihouse.co.uk

**June's Bed & Breakfast**
★★★ *Bed & Breakfast*
Cambridge CB4 2JE
**t** (01223) 572034
**e** j.nayar1@ntlworld.com
**w** tiscover.co.uk

**Kirkwood Guesthouse**
★★★★ *Guest House*
Cambridge CB4 1DA
**t** (01223) 306283
**e** info@kirkwoodhouse.co.uk
**w** kirkwoodhouse.co.uk

**Lantern House** ★★★★
*Guest House*
174 Chesterton Road,
Cambridge CB4 1DA
**t** (01223) 359980
**e** lanternhouse@msn.com
**w** lanternguesthouse.co.uk

**Leverton House**
Rating Applied For
*Guest Accommodation*
732 Newmarket Road,
Cambridge CB5 8RS
**t** (01223) 292094
**w** levertonhouse.co.uk

**The Poplars** ★★★★
*Bed & Breakfast*
12 East Drive, Highfields
Caldecote CB23 7NZ
**t** (01954) 210396
**e** thepoplars@onetel.com
**w** tiscover.co.uk

**Railway Lodge Guest House**
★★★ *Guest House*
150 Tenison Road, Cambridge
CB1 2DP
**t** (01223) 467688
**e** railwaylodge@cambridge-
guesthouse-accommodation.
co.uk
**w** cambridge-guesthouse-
accommodation.co.uk

**Rock View** ★★★
*Bed & Breakfast*
99 Cherry Hinton Road,
Cambridge CB1 7BS
**t** (01223) 573455
**w** rockviewguesthouse.co.uk

**Somerset House** ★★★
*Bed & Breakfast*
Cambridge CB4 1XE
**t** (01223) 505131
**e** somersetbedandbreakfast@
msn.com
**w** tiscover.co.uk

**Southampton Guest House**
★★★ *Guest Accommodation*
7 Elizabeth Way, Cambridge
CB4 1DE
**t** (01223) 357780
**e** southamptonhouse@
telco4u.net
**w** southamptonguesthouse.
com

**Sycamore House** ★★
*Bed & Breakfast*
56 High Street, Cambridge
CB1 5JD
**t** (01223) 880751
**e** barry@thesycamorehouse.
co.uk
**w** thesycamorehouse.co.uk

**Tudor Cottage** ★★★★
*Bed & Breakfast*
292 Histon Road, Cambridge
CB4 3HS
**t** (01223) 565212
**e** email@tudor-cottage.net
**w** tudorcottageguesthouse.co.
uk

**Upton House** ★★★★
*Bed & Breakfast*
SILVER AWARD
11b Grange Road, Cambridge
CB3 9AS
**t** (01223) 323201

**Vicarage** ★★★
*Bed & Breakfast*
15 St Pauls Road, Cambridge
CB1 2EZ
**t** (01223) 315832
**w** tiscover.co.uk

**Victoria Guest House**
★★★★ *Guest House*
57 Arbury Road, Cambridge
CB4 2JB
**t** (01223) 350086
**e** victoriahouse@ntlworld.com
**w** cambridge-accommodation.
com

**Warkworth House** ★★★★
*Guest House*
Warkworth Terrace,
Cambridge CB1 1EE
**t** (01223) 363682
**e** enquiries@warkworthhouse.
co.uk
**w** warkworthhouse.co.uk

**Woodfield House** ★★★★
*Bed & Breakfast*
Madingley Road, Coton
CB3 7PH
**t** (01954) 210265
**e** wendy-john@wsadler.
freeserve.co.uk
**w** tiscover.co.uk

**Woodhaven** ★★★★
*Bed & Breakfast*
245 Milton Road, Cambridge
CB4 1XQ
**t** (01223) 226108
**e** mike.furn@virgin.net
**w** tiscover.co.uk

**Woodview Bed & Breakfast**
★★★★ *Bed & Breakfast*
Great Cambourne CB3 6GF
**t** (01954) 710338
**e** woodviewcambridge@
tiscali.co.uk
**w** tiscover.co.uk

**Worth House** ★★★★
*Guest House* SILVER AWARD
152 Chesterton Road,
Cambridge CB4 1DA
**t** (01223) 316074
**e** enquiry@worth-house.co.uk
**w** worth-house.co.uk

CAMPSEA ASHE
Suffolk

**The Dog & Duck** ★★★
*Guest Accommodation*
Station Road, Campsea Ashe
IP13 0PT
**t** (01728) 748439

CARLTON
Suffolk

**Willow Tree Cottage** ★★★★
*Bed & Breakfast*
3 Belvedere Close, Kelsale
IP17 2RS
**t** (01728) 602161
**w** tiscover.co.uk

CASTLE ACRE
Norfolk

**Willow Cottage Tea Rooms**
★★★★
*Guest Accommodation*
Stocks Green, Castle Acre
PE32 2AE
**t** (01760) 755551
**e** info@willowcottage.biz
**w** broadland.com

CASTOR
Cambridgeshire

**Cobnut Cottage** ★★★★
*Guest Accommodation*
45 Peterborough Road, Castor,
Peterborough PE5 7AX
**t** (01733) 380745
**e** enquiries@cobnut-cottage.
co.uk
**w** cobnut-cottage.co.uk

CATFIELD
Norfolk

**The Limes** ★★★★
*Bed & Breakfast*
Limes Road, Catfield
NR29 5DG
**t** (01692) 581221
**e** info@thelimesatcatfield.com
**w** thelimesatcatfield.com

CAVENDISH
Suffolk

**Embleton House** ★★★★
*Guest Accommodation*
SILVER AWARD
Melford Road, Cavendish,
Sudbury CO10 8AA
**t** (01787) 280447
**e** silverned@aol.com
**w** embletonhouse.co.uk

CHEDGRAVE
Norfolk

**Chedgrave House B&B**
★★★★ *Bed & Breakfast*
2 Norwich Road, Chedgrave
NR14 6HB
**t** (01508) 521095
**e** june@chedgrave-house.
freeserve.co.uk
**w** chedgravehouse.co.uk

CHEDISTON
Suffolk

**Oak Lodge** ★★★★
*Guest House*
Chediston Green, Halesworth
IP19 0BB
**t** (01986) 785268
**e** oaklodgebandb@btconnect.
com
**w** tiscover.co.uk

CHELMSFORD
Essex

**Aarandale** ★★★
*Guest House*
9 Roxwell Road, Chelmsford
CM1 2LY
**t** (01245) 251713
**e** aarandaleuk@aol.com
**w** aarandale.com

**Compasses Motel** ★★★ *Inn*
141 Broomfield Road,
Chelmsford CM1 1RY
**t** (01245) 292051
**w** tiscover.co.uk

**Sherwood** ★★★
*Bed & Breakfast*
Cedar Avenue West,
Chelmsford CM1 2XA
**t** (01245) 257981
**e** jeremy.salter@btclick.com
**w** tiscover.co.uk

**Wards Farm** ★★
*Bed & Breakfast*
Loves Green, Highwood Road,
Chelmsford CM1 3QJ
**t** (01245) 248812
**e** alsnbrtn@aol.com
**w** tiscover.co.uk

CHERRY HINTON
Cambridgeshire

**Old Rosemary Branch** ★★
*Bed & Breakfast*
The Old Rosemary Branch,
Cherry Hinton CB1 3LF
**t** (01223) 247161
**e** s.anderson@
constructionplus.net
**w** theoldrosemarybranch.co.uk

CHESHUNT
Hertfordshire

**YHA Lee Valley Village**
★★★★ *Hostel*
Windmill Lane, Cheshunt,
Waltham Cross EN8 9AJ
**t** (01992) 628392
**e** leevalley@yha.org.uk
**w** yha.org.uk

CHEVELEY
Cambridgeshire

**1eleven Bed & Breakfast**
★★★★ *Bed & Breakfast*
SILVER AWARD
111 High Street, Newmarket
CB8 9DG
**t** (01638) 731177
**e** richard@1elevenbandb.co.
uk
**w** 1elevenbandb.co.uk

**Juniper** ★★★★
*Bed & Breakfast*
SILVER AWARD
9 Church Lane, Newmarket
CB8 9DJ
**t** (01638) 731244
**e** kate.auty@tiscali.co.uk
**w** tiscover.co.uk

**Old Farmhouse** ★★★★
*Bed & Breakfast*
165 High Street, Cheveley
CB8 9DG
**t** (01638) 730771 &
07909 970047
**e** amrobinson@clara.co.uk
**w** cheveleybandb.co.uk

CHIPPENHAM
Cambridgeshire

**Maltings Yard Cottage**
★★★★ *Bed & Breakfast*
20 High Street, Chippenham
CB7 5PP
**t** (01638) 720110
**w** tiscover.co.uk

CHORLEYWOOD
Hertfordshire

**Ashburton Country House**
★★★★★ *Bed & Breakfast*
SILVER AWARD
48 Berks Hill, Chorleywood
WD3 5AH
**t** (01923) 285510
**e** info@ashburtonhouse.co.uk
**w** ashburtonhouse.co.uk

**North Hill Farm** ★★★★
*Bed & Breakfast*
North Hill, Rickmansworth
WD3 6HA
**t** (01923) 284760

## CLACTON-ON-SEA
### Essex

**Adelaide Guesthouse ★★★**
*Guest House*
24 Wellesley Road, Clacton-on-Sea CO15 3PP
t (01255) 435628
e adelaide_guesthouse@yahoo.co.uk
w adelaide-guesthouse.co.uk

**Beam Guest House ★★★★**
*Guest House*
26 Nelson Road, Clacton-on-Sea CO15 1LU
t (01255) 433992
w tiscover.co.uk

**The Chudleigh ★★★★**
*Guest Accommodation*
13 Agate Road, Marine Parade West, Clacton-on-Sea CO15 1RA
t (01255) 425407
e reception@chudleighhotel.com
w tiscover.co.uk/chudleigh-hotel

**Le'Vere House ★★★**
*Guest Accommodation*
Clacton-on-Sea CO15 1RA
t (01255) 423044
e kemphotel@aol.com
w leverehotel.co.uk

**Pond House Farmhouse Bed and Breakfast ★★★★**
*Farmhouse* **SILVER AWARD**
Earls Hall Farm, St Osyth CO16 8BP
t (01255) 820458
e brenda_lord@farming.co.uk
w earlshallfarm.info

▨ ◪

## CLAPHAM
### Bedfordshire

**Narly Oak Lodge ★★★★**
*Bed & Breakfast*
Narly Oak, The Baulk, Green Lane, Bedford MK41 6AA
t (01234) 350353
e mollie.foster07@btinternet.com
w narlyoaklodge.com

## CLARE
### Suffolk

**Bell Hotel ★★★★** *Inn*
Market Hill, Clare CO10 8NN
t (01787) 277741
e info@thebellhotel-clare.com
w thebellhotel-clare.com

**Old Clare ★★★**
*Guest Accommodation*
19 Nethergate Street, Clare CO10 8NP
t (01787) 277449
e htannhauser@aol.com
w theclarehotel.co.uk

## CLAVERING
### Essex

**Brocking Farm Cottages ★★★★**
*Guest Accommodation*
Roast Green, Clavering CB11 4SH
t (01279) 777349
e t.gingell@btopenworld.com
w brockingfarmcottages.co.uk

## CLENCHWARTON
### Norfolk

**Kismet Lodge Bed and Breakfast ★★★★**
*Guest Accommodation*
15 Willow Drive, Clenchwarton PE34 4EN
t (01553) 761409
e kismetlodgebb@aol.com
w bed-and-breakfast-kismet-lodge.co.uk

## COCKFIELD
### Suffolk

**The Old Manse Barn ★★★★**
*Guest Accommodation*
**SILVER AWARD**
Chapel Road, Cockfield IP30 0HE
t (01284) 828120
e bookings@theoldmansebarn.co.uk
w theoldmansebarn.co.uk

## COLCHESTER
### Essex

**17 Roman Road ★★★★**
*Bed & Breakfast*
Roman Road, Colchester CO1 1UR
t (01206) 768898
e marianne.gilbert@btinternet.com

**Anns Bed And Breakfast ◆◆◆** *Guest Accommodation*
2 Coventry Close, Riverside Estate, Colchester CO1 2RN
t (01206) 512721
e annsb.b@ntlworld.com
w annsbedandbreakfast.co.uk

**Apple Blossom House ★★★**
*Guest Accommodation*
8 Guildford Road, Colchester CO1 2YL
t (01206) 512303
w tiscover.co.uk

**Beacon House ★★**
*Bed & Breakfast*
12 Berriman Close, Colchester CO4 3XF
t (01206) 794501
e hannahmulvey@aol.com
w tiscover.co.uk

**The Castle Inn ★★** *Inn*
92 High Street, Colchester CO1 1TH
t (01206) 563988

**Charlie Brown's ★★★★**
*Bed & Breakfast*
**SILVER AWARD**
60 East Street, Colchester CO1 2TS
t (01206) 517541
e charliebrowns@ntlworld.com

**Four Sevens Guesthouse ★★★** *Guest Accommodation*
Colchester CO3 3HU
t (01206) 546093
e calypso1@hotmail.com
w tiscover.co.uk

**Fridaywood Farm ★★★★**
*Guest Accommodation*
**SILVER AWARD**
Bounstead Road, Colchester CO2 0DF
t (01206) 573595
e lochorem8@aol.com
w tiscover.co.uk

▨ ◪

**Nutcrackers ◆◆◆**
*Guest Accommodation*
6 Mayberry Walk, Colchester CO2 8PS
t (01206) 543085
e jean123@btinternet.com
w tiscover.co.uk

**Old Courthouse Inn ★★★★**
*Inn*
Harwich Road, Great Bromley CO7 7JG
t (01206) 250322
e oldcourthouseinn@btinternet.com

**Park Hall Country House ★★★★★**
*Guest Accommodation*
**GOLD AWARD**
Park Hall, St Osyth CO16 8HG
t (01255) 820922
e trish@parkhall.fslife.co.uk
w parkhall.info

**Pescara House ◆◆◆**
*Guest Accommodation*
88 Manor Road, Colchester CO3 3LY
t (01206) 520055
e dave@pescarahouse.co.uk
w pescarahouse.co.uk

**Rutland House Bed and Breakfast ★★★★**
*Bed & Breakfast*
**SILVER AWARD**
121 Lexden Road, Colchester CO3 3RD
t (01206) 573437
e rutland121@aol.com
w rutlandhousebandb.co.uk

**Rye Farm ★★★★** *Farmhouse*
Rye Lane, Layer-de-la-Haye, Colchester CO2 0JL
t (01206) 734350
e peter@buntingp.fsbusiness.co.uk
w buntingp.fsbusiness.co.uk

▨ ◪

**Scheregate Hotel ★★**
*Guest House*
36 Osborne Street, Via St John's Street, Colchester CO2 7DB
t (01206) 573034

**Seven Arches Farm ★★**
*Guest Accommodation*
Chitts Hill, Lexden, Colchester CO3 9SX
t (01206) 574896
w tiscover.co.uk

**Tall Trees ★★★★**
*Guest Accommodation*
25 Irvine Road, Colchester CO3 3TP
t (01206) 576650
e whitehead.talltrees@ntlworld.com
w tiscover.co.uk

## COLTISHALL
### Norfolk

**Bridge House ★★★★**
*Guest House*
Coltishall NR12 7AA
t (01603) 737323
e bhbookings@talktalk.net
w bridgehouse-coltishall.co.uk

**Hedges Guesthouse ★★★★**
*Guest Accommodation*
Tunstead Road, Coltishall NR12 7AL
t (01603) 738361
e info@hedgesbandb.co.uk
w hedgesbandb.co.uk

**Old Railway Station ★★★★**
*Bed & Breakfast*
Station Road, Coltishall, Norwich NR12 7JG
t (01603) 737069
e info@theoldrailwaystation.co.uk
w theoldrailwaystation.co.uk

**Seven Acres House ★★★★★** *Bed & Breakfast*
**SILVER AWARD**
Great Hautbois, Coltishall NR12 7JZ
t (01603) 736737
e william@hautbois.plus.com
w norfolkbroadsbandb.com

## CRANFIELD
### Bedfordshire

**Croft End Bed And Breakfast ★★★**
*Guest Accommodation*
10 Hotch Croft, Cranfield, Bedford MK43 0BN
t (01234) 750753
e chambers@xalt.co.uk
w tiscover.co.uk

## CREETING ST MARY
### Suffolk

**Hungercut Hall Bed and Breakfast ★★★★**
*Guest Accommodation*
Coddenham Road, Creeting St Mary, Ipswich IP6 8NX
t (01449) 721323
w tiscover.co.uk

## CROMER
### Norfolk

**Cambridge House ★★★★**
*Guest Accommodation*
Sea Front, East Cliff NR27 9HD
t (01263) 512085
w broadland.com

**Captains House ★★★★★**
*Guest Accommodation*
**GOLD AWARD**
5 The Crescent, Cromer NR27 9EX
t (01263) 515434
e captainshouse@aol.com
w captains-house.co.uk

**Grove Guesthouse ★★★★**
*Guest Accommodation*
95 Overstrand Road, Cromer NR27 0DJ
t (01263) 512412
e enquiries@thegrovecromer.co.uk
w thegrovecromer.co.uk

**Incleborough House Luxury Bed and Breakfast ★★★★★**
*Bed & Breakfast*
East Runton, Cromer NR27 9PG
t (01263) 515939
e enquiries@incleboroughhouse.co.uk
w incleboroughhouse.co.uk

◪

**Knoll Guesthouse** ★★★
*Guest Accommodation*
23 Alfred Road, Cromer
NR27 9AN
t (01263) 512753
e ian@knollguesthouse.co.uk
w tiscover.co.uk

**Shrublands Farm** ★★★★
*Farmhouse* SILVER AWARD
Northrepps, Cromer NR27 0AA
t (01263) 579297

CULFORD
Suffolk

**Benyon Gardens 47** ★★★
*Bed & Breakfast*
47 Benyon Gardens, Culford,
Bury St Edmunds IP28 6EA
t (01284) 728763
w tiscover.co.uk

DANBURY
Essex

**Wych Elm** ★★★
*Bed & Breakfast*
Mayes Lane, Danbury,
Chelmsford CM3 4NJ
t (01245) 222674
e axonwychelm@tiscali.co.uk
w wychelmb-b.co.uk

DEDHAM
Essex

**Good Hall** ◆◆◆◆
*Guest Accommodation*
SILVER AWARD
Coggeshall Road, Dedham/
Ardleigh, Colchester CO7 7LR
t (01206) 322100
e goodhall@ic24.net
w tiscover.co.uk

DENVER
Norfolk

**Westhall Cottages** ★★★
*Bed & Breakfast*
20-22 Sluice Road, Downham
Market PE38 0DY
t (01366) 382987
w tiscover.co.uk

DEREHAM
Norfolk

**Greenbanks Country Hotel
and 3 Palms Leisure Pool**
★★★★
*Guest Accommodation*
Swaffham Road, Wendling,
Dereham NR19 2AR
t (01362) 687742
e jenny@greenbanks.co.uk

**Hunters Hall** ★★★★
*Farmhouse*
Park Farm, Swanton Morley,
Dereham NR20 4JU
t (01362) 637457
e office@huntershall.com
w huntershall.com

DERSINGHAM
Norfolk

**Ashdene House** ★★★★
*Guest Accommodation*
SILVER AWARD
60 Hunstanton Road,
Dersingham PE31 6HQ
t (01485) 540395
e mail@ashdene-house.co.uk
w ashdene-house.co.uk

**Barn House Bed And
Breakfast** ★★★★
*Guest Accommodation*
14 Station Road, Dersingham,
King's Lynn PE31 6PP
t (01485) 543086
e tom.chapman@eidosnet.co.uk
w smoothhound.co.uk/hotels/barnho

**The Corner House** ★★★★
*Bed & Breakfast*
SILVER AWARD
2 Sandringham Road,
Dersingham PE31 6LL
t (01485) 543532
e the_corner_house@btinternet.com
w tiscover.co.uk

**Dove Lodge** ★★★★
*Guest Accommodation*
SILVER AWARD
21 Woodside Avenue,
Dersingham PE31 6QB
t (01485) 540053
e dovelodgebb@fsnet.co.uk
w dovelodge.20m.com

**Holkham Cottage** ★★★★
*Guest Accommodation*
34 Hunstanton Road,
Dersingham PE31 6HQ
t (01485) 544562
e holkham.cottage@btinternet.com
w tiscover.co.uk

**St Jude's** ★★★
*Bed & Breakfast*
12 Sandringham Road,
Dersingham PE31 6LL
t (01485) 541755
e gwen@wncb.net
w tiscover.co.uk

**Tall Trees** ★★★★
*Bed & Breakfast*
Helsey House, Helsey, Nr
Hogsthorpe PE31 6JR
t (01485) 542638
e frosty-trees@classicfm.net
w talltrees-norfolk.co.uk

**White House** ★★★★
*Guest House*
Dersingham PE31 6HQ
t (01485) 541895
e firesafe@ukonline.co.uk
w tiscover.co.uk

**The Willows** ★★★★
*Bed & Breakfast*
11b Post Office Road,
Dersingham PE31 6HR
t (01485) 543602
e thewillowsbandb@hotmail.com
w thewillowsbandb.com

DISS
Norfolk

**Dickleburgh Hall** ★★★★★
*Bed & Breakfast*
GOLD AWARD
Semere Green Lane,
Dickleburgh IP21 4NT
t (01379) 741259
e johntaylor05@btinternet.com
w dickhall.co.uk

**Old Rectory Hopton** ★★★★★ *Bed & Breakfast*
GOLD AWARD
High Street, Hopton, Diss
IP22 2QX
t (01953) 688135
e llewellyn.hopton@btinternet.com
w theoldrectoryhopton.com

**Strenneth** ★★★★
*Guest Accommodation*
SILVER AWARD
Airfield Road, Fersfield
Common, Fersfield IP22 2BP
t (01379) 688182
e pdavey@strenneth.co.uk
w strenneth.co.uk

DOCKING
Norfolk

**Jubilee Lodge** ★★★★
*Guest Accommodation*
Station Road, Docking
PE31 8LS
t (01485) 518473
e eghoward62@hotmail.com
w jubilee-lodge.com

DOVERCOURT
Essex

**Homebay** ★★★
*Guest Accommodation*
9 Bay Road, Dovercourt
CO12 3JZ
t (01255) 504428
e sydiej9@btinternet.com
w tiscover.co.uk

DOWNHAM MARKET
Norfolk

**Chestnut Villa** ★★★
*Guest Accommodation*
44 Railway Road, Downham
Market PE38 9EB
t (01366) 384099
e chestnutvilla@talk21.com
w chestnutvilla-downham.com

DUNMOW
Essex

**Alberta House** ◆◆◆◆
*Guest Accommodation*
The Downs, Stebbing,
Dunmow CM6 3RA
t (01371) 856483

**Puttocks Farm B&B** ★★★★
*Farmhouse*
Philpot End, Great Dunmow
CM6 1JQ
t (01371) 872377
e roger@puttocksfarm.com
w puttocksfarm.com

**Westpoint** ★★★★
*Bed & Breakfast*
Aythorpe Roding, Dunmow
CM6 1PU
t (01279) 876462
e barbara@westpointbandb.co.uk
w westpointbandb.co.uk

EARL SOHAM
Suffolk

**Bridge House** ★★★★
*Guest Accommodation*
SILVER AWARD
Earl Soham, Woodbridge
IP13 7RT
t (01728) 685473
e bridgehouse46@hotmail.com
w tiscover.co.uk

EARLS COLNE
Essex

**Greenlands Farm** ★★★★
*Bed & Breakfast*
SILVER AWARD
Lamberts Lane, Earls Colne,
Colchester CO6 2LE
t (01787) 224895
e david@greenlandsfarm.freeserve.co.uk
w greenlandsfarm.co.uk

**Riverside Lodge** ★★★
*Guest Accommodation*
40 Lower Holt Street, Earls
Colne, Colchester CO6 2PH
t (01787) 223487
e bandb@riversidelodge-uk.com
w riversidelodge-uk.com

EAST BARSHAM
Norfolk

**White Horse Inn** ★★★★ *Inn*
Fakenham Road, East Barsham,
Fakenham NR21 0LH
t (01328) 820645

EAST BERGHOLT
Suffolk

**Rosemary** ★★★
*Guest Accommodation*
Rectory Hill, East Bergholt
CO7 6TH
t (01206) 298241
w tiscover.co.uk

EAST CARLETON
Norfolk

**Majority Cottage** ★★★★
*Guest Accommodation*
GOLD AWARD
Wymondham Road, East
Carleton NR14 8JB
t (01508) 571198
e richardphillips@majority.freeserve.co.uk
w tiscover.co.uk

EAST HYDE
Bedfordshire

**Hyde Mill** ★★★★
*Bed & Breakfast*
Lower Luton Road, Luton
LU2 9PX
t (01582) 712641
e info@hydemill.co.uk
w hydemill.co.uk

EAST MERSEA
Essex

**Bromans Farm** ★★★★
*Bed & Breakfast*
Mersea Island, East Mersea
CO5 8UE
t (01206) 383235
e bromansfarm@btopenworld.com
w tiscover.co.uk

ELMSTEAD
Essex

**Pheasant Lodge** ★★★★
*Bed & Breakfast*
SILVER AWARD
Balls Farm, Tye Road, Elmstead
Market CO7 7BB
t (01206) 822514
e lyndaevans@aol.com
w ballsfarm.net

## ELMSWELL
Suffolk

**Elmswell Hall Bed And Breakfast** ★★★★ *Farmhouse*
**SILVER AWARD**
Elmswell Hall, Elmswell
IP30 9EN
t (01359) 240215
e kate@elmswellhall.
freeserve.co.uk
w elmswellhall.co.uk

**Kiln Farm**
Rating Applied For
*Guest House*
Kiln Lane, Elmswell IP30 9QR
t (01359) 240442
w tiscover.co.uk

**Mulberry Farm** ★★★★
*Farmhouse* **SILVER AWARD**
Ashfield Road, Elmswell
IP30 9HG
t (01359) 244244
e mulberryfarm@tesco.net
w tiscover.co.uk

## ELY
Cambridgeshire

**29 Waterside** ★★★
*Bed & Breakfast*
Ely CB7 4AU
t (01353) 614329
e info@29waterside.org
w 29waterside.org

**57 Lynn Road** ★★★★
*Bed & Breakfast*
Ely CB6 1DD
t (01353) 663685
e marting7vgh@aol.com
w tiscover.co.uk

**9 Willow Walk** ★★★★
*Bed & Breakfast*
Ely CB7 4AT
t (01353) 664205
w tiscover.co.uk

**96 Lynn Road** ◆◆◆◆
*Guest Accommodation*
**SILVER AWARD**
Ely CB6 1DE
t (01353) 665044
w tiscover.co.uk

**Anchor Inn** ★★★★
*Restaurant with Rooms*
Sutton Gault, Sutton CB6 2BD
t (01353) 778537
e anchorinn@popmail.bta.com
w anchorsuttongault.co.uk

**Bowmount House** ★★★★
*Bed & Breakfast*
**SILVER AWARD**
Ely CB6 3WP
t (01353) 669943
e pauljacton@hotmail.com
w tiscover.co.uk

**Cathedral House** ★★★★
*Bed & Breakfast*
17 St Mary's Street, Ely
CB7 4ER
t (01353) 662124
e farndale@cathedralhouse.
co.uk
w tiscover.co.uk

**The Grove** ★★★★
*Bed & Breakfast*
**SILVER AWARD**
Bury Lane, Sutton Gault
CB6 2BD
t (01353) 777196
e stella.f.anderson@
btopenworld.com
w tiscover.co.uk

**Harvest House** ★★★★
*Bed & Breakfast*
122b St Johns Road, Ely
CB6 3BW
t (01353) 663517
w tiscover.co.uk

**Hill House Farm** ★★★★
*Farmhouse* **GOLD AWARD**
9 Main Street, Coveney, Ely
CB6 2DJ
t (01353) 778369
e info@hillhousefarm-ely.co.
uk
w hillhousefarm-ely.co.uk

**Little Haven** ★★★★
*Bed & Breakfast*
36 Wissey Way, Ely CB6 2WW
t (01353) 615492
w tiscover.co.uk

**Nyton Hotel** ★★★
*Guest Accommodation*
7 Barton Road, Ely CB7 4HZ
t (01353) 662459
e nytonhotel@yahoo.co.uk
w thenytonhotel.com

**Post House** ★★
*Bed & Breakfast*
12a Egremont Street, Ely
CB6 1AE
t (01353) 667184
e nora@covell.fsbusiness.co.
uk
w tiscover.co.uk

**Spinney Abbey** ★★★★
*Farmhouse*
Stretham Road, Wicken
CB7 5XQ
t (01353) 720971
e spinney.abbey@tesco.net
w spinneyabbey.co.uk

**Walnut House** ★★★★
*Bed & Breakfast*
**SILVER AWARD**
Ely CB7 4JN
t (01353) 661793
e walnuthouse1@aol.com
w ely.org.uk/walnuthouse

**Willow Fen Cottage** ★★
*Bed & Breakfast*
4 Prickwillow Road, Ely
CB7 4QP
t (01353) 665591
w tiscover.co.uk

## EPPING
Essex

**The Coach House** ★★★★
*Guest Accommodation*
**SILVER AWARD**
Wintry Park House,
Thornwood Road, Epping
CM16 6SZ
t (01992) 577407

**Pergola Lodge** ★★★★
*Guest Accommodation*
5a Buttercross Lane, Epping
CM16 5AA
t (01992) 571354
e info@stayinepping.co.uk
w stayinepping.co.uk

## ERPINGHAM
Norfolk

**Saracens Head Inn** ★★★★
*Restaurant with Rooms*
**SILVER AWARD**
Wolterton, Nr Erpingham
NR11 7LX
t (01263) 768909
e saracenshead@wolterton.
freeserve.co.uk
w saracenshead-norfolk.co.uk

## EYE
Suffolk

**Bull Auberge** ★★★★★
*Restaurant with Rooms*
**SILVER AWARD**
Ipswich Road, Yaxley IP23 8BZ
t (01379) 783604
w the-auberge.co.uk

**Camomile Cottage** ★★★★
*Bed & Breakfast*
**SILVER AWARD**
Brome Avenue, Langton Green
IP23 7HW
t (01379) 873528
e aly@camomilecottage.co.uk
w camomilecottage.co.uk

**Rookery House Bed and Breakfast** ★★★
*Bed & Breakfast*
Rookery House, Eye IP23 7AR
t (01379) 873155
w tiscover.co.uk

**The White Horse Inn**
★★★★ *Inn*
Stoke Ash, Eye IP23 7ET
t (01379) 678222
e mail@whitehorse-suffolk.co.
uk
w whitehorse-suffolk.co.uk

## EYKE
Suffolk

**Marsh Cottage** ★★
*Guest Accommodation*
Low Road, Eyke IP12 2QF
t (01394) 460203
w tiscover.co.uk

## FAKENHAM
Norfolk

**Abbott Farm** ★★★
*Farmhouse*
Walsingham Road, Binham
NR21 0AW
t (01328) 830519
e abbot.farm@btinternet.com
w abbottfarm.co.uk

**Erikas Bed And Breakfast**
★★★★ *Bed & Breakfast*
3 Gladstone Road, Fakenham
NR21 9BZ
t (01328) 863058
w erikasbandb.co.uk

**Highfield Farm** ★★★★
*Farmhouse* **SILVER AWARD**
Highfield Lane, Great Ryburgh
NR21 7AL
t (01328) 829249
e elizabethsavory@waitrose.
com
w broadland.com/highfield

**Holly Lodge** ★★★★★
*Guest Accommodation*
**GOLD AWARD**
Thursford Green, Fakenham
NR21 0AS
t (01328) 878465
e info@hollylodgeguesthouse.
co.uk
w hollylodgeguesthouse.co.uk

**The Old Brick Kilns Guesthouse** ★★★★
*Bed & Breakfast*
Little Barney Lane, Barney
NR21 0NL
t (01328) 878305
e enquiries@old-brick-kilns.co.
uk
w old-brick-kilns.co.uk

**Rosemary Cottage** ★★★
*Guest Accommodation*
The Street, West Raynham
NR21 7AD
t (01328) 838318
e francoisew@btinternet.com
w tiscover.co.uk

## FEERING
Essex

**Old Wills Farm** ★★★★
*Farmhouse*
Little Tey Road, Feering,
Colchester CO5 9RP
t (01376) 570259
e janecrayston@btconnect.
com

## FELIXSTOWE
Suffolk

**Burlington House** ★★★★
*Guest Accommodation*
7 Beach Road West, Felixstowe
IP11 2BH
t (01394) 282051
e burlington.house@tesco.net
w tiscover.co.uk

**Dolphin** ★★
*Guest Accommodation*
41 Beach Station Road,
Felixstowe IP11 2EY
t (01394) 282261
w tiscover.co.uk

**Dorincourt Guesthouse** ★★
*Guest House*
Undercliff Road West,
Felixstowe IP11 2AH
t (01394) 270447
w tiscover.co.uk

**The Grafton Guesthouse**
★★★★
*Guest Accommodation*
13 Sea Road, Felixstowe
IP11 2BB
t (01394) 284881
e info@grafton-house.com
w grafton-house.com

**The Norfolk Guest House**
★★★★ *Guest House*
1-3 Holland Road, Felixstowe
IP11 2BA
t (01394) 283160
e thenorfolk@btconnect.com
w thenorfolk.com

**Ranevale** ★★★★
*Bed & Breakfast*
96 Ranelagh Road, Felixstowe
IP11 7HU
t (01394) 270001
e joy.s@btclick.com

## FENSTANTON
Cambridgeshire

**Orchard House ★★★**
*Bed & Breakfast*
6a Hilton Road, Fenstanton
PE28 9LH
t (01480) 469208
e ascarrow@aol.com
w tiscover.co.uk

## FINCHINGFIELD
Essex

**Red Lion Inn ★★** *Inn*
Church Hill, Finchingfield
CM7 4NN
t (01371) 810400
w red-lion-finchingfield.com

## FLATFORD MILL
Suffolk

**Granary ★★★**
*Guest Accommodation*
Flatford, East Bergholt
CO7 6UL
t (01206) 298111
e flatfordmill@fsdial.co.uk
w tiscover.co.uk

## FORDHAM
Cambridgeshire

**Annes Bed And Breakfast**
**★★★★** *Bed & Breakfast*
158 Mildenhall Road, Fordham
CB7 5NS
t (01638) 720514
e annes.bnb@btinternet.com
w tiscover.co.uk

## FRAMLINGHAM
Suffolk

**High House Farm ★★★**
*Farmhouse*
Cransford, Woodbridge
IP13 9PD
t (01728) 663461
e info@highhousefarm.co.uk
w highhousefarm.co.uk

## FRECKENHAM
Suffolk

**The Golden Boar Inn ★★★★**
*Inn*
The Street, Freckenham, Bury
St. Edmunds IP28 8HZ
t (01638) 723000
e thegoldenboarinn@aol.com

## FRINTON-ON-SEA
Essex

**Russell Lodge ★★★**
*Bed & Breakfast*
47 Hadleigh Road, Frinton-on-
Sea CO13 9HQ
t (01255) 675935 &
07891 899824
e stay@russell-lodge.fsnet.co.
uk
w russell-lodge.fsnet.co.uk

**Uplands Guesthouse ★★★**
*Guest Accommodation*
41 Hadleigh Road, Frinton-on-
Sea CO13 9HQ
t (01255) 674889
e info@uplandsguesthouse.co.
uk
w uplandsguesthouse.com

## FRISTON
Suffolk

**Old School ★★★★**
*Guest Accommodation*
**SILVER AWARD**
Aldeburgh Road, Friston
IP17 1NP
t (01728) 688173
e oldschool@fristonoldschool.
freeserve.co.uk
w tiscover.co.uk

## FRITTON
Norfolk

**Decoy Barn Bed & Breakfast**
**★★★★** *Bed & Breakfast*
Beccles Road, Great Yarmouth
NR31 9AB
t (01493) 488222
e karenwilder9@aol.com
w decoybarn.co.uk

## FURNEUX PELHAM
Hertfordshire

**The White House ★★★★**
*Bed & Breakfast*
East End, Furneux Pelham,
Buntingford SG9 0JU
t (01279) 777629
e heather.spanes@talk21.com

## GAMLINGAY
Cambridgeshire

**Emplins ★★★**
*Bed & Breakfast*
Church Street, Gamlingay
SG19 3ER
t (01767) 650581
e philip.gorton@virgin.net
w smoothhound.co.uk

## GOLDHANGER
Essex

**Brent Cottage ★★★★**
*Bed & Breakfast*
18 Fish Street, Goldhanger
CM9 8AT
t (01621) 788275

## GOSFIELD
Essex

**Rare View ★★★**
*Guest Accommodation*
Shardlowes Farm, Hedingham
Road, Halstead CO9 1PL
t (01787) 474696
w rareviewholidays.com

## GREAT BADDOW
Essex

**Homecroft ★★★**
*Guest Accommodation*
Southend Road, Great Baddow
CM2 7AD
t (01245) 475070
e jesse@pryke.fsbusiness.co.
uk
w tiscover.co.uk

**Rothmans ★★**
*Bed & Breakfast*
22 High Street, Great Baddow
CM2 7HQ
t (01245) 476833
e pjaspbury@ukonline.co.uk
w rothmansbedandbreakfast.
co.uk

## GREAT BEALINGS
Suffolk

**Apple Tree Cottage ★★★**
*Bed & Breakfast*
Boot Street, Great Bealings
IP13 6PB
t (01473) 738997

## GREAT BRICETT
Suffolk

**Riverside Cottage ★★★★**
*Bed & Breakfast*
The Street, Great Bricett
IP7 7DQ
t (01473) 658266
e chasmhorne@aol.com
w riversidecottagebandb.co.uk

## GREAT CRESSINGHAM
Norfolk

**Vines ★★★★**
*Bed & Breakfast*
The Street, Great Cressingham
IP25 6NL
t (01760) 756303
e stay@thevines.fsbusiness.
co.uk
w thevines.fsbusiness.co.uk

## GREAT DUNMOW
Essex

**Harwood Guest House**
**★★★★** *Guest House*
52 Stortford Road, Great
Dunmow CM6 1DN
t (01371) 874627
e info@harwoodguesthouse.
com
w harwoodguesthouse.com

**Homelye Farm ♦♦♦♦**
*Guest Accommodation*
Homelye Chase, Braintree
Road, Great Dunmow
CM6 3AW
t (01371) 872127
e homelye@btconnect.com
w homelyefarm.co.uk

**Mallards**
Rating Applied For
*Guest Accommodation*
Star Lane, Dunmow CM6 1AY
t (01371) 872641
e millersmallardsdunmow@
tesco.net
w tiscover.co.uk

## GREAT EASTON
Essex

**The Swan Inn ★★★★** *Inn*
The Endway, Dunmow
CM6 2HG
t (01371) 870359
e theswangreateaston@tiscali.
co.uk
w theswangreateaston.co.uk

## GREAT ELLINGHAM
Norfolk

**Home Cottage Farm ★★★★**
*Farmhouse*
Penhill Road, Great Ellingham
NR17 1LS
t (01953) 483734
e maureenhcf@btinternet.com
w bandbuk.com

**Manor Farm ★★★★**
*Farmhouse* **GOLD AWARD**
Hingham Road, Great
Ellingham NR17 1JE
t (01953) 453388
e a.rivett@btconnect.com
w tiscover.co.uk

## GREAT HORMEAD
Hertfordshire

**Brick House Farm Bed And**
**Breakfast ★★★★** *Farmhouse*
**SILVER AWARD**
Great Hormead, Buntingford
SG9 0PB
t (01763) 289356
e helen@brickhousefarm.net
w brickhousefarm.net

## GREAT LEIGHS
Essex

**Acorns Bed & Breakfast**
**★★★★** *Bed & Breakfast*
3 Woodview Drive, Great
Leighs CM3 1NW
t (01245) 361403
e kathryn@
acornsbedandbreakfast.com
w acornsbedandbreakfast.co.
uk

## GREAT OAKLEY
Essex

**Zig Zag Cottage ★★★★**
*Bed & Breakfast*
**SILVER AWARD**
8 Queen Street, Great Oakley
CO12 5AS
t (01255) 880968
e ziza.lifestyle@zigzagcottage.
com
w zigzagcottage.com

## GREAT SALING
Essex

**The Mews ★★★★**
*Guest Accommodation*
The Grove, Saling Grove,
Braintree CM7 5DP
t 07747 844800
e info@thegroveestate.co.uk
w thegroveestate.co.uk

**The Orangery**
Rating Applied For
*Guest House*
The Grove, Saling Grove,
Braintree CM7 5DP
t 07867 971285
e info@thegroveestate.co.uk
w thegroveestate.co.uk

## GREAT SNORING
Norfolk

**Top Farm ★★★★** *Farmhouse*
Thursford Road, Great Snoring
NR21 0HW
t (01328) 820351
e davidperowne@aol.com
w tiscover.co.uk

## GREAT WILBRAHAM
Cambridgeshire

**Kettles Cottage ★★★★**
*Bed & Breakfast*
30 High Street, Great
Wilbraham CB21 5JD
t (01223) 880801
e kettlecottage@btopenworld.
com
w kettlescottage.co.uk

## GREAT YARMOUTH
Norfolk

**Anglia House ★★★**
*Guest House*
56 Wellesley Road, Great
Yarmouth NR30 1EX
t (01493) 844395
e angliahouse@aol.com
w tiscover.co.uk

**The Arch House** ★★★
*Guest House*
Great Yarmouth NR30 3AQ
t (01493) 854258
e barry@straw3.freeserve.co.
uk
w tiscover.co.uk

**Barnard House** ★★★★
*Bed & Breakfast*
SILVER AWARD
2 Barnard Crescent, Great
Yarmouth NR30 4DR
t (01493) 855139
e enquiries@barnardhouse.
com
w barnardhouse.com

**Barons Court** ★★★★
*Guest Accommodation*
5 Norfolk Square, Great
Yarmouth NR30 1EE
t (01493) 843987
e edward.shearing@
btopenworld.com
w baronscourthotel.co.uk

**Beaumont House** ★★★★
*Guest House* SILVER AWARD
52 Wellesley Road, Great
Yarmouth NR30 1EX
t (01493) 843957
e info@beaumonthousehotel.
com
w beaumonthousehotel.com

**Belvedere** ★★★
*Guest House*
90 North Denes Road, Great
Yarmouth NR30 4LN
t (01493) 844200
e info@stayatbelvedere.co.uk
w stayatbelvedere.co.uk

**The Bromley** ★★★★
*Guest House*
Great Yarmouth NR30 2HG
t (01493) 842321
e info@bromleyhotel.co.uk
w bromleyhotel.co.uk

**Cavendish House** ★★★
*Guest Accommodation*
19-20 Princes Road, Great
Yarmouth NR30 2DG
t (01493) 843148

**Chateau** ★★★
*Guest Accommodation*
1 North Drive, Great Yarmouth
NR30 1ED
t (01493) 859052
e info@chateau-gy.fsbusiness.
co.uk
w chateau-gy.fsbusiness.co.uk

**The Chimes** ★★★★
*Guest House*
48 Wellesley Road, Great
Yarmouth NR30 1EX
t (01493) 844610
e dilys.jones1@ntlworld.com
w thechimes.co.uk

**The Cleasewood** ★★★
*Guest Accommodation*
55 Wellesley Road, Great
Yarmouth NR30 1EX
t (01493) 843960
w tiscover.co.uk

**Dene House** ★★★
*Guest House*
89 North Denes Road, Great
Yarmouth NR30 4LW
t (01493) 844181
e denehouse@btinternet.com
w denehouse-greatyarmouth.
com

**The Fjaerland** ★★★★
*Guest Accommodation*
24-25 Trafalgar Road, Great
Yarmouth NR30 2LD
t (01493) 856339
w fjaerland.co.uk

**Great Yarmouth Yha** ★
*Hostel*
2 Sandown Road, Great
Yarmouth NR30 1EY
t (01493) 843991
e gtyarmouth@yha.org.uk
w yha.org.uk
▣▨

**Kensington** ★★★★
*Guest Accommodation*
Great Yarmouth NR30 4EW
t (01493) 844145
w tiscover.co.uk

**Kentville Guest House** ★★★
*Guest House*
5 Kent Square, Great Yarmouth
NR30 2EX
t (01493) 844783

**Kilbrannan Guest House**
★★★ *Guest House*
14 Trafalgar Road, Great
Yarmouth NR30 2LD
t (01493) 850383

**Lea Hurst Guest House**
Rating Applied For
*Guest House*
117 Wellesley Road, Great
Yarmouth NR30 2AP
t (01493) 843063

**Lynden Guest House** ★★★
*Guest House*
102 Wellesley Road, Great
Yarmouth NR30 2AR
t (01493) 844693
w tiscover.co.uk

**Maluth Lodge** ★★★★
*Guest Accommodation*
40 North Denes Road, Great
Yarmouth NR30 4LU
t (01493) 304652
e enquiries@maluthlodge.co.
uk
w maluthlodge.co.uk

**The Maryland** ★★★
*Guest House*
Great Yarmouth NR30 1EX
t (01493) 844409
e lucy@themaryland.co.uk
w themaryland.co.uk

**Merivon Guest House**
★★★★
*Guest Accommodation*
6 Trafalgar Road, Great
Yarmouth NR30 2LD
t (01493) 844419
w tiscover.co.uk

**Midland** ★★★
*Guest Accommodation*
Great Yarmouth NR30 2AP
t (01493) 330046
e info@
midlandhotelgreatyarmouth.
co.uk
w midlandhotelgreatyarmouth.
co.uk

**No. 78** ★★★★
*Guest Accommodation*
78 Marine Parade, Great
Yarmouth NR30 2DH
t (01493) 850001
e info@no78.co.uk
w no78.co.uk

**Prince Hotel** ★★★
*Guest Accommodation*
Great Yarmouth NR30 2DG
t (01493) 844033
e info@
princehotelgreatyarmouth.co.
uk
w princehotelgreatyarmouth.
co.uk

**Royston House** ★★★
*Guest House*
Great Yarmouth NR30 1DY
t (01493) 844680
e enquiries@roystonhotel.com
w roystonhotel.com

**The Ryecroft** ★★★
*Guest House*
91 North Denes Road, Great
Yarmouth NR30 4LW
t (01493) 844015
e info@ryecroftguesthouse.co.
uk
w ryecroftguesthouse.co.uk

**Sandy Acres** ★★★★
*Guest Accommodation*
80-81 Salisbury Road, Great
Yarmouth NR30 4LB
t (01493) 856553
e sandyacres@talk21.com
w sandyacres.co.uk

**The Shrewsbury Guest
House** ★★★
*Guest Accommodation*
9 Trafalgar Road, Great
Yarmouth NR30 2LD
t (01493) 844788
e shrewsbury.guesthouse@
virgin.net
w shrewsburyguesthouse.co.
uk

**Silverstone House** ★★★
*Guest Accommodation*
Great Yarmouth NR30 1EU
t (01493) 844862
e silverstonehouse@yahoo.co.
uk
w silverstone-house.co.uk

**The Southern** ★★★★
*Guest Accommodation*
46 Queens Road, Great
Yarmouth NR30 3JR
t (01493) 843313
e sally@southernhotel.co.uk
w southernhotel.co.uk

**Spindrift Guesthouse** ★★★
*Guest House*
Great Yarmouth NR30 1EU
t (01493) 843772
e spindrifthotel@btinternet.
com
w tiscover.co.uk

**Sunnydene** ★★★★
*Guest House*
83-84 North Denes Road,
Great Yarmouth NR30 4LW
t (01493) 843554
e info@sunnydenehotel.co.uk
w sunnydenehotel.co.uk

**Trevi Guest House** ★★★
*Guest House*
57 Wellesley Road, Great
Yarmouth NR30 1EX
t (01493) 842821

**Trotwood** ★★★
*Guest Accommodation*
2 North Drive, Great Yarmouth
NR30 1ED
t (01493) 843971
e richard@trotwood.
fsbusiness.co.uk
w trotwood.fsbusiness.co.uk

**Woods End Hotel** ★★★
*Guest House*
49 Wellesley Road, Great
Yarmouth NR30 1EX
t (01493) 842229

### GRIMSTON
Norfolk

**The Old Bell Guesthouse**
★★★★ *Guest House*
1 Gayton Road, Grimston
PE32 1BG
t (01485) 601156

### GUYHIRN
Cambridgeshire

**Oliver Twist Country Inn**
★★★★ *Inn*
High Road, Guyhirn PE13 4EA
t (01945) 450523
e enjoy@theolivertwist.com
w theolivertwist.com

### HADLEIGH
Suffolk

**Edge Hall** ★★★★★
*Guest Accommodation*
2 High Street, Hadleigh
IP7 5AP
t (01473) 822458
e r.rolfe@edgehall.co.uk
w edgehall.co.uk

### HAINFORD
Norfolk

**Haynford Lodge B&B** ★★
*Guest Accommodation*
Hall Road, Hainford NR10 3LX
t (01603) 898844
e info@haynfordlodge.co.uk
w haynfordlodge.co.uk

### HALESWORTH
Suffolk

**Fen-Way Guest House** ★★★
*Bed & Breakfast*
Fen-Way, School Lane,
Halesworth IP19 8BW
t (01986) 873574

**Rumburgh Farm** ★★★★
*Farmhouse*
Rumburgh, Halesworth
IP19 0RU
t (01986) 781351
e binder@rumburghfarm.co.
uk
w rumburghfarm.co.uk

**Valley Farm Vineyards**
★★★★ *Bed & Breakfast*
SILVER AWARD
Rumburgh Road, Wissett
IP19 0JJ
t (01986) 785535
e valleyfarmvineyards@tiscali.
com
w valleyfarmvineyards.com

## HALSTEAD
### Essex

**The Limes B&B @ Sible Hedingham ★★★**
*Bed & Breakfast*
Sible Hedingham CO9 3HP
t (01787) 460360
e patricia@patriciapatterson.
wanadoo.co.uk
w sudburysuffolk.com

**The White Hart ★★★** *Inn*
15 High Street, Halstead
CO9 2AA
t (01787) 475657
w innpubs.co.uk

## HALVERGATE
### Norfolk

**School Lodge Country Guesthouse ★★★★**
*Guest Accommodation*
Marsh Road, Halvergate
NR13 3QB
t (01493) 700111
e info@uk-guesthouse.com
w uk-guesthouse.com

## HARDWICK
### Cambridgeshire

**Wallis Farm ★★★★**
*Farmhouse*
98 Main Street, Hardwick
CB3 7QU
t (01954) 210347
e enquiries@wallisfarmhouse.
co.uk
w wallisfarmhouse.co.uk

## HARLESTON
### Norfolk

**Weston House Farm ★★★★**
*Farmhouse*
Mendham, Harleston IP20 0PB
t (01986) 782206
e holden@farmline.com
w westonhousefarm.co.uk

## HARLOW
### Essex

**Harlow International Hostel ★** *Hostel*
13 School Lane, Harlow
CM20 2QD
t (01279) 421702

**The Old Granary ★★★★**
*Guest Accommodation*
Holts Farm, Theshers Bush,
High Laver CM17 0NS
t (01279) 438377
e info@holtsfarm.co.uk
w holtsfarm.co.uk

## HARWICH
### Essex

**Paston Lodge ★★★**
*Guest Accommodation*
Una Road, Parkeston
CO12 4PP
t (01255) 551390
e b.b-harwich@pastonlodge.
co.uk
w tiscover.co.uk

**Stingray Freehouse ★★★**
*Guest Accommodation*
56 Church Street, Harwich
CO12 3DS
t (01255) 503507
e enquiries@thestingray.co.uk
w thestingray.co.uk

**Woodview Cottage ★★★★**
*Bed & Breakfast*
**SILVER AWARD**
Wrabness Road, Ramsey
CO12 5ND
t (01255) 886413
e annec@zetnet.co.uk
w woodview-cottage.co.uk

## HATFIELD BROAD OAK
### Essex

**Bury House ♦♦♦**
*Guest Accommodation*
High Street, Hatfield Broad
Oak, Bishop's Stortford
CM22 7HQ
t (01279) 718259
e bswandburyhouse@
wanadoo.co.uk
w tiscover.co.uk

**Cottage ★★** *Bed & Breakfast*
Dunmow Road, Hatfield Broad
Oak, Bishops Stortford
CM22 7JJ
t (01279) 718230
e elizabeth.britton@virgin.net
w tiscover.co.uk

## HATFIELD HEATH
### Essex

**Friars Farm ★★★★**
*Farmhouse* **SILVER AWARD**
Hatfield Heath, Bishop's
Stortford CM22 7AP
t (01279) 730244
w tiscover.co.uk

**Oaklands ★★★★**
*Bed & Breakfast*
Bishop's Stortford CM22 7AD
t (01279) 730240
e langman544@btinternet.
com
w tiscover.co.uk

## HAUGHLEY
### Suffolk

**Haughley House ★★★★★**
*Guest Accommodation*
**SILVER AWARD**
Haughley, Stowmarket
IP14 3NS
t (01449) 673398
e bowden@keme.co.uk
w haughleyhouse.co.uk

**Red House Farm ★★★★**
*Farmhouse*
Haughley, Stowmarket
IP14 3QP
t (01449) 673323
e mary@
redhousefarmhaughley.co.uk
w farmstayanglia.co.uk

## HAUXTON
### Cambridgeshire

**Dorset House ★★★★**
*Guest Accommodation*
35 Newton Road, Cambridge
CB2 5HL
t (01223) 844440
e dorsethouse@btopenworld.
com
w tiscover.co.uk

## HEACHAM
### Norfolk

**Holly House ★★★**
*Guest Accommodation*
3 Broadway, Heacham
PE31 7DF
t (01485) 572935
e irbusn@aol.com
w tiscover.co.uk

**Saint Annes Guest House ★★★★**
*Guest Accommodation*
53 Neville Road, Heacham
PE31 7HB
t (01485) 570021
e elaine@stannesguesthouse.
co.uk
w tiscover.co.uk

## HELHOUGHTON
### Norfolk

**Woodfarm House ★★★★★**
*Bed & Breakfast*
**SILVER AWARD**
Broomsthorpe Road,
Hellhoughton NR21 7BT
t (01485) 528586
e booking@woodfarm-house.
com
w woodfarm-house.com

## HELLESDON
### Norfolk

**Cairdean ★★★★**
*Bed & Breakfast*
71 Middletons Lane, Hellesdon
NR6 5NS
t (01603) 419041
e info@cairdean.co.uk
w cairdean.co.uk

**Old Corner Shop Guesthouse ★★★**
*Bed & Breakfast*
26 Cromer Road, Norwich
NR6 6LZ
t (01603) 419000
e info@
theoldcornershopguesthouse.
co.uk
w theoldcornershopguest
house.co.uk

## HEMEL HEMPSTEAD
### Hertfordshire

**47 Crescent Road ★★**
*Bed & Breakfast*
Hemel Hempstead HP2 4AJ
t (01442) 255137
w tiscover.co.uk

**Marsh Farm ★★★★**
*Bed & Breakfast*
Ledgemore Lane, Great
Gaddesden HP2 6HA
t (01442) 252517
e nicky@bennett-baggs.com
w marshfarm.org

**Red House Bed And Breakfast ★★★**
*Bed & Breakfast*
Alexandra Road, Hemel
Hempstead HP2 5BS
t (01442) 246665
w tiscover.co.uk

## HERTFORD
### Hertfordshire

**Castle Moat House ★★★★**
*Bed & Breakfast*
25 Castle Street, Hertford
SG14 1HH
t (01992) 584004
e thornton25@ntlworld.com

## HEVINGHAM
### Norfolk

**Marsham Arms Inn ★★★★**
*Inn*
Holt Road, Hevingham
NR10 5NP
t (01603) 754268
e info@marshamarms.co.uk
w marshamarms.co.uk

## HEYDON
### Cambridgeshire

**The End Cottage ♦♦♦♦**
*Guest Accommodation*
Fowlmere Road, Heydon
SG8 8PZ
t (01763) 838212
e d-macfayden@amserve.com
w tiscover.co.uk

## HICKLING
### Norfolk

**Black Horse Cottage ★★★**
*Bed & Breakfast*
The Green, Hickling NR12 0YA
t (01692) 598691
e info@blackhorsecottage.
com
w blackhorsecottage.com

**The Dairy Barns ★★★★**
*Farmhouse* **GOLD AWARD**
Lound Farm, Hickling, Norwich
NR12 0BE
t (01692) 598243
e enquiries@dairybarns.co.uk
w dairybarns.co.uk

## HINDRINGHAM
### Norfolk

**Field House ★★★★★**
*Bed & Breakfast*
**GOLD AWARD**
Moorgate Road, Hindringham
NR21 0PT
t (01328) 878726
e stay@
fieldhousehindringham.co.uk
w fieldhousehindringham.co.
uk

## HINTLESHAM
### Suffolk

**College Farm ★★★★**
*Farmhouse* **SILVER AWARD**
Hintlesham, Ipswich IP8 3NT
t (01473) 652253
e bandb@collegefarm.plus.
com
w collegefarm.net

## HISTON
### Cambridgeshire

**Wynwyck ★★★**
*Bed & Breakfast*
55 Narrow Lane, Histon
CB4 9HD
t (01223) 232496
e torrens@wynwyck-guest-
house.co.uk
w tiscover.co.uk

## HOLT
### Norfolk

**Byfords ★★★★★**
*Guest Accommodation*
**GOLD AWARD**
1-3 Shirehall Plain, Holt
NR25 6BG
t (01263) 711400
e queries@byfords.org.uk
w byfords.org.uk

**Hempstead Hall ★★★★**
*Farmhouse*
Hempstead, Holt NR25 6TN
t (01263) 712224

---

**Kadina** ★★★★
*Bed & Breakfast*
**SILVER AWARD**
High Kelling NR25 6QX
t (01263) 710116
e enquiries@kadinanorfolk.co.
uk
w kadinanorfolk.co.uk

**Three Corners** ★★
*Bed & Breakfast*
12 Kelling Close, Holt
NR25 6RU
t (01263) 713389
e ronvcox@aol.com
w tiscover.co.uk

**Stratford House** ★★★★
*Bed & Breakfast*
Holton St Mary CO7 6NT
t (01206) 298246
e fselleck@uwclub.net
w accomsuffolk.co.uk

**North View Guesthouse**
★★★ *Guest Accommodation*
North View, Malting Row,
Honington IP31 1RE
t (01359) 269423

**Willow Bed And Breakfast**
★★★★ *Bed & Breakfast*
Ixworth Road, Honington
IP31 1QY
t (01359) 269600
e celialawrence@talk21.com
w tiscover.co.uk

**Gable Cottage** ★★★★
*Guest Accommodation*
61 Lower Street, Horning
NR12 8AA
t (01692) 631239
e gablecottage61@aol.com
w tiscover.co.uk

**The Moorhen** ★★★★
*Bed & Breakfast*
45 Lower Street, Horning
NR12 8AA
t (01692) 631444
e themoorhenhorning@tiscali.
co.uk
w themoorhenhorning.co.uk

**The Six Bells** ★★★
*Bed & Breakfast*
The Street, Horringer, Bury St
Edmunds IP29 5SJ
t (01284) 735551
e martin@sixbellshorringer.co.
uk
w thesixbellshorringer.co.uk

**Chequer Cottage** ★★★★
*Bed & Breakfast*
43 Streetly End, Cambridge
CB1 6RP
t (01223) 891522
e stay@chequercottage.com
w chequercottage.com

**The Old Chapel** ★★★★
*Guest Accommodation*
Horsey Corner, Horsey
NR29 4EH
t (01493) 393498
e enquiries@
norfolkbedbreakfast.com
w norfolkbedbreakfast.com

**Beverley Farm** ★★★
*Guest Accommodation*
Norwich Road, Horstead
NR12 7EH
t (01603) 737279
e benton@beverleyfarm.
freeserve.co.uk
w tiscover.co.uk

**Cheriton House** ★★★★★
*Guest Accommodation*
**SILVER AWARD**
Mill Street, Houghton
PE28 2AZ
t (01480) 464004
e sales@cheritonhousecambs.
co.uk
w cheritonhousecambs.co.uk

**The Vineries Bed &
Breakfast** ★★★★
*Guest Accommodation*
72 Stalham Road, Hoveton
NR12 8DU
t (01603) 782514
e enquiries@thevineries.com
w thevineries.com

**Rectory Barn Bed and
Breakfast** ★★★★
*Bed & Breakfast*
Howe Green, Howe NR15 1HD
t (01508) 558176
e d.cuddon@btinternet.com
w rectorybarnbandb.co.uk

**The Plough Inn**
Rating Applied For
*Guest Accommodation*
Brockley Green, Sudbury
CO10 8DT
t (01440) 786789
e info@theploughhundon.co.
uk
w theploughhundon.co.uk

**Ashleigh Lodge** ★★★
*Guest Accommodation*
Austin Street, Hunstanton
PE36 6AL
t (01485) 533247
e nick.bishop1@tesco.net
w ashleighlodge.co.uk

**The Bays** ★★★★
*Guest House*
31 Avenue Road, Hunstanton
PE36 5BW
t (01485) 532079

**Belgrave House** ★★★★
*Guest Accommodation*
49 Northgate, Hunstanton
PE36 6DS
t (01485) 533007
e belgrave-house@btconnect.
com
w belgrave-housebb.co.uk

**The Burleigh** ★★★★
*Guest Accommodation*
7 Cliff Terrace, Hunstanton
PE36 6DY
t (01485) 533080
e reservations@theburleigh.
com
w theburleigh.com

**Cori House Bed & Breakfast**
★★★ *Bed & Breakfast*
Hunstanton PE36 5HA
t (01485) 533034
e corihousebandb@yahoo.co.
uk
w corihouse.co.uk

**Deepdene House** ★★★★
*Guest Accommodation*
**SILVER AWARD**
29 Avenue Road, Hunstanton
PE36 5BW
t (01485) 532460
e deepdenehouse@
btopenworld.com
w tiscover.co.uk

**Ellinbrook House** ★★★★
*Guest Accommodation*
37 Avenue Road, Hunstanton
PE36 5HW
t (01485) 532022
e ellinbrookhouse@aol.com
w ellinbrookhouse.co.uk

**Eton Lodge** ★★★★
*Bed & Breakfast*
47 Greevegate, Hunstanton
PE36 6AF
t (01485) 533783
w bbinhunstanton.co.uk

**The Gables** ★★★★
*Guest Accommodation*
Austin Street, Hunstanton
PE36 6AW
t (01485) 532514

**Garganey House** ★★★
*Guest House*
46 Northgate, Hunstanton
PE36 6DR
t (01485) 533269
e garganey1@f.s.net.co.uk
w tiscover.co.uk

**Gate Lodge** ★★★★
*Guest Accommodation*
**SILVER AWARD**
2 Westgate, Hunstanton
PE36 5AL
t (01485) 533549
e lynn@gatelodge-
guesthouse.co.uk
w gatelodge-guesthouse.co.uk

**Glenberis Bed And
Breakfast** ★★★★
*Bed & Breakfast*
**SILVER AWARD**
6 St Edmunds Avenue,
Hunstanton PE36 6AY
t (01485) 533663
e glenberis.hunstanton@
ntlworld.com
w tiscover.co.uk

**Hunstanton Yha** ★★★
*Hostel*
15 Avenue Road, Hunstanton
PE36 5BW
t (01485) 532061
e hunstanton@yha.org.uk
w yha.org.uk

**Kiama Cottage Guesthouse**
★★★★
*Guest Accommodation*
23 Austin Street, Hunstanton
PE36 6AN
t (01485) 533615
e kiamacottage@btopenworld.
com
w tiscover.co.uk

**The King William IV Country
Inn & Restaurant** ★★★★ *Inn*
**SILVER AWARD**
Heacham Road, Sedgeford,
Hunstanton PE36 5LU
t (01485) 571765
e info@
thekingwilliamsedgeford.co.uk
w thekingwilliamsedgeford.co.
uk

**Lakeside** ★★★★
*Guest Accommodation*
Waterworks Road, Old
Hunstanton PE36 6JE
t (01485) 533763
w oldwaterworks.co.uk

**Linksway Country House**
★★★★
*Guest Accommodation*
**SILVER AWARD**
Golf Course Road, Old
Hunstanton PE36 6JE
t (01485) 532209
e linksway-hotel@totalise.co.
uk
w linkswayhotel.com

**Miramar Guesthouse** ★★★
*Guest House*
7 Boston Square, Hunstanton
PE36 6DT
t (01485) 532902
w tiscover.co.uk

**Neptune Inn** ★★★★ *Inn*
**SILVER AWARD**
Old Hunstanton Road, Old
Hunstanton PE36 6HZ
t (01485) 532122
e reservations@theneptune.
co.uk
w theneptune.co.uk

**Pads** ★★★★ *Bed & Breakfast*
**SILVER AWARD**
3 Austin Street, Hunstanton
PE36 6AJ
t (01485) 533366

**Peacock House** ★★★★
*Guest Accommodation*
**SILVER AWARD**
28 Park Road, Hunstanton
PE36 5BY
t (01485) 534551
e peacockhouse@onetel.com
w peacockhouse-hunstanton.
co.uk

**Queensbury House** ★★★
*Bed & Breakfast*
Glebe Avenue, Hunstanton
PE36 6BS
t (01485) 534320
w tiscover.co.uk

**Rosamaly Guesthouse**
★★★★
*Guest Accommodation*
14 Glebe Avenue, Hunstanton
PE36 6BS
t (01485) 534187
e vacancies@rosamaly.co.uk
w tiscover.co.uk
🖼🖊

**Rose Fitt House** ★★★★
*Guest Accommodation*
40 Northgate, Hunstanton
PE36 6DR
t (01485) 534776
e andrea.rosefitt@btinternet.
com
w rose-fitt-house-hunstanton.
co.uk

**Sunningdale** ★★★★
*Guest House*
3-5 Avenue Road, Hunstanton
PE36 5BW
t (01485) 532562
e reception@
sunningdalehotel.com
w tiscover.co.uk

**Bramble Corner** ★★
*Guest Accommodation*
Bluntisham PE28 3LN
t (01487) 842646
e enquiries@bramblecorner.
co.uk
w bramblecorner.co.uk

**Shepherds Cottage** ★★★★
*Bed & Breakfast*
Grange Road, Ickleton, Saffron
Walden CB10 1TA
t (01799) 531171
e jcase@nascr.net
w shepherds-cottage.co.uk

**Pencob House** ★★★★
*Bed & Breakfast*
SILVER AWARD
56 Hill Road, Ingoldisthorpe
PE31 6NZ
t (01485) 543882
e pencob@supanet.com
w tiscover.co.uk

**Bramshaw** ★★★★
*Guest House*
77 Bucklesham Road, Ipswich
IP3 8TR
t (01473) 712379
e gill.mann@btinternet.com
w tiscover.co.uk

**Carlton** ★★★
*Guest Accommodation*
41-43 Berners Street, Ipswich
IP1 3LT
t (01473) 254955
e carltonhotel3@hotmail.com
w carlton-ipswich.co.uk

**Gables of Park Road** ♦♦♦♦
*Guest Accommodation*
17 Park Road, Ipswich IP1 3SX
t (01473) 254252
e enquiries@
gablesofparkroad.co.uk
w gablesofparkroad.co.uk

**The Gatehouse Hotel Ltd**
★★★★★
*Guest Accommodation*
SILVER AWARD
799 Old Norwich Road, Ipswich
IP1 6LH
t (01473) 741897

**Lattice Lodge Guest House**
★★★★ *Guest House*
SILVER AWARD
Ipswich IP4 4EP
t (01473) 712474
e latticelodge@btinternet.com
w latticelodge.co.uk

**Queenscliffe Bed And
Breakfast** ★★★★
*Bed & Breakfast*
2 Queenscliffe Road, Ipswich
IP2 9AS
t (01473) 686810
e queenscliffe@supanet.com
w tiscover.co.uk

**Sidegate Guesthouse**
★★★★ *Guest House*
SILVER AWARD
121 Sidegate Lane, Ipswich
IP4 4JB
t (01473) 728714
e bookings@
sidegateguesthouse.co.uk
w sidegateguesthouse.co.uk

**Hill House** ★★★★
*Bed & Breakfast*
Kelsale IP17 2NZ
t (01728) 602940
e smp@hillhousekelsale.co.uk
w hillhousekelsale.co.uk

**Highfields Farm B&B**
★★★★ *Farmhouse*
Highfields Lane, Kelvedon
CO5 9BJ
t (01376) 570334
e highfieldsfarm@
farmersweekly.net
w highfieldsfarm.co.uk

**Swan House** ★★★
*Bed & Breakfast*
3 Swan Street, Kelvedon
CO5 9NG
t (01376) 573768
e dnspiers@lineone.net
w swan-house.co.uk

**Box Tree Farm** ★★★★
*Farmhouse*
Kettlebaston IP7 7PZ
t (01449) 741318
e junecarpenter@btinternet.
com
w boxtreefarm.350.com
🖼🖊

**Church Farm** ★★★
*Farmhouse*
Kettleburgh, Woodbridge
IP13 7LF
t (01728) 723532
e jbater@suffolkonline.net

**67 Hempstead Road** ★★
*Bed & Breakfast*
Kings Langley WD4 8BS
t (01923) 400453
e ian.macpherson17@
ntlworld.com
w tiscover.co.uk

**The Bank House** ★★★★★
*Guest Accommodation*
GOLD AWARD
Kings Staithe Square, King's
Lynn PE30 1RD
t (01553) 660492
e colinbailey@
dawbarnspearson.co.uk
w thebankhouse.co.uk

**Beeches Guesthouse** ★★★
*Guest House*
2 Guanock Terrace, King's
Lynn PE30 5QT
t (01553) 766577
e kelvin.sellers@virgin.net
w beechesguesthouse.co.uk

**Fairlight Lodge** ★★★★
*Guest Accommodation*
79 Goodwins Road, King's
Lynn PE30 5PE
t (01553) 762234
e enquiries@fairlightlodge.co.
uk
w fairlightlodge.co.uk

**King's Lynn YHA** ★★ *Hostel*
Thoresby College, College
Lane, King's Lynn PE30 1JB
t 0870 770 5902
🖼🖊

**Maranatha Guesthouse**
★★★ *Guest House*
115-117 Gaywood Road,
King's Lynn PE30 2PU
t (01553) 774596
e maranathaguesthouse@
yahoo.co.uk
w maranathaguesthouse.co.uk

**Marsh Farm** ★★★★
*Farmhouse*
Wolferton, King's Lynn
PE31 6HB
t (01485) 540265
e info@
marshfarmbedandbreakfast.co.
uk
w marshfarmbedandbreakfast.
co.uk

**Old Rectory** ★★★
*Guest Accommodation*
33 Goodwins Road, King's
Lynn PE30 5QX
t (01553) 768544
e clive@theoldrectory-
kingslynn.com
w theoldrectory-kingslynn.com

**Butterley House** ★★★★
*Bed & Breakfast*
Leet Hill Farm, Kirby Cane
NR35 2HJ
t (01508) 518301
w tiscover.co.uk

**Goldhill** ★★★
*Bed & Breakfast*
10 Deards End Lane,
Knebworth SG3 6NL
t (01438) 813230
e tengoldhill@hotmail.com
w maryharris.co.uk

**Paradise Lodge** ★★★★
*Guest Accommodation*
Highbridge Gravel Road,
Lakenheath, Brandon IP27 9HD
t (01842) 862963

**Manor Farm** ★★★★
*Farmhouse*
Green End, Landbeach,
Cambridge CB4 8ED
t (01223) 860165

**Oak Apple Farm** ★★★★
*Bed & Breakfast*
Greyhound Hill, Langham
CO4 5QF
t (01206) 272234
e oak.apple.farm@btinternet.
com
w smoothhound.co.uk/hotels/
oak.html

**Home Close** ★★★★
*Guest Accommodation*
North Street, Langham
NR25 7DG
t (01328) 830348
e patallen@lineone.net

**Angel Inn** ★★★★ *Inn*
Larling, Norwich NR16 2QU
t (01953) 717963
w tiscover.co.uk

**Crouch Valley Motel** ★★★
*Guest Accommodation*
Burnham Road, Latchingdon
CM3 6EX
t (01621) 740770
e reservations@crouchvalley.
com
w crouch-valley-motel.co.uk

**Angel Gallery** ★★★★
*Bed & Breakfast*
17 Market Place, Lavenham
CO10 9QZ
t (01787) 248417
e angel-gallery@gofornet.co.
uk
w lavenham.co.uk

**Brett Farm** ★★★★
*Bed & Breakfast*
The Common, Sudbury,
Lavenham CO10 9PG
t (01787) 248533
e brettfarmbandb@aol.com
w brettfarm.com

**De Vere House ★★★★★**
*Bed & Breakfast*
SILVER AWARD
Water Street, Sudbury
CO10 9RW
t (01787) 249505
e deverehouse@aol.com
w deverehouse.co.uk

**Erindor ★★★★**
*Bed & Breakfast*
Lavenham CO10 9PY
t (01787) 249198
w erindor.co.uk

**Guinea House Bed & Breakfast ★★★★**
*Bed & Breakfast*
SILVER AWARD
16 Bolton Street, Lavenham,
Sudbury CO10 9RG
t (01787) 249046
e gdelucy@aol.com
w guineahouse.co.uk

**Lavenham Great House Restaurant with Rooms**
★★★★ *Bed & Breakfast*
SILVER AWARD
Market Place, Lavenham
CO10 9QZ
t (01787) 247431
e info@greathouse.co.uk
w greathouse.co.uk

**Lavenham Priory ★★★★★**
*Guest Accommodation*
GOLD AWARD
Water Street, Lavenham
CO10 9RW
t (01787) 247404
e mail@lavenhampriory.co.uk
w lavenhampriory.co.uk

**Old Convent ★★★★**
*Bed & Breakfast*
SILVER AWARD
The Street, Kettlebaston
IP7 7QA
t (01449) 741557
e holidays@kettlebaston.fsnet.
co.uk
w tiscover.co.uk

**Red House ★★★★**
*Bed & Breakfast*
29 Bolton Street, Lavenham
CO10 9RG
t (01787) 248074
e redhouse-lavenham@
amserve.com
w lavenham.co.uk/redhouse

### LEIGHTON BUZZARD
### Bedfordshire

**Ivy Cottage Annex ★★★**
*Guest Accommodation*
43 High Street, Leighton
Buzzard LU7 0JS
t (01296) 689132
w tiscover.co.uk

### LEISTON
### Suffolk

**Field End ★★★★**
*Guest House* SILVER AWARD
1 Kings Road, Leiston
IP16 4DA
t (01728) 833527
w fieldendbedandbreakfast.co.
uk

### LESSINGHAM
### Norfolk

**The Star Inn ★★★** *Inn*
Star Inn, School Road,
Lessingham NR12 0DN
t (01692) 580510
e info@thestarlessingham.co.
uk
w thestarlessingham.co.uk

### LEVINGTON
### Suffolk

**Lilac Cottage ★★★★**
*Bed & Breakfast*
Levington Green, Ipswich
IP10 0LE
t (01473) 659509
e lenandjo.wenham@
btinternet.com
w tiscover.co.uk

### LITCHAM
### Norfolk

**Bull Inn ★★★** *Inn*
Church Street, Litcham, King's
Lynn PE32 2NS
t (01328) 701340
e jdfrankland@btinternet.com
w northnorfolkinns.co.uk

**Hanworth House ★★★★**
*Bed & Breakfast*
Pound Lane, Litcham, King's
Lynn PE32 2QR
t (01328) 701172
e cfstewart@breathemail.net
w hanworthhouse.com

### LITTLE BEALINGS
### Suffolk

**Timbers ★★★**
*Guest Accommodation*
Martlesham Road, Little
Bealings, Woodbridge IP13 6LY
t (01473) 622713
w tiscover.co.uk

### LITTLE CRESSINGHAM
### Norfolk

**Sycamore House B&B
★★★★**
*Guest Accommodation*
Sycamore House, Little
Cressingham IP25 6NE
t (01953) 881887
w tiscover.co.uk

### LITTLE DOWNHAM
### Cambridgeshire

**Bury House Bed And Breakfast ★★★**
*Bed & Breakfast*
11 Main Street, Little
Downham CB6 2ST
t (01353) 698766
e p.ambrose@amserve.com
w tiscover.co.uk

### LITTLE EASTON
### Essex

**Roslyns ★★★★**
*Bed & Breakfast*
SILVER AWARD
Little Easton, Dunmow
CM6 2JF
t (01371) 852177
e clare@roslynsbandb.co.uk
w roslynsbandb.co.uk

### LITTLE HALLINGBURY
### Hertfordshire

**SWAY ★★★★**
*Bed & Breakfast*
Wrights Green, Little
Hallingbury, Bishop's Stortford
CM22 7RH
t (01279) 723572

### LITTLE SAMPFORD
### Essex

**Bush Farm ★★★★**
*Guest Accommodation*
SILVER AWARD
Bush Lane, Little Sampford,
Saffron Walden CB10 2RY
t (01799) 586636
e angelabushfarm@yahoo.co.
uk
w tiscover.co.uk

### LITTLE WALTHAM
### Essex

**Channels Lodge ★★★★**
*Guest Accommodation*
SILVER AWARD
Belsteads Farm Lane, Little
Waltham CM3 3PT
t (01245) 441547
e info@channelslodge.co.uk
w channelslodge.co.uk

**Little Belsteads ★★★★**
*Bed & Breakfast*
Back Lane, Little Waltham
CM3 3PP
t (01245) 360249
w tiscover.co.uk

### LITTLEPORT
### Cambridgeshire

**Glebe House ★★★★**
*Bed & Breakfast*
Littleport CB6 1RG
t (01353) 862924
e info@glebehouseuk.co.uk
w glebehouseuk.co.uk

**Killiney House ★★★★★**
*Bed & Breakfast*
GOLD AWARD
18 Barkhams Lane, Littleport
CB6 1NN
t (01353) 860404
e enquiries@killineyhouse.co.
uk
w killineyhouse.co.uk

### LODDON
### Norfolk

**Hall Green Farm B&B
★★★★**
*Guest Accommodation*
Norton Road, Loddon
NR14 6DT
t (01508) 522039
e hallgreenfarm@hotmail.com
w hallgreenfarm.cjb.net

### LONG MELFORD
### Suffolk

**Denmark House ★★★★**
*Bed & Breakfast*
Hall Street, Long Melford,
Sudbury CO10 9JD
t (01787) 378798

**High Street Farmhouse
★★★★ *Bed & Breakfast***
SILVER AWARD
High Street, Long Melford,
Sudbury CO10 9BD
t (01787) 375765
e mail@gallopingchef.co.uk
w highstreetfarmhouse.co.uk

### LONG STRATTON
### Norfolk

**Greenacres Farm ★★★★**
*Bed & Breakfast*
Wood Green, Long Stratton
NR15 2RR
t (01508) 530261
e greenacresfarm@tinyworld.
co.uk
w abreakwithtradition.co.uk

### LOUGHTON
### Essex

**9 Garden Way ★★**
*Bed & Breakfast*
Loughton IG10 2SF
t (020) 8508 6134
w tiscover.co.uk

**Epping Forest Yha ★★**
*Hostel*
Wellington Hill, High Beach,
Loughton IG10 4AG
t 0870 770 5822
w yha.org.uk

**Forest Edge ★★★**
*Bed & Breakfast*
York Hill, Loughton IG10 1HZ
t (020) 8508 9834
e arthur@catterallarthur.fsnet.
co.uk
w tiscover.co.uk

### LOWESTOFT
### Suffolk

**Fairways Bed and Breakfast**
★★★★ *Bed & Breakfast*
288 Normanston Drive, Oulton
Broad, Lowestoft NR32 2PS
t (01502) 582756
e info@fairwaysbb.co.uk
w fairwaysbb.co.uk

**Homelea Guest House ★★★**
*Guest House*
Marine Parade, Lowestoft
NR33 0QN
t (01502) 511640
e info@homeleaguesthouse.
co.uk
w homeleaguesthouse.co.uk

**Lorne Guest House ★★★**
*Guest House*
4 Pakefield Road, Lowestoft
NR33 0HS
t (01502) 568972
w tiscover.co.uk

**Saint Catherines House**
★★★ *Bed & Breakfast*
186 Denmark Road, Lowestoft
NR32 2EN
t (01502) 500951
w tiscover.co.uk

**Sandcastle ★★★★**
*Guest House*
35 Marine Parade, Lowestoft
NR33 0QN
t (01502) 511799
e susie@thesandcastle.co.uk
w thesandcastle.co.uk

## LUDHAM
### Norfolk

**Broadland Bed and Breakfast** ★★★★
*Bed & Breakfast*
West End Lodge, Norwich Road, Ludham NR29 5PB
t (01692) 678420
e westendlodge@btinternet.com
w bedbreakfast-norfolkbroads.co.uk

## MALDON
### Essex

**Anchor Guesthouse** ★★★
*Guest House*
7 Church Street, Maldon CM9 5HW
t (01621) 855706
w tiscover.co.uk

**Limes** ★★★★ *Guest House*
21 Market Hill, Maldon CM9 4PZ
t (01621) 850350
e maldonlimes@ukonline.co.uk
w smoothhound.co.uk

**Star House Bed And Breakfast** ♦♦♦
*Guest Accommodation*
72 Wantz Road, Maldon CM9 5DE
t (01621) 853527
e star.house@talk21.com
w tiscover.co.uk

**Tatoi Bed & Breakfast**
★★★★ *Bed & Breakfast*
31 Acacia Drive, Maldon CM9 6AW
t (01621) 853841 & 07860 162328
e diana.rogers2@btinternet.com

## MANNINGTREE
### Essex

**Dry Dock** ★★★
*Bed & Breakfast*
Dry Dock Quay Street, Manningtree CO11 1AU
t (01206) 392620
w tiscover.co.uk

**Emsworth House** ★★★★
*Bed & Breakfast*
Station Road, Ship Hill, Bradfield, Manningtree CO11 2UP
t (01255) 870860
e emsworthhouse@hotmail.com
w emsworthhouse.co.uk

## MARCH
### Cambridgeshire

**Causeway Guest House**
★★★ *Guest House*
6 The Causeway, March PE15 9NT
t (01354) 650823

**Willows Motel** ★★★
*Guest Accommodation*
Elm Road, March PE15 8PS
t (01354) 661292
e david.coe4@btinternet.com
w willowsmotel.co.uk

## MARKYATE
### Hertfordshire

**Beechwood Home Farm**
★★★ *Farmhouse*
Beechwood Park, Markyate AL3 8AJ
t (01582) 840209
w tiscover.co.uk

## MARSTON MORETAINE
### Bedfordshire

**Aldermans Tanglewood B&B**
★★★ *Bed & Breakfast*
35 Upper Shelton Road, Upper Shelton, Marston, Bedford MK43 0LT
t (01234) 768584
e alanalder@freenetname.co.uk
w tiscover.co.uk

**Twin Lodge** ★★★★
*Bed & Breakfast*
177 Lower Shelton Road, Lower Shelton MK43 0LP
t (01234) 767597
e pwillsmore@waitrose.co.uk
w tiscover.co.uk

**White Cottage** ★★★★
*Guest House*
Marston Hill, Cranfield MK43 0QJ
t (01234) 751766
e stay@thewhitecottage.fsbusiness.co.uk
w thewhitecottage.net

## MELTON CONSTABLE
### Norfolk

**Lowes Farm** ★★★
*Guest Accommodation*
Edgefield, Melton Constable NR24 2EX
t (01263) 712317
e davidhudson@tiscali.co.uk
w tiscover.co.uk

## MEPPERSHALL
### Bedfordshire

**Old Joe's** ★★ *Bed & Breakfast*
90 Fildyke Road, Shefford SG17 5LU
t (01462) 815585
e cih@freenet.co.uk
🖬

## MILTON
### Cambridgeshire

**Ambassador Lodge** ★★★★
*Guest Accommodation*
37 High Street, Milton CB24 6DF
t (01223) 860168
e ambassadorlodge@yahoo.co.uk
w amassadorlodge.co.uk

## MILTON BRYAN
### Bedfordshire

**Town Farm** ★★★★
*Farmhouse*
South End, Milton Bryan MK17 9HS
t (01525) 210001
e townfarm@tesco.net
w tiscover.co.uk

## MOULTON
### Suffolk

**37 Newmarket Road** ★★★★
*Bed & Breakfast*
Newmarket Road, Moulton CB8 8QP
t (01638) 750362
e dkbowes@waitrose.com
w tiscover.co.uk

## MUCH HADHAM
### Hertfordshire

**Wheatcroft** ★★★★
*Bed & Breakfast*
Hadham Cross, Much Hadham SG10 6AP
t (01279) 842206

## MUNDESLEY
### Norfolk

**The Durdans** ★★★★
*Guest Accommodation*
36 Trunch Road, Mundesley NR11 8JX
t (01263) 722225
e info@thedurdans.co.uk
w thedurdans.co.uk

**Overcliff Lodge**
Rating Applied For
*Guest House*
46 Cromer Road, Mundesley NR11 8DB
t (01263) 720016
e overclifflodge@btinternet.com
w tiscover.co.uk

## MUNDFORD
### Norfolk

**Colveston Manor** ★★★★
*Farmhouse*
Mundford IP26 5HU
t (01842) 878218
e mail@colveston-manor.co.uk
w colveston-manor.co.uk

## MUNDHAM
### Norfolk

**Grange Farm Bed & Breakfast**
Rating Applied For
*Bed & Breakfast*
Grange Road, Norwich NR14 6EP
t (01508) 550027

## NARBOROUGH
### Norfolk

**Mill View Rooms** ★★★★
*Bed & Breakfast*
Main Road, Narborough PE32 1TE
t (01760) 338005
e narfish@supanet.com
w narfish.co.uk

## NAYLAND
### Suffolk

**Gladwins Farm** ★★★★
*Farmhouse*
Harpers Hill, Nayland CO6 4NU
t (01206) 262261
e gladwinsfarm@aol.com
w gladwinsfarm.co.uk

**The Steam Mill House**
★★★★ *Bed & Breakfast*
1 Fen Street, Nayland CO6 4HT
t (01206) 262818
e brendaassing@tiscali.co.uk
w thesteammillhouse.com

**White Hart Inn** ★★★★★
*Restaurant with Rooms*
**GOLD AWARD**
High Street, Nayland CO6 4JF
t (01206) 263382
e nayhart@aol.com
w whitehart-nayland.co.uk

## NEATISHEAD
### Norfolk

**Regency Guesthouse**
★★★★ *Guest House*
**SILVER AWARD**
The Street, Neatishead NR12 8AD
t (01692) 630233
e regencywrigley@btopenworld.com
w go2norfolk.co.uk

## NEW BUCKENHAM
### Norfolk

**Pump Court Bed and Breakfast** ★★★★
*Bed & Breakfast*
**SILVER AWARD**
Church Street, New Buckenham NR16 2BA
t (01953) 861153
e enquiries@pump-court.co.uk
w pump-court.co.uk

## NEWGATE STREET
### Hertfordshire

**Mulberry Lodge** ★★★★
*Guest Accommodation*
Newgate Street, Epping Green, Hertford SG13 8NQ
t (01707) 879652
e boookings@mulberrylodge.org.uk
w mulberrylodge.org.uk

## NEWMARKET
### Suffolk

**Birdcage Walk** ★★★★
*Guest Accommodation*
**GOLD AWARD**
2 Birdcage Walk, Newmarket CB8 0NE
t (01638) 669456
e patmerry@btinternet.com
w birdcagewalk.co.uk

**Hilldown House** ★★★
*Guest Accommodation*
19 Duchess Drive, Newmarket CB8 8AG
t (01638) 664250
e angiecampbell@talktalk.net
w tiscover.co.uk

**Laurel** ★★★ *Bed & Breakfast*
40 Green Road, Newmarket CB8 9BA
t (01638) 664461
w tiscover.co.uk

**Meadow House** ★★★★
*Guest Accommodation*
2a High Street, Burwell, Cambridge CB25 0HB
t (01638) 741926
e hilary@themeadowhouse.co.uk
w themeadowhouse.co.uk

**Rosery** ★★★★
*Guest Accommodation*
15 Church Street, Exning CB8 7EH
t (01638) 577312
e roseryhotel@tiscali.co.uk
w roseryhotel.co.uk

**Sandhurst ★★★**
*Guest Accommodation*
14 Cardigan Street, Newmarket
CB8 8HZ
t (01638) 667483 &
07714 347130
e crighton@rousnewmarket.
freeserve.co.uk
w tiscover.co.uk

**The Walnuts ★★★**
*Guest House*
22 Exning Road, Newmarket
CB8 0AB
t (01638) 664121
e walnutsguesthouse@
btinternet.com
w walnuts-guesthouse.co.uk

NORTH FAMBRIDGE
Essex

**Ferry Boat Inn ★★★** *Inn*
North Fambridge CM3 6LR
t (01621) 740208
e sylviaferryboat@aol.com
w ferryboatinn.net

NORTH LOPHAM
Norfolk

**Church Farm House**
**★★★★★**
*Guest Accommodation*
GOLD AWARD
Church Road, North Lopham
IP22 2LP
t (01379) 687270
e hosts@bassetts.demon.co.
uk
w churchfarmhouse.org

NORTH WALSHAM
Norfolk

**Bradfield House ★★★★**
*Bed & Breakfast*
19 Station Road, North
Walsham NR28 0DZ
t (01692) 404352
e chrissiemike@aol.com
w bradfieldhouse.com

**Church View House Bed and
Breakfast ◆◆◆◆**
*Guest Accommodation*
Westwick Road, Worstead
NR28 9SD
t (01692) 536863
e enquiry@church-view.co.uk
w church-view.co.uk

**Pinetrees ★★★★**
*Guest Accommodation*
SILVER AWARD
45 Happisburgh Road, North
Walsham NR28 9HB
t (01692) 404213
e elizblaxell@hotmail.com
w pinetreesbnb.co.uk

NORTH WOOTTON
Norfolk

**Red Cat Hotel ★★★** *Inn*
Station Road, North Wootton
PE30 3QH
t (01553) 631244
e enquiries@redcathotel.com
w redcathotel.com

NORTHREPPS
Norfolk

**The Stables Church Farm
★★★★**
*Guest Accommodation*
SILVER AWARD
Church Farm, Northrepps
NR27 0LG
t (01263) 579790
w tiscover.co.uk

NORWICH
Norfolk

**3 Chalk Hill Road B&B ★★**
*Bed & Breakfast*
3 Chalk Hill Road, Norwich
NR1 1SL
t (01603) 619188
e talk@moiraashby.com
w 3chalkhillroadbnb.com

**Arbor Linden Lodge ★★★★**
*Guest House*
Linden House, 557 Earlham
Road, Norwich NR4 7HW
t (01603) 451303
e info@guesthousenorwich.
com
w guesthousenorwich.co.uk

**Aylwyne House ★★★**
*Guest House*
59 Aylsham Road, Norwich
NR3 2HF
t (01603) 665798
e aylwyne@firenet.uk.net
w tiscover.co.uk

**Beaufort Lodge ★★★★**
*Guest House* SILVER AWARD
62 Earlham Road, Norwich
NR2 3DF
t (01603) 627928
e beaufortlodge@aol.com
w beaufortlodge.com

**Becklands ★★★★**
*Guest Accommodation*
105 Holt Road, Norwich
NR10 3AB
t (01603) 898582
e becklands@aol.com

**Belmonte And The Light Bar
★★★** *Guest Accommodation*
60-62 Prince of Wales Road,
Norwich NR1 1LT
t (01603) 622533
e hotelbelmonte@hotmail.com
w hotelbelmonte.com

**The Blue Boar Inn ★★★★**
*Inn*
259 Wroxham Road,
Sprowston NR7 8RL
t (01603) 426802

**Blue Cedar Lodge
Guesthouse ★★★**
*Guest House*
391 Earlham Road, Norwich
NR2 3RQ
t (01603) 458331
w tiscover.co.uk

**Butterfly Guest House ★★★**
*Guest House*
240 Thorpe Road, Norwich
NR1 1TW
t (01603) 437740

**Cavell House ★★★★**
*Bed & Breakfast*
The Common, Swardeston,
Norwich NR14 8DZ
t (01508) 578195
e joljean.harris@virgin.net

**Chestnut Grove ★★★★**
*Guest House*
129 Newmarket Road, Norwich
NR4 6SZ
t (01603) 451932
w tiscover.co.uk

**Church Farm Guesthouse
★★★★**
*Guest Accommodation*
Church Street, Norwich
NR10 3DB
t (01603) 898020
e churchfarmguesthouse@
btopenworld.com
w tiscover.co.uk

**Cottage ★★★★**
*Guest Accommodation*
Rectory Lane, Bunwell
NR16 1QU
t (01953) 789226
w tiscover.co.uk

**Earlham Guesthouse ★★★**
*Guest House*
147 Earlham Road, Norwich
NR2 3RG
t (01603) 454169
e earlhamgh@hotmail.com
w earlhamguesthouse.co.uk

**Eaton Bower ★★★★**
*Bed & Breakfast*
20 Mile End Road, Norwich
NR4 7QY
t (01603) 462204

**Edmar Lodge ★★★**
*Guest Accommodation*
64 Earlham Road, Norwich
NR2 3DF
t (01603) 615599
e mail@edmarlodge.co.uk
w edmarlodge.co.uk

**Gables Guesthouse ★★★★**
*Guest House*
527 Earlham Road, Norwich
NR4 7HN
t (01603) 456666
w tiscover.co.uk

**Ivy Dene ★★** *Guest House*
12 Earlham Road, Norwich
NR2 3DB
t (01603) 762567
e theivydene@hotmail.co.uk

**Manor Barn House ★★★★**
*Guest Accommodation*
Back Lane, Rackheath, Norwich
NR13 6NN
t (01603) 783543
e jane.roger@
manorbarnhouse.co.uk
w manorbarnhouse.co.uk

**Marlborough House ★★★**
*Guest House*
22 Stracey Road, Norwich
NR1 1EZ
t (01603) 628005

**Oakbrook House – South
Norfolk's Guest House
★★★** *Guest Accommodation*
Frith Way, Great Moulton,
Norwich NR15 2HE
t (01379) 677359
e oakbrookhouse@btinternet.
com
w oakbrookhouse.co.uk

**Old Lodge ★★★★**
*Bed & Breakfast*
SILVER AWARD
New Road, Bawburgh NR9 3LZ
t (01603) 742798
e peggy@theoldlodge.
freeserve.co.uk
w theoldlodge.co.uk

**Saint Edmundsbury ★★★**
*Guest House*
The Street, Old Costessey,
Norwich NR8 5DG
t (01603) 745959
e smiths@stedmundsbury.
fsbusiness.co.uk
w stedmundsbury.co.uk

**University of East Anglia,
Guest Suite**
Rating Applied For
*Campus*
Earlham Road, Norwich
NR4 7TJ
t (01603) 591111
e guestsuite@uea.ac.uk
w uea.ac.uk/conferences

**Wedgewood House ★★★**
*Guest Accommodation*
42 St Stephens Road, Norwich
NR1 3RE
t (01603) 625730
e stay@wedgewoodhouse.co.
uk
w wedgewoodhouse.co.uk

**Wensum Guest House**
Rating Applied For
*Guest House*
225 Dereham Road, Norwich
NR2 3TF
t (01603) 621069
w tiscover.co.uk

OLD CATTON
Norfolk

**Catton Old Hall ★★★★★**
*Guest Accommodation*
SILVER AWARD
Lodge Lane, Norwich NR6 7HG
t (01603) 419379
e enquiries@catton-hall.co.uk
w tiscover.co.uk

ORSETT
Essex

**Jays Lodge ★★★★**
*Guest Accommodation*
Chapel Farm, Baker Street,
Orsett, Grays RM16 3LJ
t (01375) 891663
e info@jayslodge.co.uk
w jayslodge.co.uk

OULTON
Suffolk

**Laurel Farm ★★★★**
*Bed & Breakfast*
Hall Lane, Oulton NR32 5DL
t (01502) 568724
e janethodgkin@laurelfarm.
com
w laurelfarm.com

## OULTON BROAD
### Suffolk

**The Mill House Bed and Breakfast ★★★★**
*Guest House* SILVER AWARD
53 Bridge Road, Oulton Broad
NR32 3LN
t (01502) 565038
e penny@themillhousebedand
breakfast.co.uk
w themillhousebedand
breakfast.co.uk

## OVERSTRAND
### Norfolk

**Cliff Cottage Bed And Brea**
★★★ *Bed & Breakfast*
18 High Street, Overstrand
NR27 0AB
t (01263) 578179
e roymin@btinternet.com
w cliffcottagebandb.com

**Danum House ★★★**
*Guest Accommodation*
22 Pauls Lane, Overstrand
NR27 0PE
t (01263) 579327
w tiscover.co.uk

## PALGRAVE
### Suffolk

**Brambley House ◆◆◆**
*Guest Accommodation*
Lion Road, Palgrave IP22 1AL
t (01379) 644403
e brambley_house@
btinternet.com
w tiscover.co.uk

## PENTNEY
### Norfolk

**Little Abbey Farm ★★★★**
*Farmhouse* SILVER AWARD
Low Road, Pentney PE32 1JF
t (01760) 337348
e enquiries@littleabbeyfarm.
co.uk
w littleabbeyfarm.co.uk

## PETERBOROUGH
### Cambridgeshire

**Brandon Hotel ★★★**
*Guest Accommodation*
161 Lincoln Road,
Peterborough PE1 2PW
t (01733) 568631
e enquiries@brandonhotel.co.
uk
w tiscover.co.uk

**Graham Guesthouse ★★★**
*Guest House*
296 Oundle Road,
Peterborough PE2 9QA
t (01733) 567824
w tiscover.co.uk

**Longueville Guesthouse**
★★★★ *Guest House*
Oundle Road, Orton
Longueville, Peterborough
PE2 7DA
t (01733) 233442
e maureenglover1@aol.com
w tiscover.co.uk

**Park Road Guesthouse**
★★★ *Guest House*
67 Park Road, Peterborough
PE1 2TN
t (01733) 562220
e parkrdguesthouse@bt.
connect.com
w parkrdguesthouse.co.uk

## PETTAUGH
### Suffolk

**Abbots Hall Farmhouse**
★★★ *Farmhouse*
Framsden Road, Pettaugh,
Stowmarket IP14 6DS
t (01473) 890548
e jakiforan@aol.com
w abbots-hall.co.uk

## POLSTEAD
### Suffolk

**Polstead Lodge ★★★★**
*Bed & Breakfast*
Mill Street, Polstead CO6 5AD
t (01206) 262196
e howards@polsteadlodge.
freeserve.co.uk
w polsteadlodge.com

## PULHAM MARKET
### Norfolk

**Old Bakery ★★★★★**
*Guest Accommodation*
GOLD AWARD
The Old Bakery, Pulham
Market IP21 4SL
t (01379) 676492
e jean@theoldbakery.net
w theoldbakery.net

## RACKHEATH
### Norfolk

**Barn Court ★★★**
*Guest Accommodation*
6 Back Lane, Rackheath
NR13 6NN
t (01603) 782536
e barncourtbb@hotmail.com
w tiscover.co.uk

**Hill Farm Lodge ★★★★**
*Bed & Breakfast*
Wroxham Road, Rackheath
NR13 6NE
t (01603) 720093
e patandclive.marshall@virgin.
net
w hillfarmlodge.co.uk

## RAMSEY
### Essex

**Roborough ★★★**
*Bed & Breakfast*
Church Hill, Ramsey CO12 5EU
t (01255) 880417
w tiscover.co.uk

## RENDHAM
### Suffolk

**Rendham Hall ★★★**
*Farmhouse*
Rendham IP17 2AW
t (01728) 663440
e dcstrachan@btinternet.com
w tiscover.co.uk

## REYDON
### Suffolk

**Ridge Bed And Breakfast**
★★★★ *Bed & Breakfast*
The Ridge, 14 Halesworth
Road, Reydon IP18 6NH
t (01502) 724855
e jules.heal@btinternet.com
w tiscover.co.uk

## RIVENHALL
### Essex

**Granary B and B Apartments**
★★★★ *Farmhouse*
Clarks Farm, Cranes Lane,
Kelvedon CO5 9AY
t (01376) 570321
e enquiries@thegranary.me.uk
w tiscover.co.uk

## ROUGHAM GREEN
### Suffolk

**Oak Farm Barn ★★★★**
*Bed & Breakfast*
SILVER AWARD
Moat Lane, Rougham IP30 9JZ
t (01359) 270014
w oakfarmbarn.co.uk

## ROYDON
### Essex

**Riverside Guesthouse**
★★★★
*Guest Accommodation*
218 High Street, Roydon
CM19 5EQ
t (01279) 792332
w tiscover.co.uk

## ROYSTON
### Hertfordshire

**Hall Farm ★★★★**
*Guest Accommodation*
Hall Lane, Great Chishill Nr
Royston SG8 8SH
t (01763) 838263
e wisehall@tiscali.co.uk
w hallfarmbb.co.uk

**New Farm ★★★★**
*Farmhouse*
Hollow Road High Street,
Chrishall, Royston SG8 8RJ
t (01763) 838282
e nfwiseman@waitrose.com
w dianabb.co.uk

## SAFFRON WALDEN
### Essex

**Ashleigh House ★★★**
*Guest Accommodation*
7 Farmadine Grove, Saffron
Walden CB11 3DR
t (01799) 513611
e info@ashleighhouse.dabsol.
co.uk
w ashleighhouse.dabsol.co.uk

**Bell House ★★★★**
*Bed & Breakfast*
Castle Street, Saffron Walden
CB10 1BD
t (01799) 527857
w tiscover.co.uk

**Buriton House ★★★★**
*Bed & Breakfast*
Station Road, Newport
CB11 3PL
t (01799) 542237
e buriton_house@hotmail.com
w tiscover.co.uk

**Chapmans ★★**
*Bed & Breakfast*
30 Lambert Cross, Saffron
Walden CB10 2DP
t (01799) 527287
w tiscover.co.uk

**The Cricketers ★★★★** *Inn*
SILVER AWARD
Wicken Road, Clavering,
Saffron Walden CB11 4QT
t (01799) 550442
e cricketers@lineone.net
w thecricketers.co.uk

**Hollingate ★★★★**
*Bed & Breakfast*
Radwinter End, Radwinter
CB10 2UD
t (01799) 599184
e enquiries@hollingate.co.uk
w hollingate.co.uk

**Hornet's Nest**
Rating Applied For
*Guest Accommodation*
21 Rook End Lane, Debden,
Saffron Walden CB11 3LR
t (01799) 543726
e rookendbandb@yahoo.co.
uk

**Redgates Farmhouse**
★★★★ *Bed & Breakfast*
Redgates Lane, Ashdon Road,
Saffron Walden CB10 2LP
t (01799) 516166
w tiscover.co.uk

**Rockells Farm ★★★★**
*Farmhouse*
Duddenhoe End, Saffron
Walden CB11 4UY
t (01763) 838053
e evert.westerhuis@tiscali.co.
uk
w tiscover.co.uk

**Rowley Hill Lodge ★★★★**
*Bed & Breakfast*
SILVER AWARD
Little Walden, Saffron Walden
CB10 1UZ
t (01799) 525975
e rhlbandb@onetel.com
w tiscover.co.uk

**Saffron Walden Yha ★★**
*Hostel*
2 Myddylton Place, Saffron
Walden CB10 1BB
t (01799) 523117
e saffron@yha.org.uk
w yha.org.uk

## ST ALBANS
### Hertfordshire

**16 York Road ★★★**
*Bed & Breakfast*
St Albans AL1 4PL
t (01727) 853647
w tiscover.co.uk

**2 The Limes ★★**
*Bed & Breakfast*
Spencer Gate, St Albans
AL1 4AT
t (01727) 831080
e hunter.mitchell@virgin.net
w tiscover.co.uk

**36 Potters Field ★★**
*Bed & Breakfast*
St Albans AL3 6LJ
t (01727) 766840
e manners_smith@ntlworld.
com
w tiscover.co.uk

**5 Approach Road ★**
*Bed & Breakfast*
St Albans AL1 1SP
t 07944 837533
e eileenvkent@aol.com
w tiscover.co.uk

**55 Charmouth Road ★★**
*Bed & Breakfast*
St Albans AL1 4SE
t (01727) 860002
e tb.charmouth@virgin.net
w tiscover.co.uk

**56 Sandpit Lane ★★★★**
*Bed & Breakfast*
St Albans AL1 4BW
t (01727) 856799
e 01727856799@talktalk.net
w tiscover.co.uk

**Ardens Way 22** ★★★★
*Bed & Breakfast*
St Albans, Marshalswick
AL4 9UJ
t (01727) 861986
w tiscover.co.uk

**Avona**
Rating Applied For
*Bed & Breakfast*
478 Hatfield Road, St Albans
AL4 0SX
t (01727) 842216
e murchu@ntlworld.com
w tiscover.co.uk

**Carousel Guest House** ★★★
*Bed & Breakfast*
122 Hatfield Road, St Albans
AL1 4HY
t (01727) 850004
e sandra.woodland@ntlworld.
com
w tiscover.co.uk

**Fern Cottage** ★★★★
*Bed & Breakfast*
116 Old London Road, St
Albans AL1 1PU
t (01727) 834200
e bookinginfo@ferncottage.
uk.net
w ferncottage.uk.net

**Fleuchary House** ★★★★
*Bed & Breakfast*
SILVER AWARD
3 Upper Lattimore Road, St
Albans AL1 3UD
t (01727) 766764
e linda@fleucharyhouse.
freeserve.co.uk
w fleucharyhouse.com

**London Road 178** ★★★
*Bed & Breakfast*
178 London Road, St Albans
AL1 1PL
t (01727) 846726
e bookings_178londonroad@
btconnect.com
w 178londonroad.co.uk

**Margarets B&B** ★★
*Bed & Breakfast*
16 Broomleys, St Albans
AL4 9UR
t (01727) 862421
w tiscover.co.uk

**Marlborough Gate 7** ★★★
*Bed & Breakfast*
7 Marlborough Gate, St Albans
AL1 3TX
t (01727) 865498
e michael.jameson@
btinternet.com
w tiscover.co.uk

**Oaktree House** ★★★★
*Bed & Breakfast*
512 Hatfield Road, St Albans
AL4 0SX
t (01727) 857521
w tiscover.co.uk

**Park House** ★★
*Bed & Breakfast*
30 The Park, St Albans
AL1 4RY
t (01727) 811910
e nora@parkhouseonline.co.
uk

**Riverside** ★★★★
*Bed & Breakfast*
SILVER AWARD
24 Minister Court, St Albans
AL2 2NF
t (01727) 758780
e ellispatriciam@ntlworld.com
w tiscover.co.uk

**Tresco** ★★★ *Bed & Breakfast*
76 Clarence Road, St Albans
AL1 4NG
t (01727) 864880
e pat_leggatt@hotmail.com
w geocities.com/patleggatt/
index.htm

**White House** ★★
*Bed & Breakfast*
28 Salisbury Avenue, St Albans
AL1 4TU
t (01727) 861017
w tiscover.co.uk

### ST NEOTS
Cambridgeshire

**Nags Head** ★★★
*Guest Accommodation*
2 Berkley Street, Eynesbury, St
Neots PE19 2NA
t (01480) 476812
e nags.stneots@btconnect.
com
w stneots.co.uk/nagshead/
main.htm

### SANDY
Bedfordshire

**Highfield Farm** ★★★★★
*Farmhouse* SILVER AWARD
Tempsford Road, Great North
Road, Sandy SG19 2AQ
t (01767) 682332
e margaret@highfield-farm.co.
uk
w highfield-farm.co.uk

**Pantiles** ★★★★
*Bed & Breakfast*
6 Swaden, Sandy SG19 2DA
t (01767) 680668
e pantilesbandb@onetel.com
w thepantilesbandb.co.uk

**The Tythe Barn** ★★★★
*Bed & Breakfast*
Drove Road, Gamlingay, Sandy
SG19 2HT
t (01767) 650156
e thetythebarn@supanet.com
w tythebb.co.uk

**Village Farm** ★★★★
*Farmhouse*
Thorncote Green, Sandy
SG19 1PU
t (01767) 627345
w tiscover.co.uk

### SAWBRIDGEWORTH
Hertfordshire

**Church Walk 7** ★★
*Bed & Breakfast*
7 Church Walk,
Sawbridgeworth CM21 9BJ
t (01279) 723233
e kent@sawbridgeworth.co.uk
w ourbedandbreakfast.co.uk

### SAWTRY
Cambridgeshire

**A1 Bed And Breakfast** ★★
*Guest Accommodation*
5 High Street, Sawtry PE28 5SR
t (01487) 830201
e pat.john@
a1bedandbreakfast.co.uk
w a1bedandbreakfast.co.uk

### SAXLINGHAM THORPE
Norfolk

**Foxhole Farm** ★★★★
*Guest Accommodation*
Foxhole, Norwich NR15 1UG
t (01508) 499226
e foxholefarm@hotmail.com
w tiscover.co.uk

### SAXMUNDHAM
Suffolk

**Georgian Guest House**
★★★★★ *Guest House*
SILVER AWARD
6 North Entrance,
Saxmundham IP17 1AY
t (01728) 603337
e enquiries@thegeorgian-
house.com
w thegeorgian-house.com

**Honeypot Lodge** ★★★★
*Guest Accommodation*
Aldecar Lane, Benhall Green,
Saxmundham IP17 1HN
t (01728) 602449
e honeypotlodge@fsmail.net
w saxmundham.info

**Moat House Farm** ★★★★
*Bed & Breakfast*
GOLD AWARD
Rendham Road, Carlton, Su
IP17 2QN
t (01728) 602228
e sally@goodacres.com
w goodacres.com

### SCOTTOW
Norfolk

**Holmwood House** ★★★★
*Bed & Breakfast*
SILVER AWARD
Tunstead Road, Scottow
NR10 5DA
t (01692) 538386
e holmwoodhouse@lineone.
net
w holmwoodhouse.co.uk

### SCULTHORPE
Norfolk

**Manor Farm Bed And
Breakfast** ◆◆◆◆
*Guest Accommodation*
SILVER AWARD
Manor Farm, Sculthorpe
NR21 9NJ
t (01328) 862185
e carol@manorfarmbandb.
fsworld.co.uk
w manorfarmbandb.com

### SHERINGHAM
Norfolk

**Alverstone** ★★★
*Bed & Breakfast*
33 The Avenue, Sheringham
NR26 8DG
t (01263) 825527
w tiscover.co.uk

**Ashcroft House Bed And
Breakfast** ★★★★
*Bed & Breakfast*
15 Morris Street, Sheringham
NR26 8JY
t (01263) 822225
e carol@fenn1465.freeserve.
co.uk
w tiscover.co.uk

**Bench Mark House**
★★★★★
*Guest Accommodation*
SILVER AWARD
32 Morley Road, Sheringham
NR26 8JE
t (01263) 823551
e benchmark.house@
btinternet.com
w bench-markhouse.co.uk

**Camberley Guesthouse**
★★★★
*Guest Accommodation*
62 Cliff Road, Sheringham
NR26 8BJ
t (01263) 823101
w camberleyguesthouse.co.uk

**Claremont Bed and
Breakfast** ★★★★
*Bed & Breakfast*
Sheringham NR26 8HP
t (01263) 821889
e claremont.bb@hotmail.com
w claremont-sheringham.co.uk

**Cleat House** ★★★★★
*Bed & Breakfast*
SILVER AWARD
7 Montague Road, Sheringham
NR26 8LN
t (01263) 822765
e stay@cleathouse.co.uk
w cleathouse.co.uk

**Fairlawns** ★★★★★
*Guest House* SILVER AWARD
26 Hooks Hill Road,
Sheringham NR26 8NL
t (01263) 824717
w fairlawns-sheringham.co.uk

**Grove Farm** ★★★★★
*Guest Accommodation*
Back Lane, Roughton
NR11 8QR
t (01263) 761594
e enquiries@grove-farm.com
w grove-farm.com

**The Melrose** ★★★
*Guest House*
9 Holway Road, Sheringham
NR26 8HN
t (01263) 823299
e jparsonage@btconnect.com
w tiscover.co.uk

**Myrtle House** ★★★
*Bed & Breakfast*
27 Nelson Road, Sheringham
NR26 8BU
t (01263) 823889
e enquiries@myrtlehouse-
sheringham.co.uk
w myrtlehouse-sheringham.co.
uk

**Olivedale** ★★★★
*Guest Accommodation*
20 Augusta Street, Sheringham
NR26 8LA
t (01263) 825871
e olivedale@bt.com
w tiscover.co.uk

**Sheringham Lodge** ★★★★
*Guest House*
Cromer Road, Sheringham
NR26 8RS
t (01263) 821954
e mikewalker19@hotmail.com
w sheringhamlodge.co.uk

**Sheringham YHA** ★★ *Hostel*
1 Cremers Drift, Sheringham
NR26 8HX
t  0870 770 6024

**Squirrels Drey** ★★★★
*Guest Accommodation*
27 Holt Road, Sheringham
NR26 8NB
t  (01263) 822982
e  squirrels-drey@lyttelton.
fsnet.co.uk
w  squirrelsdrey.northnorfolk.
co.uk

**Sunrays B&B** ★★★★
*Bed & Breakfast*
SILVER AWARD
29 Holt Road, Sheringham
NR26 8NB
t  (01263) 822663
e  elainesunrays@btinternet.
com
w  tiscover.co.uk

**The Two Lifeboats Hotel**
★★★ *Inn*
High Street, Sheringham
NR26 8JR
t  (01263) 822401

**Viburnham House B&B**
★★★★
*Guest Accommodation*
SILVER AWARD
Augusta Street, Sheringham
NR26 8LB
t  (01263) 822528
e  viburnhamhouse@aol.com
w  tiscover.co.uk

### SHINGLE STREET
Suffolk

**Lark Cottage**
Rating Applied For
*Bed & Breakfast*
Shingle Street, Nr Woodbridge
IP12 3BE
t  (01394) 411292

### SHOTLEY
Suffolk

**Hill House Farm** ★★★★
*Farmhouse* SILVER AWARD
Wades Lane, Shotley IP9 1EW
t  (01473) 787318
e  richard@rjwrinch.fsnet.co.uk
w  tiscover.co.uk

### SIBTON
Suffolk

**Park Farm** ★★★★
*Farmhouse* SILVER AWARD
Yoxford Road, Sibton IP17 2LZ
t  (01728) 668324
e  margaret.gray@btinternet.
com
w  sibtonparkfarm.co.uk

**Sibton White Horse Inn**
★★★★ *Inn*
Halesworth Road, Sibton,
Saxmundham IP17 2JJ
t  (01728) 660337
e  info@sibtonwhitehorseinn.
co.uk
w  sibtonwhitehorseinn.co.uk

### SNETTERTON
Norfolk

**Holly House Guest House**
★★★★★ *Guest House*
GOLD AWARD
Holly House, Snetterton
NR16 2LG
t  (01953) 498051
e  jeffstonell@aol.com
w  hollyhouse-guesthouse.co.
uk

### SNETTISHAM
Norfolk

**The Queen Victoria** ★★★★
*Inn*
19 Lynn Road, Snettisham
PE31 7LW
t  (01485) 541344
e  bobwarburton@talk21.com
w  queenvictoriasnettisham.co.
uk

**Twitchers Retreat
(Snettisham)** ★★★★
*Bed & Breakfast*
SILVER AWARD
9 Beach Road, Snettisham
PE31 7RA
t  (01485) 543581
e  twitchers.retreat@
googlemail.com
w  twitchers-retreat.co.uk

### SOHAM
Cambridgeshire

**Greenbank** ★★
*Bed & Breakfast*
111 Brook Street, Ely CB7 5AE
t  (01353) 720929
w  tiscover.co.uk

### SOUTH CREAKE
Norfolk

**Valentine House** ★★★
*Bed & Breakfast*
62 Back Street, South Creake
NR21 9PG
t  (01328) 823413
e  ros@valentinehouse.fsnet.
co.uk
w  valentinehouse.co.uk

### SOUTH WALSHAM
Norfolk

**Leeward Bed and Breakfast**
★★★★ *Bed & Breakfast*
5 Broad Lane, South Walsham
NR13 6EE
t  (01603) 270491
e  a.horsfield@tiscali.co.uk
w  http://mysite.wanadoo-
members.co.uk/
stayawhileinnorfolk

**Old Hall Farm** ★★★★
*Guest Accommodation*
Newport Road, South
Walsham, Norwich NR13 6DS
t  (01603) 270271
e  veronica@oldhallfarm.co.uk
w  oldhallfarm.co.uk

### SOUTHEND-ON-SEA
Essex

**Gleneagles** ★★★
*Guest Accommodation*
Clifftown Parade, Southend-
on-Sea SS1 1DP
t  (01702) 333635
w  tiscover.co.uk

**Pleasant Court Guest House**
★★ *Guest House*
64/66 Pleasant Road,
Southend-on-Sea SS1 2HJ
t  (01702) 467079
e  tinapapworth@aol.com
w  tiscover.co.uk

**Waverley Guesthouse** ★★★
*Guest Accommodation*
191 Eastern Esplanade,
Southend-on-Sea SS1 3AA
t  (01702) 585212
e  waverleyguesthouse@
hotmail.com
w  waverleyguesthouse.co.uk

### SOUTHMINSTER
Essex

**New Moor Farm** ★★★★
*Farmhouse*
Tillingham Road, Southminster
CM0 7DS
t  (01621) 772840
w  tiscover.co.uk

### SOUTHWOLD
Suffolk

**Avocet House** ★★★★
*Bed & Breakfast*
1 Strickland Place, Southwold
IP18 6HN
t  (01502) 724720
e  barnett@beeb.net
w  southwold.ws/avocet-house

**Brendas B&B** ★★★
*Bed & Breakfast*
3 Strickland Place, Southwold
IP18 6HN
t  (01502) 722403
w  tiscover.co.uk

**Newlands Country House**
★★★★
*Guest Accommodation*
SILVER AWARD
72 Halesworth Road,
Southwold IP18 6NS
t  (01502) 722164
e  info@newlandsofsouthwold.
co.uk
w  tiscover.co.uk

**Northcliffe Guesthouse**
★★★★ *Guest House*
20 North Parade, Southwold
IP18 6LT
t  (01502) 724074
e  northcliffe.southwold@
virgin.net
w  northcliffe-southwold.co.uk

**Number Three** ★★★★
*Guest Accommodation*
Cautley Road, Southwold
IP18 6DD
t  (01502) 723611
e  no3collis@acc-southwold.
fsnet.co.uk
w  tiscover.co.uk

**Poplar Hall** ★★★★
*Bed & Breakfast*
Frostenden Corner,
Frostenden, Southwold
NR34 7JA
t  (01502) 578549
e  poplarhall@tiscali.co.uk
w  southwold.ws/poplar-hall

### SPELLBROOK
Hertfordshire

**Margray Guesthouse** ★★★
*Guest Accommodation*
London Road, Spellbrook,
Bishop's Stortford CM23 4BA
t  (01279) 600138
e  margal@talktalk.net
w  tiscover.co.uk

### SPORLE
Norfolk

**Corfield House** ★★★★
*Guest Accommodation*
SILVER AWARD
Swaffham PE32 2EA
t  (01760) 723636
e  corfield.house@virgin.net
w  corfieldhouse.co.uk

### SPROUGHTON
Suffolk

**Finjaro** ★★★★ *Guest House*
Valley Farm Drive, Hadleigh
Road, Sproughton IP8 3EL
t  (01473) 652581
e  jan@finjaro.freeserve.co.uk
w  s-h-systems.co.uk/hotels/
finjaro.html

### SPROWSTON
Norfolk

**Driftwood Lodge** ★★★
*Bed & Breakfast*
102 Wroxham Road,
Sprowston, Norwich NR7 8EX
t  (01603) 444908
e  info@driftwoodlodge.co.uk
w  driftwoodlodge.co.uk

### STALHAM
Norfolk

**Bramble House** ★★★★
*Guest Accommodation*
GOLD AWARD
Cat's Common, Norwich Road,
Smallburgh NR12 9NS
t  (01692) 535069
e  bramblehouse07@
btinternet.com
w  bramblehouse.com

### STANDON
Hertfordshire

**The Granary**
Rating Applied For
*Guest Accommodation*
Mill End, Ware SG11 1LR
t  (01920) 823955
e  n.e.livings@btinternet.com

### STANFORD
Bedfordshire

**Green Man** ★★★★ *Inn*
Southill Road, Stanford
SG18 9JD
t  (01462) 812293
e  info@greenmanstanford.co.
uk
w  stanfordgreenman.co.uk

### STANSTED
Essex

**The Cottage** ★★★★
*Guest Accommodation*
SILVER AWARD
71 Birchanger Lane,
Birchanger, Bishop's Stortford
CM23 5QA
t  (01279) 812349
e  bookings@
thecottagebirchanger.co.uk
w  thecottagebirchanger.co.uk

**High Trees** ★★
*Bed & Breakfast*
Parsonage Road, Takeley,
Bishop's Stortford CM22 6QX
t (01279) 871306
e jeanhightrees@aol.com
w stansted-bandb.co.uk

**The Laurels** ★★★★
*Bed & Breakfast*
84 St Johns Road, Stansted
CM24 8JS
t (01279) 813023
e info@thelaurelsstansted.co.
uk
w thelaurelsstansted.co.uk

**White House** ★★★★
*Guest Accommodation*
Smiths Green, Takeley
CM22 6NR
t (01279) 870257
e enquiries@
whitehousestansted.co.uk
w whitehousestansted.co.uk

**Chimneys** ★★★★
*Bed & Breakfast*
**SILVER AWARD**
44 Lower Street, Stansted
Mountfitchet CM24 8LR
t (01279) 813388
e info@chimneysguesthouse.
co.uk
w chimneysguesthouse.co.uk

**Penny Mead Farm** ★★★★
*Bed & Breakfast*
Upthorpe Road, Stanton
IP31 2AP
t (01359) 250819
e jane@clelandsmith.co.uk

**Loft** ★★★ *Bed & Breakfast*
Frederick House, New Road,
Stanway CO3 0HU
t (01206) 516006
e theloft@frederickhouse.co.
uk
w frederickhouse.co.uk

**Motts Cottage** ★★★★
*Bed & Breakfast*
High Street, Stebbing,
Dunmow CM6 3SE
t (01371) 856633
e dianekittow@hotmail.com
w mottsbedandbreakfast.co.uk

**The Star Inn** ★★★★ *Inn*
The Street, Steeple,
Southminster CM0 7LF
t (01621) 772646

**The Angel Inn** ★★★★ *Inn*
Polstead Street, Stoke by
Nayland, Colchester CO6 4SA
t (01206) 263245
e info@theangelinn.net
w theangelinn.net

**Highfields Farm** ★★★
*Bed & Breakfast*
Chandler Road, Upper Stoke
Holy Cross, Norwich
NR14 8RQ
t (01508) 493247
e valgolding@lineone.net

**Salamanca Farm** ★★★
*Farmhouse*
118 Norwich Road, Norwich
NR14 8QJ
t (01508) 492322
w tiscover.co.uk

**Bays Farm** ★★★★★
*Guest Accommodation*
**GOLD AWARD**
Forward Green, Stowmarket
IP14 5HU
t (01449) 711286
e info@baysfarmsuffolk.co.uk
w baysfarmsuffolk.co.uk

**Step House** ★★★★
*Bed & Breakfast*
**SILVER AWARD**
Hockey Hill, Wetheringsett
IP14 5PL
t (01449) 766476
w tiscover.co.uk

**Stricklands** ★★★
*Guest Accommodation*
Stricklands Road, Stowmarket
IP14 1AP
t (01449) 612450
e poppy@stricklandshouse.
fsnet.co.uk
w tiscover.co.uk

**Three Bears Cottage** ★★★
*Guest Accommodation*
Mulberry Tree Farm,
Middlewood Green IP14 5EU
t (01449) 711707
w aristoclassics.com

**Verandah House** ★★★★
*Guest House*
29 Ipswich Road, Stowmarket
IP14 1BD
t (01449) 676104
e info@verhandahhouse.co.uk
w verandahhouse.co.uk

**Lowlands** ★★★★
*Bed & Breakfast*
Upper Street, Stratford St Mary
CO7 6JN
t (01206) 323858
e lowlands@dersley.co.uk
w tiscover.co.uk

**The Black Boy** ★★★ *Inn*
7 Market Hill, Sudbury
CO10 2EA
t (01787) 379046

**Hill Lodge** ★★★
*Guest Accommodation*
8 Newton Road, Sudbury
CO10 2RL
t (01787) 377568
e enquiries@hilllodgehotel.co.
uk
w hilllodgehotel.co.uk

**Hillview Studio** ★★★
*Bed & Breakfast*
58 Clarence Road, Sudbury
CO10 1NJ
t (01787) 374221 &
07779 854199
e sooteapot@hotmail.com

**Millhouse Bed & Breakfast**
★★★★ *Bed & Breakfast*
Nayworth Cottages, Cross
Street, Sudbury CO10 2DS
t (01787) 881173
e mills@travelandleisure.co.uk
w millhouse-sudbury.co.uk

**St David's Hall** ★★★★
*Bed & Breakfast*
40a Friars Street, Sudbury
CO10 2AG
t (01787) 373044
e stdavidshall@tiscali.co.uk
w tiscover.co.uk

**West House** ★★
*Bed & Breakfast*
59 Ballingdon Street, Sudbury
CO10 2DA
t (01787) 375033
e aitken@westhousebb.fsnet.
co.uk
w tiscover.co.uk

**Repton House** ★★★★
*Bed & Breakfast*
Oaks Drive, Swaffham
PE37 7ER
t (01760) 336399
e booking@reptonhouse.com
w reptonhouse.com

**B&B at Martin House**
★★★★ *Bed & Breakfast*
1 Station Road, Swaffham
Bulbeck CB5 0NB
t (01223) 813115
e sally@martinhousebb.co.uk
w martinhousebb.co.uk

**Black Horse** ★★★ *Inn*
High Street, Swaffham Bulbeck
CB5 0HP
t (01223) 811366
e blackhorsepubandmotel@
hotmail.com
w blackhorsepubandmotel.
com

**Pheasant Cottage** ★★★★★
*Guest Accommodation*
Long Common Lane, Swanton
Abbott, Norwich NR10 5BH
t (01692) 538169
e melanie@pheasantcottage.
freeserve.co.uk
w tiscover.co.uk

**Frogs Hall Farm** ★★★★★
*Guest Accommodation*
**SILVER AWARD**
Frogs Hall Lane, Woodgate,
Swanton Morley, Dereham
NR20 4NX
t (01362) 638355
e mail@frogshall.e-zum.com
w frogs-hall.fsnet.co.uk

**The Old Farmhouse** ★★★★
*Bed & Breakfast*
Holden's Lane, Sweffling
IP17 2BW
t (01728) 663565
e june-bellamy@lineone.net
w tiscover.co.uk

**Crossroads B and B** ★★
*Bed & Breakfast*
2 Hawthorn Close, Takeley
CM22 6SD
t (01279) 870619
e ajcaiger884@aol.com
w tiscover.co.uk

**Jan Smiths Bandb** ★★★★
*Bed & Breakfast*
The Cottage, Jacks Lane,
Takely CM22 6NT
t (01279) 870603
e smiths-residence@fsmail.net
w thecottagebnbjackslane.co.
uk

**Little Bullocks Farm** ★★★★
*Guest Accommodation*
Bullocks Lane, Hope End,
Takeley CM22 6TA
t (01279) 870464
e julie@waterman-farm.
demon.co.uk
w littlebullocksfarm.co.uk

**Oak Lodge Bed And
Breakfast** ★★★★
*Bed & Breakfast*
**SILVER AWARD**
Oak Lodge, Jacks Lane, Takeley
CM22 6NT
t (01279) 871667
e oaklodgebb@aol.com
w oaklodgebb.com

**Pussy Willow** ★★★★
*Bed & Breakfast*
**SILVER AWARD**
Mill House, The Street,
Takeley, Bishop's Stortford
CM22 6QR
t (01279) 871609
e brian@toaddurham.fsnet.co.
uk

**San Michelle** ◆◆◆◆
*Guest Accommodation*
Jacks Lane, Takeley CM22 6NT
t (01279) 870946
e ian.mcreynolds@tesco.net
w tiscover.co.uk

**Tap Hall** ★★★
*Bed & Breakfast*
15 The Street, Takeley,
Bishop's Stortford CM22 6QS
t (01279) 871035
e carolking.taphall@amserve.
com

**Wayside Cottage B&B**
★★★★ *Bed & Breakfast*
The Street, Tendring
CO16 0BW
t (01255) 830864
e vicky@waysidecottageb-b.
co.uk
w waysidecottageb-b.co.uk

## TERRINGTON ST JOHN
### Norfolk

**White House** ★★★★
*Bed & Breakfast*
Main Road, Terrington St John
PE14 7RR
t (01945) 880741
e fieldcarol@hotmail.com
w thewhitehousebnb.co.uk

## THAXTED
### Essex

**Crossways Guesthouse**
◆◆◆◆ *Guest Accommodation*
**SILVER AWARD**
32 Town Street, Thaxted
CM6 2LA
t (01371) 830348
e info@crosswaysthaxted.co.
uk
w crosswaysthaxted.co.uk

**The Farmhouse Inn** ★★★
*Guest Accommodation*
Monk Street, Thaxted,
Dunmow CM6 2NR
t (01371) 830864

## THEBERTON
### Suffolk

**Alders** ★★★
*Guest Accommodation*
Potters Street, Theberton
IP16 4RL
t (01728) 831790
w tiscover.co.uk

**Lupin Cottage** ◆◆◆
*Guest Accommodation*
Church Road, Theberton,
Leiston IP16 4SF
t (01728) 830531
w tiscover.co.uk

## THETFORD
### Norfolk

**East Farm** ★★★★ *Farmhouse*
Euston Road, Barnham,
Thetford IP24 2PB
t (01842) 890231
w tiscover.co.uk

**Glebe Country House Bed & Breakfast** ★★★★
*Guest Accommodation*
**SILVER AWARD**
Elveden, Thetford IP24 3TL
t (01842) 890027
e deirdre@jrudderham.
freeserve.co.uk
w glebecountryhouse.co.uk

**Wereham House** ★★★★
*Guest Accommodation*
24 White Hart Street, Thetford
IP24 1AD
t (01842) 761956
e mail@werehamhouse.co.uk
w werehamhouse.co.uk

## THOMPSON
### Norfolk

**Chequers Inn** ★★★★ *Inn*
Griston Road, Thompson
IP24 1PX
t (01953) 483360
e richard@chequers-inn.
wanadoo.co.uk
w thompson-chequers.co.uk

## THORNDON
### Suffolk

**Moat Farm** ★★★★
*Farmhouse* **SILVER AWARD**
Thorndon, Eye IP23 7LX
t (01379) 678437
e gerald@moatfarm.co.uk
w moatfarm.co.uk

## THORNHAM MAGNA
### Suffolk

**The Four Horseshoes**
★★★★ *Inn*
Wickham Road, Thornham
Magna, Eye IP23 8HD
t (01379) 678777

**Red House**
Rating Applied For
*Guest Accommodation*
Red House Yard, Gislingham
Road, Eye IP23 8HH
t (01379) 783336
e ladyhenniker@tiscali.co.uk

**Thornham Hall and Restaurant** ★★★★★
*Guest Accommodation*
**SILVER AWARD**
Thornham Hall, Thornham
Magna, Eye IP23 8HA
t (01379) 783314
e hallrestaurant@aol.com
w thornhamhallandrestaurant.
com

## THORPE BAY
### Essex

**Beaches** ★★★★
*Guest House*
192 Eastern Esplanade, Thorpe
Bay, Southend-on-Sea
SS1 3AA
t (01702) 586124
e mark@beachesguesthouse.
co.uk
w beachesguesthouse.co.uk

## THORPE MARKET
### Norfolk

**Manorwood** ★★★★
Church Road, Thorpe Market
NR11 8UA
t (01263) 834938

## THORPE MORIEUX
### Suffolk

**Elm Tree Farm** ★★★★
*Bed & Breakfast*
Bury Road, Thorpe Morieux
IP30 0NT
t (01284) 827053
e liz.conibear@virgin.net
w elmtreefarmlodge.co.uk

## THURLEIGH
### Bedfordshire

**The Windmill** ★★★★
*Bed & Breakfast*
Milton Road, Thurleigh
MK44 2DF
t (01234) 771016
e wendy.armitage1@talk21.
com
w thewindmill.uk.com

## THURSTON
### Suffolk

**Chalk Pit Lodge** ★★★★
*Bed & Breakfast*
27 Barton Road, Thurston
IP31 3PA
t (01359) 232741
w tiscover.co.uk

**The Fox & Hounds** ★★★★
*Inn*
Barton Road, Bury St Edmunds
IP31 3QT
t (01359) 232228
e thurstonfox@btinternet.com
w thurstonfoxandhounds.co.
uk

## TOFT
### Cambridgeshire

**Meadowview** ★★★★
*Bed & Breakfast*
3 Brookside, Toft CB23 2RJ
t (01223) 263395
e carol@meadowview.co.uk
w meadowview.co.uk

## TOLLESBURY
### Essex

**Fernleigh** ★★★
*Bed & Breakfast*
16 Woodrolfe Farm Lane,
Maldon CM9 8SX
t (01621) 868245
e gillwillson@onetel.com
w tiscover.co.uk

## TOLLESHUNT MAJOR
### Essex

**Wicks Manor Farm** ★★★★
*Farmhouse*
Witham Road, Tolleshunt
Major CM9 8JU
t (01621) 860629
e rhowie@aspects.net
w wicksmanor.co.uk

## TOPPESFIELD
### Essex

**Harrow Hill Cottage** ★★★
*Bed & Breakfast*
Harrow Hill, Toppesfield
CO9 4LX
t (01787) 237425
w tiscover.co.uk

## TOTTENHILL
### Norfolk

**Andel Lodge** ★★★★
*Restaurant with Rooms*
48 Lynn Road, Tottenhill
PE33 0RH
t (01553) 810256
e reception@andellodge.co.uk
w tiscover.co.uk

## TRUMPINGTON
### Cambridgeshire

**Bishops Bed And Breakfast**
★★★★ *Bed & Breakfast*
80 Bishops Road, Trumpington
CB2 2NH
t (01223) 840045
e valneilm@yahoo.co.uk
w geocities.com/valneilm

## TUNSTALL
### Norfolk

**Manor House** ★★★★
*Farmhouse* **SILVER AWARD**
Tunstall Road, Halvergate
NR13 3PS
t (01493) 700279
e smore@fsmail.net
w tiscover.co.uk

## UFFORD
### Suffolk

**Strawberry Hill** ★★★★
*Bed & Breakfast*
Loudham Lane, Lower Ufford,
Woodbridge IP13 6ED
t (01394) 460252
e strawberryhilly@yahoo.co.
uk
w smoothhound.co.uk/hotels/
strawber.html

## UGGESHALL
### Suffolk

**Bankside** ★★★★
*Bed & Breakfast*
The Hills, Uggeshall NR34 8EN
t (01502) 578047
e liz@bankside19.fsnet.co.uk
w banksidebandb.co.uk

## UPPER SHERINGHAM
### Norfolk

**Lodge Cottage** ★★★★
*Guest Accommodation*
Lodge Hill, Upper Sheringham
NR26 8TJ
t (01263) 821445
e stay@visitlodgecottage.com
w visitlodgecottage.com

## WACTON
### Norfolk

**Le Grys Barn** ★★★★
*Bed & Breakfast*
**SILVER AWARD**
Wacton Common, Norwich
NR15 2UR
t (01508) 531576
e jm.franklin@virgin.net
w legrys-barn.co.uk

## WAKES COLNE
### Essex

**Rosebank Bed And Breakfast** ★★★★
*Bed & Breakfast*
Rosebank Station Road, Wakes
Colne CO6 2DS
t (01787) 223552
e peterlynn@btinternet.com
w tiscover.co.uk

## WALBERSWICK
### Suffolk

**Troy** ★★★★ *Bed & Breakfast*
Church Field, Walberswick
IP18 6TG
t (01502) 723387
w visit.walberswick.com/troy/

## WALDRINGFIELD
### Suffolk

**Thatched Farm** ★★★★
*Bed & Breakfast*
Woodbridge Road,
Waldringfield IP12 4PW
t (01473) 811755
e mailus@thatchedfarm.co.uk
w thatchedfarm.co.uk

## WALTON-ON-THE-NAZE
### Essex

**Bufo Villae Guest House**
★★★★
*Guest Accommodation*
31 Beatrice Road, Walton-on-
the-Naze CO14 8HJ
t (01255) 672644
e bufo@ukgateway.net
w bufovillae.co.uk

### WANGFORD
Suffolk

**Fluff Cottage ★★★★**
*Bed & Breakfast*
1 High Street, Wangford
NR34 8RL
t (01502) 578997
w tiscover.co.uk

**The Plough Inn ★★★★**
*Guest Accommodation*
London Road, Wangford,
Southwold, Beccles NR34 8AZ
t (01502) 578239
e enquiries@the-plough.biz
w the-plough.biz

### WANSFORD
Cambridgeshire

**Stoneacre Guest House
★★★★ *Guest House***
Elton Road, Wansford PE8 6JT
t (01780) 783283
w stoneacreguesthouse.co.uk

### WARE
Hertfordshire

**Barbaras B&B ★★**
*Guest Accommodation*
6 High Oak Road, Ware
SG12 7PG
t (01920) 484796
e truttb@aol.com
w tiscover.co.uk

### WATERDEN
Norfolk

**Old Rectory ★★★★**
*Bed & Breakfast*
Waterden, Little Walsingham
NR22 6AT
t (01328) 823298
w tiscover.co.uk

### WELLS-NEXT-THE-SEA
Norfolk

**Arch House ★★★**
*Guest Accommodation*
50 Mill Road, Wells-next-the-
Sea NR23 1DB
t (01328) 710112
e enquiries@archhouse.co.uk
w archhouse.co.uk

**Boxwood Guest House
★★★★ *Guest House***
Northfield Lane, Wells-next-
the-Sea NR23 1JZ
t (01328) 711493

**The Cobblers ★★★★**
*Guest House*
Standard Road, Wells-next-the-
Sea NR23 1JU
t (01328) 710155
e info@cobblers.co.uk
w cobblers.co.uk

**Glebe Barn ◆◆◆◆**
*Guest Accommodation*
The Glebe, Wells-next-the-Sea
NR23 1AZ
t (01328) 711809
e glebebarn@aol.com
w tiscover.co.uk

**Machrimore ★★★★**
*Bed & Breakfast*
GOLD AWARD
Burnt Street, Wells-next-the-
Sea NR23 1HS
t (01328) 711653
e dottiemac39@hotmail.com
w machrimore.co.uk

### Meadow View Guest House
★★★★
*Guest Accommodation*
GOLD AWARD
53 High Street, Wighton
NR23 1PF
t (01328) 821527
e bookings@meadowview.net
w meadow-view.net

**Normans ★★★★★**
*Guest Accommodation*
GOLD AWARD
Invaders Court, Standard Road,
Wells-next-the-Sea NR23 1JW
t (01328) 710657
w thenormansatwells.co.uk

**Old Custom House ★★★★**
*Guest Accommodation*
East Quay, Wells-next-the-Sea
NR23 1LD
t (01328) 711463
e bb@eastquay.co.uk
w eastquay.co.uk

**Wells-next-the-Sea YHA
★★★★ *Hostel***
Church Plain, Wells-next-the-
Sea NR23 1EQ
t (01328) 711748
e wellsnorfolk@yha.org.uk
w yha.org.uk

### WELWYN
Hertfordshire

**Catbells ★★★★**
*Bed & Breakfast*
40 Firs Walk, Tewin Wood
AL6 0NZ
t (01438) 798412
w tiscover.co.uk

### WENHASTON
Suffolk

**Rowan House ★★★★**
*Guest Accommodation*
Hall Road, Wenhaston
IP19 9HF
t (01502) 478407
e rowanhouse@btinternet.
com
w tiscover.co.uk

### WENTWORTH
Cambridgeshire

**Desiderata ★★★**
*Bed & Breakfast*
44 Main Street, Wentworth, Ely
CB6 3QG
t (01353) 776131
e chips.1@virgin.net
w mgraham.net

### WEST RUDHAM
Norfolk

**Oyster House ★★★★**
*Bed & Breakfast*
SILVER AWARD
Lynn Road, Nest Rudham
PE31 8RW
t (01485) 528327
e oyster-house@tiscali.co.uk
w oysterhouse.co.uk

### WEST RUNTON
Norfolk

**The Old Barn ★★★★**
*Guest Accommodation*
Cromer Road, West Runton
NR27 9QT
t (01263) 838285
w tiscover.co.uk

### WESTCLIFF-ON-SEA
Essex

**Asgard Guesthouse ★★★★**
*Guest House*
25 Cobham Road, Westcliff-on-
Sea SS0 8EG
t (01702) 345466
w tiscover.co.uk

**Pavilion ★★**
*Guest Accommodation*
1 Trinity Avenue, Westcliff-on-
Sea SS0 7PU
t (01702) 332767
w tiscover.co.uk

**Retreat Guesthouse ★★★**
*Guest Accommodation*
12 Canewdon Road, Westcliff-
on-Sea SS0 7NE
t (01702) 348217
e retreatguesthouse.co.uk@
tinyworld.co.uk
w tiscover.co.uk

**Rose House Hotel ★★★**
*Guest House*
21-23 Manor Road, Westcliff-
on-Sea SS0 7SR
t (01702) 341959

### WESTHORPE
Suffolk

**Moat Hill Farm B&B**
Rating Applied For
*Bed & Breakfast*
Church Road, Westhorpe
IP14 4SZ
t (01449) 780165
e moathillb&b@talktalk.net

### WESTLETON
Suffolk

**Pond House ★★★★**
*Bed & Breakfast*
The Hill, Westleton IP17 3AN
t (01728) 648773
w tiscover.co.uk

### WETHERSFIELD
Essex

**Church Hill House ★★★★**
*Bed & Breakfast*
High Street, Wethersfield
CM7 4BY
t (01371) 850342
e clubley@churchhillhouse.co.
uk
w churchhillhouse.co.uk

### WHEATHAMPSTEAD
Hertfordshire

**The Crosskeys ★★★ *Inn***
Gustard Wood,
Wheathampstead AL4 8LA
t (01582) 832165

### WHEPSTEAD
Suffolk

**The Old Pear Tree ★★★★**
*Bed & Breakfast*
Whepstead, Bury St Edmunds
IP29 4UD
t (01284) 850470
e jennyatpeartree@tiscali.co.
uk
w theoldpeartree.itgo.com

### WHITE NOTLEY
Essex

**Elms Farm ★★★★**
*Bed & Breakfast*
Green Lanes, White Notley
CM8 1RB
t (01376) 321559
w tiscover.co.uk

### WHITTLESEY
Cambridgeshire

**Whitmore House ★★★★**
*Bed & Breakfast*
31 Whitmore Street,
Peterborough PE7 1HE
t (01733) 203088
w tiscover.co.uk

### WICKHAM MARKET
Suffolk

**The Old Pharmacy ★★★★**
*Bed & Breakfast*
SILVER AWARD
72/74 High Street, Wickham
Market IP13 0QU
t (01728) 745012

### WIMBISH
Essex

**Beeholme House ★★★★★**
*Bed & Breakfast*
SILVER AWARD
Howlett End, Wimbish
CB10 2XP
t (01799) 599458
e beeholme@btinternet.co.uk
w wolseylodges.com

**Fieldview ★★★★**
*Bed & Breakfast*
Howlett End, Wimbish
CB10 2XW
t (01799) 599616
e mfludre@aol.com
w fieldview.eu

**Newdegate House ★★★★**
*Guest Accommodation*
SILVER AWARD
Howlett End, Wimbish
CB10 2XW
t (01799) 599748
e jacky@newdegate.co.uk
w tiscover.co.uk

### WINGFIELD
Suffolk

**Gables Farm ★★★★**
*Bed & Breakfast*
SILVER AWARD
Earsham Street, Wingfield, Diss
IP21 5RH
t (01379) 586355 &
07824 445464
e enquiries@gablesfarm.co.uk
w gablesfarm.co.uk

### WINTERTON-ON-SEA
Norfolk

**Tower Cottage ★★★★**
*Bed & Breakfast*
Black Street, Winterton-on-Sea
NR29 4AP
t (01493) 394053
e towercottage@talktalk.net
w towercottage.co.uk

### WISBECH
Cambridgeshire

**Marmion House ★★★**
*Guest Accommodation*
Lynn Road, Wisbech PE13 3DD
t (01945) 582822
w tiscover.co.uk

### WISSETT
Suffolk

**Wissett Lodge ★★★★**
*Farmhouse*
Lodge Lane, Halesworth
IP19 0JQ
t (01986) 873173
e mail@wissettlodge.co.uk
w wissettlodge.co.uk

## WITCHFORD
### Cambridgeshire

**Woodlands** ★★★★
*Guest House*
Grunty Fen Road, Ely CB6 2JE
t (01353) 663746
e uptonheath@tinyworld.co.
uk
w woodlandsbandb.co.uk

## WITHAM
### Essex

**Chestnuts** ★★★★
*Bed & Breakfast*
8 Octavia Drive, Witham
Lodge, Witham CM8 1HQ
t (01376) 515990
e janetmoya@aol.com
w tiscover.co.uk

## WIX
### Essex

**Periwinkle Cottage** ★★★★
*Bed & Breakfast*
**SILVER AWARD**
Colchester Road, Wix, Nr
Harwich CO11 2PD
t (01255) 870167
w tiscover.co.uk

## WOODBRIDGE
### Suffolk

**Cherry Tree Inn** ★★★★
*Guest Accommodation*
73 Cumberland Street,
Woodbridge IP12 4AG
t (01394) 384627

**The Coach House** ★★★★
*Guest Accommodation*
121 Ipswich Road, Woodbridge
IP12 4BY
t (01394) 385918
e rita@thecoachhouse-
woodbridge.co.uk
w thecoachhouse-woodbridge.
co.uk

**Deben Lodge** ★★
*Bed & Breakfast*
Melton Road, Woodbridge
IP12 1NH
t (01394) 382740
w smoothhound.co.uk/shs.
html
🖼️🖼️

**Fir Tree Lodge** ★★★★
*Guest Accommodation*
25 Moorfield Road,
Woodbridge IP12 4JN
t 07968 346029
e nights@debenaccom.com
w debenaccom.com

**Mill View House** ★★★
*Bed & Breakfast*
33 Mill View Close,
Woodbridge IP12 4HR
t (01394) 383010
e gregory_millview@
btinternet.com
w tiscover.co.uk

**Moat Barn** ★★★★
*Bed & Breakfast*
Dallinghoo Road, Bredfield
IP13 6BD
t (01473) 737520
w moatbarn.co.uk

**The Old Rectory** ★★★★
*Guest Accommodation*
**SILVER AWARD**
Station Road, Campsea Ashe
IP13 0PU
t (01728) 746524
e mail@theoldrectorysuffolk.
com
w theoldrectorysuffolk.com

**Pettistree House** ♦♦♦
*Guest Accommodation*
Main Road, Pettistree,
Woodbridge IP13 0HL
t (01728) 748008
e henrikay@aol.com
w pettistreereceptions-
marquees.co.uk

**Pond Farm B&B** ★★★
*Bed & Breakfast*
Pond Farm, Fingal Street,
Worlingworth IP13 7PD
t (01728) 628565
e enquiries@pond-farm.co.uk
w pond-farm.co.uk

**St Anne's School House** ★★
*Bed & Breakfast*
Crown Place, Woodbridge
IP12 1BU
t (01394) 386942
e lesleyterry@keme.co.uk

## WOODHAM MORTIMER
### Essex

**Chase Farm Bed & Breakfast**
♦♦♦ *Guest Accommodation*
Chase Farm, Hyde Chase,
Woodham Mortimer, Maldon
CM9 6TN
t (01245) 223268

## WOODHURST
### Cambridgeshire

**The Raptor Foundation**
★★★ *Guest Accommodation*
The Heath, St Ives Road,
Huntingdon PE28 3BT
t (01487) 741140
e heleowl@aol.com
w raptorfoundation.org.uk

## WOODSTON
### Cambridgeshire

**White House Guesthouse**
★★★ *Guest House*
White House, 318 Oundle
Road, Peterborough PE2 9QP
t (01733) 566650
e helmorgan@lineone.com
w tiscover.co.uk

## WOOLPIT
### Suffolk

**Bull Inn and Restaurant**
★★★ *Inn*
The Street, Woolpit, Bury St
Edmunds IP30 9SA
t (01359) 240393
e info@bullinnwoolpit.co.uk
w bullinnwoolpit.co.uk

**Grange Farm** ★★★★
*Farmhouse*
Woolpit IP30 9RG
t (01359) 241143
e grangefarm@btinternet.com
w farmstayanglia.co.uk/
grangefarm/

## WORSTEAD
### Norfolk

**Hall Farm Guesthouse**
★★★★
*Guest Accommodation*
**SILVER AWARD**
Hall Farm, Sloley Road,
Worstead NR28 9RS
t (01692) 536124
e lowehall@aol.com
w hallfarmguesthouse.co.uk

**Ollands** ★★★★
*Guest Accommodation*
**GOLD AWARD**
Swanns Loke, Worstead
NR28 9RP
t (01692) 535150
e theollands@btinternet.com
w ollandsfarm.com

## WORTHAM
### Suffolk

**Rookery Farm** ★★★★
*Farmhouse* **SILVER AWARD**
Old Bury Road, Wortham, Diss
IP22 1RB
t (01379) 783236
e russell.ling@ukgateway.net
w tiscover.co.uk

## WOTHORPE
### Cambridgeshire

**Firwood** ★★★★
*Bed & Breakfast*
First Drift, Wothorpe PE9 3JL
t (01780) 765654
w tiscover.co.uk

## WRENTHAM
### Suffolk

**Five Bells** ★★★ *Inn*
Southwold Road, Wrentham
NR34 7JF
t (01502) 675249
e victoriapub@aol.com
w five-bells.com

**The Hideaway** ★★★
*Bed & Breakfast*
68 Southwold Road, Wrentham
NR34 7JF
t (01502) 675692
e lillylady@hotmail.co.uk
w tiscover.co.uk

## WROXHAM
### Norfolk

**58 Norwich Road** ★★★★
*Bed & Breakfast*
Norwich Road, Wroxham,
Norwich NR12 8RX
t (01603) 783998

**Coach House** ★★★★
*Bed & Breakfast*
**SILVER AWARD**
96 Norwich Road, Wroxham
NR12 8RY
t (01603) 784376
e bishop@worldonline.co.uk
w coachhousewroxham.co.uk

**Wroxham Park Lodge**
★★★★ *Bed & Breakfast*
142 Norwich Road, Wroxham,
Norwich NR12 8SA
t (01603) 782991
e parklodge@computer-assist.
net
w wroxhamparklodge.com

## WYMONDHAM
### Norfolk

**Avalon Farm** ★★★★
*Guest Accommodation*
Suton Street, Suton NR18 9JQ
t (01953) 602339
w tiscover.co.uk

**Witch Hazel** ★★★★
*Bed & Breakfast*
**SILVER AWARD**
55 Church Lane, Wicklewood
NR18 9QH
t (01953) 602247
e witchhazel@tiscali.co.uk
w witchhazel-norfolk.co.uk

## YOXFORD
### Suffolk

**The Griffin** ★★★ *Inn*
Yoxford, Saxmundham
IP17 3EP
t (01728) 668229
e enquiries@thegriffin.co.uk
w thegriffin.co.uk

**Old Methodist Chapel**
★★★★ *Bed & Breakfast*
High Street, Yoxford IP17 3EU
t (01728) 668333
e browns@chapelsuffolk.co.uk
w chapelsuffolk.co.uk

## LONDON

### INNER LONDON

#### E4

**Ridgeway Hotel Limited** ★★★ *Guest House*
115 The Ridgeway, London
E4 6QU
t (020) 8529 1964
e bookings@ridgewayhotel.co.uk
w ridgewayhotel.co.uk

#### EC4

**City of London YHA** ★★★
*Hostel*
36 Carter Lane, London
EC4V 5AB
t (020) 7236 4965
e city@yha.org.uk
w yha.org.uk

#### N1

**Kandara Guest House** ★★★
*Guest Accommodation*
68 Ockendon Road, Islington,
London N1 3NW
t (020) 7226 5721
e admin@kandara.co.uk
w kandara.co.uk

**Walter Sickert Hall City University**
Rating Applied For
*Campus*
Graham Street, London N1 8LA
t (020) 7040 8822
e wsh@city.ac.uk
w city.ac.uk/ems

#### N4

**Costello Palace Hotel** ★★
*Guest Accommodation*
374 Seven Sisters Road,
London N4 2PG
t (020) 8802 6551
e costellopalace@ukonline.co.uk
w infotel.co.uk/16419

#### N7

**Europa** ★★★
*Guest Accommodation*
62 Anson Road, London
N7 0AA
t (020) 7607 5935
e info@europahotellondon.co.uk
w europahotellondon.co.uk

#### N8

**White Lodge Hotel** ★★★
*Guest Accommodation*
1 Church Lane, London
N8 7BU
t (020) 8348 9765
e info@whitelodgehornsey.co.uk
w whitelodgehornsey.co.uk

#### N10

**The Muswell Hill** ★★★
*Guest House*
73 Muswell Hill Road, London
N10 3HT
t (020) 8883 6447
e reception@muswellhillhotel.co.uk
w muswellhillhotel.co.uk

#### N22

**Pane Residence** ★★
*Bed & Breakfast*
154 Boundary Road, London
N22 6AE
t (020) 8889 3735

#### NW1

**MIC Hotel & Conference Centre** ★★★★
*Guest Accommodation*
81-103 Euston Street, London
NW1 2EZ
t (020) 7380 0001

**St Pancras YHA** ★★★★
*Hostel*
79-81 Euston Road, London
NW1 2QS
t (020) 7388 9998
e stpancras@yha.org.uk
w yha.org.uk

#### NW3

**Dillons** ★★★
*Guest Accommodation*
21 Belsize Park, London
NW3 4DU
t (020) 7794 3360
e desk@dillonshotel.com
w dillonshotel.com

#### NW8

**The New Inn** ★★★ *Inn*
2 Allitsen Road, St John's
Wood, London NW8 6LA
t (020) 7722 0726
e thenewinnlondon@aol.com
w newinnlondon.co.uk

#### NW11

**Anchor-Nova Hotel** ★★★
*Guest Accommodation*
Flat 2, 10 West Heath Drive,
London NW11 7QH
t (020) 8458 8764
e enquir@anchor-hotel.co.uk
w anchor-hotel.co.uk

#### SE3

**3 Tilbrook Road** ★★
*Bed & Breakfast*
London SE3 9QD
t (020) 8319 8843
e m.hutson@talktalk.net

**59a Lee Road, Blackheath**
★★★ *Bed & Breakfast*
London SE3 9EN
t (020) 8318 7244
e ac@blackheath318.freeserve.co.uk

**The Grovers** ★★★
*Bed & Breakfast*
96 Merriman Road, London
SE3 8RZ
t (020) 8488 7719
e james.grover13@ntlworld.com

#### SE4

**Crofton Park Holdenby** ★★
*Bed & Breakfast*
28 Holdenby Road, London
SE4 2DA
t (020) 8694 0011
e savitri.gaines@totalise.co.uk
w ukhomestay.net

**Geoffrey Bed & Breakfast**
★★ *Bed & Breakfast*
66 Geoffrey Road, London
SE4 1NT
t (020) 8691 3887
e andrea.dechamps@btclick.com

#### SE6

**The Heathers** ★★★
*Guest Accommodation*
71 Verdant Lane, London
SE6 1JD
t (020) 8698 8340
e berylheath@yahoo.co.uk
w theheathersbb.com

**Tulip Tree House** ★★
*Bed & Breakfast*
41 Minard Road, London
SE6 1NP
t (020) 8697 2596

#### SE8

**M B Guest House** ★★
*Guest Accommodation*
7 Bolden Street, London
SE8 4JF
t (020) 8692 7030
e mbguesthouse@yahoo.co.uk

#### SE9

**Boru House** ★★
*Guest Accommodation*
70 Dunvegan Road, London
SE9 1SB
t (020) 8850 0584

#### SE10

**16 St Alfeges** ★★
*Bed & Breakfast*
16 St Alfege Passage, London
SE10 9JS
t (020) 8853 4337
e nicmesure@yahoo.co.uk
w st-alfeges.co.uk

**The Corner House** ★★
*Guest Accommodation*
28 Royal Hill, London SE10 8RT
t (020) 8692 3023
e joannacourtney@aol.com

#### SE13

**8 Yeats Close** ★★
*Bed & Breakfast*
Yeats Close, 8 Eliot Park,
London SE13 7ET
t (020) 8318 3421
e pathu@tesco.net

**Manna House** ★★★
*Bed & Breakfast*
320 Hither Green Lane, London
SE13 6TS
t (020) 8461 5984
e mannahouse@aol.com
w members.aol.com/mannahouse

#### SE14

**Annemarten Pepys Road**
Rating Applied For
*Guest Accommodation*
Pepys Road, London SE14 5SE
t (020) 7639 1060
e annemarten@pepysroad.com

#### SE16

**YHA London Thameside** ★★
*Hostel*
20 Salter Road, London
SE16 5PR
t 0870 770 6010
e thameside@yha.org.uk
w yha.org.uk

#### SE20

**Melrose House** ★★★★
*Guest Accommodation*
89 Lennard Road, London
SE20 7LY
t (020) 8776 8884
e melrosehouse@supanet.com
w uk-bedandbreakfast.com

#### SW1

**30 Pavilion Road** ★★★
*Guest Accommodation*
London SW1X 0HJ
t (020) 7584 4921
e rgr@searcys.co.uk
w searcys.co.uk

**Carlton Hotel** ★★
*Guest Accommodation*
90 Belgrave Road, London
SW1V 2BJ
t (020) 7976 6634
e info@cityhotelcarlton.co.uk
w cityhotelcarlton.co.uk

**Caswell Hotel** ★★
*Guest Accommodation*
25 Gloucester Street, London
SW1V 2DB
t (020) 7834 6345
e manager@hotellondon.co.uk
w hotellondon.co.uk

**Central House Hotel** ★★★
*Guest Accommodation*
37-41 Belgrave Road, London
SW1V 2BB
t (020) 7834 8036
e info@centralhousehotel.co.uk

**Comfort Inn Buckingham Palace Road** ★★★
*Guest Accommodation*
10 St Georges Drive, Victoria,
London SW1V 4BJ
t (020) 7834 2988
e info@comfortinnbuckinghampalacerd.co.uk
w comfortinnbuckinghampalacerd.co.uk

**The Dover** ★★
*Guest Accommodation*
44 Belgrave Road, London
SW1V 1RG
t (020) 7821 9085
e reception@dover-hotel.co.uk
w dover-hotel.co.uk

**Elizabeth Hotel & Apartments** ★★★
*Guest Accommodation*
37 Eccleston Square, London
SW1V 1PB
t (020) 7828 6812
e info@elizabethhotel.com
w elizabethhotel.com

**Georgian House Hotel ★★★**
*Guest Accommodation*
35 St Georges Drive, London
SW1V 4DG
t (020) 7834 1438
e reception@
georgianhousehotel.co.uk
w georgianhousehotel.co.uk

**Huttons Hotel ★★★**
*Guest Accommodation*
55 Belgrave Road, London
SW1V 2BB
t (020) 7834 3726

**Luna-Simone Hotel ★★★★**
*Guest House*
47 Belgrave Road, London
SW1V 2BB
t (020) 7834 5897

**Melita House ★★★**
*Guest Accommodation*
35 Charlwood Street, London
SW1V 2DU
t (020) 7828 0471
e reserve@melitahotel.com
w melitahotel.com

**Stanley House ★★**
*Guest Accommodation*
19-21 Belgrave Road, London
SW1V 1RB
t (020) 7834 5042 &
(020) 7834 7292
e cmahotel@aol.com
w londonbudgethotels.co.uk

**Vandon House ★★★**
*Guest Accommodation*
1 Vandon Street, London
SW1H 0AH
t (020) 7799 6780
e info@vandonhouse.com
w vandonhouse.com

**Victor Hotel ★★★**
*Guest Accommodation*
51 Belgrave Road, London
SW1V 2BB
t (020) 7592 9853
w victorhotel.co.uk

**The Victoria Inn London**
★★★ *Guest Accommodation*
65-67 Belgrave Road, London
SW1V 2BG
t (020) 7834 6721
e welcome@victoriainn.co.uk
w victoriainn.co.uk

**Windermere Hotel ★★★★**
*Guest Accommodation*
SILVER AWARD
142-144 Warwick Way,
London SW1V 4JE
t (020) 7834 5163
e reservations@windermere-
hotel.co.uk
w windermere-hotel.co.uk

SW3

**IES Student Residence Hall**
★ *Campus*
Manresa Road, King's Road,
London SW3 6NA
t (020) 7808 9200
e info@iesreshall.com
w iesreshall.com

SW5

**Beaver Hotel ★★**
*Guest Accommodation*
57-59 Philbeach Gardens,
London SW5 9ED
t (020) 7373 4553
e hotelbeaver@hotmail.com
w beaverhotel.co.uk

**Comfort Inn Earl's Court**
★★★ *Guest Accommodation*
11-13 Penywern Road, London
SW5 9TT
t (020) 7373 6514
e info@comfortinnearlscourt.
co.uk
w comfortinnearlscourt.co.uk

**Hotel Earls Court ★**
*Guest House*
28 Warwick Road, London
SW5 9UD
t (020) 7373 7079
e info@hotelearlscourt.com
w hotelearlscourt.com

**Lord Jim Hotel ★★**
*Guest House*
25 Penywern Road, London
SW5 9TT
t (020) 7370 6071
e ljh@lgh-hotels.com
w lgh-hotels.com

**Merlyn Court Hotel ★★★**
*Guest Accommodation*
2 Barkston Gardens, London
SW5 0EN
t (020) 7370 1640
e london@merlyncourthotel.
com
w merlyncourthotel.com

**Mowbray Court ★★**
*Guest Accommodation*
28-32 Penywern Road, London
SW5 9SU
t (020) 7370 2316
e mowbraycrthot@hotmail.
com
w mowbraycourthotel.co.uk

**Rasool Court Hotel ★★**
*Guest Accommodation*
19-21 Penywern Road, London
SW5 9TT
t (020) 7373 8900
e rasool@rasool.demon.co.uk
w rasoolcourthotel.com

**YHA Earl's Court ★★★★**
*Hostel*
38 Bolton Gardens, London
SW5 0AQ
t (020) 7373 7083
e earlscourt@yha.org.uk
w yha.org.uk

SW6

**91 Langthorne Street ★★**
*Bed & Breakfast*
London SW6 6JU
t (020) 7381 0198
e brigid.touristguideuk@
virgin.net
w londonthameswalk.co.uk

SW7

**Imperial College London
Beit Hall of Residence ★★★**
*Campus*
Prince Consort Road, South
Kensington, London SW7 2BB
t (020) 7594 9507
e accommodationlink@
imperial.ac.uk
w imperial-accommodationlink.
com

**YHA South Kensington
Baden-Powell House**
★★★★ *Hostel*
65-67 Queen's Gate, London
SW7 5JS
t (020) 7590 6900
e bph.hostel@scout.org.uk
w yha.org.uk

SW8

**Comfort Inn London
Vauxhall ★★★★**
*Guest Accommodation*
87 South Lambeth Road,
London SW8 1RN
t (020) 7735 9494
e stay@comfortinnvx.co.uk
w comfortinnvx.co.uk

SW9

**Belgrave Oval Hotel ★★★**
*Guest House*
9-13 Clapham Road, London
SW9 0JD
t (020) 7793 0142
e enquiries@belgravehotel.net

SW11

**Lavender Guest House**
★★★ *Guest House*
18 Lavender Sweep, London
SW11 1HA
t (020) 7585 2767
w thelavenderguesthouse.com

SW15

**Whitelands College ★★★**
*Campus*
Holybourne Avenue, London
SW15 4JD
t (020) 8392 3505
e info@parksteadhouse.co.uk
w parksteadhouse.co.uk

SW16

**The Konyots ★**
*Guest Accommodation*
95 Pollards Hill South, London
SW16 4LS
t (020) 8764 0075

W1

**Hallam Hotel ★★★**
*Guest Accommodation*
12 Hallam Street, London
W1W 6JF
t (020) 7580 1166
e hallam-hotel@hotmail.com
w hallamhotel.com

**International Students
House**
Rating Applied For
*Campus*
229 Great Portland Street,
Regent's Park, London
W1N 5HD
t (020) 7631 8300
e accom@ish.org.uk
w ish.org.uk

**Lincoln House – Central
London ★★**
*Guest Accommodation*
33 Gloucester Place, London
W1U 8HY
t (020) 7486 7630
e reservations@lincoln-house-
hotel.co.uk
w lincoln-house-hotel.co.uk

**Marble Arch Inn ★★**
*Guest Accommodation*
49-50 Upper Berkeley Street,
London W1H 5QR
t (020) 7723 7888
e sales@marblearch-inn.co.uk
w marblearch-inn.co.uk

**Oxford Street YHA ★★**
*Hostel*
14 Noel Street, London
W1F 8GJ
t (020) 7734 1618
e oxfordst@yha.org.uk
w yha.org.uk

**Piccadilly Backpackers Hotel**
★ *Hostel*
12 Sherwood Street, Piccadilly
Circus, London W1F 7BR
t (020) 7434 9009
e bookings@
piccadillybackpackers.com
w piccadillybackpackers.com

**Wigmore Court Hotel ★★★**
*Guest Accommodation*
23 Gloucester Place, London
W1U 8HS
t (020) 7935 0928
e rec@wigmore-hotel.co.uk
w wigmore-hotel.co.uk

W2

**The Abbey Court ★★★★**
*Guest Accommodation*
20 Pembridge Gardens,
London W2 4DU
t (020) 7221 7518
e info@abbeycourthotel.co.uk
w abbeycourthotel.co.uk

**Abbey Court & Westpoint
Hotel ★★★**
*Guest Accommodation*
174 Sussex Gardens, London
W2 1TP
t (020) 7402 0281
e info@abbeycourt.com
w abbeycourthotel.com

**Alexandra Hotel ★★★**
*Guest Accommodation*
159-161 Sussex Gardens,
London W2 2RY
t (020) 7402 6471
e hotels.leventis-group@
virgin.net
w hotels-leventisgroup.co.uk

**Barry House ★★★**
*Guest Accommodation*
12 Sussex Place, London
W2 2TP
t (020) 7723 7340
e hotel@barryhouse.co.uk
w barryhouse.co.uk

**Cardiff Hotel ★★★**
*Guest Accommodation*
5-9 Norfolk Square, London
W2 1RU
t (020) 7723 9068
e stay@cardiff-hotel.com
w cardiff-hotel.com

**Elysee Hotel ★★★**
*Guest Accommodation*
25/26 Craven Terrace, London
W2 3EL
t (020) 7402 7603
e info@hotelelysee.co.uk
w hotelelysee.co.uk

**Europa House Hotel** ♦♦
*Guest Accommodation*
151 Sussex Gardens, London
W2 2RY
t (020) 7723 7343
e europahouse@enterprise.
net
w europahousehotel.com

**Hyde Park Radnor Hotel**
★★★★
*Guest Accommodation*
7-9 Sussex Place, London
W2 2SX
t (020) 7723 5969
e hydeparkradnor@btconnect.
com
w hydeparkradnor.com

**Hyde Park Rooms** ★★
*Guest Accommodation*
137 Sussex Gardens, London
W2 2RX
t (020) 7723 0225
e reception@hydeparkrooms.
com
w hydeparkrooms.com

**Kingsway Park Hotel Hyde
Park** ★★★
*Guest Accommodation*
139 Sussex Gardens, London
W2 2RX
t (020) 7723 5677
e info@kingswaypark.hotel.
com
w kingswaypark-hotel.com

**Nayland Hotel** ★★★★
*Guest Accommodation*
132-134 Sussex Gardens,
London W2 1UB
t (020) 7723 4615
e info@naylandhotel.com
w naylandhotel.com

**The Oxford** ★★★
*Guest Accommodation*
13-14 Craven Terrace, London
W2 3QD
t (020) 7402 6860
e info@oxfordhotel.freeserve.
co.uk
w oxfordhotellondon.co.uk

**Park Lodge Hotel** ★★★
*Guest Accommodation*
73 Queensborough Terrace,
London W2 3SU
t (020) 7229 6424

**The Piccolino Hotel** ★★★
*Guest Accommodation*
14 Sussex Place, London
W2 2TP
t (020) 7402 4439
e enquiries@piccolinohotel.
com
w piccolinohotel.com

**Rhodes House** ★★★
*Guest Accommodation*
195 Sussex Gardens, London
W2 2RJ
t (020) 7262 5617
e chris@rhodeshotel.com
w rhodeshotel.com

**St David's and Norfolk Court
Hotel** ★★
*Guest Accommodation*
16 Norfolk Square, London
W2 1RS
t (020) 7723 3856
e info@stdavidshotels.com
w stdavidshotels.com

## W4

**Chiswick Guest House** ★★
*Bed & Breakfast*
40 Spencer Road, Chiswick,
London W4 3SP
t (020) 8994 0876
e rooms@chiswickguesthouse.
co.uk
w chiswickguesthouse.co.uk

## W5

**Grange Lodge** ★★
*Guest House*
48-50 Grange Road, London
W5 5BX
t (020) 8567 1049
e enquiries@
londonlodgehotels.com
w londonlodgehotels.com

## W6

**The Globetrotter Inn London**
★★★★ *Hostel*
Ashlar Court, Ravenscourt
Gardens, London W6 0TU
t (020) 8746 3112
e london@globetrotterinns.
com
w globetrotterinns.com

**Hotel Orlando** ★★
*Guest Accommodation*
83 Shepherds Bush Road,
London W6 7LR
t (020) 7603 4890
e hotelorlando@btconnect.
com
w hotelorlando.co.uk

**St Peters Hotel** ★★★
*Guest Accommodation*
407 Goldhawk Road, London
W6 0SA
t (020) 8741 4239
e info@stpetershotel.co.uk
w stpetershotel.co.uk

## W7

**Boston Manor Hotel** ★★
*Guest Accommodation*
146 Boston Road, London
W7 2HJ
t (020) 8566 1534
e bmh@bostonmanor.com
w bostonmanor.com

## W8

**Holland House YHA** ★★★
*Hostel*
Holland Walk, Kensington,
London W8 7QN
t (020) 7937 0748
e hollandhouse@yha.org.uk
w yha.org.uk

## W11

**Nottinghill Guesthouse Ltd**
♦♦ *Guest Accommodation*
72 Holland Park Avenue,
London W11 3QZ
t (020) 7229 9233
e hotelondon@aol.com
w thiswaytolondon.com

## W14

**Ace Hotel** ★★★ *Hostel*
16-22 Gunterstone Road,
London W14 9BX
t (020) 7602 6600
e reception@ace-hotel.co.uk
w acehotel.co.uk

## WC1

**Arran House Hotel** ★★★
*Guest House*
77-79 Gower Street, London
WC1E 6HJ
t (020) 7636 2186
e arran@dircon.co.uk
w london-hotel.co.uk

**Comfort Inn Kings Cross**
★★★★
*Guest Accommodation*
1-6 St Chad's Street, London
WC1H 8BD
t (020) 7837 1940
e info@comfortinnkingscross.
co.uk
w comfortinnkingscross.co.uk

**Guilford House Hotel** ★★
*Guest House*
6 Guilford Street, London
WC1N 1DR
t (020) 7430 2504
e guilford-hotel@lineone.net
w guilfordhotel.co.uk

## OUTER LONDON

### BEXLEY

**66 Arcadian Avenue** ★★★
*Guest Accommodation*
Bexley DA5 1JW
t (020) 8303 5732

**Blendon Lodge** ★★★★
*Bed & Breakfast*
30 Blendon Road, Bexley
DA5 1BW
t (020) 8303 2571

**Buxted Lodge Bed and
Breakfast** ★★★
*Guest Accommodation*
40 Parkhurst Road, Bexley
DA5 1AS
t (01322) 554010
e info@buxtedlodge.co.uk
w buxtedlodge.co.uk

### BRENTFORD

**Kings Arms** ★★★
*Guest Accommodation*
19 Boston Manor Road,
Brentford TW8 8EA
t (020) 8560 5860
w kingsarmsbrentjord.co.uk

### BROMLEY

**Glendevon House Hotel**
★★★ *Guest House*
80 Southborough Road,
Bromley BR1 2EN
t (020) 8467 2183
w avishotels.com

### CHISLEHURST

**The Crown Inn** ★★★ *Inn*
School Road, Chislehurst
BR7 5PQ
t (020) 8467 7326
e crownchislehurst@
shepherdneame.co.uk
w crownchislehurst.co.uk

### COULSDON

**Aries Guest House** ★★★
*Guest Accommodation*
38 Brighton Road, Coulsdon
CR5 2BA
t (020) 8668 5744
w ariesguesthouse.co.uk

## CROYDON

**Bramley** ★★★
*Bed & Breakfast*
7 Greencourt Avenue,
Croydon CR0 7LD
t (020) 8654 6776

**Croydon Court Hotel** ★★★
*Guest Accommodation*
597-603 London Road,
Thornton Heath CR7 6AY
t (020) 8684 3947
e bookings@
croydencourthotel.co.uk

**Croydon Friendly
Guesthouse** ★★★
*Guest Accommodation*
16 St Peters Road, Croydon
CR0 1HD
t (020) 8680 4428
e admin@croydonhotel.com
w croydonhotel.com

**Foxley Mount** ★★★
*Bed & Breakfast*
44 Foxley Lane, Purley
CR8 3EE
t (020) 8660 9751
e enquiries@foxleymount.co.
uk
w foxleymount.co.uk

**Ginetta Guest House** ★★★
*Guest Accommodation*
32 Rylandes Road, South
Croydon CR2 8EA
t (020) 8657 3132

**Owlets** ★★★ *Bed & Breakfast*
112 Arundel Avenue, South
Croydon CR2 8BH
t (020) 8657 5213

**The Park** ★★★
*Bed & Breakfast*
63 Addington Road, South
Croydon CR2 8RD
t (020) 8657 8776

**The Woodstock Guest
House** ★★★ *Guest House*
30 Woodstock Road, Croydon
CR0 1JR
t (020) 8680 1489
e woodstockhotel@tiscali.co.
uk
w woodstockhotel.co.uk

### ENFIELD

**Sylvia & Roger Bed &
Breakfast** ♦♦♦
*Guest Accommodation*
1 Chinnery Close, Enfield
EN1 4AX
t (020) 8363 3887
e sylviahall@talk21.com

### HAMPTON

**The Chestnuts** ★★★★
*Guest Accommodation*
16 Chestnut Avenue, Hampton
TW12 2NU
t (020) 8979 8314
e thechestnuts_16@fsmail.net

**Houseboat Riverine** ★★★
*Guest Accommodation*
Riverine, Taggs Island,
Hampton TW12 2HA
t (020) 8979 2266
e malcolm@feedtheducks.com
w feedtheducks.com

## HARROW

**Rhondda House** ★★★
*Guest House*
16 Harrow View, Harrow
HA1 1RG
t (020) 8427 5009
w rhonddahouse.com

## HOUNSLOW

**Civic Guest House** ★★
*Guest House*
87-89 Lampton Road,
Hounslow TW3 4DP
t (020) 8572 5107
e enquiries@civicguesthouse.
freeserve.co.uk
w civicguesthouse.freeserve.
co.uk

## ILFORD

**Cranbrook Hotel** ★★
*Guest Accommodation*
22-24 Coventry Road, Ilford
IG1 4QR
t (020) 8554 6544

**Park Hotel** ★★
*Guest Accommodation*
327 Cranbrook Road, Ilford
IG1 4UE
t (020) 8554 9616
e parkhotelilford@
netscapeonline.co.uk
w expresslodging.co.uk

## KENLEY

**Appledore** ★★★
*Bed & Breakfast*
6 Betula Close, Kenley
CR8 5ET
t (020) 8668 4631

## KEW

**11 Leyborne Park** ★★★★
*Guest Accommodation*
Richmond TW9 3HB
t (020) 8948 1615
e mary@stay-in-kew.com
w stay-in-kew.com

**29 West Park Road** ★★★★
*Guest Accommodation*
Kew, Richmond TW9 4DA
t (020) 8878 0505
e aghillman@aol.com

**Arbroath** ★★★★
*Guest Accommodation*
35 Beechwood Avenue,
Richmond TW9 4DD
t (020) 8878 0049
e t.stoten@btopenworld.com

**Melbury** ★★★
*Bed & Breakfast*
33 Marksbury Avenue,
Richmond TW9 4JE
t (020) 8876 3930
e jennieallen@mac.com
w accommodation-kew-
richmond.co.uk

**West Lodge** ★★★
*Bed & Breakfast*
179 Mortlake Road, Richmond
TW9 4AW
t (020) 8876 0584
e westlodge@thakria.demon.
co.uk

## KINGSTON UPON THAMES

**40 The Bittoms** ★★
*Bed & Breakfast*
Kingston-upon-Thames
KT1 2AP
t (020) 8541 3171

**8 St Albans Road** ★★
*Bed & Breakfast*
Kingston-upon-Thames
KT2 5HQ
t (020) 8549 5910

**Ditton Lodge Hotel** ★★★★
*Guest House*
47 Lovelace Road, Long Ditton,
Kingston-upon-Thames
KT6 6NA
t (020) 8399 7482
w dittonlodge.co.uk

## PINNER

**Delcon** ★★★ *Bed & Breakfast*
468 Pinner Road, Pinner
HA5 5RR
t (020) 8863 1054
e delcon@homecall.co.uk

## PURLEY

**The Maple House** ★★★
*Bed & Breakfast*
174 Foxley Lane, Purley
CR8 3NF
t (020) 8407 5123
e trevbrgg@aol.com

**The Nook** ★★
*Bed & Breakfast*
12 Grasmere Road, Purley
CR8 1DU
t (020) 8660 1742

**Purley Cross Guest House**
★★★ *Guest House*
50 Brighton Road, Purley
CR8 2LG
t (020) 8668 4964
e bookings@purleycross.com

## RICHMOND

**Chalon House** ★★★★★
*Guest Accommodation*
GOLD AWARD
8 Spring Terrace, Richmond
TW9 1LW
t (020) 8332 1121
e chalonhouse@hotmail.com

**Hobart Hall Guest House**
★★★ *Guest Accommodation*
43-47 Petersham Road,
Richmond TW10 6UL
t (020) 8940 0435
e hobarthall@aol.com
w smoothhound.co.uk/hotels/
hobarthall.html

**Ivy Cottage** ★★★
*Guest Accommodation*
Upper Ham Road, Ham
Common, Richmond
TW10 5LA
t (020) 8940 8601 &
07742 278247
e taylor@dbta.freeserve.co.uk
w dbta.freeserve.co.uk

**Larkfield Apartments** ★★★
*Guest Accommodation*
19 Larkfield Road, Richmond
TW9 2PG
t (020) 8948 6620
e shipplets@ukgateway.net
w shipplets.com

**Pro Kew Gardens B&B** ★★
*Bed & Breakfast*
15 Pensford Avenue,
Richmond TW9 4HR
t (020) 8876 3354
e info@prokewbandb.demon.
co.uk
w prokewbandb.demon.co.uk

**The Red Cow** ★★★ *Inn*
59 Sheen Road, Richmond
TW9 1YJ
t (020) 8940 2511
e tom@redcowpub.com
w redcowpub.com

**Richmond Inn Hotel** ★★★★
*Guest Accommodation*
50-56 Sheen Road, Richmond
TW9 1UG
t (020) 8940 0171
w richmondinnhotel.com

**Riverside Hotel** ★★★
*Guest Accommodation*
23 Petersham Road, Richmond
TW10 6UH
t (020) 8940 1339
e riversidehotel@yahoo.com
w riversiderichmond.co.uk

**West Park Gardens** ★★★
*Guest Accommodation*
105 Mortlake Road, Richmond
TW9 4AA
t (020) 8876 6842
e nj.edwards@ukonline.co.uk

## SIDCUP

**Hilbert House** ★★★
*Guest Accommodation*
Halfway Street, Sidcup
DA15 8DE
t (020) 8300 0549
e annandeddie@talktalk.net

## SURBITON

**The Broadway Lodge** ★★
*Guest House*
41 The Broadway, Tolworth,
Surbiton KT6 7DJ
t (020) 8399 6555
e broadway.lodge@tiscali.co.
uk
w broadway-stgeorgeslodge.
com

**Villiers Lodge Bed and
Breakfast** ★★
*Bed & Breakfast*
1 Cranes Park, Surbiton
KT5 8AB
t (020) 8399 6000

## SUTTON

**St Margarets Guest House**
★★ *Guest Accommodation*
31 Devon Road, Sutton
SM2 7PE
t (020) 8643 0164
e margarettrotman@hotmail.
com
w stmargaretsbandb.co.uk

## TEDDINGTON

**Hazeldene** ★★★★
*Guest Accommodation*
58 Hampton Road, Teddington
TW11 0JX
t (020) 8286 8500
e glasslisa58@hotmail.com

**King Edwards Grove** ★★★
*Guest Accommodation*
Teddington TW11 9LY
t (020) 8977 7251

**Ladywood** ★★★
*Bed & Breakfast*
Teddington TW11 8AP
t (020) 8977 6066
e lyndano@hotmail.com

## TWICKENHAM

**11 Spencer Road** ★★★
*Bed & Breakfast*
Twickenham TW2 5TH
t (020) 8894 5271
e bruceduff@hotmail.com

**136 London Road** ★★★
*Bed & Breakfast*
Twickenham TW1 1HD
t (020) 8892 3158
e jenniferjfinnerty@hotmail.
com
w accommodation-in-
twickenham.co.uk/

**3 Waldegrave Gardens** ★★
*Bed & Breakfast*
Twickenham TW1 4PQ
t (020) 8892 3523

**39 Grange Avenue** ★★★★
*Bed & Breakfast*
Twickenham TW2 5TW
t (020) 8894 1055
e carole@fanfoliage.
fsbusiness.co.uk
w thewrightresidence.co.uk

**Avalon Cottage** ★★
*Bed & Breakfast*
50 Moor Mead Road,
Twickenham TW1 1JS
t (020) 8744 2178
e avaloncottage@anftel.com
w avalon-cottage.com

**Peter and Marilyn Wilkins**
★★★★
*Guest Accommodation*
37 Grange Avenue, Strawberry
Hill, Twickenham TW2 5TW
t (020) 8898 0412
e wilkins_family@blueyonder.
co.uk
w twickenham-
accommodation.co.uk

## UPMINSTER

**Corner Farm** ★★★
*Guest Accommodation*
Fen Lane, North Ockendon,
Upminster RM14 3RB
t (01708) 851310
w corner-farm.co.uk

## UXBRIDGE

**Brunel University
Conference Centre**
★★–★★★ *Campus*
Conference Office, Brunel
University, Uxbridge UB8 3PH
t (01895) 238353
e conference@brunel.ac.uk
w brunel.ac.uk/campus/
conference

## WELLING

**Danson Bed & Breakfast** ★★
*Guest Accommodation*
73 Danson Crescent, Welling
DA16 2AR
t (020) 8304 1239
e delfreda@ntlworld.com

## WHITTON

**Oscars B&B** ★★★
*Guest Accommodation*
113 Staines Road, Twickenham
TW2 5BD
t (020) 8898 3514
e grievesjam@aol.com

## SOUTH EAST ENGLAND

### ABINGDON
Oxfordshire

**Abbey Guest House ★★★★**
*Guest House*
136 Oxford Road, Abingdon
OX14 2AG
**t** (01235) 537020
**e** info@abbeyguest.com
**w** abbeyguest.com

**Barrows End ★★★★**
*Bed & Breakfast*
3 The Copse, Abingdon
OX14 3YW
**t** (01235) 523541
**e** dsharm@tesco.net

**Kingfisher Barn ★★★★**
*Guest Accommodation*
Rye Farm, Abingdon
OX14 3NN
**t** (01235) 537538
**e** info@kingfisherbarn.com
**w** kingfisherbarn.com

### ABINGER COMMON
Surrey

**Leylands Farm ★★★★**
*Guest Accommodation*
**SILVER AWARD**
Sheephouse Lane, Abinger
Common, Dorking RH5 6JU
**t** (01306) 730115 &
07818 422881
**e** annieblf@btopenworld.com
**w** leylandsfarm.co.uk

### ADDERBURY
Oxfordshire

**The Bell Inn ★★★** *Inn*
High Street, Adderbury,
Banbury OX17 3LS
**t** (01295) 810338
**e** info@the-bell.com
**w** the-bell.com

### ALBURY
Surrey

**Barn Cottage ★★★★**
*Bed & Breakfast*
Farley Green, Albury, Guildford
GU5 9DN
**t** (01483) 202571
**e** bookings@barn-cottage.com
**w** barn-cottage.com

### ALDINGBOURNE
West Sussex

**Limmer Pond House ★★★**
*Bed & Breakfast*
Church Road, Aldingbourne,
Nr Chichester PO20 3TU
**t** (01243) 543210

### ALDINGTON
Kent

**Fostums ★★★★**
*Guest Accommodation*
**SILVER AWARD**
Roman Road, Aldington,
Ashford TN25 7EP
**t** (01233) 720996
**e** fax@fostums.co.uk
**w** fostums.co.uk

**Hogben Farm ★★★★**
*Farmhouse*
Church Lane, Aldington,
Ashford TN25 7EH
**t** (01233) 720219
**e** ros@hogbenfarm.co.uk
**w** hogbenfarm.co.uk

### ALDWORTH
Berkshire

**Fieldview Cottage ★★★★**
*Bed & Breakfast*
Bell Lane, Aldworth, Reading
RG8 9SB
**t** (01635) 578964
**e** hunt@fieldvu.freeserve.co.
uk

### ALFRISTON
East Sussex

**Alfriston Youth Hostel ★★**
*Hostel*
Frog Firle, Alfriston, Polegate
BN26 5SD
**t** 0870 770 5666
**e** alfriston@yha.org.uk

**Riverdale House ★★★★**
*Guest House* **SILVER AWARD**
Seaford Road, Alfriston
BN26 5TR
**t** (01323) 871038
**e** info@riverdalehouse.co.uk
**w** riverdalehouse.co.uk

**Rose Cottage ★★★★**
*Bed & Breakfast*
North Street, Alfriston
BN26 5UQ
**t** (01323) 871534
**e** hd.rosecottage@btinternet.
com
**w** rosecott.uk.com

**Wingrove House ★★★★★**
*Restaurant with Rooms*
High Street, Alfriston
BN26 5TD
**t** (01323) 870276
**e** info@wingrovehousehotel.
com
**w** wingrovehousehotel.com

### ALRESFORD
Hampshire

**Haygarth ★★★**
*Bed & Breakfast*
John and Val Ramshaw,
82 Jacklyns Lane, Alresford
SO24 9LJ
**t** (01962) 732715 &
07986 372895

### ALTON
Hampshire

**Boundary House ★★★★**
*Bed & Breakfast*
**SILVER AWARD**
Gosport Road, Lower
Farringdon, Nr Alton
GU34 3DH
**t** (01420) 587076
**e** boundarys@messages.co.uk
**w** boundaryhouse.co.uk

**Farthings ★★★★**
*Bed & Breakfast*
**SILVER AWARD**
Powntley Copse, Alton
GU34 4DL
**t** (01256) 862427
**e** susiehare@powntleycopse.
net
**w** powntleycopse.net/
farthings

### The Granary ★★★★
*Farmhouse* **GOLD AWARD**
Stubbs Farm, South Hay,
Kingsley GU35 9NR
**t** (01420) 474906
**e** info@stubbsfarm.co.uk
**w** stubbsfarm.co.uk

**The Manor House ★★★★**
*Bed & Breakfast*
Church Lane, Holybourne,
Alton GU34 4HD
**t** (01420) 541321 &
07711 655450
**e** clare@whately.net

**Neatham Barn ★★★★**
*Bed & Breakfast*
Holybourne, Neatham, Alton
GU34 4NP
**t** (01420) 544215
**e** neathambarn@f2s.com
**w** neathambarn.com

**St Mary's Hall ★★★★**
*Bed & Breakfast*
18 Albert Road, Alton
GU34 1LP
**t** (01420) 82235

**Shepherds Court ★★★★**
*Guest Accommodation*
**SILVER AWARD**
Whitehouse Farm, Alton
GU34 3HL
**t** (01420) 83847
**e** info@shepherdscourt.co.uk
**w** shepherdscourt.co.uk

**West End Farm ★★★★**
*Farmhouse*
Upper Froyle, Alton GU34 4JG
**t** (01420) 22130
**e** butlerfroyle@btopenworld.
com
**w** hampshirebedandbreakfast.
co.uk

### ALVERSTONE GARDEN VILLAGE
Isle of Wight

**Bluebell Wood Bed & Breakfast**
Rating Applied For
*Bed & Breakfast*
13 Woodside Avenue,
Alverstone Garden Village,
Sandown PO36 0JD
**t** (01983) 401869

### AMBERLEY
West Sussex

**Brook Green Arundel ★★**
*Bed & Breakfast*
1 Hog Lane, Amberley,
Arundel BN18 9NQ
**t** (01798) 831275

### AMERSHAM
Buckinghamshire

**Cherry Trees ★★★★**
*Bed & Breakfast*
51 Longfield Drive, Amersham
HP6 5HE
**t** (01494) 729321
**e** angelicaschweiger@hotmail.
com
**w** cherrytrees-bandb.co.uk

### Rocquaine House ★★★★★
*Bed & Breakfast*
**GOLD AWARD**
36 Stanley Hill Avenue,
Amersham HP7 9BB
**t** (01494) 726671
**e** anneandray@waitrose.com

**St Catherins ★★★**
*Bed & Breakfast*
9 Parkfield Avenue, Amersham
HP6 6BE
**t** (01494) 728125
**e** jellio@talktalk.net
**w** st-catherins-bandb.co.uk

### ANDOVER
Hampshire

**Amberley Hotel**
Rating Applied For
*Guest House*
70 Weyhill Road, Andover
SP10 3NP
**t** (01264) 352224
**e** amberleyand@fsbdial.co.uk

**Amport Inn ★★★** *Inn*
Sarson, Amport, Andover
SP11 8AE
**t** (01264) 710371

**Bridge Cottage ★★★★★**
*Guest Accommodation*
**SILVER AWARD**
Upper Clatford, Andover
SP11 7LW
**t** 07831 121320
**e** enquiries@bridgecottage.
info
**w** bridgecottage.info

**Church Mews Guest House**
**★★** *Guest House*
2 Chantry Street, Andover
SP10 1DE
**t** (01264) 324323
**e** edmund@
point2pointandover.com

**May Cottage ★★★★**
*Bed & Breakfast*
**SILVER AWARD**
Thruxton, Andover SP11 8LZ
**t** (01264) 771241
**e** info@maycottage-thruxton.
co.uk
**w** maycottage-thruxton.co.uk

**Salisbury Road Bed & Breakfast ★★★★**
*Bed & Breakfast*
99 Salisbury Road, Andover
SP10 2LN
**t** (01264) 362638
**e** jenny@
andoveraccommodation.co.uk
**w** andoveraccommodation.co.
uk

### ARDINGLY
West Sussex

**Lywood House ★★★★**
*Guest House*
Lindfield Road, Ardingly,
Haywards Heath RH17 6SW
**t** (01444) 892369
**e** cleonep@btconnect.com
**w** lywoodhouse.com

### ARDLEY
Oxfordshire

**The Old Post Office ★★★**
*Bed & Breakfast*
Church Road, Ardley, Bicester
OX27 7NP
t (01869) 345958
e mail@
theoldpostofficeardley.co.uk
w theoldpostofficeardley.co.uk

### ARRETON
Isle of Wight

**Arreton Manor ♦♦♦♦**
*Guest Accommodation*
GOLD AWARD
Main Road, Arreton PO30 3AA
t (01983) 522604
e arreton@arretonmanor.co.
uk
w arretonmanor.co.uk

### ARUNDEL
West Sussex

**Arundel House Restaurant & Rooms ★★★★★**
*Restaurant with Rooms*
GOLD AWARD
11 High Street, Arundel
BN18 9AD
t (01903) 882136
w arundelhouseonline.com

**Pindars ★★★★**
*Guest Accommodation*
SILVER AWARD
Lyminster, Arundel BN17 7QF
t (01903) 882628
e pindars@btinternet.com
w pindars.co.uk

**Sandfield House ★★★**
*Bed & Breakfast*
Lyminster Road, Wick,
Littlehampton BN17 7PG
t (01903) 724129
e francesfarrerbrown@
btconnect.com
w visitsussex.org/
sandfieldhouse

**The Townhouse ★★★★**
*Restaurant with Rooms*
SILVER AWARD
65 High Street, Arundel
BN18 9AJ
t (01903) 883847
e enquiries@thetownhouse.
co.uk
w thetownhouse.co.uk

**Woodpeckers ♦♦♦♦**
*Guest Accommodation*
15 Dalloway Road, Arundel
BN18 9HJ
t (01903) 883948

### ASCOT
Berkshire

**Tanglewood ★★★**
*Bed & Breakfast*
Tanglewood Birch Lane, Long
Hill Road Chavey Down, Ascot
SL5 8RF
t (01344) 882528
e beer.tanglewood@
btinternet.com

### ASCOTT-UNDER-WYCHWOOD
Oxfordshire

**College Farm ★★★★**
*Farmhouse*
Ascott-under-Wychwood,
Chipping Norton OX7 6AL
t (01993) 831900
e walkers@collegefarmbandb.
fsnet.co.uk

**Meadowbank House ★★★★**
*Bed & Breakfast*
Shipton Road, Ascott-under-
Wychwood, Chipping Norton
OX7 6AG
t (01993) 830612
e ingrid@meadowbank-ascott.
co.uk
w meadowbank-ascott.co.uk

### ASH
Kent

**Great Weddington**
**★★★★★ Bed & Breakfast**
Weddington, Ash, Canterbury
CT3 2AR
t (01304) 813407
e traveltale@aol.com
w greatweddington.co.uk

### ASHFORD
Kent

**Dean Court Farm ★★★**
*Guest Accommodation*
Challock Lane, Westwell,
Ashford TN25 4NH
t (01233) 712924

**The New Flying Horse**
**★★★★ Inn**
Upper Bridge Street, Wye,
Ashford TN25 5AN
t (01233) 812297
e newflyhorse@
shepherdneame.co.uk
w newflyinghorsewye.co.uk

**Sue & Jim's Bed & Breakfast**
**★★★ Guest Accommodation**
31 Birling Road, Ashford
TN24 8BD
t (01233) 643069
e susan.mclaren1@ntlworld.
com

### ASHURST
Hampshire

**Forest Gate Lodge ♦♦♦♦**
*Guest Accommodation*
161 Lyndhurst Road, Ashurst,
Southampton SO40 7AW
t (023) 8029 3026
w forestgatelodge.co.uk

**Kingswood Cottage ★★★★**
*Bed & Breakfast*
SILVER AWARD
10 Woodlands Road, Ashurst,
Lyndhurst SO40 7AD
t (023) 8029 2582
e kingswoodcottage@yahoo.
co.uk
w kingswoodcottage.co.uk

### ASTON ABBOTTS
Buckinghamshire

**Windmill Hill Barns ★★★★**
*Bed & Breakfast*
Moat Lane, Aston Abbotts,
Aylesbury HP22 4NF
t (01296) 681714

### ASTON UPTHORPE
Oxfordshire

**Middle Fell ★★★★**
*Guest Accommodation*
Moreton Road, Aston
Upthorpe, Didcot OX11 9ER
t (01235) 850207
e middlefell@ic24.net

### AWBRIDGE
Hampshire

**Crofton Country Bed and Breakfast ★★★★★**
*Bed & Breakfast*
SILVER AWARD
Kents Oak, Awbridge, Romsey
SO51 0HH
t (01794) 340333
e pauline@croftonbandb.com
w croftonbandb.com

**Woodpeckers B&B ★★★★**
*Farmhouse* SILVER AWARD
1 The Prophets, Romsey
SO51 0GG
t (01794) 342400
e woodpeckersbandb@aol.
com
w woodpeckersbandb.co.uk

### AYLESBURY
Buckinghamshire

**46 Craigwell Avenue ★★★**
*Bed & Breakfast*
Buckingham HP21 7AF
t (01296) 338673

**74 Friarscroft Way ★★**
*Bed & Breakfast*
Aylesbury HP20 2TF
t (01296) 489439

**Ambleside**
Rating Applied For
*Guest Accommodation*
Aylesbury HP21 9TT
t (01296) 584395

**Applecroft ★★★**
*Bed & Breakfast*
187 Aylesbury Road, Aylesbury
HP22 5DS
t (01296) 485345
e marie.archer@applecroftbb.
co.uk
w applecroftbb.co.uk

**Bay Lodge Guest House ★★**
*Guest House*
47 Tring Road, Aylesbury
HP20 1LD
t (01296) 331404
e blodge47@hotmail.com
w bay-lodge.co.uk

**The Cottage B&B ★★★★**
*Bed & Breakfast*
Pitchcott Road, Oving,
Aylesbury HP22 4HR
t (01296) 641891
e thegeorges@btinternet.com

**Lakeside Bed & Breakfast**
**★★★★ Bed & Breakfast**
9/10 Osprey Walk, Aylesbury
HP19 0FF
t (01296) 331351
e sil@waitrose.com

**Number 19 ★★★★**
*Bed & Breakfast*
19 Castle Street, Buckingham
HP20 2RE
t (01296) 434247
e clairesamways@breathe.com
w http://myweb.tiscali.co.uk/
number19

**The Old Forge Barn ★★★**
*Bed & Breakfast*
Ridings Way, Cublington,
Leighton Buzzard LU7 0LW
t (01296) 681194
e waples@ukonline.co.uk

**Olympic Lodge Hotel ★★★**
*Guest Accommodation*
Stoke Mandeville Stadium,
Guttmann Road, Aylesbury
HP21 9PP
t (01296) 484848
e sms.events@
leisureconnection.co.uk
w stokemandevillestadium.co.
uk

**Spindleberries ★★**
*Bed & Breakfast*
331 Tring Road, Aylesbury
HP20 1PJ
t (01296) 424012

**Tanamera ★★★★**
*Bed & Breakfast*
SILVER AWARD
37 Bishopstone Village,
Bishopstone, Aylesbury
HP17 8SH
t (01296) 748551
e tanamera@tesco.net

**Town House ★★★**
*Guest House*
35 Tring Road, Aylesbury
HP20 1LD
t (01296) 395295

**Wallace Farm (B&B) ★★★**
*Farmhouse*
Upton Road, School Lane,
Dinton HP17 8UZ
t (01296) 748660
e jackiecook@wallacefarm.
freeserve.co.uk
w wallacefarm.com

### AYLESFORD
Kent

**Wickham Lodge ★★★★★**
*Guest Accommodation*
GOLD AWARD
High Street, Aylesford
ME20 7AY
t (01622) 717267
e wickhamlodge@aol.com
w wickhamlodge.co.uk

### BALCOMBE
West Sussex

**Rocks Lane Cottage ★★★★**
*Bed & Breakfast*
Rocksl Lane, Balcombe,
Haywards Heath RH17 6JG
t (01444) 811245
e angelaparry@talktalk.net

### BAMPTON
Oxfordshire

**The Granary ★★★**
*Bed & Breakfast*
Main Street, Clanfield,
Bampton OX18 2SH
t (01367) 810266

**Wheelgate House Bed & Breakfast ★★★★**
*Bed & Breakfast*
Wheelgate House, Market
Square, Bampton OX18 2JH
t (01993) 851151
e bizgooddy@hotmail.com

---

## BANBURY
### Oxfordshire

**Amberley Guest House ★★**
*Guest Accommodation*
151 Middleton Road, Banbury
OX16 3QS
**t** (01295) 255797

**Ark Guest House ★★★**
*Guest Accommodation*
120 Warwick Road, Banbury
OX16 2AN
**t** (01295) 254498

**Ashlea Guest House ★★**
*Guest Accommodation*
58 Oxford Road, Banbury
OX16 9AN
**t** (01295) 250539

**Avonlea Guest House ★★★**
*Guest Accommodation*
41 Southam Road, Banbury
OX16 2EP
**t** (01295) 267837
**e** whitforddebbie@hotmail.
com
**w** avonleaguesthouse.co.uk

**Babington Barn ★★★**
*Guest Accommodation*
Williamscot, Banbury
OX17 1AD
**t** (01295) 750546

**Banbury Cross Bed &
Breakfast ★★★★**
*Guest House* **SILVER AWARD**
1 Broughton Road, Banbury
OX16 9QB
**t** (01295) 266048
**w** banburycrossbandb.co.uk

**Cotefields Bed & Breakfast
★★ Bed & Breakfast**
Oxford Road, Bodicote,
Banbury OX15 4AQ
**t** (01295) 264977
**e** tony.stockford@ic24.net or
cheapbed@yahoo.com
**w** bedandbreakfastcotefields.
co.uk

**Easington House ★★★★**
*Guest House*
50 Oxford Road, Banbury
OX16 9AN
**t** (01295) 270181

**Hanwell House ★★★★**
*Bed & Breakfast*
2 Lapsley Drive, Banbury
OX16 1LJ
**t** (01295) 263001
**e** jmb_events@yahoo.co.uk

**Prospect House ★★★**
*Guest Accommodation*
Oxford Road, Banbury
OX16 9AN
**t** (01295) 268749

**St Martins House ★★★★**
*Bed & Breakfast*
Warkworth, Banbury
OX17 2AG
**t** (01295) 712684

**White Cross House ★★★★**
*Bed & Breakfast*
7 Broughton Road, Banbury
OX16 9QB
**t** (01295) 277932
**e** marian@kedwards50.fsnet.
co.uk

## BARNHAM
### West Sussex

**Downhills ★★**
*Bed & Breakfast*
87 Barnham Road, Barnham,
Bognor Regis PO22 0EQ
**t** (01243) 553104

**Saxby**
Rating Applied For
*Guest Accommodation*
Yapton Road, Barnham, Bognor
Regis PO22 0BQ
**t** (01243) 552996
**e** saxby-bandb@tiscali.co.uk
**w** saxbybandb.co.uk

## BARTON ON SEA
### Hampshire

**Grandco Lodge ★★★★**
*Bed & Breakfast*
**SILVER AWARD**
29 Marine Drive East, Barton
on Sea, New Milton BH25 7DU
**t** (01425) 610541

**Pebble Beach ★★★★**
*Restaurant with Rooms*
Marine Drive, Barton on Sea,
New Milton BH25 7DZ
**t** (01425) 627777
**e** mail@pebblebeach-uk.com
**w** pebblebeach-uk.com

## BASINGSTOKE
### Hampshire

**Arundel ★★**
*Guest Accommodation*
25 Linden Avenue, Old Basing,
Basingstoke RG24 7HS
**t** (01256) 327282

**The Haven ★★**
*Guest Accommodation*
8 Newnham Lane, Old Basing,
Basingstoke RG24 7AT
**t** (01256) 462892

**Millfield House ★★★★**
*Guest Accommodation*
1a Little Basing, Bartons Lane,
Basingstoke RG24 8AX
**t** (01256) 474513
**e** info@millfieldhouse.co.uk
**w** millfieldhouse.co.uk

**Wessex House ★★★**
*Guest House*
120 Winchester Road,
Basingstoke RG21 8YW
**t** (01256) 325202
**e** wessex10@hotmail.com
**w** wessexhousebandb.co.uk

## BATTLE
### East Sussex

**A White Lodge ★★★★**
*Bed & Breakfast*
**SILVER AWARD**
42 Hastings Road, Battle
TN33 0TE
**t** (01424) 772122
**e** janewhitelodge2@msn.com
**w** bedandbreakfastbattle.co.uk

**Acacia House ★★★★**
*Bed & Breakfast*
Starrs Green Lane, Battle
TN33 0TD
**t** (01424) 772416
**e** acacia.house@beamingmail.
com
**w** battlebedandbreakfast.co.uk

**Battle Golf Club ★★★**
*Guest Accommodation*
Netherfield Hill, Battle
TN33 0LH
**t** (01424) 775677
**e** clare@battlegolfclub.com
**w** battlegolfclub.com

**Heather Hill ★★★★★**
*Bed & Breakfast*
94 Hastings Road, Battle
TN33 0TQ
**t** (01424) 774746
**e** ardibley1@aol.com
**w** battlebedandbreakfast.com

**Tollgate Farm House
★★★★**
*Guest Accommodation*
**SILVER AWARD**
59 North Trade Road, Battle
TN33 0HS
**t** (01424) 777436
**e** christinemhowe@hotmail.
com
**w** tollgatefarmhouse.co.uk

## BEARSTED
### Kent

**Cherwell ★★★★**
*Guest Accommodation*
88 Ashford Road, Maidstone
ME14 4LT
**t** (01622) 738278
**e** anna.cherwell@btinternet.
com
**w** cherwellbandb.co.uk

## BEAULIEU
### Hampshire

**Dale Farm House ★★★★**
*Guest Accommodation*
Manor Road, Applemore Hill,
Dibden, Southampton
SO45 5TJ
**t** (023) 8084 9632
**w** dalefarmhouse.co.uk

**Leygreen Farm House
★★★★** *Bed & Breakfast*
Lyndhurst Road, Beaulieu,
Brockenhurst SO42 7YP
**t** (01590) 612355
**w** newforest.demon.co.uk/
leygreen.htm

## BENENDEN
### Kent

**Apple Trees B&B ★★★**
*Bed & Breakfast*
Goddards Green, Nr
Benenden, Cranbrook
TN17 4AR
**t** (01580) 240622
**e** garryblanch@aol.com
**w** appletreescentre.co.uk

**The Holt ★★★★**
*Bed & Breakfast*
**SILVER AWARD**
New Pond Road, Cranbrook
TN17 4EL
**t** (01580) 240414
**e** kate@theholt.org
**w** theholt.org

## BENHAM HILL
### Berkshire

**Chef's House ★★★★**
*Guest Accommodation*
404 London Road, Benham Hill,
Thatcham RG18 3AA
**t** (01635) 42231
**e** sean@chefshouse.co.uk
**w** chefshouse.co.uk

## BENSON
### Oxfordshire

**Brookside ★★★★**
*Bed & Breakfast*
Brook Street, Benson,
Wallingford OX10 6LJ
**t** (01491) 838289

**Fyfield Manor ★★★★**
*Bed & Breakfast*
**SILVER AWARD**
Benson, Wallingford
OX10 6HA
**t** (01491) 835184
**e** chris_fyfield@hotmail.co.uk
**w** fyfieldmanor.co.uk

## BENTLEY
### Hampshire

**Pittersfield ★★★★**
*Bed & Breakfast*
Hole Lane, Bentley, Farnham
GU10 5LT
**t** (01420) 22414
**e** jenefer@pittersfield.
wanadoo.co.uk

## BETHERSDEN
### Kent

**Anderson Potters Farm
★★★** *Guest Accommodation*
Bethersden, Ashford TN26 3JX
**t** (01233) 820341
**e** pottersfarms@aol.com
**w** smoothhound.co.uk/hotels/
potters.html

**The Old Stables ★★★★**
*Guest Accommodation*
**SILVER AWARD**
Wissenden, Bethersden,
Ashford TN26 3EL
**t** (01233) 820597
**e** pennygillespie@
theoldstables.co.uk
**w** theoldstables.co.uk

## BEXHILL-ON-SEA
### East Sussex

**Arden House ★★★★**
*Bed & Breakfast*
28 Manor Road, Bexhill-on-Sea
TN40 1SP
**t** (01424) 225068
**e** info@ardenhousebexhill.co.
uk
**w** ardenhousebexhill.co.uk

**Barkers Bed and Breakfast
★★★** *Bed & Breakfast*
16 Magdalen Road, Bexhill-on-
Sea TN40 1SB
**t** (01424) 218969

**Barrington ★★★★**
*Guest Accommodation*
14 Wilton Road, Bexhill-on-Sea
TN40 1HY
**t** (01424) 210250

**Buenos Aires Guest House
★★★★** *Guest House*
24 Albany Road, Bexhill-on-Sea
TN40 1BZ
**t** (01424) 212269
**e** buenosairesguest@hotmail.
com
**w** buenosairesguesthouse.com

**Cobwebs ★★★★**
*Guest Accommodation*
26 Collington Avenue, Bexhill-
on-Sea TN39 3QA
**t** (01424) 213464
**e** kobwebs@waitrose.com

**Collington Lodge Guest House** ★★★★ *Guest House*
41 Collington Avenue, Bexhill-on-Sea TN39 3PX
t (01424) 210024

**Dunselma** ★★★★
*Guest Accommodation*
25 Marina, Bexhill-on-Sea TN40 1BP
t (01424) 734144
e stay@dunselma.co.uk
w dunselma.co.uk

**Manor Barn Ensuite Chalets** ★★★ *Bed & Breakfast*
Ninfield Road, Lunsford Cross, Bexhill-on-Sea TN39 5JJ
t (01424) 893018
e bsgillingham@yahoo.co.uk

**The Old Manse** ★★★★★
*Bed & Breakfast*
**SILVER AWARD**
Terminus Avenue, Bexhill-on-Sea TN39 3LS
t (01424) 216151
e debbie.march@virgin.net
w theoldmansebexhill.co.uk

**The Old Vicarage** ★★★★
*Bed & Breakfast*
**GOLD AWARD**
5 Brassey Road, Bexhill-on-Sea TN40 1LD
t (01424) 213498

**Park Lodge** ★★★★
*Guest Accommodation*
16 Egerton Road, Bexhill-on-Sea TN39 3HH
t (01424) 216547
e info@parklodgehotel.co.uk
w parklodgehotel.co.uk

**Waveney** ★★★★
*Guest Accommodation*
20 Hastings Road, Bexhill-on-Sea TN40 2HH
t (01424) 733268

**The York Hotel** ★★★
*Guest Accommodation*
92 London Road, Bexhill-on-Sea TN39 4AE
t (01424) 224275

### BICESTER
Oxfordshire

**Home Farm** ★★★ *Farmhouse*
Mansmoor Lane, Charlton on Otmoor, Kidlington OX5 2US
t (01865) 331267 & 07774 710305

**Manor Farm Bed & Breakfast** ★★★ *Farmhouse*
Main Street, Poundon, Bicester OX27 9BB
t (01869) 277212
e jeannettecollett@aol.com
w smoothhound.co.uk/hotels/manor3.html

### BIDDENDEN
Kent

**Barclay Farmhouse** ★★★★★
*Guest Accommodation*
**GOLD AWARD**
Woolpack Corner, Biddenden, Ashford TN27 8BQ
t (01580) 292626
e info@barclayfarmhouse.co.uk
w barclayfarmhouse.co.uk

**Birchley Bed & Breakfast** ★★★★★
*Guest Accommodation*
**GOLD AWARD**
Fosten Lane, Biddenden, Ashford TN27 8DZ
t (01580) 291413
e bookings@birchleyhouse.co.uk
w birchleyhouse.co.uk

**Bishopsdale Oast** ★★★★
*Guest Accommodation*
**SILVER AWARD**
Biddenden, Ashford TN27 8DR
t (01580) 291027
e drysdale@bishopsdaleoast.co.uk
w bishopsdaleoast.co.uk

**Heron Cottage** ★★★★
*Guest Accommodation*
Biddenden, Ashford TN27 8HH
t (01580) 291358
w heroncottage.info

**Tudor Cottage** ★★★★
*Guest Accommodation*
25 High Street, Biddenden, Ashford TN27 8AL
t (01580) 291913
e suemorris.biddenden@virgin.net
w tudorcottagebiddenden.co.uk

**Whitfield Farm** ★★★★
*Guest Accommodation*
**SILVER AWARD**
Dashmonden Lane, Biddenden, Ashford TN27 8BZ
t (01580) 291092
e enquiries@whitfieldfarm.co.uk
w whitfieldfarm.co.uk

### BILSINGTON
Kent

**Willow Farm B&B** ★★★
*Guest Accommodation*
Bilsington, Ashford TN25 7JJ
t (01233) 721700
e renee@willowfarmenterprises.co.uk
w willowfarmenterprises.co.uk

### BINFIELD
Berkshire

**Berkshire Rooms** ◆◆◆◆
*Guest Accommodation*
The Ridges, Murrell Hill Lane, Bracknell RG42 4DA
t (01344) 360077
e info@berkshirerooms.com
w berkshirerooms.com

### BINSTEAD
Isle of Wight

**Newnham Farm** ★★★★★
*Farmhouse* **SILVER AWARD**
Newnham Lane, Ryde PO33 4ED
t (01983) 882423
e di@newnhamfarm.co.uk
w newnhamfarm.co.uk

### BIRDHAM
West Sussex

**Croftside Cottage** ★★★★
*Bed & Breakfast*
Main Road, Birdham, Chichester PO20 7HS
t (01243) 512864
e info@croftside.com
w croftside.com

### BISHOP'S WALTHAM
Hampshire

**Post Mead** ★★★★
*Bed & Breakfast*
**SILVER AWARD**
Shore Lane, Southampton SO32 1DY
t (01489) 895795
e ian_leesmith@attglobal.net

### BISHOPSTONE
Buckinghamshire

**Standalls Farm** ★★
*Bed & Breakfast*
Bishopstone, Aylesbury HP17 8SL
t (01296) 612687
e rogergoodchild@tesco.net

### BLACKBOYS
East Sussex

**Rangers Cottage** ★★★★
*Bed & Breakfast*
Terminus Road, Blackboys, Uckfield TN22 5LX
t (01825) 890463
e rangers.cottage@btinternet.com

### BLACKTHORN
Oxfordshire

**Lime Trees Farm** ★★★★
*Farmhouse*
Lower Road, Blackthorn, Bicester OX25 1TG
t (01869) 248435
e caroline@limetreesfarm.co.uk
w limetreesfarm.co.uk

### BLACKWATER
Hampshire

**Abacus** ★★★
*Guest Accommodation*
7 Woodside, Blackwater, Camberley GU17 9JJ
t (01276) 38339
e jane@abacusbedandbreakfast.co.uk
w abacusbedandbreakfast.co.uk

### BLADBEAN
Kent

**Molehills** ★★★★
*Guest Accommodation*
Bladbean, Canterbury CT4 6LU
t (01303) 840051
e molehills84@hotmail.com

### BLADON
Oxfordshire

**Park House** ★★★★
*Bed & Breakfast*
26 Park Street, Woodstock OX20 1RW
t (01993) 813888
e info@parkhouseantiques.co.uk
w parkhouseantiques.co.uk/bandb

### BOGNOR REGIS
West Sussex

**Alderwasley Cottage** ★★★★ *Bed & Breakfast*
**SILVER AWARD**
Off West Street, Bognor Regis PO21 1XH
t (01243) 821339
e alderwasley@btinternet.com
w alderwasleycottage.co.uk

**Bognor Regis Campus University College Chichester** ★–★★ *Campus*
Accommodation Office, Upper Bognor Road, Bognor Regis PO21 1HR
t (01243) 812140
w ucc.ac.uk

**Homestead Guest House** ★★★ *Guest House*
90 Aldwick Road, Bognor Regis PO21 2PD
t (01243) 823443

**Jubilee Guest House** ★★★
*Guest Accommodation*
5 Gloucester Road, Bognor Regis PO21 1NU
t (01243) 863016
e jubileeguesthouse@tiscali.co.uk
w jubileeguesthouse.com

**Regis Lodge** ★★
*Guest Accommodation*
3 Gloucester Road, Bognor Regis PO21 1NU
t (01243) 827110
e frank.regislodge@btinternet.com
w regislodge.co.uk

**Sea Crest Private Hotel** ★★★ *Guest Accommodation*
Nyewood Lane, Bognor Regis PO21 2QB
t (01243) 821438

**Selwood Lodge** ★★★
*Guest House*
93 Victoria Drive, Bognor Regis PO21 2DZ
t (01243) 865071
e mail@selwoodlodge.com
w selwoodlodge.com

**Swan Guest House** ★★★★
*Guest Accommodation*
17 Nyewood Lane, Aldwick, Bognor Regis PO21 2QB
t (01243) 826880
e swanhse@globalnet.co.uk
w swanguesthousebognor.co.uk

**Trevali Guest House** ★★★★
*Guest Accommodation*
Belmont Street, Bognor Regis PO21 1LE
t (01243) 862203
e info@trevaliguesthouse.co.uk
w trevaliguesthouse.co.uk

**Tudor Cottage Guest House** ◆◆◆◆ *Guest Accommodation*
194 Chichester Road, Bognor Regis PO21 5BJ
t (01243) 821826
e tudorcottage@supernet.com

**White Horses Felpham Bed & Breakfast** ★★★★
*Bed & Breakfast*
Clyde Road, Felpham, Bognor Regis PO22 7AH
t (01243) 824320
e info@whitehorsesfelpham.co.uk
w whitehorsesfelpham.co.uk

## BOLNEY
### West Sussex

**Bramble Cottage ★★★★**
*Bed & Breakfast*
The Street, Bolney, Haywards
Heath RH17 5PG
t (01444) 881643
e enquiries@
bramblecottagebb.co.uk
w bramblecottagebb.co.uk

**Broxmead Paddock ★★★★**
*Bed & Breakfast*
Broxmead Lane, Bolney,
Haywards Heath RH17 5RG
t (01444) 881458
e broxmeadpaddock@hotmail.
com
w broxmeadpaddock.eclipse.
co.uk

## BOLTER END
### Buckinghamshire

**Trillium House ★★★★**
*Bed & Breakfast*
Bolter End Lane, Bolter End
HP14 3LU
t (01494) 881627
e terence.mcgibbon@
btopenworld.com

## BONCHURCH
### Isle of Wight

**The Lake ★★★★**
*Guest Accommodation*
Shore Road, Bonchurch,
Ventnor PO38 1RF
t (01983) 852613
e enquiries@lakehotel.co.uk
w lakehotel.co.uk

**Under Rock Country House
★★★★**
*Guest Accommodation*
Shore Road, Bonchurch
PO38 1RF
t (01983) 855274
w under-rock.co.uk

**Winterbourne Country
House ★★★★★**
*Guest House* **SILVER AWARD**
Bonchurch Village Road,
Ventnor PO38 1RQ
t (01983) 852535
e info@winterbournehouse.
co.uk
w winterbournehouse.co.uk

## BORDEN
### Kent

**Holly House Bed & Breakfast
★★★★** *Bed & Breakfast*
**SILVER AWARD**
Wises Lane, Borden,
Sittingbourne ME9 8LR
t (01795) 426953

## BORDON
### Hampshire

**Groomes ★★★★★**
*Guest Accommodation*
**GOLD AWARD**
Frith End, Bordon GU35 0QR
t (01420) 489858
e pete@groomes.co.uk
w groomes.co.uk

## BOSHAM
### West Sussex

**Good Hope ★★★★**
*Bed & Breakfast*
**SILVER AWARD**
Delling Lane, Bosham,
Chichester PO18 8NR
t (01243) 572487
e goodhope_bosham@yahoo.
co.uk
w visitsussex.org/goodhope

## BOUGHTON
### Kent

**The Lees ★★★**
*Bed & Breakfast*
Horselees Road, Boughton-
under-Blean, Faversham
ME13 9TG
t (01227) 751332
e keith@theleesbb.co.uk
w theleesbb.fsnet.co.uk

**Tenterden House ♦♦♦**
*Guest Accommodation*
209 The Street, Boughton,
Faversham ME13 9BL
t (01227) 751593
e platham@tesco.net
w faversham.org/
tenterdenhouse

## BOUGHTON MONCHELSEA
### Kent

**Wierton Hall Farm ★★★**
*Guest Accommodation*
East Hall Hill, Maidstone
ME17 4JU
t (01622) 743535
e lorraine@aspentreeservices.
co.uk
w wiertonhallfarm.co.uk

## BOURNE END
### Buckinghamshire

**Hollands Farm ★★★★**
*Farmhouse*
Hedsor Road, Bourne End
SL8 5EE
t (01628) 520423
e info@hollands-farm.co.uk
w hollands-farm.co.uk

**Lower Martins ★★★★**
*Bed & Breakfast*
Coldmoorholme Lane, Bourne
End SL8 5PS
t (01628) 521730
e marianiwills@supanet.com
w marianiwills.supanet.com

## BOXGROVE
### West Sussex

**Brufords ★★★★**
*Guest Accommodation*
66/66a The Street, Boxgrove,
Chichester PO18 0EE
t (01243) 774085
e room4me@brufords.org
w brufords.org

## BOXLEY
### Kent

**Styles House ★★**
*Guest Accommodation*
Style Cottage, Styles Lane,
Maidstone ME14 3DZ
t (01622) 757567
e sue@stylescottage.co.uk
w stylescottage.co.uk

## BRACKNELL
### Berkshire

**The Admirals Inn ★★★**
*Guest Accommodation*
27 Stoney Road, Bracknell
RG42 1XY
t (01344) 483052
e cunninghambarry@tiscali.co.
uk
w theadmiralsinnguesthouse.
com

**Elizabeth House Ltd.
★★★★**
*Guest Accommodation*
Rounds Hill, Wokingham Road,
Bracknell RG42 1PB
t (01344) 868480
e admin@lizhotel.co.uk
w lizhotel.co.uk

**Tenterden ★★★**
*Guest Accommodation*
Rounds Hill, Wokingham Road,
Bracknell RG42 1PB
t (01344) 483052
e cunninghambarry@tiscali.co.
uk
w tenterdenguesthouse.co.uk

## BRADWELL
### Buckinghamshire

**YHA Bradwell Village ★★**
*Hostel*
Manor Farm, Vicarage Road,
Milton Keynes MK13 9AG
t 0870 770 5716
e bradwellvillage@yha.org.uk
w yha.org.uk

## BRAMSHAW
### Hampshire

**Wych Green Cottage**
**★★★★** *Bed & Breakfast*
Bramshaw, Lyndhurst SO43 7JF
t (023) 8081 2561
e suniverseone@aol.com
w newforest-uk.com

## BRANSGORE
### Hampshire

**The Corner House ★★★★**
*Bed & Breakfast*
Betsy Lane, Bransgore,
Christchurch BH23 8AQ
t (01425) 673201

## BRASTED
### Kent

**The Mount House ★★★★**
*Bed & Breakfast*
Brasted, Westerham TN16 1JB
t (01959) 563611
e diana@themounthouse.com
w themounthouse.com

**The Orchard House ★★**
*Bed & Breakfast*
Brasted Chart, Westerham
TN16 1LR
t (01959) 563702
e david.godsal@tesco.net

## BREDE
### East Sussex

**2 Stonelink Cottages ★★★**
*Bed & Breakfast*
Stubb Lane, Brede, Rye
TN31 6BL
t (01424) 882943 &
07802 573612
e stonelinkC@aol.com
w visit-rye.co.uk

## Brede Court Country House
**★★★★** *Guest House*
Brede Hill, Brede, Rye
TN31 6EJ
t (01424) 883105
e bredecrt@globalnet.co.uk
w bredecourt.co.uk

**The Mill House ★★★★**
*Bed & Breakfast*
**SILVER AWARD**
Pottery Lane, Brede TN31 6EA
t (01424) 883096
e michaelt@euphonyzone.
com
w themillhousebandb.co.uk

## BRENCHLEY
### Kent

**Hononton Cottage ★★★★**
*Bed & Breakfast*
**SILVER AWARD**
Palmers Green Lane, Nr
Brenchley, Tonbridge
TN12 7BJ
t (01892) 722483
e marston.brenchley@
tinyworld.co.uk
w smoothhound.co.uk/hotels/
hononton.html

**Woodlands Cottage ★★★★**
*Guest Accommodation*
Fairmans Lane, Nr Brenchley,
Tonbridge TN12 7BB
t (01892) 722707
e chris.omalley@zen.co.uk

## BRIGHSTONE
### Isle of Wight

**Brighstone Tea Rooms Bed
& Breakfast**
Rating Applied For
*Guest House*
Main Road, Brighstone
PO30 4AH
t (01983) 740370
w brighstone-tearooms-bb.co.
uk

**Chilton Farm B&B ★★★★**
*Farmhouse*
Chilton Farm, Chilton Lane,
Newport PO30 4DS
t (01983) 740338
e info@chiltonfarm.co.uk
w chiltonfarm.co.uk

**The Lodge Brighstone
★★★★**
*Guest Accommodation*
Main Road, Brighstone
PO30 4DJ
t (01983) 741272
e paul@thelodgebrighstone.
com
w thelodgebrighstone.com

## BRIGHTLING
### East Sussex

**Orchard Barn ★★★**
*Bed & Breakfast*
3 Twelve Oaks Cottages,
Brightling, Robertsbridge
TN32 5HS
t (01424) 838263

## BRIGHTON & HOVE
### East Sussex

**3 The Red House**
Rating Applied For
*Guest Accommodation*
21 Lansdowne Road, Hove
BN3 1FE
t (01273) 773700
e dianabundy@hotmail.com

**The Abbey** ★★★
*Guest Accommodation*
14-19 Norfolk Terrace,
Brighton BN1 3AD
t (01273) 778771
e reception@abbeyhotel.biz
w abbeyhotel.biz

**Adelaide Hotel** ★★★★
*Guest Accommodation*
51 Regency Square, Brighton
BN1 2FF
t (01273) 205286
e info@adelaidehotel.co.uk
w adelaidehotel.co.uk

**Andorra Guest
Accommodation** ★★★
*Guest Accommodation*
15-16 Oriental Place, Brighton
BN1 2LJ
t (01273) 321787
w andorrahotelbrighton.co.uk

**Atlantic Seafront** ★★★
*Guest Accommodation*
16 Marine Parade, Brighton
BN2 1TL
t (01273) 695944
e majanatlantic@hotmail.com
w atlantichotelbrighton.co.uk

**Aymer Guest House** ★★★★
*Guest Accommodation*
13 Aymer Road, Hove
BN3 4GB
t (01273) 271165
e michelle@aymerguesthouse.
co.uk
w aymerguesthouse.co.uk

**Blanch House**
Rating Applied For
*Guest Accommodation*
17 Atlingworth Street, Brighton
BN2 1PL
t (01273) 603504
e info@blanchhouse.co.uk
w blanchhouse.co.uk

**brightonwave** ★★★★
*Guest Accommodation*
**SILVER AWARD**
10 Madeira Place, Brighton
BN2 1TN
t (01273) 676794
e info@brightonwave.co.uk
w brightonwave.co.uk

**Brightside** ★★★★
*Guest Accommodation*
4 Shirley Road, Hove BN3 6NN
t (01273) 552557

**C Breeze Hotel** ★★★
*Guest House*
12a Upper Rock Gardens,
Brighton BN2 1QE
t (01273) 602608
e bookings@c-breezehotel.co.
uk
w c-breezehotel.co.uk

**The Cavalaire** ★★★★
*Guest Accommodation*
**SILVER AWARD**
34 Upper Rock Gardens,
Brighton BN2 1QF
t (01273) 696899
e welcome@cavalaire.co.uk
w cavalaire.co.uk

**Chatsworth Hotel** ★★
*Guest House*
9 Salisbury Road, Hove
BN3 3AB
t (01273) 737360

**Christina Guest House** ★★★
*Guest Accommodation*
20 St Georges Terrace,
Brighton BN2 1JH
t (01273) 690862
e christinaguesthouse@yahoo.
co.uk
w christinaguesthouse
brighton.co.uk

**Churchill Guest House** ★★★
*Guest Accommodation*
44 Russell Square, Brighton
BN1 2EF
t (01273) 700777
e stay@valentinehousehotel.
com

**The Claremont** ★★★★★
*Guest Accommodation*
13 Second Avenue, Hove,
Brighton BN3 2LL
t (01273) 735161
e info@theclaremont.eu
w theclaremont.eu

**Cosmopolitan** ★★★
*Guest Accommodation*
29-31 New Steine, Brighton
BN2 1PD
t (01273) 682461
e cosmopolitan2@btconnect.
com
w cosmopolitanhotel.co.uk

**The Dove** ★★★
*Guest Accommodation*
18 Regency Square, Brighton
BN1 2FG
t (01273) 779222
e enquiries@thedovehotel.co.
uk
w thedovehotel.co.uk

**Funchal Guest House** ★★
*Guest Accommodation*
17 Madeira Place, Brighton
BN2 1TN
t (01273) 603975

**Hudsons** ★★★★
*Guest Accommodation*
22 Devonshire Place, Brighton
BN2 1QA
t (01273) 683642
e info@hudsonshotel.com
w hudsonsinbrighton.co.uk

**Leona House** ★★★★
*Guest Accommodation*
74 Middle Street, Brighton
BN1 1AL
t (01273) 327309
e hazel.eastman@btconnect.
com
w leonahousebrighton.com

**Lichfield House** ★★★
*Guest Accommodation*
30 Waterloo Street, Hove
BN3 1AN
t (01273) 777740
e bookings@fieldhousehotels.
co.uk
w fieldhousehotels.co.uk

**Marine View** ★★★
*Guest Accommodation*
24 New Steine, Brighton
BN2 1PD
t (01273) 603870
e info@mvbrighton.co.uk
w mvbrighton.co.uk

**Neo** ★★★★
*Guest Accommodation*
19 Oriental Place, Brighton
BN1 2LL
t (01273) 711104
e info@neohotel.com
w neohotel.com

**New Madeira Hotel** ★★★★
*Guest Accommodation*
19-23 Marine Parade, Brighton
BN2 1TL
t (01273) 698331
e info@newmadeirahotel.com
w newmadeirahotel.com

**Regency Hotel** ★★★★
*Guest House*
28 Regency Square, Brighton
BN1 2FH
t (01273) 202690
e info@regencybrighton.co.uk
w regencybrighton.co.uk

**Russell Guest House** ★★★
*Guest Accommodation*
19 Russell Square, Brighton
BN1 2EE
t (01273) 327969
e info@therussell.co.uk
w smoothhound.co.uk/hotels/
russellgh

**Sandpiper Guest House**
★★★ *Guest Accommodation*
11 Russell Square, Brighton
BN1 2EE
t (01273) 328202
e sandpiper@brighton.co.uk

**Sea Spray** ★★★★
*Guest Accommodation*
25 New Steine, Brighton
BN2 1PD
t (01273) 680332
e seaspray@brighton.co.uk
w seaspraybrighton.co.uk

**Seafield House** ★★★★
*Guest Accommodation*
23 Seafield Road, Hove
BN3 2TP
t (01273) 777740
e enquiries@fieldhousehotels.
co.uk
w fieldhousehotels.co.uk

**Strawberry Fields**
Rating Applied For
*Guest Accommodation*
6-7 New Steine, Brighton
BN2 1PB
t (01273) 681576
w strawberry-fields-hotel.com

**The Townhouse Brighton**
★★★★
*Guest Accommodation*
19 New Steine, Brighton
BN2 1PD
t (01273) 607456
e info@
thetownhousebrighton.com
w thetownhousebrighton.com

**University of Brighton**
★★–★★★ *Campus*
Conference Office, Room 228,
Brighton BN2 4AT
t (01273) 643 1678
e conferences@brighton.ac.uk
w brighton.ac.uk/conferences

**Valentine House Hotel** ★★★
*Guest House*
38 Russell Square, Brighton
BN1 2EF
t (01273) 700800
e stay@valentinehousehotel.
com
w valentinehousehotel.com

**Whitburn Lodge** ★★★
*Guest House*
Montpelier Road, Brighton
BN1 2LQ
t (01273) 729005
e info@whitburnlodge.com

**BRIGHTWELL-CUM-SOTWELL**
Oxfordshire

**Hope Cottage** ★★★★
*Guest Accommodation*
Mackney Lane, Brightwell-
cum-Sotwell, Wallingford
OX10 0SQ
t (01491) 837100
e sue@hopecottagetours.co.
uk
w hopecottagetours.co.uk

**BRILL**
Buckinghamshire

**Poletrees Farm** ★★★★
*Farmhouse*
Ludgersall Road, Aylesbury
HP18 9TZ
t (01844) 238276

**BRIMPTON COMMON**
Berkshire

**Wasing Wood Edge** ★★★
*Bed & Breakfast*
Brimpton Common, Reading
RG7 4RY
t (0118) 981 3843
e pennyevanswwe@
btinternet.com

**BRIZE NORTON**
Oxfordshire

**The Priory** ★★★
*Guest Accommodation*
Manor Farm, Manor Road,
Brize Norton OX18 3NA
t (01993) 843062
e mail@priorymanor.wanadoo.
co.uk
w priorymanor.co.uk

**BROAD OAK**
East Sussex

**Hazelhurst** ★★★★
*Guest Accommodation*
**SILVER AWARD**
Chitcombe Road, Broad Oak,
Rye TN31 6EU
t (01424) 883411

**Platts Cottage** ★★★★
*Bed & Breakfast*
**SILVER AWARD**
Chitcombe Road, Rye
TN31 6EX
t (01424) 882551

**BROADSTAIRS**
Kent

**Anchor House** ★★★★
*Guest Accommodation*
**SILVER AWARD**
10 Chandos Road, Broadstairs
CT10 1QP
t (01843) 863347
e stay@anchorhouse.net
w anchorhouse.net

**Anchor Lodge** ★★★★
*Bed & Breakfast*
**SILVER AWARD**
57 Dumpton Park Drive,
Broadstairs CT10 1RH
t (01843) 602564
e enquiries@anchorlodge.net
w anchorlodge.net

**The Bay Tree** ★★★★
*Guest Accommodation*
12 Eastern Esplanade,
Broadstairs CT10 1DR
t (01843) 862502

**Burrow House** ★★★★★
*Guest Accommodation*
Granville Road, Broadstairs
CT10 1QD
t (01843) 601817
e enquiries@burrowhouse.
com
w burrowhouse.com

**Cintra** ★★★
*Guest Accommodation*
24 Victoria Parade, Broadstairs
CT10 1QL
t (01843) 862253
e visit@cintrabb.com
w cintrabb.com

**Copperfields Guest House**
★★★★ *Guest House*
**SILVER AWARD**
Queens Road, Broadstairs
CT10 1NU
t (01843) 601247
e copperfieldsbb@btinternet.
com
w copperfieldsbb.co.uk

**The Devonhurst** ★★★★
*Guest Accommodation*
**SILVER AWARD**
Eastern Esplanade, Broadstairs
CT10 1DR
t (01843) 863010
e info@devonhurst.co.uk
w devonhurst.co.uk

**East Horndon** ★★★★
*Guest Accommodation*
**SILVER AWARD**
4 Eastern Esplanade,
Broadstairs CT10 1DP
t (01843) 868306
e easthorndon@hotmail.com
w easthorndonhotel.com
▣✦

**The Hanson** ★★★
*Guest Accommodation*
41 Belvedere Road, Broadstairs
CT10 1PF
t (01843) 868936
e hotelhanson@tiscali.co.uk
w hansonhotel.co.uk

**Merriland** ★★★★
*Guest House*
13 The Vale, Broadstairs
CT10 1RB
t (01843) 861064
e merrilandhotel@aol.com

**Number 68** ★★★★
*Guest Accommodation*
**SILVER AWARD**
68 West Cliff Road, Broadstairs
CT10 1PY
t (01843) 609459
e number68@btinternet.com
w number68.co.uk

**Pierremont** ★★★
*Guest Accommodation*
102 Pierremont Avenue,
Broadstairs CT10 1NT
t (01843) 600462
e peter@
pierremontguesthouse.co.uk
w pierremontguesthouse.co.uk

**South Lodge Guest House**
★★★★ *Guest House*
**SILVER AWARD**
19 The Vale, Broadstairs
CT10 1RB
t (01843) 600478
e contactus@visitsouthlodge.
co.uk
w visitsouthlodge.co.uk

**Torwood House B&B**
Rating Applied For
*Guest Accommodation*
41 West Cliff Road, Broadstairs
CT10 1PU
t (01843) 863953
e zaholness@btinternet.com

**The Victoria** ★★★★★
*Guest Accommodation*
**SILVER AWARD**
23 Victoria Parade, Broadstairs
CT10 1QL
t (01843) 871010
e mullin@
thevictoriabroadstairs.co.uk
w thevictoriabroadstairs.co.uk

BROCKENHURST
Hampshire

**Goldenhayes** ★★
*Bed & Breakfast*
9 Chestnut Road, Brockenhurst
SO42 7RF
t (01590) 623743

**Poppy Cottage** ★★★★
*Bed & Breakfast*
2 Fathersfield, Brockenhurst
SO42 7TH
t (01590) 624423
e pat@poppy-cottage.co.uk
w poppy-cottage.co.uk

**Rose And Crown** ★★★ *Inn*
Lyndhurst Road, Brockenhurst
SO42 7RH
t (01590) 622225
e roseandcrown@ep-ltd.com
w roomattheinn.info

BROOK
Isle of Wight

**The Clock House** ★★★
*Guest Accommodation*
Brook Village Road, Brook
PO30 4EJ
t (01983) 741212
e ridlerlee@btinternet.com
w clockhousebrook.co.uk

BROOKLAND
Kent

**The Royal Oak** ★★★★ *Inn*
High Street, Brookland,
Romney Marsh TN29 9QR
t (01797) 344215

BUCKINGHAM
Buckinghamshire

**Churchwell** ★★
*Bed & Breakfast*
23 Church Street, Buckingham
MK18 1BY
t (01280) 815415
w churchwell.co.uk

**Folly Farm** ★★★★
*Farmhouse*
Buckingham Road, Adstock,
Buckingham MK18 2HS
t (01296) 712413

**Huntsmill Farm B&B** ★★★★
*Bed & Breakfast*
Nr Buckingham, Shalstone
MK18 5ND
t (01280) 704852
e fiona@huntsmill.com
w huntsmill.com

**Radclive Dairy Farm** ★★★★
*Farmhouse*
Radclive Road, Buckingham
MK18 4AA
t (01280) 813433
e rosalind.fisher@
radclivedairyfarm.co.uk
w radclivedairyfarm.co.uk

BURFORD
Oxfordshire

**Barley Park** ★★★★
*Bed & Breakfast*
**SILVER AWARD**
Shilton Road, Burford
OX18 4PD
t (01993) 823573
e barley_park@hotmail.com
w burford-bed-and-breakfast.
co.uk

**Burford House Hotel**
★★★★★
*Guest Accommodation*
**GOLD AWARD**
99 High Street, Burford
OX18 4QA
t (01993) 823151
e stay@burfordhouse.co.uk
w burfordhouse.co.uk

**Cotland House B&B** ★★★★
*Guest Accommodation*
Fulbrook Hill, Burford
OX18 4BH
t (01993) 822382
e info@cotlandhouse.com
w otlandhouse.com
▣✦

**Courtlands B&B** ★★★★
*Bed & Breakfast*
6 Courtlands Road, Shipton-
under-Wychwood, Chipping
Norton OX7 6DF
t (01993) 830551
e j-jfletcher@which.net
w cotswoldsbandb.com

**Westview House** ★★★★
*Bed & Breakfast*
**GOLD AWARD**
151 The Hill, Burford
OX18 4RE
t (01993) 824723
e titcombe@aol.com
w westview-house.co.uk

BURGESS HILL
West Sussex

**Daisy Lodge B&B** ★★★
*Guest Accommodation*
26 Royal George Road, Burgess
Hill RH15 9SE
t (01444) 870570
e daisylodge@btinternet.com

**Meadows** ★★★
*Bed & Breakfast*
87 Meadow Lane, Burgess Hill
RH15 9JD
t (01444) 248421
e bsayers@onetel.net.uk

**St Owens** ★★★★
*Bed & Breakfast*
11 Silverdale Road, Burgess Hill
RH15 0ED
t (01444) 236435
e nevillebaker@btinternet.com
w visitsussex.org/stowens

**Wellhouse** ★★★★
*Guest Accommodation*
**SILVER AWARD**
Wellhouse Lane, Burgess Hill
RH15 0BN
t (01444) 233231
e amhallen@onetel.com
w visitsussex.org/wellhouse

BURGHCLERE
Berkshire

**The Carnarvon Arms**
★★★★ *Inn*
Winchester Road, Whitway,
Burghclere, Newbury
RG20 9LE
t (01635) 278222
e info@carnarvonarms.com
w carnarvonarms.com

BURLEY
Hampshire

**The Burley Inn** ★★★ *Inn*
The Cross, Burley, Ringwood
BH24 4AB
t (01425) 403448
e info@theburleyinn.co.uk
w theburleyinn.co.uk

**Burley YHA** ★★★ *Hostel*
Cottesmore House, Cott Lane,
Ringwood BH24 4BB
t (01425) 403233
▣✦

**Holmans** ★★★★
*Bed & Breakfast*
**GOLD AWARD**
Bisterne Close, Burley,
Ringwood BH24 4AZ
t (01425) 402307
e holmans@talktalk.net

**Wayside Cottage** ★★★★
*Bed & Breakfast*
27 Garden Road, Burley,
Ringwood BH24 4EA
t (01425) 403414
e jwest@wayside-cottage.co.
uk
w wayside-cottage.co.uk
▣✦

**The White Buck Inn** ★★★★
*Inn*
Bisterne Close, Burley,
Ringwood BH24 4AT
t (01425) 402264
e whitebuckinn@
accommodating-inns.co.uk
w accommodating-inns.co.uk

BURMARSH
Kent

**Dolly Plum Cottage Guest
House** ◆◆◆◆
*Guest Accommodation*
Burmarsh Road, Dymchurch,
Romney Marsh TN29 0JT
t (01303) 874558
e dollyplumcottage@aol.com
w s-h-systems.co.uk/hotels/
dollyplum.html

**Haguelands Farm** ★★★★★
*Guest Accommodation*
**GOLD AWARD**
Burmarsh, Romney Marsh
TN29 0JR
t (01303) 872273
e anne@aaclifton.ltd.uk
w haguelandsfarm.co.uk

**Buscot Manor** ★★★★★
*Bed & Breakfast*
**GOLD AWARD**
Buscot, Oxon SN7 8DA
t (01367) 252431
e enquiries@buscotmanor.com
w buscotmanor.com

**Weston Farm** ★★★★
*Farmhouse* **SILVER AWARD**
Buscot Wick, Faringdon
SN7 8DJ
t (01367) 252222
e westonfarmbandb@amserve.com
w country-accom.co.uk/weston-farm

**South Fields** ★★
*Bed & Breakfast*
High Wycombe HP14 3PJ
t (01494) 881976
e crichtons@crichtonville.freeserve.co.uk
w crichtonville.freeserve.co.uk

**Kingsbridge House** ★★★★
*Guest Accommodation*
Southampton Road, Cadnam
SO40 2NH
t (023) 8081 1161
e linda@kingsbridgehouse.freeserve.co.uk
w kingsbridgehousebandb.co.uk

**Abberley House** ★★★
*Bed & Breakfast*
115 Whitstable Road,
Canterbury CT2 8EF
t (01227) 450265
e r.allcorn@discovercanterbury.co.uk

**Alexandra House** ★★★★
*Guest Accommodation*
1 Roper Road, Canterbury
CT2 7EH
t (01227) 786617
e reservations@alexandrahouse.net
w alexandrahouse.net

**Alicante Guest House**
★★★★
*Guest Accommodation*
4 Roper Road, Canterbury
CT2 7EH
t (01227) 766277

**Anns House** ★★★
*Guest House*
63 London Road, Canterbury
CT2 8JZ
t (01227) 768767
e info@annshousecanterbury.co.uk
w annshousecanterbury.co.uk

**Ashley Guest House** ★★
*Bed & Breakfast*
9 London Road, Canterbury
CT2 8LR
t (01227) 455863

**Bluebells Guest House** ★★★
*Guest House*
248 Wincheap, Canterbury
CT1 3TY
t (01227) 478842
e canterburybluebells@yahoo.co.uk
w smoothhound.co.uk/hotels/bluebells.html

**Bower Farm House** ★★★★
*Bed & Breakfast*
**SILVER AWARD**
Bossingham Road, Stelling
Minnis, Canterbury CT4 6BB
t (01227) 709430
e anne@bowerbb.freeserve.co.uk
w bowerfarmhouse.co.uk

**Canterbury YHA** ★★ *Hostel*
54 New Dover Road,
Canterbury CT1 3DT
t (01227) 462911
e canterbury@yha.org.uk
w yha.org.uk

**Carena** ★★★ *Guest House*
250 Wincheap, Canterbury
CT1 3TY
t (01227) 765630
e carena.house@btconnect.com
w smoothhound.co.uk/hotels/carena.html

**Castle House** ★★★★
*Guest Accommodation*
**SILVER AWARD**
28 Castle Street, Canterbury
CT1 2PT
t (01227) 761897
e enquries@castlehousehotel.co.uk
w castlehousehotel.co.uk

**Chaucer Lodge** ★★★
*Guest House*
62 New Dover Road,
Canterbury CT1 3DT
t (01227) 459141
e enquiries@chaucerlodge.co.uk
w chaucerlodge.co.uk

**Clare Ellen Guest House**
Rating Applied For
*Guest House*
9 Victoria Road, Wincheap,
Canterbury CT1 3SG
t (01227) 760205
e loraine.williams@clareellenguesthouse.co.uk
w clareellenguesthouse.co.uk

**Elmstone Court** ◆◆◆◆◆
*Guest Accommodation*
**SILVER AWARD**
Out Elmstead Lane, Barham,
Canterbury CT4 6PH
t (01227) 830433
e enquiries@elmstonecourt.com
w elmstonecourt.com

**Four Seasons** ★★★
*Guest Accommodation*
77 Sturry Road, Canterbury
CT1 1BU
t (01227) 787078
e fourseasonsbnb@aol.com
w fourseasonscanterbury.co.uk

**Greyfriars House** ★★★
*Guest House*
6 Stour Street, Canterbury
CT1 2NR
t (01227) 456255
e christine@greyfriars-house.co.uk
w greyfriars-house.co.uk

**Harriet House** ★★★★
*Guest Accommodation*
**SILVER AWARD**
3 Broad Oak Road, Canterbury
CT2 7PL
t (01227) 457363
e merryjb@supanet.com
w harriethouse.co.uk

**Hornbeams** ★★★★
*Farmhouse*
Jesses Hill, Kingston,
Canterbury CT4 6JD
t (01227) 830119
e bandb@hornbeams.co.uk
w hornbeams.co.uk

**Iffin Farmhouse** ★★★★
*Guest Accommodation*
Iffin Lane, Canterbury CT4 7BE
t (01227) 462776
e sarah@iffin.co.uk
w iffin.co.uk

**Kent Hospitality** ★★–★★★
*Campus*
Tanglewood, Giles Lane, The
University, Canterbury
CT2 7LX
t (01227) 828000
e hospitality-enquiry@kent.ac.uk
w kent.ac.uk/hospitality/

**The Kings Head** ★★★ *Inn*
204 Wincheap, Canterbury
CT1 3RY
t (01227) 462885
e thekingshead@wincheap.wanadoo.co.uk
w smoothhound.co.uk/hotels/thekingshead.html

**Kingsbridge Villa** ★★★★
*Guest House*
15 Best Lane, Canterbury
CT1 2JB
t (01227) 766415
e info@canterburyguesthouse.com
w canterburyguesthouse.com

**Kingsmead House** ★★★
*Bed & Breakfast*
68 St Stephens Road,
Canterbury CT2 7JF
t (01227) 760132
e john.clark52@btopenworld.com
w kingsmeadhouse.com

**Kipps Independent Hostel**
★★ *Backpacker*
40 Nunnery Fields, Canterbury
CT1 3JT
t (01227) 786121

**Magnolia House** ★★★★★
*Guest Accommodation*
**GOLD AWARD**
36 St Dunstans Terrace,
Canterbury CT2 8AX
t (01227) 765121
e info@magnoliahousecanterbury.co.uk
w magnoliahousecanterbury.co.uk

**The Millers Arms** ★★★★ *Inn*
2 Mill Lane, St Radigunds,
Canterbury CT1 2AW
t (01227) 456057
w shepherdneame.co.uk

**Oak Cottage** ★★★★
*Guest Accommodation*
Elmsted, Ashford TN25 5JT
t (01233) 750272
e oakcottage@invictanet.co.uk
w oakcottage-elmsted.co.uk

**The Old Kent Barn** ★★★★★
*Bed & Breakfast*
**GOLD AWARD**
Smersole Farm, Swingfield,
Dover CT15 7HF
t (01303) 844270
e hilaryjanesimmons@zoom.co.uk
w theoldkentbarn.co.uk

**The Plantation** ★★★★
*Bed & Breakfast*
Iffin Lane, Canterbury CT4 7BD
t (01227) 472104
e plantation@lycos.co.uk
w theplantation.biz

**Renville Oast** ★★★★
*Bed & Breakfast*
Renville, Bridge, Canterbury
CT4 5AD
t (01227) 830215
e renville.oast@virgin.net
w renvilleoast.co.uk

**Thanington** ★★★★★
*Guest Accommodation*
140 Wincheap, Canterbury
CT1 3RY
t (01227) 453227
e enquiries@thanington-hotel.co.uk
w thanington-hotel.co.uk

**Tudor House** ★★★
*Guest Accommodation*
6 Best Lane, Canterbury
CT1 2JB
t (01227) 765650

**White Horse Inn** ★★★
*Guest Accommodation*
The Street, Boughton-under-
Blean, Faversham ME13 9AX
t (01227) 751700
e whitehorse@shepherd-neame.co.uk
w shepherd-neame.co.uk

**Wincheap Guest House**
★★★ *Guest House*
94 Wincheap, Canterbury
CT1 3RS
t (01227) 762309
e wincheapguesthouse@tiscali.co.uk
w wincheapguesthouse.com

**The Woolpack Inn** ★★★★
*Inn*
The Street, Chilham,
Canterbury CT4 8DL
**t** (01227) 730351
**e** woolpack@shepherdneame.
co.uk
**w** woolpackchilham.co.uk

**Yorke Lodge** ★★★★
*Guest House* **SILVER AWARD**
50 London Road, Canterbury
CT2 8LF
**t** (01227) 451243
**e** enquiries@yorkelodge.com
**w** yorkelodge.com

### CAPEL
Surrey

**Nightless Copse** ★★★★
*Bed & Breakfast*
Rusper Road, Capel, Dorking
RH5 5HE
**t** (01306) 713247
**e** bb@nightlesscopse.co.uk
**w** nightlesscopse.co.uk

### CARISBROOKE
Isle of Wight

**Alvington Manor Farm** ♦♦♦
*Guest Accommodation*
Manor Farm Lane, Off
Calbourne Road, Carisbrooke
PO30 5SP
**t** (01983) 523463

### CARTERTON
Oxfordshire

**The Jays** ★★★★
*Bed & Breakfast*
23 The Crescent, Carterton,
Oxon OX18 3SJ
**t** (01993) 843301
**e** info@thejays-carterton.co.uk
**w** thejays-carterton.co.uk

### CASSINGTON
Oxfordshire

**Burleigh Farm** ★★★★
*Farmhouse*
Bladon Road, Nr Cassington,
Oxford OX29 4EA
**t** (01865) 881352
**e** cook_jane@btconnect.com
**w** oxfordcity.co.uk/accom/
burleighfarm

### CASTLETHORPE
Buckinghamshire

**A Village B&B** ★★
*Guest Accommodation*
Manor Farm House, South
Street, Milton Keynes
MK19 7EL
**t** (01908) 510216
**e** manorfarmhouse@aol.com
**w** mkweb.co.uk

### CATHERINGTON
Hampshire

**Flowerdown** ★★★
*Bed & Breakfast*
82 Downhouse Road,
Catherington PO8 0TY
**t** (023) 9259 8029
**e** madeingb1@tiscali.co.uk

**Lone Barn** ★★★★
*Bed & Breakfast*
**SILVER AWARD**
Catherington, Waterlooville
PO8 0SF
**t** (023) 9263 2911
**e** marchburn@ukonline.co.uk
**w** lonebarn.net

### CHACKMORE
Buckinghamshire

**Ivy Cottage** ★★★
*Bed & Breakfast*
Main Street, Buckingham
MK18 5JE
**t** (01280) 812130
**e** timandtish@hotmail.com

### CHALFONT ST GILES
Buckinghamshire

**Gorelands Corner** ★★★★
*Bed & Breakfast*
Gorelands Lane, Chalfont St
Giles HP8 4HQ
**t** (01494) 872689
**e** bickfordcsg@onetel.com

**The Ivy House** ★★★★ *Inn*
**SILVER AWARD**
London Road, Chalfont St Giles
HP8 4RS
**t** (01494) 872184

**The White Hart Inn** ★★★★
*Inn*
Three Households, Chalfont St
Giles HP8 4LP
**t** (01494) 872441
**e** enquiries@
thewhitehartstgiles.co.uk

### CHALFONT ST PETER
Buckinghamshire

**Hebron** ★★★
*Guest Accommodation*
128 Rickmansworth Lane,
Chalfont St Peter, Gerrards
Cross SL9 0RQ
**t** (01494) 873533
**e** sheppee@btinternet.com

### CHALGROVE
Oxfordshire

**Cornerstones** ★★
*Bed & Breakfast*
1 Cromwell Close, Chalgrove,
Oxford OX44 7SE
**t** (01865) 890298
**e** corner.stones@virgin.net
**w** http://freespace.virgin.net/
corner.stones

### CHARLBURY
Oxfordshire

**Banbury Hill Farm** ★★★★
*Guest Accommodation*
Enstone Road, Charlbury,
Chipping Norton OX7 3JH
**t** (01608) 810314
**e** beds@gfwiddows.f9.co.uk
**w** charlburyoxfordaccom.co.uk

**The Bull** ★★★★ *Inn*
Sheep Street, Charlbury,
Chipping Norton OX7 3RR
**t** (01608) 810689
**e** info@bullinn-charlbury.com
**w** bullinn-charlbury.com

### CHARLWOOD
Surrey

**Trumbles Guest House**
★★★★
*Guest Accommodation*
Stan Hill, Charlwood, Horley
RH6 0EP
**t** (01293) 863418
**e** info@trumbles.co.uk
**w** trumbles.co.uk

### CHART SUTTON
Kent

**White House Farm** ★★★★
*Guest Accommodation*
Green Lane, Maidstone
ME17 3ES
**t** (01622) 842490
**e** info@whitehousefarm-kent.
co.uk
**w** whitehousefarm-kent.co.uk

### CHARTHAM HATCH
Kent

**Wisteria Lodge** ★★★★
*Bed & Breakfast*
New Town Street, Canterbury
CT4 7LT
**t** (01227) 738654
**e** wisteriabandb@yahoo.co.uk

### CHATHAM
Kent

**Normandy House** ★★★
*Guest Accommodation*
Maidstone Road, Chatham
ME4 6JE
**t** (01634) 843047

**Officers Hill** ★★★★★
*Bed & Breakfast*
**GOLD AWARD**
7 College Road, The Historic
Dockyard, Chatham ME4 4QX
**t** (01634) 828436
**e** gmchambers@btopenworld.
com

**Ship & Trades** ★★★
*Guest Accommodation*
Maritime Way, St Marys Island,
Chatham ME4 3ER
**t** (01634) 895200
**e** ship&trades@shepherd-
neame.co.uk
**w** shepherd-neame.co.uk

### CHATTENDEN
Kent

**Windwhistle** ♦♦♦♦
*Guest Accommodation*
Chattenden Farm, Lodge Hill
Lane, Chattenden, Rochester
ME3 8NY
**t** (01634) 252859
**e** windwhistlebandb@hotmail.
co.uk

### CHECKENDON
Oxfordshire

**Larchdown Farm** ★★★★
*Guest Accommodation*
**SILVER AWARD**
Whitehall Lane, Checkendon,
Reading RG8 0TT
**t** (01491) 682282
**e** larchdown@onetel.com
**w** larchdown.com

### CHELWOOD GATE
East Sussex

**Holly House** ★★★★
*Guest House*
Beaconsfield Road, Chelwood
Gate RH17 7LF
**t** (01825) 740484
**e** deebirchell@hollyhousebnb.
demon.co.uk
**w** hollyhousebnb.demon.co.uk

**Laurel Cottage** ★★★
*Bed & Breakfast*
Baxters Lane, Chelwood Gate,
Haywards Heath RH17 7LU
**t** (01825) 740547
**e** smartin@chelwood.fsnet.co.
uk
**w** visitsussex.org/laurelcottage

### CHERITON
Hampshire

**Old Kennets Cottage**
★★★★
*Guest Accommodation*
Cheriton, Alresford SO24 0PX
**t** (01962) 771863
**e** dglssmith@aol.com

### CHESHAM
Buckinghamshire

**49 Lowndes Avenue** ★★★
*Bed & Breakfast*
Chesham HP5 2HH
**t** (01494) 792647
**e** bbormelowndes@tiscali.co.
uk

**Katsina** ★★ *Bed & Breakfast*
Broomstick Lane, Botley,
Chesham HP5 1XU
**t** (01494) 773110

### CHICHESTER
West Sussex

**21 Brandyhole Lane** ★★
*Guest Accommodation*
Brandy Hole Lane, Chichester
PO19 5RL
**t** (01243) 528201
**e** anne@anneparry.me.uk

**5a Little London** ★★★
*Bed & Breakfast*
Little London, Chichester
PO19 1PH
**t** (01243) 788405

**Anna's** ★★★ *Bed & Breakfast*
27 Westhampnett Road,
Chichester PO19 7HW
**t** (01243) 788522
**e** judiths@fsmail.net
**w** annasofchichester.co.uk

**Apiary Cottage** ★★★
*Bed & Breakfast*
Compton, Chichester
PO18 9EX
**t** (023) 9263 1306

**Bayleaf** ★★★
*Bed & Breakfast*
Whyke Road, Chichester
PO19 7AN
**t** (01243) 774330

**Brandram House** ★★★
*Bed & Breakfast*
200 Whyke Road, Chichester
PO19 7AQ
**t** (01243) 781335
**e** brandramhouse@boltblue.
com
**w** brandramhouse.co.uk

**Cherry End** ★★★★
*Bed & Breakfast*
3 Clydesdale Avenue,
Chichester PO19 7PW
**t** (01243) 531397
**e** cherryendbb@yahoo.co.uk
**w** cherryend.2ya.com

**The Cottage** ★★★
*Bed & Breakfast*
22b Westhampnett Road,
Chichester PO19 7HW
**t** (01243) 774979
**e** mbc.technical@virgin.net

**Englewood** ★★★★
*Bed & Breakfast*
East Ashling, West Sussex,
Chichester PO18 9AS
t (01243) 575407
e sjenglewood@hotmail.co.uk
w smoothhound.co.uk/hotels/
englewood.html

**Finisterre** ★★★
*Bed & Breakfast*
9 Albert Road, Chichester
PO19 3JE
t (01243) 532680
e leonard9@tiscali.co.uk
w http://myweb.tiscali.co.uk/
finisterre

**Fox Goes Free (B&B)** ★★★
*Inn*
Charlton, Chichester
PO18 0HU
t (01243) 811461
e thefoxgoesfree.always@
virgin.net
w thefoxgoesfree.com

**Friary Close** ★★★★
*Bed & Breakfast*
SILVER AWARD
Friary Lane, Chichester
PO19 1UF
t (01243) 527294
e mail@friaryclose.co.uk
w friaryclose.co.uk

**Kia-ora** ★★★ *Bed & Breakfast*
Main Road, Nutbourne,
Chichester PO18 8RT
t (01243) 572858
e ruthiefp@tiscali.co.uk

**Litten House** ★★★
*Bed & Breakfast*
148 St Pancras, Chichester
PO19 7SH
t (01243) 774503
e victoria@littenho.demon.co.
uk
w littenho.demon.co.uk

**Longmeadow** ★★
*Bed & Breakfast*
Pine Grove, Chichester
PO19 3PN
t (01243) 782063
e bbeeching@lineone.net
w longmeadowguesthouse.
com

**Old Store Guest House**
★★★★
*Guest Accommodation*
Stane Street, Halnaker,
Chichester PO18 0QL
t (01243) 531977
e info@
theoldstoreguesthouse.com
w theoldstoreguesthouse.com

**Pen Cottage** ★★★
*Bed & Breakfast*
The Drive, Summersdale,
Chichester PO19 5QA
t (01243) 783667
e monicaandcolinkaye@
talktalk.net
w visitsussex.org/pencottage

**Sherwood House Guests**
Rating Applied For
*Bed & Breakfast*
Drayton Lane, Chichester
PO20 2BN
t (01243) 778005

**Spooners** ★★★★
*Bed & Breakfast*
1 Maplehurst Road, Chichester
PO19 6QL
t (01243) 528467
e sue-spooner@tiscali.co.uk

**West Faldie** ★★★★
*Bed & Breakfast*
Lavant, Chichester PO18 0BW
t (01243) 527450
e hilary@mitten.fsnet.co.uk

**Woodstock House Hotel**
★★★★ *Guest House*
SILVER AWARD
Charlton, Chichester
PO18 0HU
t (01243) 811666
e info@woodstockhousehotel.
co.uk
w woodstockhousehotel.co.uk

### CHIDDINGSTONE
### Kent

**Hoath House** ★★★
*Guest Accommodation*
Chiddingstone, Edenbridge
TN8 7DB
t (01342) 850362
e janestreatfield@hoath-
house.freeserve.co.uk

### CHIEVELEY
### Berkshire

**Thatched House B&B**
★★★★ *Bed & Breakfast*
High Street, Newbury
RG18 8TE
t (01635) 248295
e s.malty@btinternet.com
w geocities.com/
thatchedhouseandb

### CHILCOMB
### Hampshire

**Complyns B&B** ★★★★
*Bed & Breakfast*
Chilcomb, Winchester
SO21 1HT
t (01962) 861600
w complyns.co.uk

### CHILGROVE
### West Sussex

**Chilgrove Farm** ★★★★
*Bed & Breakfast*
Chilgrove Park Road,
Chichester PO18 9HU
t (01243) 519436
e simonrenwick@aol.com

### CHILHAM
### Kent

**Castle Cottage Chilham Bed**
**& Breakfast** ★★★★
*Bed & Breakfast*
School Hill, Canterbury
CT4 8DE
t (01227) 730330
e l.frankel@btinternet.com
w castlecottagechilham.co.uk

### CHINEHAM
### Hampshire

**Ashfields** ★★★
*Guest Accommodation*
51a Reading Road, Chineham,
Basingstoke RG24 8LT
t (01256) 324629

### CHINNOR
### Oxfordshire

**The Croft** ★★★★
*Bed & Breakfast*
Chinnor Hill, Chinnor
OX39 4BS
t (01844) 353654
e beth@acornhomesltd.co.uk
w bethatthecroft.co.uk

**Manor Farm Cottage** ★★★
*Bed & Breakfast*
Henton, Chinnor OX39 4AE
t (01844) 353301
e dixonhenton@aol.com
w manorfarmcottage.info

### CHIPPING NORTON
### Oxfordshire

**The Forge** ★★★★
*Guest Accommodation*
SILVER AWARD
Church Road, Churchill,
Chipping Norton OX7 6NJ
t (01608) 658173
e enquiries@cotswolds-
accommodation.com
w cotswolds-accommodation.
com

**Rectory Farm** ★★★★★
*Farmhouse* SILVER AWARD
Golden Lane, Salford, Chipping
Norton OX7 5YZ
t (01608) 643209
e colston@rectoryfarm75.
freeserve.co.uk
w rectoryfarm.info

### CHIPSTEAD
### Kent

**Windmill Farm** ★★★★
*Guest Accommodation*
Chevening Road, Sevenoaks
TN13 2SA
t (01732) 452054

### CHURT
### Surrey

**The Retreat** ★★★★
*Bed & Breakfast*
New Farm Cottage, Frensham
Lane, Churt, Farnham
GU10 2QG
t (01252) 792998
e suzy.johnson@tiscali.co.uk

### CLIFFE WOODS
### Kent

**Orchard Cottage** ★★★★
*Guest Accommodation*
SILVER AWARD
11 View Road, Cliffe Woods,
Rochester ME3 8JQ
t (01634) 222780

### CLIFTONVILLE
### Kent

**The Bay** ♦♦
*Guest Accommodation*
23 Fort Crescent, Cliftonville,
Margate CT9 1HX
t (01843) 290889

### COLD ASH
### Berkshire

**2 Woodside** ★★★★
*Bed & Breakfast*
Woodside, Cold Ash,
Thatcham RG18 9JF
t (01635) 860028
e anita.rhiggs@which.net

### COLEMANS HATCH
### East Sussex

**Gospel Oak** ★★★
*Bed & Breakfast*
Sandy Lane, Colemans Hatch,
Hartfield TN7 4ER
t (01342) 823840

### COLWELL BAY
### Isle of Wight

**Rockstone Cottage** ★★★★
*Guest House*
Colwell Chine Road, Colwell
Bay, Freshwater PO40 9NR
t (01983) 753723
e enquiries@
rockstonecottage.co.uk
w rockstonecottage.co.uk

### COLWORTH
### West Sussex

**Glencroft** ★★★
*Bed & Breakfast*
Colworth PO20 2DS
t (01243) 532929
e glencroft.b_and_b@
btinternet.com
w glencroft.biz

### COOKSBRIDGE
### East Sussex

**Lower Tulleys Wells Farm**
★★★ *Guest Accommodation*
Beechwood Lane,
Cooksbridge, Lewes BN7 3QG
t (01273) 472622
e jmpnzr@aol.com

### COPTHORNE
### West Sussex

**The Gatwick Grove Guest**
**House** ★★★★ *Guest House*
Copthorne Common,
Copthorne, Crawley RH10 3LA
t (01342) 719463
e info@thegatwickgrove.co.uk
w thegatwickgrove.co.uk

### COWDEN
### Kent

**Southernwood House**
★★★★ *Bed & Breakfast*
Church Street, Edenbridge
TN8 7JE
t (01342) 850880
e info@southernwoodhouse.
org.uk
w southernwoodhouse.org.uk

**White Horse Inn** ★★★ *Inn*
Holtye, Cowden, Edenbridge
TN8 7ED
t (01342) 850640
e whitehorse@greatpubs.net
w whitehorse.greatpubs.net

### COWES
### Isle of Wight

**Anchorage Guest House**
★★★★
*Guest Accommodation*
23 Mill Hill Road, Cowes
PO31 7EE
t (01983) 247975
e peterandjenni@
anchoragecowes.co.uk
w anchoragecowes.co.uk

**Halcyone Villa** ★★★
*Guest Accommodation*
Grove Road, West Cowes
PO31 7JP
t (01983) 291334
e sandraonwight@btinternet.
com

## CRANBROOK
### Kent

**Bargate House ★★★★**
*Guest Accommodation*
Angley Road, Cranbrook
TN17 2PQ
t (01580) 714254
e pennylane@bargatehouse.
co.uk
w bargatehouse.co.uk

**Guernsey Cottage ★★★**
*Guest Accommodation*
Wilsley Green, Cranbrook
TN17 2LG
t (01580) 712542
e grahamstarkey@waitrose.
com

**Tolehurst Barn ★★★★**
*Guest Accommodation*
Cranbrook Road, Frittenden,
Cranbrook TN17 2BP
t (01580) 714385
e info@tolehurstbarn.co.uk
w tolehurstbarn.co.uk

## CRANLEIGH
### Surrey

**Long Copse ★★★**
*Bed & Breakfast*
Pitch Hill, Ewhurst, Cranleigh
GU6 7NN
t (01483) 277458
e shhandley@btinternet.com

## CROSS-IN-HAND
### East Sussex

**High Brow ★★★★**
*Bed & Breakfast*
SILVER AWARD
Back Lane, Cross in Hand,
Heathfield TN21 0QD
t (01435) 868406
e jrossm@gmail.com
w smoothhound.co.uk/hotels/
high-brow.html

## CROSSBUSH
### West Sussex

**April Cottage ★★★★**
*Bed & Breakfast*
SILVER AWARD
Crossbush Lane, Arundel
BN18 9PQ
t (01903) 885401
e april.cott@btinternet.com
w april-cottage.co.uk

## CROWBOROUGH
### East Sussex

**Bathurst ★★★★**
*Bed & Breakfast*
Fielden Road, Crowborough
TN6 1TR
t (01892) 665476
e annslender1@hotmail.com

**Braemore ★★★★**
*Bed & Breakfast*
SILVER AWARD
Eridge Road, Crowborough
TN6 2SS
t (01892) 665700

**Yew House Bed & Breakfast
★★★★**
*Guest Accommodation*
SILVER AWARD
Crowborough Hill,
Crowborough TN6 2EA
t (01892) 610522
e yewhouse@yewhouse.com
w yewhouse.com

## CRUNDALE
### Kent

**The Man of Kent ★★★★**
*Bed & Breakfast*
Denwood Street, Crundale,
Canterbury CT4 7EF
t (01227) 730743
e lewisgerol@hotmail.com

## CUBLINGTON
### Buckinghamshire

**Manor Farm B&B ★★★**
*Bed & Breakfast*
Whitchurch Road, Cublington,
Leighton Buzzard LU7 0LP
t (01296) 681107
e honor.vale@tesco.net

## CUCKFIELD
### West Sussex

**Highbridge Mill ★★★★**
*Bed & Breakfast*
SILVER AWARD
Cuckfield Road, Haywards
Heath RH17 5AE
t (01444) 450881
w highbridgemill.com

## DAMERHAM
### Hampshire

**The Compasses Inn ★★★★**
*Inn*
East End, Damerham,
Fordingbridge SP6 3HQ
t (01725) 518231

## DANEHILL
### East Sussex

**New Glenmore ★★★★**
*Guest Accommodation*
Sliders Lane, Furners Green,
Uckfield TN22 3RU
t (01825) 790783
e alan.robinson@bigfoot.com

## DEAL
### Kent

**Beachbrow Hotel ★★★**
*Guest Accommodation*
29 Beach Street, Deal
CT14 6HY
t (01304) 374338
e beachbrowh@aol.com
w beachbrow-hotel.com

**The Clarendon ★★★★**
*Guest Accommodation*
51-55 Beach Street, Deal
CT14 6HY
t (01304) 374748
e admin@clarendonhoteldeal.
co.uk
w shepherd-neame.co.uk

**Ilex Cottage ★★★★**
*Guest Accommodation*
Temple Way, Worth, Deal
CT14 0DA
t (01304) 617026
e info@ilexcottage.com
w ilexcottage.com

**Keep House ★★★**
*Guest Accommodation*
1 Deal Castle Road, Deal
CT14 7BB
t (01304) 368162
e keephouse@talk21.com
w keephouse.co.uk

**Kings Head Public House
★★★ Inn**
9 Beach Street, Deal CT14 7AH
t (01304) 368194

**The Malvern ★★★**
*Guest House*
5-7 Ranelagh Road, Deal
CT14 7BG
t (01304) 372944

**The Roast House Lodge
★★★ Guest Accommodation**
224 London Road, Deal
CT14 9PW
t (01304) 380824
e theroasthouse@amserve.
com

**St Crispin Inn ★★★★ Inn**
The Street, Worth, Deal
CT14 0DF
t (01304) 612081
w stcrispininn.com

## DEDDINGTON
### Oxfordshire

**Hill Barn ★★★**
*Bed & Breakfast*
Banbury Road, Deddington,
Banbury OX15 0TS
t (01869) 338631
e hillbarn-bb@supanet.com

**Stonecrop Guest House ★★**
*Guest House*
Hempton Road, Deddington,
Banbury OX15 0QH
t (01869) 338335
e info@stonecropguesthouse.
co.uk
w stonecropguesthouse.co.uk

## DIDCOT
### Oxfordshire

**Prospect House ★★★**
*Bed & Breakfast*
Upton, Didcot OX11 9HU
t (01235) 850268

**The White House ♦♦♦♦**
*Guest Accommodation*
Reading Road, Upton, Didcot
OX11 9HP
t (01235) 850289

## DINTON
### Buckinghamshire

**Dinton Cottage ★★★**
*Guest Accommodation*
Biggs Lane, Dinton, Aylesbury
HP17 8UH
t (01296) 748270
e lesley@dintoncottage.co.uk
w dintoncottage.co.uk

## DODDINGTON
### Kent

**Palace Farm Hostel ★★★**
*Hostel*
Doddington, Sittingbourne
ME9 0AU
t (01795) 886200
e info@palacefarm.com
w palacefarm.com

**Palace Farmhouse ★★★**
*Guest Accommodation*
Chequers Hill, Doddington,
Sittingbourne ME9 0AU
t (01795) 886820

## DORCHESTER ON THAMES
### Oxfordshire

**Buena Vista B&B ★★★★★**
*Guest Accommodation*
SILVER AWARD
34 Watling Lane, Dorchester-
on-Thames, Wallingford
OX10 7JG
t (01865) 340903
e enquiries@buenavistabnb.
co.uk
w buenavistabnb.co.uk

## DORKING
### Surrey

**Ballantrae ★★★**
*Bed & Breakfast*
55 Ashcombe Road, Dorking
RH4 1LZ
t (01306) 875873
e morris@mabadanfsnet.co.uk

**Broomhill ★★★**
*Bed & Breakfast*
15 Broomfield Park, Dorking
RH4 3QQ
t (01306) 885565
e suzanne.willis@virgin.net

**Chart House B and B
★★★★**
*Guest Accommodation*
Chart Lane, Dorking RH4 2BU
t (01306) 882040
e bedandbreakfast@
charthouse.uk.com
w charthouse.org.uk

**Claremont Cottage**
Rating Applied For
*Bed & Breakfast*
Rose Hill, Dorking RH4 2ED
t (01306) 885487
e claremontcott@btinternet.
com
w claremontcott.co.uk

**Deepdene B&B ★★★★**
*Bed & Breakfast*
24 Deepdene Avenue, Dorking
RH4 1SR
t (01306) 877332
e deepdenedorking@yahoo.
co.uk
w deepdene.talktalk.net

**Denbies Farmhouse ★★★★**
*Farmhouse*
Denbies Wine Estate, London
Road, Dorking RH5 6AA
t (01306) 876777
e bandb@denbiesvineyard.co.
uk
w denbiesvineyard.co.uk

**Fairdene Guest House ★★★**
*Guest Accommodation*
Moores Road, Dorking
RH4 2BG
t (01306) 888337
e zoe.richardson@ntlworld.
com

**Stylehurst Farm ★★★★**
*Bed & Breakfast*
SILVER AWARD
Weare Street, Capel, Dorking
RH5 5JA
t (01306) 711259
e rosemary.goddard@virgin.
net
w stylehurstfarm.com

**Tanners Hatch YHA** ★ *Hostel*
Off Ranmore Road, Dorking
RH5 6BE
t (01306) 877964
e tanners@yha.org.uk
w yha.org.uk

**The Waltons** ★★★★
*Guest Accommodation*
5 Rose Hill, Dorking RH4 2EG
t (01306) 883127
e thewaltons@rosehill5.
demon.co.uk
w a1tourism.com/uk/walt.html

### DOVER
### Kent

**Alkham Court** ★★★★★
*Farmhouse* **GOLD AWARD**
Meggett Lane, South Alkham,
Dover CT15 7DG
t (01303) 892056
e wendy.burrows@
alkhamcourt.co.uk
w alkhamcourt.co.uk

**Amanda Guest House** ★★★
*Guest House*
4 Harold Street, Dover
CT16 1SF
t (01304) 201711
e amandaguesthouse@
hotmail.com
w amandaguesthouse.
homestead.com

**Blakes of Dover** ★★★★
*Guest Accommodation*
52 Castle Street, Dover
CT16 1PJ
t (01304) 202194
w blakesofdover.com

**Castle Guest House** ★★★★
*Guest House*
10 Castle Hill Road, Dover
CT16 1QW
t (01304) 201656
e dimechr@aol.com
w castle-guesthouse.co.uk

**Chrislyn's Guest House**
★★★★ *Bed & Breakfast*
104 Maison Dieu Road, Dover
CT16 1RU
t (01304) 203317

**Clare Guest House** ★★★
*Guest House*
167 Folkestone Road, Dover
CT17 9SJ
t (01304) 204553
e stay@clarehouse-dover.co.
uk
w clarehouse-dover.co.uk

**Cleveland Guest House** ♦♦♦
*Guest Accommodation*
2 Laureston Place, Dover
CT16 1QX
t (01304) 204622
e albetcleve@aol.com
w clevelandguesthouse.
homestead.com

**Colret House** ★★★★
*Bed & Breakfast*
The Green, Coldred, Dover
CT15 5AP
t (01304) 830388
e jackiecolret@aol.com
w colrethouse.co.uk

**Dover's Restover Bed &
Breakfast** ★★★
*Guest Accommodation*
69 Folkestone Road, Dover
CT17 9RZ
t (01304) 206031
e enquiries@doversrestover.
co.uk
w doversrestover.co.uk

**East Lee Guest House**
Rating Applied For
*Guest Accommodation*
Maison Dieu Road, Dover
CT16 1RT
t (01304) 210176
e elgh@eclipse.co.uk
w eastlee.co.uk

**Frith Lodge** ★★★
*Bed & Breakfast*
14 Frith Road, Dover CT16 2PY
t (01304) 208139
e frithlodge@yahoo.co.uk
w frithlodge.co.uk

**Hubert House Guest House
& Licensed Coffee House**
★★★★ *Guest House*
9 Castle Hill Road, Dover
CT16 1QW
t (01304) 202253
e huberthouse@btinternet.
com
w huberthouse.co.uk

**Lenox House** ★★★★
*Bed & Breakfast*
Granville Road, St Margarets
Bay, Dover CT15 6DS
t (01304) 853253

**Loddington House Hotel**
★★★★
*Guest Accommodation*
East Cliff, Dover CT16 1LX
t (01304) 201947
e loddingtonhotel@btconnect.
com
w loddingtonhousehotel.com

**Longfield Guest House**
★★★ *Guest Accommodation*
203 Folkestone Road, Dover
CT17 9SL
t (01304) 204716
e res@longfieldguesthouse.co.
uk
w longfieldguesthouse.co.uk

**Maison Dieu Guest House**
★★★★ *Guest House*
89 Maison Dieu Road, Dover
CT16 1RU
t (01304) 204033
e info@maisondieu.co.uk
w maisondieu.com

**The Norman Guest House**
★★★ *Guest House*
Folkestone Road, Dover
CT17 9RZ
t (01304) 207803
e thenorman@btopenworld.
com
w thenorman-guesthouse.co.
uk

**Number One Guest House**
★★★★ *Guest House*
1 Castle Street, Dover
CT16 1QH
t (01304) 202007
e res@number1guesthouse.
co.uk
w number1guesthouse.co.uk

**Number Twenty- Four Bed &
Breakfast** ★★★★
*Bed & Breakfast*
24 East Cliff, Marine Parade,
Dover CT16 1LU
t (01304) 330549
e number24dover@aol.com

**Westbank Guest House**
★★★★ *Guest House*
239-241 Folkestone Road,
Dover CT17 9LL
t (01304) 201061
e thewestbank@aol.com
w westbankguesthouse.co.uk

### DUCKLINGTON
### Oxfordshire

**Ducklington Farm** ★★★
*Farmhouse*
Course Hill Lane, Ducklington,
Witney OX29 7YL
t (01993) 772175
w countryaccom.co.uk

### DUDDLESWELL
### East Sussex

**Duddleswell Manor** ♦♦♦♦
*Guest Accommodation*
**SILVER AWARD**
Duddleswell, East Sussex,
Uckfield TN22 3JL
t (01825) 712701
e smithduddleswell@tiscali.co.
uk

### DUMMER
### Hampshire

**Oakdown Farm Bungalow**
★★★ *Farmhouse*
Oakdown Farm, Dummer,
Basingstoke RG23 7LR
t (01256) 397218

### DYMCHURCH
### Kent

**Waterside Guest House**
★★★★
*Guest Accommodation*
15 Hythe Road, Dymchurch,
Romney Marsh TN29 0LN
t (01303) 872253
e info@watersideguesthouse.
co.uk
w watersideguesthouse.co.uk

### EARNLEY
### West Sussex

**Millstone** ★★★★
*Bed & Breakfast*
**GOLD AWARD**
Clappers Lane, Earnley,
Chichester PO20 7JJ
t (01243) 670116
e michaelharrington@
btinternet.com
w visitsussex.org/millstone

### EAST ASHLING
### West Sussex

**The Dairy Farm** ★★★★
*Bed & Breakfast*
**SILVER AWARD**
East Ashling, Chichester
PO18 9AR
t (01243) 575544
e david.ash1@virgin.net

**Horse & Groom** ★★★★ *Inn*
East Ashling, Chichester
PO18 9AX
t (01243) 575339
e info@thehorseandgroom
chichester.co.uk
w thehorseandgroom
chichester.co.uk

### EAST COWES
### Isle of Wight

**Crossways House** ★★★★
*Guest Accommodation*
**SILVER AWARD**
Crossways Road, East Cowes
PO32 6LJ
t (01983) 298282
e enquiries@bedbreakfast-
cowes.co.uk
w bedbreakfast-cowes.co.uk

**Wisteria House** ★★★★
*Bed & Breakfast*
191 York Avenue, East Cowes
PO32 6BE
t (01983) 295999
e philgillan@hotmail.co.uk

### EAST DEAN
### West Sussex

**The Star and Garter** ★★★★
*Inn*
East Dean, Chichester
PO18 0JG
t (01243) 811318
w singletonvillage.com

### EAST GRINSTEAD
### West Sussex

**Coach House** ★★★
*Bed & Breakfast*
Courtlands, Chilling Street, East
Grinstead RH19 4JF
t (01342) 810512
e friends@mmarshall.vispa.
com
w visitsussex.org/
coachhousesharpthorne

**Moat House X** ★★★★
*Guest Accommodation*
**SILVER AWARD**
Moat Road, East Grinstead
RH19 3JZ
t (01342) 326785
e moathouse@freenet.co.uk
w moathouse-eastgrinstead.co.
uk

**Saxons** ★★★★
*Guest Accommodation*
Horsted Lane, Sharpthorne,
East Grinstead RH19 4HY
t (01342) 810821
e saxonsbandb@btinternet.
com
w saxons.freeuk.com

### EAST HAGBOURNE
### Oxfordshire

**Hagbourne Mill Farm** ★★★
*Guest Accommodation*
East Hagbourne, Didcot
OX11 9EA
t (01235) 813140
e corderoy@hagmill.freeserve.
co.uk

### EAST HANNEY
### Oxfordshire

**Mill Cottage** ★★★
*Bed & Breakfast*
East Hanney, Wantage
OX12 0JJ
t (01235) 868507
e ormehanney@aol.com

## EAST HENDRED
### Oxfordshire

**A Monks Court ★★★**
*Bed & Breakfast*
Newbury Road, East Hendred,
Wantage OX12 8LG
t (01235) 833797

**Cowdrays ★★★**
*Bed & Breakfast*
Cat Street, East Hendred,
Wantage OX12 8JT
t (01235) 833313

## EAST HOATHLY
### East Sussex

**Old Whyly ★★★★**
*Bed & Breakfast*
SILVER AWARD
Halland Road, East Hoathly,
Lewes BN8 6EL
t (01825) 840216
e stay@oldwhyly.co.uk
w oldwhyly.co.uk

## EAST LAVANT
### West Sussex

**The Flint House ★★★★★**
*Bed & Breakfast*
SILVER AWARD
Pook Lane, East Lavant,
Chichester PO18 0AS
t (01243) 773482
e theflinthouse@ukonline.co.uk
w visitsussex.org/theflinthouse

**Royal Oak ★★★★★ Inn**
GOLD AWARD
East Lavant, Chichester
PO18 0AX
t (01243) 527434
e nickroyaloak@aol.com
w thesussexpub.com

## EAST PRESTON
### West Sussex

**Roselea Cottage ★★★**
*Bed & Breakfast*
2 Elm Avenue, East Preston,
Littlehampton BN16 1HJ
t (01903) 786787
e roselea.cottage@tesco.net
w roseleacottage.co.uk

## EAST WELLOW
### Hampshire

**Country Views B&B ★★★★**
*Guest Accommodation*
Willowbend, Dunwood Hill,
Shootash, Romsey SO51 6FD
t (01794) 514735
e sue@countryviewsbandb.
freeserve.co.uk
w countryviewsbandb.
freeserve.co.uk

## EASTBOURNE
### East Sussex

**Atlanta Hotel ★★★**
*Guest House*
10 Royal Parade, Eastbourne
BN22 7AR
t (01323) 730486

**The Berkeley ★★★★★**
*Guest Accommodation*
3 Lascelles Terrace, Eastbourne
BN21 4BJ
t (01323) 645055
e info@theberkeley.net
w theberkeley.net/

**The Birling Gap ★★★**
*Guest Accommodation*
Birling Gap, Seven Sisters
Cliffs, Eastbourne BN20 0AB
t (01323) 423197
e reception@birlinggaphotel.
co.uk
w birlinggaphotel.co.uk

**Boyne House ★★★★**
*Guest Accommodation*
12 St Aubyn's Road,
Eastbourne BN22 7AS
t (01323) 430245

**Bramble Guest House ★★★**
*Guest House*
16 Lewes Road, Eastbourne
BN21 2BT
t (01323) 722343
e bramble@
eastbourneguesthouse.co.uk
w brambleguesthouse.co.uk

**Brayscroft House ★★★★**
*Guest House* GOLD AWARD
13 South Cliff Avenue,
Eastbourne BN20 7AH
t (01323) 647005
e brayscroft@hotmail.com
w brayscrofthotel.co.uk

**Cambridge House ★★★**
*Guest House*
6 Cambridge Road, Eastbourne
BN22 7BS
t (01323) 721100

**The Cherry Tree ★★★★**
*Guest House*
15 Silverdale Road, Lower
Meads, Eastbourne BN20 7AJ
t (01323) 722406
e lynda@cherrytree-
eastbourne.co.uk
w cherrytree-eastbourne.co.uk

**Ebor Lodge ★★★★**
*Guest House*
71 Royal Parade, Eastbourne
BN22 7AQ
t (01323) 640792
e info@eborlodge.co.uk
w eborlodge.co.uk

**The Gladwyn ★★★★**
*Guest House*
16 Blackwater Road,
Eastbourne BN21 4JD
t (01323) 733142
e gladwynhotel@aol.com
w gladwynhotel.com

**The Guesthouse East ★★★★**
*Guest Accommodation*
SILVER AWARD
13 Hartington Place,
Eastbourne BN21 3BS
t (01323) 722774
e fiona.bugler1@btinternet.
com
w theguesthouseeastbourne.
co.uk

**Little Foxes ★★★**
*Bed & Breakfast*
24 Wannock Road, Eastbourne
BN22 7JU
t (01323) 640670 &
07957 565951
e Gunnersmith2001@yahoo.
co.uk
w thelittlefoxes.com

**Loriston Guest House ★★★★**
*Guest Accommodation*
GOLD AWARD
17 St Aubyns Road, Eastbourne
BN22 7AS
t (01323) 726193

**Nirvana Hotel ★★★**
*Guest House*
32 Redoubt Road, Eastbourne
BN22 7DL
t (01323) 722603

**Hotel Pavilion ★★★★**
*Guest House*
60 Royal Parade, Eastbourne
BN22 7AQ
t (01323) 736988
e info@hotelpavilion.co.uk
w hotelpavilion.co.uk

**The Pier Hotel ★★★★**
*Guest Accommodation*
2-4 Grand Parade, Eastbourne
BN21 3EH
t (01323) 649544

**The Reymar ★★★**
*Guest Accommodation*
2 Cambridge Road, Eastbourne
BN22 7BS
t (01323) 724649
e info@reymar.co.uk
w reymarhotel.co.uk

**St Omer's ★★★★**
*Guest House*
13 Royal Parade, Eastbourne
BN22 7AR
t (01323) 722152
e stomerhotel@hotmail.com
w st-omer.co.uk

**Southcroft ★★★★**
*Guest House* SILVER AWARD
15 South Cliff Avenue,
Eastbourne BN20 7AH
t (01323) 729071
e southcroft@eastbourne34.
freeserve.co.uk
w southcrofthotel.co.uk

## EASTCHURCH
### Kent

**Dunmow House ★★★★**
*Guest Accommodation*
9 Church Road, Eastchurch,
Sheerness ME12 4DG
t (01795) 880576
e mep4@btinternet.com

**Sheppey Island Guest House ★★★★** *Guest House*
High Street, Sheerness
ME12 4DF
t (01795) 880454
e info@sheppeyisland.co.uk
w sheppeyisland.co.uk

## EASTERGATE
### West Sussex

**Eastmere House ★★★**
*Bed & Breakfast*
Eastergate Lane, Eastergate,
Chichester PO20 3SJ
t (01243) 544204
e bernardlane@hotmail.com
w eastmere.com

**Mount Pleasant House ★★★★** *Bed & Breakfast*
Level Mare Lane, Eastergate,
Chichester PO20 3SB
t (01243) 545368

## EASTLEIGH
### Hampshire

**Carinya B&B ★★★**
*Bed & Breakfast*
38 Sovereign Way, Eastleigh
SO50 4SA
t (023) 8061 3128
e carinya38@talktalk.net

## EDENBRIDGE
### Kent

**Mowshurst Farm House ★★★★** *Bed & Breakfast*
SILVER AWARD
Swan Lane, Edenbridge
TN8 6AH
t (01732) 862064
w mowshurstfarmhouse.co.uk

**Starborough Manor ★★★★**
*Guest Accommodation*
GOLD AWARD
Moor Lane, Marsh Green,
Edenbridge TN8 5QY
t (01732) 862152
e lynn@starboroughmanor.co.
uk
w starboroughmanor.co.uk

## EDGCOTT
### Buckinghamshire

**Perry Manor Farm ★★**
*Farmhouse*
Buckingham Road, Edgcott,
Aylesbury HP18 0TR
t (01296) 770257

## EFFINGHAM
### Surrey

**Cornerways Cottage ★★★**
*Bed & Breakfast*
Orestan Lane, Effingham,
Leatherhead KT24 5SN
t (01372) 451990
e carolinegatford@fsmail.net

## EGHAM
### Surrey

**Bulkeley House ★★★**
*Guest Accommodation*
Englefield Green, Egham
TW20 0JU
t (01784) 431287

**Royal Holloway University of London ★★★–★★★★**
*Campus*
Egham Hill, Egham TW20 0EX
t (01784) 443045
e sales-office@rhul.ac.uk
w rhul.ac.uk/fm

## ELMSTED
### Kent

**Elmsted Court Farm ★★★★**
*Farmhouse*
Elmsted, Ashford TN25 5JN
t (01233) 750269
e carol@elmsted-court-farm.
co.uk
w elmsted-court-farm.co.uk

## ELSTEAD
### Surrey

**Anstey's Bed and Breakfast ★★★** *Bed & Breakfast*
10 Springhill, Elstead,
Godalming GU8 6EL
t (01252) 706995
e nickyanstey@aol.com
w hometown.aol.co.uk/
nickyanstey/bedandbreakfast.
html

Look out for establishments participating in the National Accessible Scheme

**EPWELL**
Oxfordshire

**Yarnhill Farm** ★★★
*Farmhouse*
Shenington Road, Epwell,
Banbury OX15 6JA
t (01295) 780250
e bedandbreakfast@
yarnhillfarm.freeserve.co.uk

**EVERTON**
Hampshire

**Glenhurst B&B** ★★★★
*Bed & Breakfast*
86 Wainsford Road, Everton,
Lymington SO41 0UD
t (01590) 644256

**Trees Cottage B&B** ♦♦♦
*Guest Accommodation*
East Lane, Everton, Lymington
SO41 0JL
t (01590) 641622
e sidcrowton@yahoo.com

**EWELME**
Oxfordshire

**Mays Farm** ★★★★
*Bed & Breakfast*
Ewelme, Wallingford
OX10 6QF
t (01491) 641294
e trish.passmore@btinternet.
com

**EWHURST**
Surrey

**Malricks** ★★★
*Bed & Breakfast*
The Street, Ewhurst, Cranleigh
GU6 7RH
t (01483) 277575
e malricks@tesco.net
w http://malricks.mysite.
wanadoo-members.co.uk

**EWHURST GREEN**
East Sussex

**Clouds** ★★★★★
*Bed & Breakfast*
SILVER AWARD
9 Dagg Lane, Robertsbridge
TN32 5RD
t (01580) 830677
e jandfwouters@aol.com
w cloudsbedandbreakfast.co.
uk

**EWSHOT**
Hampshire

**Dares Farm House** ★★★★
*Guest House*
Farnham Road, Ewshot,
Farnham GU10 5BB
t (01252) 851631
e daresfarm@tiscali.co.uk

**FAIRLIGHT**
East Sussex

**Fairlight Cottage** ★★★★
*Guest Accommodation*
Warren Road, Fairlight,
Hastings TN35 4AG
t (01424) 812545

**FAREHAM**
Hampshire

**Bridge House** ★★★★
*Bed & Breakfast*
1 Waterside Gardens,
Wallington, Fareham
PO16 8SD
t (01329) 287775
e maryhb8@aol.com

**Catisfield Cottage Guest
House** ★★ *Bed & Breakfast*
1 Catisfield Lane, Fareham
PO15 5NW
t (01329) 843301

**Harbour View** ★★
*Bed & Breakfast*
85 Windmill Grove, Fareham
PO16 9HH
t (023) 9237 6740

**Seven Sevens Guest House**
★★★ *Guest Accommodation*
56 Hill Head Road, Hill Head,
Fareham PO14 3JL
t (01329) 662408

**Springfield Hotel** ★★★
*Guest Accommodation*
67 The Avenue, Fareham
PO14 1PE
t (01329) 828325
w springfieldhotelfareham.co.
uk

**Trafalgar Guest House** ★★★
*Guest Accommodation*
63 High Street, Fareham
PO16 7BG
t (01329) 235010
e enquiries@
trafalgarguesthouse.co.uk
w trafalgarguesthouse.co.uk

**Travelrest Fareham** ★★★
*Guest Accommodation*
22 The Avenue, Fareham
PO14 1NS
t (01329) 232175
e solentreservations@
travelrest.co.uk
w travelrest.co.uk/fareham

**FARINGDON**
Oxfordshire

**Bridge Farm** ★★★
*Bed & Breakfast*
Thrupp, Nr Faringdon, Oxon
SN7 8JY
t (01367) 244774
e sally@dodd-noble.fsnet.co.
uk

**FARNBOROUGH**
Hampshire

**Langfords Bed & Breakfast**
★★★ *Bed & Breakfast*
165 Cheyne Way, Farnborough
GU14 8SD
t (01252) 547311
e bookings@langfordsbandb.
co.uk
w langfordsbandb.co.uk

**The Oak Tree Guest House**
★★★★
*Guest Accommodation*
112 Farnborough Road,
Farnborough GU14 6TN
t (01252) 545491
e joanne.dickinson21@
ntlworld.com
w theoaktreeguesthouse.com

**FARNHAM**
Surrey

**High Wray** ★★★
*Bed & Breakfast*
73 Lodge Hill Road, Lower
Bourne, Farnham GU10 3RB
t (01252) 715589
e alexine@highwray73.co.uk
w highwray73.co.uk

**Kernel Cottage** ★★★
*Bed & Breakfast*
14 Nutshell Lane, Upper Hale,
Farnham GU9 0HG
t (01252) 710147

**St Gallen** ★★★★
*Bed & Breakfast*
Old Frensham Road, Lower
Bourne, Farnham GU10 3PT
t (01252) 793412
e cary_wilkins@cw1999.
freeserve.co.uk

**FAVERSHAM**
Kent

**Barnsfield** ★★★
*Guest Accommodation*
Fostall, Hernhill, Faversham
ME13 9JG
t (01227) 750973
e barnsfield@yahoo.com
w barnsfield.co.uk

**Brenley Farm House** ★★★★
*Farmhouse*
Brenley Lane, Boughton-under-
Blean, Faversham ME13 9LY
t (01227) 751203
e info@brenley-farm.co.uk
w brenley-farm.co.uk

**Fairlea**
Rating Applied For
*Bed & Breakfast*
27 Preston Avenue, Faversham
ME13 8NH
t (01795) 539610
e davidfairlie@supanet.com

**Gladstone House** ★★
*Guest Accommodation*
SILVER AWARD
60 Newton Road, Faversham
ME13 8DZ
t (01795) 536432
e maryjmackay@hotmail.com
w faversham.org/wheretostay/
gladstone.asp

**Leaveland Court** ★★★★
*Guest Accommodation*
SILVER AWARD
Leaveland, Faversham
ME13 0NP
t (01233) 740596
e info@leavelandcourt.co.uk
w leavelandcourt.co.uk

**March Cottage** ★★★
*Bed & Breakfast*
5 Preston Avenue, Faversham
ME13 8NH
t (01795) 536514
e sarah@marchcottagebandb.
co.uk
w marchcottagebandb.co.uk

**Owens Court Farm** ★★★★
*Guest Accommodation*
SILVER AWARD
Selling, Faversham ME13 9QN
t (01227) 752247
e enquiries@owenscourt.com
w owenscourt.com

**The Sun Inn** ★★★ *Inn*
10 West Street, Faversham
ME13 7JE
t (01795) 535098
w shepherdneame.co.uk

**FAWLEY**
Hampshire

**Walcot Guest House** ★★★★
*Guest House*
Blackfield Road, Fawley,
Beaulieu SO45 1ED
t (023) 8089 1344
e stephenjbrown@tiscali.co.uk
w walcothousehotel.com

**FIFIELD**
Berkshire

**Victoria Cottage** ★★
*Bed & Breakfast*
2 Victoria Cottages, Fifield
Road, Fifield SL6 2NZ
t (01628) 623564

**FIFIELD**
Oxfordshire

**Merryfield** ★★★
*Bed & Breakfast*
High Street, Fifield, Chipping
Norton OX7 6HL
t (01993) 830517
e john714@btinternet.com
w merryfieldbandb.co.uk

**FINDON**
West Sussex

**John Henry's Inn** ★★★★ *Inn*
The Forge, Nepcote Lane,
Findon, Worthing BN14 0SE
t (01903) 877277
e enquiries@john-henrys.com
w john-henrys.com

**FINGLESHAM**
Kent

**Orchard Lodge** ★★★★
*Guest Accommodation*
The Street, Finglesham, Deal
CT14 0NA
t (01304) 620192
e hutsonbob@aol.com
w orchardlodge.co.uk

**FITTLEWORTH**
West Sussex

**Old Post Office** ★★★★
*Bed & Breakfast*
Fittleworth, Pulborough
RH20 1JE
t (01798) 865315
e sue.moseley@ukgateway.
net
w visitsussex.org/oldpostoffice

**Swan Inn** ★★★★ *Inn*
Lower Street, Fittleworth,
Petworth RH20 1EN
t (01798) 865429
e hotel@swaninn.com
w swaninn.com

**FIVE OAK GREEN**
Kent

**Ivy House** ★★★
*Bed & Breakfast*
Tonbridge TN12 6RB
t (01892) 832041

**FLEET**
Hampshire

**Copperfield** ★★★
*Bed & Breakfast*
16 Glen Road, Fleet GU51 3QR
t (01252) 616140
e bill@copperfieldbnb.co.uk
w copperfieldbnb.co.uk

**Tinkers Furze ★★★★**
*Bed & Breakfast*
Gough Road, Fleet GU51 4LL
t (01252) 615995
e judykeep@yahoo.co.uk
w tinkersfurze.co.uk

**Tundry House Bed & Breakfast ★★★★**
*Bed & Breakfast*
Church Lane, Dogmersfield,
Hook RG27 8SZ
t (01252) 614677
e sally@tundry.co.uk
w tundryhouse.co.uk

### FLIMWELL
Kent

**Forest Edge Motel**
Rating Applied For
*Guest Accommodation*
Rosaem House, London Road,
Wadhurst TN5 7PL
t (01580) 879222
w forestedgemotel.co.uk

### FOLKESTONE
Kent

**Beachborough Park ♦♦♦**
*Guest Accommodation*
Beachborough, Newington,
Folkestone CT18 8BW
t (01303) 275432
w kentaccess.org.uk

**Garden Lodge ★★★★**
*Guest Accommodation*
324 Canterbury Road, Densole,
Folkestone CT18 7BB
t (01303) 893147
e stay@garden-lodge.com
w garden-lodge.com

**Kentmere Guest House ★★★** *Guest House*
76 Cheriton Road, Folkestone
CT20 1DG
t (01303) 259661
e enquiries@kentmere-guesthouse.co.uk
w kentmere-guesthouse.co.uk

**The Rob Roy Guest House ★★★** *Guest House*
227 Dover Road, Folkestone
CT19 6NH
t (01303) 253341
e robroy.folkestone@ntlworld.com
w therobroyguesthouse.co.uk

**Seacliffe ♦♦♦**
*Guest Accommodation*
3 Wear Bay Road, Folkestone
CT19 6AT
t (01303) 254592

**Sunny Lodge Guest House ★★★** *Guest Accommodation*
85 Cheriton Road, Folkestone
CT20 2QL
t (01303) 251498
e linda.dowsett@btclick.com
w s-h-systems.co.uk/hotels/sunnyl.html

**Windsor Hotel ★★**
*Guest Accommodation*
5-6 Langhorne Gardens,
Folkestone CT20 2EA
t (01303) 251348
e windsorhotel_folkestone@hotmail.com

### FONTWELL
West Sussex

**Park Cottage ★★★★**
*Bed & Breakfast*
London Road, Fontwell, Nr
Arundel BN18 0SG
t (01243) 544133

**Woodacre ★★★★**
*Guest Accommodation*
Arundel Road, Fontwell,
Arundel BN18 0QP
t (01243) 814301
e wacrebb@aol.com
w woodacre.co.uk

### FORDINGBRIDGE
Hampshire

**Broomy ★★★★**
*Bed & Breakfast*
Ogdens, Fordingbridge
SP6 2PY
t (01425) 653264

**The Three Lions ★★★★**
*Restaurant with Rooms*
Stuckton, Fordingbridge
SP6 2HF
t (01425) 652489

### FOREST ROW
East Sussex

**Brambletye Hotel ★★★** *Inn*
The Square, Forest Row
RH18 5EZ
t (01342) 824144
e brambletyehotel@accommodating-inns.co.uk
w accommodating-inns.co.uk

### FRAMFIELD
East Sussex

**Beggars Barn ★★★★**
*Guest Accommodation*
SILVER AWARD
Barn Lane, Framfield, Uckfield
TN22 5RX
t (01825) 890868
e caroline@beggarsbarn.co.uk
w beggarsbarn.co.uk

### FREEFOLK
Hampshire

**The Old Rectory ★★★**
*Bed & Breakfast*
Freefolk, Whitchurch
RG28 7NW
t (01256) 895408
w theoldrectoryfreefolk.co.uk

### FRESHWATER
Isle of Wight

**Braewood ★★★★**
*Bed & Breakfast*
Afton Road, Freshwater
PO40 9TP
t (01983) 759910
e enquiries@braewood-iow.co.uk
w braewood-iow.co.uk

**Heather Cottage B&B ★★★★** *Bed & Breakfast*
Afton Road, Freshwater Bay
PO40 9TP
t (01983) 754319
e heathercottbb@aol.com

**Royal Standard ★★★★**
*Guest House*
School Green Road,
Freshwater PO40 9AJ
t (01983) 753227
e theroyalstandard@turboweb.org
w theroyalstandardhotel.com

**Seahorses ★★★★**
*Guest Accommodation*
Victoria Road, Freshwater
PO40 9PP
t (01983) 752574
e seahorses-iow@tiscali.co.uk
w seahorsesisleofwight.com

### FROXFIELD GREEN
Hampshire

**The Trooper Inn and Hotel ★★★★** *Inn*
Froxfield, Petersfield
GU32 1BD
t (01730) 827293
e troopersec@btconnect.com
w trooperinn.com

### FULBROOK
Oxfordshire

**Star Cottage ★★★★**
*Bed & Breakfast*
SILVER AWARD
Meadow Lane, Fulbrook,
Burford OX18 4BW
t (01993) 822032
e peterwyatt@tesco.net

### GARSINGTON
Oxfordshire

**Hill Copse Cottage ★★★**
*Bed & Breakfast*
Wheatley Road, Garsington,
Oxford OX44 9DT
t (01865) 361478

### GATCOMBE
Isle of Wight

**Freewaters ★★★★**
*Guest Accommodation*
SILVER AWARD
New Barn Lane, Gatcombe
PO30 3EQ
t (01983) 721439
e john@pitstopmodels.demon.co.uk
w colourpointdesign.co.uk/freewaters

**Little Gatcombe Farm ★★★★** *Bed & Breakfast*
SILVER AWARD
Newbarn Lane, Gatcombe
PO30 3EQ
t (01983) 721580
e anita@littlegatcombefarm.co.uk
w littlegatcombefarm.co.uk

### GATWICK
West Sussex

**The Corner House ★★★★**
*Guest Accommodation*
72 Massetts Road, Horley
RH6 7ED
t (01293) 784574
e info@thecornerhouse.co.uk
w thecornerhouse.co.uk

**The Lawn Guest House ★★★★** *Guest House*
SILVER AWARD
30 Massetts Road, Horley
RH6 7DF
t (01293) 775751
e info@lawnguesthouse.co.uk
w lawnguesthouse.co.uk

**Southbourne Guest House Gatwick ★★★★**
*Guest House*
34 Massetts Road, Horley
RH6 7DS
t (01293) 771991
e reservations@southbournegatwick.com
w southbournegatwick.com

### GERRARDS CROSS
Buckinghamshire

**The Rowans ★★★**
*Bed & Breakfast*
15 Howards Wood Drive,
Gerrards Cross SL9 7HR
t (01753) 884911
e sylvia.crosby@ntlworld.com

### GILLINGHAM
Kent

**King Charles Hotel ★★★**
*Guest Accommodation*
Brompton Road, Gillingham
ME7 5QT
t (01634) 830303
e enquiries@kingcharleshotel.co.uk
w kingcharleshotel.co.uk

**Medway YHA ★★★** *Hostel*
351 Capstone Road, Gillingham
ME7 3JE
t (01634) 400788
e medway@yha.org.uk
w yha.org.uk

**Ramsey House ★★★★**
*Guest Accommodation*
228a Barnsole Road,
Gillingham ME7 4JB
t (01634) 854193

### GLYNDE
East Sussex

**Ranscombe House ★★★**
*Guest Accommodation*
Ranscombe Lane, Glynde, Nr
Glyndebourne, Lewes
BN8 6AA
t (01273) 858538
w ranscombehouse.co.uk

### GODALMING
Surrey

**24 Croft Road**
Rating Applied For
*Guest House*
Croft Road, Godalming
GU7 1BY
t (01483) 429982
e alanbishop@mac.com

**Combe Ridge ★★★**
*Bed & Breakfast*
Pook Hill, Chiddingfold,
Godalming GU8 4XR
t (01428) 682607
e brendaessex@btinternet.com

**Heath Hall Farm ★★★**
*Farmhouse*
Bowlhead Green, Godalming
GU8 6NW
t (01428) 682808
e heathhallfarm@btinternet.com
w heathhallfarm.co.uk

**Heath House ★★★★**
*Bed & Breakfast*
SILVER AWARD
Alldens Lane, Godalming
GU8 4AP
t (01483) 416961
e csh@gofast.co.uk
w heathhouse.eu

**Highview** ★★
*Bed & Breakfast*
SILVER AWARD
39 Nightingale Road,
Godalming GU7 2HU
t  (01483) 861974
e  highview@which.net
w  highview-bedbreakfast.co.uk

## GODSHILL
Hampshire

**Croft Cottage** ★★★
*Bed & Breakfast*
Southampton Road, Godshill,
Fordingbridge SP6 2LE
t  (01425) 657955
e  croftcottage@btopenworld.com
w  croftcottagenewforest.co.uk

## GODSHILL
Isle of Wight

**Koala Cottage Retreat**
★★★★★
*Guest Accommodation*
GOLD AWARD
Church Hollow, Godshill,
Ventnor PO38 3DR
t  (01983) 842031
e  info@koalacottage.co.uk
w  koalacottage.co.uk

## GOODWOOD
West Sussex

**The Coach House** ★★★★
*Bed & Breakfast*
SILVER AWARD
1 Pilleygreen Lodge,
Goodwood, Chichester
PO18 0QE
t  (01243) 811467 &
07776 417709
e  enquiries@coachousegoodwood.co.uk
w  coachousegoodwood.co.uk

## GORING
Oxfordshire

**Beverlley B&B** ★★★
*Bed & Breakfast*
69 Wallingford Road, Reading
RG8 0HL
t  (01491) 872659
e  janet@beverleybandb.nanadoo.co.uk
w  beverleybandb.nanadoo.co.uk

## GOSPORT
Hampshire

**Anglesey Hotel** ★★★★
*Guest House*
24 Crescent Road, Alverstoke,
Gosport PO12 2DH
t  (023) 9258 2157
e  reservations@angleseyhotel.co.uk
w  angleseyhotel.co.uk

**Ellachie Guest House**
★★★★ *Bed & Breakfast*
1 Ellachie Road, Alverstoke,
Gosport PO12 2DP
t  (023) 9258 6258
e  info@ellachie.co.uk
w  ellachie.co.uk

## GOUDHURST
Kent

**The South Oast** ★★★★
*Bed & Breakfast*
Bedgebury Road, Goudhurst,
Cranbrook TN17 2QU
t  (01580) 211457
e  judith.farnfield@goudhurst.co.uk

## GRAFFHAM
West Sussex

**Brook Barn** ★★★★
*Bed & Breakfast*
SILVER AWARD
Selham Road, Graffham,
Petworth GU28 0PU
t  (01798) 867356
e  brookbarn@hotmail.com
w  visitsussex.org/brookbarn

**Withy** ★★★★★
*Guest Accommodation*
SILVER AWARD
Graffham, Petworth GU28 0PY
t  (01798) 867000
e  jacquelinewoods@hotmail.com
w  withy.uk.com

## GRAFTY GREEN
Kent

**Foxes Earth Bed & Breakfast**
★★★★
*Guest Accommodation*
SILVER AWARD
Headcorn Road, Grafty Green,
Maidstone ME17 2AP
t  (01622) 858350
e  foxesearth@btinternet.com
w  foxesearthbedandbreakfast.co.uk

**Who'd A Thought It** ★★★★
*Guest Accommodation*
Headcorn Road, Grafty Green,
Maidstone ME17 2AR
t  (01622) 858951
e  joe@whodathoughtit.com
w  whodathoughtit.com

## GRAVESEND
Kent

**Briars Court B&B** ★★★★
*Bed & Breakfast*
90 Windmill Street, Gravesend
DA12 1LH
t  (01474) 363788
e  bandb@briarscourt.co.uk
w  briarscourt.co.uk

**Eastcourt Oast** ★★★★
*Guest Accommodation*
14 Church Lane, Gravesend
DA12 2NL
t  (01474) 823937
e  mary.@eastcourtoast.co.uk
w  eastcourtoast.co.uk

## GREAT BOOKHAM
Surrey

**Selworthy** ★★
*Bed & Breakfast*
310 Lower Road, Bookham,
Leatherhead KT23 4DW
t  (01372) 453952
e  bnb.selworthy@btinternet.com

## GOUDHURST — GREAT MISSENDEN
Buckinghamshire

**Forge House** ★★★★
*Bed & Breakfast*
10 Church Street, Great
Missenden HP16 0AX
t  (01494) 867347

**The Rising Sun** ★★★ *Inn*
Great Missenden HP16 9PS
t  (01494) 488393
e  sunrising@rising-sun.demon.co.uk
w  rising-sun.demon.co.uk

## GREATSTONE
Kent

**White Horses Cottage**
★★★★
*Guest Accommodation*
SILVER AWARD
180 The Parade, Greatstone,
New Romney TN28 8RS
t  (01797) 366626
e  whitehorses@tesco.net
w  horses-cottage.co.uk

## GREENHAM
Berkshire

**Cumorah** ★★★★
*Guest Accommodation*
7 Spa Meadow Close,
Greenham, Thatcham
RG19 8ST
t  (01635) 34464
e  pam.wiltshire@telco4u.net
w  freeweb.telco4u.net/cumorah

## GUESTLING
East Sussex

**Mount Pleasant Farm**
★★★★ *Bed & Breakfast*
White Hart Hill, Guestling,
Hastings TN35 4LR
t  (01424) 813108
e  angelajohn@mountpleasantfarm.fsbusiness.co.uk
w  mountpleasantfarm.fsbusiness.co.uk

## GUILDFORD
Surrey

**Abeille House** ★★★★
*Bed & Breakfast*
119 Stoke Road, Guildford
GU1 1ET
t  (01483) 532200
e  abeille.house119@ntlworld.com
w  abeillehouse.co.uk

**Amberley** ★★★
*Bed & Breakfast*
Maori Road, Guildford
GU1 2EL
t  (01483) 573198
e  amberleyjoyners@connectfree.co.uk

**Bluebells** ★★★
*Guest Accommodation*
21 Coltsfoot Drive, Guildford
GU1 1YH
t  (01483) 826124
e  hughes.a@ntlworld.com
w  bluebellsbedandbreakfast.co.uk

**Cherry Trees** ★★★★
*Bed & Breakfast*
Gomshall Lane, Shere,
Guildford GU5 9HE
t  (01483) 202288

**East Woodhay** ★★★
*Bed & Breakfast*
86a Epsom Road, Guildford
GU1 2DH
t  (01483) 575986
e  eastwoodhaybandb@hotmail.co.uk

**Field Villa** ★★
*Bed & Breakfast*
Liddington New Road,
Guildford GU3 3AH
t  (01483) 233961

**Guildford YMCA** ★★★★
*Hostel*
Bridge Street, Guildford
GU1 4SB
t  (01483) 532555
e  accom@guildfordymca.org.uk
w  guildfordymca.org.uk

**Holroyd Arms Pubotel** ★★
*Inn*
36 Aldershot Road, Guildford
GU2 8AF
t  (01483) 560215

**The Homestead BNB** ★★★
*Bed & Breakfast*
75 Bray Road, Guildford
GU2 7LJ
t  (01483) 828663
w  thehomesteadbnb.co.uk

**The Laurels** ★★★
*Bed & Breakfast*
Dagden Road, Shalford,
Guildford GU4 8DD
t  (01483) 565753

**Lavender House B&B** ★★
*Bed & Breakfast*
4 Medlar Close, Guildford
GU1 1LS
t  07709 760000
e  ayse.stevenson@ntlworld.com

**Littlefield Manor** ★★★
*Farmhouse*
Littlefield Common, Guildford
GU3 3HJ
t  (01483) 233068
e  john@littlefieldmanor.co.uk
w  littlefieldmanor.co.uk

**Matchams** ★★★
*Guest Accommodation*
35 Boxgrove Avenue,
Guildford GU1 1XQ
t  (01483) 567643

**The Old Malt House** ★★★
*Bed & Breakfast*
Bagshot Road, Worplesdon,
Guildford GU3 3PT
t  (01483) 232152

**Patcham** ★★ *Bed & Breakfast*
44 Farnham Road, Guildford
GU2 4LS
t  (01483) 570789

**Plaegan House** ★★★★
*Bed & Breakfast*
SILVER AWARD
96 Wodeland Avenue,
Guildford GU2 4LD
t  (01483) 822181 &
07961 919430
e  froxanphillips@yahoo.co.uk
w  plaeganhouse.co.uk

**Stoke House** ★★★
*Guest House*
113 Stoke Road, Guildford
GU1 1ET
**t** (01483) 453025 &
07714 339588
**e** bookings@stokehouse.net
**w** stokehouse.net

**Yew Tree House** ★★★★
*Bed & Breakfast*
2 The Paddock, Guildford
GU1 2RQ
**t** (01483) 573735
**e** rooms@yewtreehouse.info
**w** yewtreehouse.info

### GURNARD
### Isle of Wight

**Hillbrow House** ★★★★
*Guest Accommodation*
Tuttons Hill, Cowes PO31 8JA
**t** (01983) 297240

### HADDENHAM
### Buckinghamshire

**New Hadden**
Rating Applied For
*Bed & Breakfast*
3a High Street, Haddenham,
Aylesbury HP17 8ES
**t** (01844) 291347

### HADLOW
### Kent

**Ferndale House** ★★★★
*Bed & Breakfast*
Maidstone Road, Tonbridge
TN11 0DN
**t** (01732) 850876
**e** mikeanniereynolds@
btopenworld.com

### HAILEY
### Oxfordshire

**Hunter Close Farm** ★★★★
*Bed & Breakfast*
Middletown, Hailey, Witney
OX29 9UB
**t** (01993) 772332
**e** felicity@huntersclosefarm.
freeserve.co.uk

### HAILSHAM
### East Sussex

**The Corn Exchange** ★★★
*Inn*
19 High Street, Hailsham
BN27 1AL
**t** (01323) 442290

**Hailsham Grange** ★★★★★
*Guest Accommodation*
Vicarage Road, Hailsham
BN27 1BL
**t** (01323) 844248
**e** noel-hgrange@amserve.com
**w** hailshamgrange.co.uk

**Longleys Farm Cottage**
★★★ *Guest Accommodation*
Harebeating Lane, Hailsham
BN27 1ER
**t** (01323) 841227
**e** longleysfarmcottagebb@dsl.
pipex.com
**w** longleysfarmcottage.co.uk

**Windesworth** ★★★★
*Bed & Breakfast*
Carters Corner, Hailsham
BN27 4HT
**t** (01323) 847178
**e** windesworth.
bedandbreakfast@virgin.net
**w** visitsussex.org/windesworth

### HALE
### Hampshire

**Finches Hatch** ★★★
*Bed & Breakfast*
Forest Road, Hale,
Fordingbridge SP6 2NP
**t** (01725) 510529
**e** suesutherland@ssla.demon.
co.uk
**w** finceshatch.co.uk

### HALLAND
### East Sussex

**Shortgate Manor Farm**
★★★★
*Guest Accommodation*
GOLD AWARD
Halland, East Sussex, Uckfield
BN8 6PJ
**t** (01825) 840320
**e** david@shortgate.co.uk
**w** shortgate.co.uk

### HAMBLEDON
### Hampshire

**Forestside** ★★★
*Bed & Breakfast*
Hambledon, Waterlooville
PO7 4RA
**t** (023) 9263 2672

### HAMBROOK
### West Sussex

**Willowbrook Riding Centre**
★★ *Bed & Breakfast*
Hambrook Hill South,
Hambrook, Chichester
PO18 8UJ
**t** (01243) 572683
**e** info@willowbrook-stables.
co.uk

### HAMPTON POYLE
### Oxfordshire

**Hawks Bed and Breakfast**
◆◆◆◆ *Guest Accommodation*
6 Oxford Road, Hampton
Poyle, Kidlington OX5 2QE
**t** (01865) 378387
**e** nigfinch@aol.com
**w** oxfordcity.co.uk/accom/
hawks/

### HANSLOPE
### Buckinghamshire

**Woad Farm** ★★ *Farmhouse*
Tathall End, Hanslope, Milton
Keynes MK19 7NE
**t** (01908) 510985
**e** s.stacey@btconnect.com

### HARTFIELD
### East Sussex

**Dorset House B&B** ★★★
*Bed & Breakfast*
Dorset House, Hartfield
TN7 4BD
**t** (01892) 770035
**e** meg@rosneathengineering.
co.uk
**w** dorset-house.co.uk

### HASLEMERE
### Surrey

**Deerfell** ★★★★
*Bed & Breakfast*
Blackdown, Haslemere
GU27 3BU
**t** (01428) 653409
**e** deerfell@tesco.net
**w** deerfell.co.uk

**Sheps Hollow** ★★★
*Bed & Breakfast*
Henley Common, Henley,
Haslemere GU27 3HB
**t** (01428) 653120

**Strathire** ★★★★
*Bed & Breakfast*
Grayswood Road, Haslemere
GU27 2BW
**t** (01428) 642466

**The Wheatsheaf Inn** ★★★
*Inn*
Grayswood Road, Haslemere
GU27 2DE
**t** (01428) 644440
**e** ken@
thewheatsheafgrayswood.co.
uk

### HASTINGS
### East Sussex

**The Astral Lodge** ★★
*Guest Accommodation*
4 Carlisle Parade, Hastings
TN34 1JG
**t** (01424) 445599

**Castle Hill Guest House**
★★★ *Bed & Breakfast*
113 Castle Hill Road, Hastings
TN34 3RD
**t** (01424) 720787
**e** info@castlehillguesthouse.
co.uk
**w** castlehillguesthouse.co.uk

**Castle View Guest House**
★★ *Guest House*
Devonshire Road, Hastings
TN34 1NE
**t** (01424) 434046
**e** barbararankine@googlemail.
com

**Churchills Hotel** ★★★
*Guest Accommodation*
3 St Helens Crescent, Hastings
TN34 2EN
**t** (01424) 439359
**e** enquiries@
churchillshotelhastings.co.uk
**w** churchillshotelhastings.co.uk

**Croft Place** ★★★★
*Guest Accommodation*
2 The Croft, Hastings
TN34 3HH
**t** (01424) 433004

**The Elms** ★★★ *Guest House*
9 St Helens Park Road,
Hastings TN34 2ER
**t** (01424) 429979
**e** jmktbriggs@btinternet.com

**Hotel Europa** ★★★★
*Guest Accommodation*
2 Carlisle Parade, Hastings
TN34 1JG
**t** (01424) 717329
**e** info@europahotelhastings.
co.uk
**w** europahotelhastings.co.uk

**Four Winds** ★★★★
*Bed & Breakfast*
Parsonage Lane, Westfield,
Hastings TN35 4SH
**t** (01424) 752585
**e** stewarts@4-winds.fsnet.co.
uk
**w** 4-winds.org

**Gallery 53** ★★★★
*Guest Accommodation*
53 High Street, Hastings
TN34 3EN
**t** (01424) 433486

**The Laindons** ★★★★
*Bed & Breakfast*
23 High Street, Hastings
TN34 3EY
**t** (01424) 437710
**e** janebrumfield@mac.com
**w** laindons.co.uk

**Lavendar and Lace** ★★★★
*Bed & Breakfast*
106 All Saints Street, Hastings
TN34 3BE
**t** (01424) 716290
**e** lavendarlace1066@
btinternet.com
**w** lavendarlace1066.co.uk

**Hotel Lindum** ★★★★
*Guest Accommodation*
1a Carlisle Parade, Hastings
TN34 1JG
**t** (01424) 434070
**e** hotellindum@aol.com
**w** hotellindum.co.uk

**The Lookout** ★★★★
*Bed & Breakfast*
SILVER AWARD
Pett Level, Hastings TN35 4EQ
**t** (01424) 812070

**Medieval Lodge** ★★★
*Bed & Breakfast*
51 All Saints Street, Hastings
TN34 3BN
**t** (01424) 729104

**Millifont Guest House** ★★★
*Guest Accommodation*
8/9 Cambridge Gardens,
Hastings TN34 1EH
**t** (01424) 425645
**e** millifont@yahoo.com
**w** millifont.co.uk

**Minstrel's Rest** ★★★★
*Bed & Breakfast*
21 Greville Road, Hastings
TN35 5AL
**t** (01424) 443500
**e** minstrelsrest@hotmail.com

**The Old Town Guest House**
Rating Applied For
*Guest Accommodation*
1a George Street, Hastings
TN34 3EG
**t** (01424) 423342 &
07870 163818
**e** sophiejlw@tiscali.co.uk

**Pissarro's** ★★★ *Inn*
9/10 South Terrace, Hastings
TN34 1SA
**t** (01424) 421363

**Seaspray Guest House**
★★★★
*Guest Accommodation*
SILVER AWARD
54 Eversfield Place, St
Leonards-on-Sea TN37 6DB
**t** (01424) 436583
**e** jo@seaspraybb.co.uk
**w** seaspraybb.co.uk

**South Riding Guest House**
★★★ *Guest House*
96 Milward Road, Hastings
TN34 3RT
**t** (01424) 420805

**Summerfields House**
★★★★
*Guest Accommodation*
Bohemia Road, Hastings
TN34 1EX
t (01424) 718142
e liz.summerfields@btinternet.
com
w summerfieldshouse.co.uk

**Swan House ★★★★★**
*Guest Accommodation*
**SILVER AWARD**
1 Hill Street, Old Town,
Hastings TN34 3HU
t (01424) 430014
e res@swanhousehastings.co.
uk
w swanhousehastings.co.uk

**Tower House ★★★★**
*Guest Accommodation*
**SILVER AWARD**
Hilders Cliff, St Leonards-on-
Sea TN31 7LD
t (01797) 226865
w towerhouse-rye.co.uk

HAVANT
Hampshire

**High Towers ★★★**
*Guest Accommodation*
14 Portsdown Hill Road,
Havant PO9 3JY
t (023) 9247 1748
e hightowers14@aol.com
w hightowers.co.uk

HAWKINGE
Kent

**Braeheid Bed & Breakfast**
★★★★ *Bed & Breakfast*
2 Westland Way, Hawkinge,
Folkestone CT18 7PW
t (01303) 893928
e bill@forrest68.fsnet.co.uk

HAWKLEY
Hampshire

**Scotland Farm Countryside
Bed and Breakfast ★★★★**
*Farmhouse* **SILVER AWARD**
Hawkley, Liss GU33 6NH
t (01730) 827473
e admin@scotlandfarm.com
w scotlandfarm.com

HAYLING ISLAND
Hampshire

**16 Charleston Close ★★**
*Bed & Breakfast*
Hayling Island PO11 0JY
t (023) 9246 2527

**Ann's Cottage ★★**
*Bed & Breakfast*
45 St Andrews Road, Hayling
Island PO11 9JN
t (023) 9246 7048
e ann.jay@virgin.net

**The Coach House ★★★★**
*Guest Accommodation*
**SILVER AWARD**
Church Lane, Hayling Island
PO11 0SB
t (023) 9246 6266
e jenny.stenning1@btinternet.
com
w wakeup.to/coachhouse

**Copsewood House ★★★★**
*Bed & Breakfast*
Copse Lane, Hayling Island
PO11 0QD
t (023) 9246 9294
e jillgoulding@hotmail.com
w copsewoodhouse.piczo.com

**White House ★★★★**
*Bed & Breakfast*
250 Havant Road, Hayling
Island PO11 0LN
t (023) 9246 3464

HAYWARDS HEATH
West Sussex

**Copyhold Hollow Bed &
Breakfast ★★★★**
*Bed & Breakfast*
**GOLD AWARD**
Copyhold Lane, Borde Hill,
Haywards Heath RH16 1XU
t (01444) 413265
e vs@copyholdhollow.co.uk
w copyholdhollow.co.uk

**Oakfield Cottage ★★★★**
*Guest Accommodation*
Brantridge Lane, Staplefield,
Haywards Heath RH17 6JR
t (01444) 401121
e joydougoakfield@btinternet.
com
w smoothhound.co.uk/hotels/
oakfieldcottage.html

**The Old Forge ★★★**
*Bed & Breakfast*
16 Lucastes Avenue, Haywards
Heath RH16 1JH
t (01444) 451905

HEADCORN
Kent

**Curtis Farm ★★★★**
*Guest Accommodation*
Waterman Quarter, Headcorn,
Ashford TN27 9JJ
t (01622) 890393
e curtis.farm@btopenworld.
com
w curtis-farm-kent.co.uk

**Four Oaks ★★★★**
*Guest Accommodation*
Four Oaks Road, Headcorn
TN27 9PB
t (01622) 891224
e info@fouroaks.uk.com
w fouroaks.uk.com

**Wilderness Bed & Breakfast**
★★★★ *Bed & Breakfast*
Waterman Quarter, Headcorn,
Maidstone TN27 9JJ
t (01622) 891757
e vhonychurch@toucansurf.
com
w wildernessbandb.co.uk

HEADINGTON
Oxfordshire

**Oxford YHA ★★★★** *Hostel*
2a Botley Road, Oxford
OX2 0AB
t (01865) 727275
e oxford@yha.org.uk
w yha.org.uk

HEATHFIELD
East Sussex

**Iwood Bed & Breakfast**
★★★★
*Guest Accommodation*
**GOLD AWARD**
Mutton Hall Lane, Heathfield
TN21 8NR
t (01435) 863918
e iwoodbb@aol.com
w iwoodbb.com

**Spicers ★★★★**
*Bed & Breakfast*
Spicers Cottages, 21 Cade
Street, Heathfield TN21 9BS
t (01435) 866363
e spicersbb@btinternet.com
w spicersbb.co.uk

**Woodbine Farm ★★★★**
*Bed & Breakfast*
Cross in Hand, Heathfield
TN21 0QA
t (01435) 867458
e poppyflower668@hotmail.
com
w woodbine-farm.co.uk

HEDGE END
Hampshire

**Lakeside B&B ★★★★**
*Bed & Breakfast*
48 Stag Drive, Hedge End,
Southampton SO30 2QN
t (01489) 780618
e enquiries@lakesidebandb.
co.uk
w lakesidebandb.co.uk

HENFIELD
West Sussex

**1 The Laurels ★★★★**
*Bed & Breakfast*
Martyn Close, Henfield
BN5 9RQ
t (01273) 493518
e malc.harrington@lineone.net
w no1thelaurels.co.uk

**The George Hotel ★★★★**
*Inn*
High Street, Henfield BN5 9DB
t (01273) 492296
e info@thegeorgehotel.net
w thegeorgehotel.net

HENLEY-ON-THAMES
Oxfordshire

**61 Deanfield Road ★★★**
*Guest Accommodation*
Henley-on-Thames RG9 1UU
t (01491) 576784

**Abbottsleigh ★★★**
*Guest Accommodation*
107 St Marks Road, Henley-on-
Thames RG9 1LP
t (01491) 572982
e abbottsleigh@hotmail.com

**Alftrudis ★★★★**
*Bed & Breakfast*
8 Norman Avenue, Henley-on-
Thames RG9 1SG
t (01491) 573099

**Alushta ★★★★**
*Guest Accommodation*
23 Queen Street, Henley-on-
Thames RG9 1AR
t (01491) 636041
e sdr@alushta.co.uk
w alushta.co.uk

**Amanchris ★★★★**
*Bed & Breakfast*
**SILVER AWARD**
16 Baronsmead, Henley-on-
Thames RG9 2DL
t (01491) 578044
e pamelajstuart@aol.com
w amanchris.co.uk

**Apple Ash ★★★★**
*Guest House* **SILVER AWARD**
Woodlands Road, Harpsden,
Henley-on-Thames RG9 4AB
t (01491) 574198

**Avalon ★★★** *Bed & Breakfast*
36 Queen Street, Henley-on-
Thames RG9 1AP
t (01491) 577829
e avalon@henleybb.fsnet.co.
uk
w henleybb.fsnet.co.uk

**Azalea House ★★★★**
*Bed & Breakfast*
55 Deanfield Road, Henley-on-
Thames RG9 1UU
t (01491) 576407
w azaleahouse.co.uk

**Badgemore Park Golf Club**
★★★ *Guest Accommodation*
Badgemore, Henley-on-
Thames RG9 4NR
t (01491) 637300
e info@badgemorepark.com
w badgemorepark.com

**Bank Farm ★★** *Farmhouse*
The Old Road, Pishill, Henley-
on-Thames RG9 6HS
t (01491) 638601
e e.f.lakey@btinternet.com

**The Baskerville ★★★★**
*Guest Accommodation*
Station Road, Lower Shiplake,
Henley-on-Thames RG9 3NY
t (0118) 940 3332
e enquiries@thebaskerville.
com
w thebaskerville.com

**The Beeches ★★★★**
*Bed & Breakfast*
3a Coldharbour Close, Henley-
on-Thames RG9 1QF
t (01491) 579344
e henleyduddies@talktalk.net
w beechesbandbhenley.co.uk

**Brackenhurst ★★★**
*Bed & Breakfast*
Russells Water, Henley-on-
Thames RG9 6EU
t (01491) 642399
e info@foolonthehill.co.uk
w foolonthehill.co.uk

**Coldharbour House ★★★★**
*Bed & Breakfast*
3 Coldharbour Close, Henley-
on-Thames RG9 1QF
t (01491) 575229
w coldharbourhouse.co.uk

**Denmark House ★★★★**
*Guest Accommodation*
**SILVER AWARD**
Northfield End, Henley-on-
Thames RG9 2HN
t (01491) 572028
e ds.hutchings@virgin.net
w denmark-house.net

**Falaise House ★★★★**
*Guest Accommodation*
37 Market Place, Henley-on-
Thames RG9 2AA
t (01491) 573388

**Glenroy ★★★**
*Bed & Breakfast*
27 Makins Road, Henley-on-
Thames RG9 1PU
t (01491) 574403
e glenis.welch@virgin.net

---

**Lenwade ★★★★★**
*Bed & Breakfast*
3 Western Road, Henley-on-Thames RG9 1JL
t (01491) 573468
e lenwadeuk@aol.com
w w3b-ink.com/lenwade

**Little Parmoor Farm ★★★★**
*Farmhouse*
Parmoor, Frieth RG9 6NL
t (01494) 881600
e frances@francesemmett.com
w parmoor.com

**Old School House ★★★★**
*Bed & Breakfast*
42 Off Hart Street, Henley-on-Thames RG9 2AU
t (01491) 573929
e adrian.lake@btinternet.com

**The Old Wood ★★★**
*Bed & Breakfast*
197 Greys Road, Henley-on-Thames RG9 1QU
t (01491) 573930
e janice@janicejones.co.uk

**Orchard Dene Cottage**
**★★★★ Bed & Breakfast**
Lower Assendon, Henley-on-Thames RG9 6AG
t (01491) 575490
e info@orcharddenecottage.co.uk
w orcharddenecottage.co.uk

**Riverside Guest House**
**★★★ Guest Accommodation**
4 River Terrace, Henley-on-Thames RG9 1BG
t (01491) 571133
e no4.riverside@virgin.net
w no4riverside.co.uk

**Robhill ★★★★**
*Bed & Breakfast*
267 Greys Road, Henley-on-Thames RG9 1QS
t (01491) 577391

**Slaters Farm ★★★**
*Bed & Breakfast*
Church Lane, Rotherfield Peppard, Henley-on-Thames RG9 5JL
t (01491) 628675
e stay@slatersfarm.co.uk

**Stag Hall ★★★**
*Bed & Breakfast*
Stoke Row Road, Kingwood, Henley-on-Thames RG9 5NX
t (01491) 680338
e stag_hall@hotmail.com

**The Unicorn ★★★★ Inn**
**SILVER AWARD**
Colmore Lane, Kingwood RG9 5LX
t (01491) 628452
e the-unicorn-pub@hotmail.com
w the-unicorn.co.uk

**The Walled Garden ★★★★**
*Bed & Breakfast*
Bell Lane, Henley-on-Thames RG9 2HR
t (01491) 573142
e walledgard@aol.com

## HERNE BAY
### Kent

**Evening Tide ★★★★**
*Guest House*
Central Parade, Herne Bay CT6 5JJ
t (01227) 365014
e info@eveningtide.co.uk
w eveningtide.co.uk

**Priory B&B ★★★★**
*Guest Accommodation*
203 Canterbury Road, Herne Bay CT6 5UG
t (01227) 366670
e stephen@guy200.demon.co.uk
w thepriorybandb.co.uk

**Seahaven ★★★★**
*Bed & Breakfast*
64 Linden Avenue, Herne Bay CT6 8TZ
t (01227) 366582
e marilynbudd@hotmail.co.uk

**Summer House ★★★★**
*Bed & Breakfast*
15 Glenbervie Drive, Beltinge, Herne Bay CT6 6QL
t (01227) 363192
e cpye@tesco.net
w beltingesummerhouse.co.uk

**Westgrange House Bed and Breakfast ★★★★**
*Bed & Breakfast*
42 Busheyfield Road, Herne Bay CT6 7LJ
t (01227) 740663

## HERNHILL
### Kent

**Church Oast ★★★★**
*Bed & Breakfast*
Faversham ME13 9JW
t (01227) 750974
e jill@geliot.plus.com

## HERSHAM
### Surrey

**Bricklayers Arms ★★★★ Inn**
6 Queens Road, Walton-on-Thames KT12 5LS
t (01932) 220936
e ff@bricklayers-arms.fsworld.co.uk

## HERSTMONCEUX
### East Sussex

**Sandhurst ★★★★**
*Guest Accommodation*
Church Road, Herstmonceux, Hailsham BN27 1RG
t (01323) 833088
e junealanruss@aol.com

**The Stud Farm ★★★**
*Farmhouse*
Bodle Street Green, Hailsham BN27 4RJ
t (01323) 832647
e timkatemills@aol.com
w studfarmsussex.co.uk

**Waldenheath Country House ★★★★**
*Bed & Breakfast*
Hailsham Road, Amberstone, Hailsham BN27 1PJ
t (01323) 442259
e waldenheath.c.h@btinternet.com
w visitsussex.org/waldenheathcountryhouse

## HEVER
### Kent

**Becketts ★★★★**
*Bed & Breakfast*
**SILVER AWARD**
Pylegate Farm, Hartfield Road, Cowden, Edenbridge TN8 7HE
t (01342) 850514
e jacqui@becketts-bandb.co.uk
w becketts-bandb.co.uk

## HEYSHOTT
### West Sussex

**Little Hoyle ◆◆◆◆**
*Guest Accommodation*
Hoyle Lane, Heyshott, Midhurst GU29 0DX
t (01798) 867359
e ralphs.littlehoyle@btopenworld.com
w smoothhound.co.uk/hotels/littlehoyle

## HIGH HURSTWOOD
### East Sussex

**Chillies Granary ★★★★**
*Guest Accommodation*
Chillies Lane, High Hurstwood, Crowborough TN6 3TB
t (01892) 655560

**The Orchard ★★★★**
*Bed & Breakfast*
Rocks Lane, High Hurstwood, Uckfield TN22 4BN
t (01825) 732946
e turtonorchard@aol.com
w theorchardbandb.co.uk

## HIGH WYCOMBE
### Buckinghamshire

**9 Green Road ★★★★**
*Bed & Breakfast*
High Wycombe HP13 5BD
t (01494) 437022
w lovetostayat9.co.uk

**9 Sandford Gardens ★★★**
*Bed & Breakfast*
Daws Hill, High Wycombe HP11 1QT
t (01494) 441723 & 07980 439 560

**Amersham Hill Guest House**
**★★★ Guest House**
52 Amersham Hill, High Wycombe HP13 6PQ
t (01494) 520635

**The Bell ★★★ Inn**
41 Frogmoor, High Wycombe HP13 5DQ
t (01494) 525588
e info@thebellonline.co.uk
w thebellonline.co.uk

**Longforgan Bed and Breakfast ★★**
*Bed & Breakfast*
**SILVER AWARD**
Magpie Lane, Flackwell Heath, High Wycombe HP10 9EA
t (01628) 525178
e carol@bedandbreakfasthighwycombe.co.uk
w bedandbreakfasthighwycombe.co.uk

**The Three Horseshoes Inn**
**★★★★ Inn GOLD AWARD**
Horseshoe Road, Bennett End, Radnage, High Wycombe HP14 4EB
t (01494) 483273
e threehorseshoe@btconnect.com
w thethreehorseshoes.net

## HILDENBOROUGH
### Kent

**The Barn at Woodview**
**★★★★ Bed & Breakfast**
**SILVER AWARD**
London Road, Watts Cross, Tonbridge TN11 8NQ
t (01732) 833167
e woodview.barn@ntlworld.com

## HINTON WALDRIST
### Oxfordshire

**The Old Rectory ★★★★**
*Bed & Breakfast*
Hinton Waldrist, Faringdon SN7 8SA
t (01865) 821228

## HOLMBURY ST MARY
### Surrey

**Holmbury Farm ★★★★**
*Guest Accommodation*
Holmbury St Mary, Dorking RH5 6NB
t (01306) 621443
e virginialloyd@onetel.com
w smoothhound.co.uk/hotels/holmbury.html

**Holmbury St Mary YHA ★★**
*Hostel*
Radnor Lane, Dorking RH5 6NW
t (01306) 730777
e holmbury@yha.org.uk
w yha.org.uk

**The Royal Oak**
*Rating Applied For*
*Inn*
Felday Glade, Felday Road, Dorking RH5 6PF
t (01306) 730120
e the.royaloak@btconnect.com

## HOLYBOURNE
### Hampshire

**Upper Neatham Mill Farm Guest House ★★★★**
*Guest House*
Upper Neatham Mill Lane, Holybourne, Alton GU34 4EP
t (01420) 542908
e upperneatham@btinternet.com
w upperneatham.co.uk

## HOOK NORTON
### Oxfordshire

**Manor Farm ★★★**
*Farmhouse*
Hook Norton, Banbury OX15 5LU
t (01608) 737204
e jdyhughes@aol.com

## HORLEY
### Oxfordshire

**Sor Brook House Farm**
**★★★★ Bed & Breakfast**
**SILVER AWARD**
Hornton Lane, Banbury OX15 6BL
t (01295) 738121

## HORLEY
### Surrey

**Berrens Guest House ★★★**
*Guest Accommodation*
62 Massetts Road, Horley
RH6 7DS
t (01293) 430800

**Melville Lodge Guest House**
★★★ *Guest House*
15 Brighton Road, Horley
RH6 7HH
t (01293) 784951
e melvillelodge.guesthouse@
tesco.net
w melvillelodgegatwick.co.uk

**Rosemead Guest House**
★★★★ *Guest House*
SILVER AWARD
19 Church Road, Horley
RH6 7EY
t (01293) 784965
e info@rosemeadguesthouse.
co.uk
w rosemeadguesthouse.co.uk

**The Turret Guest House**
★★★ *Guest Accommodation*
48 Massetts Road, Horley
RH6 7DS
t (01293) 782490 &
07970 066471
e info@theturret.com
w theturret.com

## HORNDEAN
### Hampshire

**The Ship & Bell Hotel ★★★**
*Inn*
6 London Road, Horndean,
Waterlooville PO8 0BZ
t (023) 9259 2107
e shipandbell@
accommodating-inns.co.uk
w accommodating-inns.co.uk

## HORSHAM
### West Sussex

**The Deans ★★★**
*Guest Accommodation*
8 Wimblehurst Road, Horsham
RH12 2ED
t (01403) 268166
e contact@thedeans.co.uk
w thedeans.com

**The Larches ★★★**
*Bed & Breakfast*
28 Rusper Road, Horsham
RH12 4BD
t (01403) 263392
e ericjanelane@aol.com

**The Wirrals ★★**
*Bed & Breakfast*
1 Downsview Road, Horsham
RH12 4PF
t (01403) 269400
e thewirralsarchibald@
btinternet.com
w visitsussex.org/thewirrals

## HULVERSTONE
### Isle of Wight

**The Elms ★★★★**
*Bed & Breakfast*
Hulverstone PO30 4EH
t (01983) 741528
e theelmsbnb@aol.com
w theelmsbnb.co.uk

## HUNGERFORD
### Berkshire

**The Garden House ★★★★**
*Bed & Breakfast*
Rear of 34 High Street,
Hungerford RG17 0NF
t (01488) 685369
e bevjess@openscreen.co.uk
w openscreen.co.uk/
thegardenhouse

**Wilton House ★★★★**
*Bed & Breakfast*
SILVER AWARD
33 High Street, Hungerford
RG17 0NF
t (01488) 684228
e welfares@hotmail.com
w wiltonhouse-hungerford.co.
uk

## HUNSTON
### West Sussex

**Spire Cottage ★★★★**
*Bed & Breakfast*
Church Lane, Hunston,
Chichester PO20 1AJ
t (01243) 778937
e jan@spirecottage.co.uk
w spirecottage.co.uk

## HURLEY
### Berkshire

**Meadow View ★★★★★**
*Bed & Breakfast*
SILVER AWARD
Henley Road, Hurley,
Maidenhead SL6 5LW
t (01628) 829764
e info@meadowviewbedand
breakfast.co.uk
w meadowviewbedand
breakfast.co.uk

## HURST
### Hampshire

**Copper Beeches ★★★**
*Bed & Breakfast*
Torberry Farm, Hurst, Midhurst
GU31 5RG
t (01730) 826662
e ianchew@torberry212.fsnet.
co.uk
w copperbeeches.homecall.co.
uk

## HURSTPIERPOINT
### West Sussex

**Wickham Place ★★★★**
*Guest Accommodation*
SILVER AWARD
Wickham Drive,
Hurstpierpoint, Hassocks
BN6 9AP
t (01273) 832172
e accommodation@wickham-
place.co.uk
w smoothhound.co.uk/hotels/
wickham

## HYTHE
### Kent

**The Shrubsoles B&B ★★★**
*Bed & Breakfast*
62 Brockhill Road, Hythe
CT21 4AG
t (01303) 238832
e info@theshrubsoles.co.uk
w theshrubsoles.co.uk

## IBTHORPE
### Hampshire

**Staggs Cottage ★★★★**
*Guest Accommodation*
Windmill Hill, Ibthorpe,
Andover SP11 0BP
t (01264) 736235
e staggscottage@aol.com
w staggscottage.co.uk

## IDEN
### East Sussex

**Iden Coach House ★★★★**
*Bed & Breakfast*
Wittersham Road, Rye
TN31 7XB
t (01797) 280118
e p.abrams@virgin.net
w idencoachhouse.co.uk

## ITCHEN ABBAS
### Hampshire

**Hatch End ★★★★**
*Bed & Breakfast*
Main Road, Itchen Abbas,
Winchester SO21 1AT
t (01962) 779279
e allen@hatchend.freeserve.
co.uk

## IVINGHOE
### Buckinghamshire

**Bull Lake B&B ★★★★**
*Bed & Breakfast*
Ford End, Ivinghoe, Leighton
Buzzard LU7 9EA
t (01296) 668834
e enquiries@bull-lake.co.uk
w bull-lake.co.uk

## JORDANS
### Buckinghamshire

**Jordans YHA ★ *Hostel***
Welders Lane, Beaconsfield
HP9 2SN
t (01494) 873135
e jordans@yha.org.uk
w yha.org.uk

## KENNINGTON
### Kent

**The Conningbrook Hotel**
★★★★
*Guest Accommodation*
Canterbury Road, Kennington,
Ashford TN24 9QR
t (01233) 636863
e conningbrook@
shepherdneame.co.uk
w conningbrookashford.co.uk

## KIDLINGTON
### Oxfordshire

**Breffni House ★★★**
*Bed & Breakfast*
9 Lovelace Drive, Kidlington
OX5 2LY
t (01865) 372569

**Colliers B&B ★★★**
*Bed & Breakfast*
55 Nethercote Road, Tackley,
Kidlington OX5 3AT
t (01869) 331255
e colliersbnb@virgin.net
w colliersbnb.co.uk

**Warsborough House**
★★★★ *Bed & Breakfast*
52 Mill Street, Kidlington
OX5 2EF
t (01865) 370316

## KILMESTON
### Hampshire

**Dean Farm ★★★★**
*Guest Accommodation*
Kilmeston, Alresford SO24 0NL
t (01962) 771286
e warrdeanfarm@btinternet.
com
w warrdeanfarm.btinternet.co.
uk

## KINGHAM
### Oxfordshire

**The Tollgate Inn &
Restaurant ★★★★ *Inn***
Church Street, Chipping
Norton OX7 6YA
t (01608) 658389
e info@thetollgate.com
w thetollgate.com

## KINGSDOWN
### Kent

**The Gardeners Rest**
★★★★★
*Guest Accommodation*
GOLD AWARD
Nemesis, Queensdown Road,
Kingsdown, Deal CT14 8EF
t (01304) 371449
e palmers3@freenetname.co.
uk

**Sparrow Court ★★★★**
*Bed & Breakfast*
Chalk Hill Road, Kingsdown,
Deal CT14 8DP
t (01304) 389253
e gmaude@waitrose.com
w farm-stay-kent.co.uk

## KINGSLEY
### Hampshire

**Spring Cottage ★★★**
*Bed & Breakfast*
Main Road, Kingsley, Bordon
GU35 9NA
t (01420) 472703

## KINGSTON BLOUNT
### Oxfordshire

**The Cherry Tree ★★★**
*Guest Accommodation*
High Street, Kingston Blount,
Chinnor OX39 4SJ
t (01844) 352273
e cherrytreepub@btconnect.
com
w thecherrytreepub.com

## KINTBURY
### Berkshire

**The Dundas Arms ★★★ *Inn***
Station Road, Kintbury,
Hungerford RG17 9UT
t (01488) 658263
e info@dundasarms.co.uk
w dundasarms.co.uk

## LADDINGFORD
### Kent

**Chequers Inn ★★★★ *Inn***
Yalding, Maidstone ME18 6BP
t (01622) 871266

## LAKE
### Isle of Wight

**Ashleigh House ★★★★**
*Guest Accommodation*
81 Sandown Road, Lake,
Sandown PO36 9LE
t (01983) 402340
e richard@
ashleighhousehotel.com
w ashleighhousehotel.com

**Haytor Lodge** ★★★★
*Guest Accommodation*
16 Cliff Path, Lake PO36 8PL
**t** (01983) 402969

**Osterley Lodge** ★★★★
*Guest Accommodation*
62 Sandown Road, Sandown
PO36 9JX
**t** (01983) 402017
**e** osterleylodgeiw@aol.com
**w** netguides.co.uk/wight/
basic/osterley.html

**Piers View Guest House**
★★★★
*Guest Accommodation*
20 Cliff Path, Lake PO36 8PL
**t** (01983) 404646

### LAMBERHURST
Kent

**Woodpecker Barn** ★★★★★
*Bed & Breakfast*
SILVER AWARD
Wickhurst Farm, Tunbridge
Wells TN3 8BH
**t** (01892) 891958
**e** martinloveday@btinternet.
com
**w** woodpeckerbarn.co.uk

### LANCING
West Sussex

**Edelweiss Guest House** ◆◆◆
*Guest Accommodation*
Kings Road, Lancing BN15 8EB
**t** (01903) 753412

### LANE END
Buckinghamshire

**Rances** ★★★★
*Bed & Breakfast*
Moor Common, Lane End
HP14 3HR
**t** (01494) 881294
**e** d.is@btopenworld.com

### LANGLEY
Kent

**Orchard House** ★★★★
*Bed & Breakfast*
Sutton Road, Maidstone
ME17 3LZ
**t** (01622) 862694
**e** orchard_house2004@yahoo.
co.uk

### LANGRISH
Hampshire

**Upper Parsonage Farm**
★★★★ *Farmhouse*
SILVER AWARD
Harvesting Lane, East Meon,
Petersfield GU32 1QR
**t** (01730) 823490
**e** sue@atko.demon.co.uk

**Yew Tree Farm House** ★★★
*Bed & Breakfast*
Langrish, Petersfield GU32 1RB
**t** (01730) 264959
**e** jane.sprinks@tesco.net

### LAUGHTON
East Sussex

**The Roebuck Inn** ★★★★ *Inn*
Lewes Road, Lewes BN8 6BG
**t** (01323) 811464
**e** p@mundy6083.fsnet.co.uk

### LAVANT
West Sussex

**Flint Cottage** ★★★★
*Bed & Breakfast*
47 Mid Lavant, Lavant,
Chichester PO18 0AA
**t** (01243) 785883
**e** chriskemble2@tiscali.co.uk
**w** smoothhound.co.uk/hotels/
flint.html

### LECKHAMPSTEAD
Buckinghamshire

**Weatherhead Farm** ★★★★
*Farmhouse*
Leckhampstead, Buckingham
MK18 5NP
**t** (01280) 860502
**e** weatherheadfarm@aol.com

### LEDBURN
Buckinghamshire

**Bee Hive Cottage** ★★★★
*Bed & Breakfast*
2 Ledburn, Leighton Buzzard
LU7 0PX
**t** (01525) 374615
**e** the-naylors@hotmail.co.uk

### LEE COMMON
Buckinghamshire

**Lower Bassibones Farm B&B**
★★★★
*Guest Accommodation*
Ballinger Road, Great
Missenden HP16 9LA
**t** (01494) 837798
**e** lowerbassibones@yahoo.co.
uk
**w** discover-real-england.com

### LEE-ON-THE-SOLENT
Hampshire

**Avon Manor Guest House**
★★★ *Guest House*
12 South Place, Lee-on-the-
Solent PO13 9AS
**t** (023) 9255 2773
**e** karen@avonmanor.co.uk
**w** avonmanor.co.uk

**Chester Lodge** ★★★★
*Bed & Breakfast*
20 Chester Crescent, Lee-on-
the-Solent PO13 9BH
**t** (023) 9255 0894
**e** chesterlodge@btinternet.
com

**Leeward House B&B** ★★★★
*Bed & Breakfast*
18 Russell Road, Lee-on-the-
Solent PO13 9HP
**t** (023) 9255 6090
**e** enq@leewardhouse.co.uk
**w** leewardhouse.co.uk

**Milvil Corner** ★★★★
*Guest Accommodation*
SILVER AWARD
41 Milvil Road, Lee-on-the-
Solent PO13 9LU
**t** (023) 9255 3489
**e** enquiries@milvilcorner.co.
uk
**w** milvilcorner.co.uk

### LEEDS
Kent

**Further Fields** ★★★
*Guest Accommodation*
Caring Lane, Maidstone
ME17 1TJ
**t** (01622) 861288
**e** furtherfields@aol.com
**w** furtherfields.co.uk

**West Forge** ★★★
*Guest Accommodation*
Back Street, Maidstone
ME17 1TF
**t** (01622) 861428

### LEIGH
Kent

**Charcott Farmhouse** ★★★★
*Bed & Breakfast*
Charcott, Tonbridge TN11 8LG
**t** (01892) 870024
**e** charcottfarmhouse@
btinternet.com
**w** smoothhound.co.uk/hotels/
charcott

### LENHAM
Kent

**Bramley Knowle Farm**
★★★★
*Guest Accommodation*
Eastwood Road, Maidstone
ME17 1ET
**t** (01622) 858878
**e** diane@bramleyknowlefarm.
co.uk
**w** bramleyknowlefarm.co.uk

**The Dog & Bear Hotel**
★★★★ *Inn*
The Square, Lenham,
Maidstone ME17 2PG
**t** (01622) 858219
**e** dogbear@shepherd-neame.
co.uk
**w** shepherd-neame.co.uk

**East Lenham Farm** ★★★★
*Guest Accommodation*
SILVER AWARD
Lenham, Maidstone ME17 2DP
**t** (01622) 858686
**e** eastlenham@farmline.com
**w** eastlenhamfarm.co.uk

### LEWES
East Sussex

**13 Hill Road** ★★★
*Bed & Breakfast*
Lewes BN7 1DB
**t** (01273) 477723
**e** kmyles@btclick.com

**Berkeley House** ★★★★
*Guest Accommodation*
2 Albion Street, Lewes
BN7 2ND
**t** (01273) 476057
**e** enquiries@
berkeleyhouselewes.co.uk
**w** berkeleyhouselewes.co.uk

**The Blacksmiths Arms**
★★★★ *Inn* SILVER AWARD
London Road, Offham, Lewes
BN7 3QD
**t** (01273) 472971
**e** blacksmithsarms@tiscali.co.
uk
**w** theblacksmithsarms-offham.
co.uk

**The Crown Inn** ★★★ *Inn*
191 High Street, Lewes
BN7 2NA
**t** (01273) 480670
**e** crowninnlewes@yahoo.co.
uk
**w** crowninn-lewes.co.uk

**Eckington House** ★★★★
*Guest Accommodation*
SILVER AWARD
Ripe, Nr Glyndebourne, Lewes
BN8 6AR
**t** (01323) 811274
**e** suebrianhill@btopenworld.
com
**w** eckingtonhouse.co.uk

**Hale Farm House** ★★★★
*Guest Accommodation*
Hale Green, Lewes BN8 6HQ
**t** (01825) 872619
**e** s.burrough@virgin.net
**w** halefarmhouse.co.uk

**Langtons House** ★★★★
*Guest Accommodation*
SILVER AWARD
143b High Street, Lewes
BN7 1XT
**t** (01273) 476644
**e** info@langtonshouse.com
**w** langtonshouse.com

**Millers** ★★★★
*Guest Accommodation*
SILVER AWARD
134 High Street, Lewes
BN7 1XS
**t** (01273) 475631
**e** millers134@aol.com
**w** hometown.aol.com/
millers134

**Pelham House** ★★★★
*Guest Accommodation*
SILVER AWARD
St Andrews Lane, Lewes
BN7 1UW
**t** (01273) 488600
**e** reception@pelhamhouse.
com
**w** pelhamhouse.com

**Tamberry Hall** ★★★★★
*Guest Accommodation*
GOLD AWARD
Eastbourne Road, Halland,
Lewes BN8 6PS
**t** (01825) 880090
**e** bedandbreakfast@
tamberryhall.fsbusiness.co.uk
**w** tamberryhall.co.uk

### LEYSDOWN ON SEA
Kent

**Muswell Manor Holiday Park**
★★★ *Guest Accommodation*
Shellness Road, Leysdown,
Sheerness ME12 4RJ
**t** (01795) 510245
**e** mail@muswellmanor.co.uk
**w** muswellmanorholidaypark.
com

### LINDFIELD
West Sussex

**Little Lywood** ★★★★
*Guest Accommodation*
Ardingly Road, Lindfield,
Haywards Heath RH16 2QX
**t** (01444) 892571
**e** nick@littlelywood.freeserve.
co.uk

## LITTLE MARLOW
### Buckinghamshire

**The Barn @ The Old Cottage**
★★★★ *Bed & Breakfast*
Church Road, Marlow SL7 3RT
t (01628) 483019
e porridgepiggy@hotmail.com

## LITTLEBOURNE
### Kent

**The Evenhill** ★★★★ *Inn*
62 The Hill, Littlebourne,
Canterbury CT3 1TA
t (01227) 728073
w shepherdneame.co.uk

## LITTLEHAMPTON
### West Sussex

**Amberley Court** ★★★★
*Guest Accommodation*
SILVER AWARD
Crookthorn Lane, Nr
Littlehampton BN17 5SN
t (01903) 725131
e msimmonds06@aol.com
w visitsussex.org

**Arun Sands** ★★★
*Guest Accommodation*
84 South Terrace,
Littlehampton BN17 5LJ
t (01903) 732489
e info@arun-sands.co.uk
w arun-sands.co.uk

**Arun View Inn** ★★ *Inn*
Wharf Road, Littlehampton
BN17 5DD
t (01903) 722335
w thearunview.co.uk

**Selborne House** ★★★
*Bed & Breakfast*
21 Selborne Road,
Littlehampton BN17 5LZ
t (01903) 726064
e fipickett@hotmail.com
w selbornehouse.net

**YHA Littlehampton** ★★★★
*Hostel*
63 Surrey Street, Littlehampton
BN17 5AW
t (01903) 733177
e littlehampton@yha.org.uk
w yha.org.uk
▣◪

## LONG HANBOROUGH
### Oxfordshire

**The Close Guest House**
★★★ *Guest House*
Witney Road, Long
Hanborough, Witney
OX29 8HF
t (01993) 882485

**Old Farmhouse** ★★★★
*Bed & Breakfast*
Station Hill, Long Hanborough,
Witney OX29 8JZ
t (01993) 882097
e rvmaundrell@btinternet.com
w countryaccom.co.uk/old-
farmhouse

## LONG WITTENHAM
### Oxfordshire

**The Grange** ★★★
*Bed & Breakfast*
High Street, Long Wittenham,
Abingdon OX14 4QH
t (01865) 407808
e grahamneil@talk21.com
w smoothhound.co.uk/hotels/
grange5.html
▣◪

**Witta's Ham Cottage** ◆◆◆◆
*Guest Accommodation*
SILVER AWARD
High Street, Long Wittenham,
Abingdon OX14 4QH
t (01865) 407686
e bandb@wittenham.com

## LONGFIELD
### Kent

**The Rising Sun Inn** ★★★ *Inn*
Fawkham Green, Fawkham,
Longfield DA3 8NL
t (01474) 872291

## LONGPARISH
### Hampshire

**Yew Cottage Bed &
Breakfast** ★★★
*Bed & Breakfast*
Longparish, Andover SP11 6QE
t (01264) 720325
e yewcottage@ukgateway.net

## LOWER BOURNE
### Surrey

**Kiln Farm Bed and Breakfast**
★★★★ *Bed & Breakfast*
8 Kiln Lane, Lower Bourne
GU10 3LR
t (01252) 726083
e raphe_palmer@tiscali.co.uk
w kilnfarm.plus.com

## LYDD ON SEA
### Kent

**Plovers** ★★★★
*Bed & Breakfast*
Toby Road, Lydd-on-Sea
TN29 9PG
t (01797) 366935
e troddy@plovers.co.uk
w plovers.co.uk
▣◪

## LYMINGE
### Kent

**Roundwood Hall Bed &
Breakfast** ★★★★
*Bed & Breakfast*
Stone Street, Lyminge
CT18 8DJ
t (01303) 862260
e bnb@roundwoodhall.co.uk
w roundwoodhall.co.uk

## LYMINGTON
### Hampshire

**Bluebird Restaurant** ★★★
*Bed & Breakfast*
4 - 5 Quay Street, Lymington
SO41 3AS
t (01590) 676908
w bluebirdrestaurant.co.uk

**Britannia House** ★★★★★
*Guest Accommodation*
SILVER AWARD
Mill Lane, Lymington
SO41 9AY
t (01590) 672091

**Durlston House** ★★★
*Guest Accommodation*
Gosport Street, Lymington
SO41 9EG
t (01590) 677364
e durlstonhouse@aol.com
w durlstonhouse.co.uk

**Gorse Meadow Guest House**
★★★ *Guest House*
Sway Road, Pennington,
Lymington SO41 8LR
t (01590) 673354

**Moonraker Cottage** ★★★★
*Bed & Breakfast*
62 Milford Road, Lymington
SO41 8DU
t (01590) 678677
e moonraker62@tiscali.co.uk

**Pennavon House** ★★★★
*Bed & Breakfast*
SILVER AWARD
Lower Pennington Lane,
Pennington, Lymington
SO41 8AL
t (01590) 673984
w pennavon.co.uk

**The Pink House** ★★★★
*Bed & Breakfast*
8 Keyhaven Road, Milford-on-
Sea, Lymington SO41 0QY
t (01590) 641358
e petethepinkhouse@aol.com

**The Rowans** ◆◆◆
*Guest Accommodation*
76 Southampton Road,
Lymington SO41 9GZ
t (01590) 672276
e the.rowans@totalise.co.uk

## LYNDHURST
### Hampshire

**Burwood Lodge** ★★★★
*Guest Accommodation*
27 Romsey Road, Lyndhurst
SO43 7AA
t (023) 8028 2445
e burwoodlodge@yahoo.co.
uk
w burwoodlodge.co.uk

**Clayhill House** ★★★★
*Bed & Breakfast*
Clay Hill, Lyndhurst SO43 7DE
t (023) 8028 2304
e clayhillhouse@tinyworld.co.
uk
w clayhillhouse.co.uk
▣◪

**Englefield** ◆◆◆◆
*Guest Accommodation*
Chapel Lane, Lyndhurst
SO43 7FG
t (023) 8028 2685
e chris.salmon@virgin.net

**Hurst End** ★★★
*Bed & Breakfast*
Clayhill, Lyndhurst SO43 7DE
t (023) 8028 2606
e hurst.end@btinternet.com
w hurstend.co.uk

**Lyndhurst House** ★★★★
*Guest Accommodation*
35 Romsey Road, Lyndhurst
SO43 7AR
t (023) 8028 2230
e enquiries@
lyndhursthousebb.co.uk
w lyndhursthousebb.co.uk

**The Mailmans Arms** ★★★★
*Inn*
71 High Street, Lyndhurst
SO43 7BE
t (023) 8028 4196
e info@mailmans-arms.co.uk

**Okeover** ★★★
*Bed & Breakfast*
12 Forest Gardens, Lyndhurst
SO43 7AF
t (023) 8028 2406
e info@
okeoveraccommodation.co.uk
w okeoveraccommodation.co.
uk

**The Penny Farthing Hotel**
★★★★
*Guest Accommodation*
Romsey Road, Lyndhurst
SO43 7AA
t (023) 8028 4422
e stay@pennyfarthinghotel.co.
uk
w pennyfarthinghotel.co.uk

**Rose Cottage** ◆◆◆◆
*Guest Accommodation*
Chapel Lane, Lyndhurst
SO43 7FG
t (023) 8028 3413
e cindy@rosecottageb-b.co.uk
w rosecottageb-b.co.uk

**Rosedale Bed & Breakfast**
★★★ *Bed & Breakfast*
24 Shaggs Meadow, Lyndhurst
SO43 7BN
t (023) 8028 3793 &
(023) 8013 4253
e rosedalebandb@btinternet.
com

## MAIDENHEAD
### Berkshire

**The Black Boys Inn** ★★★★
*Restaurant with Rooms*
SILVER AWARD
Henley Road, Hurley,
Maidenhead SL6 5NQ
t (01628) 824212

**Braywick Grange** ★★★★
*Bed & Breakfast*
100 Braywick Road,
Maidenhead SL6 1DJ
t (01628) 625915
e reception@braywickgrange.
co.uk
w braywickgrange.co.uk

**Cartlands Cottage** ★★
*Bed & Breakfast*
Kings Lane, Cookham Dean,
Maidenhead SL6 9AY
t (01628) 482196

**Clifton Guest House** ◆◆◆
*Guest Accommodation*
21 Craufurd Rise, Maidenhead
SL6 7LR
t (01628) 620086
e reservation@
cliftonguesthouse.co.uk
w cliftonguesthouse.co.uk

**Gables End** ★★
*Bed & Breakfast*
4 Gables Close, Maidenhead
SL6 8QD
t (01628) 639630
e christablight@onetel.com

**Hillcrest** ★★★ *Guest House*
19 Craufurd Rise, Maidenhead
SL6 7LR
t (01628) 620086
e reservation@
cliftonguesthouse.co.uk
w cliftonguesthouse.co.uk

**Ray Corner Guest House**
★★★ *Guest House*
141 Bridge Road, Maidenhead
SL6 8NQ
t (01628) 632784
e info@raycornerguesthouse.
co.uk
w raycornerguesthouse.co.uk

**Sheephouse Manor** ★★★
*Bed & Breakfast*
Sheephouse Road,
Maidenhead SL6 8HJ
t (01628) 776902
e info@sheephousemanor.co.
uk
w sheephousemanor.co.uk

**Sunny Cottage** ★★★★
*Guest House*
Manor Lane, Maidenhead
SL6 2QW
t (01628) 770731
e beadvr@aol.com
w sunnycottagebb.co.uk

MAIDSTONE
Kent

**29 Pickering Street** ★★★
*Guest Accommodation*
Maidstone ME15 9RS
t (01622) 747453
e ron@camcorder.plus.com

**At Home** ★★★★
*Guest Accommodation*
39 Marston Drive, Vinters Park,
Maidstone ME14 5NE
t (01622) 202196
e steveandlesley@
steleybrown.freeserve.co.uk

**The Granary** ★★★★
*Guest Accommodation*
Lower Farm Road, Boughton
Monchelsea, Maidstone
ME17 4DD
t (01622) 743532
e sue@granarybandb.co.uk
w granarybandb.co.uk

**Grove House** ★★★★
*Bed & Breakfast*
SILVER AWARD
Grove Green Road, Maidstone
ME14 5JT
t (01622) 738441

**The Hazels** ★★★★
*Guest Accommodation*
13 Yeoman Way, Maidstone
ME15 8PQ
t (01622) 737943
e carolbuse@hotmail.com
w the-hazels.co.uk

**Howard Hotel** ★★★
*Guest Accommodation*
22/24 London Road,
Maidstone ME16 8QL
t (01622) 758778
e howardhotel@btopenworld.
com
w thehowardhotel.net

**The Limes** ★★★★
*Guest Accommodation*
118 Boxley Road, Maidstone
ME14 2BD
t (01622) 750629

**Oakwood House** ★★★
*Guest Accommodation*
Oakwood Park, Maidstone
ME16 8AE
t (01622) 626600
e oakwoodhouse@kent.gov.
uk
w oakwoodhouse-kcc.com

**Penenden Heath Lodge**
★★★★ *Bed & Breakfast*
2 Penenden Heath Road,
Penenden Heath, Maidstone
ME14 2DA
t (01622) 672562
e penendenheathlodge@
blueyonder.co.uk
w penendenheathlodge.com

**Ringlestone House**
★★★★★
*Guest Accommodation*
Ringlestone Road, Harrietsham,
Maidstone ME17 1NX
t (01622) 859911
e bookings@
ringlestonehouse.co.uk
w ringlestone.co.uk

**Roslin Villa** ★★★★
*Guest House*
11 St Michaels Road,
Maidstone ME16 8BS
t (01622) 758301
e info@roslinvillaguesthouse.
com
w roslinvillaguesthouse.com

MARDEN
Kent

**3 Chainhurst Cottages**
★★★★ *Bed & Breakfast*
SILVER AWARD
Dairy Lane, Tonbridge
TN12 9SU
t (01622) 820483
e member@heatherscott0.
wanadoo.co.uk

**Tanner House** ★★★★
*Farmhouse*
Tanner Farm, Goudhurst Road,
Tonbridge TN12 9ND
t (01622) 831214
e enquiries@tannerfarmpark.
co.uk
w tannerfarmpark.co.uk

MARGATE
Kent

**The Hussar** ★★★★ *Inn*
219 Canterbury Road, Margate
CT9 5JP
t (01843) 836296
e rdobbs@ukgateway.net
w hussarhotel.com

**Innsbrook House** ★★★
*Guest Accommodation*
Dalby Square, Cliftonville,
Margate CT9 2ER
t (01843) 298946
e info@innsbrookhouse.co.uk
w innsbrookhouse.co.uk

**The Malvern Guest House
and Blues Grill** ★★★
*Guest House*
29 Eastern Esplanade,
Cliftonville, Margate CT9 2HL
t (01843) 290192
e themalvern@aol.com
w malvern-hotel.co.uk

**YHA Margate The
Beachcomber** ★★ *Hostel*
3-4 Royal Esplanade,
Westbrook Bay, Margate
CT9 5DL
t (01843) 221616
e margate@yha.org.uk
w yha.org.uk

MARK CROSS
East Sussex

**Rose Cottage** ★★★★
*Bed & Breakfast*
Mill Lane, Mark Cross,
Crowborough TN6 3PJ
t (01892) 852592

MARLOW
Buckinghamshire

**10 Lock Road** ★★★
*Bed & Breakfast*
Lock Road, Marlow SL7 1QP
t (01628) 473875
w marlow-bed-breakfast.co.uk

**18 Rookery Court** ★★★★
*Bed & Breakfast*
SILVER AWARD
Marlow SL7 3HR
t (01628) 486451
e gillbullen@rookerycourt.
fsnet.co.uk
w bandb-marlow.co.uk

**Acorn Lodge** ◆◆◆◆
*Guest Accommodation*
79 Marlow Bottom Road,
Marlow Bottom SL7 3NA
t (01628) 472197
e acornlodge@btconnect.com
w smoothhound.co.uk/hotels/
acornlodge1.html

**Glade End** ★★★★★
*Guest Accommodation*
2 Little Marlow Road, Marlow
SL7 1HD
t (01628) 471334
e sue@gladeend.com
w gladeend.com

**Granny Anne's** ★★★
*Bed & Breakfast*
54 Seymour Park Road, Marlow
SL7 3EP
t (01628) 473086
e enquiries@grannyannes.
com
w marlowbedbreakfast.co.uk

**Hazeldene** ★★
*Bed & Breakfast*
53 Stapleton Close, Marlow
SL7 1TZ
t (01628) 482183

**Heathercroft** ★★★★
*Bed & Breakfast*
Marlow SL7 2QR
t (01628) 473641
e ellimarlow@aol.com
w heathercroft-marlow.com

**Little Burford** ★★★★
*Bed & Breakfast*
19 Gypsy Lane, Marlow
SL7 3JT
t (01628) 485959
e gypsylanebnb@aol.com

**Malvern House** ★★★★
*Guest Accommodation*
Fernie Fields, New Road
HP12 4SP
t 07792 815846
e office@malvernguesthouse.
co.uk
w malvernguesthouse.co.uk

**Old Barn Cottage** ★★★★
*Bed & Breakfast*
Church Road, Little Marlow
SL7 3RZ
t (01628) 483817
e anthea@oldbarncottage.co.
uk
w oldbarncottage.co.uk

**Red Barn Farm** ★★★
*Farmhouse*
Marlow Road, Marlow
SL7 3DQ
t (01494) 882820
e redbarnfarm@btinternet.
com

**Riverdale** ★★★★
*Bed & Breakfast*
Marlow Bridge Lane, Marlow
SL7 1RH
t (01628) 485206
e chrisrawlings@onetel.com
w bed-breakfast-marlow.co.uk

**Swiss Cottage B&B** ★★★★
*Bed & Breakfast*
New Road, Marlow SL7 3NG
t 07752 032407
e swisscottagebb@hotmail.
com
w swisscottagemarlow.co.uk

MARLOW BOTTOM
Buckinghamshire

**Sue Simmons Bed &
Breakfast** ★★
*Bed & Breakfast*
61 Hill Farm Road, Marlow
Bottom, Marlow SL7 3LX
t (01628) 475145
e suesimmons@
accommodationmarlow.com
w accommodationmarlow.com

**T J O'Reilly's** ★★★ *Inn*
61 Marlow Bottom Road,
Marlow SL7 3NA
t (01628) 484926

MARSH GIBBON
Buckinghamshire

**Judges Close** ★★★
*Farmhouse*
West Edge, Marsh Gibbon,
Bicester OX27 0HA
t (01869) 278508

MARSHBOROUGH
Kent

**Honey Pot Cottage** ★★★★
*Guest Accommodation*
Marshborough Road,
Marshborough, Sandwich
CT13 0PQ
t (01304) 813374
e honeypotcottage@lycos.
com
w honeypotcottage.co.uk

**Southside Bed & Breakfast**
★★★★ *Bed & Breakfast*
Southside, Marshborough
Road, Sandwich CT13 0PQ
t (01304) 812802
e reservations.
southsidebandb@yahoo.co.uk
w southsidebandb.co.uk

## MEOPHAM
### Kent

**Ashbank**
Rating Applied For
*Bed & Breakfast*
White Hill Road, Meopham,
Gravesend DA13 0PA
t (01474) 812142
e ashbank_bandb@yahoo.co.
uk
w ashbankbandb.co.uk

## MERSHAM
### Kent

**Garden Cottage at Munday Manor**
Rating Applied For
*Guest Accommodation*
Munday Manor, Mersham,
Ashford TN25 7HU
t (01233) 720353
e johnrais@aol.com
w mundaymanor.co.uk

## MICHELDEVER
### Hampshire

**Willow Cottage (Micheldever)** ★★★
*Bed & Breakfast*
Duke Street, Micheldever,
Winchester SO21 3DF
t (01962) 774520
e willcott@globalnet.co.uk
w winchesterbedandbreakfast.
co.uk

## MIDDLE ASTON
### Oxfordshire

**Home Farm House** ★★★
*Bed & Breakfast*
Middle Aston, Bicester
OX25 5PX
t (01869) 340666
e carolineparsons@tiscali.co.
uk
w countryaccom.co.uk/
homefarmhouse

## MIDGHAM
### Berkshire

**Eastfield** ★★★
*Bed & Breakfast*
Birds Lane, Midgham, Nr
Reading RG7 5UL
t (0118) 971 3160

## MIDHURST
### West Sussex

**18 Pretoria Avenue** ★★★
*Bed & Breakfast*
Pretoria Avenue, Midhurst
GU29 9PP
t (01730) 814868

**20 Guillards Oak** ★★★★
*Bed & Breakfast*
Midhurst GU29 9JZ
t (01730) 812550
e coljenmidhurst@tiscali.co.uk
w visitsussex.org/
20guillardsoak

**Carron Dune** ★★★
*Bed & Breakfast*
Carron Lane, Midhurst
GU29 9LD
t (01730) 813558

**Oakhurst Cottage** ★★★
*Bed & Breakfast*
Carron Lane, Midhurst
GU29 9LF
t (01730) 813523

**Pear Tree Cottage** ★★★
*Bed & Breakfast*
Lamberts Lane, Midhurst
GU29 9EF
t (01730) 817216

**Sunnyside** ★★★
*Bed & Breakfast*
Cocking Causeway, Midhurst
GU29 9QH
t (01730) 814370

**Ye Olde Tea Shoppe** ★★★
*Guest Accommodation*
North Street, Midhurst
GU29 9DY
t (01730) 817081
e yeoldeteashoppe@
btconnect.com

## MILFORD ON SEA
### Hampshire

**Alma Mater** ★★★★
*Bed & Breakfast*
4 Knowland Drive, Milford on
Sea, Lymington SO41 0RH
t (01590) 642811
e bandbalmamater@aol.com
w almamater.org.uk

**The Bay Trees** ★★★★
*Bed & Breakfast*
GOLD AWARD
8 High Street, Milford-on-Sea,
Lymington SO41 0QD
t (01590) 642186
e rp.fry@virgin.net
w baytreebedandbreakfast.co.
uk

**Ha'penny House** ★★★★★
*Guest Accommodation*
SILVER AWARD
Whitby Road, Milford-on-Sea,
Lymington SO41 0ND
t (01590) 641210

## MILTON COMMON
### Oxfordshire

**Byways** ★★★★
*Bed & Breakfast*
Old London Road, Milton
Common, Thame OX9 2JR
t (01844) 279386
w bywaysbedandbreakfast.co.
uk

## MILTON KEYNES
### Buckinghamshire

**Chantry Farm** ★★★
*Bed & Breakfast*
Pindon End, Hanslope, Milton
Keynes MK19 7HL
t (01908) 510269
e chuff.wake@tiscali.co.uk
w chantryfarmbandb.com

**Fairview Cottage** ★★★★
*Bed & Breakfast*
SILVER AWARD
1 Newport Road, Woughton on
the Green, Milton Keynes
MK6 3BS
t (01908) 665520
e info@fairviewmk.com

**Furtho Manor Farm** ★★★
*Farmhouse*
Northampton Road, Old
Stratford, Milton Keynes
MK19 6NR
t (01908) 542139
e furtho@farming.co.uk
w furthomanorfarm.co.uk

**Kingfishers** ★ *Guest House*
9 Rylstone Close, Heelands,
Milton Keynes MK13 7QT
t 07866 424417 &
07866 424417
e enquiry@kingfishersmk.co.
uk
w kingfishersmk.co.uk

**Spinney Lodge Farm** ★★★
*Farmhouse*
Forest Road, Hanslope, Milton
Keynes MK19 7DE
t (01908) 510267

**The White Hart** ★★★★ *Inn*
1 Gun Lane, Sherington,
Newport Pagnell MK16 9PE
t (01908) 611953
e whitehartresort@aol.com
w whitehartsherington.com

## MINSTER-IN-SHEPPEY
### Kent

**Glen Haven** ★★
*Bed & Breakfast*
Lower Road, Minster-on-Sea,
Sheerness ME12 3ST
t (01795) 877064
e johnstanford@btinternet.
com

## MINSTER LOVELL
### Oxfordshire

**Hill Grove Farm** ★★★★
*Farmhouse*
Crawley Dry Lane, Minster
Lovell, Witney OX29 0NA
t (01993) 703120
e kbrown@eggconnect.net
w countryaccom.co.uk/hill-
grove-farm/

## MORETON
### Oxfordshire

**Elm Tree Farmhouse** ★★★★
*Farmhouse*
Moreton, Thame OX9 2HR
t (01844) 213692
e wavb@btinternet.com
w elmtreefarmhouse.co.uk

## MOTTISTONE
### Isle of Wight

**Mottistone Manor Farmhouse** ★★★★
*Bed & Breakfast*
Mottistone PO30 4ED
t (01983) 740207
e bookings@bolthols.co.uk
w bolthols.co.uk

## MOULSOE
### Buckinghamshire

**The Old Stables** ★★★★
*Guest House*
Newport Road, Moulsoe,
Newport Pagnell MK16 0HR
t (01908) 217766
e hermitage.moulsoe@tiscali.
co.uk

## NETTLEBED
### Oxfordshire

**Parkcorner Farm House**
★★★ *Bed & Breakfast*
Park Corner, Nettlebed,
Henley-on-Thames RG9 6DX
t (01491) 641450
e parkcorner_farmhouse@
hotmail.com

## NETTLESTEAD
### Kent

**Rock Farm House** ★★★★
*Guest Accommodation*
Rock Farm, Gibbs Hill,
Maidstone ME18 5HT
t (01622) 812244
w rockfarmhousebandb.co.uk

## NEW MILTON
### Hampshire

**Bashley House** ★★★
*Bed & Breakfast*
Bashley Common Road, New
Milton BH25 5SQ
t 07919 094390
e burleyv@globalnet.co.uk
w bashleyhouse.co.uk

**Beech Lodge** ★★★★
*Guest House*
16 Mount Avenue, New Milton
BH25 6NT
t (01425) 622130
e johnevans856@aol.com
w beechlodge.org.uk

**Jobz-A-Gudn** ★★★★
*Bed & Breakfast*
169 Stem Lane, New Milton
BH25 5ND
t (01425) 615435

**Nyewood Cottage Bed & Breakfast** ◆◆◆◆
*Guest Accommodation*
37 Barton Court Road, New
Milton BH25 6NW
t (01425) 615321

**The Old Barn** ★★★
*Guest Accommodation*
Gore Road, New Milton
BH25 6SJ
t (01425) 618800
e enquiries@
oldbarnnewmilton.co.uk
w oldbarnnewmilton.co.uk

**St Ursula** ★★★
*Bed & Breakfast*
30 Hobart Road, New Milton
BH25 6EG
t (01425) 613515

**Taverners Cottage** ★★★★
*Bed & Breakfast*
SILVER AWARD
Bashley Cross Road, Bashley,
New Milton BH25 5SZ
t (01425) 615403
e judith@tavernerscottage.co.
uk
w tavernerscottage.co.uk

**Willy's Well** ★★★★
*Bed & Breakfast*
Bashley Common Road,
Bashley, New Milton BH25 5SF
t (01425) 616834
e moyramac2@hotmail.com

**Woodlands** ★★★★
*Bed & Breakfast*
Ashley Lane, New Milton
BH25 5AQ
t (01425) 616425

## NEWBURY
### Berkshire

**160 Craven Road** ★★
*Bed & Breakfast*
Newbury RG14 5NR
t (01635) 40522

**19 Kimbers Drive ★★**
*Bed & Breakfast*
Speen, Newbury RG14 1RQ
t   (01635) 521571
w  the-process.com/sandra

**93 Gloucester Road ★★★★**
*Guest Accommodation*
Newbury RG14 5JJ
t   (01635) 32376
e  maggie@newbury2.demon.
co.uk

**The Bell at Boxford ★★★**
*Guest Accommodation*
Boxford, Newbury RG20 8DD
t   (01488) 608721
e  paul@bellatboxford.com
w  bellatboxford.com

**East End Farm ★★★★**
*Guest Accommodation*
East End, Newbury RG20 0AB
t   (01635) 254895
e  mp@eastendfarm.co.uk
w  eastendfarm.co.uk

**Highclere Farm ★★★★**
*Bed & Breakfast*
Highclere, Newbury RG20 9PY
t   (01635) 255013
e  walshhighclere@
newburyweb.net

**Ingledene Bed and Breakfast
★★★★**
*Guest Accommodation*
225 Andover Road, Newbury
RG14 6NG
t   (01635) 43622
e  info@ingledenebnb.co.uk

**Livingstone House ★★★★**
*Bed & Breakfast*
48 Queens Road, Newbury
RG14 7PA
t   (01635) 45444
e  info@livingstone-house.co.
uk
w  livingstone-house.co.uk

**Manor Farm House ★★★★**
*Farmhouse* **SILVER AWARD**
Church Street, Hampstead
Norreys, Newbury RG18 0TD
t   (01635) 201276
e  bettsbedandbreakfast@
hotmail.com
w  bettsbedandbreakfast.co.uk

**The Old Farmhouse ★★★★**
*Bed & Breakfast*
Downend Lane, Chieveley,
Newbury RG20 8TN
t   (01635) 248361
e  palletts@aol.com
w  smoothhound.co.uk/hotels/
oldfarmhouse

**The Paddock ★★★**
*Bed & Breakfast*
Midgham Green, Reading
RG7 5TT
t   (0118) 971 3098
e  midghamgreen@yahoo.co.
uk
w  midghamgreen.co.uk

**St Ann's ★★**
*Guest Accommodation*
32 Craven Road, Newbury
RG14 5NE
t   (01635) 41353

### NEWFOUND
Hampshire

**Rose Cottage Bed &
Breakfast ★★★★**
*Guest Accommodation*
Newfound, Basingstoke
RG23 7HF
t   (01256) 780949
w  rosecottage.bravepages.com

### NEWHAVEN
East Sussex

**Newhaven Lodge Guest
House ★★★** *Guest House*
12 Brighton Road, Newhaven
BN9 9NB
t   (01273) 513736
e  newhavenlodge@aol.com
w  newhavenlodge.co.uk

### NEWICK
East Sussex

**Holly Lodge ★★★★**
*Bed & Breakfast*
Oxbottom Lane, Newick,
Lewes BN8 4RA
t   (01825) 722738
e  lallie@waitrose.com

### NEWINGTON
Oxfordshire

**Hill Farm ★★★** *Farmhouse*
Newington, Wallingford
OX10 7AL
t   (01865) 891173

### NEWPORT
Isle of Wight

**Forest View B&B ★★★★**
*Bed & Breakfast*
1 Forest View, Marks Corner,
Newport PO30 5UD
t   (01983) 295578
e  janet.groundsell@virgin.net

**Litten Park Guest House
★★★★** *Guest House*
48 Medina Avenue, Newport
PO30 1EL
t   (01983) 526836

**Newport Quay ★★★★**
*Guest Accommodation*
**SILVER AWARD**
41 Quay Street, Newport
PO30 5BA
t   (01983) 528544
e  enquiries@
newportquayhotel.co.uk
w  newportquayhotel.co.uk

**Wheatsheaf Hotel ★★★**
*Guest Accommodation*
St Thomas Square, Newport
PO30 1SG
t   (01983) 523865
e  information@wheatsheaf-
iow.co.uk
w  wheatsheaf-iow.co.uk

### NEWPORT PAGNELL
Buckinghamshire

**The Clitheroes ★★**
*Bed & Breakfast*
5 Walnut Close, Newport
Pagnell MK16 8JH
t   (01908) 611643
e  shirleyderek.clitheroe@
btinternet.com

**Rectory Farm ★★★**
*Farmhouse*
Brook End, North Crawley,
Newport Pagnell MK16 9HH
t   (01234) 391213

**Rosemary House ★★★★**
*Bed & Breakfast*
7 Hill View, Newport Pagnell
MK16 8BE
t   (01908) 612198
e  rosemaryhouse@btinternet.
com

### NINGWOOD
Isle of Wight

**Brookside Farm Cottage Bed
& Breakfast**
Rating Applied For
*Guest Accommodation*
Main Road, Ningwood,
Newport PO30 4NW
t   (01983) 761832
e  brookside@isleofwight.com
w  isleofwight.com/brookside

### NORTH BERSTED
West Sussex

**Willow Rise ★★★★**
*Bed & Breakfast*
131 North Bersted Street,
Bognor Regis PO22 9AG
t   (01243) 829544
e  gillboon@aol.com
w  visitsussex.org

### NORTH LEIGH
Oxfordshire

**Elbie House ★★★★**
*Guest Accommodation*
**SILVER AWARD**
East End, North Leigh, Witney
OX29 6PX
t   (01993) 880166
e  mandy@cotswoldbreak.co.
uk
w  cotswoldbreak.co.uk

### NORTH MUNDHAM
West Sussex

**The Cottage ♦♦♦♦**
*Guest Accommodation*
**SILVER AWARD**
Church Road, North
Mundham, Chichester
PO20 1JU
t   (01243) 784586
e  lambrinudi-bandb@supanet.
com
w  the-thatched-cottage.co.uk

### NORTH NEWINGTON
Oxfordshire

**The Blinking Owl Country
Inn ★★★** *Inn*
Main Street, North Newington,
Banbury OX15 6AE
t   (01295) 730650

**The Mill House**
Rating Applied For
*Guest Accommodation*
North Newington, Banbury
OX15 6AA
t   (01295) 730212
e  lamadonett@aol.com
w  themillhousebanbury.com

### NORTON
West Sussex

**Norton Cottage ★★★★**
*Bed & Breakfast*
**SILVER AWARD**
Norton Lane, Norton,
Chichester PO20 3NH
t   (01243) 544805
e  nortoncottagebb@
btinternet.com
w  nortoncottage.co.uk

### NUTLEY
East Sussex

**West Meadows ★★★★**
*Bed & Breakfast*
**SILVER AWARD**
Bell Lane, Nutley, Forest Row
TN22 3PD
t   (01825) 712434
e  west.meadows@virgin.net
w  westmeadows.co.uk

### OAKLEY
Buckinghamshire

**New Farm ★★** *Farmhouse*
Oxford Road, Oakley,
Aylesbury HP18 9UR
t   (01844) 237360

### OAKLEY GREEN
Berkshire

**Rainworth House ★★★★**
*Guest Accommodation*
Oakley Green Road, Oakley
Green, Windsor SL4 5UL
t   (01753) 856749
e  info@rainworthhouse.com
w  rainworthguesthouse.com

### OARE
Kent

**Uplees Lodge ★★★★**
*Guest Accommodation*
Uplees Road, Faversham
ME13 0QR
t   (01795) 535014
e  upleeslodge@aol.com

### OCKLEY
Surrey

**The Kings Arms Inn ★★★★**
*Inn*
Stane Street, Ockley, Dorking
RH5 5TS
t   (01306) 711224
e  enquiries@
thekingsarmsockley.co.uk
w  thekingsarmsockley.co.uk

### OLD WINDSOR
Berkshire

**Union Inn ★★★** *Inn*
Crimp Hill Road, Windsor
SL4 2QY
t   (01753) 861955
w  unioninnwindsor.co.uk

### OLNEY
Buckinghamshire

**Colchester House ★★★★**
*Guest Accommodation*
**SILVER AWARD**
26 High Street, Olney
MK46 4BB
t   (01234) 712602
e  peter.blenkinsop@
btopenworld.com
w  olneybucks.co.uk

**The Lindens ★★★★**
*Guest Accommodation*
30a High Street, Olney
MK46 4BB
t   (01234) 712891
e  accommodation@
thelindens.com
w  thelindens.com

### OTFORD
Kent

**Darenth Dene ★★★**
*Bed & Breakfast*
Shoreham Road, Sevenoaks
TN14 5RP
t   (01959) 522293

## OXFORD
### Oxfordshire

**21 Lincoln Road** ★★★
*Bed & Breakfast*
Oxford OX1 4TB
t (01865) 246944
e gbaleham@hotmail.com

**Adams Guest House** ★★
*Guest Accommodation*
302 Banbury Road, Oxford
OX2 7ED
t (01865) 556118
e oxfordadamsguesthouse@
hotmail.com

**Arden Lodge** ★★★
*Guest Accommodation*
34 Sunderland Avenue, Off
Banbury Road, Oxford
OX2 8DX
t (01865) 552076

**Beaumont Guest House** ◆◆◆
*Guest Accommodation*
234 Abingdon Road, Oxford
OX1 4SP
t (01865) 241767
e info@beaumont.sagehost.
co.uk
w oxfordcity.co.uk/accom/
beaumont

**Becket House** ★★
*Guest Accommodation*
5 Becket Street, Oxford
OX1 1PP
t (01865) 724675
e becketguesthouse@yahoo.
co.uk

**Brenal Guest House** ★★★
*Guest House*
307 Iffley Road, Oxford
OX4 4AG
t (01865) 721561
e brenalguesthouse@hotmail.
co.uk

**Broomhill** ★★★★
*Bed & Breakfast*
Lincombe Lane, Boars Hill,
Oxford OX1 5DZ
t (01865) 735339
e sara@broomhill-oxford.co.uk
w broomhill-oxford.co.uk

**Brown's Guest House** ★★★
*Guest Accommodation*
281 Iffley Road, Oxford
OX4 4AQ
t (01865) 246822
e brownsgh@hotmail.com
w brownsguesthouse.co.uk

**The Bungalow** ★★★
*Guest Accommodation*
Mill Lane, Marston, Oxford
OX3 0QF
t (01865) 557171
e ros.bungalowbb@btinternet.
com
w cherwellfarm-oxford-accom.
com

**Central Backpackers Oxford**
★★ *Backpacker*
13 Park End Street, Oxford
OX1 1HH
t (01865) 242288
e oxford@centralbackpackers.
co.uk
w centralbackpackers.co.uk

**Chestnuts** ★★★
*Bed & Breakfast*
72 Cumnor Hill, Oxford
OX2 9HU
t (01865) 863602

**Cornerways Guest House**
★★★★
*Guest Accommodation*
282 Abingdon Road, Oxford
OX1 4TA
t (01865) 240135
e jeakings@btopenworld.com

**Cotswold House** ★★★★
*Guest Accommodation*
363 Banbury Road, Oxford
OX2 7PL
t (01865) 310558
e d.r.walker@talk21.com
w cotswoldhouse.co.uk

**Department for Continuing
Education** ★★★ *Campus*
Rewley House, 1 Wellington
Square, Oxford OX1 2JA
t (01865) 280166
e res-ctr@conted.ox.ac.uk
w conted.ox.ac.uk

**Dial House** ★★★★
*Guest House*
25 London Road, Headington,
Oxford OX3 7RE
t (01865) 425100
e dialhouse@ntlworld.com
w dialhouseoxford.co.uk

**Euro Bar & Hotel Oxford**
★★★ *Inn*
48 George Street, Oxford
OX1 2AQ
t (01865) 725087
e eurobarox@aol.com
w oxfordcity.co.uk/accom/
eurobar/

**Falcon Private Hotel** ★★★
*Guest Accommodation*
88-90 Abingdon Road, Oxford
OX1 4PX
t (01865) 511122
e stay@falconoxford.co.uk
w oxfordcity.co.uk/hotels/
falcon

**Five Mile View Guest House**
◆◆◆ *Guest Accommodation*
528 Banbury Road, Oxford
OX2 8EG
t (01865) 558747
e 5mile@cav.demon.co.uk
w oxfordcity.co.uk/accom/
fivemileview

**Gables Guest House**
★★★★★
*Guest Accommodation*
SILVER AWARD
6 Cumnor Hill, Oxford
OX2 9HA
t (01865) 862153
e stay@gables-oxford.co.uk
w gables-guesthouse.co.uk

**Gorselands Hall** ★★★★
*Guest Accommodation*
SILVER AWARD
Boddington Lane, North Leigh,
Witney OX29 6PU
t (01993) 882292
e hamilton@gorselandshall.
com
w gorselandshall.com

**Head of the River** ★★★★
*Inn*
Folly Bridge, Oxford OX1 4LB
t (01865) 721600
e headoftheriver@fullers.co.uk

**Hollybush Guest House**
★★★ *Guest Accommodation*
530 Banbury Road, Oxford
OX2 8EG
t (01865) 554886
e heather@hollybush.
fsbusiness.co.uk
w angelfire.com/on/hollybush

**Home Farm House** ◆◆◆◆
*Guest Accommodation*
SILVER AWARD
Holton, Oxford OX33 1QA
t (01865) 872334
e sonja.barter@tiscali.co.uk
w homefarmholton.co.uk

**Homelea Guest House**
★★★★
*Guest Accommodation*
356 Abingdon Road, Oxford
OX1 4TQ
t (01865) 245150
e homelea@talk21.com
w oxford-guesthouse.co.uk

**Isis Guest House** ★★
*Guest House*
45-53 Iffley Road, Oxford
OX4 1ED
t (01865) 248894
e isis@herald.ox.ac.uk
w isisguesthouse.co.uk

**Lakeside Guest House** ★★★
*Guest Accommodation*
118 Abingdon Road, Oxford
OX1 4PZ
t (01865) 244725
e danielashirley@btclick.com

**Lonsdale Guest House** ★★★
*Guest House*
312 Banbury Road, Oxford
OX2 7ED
t (01865) 554872
e lons.dale.bb@amserve.com

**Milka's Guest House** ★★★
*Guest Accommodation*
379 Iffley Road, Oxford
OX4 4DP
t (01865) 778458
e reservations@milkas.co.uk
w milkas.co.uk

**Mulberry Guest House**
★★★ *Guest Accommodation*
265 London Road, Headington,
Oxford OX3 9EH
t (01865) 767114
e reservations@
mulberryguesthouse.co.uk
w mulberryguesthouse.co.uk

**Newton House** ★★★
*Guest Accommodation*
82-84 Abingdon Road, Oxford
OX1 4PL
t (01865) 240561
e newton.house@btinternet.
com
w oxfordcity.co.uk/accom/
newton

**The Old Black Horse Hotel**
★★★★ *Inn*
102 St Clements Street, Oxford
OX4 1AR
t (01865) 244691
e info@oldblackhorse.com
w oldblackhorse.com

**Park House** ★★★
*Bed & Breakfast*
7 St Bernard's Road, Oxford
OX2 6EH
t (01865) 310824
e krynpark@hotmail.com

**Parklands Hotel** ★★★★
*Guest Accommodation*
100 Banbury Road, Oxford
OX2 6JU
t (01865) 554374
e stay@parklandsoxford.co.uk
w oxfordcity.co.uk/hotels/
parklands

**Pickwicks Guest House**
★★★★ *Guest House*
15-17 London Road,
Headington, Oxford OX3 7SP
t (01865) 750487
e pickwicks@tiscali.co.uk
w pickwicksguesthouse.co.uk

**Remont Guest House**
★★★★
*Guest Accommodation*
367 Banbury Road,
Summertown, Oxford OX2 7PL
t (01865) 311020
e info@remont-guesthouse.
co.uk
w remont-guesthouse.co.uk

**The Ridings** ★★★
*Guest Accommodation*
280 Abingdon Road, Oxford
OX1 4TA
t (01865) 248364
e stay@theridingsguesthouse.
co.uk
w theridingsguesthouse.co.uk

**River Hotel** ★★★
*Guest Accommodation*
17 Botley Road, Oxford
OX2 0AA
t (01865) 243475
e reception@riverhotel.co.uk
w riverhotel.co.uk

**Sportsview Guest House**
★★★ *Guest Accommodation*
106-110 Abingdon Road,
Oxford OX1 4PX
t (01865) 244268
e stay@
sportsviewguesthouse.co.uk
w sportsviewguesthouse.co.uk

**Tilbury Lodge** ★★★★
*Guest Accommodation*
5 Tilbury Lane, Oxford
OX2 9NB
t (01865) 862138

**The Tower House Hotel**
★★★★
*Guest Accommodation*
15 Ship Street, Oxford
OX1 3DA
t (01865) 246828
e thetowerhouse@btconnect.
com
w towerhouseoxford.co.uk

**The Westgate Hotel** ★★
*Guest Accommodation*
1 Botley Road, Oxford
OX2 0AA
t (01865) 726721
e westgatehotel.2@
btopenworld.com

**White House View** ★★
*Guest House*
9 White House Road, Oxford
OX1 4PA
t (01865) 721626

---

## OXTED
### Surrey

**The New Bungalow ★★★**
*Guest Accommodation*
Old Hall Farm, Tandridge Lane,
Tandridge RH8 9NS
**t** (01342) 892508
**e** don.nunn@tesco.net

## PADDOCK WOOD
### Kent

**Pinto ★★★★** *Bed & Breakfast*
Chantlers Hill, Brenchley,
Tonbridge TN12 6LX
**t** (01892) 836254
**e** janemoor@supanet.com

## PANGBOURNE
### Berkshire

**Weir View House ★★★★**
*Guest Accommodation*
9 Shooters Hill, Pangbourne,
Reading RG8 7DZ
**t** (0118) 984 2120
**e** info@weirview.co.uk
**w** weirview.co.uk

## PARTRIDGE GREEN
### West Sussex

**Pound Cottage ★★★**
*Bed & Breakfast*
Mill Lane, Littleworth, Horsham
RH13 8JU
**t** (01403) 710218
**e** thegeo@poundcott.
freeserve.co.uk

## PENNINGTON
### Hampshire

**Little Gem ★★★★**
*Bed & Breakfast*
1 Pennington Close, Lymington
SO41 8EU
**t** (01590) 672799
**e** ianandelainem@hotmail.com

## PETERSFIELD
### Hampshire

**1 The Spain ★★★★**
*Bed & Breakfast*
Sheep Street, Petersfield
GU32 3JZ
**t** (01730) 263261
**e** allantarver@ntlworld.com
**w** 1thespain.com

**80 Rushes Road ★★★**
*Bed & Breakfast*
Petersfield GU32 3BP
**t** (01730) 261638
**e** collinstudor@waitrose.com
**w** rushes-road.co.uk

**Border Cottage ★★★★**
*Bed & Breakfast*
4 Heath Road, Petersfield
GU31 4DU
**t** (01730) 263179
**e** lawrence@bordercottage.co.
uk
**w** bordercottage.co.uk

**The Corner House ★★★**
*Bed & Breakfast*
1a Sandringham Road,
Petersfield GU32 2AA
**t** (01730) 261028
**e** pat.elborough@ukonline.co.
uk

**Downsview (Petersfield)**
**★★★★** *Bed & Breakfast*
58 Heath Road, Petersfield
GU31 4EJ
**t** (01730) 264171
**e** info@downsview58.co.uk
**w** downsview58.co.uk

**Heath Farmhouse ★★★★**
*Bed & Breakfast*
Sussex Road, Petersfield
GU31 4HU
**t** (01730) 264709
**e** info@heathfarmhouse.co.uk
**w** heathfarmhouse.co.uk

**The Holt ★★★★**
*Bed & Breakfast*
60 Heath Road, Petersfield
GU31 4EJ
**t** (01730) 262836

**Pipers ★★★** *Bed & Breakfast*
1 Oaklands Road, Petersfield
GU32 2EY
**t** (01730) 262131

**Quinhay Farmhouse ★★★★**
*Bed & Breakfast*
Alton Road, Froxfield,
Petersfield GU32 1BZ
**t** (01730) 827183
**e** janerothery@quinhaybandb.
co.uk
**w** quinhaybandb.co.uk

**South Gardens Cottage**
**★★★** *Bed & Breakfast*
South Harting, Petersfield
GU31 5QJ
**t** (01730) 825040

## PETHAM
### Kent

**South Wootton House ★★★**
*Farmhouse*
Capel Lane, Petham,
Canterbury CT4 5RG
**t** (01227) 700643
**e** mountfrances@farming.co.
uk

## PETWORTH
### West Sussex

**Burton Park Farm ★★★**
*Farmhouse*
Burton Park Road, Petworth
GU28 0JT
**t** (01798) 342431

**Eedes Cottage ★★★★**
*Bed & Breakfast*
Bignor Park Road, Bury Gate,
Pulborough RH20 1EZ
**t** (01798) 831438
**e** eedes.bandb.hare@
amserve.com
**w** visitsussex.org/
eedescottage

**Garden Cottage ★★★★**
*Bed & Breakfast*
Park Road, Petworth
GU28 0DS
**t** (01798) 342414
**e** a.wolseley@ukonline.co.uk

**Halfway Bridge Inn**
**★★★★★** *Inn*
**GOLD AWARD**
Halfway Bridge, Lodsworth,
Petworth GU28 9BP
**t** (01798) 861281
**e** halfwaybridge@btconnect.
com
**w** thesussexpub.co.uk

**Old Railway Station ★★★★**
*Guest Accommodation*
Station Road, Petworth
GU28 0JF
**t** (01798) 342346
**e** info@old-station.co.uk
**w** old-station.co.uk

**Rectory Cottage ★★★**
*Guest Accommodation*
Rectory Lane, Petworth
GU28 0DB
**t** (01798) 342380
**e** dcradd@aol.com
**w** visitsussex.org/
rectorycottage

## PEVENSEY BAY
### East Sussex

**The Bay Hotel ★★★** *Inn*
2-4 Eastbourne Road,
Pevensey Bay, Pevensey
BN24 6EJ
**t** (01323) 768645

## PISHILL
### Oxfordshire

**Orchard House ★★★★**
*Guest Accommodation*
Pishill, Henley-on-Thames
RG9 6HJ
**t** (01491) 638351

## PITT
### Hampshire

**Enmill Barn ★★★★★**
*Bed & Breakfast*
**SILVER AWARD**
Enmill Lane, Winchester
SO22 5QR
**t** (01962) 856740
**e** jennywray21@hotmail.com
**w** enmill-barn.co.uk

## PLAITFORD
### Hampshire

**The shoe Inn ★★★★** *Inn*
Salisbury Road, Romsey
SO51 6EE
**t** (01794) 322397
**e** theshoeinn@btinteenet.com
**w** shoeinn.co.uk

**Southernwood B&B ★★★**
*Bed & Breakfast*
Plaitford Village Hall, Salisbury
Road, Romsey SO51 6EE
**t** (01794) 323255
**e** southernwood@lycos.co.uk

## PLAY HATCH
### Oxfordshire

**The Crown at Playhatch**
**★★★★** *Inn*
The Crown, Playhatch
RG4 9QN
**t** (0118) 947 2872
**e** info@thecrown.co.uk
**w** thecrown.co.uk

## PLAYDEN
### East Sussex

**The Corner House ★★★★**
*Guest Accommodation*
Rye Road, Rye TN31 7UL
**t** (01797) 280439
**e** richard.turner5@virgin.net
**w** thecornerhouse-bed-
breakfast.co.uk

**Playden Oasts Hotel & Inn**
**★★★** *Inn*
Rye Road, Playden, Rye
TN31 7UL
**t** (01797) 223502

## PLUCKLEY
### Kent

**Elvey Farm ★★★★**
*Guest Accommodation*
Elvey Lane, Ashford TN27 0SU
**t** (01233) 840442
**e** bookings@elveyfarm.co.uk
**w** elveyfarm.co.uk

## PORCHFIELD
### Isle of Wight

**Youngwoods Farm ★★★**
*Farmhouse*
Whitehouse Road, Porchfield
PO30 4LJ
**t** (01983) 522170
**e** judith@youngwoods.com
**w** youngwoods.com

## PORTSMOUTH & SOUTHSEA
### Hampshire

**Abbey Lodge ★★★**
*Guest House*
30 Waverley Road, Southsea
PO5 2PW
**t** (023) 9282 8285
**e** linda@abbeylodge.co.uk
**w** abbeylodge.co.uk

**The Albatross Guest House**
**★★★** *Guest Accommodation*
51 Waverley Road, Southsea
PO5 2PJ
**t** (023) 9282 8325

**Arden Guest House ♦♦♦**
*Guest Accommodation*
14 Herbert Road, Southsea
PO4 0QA
**t** (023) 9282 6409

**Bembell Court ★★★**
*Guest House*
69 Festing Road, Southsea
PO4 0NQ
**t** (023) 9273 5915
**e** keith@bembell.co.uk
**w** bembell.co.uk

**Esk Vale Guest House**
Rating Applied For
*Guest Accommodation*
39 Granada Road, Southsea
PO4 0RD
**t** (023) 9286 2639
**e** enquiries@
eskvaleguesthouse.co.uk
**w** eskvaleguesthouse.co.uk

**Everley Guest House ★★★**
*Guest House*
33 Festing Road, Southsea
PO4 0NG
**t** (023) 9273 1001
**e** everleyguesthouse@
ntlworld.com

**Fortitude Cottage ★★★★**
*Guest Accommodation*
51 Broad Street, Portsmouth
PO1 2JD
**t** (023) 9282 3748
**e** info@fortitudecottage.co.uk
**w** fortitudecottage.co.uk

**Gainsborough House ♦♦♦**
*Guest Accommodation*
9 Malvern Road, Southsea
PO5 2LZ
**t** (023) 9282 2604

**Greenacres Guest House**
**★★★** *Guest Accommodation*
12 Marion Road, Southsea
PO4 0QX
**t** (023) 9235 3137

**Hamilton House Bed &**
**Breakfast ★★★★**
*Guest Accommodation*
95 Victoria Road North,
Portsmouth PO5 1PS
**t** (023) 9282 3502
**e** sandra@hamiltonhouse.co.
uk
**w** hamiltonhouse.co.uk

**Homestead Guest House**
★★★ *Guest Accommodation*
11 Bembridge Crescent,
Southsea PO4 0QT
t (023) 9273 2362
e b.currie1@ntlworld.com
w homesteadguesthouse-
southsea.com

**Lamorna Guest House** ★★
*Bed & Breakfast*
23 Victoria Road South,
Southsea PO5 2BX
t (023) 9281 1157

**Victoria Court** ★★★
*Guest Accommodation*
29 Victoria Road North,
Southsea PO5 1PL
t (023) 9282 0305
e stay@victoriacourt.co.uk
w victoriacourt.co.uk

**Waverley Park Lodge Guest
House** ★★★
*Guest Accommodation*
99 Waverley Road, Southsea
PO5 2PL
t (023) 9273 0402
e waverleyparklodge@yahoo.
co.uk
w waverleyparklodge.co.uk

**Woodville Hotel** ★★★
*Guest Accommodation*
6 Florence Road, Southsea
PO5 2NE
t (023) 9282 3409
e woodvillehotel@boltblue.
com

PRESTON
Kent

**Look Cottage** ★★★★
*Bed & Breakfast*
**SILVER AWARD**
The Forstal, Preston,
Canterbury CT3 1DT
t (01227) 722518
e sales@lookcottage.co.uk
w lookcottage.co.uk/

PRINCES RISBOROUGH
Buckinghamshire

**Coppins** ★★★★
*Bed & Breakfast*
New Road, Princes Risborough
HP27 0LA
t (01844) 344508
e jillthomas@thecoppins.co.uk
w thecoppins.co.uk

**Drifters Lodge** ★★★★
*Bed & Breakfast*
Picts Lane, Princes Risborough
HP27 9DX
t (01844) 274773
e info@drifterslodge.co.uk
w drifterslodge.co.uk

**The Old Station** ★★★★★
*Bed & Breakfast*
Sandpit Lane, Princes
Risborough HP27 9QQ
t (01844) 345086
e ianmackinson@hotmail.com
w theoldstation-bledlow.co.uk

**Solis Ortu** ★★★
*Bed & Breakfast*
Aylesbury Road, Askett,
Princes Risborough HP27 9LY
t (01844) 344175
e pamela@crockettandson.
com

PULBOROUGH
West Sussex

**Barn House Lodge** ★★★★
*Bed & Breakfast*
Barn House Lane, Pulborough
RH20 2BS
t (01798) 872682
e suehj@aol.com

**The Labouring Man** ★★★★
*Inn*
Old London Road, Pulborough
RH20 1LF
t (01798) 872215
e philip.beckett@btconnect.
com
w thelabouringman.co.uk

**Lyon Cottage** ★★
*Bed & Breakfast*
Bury Gate, Pulborough
RH20 1EY
t (01798) 865295

**St Cleather** ★★★★
*Bed & Breakfast*
**SILVER AWARD**
Rectory Lane, Pulborough
RH20 2AD
t (01798) 873038
e enquiries@stcleather.me.uk
w stcleather.me.uk

RADNAGE
Buckinghamshire

**Rosling House** ★★★★
*Bed & Breakfast*
Radnage Common Road,
Radnage HP14 4DD
t (01494) 482724
e c.wheeler1@btinternet.com
w roslinghouse.co.uk

RAINHAM
Kent

**Abigails** ★★
*Guest Accommodation*
17 The Maltings, Rainham,
Gillingham ME8 8JL
t (01634) 365427
e davidjpenfold@
btopenworld.com

RAMSGATE
Kent

**Abbeygail Guest House**
★★★★ *Guest House*
17 Penshurst Road, Ramsgate
CT11 8RG
t (01843) 594154
e abbeygail2004@aol.com
w abbeygail.co.uk

**Belvidere Guest House**
Rating Applied For
*Guest Accommodation*
26 Augusta Road, Ramsgate
CT11 8JS
t (01843) 588809

**Glendevon Guest House**
★★★★ *Guest House*
8 Truro Road, Ramsgate
CT11 8DB
t (01843) 570909
e rebekah.smith1@btinternet.
com
w glendevonguesthouse.co.uk

**Glenholme Guest House**
★★★ *Guest Accommodation*
6 Crescent Road, Ramsgate
CT11 9QU
t (01843) 595149

**Grove End** ★★★★
*Guest Accommodation*
2 Grange Road, Ramsgate
CT11 9NA
t (01843) 587520
e reservations@
groveendhotel.demon.co.uk
w groveendhotel.demon.co.uk

**The Royale Guest House**
★★★ *Guest Accommodation*
7 Royal Road, Ramsgate
CT11 9LE
t (01843) 594712
e sylvbarry@aol.com
w theroyaleguesthouse.co.uk

**Spencer Court** ★★★
*Guest Accommodation*
37 Spencer Square, Ramsgate
CT11 9LD
t (01843) 594582
e glendaandken@hotmail.com
w smoothhound.co.uk/hotels/
spencer.ltml

READING
Berkshire

**Beech House** ★★★★
*Guest Accommodation*
60 Bath Road, Reading
RG30 2AY
t (0118) 959 1901

**Belle Vue House** ★★★★
*Guest Accommodation*
2 Tilehurst Road, Reading
RG1 7TN
t (0118) 959 4445
e bellevuehotel@btconnect.
com
w bellevuehousehotel.co.uk

**Caversham Lodge** ★★
*Guest House*
133a Caversham Road,
Reading RG1 8AS
t (0118) 961 2110
e raj.roy@hotmail.co.uk

**Dittisham Guest House**
★★★ *Guest Accommodation*
63 Tilehurst Road, Reading
RG30 2JL
t (0118) 956 9483
e dittishamgh@aol.com

**Great Expectations Hotel
and Bar** ★★★
*Guest Accommodation*
33 London Street, Reading
RG1 4PS
t (0118) 950 3925

RINGMER
East Sussex

**Bethany** ★★★
*Bed & Breakfast*
25 Ballard Drive, Ringmer,
Lewes BN8 5NU
t (01273) 812025
e dimeadows@rockuk.net

**Bryn-Clai** ★★★★
*Guest Accommodation*
Uckfield Road, Ringmer, Lewes
BN8 5RU
t (01273) 814042
w brynclai.co.uk

RINGWOOD
Hampshire

**The Auld Kennels** ★★★
*Bed & Breakfast*
215 Christchurch Road,
Ringwood BH24 3AN
t (01425) 475170
e auldkennels@aol.com

**Avonmead House** ★★★★
*Bed & Breakfast*
16 Salisbury Road, Ringwood
BH24 1AS
t (01425) 475531
e chrissie.peckham@virgin.net
w avonmeadhouse.co.uk

**Fraser House** ★★★★
*Guest House*
Salisbury Road, Blashford,
Ringwood BH24 3PB
t (01425) 473958
e mail@fraserhouse.net
w fraserhouse.net

**High Corner Inn** ★★★ *Inn*
Linwood, Ringwood BH24 3QY
t (01425) 473973

**Moortown Lodge** ★★★★
*Guest Accommodation*
244 Christchurch Road,
Ringwood BH24 3AS
t (01425) 471404
e enquiries@moortownlodge.
co.uk
w moortownlodge.co.uk

**The Star Inn** ★★★★ *Inn*
**SILVER AWARD**
Market Place, Ringwood
BH24 1AW
t (01425) 473105
w thestarringwood.co.uk

**Torre Avon** ★★★★
*Bed & Breakfast*
21 Salisbury Road, Ringwood
BH24 1AS
t (01425) 472769
e b&b@torreavon.freeserve.
co.uk
w torreavon.freeserve.co.uk

RINGWOULD
Kent

**Rippledown Environmental
Education Centre** ★★★
*Group Hostel*
Ripple Down House, Dover
Road, Deal CT14 8HE
t (01304) 364854
e office@rippledown.com
w rippledown.com

RIPE
East Sussex

**Hall Court Farm** ★★★★★
*Bed & Breakfast*
**SILVER AWARD**
Ripe, Lewes BN8 6AY
t (01323) 811496
e johnhecks@btconnect.com
w hallcourtfarm.co.uk

RIPLEY
Surrey

**Four Oaks Cottage** ★★★
*Bed & Breakfast*
Polesden Lane, Ripley, Woking
GU23 6DX
t (01483) 225251
e fouroaksbb@aol.com
w fouroaksbb.co.uk

## RIVER
### Kent

**Woodlands ★★★**
*Guest Accommodation*
29 London Road, River, Dover
CT17 0SF
**t** (01304) 823635

## ROBERTSBRIDGE
### East Sussex

**Glenferness ★★★★**
*Bed & Breakfast*
Brightling Road, Robertsbridge
TN32 5DP
**t** (01580) 881841
**e** info@glenferness.co.uk
**w** glenferness.co.uk

## ROCHESTER
### Kent

**Ambleside Lodge ★★★★**
*Guest Accommodation*
12 Abbotts Close, Priestfields,
Rochester ME1 3AZ
**t** (01634) 815926
**e** bryanmills@blueyonder.co.
uk

**Churchfields ★★**
*Bed & Breakfast*
SILVER AWARD
Churchfields Terrace, St
Margarets Street, Rochester
ME1 1TQ
**t** (01634) 400679
**e** sian-smiles@supanet.com
**w** churchfields.co.uk

**The Cottage ★★★★**
*Bed & Breakfast*
66 Borstal Road, Rochester
ME1 3BD
**t** (01634) 403888

**Greystones ★★★★**
*Guest Accommodation*
25 Watts Avenue, Rochester
ME1 1RX
**t** (01634) 409565

**Guinea Lodge ★★★**
*Guest Accommodation*
435 Maidstone Road,
Rochester ME1 3PQ
**t** (01634) 306716

**North Downs Barn ★★★★**
*Bed & Breakfast*
Bush Road, Cuxton, Rochester
ME2 1HF
**t** (01634) 296829
**e** alison@northdownsbarn.
wanadoo.co.uk
**w** northdownsbarn.co.uk

**Salisbury House ★★★★**
*Guest Accommodation*
29 Watts Avenue, Rochester
ME1 1RX
**t** (01634) 400182

## RODMELL
### East Sussex

**Garden Studio ★★★★**
*Guest Accommodation*
Robin Hill, Mill Lane, Rodmell,
Lewes BN7 3HS
**t** (01273) 476715 &
07775 624235

## ROLVENDEN
### Kent

**Duck & Drake Cottage ★★★**
*Guest Accommodation*
Sandhurst Lane, Rolvenden,
Cranbrook TN17 4PQ
**t** (01580) 241533
**e** duckanddrake@supanet.
com

**Green Cottage B&B ★★**
*Bed & Breakfast*
5 Sparkes Wood Avenue,
Rolvenden, Nr Tenterden
TN17 4LU
**t** (01580) 241765
**e** stevree@onetel.com

## ROMNEY MARSH
### Kent

**Coxell House ★★★★**
*Guest Accommodation*
SILVER AWARD
Manor Road, Lydd TN29 9HR
**t** (01797) 322037
**e** coxellhouse@btopenworld.
com
**w** coxellhouse.co.uk

**Stable Cottage ★★★★**
*Bed & Breakfast*
The Sheiling, Donkey Street,
Burmarsh, Romney Marsh
TN29 0JN
**t** (01303) 872335 &
07870 918387
**e** eric777@tiscali.co.uk
**w** stablecottageburmarsh.co.
uk

## ROMSEY
### Hampshire

**The Chalet Guest House ★★**
*Bed & Breakfast*
105 Botley Road, Whitenap,
Romsey SO51 5RQ
**t** (01794) 517299
**e** thechalet@ntlworld.com

**The Dairy at Packridge Farm
★★★★**
*Guest Accommodation*
Packridge Lane, Romsey
SO51 9LL
**t** 0845 257 2660
**e** thedairy@packridgeestate.
com
**w** packridgeestate.com

**Mortimer Arms ★★★★** *Inn*
Romsey Road, Ower, Romsey
SO51 6AF
**t** (023) 8081 4379

**Nursery Cottage ★★**
*Bed & Breakfast*
East Tytherley, Nr Romsey,
Salisbury SP5 1LF
**t** (01794) 341060
**e** nursery-cottage@waitrose.
com
**w** nursery-cottage.com

**Pauncefoot House ★★★★**
*Guest Accommodation*
Pauncefoot Hill, Romsey
SO51 6AA
**t** (01794) 513139
**e** lendupont@aol.com

**Pyesmead Farm ★★★★**
*Farmhouse*
Plaitford, Romsey SO51 6EE
**t** (01794) 323386
**e** pyesmead@talk21.com
**w** pyesmeadfarm.co.uk

**Ranvilles Farm House**
**★★★★★** *Bed & Breakfast*
Pauncefoot Hill, Romsey
SO51 6AA
**t** (023) 8081 4481
**e** info@ranvilles.com
**w** ranvilles.com

**St Brelades House ★★★★**
*Bed & Breakfast*
Mill Lane, Sherfield English,
Romsey SO51 6FN
**t** (01794) 324766
**e** b&b@st-brelades.freeserve.
co.uk
**w** stbrelades.com

**Stoneymarsh Bed &
Breakfast ★★★**
*Bed & Breakfast*
Stoneymarsh Cottage,
Stoneymarsh, Michelmersh
SO51 0LB
**t** (01794) 368867
**e** m.m.moran@btinternet.com

**Wessex Guest House ★★★**
*Guest Accommodation*
5 Palmerston Street, Romsey
SO51 8GF
**t** (01794) 512038

## ROOKLEY
### Isle of Wight

**Kennerley House – B&B**
**★★★★** *Bed & Breakfast*
Main Road, Rookley PO38 3NB
**t** (01983) 842001
**e** carolfoote@btinternet.com
**w** kennerleyhouse.com

## ROUND GREEN
### Kent

**Cordons ★★★**
*Bed & Breakfast*
Round Green Lane, Colliers
Green, Cranbrook TN17 2NB
**t** (01580) 211633

## ROWLEDGE
### Surrey

**Rosebarton ★★★★**
*Bed & Breakfast*
Cherry Tree Walk, Rowledge,
Farnham GU10 4AD
**t** (01252) 793580
**e** rosebarton@btinternet.com

## ROYAL TUNBRIDGE WELLS
### Kent

**191 Upper Grosvenor Road
★★★** *Bed & Breakfast*
Royal Tunbridge Wells
TN1 2EF
**t** (01892) 537305

**40 York Road ★★★★**
*Bed & Breakfast*
York Road, Tunbridge Wells
TN1 1JY
**t** (01892) 531342
**e** info@yorkroad.co.uk
**w** yorkroad.co.uk

**Alconbury Guest House
★★★★★** *Bed & Breakfast*
SILVER AWARD
41 Molyneux Park Road, Royal
Tunbridge Wells TN4 8DX
**t** (01892) 511279
**e** wisepig@telecomplus.org.uk
**w** palace4u.co.uk

**Ash Tree Cottage ★★★★**
*Bed & Breakfast*
SILVER AWARD
7 Eden Road, Tunbridge Wells
TN1 1TS
**t** (01892) 541317
**e** rogersashtree@excite.com

**Badgers End ★★**
*Bed & Breakfast*
47 Thirlmere Road, Tunbridge
Wells TN4 9SS
**t** (01892) 533176

**Bankside ★★★★**
*Bed & Breakfast*
6 Scotts Way, Tunbridge Wells
TN2 5RG
**t** (01892) 531776
**e** amkib1@yahoo.co.uk
**w** banksidebedandbreakfast-
tunbridgewells.co.uk

**The Beacon ★★★★**
*Guest Accommodation*
Tea Garden Lane, Tunbridge
Wells TN3 9JH
**t** (01892) 524252
**e** beaconhotel@btopenworld.
com
**w** beacon-hotel.co.uk

**Bethany House ★★★★**
*Guest Accommodation*
SILVER AWARD
170 St Johns Road, Tunbridge
Wells TN4 9UY
**t** (01892) 684363
**e** info@bethanyhousetwells.
co.uk
**w** bethanyhousetwells.co.uk

**Blundeston ★★★★**
*Guest Accommodation*
Eden Road, Royal Tunbridge
Wells TN1 1TS
**t** (01892) 513030
**e** daysblundeston@excite.com

**The Brick House ★★★★**
*Bed & Breakfast*
SILVER AWARD
21 Mount Ephraim Road,
Tunbridge Wells TN1 1EN
**t** (01892) 516517
**e** info@thebrickhousebandb.
co.uk
**w** thebrickhousebandb.co.uk

**Broadwater ★★★★**
*Bed & Breakfast*
24 Clarendon Way, Tunbridge
Wells TN2 5LD
**t** (01892) 528161
**e** david.thompson4@which.
net

**Clarken Guest House ★★★**
*Guest House*
61 Frant Road, Tunbridge
Wells TN2 5LH
**t** (01892) 533397
**e** suekench@hotmail.com

**Danehurst House ★★★★★**
*Bed & Breakfast*
SILVER AWARD
41 Lower Green Road,
Tunbridge Wells TN4 8TW
**t** (01892) 527739
**e** info@danehurst.net
**w** danehurst.net

**Ford Cottage** ★★★★
*Guest Accommodation*
Linden Park Road, Tunbridge
Wells TN2 5QL
t (01892) 531419
e fordcottage@tinyworld.co.
uk

**Great Oaks** ★★
*Bed & Breakfast*
163 St Johns Road, Tunbridge
Wells TN4 9UP
t (01892) 539876
e greatoaks163@tiscali.co.uk

**Hawkenbury Farm** ★★★★
*Bed & Breakfast*
Hawkenbury Road, Royal
Tunbridge Wells TN3 9AD
t (01892) 536977
e rhwright1@aol.com

**Hazelwood House** ★★
*Bed & Breakfast*
Bishop's Down Park Road,
Tunbridge Wells TN4 8XS
t (01892) 545924
e judith@hurcomb3.wanadoo.
co.uk

**Manor Court Farm** ★★★
*Farmhouse*
Ashurst Road, Ashurst,
Tunbridge Wells TN3 9TB
t (01892) 740279
e jsoyke@jsoyke.freeserve.co.
uk
w manorcourtfarm.co.uk

**The Nightingales** ★★★★
*Bed & Breakfast*
London Road, Southborough,
Tunbridge Wells TN4 0UJ
t (01892) 522384
e milliken61@oal.com

**Rosnaree** ★★★
*Bed & Breakfast*
189 Upper Grosvenor Road,
Tunbridge Wells TN1 2EF
t (01892) 524017
e david@rosnaree.freeserve.
co.uk

**Salomons** ★★★ *Campus*
David Salomons Estate,
Broomhill Road, Royal
Tunbridge Wells TN3 0TG
t (01892) 515152
e m.salomonson@salomons.
org.uk
w salomonscentre.org.uk

**Studley Cottage** ◆◆◆◆
*Guest Accommodation*
GOLD AWARD
Bishop's Down Park Road,
Tunbridge Wells TN4 8XX
t (01892) 539854
e cook@studleycottage.co.uk
w studleycottage.co.uk

**Swan Cottage** ★★★★
*Bed & Breakfast*
17 Warwick Road, Royal
Tunbridge Wells TN1 1YL
t (01892) 525910
e swancot@btinternet.com
w swancottage.co.uk

RUDGWICK
West Sussex

**Alliblaster House** ★★★★★
*Bed & Breakfast*
SILVER AWARD
Hillhouse Lane, Horsham
RH12 3BD
t (01403) 822860
e info@alliblasterhouse.com
w alliblasterhouse.com

**Mucky Duck Inn** ★★★★ *Inn*
Tismans Common, Loxwood
Road, Horsham RH12 3BW
t (01403) 822300
e mucky_duck_pub@msn.
com
w mucky-duck-inn.co.uk

RUSTINGTON
West Sussex

**Kenmore** ★★★★
*Guest Accommodation*
SILVER AWARD
Claigmar Road, Rustington,
Littlehampton BN16 2NL
t (01903) 784634
e thekenmore@amserve.net
w kenmoreguesthouse.co.uk

**Mallon Dene** ★★★★
*Bed & Breakfast*
SILVER AWARD
Littlehampton BN16 2JP
t (01903) 775383
e jenny@mallondene.co.uk
w mallondene.co.uk

RYDE
Isle of Wight

**Claverton House Bed and
Breakfast** ★★★★
*Bed & Breakfast*
Claverton House, 12 The
Strand, Ryde PO33 1JE
t (01983) 613015
e clavertonhouse@aol.com
w clavertonhouse.co.uk

**Dorset House** ★★★
*Guest Accommodation*
31 Dover Street, Ryde
PO33 2BW
t (01983) 564327
e hoteldorset@aol.com
w thedorsethotel.co.uk

**Fern Cottage** ★★★★
*Bed & Breakfast*
8 West Street, Ryde
PO33 2NW
t (01983) 565856
e sandra@psdferguson.
freeserve.co.uk

**Kasbah** ★★★★
*Guest Accommodation*
76 Union Street, Ryde
PO33 2LN
t (01983) 810088
e newkasbah@btconnect.com
w kas-bah.co.uk

**Pencombe House** ★★★★
*Bed & Breakfast*
Newnham Road, Ryde
PO33 3TH
t (01983) 567910

**Seahaven House** ★★★
*Guest Accommodation*
36 St Thomas Street, Ryde
PO33 2DL
t (01983) 563069
e seahaven@netguides.co.uk

**Seaward Guest House** ★★
*Guest House*
14-16 George Street, Ryde
PO33 2EW
t (01983) 563168
e seaward@fsbdial.co.uk

**Sillwood Acre** ★★★★
*Bed & Breakfast*
SILVER AWARD
Church Road, Binstead
PO33 3TB
t (01983) 563553
e debbie@sillwood-acre.co.uk
w sillwood-acre.co.uk

**Trentham Guest House** ◆◆◆
*Guest Accommodation*
38 The Strand, Ryde PO33 1JF
t (01983) 563418
e info@trentham-guesthouse.
co.uk
w trentham-guesthouse.co.uk

RYE
East Sussex

**11 High Street** ◆◆◆
*Guest Accommodation*
High Street, Rye TN31 7JF
t (01797) 223952

**At Wisteria Corner** ★★★★
*Bed & Breakfast*
47 Ferry Road, Rye TN31 7DJ
t (01797) 225011
e mmpartridge@lineone.net
w wisteriacorner.co.uk

**Aviemore Guest House**
★★★ *Guest House*
28-30 Fishmarket Road, Rye
TN31 7LP
t (01797) 223052
e info@aviemorerye.co.uk
w aviemorerye.co.uk

**Durrant House** ★★★★★
*Guest Accommodation*
GOLD AWARD
2 Market Street, Rye TN31 7LA
t (01797) 223182
e Info@durranthouse.com
w durranthouse.com

**Fairacres** ★★★★★
*Bed & Breakfast*
GOLD AWARD
Udimore Road, Broad Oak, Rye
TN31 6DG
t (01424) 883236
e shelagh-john@fairacres.
fsworld.co.uk
w smoothhound.co.uk/hotels/
fairacres

**Four Seasons** ★★★★
*Guest Accommodation*
SILVER AWARD
96 Udimore Road, Rye
TN31 7DY
t (01797) 224305

**Hayden's** ★★★★★
*Bed & Breakfast*
108 High Street, Rye TN31 7JE
t (01797) 224501
e richard.hayden@mac.com
w cheynehouse.co.uk

**Jeake's House** ★★★★★
*Guest Accommodation*
GOLD AWARD
Mermaid Street, Rye TN31 7ET
t (01797) 222828
e stay@jeakeshouse.com
w jeakeshouse.com

**Kimbley Cottage** ★★★★
*Bed & Breakfast*
Main Street, Peasmarsh, Rye
TN31 6UL
t (01797) 230514
e kimbleycot@aol.com
w kimbleycottage.co.uk

**Layces B&B** ★★★★
*Bed & Breakfast*
SILVER AWARD
Chitcombe Road, Broad Oak
Brede, Rye TN31 6EU
t (01424) 882836
e stephens@layces.co.uk
w layces.co.uk

**Leswinton B&B** ★★★★
*Bed & Breakfast*
Leswinton, West Undercliff,
Rye TN31 7DX
t (01797) 224710
e leswintonbandb@yahoo.co.
uk

**The Mill House, Holmdale**
★★★★
*Guest Accommodation*
Holmdale Farm, Peasmarsh
Road, Rye TN31 7UN
t (01797) 280154
e jen@pay7900.freeserve.co.
uk

**Oaklands** ★★★★★
*Guest Accommodation*
SILVER AWARD
Udimore Road, Rye TN31 6AB
t (01797) 229734
e info@oaklands-rye.co.uk
w oaklands-rye.co.uk

**The Place Camber Sands**
★★★★
*Guest Accommodation*
New Lydd Road, Rye
TN31 7RB
t (01797) 225057
e enquiries@
theplacecambersands.co.uk
w theplacecambersands.co.uk

**The Rise** ★★★★
*Bed & Breakfast*
GOLD AWARD
82 Udimore Road, Rye
TN31 7DY
t (01797) 222285
e theriserye@aol.com
w therise-rye.co.uk

**Ship Inn** ★★★ *Inn*
The Strand, Rye TN31 7DB
t (01797) 222233

**The Strand House** ★★★★
*Guest Accommodation*
SILVER AWARD
Tanyards Lane, The Strand,
Winchelsea TN36 4JT
t (01797) 226276
e info@thestrandhouse.co.uk
w thestrandhouse.co.uk

**Top o'The Hill at Rye** ★★★
*Inn*
Rye Hill, Rye TN31 7NH
t (01797) 223284

**Vine-Cottage** ★★★
*Bed & Breakfast*
25a Udimore Road, Rye
TN31 7DS
t (01797) 222822

**Willow Tree House**
★★★★★
*Guest Accommodation*
**SILVER AWARD**
113 Winchelsea Road, Rye
TN31 7EL
t (01797) 227820
e info@willow-tree-house.com
w willow-tree-house.com

RYE FOREIGN
East Sussex

**The Hare & Hounds** ★★★★
*Inn*
Rye Road, Rye TN31 7ST
t (01797) 230483

ST CROSS
Hampshire

**Dolphin House Studios**
★★★★ *Bed & Breakfast*
**SILVER AWARD**
3 Compton Road, Winchester
SO23 9SL
t (01962) 853284
e lizsandes@hotmail.co.uk
w dolphinhousestudios.co.uk

ST LAWRENCE
Isle of Wight

**Lisle Combe** ★★★
*Guest Accommodation*
Bank End Farm, Undercliff
Drive, St Lawrence PO38 1UW
t (01983) 852582
e lislecombe@yahoo.com
w lislecombe.co.uk

**Little Orchard** ★★★★
*Guest Accommodation*
Undercliff Drive, St Lawrence
PO38 1YA
t (01983) 731106

ST LEONARDS
East Sussex

**Hastings House** ★★★
*Guest Accommodation*
9 Warrior Square, St Leonards-
on-Sea, Hastings TN37 6BA
t (01424) 422709
e sengloy@btconnect.com
w hastingshouse.co.uk

**Hollington Croft** ★★★
*Bed & Breakfast*
272 Battle Road, St Leonards-
on-Sea TN37 7BA
t (01424) 851795

**Marina Lodge** ★★★
*Guest House*
123 Marina, St Leonards-on-
Sea TN38 0BN
t (01424) 715067
e marinalodgeguesthse@
tiscali.co.uk
w marinalodge.co.uk

**Melrose Guest House**
★★★★ *Guest House*
18 de Cham Road, St
Leonards-on-Sea TN37 6JP
t (01424) 715163
e melrose18@hotmail.com

**Rutland** ★★★ *Guest House*
17 Grosvenor Crescent, St
Leonards-on-Sea TN38 0AA
t (01424) 714720
e rut1land@aol.com

**Sherwood Guest House**
★★★★ *Guest House*
15 Grosvenor Crescent, St
Leonards-on-Sea TN38 0AA
t (01424) 433331
e wendy@sherwoodhastings.
co.uk
w sherwoodhastings.co.uk

ST-MARGARETS-AT-CLIFFE
Kent

**Holm Oaks** ★★★★
*Guest Accommodation*
**SILVER AWARD**
Dover Road, St Margarets-at-
Cliffe, Dover CT15 6EP
t (01304) 852090
e holmoaks@invictawiz.co.uk

ST MARGARET'S BAY
Kent

**Small Acre** ★★★★
*Guest Accommodation*
**SILVER AWARD**
Sea View Road, Dover
CT15 6EE
t (01304) 851840
e marion@smallacre.co.uk
w smallacre.co.uk

SANDFORD
Isle of Wight

**The Barn** ★★★★ *Farmhouse*
Pound Farm, Shanklin Road,
Sandford PO38 3AW
t (01983) 840047
e barnpoundfarm@
barnpoundfarm.free-online.co.
uk

SANDHURST
Berkshire

**The Wellington Arms** ★★★
*Inn*
203 Yorktown Road, Sandhurst
GU47 9BN
t (01252) 872408
w thewellingtonarms.co.uk

SANDHURST
Kent

**Lamberden Cottage** ★★★★
*Bed & Breakfast*
Rye Road, Cranbrook
TN18 5PH
t (01580) 850743
e thewalledgarden@hotmail.
co.uk
w lamberdencottage.co.uk

SANDOWN
Isle of Wight

**Alendel Hotel** ★★★
*Guest House*
1 Leed Street, Sandown
PO36 9DA
t (01983) 402967
e info@alendelhotel.co.uk
w alendelhotel.co.uk

**Beaufort House**
Rating Applied For
*Guest House*
30 Broadway, Sandown
PO36 9BY
t (01983) 403672
e enquiries@
thebeaufortsandown.co.uk
w thebeaufortsandown.co.uk

**Belgrave Hotel** ★★
*Guest Accommodation*
14-16 Beachfield Road,
Sandown PO36 8NA
t (01983) 404550

**The Bernay** ★★★
*Guest Accommodation*
24 Victoria Road, Sandown
PO36 8AL
t (01983) 402205
e info@thebernayhotel.co.uk
w thebernayhotel.co.uk

**Bertram Lodge**
Rating Applied For
*Guest House*
3 Leed Street, Sandown
PO36 9DA
t (01983) 402551
e gazz@blodge.fslife.co.uk
w bertramlodge.co.uk

**The Caprera** ★★★
*Guest House*
Melville Street, Sandown
PO36 8LE
t (01983) 402482
e the.caprera@virgin.net
w thecaprera.com

**Copperfield Lodge** ★★★★
*Bed & Breakfast*
**SILVER AWARD**
Newport Road, Apse Heath,
Sandown PO36 9PJ
t 07733 262889
e copperfieldlodge@aol.com

**The Danebury Hotel** ♦♦♦
*Guest Accommodation*
26 Victoria Road, Sandown
PO36 8AL
t (01983) 403795
e danebury@onetel.com
w daneburyhotel.com

**The Denewood** ★★★★
*Guest Accommodation*
7-9 Victoria Road, Sandown
PO36 8AL
t (01983) 402980
e holidays@denewoodhotel.
co.uk
w denewood-hotel.co.uk

**Heathfield House** ★★★★
*Guest Accommodation*
52 Melville Street, Sandown
PO36 8LF
t (01983) 400002
e mail@heathfieldhousehotel.
com
w heathfieldhousehotel.com

**Inglewood Guest House**
★★★ *Guest House*
15 Avenue Road, Sandown
PO36 8BN
t (01983) 403485
e inglewooduk@yahoo.co.uk

**The Montpelier** ★★★
*Guest Accommodation*
Pier Street, Sandown PO36 8JR
t (01983) 403964
e enquiries@themontpelier.co.
uk
w themontpelier.co.uk

**Mount Brocas Guest House**
★★★ *Guest House*
15 Beachfield Road, Sandown
PO36 8LT
t (01983) 406276
e mountbrocas1@btconnect.
com
w wightstay.co.uk/brocas.html

**The Philomel** ★★★
*Guest House*
21 Carter Street, Sandown
PO36 8BL
t (01983) 406413
e enquiries@philomel-hotel.
co.uk
w philomel-hotel.co.uk

**Rooftree Guesthouse**
★★★★ *Guest House*
26 Broadway, Sandown
PO36 9BY
t (01983) 403175
e rooftree@btconnect.com
w rooftree-hotel.co.uk

**Southwood House** ★★★
*Guest Accommodation*
26 Albert Road, Sandown
PO36 8AW
t (01983) 407297
e southwoodhouse@aol.com
w southwoodhouse.co.uk

**Treval Guest House** ★★★★
*Bed & Breakfast*
46 Culver Way, Yaverland,
Sandown PO36 8QJ
t (01983) 407910
e val-newton@tiscali.co.uk
w treval-sandown.co.uk

**Winchester Park** ★★
*Guest House*
Fitzroy Street, Sandown
PO36 8HQ
t (01983) 402619
e reception@
winchesterparkhotel.co.uk
w winchesterparkhotel.co.uk

SANDWICH
Kent

**Molland House** ★★★★★
*Guest Accommodation*
**GOLD AWARD**
Molland Lane, Ash, Canterbury
CT3 2JB
t (01304) 814210
e tracy@mollandhouse.co.uk
w mollandhouse.co.uk

SARRE
Kent

**Crown Inn (The Famous
Cherry Brandy House)**
★★★★ *Inn*
Ramsgate Road, Sarre,
Birchington CT7 0LF
t (01843) 847808
e crown@shepherd-neame.co.
uk
w shepherd-neame.co.uk

SEAFORD
East Sussex

**Cornerways** ★★★
*Guest Accommodation*
10 The Covers, Seaford
BN25 1DF
t (01323) 492400

**Malvern House** ★★★
*Bed & Breakfast*
Alfriston Road, Seaford
BN25 3QG
t (01323) 492058
e malvernbandb@aol.com
w malvernhouse.gb.com

**The Silverdale ★★★★**
*Guest House*
21 Sutton Park Road, Seaford
BN25 1RH
t (01323) 491849
e silverdale@mistral.co.uk
w silverdaleseaford.co.uk

### SEAVIEW
### Isle of Wight

**1 Cluniac Cottages ★★★**
*Bed & Breakfast*
Priory Road, Seaview
PO34 5BU
t (01983) 812119
e bill.elfenjay@virgin.net
w cluniaccottages.co.uk

**Clover Ridge ★★★★**
*Bed & Breakfast*
18 Horestone Rise, Seaview
PO34 5DB
t (01983) 617377
e cloverridge.seaviewiow@
virgin.net
w cloverridge.co.uk

**Maple Villa B&B ★★**
*Bed & Breakfast*
Oakhill Road, Seaview
PO34 5AP
t (01983) 614826
e mail@maplevilla.co.uk
w maplevilla.co.uk

### SEDLESCOMBE
### East Sussex

**Forge House ★★★★**
*Bed & Breakfast*
The Green, Sedlescombe,
Battle TN33 0QA
t (01424) 870054
e jean@bridgetvaughan.
wannado.co.uk

**Luff's Farm ★★★★**
*Guest Accommodation*
Chapel Hill, Sedlescombe,
Battle TN33 0QX
t (01424) 870349
e amandapollard32@hotmail.
com
w luffsfarm.co.uk

### SEER GREEN
### Buckinghamshire

**Highclere Farm ★★★**
*Guest Accommodation*
Newbarn Lane, Beaconsfield
HP9 2QZ
t (01494) 874505
e highclerepark@aol.com
w highclerefarm.co.uk

### SELBORNE
### Hampshire

**Ivanhoe ★★★★**
*Bed & Breakfast*
Oakhanger, Selborne, Bordon
GU35 9JG
t (01420) 473464
w ivanhoe-bnb.co.uk

### SELSEY
### West Sussex

**Greenacre Bed & Breakfast**
**★★★★** *Bed & Breakfast*
Manor Farm Court, Selsey
PO20 0LY
t (01243) 602912
e greenacre@zoom.co.uk
w visitsussex.org/greenacre

**Keston House ★★★★**
*Bed & Breakfast*
16 Beacon Drive, Chichester
PO20 0TW
t (01243) 604513
e mrt@mercedes553.
wanadoo.co.uk
w kestonhouseselsey.co.uk

**Norton Lea Guest House**
**★★★** *Bed & Breakfast*
Chichester Road, Selsey,
Chichester PO20 9EA
t (01243) 605454
e nortonlea@aol.com
w nortonlea.com

**St Andrews Lodge Guest**
**Accommodation ★★★★**
*Guest Accommodation*
Chichester Road, Selsey,
Chichester PO20 0LX
t (01243) 606899
e info@standrewslodge.co.uk
w standrewslodge.co.uk

### SEND
### Surrey

**Sommerhay Barn ★★★★**
*Bed & Breakfast*
Church Lane, Send, Woking
GU23 7JL
t (01483) 210107
e angey_watson@hotmail.com

### SEVENOAKS
### Kent

**40 Robyns Way ★★★**
*Bed & Breakfast*
Sevenoaks TN13 3EB
t (01732) 452401
e ingram7oaks@onetel.com
w http://web.onetel.com/
~ingram7oaks/

**56 The Drive ★★★**
*Bed & Breakfast*
Sevenoaks TN13 3AF
t (01732) 453236
e shirley.lloyd@7oaks.net

**Bramber ★★** *Bed & Breakfast*
45 Shoreham Lane, Sevenoaks
TN13 3DX
t (01732) 457466

**Crofters ★★★★**
*Bed & Breakfast*
67 Oakhill Road, Sevenoaks
TN13 1NU
t (01732) 460189
e ritamarfry@talk21.com

**The Heathers ★★★★**
*Guest Accommodation*
29 White Hart Wood,
Sevenoaks TN13 1RS
t (01732) 454061
e ken@beaumontk.fslife.co.uk
w http://the-heathers.mysite.
wanadoo-members.co.uk

**Hornshaw House ★★★★**
*Bed & Breakfast*
47 Mount Harry Road,
Sevenoaks TN13 3JN
t (01732) 465262
e elizabeth.bates4@btinternet.
com
w hornshaw-house.co.uk

**Old Timbertop Cottage**
**★★★★** *Bed & Breakfast*
**SILVER AWARD**
4 Old Timbertop Cottages,
Bethel Road, Sevenoaks
TN13 3UE
t (01732) 460506
e timbertopcottage@tiscali.co.
uk
w timbertopcottage.co.uk

**The Pightle ★★★★**
*Guest Accommodation*
21 White Hart Wood,
Sevenoaks TN13 1RS
t (01732) 451678
e emtess@tiscali.co.uk
w thepightle.co.uk

**Robann ★★★**
*Bed & Breakfast*
5 Vestry Cottages, Old Otford
Road, Sevenoaks TN14 5EH
t (01732) 456272
e info@robannbandb.co.uk
w robannbandb.co.uk

**The Studio At Double Dance**
**★★★★** *Bed & Breakfast*
**SILVER AWARD**
Penny Cracknell, Double
Dance, Bates Hill, Ightham
TN15 9AT
t (01732) 884198
e pennycracknell@
doubledance.co.uk
w doubledance.co.uk

**Wendy Wood Bed &**
**Breakfast ★★★★**
*Bed & Breakfast*
86 Childsbridge Lane, Seal,
Sevenoaks TN15 0BW
t (01732) 763755
e bandb@f2s.com
w wendywood.co.uk

### SHALFORD
### Surrey

**2 Northfield ★★★**
*Bed & Breakfast*
Off Summersbury Drive,
Shalford, Guildford GU4 8JN
t (01483) 570431
e themordens@tiscali.co.uk
w northfieldbnb.net

### SHALSTONE
### Buckinghamshire

**Barnita ★★★** *Bed & Breakfast*
Wood Green, Buckingham
MK18 5DZ
t (01280) 850639

### SHANKLIN
### Isle of Wight

**The Appley ★★★★**
*Guest House*
13 Queens Road, Shanklin
PO37 6AW
t (01983) 862666
e rod.folds@virgin.net
w appleyhotel.com

**Atholl Court ★★★**
*Guest House*
1 Atherley Road, Shanklin
PO37 7AT
t (01983) 862414
e info@atholl-court.co.uk
w atholl-court.co.uk

**The Birkdale ★★★★**
*Guest House* **SILVER AWARD**
5 Grange Road, Shanklin
PO37 6NN
t (01983) 862949
e birkdale-iow@hotmail.co.uk
w birkdalehotel.com

**Brooke House ★★★**
*Guest House*
2 St Pauls Avenue, Shanklin
PO37 7AL
t (01983) 863162
e brookehousehotel@
btconnect.com
w brookehousehotel.co.uk

**The Burlington (Shanklin)**
**★★★** *Guest House*
6 Chine Avenue, Shanklin
PO37 6AG
t (01983) 862090
e burlingtonshanklin@
isleofwight.com
w isleofwighthotels.org.uk

**The Chestnuts ★★★★**
*Guest House*
4 Hope Road, Shanklin
PO37 6EA
t (01983) 862162
e chrischestnuts@yahoo.co.uk
w thechestnutsshanklin.co.uk

**Claremont Guest House**
**★★★★** *Guest House*
4 Eastmount Road, Shanklin
PO37 6DN
t (01983) 862083
e claremont@dsl.pipex.com
w southernuk.com/claremont.
htm

**Cliftonville Guest House**
**★★★** *Guest House*
6 Hope Road, Shanklin
PO37 6EA
t (01983) 862197
e info@cliftonvillehotel.
wanadoo.co.uk
w cliftonvillehotel.com

**Dolphin House ★★★**
*Bed & Breakfast*
Luccombe Road, Shanklin
PO37 6RR
t (01983) 864434
e info@dolphin-house.net
w dolphin-house.net

**The Edgecliffe ★★★★**
*Guest Accommodation*
7 Clarence Gardens, Shanklin
PO37 6HA
t (01983) 866199
e edgecliffehtl@aol.com
w wightonline.co.uk/
edgecliffehotel

**Farringford Hotel – Shanklin**
**★★★★** *Guest House*
19 Hope Road, Shanklin
PO37 6EA
t (01983) 862176
e annette.hill@sky.com
w farringfordhotel.com

**The Fawley Guest House**
**★★★★** *Guest House*
12 Hope Road, Shanklin
PO37 6EA
t (01983) 868898
e enquiries@the-fawley.co.uk
w the-fawley.co.uk

**Foxhills** ★★★★★
*Guest Accommodation*
**GOLD AWARD**
30 Victoria Avenue, Shanklin
PO37 6LS
t (01983) 862329
e info@foxhillshotel.co.uk
w foxhillshotel.co.uk

**Grange Bank House** ★★★★
*Guest Accommodation*
**SILVER AWARD**
Grange Road, Shanklin
PO37 6NN
t (01983) 862337
e grangebank@btinternet.com
w grangebank.co.uk

**Hambledon** ★★★★
*Guest Accommodation*
11 Queens Road, Shanklin
PO37 6AW
t (01983) 862403
e enquiries@hambledon-
hotel.co.uk
w hambledon-hotel.co.uk

**The Havelock** ★★★★
*Guest Accommodation*
**GOLD AWARD**
2 Queens Road, Shanklin
PO37 6AN
t (01983) 862747
e enquiries@havelockhotel.co.
uk
w havelockhotel.co.uk

**The Hazelwood** ★★★
*Guest House*
14 Clarence Road, Shanklin
PO37 7BH
t (01983) 862824
e hazelwoodiow@aol.com
w hazelwoodiow.co.uk

**The Heatherleigh** ★★★★
*Guest House*
17 Queens Road, Shanklin
PO37 6AW
t (01983) 862503
e enquiries@heatherleigh.co.
uk
w heatherleigh.co.uk

**Holly Lodge** ★★★
*Guest Accommodation*
29 Queens Road, Shanklin
PO37 6DQ
t (01983) 863604
e hollylodge.iow@btinternet.
com

**Hope Lodge** ♦♦♦♦
*Guest Accommodation*
**GOLD AWARD**
21 Hope Road, Shanklin
PO37 6EA
t (01983) 863140
e janetwf@aol.com
w wight365.com/dart/
hopelodge/index.htm

**The Kenbury** ★★★★
*Guest Accommodation*
Clarence Road, Shanklin
PO37 7BH
t (01983) 862085
e kenbury@isleofwighthotel.
co.uk
w isleofwighthotel.co.uk

**The Lincoln** ★★★★
*Guest House*
30 Littlestairs Road, Shanklin
PO37 6HS
t (01983) 861171
e enquiries@thelincolnhotel.
org.uk
w thelincolnhotel.org.uk

**Miclaran** ★★★ *Guest House*
37 Littlestairs Road, Shanklin
PO37 6HS
t (01983) 862726
e miclaran@btinternet.com

**Mount House** ★★★
*Guest House*
20 Arthurs Hill, Shanklin
PO37 6EE
t (01983) 862556
e graham.mounthouse@
btopenworld.com
w wightstay.co.uk/mount.html

**Overstrand** ★★★★
*Guest Accommodation*
5 Howard Road, Shanklin
PO37 6HD
t (01983) 862100
e enquiries@overstrand-hotel.
co.uk
w overstrand-hotel.co.uk

**The Palmerston** ★★★
*Guest Accommodation*
16 Palmerston Road, Shanklin
PO37 6AS
t (01983) 865547
e info@palmerston-hotel.co.uk
w palmerston-hotel.co.uk

**Parkway Hotel**
Rating Applied For
*Guest Accommodation*
6 Park Road, Shanklin
PO37 6AZ
t (01983) 862740
e info@parkwayhotelshanklin.
co.uk
w parkwayhotelshanklin.co.uk

**The Pink Beach Guest House**
★★★ *Guest House*
20 The Esplanade, Shanklin
PO37 6BN
t (01983) 862501
e pinkbeach@btopenworld.
com
w pink-beach-hotel.co.uk

**Roseberry** ★★★★
*Guest Accommodation*
3 Alexandra Road, Shanklin
PO37 6AF
t (01983) 862805
e herm-beach@tinyworld.co.
uk
w roseberryhotel-isleofwight.
co.uk

**Royson Hotel**
Rating Applied For
*Guest House*
26 Littlestairs Road, Shanklin
PO37 6HS
t (01983) 862163
e enquiries@theroyson.co.uk
w theroyson.co.uk

**Rozelle Hotel** ♦♦♦
*Guest Accommodation*
Atherley Road, Shanklin
PO37 7AT
t (01983) 862745
e rozelle@fsmail.net

**The Ryedale** ★★★
*Guest Accommodation*
3 Atherley Road, Shanklin
PO37 7AT
t (01983) 862375
e hayley@ryedale-hotel.co.uk
w ryedale-hotel.co.uk

**St Leonards Hotel** ★★★★
*Guest Accommodation*
**SILVER AWARD**
22 Queens Road, Shanklin
PO37 6AW
t (01983) 862121
e info@thestleonards.co.uk
w thestleonards.co.uk

**Snowdon House** ★★★★
*Guest Accommodation*
**SILVER AWARD**
19 Queens Road, Shanklin
PO37 6AW
t (01983) 862853
e info@snowdonhotel.fsnet.
co.uk
w thesnowdonhotel.co.uk

**Somerville** ★★★
*Guest Accommodation*
14 St Georges Road, Shanklin
PO37 6BA
t (01983) 862821
e somerville@fsmail.net

**Steamer Inn – Quayside
Leisure** ♦♦♦♦
*Guest Accommodation*
18 The Esplanade, Shanklin
PO37 6BS
t (01983) 862641
e info@thesteamer.co.uk
w steamerinn.co.uk

**The Suncliffe** ★★★
*Guest House*
8 Hope Road, Shanklin
PO37 6EA
t (01983) 863009
e kenandlinda@wanadoo.co.
uk
w suncliffe.co.uk

**Swiss Cottage Guest House**
Rating Applied For
*Guest House*
10 St Georges Road, Shanklin
PO37 6BA
t (01983) 862333
e mail@swisscottagehotel.
fsnet.co.uk
w swiss-cottage.co.uk

**Westbury Lodge** ★★★★
*Guest Accommodation*
25 Queens Road, Shanklin
PO37 6AW
t (01983) 864926
e enquiries@westburylodge.
co.uk
w westburylodge.co.uk

SHARPTHORNE
West Sussex

**Courtlands Nurseries**
★★★★ *Bed & Breakfast*
Chilling Street, Sharpthorne,
East Grinstead RH19 4JF
t (01342) 810780
e lindsay.shurvell@virgin.net
w courtlandsnurseries.co.uk

SHAWFORD
Hampshire

**Greenmead Cottage** ★★★★
*Bed & Breakfast*
**SILVER AWARD**
Fairfield Road, Shawford
SO21 2DA
t (01962) 713172
e junetice@yahoo.com
w greenmeadcottage.co.uk

**Orchard House** ★★★
*Bed & Breakfast*
40 Castle Street, Steventon,
Winchester OX13 6SR
t (01235) 821351
e orchardhouse.40@ntlworld.
com
w homepage.ntlworld.com/
orchardhouse40/

SHEERNESS
Kent

**The Croft Guesthouse** ★★★
*Guest House*
89 Queenborough Road,
Sheerness ME12 3DB
t (01795) 662003
e thecroftguesthouse@
hotmail.com
w thecroftguesthouse.co.uk

**The Ferry House Inn** ★★★★
*Guest Accommodation*
Harty Ferry Road, Leysdown-
on-Sea, Sheerness ME12 4BQ
t (01795) 510214
e info@ferryhouseinn.com
w ferryhouseinn.com

**Invicta Guest House** ★★★
*Guest House*
6 Marine Parade, Sheerness
ME12 2AL
t (01795) 661731
w invictaguesthouse.co.uk

SHENINGTON
Oxfordshire

**Top Farm House** ★★★
*Bed & Breakfast*
Shenington, Banbury
OX15 6LZ
t (01295) 670226
e info@topfarmhouse.co.uk
w topfarmhouse.co.uk

SHENLEY CHURCH END
Buckinghamshire

**The Malt House** ♦♦♦♦
*Guest Accommodation*
Oakhill Road, Shenley Church
End, Milton Keynes MK5 6AE
t (01908) 501619
e pat.morris11@btopenworld.
com

SHERBORNE ST JOHN
Hampshire

**Manor Farm Stables** ★★★★
*Bed & Breakfast*
Vyne Road, Sherborne St John,
Basingstoke RG24 9HX
t (01256) 851324

SHERE
Surrey

**Lockhurst Hatch Farm**
★★★★ *Farmhouse*
Lockhurst Hatch Lane, Shere,
Guildford GU5 9JN
t (01483) 202689
e gill@lockhurst-hatch-farm.
co.uk
w users.waitrose.com/
~gmgellatly

**Rookery Nook Bed and
Breakfast** ★★
*Guest Accommodation*
The Square, Shere, Guildford
GU5 9HG
t (01483) 209399
e info@rookerynook.info
w rookerynook.info

**The Sanctuary** ★★★★
*Guest Accommodation*
Burrows Lea, Hook Lane,
Shere, Guildford GU5 9QG
t   (01483) 205620
e   accommodation@
burrowslea.org.uk
w  sanctuary-burrowslea.org.uk

**Alouette Bed & Breakfast**
★★★★ *Bed & Breakfast*
2 Caldicot Close, Shillingford,
Wallingford OX10 7HF
t   (01865) 858600
e   wendy@alouettebandb.co.
uk
w  alouettebandb.co.uk

**The Kingfisher Inn** ★★★★
*Inn*
27 Henley Road, Shillingford,
Wallingford OX10 7EL
t   (01865) 858595
e   enquiries@kingfisher-inn.co.
uk
w  kingfisher-inn.co.uk

**Goffsland Farm (B & B)**
◆◆◆◆ *Guest Accommodation*
Shipley, Horsham RH13 9BQ
t   (01403) 730434

**The White House** ★★
*Bed & Breakfast*
Faringdon Road, Shippon,
Abingdon OX13 6LW
t   (01235) 521998
e   judymccairns@freeuk.com

**Court Farm** ★★★★
*Bed & Breakfast*
Mawles Lane, Shipton-under-
Wychwood, Chipping Norton
OX7 6DA
t   (01993) 831515
e   enquiries@courtfarmbb.com
w  courtfarmbb.com

**Garden Cottage** ★★★
*Bed & Breakfast*
Fiddlers Hill, Shipton-under-
Wychwood, Chipping Norton
OX7 6DR
t   07803 399697
e   charmian@gardencottage.
wanadoo.co.uk

**Lodge Cottage** ★★★
*Bed & Breakfast*
High Street, Shipton-under-
Wychwood, Chipping Norton
OX7 6DG
t   (01993) 830811
e   h.a.savill@tiscali.co.uk

**Shipton Grange House**
★★★★★ *Bed & Breakfast*
High Street, Shipton-under-
Wychwood, Chipping Norton
OX7 6DG
t   (01993) 831298
e   veronica@
shiptongrangehouse.com
w  shiptongrangehouse.com

**Preston Farmhouse** ★★★★
*Farmhouse*
Shoreham Road, Shoreham,
Sevenoaks TN14 7UD
t   (01959) 522029

**Rutland House** ★★★★
*Guest Accommodation*
418 Upper Shoreham Road,
Shoreham-by-Sea BN43 5NE
t   (01273) 461681
e   info@rutlandhouse.net
w  rutlandhouse.net

**Truleigh Hill YHA** ★★★
*Hostel*
Tottington Barn, Truleigh Hill,
Shoreham-by-Sea BN43 5FB
t   (01903) 813419
e   truleighhill@yha.org.uk
w  yha.org.uk

**Northcourt** ★★★★
*Guest Accommodation*
SILVER AWARD
Shorwell PO30 3JG
t   (01983) 740415
e   enquiries@northcourt.info
w  northcourt.info

**Westcourt Farm** ★★★★
*Farmhouse* SILVER AWARD
Limerstone Road, Shorwell
PO30 3LA
t   (01983) 740233
e   julie@westcourt-farm.co.uk
w  westcourt-farm.co.uk

**The Horse and Groom Inn**
★★★★ *Inn*
Milcombe, Banbury OX15 5RS
t   (01295) 722142

**Brimfast House** ★★★
*Bed & Breakfast*
Brimfast Lane, Sidlesham
Common, Chichester
PO20 7PZ
t   (01243) 641841
e   bookings@brimfastbandb.
co.uk
w  brimfastbandb.co.uk

**1 Rose Cottage**
Rating Applied For
*Guest Accommodation*
Singleton, Chichester
PO18 0HP
t   (01243) 811607
e   rosecottagesingleton@yahoo.
co.uk
w  1rosecottage.com

**Scuttington Manor Guest
House** ★★★★ *Guest House*
Dully Road, Tonge,
Sittingbourne ME9 9PA
t   (01795) 521316

**Woodstock Guest House**
★★★★ *Bed & Breakfast*
SILVER AWARD
25 Woodstock Road,
Sittingbourne ME10 4HJ
t   (01795) 421516
e   woodstockbnb@
blueyonder.co.uk
w  woodstockguesthouse.com

**The Old Bakery** ★★★★
*Guest Accommodation*
Skirmett RG9 6TD
t   (01491) 638309
e   lizzroach@aol.com

**Magpies** ★★★
*Bed & Breakfast*
Stane Street, Slinfold, Horsham
RH13 0QX
t   (01403) 790764

**The Red Lyon** ★★★ *Inn*
The Street, Slinfold, Horsham
RH13 0RR
t   (01403) 790339
e   smarkham@theredlyon.co.
uk
w  theredlyon.co.uk

**Furnival Lodge** ★★★★
*Guest House*
53-55 Furnival Avenue, Slough
SL2 1DH
t   (01753) 570333
e   info@furnival-lodge.co.uk
w  furnival-lodge.co.uk

**Hereford Oast** ★★★★
*Bed & Breakfast*
SILVER AWARD
Smarden Bell Road, Smarden,
Ashford TN27 8PA
t   (01233) 770541
e   suzy@herefordoast.fsnet.co.
uk
w  herefordoast.co.uk

**Snap Mill** ★★★★
*Guest Accommodation*
SILVER AWARD
Romden Road, Smarden,
Ashford TN27 8RB
t   (01233) 770333
e   snapmill@aol.com
w  snapmill.co.uk

**Tower Fields** ★★★
*Farmhouse*
Souldern, Bicester OX27 7HY
t   (01869) 346554
e   toddyclive@towerfields.com
w  towerfields.com

**Harts Lane Cottage** ★★★★
*Guest Accommodation*
Harts Lane, South Godstone,
Godstone RH9 8LZ
t   (01342) 892162
e   beacronk@hotmail.com

**A D's B&B** ★★★
*Bed & Breakfast*
37 Whitehouse Gardens,
Southampton SO15 0SB
t   (023) 8070 3969
e   angela.davies37@btinternet.
com

**Alcantara Guest House**
★★★★
*Guest Accommodation*
20 Howard Road, Shirley,
Southampton SO15 5BN
t   (023) 8033 2966
e   alcantara@btconnect.com
w  alcantaraguesthouse.co.uk

**Amberley Lodge Guest
House** ★★★
*Guest Accommodation*
1 Howard Road, Shirley,
Southampton SO15 5BB
t   (023) 8022 3789
e   contact@
amberleyguesthouse.co.uk
w  amberleyguesthouse.co.uk

**Argyle Lodge Guest House**
★★★★
*Guest Accommodation*
13 Landguard Road, Shirley,
Southampton SO15 5DL
t   (023) 8022 4063
e   judith@higgs1236.freeserve.
co.uk
w  argylelodge.com

**Banister Guest House** ★★★
*Guest Accommodation*
11 Brighton Road,
Southampton SO15 2JJ
t   (023) 8022 1279
e   info@banisterhotel.co.uk
w  banisterhotel.co.uk

**Brunswick Lodge** ★★★★
*Guest Accommodation*
100 Anglesea Road, Shirley,
Southampton SO15 5QS
t   (023) 8077 4777
w  brunswicklodge.co.uk

**Dormy House Guest
Accommodation** ★★★★
*Guest Accommodation*
21 Barnes Lane, Sarisbury
Green, Southampton
SO31 7DA
t   (01489) 572626
e   dormyhousehotel@warsash.
globalnet.co.uk
w  dormyhousehotel.net

**Eaton Court** ★★★
*Guest Accommodation*
32 Hill Lane, Southampton
SO15 5AY
t   (023) 8022 3081
e   ecourthot@aol.com
w  eatoncourtsouthampton.co.
uk

**Ellenborough House** ★★★
*Guest Accommodation*
172 Hill Lane, Southampton
SO15 5DB
t   (023) 8022 1716
e   ellenboroughhse@aol.com
w  ellenboroughhouse.co.uk

**Fenland Guest House** ★★★
*Guest Accommodation*
79 Hill Lane, Southampton
SO15 5AD
t (023) 8022 0360
e fenland@btconnect.com
w fenlandguesthouse.co.uk

**Lakeside** ★★★★
*Bed & Breakfast*
West Common, Blackfield,
New Forest SO45 1XJ
t (023) 8089 8926
e tonycavell@aol.com
w lakesidebandb.net

**Landguard House** ★★★
*Guest House*
44 Landguard Road,
Southampton SO15 5DP
t (023) 8022 9708
e vonmilne@aol.com
w landguardhouse.co.uk

**Linden Guest House** ★★★
*Guest Accommodation*
51-53 The Polygon,
Southampton SO15 2BP
t (023) 8022 5653
e trisha@lindenguesthouse.
net
w lindenguesthouse.net

**Mayfair Guest House**
★★★★
*Guest Accommodation*
11 Landguard Road,
Southampton SO15 5DL
t (023) 8022 9861
e info@themayfairguesthouse.
co.uk
w themayfairguesthouse.co.uk

**Mayview Guest House** ★★★
*Guest Accommodation*
30 The Polygon, Southampton
SO15 2BN
t (023) 8022 0907
e info@mayview.co.uk
w mayview.co.uk

**Rivendell Guest House**
★★★★
*Guest Accommodation*
19 Landguard Road, Hill Lane,
Southampton SO15 5DL
t (023) 8022 3240
e rivendelllalley@
talktalkbusiness.net

**The Spinnaker** ★★★★ *Inn*
Bridge Road, Lower Swanwick,
Southampton SO31 7EB
t (01489) 572123

**Bramble Barn** ★★★★
*Bed & Breakfast*
Southerham, Lewes BN8 6JN
t (01273) 474924

**Birchwood Guest House**
★★★★
*Guest Accommodation*
44 Waverley Road, Southsea
PO5 2PP
t (023) 9281 1337
e enquiries@birchwood.uk.
com
w birchwood.uk.com

**Ferryman Guest House**
★★★ *Guest Accommodation*
16 Victoria Road South,
Southsea PO5 2BZ
t (023) 9287 5824
e theferrymanhotel@hotmail.
com
w ferryman-southsea.co.uk

**No. 32** ★★★★
*Bed & Breakfast*
32 Albert Grove, Southsea
PO5 1NG
t (023) 9229 7238
e jagoah2003@yahoo.co.uk

**Portsmouth & Southsea
Backpackers Lodge** ★
*Backpacker*
4 Florence Road, Southsea
PO5 2NE
t (023) 9283 2495
e portsmouthbackpackers@
hotmail.com
w portsmouthbackpackers.co.
uk

**University of Portsmouth**
★★ *Guest Accommodation*
Queen Elizabeth the Queen
Mother Hall, Furze Lane,
Southsea PO4 8LW
t (023) 92844884

**Cox's Hall** ★★★★
*Bed & Breakfast*
High Street, Stanford-in-the-
Vale, Faringdon SN7 8NQ
t (01367) 710248

**The Black Horse** ★★★ *Inn*
Tumblefield Road, Stansted
TN15 7PR
t (01732) 822355
e blackhorsekent@tiscali.co.uk

**Travelrest-London
Heathrow** ★★★
*Guest Accommodation*
171 Town Lane, Staines
TW19 7PW
t (01784) 252292

**The Black Pig** ★★★ *Inn*
Barnsole Road, Staple,
Canterbury CT3 1LE
t (01304) 813000
e info@theblackpig.co.uk
w theblackpig.co.uk

**White Cottage** ★★★★
*Bed & Breakfast*
Headcorn Road, Hawkenbury,
Tonbridge TN12 0DU
t (01580) 891480
e john.batten@macunlimited.
net
w the-whitecottage.co.uk

**Old Toms** ★★★
*Bed & Breakfast*
North Side, Steeple Aston,
Bicester OX25 4SE
t (01869) 340212
e marymlloyd@aol.com

**Great Field Farm** ★★★★
*Farmhouse* **SILVER AWARD**
Misling Lane, Stelling Minnis,
Canterbury CT4 6DE
t (01227) 709223
e Greatfieldfarm@aol.com
w great-field-farm.co.uk

**Ascari House B&B** ★★★
*Bed & Breakfast*
23 High Street, Steventon,
Abingdon OX16 6RZ
t (01235) 831435
e ascarihouse@yahoo.com
w ascarihouse.com

**Bramble Grange** ★★★★
*Farmhouse*
Hanney Road, Abingdon
OX13 6AP
t (01235) 834664
e helen@bramblegrange.com
w bramblegrange.com

**Tethers End** ★★★
*Bed & Breakfast*
Abingdon Road, Steventon,
Abingdon OX13 6RW
t (01235) 834015

**Nash Manor** ★★★★
*Guest Accommodation*
**SILVER AWARD**
Horsham Road, Steyning
BN44 3AA
t (01903) 814988
e info@nashmanor.co.uk
w nashmanor.co.uk
▷▮ ⫽

**Penfold Gallery Guest House**
★★★★★ *Guest House*
**SILVER AWARD**
30 High Street, Steyning
BN44 3GG
t (01903) 815595
e johnturner57@aol.com
w artyguesthouse.co.uk

**The Cherry Tree Inn** ★★★★
*Inn*
Stoke Row, Henley-on-Thames
RG9 5QA
t (01491) 680430
e info@thecherrytreeinn.com
w thecherrytreeinn.com

**Tighe Farmhouse** ★★★★
*Farmhouse*
Stone-in-Oxney, Tenterden
TN30 7JU
t (01233) 758251
e robin.kingsley@ndierct.co.
uk
w accommodationrye.co.uk

**Chardonnay** ★★★★
*Bed & Breakfast*
Hampers Lane, Storrington,
Pulborough RH20 3HZ
t (01903) 746688
e annsearancke@bigfoot.com
▷▮ ⫽

**The White Horse Inn** ★★★
*Inn*
2 The Square, Storrington,
Pulborough RH20 4DJ
t (01903) 743451

**Pine Hill** ★★★★
*Guest Accommodation*
**SILVER AWARD**
Stowting, Ashford TN25 6BD
t (01303) 863708
e sarahjanem@msn.com
w pine-hill.co.uk

**West Farm** ★★★★
*Farmhouse*
Launton Road, Bicester
OX27 9AS
t (01869) 278344

**Streatley On Thames YHA**
★★★ *Hostel*
Hill House, Reading Road,
Streatley, Reading RG8 9JJ
t (01491) 872278
e streatley@yha.org.uk
w yhastreatley.org.uk
▷▮ ⫽

**The Sundial** ★★
*Guest Accommodation*
18 Ranscombe Close,
Rochester ME2 2PB
t (01634) 721831
e sean@company8234.
freeserve.co.uk

**The White Cottage** ★★★★
*Guest Accommodation*
41 Rede Court Road, Rochester
ME2 3SP
t (01634) 719988

**Beaufort House** ★★★★
*Bed & Breakfast*
Broomfield Park, Ascot SL5 0JT
t (01344) 622991
e jenny@beaufort-house.com
w beaufort-house.com

**Forge House** ★★★★
*Bed & Breakfast*
5 Old Forge Yard, Swalcliffe,
Banbury OX15 5EH
t (01295) 788677

**Grange Farm Bed &
Breakfast** ★★★ *Farmhouse*
Swalcliffe Grange, Banbury
OX15 5EX
t (01295) 780206
e taylor@swalcliffe-grange.
freeserve.co.uk
w swalcliffegrange.com

**Greenacres** ★★★★
*Bed & Breakfast*
15 Greenacre Close, Swanley
BR8 8HT
t (01322) 613656
e pauline.snow1@btinternet.
com
w greenacrebandb.co.uk

## SWAY
### Hampshire

**The Arches** ★★★★
*Bed & Breakfast*
Station Road, Lymington
SO41 6AA
t (01590) 681339
e lynn@thenewforest.
wanadoo.co.uk
w the-arches.co.uk

**Manor Farm** ★★★
*Bed & Breakfast*
Coombe Lane, Sway SO41 6BP
t (01590) 683542

**The Nurse's Cottage** ★★★★
*Guest Accommodation*
Station Road, Sway, Lymington
SO41 6BA
t (01590) 683402

**Tiverton** ★★★★
*Bed & Breakfast*
9 Cruse Close, Sway,
Lymington SO41 6AY
t (01590) 683092
e ronrowe@talk21.com
w tivertonnewforest.co.uk

## TAPLOW
### Buckinghamshire

**Bridge Cottage Guest House**
★★★ *Guest House*
Bath Road, Taplow SL6 0AR
t (01628) 626805
e bridgecottagebb@aol.com
w bridgecottagebb.co.uk

## TELSCOMBE
### East Sussex

**TelscombeYouth Hostel** ★★
*Hostel*
Bank Cottages, Telscombe
Village, Newhaven BN7 3HZ
t (01273) 301357
e reservations@yha.org.uk
w yha.org.uk

## TENTERDEN
### Kent

**Collina House Hotel** ★★★★
*Guest Accommodation*
5 East Hill, Tenterden
TN30 6RL
t (01580) 764852
e enquiries@
collinahousehotel.co.uk
w collinahousehotel.co.uk

**Old Burren** ★★★★
*Guest Accommodation*
SILVER AWARD
25 Ashford Road, Tenterden
TN30 6LL
t (01580) 764442
e gill@burren.plus.com
w oldburren.co.uk

**Signal Cottage Bed &
Breakfast** ★★★★
*Bed & Breakfast*
3 Rogersmead, Tenterden
TN30 6LF
t (01580) 761806

**The Tower House** ◆◆◆◆
*Guest Accommodation*
SILVER AWARD
27 Ashford Road, Tenterden
TN30 6LL
t (01580) 761920
e pippa@towerhouse.biz
w towerhouse.biz

**The White Cottage** ★★★
*Bed & Breakfast*
London Beach, Ashford Road,
Tenterden TN30 6SR
t (01233) 850583
e ruth@
thewhitecottagebedand
breakfast.co.uk
w thewhitecottagebedand
breakfast.co.uk

## THAME
### Oxfordshire

**Field Farm** ★★★★
*Farmhouse*
North Weston, Thame
OX9 2HQ
t (01844) 215428
e colin.quartly@talk21.com
w fieldfarmbandb.co.uk

**Langsmeade House** ★★★★
*Bed & Breakfast*
SILVER AWARD
Milton Common, Thame
OX9 2JY
t (01844) 278727
e enquiries@
langsmeadehouse.co.uk
w langsmeadehouse.co.uk

**Oakfield** ★★★★ *Farmhouse*
SILVER AWARD
Thame Park Road, Thame
OX9 3PL
t (01844) 213709

## THATCHAM
### Berkshire

**One Church Lane** ★★★★
*Guest Accommodation*
1 Church Lane, Thatcham
RG19 3JL
t (01635) 869098
e johnhousemaster@aol.com

## THURNHAM
### Kent

**Black Horse Inn** ★★★★ *Inn*
Pilgrims Way, Thurnham,
Maidstone ME14 3LD
t (01622) 737185
e info@wellieboot.net
w wellieboot.net

**Coldblow Farm Bunkbarns**
*Bunkhouse*
Cold Blow Lane, Thurnham,
Maidstone ME14 3LR
t (01622) 735038
e campingbarns@yha.org.uk
w coldblow-camping.co.uk

## THURSLEY
### Surrey

**Hindhead YHA** ★ *Hostel*
Devil's Punchbowl, Off
Portmouth Road, Godalming
GU8 6NS
t (01428) 604285
w yha.org.uk

## TONBRIDGE
### Kent

**86 Hadlow Road** ★★
*Bed & Breakfast*
Tonbridge TN9 1PA
t (01732) 357332
e aurelia.gemini@virgin.net

**Fieldswood** ★★★★
*Bed & Breakfast*
SILVER AWARD
Hadlow Park, Hadlow,
Tonbridge TN11 0HZ
t (01732) 851433
e info@fieldswood.co.uk
w fieldswood.co.uk

## TOTLAND BAY
### Isle of Wight

**Chart House** ★★★★
*Guest Accommodation*
SILVER AWARD
Madeira Road, Totland Bay,
Totland PO39 0BJ
t (01983) 755091

**Clifton House**
Rating Applied For
*Bed & Breakfast*
Colwell Common Road,
Totland Bay PO39 0DD
t (01983) 753237
e clifton.house@btinternet.
com

**Littledene Lodge** ★★★
*Guest House*
Granville Road, Totland Bay
PO39 0AX
t (01983) 752411
e littledenehotel@aol.com

**Sandy Lane Bed and
Breakfast** ★★★★
*Guest House*
Sandy Lane, Colwell Common
Road, Totland Bay PO39 0DD
t (01983) 752240
e louise@sandylane-iow.co.uk
w sandylane-iow.co.uk

**Totland Bay YHA** ★★★
*Hostel*
Hurst Hill, Totland Bay
PO39 0HD
t (01983) 752165
e totland@yha.org.uk
w yha.org.uk

## TROTTON
### West Sussex

**Orchard House** ★★★★
*Bed & Breakfast*
SILVER AWARD
Mill Lane, Trotton, Midhurst
GU31 5JT
t (01730) 812530
e orchardhouse.trotton@
btinternet.com
w orchardhouse.cabanova.com

## TWYFORD
### Hampshire

**Highfield Cottage** ★★★★
*Bed & Breakfast*
Old Rectory Lane, Twyford,
Winchester SO21 1NR
t (01962) 712921
e reescj@hotmail.com
w smoothhound.co.uk

**Twyford House** ★★★★
*Bed & Breakfast*
High Street, Twyford,
Winchester SO21 1NU
t (01962) 713114
e crchtwyho@aol.com
w twyfordhousebnb.co.uk

## UCKFIELD
### East Sussex

**Old Mill Farm B&B** ★★★★
*Farmhouse*
Chillies Lane, High Hurstwood,
Uckfield TN22 4AD
t (01825) 732279

**South Paddock** ★★★★★
*Bed & Breakfast*
SILVER AWARD
Maresfield Park, Uckfield
TN22 2HA
t (01825) 762335

## UFFINGTON
### Oxfordshire

**Norton House** ★★★★
*Guest Accommodation*
SILVER AWARD
Broad Street, Faringdon
SN7 7RA
t (01367) 820230
e carloberman@aol.com

## UPNOR
### Kent

**Arethusa Venture Centre**
★★ *Activity Accommodation*
Rochester ME2 4XB
t (01634) 719933
e lwright@shaftesbury.org.uk
w arethusa.org.uk

## UPPER FARRINGDON
### Hampshire

**Old Timbers** ★★★★
*Bed & Breakfast*
Crows Lane, Upper Farringdon,
Alton GU34 3ED
t (01420) 588449
e info@oldtimberscottage.co.
uk
w oldtimberscottage.co.uk

## UPPER LAMBOURN
### Berkshire

**Saxon Cottage** ★★★★
*Guest Accommodation*
Upper Lambourn, Hungerford
RG17 8QN
t (01488) 71503
e judy.gaselee@virgin.net

## VENTNOR
### Isle of Wight

**Bonchurch Manor** ★★★★
*Guest Accommodation*
Bonchurch Shute, Bonchurch
PO38 1NU
t (01983) 852868
e reception@
bonchurchmanor.com
w bonchurchmanor.com

**Brunswick House**
Rating Applied For
*Guest House*
Victoria Street, Ventnor
PO38 1ET
t (01983) 852656
e brunswick.house.services.
ltd@unicombox.co.uk
w brunswickhouse-web.co.uk

**The Enchanted Manor**
★★★★★
*Guest Accommodation*
GOLD AWARD
St Catherine's Point, Sandrock
Road, Niton PO38 2NG
t (01983) 730215
e info@enchantedmanor.co.uk
w enchantedmanor.co.uk

**The Hermitage Country House ★★★★★**
*Guest Accommodation*
**GOLD AWARD**
St Catherines Down, Ventnor
PO38 2PD
t (01983) 730010
e enquiries@hermitage-iow.
co.uk
w hermitage-iow.co.uk

**Hill House ★★★**
*Guest Accommodation*
22 Spring Hill, Ventnor
PO38 1PF
t (01983) 854581
e hillhouseventnor@aol.com
w hillhouse-ventnor.co.uk

**The Leconfield ★★★★★**
*Guest Accommodation*
**SILVER AWARD**
85 Leeson Road, Upper
Bonchurch, Ventnor PO38 1PU
t (01983) 852196
e enquiries@leconfieldhotel.
com
w leconfieldhotel.com

### WADDESDON
Buckinghamshire

**The Lion ★★★★** *Inn*
70a High Street, Aylesbury
HP18 0JD
t (01296) 651227
e info@thelionwaddesdon.co.
uk
w thelionwaddesdon.co.uk

**The Old Dairy ★★★**
*Bed & Breakfast*
4 High Street, Waddesdon
HP18 0JA
t (01296) 658627
e hconyard@tesco.net
w theolddairywaddesdon.co.
uk

### WADHURST
East Sussex

**The Greyhound ★★★** *Inn*
St James Square, Wadhurst
TN5 7EN
t (01892) 783224
e jharrold@lineone.net

**Spring Cottage ★★★**
*Bed & Breakfast*
90 Felpham Road, Felpham,
Bognor Regis PO22 7PD
t (01243) 868500
e springcottage.bb@virgin.net
w springcottagebb.co.uk

### WALBERTON
West Sussex

**Longacre ★★★★**
*Bed & Breakfast*
The Street, Walberton, Nr
Arundel BN18 0PY
t (01243) 543542
e longacrebandb@tinyworld.
co.uk
w visitsussex.org/longacre

### WALDERTON
West Sussex

**Hillside Cottages ★★★**
*Bed & Breakfast*
Cooks Lane, Walderton,
Chichester PO18 9EF
t (023) 9263 1260
e info@hillside-cottages.co.uk
w hillside-cottages.co.uk

### WALLINGFORD
Oxfordshire

**Fords Farm ★★★★**
*Farmhouse* **SILVER AWARD**
Ewelme, Wallingford
OX10 6HU
t (01491) 839272

**Huntington House ★★★**
*Bed & Breakfast*
18 Wood Street, Wallingford
OX10 0AX
t (01491) 839201
e hunting311@aol.com

**Little Gables ★★★★**
*Bed & Breakfast*
166 Crowmarsh Hill,
Crowmarsh Gifford,
Wallingford OX10 8BG
t (01491) 837834 &
07860 148882
e jill@stayingaway.com
w stayingaway.com

**Marsh House ★★★**
*Bed & Breakfast*
7 Court Drive, Shillingford,
Wallingford OX10 7ER
t (01865) 858496
e marsh.house@talk21.com
w marshhousebandb.co.uk

**North Moreton House ★★★★★**
*Guest Accommodation*
**SILVER AWARD**
High Street, North Moreton,
Didcot OX11 9AT
t (01235) 813283
e katie@northmoretonhouse.
co.uk
w northmoretonhouse.co.uk

### WALMER
Kent

**Hardicot Guest House ★★★★** *Bed & Breakfast*
Kingsdown Road, Walmer,
Deal CT14 8AW
t (01304) 373867
e guestboss@btopenworld.
com
w hardicot-guest-house.co.uk

### WANTAGE
Oxfordshire

**B&B in Wantage ★★★★**
*Bed & Breakfast*
50 Foliat Drive, Wantage
OX12 7AL
t (01235) 760495
e eleanor@eaturner.freeserve.
co.uk
w geocities.com/
bandbinwantage

**Hazelwood ★★★★**
*Bed & Breakfast*
Main Street, Wantage
OX12 0JF
t (01235) 868412
e len.firth@virgin.net

**Old Yeomanry House ★★★★**
*Guest Accommodation*
27 Wallingford Street,
Wantage OX12 8AU
t (01235) 772778
e jenny@yeomanryhouse.co.
uk
w yeomanryhouse.co.uk

**Regis Bed and Breakfast ★★★★** *Guest House*
**SILVER AWARD**
12 Charlton Road, Wantage
OX12 8ER
t (01235) 762860
e millie_rastall@hotmail.com

### WARNHAM
West Sussex

**Nowhere House ★★★**
*Bed & Breakfast*
Dorking Road, Durfold Hill,
Horsham RH12 3RZ
t (01306) 627272

### WARNINGCAMP
West Sussex

**Furzetor ★★★★**
*Bed & Breakfast*
Clay Lane, Warningcamp,
Arundel BN18 9QN
t (01903) 882974
e furzetor@hotmail.com

**YHA Arundel ★★★** *Hostel*
Warningcamp, Arundel
BN18 9QY
t (01903) 882204
e arundel@yha.org.uk
w yha.org.uk

### WASH WATER
Berkshire

**The Chase Guest House ★★★★** *Bed & Breakfast*
Waterbourne, Andover Drove,
Newbury RG20 0LZ
t (01635) 231441
e chaseguesthouse@
btconnect.com
w thechaseguesthouse.com

### WATER STRATFORD
Buckinghamshire

**The Rolling Acres ★★★★**
*Bed & Breakfast*
Water Stratford, Buckingham
MK18 5DX
t (01280) 847302
e info@rolling-acres.co.uk

### WATERLOOVILLE
Hampshire

**Ashdown ★★★★**
*Bed & Breakfast*
33 Ferndale, Waterlooville
PO7 7PH
t (023) 9226 2607
e ashdown.jennyancill@
btopenworld.com

**Holly Dale ★★**
*Bed & Breakfast*
11 Lovedean Lane,
Waterlooville PO8 8HH
t (023) 9259 2047
e pwengland@uku.co.uk

**New Haven Bed & Breakfast ★★★** *Bed & Breakfast*
193 London Road,
Waterlooville PO7 7RN
t (023) 9226 8559
e newhaven@toucansurf.com
w smoothhound.co.uk/hotels/
newhavenbedandbreakfast.
html

### WATERSFIELD
West Sussex

**The Willows ★★★★**
*Bed & Breakfast*
London Road, Watersfield,
Pulborough RH20 1NB
t (01798) 831576
e mount@ukonline.co.uk
w mountbandb.co.uk

### WATLINGTON
Oxfordshire

**The Fox and Hounds Inn ★★★★** *Inn*
13 Shirburn Street, Watlington
OX49 5BU
t (01491) 613040
e info@foxandhounds.net
w foxandhounds.net

**Woodgate Orchard Cottage ◆◆◆◆** *Guest Accommodation*
Howe Road, Watlington
OX49 5EL
t (01491) 612675
e mailbox@wochr.freeserve.
co.uk

### WEALD
Oxfordshire

**The Coach House ★★★★**
*Bed & Breakfast*
College Farm, Bridge Street,
Bampton OX18 2HG
t (01993) 851041
e robinshuck@btinternet.com
w thecoachhousebampton.co.
uk

### WENDOVER
Buckinghamshire

**17 Icknield Close ★★★**
*Guest Accommodation*
Wendover, Aylesbury
HP22 6HG
t (01296) 583285
e grbr.samuels@ntlworld.com

**25 Witchell ★★**
*Bed & Breakfast*
Witchell, Wendover, Aylesbury
HP22 6EG
t (01296) 623426

**Dunsmore Edge ★★★**
*Bed & Breakfast*
Dunsmore Lane, London Road,
Wendover, Aylesbury
HP22 6PN
t (01296) 623080
e uron@lineone.net

### WEST BRABOURNE
Kent

**Bulltown Farmhouse Bed & Breakfast ★★★★**
*Guest Accommodation*
Bulltown Lane, West
Brabourne, Ashford TN25 5NB
t (01233) 813505
e wiltons@bulltown.fsnet.co.
uk

### WEST CLANDON
Surrey

**The Oaks ★★★**
*Guest Accommodation*
Highcotts Lane, West Clandon,
Guildford GU4 7XA
t (01483) 222531
e kate_broad@yahoo.co.uk

## WEST DEAN
### West Sussex

**Lodge Hill Farm ★★**
*Farmhouse*
West Dean, Chichester
PO18 0RT
t (01243) 535245

## WEST HARTING
### West Sussex

**Three Quebec ★★★★**
*Bed & Breakfast*
West Harting, Nr Petersfield,
Midhurst GU31 5PG
t (01730) 825386
e patriciastevens@
threequebec.co.uk
w threequebec.co.uk

## WEST HORSLEY
### Surrey

**Silkmore ★★★★**
*Bed & Breakfast*
Silkmore Lane, West Horsley,
Leatherhead KT24 6JQ
t (01483) 282042
e carolyn@leporello.co.uk

## WEST MALLING
### Kent

**Appledene ★★★★**
*Guest Accommodation*
164 Norman Road, West
Malling ME19 6RW
t (01732) 842071
e appledene@westmalling.
freeserve.co.uk
w smoothhound.co.uk/
hotelsappledene

## WEST STOKE
### West Sussex

**West Stoke House ★★★★★**
*Restaurant with Rooms*
**GOLD AWARD**
Downs Road, West Stoke,
Chichester PO18 9BN
t (01243) 575226
e info@weststokehouse.co.uk
w weststokehouse.co.uk

## WEST WITTERING
### West Sussex

**The Beach House ★★★**
*Guest House*
Rookwood Road, West
Wittering, Witterings PO20 8LT
t (01243) 514800
e info@beachhse.co.uk
w beachhse.co.uk

**Thornton Cottage ★★★★**
*Bed & Breakfast*
**SILVER AWARD**
Chichester Road, West
Wittering, Chichester
PO20 8QA
t (01243) 512470
e thornton@b-and-b.
fsbusiness.co.uk

## WESTCOTT
### Surrey

**Corner House Bed &
Breakfast ★★**
*Guest Accommodation*
Guildford Road, Westcott,
Dorking RH4 3QE
t (01306) 888798
e ktnyman@tiscali.co.uk

## WESTGATE ON SEA
### Kent

**White Lodge Guest House
★★★** *Guest House*
12 Domneva Road, Westgate-
on-Sea CT8 8PE
t (01843) 831828
e whitelodge.thanet@
btinternet.com
w whitelodge.co.uk

## WESTON-ON-THE-GREEN
### Oxfordshire

**Westfield Court House
★★★★** *Bed & Breakfast*
North Lane, Weston-on-the-
Green, Bicester OX25 3RG
t (01869) 350777

**Weston Grounds Farm ★★★**
*Farmhouse*
Northampton Road, Weston-
on-the-Green, Bicester
OX25 3QX
t (01869) 351168

## WESTON TURVILLE
### Buckinghamshire

**Loosley House B&B ★★★★**
*Guest House*
87 New Road, Weston Turville,
Aylesbury HP22 5QT
t (01296) 484157
w loosleyhouse.co.uk

## WESTWELL
### Kent

**Tylers ★★★★★**
*Bed & Breakfast*
**SILVER AWARD**
The Street, Westwell, Ashford
TN25 4LQ
t (01233) 713152
e info@tylerswestwell.com
w tylerswestwell.com

## WEYBRIDGE
### Surrey

**Riverdene Gardens
★★★★★**
*Guest Accommodation*
**SILVER AWARD**
1 Oatlands Drive, Weybridge
KT13 9NA
t (01932) 223574
e riverdenegardens@
btinternet.com
w riverdenegardens.co.uk

## WHATLINGTON
### East Sussex

**Woodmans ★★★★**
*Bed & Breakfast*
Whatlington, Battle TN33 0NN
t (01424) 870342

## WHITCHURCH
### Hampshire

**Peak House Farm ★★★**
*Farmhouse*
Cole Henley, Whitchurch
RG28 7QJ
t (01256) 892052
e info@peakhousefarm.co.uk
w peakhousefarm.co.uk

## WHITSTABLE
### Kent

**Alliston House ★★★★**
*Bed & Breakfast*
**SILVER AWARD**
1 Joy Lane, Whitstable CT5 4LS
t (01227) 779066
e bobgough57@aol.com
w stayinwhitstable.co.uk

**The Captain's House Bed
and Breakfast ★★★**
*Bed & Breakfast*
56 Harbour Street, Whitstable
CT5 1AQ
t (01227) 275156
e captainshouse-56@tiscali.co.
uk

**Copeland House ★★★★**
*Guest House*
4 Island Wall, Whitstable
CT5 1EP
t (01227) 266207
e mail@copelandhouse.co.uk
w copelandhouse.co.uk

**The Duke of Cumberland
★★★** *Inn*
High Street, Whitstable
CT5 1AP
t (01227) 280617
e enquiries@
thedukeinwhitstable.co.uk
w thedukeinwhitstable.co.uk

**The Pearl Fisher ★★★★**
*Guest Accommodation*
**SILVER AWARD**
103 Cromwell Road,
Whitstable CT5 1NL
t (01227) 771000
e stay@thepearlfisher.co.uk
w thepearlfisher.com

**The Townhouse ★★★★★**
*Guest Accommodation*
26 Oxford Street, Whitstable
CT5 1DD
t (01227) 262384
e townhousewhitstable@
yahoo.co.uk
w townhousewhitstable.co.uk

**Victoria Villa ★★★★**
*Guest Accommodation*
**GOLD AWARD**
Victoria Street, Whitstable
CT5 1JB
t (01227) 779191
e victoria.villa@virgin.net
w victoria-villa.i12.com

**Windyridge Guest House
★★★★**
*Guest Accommodation*
Wraik Hill, Whitstable CT5 3BY
t (01227) 263506
e scott@windyridgewhitstable.
co.uk

## WHITWELL
### Isle of Wight

**The Old Rectory (B&B)
★★★★**
*Guest Accommodation*
**GOLD AWARD**
Ashknowle Lane, Whitwell
PO38 2PP
t (01983) 731242
e rectory@ukonline.co.uk
w isleofwightbandb.com

## WIDLEY
### Hampshire

**Roughay ★★** *Bed & Breakfast*
96 The Brow, Widley,
Waterlooville PO7 5DA
t (023) 9237 9341
e gillcross@gilbertgrapevine.
org
w roughay.co.uk

## WIGGINTON
### Oxfordshire

**Pretty Bush Barn ★★★★**
*Bed & Breakfast*
Pretty Bush Lane, Wigginton,
Banbury OX15 4LD
t (01608) 738262

## WILLESBOROUGH
### Kent

**Boys Hall ★★★★**
*Guest Accommodation*
Boys Hall Road, Ashford
TN24 0LA
t (01233) 633772
e enquiries@boyshall.co.uk
w boyshall.co.uk

## WINCHELSEA
### East Sussex

**Winchelsea Lodge Motel
★★★★**
*Guest Accommodation*
Hastings Road, Winchelsea
TN36 4AD
t (01797) 226211
e rooms@1066motels.co.uk
w winchelsea-lodge-motel.co.
uk

## WINCHESTER
### Hampshire

**12 Christchurch Road ★★★**
*Bed & Breakfast*
Winchester SO23 9SR
t (01962) 854272
e pjspatton@yahoo.co.uk

**152 Teg Down Meads ★★★**
*Bed & Breakfast*
Winchester SO22 5NS
t (01962) 862628

**21 Rosewarne Court ★★★**
*Guest Accommodation*
Hyde Street, Winchester
SO23 7HL
t (01962) 863737

**29 Christchurch Road**
**★★★★★** *Bed & Breakfast*
**SILVER AWARD**
Christchurch Road, Winchester
SO23 9SU
t (01962) 868661
e dilke@waitrose.com
w fetherstondilke.com

**5 Clifton Terrace ★★★★**
*Bed & Breakfast*
**SILVER AWARD**
Winchester SO23 5BJ
t (01962) 890053
e chrissiejohnston@hotmail.
com

**53A Parchment Street ★★★**
*Bed & Breakfast*
Winchester SO23 8BA
t (01962) 849962

**58 Hyde Street ★★★**
*Bed & Breakfast*
Hyde Street, Winchester
SO23 7DY
t (01962) 854646
e gj.harvey@ntlworld.com
w 58hydestreet.co.uk

**Acacia ★★★★**
*Bed & Breakfast*
**SILVER AWARD**
44 Kilham Lane, Winchester
SO22 5PT
t (01962) 852259
e eric.buchanan@btinternet.
com

**Cheriton House** ★★★
*Bed & Breakfast*
61 Cheriton Road, Winchester
SO22 5AY
t (01962) 620374
e cheritonhouse@hotmail.com

**Dawn Cottage** ★★★★★
*Bed & Breakfast*
**SILVER AWARD**
99 Romsey Road, Winchester
SO22 5PQ
t (01962) 869956
e dawncottage@hotmail.com

**Giffard House** ★★★★★
*Guest Accommodation*
**GOLD AWARD**
50 Christchurch Road,
Winchester SO23 9SU
t (01962) 852628
e giffardhotel@aol.com
w giffardhotel.co.uk

**Gillian Davies** ★★
*Bed & Breakfast*
5 Compton Road, Winchester
SO23 9SL
t (01962) 869199
e vicb@csma-netlink.co.uk

**Lainston** ★★★
*Bed & Breakfast*
Lainston Close, Winchester
SO22 5LJ
t (01962) 866072
e bedandbreakfast@lainston.
co.uk
w lainston.co.uk

**The Lilacs** ★★
*Bed & Breakfast*
1 Harestock Close, Off
Andover Road North,
Winchester SO22 6NP
t (01962) 884122
e susanm.pell@ntlworld.com
w smoothhound.co.uk/hotels/
lilacs.html

**R J and V J Weller** ★★★
*Bed & Breakfast*
63 Upper Brook Street,
Winchester SO23 8DG
t (01962) 620367
e robert.weller@ntlworld.com

**Rowanhurst** ★★★★
*Bed & Breakfast*
Northbrook Avenue,
Winchester SO23 0JW
t (01962) 862433
e joanne.kingswell@talk21.
com

**St Johns Croft** ★★★
*Bed & Breakfast*
St Johns Street, Winchester
SO23 0HF
t (01962) 859976
e dottyfraser@gmail.com

**St Margaret's** ★★★
*Bed & Breakfast*
3 St Michael's Road,
Winchester SO23 9JE
t (01962) 861450
e brigid@bbrett.f2s.com
w winchesterbandb.com

**Staddle-Stones** ★★★★
*Bed & Breakfast*
15b Bereweeke Avenue,
Winchester SO22 6BH
t (01962) 877883
e sheila@staddle-stones.
freeserve.co.uk
w staddle-stones.co.uk

**Sullivans** ♦♦
*Guest Accommodation*
29 Stockbridge Road,
Winchester SO22 6RW
t (01962) 862027
e sullivans_bandb@amserve.
net

**Sycamores** ★★★
*Bed & Breakfast*
4 Bereweeke Close,
Winchester SO22 6AR
t (01962) 867242
e sycamores.b-and-b@virgin.
net

**The University of
Winchester** ★★★ *Campus*
West Hill, Winchester
SO22 4NR
t (01962) 827332
e conferences@winchester.ac.
uk

**Windy Ridge** ★★
*Bed & Breakfast*
99 Andover Road, Winchester
SO22 6AX
t (01962) 882527
e angela.westall@virgin.net

**22 York Avenue** ★★★
*Bed & Breakfast*
Windsor SL4 3PD
t (01753) 865775

**3 York Road** ★★★
*Bed & Breakfast*
Windsor SL4 3NX
t (01753) 861741
e kerrin@tiscali.co.uk

**76 Duke Street** ★★★★
*Bed & Breakfast*
Windsor SL4 1SQ
t (01753) 620636
e admin@76dukestreet.co.uk
w 76dukestreet.co.uk

**Alma Lodge Guest House**
★★★ *Guest House*
58 Alma Road, Windsor
SL4 3HA
t (01753) 855620
e info@almalodge.co.uk
w almalodge.co.uk

**Barbara's Bed & Breakfast**
★★★ *Bed & Breakfast*
16 Maidenhead Road, Windsor
SL4 5EQ
t (01753) 840273
e bbandb@btinternet.com

**Bluebell House** ★★★★
*Guest Accommodation*
Lovel Lane, Woodside,
Winkfield, Windsor SL4 2DG
t (01344) 886828
e registrations@
bluebellhousehotel.co.uk
w bluebellhousehotel.co.uk

**The Clarence** ★★★
*Guest House*
9 Clarence Road, Windsor
SL4 5AE
t (01753) 864436
w clarence-hotel.co.uk

**The Cottage Inn** ★★★★ *Inn*
Winkfield Street, Winkfield,
Windsor SL4 4SW
t (01344) 882242
e cottage@btconnect.com
w cottage-inn.co.uk

**The Dorset** ♦♦♦♦
*Guest Accommodation*
4 Dorset Road, Windsor
SL4 3BA
t (01753) 852669

**Langton House** ★★★★
*Guest Accommodation*
46 Alma Road, Windsor
SL4 3HA
t (01753) 858299
e enquiries@langtonhouse.co.
uk
w langtonhouse.co.uk

**Melrose House** ★★★
*Guest House*
53 Frances Road, Windsor
SL4 3AQ
t (01753) 865328
e info@melrosehousewindsor.
com

**The Oast Barn** ★★★★
*Bed & Breakfast*
Staines Road, Wraysbury,
Staines TW19 5BS
t (01784) 481598
e bandb@oastbarn.com
w oastbarn.com

**The Old Farmhouse** ★★★★
*Bed & Breakfast*
Dedworth Road, Oakley Green,
Windsor SL4 4LH
t (01753) 850411
e debbie@theoldfarmhouse.
fslife.co.uk
w theoldfarmhousewindsor.
com

**Oscar Lodge** ★★
*Guest House*
65 Vansittart Road, Windsor
SL4 5DB
t (01753) 830613
e oscarhotel@btconnect.com
w oscarhotel.co.uk

**The Prince Albert** ★★★ *Inn*
2 Clewer Hill Road, Windsor
SL4 4BS
t (01753) 864788
e theprincealbert@tiscali.co.uk
w theprincealbertpub.com

**The Trooper** ★★★ *Inn*
97 St Leonard's Road, Windsor
SL4 3BZ
t (01753) 670123
e trooper@fullers.co.uk
w accommodating-inns.co.uk

**Windsor Edwardian** ★★★★
*Bed & Breakfast*
21 Osborne Road, Windsor
SL4 3EG
t (01753) 858995
e info@windsoredwardian.co.
uk
w windsoredwardian.co.uk

**Witsend** ★★★
*Bed & Breakfast*
9 Buckingham Road, Winslow,
Buckingham MK18 3DT
t (01296) 712503
e sheila.spatcher@tesco.net
w witsendwinslow.co.uk

**Crofters Guest House**
★★★★
*Guest Accommodation*
29 Oxford Hill, Witney
OX28 3JU
t (01993) 778165
e crofers.ghouse@virgin.net

**The Laurels** ★★★
*Guest House*
53 Burford Road, Witney
OX28 6DR
t (01993) 702193
e thelaurelsbandb@fsmail.net
w thelaurelsguesthouse.co.uk

**Pinkhill Cottage** ★★★★
*Bed & Breakfast*
45 Rack End, Standlake,
Witney OX29 7SA
t (01865) 300544
e jane@pinkhill.plus.com
w smoothhound.co.uk/hotels/
pinkhill

**Quarrydene** ♦♦♦
*Guest Accommodation*
17 Dene Rise, Witney
OX28 6LU
t (01993) 772152
e jeanniemarshall@
quarrydene.fsworld.co.uk

**Springhill Farm Bed &
Breakfast** ★★★
*Guest Accommodation*
Cogges, Witney OX29 6UL
t (01993) 704919
e jan@strainge.fsnet.co.uk
⚘

**The Witney** ★★★
*Guest Accommodation*
7 Church Green, Witney
OX28 4AZ
t (01993) 702137
e bookings@thewitneyhotel.
co.uk
w thewitneyhotel.co.uk

**Halketts** ★★★★
*Bed & Breakfast*
72 Kings Hill, Beech, Alton
GU34 4AN
t (01420) 562258

**The Old Stables** ★★★★
*Guest House*
Bow Brickhill Road, Woburn
Sands, Milton Keynes
MK17 8DE
t (01908) 281340
e info@oldstables.co.uk
w oldstables.co.uk

**Grantchester** ★★
*Bed & Breakfast*
Boughton Hall Avenue, Send,
Woking GU23 7DF
t (01483) 225383
e gary@hotpotmail.com

**St Columba's House** ♦♦♦
*Guest Accommodation*
Maybury Hill, Woking
GU22 8AB
t (01483) 766498
e retreats@st.columba.org.uk
w stcolumbashouse.org.uk

## WOKINGHAM
### Berkshire

**The Dukes Head ★★★** *Inn*
56 Denmark Street,
Wokingham RG40 2BQ
t (0118) 978 0316
w dukes-head.com

## WONERSH
### Surrey

**Woodyers Farm ★★★★**
*Bed & Breakfast*
Barnett Lane, Wonersh,
Guildford GU5 0RX
t (01483) 892862
e sj@wcjeng.com

## WOODFALLS
### Hampshire

**The Woodfalls Inn ★★** *Inn*
The Ridge, Redlynch, Salisbury
SP5 2LN
t (01725) 513222
e woodfallsi@aol.com
w woodfallsinn.co.uk

## WOODGREEN
### Hampshire

**Cottage Crest**
Rating Applied For
*Bed & Breakfast*
Castle Hill, Woodgreen,
Fordingbridge SP6 2AX
t (01725) 512009
e lupita_cadman@yahoo.co.uk
w cottage-crest.co.uk

## WOODSTOCK
### Oxfordshire

**Blenheim Guest House &
Tea Rooms ★★★★**
*Guest House*
17 Park Street, Woodstock
OX20 1SJ
t (01993) 813814
e theblenheim@aol.com
w theblenheim.com

**The Duke of Marlborough
★★★★** *Inn*
A44 Woodleys, Woodstock
OX20 1HT
t (01993) 811460
e sales@dukeofmarlborough.
co.uk
w dukeofmarlborough.co.uk

**The Laurels ★★★★**
*Bed & Breakfast*
**SILVER AWARD**
40 Hensington Road,
Woodstock OX20 1JL
t (01993) 812583
e stay@laurelsguesthouse.co.
uk
w laurelsguesthouse.co.uk

**Shepherds Hall ★★★**
*Guest House*
Witney Road, Freeland, Oxford
OX29 8HQ
t (01993) 881256
w shepherdshall.co.uk

## WOOTTON BRIDGE
### Isle of Wight

**Grange Farm B&B ★★★★**
*Farmhouse*
Grange Farm, Staplers Road,
Wootton PO33 4RW
t (01983) 882147
e info@grange-farm-holidays.
co.uk
w grange-farm-holidays.co.uk

## WORMINGHALL
### Buckinghamshire

**Crabtree Barn ★★★★**
*Farmhouse*
Menmarsh Road, Worminghall,
Aylesbury HP18 9JY
t (01844) 339719
e issy@crabtreebarn.co.uk
w crabtreebarn.co.uk

## WORTH
### Kent

**Solley Farm House ★★★★★**
*Bed & Breakfast*
**GOLD AWARD**
The Street, Worth, Deal
CT14 0DG
t (01304) 613701
e solleyfarmhouse@tiscali.co.
uk
w solleyfarmhouse.co.uk

## WORTHING
### West Sussex

**Benson's ★★★★**
*Guest Accommodation*
**GOLD AWARD**
Brighton Road, Worthing
BN11 2EU
t (01903) 206623
e 15bgh4vw@f2s.com
w bensonstheguesthouse.co.
uk

**Blair House Hotel ★★★★**
*Guest House*
11 St Georges Road, Worthing
BN11 2DS
t (01903) 234071
e stay@blairhousehotel.co.uk
w blairhousehotel.co.uk

**The Brunswick ★★** *Inn*
Thorn Road, Worthing
BN11 3ND
t (01903) 202141
e pub@thebrunswick.co.uk
w thebrunswick.co.uk

**Camelot House ★★★★**
*Guest Accommodation*
20 Gannon Road, Worthing
BN11 2DT
t (01903) 204334
e stay@camelothouse.co.uk
w camelothouse.co.uk

**Edwardian Dreams ★★★★**
*Guest Accommodation*
**SILVER AWARD**
77 Manor Road, Worthing
BN11 4SL
t (01903) 218565
e info@edwardiandreams.co.
uk
w edwardiandreams.co.uk

**Glenhill ★★★**
*Guest Accommodation*
21 Alexandra Road, Worthing
BN11 2DX
t (01903) 202756
e linda@filmersankey.
wanadoo.co.uk

**The Grand Victorian Hotel
★★★** *Guest Accommodation*
27 Railway Approach,
Worthing BN11 1UR
t (01903) 230690
e grandvictorian@
thechapmansgroup.co.uk
w chapmansgroup.co.uk

**Haytor Guest House ♦♦♦**
*Guest Accommodation*
5 Salisbury Road, Worthing
BN11 1RB
t (01903) 235287
e linda.shipley@homecall.co.
uk

**Heenefields Guest House
★★★★**
*Guest Accommodation*
98 Heene Road, Worthing
BN11 3RE
t (01903) 538780
e heenefields.guesthouse@
virgin.net
w heenefields.com

**High Beach Guest House
★★★★**
*Guest Accommodation*
201 Brighton Road, Worthing
BN11 2EX
t (01903) 236389
e infot@highbeachworthing.
com
w highbeachworthing.com

**High Trees Guest House
★★★** *Guest House*
2 Warwick Gardens, Worthing
BN11 1PE
t (01903) 236668
e bill@hightreesguesthouse.
co.uk
w hightreesguesthouse.co.uk

**Highdown Hotel ★★★** *Inn*
Littlehampton Road, Worthing
BN12 6PF
t (01903) 700152
e highdownhotel@
thechapmansgroup.co.uk
w highdownhotel.co.uk

**Marine View Inn ★★★**
*Guest Accommodation*
111 Marine Parade, Worthing
BN11 3QG
t (01903) 238413
e reservations@
marineviewhotel.co.uk
w marineviewhotel.co.uk

**Merton House ★★★★**
*Guest House*
96 Broadwater Road, Worthing
BN14 8AW
t (01903) 238222
e stay@mertonhouse.co.uk
w mertonhouse.co.uk

**Moorings ★★★★**
*Guest Accommodation*
4 Selden Road, Worthing
BN11 2LL
t (01903) 208882
e themooringsworthing@
hotmail.co.uk
w mooringsworthing.co.uk

**The Old Guard House
★★★★** *Bed & Breakfast*
55 Poulters Lane, Worthing
BN14 7ST
t (01903) 527470
e eddie442002@tiscali.co.uk

**Pebble Beach ★★★**
*Guest Accommodation*
281 Brighton Road, Worthing
BN11 2HG
t (01903) 210766
e pebblebeach281@aol.com
w pebblebeach-worthing.co.uk

**Rosedale House ★★**
*Guest House*
12 Bath Road, Worthing
BN11 3NU
t (01903) 233181
e rosedale@amserve.net

**Tamara Guest House ★★★**
*Bed & Breakfast*
19 Alexandra Road, Worthing
BN11 2DX
t (01903) 520332
w tamara-worthing.co.uk

## WROXALL
### Isle of Wight

**Little Span Farm B&B ★★★**
*Farmhouse*
Rew Lane, Ventnor PO38 3AU
t (01983) 852419
e info@spanfarm.co.uk
w spanfarm.co.uk

## WYE
### Kent

**Mistral ★★★★**
*Bed & Breakfast*
3 Oxenturn Road, Wye,
Ashford TN25 5BH
t (01233) 813011
e geoff@chapman.invictanet.
co.uk
w chapman.invictanet.co.uk

## YARMOUTH
### Isle of Wight

**Homestead Farmhouse
★★★** *Bed & Breakfast*
Caulbourne Lane, Newbridge
PO41 0TZ
t (01983) 531270
e homesteadfarmiow@
hotmail.co.uk
w homesteadfarmbandb.co.uk

**Medlars ★★★**
*Bed & Breakfast*
Halletts Shute, Norton,
Yarmouth PO41 0RH
t (01983) 761541
e greye@tiscali.co.uk
w milford.co.uk

## SOUTH WEST ENGLAND

### ABBOTSBURY
Dorset

**Swan Lodge ★★★**
*Guest Accommodation*
Rodden Row, Abbotsbury,
Weymouth DT3 4JL
t (01305) 871249

### ABBOTSKERSWELL
Devon

**The Coachman's Cottage
★★★★**
*Guest Accommodation*
Whiddon, Abbotskerswell,
Newton Abbot TQ12 5LG
t (01803) 872451
w thecoachmanscottage.co.uk

### ADVENT
Cornwall

**Higher Trezion ★★★★**
*Farmhouse*
Tresinney, Advent, Camelford
PL32 9QW
t (01840) 213761
e higher.trezion@btinternet.
com
w highertrezion.co.uk

### ALDERHOLT
Dorset

**Desford Cottage ★★★**
*Bed & Breakfast*
3 Park Lane, Alderholt SP6 3AJ
t (01425) 652434
e shirleyhooley@aol.com

### ALDERTON
Gloucestershire

**Moors Farm House
★★★★★ Bed & Breakfast
GOLD AWARD**
32 Beckford Road, Alderton,
Tewkesbury GL20 8NL
t (01242) 620523
e moorsfarmhouse@ukworld.
net
w ukworld.net/
moorsfarmhouse

### ALMONDSBURY
Gloucestershire

**Royland Cottage ★★★**
*Farmhouse*
Fernhill, Almondsbury, Bristol
BS32 4LU
t (01454) 610123

### ALTON PANCRAS
Dorset

**Whiteways Farmhouse
Accommodation ★★★★**
*Bed & Breakfast*
**SILVER AWARD**
Bookham, Dorchester DT2 7RP
t (01300) 345511
e andy.foot1@btinternet.com
w bookhamcourt.co.uk

### ALVERTON
Cornwall

**Penzance Youth Hostel –
Al124 ★★ Hostel**
Castle Horneck, Alverton,
Penzance TR18 4LP
t (01736) 362666
e penzance@yha.co.uk

### AMESBURY
Wiltshire

**Fairlawn ★★★ Guest House**
42 High Street, Salisbury
SP4 7DL
t (01980) 622103
e fairlawnhotel@hotmail.com
w fairlawnhotel.co.uk

**The George Hotel ★★★ Inn**
High Street, Amesbury,
Salisbury SP4 7ET
t (01980) 622108
w chapmansgroup.com

**The Old Bakery ★★★**
*Bed & Breakfast*
Netton, Salisbury SP4 6AW
t (01722) 782351
e valahen@aol.com
w members.aol.com/valahen

### APPLEDORE
Devon

**West Farm ★★★★★**
*Bed & Breakfast*
**SILVER AWARD**
Irsha Street, Appledore,
Bideford EX39 1RY
t (01237) 425269
e gail@appledore-devon.co.uk
w appledore-devon.co.uk

### ASHBRITTLE
Somerset

**Lower Westcott Farm
★★★★ Farmhouse**
Ashbrittle, Nr Wellington
TA21 0HZ
t (01398) 361296
e lowerwestcott@aol.com

### ASHTON KEYNES
Wiltshire

**Wheatleys Farm ★★★★**
*Farmhouse* **SILVER AWARD**
High Road, Ashton Keynes,
Swindon SN6 6NX
t (01285) 861310
e gill@wheatleysfarm.co.uk
w wheatleysfarm.co.uk

### ATHELHAMPTON
Dorset

**White Cottage ★★★★**
*Bed & Breakfast*
**SILVER AWARD**
Dorchester DT2 7LG
t (01305) 848622
e markjamespiper@aol.com
w freewebs.com/
whitecottagebandb

### ATWORTH
Wiltshire

**Church Farm ★★★★**
*Farmhouse*
Church Street, Atworth,
Melksham SN12 8JA
t (01225) 702215
e churchfarm@tinyonline.co.
uk
w churchfarm-atworth.
freeserve.co.uk

### AVEBURY
Wiltshire

**Manor Farm ★★★★**
*Bed & Breakfast*
High Street, Avebury,
Marlborough SN8 1RF
t (01672) 539294

**The New Inn ★★★**
*Guest Accommodation*
Winterbourne Monkton,
Swindon SN4 9NW
t (01672) 539240
e enquiries@thenewinn.net
w thenewinn.net

### AVETON GIFFORD
Devon

**Helliers Farm ★★★★**
*Farmhouse*
Ashford, Kingsbridge TQ7 4NB
t (01548) 550689
e helliersfarm@ukonline.co.uk
w helliersfarm.co.uk

### AXMINSTER
Devon

**Beckford Cottage ♦♦♦♦**
*Guest Accommodation*
Dalwood, Axminster EX13 7HQ
t (01404) 881641
e beckfordcottage@hotmail.
com
w beckford-cottage.co.uk

**Hedgehog Corner ★★★★**
*Guest Accommodation*
**SILVER AWARD**
Lyme Road, Axminster
EX13 5SU
t (01297) 32036
e info@hedgehogcorner.co.uk
w hedgehogcorner.co.uk

**Kerrington House Hotel
★★★★★**
*Guest Accommodation*
**GOLD AWARD**
Musbury Road, Axminster
EX13 5JR
t (01297) 35333
e ja.reaney@kerringtonhouse.
com
w kerringtonhouse.com

**Prestoller House ★★★★**
*Guest Accommodation*
Beaver Lane, Axminster
EX13 5EQ
t (01297) 33659
e prestollerhouse@btinternet.
com
w prestollerbedandbreakfast.
co.uk

### AYLBURTON
Gloucestershire

**Trimwood House Bed &
Breakfast ★★**
*Guest Accommodation*
39 High Street, Aylburton,
Lydney GL15 6DE
t (01594) 842163
e jackicollie@aol.com

### BABBACOMBE
Devon

**Seabury ★★★★**
*Guest Accommodation*
Manor Road, Babbacombe,
Torquay TQ1 3JX
t (01803) 327255

### BAMPTON
Devon

**Lodfin Farm Bed & Breakfast
★★★★ Bed & Breakfast
SILVER AWARD**
Morebath, Bampton, Tiverton
EX16 9DD
t (01398) 331400
e info@lodfinfarm.com
w lodfinfarm.com

### BARFORD ST MARTIN
Wiltshire

**Briden House ★★★★**
*Bed & Breakfast*
West Street, Salisbury SP3 4AH
t (01722) 743471
e bridenhouse@barford25.
freeserve.co.uk
w smoothhound.co.uk/hotels/
bridenho.html

### BARNSTAPLE
Devon

**Acland Barton ★★★**
*Farmhouse*
Acland Road, Barnstaple
EX32 0LD
t (01271) 830253

**Broomhill Farm ★★★★**
*Farmhouse*
Muddiford, Barnstaple
EX31 4EX
t (01271) 850676

**Field House ★★★★**
*Bed & Breakfast*
Lower Blakewell, Barnstaple
EX31 4ET
t (01271) 376205

**Little Orchard ★★★**
*Guest Accommodation*
Braunton Road, Barnstaple
EX31 1GA
t (01271) 371714
e terrychaplin@accanet.com

**Lower Yelland Farm B&B
★★★★ Farmhouse**
Fremington, Barnstaple
EX31 3EN
t (01271) 860101
e peterday@loweryellandfarm.
co.uk
w loweryellandfarm.co.uk

**The Red House ★★★★**
*Bed & Breakfast*
Roundswell, Barnstaple
EX31 3NP
t (01271) 345966
e booking@
theredhousenorthdevon.co.uk
w theredhousenorthdevon.co.
uk

**The Spinney ★★★★**
*Guest House* **SILVER AWARD**
Shirwell, Barnstaple EX31 4JR
t (01271) 850282
e thespinney@shirwell.fsnet.
co.uk
w thespinneyshirwell.co.uk

**Waytown Farm ★★★★**
*Farmhouse*
Shirwell, Barnstaple EX31 4JN
t (01271) 850396
e info@waytownholidays.co.
uk
w waytownholidays.co.uk

**Westcott Barton** ★★★★
*Guest Accommodation*
Middle Marwood, Barnstaple
EX31 4EF
t (01271) 812842
e westcott_barton@yahoo.co.
uk
w westcottbarton.co.uk

### BARWICK
Somerset

**Barwick Farm House** ★★★
*Farmhouse*
Rexs Lane, Nr Yeovil BA22 9TD
t (01935) 410779
e angelaml.nicoll@btinternet.
com
w barwickfarmhouse.co.uk

### BATCOMBE
Somerset

**Valley View Farm** ★★★★
*Guest Accommodation*
Hincombe Hill, Nr Shepton
Mallet BA4 6AJ
t (01749) 850302
e valleyviewfarm@lineone.net
w http://mysite.wanadoo-
members.co.uk/valleyviewfarm

### BATH
Somerset

**139 @ Leighton House**
★★★★
*Guest Accommodation*
Leighton House, 139 Wells
Road, Bath BA2 3AL
t (01225) 314769
e info@139bath.co.uk
w 139bath.co.uk

**14 Raby Place** ★★★★
*Bed & Breakfast*
Bath BA2 4EH
t (01225) 465120

**16 Bloomfield Road** ★★★
*Bed & Breakfast*
Bear Flat, Bath BA2 2AB
t (01225) 337804
e pamela.beresford@
homecall.co.uk
w 16bloomfieldroad.co.uk

**Abbey Rise** ★★★★
*Guest Accommodation*
97 Wells Road, Bath BA2 3AN
t (01225) 316177
e b&b@abbeyrise.co.uk
w abbeyrise.co.uk

**Amberley House Bed &
Breakfast** ★★★
*Guest Accommodation*
25 Pulteney Gardens, Bath
BA2 4HG
t (01225) 310033
e info@amberleyhouse.net
w amberleyhouse.net

**Anabelle's Guest House**
★★★ *Guest House*
6 Manvers Street, Bath
BA1 1JQ
t (01225) 330133
e dmlotfibath@yahoo.co.uk
w anabellesguesthouse.com

**Aquae Sulis** ★★★★
*Guest Accommodation*
174/176 Newbridge Road,
Bath BA1 3LE
t (01225) 420061
e enquiries@aquaesulishotel.
co.uk
w aquaesulishotel.co.uk

**Ashgrove Guest House**
★★★★ *Bed & Breakfast*
39 Bathwick Street, Bath
BA2 6PA
t (01225) 421911

**Ashley Villa** ★★★★
*Guest Accommodation*
26 Newbridge Road, Bath
BA1 3JZ
t (01225) 421683
e reservations@ashleyvilla.co.
uk
w ashleyvilla.co.uk

**Astor House** ★★★★
*Bed & Breakfast*
14 Oldfield Road, Bath
BA2 3ND
t (01225) 429134
e astorhouse.visitus@virgin.
net
w visitus.co.uk

**Athole Guest House**
★★★★★ *Bed & Breakfast*
**GOLD AWARD**
33 Upper Oldfield Park, Bath
BA2 3JX
t (01225) 320000
e info@atholehouse.co.uk
w atholehouse.co.uk

**Avon Guest House** ★★★
*Guest House*
1 Pulteney Gardens, Bath
BA2 4HG
t (01225) 313009
e julie@avonguesthousebath.
co.uk
w avonguesthousebath.co.uk

**The Ayrlington** ★★★★★
*Guest Accommodation*
**GOLD AWARD**
24/25 Pulteney Road, Bath
BA2 4EZ
t (01225) 425495
e mail@ayrlington.com
w ayrlington.com

**Badminton Villa** ★★★★
*Guest House* **SILVER AWARD**
10 Upper Oldfield Park, Bath
BA2 3JZ
t (01225) 426347
e badmintonvilla@blueyonder.
co.uk
w s-h-systems.co.uk/hotels/
badminton.html

**Bath YHA** ★★★ *Hostel*
Bathwick Hill, Bath BA2 6JZ
t (01225) 465674
e bath@yha.org.uk
w yha.org.uk

**Bay Tree House** ◆◆◆◆
*Guest Accommodation*
**SILVER AWARD**
12 Crescent Gardens, Bath
BA1 2NA
t (01225) 483699
e stay@baytreehousebath.co.
uk
w baytreehousebath.co.uk/
vbath

**The Belmont** ★★★
*Bed & Breakfast*
7 Belmont, Lansdown Road,
Bath BA1 5DZ
t (01225) 423082
e archie_watson@hotmail.com
w belmontbath.co.uk

**Belvedere Bed & Breakfast**
★★★ *Guest Accommodation*
25 Belvedere, Lansdown Road,
Bath BA1 5ED
t (01225) 330264
e info@belvederewinevaults.
co.uk
w belvederewinevaults.co.uk

**Braemar Guest House**
★★★★ *Bed & Breakfast*
43 Wellsway, Bath BA2 4RS
t (01225) 422743
e info@bathbraemar.co.uk
w bathbraemar.co.uk

**Bridgnorth House** ★★★
*Bed & Breakfast*
2 Crescent Gardens, Bath
BA1 2NA
t (01225) 331186
w bridgnorthhouse.co.uk

**The Carfax** ★★★★★
*Guest Accommodation*
13-15 Great Pulteney Street,
Bath BA2 4BS
t (01225) 462089
e reservations@carfaxhotel.co.
uk
w carfaxhotel.co.uk

**Chestnuts House** ★★★★
*Guest Accommodation*
16 Henrietta Road, Bath
BA2 6LY
t (01225) 334279
e reservations@
chestnutshouse.co.uk
w chestnutshouse.co.uk

**Church Farm** ★★★
*Farmhouse*
Monkton Farleigh, Bradford-
on-Avon BA15 2QJ
t (01225) 858583
e reservations@
churchfarmmonktonfarleigh.co.
uk
w churchfarmmonktonfarleigh.
co.uk

**Corston Fields Farm** ★★★★
*Farmhouse* **SILVER AWARD**
Corston Fields, Corston, Bath
BA2 9EZ
t (01225) 873305
e info@corstonfields.com
w corstonfields.co.uk

**The Edgar Hotel** ★★★
*Guest Accommodation*
64 Great Pulteney Street, Bath
BA2 4DN
t (01225) 420619
e edgar-hotel@btconnect.com
w edgar-hotel.co.uk

**The Firs** ★★★★
*Bed & Breakfast*
2 Newbridge Hill, Bath
BA1 3PU
t (01225) 334575
e dawnsandora@gmail.com

**Flaxley Villa** ★★★
*Bed & Breakfast*
9 Newbridge Hill, Bath
BA1 3PW
t (01225) 313237
e flaxleyvilla@fsmail.net

**Forres House** ★★★★
*Guest House*
172 Newbridge Road, Bath
BA1 3LE
t (01225) 427698
e jj.forres@btinternet.co.uk
w forreshouse.co.uk

**The Garden House** ★★★★
*Bed & Breakfast*
Adelaide Place, Bath BA2 6BU
t 07769 658453
e carolinehart@btopenworld.
com

**Glen View** ★★★★
*Guest Accommodation*
162 Newbridge Road, Bath
BA1 3LE
t (01225) 421376
e info@glenviewbath.co.uk
w glenviewbath.co.uk

**Grove Lodge** ★★★★
*Bed & Breakfast*
11 Lambridge, Bath BA1 6BJ
t (01225) 310860
e stay@grovelodgebath.co.uk
w grovelodgebath.co.uk

**The Grove** ★★★★★
*Bed & Breakfast*
Lyncombe Vale Road, Bath
BA2 4LR
t (01225) 484282
e rhstower@aol.com
w bathbandb.com

**Hatt Farm** ★★★★
*Farmhouse*
Old Jockey, Box, Corsham
SN13 8DJ
t (01225) 742989
e b&b@hattfarm.co.uk
w hattfarm.co.uk

**Haydon House** ★★★★★
*Guest House*
9 Bloomfield Park, Bath
BA2 2BY
t (01225) 444919
e stay@haydonhouse.co.uk
w haydonhouse.co.uk

**Hermitage** ★★★
*Guest House*
Bath Road, Box, Corsham
SN13 8DT
t (01225) 744187
e hermitagebb@btconnect.
com

**The Hollies** ★★★★
*Guest Accommodation*
**SILVER AWARD**
Hatfield Road, Bath BA2 2BD
t (01225) 313366
e davcartwright@lineone.net
w theholliesbath.co.uk

**Lamp Post Villa** ★★★
*Bed & Breakfast*
3 Crescent Gardens, Bath
BA1 2NA
t (01225) 331221
e lamppostvilla@aol.com

**Lindisfarne Guest House**
★★★★ *Bed & Breakfast*
41a Warminster Road, Bath
BA2 6XJ
t (01225) 466342
e lindisfarne-bath@talk21.com
w bath.org/hotel/lindisfarne.
htm

**Lynwood House** ◆◆◆◆
*Guest Accommodation*
6 Pulteney Gardens, Bath
BA2 4HG
t (01225) 426410
e post@lynwood-house.com
w lynwood-house.com

**Marisha's Guest House**
★★★ *Guest House*
68 Newbridge Hill, Bath
BA1 3QA
t (01225) 446881
e marishasguesthouse@tiscali.
co.uk
w marishasinbath.co.uk

**Marlborough House** ★★★★
*Guest House*
1 Marlborough Lane, Bath
BA1 2NQ
t (01225) 318175
e mars@manque.dircon.co.uk
w marlborough-house.net

**Membland Guest House**
★★★ *Bed & Breakfast*
7 Pulteney Terrace, Bath
BA2 4HJ
t 07958 599572
e membland@tiscali.co.uk

**Milton House** ★★★★
*Guest House*
75 Wellsway, Bath BA2 4RU
t (01225) 335632
e info@milton-house.fsnet.co.
uk
w milton-house.fsnet.co.uk

**Parkside** ★★★★
*Guest Accommodation*
11 Marlborough Lane, Bath
BA1 2NQ
t (01225) 429444
e post@parksidebandb.co.uk
w parksidebandb.co.uk

**Pulteney House** ★★★
*Guest House*
14 Pulteney Road, Bath
BA2 4HA
t (01225) 460991
e pulteney@tinyworld.co.uk
w pulteneyhotel.co.uk

**Radnor Guesthouse** ★★★★
*Guest House*
9 Pulteney Terrace, Pulteney
Road, Bath BA2 4HJ
t (01225) 316159
e info@radnorguesthouse.co.
uk
w radnorguesthouse.co.uk

**Ravenscroft (Sydney Road)**
★★★★ *Bed & Breakfast*
SILVER AWARD
Sydney Road, Bath BA2 6NT
t (01225) 469267
e rav.bath@ukonline.co.uk

**The Residence** ★★★★★
*Guest Accommodation*
GOLD AWARD
Weston Road, Bath BA1 2XZ
t (01225) 750180
e info@theresidencebath.com
w theresidencebath.com

**Roban House** ★★★★★
*Hostel*
26 Lower Oldfield Park, Bath
BA2 3HP
t (01225) 445390
e info@bathholidayrooms.co.
uk
w bathholidayrooms.co.uk

**Royal Park Guest House**
★★★★
*Guest Accommodation*
16 Crescent Gardens, Bath
BA1 2NA
t (01225) 317651
e info@royalparkbath.co.uk
w royalparkbath.co.uk

**St Leonards** ★★★★
*Guest Accommodation*
SILVER AWARD
Warminster Road, Bath
BA2 6SQ
t (01225) 465838
e stay@stleonardsbath.co.uk
w stleonardsbath.co.uk

**Tasburgh House Hotel**
★★★★★
*Guest Accommodation*
Warminster Road, Bath
BA2 6SH
t (01225) 425096
e hotel@bathtasburgh.co.uk
w bathtasburgh.co.uk

**Three Abbey Green** ★★★★
*Guest House* SILVER AWARD
3 Abbey Green, Bath
BA1 1NW
t (01225) 428558
e stay@threeabbeygreen.com
w threeabbeygreen.com

**Toghill House Farm** ★★★★
*Farmhouse*
Freezing Hill, Wick, Bristol
BS30 5RT
t (01225) 891261
e accommodation@
toghillhousefarm.co.uk
w toghillhousefarm.co.uk

**Tolley Cottage** ★★★★
*Bed & Breakfast*
SILVER AWARD
23 Sydney Buildings, Bath
BA2 6BZ
t (01225) 463365
e jj@judyj.plus.com
w tolleycottage.co.uk

**Villa Claudia** ★★★★
*Bed & Breakfast*
19 Forester Road, Bathwick,
Bath BA2 6QE
t (01225) 329670
e claudiaamato77@aol.com

**Villa Magdala Hotel**
★★★★
*Guest Accommodation*
Henrietta Road, Bath BA2 6LX
t (01225) 466329
e office@villamagdala.co.uk
w villamagdala.co.uk

**Walton Villa** ★★★★
*Guest Accommodation*
3 Newbridge Hill, Bath
BA1 3PW
t (01225) 482792
e walton.villa@virgin.net
w walton.izest.com

**Wellsway Guest House** ★★
*Guest Accommodation*
51 Wellsway, Bath BA2 4RS
t (01225) 423434

**Weston Lawn** ★★★★
*Guest Accommodation*
Lucklands Road, Weston, Bath
BA1 4AY
t (01225) 421362
e reservations@westonlawn.
co.uk
w westonlawn.co.uk

**Wheelwrights Arms** ★★★★
*Inn*
Monkton Combe, Bath
BA2 7HB
t (01225) 722287
e bookings@
wheelwrightsarms.co.uk
w wheelwrightsarms.co.uk/

**BATHEALTON**
Somerset

**Hagley Bridge Farm** ★★★★
*Farmhouse*
Ridge Highway, Nr
Wiveliscombe TA4 2BQ
t (01984) 629026

**BATHFORD**
Somerset

**Bridge Cottage** ★★★★
*Guest Accommodation*
Ashley Road, Bathford
BA1 7TT
t (01225) 852399
e daphne@bridge-cottages.co.
uk
w bridge-cottages.co.uk

**BAWDRIP**
Somerset

**Kings Farm** ★★ *Farmhouse*
10 Eastside Lane, Nr
Bridgwater TA7 8QB
t (01278) 683233

**BEAMINSTER**
Dorset

**Headington Bed & Breakfast**
★★★★ *Bed & Breakfast*
Down Road, Mosterton,
Beaminster DT8 3JF
t (01308) 867312
e headingtonbandb@hotmail.
com
w beaminsterbedandbreakfast.
co.uk

**Kitwhistle Farm** ★★★
*Farmhouse*
Beaminster Down, Beaminster
DT8 3SG
t (01308) 862458

**North Buckham Farm** ★★★
*Farmhouse*
Beaminster DT8 3SH
t (01308) 863054
e trish@northbuckham.fsnet.
co.uk
w northbuckhamfarm.co.uk

**The Walnuts** ★★★★
*Guest Accommodation*
2 Prout Bridge, Beaminster
DT8 3AY
t (01308) 862211
e caroline@thewalnuts.co.uk
w thewalnuts.co.uk

**Watermeadow House**
★★★★★ *Farmhouse*
SILVER AWARD
Hooke, Beaminster DT8 3PD
t (01308) 862619
e enquiries@
watermeadowhouse.co.uk
w watermeadowhouse.co.uk

**BECKINGTON**
Somerset

**Eden Vale Farm** ★★★
*Farmhouse*
Mill Lane, Nr Frome BA11 6SN
t (01373) 830371
e bandb@edenvalefarm.co.uk
w edenvalefarm.co.uk

**BEER**
Devon

**Belmont House B&B** ★★★★
*Bed & Breakfast*
Gordon Terrace, Clapps Lane,
Beer EX12 3EN
t (01297) 24415
e simongooch12345@aol.com
w belmonthousebedand
breakfast.co.uk

**YHA Beer** ★★★ *Hostel*
Bovey Combe, Townsend,
Seaton EX12 3LL
t 0870 770 5690
e beer@yha.org.uk
w yha.org.uk

**BELSTONE**
Devon

**The Cleave House** ★★★★
*Guest Accommodation*
Belstone, Okehampton
EX20 1QY
t (01837) 840055
e mail@thecleavehouse.co.uk
w thecleavehouse.co.uk

**BERE REGIS**
Dorset

**The Dorset Golf Resort**
★★★★
*Guest Accommodation*
The Dorset Golf & Country
Club, Hyde, Wareham
BH20 7NT
t (01929) 472244
e admin@dorsetgolfresort.
com
w dorsetgolfresort.com

**BERKELEY**
Gloucestershire

**Pickwick Farm** ★★★
*Farmhouse*
A38, Berkeley Heath, Berkeley
GL13 9EU
t (01453) 810241

**BERROW**
Somerset

**Berrow Links House** ★★★★
*Bed & Breakfast*
SILVER AWARD
Coast Road, Berrow TA8 2QS
t (01278) 751422
e afnt@towens.co.uk

**BERRY HILL**
Gloucestershire

**Berry Hill House** ★★★
*Bed & Breakfast*
Park Road, Berry Hill, Coleford
GL16 7AG
t (01594) 832325
e glynis@berryhillhouse.co.uk
w berryhillhouse.co.uk

**BERRY POMEROY**
Devon

**Berry Farm** ★★★★
*Farmhouse*
Berry Pomeroy, Totnes
TQ9 6LG
t (01803) 863231

## BERRYNARBOR
### Devon

**Langleigh Guest House**
★★★★
*Guest Accommodation*
The Village, Berrynarbor
EX34 9SG
t (01271) 883410
e relax@langleighguesthouse.
co.uk
w langleighguesthouse.co.uk

**The Lodge** ★★★★
*Guest Accommodation*
Pitt Hill, Ilfracombe EX34 9SG
t (01271) 883246
e philbridle@aol.com
w lodge-country-house-hotel.
co.uk

## BIBURY
### Gloucestershire

**Catherine Wheel** ★★★ *Inn*
Arlington, Bibury, Cirencester
GL7 5ND
t (01285) 740250
e catherinewhhel.bibury@
eldridge-pope.co.uk

**Cotteswold House** ★★★★
*Bed & Breakfast*
**GOLD AWARD**
Arlington, Bibury, Cirencester
GL7 5ND
t (01285) 740609
e enquiries@cotteswoldhouse.
org.uk
w cotteswoldhouse.org.uk

**The William Morris Bed &**
**Breakfast** ★★★★
*Bed & Breakfast*
11 The Street, Bibury GL7 5NP
t (01285) 740555
e ian@ianhoward8.wanadoo.
co.uk
w thewilliammorris.com

## BIDEFORD
### Devon

**Bulworthy Cottage** ★★★★
*Guest House* **SILVER AWARD**
Stoney Cross, Bideford
EX39 4PY
t (01271) 858441
e bulworthy@aol.com
w bulworthycottage.co.uk

**The Mount** ★★★★
*Guest House* **SILVER AWARD**
Northdown Road, Bideford
EX39 3LP
t (01237) 473748
e andrew@themountbideford.
fsnet.co.uk
w themountbideford.co.uk

## BILBROOK
### Somerset

**The Wayside B&B** ★★★★
*Guest Accommodation*
**SILVER AWARD**
Bilbrook, Minehead TA24 6HE
t (01984) 641669
e thewayside@tiscali.co.uk
w thewayside.co.uk

## BINEGAR
### Somerset

**Mansfield House** ★★★★
*Guest Accommodation*
**SILVER AWARD**
Binegar, Radstock BA3 4UG
t (01749) 840568
e mansfieldhouse@aol.com

## BISHOP SUTTON
### Somerset

**Centaur** ★★★
*Bed & Breakfast*
Ham Lane, Bishop Sutton
BS39 5TZ
t (01275) 332321

## BISHOP'S CLEEVE
### Gloucestershire

**Manor Cottage** ★★★
*Guest Accommodation*
41 Station Road, Bishops
Cleeve, Cheltenham GL52 8HH
t (01242) 673537

## BISHOPS HULL
### Somerset

**The Old Mill** ★★★★★
*Guest Accommodation*
**SILVER AWARD**
Netherclay, Taunton TA1 5AB
t (01823) 289732
w theoldmillbandb.co.uk

## BISHOP'S LYDEARD
### Somerset

**West View** ★★★★
*Guest Accommodation*
Minehead Road, Taunton
TA4 3BS
t (01823) 432223
e westview@pattemore.
freeserve.co.uk
w westviewbandb.co.uk

## BISHOPSTON
### City of Bristol

**Basca House**
Rating Applied For
*Bed & Breakfast*
19 Broadway Road, Bishopston
BS7 8ES
t (0117) 942 2182

## BISHOPSTONE
### Wiltshire

**Cheney Thatch** ★★★
*Bed & Breakfast*
Oxon Place, Bishopstone,
Swindon SN6 8PS
t (01793) 790508

## BLAKENEY
### Gloucestershire

**The Old Tump House** ★★★
*Bed & Breakfast*
New Road, Blakeney
GL15 4DG
t (01594) 517333
e georginadangelo@
btinternet.com
w oldtumphouse.co.uk

## BLANDFORD FORUM
### Dorset

**Farnham Farm House**
★★★★★
*Guest Accommodation*
**GOLD AWARD**
Blandford Forum DT11 8DG
t (01725) 516254
e info@farnhamfarmhouse.co.
uk
w farnhamfarmhouse.co.uk

**Lower Bryanston Farm B&B**
★★★★ *Bed & Breakfast*
Lower Bryanston, Blandford
Forum DT11 0LS
t (01258) 452009
e andrea@bryanstonfarm.co.
uk
w brylow.co.uk

**St Leonards Farmhouse**
★★★★ *Bed & Breakfast*
Wimborne Road, Blandford
Forum DT11 7SB
t (01258) 456635
e info.stleonardsfarmhouse@
fsmail.net
w stleonardsfarmhouse.com

**The Anvil** ★★★★ *Inn*
Salisbury Road, Pimperne,
Blandford Forum DT11 8UQ
t (01258) 453431
e theanvil.inn@btconnect.com
w anvilinn.co.uk

## BLEDINGTON
### Gloucestershire

**Kings Head Inn and**
**Restaurant** ★★★★ *Inn*
The Green, Bledington,
Chipping Norton OX7 6XQ
t (01608) 658365
e kingshead@orr-ewing.com
w kingsheadinn.net

## BLOCKLEY
### Gloucestershire

**Arreton House** ◆◆◆◆
*Guest Accommodation*
**SILVER AWARD**
Station Road, Blockley,
Moreton-in-Marsh GL56 9DT
t (01386) 701077
e bandb@arreton.demon.uk
w arreton.demon.co.uk

**Mill Dene Garden Country**
**Bed & Breakfast** ★★★★
*Bed & Breakfast*
**SILVER AWARD**
School Lane, Blockley,
Moreton-in-Marsh GL56 9HU
t (01386) 700457
e wendy@milldene.co.uk
w milldene.co.uk

## BLUE ANCHOR
### Somerset

**The Langbury** ★★★★
*Guest Accommodation*
Carhampton Road, Blue
Anchor TA24 6LB
t (01643) 821375
e post@langbury.co.uk
w langbury.co.uk

## BLUNSDON
### Wiltshire

**The Cott** ★★★
*Bed & Breakfast*
24 High Street, Blunsdon,
Swindon SN26 7AF
t (01793) 721246

## BODMIN
### Cornwall

**Bedknobs** ◆◆◆◆
*Guest Accommodation*
**SILVER AWARD**
Polgwyn, Castle Street, Bodmin
PL31 2DX
t (01208) 75533
e gilly@bedknobs.co.uk
w bedknobs.co.uk

**Bokiddick Farm** ★★★★★
*Farmhouse* **SILVER AWARD**
Bokiddick, Lanivet, Bodmin
PL30 5HP
t (01208) 831481
e gillhugo@bokiddickfarm.co.
uk
w bokiddickfarm.co.uk

**Hotel Casi Casa** ★★★
*Guest Accommodation*
11 Higher Bore Street, Bodmin
PL31 1JS
t (01208) 77592
e bookings@hotelcasicasa.co.
uk
w hotelcasicasa.co.uk

**Colliford Tavern** ★★★ *Inn*
Bodmin PL14 6PZ
t (01208) 821335
e info@colliford.com
w colliford.com

**Elm Grove** ★★★
*Bed & Breakfast*
2 Elm Grove, Cardell Road,
Bodmin PL31 2NJ
t (01208) 74044

**Kemsing** ◆◆◆◆
*Guest Accommodation*
44 Crabtree Lane, Bodmin
PL31 1BL
t (01208) 73343
e dianagoom@sagainternet.
co.uk

**Many Views House** ★★★
*Bed & Breakfast*
Launceston Road, Cooksland,
Bodmin PL31 2AR
t (01208) 269991
e chris@manyviewshouse.co.
uk
w manyviewshouse.co.uk

**Meadow Oak B&B** ★★★★
*Bed & Breakfast*
Lostwithiel Road, Bodmin
PL30 5AB
t (01208) 74828
e enquiry@meadowoakbandb.
co.uk
w meadowoakbandb.co.uk

**Milobel House** ★★★
*Bed & Breakfast*
20 Lower Bore Street, Bodmin
PL31 2JY
t (01208) 269818

**The Old School House**
★★★★ *Bed & Breakfast*
Averys Green, Cardinham,
Bodmin PL30 4EA
t (01208) 821303
e libby@cardinhambb.co.uk
w visitbodminmoor.co.uk

**Priory Cottage** ★★★
*Bed & Breakfast*
34 Rhind Street, Bodmin
PL31 2EL
t (01208) 73064
e jackiedingle@yahoo.com
w bodminlive.com

**Rocquaine B&B** ★★★★
*Bed & Breakfast*
Westheath Road, Bodmin
PL31 1QQ
t (01208) 72368
e pam@robilliard.freeserve.co.
uk

**Scrumptious** ★★
*Bed & Breakfast*
26 Berrycombe Hill, Bodmin
PL31 2PW
t (01208) 75939
e rosmcnary@scrumptious.
fsnet.co.uk
w cornwall-online.co.uk/
scrumpt

**Suncroft** ★★★★
*Bed & Breakfast*
12 Boxwell Park, Bodmin
PL31 2BG
t (01208) 73408
e tbugdale2000@yahoo.co.uk

**Trebray House** ★★★★
*Bed & Breakfast*
8 Cross Lane, Bodmin PL31 2EJ
t (01208) 73007
e dianelewis@vodafone.net
w bodminaccommodation.com

**Trewint Farm** ★★★★
*Bed & Breakfast*
Blisland, Bodmin PL30 4HX
t (01208) 851190
e johntipler@btinternet.com

### BOLVENTOR
### Cornwall

**Jamaica Inn** ★★★ *Inn*
Bolventor, Launceston
PL15 7TS
t (01566) 86250
e enquiry@jamaicainn.co.uk
w jamaicainn.co.uk

### BOSCASTLE
### Cornwall

**Boscastle Harbour Youth
Hostel – AB045** ★★★★
*Hostel*
Palace Stables, Boscastle
PL35 0HD
t (01840) 250287
e customerservices@yha.org.
uk

**Bridge House** ★★★
*Guest Accommodation*
The Bridge, Boscastle
PL35 0HE
t (01840) 250011
e simon@buxton01.wanadoo.
co.uk
w cornwall-online.com

**Home Farm Bed and
Breakfast** ◆◆◆◆
*Guest Accommodation*
SILVER AWARD
Boscastle PL35 0BN
t (01840) 250195
e homefarm.boscastle@tisali.
co.uk
w homefarm-boscastle.co.uk

**Lower Meadows** ★★★★
*Guest Accommodation*
Penally Hill, Boscastle
PL35 0HF
t (01840) 250570
e stay@lowermeadows.co.uk
w lowermeadows.co.uk

**The Old Coach House**
Rating Applied For
*Guest Accommodation*
Tintagel Road, Boscastle
PL35 0AS
t (01840) 250398
e jackiefarm@btinternet.com
w old-coach.co.uk

**Orchard Lodge** ★★★★
*Guest Accommodation*
Gunpool Lane, Boscastle
PL35 0AT
t (01840) 250418
e orchardlodge@fsmail.net
w orchardlodgeboscastle.co.uk

**Reddivallen Farm** ★★★★★
*Farmhouse* SILVER AWARD
Trevalga, Boscastle PL35 0EE
t (01840) 250854
e reddivallen@tiscali.co.uk
w reddivallenfarm.co.uk

**The Riverside** ★★★★★
*Guest Accommodation*
The Bridge, Boscastle
PL35 0HE
t (01840) 250216
e reception@hotelriverside.co.
uk
w hotelriverside.co.uk

**Trefoil Farm** ★★★
*Farmhouse*
Camelford Road, Boscastle
PL35 0AD
t (01840) 250606
e trefoil.farm@tiscali.co.uk

**Valency Bed and Breakfast**
★★★★
*Guest Accommodation*
SILVER AWARD
Penally Hill, Boscastle
PL35 0HF
t (01840) 250397
e tillinghast@btinternet.com
w valencybandb.com

### BOSSINGTON
### Somerset

**Buckley Lodge** ★★★★
*Bed & Breakfast*
Bossington, Minehead
TA24 8HQ
t (01643) 862521
e bucklodgeuk@yahoo.co.uk

**Tudor Cottage** ★★★★
*Bed & Breakfast*
SILVER AWARD
Bossington Lane, Nr Porlock
TA24 8HQ
t (01643) 862255
e bookings@tudorcottage.net
w tudorcottage.net

### BOSWINGER
### Cornwall

**Boswinger YHA** ★★★ *Hostel*
Boswinger, St Austell PL26 6LL
t (01726) 844527

### BOURNEMOUTH
### Dorset

**Alexander Lodge Hotel**
★★★★ *Guest House*
21 Southern Road,
Southbourne, Bournemouth
BH6 3SR
t (01202) 421662
e alexanderlodge@yahoo.com
w alexanderlodgehotel.co.uk

**Balincourt Hotel** ★★★★★
*Guest Accommodation*
SILVER AWARD
58 Christchurch Road,
Bournemouth BH1 3PF
t (01202) 552962
e rooms@balincourt.co.uk
w balincourt.co.uk

**Beach Lodge** ★★★★
*Guest Accommodation*
61 Grand Avenue,
Southbourne, Bournemouth
BH6 3TA
t (01202) 423396
e stay@beach-lodge.co.uk
w beach-lodge.co.uk

**The Blue Palms** ★★★★
*Guest Accommodation*
26 Tregonwell Road,
Bournemouth BH2 5NS
t (01202) 554968
e bluepalmshotel@
btopenworld.com
w bluepalmshotel.com

**Bonnington Hotel** ★★★
*Guest Accommodation*
44 Tregonwell Road,
Bournemouth BH2 5NT
t (01202) 553621
e john@thebonningtonhotel.
com
w thebonningtonhotel.com

**Cavendish** ★★★★
*Guest Accommodation*
20 Durley Chine Road, West
Cliff, Bournemouth BH2 5LF
t (01202) 290489
e info@cavendishhotel.uk.net
w cavendishhotel.uk.net

**Charlton Lodge** ★★★
*Bed & Breakfast*
826 Ringwood Road,
Bournemouth BH11 8NF
t (01202) 249977
e friggs@cwctv.net

**Claremont Hotel** ★★★★
*Guest Accommodation*
89 St Michaels Road,
Bournemouth BH2 5DR
t (01202) 290875
e info@claremonthotel
bournemouth.co.uk
w claremonthotel
bournemouth.co.uk

**Cransley Hotel** ★★★★
*Guest Accommodation*
11 Knyveton Road, East Cliff,
Bournemouth BH1 3QG
t (01202) 290067
e info@cransley.com
w cransley.com

**Denewood** ★★★
*Guest Accommodation*
1 Percy Road, Bournemouth
BH5 1JE
t (01202) 394493
e info@denewood.co.uk
w denewood.co.uk

**Earlham Lodge** ★★★★
*Guest House*
91 Alumhurst Road, Alum
Chine, Bournemouth BH4 8HR
t (01202) 761943
e earlhamlodge@hotmail.com
w earlhamlodge.com

**Fielden Court Hotel** ★★★★
*Guest House*
20 Southern Road,
Bournemouth BH6 3SR
t (01202) 427459
e enquiries@
fieldencourthotel.co.uk
w fieldencourthotel.co.uk

**The Fircliff**
Rating Applied For
*Guest House*
Studland Road, Bournemouth
BH4 8HZ
t (01202) 765307
e coastl@tiscali.co.uk

**The Golden Sovereign Hotel**
★★★★ *Guest House*
97 Alumhurst Road,
Bournemouth BH4 8HR
t (01202) 762088
e scott.p@talk21.com
w goldensovereignhotel.com

**Ingledene Guest House** ★★
*Guest House*
20 Gardens View,
Bournemouth BH1 3QA
t (01202) 291914
e ingledenehouse@yahoo.
com
w ingledenehouse.co.uk

**The Kings Langley** ★★★
*Guest Accommodation*
1 West Cliff Road,
Bournemouth BH2 5ES
t (01202) 557349
e john@kingslangleyhotel.com
w kingslangleyhotel.com

**Marlins Hotel** ★★★★
*Guest Accommodation*
2 West Cliff Road, West Cliff,
Bournemouth BH2 5EY
t (01202) 299645
e marlinshotel@aol.com
w marlinhotel.com

**Mount Lodge Guest
Accommodation** ★★
*Guest Accommodation*
19 Beaulieu Road, Alum Chine,
Bournemouth BH4 8HY
t (01202) 761173
e mountlodgehotel@yahoo.co.
uk

**Silver How Hotel** ★★★
*Guest Accommodation*
5 West Cliff Gardens,
Bournemouth BH2 5HN
t (01202) 551537
e reservations@
silverhowhotel.co.uk
w silverhowhotel.co.uk

**Southernhay Guest House**
★★★ *Guest Accommodation*
42 Alum Chine Road,
Westbourne, Bournemouth
BH4 8DX
t (01202) 761251
e enquiries@
southernhayhotel.co.uk
w southernhayhotel.co.uk

**Sun Haven Guest House**
★★★ *Guest Accommodation*
39 Southern Road,
Southbourne, Bournemouth
BH6 3SS
t (01202) 427560

**Wenrose** ★★★★
*Guest Accommodation*
23 Drummond Road,
Boscombe, Bournemouth
BH1 4DP
t (01202) 396451 &
07778 800804
e wenrose@bigfoot.com
w bournemouthbedand
breakfast.com

**West Cliff Sands** ★★
*Guest House*
9 Priory Road, Bournemouth
BH2 5DF
t (01202) 557013
e wst.clff-sds@virgin.net
w westcliffsands.sageweb.co.
uk

**Whitley Court** ★
*Guest Accommodation*
West Cliff Gardens,
Bournemouth BH2 5HL
**t** (01202) 551302

**Winter Dene Guest House**
★★★★
*Guest Accommodation*
11 Durley Road South, West
Cliff, Bournemouth BH2 5JH
**t** (01202) 554150
**e** info@winterdenehotel.com
**w** winterdenehotel.com

**Wood Lodge** ★★★★
*Guest House*
10 Manor Road, Bournemouth
BH1 3EY
**t** (01202) 290891
**e** enquiries@woodlodgehotel.
co.uk
**w** woodlodgehotel.co.uk

🅰

**The Woodlands Hotel** ★★★
*Guest House*
28 Percy Road, Boscombe
Manor, Bournemouth BH5 1JG
**t** (01202) 396499
**e** thewoodlandshotel@
tinyworld.co.uk
**w** the-woodlands-hotel.co.uk

BOURTON-ON-THE-WATER
Gloucestershire

**Alderley Guesthouse**
★★★★
*Guest Accommodation*
SILVER AWARD
Rissington Road, Bourton-on-
the-Water, Cheltenham
GL54 2DX
**t** (01451) 822788
**e** alderleyguesthouse@
hotmail.com
**w** alderleyguesthouse.com

**Broadlands Guest House**
★★★ *Guest Accommodation*
Clapton Row, Bourton-on-the-
Water, Cheltenham GL54 2DN
**t** (01451) 822002
**e** marco@broadlands-guest-
house.co.uk
**w** broadlands-guest-house.co.
uk

**Coombe House** ★★★★
*Guest Accommodation*
GOLD AWARD
Rissington Road, Bourton-on-
the-Water, Cheltenham
GL54 2DT
**t** (01451) 821966
**e** info@coombehouse.net
**w** coombehouse.net

**Cotswold Carp Farm** ★★★★
*Bed & Breakfast*
Bury Barn Lane, Bourton-on-
the-Water, Cheltenham
GL54 2HB
**t** (01451) 821795

**Elvington Bed and Breakfast**
★★★★ *Bed & Breakfast*
Rissington Road, Bourton-on-
the-Water, Cheltenham
GL54 2DX
**t** (01451) 822026
**e** the@tuckwells.freeserve.co.
uk
**w** bandb.fsnet.co.uk

**Farncombe** ★★★★
*Bed & Breakfast*
Clapton, Cheltenham
GL54 2LG
**t** (01451) 820120
**e** julia@farncombecotswold.
com
**w** smoothhound.co.uk/hotels/
farncomb.
htmlandfarncombecotswolds.
com

**Holly House** ★★★★
*Guest Accommodation*
Station Road, Bourton-on-the-
Water, Cheltenham GL54 2ER
**t** (01451) 821302
**e** paula@hollyhousebourton.
co.uk
**w** hollyhousebourton.co.uk

**Lamb Inn** ★★★★ *Inn*
Great Rissington, Cheltenham
GL54 2LP
**t** (01451) 820388
**w** thelambinn.com

**Lansdowne Villa Guest
House** ★★★★ *Guest House*
Lansdown, Bourton-on-the-
Water, Cheltenham GL54 2AR
**t** (01451) 820673
**e** lansdownevilla@aol.com
**w** lansdownevilla.co.uk

**Manor Close** ★★★★
*Bed & Breakfast*
High Street, Bourton-on-the-
Water, Cheltenham GL54 2AP
**t** (01451) 820339

**Meadow View** ★★★★
*Bed & Breakfast*
GOLD AWARD
Pock Hill Lane, Bourton-on-the-
Water, Cheltenham GL54 2DD
**t** (01451) 821860
**e** info@meadow-rise.co.uk
**w** meadow-rise.co.uk

**Old New Inn** ★★ *Inn*
The Old New Inn, Bourton-on-
the-Water, Cheltenham
GL54 2AF
**t** (01451) 820467
**e** reception@theoldnewinn.co.
uk
**w** theoldnewinn.co.uk

**The Ridge Guesthouse**
★★★★
*Guest Accommodation*
Whiteshoots Hill, Bourton-on-
the-Water, Cheltenham
GL54 2LE
**t** (01451) 820660
**e** info@theridge-guesthouse.
co.uk
**w** theridge-guesthouse.co.uk

**Southlands** ★★★★
*Guest Accommodation*
Rissington Road, Bourton-on-
the-Water, Cheltenham
GL54 2DT
**t** (01451) 821987
**e** christine.hutchman@
btopenworld.com
**w** southlands-bb.co.uk

**Touchstone** ★★★★
*Bed & Breakfast*
SILVER AWARD
Little Rissington, Cheltenham
GL54 2ND
**t** (01451) 822481
**e** touchstone.bb@lineone.net
**w** http://website.lineone.net/
~touchstone.bb

BOVEY TRACEY
Devon

**Brookfield House** ★★★★★
*Bed & Breakfast*
GOLD AWARD
Challabrook Lane, Bovey
Tracey TQ13 9DF
**t** (01626) 836181
**e** enquiries@brookfield-house.
com
**w** brookfield-house.com

**Oaklands** ★★★★
*Bed & Breakfast*
Challabrook Lane, Newton
Abbot TQ13 9DF
**t** (01626) 832602
**e** kathleen.stephens@virgin.
net
**w** oaklandsholidaysdevon.co.
uk

BOWERHILL
Wiltshire

**Springfield Gardens B&B**
★★★★ *Bed & Breakfast*
29 Kingfisher Drive, Bowerhill,
Melksham SN12 6FH
**t** (01225) 703694
**e** janet@jory3862.freeserve.
co.uk
**w** visitwiltshire.co.uk/
springfield

BOX
Wiltshire

**Lorne House** ★★★★
*Guest House*
London Road, Box, Corsham
SN13 8NA
**t** (01225) 742597
**e** lornehouse2003@yahoo.co.
uk
**w** lornehouse.net

**Norbin Farmhouse** ★★★★
*Farmhouse*
Norbin, Box, Corsham SN13 8JJ
**t** (01225) 866907
**e** gillhillier@yahoo.co.uk

BRADFORD-ON-AVON
Wiltshire

**The Beeches Farmhouse**
★★★★ *Farmhouse*
Holt Road, Bradford-on-Avon
BA15 1TS
**t** (01225) 865170
**e** beeches-farmhouse@
netgates.co.uk
**w** beeches-farmhouse.co.uk

**The Georgian Lodge Hotel**
★★★ *Guest Accommodation*
25 Bridge Street, Bradford-on-
Avon BA15 1BY
**t** (01225) 862268
**e** georgianlodge@btconnect.
com
**w** georgianlodgehotel.com

**Great Ashley Farm** ★★★★
*Bed & Breakfast*
SILVER AWARD
Great Ashley, Bradford-on-
Avon BA15 2PP
**t** (01225) 864563
**e** info@greatashley.co.uk
**w** greatashley.co.uk

**Honeysuckle Cottage**
★★★★ *Bed & Breakfast*
SILVER AWARD
95 The Common, Broughton
Gifford, Melksham SN12 8ND
**t** (01225) 782463
**e** info@honeysuckle-cottage.
org.uk
**w** honeysuckle-cottage.org.uk

**Springfields** ★★★★
*Guest Accommodation*
Great Ashley, Bradford-on-
Avon BA15 2PP
**t** (01225) 866125
**e** christine.rawlings@
farmersweekly.net
**w** bed-and-breakfast.org

BRADPOLE
Dorset

**Orchard Barn** ★★★★★
*Guest Accommodation*
SILVER AWARD
Off Lee Lane, Bradpole,
Bridport DT6 4AR
**t** (01308) 455655
**e** corbett@
lodgeatorchardbarn.co.uk
**w** lodgeatorchardbarn.co.uk

**Spray Copse Farm** ★★★★
*Bed & Breakfast*
Lee Lane, Bridport DT6 4AP
**t** (01308) 458510

BRADWORTHY
Devon

**Lew Barn** ★★★
*Guest Accommodation*
Bradworthy, Holsworthy
EX22 7SQ
**t** (01409) 241964
**e** lewmillington@btinternet.
com
**w** lewbarn.co.uk

📷🖼

BRATTON CLOVELLY
Devon

**Eversfield Lodge and Coach
House** ★★★★
*Guest Accommodation*
Ellacott Barton, Bratton
Clovelly, Okehampton
EX20 4LB
**t** (01837) 871480
**e** bookings@eversfieldlodge.
co.uk
**w** eversfieldlodge.co.uk

BRATTON FLEMING
Devon

**Bracken House Country
Hotel** ★★★★★
*Guest Accommodation*
Bratton Fleming, Barnstaple
EX31 4TG
**t** (01598) 710320
**e** steve@brackenhousehotel.
co.uk
**w** brackenhousehotel.co.uk

🅰

**Haxton Down Farm** ★★★★
*Farmhouse*
Bratton Fleming, Barnstaple
EX32 7JL
**t** (01598) 710275
**e** haxtondown@tiscali.co.uk
**w** haxton-down-farm-holidays.
co.uk

---

## BRAUNTON
### Devon

**The George Hotel ★★★** *Inn*
Exeter Road, Braunton
EX33 2JJ
**t** (01271) 812029
**e** georgehoteldevon@
btconnect.com
**w** georgehotel-braunton.co.uk

## BRAYFORD
### Devon

**Kimbland Farm ★★★**
*Farmhouse*
Brayford, Barnstaple EX32 7PS
**t** (01598) 710352
**w** kimblandfarmholidays.co.uk

## BREAM
### Gloucestershire

**Lindum House ★★★**
*Bed & Breakfast*
Oakwood Road, Bream,
Lydney GL15 6HS
**t** (01594) 560378
**e** lynne@lindumhouse.
fsworld.co.uk
**w** lindum-house.co.uk

**Rising Sun ★★★** *Inn*
High Street, Bream, Lydney
GL15 6JF
**t** (01594) 564555
**e** jonjo_risingsun@msn.com
**w** therisingsunbream.co.uk

## BREAN
### Somerset

**The Old Rectory Motel
★★★★**
*Guest Accommodation*
Church Road, Brean, Burnham-
on-Sea TA8 2SF
**t** (01278) 751447
**e** helen@old-rectory.
fsbusiness.co.uk
**w** old-rectory.fsbusiness.co.uk

**Yew Tree House ★★★★**
*Guest Accommodation*
Hurn Lane, Berrow, Nr Brean,
Burnham-on-Sea TA8 2QT
**t** (01278) 751382
**e** yewtree@yewtree-house.co.
uk
**w** yewtree-house.co.uk

## BRENTOR
### Devon

**Burnville House ★★★★★**
*Farmhouse* **SILVER AWARD**
Burnville Farm, Brentor,
Tavistock PL19 0NE
**t** (01822) 820443
**e** burnvillef@aol.com
**w** burnville.co.uk

## BRIDESTOWE
### Devon

**Fox & Hounds** *Camping Barn*
Fox & Hounds Hotel,
Bridestowe, Okehampton
EX20 4HF
**t** (01822) 820206
**w** foxandhoundshotel.com

## BRIDGWATER
### Somerset

**Admirals Rest ♦♦♦**
*Guest Accommodation*
5 Taunton Road, Bridgwater
TA6 3LW
**t** (01278) 458580
**e** susanparker57@hotmail.com
**w** admiralsrest.co.uk

**The Boat & Anchor Inn
★★★** *Inn*
Meads Crossing, Huntworth,
Bridgwater TA7 0AQ
**t** (01278) 662473
**e** andrea@theboatandanchor.
co.uk
**w** theboatandanchor.co.uk

**Brookland Hotel ♦♦♦♦**
*Guest Accommodation*
56 North Street, Bridgwater
TA6 3PN
**t** (01278) 423263
**w** brooklandhotel.com

**Chestnut House ★★★★★**
*Guest Accommodation*
**SILVER AWARD**
Hectors Stones, Lower Road,
Nr Bridgwater TA7 8EF
**t** (01278) 683658
**e** paul@chestnuthousehotel.
com
**w** chestnuthousehotel.com

**Cokerhurst Farm ★★★★**
*Farmhouse*
87 Wembdon Hill, Wembdon,
Bridgwater TA6 7QA
**t** (01278) 422330
**e** diana@cokerhurst.co.uk
**w** cokerhurst.co.uk

**Manor Farm ★★★**
*Farmhouse*
Waterpits, Taunton TA5 1AT
**t** (01823) 451266
**w** manorfarmbreaks.co.uk

**The Olive Mill ★★★★**
*Restaurant with Rooms*
Chilton Polden Hill, Bridgwater
TA7 9AH
**t** (01278) 722202
**e** enquiries@theolivemill.co.uk
**w** theolivemill.co.uk

## BRIDPORT
### Dorset

**Britmead House ★★★★**
*Guest Accommodation*
West Bay Road, Bridport
DT6 4EG
**t** (01308) 422941
**e** britmead@talk21.com
**w** britmeadhouse.co.uk

**Candida House ★★★★**
*Guest Accommodation*
Whitchurch Canonicorum,
Bridport DT6 6RQ
**t** (01297) 489629
**e** cbain@globalnet.co.uk
**w** candidahouse.co.uk

**Durbeyfield Guest House
★★★** *Guest Accommodation*
10 West Bay, Bridport DT6 4EL
**t** (01308) 423307
**e** manager@durbeyfield.co.uk
**w** durbeyfield.co.uk

**Eypeleaze ★★★★**
*Bed & Breakfast*
117 West Bay Road, Bridport
DT6 4EQ
**t** (01308) 423363
**e** enquiries@eypeleaze.co.uk
**w** eypeleaze.co.uk

**The Gables ★★★★**
*Bed & Breakfast*
West Allington, Bridport
DT6 5BH
**t** (01308) 459963
**e** donaldbroadley@hotmail.
com
**w** thegablesbridport.co.uk

**Highway Farm ★★★★**
*Guest Accommodation*
**SILVER AWARD**
West Road, Bridport DT6 6AE
**t** (01308) 424321
**e** bale@highwayfarm.co.uk
**w** highwayfarm.co.uk

**New House Farm ★★★**
*Farmhouse*
Mangerton Lane, Bridport
DT6 3SF
**t** (01308) 422884
**e** jane@mangertonlake.
freeserve.co.uk
**w** mangertonlake.co.uk

**Patchwork House ★★★★**
*Guest Accommodation*
47 Burton Road, Bridport
DT6 4JE
**t** (01308) 456515
**e** loveridge1@supanet.com
**w** patchworkhouse.co.uk

**The Roundham House
★★★★★**
*Guest Accommodation*
**GOLD AWARD**
Roundham Gardens, West Bay
Road, Bridport DT6 4BD
**t** (01308) 422753
**e** cyprencom@compuserve.
com
**w** roundhamhouse.co.uk

**Southcroft ♦♦♦♦**
*Guest Accommodation*
**GOLD AWARD**
Park Road, Bridport DT6 5DA
**t** (01308) 423335
**e** info@southcroftguesthouse.
com
**w** southcroftguesthouse.com

**Southfield ★★★★**
*Bed & Breakfast*
Marsh Gate, Burton Road,
Bridport DT6 4JB
**t** (01308) 458910
**e** wam.1@btinternet.com
**w** southfield-westbay.co.uk

**The Well ★★★**
*Bed & Breakfast*
St Andrews Well, Bridport
DT6 3DL
**t** (01308) 424156
**e** thewellbandb@yahoo.co.uk
**w** thewellbedandbreakfast.co.
uk

## BRISLINGTON
### City of Bristol

**Woodstock Guest House
★★★★** *Guest House*
534 Bath Road, Brislington,
Bristol BS4 3JZ
**t** (0117) 987 1613
**e** woodstock@blueyonder.co.
uk
**w** woodstockguesthouse.org

## BRISTOL
### City of Bristol

**Arches House ★★★**
*Guest Accommodation*
132 Cotham Brow, Bristol
BS6 6AE
**t** (0117) 924 7398
**e** ml@arches-hotel.co.uk
**w** arches-hotel.co.uk

**Bristol YHA ★★★** *Hostel*
14 Narrow Quay, Harbourside
BS1 4QA
**t** (0117) 922 1659
**e** bristol@yha.org.uk
**w** yha.org.uk

**Downs View Guest House
★★★** *Guest House*
38 Upper Belgrave Road,
Bristol BS8 2XN
**t** (0117) 973 7046
**e** bookings@
downsviewguesthouse.co.uk
**w** downsviewguesthouse.co.
uk

**Norfolk House ★★★**
*Guest Accommodation*
577 Gloucester Road, Bristol
BS7 0BW
**t** (0117) 951 3191

**The Paddock ★★★**
*Guest Accommodation*
Hung Road, Shirehampton,
Bristol BS11 9XJ
**t** (0117) 923 5140

**Treborough ★★**
*Bed & Breakfast*
3 Grove Road, Coombe Dingle,
Bristol BS9 2RQ
**t** (0117) 968 2712

**Tyndall's Park ★★**
*Guest Accommodation*
4 Tyndall's Park Road, Clifton,
Bristol BS8 1PG
**t** (0117) 973 5407
**e** contactus@
tyndallsparkhotel.co.uk
**w** tyndallsparkhotel.co.uk

**Wesley College ★★** *Campus*
College Park Drive, Henbury
Road, Bristol BS10 7QD
**t** (0117) 959 1200
**e** admin@wesley-college-
bristol.ac.uk
**w** wesley-college-bristol.ac.uk

**Westfield House ★★★★**
*Bed & Breakfast*
37 Stoke Hill, Sneyd Park,
Bristol BS9 1LQ
**t** (0117) 962 6119
**e** admin@westfieldhouse.net
**w** westfieldhouse.net

### BRIXHAM
Devon

**1 Hillhead Park** ★★★★
*Bed & Breakfast*
Brixham TQ5 0HG
t (01803) 854010

**Anchorage Guest House**
★★★★ *Guest House*
170 New Road, Brixham
TQ5 8DA
t (01803) 852960
e enquiries@brixham-anchorage.co.uk
w brixham-anchorage.co.uk

**Brioc Hotel** ★★★★
*Guest Accommodation*
11 Prospect Road, Brixham
TQ5 8HS
t (01803) 853540
e bill@brioc-hotel.fsnet.co.uk
w brioc-hotel.fsnet.co.uk

**Brookside Guest House**
★★★★
*Guest Accommodation*
GOLD AWARD
160 New Road, Brixham
TQ5 8DA
t (01803) 858858
e holidays@brooksidebrixham.co.uk
w brookside brixham.co.uk

**Churston Way Lodge** ★★★
*Guest Accommodation*
2 Churston Way, Brixham
TQ5 8DD
t (01803) 853315
e info@churchstonwaylodge.co.uk
w churstonwaylodge.co.uk

**Cumberland House** ★★★
*Bed & Breakfast*
Vicarage Road, Brixham
TQ5 9RE
t (01803) 853912
e susan.cranston@btinternet.com

**Lamorna Guest House**
★★★★ *Guest House*
130 New Road, Brixham
TQ5 8DA
t (01803) 853954
e caroline@lamorna.orangehome.co.uk
w lamornabedandbreakfast.co.uk

**Melville Guest House** ★★★
*Guest House*
45 New Road, Brixham
TQ5 8NL
t (01803) 852033
e melvillehotel@brixham45.fsnet.co.uk
w smoothhound.co.uk/hotels/melville2.html

**Midhurst Bed & Breakfast**
★★★★
*Guest Accommodation*
132 New Road, Brixham
TQ5 8DA
t (01803) 857331
w midhurstbnb.co.uk

**Raddicombe Lodge** ★★★★
*Guest Accommodation*
Kingswear Road, Brixham
TQ5 0EX
t (01803) 882125
e stay@raddicombelodge.co.uk
w raddicombelodge.co.uk

**Ranscombe House Hotel**
★★★★ *Hotel*
Ranscombe Road, Brixham
TQ5 9UP
t (01803) 882337
e ranscombe@lineone.net
w ranscombehousehotel.co.uk

**Redlands** ★★★★
*Guest House*
136 New Road, Brixham
TQ5 8DA
t (01803) 853813
e redlandsbrixham@aol.com
w redlandsbrixham.co.uk

**Sampford House** ★★★
*Guest Accommodation*
57-59 King Street, Brixham
TQ5 9TH
t (01803) 857761
e sampfordhouse@yahoo.co.uk
w sampfordhouse.co.uk

**The Shoalstone** ★★★
*Guest Accommodation*
105 Berry Head Road, Brixham
TQ5 9AG
t (01803) 857919

**Sunnybrook Guest House**
★★★ *Guest House*
156 New Road, Brixham
TQ5 8DA
t (01803) 854386
e info@sunnybrook.co.uk
w sunnybrook.co.uk

**Trefoil Guest House** ★★★★
*Guest House*
134 New Road, Brixham
TQ5 8DA
t (01803) 855266
e david.harmer@virgin.net
w trefoilguesthouse.co.uk

**Westbury Guest House**
★★★ *Guest House*
51 New Road, Brixham
TQ5 8NL
t (01803) 851684
e info@westburyguesthouse.co.uk
w westburyguesthouse.co.uk

**White Horse Guesthouse**
★★★★
*Guest Accommodation*
Dartmouth Road, Churston
Ferrers, Brixham TQ5 0LL
t (01803) 842381
e bookings@thewhitehorsehotel.co.uk
w thewhitehorsehotel.co.uk

**Woodlands Guest House**
★★★ *Guest House*
Parkham Road, Brixham
TQ5 9BU
t (01803) 852040
e woodlandsbrixham@btinternet.com
w woodlandsdevon.co.uk

### BRIXTON
Devon

**Venn Farm** ★★★★
*Guest Accommodation*
Brixton, Plymouth PL8 2AX
t (01752) 880378
e info@vennfarm.co.uk
w vennfarm.co.uk

### BROAD CHALKE
Wiltshire

**Lodge Farmhouse Bed & Breakfast** ★★★★
*Bed & Breakfast*
Lodge Farmhouse, Broad
Chalke, Salisbury SP5 5LU
t (01752) 519242
e mj.roe@virgin.net
w lodge-farmhouse.co.uk

### BROADCLYST
Devon

**Heath Gardens** ★★★★
*Bed & Breakfast*
Broadclyst, Exeter EX5 3HL
t (01392) 462311
e info@heathgardens.co.uk
w heathgardens.co.uk

### BROADHEMBURY
Devon

**Stafford Barton Farm**
★★★★ *Farmhouse*
Broadhembury, Honiton
EX14 3LU
t (01404) 841403
e jean.walters1@tesco.net

### BROADOAK
Dorset

**Dunster Farm** ★★★★
*Farmhouse*
Broadoak, Bridport DT6 5NR
t (01308) 424626
e dunsterfarm@ukonline.co.uk
w dunsterfarm.co.uk

### BROADSTONE
Dorset

**Ashdell** ★★★
*Bed & Breakfast*
85 Dunyeats Road, Broadstone
BH18 8AF
t (01202) 692032
e ian@ashdell.fsnet.co.uk
w ashdell.co.uk

**Heathcote House** ★★★★
*Bed & Breakfast*
SILVER AWARD
69a Dunyeats Road,
Broadstone BH18 8AE
t (01202) 602024
e lucy.home@btopenworld.com

**Honey Lodge** ★★★★
*Bed & Breakfast*
SILVER AWARD
41 Dunyeats Road, Broadstone
BH18 8AB
t (01202) 694247

**Tarven** ★★ *Bed & Breakfast*
Corfe Lodge Road, Broadstone
BH18 9NF
t (01202) 694338
e browning@tarvencorfe.fsnet.co.uk
w tarven.co.uk

**Weston Cottage** ★★★★
*Bed & Breakfast*
6 Macaulay Road, Broadstone
BH18 8AR
t (01202) 699638
e westoncot@aol.com
w westoncottage.org.uk

### BROAD CHALKE
Wiltshire

### BROADWELL
Gloucestershire

**The White House** ★★★
*Bed & Breakfast*
2 South Road, Broadwell,
Coleford GL16 7BH
t (01594) 837069
e info@whitehousebroadwell.co.uk
w whitehousebroadwell.co.uk

### BROADWINDSOR
Dorset

**Crosskeys House** ★★★★★
*Bed & Breakfast*
SILVER AWARD
High Street, Broadwindsor,
Beaminster DT8 3QP
t (01308) 868063
e robin.ademey@care4free.net

### BROMHAM
Wiltshire

**Wayside** ★★★★
*Bed & Breakfast*
Chittoe Heath, Bromham,
Chippenham SN15 2EH
t (01380) 850695
e enquiries@waysideofwhiltshire.co.uk
w waysideofwiltshire.co.uk

### BROMPTON REGIS
Somerset

**The George Inn** ★★★ *Inn*
Nr Dulverton TA22 9NL
t (01398) 371273
e thegeorgeexmoor@btconnect.com
w thegeorgeexmoor.co.uk

### BRUTON
Somerset

**Gants Mill & Garden** ★★★★
*Farmhouse*
Gants Mill Lane, Bruton
BA10 0DB
t (01749) 812393
w gantsmill.co.uk

### BRYHER
Isles of Scilly

**Bank Cottage Guest House**
★★★★ *Guest House*
Bryher TR23 0PR
t (01720) 422612
e macmace@patrol.i-way.co.uk

**Soleil D'or** ★★★★
*Bed & Breakfast*
Bryher TR23 0PR
t (01720) 422003

### BUCKERELL
Devon

**Broadlands** ★★★★
*Bed & Breakfast*
Buckerell, Honiton EX14 3EP
t (01404) 850894

### BUCKLAND NEWTON
Dorset

**Holyleas House** ★★★★★
*Guest Accommodation*
Buckland Newton, Dorchester
DT2 7DP
t (01300) 345214
e tiabunkall@holyleas.fsnet.co.uk
w holyleashouse.co.uk

**Rew Cottage** ★★★★
*Bed & Breakfast*
Buckland Newton, Dorchester
DT2 7DN
t (01300) 345467

## BUDE
### Cornwall

**Beach House** ★★★
*Guest Accommodation*
Marine Drive, Widemouth Bay,
Bude EX23 0AW
t (01288) 361256
e beachhousebookings@
tiscali.co.uk
w beachhousewidemouth.co.
uk

**Bentley House** ★★★★
*Guest Accommodation*
Killerton Road, Bude
EX23 8EW
t (01288) 353698
e amanda@
bentleyhousebude.com
w bentleyhousebude.com

**Brendon Arms** ★★★ *Inn*
Vicarage Road, Bude EX23 8SD
t (01288) 354542
e enquiries@brendonarms.co.
uk
w brendonarms.co.uk

**Creathorne Farm Bed &
Breakfast** ★★★★★
*Farmhouse*
The Granary, Creathorne Farm,
Bude EX23 0NE
t (01288) 361077
e alisonnicklen@tiscali.co.uk
w creathornefarm.co.uk
▨▧

**East Woolley Farm** ★★★★
*Guest Accommodation*
SILVER AWARD
Woolley, Bude EX23 9PP
t (01288) 331525
e julia@eastwoolleyfarm.plus.
com
w eastwoolleyfarm.co.uk

**Edgcumbe Hotel** ★★★★
*Guest Accommodation*
Summerleaze Crescent, Bude
EX23 8HJ
t (01288) 353846
e info@edgcumbe-hotel.co.uk
w edgcumbe-hotel.co.uk

**The Elms** ★★★
*Bed & Breakfast*
37 Lynstone Road, Bude
EX23 8LR
t (01288) 353429

**Grosvenor Hotel – Bude**
★★★ *Guest House*
10 Summerleaze Crescent,
Bude EX23 8HH
t (01288) 352062
e mail@grosvenorhotel.plus.
com
w grosvenorhotel-bude.co.uk

**Harefield Cottage** ★★★★
*Guest House* SILVER AWARD
Upton, Bude EX23 0LY
t (01288) 352350
e sales@coast-countryside.co.
uk
w coast-countryside.co.uk

**Highbre Crest** ★★★★
*Guest Accommodation*
SILVER AWARD
Whitstone, Holsworthy
EX22 6UF
t (01288) 341002
e lindacole285@btinternet.
com
w highbrecrest.co.uk

**Hillbrook** ★★★
*Guest Accommodation*
37 Killerton Road, Bude
EX23 8EL
t (01288) 353156
e cathyrushbrook@tiscali.co.
uk

**Kings Hill Meadow** ★★★★★
*Guest Accommodation*
SILVER AWARD
Bagbury Road, Bude EX23 8SR
t (01288) 355004
e kingshillmeadow@
btinternet.com
w kingshillmeadow.co.uk
▨▧

**Langaton Farm** ★★★★
*Farmhouse*
Whitstone, Bude EX22 6TS
t (01288) 341215
e langatonfarm@hotmail.com
w langaton-farm-holidays.co.
uk

**Links Side** ★★★★
*Guest House*
7 Burn View, Bude EX23 8BY
t (01288) 352410
e linksidebude@hotmail.com
w linkssidebude.co.uk

**Little Haven** ★★★★
*Bed & Breakfast*
SILVER AWARD
Silverton Road, Bude EX23 8EY
t (01288) 354719

**Meadow View** ★★★★
*Bed & Breakfast*
6 Kings Hill Close, Bude
EX23 8RR
t (01288) 355095

**The Palms Guest House**
★★★★ *Guest House*
17 Burn View, Bude EX23 8BZ
t (01288) 353962
e palmsguesthouse@tiscali.co.
uk
w palms-bude.co.uk

**Riverview** ★★★
*Bed & Breakfast*
Granville Terrace, Bude
EX23 8JZ
t (01288) 359399
e vennings@beeb.net

**Scadghill Farm** ★★★★
*Guest Accommodation*
SILVER AWARD
Stibb, Bude EX23 9HW
t (01288) 352373
e scadghillfarm@btconnect.
com
w scadghillfarm.co.uk

**Strands** ★★★
*Guest Accommodation*
Stibb, Bude EX23 9HW
t (01288) 353514
e brendadunstanbude@
yahoo.co.uk

**Stratton Gardens** ★★★★
*Guest Accommodation*
Cot Hill, Stratton, Bude
EX23 9DN
t (01288) 352500
e moira@stratton-gardens.co.
uk
w stratton-gardens.co.uk

**Sunrise Guest House**
★★★★ *Guest House*
6 Burn View, Bude EX23 8BY
t (01288) 353214
e sunriseguest@btconnect.
com
w sunrise-bude.co.uk

**Surf Haven** ★★★★
*Guest House*
31 Downs View, Bude
EX23 8RG
t (01288) 353923
e info@surfhaven.co.uk
w surfhaven.co.uk

**Tee-Side** ★★★★
*Guest House*
2 Burn View, Bude EX23 8BY
t (01288) 352351
e info@tee-side.co.uk
w tee-side.co.uk

**Tresillian** ★★★★
*Guest Accommodation*
10 Killerton Road, Bude
EX23 8EL
t (01288) 356199
e linda.shelvin@btinternet.
com
w tresillian-bude.co.uk

**Wyvern Guest House**
★★★★ *Guest House*
7 Downs View, Bude EX23 8RF
t (01288) 352205
e eileen@wyvernhouse.co.uk
w wyvernhouse.co.uk

## BUDLEIGH SALTERTON
### Devon

**Downderry House** ★★★★★
*Guest Accommodation*
SILVER AWARD
10 Exmouth Road, Budleigh
Salterton EX9 6AQ
t (01395) 442663
e info@downderryhouse.co.
uk
w downderryhouse.co.uk

**Hansard House** ★★★★
*Guest Accommodation*
3 Northview Road, Budleigh
Salterton EX9 6BY
t (01395) 442773
e enquiries@hansardhotel.co.
uk
w hansardhousehotel.co.uk

## BUDOCK WATER
### Cornwall

**Home Country House Hotel**
★★★ *Guest Accommodation*
Penjerrick, Falmouth TR11 5EE
t (01326) 250427

## BUGLE
### Cornwall

**The Bugle Inn** ★★★ *Inn*
57 Fore Street, Bugle, St
Austell PL26 8PB
t (01726) 850307
e bugleinn@aol.com
w bugleinn.co.uk

## BULFORD
### Wiltshire

**The Dovecot** ★★★★
*Bed & Breakfast*
SILVER AWARD
Watergate Lane, Salisbury
SP4 9DY
t (01980) 632625
e bandb@thedovecot.com
w thedovecot.com

## BULLO PILL
### Gloucestershire

**Grove Farm** ★★★★
*Farmhouse*
Bullo Pill, Newnham GL14 1DZ
t (01594) 516304
e davidandpennyhill@
btopenworld.com
w grovefarm-uk.com
▨▧

## BURLAWN
### Cornwall

**Burlawn Farm** ★★★★
*Farmhouse*
Higher Pengelly Cross,
Wadebridge PL27 7LA
t (01208) 815548
e burlawnfarm@tiscali.co.uk

**Pengelly Farm** ◆◆◆◆
*Guest Accommodation*
SILVER AWARD
Burlawn, Wadebridge
PL27 7LA
t (01208) 814217
e hodgepete@hotmail.com
w pengellyfarm.co.uk

## BURNHAM-ON-SEA
### Somerset

**Ashbourne House** ★★★★
*Guest House*
17 Berrow Road, Burnham-on-
Sea TA8 2EY
t (01278) 783217
w ashbournehouse.biz

**Cheriton Lodge** ★★★★
*Guest Accommodation*
4 Allandale Road, Burnham-on-
Sea TA8 2HG
t (01278) 781423
e enquires@cheritonlodge.
com
w cheritonlodge.com

**Cloisters** ★★★
*Guest Accommodation*
94 Berrow Road, Burnham-on-
Sea TA8 2HN
t (01278) 789280

**Knights Rest** ★★★
*Bed & Breakfast*
9 Dunstan Road, Burnham-on-
Sea TA8 1ER
t (01278) 782318

**Magnolia House** ★★★★
*Guest House*
26 Manor Road, Burnham-on-
Sea TA8 2AS
t (01278) 792460
e enquiries@magnoliahouse.
gb.com
w magnoliahouse.gb.com

**St Aubyns** ★★★★
*Guest House*
11 Berrow Road, Burnham-on-
Sea TA8 2ET
t (01278) 773769
e markhowes@stevejefferies.
fsnet.co.uk
w staubyns-guesthouse.co.uk

**Sandhills Guest House ★★★**
*Guest House*
3 Poplar Road, Burnham-on-Sea TA8 2HD
t (01278) 781208

**Shalimar Guest House ★★★**
*Guest Accommodation*
174 Berrow Road, Burnham-on-Sea TA8 2JE
t (01278) 785898

**Walton House ★★★★**
*Guest Accommodation*
148 Berrow Road, Burnham-on-Sea TA8 2PN
t (01278) 780034
e waltonhousebnb@aol.com
w waltonhousebnb.co.uk

**The Warren Guest House
★★★★** *Guest House*
29 Berrow Road, Burnham-on-Sea TA8 2EZ
t (01278) 786726
e info@thewarrenguesthouse.co.uk
w thewarrenguesthouse.co.uk

### BURTON BRADSTOCK
Dorset

**Norburton Hall ★★★★★**
*Guest Accommodation*
**GOLD AWARD**
Shipton Lane, Burton Bradstock, Bridport DT6 4NQ
t (01308) 897007
e info@norburtonhall.com
w norburtonhall.com

**Pebble Beach Lodge ★★★★**
*Guest Accommodation*
Coast Road, Burton Bradstock, Bridport DT6 4RJ
t (01308) 897428
e pebblebeachlodge@supanet.com
w burtonbradstock.org.uk/pebblebeachlodge

### BUTCOMBE
Somerset

**Butcombe Farm ★★★★**
*Guest Accommodation*
Aldwick Lane, Bristol BS40 7UW
t (01761) 462380

### CALLINGTON
Cornwall

**Hampton Manor ★★★★**
*Guest House*
Alston, Callington PL17 8LX
t (01579) 370494
e hamptonmanor@supanet.com
w hamptonmanor.co.uk

**Higher Manaton ★★★★**
*Farmhouse*
Callington PL17 8PX
t (01579) 370460
e dtrewin@manaton.fsnet.co.uk
w cornwall-devon-bandb.co.uk

**Lower House Guest House
★★★★** *Guest House*
9 Church Street, Callington PL17 7AN
t (01579) 383491
e info@lower-house.com
w lower-house.com

### CALNE
Wiltshire

**Chilvester Hill House
★★★★★**
*Guest Accommodation*
**SILVER AWARD**
Chilvester Hill, Calne SN11 0LP
t (01249) 813981
e gill.dilley@talk21.com
w chilvesterhillhouse.co.uk

**Queenwood Lodge
★★★★★**
*Guest Accommodation*
**GOLD AWARD**
Bowood Golf & Country Club, Derry Hill, Calne SN11 9PQ
t (01249) 822228
e queenwood@bowood.org
w bowood.org

### CAMELFORD
Cornwall

**Countryman Hotel ★★★**
*Guest Accommodation*
7 Victoria Road, Camelford PL32 9XA
t (01840) 212250
e countrymanhotel@btopenworld.com
w cornwall-online.co.uk/countryman

**Culloden Farmhouse
★★★★** *Bed & Breakfast*
Victoria Road, Camelford PL32 9XA
t (01840) 211128
e debbie_balaam@msn.com
w cullodenfarmhouse.co.uk

**Penlea House ★★★**
*Bed & Breakfast*
Station Road, Camelford PL32 9UR
t (01840) 212194
e jandrews04@supanet.com

### CANNINGTON
Somerset

**Blackmore Farm ★★★**
*Farmhouse*
Blackmore Lane, Nr Bridgwater TA5 2NE
t (01278) 653442
e dyerfarm@aol.com
w dyerfarm.co.uk

**Gurney Manor Mill ★★★★**
*Bed & Breakfast*
**SILVER AWARD**
Gurney Street, Nr Bridgwater TA5 2HW
t (01278) 653582
e gurneymill@yahoo.co.uk
w gurneymill.freeserve.co.uk

### CARBIS BAY
Cornwall

**Beechwood House ★★★★**
*Guest Accommodation*
St Ives Road, Carbis Bay, St Ives TR26 2SX
t (01736) 795170
e beechwood@carbisbay.wanadoo.co.uk

**Chy An Gweal House ◆◆◆**
*Guest Accommodation*
St Ives Road, Carbis Bay, St Ives TR26 2RS
t (01736) 798441
e j.butterworth548@btinternet.com

**Endsleigh Guest House
★★★★**
*Guest Accommodation*
St Ives Road, Carbis Bay, St Ives TR26 2SF
t (01736) 795777
e endsleighguesthouse@tiscali.co.uk
w endsleighguesthouse.co.uk

**Howards Hotel ★★★**
*Guest Accommodation*
St Ives Road, Carbis Bay, St Ives TR26 2SB
t (01736) 795651
e info@howards-hotel.com
w howards-hotel.com

**The Lighthouse B&B
★★★★★** *Bed & Breakfast*
**SILVER AWARD**
Pannier Lane, St Ives TR26 2RF
t (01736) 793830
e info@thelighthousebedandbreakfast.co.uk
w thelighthousebedandbreakfast.co.uk

**Tradewinds ★★★★★**
*Guest Accommodation*
**SILVER AWARD**
Pannier Lane, Carbis Bay, St Ives TR26 2RF
t (01736) 799114
e enquiries@tradewinds.co.uk
w tradewindsstives.co.uk

### CARNON DOWNS
Cornwall

**Chycara ★★★★**
*Bed & Breakfast*
Chyreen Lane, Carnon Downs, Truro TR3 6LG
t (01872) 865447
e info@chycara.co.uk
w chycara.co.uk

**Woodsedge ★★★**
*Bed & Breakfast*
10 Gig Lane, Carnon Downs, Truro TR3 6JS
t (01872) 870269

### CASHMOOR
Dorset

**Cashmoor House ★★★★**
*Farmhouse*
Cashmoor, Blandford Forum DT11 8DN
t (01725) 552339
e spencer.jones@ukonline.co.uk
w cashmoorhouse.cjb.net

### CASTLE CARY
Somerset

**Clanville Manor B&B
★★★★** *Guest House*
**SILVER AWARD**
B3153, Nr Castle Cary BA7 7PJ
t (01963) 350124
e info@clanvillemanor.co.uk
w clanvillemanor.co.uk

**The Coach House ★★★★**
*Farmhouse* **SILVER AWARD**
Main Road, Nr Castle Cary BA7 7PN
t (01963) 240315
e liz@alfordcoachhouse.co.uk
w alfordcoachhouse.co.uk

### CASTLE COMBE
Wiltshire

**Fosse Farmhouse ★★★★**
*Bed & Breakfast*
**SILVER AWARD**
Nettleton Shrub, Chippenham SN14 7NJ
t (01249) 782286
e caroncooper@compuserve.com
w fossefarmhouse.com

**Thorngrove Cottage ★★★★**
*Guest House*
Summer Lane, Castle Combe, Chippenham SN14 7NG
t (01249) 782607
e chrisdalene@sn147ng.fsnet.co.uk

### CATCOTT
Somerset

**West Barton House ★★★★**
*Bed & Breakfast*
52 Manor Road, Nr Bridgwater TA7 9HD
t (01278) 723533
e i.ihpp@btinternet.com

### CERNE ABBAS
Dorset

**Badger Hill ★★★★**
*Bed & Breakfast*
11 Springfield, Cerne Abbas, Dorchester DT2 7JZ
t (01300) 341698

### CHALFORD
Gloucestershire

**The Ragged Cot Inn ★★★**
*Inn*
Stroud GL6 8PE
t (01453) 884643
e raggedcotinn.hyde@pathfinder.co.uk

### CHALLACOMBE
Devon

**Twitchen Farm ★★★★**
*Farmhouse*
Challacombe, Barnstaple EX31 4TT
t (01598) 763568
e holidays@twitchen.co.uk
w twitchen.co.uk

### CHARD
Somerset

**Ammonite Lodge ★★★★**
*Guest Accommodation*
43 High Street, Chard TA20 1QL
t (01460) 63839
e info@ammonitelodge.co.uk
w ammonitelodge.co.uk

**Home Farm ★★★**
*Guest Accommodation*
Hornsbury Hill, Nr Chard TA20 3DB
t (01460) 63731

**Hornsbury Mill**
Rating Applied For
*Guest Accommodation*
Eleighwater, Chard TA20 3AQ
t (01460) 63317
e hornsburymill@btclick.com
w hornsburymill.co.uk

**Lindens House** ★★★
*Bed & Breakfast*
Snowden Cottage Lane, Chard
TA20 1QS
t (01460) 61137
e joan@lindenshouse.fsnet.co.
uk
w lindenshouse.co.uk

**Wambrook Farm** ★★★★
*Farmhouse*
Wambrook, Nr Chard
TA20 3DF
t (01460) 62371
e wambrookfarm@aol.com
w wambrookfarm.co.uk

CHARLTON HORETHORNE
Somerset

**Longbar** ★★★
*Bed & Breakfast*
Level Lane, Nr Sherborne
DT9 4NN
t (01963) 220266
e longbar@tinyworld.co.uk
w longbarfarm.co.uk

CHARLTON KINGS
Gloucestershire

**Detmore House** ★★
*Bed & Breakfast*
London Road, Charlton Kings,
Cheltenham GL52 6UT
t (01242) 582868

CHARMINSTER
Dorset

**Slades Farm** ★★★★
*Bed & Breakfast*
North Street, Charminster,
Dorchester DT2 9QZ
t (01305) 264032
e info@bandbdorset.org.uk
w bandbdorset.org.uk

**Three Compasses Inn** ★★★
*Inn*
The Square, Charminster,
Dorchester DT2 9QT
t (01305) 263618

CHARMOUTH
Dorset

**Broadlands Bed and
Breakfast** ★★★
*Bed & Breakfast*
Lower Sea Lane, Charmouth,
Bridport DT6 6LR
t (01297) 561181
e angela@bandbcharmouth.
co.uk
w bandbcharmouth.co.uk/

**Cardsmill Farm** ★★★
*Farmhouse*
Whitchurch Canonicorum,
Bridport DT6 6RP
t (01297) 489375
e cardsmill@aol.com
w farmhousedorset.com

**Cliffend** ★★★★
*Guest Accommodation*
Higher Sea Lane, Charmouth,
Bridport DT6 6BD
t (01297) 561047
w cliffend.co.uk

CHEDDAR
Somerset

**Applebee South Barns B&B**
★★ *Bed & Breakfast*
The Hayes, Cheddar BS27 3AN
t (01934) 743146

**Arundel House** ★★★
*Guest Accommodation*
Church Street, Cheddar
BS27 3RA
t (01934) 742264

**Bay Rose House** ★★★★
*Bed & Breakfast*
The Bays, Cheddar BS27 3QN
t (01934) 741377
e martin@bayrose.co.uk
w bayrose.co.uk

**Cheddar YHA** ★★★ *Hostel*
Hillfield, Cheddar BS27 3HN
t (01934) 742494

**Chedwell Cottage** ★★★★
*Guest Accommodation*
59 Redcliffe Street, Cheddar
BS27 3PF
t (01934) 743268

**Constantine** ★★★
*Guest Accommodation*
Lower New Road, Cheddar
BS27 3DY
t (01934) 741339

**Cricklake Farm** ★★★
*Farmhouse*
Nyland Drove, Nr Wells
BS28 4HH
t (01934) 712736

**Gordon's** ★★★
*Guest Accommodation*
Cliff Street, Cheddar BS27 3PT
t (01934) 742497

**Neuholme** ★★★★
*Guest Accommodation*
The Barrows, Cheddar
BS27 3BG
t (01934) 742841

**Wassells House** ★★★★
*Bed & Breakfast*
Upper New Road, Cheddar
BS27 3DW
t (01934) 744317
w wassellshouse.co.uk

**Waterside** ★★
*Bed & Breakfast*
Cheddar Road, Axbridge
BS26 2DP
t (01934) 743182
e gillianaldridge@hotmail.com
w watersidecheddar.co.uk

**Yew Tree Farm** ★★
*Bed & Breakfast*
Theale, Wedmore BS28 4SN
t (01934) 712475
e enquiries@
yewtreefarmbandb.co.uk
w yewtreefarmbandb.co.uk

CHEDZOY
Somerset

**Apple View** ★★★★
*Farmhouse* SILVER AWARD
Chedzoy Lane, Nr Bridgwater
TA7 8QR
t (01278) 423201
e temple_farm@hotmail.com
w apple-view.com

CHELSTON
Devon

**Elmdene Hotel** ★★★★
*Guest Accommodation*
Rathmore Road, Torquay
TQ2 6NZ
t (01803) 294940
e enquiries@elmdenehotel.co.
uk
w elmdenehotel.co.uk

**Millbrook House Hotel**
★★★★
*Guest Accommodation*
Old Mill Road, Torquay
TQ2 6AP
t (01803) 297394
e millbrookhotel@virgin.net
w millbrook-house-hotel.co.uk

CHELTENHAM
Gloucestershire

**The Abbey** ★★★★
*Guest Accommodation*
Bath Parade, Cheltenham
GL53 7HN
t (01242) 516053
e office@abbeyhotel-
cheltenham.com
w abbeyhotel-cheltenham.com

**Beaumont House** ★★★★★
*Guest Accommodation*
SILVER AWARD
56 Shurdington Road,
Cheltenham GL53 0JE
t (01242) 223311
e reservations@bhhotel.co.uk
w bhhotel.co.uk

**Bentons** ★★★
*Guest Accommodation*
71 Bath Road, Cheltenham
GL53 7LH
t (01242) 517417

**Brennan Guest House** ★★★
*Guest Accommodation*
21 St Lukes Road, Cheltenham
GL53 7JF
t (01242) 525904
e colintaylor@blueyonder.co.
uk

**Bridge House** ★★★★
*Guest Accommodation*
88 Lansdown Road,
Cheltenham GL51 6QR
t (01242) 583559
e bridgehouse@freeuk.com

**Burlington House**
Rating Applied For
*Bed & Breakfast*
418 Gloucester Road,
Cheltenham GL51 7TB
t (01242) 526665
e info@burlingtonhouse.net
w burlingtonhouse.net

**Butlers** ★★★★
*Guest Accommodation*
SILVER AWARD
Western Road, Cheltenham
GL50 3RN
t (01242) 570771
e info@butlers-hotel.co.uk
w butlers-hotel.co.uk

**Cheltenham Guest House**
★★★ *Guest Accommodation*
145 Hewlett Road, Cheltenham
GL52 6TS
t (01242) 521726
e info@
cheltenhamguesthouse.biz
w cheltenhamguesthouse.biz

**Cheltenham Lawn & Pitville
Gallery** ★★★★
*Guest Accommodation*
Pittville Lawn, Cheltenham
GL52 2BE
t (01242) 526638
e anthea.miller@
cheltenhamlawn.com
w cheltenhamlawn.com

**The Cheltenham Townhouse**
★★★★
*Guest Accommodation*
12-14 Pittville Lawn,
Cheltenham GL52 2BD
t (01242) 221922
e info@
cheltenhamtownhouse.co.uk
w cheltenhamtownhouse.co.
uk

**Colesbourne Inn**
Rating Applied For
*Inn*
Colesbourne, Cheltenham
GL53 9NP
t (01242) 870376
e info@thecolesbourneinn.co.
uk
w thecolesbourneinn.co.uk

**Crossways Guest House**
★★★★
*Guest Accommodation*
Bath Road, Cheltenham
GL53 7LH
t (01242) 527683
e cross.ways@btinternet.com
w crosswaysguesthouse.com

**Gambles Farm B&B** ◆◆◆◆◆
*Guest Accommodation*
Gambles Farm, Gambles Lane'',
Woodmancote, Cheltenham
GL52 9PU
t (01242) 677719
e ndeackes@blueyonder.co.
uk

**Garden House** ★★★★
*Guest Accommodation*
24 Christ Church Road,
Cheltenham GL50 2PL
t (01242) 522525
e miggilorraine@hotmail.com

**Hannaford's** ★★★★
*Guest Accommodation*
20 Evesham Road, Cheltenham
GL52 2AB
t (01242) 524190
e sue@hannafords.icom43.net
w hannafords.icom43.net

**Hanover House**
Rating Applied For
*Guest Accommodation*
65 St Georges Road,
Cheltenham GL50 3DU
t (01242) 541297
e info@hanoverhouse.org
w hanoverhouse.org

**Home Farm** ◆◆◆◆
*Guest Accommodation*
Stockwell Lane, Woodmancote,
Cheltenham GL52 9QE
t (01242) 675816
e info@homefarmbb.co.uk
w homefarmbb.co.uk

**Leeswood** ★★
*Guest Accommodation*
14 Montpellier Drive,
Cheltenham GL50 1TX
t (01242) 524813
e leeswood@hotmail.com
w leeswood.org.uk

**33 Montpellier** ★★★
*Guest House*
33 Montpellier Terrace,
Cheltenham GL50 1UX
t (01242) 526009
e montpellierhotel@
btopenworld.com
w montpellier-hotel.co.uk

**Moorend Park Hotel** ★★★★
*Guest Accommodation*
Moorend Park Road,
Cheltenham GL53 0LA
t (01242) 224441
e moorendpark@freeuk.com
w moorendpark.freeuk.com

**Oak Tree House** ★★★
*Bed & Breakfast*
26 Swindon Lane, Cheltenham
GL50 4NY
t (01242) 248831
e oaktreehouse1@activemail.
co.uk
w cotswolds.info/webpage/
oaktreehouse-cheltenham.htm

**The Old Station** ★★★★
*Bed & Breakfast*
Westfield, Notgrove,
Cheltenham GL54 3BU
t (01451) 850305

**Thirty Two** ★★★★★
*Bed & Breakfast*
GOLD AWARD
Imperial Square, Cheltenham
GL50 1QZ
t (01242) 771110
e stay@thirtytwoltd.com
w thirtytwoltd.com

**Westcourt** ★★★★
*Guest Accommodation*
14 Old Bath Road, Cheltenham
GL53 7QD
t (01242) 241777
e michael-seston@btconnect.
com

**Whittington Lodge Farm**
★★★★ *Farmhouse*
SILVER AWARD
Whittington, Cheltenham
GL54 4HB
t (01242) 820603
e cathy@whittlodgefarm.fslife.
co.uk
w whittlodgefarm.fslife.co.uk

**Wishmoor House** ★★★★
*Guest Accommodation*
147 Hales Road, Cheltenham
GL52 6TD
t (01242) 238504
e wishmoor@hotmail.co.uk
w wishmoor.co.uk

**The Wynyards** ★★★★
*Bed & Breakfast*
Butts Lane, Woodmancote,
Cheltenham GL52 9QH
t (01242) 673876
e smoothhound.co.uk/hotels/
wynyards

### CHELYNCH
### Somerset

**The Old Stables** ★★★★
*Bed & Breakfast*
Chelynch Road, Nr Shepton
Mallet BA4 4PY
t (01749) 880098
e maureen.keevil@amserve.
net
w the-oldstables.co.uk

### CHENSON
### Devon

**Chenson Farm** *Camping Barn*
Chenson, Chulmleigh EX18 7LF
t (01363) 83236

### CHERITON FITZPAINE
### Devon

**The Devon Wine School**
★★★★★ *Bed & Breakfast*
SILVER AWARD
Redyeates Farm, Crediton
EX17 4HG
t (01363) 866742
e alastair@devonwineschool.
co.uk
w devonwineschool.co.uk

### CHEW MAGNA
### Somerset

**Valley Farm** ★★★★
*Bed & Breakfast*
Sandy Lane, Stanton Drew,
Bristol BS39 4EL
t (01275) 332723
e valleyfarm2000@tiscali.co.uk
w smoothhound.co.uk

**Woodbarn Farm** ★★★★
*Farmhouse*
Denny Lane, Chew Magna,
Bristol BS40 8SZ
t (01275) 332599
e woodbarnfarm@hotmail.
com
w smoothhound.co.uk/hotels/
woodbarn.html

### CHEW STOKE
### Somerset

**Orchard House** ★★★
*Guest Accommodation*
Bristol Road, Chew Stoke,
Bristol BS40 8UB
t (01275) 333143
e orchardhse@ukgateway.net
w orchardhouse-chewstoke.
co.uk

### CHEWTON MENDIP
### Somerset

**Copper Beeches** ★★★★
*Guest Accommodation*
Lower Street, Chewton Mendip
BA3 4GP
t (01761) 241496
e copperbeechesbandb@
tiscali.co.uk
w copperbeechesbandb.co.uk

### CHICKERELL
### Dorset

**Stonebank** ★★★★★
*Bed & Breakfast*
GOLD AWARD
14 West Street, Chickerell,
Weymouth DT3 4DY
t (01305) 760120
e stonebanksc@btinternet.
com
w stonebank-chickerell.co.uk

### CHIDEOCK
### Dorset

**Bay Tree House** ★★★★
*Bed & Breakfast*
SILVER AWARD
Duck Street, Chideock,
Bridport DT6 6JW
t (01297) 489336
e jane@baytreechideock.co.uk
w baytreechideock.co.uk

### CHILD OKEFORD
### Dorset

**Manor Barn Bed & Breakfast**
★★★★★ *Bed & Breakfast*
SILVER AWARD
Upper Street, Child Okeford,
Blandford Forum DT11 8EF
t (01258) 860638
e carisorby@btinternet.com
w manorbarnbedandbreakfast.
co.uk

### CHILTON CANTELO
### Somerset

**Higher Farm** ★★★★
*Bed & Breakfast*
C Cantelo, Nr Yeovil BA22 8BE
t (01935) 850213
e susankerton@tinyonline.co.
uk

### CHIPPENHAM
### Wiltshire

**Church Farm** ★★★★
*Farmhouse*
Hartham, Corsham SN13 0PU
t (01249) 715180
e churchfarmbandb@hotmail.
com
w churchfarm.cjb.net

**Glebe House** ★★★★
*Bed & Breakfast*
Chittoe, Chippenham
SN15 2EL
t (01380) 850864
e info@glebehouse-chittoe.co.
uk
w glebehouse-chittoe.co.uk

**New Road Guest House**
★★★ *Guest House*
31 New Road, Chippenham
SN15 1HP
t (01249) 657259
e mail@newroadguesthouse.
co.uk
w newroadguesthouse.co.uk

**Teresa Lodge (Glen Avon)**
★★★ *Bed & Breakfast*
43 Bristol Road, Chippenham
SN15 1NT
t (01249) 653350

### CHIPPING CAMPDEN
### Gloucestershire

**Bran Mill Cottage** ★★★
*Bed & Breakfast*
Aston Magna, Moreton-in-
Marsh GL56 9QW
t (01386) 593517
e enquiries@branmillcottage.
co.uk
w branmillcottage.co.uk

**Brymbo B&B** ★★★★
*Guest Accommodation*
Honeybourne Lane, Mickleton,
Chipping Campden GL55 6PU
t (01386) 438890
e enquiries@brymbo.com
w brymbo.com

**Dragon House** ★★★★
*Bed & Breakfast*
High Street, Chipping
Campden GL55 6AG
t (01386) 840734
e info@dragonhouse-
chipping-campden.co.uk
w dragonhouse-chipping-
campden.com

**The Eight Bells** ★★★★ *Inn*
Church Street, Chipping
Campden GL55 6JG
t (01386) 840371
e neilhargreaves@bellinn.
fsnet.co.uk
w eightbellsinn.co.uk

**Gainsborough Cottage**
★★★ *Bed & Breakfast*
Pear Tree Close, Chipping
Campden GL55 6DB
t (01386) 849148
e janeayton@btinternet.com
w gainsboroughcottage.co.uk

**Home Farm House** ★★★★
*Farmhouse* SILVER AWARD
Ebrington, Chipping Campden
GL55 6NL
t (01386) 593309
e willstanley@farmersweekly.
net
w homefarminthecotswolds.
co.uk

**The Malins** ★★★★
*Bed & Breakfast*
21 Station Road, Blockley,
Moreton-in-Marsh GL56 9ED
t (01386) 700402
e johnmalin@btinternet.com
w chippingcampden.co.uk/
themalins.htm

**Manor Farm** ★★★★
*Bed & Breakfast*
Weston-Subedge, Chipping
Campden GL55 6QH
t (01386) 840390
e lucy@manorfarmbnb.
demon.co.uk
w manorfarmbnb.demon.co.uk

**Nineveh Farm** ◆◆◆◆◆
*Guest Accommodation*
GOLD AWARD
Mickleton, Chipping Campden
GL55 6PS
t (01386) 438923
e stay@ninevehfarm.co.uk
w ninevehfarm.co.uk

**Sandalwood House** ◆◆◆◆
*Guest Accommodation*
SILVER AWARD
Back Ends, Chipping Campden
GL55 6AU
t (01386) 840091
e sandalwoodhouse@hotmail.
com

**Taplins** ★★★★
*Bed & Breakfast*
5 Aston Road, Chipping
Campden GL55 6HR
t (01386) 840927
e info@cotswoldstay.co.uk

**Weston Park Farm** ★★★
*Bed & Breakfast*
Dovers Hill, Chipping
Campden GL55 6UW
t (01386) 840835
e jane_whitehouse@hotmail.
com
w cotswoldcottages.uk.com

### CHISELDON
### Wiltshire

**Norton House** ★★★★
*Bed & Breakfast*
SILVER AWARD
46 Draycott Road, Chiseldon,
Swindon SN4 0LS
t (01793) 741210
e sharian@clara.co.uk
w nortonhouse.uk.com

## CHITTLEHAMPTON
### Devon

**Higher Biddacott Farm**
★★★ *Farmhouse*
Chittlehampton, Umberleigh
EX37 9PY
t (01769) 540222
e waterers@sosi.net
w heavyhorses.net

## CHOLDERTON
### Wiltshire

**Parkhouse Motel ★★★★**
*Guest Accommodation*
Cholderton, Salisbury SP4 0EG
t (01980) 629256

## CHRISTCHURCH
### Dorset

**Belvedere Guest House**
Rating Applied For
*Guest Accommodation*
3 Twynham Avenue,
Christchurch BH23 1QU
t (01202) 485978
e belvederety@clara.co.uk

**Druid House ★★★★★**
*Guest Accommodation*
26 Sopers Lane, Christchurch
BH23 1JE
t (01202) 485615
e reservations@druid-house.
co.uk
w druid-house.co.uk

**Fisherman's Haunt ★★★** *Inn*
Salisbury Road, Winkton,
Christchurch BH23 7AS
t (01202) 477283
e fishermanshaunt@
accommodating-inns.co.uk
w accommodating-inns.co.uk

**Four Seasons B&B ★★★★**
*Bed & Breakfast*
2 Nea Road, Christchurch
BH23 4NA
t (01425) 273408
e melbar1940@aol.com
w 4seasonshighcliffe.co.uk

**Golfers Reach ★★★**
*Bed & Breakfast*
88 Lymington Road, Highcliffe,
Christchurch BH23 4JU
t (01425) 272903
e caoy@amserve.com

**Laburnum Lodge ★★★★**
*Bed & Breakfast*
33 Albion Road, Christchurch
BH23 2JQ
t (01202) 471664
e mail@laburnumlodge.info
w laburnumlodge.info

**Marshwalk ★★★**
*Bed & Breakfast*
28 Asquith Close, Christchurch
BH23 3DX
t 07818 080014
e enq@marshwalk.co.uk
w marshwalkaccommodation.
co.uk

**Salmons Reach Guest House**
★★★ *Guest Accommodation*
28 Stanpit, Christchurch
BH23 3LZ
t (01202) 477315
e info@salmonsreach.com
w salmonsreach.com

**Seawards ★★★★★**
*Bed & Breakfast*
**GOLD AWARD**
13 Avon Run Close,
Christchurch BH23 4DT
t (01425) 273188
e seawards13@hotmail.com
w seawards13.plus.com

**Stour Lodge Guest House**
★★★★ *Guest House*
54 Stour Road, Christchurch
BH23 1LW
t (01202) 486902
e enquiries@stourlodge.co.uk
w stourlodge.co.uk

## CHRISTIAN MALFORD
### Wiltshire

**Beanhill Farm ★★★★**
*Farmhouse*
Main Road, Christian Malford,
Chippenham SN15 4BS
t (01249) 720672
e bb@beanhillfarm.fsbusiness.
co.uk
w beanhillfarmwiltshire.co.uk

## CHUDLEIGH
### Devon

**Higher Rixdale Farm ★★★★**
*Farmhouse*
Newton Abbot TQ13 0BW
t (01626) 867980
e info@higher-rixdale-farm.
com
w higher-rixdale-farm.com

## CIRENCESTER
### Gloucestershire

**Abbeymead Guest House**
★★★★ *Guest House*
Victoria Road, Cirencester
GL7 1ES
t (01285) 653740
e land0603@aol.com
w abbeymeadguesthouse.com

**Apsley Villa ★★★**
*Guest House*
Victoria Road, Cirencester
GL7 1ES
t (01285) 653489

**Brooklands Farm ★★**
*Farmhouse*
Ewen, Cirencester GL7 6BU
t (01285) 770487 &
07790 948931
w glosfarmhols.co.uk

**The Bungalow ★★★★**
*Guest Accommodation*
**SILVER AWARD**
93 Victoria Road, Cirencester
GL7 1ES
t (01285) 654179
e bob_joan.lamb@virgin.net
w bandbcirencester.co.uk

**Columbrae ★★★★**
*Bed & Breakfast*
School Hill, Stratton,
Cirencester GL7 2LS
t (01285) 653114
e margaret@columbraebandb.
co.uk
w columbraebandb.co.uk

**Dixs Barn ★★★★**
*Bed & Breakfast*
Duntisbourne Abbotts,
Cirencester GL7 7JN
t (01285) 821249
e wilcox@dixsbarn.freeserve.
co.uk

**The Ivy House ★★★★**
*Guest House*
2 Victoria Road, Cirencester
GL7 1EN
t (01285) 656626
e info@ivyhousecotswolds.
com
w ivyhousecotswolds.com

**The Leauses ★★★★**
*Guest Accommodation*
101 Victoria Road, Cirencester
GL7 1EU
t (01285) 653643
e info@theleauses.co.uk
w theleauses.co.uk

**Manor Farm ★★★**
*Farmhouse*
Middle Duntisbourne,
Cirencester GL7 7AR
t (01285) 658145
e enquiries@duntisbourne.
com
w duntisbourne.com

**The Oldbrew House ★★★★**
*Guest Accommodation*
7 London Road, Cirencester
GL7 2PU
t (01285) 656099
e info@theoldbrewhouse.com
w theoldbrewhouse.com

**Raydon House Hotel ★★★**
*Guest House*
The Avenue, Cirencester
GL7 1EH
t (01285) 653485

**Riverside House ★★★★**
*Guest Accommodation*
Watermoor Road, Cirencester
GL7 1LF
t (01285) 647642
e riversidehouse@mitsubishi-
cars.co.uk
w riversidehouse.org.uk

**The Royal Agricultural
College ★★★** *Campus*
Stroud Road, Cirencester
GL7 6JS
t (01285) 652531
e commercial.services@rac.ac.
uk
w rac.ac.uk

**Le Spa ★★★★**
*Guest Accommodation*
Gloucester Road, Cirencester
GL7 2LA
t (01285) 653840
e mail@lespa.com
w lespa.com

**The Talbot Inn ★★★★** *Inn*
14 Victoria Road, Cirencester
GL7 1EN
t (01285) 653760
e info@talbotinncotswolds.co.
uk
w talbotinncotswolds.co.uk

**The White Lion Inn ★★★**
*Inn*
8 Gloucester Street,
Cirencester GL7 2DG
t (01285) 654053
e mutlow@ashtonkeynes.
fsnet.co.uk
w whitelioncirencester.co.uk

## CLAPHAM
### Devon

**Hyperion Stud ★★★★**
*Farmhouse*
Clapham Stud, Clapham,
Exeter EX6 7YQ
t (01392) 833794
e hyperwell@aol.com
w hyperion-stud.co.uk

**Yeo's Farm ★★★★**
*Farmhouse*
Dunchideock, Exeter EX2 9UJ
t (01392) 883927
e killinger.legg@tiscali.co.uk
w yeos-farm-exeter.co.uk

## CLAVERTON DOWN
### Somerset

**University of Bath**
★★–★★★ *Campus*
The Avenue, Claverton Down
BA2 7AY
t (01225) 383926
e beds@bath.ac.uk
w bath.ac.uk/salesandevents

## CLOVELLY
### Devon

**Fuchsia Cottage ★★★★**
*Bed & Breakfast*
Higher Clovelly, Clovelly,
Bideford EX39 5RR
t (01237) 431398
e tom@clovelly-holidays.co.uk
w clovelly-holidays.co.uk

**Pillowery Park ★★★★**
*Bed & Breakfast*
Burscott, Higher Clovelly,
Bideford EX39 5RR
t (01237) 431668
e info@
clovellyaccommodation.com
w clovellyaccommodation.com

## CLYFFE PYPARD
### Wiltshire

**The Goddard Arms**
*Bunkhouse*
Clyffe Pypard SN4 7PY
t (01793) 731386
e clyffepypard@yha.org.uk

## COALEY
### Gloucestershire

**Water End Farm B&B**
Rating Applied For
*Farmhouse*
Waterend Farm, Coaley
GL11 5DR
t (01453) 899141
e enquiries@waterendfarm.co.
uk
w waterendfarm.co.uk

## CODFORD ST MARY
### Wiltshire

**Glebe Cottage ★★★★**
*Bed & Breakfast*
Church Lane, Codford,
Warminster BA12 0PJ
t (01985) 850565
e bob.ra@woolrych.net

## COLEFORD
### Gloucestershire

**Braceland Adventure Centre**
*Bunkhouse*
Braceland, Coleford GL16 7NP
t (01594) 833820
e allison839@btinternet.com

**Forest House ★★★★**
*Guest Accommodation*
Cinderhill, Coleford GL16 8HQ
t  (01594) 832424
e  suesparkes@turnphouse.
fsnet.co.uk
w  forest-house-hotel.co.uk

**Symonds Yat Rock Lodge**
**★★★★**
*Guest Accommodation*
Hillersland, Coleford GL16 7NY
t  (01594) 836191
e  david@rocklodge.co.uk
w  rocklodge.co.uk

### COLLINGBOURNE KINGSTON
Wiltshire

**Manor Farm B&B ★★★★**
*Farmhouse*
Collingbourne Kingston,
Marlborough SN8 3SD
t  (01264) 850859
e  stay@manorfm.com
w  manorfm.com

### COLN ST ALDWYNS
Gloucestershire

**Deer Park Cottage ★★★★**
*Bed & Breakfast*
Hatherop Road, Coln St
Aldwyns, Cirencester GL7 5AR
t  (01285) 750692

### COLYFORD
Devon

**Swan Hill House ★★★★**
*Guest Accommodation*
Colyford, Colyton EX24 6QQ
t  (01297) 553387
e  hello@swanhillhouse.com
w  swanhillhouse.com

### COLYTON
Devon

**The Old Bakehouse ★★★★**
*Bed & Breakfast*
Lower Church Street, Colyton
EX24 6ND
t  (01297) 552518
e  france.bakehouse@hotmail.
co.uk
w  theoldbakehousebandb.co.
uk

**Smallicombe Farm ★★★★**
*Guest Accommodation*
**SILVER AWARD**
Northleigh, Colyton EX24 6BU
t  (01404) 831310
e  maggie_todd@yahoo.com
w  smallicombe.com

### COMBE DOWN
Somerset

**Beech Wood ★★★★**
*Bed & Breakfast*
Shaft Road, Combe Down
BA2 7HP
t  (01225) 832242
e  relax@beechwoodbath.co.
uk
w  beechwoodbath.co.uk

**Grey Lodge ★★★★**
*Bed & Breakfast*
**SILVER AWARD**
Summer Lane, Combe Down,
Bath BA2 7EU
t  (01225) 832069
e  greylodge@freenet.co.uk
w  greylodge.co.uk

### COMBE MARTIN
Devon

**Acorns Guest House ★★★★**
*Guest Accommodation*
2 Woodlands, Combe Martin
EX34 0AT
t  (01271) 882769
e  info@acorns-guesthouse.co.
uk
w  acorns-guesthouse.co.uk

**Blair Lodge Guest House**
**★★★★** *Guest House*
Moory Meadow, Seaview,
Combe Martin EX34 0DG
t  (01271) 882294
e  info@blairlodge.co.uk
w  blairlodge.co.uk

**Mellstock House ★★★★**
*Guest Accommodation*
Woodlands, Combe Martin
EX34 0AR
t  (01271) 882592
e  enquiries@mellstockhouse.
co.uk
w  mellstockhouse.co.uk

**Saffron House ★★★**
*Guest Accommodation*
King Street, Combe Martin,
Ilfracombe EX34 0BX
t  (01271) 883521
e  stay@saffronhousehotel.co.
uk
w  saffronhousehotel.co.uk

### COMPTON DUNDON
Somerset

**Rickham House ★★★★**
*Farmhouse*
Main Road, Nr Street
TA11 6QA
t  (01458) 445056
e  rickham.house@btconnect.
com
w  rickhamhouse.co.uk

### CONNOR DOWNS
Cornwall

**Nanterrow Farm ★★★**
*Farmhouse*
Gwithian, Hayle TR27 5BP
t  (01209) 712282
e  nanterrow@hotmail.com
w  nanterrowfarm.co.uk

### CONSTANTINE
Cornwall

**The Old Chapel ★★★★**
*Bed & Breakfast*
Seworgan, Constantine,
Falmouth TR11 5QN
t  (01326) 341418
e  theoldchapelcornwall.co.uk

### COOMBE BISSETT
Wiltshire

**Evening Hill ★★**
*Bed & Breakfast*
Blandford Road, Coombe
Bissett, Salisbury SP5 4LH
t  (01722) 718561
e  henrys@eveninghill.com
w  eveninghill.com

### COOMBE KEYNES
Dorset

**Highfield ★★★**
*Guest Accommodation*
Coombe Keynes, Lulworth
Cove BH20 5PS
t  (01929) 463208
e  jmitchell@coombekeynes.
freeserve.co.uk
w  highfield-bb.co.uk

### COPPLESTONE
Devon

**Harebell ★★★★**
*Guest Accommodation*
Copplestone, Crediton
EX17 5LA
t  (01363) 84771
e  kenjwarren@aol.com
w  harebellbandb.co.uk

### CORFE CASTLE
Dorset

**Bradle Farmhouse ★★★★**
*Farmhouse* **GOLD AWARD**
Bradle Farm, Church Knowle,
Wareham BH20 5NU
t  (01929) 480712
e  info@bradlefarmhouse.co.uk
w  bradlefarmhouse.co.uk

**Kingston Country Courtyard**
**Farmhouse ★★★★**
*Guest Accommodation*
Langton Road, Kingston,
Wareham BH20 5LR
t  (01929) 481066
e  annfry@
kingstoncountrycourtyard.com
w  kingstoncountrycourtyard.
com

**Norden House ★★★**
*Guest House*
Corfe Castle, Wareham
BH20 5DS
t  (01929) 480177
e  nordenhouse@fsmail.net
w  nordenhouse.com

**Rollington Farmhouse**
**★★★★** *Farmhouse*
**SILVER AWARD**
Studland Road, Wareham
BH20 5JG
t  (01929) 481423
e  sarah@rollington.co.uk
w  rollington.co.uk

**Westaway ★★★★**
*Bed & Breakfast*
88 West Street, Corfe Castle,
Wareham BH20 5HE
t  (01929) 480188
e  ray_hendes@btinternet.com
w  westaway-corfecastle.co.uk

### CORFE MULLEN
Dorset

**Bless this Nest ★★**
*Bed & Breakfast*
21 Moorside Road, Corfe
Mullen, Wimborne BH21 3NB
t  (01202) 602534
e  janet@blessthisnest.co.uk
w  blessthisnest.co.uk

**Elms Lodge ★★★★**
*Bed & Breakfast*
**GOLD AWARD**
7 Cogdean Way, Corfe Mullen,
Wimborne BH21 3XD
t  (01202) 699669
e  elmslodge@hotmail.com
w  elmslodge.co.uk

### CORSHAM
Wiltshire

**Ashley Wood Farm ★★★★**
*Farmhouse* **SILVER AWARD**
Lower Kingsdown Road,
Kingsdown, Corsham
SN13 8BG
t  (01225) 742288
e  ashleywoodfarm@hotmail.
com
w  ashleywoodfarm.co.uk

**Boyds Farm ★★★★★**
*Farmhouse*
Chapel Knapp, Gastard,
Corsham SN13 9PT
t  (01249) 713146
e  dorothyboydsfarm@aol.com
w  smoothhound.co.uk/hotels/
boydsfarm.html

**Heatherly Cottage ★★★★**
*Bed & Breakfast*
**GOLD AWARD**
Ladbrook Lane, Gastard,
Corsham SN13 9PE
t  (01249) 701402
e  pandj@heatherly.plus.com
w  heatherlycottage.co.uk

**Pickwick Lodge Farm**
**★★★★** *Farmhouse*
**SILVER AWARD**
Guyers Lane, Pickwick,
Corsham SN13 0PS
t  (01249) 712207
e  b&b@pickwickfarm.co.uk
w  pickwickfarm.co.uk

**Saltbox Farm ★★★★**
*Farmhouse*
Box, Corsham SN13 8PT
t  (01225) 742608
e  bbsaltboxfarm@yahoo.co.uk
w  saltboxfarm.verypretty.co.uk

### CORTON DENHAM
Somerset

**The Queens Arms**
Rating Applied For
*Guest Accommodation*
Sherborne DT9 4LR
t  (01963) 220317
e  relax@thequeensarms.com
w  thequeensarms.com

### COSSINGTON
Somerset

**Brookhayes Farm ★★★★**
*Farmhouse*
Bell Lane, Nr Bridgwater
TA7 8LR
t  (01278) 722559
e  brookhayesfm@tiscali.co.uk
w  brookhayes-farm.co.uk

### COVERACK
Cornwall

**Coverack Youth Hostel –**
**AJ061 ★★★** *Hostel*
Parc Behan, School Hill,
Helston TR12 6SA
t  (01326) 280687
e  coverack@yha.org.uk

### CRANBORNE
Dorset

**Chaseborough Farm ★★★**
*Bed & Breakfast*
Gotham, Cranborne,
Wimborne BH21 5QY
t  (01202) 813166
e  jim.ghinn@tiscali.co.uk
w  chaseboroughfarm.co.uk

## CRANTOCK
### Cornwall

**Tregenna House** ★★★★
*Guest House*
West Pentire Road, Crantock,
Newquay TR8 5RZ
t (01637) 830222
e info@tregennahouse.co.uk
w tregennahouse.co.uk

## CREWKERNE
### Somerset

**The George & Courtyard Restaurant** ★★★
*Guest Accommodation*
Market Square, Crewkerne
TA18 7LP
t (01460) 73650
e georgecrewkerne@
btconnect.com
w thegeorgehotelcrewkerne.
co.uk

**Honeydown Farm** ★★★★
*Farmhouse*
Seaborough Hill, Crewkerne
TA18 8PL
t (01460) 72665
e c.bacon@honeydown.co.uk
w honeydown.co.uk

**The Manor Arms** ★★★ *Inn*
Middle Street, North Perrott,
Crewkerne TA18 7SG
t (01460) 72901
e bookings@manorarmshotel.
co.uk
w manorarmshotel.co.uk

## CRICKLADE
### Wiltshire

**Waterhay Farm** ★★★★
*Farmhouse*
Waterhay, Leigh, Swindon
SN6 6QY
t (01285) 861253

## CROWCOMBE
### Somerset

**Home Leigh House** ★★★★
*Bed & Breakfast*
Crowcombe, Taunton TA4 4BL
t (01984) 618439
w quantockonline.co.uk/
adverts/homeleigh/
homeleigh_hughesea.html

## CROYDE
### Devon

**Baggy Lodge**
Rating Applied For
*Guest House*
Braunton EX33 1PA
t (01271) 890078
e swell@baggys.co.uk
w baggys.co.uk

**Combas Farm** ★★★★
*Farmhouse*
Croyde, Braunton EX33 1PH
t (01271) 890398
w combasfarm.co.uk

**Denham House & Cottages**
★★★★ *Guest House*
North Buckland, Braunton
EX33 1HY
t (01271) 890297
e info@denhamhouse.co.uk
w denhamhouse.co.uk

**Moorsands** ★★★
*Guest Accommodation*
34 Moor Lane, Croyde Bay,
Braunton EX33 1NP
t (01271) 890781
e paul@moorsands.co.uk
w croyde-bay.com/moorsands.
htm

## CULLOMPTON
### Devon

**Langford Court North**
★★★★ *Farmhouse*
Langford, Cullompton
EX15 1SQ
t (01884) 277234
e tchattey@yahoo.co.uk

**Newcourt Barton** ★★★★
*Farmhouse* SILVER AWARD
Langford, Cullompton
EX15 1SE
t (01884) 277326
e newcourtbarton@btinternet.
com
w newcourtbarton-devon.co.
uk

## CURRY RIVEL
### Somerset

**Orchard Cottage** ★★★★★
*Bed & Breakfast*
Townsend, Curry Rivel
TA10 0HT
t (01458) 251511

## CURY
### Cornwall

**Nanplough Farm** ◆◆◆
*Guest Accommodation*
Cury Cross Lanes, Helston
TR12 7BQ
t (01326) 241088

## DAGLINGWORTH
### Gloucestershire

**Windrush Cottage** ★★★
*Bed & Breakfast*
Itlay, Daglingworth,
Cirencester GL7 7HZ
t (01285) 652917
e louisewigfield@hotmail.co.
uk

## DALWOOD
### Devon

**Burrow Way** ★★★★
*Farmhouse*
Dalwood, Axminster EX13 7ES
t (01404) 831802
e burrow.way@tiscali.co.uk

## DARTMOUTH
### Devon

**Browns** ★★★★★
*Guest Accommodation*
27-29 Victoria Road,
Dartmouth TQ6 9RT
t (01803) 832572
e enquiries@
brownshoteldartmouth.co.uk
w brownshoteldartmouth.co.
uk

**Cladda** ★★★★
*Guest Accommodation*
88-90 Victoria Road,
Dartmouth TQ6 9EF
t (01803) 835957
w cladda-guesthouse.co.uk

**Hill View House** ★★★★
*Guest Accommodation*
GOLD AWARD
76 Victoria Road, Dartmouth
TQ6 9DZ
t (01803) 839372
e enquiries@
hillviewdartmouth.co.uk
w hillviewdartmouth.co.uk

**Lower Collaton Farm**
★★★★ *Bed & Breakfast*
Blackawton, Dartmouth
TQ9 7DW
t (01803) 712260
e mussen@lower-collaton-
farm.co.uk
w lower-collaton-farm.co.uk

**Skerries Bed & Breakfast**
★★★★
*Guest Accommodation*
SILVER AWARD
Strete, Dartmouth TQ6 0RH
t (01803) 770775
e jam.skerries@rya-online.net
w skerriesbandb.co.uk

**Strete Barton House** ★★★★
*Guest House* SILVER AWARD
Totnes Road, Strete,
Dartmouth TQ6 0RN
t (01803) 770364
e info@stretebarton.co.uk
w stretebarton.co.uk
♿ ☕

**Valley House** ★★★★
*Bed & Breakfast*
46 Victoria Road, Dartmouth
TQ6 9DZ
t (01803) 834045
e enquiries@
valleyhousedartmouth.com
w valleyhousedartmouth.com

**The Victorian House** ★★★★
*Bed & Breakfast*
SILVER AWARD
1 Vicarage Hill, Dartmouth
TQ6 9EW
t (01803) 832766
e sue@victorianhouse.org.uk
w victorianhouse.org.uk

**Westbourne House**
★★★★★ *Bed & Breakfast*
SILVER AWARD
4 Vicarage Hill, Dartmouth
TQ6 9EW
t (01803) 832213
e peterwalton@westbourne-
house.co.uk
w westbourne-house.co.uk

## DAWLISH
### Devon

**Channel View Guest House**
★★★★ *Guest House*
14 Teignmouth Hill, West Cliff,
Dawlish EX7 9DN
t (01626) 866973
e channelviewguesthouse@
fsmail.net
w channelviewguesthouse.co.
uk
♿ ☕

**Lammas Park House**
★★★★★
*Guest Accommodation*
GOLD AWARD
3 Priory Road, Dawlish EX7 9JF
t (01626) 888064
e lammaspark@hotmail.com
w lammasparkhouse.co.uk

## DEERHURST
### Gloucestershire

**Deerhurst Bed & Breakfast**
★★★★ *Farmhouse*
Deerhurst Priory, Deerhurst,
Gloucester GL19 4BX
t (01684) 293358
e timandcate@aol.com
w deerhurstbandb.co.uk

**Green Orchard**
Rating Applied For
*Bed & Breakfast*
Deerhurst Walton, Deerhurst,
Gloucester GL19 4BS
t (01242) 680362
e w.feakins@btinternet.com
w greenorchardbandb.com

## DEVIZES
### Wiltshire

**Asta B&B** ★★
*Bed & Breakfast*
66 Downlands Road, Devizes
SN10 5EF
t (01380) 722546

**Bramley House** ★★★★
*Bed & Breakfast*
SILVER AWARD
5 The Breach, Devizes
SN10 5BJ
t (01380) 729444

**Byde a Whyle** ★★★
*Bed & Breakfast*
29 Roundway Park, Devizes
SN10 2ED
t (01380) 723288

**Eastleigh House** ★★★★
*Bed & Breakfast*
3 Eastleigh Road, Devizes
SN10 3EE
t (01380) 726918
e barbara@eastleighhouse.
fsnet.co.uk
w eastleighhouse.co.uk

**The Gables** ★★★★
*Bed & Breakfast*
Bath Road, Devizes SN10 1PH
t (01380) 723086
e enquiries@
thegablesdevizes.co.uk
w thegablesdevizes.co.uk

**The Gate House** ★★★
*Bed & Breakfast*
Wick Lane, Devizes SN10 5DW
t (01380) 725283
e info@visitdevizes.co.uk
w visitdevizes.co.uk

**Longwater** ★★★
*Bed & Breakfast*
Lower Road, Erlestoke, Devizes
SN10 5UE
t (01380) 830095
e pam.hampton@talk21.com
♿

**The Old Manor** ★★★★
*Bed & Breakfast*
The Street, Chirton, Devizes
SN10 3QS
t (01380) 840777
e bandb@theoldmanor.biz
w theoldmanor.biz

**Rosemundy Cottage** ★★★★
*Guest Accommodation*
London Road, Devizes
SN10 2DS
t (01380) 727122
e info@rosemundycottage.co.
uk
w rosemundycottage.co.uk

## DINTON
### Wiltshire

**Honeysuckle Homestead**
★★★ *Guest Accommodation*
Dinton, Salisbury SP3 5HA
t (01722) 717887
e honeysuckle@dinton21.
freeserve.co.uk

**Marshwood Farm B&B**
★★★★ *Bed & Breakfast*
Dinton, Salisbury SP3 5ET
t (01722) 716334
e marshwood1@btconnect.
com
w marshwoodfarm.co.uk
▨☑

**The Penruddocke Arms** ★
*Inn*
Hindon Road, Salisbury
SP3 5EL
t (01722) 716253
e nosh4@btconnect.com
w penryddockearms.co.uk

## DIPTFORD
### Devon

**Old Rectory Bed and
Breakfast** ★★★★★
*Bed & Breakfast*
SILVER AWARD
Diptford, Totnes TQ9 7NY
t (01548) 821575
e hitchins@oldrectorydiptford.
co.uk
w oldrectorydiptford.co.uk

## DOLTON
### Devon

**Rams Head Inn** ★★★ *Inn*
South Street, Dolton,
Winkleigh EX19 8QS
t (01805) 804255
e ramsheadinn@btinternet.
com
w ramsheadinn.co.uk

## DONHEAD ST ANDREW
### Wiltshire

**Oakdale House** ★★★
*Bed & Breakfast*
New Road, Donhead St
Andrew, Shaftesbury SP7 9EG
t (01747) 828767
e ella@oakdalehouse.co.uk
w oakdalehouse.co.uk

## DONHEAD ST MARY
### Wiltshire

**Cedar Lodge** ★★★
*Bed & Breakfast*
5 Deweys Place, Donhead St
Mary, Shaftesbury SP7 9LW
t (01747) 829240
e cedarlodge@onetel.com
w cedarlodge.org.uk
▨☑

## DORCHESTER
### Dorset

**Aquila Heights** ★★★★
*Guest Accommodation*
44 Maiden Castle Road,
Dorchester DT1 2ES
t (01305) 267145
e aquila.heights@tiscali.co.uk
w aquilaheights.co.uk

**Baytree House** ★★★★
*Bed & Breakfast*
SILVER AWARD
4 Athelstan Road, Dorchester
DT1 1NR
t (01305) 263696
e info@baytreedorchester.
com
w bandbdorchester.co.uk

**Churchview Guest House**
★★★★ *Guest House*
SILVER AWARD
Winterbourne Abbas,
Dorchester DT2 9LS
t (01305) 889296
e stay@churchview.co.uk
w churchview.co.uk

**Higher Came Farmhouse**
★★★★
*Guest Accommodation*
SILVER AWARD
Higher Came, Dorchester
DT2 8NR
t (01305) 268908
e enquiries@highercame.co.
uk
w highercame.co.uk

**Hillfort View** ★★
*Bed & Breakfast*
10 Hillfort Close, Dorchester
DT1 2QT
t (01305) 268476
e maurice_d55@talktalk.net

**Sunrise Guest House** ★★★
*Guest House*
34 London Road, Dorchester
DT1 1NE
t (01305) 262425
w sunriseguesthouse
dorchester.com

**Tarkaville** ★★★★
*Bed & Breakfast*
30 Shaston Crescent,
Dorchester DT1 2EB
t (01305) 266253
e tarkaville@lineone.net

**Westwood House** ★★★★
*Guest Accommodation*
29 High West Street,
Dorchester DT1 1UP
t (01305) 268018
e reservations@
westwoodhouse.co.uk
w westwoodhouse.co.uk

**The White House** ★★★
*Bed & Breakfast*
9 Queens Avenue, Dorchester
DT1 2EW
t (01305) 266714
e sandratwh@yahoo.co.uk
w rynhorn.tripod.com/
whitehouse/index.htm

**Yalbury Park** ★★★★
*Farmhouse*
Frome Whitfield Farm,
Dorchester DT2 7SE
t (01305) 250336
e yalburypark@tesco.net

**Yellowham Farm** ★★★★
*Guest Accommodation*
SILVER AWARD
Yellowham Wood, Dorchester
DT2 8RW
t (01305) 262892
e mail@yellowham.freeserve.
co.uk
w yellowham.co.uk

## DOWNTON
### Wiltshire

**Witherington Farm Bed &
Breakfast** ★★★★★
*Bed & Breakfast*
GOLD AWARD
Witherington, Nr Downton,
Salisbury SP5 3QT
t (01722) 710222
e bandb@witheringtonfarm.
co.uk
w witheringtonfarm.co.uk

## DRAKEWALLS
### Cornwall

**Drakewalls House** ★★★
*Bed & Breakfast*
Gunnislake PL18 9EG
t (01822) 833617
e patsmyth_53@hotmail.com
w drakewallsbedandbreakfast.
co.uk

## DULOE
### Cornwall

**Carglonnon Farm** ★★★★
*Farmhouse*
Duloe, Liskeard PL14 4QA
t (01579) 320210

**Tremadart House** ★★★★
*Bed & Breakfast*
Tremadart Road, Liskeard
PL14 4PE
t (01503) 262766
e philipparead@hotmail.com
w tremadart.co.uk

## DULVERTON
### Somerset

**Hawkwell Farm House**
★★★★★ *Bed & Breakfast*
Dulverton, Somerset
TA22 9RU
t (01398) 341708
e jan@hawkwellfarmhouse.co.
uk
w hawkwellfarmhouse.co.uk

**Northcombe** *Bunkhouse*
Northcombe Farm, Nr
Dulverton TA22 9JH
t (01398) 323602
e sally@
northcombecampingbarns.
fsnet.co.uk

**Springfield Farm** ★★★★
*Farmhouse*
Ashwick Lane, Dulverton
TA22 9QD
t (01398) 323722
e stay@springfieldfarms.co.uk
w springfieldfarms.co.uk

**Three Acres Country House**
★★★★★
*Guest Accommodation*
GOLD AWARD
Brushford New Road,
Dulverton TA22 9AR
t (01398) 323730
e enquiries@
threeacrescountryhouse.co.uk
w threeacrescountryhouse.co.
uk
▨☑

**Town Mills** ★★★★
*Guest Accommodation*
SILVER AWARD
High Street, Dulverton
TA22 9HB
t (01398) 323124
e townmillsdulverton@
btinternet.com
w townmillsdulverton.co.uk

## WINSBERE HOUSE ★★★
*Bed & Breakfast*
64 Battleton, Dulverton
TA22 9HU
t (01398) 323278
e info@winsbere.co.uk
w winsbere.co.uk

*(heading:)* **Winsbere House** ★★★

## DUNKESWELL
### Devon

**The Old Kennels** ★★★★
*Guest Accommodation*
Stentwood, Honiton EX14 4RW
t (01823) 681138
e info@theoldkennels.co.uk
w theoldkennels.co.uk
▨☑

## DUNMERE
### Cornwall

**St Anne's Chapel Hayes**
★★★ *Guest Accommodation*
Dunmere, Bodmin PL31 2RD
t (01208) 77003
e jeremy@stannes.demon.co.
uk
w st-annes-chapel-cornwall.co.
uk

## DUNSTER
### Somerset

**Cedar House** ★★★★★
*Guest Accommodation*
SILVER AWARD
Old Cleeve, Nr Minehead
TA24 6HH
t (01984) 640437 &
07775 821535
e enquiries@
cedarhousesomerset.co.uk
w cedarhousesomerset.co.uk

**Conygar House** ★★★★
*Bed & Breakfast*
SILVER AWARD
2a The Ball, Dunster TA24 6SD
t (01643) 821872
e bale.dunster@virgin.net
w conygarhouse.co.uk

**Exmoor House Dunster**
★★★★
*Guest Accommodation*
SILVER AWARD
12 West Street, Dunster
TA24 6SN
t (01643) 821268
e stay@exmoorhousedunster.
co.uk
w exmoorhousedunster.co.uk

**Millstream Cottages** ★★★★
*Bed & Breakfast*
2 Mill Lane, Minehead
TA24 6SW
t (01643) 821966
w millstreamcottagedunster.
co.uk

**Spears Cross Hotel** ★★★★
*Guest Accommodation*
SILVER AWARD
1 West Street, Dunster
TA24 6SN
t (01643) 821439
e hotel@spearscross.demon.
co.uk
w spearscrosshotel.co.uk

## DURSLEY
### Gloucestershire

**Foresters** ★★★★
*Bed & Breakfast*
Chapel Street, Cam, Dursley
GL11 5NX
t (01453) 549996
e foresters@freeuk.com

### EAST CHINNOCK
Somerset

**Barrows Farmhouse ★★★★**
*Bed & Breakfast*
Weston Street, Nr Yeovil
BA22 9EJ
t (01935) 862237
e barrowsfarmhouse@aol.com
w barrowsfarmhouse.com

**Gables Guest House ★★★**
*Guest House*
East Chinnock, Nr Yeovil
BA22 9DR
t (01935) 862237
e tony@whitehead7877.
freeserve.co.uk

### EAST COKER
Somerset

**Granary House ★★★★**
*Bed & Breakfast*
SILVER AWARD
East Coker, Nr Yeovil BA22 9LY
t (01935) 862738
e stay@granaryhouse.co.uk
w granaryhouse.co.uk

### EAST HARPTREE
Somerset

**Harptree Court ★★★★★**
*Guest Accommodation*
SILVER AWARD
East Harptree, Bristol
BS40 6AA
t (01761) 221729
e location.harptree@tiscali.co.
uk
w harptreecourt.co.uk

### EAST KENNETT
Wiltshire

**The Old Forge ★★★★**
*Bed & Breakfast*
SILVER AWARD
East Kennett, Marlborough
SN8 4EY
t (01672) 861686
e laura@feeleyfamily.fsnet.co.
uk
w theoldforge-avebury.co.uk

### EAST LOOE
Cornwall

**Bridgeside Guest House
★★★** *Guest House*
Fore Street, East Looe, Looe
PL13 1HH
t (01503) 263113

**Pine Lodge B&B ★★★★**
*Bed & Breakfast*
Widegates, Looe PL13 1QB
t (01503) 240857
e bandb@pinelodgelooe.fsnet.
co.uk
w pinelodgelooe.co.uk

**Sea Breeze Guest House
★★★** *Guest House*
Lower Chapel Street, East
Looe, Looe PL13 1AT
t (01503) 263131
e annette@seabreeze.
wanadoo.co.uk
w cornwallexplore.co.uk/
seabreeze

### EAST STOUR
Dorset

**Aysgarth ★★★★**
*Bed & Breakfast*
SILVER AWARD
Back Street, East.Stour,
Gillingham SP8 5JY
t (01747) 838351
e aysgarth@lineone.net

### EAST TYTHERTON
Wiltshire

**Barnbridge ★★**
*Bed & Breakfast*
East Tytherton, Chippenham
SN15 4LT
t (01249) 740280
e bgiffard@aol.com
w barnbridge.co.uk

### EASTON ROYAL
Wiltshire

**Follets B&B ★★★★**
*Bed & Breakfast*
SILVER AWARD
Easton Royal, Pewsey SN9 5LZ
t (01672) 810619
e margaret@folletsbb.com
w folletsbb.com

### EBRINGTON
Gloucestershire

**The Ebrington Arms ★★★★**
*Inn*
Ebrington, Chipping Campden
GL55 6NH
t (01386) 593223
e info@theebringtonarms.co.
uk
w theebringtonarms.co.uk

**Little Gidding ★★★★**
*Bed & Breakfast*
SILVER AWARD
Chipping Campden GL55 6NL
t (01386) 593302
e bookings@ebrington.com
w ebrington.com

### EDGE
Gloucestershire

**The Withyholt ★★★★**
*Bed & Breakfast*
Paul Mead, Edge, Stroud
GL6 6PG
t (01452) 813618

### ENFORD
Wiltshire

**Three Horseshoes Cottage
★★★★** *Bed & Breakfast*
Enford, Pewsey SN9 6AW
t (01980) 670459
e jcjonkler@aol.com
w threehorseshoescottage.
com

### EVERCREECH
Somerset

**43 Maesdown Road ★★**
*Bed & Breakfast*
Maesdown Road, Evercreech
BA4 6LE
t (01749) 830721

**Crossdale Cottage ★★★**
*Bed & Breakfast*
Pecking Mill, Evercreech
BA4 6PQ
t (01749) 830293
e info@crossdalecottage.co.uk
w crossdalecottage.co.uk

**The Old Dairy Rooms
★★★★** *Farmhouse*
Rodmore Farm, Evercreech
BA4 6DW
t (01749) 830531
e olddairyrooms.co.uk

### EXETER
Devon

**Bendene ★★★★**
*Guest Accommodation*
15-16 Richmond Road, Exeter
EX4 4JA
t (01392) 213526
e reservations@bendene.co.
uk
w bendene.co.uk

**Braeside Guest House
★★★★** *Guest House*
21 New North Road, Exeter
EX4 4HF
t (01392) 256875

**The Clock Tower ★★★★**
*Guest Accommodation*
16/17 New North Road, Exeter
EX4 4HF
t (01392) 424545
e reservations@
clocktowerhotel.co.uk
w clocktowerhotel.co.uk

**Culm Vale Country House
★★★** *Bed & Breakfast*
Culm Vale, Stoke Canon,
Exeter EX5 4EG
t (01392) 841615
e culmvale@hotmail.com

**Exeter YHA ★★★** *Hostel*
47 Countess Wear Road,
Exeter EX2 6LR
t (01392) 873329
e exeter@yha.org.uk
w yha.org.uk

**The Galley 'Fish and
Seafood' Restaurant & Spa
with Cabins ★★★★★**
*Restaurant with Rooms*
GOLD AWARD
41 Fore Street, Topsham,
Exeter EX3 0HU
t (01392) 876078
e fish@galleyrestaurant.co.uk
w galleyrestaurant.co.uk

**The Garden House ★★★★**
*Bed & Breakfast*
SILVER AWARD
4 Hoopern Avenue,
Pennsylvania, Exeter EX4 6DN
t (01392) 256255
e stay@exeterbedandbeakfst.
co.uk
w exeterbedandbreakfast.co.
uk

**The Georgian Lodge ★★★★**
*Guest Accommodation*
5 Bystock Terrace, Exeter
EX4 4HY
t (01392) 213079
e reservations@
georgianlodge.com
w georgianlodge.com

**The Grange ★★★★**
*Guest Accommodation*
Stoke Hill, Exeter EX4 7JH
t (01392) 259723
e dudleythegrange@aol.com

**Hayne Barton Milverton
Country Holidays ★★**
*Bed & Breakfast*
Whitestone, Exeter EX4 2JN
t (01392) 811268
e g_milverton@hotmail.com
w milvertoncountryholidays.
com

**Home Farm ★★★★**
*Farmhouse*
Farringdon, Exeter EX5 2HY
t (01395) 232293

**Jades Guest House ◆◆◆**
*Guest Accommodation*
65 St Davids Hill, Exeter
EX4 4DW
t (01392) 435610
e jllbkrb@aol.com

**Lower Thornton Farm
★★★★** *Farmhouse*
SILVER AWARD
Kenn, Exeter EX6 7XH
t (01392) 833434
e will@willclack.plus.com

**Oakcliffe ★★★** *Guest House*
73 St Davids Hill, Exeter
EX4 4DW
t (01392) 258288
e oakcliffe@excite.com

**Park View Hotel ★★★**
*Guest Accommodation*
8 Howell Road, Exeter EX4 4LG
t (01392) 271772
e enquiries@parkviewexeter.
co.uk
w parkviewexeter.co.uk

**The Radnor ★★★**
*Bed & Breakfast*
St Davids Hill, Exeter EX4 4DW
t (01392) 272004
e ddweeks@radnorhotel.
eclipse.co.uk

**Raffles ★★★★**
*Guest Accommodation*
11 Blackall Road, Exeter
EX4 4HD
t (01392) 270200
e raffleshtl@btinternet.com
w raffles-exeter.co.uk

**Road Lodge ★★★**
*Guest Accommodation*
East Wonford Lodge, 42 East
Wonford Hill, Exeter EX1 3TF
t (01392) 438200
e tours@roadtrip.co.uk
w roadlodge.co.uk

**Rydon Farm ★★★★**
*Farmhouse*
Woodbury, Exeter EX5 1LB
t (01395) 232341
e sallyglanvill@aol.com
w rydonfarmwoodbury.co.uk

**Silversprings ★★★★**
*Guest Accommodation*
SILVER AWARD
12 Richmond Road, St Davids,
Exeter EX4 4JA
t (01392) 494040
e juliet@silversprings.co.uk
w silversprings.co.uk

**Strete Ralegh Farm ★★★★**
*Bed & Breakfast*
Whimple, Exeter EX5 2PP
t (01404) 822464
e info@streteraleghfarm.co.uk
w streteraleghfarm.co.uk

**The Telstar ★★★★**
*Guest House*
75-77 St Davids Hill, Exeter
EX4 4DW
t (01392) 272466
e reception@telstar-hotel.co.
uk
w telstar-hotel.co.uk

**Thorverton Arms** ★★ *Inn*
Thorverton, Exeter EX5 5NS
t (01392) 860205
e info@thethorvertonarms.co.
uk
w thethorvertonarms.co.uk

**Town House** ★★★
*Guest Accommodation*
54 St Davids Hill, Exeter
EX4 4DT
t (01392) 494994
e info@townhouseexeter.co.
uk
w townhouseexeter.co.uk

**White Hart Hotel** ★★★
*Guest Accommodation*
66 South Street, Exeter
EX1 1EE
t (01392) 279897
e booking.whexeter@
eldridge-pope.co.uk
w roomattheinn.info

**Woodbine Guesthouse**
★★★★
*Guest Accommodation*
1 Woodbine Terrace, Exeter
EX4 4LJ
t (01392) 203302
e bookings@
woodbineguesthouse.co.uk
w woodbineguesthouse.co.uk

### EXFORD
Somerset

**Exford YHA** ★★★ *Hostel*
Exe Mead, Exford TA24 7PU
t (01643) 831288
w yha.org.uk

**Exmoor Lodge Guest House**
★★★ *Guest House*
Chapel Street, Exford
TA24 7PY
t (01643) 831694
e exmoor-lodge@talktalk.net
w smoothhound.co.uk/hotels/
exmoorlodge.html

**Newland House** ★★
*Guest Accommodation*
Exford TA24 7NF
t (01643) 831199
e info@newlandhouse-
exmoor.co.uk
w newlandhouse-exmoor.co.
uk

**Stockleigh Lodge** ★★★★
*Guest Accommodation*
B3224, Exford TA24 7PZ
t (01643) 831500
e myra@stockleighexford.
freeserve.co.uk
w stockleighexford.freeserve.
co.uk

### EXMOUTH
Devon

**The Devoncourt Hotel**
★★★★
*Guest Accommodation*
Douglas Avenue, Exmouth
EX8 2EX
t (01395) 272277
e enquiries@devoncourt.com
w devoncourt.com

**New Moorings** ★★★★
*Guest Accommodation*
1 Morton Road, Exmouth
EX8 1AZ
t (01395) 223073
e anneanddave@
newmoorings.wanadoo.co.uk
w exmouthguide.co.uk/
newmoorings.htm

**The Swallows** ★★★★
*Guest Accommodation*
11 Carlton Hill, Exmouth
EX8 2AJ
t (01395) 263937
e p.russo@btclick.com
w exmouth-guide.co.uk/
swallows.htm

**Victoria Guest House**
★★★★
*Guest Accommodation*
SILVER AWARD
131 Victoria Road, Exmouth
EX8 1DR
t (01395) 222882
e alfred@exmouth.net
w exmouth.net

### FAIRFORD
Gloucestershire

**Hathaway** ★★★★
*Bed & Breakfast*
SILVER AWARD
London Road, Fairford
GL7 4AR
t (01285) 712715
e lizian.spurway@btinternet.
com

**Waiten Hill Farm** ★★★
*Bed & Breakfast*
Mill Lane, Fairford GL7 4JG
t (01285) 712652

### FALMOUTH
Cornwall

**The Beach House** ★★★★
*Guest Accommodation*
1 Boscawen Road, Falmouth
TR11 4EL
t (01326) 210407
e beachhousefalmouth@
hotmail.com
w beachhousefalmouth.co.uk

**Camelot** ★★★★
*Guest Accommodation*
5 Avenue Road, Falmouth
TR11 4AZ
t (01326) 312480
e camelotfalmouth@aol.com
w camelot-guest-house.co.uk

**Castleton Guest House**
★★★ *Guest House*
68 Killigrew Street, Falmouth
TR11 3PR
t (01326) 372644
e dawnemmerson@aol.com

**Chellowdene** ★★★★
*Guest House*
Gyllyngvase Hill, Falmouth
TR11 4DN
t (01326) 314950
e info@chellowdene.co.uk
w chellowdene.co.uk

**Chelsea House** ★★★★
*Guest Accommodation*
SILVER AWARD
2 Emslie Road, Falmouth
TR11 4BG
t (01326) 212230
e info@chelseahousehotel.
com
w chelseahousehotel.com

**Dolvean House** ★★★★★
*Guest Accommodation*
GOLD AWARD
50 Melvill Road, Falmouth
TR11 4DQ
t (01326) 313658
e reservations@dolvean.co.uk
w dolvean.co.uk

**Engleton House Guest
House** ★★★
*Guest Accommodation*
67/68 Killigrew Street,
Falmouth TR11 3PR
t (01326) 372644 &
07736 684666
e dawnemmerson@aol.com
w falmouth-bandb.co.uk

**Grove Hotel** ★★★
*Guest Accommodation*
Grove Place, Falmouth
TR11 4AU
t (01326) 319577
e grovehotel@btconnect.com
w thegrovehotel.net

**Gyllyngvase House** ★★★★
*Guest Accommodation*
Gyllyngvase Road, Falmouth
TR11 4GH
t (01326) 312956
e info@gyllyngvase.co.uk
w gyllyngvase.co.uk

**Hawthorne Dene** ★★★★
*Guest Accommodation*
SILVER AWARD
12 Pennance Road, Falmouth
TR11 4EA
t (01326) 311427
e enquiries@
hawthornedenehotel.co.uk
w hawthornedenehotel.com

**Headlands Hotel** ★★★★
*Guest Accommodation*
4 Avenue Road, Falmouth
TR11 4AZ
t (01326) 311141
e headlandsfalmouth@
hotmail.co.uk
w headlandsfalmouth.co.uk

**Highcliffe** ★★★★
*Guest Accommodation*
22 Melvill Road, Falmouth
TR11 4AR
t (01326) 314466
e info@highcliffe-falmouth.co.
uk
w stayinfalmouth.co.uk

**Lugo Rock** ★★★★
*Guest Accommodation*
59 Melvill Road, Falmouth
TR11 4DF
t (01326) 311344
e info@lugorockhotel.co.uk
w lugorockhotel.co.uk

**The Palms Guest House**
★★★★
*Guest Accommodation*
11 Castle Drive, Falmouth
TR11 4NR
t (01326) 314007
e j_miller99@hotmail.com
w thepalmsguesthouse.co.uk

**Penwarren – AK074** ★★★★
*Guest Accommodation*
SILVER AWARD
3 Avenue Road, Falmouth
TR11 4AZ
t (01326) 314216
e penwarren@btconnect.com
w penwarren.co.uk

**Poltair** ★★★★ *Guest House*
SILVER AWARD
4 Emslie Road, Falmouth
TR11 4BG
t (01326) 313158
e info@poltair.co.uk
w poltair.co.uk

**The Red House** ★★★★
*Guest Accommodation*
24 Melvill Road, Falmouth
TR11 4AR
t (01326) 311172
e info@theredhousefalmouth.
co.uk
w thered-house.com

**Tregedna Lodge – AK079**
★★★★ *Hostel*
Maenporth, Falmouth
TR11 5HL
t (01326) 250529
e tregednafarm@btinternet.
com
w tregednafarmholidays.co.uk

**Tregenna Guest House**
★★★ *Guest Accommodation*
28 Melvill Road, Falmouth
TR11 4AR
t (01326) 313881
e info@tregennafalmouth.co.
uk
w tregennafalmouth.co.uk

**Trevaylor** ★★★★
*Guest Accommodation*
8 Pennance Road, Falmouth
TR11 4EA
t (01326) 313041
e trevaylorhotel@aol.com
w trevaylorhotel.com

**Wellington House** ★★★★
*Guest Accommodation*
26 Melvill Road, Falmouth
TR11 4AR
t (01326) 319947
e wellingtonhouse@msn.com
w wellingtonhousefalmouth.
co.uk

**Westcott Hotel** ★★★★
*Guest Accommodation*
Gyllyngvase Hill, Falmouth
TR11 4DN
t (01326) 311309
e westcotthotel@btinternet.
com

**Wickham Guest House**
★★★ *Guest Accommodation*
21 Gyllyngvase Terrace,
Falmouth TR11 4DL
t (01326) 311140
e enquiries@wickhamhotel.
freeserve.co.uk
w wickham-hotel.co.uk

### FARMBOROUGH
Somerset

**Barrow Vale Farm** ★★★★
*Farmhouse*
Farmborough, Bath BA2 0BL
t (01761) 470300
e cherilynlangley@hotmail.
com

### FARRINGTON GURNEY
Somerset

**The Croft Bed & Breakfast**
Rating Applied For
*Bed & Breakfast*
The Croft, Bristol Road, Bristol
BS39 6TJ
t (01761) 453479
w thecroftbandb.com

## FAULKLAND
### Somerset

**Lime Kiln Farm** ★★★★
*Bed & Breakfast*
A366, Nr Radstock BA3 5XE
t (01373) 834305
e lime_kiln@hotmail.com
w limekilnfarm.co.uk

**Old Farm Cottages** ★★★★
*Bed & Breakfast*
The Green, Nr Radstock
BA3 5UZ
t (01373) 834597
e maryclark1@hotmail.co.uk

## FENNY BRIDGES
### Devon

**Skinners Ash Farm B&B**
★★★ *Farmhouse*
Fenny Bridges, Honiton
EX14 3BH
t (01404) 850231
w skinners-ash-farm.co.uk

## FEOCK
### Cornwall

**Come-To-Good Farm**
★★★★ *Farmhouse*
Come-To-Good, Feock, Truro
TR3 6QS
t (01872) 863828
e info@cometogoodfarm.co.uk
w cometogoodfarm.co.uk

## FIDDINGTON
### Gloucestershire

**Hillview B and B** ★★★★
*Guest Accommodation*
SILVER AWARD
Fiddington, Nr Ashchurch,
Tewkesbury GL20 7BJ
t (01684) 293231
e info@tewkesburybandb.co.uk

## FLEET
### Dorset

**Highfield** ★★★★ *Farmhouse*
SILVER AWARD
Fleet Road, Fleet, Weymouth
DT3 4EB
t (01305) 776822
e sue@highfield-fleet.co.uk
w highfield-fleet.co.uk

## FLUSHING
### Cornwall

**An Chy Coth** ★★★★
*Bed & Breakfast*
37 Kersey Road, Flushing,
Falmouth TR11 5TR
t (01326) 377028
e anchycoth@hotmail.com

## FORD
### Gloucestershire

**The Plough** ★★★★ *Inn*
SILVER AWARD
Ford, Temple Guiting,
Cheltenham GL54 5RU
t (01386) 584215
e info@theploughinnatford.co.uk
w theploughinnatford.co.uk

## FORTHAMPTON
### Gloucestershire

**Lower Lode Inn** ★★ *Inn*
Forthampton GL19 4RE
t (01684) 293224
e lowerlode@tiscali.co.uk

## FOWEY
### Cornwall

**Coombe Farm B&B** ★★★
*Farmhouse*
Fowey PL23 1HW
t (01726) 833123
e tessapaull@hotmail.com

**Fowey Marine Guest House**
★★★★ *Guest House*
21/27 Station Road, Fowey
PL23 1DF
t (01726) 833920
e enquiries@foweymarine.com
w foweymarine.com

**Old Ferry Inn** ★★★ *Inn*
Bodinnick-by-Fowey, Fowey
PL23 1LX
t (01726) 870237
e oldferryinn@bodinnick.fsnet.co.uk
w oldferryinn.com

## FRAMPTON-ON-SEVERN
### Gloucestershire

**The Bell** ★★★★ *Inn*
The Green, Frampton-on-
Severn, Gloucester GL2 7EP
t (01452) 740346
e hoqben@qotadsl.co.uk

## FRANCE LYNCH
### Gloucestershire

**The Brambles**
Rating Applied For
*Bed & Breakfast*
Avenis Green, France Lynch,
Stroud GL6 8LX
t (01453) 884307
e info@thebrambles accommodation.com
w thebramblesbedand breakfast.com

## FRIAR WADDON
### Dorset

**Corton Farm** ★★★★
*Bed & Breakfast*
SILVER AWARD
Friar Waddon, Weymouth
DT3 4EP
t (01305) 815784
e hollylasseter@corton.org

**Pump Cottage** ★★★
*Bed & Breakfast*
Friar Waddon Road, Upwey
DT3 4EW
t (01305) 816002
e ronjamsden@hotmail.com

## FROME
### Somerset

**Abergele Guest House**
★★★★ *Guest House*
2 Fromefield, Frome BA11 2HA
t (01373) 463998

**The Full Moon** ★★★★ *Inn*
Rudge Lane, Nr Frome
BA11 2QF
t (01373) 830936
e info@thefullmoon.co.uk
w thefullmoon.co.uk

**Granados** ★★★
*Bed & Breakfast*
Blatchbridge, Frome BA11 5EL
t (01373) 465317
e granadosbandb@aol.com

**The Lodge** ★★★★
*Bed & Breakfast*
Monkley Lane, Rode Common,
Nr Frome BA11 6QQ
t (01373) 830071
e juliemcdougal@btinternet.com

**Lower Grange Farm** ★★★★
*Farmhouse*
Feltham Lane, Frome BA11 5LL
t (01373) 452938
e bandb@thelowergrangefarm.fsnet.com

**Mount Grange** ★★★★
*Guest Accommodation*
25 Bath Road, Frome BA11 2HJ
t (01373) 300159
e mountgrange@blueyonder.co.uk
w mount-grange.co.uk
▶️🖊️

**Seymours Court** ★★★★
*Farmhouse*
Green Park Lane, Nr Frome
BA11 6TT
t (01373) 830466
e seymourscourt@btinternet.com
w seymourscourt.co.uk

## GILLINGHAM
### Dorset

**The Glen** ★★★
*Bed & Breakfast*
Fern Hill, East Stour, Gillingham
SP8 5ND
t (01747) 839819
e b&b@theglen-dorset.co.uk
w theglen-dorset.co.uk

**Lyde Hill Farmhouse** ★★
*Bed & Breakfast*
Woodville, Stour Provost,
Gillingham SP8 5LX
t (01747) 838483

## GITTISHAM
### Devon

**Catshayes Farm** ★★★
*Farmhouse*
Gittisham, Honiton EX14 3AE
t (01404) 850302
e catshayesfarm@aol.com
w catshayes-farm-honiton.co.uk

**Meriden House Bed &
Breakfast** ★★★★
*Bed & Breakfast*
Gittisham, Honiton EX14 3AW
t (01404) 44155
e stay@meridenhousedevon.co.uk
w meridenhousedevon.co.uk

## GLASTONBURY
### Somerset

**37 Chilkwell Street**
Rating Applied For
*Bed & Breakfast*
Chilkwell Street, Glastonbury
BA6 8DE
t (01458) 832390

**46 Bove Town** ★★★
*Bed & Breakfast*
Glastonbury BA6 8JE
t (01458) 833684

**Appletree House** ★★★★
*Bed & Breakfast*
27 Bere Lane, Glastonbury
BA6 8BD
t (01458) 830803
e sue@appletreehouse.org.uk
w appletreehouse.org.uk

**ARP** ★★★★ *Bed & Breakfast*
4 Chalice Way, Glastonbury
BA6 8EX
t (01458) 830794
e ann@arp-b-and-b.freeserve.co.uk
w arp-b-and-b.freeserve.co.uk

**The Barn** ★★★
*Bed & Breakfast*
84b Bove Town, Glastonbury
BA6 8JG
t (01458) 832991
e adriangoolden@yahoo.co.uk

**Belle-Vue** ★★★
*Bed & Breakfast*
2 Bere Lane, Glastonbury
BA6 8BA
t (01458) 830385
e belle_vueglastonbury@tiscali.co.uk
w bellevueglastonbury.co.uk

**Chalice Hill House** ★★★★
*Bed & Breakfast*
Dod Lane, Glastonbury
BA6 8BZ
t (01458) 830828
e mail@chalicehill.co.uk
w chalicehill.co.uk

**Cherrywood** ★★★
*Bed & Breakfast*
11 Rowley Road, Glastonbury
BA6 8HU
t (01458) 833115

**Chestnuts Boutique Bed and
Breakfast** ★★★★
*Bed & Breakfast*
Bove Town, Glastonbury
BA6 8JG
t (01458) 830562
e info@glastonburyaccommodation.com
w glastonburyaccommodation.com

**Coig Deug** ★★
*Bed & Breakfast*
15 Helyar Close, Glastonbury
BA6 9LQ
t (01458) 835945
e kath@coigdeug.freeserve.co.uk
w glastonbury.co.uk/accommodation/coigdeug

**Coxwithy House B&B**
★★★★ *Bed & Breakfast*
Coxwithy Lane, Edgarley,
Glastonbury BA6 8LA
t (01458) 833021
e jo@coxwithyhouse.co.uk
w coxwithyhouse.co.uk

**Daisy Centre Retreat** ★★
*Bed & Breakfast*
6 Church Lane, Glastonbury
BA6 9JQ
t (01458) 834587
e daisyfoss@haloangels.co.uk
w daisycentres.com

**The Flying Dragon** ★★★★
*Guest Accommodation*
12 Hexton Road, Glastonbury
BA6 8HL
t (01458) 830321
e rench.ness@virgin.net
w flyingdragon.co.uk

**Havyatt Cottage** ★★★
*Guest Accommodation*
2 Havyatt, Glastonbury
BA6 8LF
t (01458) 832520
e oxley1165@hotmail.com
w havyattcottage.co.uk

**Hillclose** ★★★★
*Guest Accommodation*
Street Road, Glastonbury
BA6 9EG
t (01458) 831040
w hillclose.co.uk

**Kylemore House** ★★★
*Bed & Breakfast*
16 Lambrook Street,
Glastonbury BA6 8BX
t (01458) 831612
e enquiries@kylemorehouse.
co.uk
w kylemorehouse.co.uk

**Little Orchard** ★★★
*Guest Accommodation*
Ashwell Lane, Glastonbury
BA6 8BG
t (01458) 831620
e the.littleorchard@lineone.
net
w smoothhound.co.uk/hotels/
orchard.html

**Lower Farm** ★★★★
*Farmhouse* **SILVER AWARD**
High Street, Somerton
TA11 6BA
t (01458) 223237
e lowerfarm@btconnect.com
w lowerfarm.net

**Mapleleaf Middlewick**
★★★★ *Bed & Breakfast*
Wick Lane, Glastonbury
BA6 8JW
t (01458) 832351
e middlewick@btconnect.com
w middlewickholidaycottages.
co.uk

**Meare Manor** ★★★★
*Guest Accommodation*
60 St Marys Road, Glastonbury
BA6 9SR
t (01458) 860449
e reception@mearemanor.
com
w mearemanor.com

**Melrose** ★★★★
*Bed & Breakfast*
Coursing Batch, Glastonbury
BA6 8BH
t (01458) 834706
e melrose@underthetor.
freeserve.co.uk

**Pippin** ★★★ *Bed & Breakfast*
4 Ridgeway Gardens,
Glastonbury BA6 8ER
t (01458) 834262
e daphne.slater@talktalk.net
w smoothhound.co.uk/hotels/
pippin.html

**Three Magdalene St**
★★★★★
*Guest Accommodation*
3 Magdalene Street,
Glastonbury BA6 9EW
t (01458) 832129
e info@numberthree.co.uk
w numberthree.co.uk

**Tordown B&B and Healing Centre** ★★★★
*Guest Accommodation*
5 Ashwell Lane, Glastonbury
BA6 8BG
t (01458) 832287
e torangel@aol.com
w tordown.com

**Who'd A Thought It Inn**
★★★ *Inn*
17 Northload Street,
Glastonbury BA6 9JJ
t (01458) 834460
e enquiries@whodathoughtit.
co.uk
w whodathoughtit.co.uk

### GLOUCESTER
Gloucestershire

**Albert House** ★★★
*Guest Accommodation*
56-58 Worcester Street,
Gloucester GL1 3AG
t (01452) 502081
e enquiries@alberthotel.com
w alberthotel.com

**Brookthorpe Lodge** ★★★
*Guest House*
Stroud Road, Gloucester
GL4 0UQ
t (01452) 812645
e enq@brookthorpelodge.
demon.co.uk
w brookthorpelodge.demon.
co.uk

**Kilmorie Small Holding**
★★★★
*Guest Accommodation*
Gloucester Road, Corse,
Gloucester GL19 3RQ
t (01452) 840224
e sheila-barnfield@supanet.
com
w smoothhound.co.uk/hotels/
kilmorie.html

**Longford Lodge** ★★★
*Guest Accommodation*
Tewkesbury Road, Longford,
Gloucester GL2 9EH
t (01452) 526380
e jens_eberhardt_uk@hotmail.
com
w longfordlodge.co.uk

**Lulworth** ★★
*Guest Accommodation*
12 Midland Road, Gloucester
GL1 4UF
t (01452) 521881
e lulworth-guest@tiscali.co.uk
w http://myweb.tiscali.co.uk/
lulworth

**The New Inn Hotel**
Rating Applied For
*Inn*
16 Northgate Street,
Gloucester GL1 1SF
t (01452) 522177
e new_inn_hotel@hotmail.
com
w newinnglos.com

**Nicki's Guesthouse & Taverna** ★ *Guest House*
105-107 Westgate Street,
Gloucester GL1 2PG
t (01452) 301359

**The Spalite** ★★★
*Guest House*
121 Southgate Street,
Gloucester GL1 1XQ
t (01452) 380828
e marsh@spalitehotel.fsnet.co.
uk
w spalitehotel.co.uk

**Springfields Farm** ★★
*Farmhouse*
Little Witcombe, Gloucester
GL3 4TU
t (01452) 863532

**Town Street Farm** ★★★
*Farmhouse*
Town Street, Tirley, Gloucester
GL19 4HG
t (01452) 780442
e townstreetfarm@hotmail.
com
w townstreetfarm.co.uk

### GODNEY
Somerset

**Double-Gate Farm** ★★★★
*Farmhouse* **GOLD AWARD**
Godney Drove, Glastonbury
BA5 1RX
t (01458) 832217
e doublegatefarm@aol.com
w doublegatefarm.com

### GOLANT
Cornwall

**Golant YHA** ★★★ *Hostel*
Penquite House, Fowey
PL23 1LA
t (01726) 833507

### GONVENA
Cornwall

**St Giles Cottage** ★★★★
*Bed & Breakfast*
**SILVER AWARD**
Gonvena Hill, Wadebridge
PL27 6DP
t (01208) 813695
e info@stgilescottage.co.uk
w stgilescottage.co.uk

### GOONHILLY DOWNS
Cornwall

**County Cottage** ★★★★
*Bed & Breakfast*
Goonhilly Downs, Helston,
Falmouth TR12 6LQ
t (01326) 221810
w countycottage.co.uk

### GORRAN
Cornwall

**Mount Pleasant B&B** ★★★
*Farmhouse*
Mount Pleasant Farm, Gorran,
St Austell PL26 6LR
t (01726) 843918

### GORRAN HAVEN
Cornwall

**Bumble Bees** ★★★★
*Bed & Breakfast*
Foxhole Lane, St Austell
PL26 6JP
t (01726) 842219
e bamford@foxhole.vispa.com

### GRAMPOUND
Cornwall

**Perran House** ★★★
*Guest Accommodation*
Fore Street, Grampound, Truro
TR2 4RS
t (01726) 882066

### GREAT RISSINGTON
Gloucestershire

**The Granary Guesthouse**
★★★★ *Bed & Breakfast*
7 Cotswold Meadows, Great
Rissington, Cheltenham
GL54 2LN
t (01451) 821898
e info@cotswolds-bed-and-
breakfasts.co.uk
w cotswolds-bed-and-
breakfasts.co.uk

### GREENHAM
Somerset

**Greenham Hall** ★★★★
*Bed & Breakfast*
Bishops Hill, Nr Wellington
TA21 0JJ
t (01823) 672603
e greenhamhall@
btopenworld.com
w greenhamhall.co.uk

### GRETTON
Gloucestershire

**Elms Farm** ★★★★
*Farmhouse*
Gretton Fields, Gretton,
Cheltenham GL54 5HQ
t (01242) 620150
e rose@elmsfarm.wanadoo.co.
uk

### GRITTLETON
Wiltshire

**The Neeld Arms Inn** ★★★
*Inn*
The Street, Grittleton,
Chippenham SN14 6AP
t (01249) 782470
e info@neeldarms.co.uk
w neeldarms.co.uk

### GUITING POWER
Gloucestershire

**Castlett Bank** ★★★★
*Bed & Breakfast*
Castlett Street, Guiting Power,
Cheltenham GL54 5US
t (01451) 850300
e wilderspin@btconnect.com
w smoothhound.co.uk/hotels/
castlett.html

**Cobnutt Cottage** ★★★
*Bed & Breakfast*
Guiting Power, Cheltenham
GL54 5UX
t (01451) 850658

**The Guiting Guest House**
★★★★ *Guest House*
**SILVER AWARD**
Post Office Lane, Guiting
Power, Cheltenham GL54 5TZ
t (01451) 850470
e info@guitingguesthouse.
com
w guitingguesthouse.com

**The Hollow Bottom** ★★★★
*Inn*
Winchcombe Road, Guiting
Power, Cheltenham GL54 5UX
t (01451) 850392
e hello@hollowbottom.com
w hollowbottom.com

## GULWORTHY
### Devon

**Colcharton Farm ★★★★**
*Farmhouse* **SILVER AWARD**
Gulworthy, Tavistock
PL19 8HU
t (01822) 616435
e colchartonfarm@agriplus.net
w visit-dartmoor.co.uk

**Hele Farm ★★★★**
*Guest Accommodation*
Gulworthy, Tavistock PL19 8PA
t (01822) 833084

## GUNWALLOE
### Cornwall

**Glendower ★★★★**
*Guest Accommodation*
**SILVER AWARD**
Gunwalloe, Helston, Falmouth
TR12 7QG
t (01326) 561282
e ian.mandy.turner@virgin.net

## GWEEK
### Cornwall

**Little Australia ★★★★**
*Guest Accommodation*
Nr Gweek, Helston, Falmouth
TR12 6BG
t (01326) 221245
e wrightlittleoz@hotmail.com
w littleaustraliafarm.co.uk

## HALBERTON
### Devon

**The Priory**
Rating Applied For
*Guest Accommodation*
11 High Street, Halberton,
Tiverton EX16 7AF
t (01884) 821234
e dawn.riggs@threads-of-
time.co.uk

## HALSE
### Somerset

**Rock House ★★★★**
*Bed & Breakfast*
**SILVER AWARD**
Main Road, Nr Taunton
TA4 3AF
t (01823) 432956
e dwolverson@
rockhousesomerset.co.uk
w rockhousesomerset.co.uk

## HALSTOCK
### Dorset

**Quiet Woman House**
Rating Applied For
*Bed & Breakfast*
Halstock, Yeovil BA22 9RX
t (01935) 891218
e paulandlisapovey@
btinternet.com.
w quietwomanhouse.co.uk

## HALWELL
### Devon

**The Old Inn ★★★★** *Inn*
Halwell, Totnes TQ9 7JA
t (01803) 712329

**Orchard House ★★★★★**
*Bed & Breakfast*
**SILVER AWARD**
Horner, Hallwell, Totnes
TQ9 7LB
t (01548) 821448
w orchard-house-halwell.co.uk

## HAMBROOK
### Gloucestershire

**The Coach House ★★★**
*Guest Accommodation*
Bristol Road, Hambrook, Bristol
BS16 1RY
t (0117) 956 6901
e info@bristolcoachhouse.co.
uk
w bristolcoachhouse.co.uk

## HAMWORTHY
### Dorset

**Holes Bay B&B ★★**
*Bed & Breakfast*
365 Blandford Road, Poole
BH15 4JL
t (01202) 672069
e maggie.dixon1@ntlworld.
com

**Jessimine B&B ★★★**
*Bed & Breakfast*
77 Lake Road, Hamworthy,
Poole BH15 4LF
t (01202) 257726
e anita.saville@ntlworld.com

**Sarnia Cherie ★★★★**
*Bed & Breakfast*
375 Blandford Road,
Hamworthy, Poole BH15 4JL
t (01202) 679470
e criscollier@aol.com
w sarniacherie.co.uk

**Seashells ★★★**
*Bed & Breakfast*
4 Lake Road, Poole BH15 4LH
t (01202) 671921
e chris.tony@ntlworld.com
w 4seashells.co.uk

## HARBERTONFORD
### Devon

**Pound Court Cottage
★★★★**
*Guest Accommodation*
Old Road, Harbertonford,
Totnes TQ9 7TA
t (01803) 732441
e poundcourtcottage@tiscali.
co.uk
w poundcourtcottage.co.uk

## HARLYN BAY
### Cornwall

**The Harlyn Inn ★★★** *Inn*
Harlyn Bay, Padstow PL28 8SB
t (01841) 520207
e mail@harlyn-inn.com
w harlyn-inn.com

## HARTLAND
### Devon

**Elmscott Farm ★★★★**
*Farmhouse*
Hartland, Bideford EX39 6ES
t (01237) 441276

**Gawlish Farm ★★★★**
*Farmhouse*
Hartland, Bideford EX39 6AT
t (01237) 441320

**Golden Park ★★★★★**
*Bed & Breakfast*
**GOLD AWARD**
Hartland, Bideford EX39 6EP
t (01237) 441254
e lynda@goldenpark.co.uk
w goldenpark.co.uk

**Trutrese ★★★**
*Guest Accommodation*
Harton Cross, Hartland,
Bideford EX39 6AE
t (01237) 441274

## HATHERLEIGH
### Devon

**Thomas Roberts House
★★★★** *Bed & Breakfast*
2 Higher Street, Okehampton
EX20 3JD
t (01837) 811278
e relax@thomasrobertshouse.
com
w thomasrobertshouse.com

## HELSTON
### Cornwall

**Jentone ★★★★**
*Guest Accommodation*
Carnkie, Helston, Falmouth
TR13 0DZ
t (01209) 860883
e johns@jentone.net
w jentone.net

**Little Pengwedna Farm
★★★★** *Farmhouse*
Nancegollan, Helston,
Falmouth TR13 0AY
t (01736) 850649
e ray@good-holidays.co.uk
w good-holidays.co.uk

**Lyndale Cottage Guest
House ★★★★** *Guest House*
4 Greenbank, Meneage Road,
Helston TR13 8JA
t (01326) 561082
e enquiries@lyndalecottage.
co.uk
w lyndalecottage.co.uk

**Mandeley Guesthouse ★★★**
*Guest House*
Clodgey Lane, Helston
TR13 8PJ
t (01326) 572550
e mandeley@btconnect.com
w mandeley.co.uk

**Strathallan Guest House
★★★★**
*Guest Accommodation*
6 Monument Road, Helston,
Falmouth TR13 8HF
t (01326) 573683
e strathallangh@aol.com
w connexions.co.uk/strathallan

**Tregathenan House ★★★★**
*Bed & Breakfast*
The Old Farmhouse,
Tregathenan, Helston
TR13 0RZ
t (01326) 569840
e tregathenan@hotmail.com
w tregathenan.co.uk

## HEMYOCK
### Devon

**Pounds Farm ★★★★**
*Farmhouse*
Hemyock EX15 3QS
t (01823) 680802
e shillingscottage@yahoo.co.
uk
w poundsfarm.co.uk

## HENLADE
### Somerset

**Barn Close Nurseries ★★★**
*Guest Accommodation*
Stoke Road, Nr Taunton
TA3 5DH
t (01823) 443507
e jujuat66@hotmail.co.uk

## HEXWORTHY
### Devon

**The Forest Inn ★★★** *Inn*
Hexworthy, Dartmoor,
Yelverton PL20 6SD
t (01364) 631211
e info@theforestinn.co.uk
w theforestinn.co.uk

## HEYTESBURY
### Wiltshire

**The Red Lion ★★★★**
*Guest Accommodation*
42a High Street, Heytesbury
BA12 0EA
t (01985) 840315
e donna.pease@btinternet.
com

**The Resting Post ★★★★**
*Bed & Breakfast*
High Street, Heytesbury,
Warminster BA12 0ED
t (01985) 840204
e enquiries@therestingpost.
co.uk
w therestingpost.co.uk

## HEYWOOD
### Wiltshire

**Redwood Lodge ★★★★**
*Guest Accommodation*
Capps Lane, Westbury
BA13 4NE
t (01373) 823949
w redwoodlodgeuk.com

## HIGH PENN
### Wiltshire

**High Penn House ★★★★**
*Bed & Breakfast*
High Penn Coach House, Calne
SN11 8RU
t (01249) 816458
e mandyha@btinternet.com

## HIGHBRIDGE
### Somerset

**46 Church Street ★★★**
*Bed & Breakfast*
Highbridge TA9 3AQ
t (01278) 788365

## HIGHCLIFFE
### Dorset

**10 Brook Way ★★**
*Bed & Breakfast*
Fiars Cliff, Christchurch
BH23 4HA
t (01425) 276738
e midgefinn@hotmail.com

**The Beech Tree**
Rating Applied For
*Guest Accommodation*
2 Stuart Road, Highcliffe,
Christchurch BH23 5JS
t (01425) 272038

**Beechcroft Place ★★★★**
*Bed & Breakfast*
**SILVER AWARD**
106 Lymington Road,
Highcliffe, Christchurch
BH23 4JX
t (01425) 277171
e info@beachmeetsforest.co.
uk
w beachmeetsforest.co.uk

**Castle Lodge** ★★★★
*Guest House*
173 Lymington Road,
Highcliffe, Christchurch
BH23 4JS
t (01425) 275170
e sharon@castlelodge-
highcliffe.co.uk
w castlelodge-highcliffe.co.uk

### HILLERSLAND
Gloucestershire

**Ivydene** ★★★
*Bed & Breakfast*
Ready Penny, Hillersland,
Coleford GL16 7NX
t (01594) 834994
e ivydenebandb@btinternet.
com

**The Rock** ★★★★
*Guest Accommodation*
Hillersland, Coleford GL16 7NY
t (01594) 837893
e dinahbarrand@hotmail.com
w stayattherock.com

### HILMARTON
Wiltshire

**Burfoots** ★★★★
*Bed & Breakfast*
1 The Close, Hilmarton, Calne
SN11 8TH
t (01249) 760492
e info@burfoots.co.uk
w burfoots.co.uk

### HOLBETON
Devon

**Bugle Rocks** ★★★★
*Bed & Breakfast*
Battisborough Cross, Plymouth
PL8 1JX
t (01752) 830422
e stay@buglerocks.co.uk
w buglerocks.co.uk

### HOLCOMBE
Devon

**Manor Farm** ★★★★
*Farmhouse*
Holcombe Village, Holcombe,
Dawlish EX7 0JT
t (01626) 863020
e humphreyclem@aol.com
w farmaccom.com

### HOLMEBRIDGE
Dorset

**Holmebridge House** ★★★
*Bed & Breakfast*
Wareham BH20 6AF
t (01929) 550599
e holmebridge@googlemail.
com
w holmebridgehouse.co.uk

### HOLSWORTHY
Devon

**Bason Farm** ★★★★
*Farmhouse*
Bradford, Holsworthy
EX22 7AW
t (01409) 281277
e info@basonfarmholidays.co.
uk
w basonfarmholidays.co.uk

### HONITON
Devon

**Barn Park Farm** ★★★★
*Farmhouse*
Stockland Hill, Nr Stockland,
Honiton EX14 9JA
t 0800 328 2605
e pab@barnparkfarm.fsnet.co.
uk
w lymeregisholiday.co.uk

**Claypits Farm** ★★★★
*Guest House*
Rawridge, Honiton EX14 9QP
t (01404) 861384
e heather.lockyer@
claypitsfarm.co.uk
w claypitsfarm.co.uk

**The Cottage** ★★★★
*Guest Accommodation*
Marsh, Honiton EX14 9AJ
t (01460) 234240
e buttonstephens@
btopenworld.com
w cattagemarsh.co.uk

**Wessington Farm** ★★★★
*Guest Accommodation*
SILVER AWARD
Awliscombe, Honiton
EX14 3NU
t (01404) 42280
e bandb@lre9.com
w eastdevon.com/
bedandbreakfast

### HOPE COVE
Devon

**The Cottage** ★★★
*Guest Accommodation*
Hope Cove, Salcombe TQ7 3HJ
t (01548) 561555
e info@hopecove.com
w hopecove.com

**Sand Pebbles** ★★★★
*Guest Accommodation*
Hope Cove, Kingsbridge
TQ7 3HF
t (01548) 561673
e andrew@sandpebbles.fsnet.
co.uk
w sandpebbleshotel.co.uk

### HORSINGTON
Somerset

**Half Moon Inn** ★★★ *Inn*
Off Higher Road, Nr
Templecombe BA8 0EF
t (01963) 370140
e halfmoon@horsington.co.uk
w horsington.co.uk

### HORTON
Wiltshire

**Partacre** ★★ *Bed & Breakfast*
Horton, Devizes SN10 3NB
t (01380) 860261

### HUCCLECOTE
Gloucestershire

**Notley House and The
Coach House** ★★★
*Guest Accommodation*
93 Hucclecote Road,
Gloucester GL3 3TR
t (01452) 611584
e notleyhouse@blueyonder.
co.uk
w notleyhouse.co.uk

### HULLAVINGTON
Wiltshire

**Serendipity Bed and
Breakfast** ★★★★
*Bed & Breakfast*
15 The Street, Hullavington,
Chippenham SN14 6EF
t (01666) 837661
e alison.reed@
serendipitybedandbreakfast.co.
uk

### HUNTLEY
Gloucestershire

**Birdwood Villa Farm** ★★★
*Farmhouse*
Main Road, Birdwood,
Gloucester GL19 3EQ
t (01452) 750451
e birdwood.villafarm@virgin.
net
w birdwoodvillafarm.co.uk

**Kings Head Inn** ★★★ *Inn*
Birdwood, Gloucester
GL19 3EF
t (01452) 750348
e enquiries@
kingsheadbirdwood.co.uk
w kingsheadbirdwood.co.uk

### HURN
Dorset

**Avon Causeway Inn** ★★★★
*Inn*
Hurn, Christchurch BH23 6AS
t (01202) 482714
e avoncauseway@wadworth.
co.uk
w avoncauseway.co.uk

### IDDESLEIGH
Devon

**Parsonage Farm** ★★★★
*Farmhouse* SILVER AWARD
Iddesleigh, Winkleigh
EX19 8SN
t (01837) 810318
e roseward01@yahoo.co.uk

### IDE
Devon

**Drakes Farm House** ★★★
*Bed & Breakfast*
Drakes Farm, Exeter EX2 9RL
t (01392) 256814
e drakesfarm@hotmail.com
w drakesfarm-devon.co.uk

### ILFRACOMBE
Devon

**Burnside** ★★★★
*Bed & Breakfast*
34 St Brannocks Road,
Ilfracombe EX34 8EQ
t (01271) 863097
e san-dave@meekb.freeserve.
co.uk

**Cairn House** ★★★
*Guest Accommodation*
43 St Brannocks Road,
Ilfracombe EX34 8EH
t (01271) 863911
e info@cairnhousehotel.co.uk
w cairnhousehotel.co.uk

**Capstone Restaurant (Guest
Accommodation)** ★★
*Guest Accommodation*
St James Place, Ilfracombe
EX34 9BJ
t (01271) 863540
e steve@capstone.freeserve.
co.uk
w ilfracombe2000.freeserve.
co.uk

**Combe Lodge Hotel** ★★★
*Guest House*
Chambercombe Park Road,
Ilfracombe EX34 9QW
t (01271) 864518
e combelodgehotel@
tinyworld.co.uk

**Dorchester Guest House**
★★★★ *Guest House*
59 St Brannocks Road,
Ilfracombe EX34 8EQ
t (01271) 866949
e edwardsrl@tinyworld.co.uk
w the-dorchester.co.uk

**Lyncott House** ★★★★
*Guest Accommodation*
56 St Brannocks Road,
Ilfracombe EX34 8EQ
t (01271) 862425
w lyncotthouse.co.uk

**Mullacott** *Camping Barn*
Mullacott Farm, Mullacott
Cross, Ilfracombe EX34 8NA
t (01271) 866877
e relax@mullacottfarm.co.uk
w mullacottfarm.co.uk

**Varley House** ★★★★
*Guest Accommodation*
Chambercombe Park,
Ilfracombe EX34 9QW
t (01271) 863927
e info@varleyhouse.co.uk
w varleyhouse.co.uk

**Wellbeing** ★★★★
*Guest Accommodation*
SILVER AWARD
Torrs Park, Ilfracombe
EX34 8AZ
t (01271) 863663
e info@wellbeingbandb.co.uk
w wellbeingbandb.com

**Westaway** ★★★★★
*Guest Accommodation*
SILVER AWARD
Torrs Park, Ilfracombe
EX34 8AY
t (01271) 864459
e mail@westawayhotel.co.uk
w westawayhotel.co.uk

**The Woodlands** ★★★
*Guest Accommodation*
Torrs Park, Ilfracombe
EX34 8AZ
t (01271) 863098
e info@woodlandsdevon.com
w woodlandsdevon.com

### ILLOGAN
Cornwall

**Portreath Camping Barn**
*Bunkhouse*
Nance Farm, Illogan, Redruth
TR16 4QX
t (01629) 592682

### ILLOGAN HIGHWAY
Cornwall

**Lyndhurst Guest House**
★★★ *Guest House*
80 Agar Road, Redruth
TR15 3NB
t (01209) 215146
e sales@lyndhurst-
guesthouse.net
w lyndhurst-guesthouse.net

---

Establishments in bold have a detailed entry in this guide – use the property index to find the page numbers

## ILMINSTER
### Somerset

**Dillington House ★★★★★**
*Campus*
Off Bay Hill, Ilminster
TA19 9DT
t (01460) 52427
e ccrocker@somerset.gov.uk
w dillington.com

**Graden ★★★**
*Bed & Breakfast*
Peasmarsh, Ilminster TA19 0SG
t (01460) 52371

## ISLES OF SCILLY
### Isles of Scilly

**Browarth ★★★**
*Bed & Breakfast*
Rams Valley, St Mary's
TR21 0JX
t (01720) 422353

**Covean Cottage ★★★**
*Guest House*
St Agnes TR22 0PL
t (01720) 422620
e coveancottage@fsmail.net

**Demelza Bed & Breakfast**
Rating Applied For
*Bed & Breakfast*
Demelza, Jackson's Hill, St
Marys TR21 0JZ
t (01720) 422803
e sibleysonscilly@tiscali.co.uk

**Nornour ★★★**
*Bed & Breakfast*
Mount Flagon, St Mary's
TR21 0NE
t (01720) 423901
e mjsenior26@hotmail.com
w nornourbandb.co.uk

**Nundeeps ★★★**
*Bed & Breakfast*
Rams Valley, St Mary's
TR21 0JX
t (01720) 422517
e cook@nundeeps.freeserve.
co.uk

**The Old Town Inn ★★★** *Inn*
Old Town, St Mary's
TR21 0NN
t (01720) 422301

**Pelistry Cottage ★★★★**
*Bed & Breakfast*
The Parade, St Marys TR21 0LP
t (01720) 422506
e scillyhols@hotmail.com
w scillyholidays.com

**Polreath Guest House**
**★★★★** *Bed & Breakfast*
Higher Town TR25 0QL
t (01720) 422046
e s.poat@ntlworld.com
w polreath.com

## IVYBRIDGE
### Devon

**Higher Coarsewell Farm**
**★★★★** *Bed & Breakfast*
Ugborough, Ivybridge
PL21 0HP
t (01548) 821560
e sue@highercoarsewellfarm.
co.uk
w highercoarsewellfarm.co.uk

**Hillhead Farm ★★★★**
*Farmhouse* **SILVER AWARD**
Ugborough, Ivybridge
PL21 0HQ
t (01752) 892674
e info@hillhead-farm.co.uk
w hillhead-farm.co.uk

**Venn Farm ★★★** *Farmhouse*
Ugborough, Ivybridge
PL21 0PE
t (01364) 73240
w smoothhound.co.uk/hotels/
vennfarm

## JACOBSTOW
### Cornwall

**Broad Langdon B&B ★★★★**
*Guest Accommodation*
**SILVER AWARD**
Jacobstow, Bude EX23 0BZ
t (01566) 781656
e johnnjo@btinternet.com
w broadlangdon.co.uk

## KEMBLE
### Gloucestershire

**Willows ★★** *Bed & Breakfast*
2 Glebe Lane, Kemble,
Cirencester GL7 6BD
t (01285) 770667
w willowskemble.co.uk

## KEMPLEY
### Gloucestershire

**The Granary ★★★★**
*Farmhouse*
Lower House Farm, Kempley,
Dymock GL18 2BS
t (01531) 890301

## KEYBRIDGE
### Cornwall

**Robin's Nest ★★★★**
*Bed & Breakfast*
Riverdale, Keybridge, Bodmin
PL30 4QL
t (01208) 851390
e john.gerring@telco4u.net
w riverdale.me.uk

## KILCOT
### Gloucestershire

**Withyland Heights ★★★★**
*Farmhouse*
Beavans Hill, Kilcot, Newent
GL18 1PG
t (01989) 720582

## KILKHAMPTON
### Cornwall

**Heatham Farmhouse**
**★★★★** *Farmhouse*
**SILVER AWARD**
Kilkhampton, Bude EX23 9RH
t (01288) 321325
e heathamfarm@btconnect.
com
w heathamfarm.co.uk

## KILVE
### Somerset

**The Old Mill ★★★★**
*Bed & Breakfast*
A39, Nr Williton TA5 1EB
t (01278) 741571

## KILWORTHY
### Devon

**Kilworthy Farm B&B ★★★**
*Farmhouse*
Kilworthy, Tavistock PL19 0JN
t (01822) 614477
e sandra@kilworthy.co.uk

## KIMMERIDGE
### Dorset

**Chaldecotts ★★★**
*Farmhouse*
Swalland Farm, Kimmeridge,
Wareham BH20 5PD
t (01929) 480936
w chaldecotts.co.uk

**Kimmeridge Farmhouse**
**★★★★** *Farmhouse*
**GOLD AWARD**
Kimmeridge, Wareham
BH20 5PE
t (01929) 480990
e kimmeridgefarmhouse@
hotmail.com
w kimmeridgefarmhouse.co.uk

## KINGSBRIDGE
### Devon

**Ashleigh House ★★★**
*Guest Accommodation*
Ashleigh Road, Kingsbridge
TQ7 1HB
t (01548) 852893
e reception@ashleigh-house.
co.uk
w ashleigh-house.co.uk

**Globe Inn ♦♦**
*Guest Accommodation*
Frogmore, Kingsbridge
TQ7 2NR
t (01548) 531351
e enquiries@theglobeinn.co.
uk
w theglobeinn.co.uk

**Mountain Water Experience**
**★★** *Group Hostel*
Courtlands, Kingsbridge
TQ7 4BN
t (01548) 550675
e mwe@mountainwaterexp.
demon.co.uk
w mountainwaterexperience.
com

**Shute Farm ★★★**
*Guest Accommodation*
South Milton, Kingsbridge
TQ7 3JL
t (01548) 560680
e luscombe@shutefarm.fsnet.
co.uk
w shutefarm.co.uk

**South Allington House**
**★★★★**
*Guest Accommodation*
South Allington, Chivelstone,
Kingsbridge TQ7 2NB
t (01548) 511272
e barbara@sthallingtonbnb.
demon.co.uk
w sthallingtonbnb.demon.co.
uk

## KINGSKERSWELL
### Devon

**Harewood Guesthouse**
**★★★** *Guest House*
17 Torquay Road,
Kingskerswell, Newton Abbot
TQ12 5HH
t (01803) 872228
e correneandbill1@
blueyonder.co.uk

**Rock House Bed & Breakfast**
**★★★★★** *Bed & Breakfast*
Maddacombe Road,
Kingskerswell, Newton Abbot
TQ12 5LF
t (01803) 404990
e alison.rockhouse@
blueyonder.co.uk
w rockhouse-cottage.co.uk

## KINGSTON ST MARY
### Somerset

**Fulford Grange ★★★★★**
*Bed & Breakfast*
**SILVER AWARD**
Kingston Road, Nr Taunton
TA2 8AJ
t (01823) 451206
e enquiries@fulfordgrange.co.
uk
w fulfordgrange.co.uk

## KINGTON LANGLEY
### Wiltshire

**The Moors ★★★**
*Bed & Breakfast*
Malmesbury Road, Kington
Langley, Chippenham
SN14 6HT
t (01249) 750288
e carolinetayler@hotmail.com

## KINGTON ST MICHAEL
### Wiltshire

**Arch House ★★★★**
*Bed & Breakfast*
Manor Court, Kington St
Michael SN14 6JA
t (01249) 758377
e christine@jago9440.fsnet.co.
uk
w archhousebandb.co.uk

## KNOWSTONE
### Devon

**West Bowden Farm ★★★★**
*Farmhouse*
Knowstone, South Molton
EX36 4RP
t (01398) 341224
e west.bowden@ukf.net
w westbowden.ukf.net

## LACOCK
### Wiltshire

**King John's Hunting Lodge**
**★★★★** *Bed & Breakfast*
**SILVER AWARD**
21 Church Street, Lacock,
Chippenham SN15 2LB
t (01249) 730313
e kingjohns@amserve.com

**Lacock Pottery Bed &**
**Breakfast ★★★★**
*Bed & Breakfast*
1 The Tanyard, Church Street,
Chippenham SN15 2LB
t (01249) 730266
e simonemcdowell@
lacockbedandbreakfast.com
w lacockbedandbreakfast.com

**The Old Rectory ★★★★**
*Guest Accommodation*
Cantax Hill, Lacock,
Chippenham SN15 2JZ
t (01249) 730335
e sexton@oldrectorylacock.co.
uk
w oldrectorylacock.co.uk

**Pen-Y-Brook House ★★★**
*Bed & Breakfast*
Notton, Lacock, Chippenham
SN15 2NF
t (01249) 730376

### LANDFORD
#### Wiltshire

**Planners Folly** ★★★
*Guest House*
Lyndhurst Road, Landford,
Salisbury SP5 2AF
t  (01794) 390210
e  lorddigweed@aol.com
w  plannersfolly.co.uk

### LANDKEY
#### Devon

**Downrew House** ★★★
*Guest Accommodation*
Bishops Tawton, Barnstaple
EX32 0DY
t  (01271) 342497
e  downrew@globalnet.co.uk
w  downrew.co.uk

### LANDRAKE
#### Cornwall

**Lantallack Farm** ★★★★★
*Bed & Breakfast*
**GOLD AWARD**
Landrake, Saltash PL12 5AE
t  (01752) 851281
e  enquiries@lantallack.co.uk
w  lantallack.co.uk

### LANEAST
#### Cornwall

**Stitch Park** ★★★★
*Bed & Breakfast*
**SILVER AWARD**
Laneast, Launceston PL15 8PN
t  (01566) 86687
e  stitchpark@hotmail.com

### LANESCOT
#### Cornwall

**Great Pelean Farm** ★★★★
*Farmhouse* **SILVER AWARD**
Tywardreath, Par PL24 2RX
t  (01726) 812106
e  andyjones74@hotmail.com
w  greatpeleanfarm.com

### LANGFORD BUDVILLE
#### Somerset

**The Martlet Inn** ★★★★ *Inn*
Main Road, Nr Wellington
TA21 0QZ
t  (01823) 400262
e  enquiries@martletinn.co.uk
w  martletinn.co.uk

### LANGPORT
#### Somerset

**Amberley** ★★★
*Guest Accommodation*
Martock Road, Nr Langport
TA10 9LD
t  (01458) 241542
e  jean.atamberley@talk21.com

**Muchelney Ham Farm**
★★★★ *Farmhouse*
**SILVER AWARD**
Muchelney Ham, Nr Langport
TA10 0DJ
t  (01458) 250737
w  muchelneyhamfarm.co.uk

**The Old Pound Inn** ★★★ *Inn*
High Street, Nr Langport
TA10 0RA
t  (01458) 250469

**Orchard Barn** ★★★★
*Bed & Breakfast*
Law Lane, Drayton, Langport
TA10 0LS
t  (01458) 252310
e  orchardbarn@zoom.co.uk
w  orchard-barn.com

### LANHYDROCK
#### Cornwall

**Treffry Farmhouse** ★★★
*Bed & Breakfast*
Treffry Lane, Lanhydrock,
Bodmin PL30 5AF
t  (01208) 77982
e  cashmorewendy@hotmail.
com
w  treffry.biz

### LANIVET
#### Cornwall

**St Benets Abbey** ★★★★
*Guest Accommodation*
Truro Road, Lanivet, Truro
PL30 5HF
t  (01208) 831352
e  stbenetsabbey@btconnect.
com
w  stbenetsabbey.com

**Willowbrook** ★★★★
*Guest Accommodation*
Lamorick, Lanivet, Bodmin
PL30 5HB
t  (01208) 831670
e  willowbrookbandb@aol.com
w  welcomingyou.co.uk/
willowbrook

### LANLIVERY
#### Cornwall

**Millbeam Farmhouse**
Rating Applied For
*Farmhouse*
Lanlivery, Bodmin PL30 5BZ
t  (01208) 873454
e  jo@worth11.fsnet.co.uk

### LANREATH-BY-LOOE
#### Cornwall

**Bocaddon Farm** ★★★★
*Bed & Breakfast*
Looe PL13 2PG
t  (01503) 220192
e  holidays@bocaddon.com
w  bocaddon.com

### LANSALLOS
#### Cornwall

**Lesquite Farm** ★★★★
*Farmhouse* **SILVER AWARD**
Peaswater, Lansallos, Looe
PL13 2QE
t  (01503) 220315
e  tolputt@lesquitepolperro.
fsnet.co.uk
w  lesquite-polperro.fsnet.co.uk

**West Kellow Farm** ★★★★
*Farmhouse*
Lansallos, Looe PL13 2QL
t  (01503) 272089
e  westkellow@aol.com
w  westkellow.co.uk

### LANSDOWN
#### Somerset

**The Blathwayt** ★★★★ *Inn*
Lansdown, Bath BA1 9BT
t  (01225) 421995
e  info@theblathwayt-bath.co.
uk
w  theblathwayt-bath.co.uk

### LANTEGLOS
#### Cornwall

**Trehaida** ★★★★ *Farmhouse*
Whitecross, Fowey PL23 1NF
t  (01726) 870880
e  trehaida@btopenworld.com
w  trehaida.co.uk

🖼️ ✏️

### LAUNCESTON
#### Cornwall

**Berrio Bridge House** ★★★★
*Bed & Breakfast*
North Hill, Launceston
PL15 7NL
t  (01566) 782714
e  helen@berriobridge.
freeserve.co.uk

**Glencoe Villa** ★★★
*Guest Accommodation*
13 Race Hill, Launceston
PL15 9BB
t  (01566) 775819

**Lynher Farmhouse** ★★★
*Bed & Breakfast*
Lynher Farm, North Hill,
Launceston PL15 7NR
t  (01566) 782273
e  pam@lynherfarm.fsnet.co.uk
w  lynherfarm.co.uk

**Middle Tremollett** ★★★★
*Farmhouse*
Coads Green, Launceston
PL15 7NA
t  (01566) 782416
e  btrewin@btinternet.com
w  tremollett.com

**Oakside** ★★★★
*Bed & Breakfast*
South Petherwin, Launceston
PL15 7JL
t  (01566) 86733
e  janet.crossman@tesco.net

**Primrose Cottage** ★★★★★
*Bed & Breakfast*
**SILVER AWARD**
Lawhitton, Launceston
PL15 9PE
t  (01566) 773645
e  enquiry@
primrosecottagesuites.co.uk
w  primrosecottagesuites.co.uk

**Thornbank Bed and
Breakfast** ★★★
*Guest Accommodation*
6 Highfield Park Road,
Launceston PL15 7DY
t  (01566) 776136
e  bkressinger@btopenworld.
com
w  thornbank.plus.com

**Tregood Farm** ★★★
*Bed & Breakfast*
Congdon's Shop, Launceston
PL15 7PN
t  (01566) 782263 &
07976 239893

**Trekenner Court** ★★★★
*Bed & Breakfast*
Pipers Pool, Nr Bodmin Moor,
Launceston PL15 8QG
t  (01566) 880118
e  trekennercourt@hotmail.co.
uk
w  trekennercourt.co.uk

**Trevadlock Farm** ★★★★★
*Farmhouse* **SILVER AWARD**
Congdon Shop, Launceston
PL15 7PW
t  (01566) 782239
e  trevadlock@farming.co.uk
w  trevadlock.co.uk

### Wheatley Farm ★★★★★
*Farmhouse* **GOLD AWARD**
Maxworthy, Launceston
PL15 8LY
t  (01566) 781232
e  valerie@wheatley-farm.co.
uk
w  wheatley-farm.co.uk

### LAVERSTOCK
#### Wiltshire

**1 Riverside Close**
Rating Applied For
*Bed & Breakfast*
Riverside Close, Laverstock,
Salisbury SP1 1QW
t  (01722) 320287
e  marytucker2001@yahoo.
com

**20 Potters Way** ★★★
*Bed & Breakfast*
Potters Way, Laverstock,
Salisbury SP1 1PY
t  (01722) 335031

### LECHLADE-ON-THAMES
#### Gloucestershire

**Cambrai Lodge** ★★★★
*Guest Accommodation*
Oak Street, Lechlade,
Lechlade-on-Thames GL7 3AY
t  (01367) 253173
e  cambrailodge@btconnect.
com
w  cambrailodgeguesthouse.co.
uk

**New Inn Hotel** ★★★ *Inn*
Market Square, Lechlade-on-
Thames GL7 3AB
t  (01367) 252296
e  info@newinnhotel.co.uk
w  newinnhotel.co.uk

### LEEDSTOWN
#### Cornwall

**Little Pengelly** ★★★★
*Guest Accommodation*
**SILVER AWARD**
Trenwheal, Leedstown, Hayle
TR27 6BP
t  (01736) 850452

### LEIGHTON
#### Somerset

**Broadgrove House** ★★★★
*Bed & Breakfast*
Leighton, Frome BA11 4PP
t  (01373) 836296
e  broadgrove836@tiscali.co.uk

### LELANT
#### Cornwall

**Hindon Hall** ★★★★★
*Guest Accommodation*
**SILVER AWARD**
Lelant, St Ives TR26 3EN
t  (01736) 753046
e  enquiries@hindonhall.co.uk

### LISKEARD
#### Cornwall

**Hyvue House** ★★★
*Bed & Breakfast*
Endsleigh Terrace, Liskeard
PL14 6BN
t  (01579) 348175

**Lampen Farm** ★★★★
*Farmhouse*
St Neot, Liskeard PL14 6PB
t  (01579) 320284
e  joan@lampenfarm.fsnet.co.
uk
w  lampen-farm.co.uk

**Nebula Hotel** ★★★
*Guest House*
27 Higher Lux Street, Liskeard
PL14 3JU
t (01579) 343989
e info@nebula-hotel.com
w nebula-hotel.com

**Trecorme Barton** ★★★★
*Farmhouse*
Quethiock, Liskeard PL14 3SH
t (01579) 342646
e renfree@trecormebarton.
fsnet.co.uk
w trecormebarton.co.uk

**Tregondale Farm** ★★★★
*Farmhouse* SILVER AWARD
Menheniot, Liskeard PL14 3RG
t (01579) 342407
e tregondalefarm@btconnect.
com
w tregondalefarm.co.uk

**Trewint Farm** ★★★★
*Farmhouse* SILVER AWARD
Menheniot, Liskeard PL14 3RG
t (01579) 347155
e holidays@trewintfarn.co.uk
w trewintfarm.co.uk

LITTLE LANGFORD
Wiltshire

**Little Langford Farmhouse** ★★★★★ *Farmhouse*
GOLD AWARD
Little Langford, Salisbury
SP3 4NP
t (01722) 790205
e bandb@littlelangford.co.uk
w littlelangford.co.uk

LITTLEHEMPSTON
Devon

**Post Cottage** ★★★
*Guest Accommodation*
Littlehempston, Totnes
TQ9 6LU
t (01803) 868192
e hjgf@onetel.com
w postcottage.co.uk

LITTON CHENEY
Dorset

**Litton Cheney YHA** ★★★
*Hostel*
Litton Cheney, Dorchester
DT2 9AT
t (01308) 482340

🏠🅿️

LIZARD
Cornwall

**Atlantic House** ★★★★★
*Guest Accommodation*
SILVER AWARD
Pentreath Lane, The Lizard,
Helston TR12 7NY
t (01326) 290399
e jayne@atlantichouselizard.
co.uk
w atlantichouselizard.co.uk

**Lizard Point Youth Hostel** ★★★★ *Hostel*
Yha Lizard, Helston TR12 7NT
t 0870 770 6120

🅿️🏠🅿️

**The Top House Inn**
Rating Applied For
*Inn*
The Top House, Helston
TR12 7NQ
t (01326) 290974
w thetophouselizard.co.uk

**Trethvas Farmhouse** ★★★★
*Farmhouse*
Lizard Village, Helston,
Falmouth TR12 7AR
t (01326) 290720
e trethvasfarm@amserve.com

LONGBOROUGH
Gloucestershire

**Luckley Holidays** ★★★
*Farmhouse*
Longborough, Moreton-in-
Marsh GL56 0RD
t (01451) 870885
e info@luckley-holidays.co.uk
w luckley-holidays.co.uk

LONGBURTON
Dorset

**Manor Farm House** ★★★★
*Guest Accommodation*
Longburton, Sherborne
DT9 5PG
t (01963) 210457
e dann.bunnage@btinternet.
com
w manorfarmhouse.net

LONGHOPE
Gloucestershire

**The Farmers Boy Inn** ★★★
*Inn*
Ross Road, Longhope
GL17 0LP
t (01452) 831300
e info@thefarmersboyinn.co.
uk
w thefarmersboyinn.co.uk

LOOE
Cornwall

**Bucklawren Farm** ★★★★
*Farmhouse* SILVER AWARD
St Martin, Looe PL13 1NZ
t (01503) 240738
e bucklawren@btopenworld.
com
w bucklawren.com

**Coombe Farm** ★★★★
*Guest House*
Widegates, Looe PL13 1QN
t (01503) 240223
e coombe_farm@hotmail.com
w coombefarmhotel.co.uk

**The Deganwy** ★★★★
*Guest House*
Station Road, East Looe, Looe
PL13 1HL
t (01503) 262984
e enquiries@deganwyhotel.
co.uk
w deganwyhotel.co.uk

**Dolphin Guest House** ★★★
*Guest House*
Station Road, East Looe, Looe
PL13 1HL
t (01503) 262578
e dolphinhouse@btconnect.
com
w dolphin-house.co.uk

**Dovers House** ★★★★
*Guest House* SILVER AWARD
St Martins Road, St Martin,
Looe PL13 1PB
t (01503) 265468
e twhyte@btconnect.com
w dovershouse.co.uk

**Driftwood** ★★★★
*Bed & Breakfast*
Portuan Road, Hannafore, Looe
PL13 2ND
t (01503) 262990
e picko@westlooe.fsnet.co.uk

**Haven House** ★★★
*Guest Accommodation*
Barbican Hill, East Looe, Looe
PL13 1BQ
t (01503) 264160
e enquiries@visitlooe.co.uk
w visitlooe.co.uk

**The Hill House** ★★★★
*Guest House*
St Martins Road, Looe
PL13 1LP
t (01503) 262556
e thehillhouse@fsmail.net
w thehillhouse.webeden.co.uk

**Hillingdon** ★★★
*Guest House*
Portuan Road, Looe PL13 2DW
t (01503) 262906
e ann.mike@tinyonline.co.uk
w hillingdonguesthouse.co.uk

**Little Larnick Farm** ★★★★
*Farmhouse* SILVER AWARD
Pelynt, Looe PL13 2NB
t (01503) 262837
e littlelarnick@btclick.com
w littlelarnick.co.uk

**Schooner Point B&B** ★★★
*Guest House*
1 Trelawney Terrace, Polperro
Road, Looe PL13 2AG
t (01503) 262670
e enquiries@schoonerpoint.
co.uk
w schoonerpoint.co.uk

**Seaview** ★★★
*Bed & Breakfast*
Portuan Road, Looe PL13 2DW
t (01503) 265837
e sharon@seaviewlooe.
fsworld.co.uk
w seaview-looe.co.uk

**Trelren** ★★★ *Bed & Breakfast*
Polperro Road, Looe PL13 2JS
t (01503) 263918
e enquiries@trelren.co.uk
w trelren.co.uk

**Trevanion Hotel** ★★★
*Guest House*
Hannafore Road, Looe
PL13 2DE
t (01503) 262003
e hotel@looecornwall.co.uk
w looecornwall.co.uk

**The Watermark** ★★★★
*Guest House*
Hannafore Road, Looe
PL13 2DE
t (01503) 262123
e ash@looe.co.uk
w looe.co.uk

LOPCOMBE
Wiltshire

**Downs View Bed and Breakfast** ★★★
*Bed & Breakfast*
Stockbridge Road, Lopcombe
Corner, Salisbury SP5 1BW
t 07808 572671
w walkersatlopcombecorner@
btinternet.com

LOSTWITHIEL
Cornwall

**Tremont House** ★★★★
*Bed & Breakfast*
2 The Terrace, Lostwithiel
PL22 0DT
t (01208) 873055

LOWER GODNEY
Somerset

**Willow Bridge Farm's Country Guesthouse**
★★★★★ *Guest House*
SILVER AWARD
Tilleys Drove, Wells BA5 1RZ
t (01458) 835371
e julie@willowbridgefarm.co.
uk
w willowbridgefarm.co.uk

LOWER WRAXALL
Dorset

**Lower Wraxall Farmhouse**
★★★★ *Bed & Breakfast*
Lower Wraxall, Dorchester
DT2 0HL
t (01935) 83218
e judy-thompson@beeb.net

LYDBROOK
Gloucestershire

**Rocksdale Bed & Breakfast**
★★★★ *Bed & Breakfast*
Coppice Road, Lydbrook
GL17 9RJ
t 07930 395563 &
07930 395563

LYDFORD
Devon

**Lydford House** ★★★★
*Guest House*
Lydford, Okehampton
EX20 4AU
t (01822) 820347
e info@lydfordhouse.com
w lydfordhouse.com

LYDIARD TREGOZE
Wiltshire

**Park Farm** ★★★ *Farmhouse*
Hook Street, Lydiard Tregoze,
Swindon SN5 3NY
t (01793) 853608

LYDNEY
Gloucestershire

**Millingbrook Lodge** ★★★★
*Inn*
George Inn, High Street,
Aylburton, Lydney GL15 6DE
t (01594) 845522 &
(01594) 842163
e jackicollie@aol.com
w millingbrooklodge.com

LYME REGIS
Dorset

**Charnwood Guest House**
★★★★
*Guest Accommodation*
21 Woodmead Road, Lyme
Regis DT7 3AD
t (01297) 445281
e enquiries@
lymeregisaccommodation.com
w lymeregisaccommodation.
com

**Clappentail House** ★★★★★
*Bed & Breakfast*
GOLD AWARD
Uplyme Road, Lyme Regis
DT7 3LP
t (01297) 445739
e pountain@clappentail.
freeserve.co.uk

**Clovelly Guest House**
★★★★
Guest Accommodation
SILVER AWARD
View Road, Lyme Regis
DT7 3AA
t (01297) 444052
e clovelly@lymeregisbnb.com
w lymeregisbnb.com

**Devonia Guest House**
★★★★ Guest House
2 Woodmead Road, Lyme
Regis DT7 3AB
t (01297) 442869
e booking@devoniaguest.co.uk
w devoniaguest.co.uk

**Kersbrook Hotel** ★★★
Guest Accommodation
Pound Road, Lyme Regis
DT7 3HX
t (01297) 442596
e alex@kersbrook.co.uk
w kersbrook.co.uk

**The London** ★★★★
Guest Accommodation
40 Church Street, Lyme Regis
DT7 3DA
t (01297) 442083
e info@londonlymeregis.co.uk
w londonlymeregis.co.uk

**Lucerne** ★★★★
Guest Accommodation
View Road, Lyme Regis
DT7 3AA
t (01297) 443752
e lucerne@lineone.net

**Manaton** ★★★★
Guest Accommodation
Hill Road, Lyme Regis DT7 3PE
t (01297) 445138
e enquiries@manaton.net
w manaton.net

**Ocean View** ★★★★
Guest Accommodation
2 Hadleigh Villas, Silver Street,
Lyme Regis DT7 3HR
t (01297) 442567
e jaybabe@supanet.com
w lymeregis.com/ocean/view

**Old Lyme Guest House**
★★★★ Guest House
GOLD AWARD
29 Coombe Street, Lyme Regis
DT7 3PP
t (01297) 442929
e oldlyme.guesthouse@virgin.net
w oldlymeguesthouse.co.uk

**The Red House** ★★★★
Bed & Breakfast
Sidmouth Road, Lyme Regis
DT7 3ES
t (01297) 442055
e red.house@virgin.net
w smoothhound.co.uk/hotels/redhous2.html

**Rotherfield** ★★★★
Guest Accommodation
View Road, Lyme Regis
DT7 3AA
t (01297) 445585
e rotherfield@lymeregis.com
w rotherfieldguesthouse.com

**St Andrews House** ★★★★
Guest Accommodation
Uplyme Road, Lyme Regis
DT7 3LP
t (01297) 445495

**Southernhaye** ★★★
Bed & Breakfast
Pound Road, Lyme Regis
DT7 3HX
t (01297) 443077
w southernhaye.co.uk

**Springfield** ★★★★
Guest Accommodation
Woodmead Road, Lyme Regis
DT7 3LJ
t (01297) 443409
e springfield@lymeregis.com
w lymeregis.com/springfield

**Thatch** ★★★★
Bed & Breakfast
Uplyme Road, Lyme Regis
DT7 3LP
t (01297) 442212
e thatchbb@btinternet.com

**Brendon House** ★★★★
Guest House
Brendon, Exmoor, Lynton
EX35 6PS
t (01598) 741206
e brendonhouse4u@aol.com
w brendonhouse4u.com

**Coombe Farm** ★★★
Guest Accommodation
Countisbury, Lynton EX35 6NF
t (01598) 741236
e coombefarm@freeuk.com
w brendonvalley.co.uk/coombe_farm.htm

**The Heatherville Hotel**
★★★★★
Guest Accommodation
SILVER AWARD
3 Tors Park, Lynmouth
EX35 6NB
t (01598) 752327
w heatherville.co.uk

**The Village Inn** ★★★★ Inn
19 Lynmouth Street, Lynmouth
EX35 6EH
t (01598) 752354
e info@villageinnlynmouth.co.uk
w villageinnlynmouth.co.uk

**Croft House** ★★★★
Guest Accommodation
Lydiate Lane, Lynton EX35 6HE
t (01598) 752391
e relax@crofthotel.uk.com
w crofthotel.uk.com

**The Denes Guest House**
★★★★ Guest House
SILVER AWARD
15 Longmead, Lynton
EX35 6DQ
t (01598) 753573
e j.e.mcgowan@btinternet.com
w thedenes.com

**Fernleigh Guest House**
★★★★ Guest House
Park Street, Lynton EX35 6BY
t (01598) 753575
e bookings@fernleigh.net
w fernleigh.net

**Gable Lodge Guest House**
★★★★ Guest House
35 Lee Road, Lynton EX35 6BS
t (01598) 752367
e gablelodge@btconnect.com
w gablelodgelynton.co.uk

**Highcliffe House** ★★★★★★
Guest Accommodation
SILVER AWARD
Sinai Hill, Lynton EX35 6AR
t (01598) 752235
e info@highcliffehouse.co.uk
w highcliffehouse.co.uk

**Ingleside Hotel** ★★★★
Guest Accommodation
SILVER AWARD
Lee Road, Lynton EX35 6HW
t (01598) 752223
e keithdiana@supanet.com
w ingleside-hotel.co.uk

**Kingford House** ★★★★
Guest Accommodation
SILVER AWARD
Longmead, Lynton EX35 6DQ
t (01598) 752361
e tricia@kingfordhouse.co.uk
w kingfordhouse.co.uk

**Lee House** ★★★★
Guest Accommodation
Lee Road, Lynton EX35 6BP
t (01598) 752364
e info@leehouselynton.co.uk
w leehouselynton.co.uk

**Longmead House Hotel**
★★★★
Guest Accommodation
SILVER AWARD
9 Longmead, Lynton
EX35 6DQ
t (01598) 752523
e info@longmeadhouse.co.uk
w longmeadhouse.co.uk

**South View Guest House**
★★★★
Guest Accommodation
23 Lee Road, Lynton EX35 6BP
t (01598) 752289
e maureenroper@hotmail.com
w southview-lynton.co.uk

**Southcliffe** ★★★★
Guest Accommodation
SILVER AWARD
34 Lee Road, Lynton EX35 6BS
t (01598) 753328
e info@southcliffe.co.uk
w southcliffe.co.uk

**The Turret** ★★★★
Guest Accommodation
33 Lee Road, Lynton EX35 6BS
t (01598) 753284
w turrethotel.co.uk

**Valley House** ★★★★
Guest House
Lynbridge Road, Lynton
EX35 6BD
t (01598) 752285
e info@valley-house.co.uk
w valley-house.co.uk

**Waterloo House** ★★★★
Guest House
Lydiate Lane, Lynton EX35 6AJ
t (01598) 753391
e relax@waterloohousehotel.com
w waterloohousehotel.com

**Kinfield** ★★★
Guest Accommodation
Bremilham Road, Malmesbury
SN16 0DQ
t (01666) 825041
e jennifer.warner1@tesco.net

**Lovett Farm** ★★★★
Farmhouse
Little Somerford, Chippenham
SN15 5BP
t (01666) 823268
e lovettfarm@btinternet.com
w lovettfarm.co.uk

**Manor Farm** ★★★★
Farmhouse
Corston, Malmesbury
SN16 0HF
t (01666) 822148
e ross@manorfarmbandb.fsnet.co.uk
w manorfarmbandb.co.uk

**Marsh Farmhouse** ★★★
Guest House
Crudwell Road, Malmesbury
SN16 9JL
t (01666) 822208

**Oakwood Farm** ★★★
Farmhouse
Upper Minety, Malmesbury
SN16 9PY
t (01666) 860286

**Woodbury** ★★★★
Bed & Breakfast
Truro TR1 1SQ
t (01872) 271466

**Great Houndtor** Bunkhouse
Manaton, Newton Abbot
TQ13 9UW
t (01647) 221202

**Fern Cottage Bed &
Breakfast** ★★★★ Farmhouse
SILVER AWARD
188 Shortwood Hill,
Pucklechurch BS16 9PG
t (0117) 937 4966
e sueandpete@ferncottagebedandbreakfast.co.uk
w ferncottagebedandbreakfast.co.uk

**Huntlys** ★★★★ Farmhouse
Manningford Abbots, Pewsey
SN9 6HZ
t (01672) 563663
e meg@gimspike.fsnet.co.uk

**Northwood Cottages B&B**
★★★★
Guest Accommodation
SILVER AWARD
2 Northwood Cottages,
Manston, Sturminster Newton
DT10 1HD
t (01258) 472666
e info@northwoodcottages.co.uk
w northwoodcottages.co.uk

---

## MARAZION
### Cornwall

**Chymorvah Private Hotel**
◆◆◆◆ *Guest Accommodation*
Marazion, Penzance TR17 0DQ
t (01736) 710497
e info@chymorvah.co.uk
w chymorvah.co.uk

**Rosario ★★★★**
*Guest Accommodation*
The Square, Marazion
TR17 0BH
t (01736) 711998
w marazion.net

## MARK
### Somerset

**Burnt House Farm ★★★**
*Guest Accommodation*
Yarrow Road, Nr Highbridge
TA9 4LR
t (01278) 641280
e carmenburnthouse@yahoo.
co.uk

## MARKET LAVINGTON
### Wiltshire

**The Green Dragon ★★★** *Inn*
26-28 High Street, Market
Lavington, Devizes SN10 4AG
t (01380) 813235
e greendragonlavington@
tiscali.co.uk
w greendragonlavington.co.uk

## MARLBOROUGH
### Wiltshire

**Crofton Lodge ★★★★**
*Bed & Breakfast*
**SILVER AWARD**
Crofton, Marlborough
SN8 3DW
t (01672) 870328
e ali@croftonlodge.co.uk
w croftonlodge.co.uk

**The Inn with the Well ★★★**
*Inn*
Marlborough Road, Ogbourne
St George, Marlborough
SN8 1SQ
t (01672) 841445
e info@theinnwiththewell.co.
uk
w theinnwiththewell.co.uk

**The Merlin Bed and
Breakfast ★★★**
*Guest Accommodation*
High Street, Marlborough
SN8 1LW
t (01672) 512151
e info@merlinhotel.co.uk
w merlinhotel.co.uk

**Upper Westcourt ★★★★**
*Bed & Breakfast*
Westcourt, Burbage,
Marlborough SN8 3BW
t (01672) 810307
e prhill@onetel.com
w upperwestcourt.co.uk

**Wernham Farm**
Rating Applied For
*Farmhouse*
Clench Common, Marlborough
SN8 4DR
t (01672) 512236
e margglvsf@aol.com

## MARTOCK
### Somerset

**Bartletts Farm ★★★★**
*Farmhouse*
Isle Brewers, Nr Taunton
TA3 6QN
t (01460) 281423
e sandjpeach@tesco.net
w bartlettsfarm.net

**The White Hart Hotel
★★★★** *Inn*
East Street, Martock TA12 6JQ
t (01935) 822005
e enquiries@
whitehartotelmartock.co.uk
w whitehartotelmartock.co.uk

**Wychwood ★★★**
*Bed & Breakfast*
7 Bearley Road, Martock
TA12 6PG
t (01935) 825601
e wychwoodmartock@yahoo.
co.uk

## MATCHAMS
### Dorset

**Little Paddock**
Rating Applied For
*Bed & Breakfast*
218 Hurn Road, Ringwood
BH24 2BT
t (01425) 470889
e enquiries@little-paddock.
com
w little-paddock.com

## MAWGAN PORTH
### Cornwall

**Bre-Pen Farm ★★★★**
*Farmhouse*
Mawgan Porth, Newquay
TR8 4AL
t (01637) 860420
e jill.brake@virgin.net
w bre-penfarm.co.uk

**Trevarrian Lodge ★★★**
*Guest House*
Trevarrian, Mawgan Porth,
Newquay TR8 4AQ
t (01637) 860156
e trevarrian@aol.com
w trevarrianlodge.co.uk

## MAYPOOL
### Devon

**Maypool YHA ★★** *Hostel*
Maypool, Brixham TQ5 0ET
t (01803) 842444
e maypool@yha.org.uk
w yha.org.uk

## MELKSHAM
### Wiltshire

**Longhope Guest House
★★★** *Guest House*
9 Beanacre Road, Melksham
SN12 8AG
t (01225) 706737

## MELLS
### Somerset

**Claveys Farm ★★** *Farmhouse*
Mells Green, Nr Frome
BA11 3QP
t (01373) 814651
e b&b@fleurkelly.com
w fleurkelly.com/bandb

## MERE
### Wiltshire

**The Old Police House ★★★**
*Bed & Breakfast*
North Street, Mere,
Warminster BA12 6HH
t (01747) 861768
e gilly.gristwood@
btopenworld.com

## MERRYMEET
### Cornwall

**Higher Trevartha Farm
★★★★** *Farmhouse*
**SILVER AWARD**
Pengover, Liskeard PL14 3NJ
t (01579) 343382
e tandksobey@hotmail.co.uk

## MEVAGISSEY
### Cornwall

**Bacchus B&B ★★★**
*Bed & Breakfast*
Bacchus, Trevarth, St Austell
PL26 6RX
t (01726) 843473
e susiecannone@yahoo.co.uk

**Buckingham House ★★★**
*Guest House*
17 Tregoney Hill, Mevagissey,
St Austell PL26 6RD
t (01726) 843375
e housead07@aol.com
w buckinghamhouse
mevagissey.co.uk

**Corran Farm B&B ★★★★**
*Farmhouse* **SILVER AWARD**
St Ewe, Mevagissey, St Austell
PL26 6ER
t (01726) 842159
e terryandkathy@corranfarm.
fsnet.co.uk
w corranfarm.co.uk

**Eden B&B ★★★★**
*Guest Accommodation*
**SILVER AWARD**
Omega, Bodrugan Hill,
Portmellon PL26 6PS
t (01726) 842836
e edenbandbcornwall@
hotmail.com
w eden-bed-and-breakfast.co.
uk

**Honeycombe House ★★★★**
*Guest House*
61 Polkirt Hill, Mevagissey, St
Austell PL26 6UR
t (01726) 843750
e enquiries@
honeycombehouse.co.uk
w honeycombehouse.co.uk

**Portmellon Cove Guest
House ★★★★★**
*Guest House* **SILVER AWARD**
121 Portmellon Park,
Portmellon, St Austell
PL26 6XD
t (01726) 843410
e stay@portmellon-cove.com
w portmellon-cove.com

**Tregilgas Farm ★★★★**
*Farmhouse*
Gorran, St Austell PL26 6ND
t (01726) 842342
e Dclemes88@aol.com
w tregilgasfarmbedand
breaksfast.co.uk

## TREGONEY HOUSE ★★★
*Bed & Breakfast*
Tregoney Hill, Mevagissey, St
Austell PL26 6RD
t (01726) 842760
e dianne.young@hotmail.co.
uk
w tregoneyhouse.co.uk

**Tregorran House ★★★★**
*Guest House*
Cliff Street, Mevagissey, St
Austell PL26 6QW
t (01726) 842319
e helen@tregorran.co.uk
w tregorran.co.uk

**The Wheelhouse
Guesthouse ★★★**
*Guest House*
West Wharf, Mevagissey, St
Austell PL26 6UJ
t (01726) 843404
e wheel-house@btconnect.
com
w wheelhouse.me.uk

## MIDDLECOMBE
### Somerset

**Highlands ★★★**
*Activity Accommodation*
Porlock Road, Minehead
TA24 8SW
t (01643) 705079
e helen@
exmoormtbexperiences.co.uk
w exmoormtbexperiences.co.
uk

## MILLBROOK
### Cornwall

**Stone Farm ◆◆◆◆**
*Guest Accommodation*
**SILVER AWARD**
Whitsand Bay, Millbrook,
Torpoint PL10 1JJ
t (01752) 822267
e blake@stone-farm.fsnet.co.
uk
w stone-farm.co.uk

## MILTON ABBAS
### Dorset

**Dunbury Heights ★★★★**
*Bed & Breakfast*
Milton Abbas, Blandford Forum
DT11 0DH
t (01258) 880445

## MILTON DAMEREL
### Devon

**Buttermoor Farm ★★★★**
*Farmhouse*
Milton Damerel, Holsworthy
EX22 7PB
t (01409) 261314
e info@buttermoorfarm.co.uk
w buttermoorfarm.co.uk

## MINEHEAD
### Somerset

**Avondale ★★★★**
*Guest House*
Martlet Road, Minehead
TA24 5QD
t (01643) 706931

**Bactonleigh ★★★**
*Guest Accommodation*
20 Tregonwell Road, Minehead
TA24 5DU
t (01643) 702147

**Baytree** ★★★★
*Bed & Breakfast*
29 Blenheim Road, Minehead
TA24 5PZ
t (01643) 703374
e derekcole@onetel.com

**Beverleigh** ★★★★
*Bed & Breakfast*
Beacon Road, Minehead
TA24 5SE
t (01643) 708450

**Edgcott House** ★★★★
*Guest Accommodation*
Porlock Road, Exford
TA24 7QG
t (01643) 831495
e enquiries@edgcotthouse.co.
uk
w edgcotthouse.co.uk

**Glendower House** ★★★★
*Guest House*
30-32 Tregonwell Road,
Minehead TA24 5DU
t (01643) 707144
e info@glendower-house.co.
uk
w glendower-house.co.uk

**The Kingsway** ★★★★
*Guest Accommodation*
36 Ponsford Road, Minehead
TA24 5DY
t (01643) 702313
e kingswayhotel@msn.com
w kingswayhotelminehead.co.
uk

**Marston Lodge** ★★★
*Guest Accommodation*
St Michaels Road, Minehead
TA24 5JP
t (01643) 702510
e enquiry@
marstonlodgehotel.co.ik
w marstonlodgehotel.co.uk

**Montrose Guest House**
★★★★ *Guest House*
14 Tregonwell Road, Minehead
TA24 5DU
t (01643) 706473
e montroseminehead@
btinternet.com
w montroseminehead.co.uk

**Oakfield Guest House**
★★★★★ *Bed & Breakfast*
SILVER AWARD
Northfield Road, Minehead
TA24 5QH
t (01643) 704911
e oakfieldminehead@yahoo.
com

**The Parks** ★★★★
*Guest House* SILVER AWARD
26 The Parks, Minehead
TA24 8BT
t (01643) 703547
e info@parksguesthouse.co.uk
w parksguesthouse.co.uk
🔲🔲

**Promenade Hotel** ★★★
*Guest Accommodation*
Esplanade, Minehead
TA24 5QS
t (01643) 702572
e jgph@globalnet.co.uk
w johngroons.org.uk

**Sunfield** ★★★
*Guest Accommodation*
83 Summerland Avenue,
Minehead TA24 5BW
t (01643) 703565
e stay@sunfieldminehead.co.
uk
w sunfieldminehead.co.uk

**Tranmere House** ★★★★
*Guest Accommodation*
24 Tregonwell Road, Minehead
TA24 5DU
t (01643) 702647

**Tregonwell House** ★★★
*Guest House*
1 Tregonwell Road, Minehead
TA24 5DT
t (01643) 709287
w tregonwellhouse.co.uk

**YHA Minehead** ★★★ *Hostel*
Manor Road, Minehead
TA24 6EW
t (01643) 702595
e minehead@yha.org.uk
w yha.org.uk

### MINSTERWORTH
### Gloucestershire

**Severn Bank** ★★★
*Guest Accommodation*
Minsterworth, Gloucester
GL2 8JH
t (01452) 750146
e info@severn-bank.com
w severn-bank.com

### MODBURY
### Devon

**Weeke Farm** ★★★
*Farmhouse*
Modbury, Ivybridge PL21 0TT
t (01548) 830219

### MOLLAND
### Devon

**West Lee Farm** ★★★★
*Farmhouse*
Molland, South Molton
EX36 3NJ
t (01398) 341751
e maggi.woodward@ukonline.
co.uk
w westleefarm.co.uk

### MONTACUTE
### Somerset

**Carents House** ★★★★
*Bed & Breakfast*
7a Middle Street, Montacute
TA15 6UZ
t (01935) 824914
e dianasloan@onetel.net
w carentshouse.co.uk

**Montacute Country
Tearooms** ★★★
*Bed & Breakfast*
1 South Street, Montacute
TA15 6XD
t (01935) 823024
e info@montacutemuseum.co.
uk
w montacutemuseum.co.uk
🔲🔲

### MORCOMBELAKE
### Dorset

**Wisteria Cottage** ★★★★
*Guest Accommodation*
Taylors Lane, Morcombelake,
Bridport DT6 6ED
t (01297) 489019
e dave@dorsetcottage.org.uk
w dorsetcottage.org.uk

### MORETON-IN-MARSH
### Gloucestershire

**Acacia** ★★
*Guest Accommodation*
New Road, Moreton-in-Marsh
GL56 0AS
t (01608) 650130

**Fosseway Farm B&B** ★★★★
*Farmhouse*
Stow Road, Moreton-in-Marsh
GL56 0DS
t (01608) 650503

**Jasmine Cottage** ★★★
*Bed & Breakfast*
Stretton-on-Fosse, Moreton-in-
Marsh GL56 9SA
t (01608) 661972
e ann@jasminecottage.
wanadoo.co.uk
w http://jasmine-cottage.
mysite.wanadoo-members.co.
uk/

**Kymalton House** ★★★★
*Bed & Breakfast*
Todenham Road, Moreton-in-
Marsh GL56 9NJ
t (01608) 650487
e kymalton@uwclub.net

**New Farm** ★★★ *Farmhouse*
Dorn, Moreton-in-Marsh
GL56 9NS
t (01608) 650782 &
07811 646320
e catherinerighton@
btinternet.com
w newfarmbandb.co.uk

**Old Farm** ★★★ *Farmhouse*
Dorn, Moreton-in-Marsh
GL56 9NS
t (01608) 650394
e info@oldfarmdorn.co.uk
w oldfarmdorn.co.uk

**Staddle Stones Guest House**
★★★ *Bed & Breakfast*
Rowborough, Stretton-on-
Fosse, Moreton-in-Marsh
GL56 9RE
t (01608) 662774

**Treetops** ★★★★
*Guest House*
London Road, Moreton-in-
Marsh GL56 0HE
t (01608) 651036
e treetops1@talk21.com
w treetopscotswolds.co.uk

**Windy Ridge House**
★★★★★ *Bed & Breakfast*
SILVER AWARD
The Crook, Longborough,
Moreton-in-Marsh GL56 0QY
t (01451) 830465
e nick@windy-ridge.co.uk
w windy-ridge.co.uk

### MORETONHAMPSTEAD
### Devon

**Great Sloncombe Farm**
★★★★ *Farmhouse*
SILVER AWARD
Moretonhampstead, Newton
Abbot TQ13 8QF
t (01647) 440595
e hmerchant@sloncombe.
freeserve.co.uk
w greatsloncombefarm.co.uk

**Great Wooston Farm**
★★★★ *Farmhouse*
Moretonhampstead, Newton
Abbot TQ13 8QA
t (01647) 440367 &
07798 670590
e info@greatwoostonfarm.
com
w greatwoostonfarm.com

**Little Wooston Farm** ★★★
*Guest Accommodation*
Moretonhampstead, Newton
Abbot TQ13 8QA
t (01647) 440551
e jeannecuming@tesco.net

### MORWENSTOW
### Cornwall

**Cornakey Farm** ★★★
*Farmhouse*
Morwenstow, Bude EX23 9SS
t (01288) 331260
w cornakey-farm.co.uk

**Willow Tree Cottage** ★★★★
*Bed & Breakfast*
SILVER AWARD
Morwenstow, Bude EX23 9SJ
t (01288) 331100
e rfsphillips@tiscali.co.uk
w willowtreecottage.co.uk

### MOTCOMBE
### Dorset

**The Coppleridge Inn** ★★★
*Inn*
Motcombe, Shaftesbury
SP7 9HW
t (01747) 851980
e thecoppleridgeinn@
btinternet.com
w coppleridge.com

**Pear Tree House** ★★★
*Bed & Breakfast*
Bittles Green, Motcombe,
Shaftesbury SP7 9NX
t (01747) 852647
e pocock@motcombe.eclipse.
co.uk

### MOUSEHOLE
### Cornwall

**Kerris Farm** ★★★★
*Farmhouse*
Kerris, Paul, Penzance
TR19 6UY
t (01736) 731309
e kerrisfarm@btconnect.com
w kerrisfarm.co.uk

**Mousehole B&B** ★★★
*Bed & Breakfast*
Two Foxes Lane, Mousehole,
Penzance TR19 6QQ
t (01736) 731882
e twofoxes.m@btopenworld.
com

**Tremayne** ★★★
*Guest Accommodation*
Tremayne Restaurant
Accommodation, The Parade,
Penzance TR19 6PS
t (01736) 731214
e tremayne@
mouseholecornwall.fsnet.co.uk

## MUCHELNEY
### Somerset

**The Parsonage ★★★★★**
*Guest Accommodation*
**GOLD AWARD**
Silver Street, Nr Langport
TA10 0DL
t (01458) 259058
e valerie@breathe.co.uk
w parsonagesouthsomerset.co.uk

## MUDFORD
### Somerset

**Half Moon Inn and Country Lodge ★★★★**
*Guest Accommodation*
Main Street, Nr Yeovil
BA21 5TF
t (01935) 850289
e thehalfmoon@dclonline.net
w visitwestcountry.com/thehalfmoon

## MULLION
### Cornwall

**The Mounts Bay Guest House ★★★**
*Guest Accommodation*
Churchtown, Helston
TR12 7HN
t (01326) 241761
e jan@mountsbayguesthouse.wanadoo.co.uk

**Polhormon Farm ★★★★**
*Guest Accommodation*
Polhormon Lane, Mullion,
Helston TR12 7JE
t (01326) 240304
e aliceharry@polhormonfarm.co.uk
w farmholidaycornwall.co.uk

**Tregaddra Farmhouse ♦♦♦♦**
*Guest Accommodation*
**SILVER AWARD**
Cury Cross Lanes, Helston,
Falmouth TR12 7BB
t (01326) 240235
e june@tregaddra.co.uk
w tregaddra.co.uk

**Trenance Farmhouse ★★★★**
*Guest Accommodation*
Mullion, Helston, Falmouth
TR12 7HB
t (01326) 240639
e info@trenancefarmholidays.co.uk
w trenancefarmholidays.co.uk

## MUSBURY
### Devon

**Kate's Farm Bed & Breakfast**
**★★★** *Bed & Breakfast*
Lower Bruckland Farm,
Musbury, Axminster EX13 8ST
t (01297) 552861
e katesatterley@hotmail.com

## NAILSWORTH
### Gloucestershire

**1 Orchard Mead ★★**
*Bed & Breakfast*
Nailsworth, Stroud GL6 0RE
t (01453) 833581

## NAUNTON
### Gloucestershire

**Aylworth Manor ★★★★**
*Bed & Breakfast*
Naunton, Cheltenham
GL54 3AH
t (01451) 850850
e jeaireland@aol.com
w aylworthmanor.co.uk

**Fox Hill ★★★★**
*Guest Accommodation*
**SILVER AWARD**
Stow Road, Andoversford,
Cheltenham GL54 5RL
t (01451) 850496

## NETHER STOWEY
### Somerset

**Castle of Comfort Country House ★★★★★**
*Guest Accommodation*
**SILVER AWARD**
Dodington, Nether Stowey,
Bridgwater TA5 1LE
t (01278) 741264
e reception@castle-of-comfort.co.uk
w castle-of-comfort.co.uk

**Keenthorne House ★★★**
*Bed & Breakfast*
A39, Nr Nether Stowey
TA5 1HZ
t (01278) 733118
e nirmala4@btinternet.com

**The Old Cider House ★★★★**
*Guest Accommodation*
25 Castle Street, Nr Bridgwater
TA5 1LN
t (01278) 732228
e info@theoldciderhouse.co.uk
w theoldciderhouse.co.uk

**The Old House ★★★★**
*Bed & Breakfast*
**SILVER AWARD**
St Mary Street, Bridgwater
TA5 1LJ
t (01278) 732392
e scourfieldfarm@yahoo.co.uk

**Stowey Brooke House ★★★★★**
*Guest Accommodation*
18 Castle Street, Nr Bridgwater
TA5 1LN
t (01278) 733356
e markandjackie@stoweybrookehouse.co.uk
w stoweybrookehouse.co.uk

## NETHERBURY
### Dorset

**Jasmine Cottage ★★★★**
*Bed & Breakfast*
**SILVER AWARD**
St James Road, Netherbury,
Bridport DT6 5LP
t (01308) 488767

**Parnham Farm ★★★★**
*Guest Accommodation*
Crook Hill, Netherbury,
Bridport DT6 5LY
t (01308) 488214
e rbbowditch@aol.com

## NEWENT
### Gloucestershire

**The George ★★★** *Inn*
Church Street, Newent
GL18 1PU
t (01531) 820203
e enquiries@georgehotel.uk.com
w georgehotel.uk.com

**Newent Golf and Lodges**
**★★★** *Guest Accommodation*
Newent Golf Course, Cold
Harbour Lane, Newent
GL18 1DJ
t (01531) 820478
e tomnewentgolf@aol.com
w short-golf-break.com

**Three Ashes House**
Rating Applied For
*Bed & Breakfast*
Ledbury Road, Newent
GL18 1DE
t (01531) 820226
e judith@threeasheshouse.co.uk

## NEWLAND
### Gloucestershire

**Tan House Farm ★★★**
*Bed & Breakfast*
Laundry Lane, Newland,
Coleford GL16 8NQ
t (01594) 832222
e christiearno@talktalk.net
w tanhousefarm.org.uk

## NEWNHAM-ON-SEVERN
### Gloucestershire

**Swan House Guest House**
**★★★★**
*Guest Accommodation*
High Street, Newnham
GL14 1BY
t (01594) 516504
e stay@swanhousenewnham.co.uk
w swanhousenewnham.co.uk

## NEWQUAY
### Cornwall

**The Alex Guesthouse ★★★**
*Guest House*
19 Alexandra Road, Newquay
TR7 3ND
t (01637) 875311
e enquiries@alexguesthouse.co.uk
w alexguesthouse.co.uk

**Alicia ★★★★** *Guest House*
136 Henver Road, Newquay
TR7 3EQ
t (01637) 874328
e aliciaguesthouse@mlimer.fsnet.co.uk
w alicia-guesthouse.co.uk

**The Carlton ★★★★**
*Guest Accommodation*
6 Dane Road, Newquay
TR7 1HL
t (01637) 872658
e enquiries@carltonhotelnewquay.co.uk
w carltonhotelnewquay.co.uk

**Chichester Interest Holidays**
**★★** *Guest Accommodation*
14 Bay View Terrace, Newquay
TR7 2LR
t (01637) 874216
e sheila.harper@virgin.net
w http://freespace.virgin.net/sheila.harper

**Chynoweth Lodge ★★★★**
*Guest Accommodation*
1 Eliot Gardens, Newquay
TR7 2QE
t (01637) 876684
e chynowethlodge@btconnect.com
w chynowethlodge.co.uk

**Gannel View Lodge ★★★**
*Guest Accommodation*
91 Pentire Avenue, Newquay
TR7 1PE
t (01637) 875013
e ken_pyrah@compuserve.com
w ourworld.compuserve.com/homepages/ken_pyrah

**The Glendeveor ★★★**
*Guest Accommodation*
25 Mount Wise, Newquay
TR7 2BQ
t (01637) 872726
e enquiries@glendeveorhotel.co.uk
w glendeveorhotel.co.uk

**Godolphin Arms Hotel ★★★**
*Guest Accommodation*
86-88 Henver Road, Newquay
TR7 3BL
t (01637) 872572
e godolphin.arms@btconnect.com
w godolphinarmshotel.co.uk

**Gratton Lodge ★★★**
*Guest House*
119 Mount Wise, Newquay
TR7 1QR
t (01637) 877011
e grattonlodge@fsmail.net
w grattonlodge.co.uk

**The Harbour Hotel ★★★★**
*Guest Accommodation*
**SILVER AWARD**
North Quay Hill, Newquay
TR7 1HF
t (01637) 873040

**Harrington Guest House**
**★★★** *Guest House*
25 Tolcarne Road, Newquay
TR7 2NQ
t (01637) 873581
e harringtonguesthouse@yahoo.co.uk
w harringtonguesthouse.com

**Lynton Hotel ★★★**
*Guest House*
4 The Crescent, Newquay
TR7 1DT
t (01637) 873048
e info@lyntonhotel.wanadoo.co.uk
w lynton-hotel-newquay.co.uk

**The Metro ★★★★**
*Guest Accommodation*
142 Henver Road, Newquay
TR7 3EQ
t (01637) 871638
e info@metronewquay.co.uk
w metronewquay.co.uk

**Pengilley Guest House ★★★**
*Guest House*
12 Trebarwith Crescent,
Newquay TR7 1DX
t (01637) 872039
e jan@pengilley-guesthouse.co.uk
w pengilley-guesthouse.co.uk

**Pensalda Guest House ★★★**
*Guest House*
98 Henver Road, Newquay
TR7 3BL
t (01637) 874601
e karen_pensalda@yahoo.co.
uk
w pensalda-guesthouse.co.uk

**Pine Lodge ★★★★**
*Guest Accommodation*
Henver Road, Newquay
TR7 3DJ
t (01637) 850891
e enquiries@pinelodgehotel.
co.uk
w pinelodgehotel.co.uk

**Reef Surf Lodge ★★★★**
*Hostel*
10-12 Berry Road, Newquay
TR7 1AR
t (01637) 879058

**Roma Guest House ★★★★**
*Guest Accommodation*
1 Atlantic Road, Newquay
TR7 1QJ
t (01637) 875085
e romaghnewquay@aol.com
w romaguesthouse.co.uk

**St Andrews ★★★★**
*Guest Accommodation*
Island Crescent, Newquay
TR7 1DZ
t (01637) 873556
e enquiries@
standrewsnewquay.co.uk
w standrewsnewquay.co.uk

**Surfside B&B ★★★**
*Bed & Breakfast*
35 Mount Wise, Newquay
TR7 2BH
t (01637) 872707 &
07813 330609
e surfsidehotel@btconnect.
com
w surfsidenewquay.co.uk

**Three Beaches ★★★**
*Guest Accommodation*
17 Godophin Way, Newquay
TR7 3BU
t (01637) 873931
e graham@threebeacheshotel.
fsnet.co.uk
w threebeacheshotel.co.uk

**Tir Chonaill Lodge Hotel
★★★** *Guest Accommodation*
106 Mount Wise, Newquay
TR7 1QP
t (01637) 876492
e tirchonaillhotel@talk21.com
w tirchonaill.co.uk

**Wheal Treasure ★★★**
*Guest Accommodation*
72 Edgcumbe Avenue,
Newquay TR7 2NN
t (01637) 874136
w whealtreasurehotel.co.uk

### NEWTON ABBOT
Devon

**Travellers Rest ★★★**
*Guest Accommodation*
19 Torquay Road,
Kingskerswell, Newton Abbot
TQ12 5HH
t (01803) 873143
e patrick.beacroft@ntlworld.
com

### NEWTON POPPLEFORD
Devon

**Milestone Cottage ★★★**
*Bed & Breakfast*
High Street, Sidmouth
EX10 0DU
t (01395) 568267
e stay@a1-guesthouse.co.uk
w a1-guesthouse.co.uk

▨ ◪

### NEWTON ST LOE
Somerset

**Pennsylvania Farm B&B
★★★★** *Farmhouse*
Newton St Loe, Bath BA2 9JD
t (01225) 314912
e info@pennsylvaniafarm.co.
uk
w pennsylvaniafarm.co.uk

### NORTH BRADLEY
Wiltshire

**49a Church Lane ★★★★**
*Bed & Breakfast*
SILVER AWARD
North Bradley, Trowbridge
BA14 0TA
t (01225) 762558
e m-wise@amserve.com

### NORTH CADBURY
Somerset

**Ashlea House ★★★★**
*Guest Accommodation*
SILVER AWARD
High Street, Nr Wincanton
BA22 7DP
t (01963) 440891
e ashlea@btinternet.com
w ashleahouse.co.uk

### NORTH CERNEY
Gloucestershire

**The Bathurst Arms ★★★★**
*Inn*
Cirencester GL7 7BZ
t (01285) 831281
e james@bathurstarms.com
w bathurstarms.com

### NORTH WOOTTON
Dorset

**Stoneleigh Barn ★★★★**
*Bed & Breakfast*
SILVER AWARD
North Wootton, Sherborne
DT9 5JW
t (01935) 815964
e stoneleighbarn@aol.com
w stoneleighbarn.com

### NORTHLEACH
Gloucestershire

**Cotteswold House &
Cottage ★★★★**
*Bed & Breakfast*
SILVER AWARD
Market Place, Northleach,
Cheltenham GL54 3EG
t (01451) 860493
w cotteswoldhouse.com

**Northfield Bed and
Breakfast ★★★★**
*Guest Accommodation*
SILVER AWARD
Northleach, Cheltenham
GL54 3JL
t (01451) 860427
e nrthfield0@aol.com
w northfieldbandb.co.uk

### NORTON FITZWARREN
Somerset

**The Old Rectory ★★★★**
*Bed & Breakfast*
Rectory Road, Taunton
TA2 6SE
t (01823) 330081
e jw@oldrectorynorton.net
w oldrectorynorton.net

### NORTON ST PHILIP
Somerset

**The Plaine ★★★★**
*Guest Accommodation*
Bell Hill, Nr Radstock BA2 7LT
t (01373) 834723
e theplaine@easynet.co.uk
w theplaine.co.uk

### OAKDALE
Dorset

**Heathwood Guest House
★★★** *Guest House*
266 Wimborne Road, Oakdale,
Poole BH15 3EF
t (01202) 679176
e heathwoodhotel@tiscali.co.
uk
w heathwoodhotel.co.uk

### OAKFORD
Devon

**Harton Farm ★★★**
*Farmhouse*
Oakford, Tiverton EX16 9HH
t (01398) 351209
e lindy@hartonfarm.co.uk
w hartonfarm.co.uk

### OGBOURNE ST GEORGE
Wiltshire

**Blue Barn ★★★★**
*Bed & Breakfast*
Ogbourne St George,
Marlborough SN8 2NT
t (01672) 841082
e jaxs@capalmer.com

**The Sanctuary ★★★★**
*Bed & Breakfast*
Ogbourne St George,
Marlborough SN8 1SQ
t (01672) 841473
e rebecca.macdonald@core-
support.co.uk

### OKEFORD FITZPAINE
Dorset

**Oke Apple House ★★★★**
*Bed & Breakfast*
Okeford Fitzpaine, Blandford
Forum DT11 0RS
t (01258) 861126
e 51fairmount@tiscali.co.uk

### OKEHAMPTON
Devon

**Charlecott Lodge ★★★★**
*Bed & Breakfast*
38 Station Road, Okehampton
EX20 1EA
t (01837) 53998
e susan@charlecott.freeserve.
co.uk

**The Knole Farm ★★★★★**
*Farmhouse* SILVER AWARD
Bridestowe, Okehampton
EX20 4HA
t (01837) 861241
e mavis.bickle@btconnect.
com
w knolefarm-dartmoor-
holidays.co.uk

**Lower Trecott Farm ★★★★**
*Bed & Breakfast*
SILVER AWARD
Wellsprings Lane, Sampford
Courtenay, Okehampton
EX20 2TD
t (01837) 880118
e craig@trecott.fsnet.co.uk

**Week Farm Country
Holidays ★★★★** *Farmhouse*
Bridestowe, Okehampton
EX20 4HZ
t (01837) 861221
e accom@weekfarmonline.
com
w weekfarmonline.com

**YHA Okehampton ★★★**
*Activity Accommodation*
Klondyke Road, Okehampton
EX20 1EW
t (01837) 53916
e okehampton@yha.org.uk
w okehampton-yha.co.uk

### OLD CLEEVE
Somerset

**Binham Grange ★★★★★**
*Guest Accommodation*
SILVER AWARD
Nr Williton TA24 6HX
t (01984) 640056
e mariethomas9@hotmail.co.
uk

### OLD TOWN
Isles of Scilly

**Carn Ithen ★★★★**
*Bed & Breakfast*
SILVER AWARD
Trench Lane, Old Town, St
Mary's TR21 0PA
t (01720) 422917
e roz-alfred@carn-ithen.fsnet.
co.uk
w scilly-oldtown.com

**The Greenlaws ★★★★**
*Bed & Breakfast*
Old Town, St Mary's
TR21 0NH
t (01720) 422045

### OTTERY ST MARY
Devon

**Pitt Farm ◆◆◆◆**
*Guest Accommodation*
Coombelake, Ottery St Mary
EX11 1NL
t (01404) 812439
e pittfarm@tiscali.co.uk
w pitt-farm-devon.co.uk

### OVER STOWEY
Somerset

**Parsonage Farm ★★★★**
*Bed & Breakfast*
Adscombe Lane, Nr Bridgwater
TA5 1HA
t (01278) 733237
e sukie@parsonfarm.co.uk
w parsonfarm.co.uk

### PADSTOW
Cornwall

**1 Caswarth Terrace ★★**
*Bed & Breakfast*
Padstow PL28 8EE
t (01841) 532025

**50 Church Street ★★★★**
*Bed & Breakfast*
**SILVER AWARD**
Padstow PL28 8BG
t (01841) 532121
e churchstreet50@hotmail.com
w 50churchstreet.co.uk

**Althea House ★★★★★**
*Bed & Breakfast*
**SILVER AWARD**
64 Church Street, Padstow
PL28 8BG
t (01841) 532579
e zooat14@aol.com
w altheahouse.co.uk

**Althea Library ★★★★★**
*Guest Accommodation*
**SILVER AWARD**
27 High Street, Padstow
PL28 8BB
t (01841) 532717
e enquiries@althealibrary.co.uk
w althealibrary.co.uk

**Cally Croft ★★★★**
*Bed & Breakfast*
**SILVER AWARD**
26 Raleigh Close, Padstow
PL28 8BQ
t (01841) 533726
e callycroft@btinternet.com
w padstow-callycroft.co.uk

**Chyloweth ★★★★**
*Bed & Breakfast*
Constantine Bay, Padstow
PL28 8JQ
t (01841) 521012
e roger.vivian@tiscali.co.uk
w padstowlive.com

**Coswarth House Bed & Breakfast ★★★★★**
*Bed & Breakfast*
**SILVER AWARD**
12 Dennis Road, Padstow
PL28 8DD
t (01841) 534755
e coswarthhouse@btinternet.com
w coswarthhouse.com

**Cyntwell ★★★★**
*Bed & Breakfast*
4 Cross Street, Padstow
PL28 8AT
t (01841) 533447
e wendy@wgidlow.fsnet.co.uk
w cyntwell.co.uk

**Damara House ★★★**
*Guest Accommodation*
1 Grenville Road, Padstow
PL28 8EX
t (01841) 532653
e info@sianhowells.com
w sianhowells.com

**Garslade Guest House**
**★★★★ Bed & Breakfast**
52 Church Street, Padstow
PL28 8BG
t (01841) 533804
e garsladeguest@btconnect.com
w garslade.com

**Lamorva House ★★★★**
*Guest Accommodation*
3 Sarahs Meadow, Padstow
PL28 8LX
t (01841) 533841
e lamorva@aol.com
w padstowlive.com

**Lellizzick Farm ★★★★**
*Farmhouse*
Lellizzick, Padstow PL28 8HR
t (01841) 532838
e lellizzick1@aol.com
w padstowfarmfoods.biz

**Mena-Gwins Padstow**
**★★★★ Bed & Breakfast**
6 Raleigh Close, Padstow
PL28 8BQ
t (01841) 533396
e jenniferivivian@talktalk.net

**Molesworth Manor ★★★★**
*Guest Accommodation*
Little Petherick, Wadebridge
PL27 7QT
t (01841) 540292
e molesworthmanor@aol.com
w molesworthmanor.co.uk

**Number Eight ★★★★**
*Bed & Breakfast*
8 Drake Road, Padstow
PL28 8ES
t (01841) 532541

**Pendeen House ★★★★**
*Bed & Breakfast*
28 Dennis Road, Padstow
PL28 8DE
t (01841) 532 724
e enquire@pendeenhousepadstow.co.uk
w pendeenhousepadstow.co.uk

**Petrocstowe ★★★★**
*Guest Accommodation*
**SILVER AWARD**
30 Treverbyn Road, Padstow
PL28 8DW
t (01841) 532429
e andrearichards@btinternet.com
w stayinpadstow.co.uk

**Rosevanion ♦♦♦**
*Guest Accommodation*
Sarahs Lane, Padstow PL28 8EL
t (01841) 532227
e mary@haller250.freeserve.co.uk
w padstow-rosevanion.wanadoo.co.uk

**Rosmarinus ★★★★**
*Guest Accommodation*
8 Raleigh Close, Padstow
PL28 8BQ
t (01841) 533712
e richardellis8@aol.com
w padstowbb.co.uk

**Tamarisk ★★★★**
*Bed & Breakfast*
13 Grenville Road, Padstow
PL28 8EX
t (01841) 532272

**Trealaw Bed & Breakfast**
**★★★★ Bed & Breakfast**
22 Duke Street, Padstow
PL28 8AB
t (01841) 533161
w trealaw.com

**Treann ★★★★**
*Guest Accommodation*
Dennis Road, Padstow
PL28 8DE
t (01841) 533855
e emmacaddis@yahoo.co.uk
w treverbynhouse.com/treann.html

**Treverbyn House – Padstow**
**★★★★**
*Guest Accommodation*
Treverbyn House, Station
Road, Padstow PL28 8DA
t (01841) 532855
w treverbynhouse.com

**Trevorrick Farm – B&B**
**★★★ Farmhouse**
St Issey, Padstow PL27 7QH
t (01841) 540574
e info@trevorrick.co.uk
w trevorrick.co.uk

**West House ★★★★**
*Bed & Breakfast*
Grenville Rd, Padstow
PL28 8EX
t (01841) 533479
e willis@bun.com
w westhouse-padstow.co.uk

**The White Hart Apartment**
**★★★★ Bed & Breakfast**
**SILVER AWARD**
30 New Street, Padstow
PL28 8EA
t (01841) 532350
e whthartpad@aol.com
w whitehartpadstow.co.uk

**Woodlands Country House**
**★★★★★**
*Guest Accommodation*
**SILVER AWARD**
Treator, Padstow PL28 8RU
t (01841) 532426
e info@woodlands-padstow.co.uk
w woodlands-padstow.co.uk

### PAIGNTON
Devon

**Amber House ★★★★**
*Guest Accommodation*
**SILVER AWARD**
6 Roundham Road, Paignton
TQ4 6EZ
t (01803) 558372
e enquiries@amberhousehotel.co.uk
w amberhousehotel.co.uk

**Arden House ★★★**
*Guest House*
10 Youngs Park Road, Paignton
TQ4 6BU
t (01803) 558443
e info@ardenhousehotel.com
w ardenhousehotel.com

**The Ashleigh Hotel ♦♦♦**
*Guest Accommodation*
15 Queens Road, Paignton
TQ4 6AT
t (01803) 558923
e ashleighhotel4@aol.com
w ashleigh-hotel.co.uk

**Bay Sands Hotel ♦♦♦♦**
*Guest Accommodation*
14 Colin Road, Paignton
TQ3 2NR
t (01803) 524877
e enquiries@baysands.co.uk
w baysands.co.uk

**Beach House ★★★★**
*Guest Accommodation*
39 Garfield Road, Paignton
TQ4 6AX
t (01803) 525742
e beachhouse@l2222.fsbusiness.co.uk

**Beecroft Lodge ★★★**
*Guest Accommodation*
10 St Andrews Road, Paignton
TQ4 6HA
t (01803) 558702
e info@beecrofthotel.co.uk
w beecrofthotel.co.uk

**Bella Vista Guest House**
**★★★ Guest Accommodation**
Berry Square, Paignton
TQ4 6AZ
t (01803) 558122
e bellavista@berrysquare.fsbusiness.co.uk
w english-riviera.co.uk/accommodation/guest-houses/bella-vista/index.htm

**Benbows ★★★ Guest House**
1 Alta Vista Road, Roundham,
Paignton TQ4 6DB
t (01803) 558128
e benbowshotel@btinternet.com
w benbowshotel.co.uk

**The Beresford ★★★★**
*Guest Accommodation*
**SILVER AWARD**
5 Adelphi Road, Paignton
TQ4 6AW
t (01803) 551560
e info@beresfordhotel.co.uk
w beresfordhotel.co.uk

**Birchwood House ★★★★**
*Guest House*
33 St Andrews Road, Paignton
TQ4 6HA
t (01803) 551323
e dawnbowbeer@hotmail.co.uk
w birchwoodhouse.net

**Birklands Guest House**
**★★★ Guest House**
33 Garfield Road, Paignton
TQ4 6AX
t (01803) 556970
e trevor@trevor27.freeserve.co.uk
w birklands.co.uk

**Blue Waters Lodge**
Rating Applied For
*Guest Accommodation*
4 Leighon Road, Paignton
TQ3 2BQ
t (01803) 557749
e bluewaters.lodge@virgin.net
w bluewaterslodge.co.uk

**Braedene Hotel ★★★**
*Guest House*
22 Manor Road, Paignton
TQ3 2HR
t (01803) 551079
e stay@braedenehotel.fsnet.co.uk
w braedenehotel.co.uk

**Briars ★★★★**
*Guest Accommodation*
Sands Road, Paignton TQ4 6EJ
t (01803) 557729
e enquiries@briarshotel.com
w briarshotel.com

**Bristol House ★★**
*Guest House*
Garfield Road, Paignton
TQ4 6AU
t (01803) 558282
e info@bristolhousehotel.com
w bristolhousehotel.com

**Carrington Guest House**
★★★ *Guest House*
10 Beach Road, Paignton
TQ4 6AY
t (01803) 558785
e info@carringtonguesthouse.
co.uk
w carringtonguesthouse.co.uk

**Charnwood House** ★★★★
*Guest Accommodation*
Queens Road, Paignton
TQ4 6AT
t (01803) 558889

**The Cherra** ★★★
*Guest Accommodation*
15 Roundham Road, Paignton
TQ4 6DN
t (01803) 550723
e info@cherra-hotel.co.uk
w cherra-hotel.co.uk

**Cherwood Hotel** ★★★★
*Guest Accommodation*
SILVER AWARD
26 Garfield Road, Paignton
TQ4 6AX
t (01803) 556515
e pauline@cherwood-hotel.co.
uk
w cherwood-hotel.co.uk

**Cleve Court Hotel** ◆◆◆◆
*Guest Accommodation*
3 Cleveland Road, Paignton
TQ4 6EN
t (01803) 551444
e info@clevecourthotel.co.uk
w clevecourthotel.co.uk

**Cliveden** ★★★★
*Guest Accommodation*
27 Garfield Road, Paignton
TQ4 6AX
t (01803) 557461
e ros.mager@btconnect.com
w clivedenguesthouse.co.uk

**Colin House** ★★★★
*Guest Accommodation*
2 Colin Road, Paignton
TQ3 2NR
t (01803) 550609
e colin_house2@fsmail.net
w colinhouse.co.uk

**The Cosmopolitan** ★★★★
*Guest Accommodation*
2 Kernou Road, Paignton
TQ4 6BA
t (01803) 523118
e mail@paignton-
cosmopolitan.com
w paignton-cosmopolitan.com

**Craigmore Guest House**
★★★ *Guest House*
54 Dartmouth Road, Paignton
TQ4 5AN
t (01803) 557373
e cgh@excite.co.uk

**Culverden Guest House**
★★★ *Guest Accommodation*
4 Colin Road, Preston, Paignton
TQ3 2NR
t (01803) 559786
e info@culverdenhotel.co.uk
w culverdenhotel.co.uk
▨◪

**Earlston House** ★★★★
*Guest Accommodation*
31 St Andrews Road, Paignton
TQ4 6HA
t (01803) 558355
e stay@earlstonhouse.co.uk
w earlstonhouse.co.uk

**Easton Court** ★★★
*Guest House*
5 St Andrews Road, Paignton
TQ4 6HA
t (01803) 555810
e info@eastoncourt.co.uk
w eastoncourt.co.uk

**The Florida** ★★★★
*Guest Accommodation*
9 Colin Road, Paignton
TQ3 2NR
t (01803) 551447
e stay@floridahotelpaignton.
co.uk
w floridahotelpaignton.co.uk

**Harbour Lodge** ★★★
*Guest Accommodation*
4 Cleveland Road, Paignton
TQ4 6EN
t (01803) 556932
e enquiries@harbourlodge.co.
uk
w harbourlodge.co.uk

**The Mayfield** ★★★★
*Guest Accommodation*
8 Queens Road, Paignton
TQ4 6AT
t (01803) 556802

**Middlepark Hotel** ◆◆◆
*Guest Accommodation*
3 Marine Drive, Paignton
TQ3 2NJ
t (01803) 559025

**Norbreck** ★★★ *Guest House*
New Street, Paignton TQ3 3HL
t (01803) 558033
e norbreckguesthouse@
hotmail.com
w norbreck.com

**The Old School House Bed &
Breakfast** ★★★★★
*Bed & Breakfast*
Blagdon Road, Collaton St
Mary, Paignton TQ3 3YA
t (01803) 523011
e abdy13@tiscali.co.uk
w theoldschoolhousedevon.co.
uk

**Paignton Court** ★★★
*Guest Accommodation*
17-19 Sands Road, Paignton
TQ4 6EG
t (01803) 553111
e paigntoncourt@aol.com
w paignton-court-hotel.co.uk

**Park Lodge Hotel** ★★★
*Guest House*
16-18 Adelphi Road, Paignton
TQ4 6AW
t (01803) 551232

**Rockview Guest House**
★★★ *Guest House*
13 Queens Road, Paignton
TQ4 6AT
t (01803) 556702
e rockview@blueyonder.co.uk
w rockview.co.uk

**Rosemead Guest House**
★★★ *Guest Accommodation*
22 Garfield Road, Paignton
TQ4 6AX
t (01803) 557944
e rosemeadhotel@aol.com
w rosemeadpaignton.co.uk

**Rougemont Hotel** ★★★
*Guest Accommodation*
23 Roundham Road, Paignton
TQ4 6DN
t (01803) 556570
e beds@rougemonthotel.co.
uk
w rougemonthotel.co.uk

**Roundham Lodge** ★★★★★
*Guest Accommodation*
SILVER AWARD
16 Roundham Road, Paignton
TQ4 6DN
t (01803) 558485
e enquiries@roundham-lodge.
co.uk
w roundham-lodge.co.uk

**The Rowcroft** ★★★★
*Guest Accommodation*
14 Youngs Park Road,
Goodrington Sands, Paignton
TQ4 6BU
t (01803) 559420
e enquiries@rowcroft-hotel.
com
w rowcroft-hotel.com

**St Edmunds** ★★★
*Guest Accommodation*
25 Sands Road, Paignton
TQ4 6EG
t (01803) 558756
e stedmunds@lycos.co.uk
w stedmundshotel.com

**San Brelade** ★★★
*Guest House*
3 Alta Vista Road, Paignton
TQ4 6DB
t (01803) 553725
e info@hotelsanbrelade.co.uk
w hotelsanbrelade.co.uk

**The Sands Hotel** ★★★★
*Guest Accommodation*
32 Sands Road, Paignton
TQ4 6EJ
t (01803) 551282
e hotel.sands@virgin.net
w hotelsands.co.uk

**Sea Spray Hotel** ★★★
*Guest Accommodation*
1 Beach Road, Paignton
TQ4 6AY
t (01803) 553141
e mail@seasprayhotel.co.uk
w seasprayhotel.co.uk

**Seacroft Guest House**
★★★★
*Guest Accommodation*
41 Sands Road, Paignton
TQ4 6EG
t (01803) 523791
e enquiries@
seacroftguesthouse.co.uk
w seacroftguesthouse.co.uk

**Seaford Sands** ★★★
*Guest Accommodation*
Roundham Road, Paignton
TQ4 6DN
t (01803) 557722
w seafordsandshotel.co.uk

**Sonachan House** ★★★★
*Guest Accommodation*
35 St Andrews Road, Paignton
TQ4 6HA
t (01803) 558021
e info@sonachan.co.uk
w sonachan.co.uk

**The Sundale** ★★
*Guest Accommodation*
10 Queens Road, Paignton
TQ4 6AT
t (01803) 557431
e sundalehotel@tiscali.co.uk
w sundalehotelpaignton.co.uk

**Two Beaches** ★★★★
*Guest Accommodation*
27 St Andrews Road, Paignton
TQ4 6HA
t (01803) 522164
e 2beaches@tiscali.co.uk
w twobeaches.co.uk

**The Wynncroft** ★★★
*Guest Accommodation*
Elmsleigh Park, Paignton
TQ4 5AT
t (01803) 525728
e wynncroft@fsbdial.co.uk
w wynncroft.co.uk

## PAINSWICK
### Gloucestershire

**Cardynham House** ★★★★
*Guest Accommodation*
The Cross, Painswick, Stroud
GL6 6XX
t (01452) 814006
e info@cardynham.co.uk
w cardynham.co.uk

**Hambutts Mynd** ★★★
*Guest Accommodation*
Edge Road, Painswick, Stroud
GL6 6UP
t (01452) 812352
e ewarland@aol.com
w accommodation.uk.net/
hambutts.htm

**Meadowcote** ★★★★
*Bed & Breakfast*
Stroud Road, Painswick, Stroud
GL6 6UT
t (01452) 813565
e lockmeadowcote@talktalk.
net

**St Annes** ★★★
*Bed & Breakfast*
Gloucester Street, Painswick,
Stroud GL6 6QN
t (01452) 812879
e greg-iris@supanet.com
w st-annes-painswick.co.uk

**St Michaels Restaurant**
★★★★
*Restaurant with Rooms*
Victoria Street, Painswick
GL6 6QA
t (01452) 814555
e info@stmickshouse.co.uk
w stmickshouse.co.uk

**Skyrack** ★★★
*Bed & Breakfast*
The Highlands, Painswick,
Stroud GL6 6SL
t (01452) 812029
e wendyskyrack@hotmail.com

**Thorne** ★★★ *Bed & Breakfast*
Friday Street, Painswick, Stroud
GL6 6QJ
t (01452) 812476

**Troy House** ★★★
*Bed & Breakfast*
Gloucester Street, Painswick,
Stroud GL6 6QN
t (01452) 812339
e simonnefrissen@microdia.
co.uk
w troyhousepainswick.co.uk

**Upper Doreys Mill** ★★★
*Bed & Breakfast*
Edge, Painswick, Stroud
GL6 6NF
t (01452) 812459
e sylvia@doreys.co.uk
w doreys.co.uk

### PAMINGTON
Gloucestershire

**Pamington Court Farm**
★★★★ *Farmhouse*
Pamington, Aschurch,
Tewkesbury GL20 8LY
t (01684) 772301
e mhill@uwclub.net
w pamingtoncourtfarm.co.uk

### PANBOROUGH
Somerset

**Garden End Farm** ★★★
*Farmhouse*
Wells Road, Nr Wells BA5 1PN
t (01934) 712414
e sheila@gardenendfarm.
freeserve.co.uk
w gardenendfarm.freeserve.
co.uk

### PAR
Cornwall

**Reynards Rest** ★★★★
*Bed & Breakfast*
The Mount, Par, St Austell
PL24 2BZ
t (01726) 815770
e carol@reynardsrest.co.uk
w reynardsrest.co.uk

**The Royal Inn** ★★★★ *Inn*
66 Eastcliffe Road, Par
PL24 2AJ
t (01726) 815601
e info@royal-inn.co.uk
w royal-inn.co.uk

### PARKEND
Gloucestershire

**Deanfield** ★★★★
*Guest Accommodation*
Folly Road, Parkend, Lydney
GL15 4JF
t (01594) 562256
e deanfieldbb@aol.com
w deanfield.org.uk

**Edale House** ★★★★
*Guest House*
Folly Road, Parkend, Lydney
GL15 4JP
t (01594) 562835
e enquiry@edalehouse.co.uk
w edalehouse.co.uk

**The Fountain Inn** ★★★ *Inn*
Parkend, Lydney GL15 4JD
t (01594) 562189
e thefountaininn@aol.com

### PARKSTONE
Dorset

**Viewpoint Guest House**
★★★★ *Guest House*
11 Constitution Hill Road,
Poole BH14 0QB
t (01202) 733586
e heather@viewpoint-gh.co.uk
w viewpoint-gh.co.uk

### PARRACOMBE
Devon

**Higher Bodley Farm** ★★★★
*Farmhouse*
Parracombe EX31 4QN
t (01598) 763798
e higherbodley@hotmail.co.uk
w higherbodleyfarm.co.uk

### PAXFORD
Gloucestershire

**1 The Old Manor Paxford**
★★★★ *Bed & Breakfast*
Old Manor Cottages, Paxford,
Chipping Campden GL55 6XL
t (01386) 593130
e jankirton@hotmail.co.uk

### PAYHEMBURY
Devon

**Luton Barn** ★★★★
*Bed & Breakfast*
Luton, Payhembury, Honiton
EX14 3HZ
t (01404) 841498
e lutonbarn@talktalk.net
w lutonbarn.co.uk

**Yellingham Farm** ★★★★
*Farmhouse* SILVER AWARD
Payhembury, Honiton
EX14 3HE
t (01404) 850272
e janeteast@yellinghamfarm.
co.uk
w yellinghamfarm.co.uk

### PEDWELL
Somerset

**Polden Vale** ★★★★
*Bed & Breakfast*
Taunton Road, Nr Street
TA7 9BG
t (01458) 211114
e paul.malabar@onetel.net

**Sunnyside** ★★★★
*Bed & Breakfast*
SILVER AWARD
34 Taunton Road, Nr Street
TA7 9BG
t (01458) 210097
e sunnyside@pedwell.freeuk.
com
w pedwell.freeuk.com

### PELYNT
Cornwall

**Bake Farm** ★★★★
*Farmhouse*
Pelynt, Looe PL13 2QQ
t (01503) 220244
e bakefarm@btopenworld.
com

**Cardwen Farm** ★★★★
*Farmhouse*
Pelynt, Looe PL13 2LU
t (01503) 220213
e cardwenfarm@freenet.co.uk
w cardwenfarm.com

**Trenderway Farm** ★★★★★
*Farmhouse* SILVER AWARD
Pelynt, Looe PL13 2LY
t (01503) 272214
e trenderwayfarm@hotmail.
com
w trenderwayfarm.co.uk

### PENHALLOW
Cornwall

**Lambriggan Court** ★★★★
*Guest Accommodation*
Lambriggan, Penhallow,
Perranporth TR4 9LU
t (01872) 571636
e lynn_c_churchill@hotmail.
com
w lambriggancourt.co.uk

### PENRYN
Cornwall

**Bay View** ★★★
*Bed & Breakfast*
Busvannah, Penryn TR10 9LQ
t (01326) 372644
e dawnemmerson@aol.com
w falmouth-bandb.co.uk

**Sunnyside Bed and
Breakfast** ★★★★
*Bed & Breakfast*
Treluswell, Penryn TR10 9AN
t (01326) 379254
e enquiries.sunnyside@
btinternet.com
w sunnysidebedandbreakfast.
co.uk

### PENSFORD
Somerset

**Green Acres** ★★
*Guest Accommodation*
Stanton Wick, Pensford, Bristol
BS39 4BX
t (01761) 490397

**Leigh Farm** ★★ *Farmhouse*
Old Road, Pensford, Bristol
BS39 4BA
t (01761) 490281

### PENSILVA
Cornwall

**Langstone** ★★
*Bed & Breakfast*
Lower Middle Hill Lane,
Pensilva, Liskeard PL14 5QS
t (01579) 362719
e senatore945@btinternet.
com
w langstone.me.uk

**Penharget Farm** ★★★★
*Farmhouse*
Pensilva, Liskeard PL14 5RJ
t (01579) 362221
e penhargetfarm@ukonline.
co.uk
w penharget-farm-cornwall.co.
uk

### PENTEWAN
Cornwall

**Ancient Shipbrokers**
★★★★ *Bed & Breakfast*
1 Higher West End, Pentewan,
St Austell PL26 6BY
t (01726) 843370
e wendy@shipbrokers.
orangehome.co.uk
w mevagissey.net

### PENZANCE
Cornwall

**Carnson House** ★★★
*Guest Accommodation*
2 East Terrace, Penzance
TR18 2TD
t (01736) 365589
e carnsonhouse@btconnect.
com
w carnson-house.co.uk

**Castallack Farm** ★★★★
*Farmhouse*
Castallack, Lamorna, Penzance
TR19 6NL
t (01736) 731969
e info@castallackfarm.co.uk
w castallackfarm.co.uk

**Chiverton House B&B**
★★★★
*Guest Accommodation*
SILVER AWARD
Mennaye Road, Penzance
TR18 4NG
t (01736) 332733
e alan.waller@sky.com

**Con Amore, Penzance**
★★★★
*Guest Accommodation*
38 Morrab Road, Penzance
TR18 4EX
t (01736) 363423
e krich30327@aol.com
w con-amore.co.uk

**The Corner House** ★★★★
*Guest Accommodation*
20 Marine Terrace, Penzance
TR18 4DL
t (01736) 351324
e info@
thecornerhousepenzance.co.uk
w thecornerhousepenzance.
co.uk

**Cornerways Guest House**
★★★ *Guest Accommodation*
5 Leskinnick Street, Penzance
TR18 2HA
t (01736) 364645
e enquiries@cornerways-
penzance.co.uk
w penzance.co.uk/cornerways

**Georgian House Hotel**
Rating Applied For
*Guest Accommodation*
20 Chapel Street, Penzance
TR18 4AW
t (01736) 365664
e georgianhouse@
btopenworld.com
w theaa.co.uk/hotels

**Glencree House** ★★★★
*Guest Accommodation*
2 Mennaye Road, Penzance
TR18 4NG
t (01736) 362026
e stay@glencreehouse.co.uk
w glencreehouse.co.uk

**Halcyon Guest House**
★★★★ *Guest House*
6 Chyandour Square, Penzance
TR18 3LW
t (01736) 366302
e pat+bob@halcyon1.co.uk
w halcyon1.co.uk

**Harbour Heights Bed and Breakfast** ★★★
*Bed & Breakfast*
Boase Street, Newlyn, Penzance TR18 5JE
**t** (01736) 350976
**e** anneofnewlyn@aol.com
**w** harbour-heights.co.uk

**Lombard House Hotel** ◆◆◆◆
*Guest Accommodation*
SILVER AWARD
16 Regent Terrace, Penzance TR18 4DW
**t** (01736) 364897
**e** lombardhouse@btconnect. com
**w** lombardhousehotel.com

**Lowenna, Mousehole**
◆◆◆◆◆ *Guest Accommodation*
GOLD AWARD
Lowenna, Raginnis Hill, Penzance TR19 6SL
**t** (01736) 731077
**e** mm4lowenna@aol.com

**Lynwood Guest House**
★★★ *Guest Accommodation*
Morrab Road, Penzance TR18 4EX
**t** (01736) 365871
**e** lynwoodpz@aol.com
**w** lynwood-guesthouse.co.uk

**Menwidden Farm** ★★★
*Farmhouse*
Ludgvan, Penzance TR20 8BN
**t** (01736) 740415
**e** cora@menwidden.freeserve. co.uk

**The Pendennis** ★★★★
*Guest Accommodation*
Alexandra Road, Penzance TR18 4LZ
**t** (01736) 363823
**e** thependennis@googlemail. com
**w** thependennis.co.uk

**Penrose Guest House** ★★★
*Guest House*
8 Penrose Terrace, Penzance TR18 2HQ
**t** (01736) 362782
**e** enquiries@penrosegsthse. co.uk
**w** penrosegsthse.co.uk

**Rose Farm** ★★★★
*Farmhouse*
Chyenhal, Buryas Bridge, Penzance TR19 6AN
**t** (01736) 731808
**e** lally@rosefarmcornwall.co. uk

**Shoreline Guest House**
★★★★
*Guest Accommodation*
17 Marine Terrace, Promenade, Penzance TR18 4DL
**t** (01736) 366821
**e** enquiries@shoreline-penzance.com
**w** shoreline-penzance.com

**Stanley (The)** ★★★
*Guest Accommodation*
The Promenade, Penzance TR18 4DW
**t** (01736) 362146
**e** info@stanley-hotel.co.uk
**w** stanley-hotel.co.uk

**Summer House (The)**
★★★★★
*Guest Accommodation*
Cornwall Terrace, Penzance TR18 4HL
**t** (01736) 363744
**e** reception@summerhouse. cornwall.com
**w** summerhouse-cornwall.com

**Torwood House Hotel** ★★★
*Guest House*
Alexandra Road, Penzance TR18 4LZ
**t** (01736) 360063
**e** lyndasowerby@aol.com
**w** torwoodhousehotel.co.uk

**Tremont Hotel** ★★★★
*Guest Accommodation*
Alexandra Road, Penzance TR18 4LZ
**t** (01736) 362614
**e** info@tremonthotel.co.uk
**w** tremonthotel.co.uk

**Treventon** ★★★
*Guest House*
Alexandra Place, Penzance TR18 4NE
**t** (01736) 363521

**Warwick House Hotel, Penzance** ★★★★
*Guest House*
17 Regent Terrace, Penzance TR18 4DW
**t** (01736) 363881
**e** reception@warwickhouse penzance.co.uk
**w** warwickhousepenzance.co. uk

**Woodstock Guest House**
Rating Applied For
*Guest House*
29 Morrab Road, Penzance TR18 4EZ
**t** (01736) 369049
**e** info@ woodstockguesthouse.co.uk
**w** woodstockguesthouse.co.uk

**Wymering** ★★★
*Guest Accommodation*
Regent Square, Penzance TR18 4BG
**t** (01736) 362126
**e** pam@wymering.com
**w** wymering.com

### PERRANPORTH
Cornwall

**Perranporth Youth Hostel – AF033** ★★ *Hostel*
Droskyn Point, Perranporth TR6 0GS
**t** (01872) 573812
**e** perranporth@yha.org.uk

**Tides Reach** ★★★★
*Guest House*
Ponsmere Road, Perranporth TR6 0BW
**t** (01872) 572188
**e** jandf.boyle@virgin.net
**w** tidesreachhotel.com

**The Whitehouse Inn & Luxury Lodge** ★★★★ *Inn*
Penhallow, Nr Truro, St Agnes TR4 9LQ
**t** (01872) 573306
**e** whitehouseinn@btconnect. com
**w** whitehousecornwall.co.uk

### PIDDLETRENTHIDE
Dorset

**The European Inn** ★★★★
*Inn* SILVER AWARD
Dorchester DT2 7QT
**t** (01300) 348308
**e** info@european-inn.co.uk
**w** european-inn.co.uk

**The Poachers Inn** ★★★★
*Inn*
Piddletrenthide, Dorchester DT2 7QX
**t** (01300) 348358
**e** thepoachersinn@ piddletrenthide.fsbusiness.co. uk
**w** thepoachersinn.co.uk

### PILSDON
Dorset

**Gerrards Farm** ★★★★
*Farmhouse* SILVER AWARD
Pilsdon, Bridport DT6 5PA
**t** (01308) 867474
**e** chrisrabbetts@btinternet. com
**w** gerrardsfarm.co.uk

### PILTON
Somerset

**Bowermead House** ★★★★
*Guest Accommodation*
Whitstone Hill, Nr Shepton Mallet BA4 4DT
**t** (01749) 890744
**e** w.southcombe@ btopenworld.com
**w** bowermeadhouse.co.uk

### PITCHCOMBE
Gloucestershire

**Gable End** ★★★
*Bed & Breakfast*
Pitchcombe, Stroud GL6 6LN
**t** (01452) 812166

### PLYMOUTH
Devon

**Athenaeum Lodge** ★★★★
*Guest Accommodation*
4 Athenaeum Street, The Hoe, Plymouth PL1 2RQ
**t** (01752) 665005 & (01752) 670090
**e** us@athenaeumlodge.com
**w** athenaeumlodge.com

**Berkeleys of St James**
★★★★
*Guest Accommodation*
4 St James Place East, Plymouth PL1 3AS
**t** (01752) 221654
**e** enquiry@onthehoe.co.uk
**w** onthehoe.co.uk

**Bowling Green Hotel**
★★★★
*Guest Accommodation*
SILVER AWARD
9-10 Osborne Place, Plymouth PL1 2PU
**t** (01752) 209090
**e** info@bowlingreenhotel.com
**w** bowlingreenhotel.com

**Brittany Guest House** ★★★
*Guest House*
28 Athenaeum Street, The Hoe, Plymouth PL1 2RQ
**t** (01752) 262247
**e** enquiries@ brittanyguesthouse.com
**w** brittanyguesthouse.co.uk

**Caledonia Guest House**
★★★★ *Guest House*
27 Athenaeum Street, Plymouth PL1 2RQ
**t** (01752) 229052
**e** info@thecaledonia.co.uk
**w** thecaledonia.co.uk

**Casa Mia Guest House** ★★★
*Guest House*
201 Citadel Road East, The Hoe, Plymouth PL1 2JF
**t** (01752) 265742
**e** fletcher@cons10.freeserve. co.uk
**w** casa-mia-onthehoe.com

**Citadel House** ★★
*Guest House*
55 Citadel Rd, The Hoe, Plymouth PL1 3AU
**t** (01752) 661712
**w** citadelhouse.co.uk

**Crescent House Hotel** ★★★
*Guest House*
18 Garden Crescent, West Hoe, Plymouth PL1 3DA
**t** (01752) 266424

**Four Seasons** ★★★★
*Guest House*
207 Citadel Road East, Plymouth PL1 2JF
**t** (01752) 223591
**e** bobkatecarter@btconnect. com
**w** fourseasonsguesthouse.co. uk

**Gabber Farm** ★★★
*Farmhouse*
Gabber Lane, Down Thomas, Plymouth PL9 0AW
**t** (01752) 862269
**e** gabberfarm@tiscali.co.uk

**Homeleigh Bed & Breakfast**
★★ *Bed & Breakfast*
5 George Lane, Plympton, Plymouth PL7 1LJ
**t** (01752) 330478
**e** homeleighbandb@ blueyonder.co.uk
**w** homeleighbandb.co.uk

**Hotspur Guest House** ★★★
*Guest House*
108 North Road East, Plymouth PL4 6AW
**t** (01752) 663928
**e** info@hotspurguesthouse.co. uk
**w** hotspurguesthouse.co.uk

**The Imperial** ★★★
*Guest Accommodation*
Lockyer Street, Plymouth PL1 2QD
**t** (01752) 227311
**e** info@imperialplymouth.co. uk
**w** imperialplymouth.co.uk

**Kynance House** ★★
*Guest Accommodation*
113 Citadel Road West, The Hoe, Plymouth PL1 2RN
**t** (01752) 266821
**e** info@kynancehotel.co.uk
**w** kynancehotel.co.uk

**Mariners Guest House ★★★**
*Guest House*
11 Pier Street, West Hoe,
Plymouth PL1 3BS
t (01752) 261778
e marinersguesthouse@
blueyonder.co.uk
w marinersguesthouse.co.uk

**Mayflower Guest House**
**★★★ Guest House**
209 Citadel Road East,
Plymouth PL1 2JF
t (01752) 667496
e mayflower.guest.house@
gmail.com
w mayflowerguesthouse.co.uk

**The Moorings Guest House**
**★★★ Guest Accommodation**
4 Garden Crescent, West Hoe,
Plymouth PL1 3DA
t (01752) 250128
e enquiries@
themooringsguesthouse
plymouth.com
w themooringsguesthouse
plymouth.com

**Osmond Guest House**
**★★★★ Guest House**
42 Pier Street, Plymouth
PL1 3BT
t (01752) 229705
e info@osmondguesthouse.
co.uk
w osmondguesthouse.co.uk

**Poppy's Guest House ★★★**
*Guest House*
4 Alfred Street, The Hoe,
Plymouth PL1 2RP
t (01752) 670452
w poppysguesthouse.co.uk

**Seymour Guest House ★★**
*Guest House*
211 Citadel Road East, The
Hoe, Plymouth PL1 2JF
t (01752) 667002
e peter@seymourguesthouse.
co.uk
w seymourguesthouse.co.uk

**Sydney Guest House ★★**
*Guest House*
181 North Road West,
Plymouth PL1 5DE
t (01752) 266541

**Tudor House ★★★**
*Guest Accommodation*
105 Citadel Road, The Hoe,
Plymouth PL1 2RN
t (01752) 661557
e tudorhouse.plymouth@
tiscali.co.uk
w tudorhouseplymouth.co.uk

**University of Plymouth**
**★★★ Campus**
Drake Circus, Plymouth
PL4 8AA
t (01752) 232061
e summer-accommodation@
plymouth.ac.uk
w plymouth.ac.uk/
holidayaccommodation

POLBATHIC
Cornwall

**Buttervilla Farm ★★★★**
*Farmhouse* SILVER AWARD
Polbathic, St Germans, Looe
PL11 3EY
t (01503) 230315
e info@buttervilla.com
w buttervilla.com

POLGOOTH
Cornwall

**Hunters Moon ★★★★**
*Guest House*
Chapel Hill, Polgooth, St
Austell PL26 7BU
t (01726) 66445
e enquiries@
huntersmooncornwall.co.uk
w huntersmooncornwall.co.uk

POLPERRO
Cornwall

**Chyavallon ★★★★**
*Bed & Breakfast*
Landaviddy Lane, Polperro,
Looe PL13 2RT
t (01503) 272788
w polperro.org/chyavallon

**The Cottage Restaurant**
**★★★★**
*Restaurant with Rooms*
SILVER AWARD
The Coombes, Polperro, Looe
PL13 2RG
t (01503) 272217
w cornwalltouristboard.co.uk/
thecottagerestaurant

**Crumplehorn Inn and Mill**
**★★★ Inn**
Crumplehorn, Polperro, Looe
PL13 2RJ
t (01503) 272348
e host@crumplehorn-inn.co.
uk
w crumplehorn-inn.co.uk

**Millie's ★★★ Bed & Breakfast**
Crumplehorn, Looe PL13 2RJ
t (01503) 272492

POLZEATH
Cornwall

**White Heron ★★★★**
*Guest House*
Polzeath, Wadebridge
PL27 6TJ
t (01208) 863623
e info@whiteheronhotel.co.uk
w whiteheronhotel.co.uk

POOLE
Dorset

**Alice Sea Guest House B&B**
**★★★ Bed & Breakfast**
17 Burngate Road, Hamworthy,
Poole BH15 4HS
t (01202) 679840
e alice.sea@ntlworld.com

**Cherry Tree B&B ★★★**
*Bed & Breakfast*
84 Parkstone Heights, Poole
BH14 0RZ
t (01202) 723494
e cherrytree_poole@
btinternet.com

**Corkers Restaurant & Cafe
Bar with Guest Rooms**
**★★★★ Guest House**
SILVER AWARD
1 High Street, Poole BH15 1AB
t (01202) 681393
e corkers@corkers.co.uk
w corkers.co.uk/corkers

**Cranborne House ★★★★**
*Guest Accommodation*
SILVER AWARD
45 Shaftesbury Road, Poole
BH15 2LU
t (01202) 685200
w cranborne-house.co.uk

**Danecourt Lodge ★★★★**
*Bed & Breakfast*
GOLD AWARD
58 Danecourt Road, Poole
BH14 0PQ
t (01202) 730957

**Fleetwater Guest House**
**★★★★**
*Guest Accommodation*
161 Longfleet Road, Poole
BH15 2HS
t (01202) 682509
e fleetwater161@yahoo.co.uk
w fleetwaterguesthouse.co.uk

**Foxes B&B ★★**
*Bed & Breakfast*
SILVER AWARD
13 Sandbanks Road, Poole
BH14 8AG
t (01202) 269633
e sue.fox@foxesbandb.co.uk
w foxesbandb.co.uk

**Harbourside Guest House**
**★★ Bed & Breakfast**
195 Blandford Road, Poole
BH15 4AX
t (01202) 673053
e harboursideguest@amserve.
com

**Highways ★★★**
*Bed & Breakfast*
29 Fernside Road, Poole
BH15 2QU
t (01202) 677060

**Hoveto B&B ★★★★**
*Bed & Breakfast*
Salterns Road, Poole BH14 8BJ
t (01202) 241430
e hoveto3@hotmail.com

**Lytchett Mere ★★★★**
*Bed & Breakfast*
SILVER AWARD
191 Sandy Lane, Upton, Poole
BH16 5LU
t (01202) 622854

**Mariners Guest House ★★★**
*Guest House*
26 Sandbanks Road, Poole
BH14 8AQ
t (01202) 247218
e admin@
themarinersguesthouse.co.uk
w themarinersguesthouse.co.
uk

**Oakborne ★★★★**
*Bed & Breakfast*
116 Ringwood Road, Poole
BH14 0RW
t (01202) 678211
e absmurrey@aol.com
w oakborne.co.uk

**Quay House ★★**
*Bed & Breakfast*
3a Thames Street, Poole
BH15 1JN
t (01202) 686335
w poole-bed-and-breakfast.
com

**Quayside Bed & Breakfast**
**★★ Guest Accommodation**
9 High Street, Poole BH15 1AB
t (01202) 683733

**The Saltings ★★★★**
*Bed & Breakfast*
SILVER AWARD
5 Salterns Way, Poole
BH14 8JR
t (01202) 707349
e saltings_poole@yahoo.co.uk
w the-saltings.com

**Tideway ★★★★**
*Bed & Breakfast*
Beach Road, Upton, Poole
BH16 5NA
t (01202) 621293
e tideway@tiscali.co.uk
w tidewaybb.co.uk

**Vernon ★★ Bed & Breakfast**
96 Blandford Road North,
Beacon Hill, Poole BH16 6AD
t (01202) 625185
e fred@vernonbnb.co.uk
w vernonbnb.co.uk

PORLOCK
Somerset

**Exmoor House ★★★★★**
*Guest Accommodation*
SILVER AWARD
Minehead Road, Porlock
TA24 8EY
t (01643) 863599
e ann@exmoor-house.co.uk
w exmoor-house.co.uk

**Leys ★★★ Bed & Breakfast**
The Ridge, Bossington Lane,
Porlock TA24 8HA
t (01643) 862477

**Myrtle Cottage ★★★**
*Bed & Breakfast*
High Street, Porlock TA24 8PU
t (01643) 862978
e bob.steer@virgin.net
w myrtleporlock.co.uk

**Rose Bank Guest House**
**★★★★ Guest House**
SILVER AWARD
High Street, Porlock TA24 8PY
t (01643) 862728
e info@rosebankguesthouse.
co.uk
w rosebankguesthouse.co.uk

**Sea View ★★★★**
*Bed & Breakfast*
High Street, Porlock TA24 8NP
t (01643) 863456
e seaview.porlock@btconnect.
com

PORT ISAAC
Cornwall

**Anchorage – Port Isaac**
**★★★★**
*Guest Accommodation*
12 The Terrace, Port Isaac
PL29 3SG
t (01208) 880629
w anchorageportisaac.co.uk

**Cornish Arms ★★★ Inn**
Pendoggett, Port Isaac
PL30 3HH
t (01208) 880263
e info@cornisharms.com
w cornisharms.com

**Hathaway Bed and Breakfast** ◆◆◆◆
*Guest Accommodation*
Roscarrock Hill, Port Isaac
PL29 3RG
t (01208) 880416
e marion.andrews1@
btopenworld.com
w cornwall-online.co.uk/
hathaway

**The Longcross Hotel** ★★★★
*Guest Accommodation*
Trelights, Port Isaac PL29 3TF
t (01208) 880243
e longcross@portisaac.com
w portisaac.com

**The Slipway** ★★★★ *Inn*
Harbour Front, Port Isaac
PL29 3RH
t (01208) 880264
e slipway@portisaachotel.com
w portisaachotel.com

**Westaway** ★★★★★
*Guest Accommodation*
Trelights, Port Isaac PL29 3TF
t (01208) 881156
e info@westawaycornwall.
com
w westawaycornwall.com

### PORTHCRESSA
### Isles of Scilly

**The Lookout** ★★★★
*Bed & Breakfast*
Porthcressa, St Mary's
TR21 0JQ
t (01720) 422132

### PORTHLEVEN
### Cornwall

**The Copper Kettle** ★★★★
*Guest Accommodation*
33 Fore Street, Porthleven,
Helston TR13 9HQ
t (01326) 565660
e terry@davis9658.fsnet.co.uk
w cornishcopperkettle.com

### PORTLAND
### Dorset

**Alessandria House** ★★
*Guest Accommodation*
71 Wakeham Easton, Portland
DT5 1HW
t (01305) 822270

**Brackenbury House** ★★★
*Bed & Breakfast*
Fortuneswell, Portland DT5 1LP
t (01305) 826509
e enquiries@
brackenburyhouse.co.uk
w brackenburyhouse.co.uk

**YHA Portland** ★★★ *Hostel*
Hardy House, Portland
DT5 1AU
t 0870 770 6000
e portland@yha.org.uk
w yha.org.uk

### PORTON
### Wiltshire

**The Porton** ★★★ *Inn*
Station Approach, Porton
SP4 0LA
t (01980) 610203
e info@portonhotel.com
w portonhotel.com

### PORTREATH
### Cornwall

**Fountain Springs** ★★★
*Guest Accommodation*
Glenfeadon House, Portreath,
Redruth TR16 4JU
t (01209) 842650
e glenfeadonhouse@aol.com
w fountainsprings.co.uk

### PORTSCATHO
### Cornwall

**Trewithian Farm B&B**
★★★★
*Guest Accommodation*
Trewithian, Portscatho, St
Mawes TR2 5EJ
t (01872) 580293
e penhaligon@trewithian.
freeserve.co.uk
w trewithianfarm.co.uk

### POSTBRIDGE
### Devon

**Bellever YHA** ★★ *Hostel*
Bellever, Postbridge, Yelverton
PL20 6TU
t (01822) 880227
e bellever@yha.org.uk
w yha.org.uk

**Runnage** *Bunkhouse*
Runnage Farm, Postbridge,
Yelverton PL20 6TN
t (01822) 880222
e christine@
runnagecampingbarns.fsnet.co.uk
w runnagecampingbarns.co.uk

### POTTERNE
### Wiltshire

**Four Winds** ★★★
*Bed & Breakfast*
11 Silver Street, Potterne,
Devizes SN10 5NQ
t (01380) 730334
e angelahousehold@hotmail.
com

**Frogsleap** ★★★★
*Bed & Breakfast*
10 Blounts Court, Potterne,
Devizes SN10 5QA
t (01380) 727761
e crisp@frogsleap.freeserve.
co.uk

### POULSHOT
### Wiltshire

**Poulshot Lodge Farm** ★★
*Farmhouse*
Poulshot Road, Poulshot,
Devizes SN10 1RQ
t (01380) 828255

### POUNDSTOCK
### Cornwall

**Outdoor Adventure Ltd**
★★★ *Activity Accommodation*
Atlantic Court, Widemouth
Bay, Bude EX23 0DF
t (01288) 361312

### POWERSTOCK
### Dorset

**Three Horseshoes Inn**
★★★★ *Inn*
Powerstock, Bridport DT6 3TF
t (01308) 485328
e info@threehorseshoesinn.
com
w threehorseshoesinn.com

### PRAA SANDS
### Cornwall

**Mzima** ★★★
*Guest Accommodation*
Penlee Close, Praa Sands,
Penzance TR20 9SR
t (01736) 763856

### PRIDDY
### Somerset

**Ebborways Farm** ★★★
*Guest Accommodation*
Pelting Drove, Nr Wells
BA5 3BA
t (01749) 676339
e chrisdyke@
ebborwayspriddy.eclipse.co.uk

### QUEEN CAMEL
### Somerset

**Dairy Court** ★★★★
*Guest Accommodation*
Wales, Yeovil BA22 7PA
t (01935) 850003
e enquiries@dairycourt.com
w dairycourt.com

### RADSTOCK
### Somerset

**Hollow Hole Barn** ★★★★
*Guest Accommodation*
Binegar Lane, Binegar BA3 4TR
t (01749) 841200
e hhbarn@fsmail.net
w hollowholebarn.co.uk

**Radstock Hotel & Bar** ★★★
*Inn*
Market Place, Radstock
BA3 3AD
t (01761) 420776
e samantha.smith22@tesco.
net
w radstockhotel.co.uk/

### RAMSBURY
### Wiltshire

**Marridge Hill Cottage** ★★★
*Bed & Breakfast*
Marridge Hill, Ramsbury,
Marlborough SN8 2HG
t (01672) 520486

### REDLYNCH
### Wiltshire

**Forest Edge B&B** ★★★★
*Bed & Breakfast*
Lower Windyeats Cottage,
Forest Road, Salisbury SP5 2PU
t (01725) 511516
e forestedge@hotmail.co.uk
w newforestedge.co.uk

### REDRUTH
### Cornwall

**GooNearl Cottage** ★★★★
*Guest House*
Wheal Rose, Scorrier, Redruth
TR16 5DF
t (01209) 891571
e goonearl@onetel.com
w goonearlcottage.com

**Tumblydown Farm** ★★★
*Guest Accommodation*
Tolgus Mount, Redruth
TR15 3TA
t (01209) 211191
w tumblydownfarm.co.uk

### REZARE
### Cornwall

**Rezare Farmhouse** ★★★★
*Guest Accommodation*
SILVER AWARD
Rezare, Launceston PL15 9NX
t (01579) 371214
e info@rezarefarmhouse.co.uk
w rezarefarmhouse.co.uk

### ROADWATER
### Somerset

**Woodadvent Farm**
*Camping Barn*
Watchet TA23 0RR
t (01984) 640920
e info@woodadventfarm.co.
uk
w woodadventfarm.co.uk

### ROBOROUGH
### Devon

**Lopwell Camping Barn**
*Camping Barn*
Roborough, Plymouth PL6 7BZ
t 0870 770 6113
e campingbarns@yha.org.uk
w yha.org.uk

### ROCK
### Cornwall

**Silvermead** ★★★
*Guest House*
Wadebridge PL27 6LB
t (01208) 862425
w silvermeadguesthouse.co.uk

### ROSCROGGAN
### Cornwall

**Roscroggan Chapel** ★★★
*Guest House*
Roscroggan, Camborne
TR14 0JA
t (01209) 714696
e enquiries@accommodation-
in-cornwall.com
w accommodation-in-cornwall.
com

### RUAN HIGH LANES
### Cornwall

**New Gonitor Farm** ★★★★
*Farmhouse*
Ruan High Lanes, Truro
TR2 5LE
t (01872) 501345
e rosemary@newgonitorfarm.
wanadoo.co.uk

**Trenona Farm Holidays**
★★★ *Farmhouse*
Ruan High Lanes, Truro
TR2 5JS
t (01872) 501339
e info@trenonafarmholidays.
co.uk
w trenonafarmholidays.co.uk

### RUAN MINOR
### Cornwall

**Skyber** ★★★★
*Bed & Breakfast*
Treal, Ruan Minor, Helston
TR12 7LS
t (01326) 290684

### RUDDLE
### Gloucestershire

**Underhill House** ★★★★
*Farmhouse*
Newnham GL14 1DS
t (01594) 510621
e info@underhill-house.co.uk
w underhill-house.co.uk

---

## RUDFORD
### Gloucestershire

**The Dark Barn Cottages**
★★★★
*Guest Accommodation*
Barbers Bridge, Rudford,
Gloucester GL2 8DX
t (01452) 790412
e info@barbersbridge.co.uk
w barbersbridge.co.uk

## RUSHALL
### Wiltshire

**Chestnuts Cottage** ★★★★
*Bed & Breakfast*
Church Lane, Rushall, Pewsey
SN9 6EH
t (01980) 630976
e richard@chestnuts.
fsbusiness.co.uk

**Little Thatch** ★★★
*Bed & Breakfast*
Rushall, Pewsey SN9 6EN
t (01980) 635282

## ST AGNES
### Cornwall

**Penkerris** ★★ *Guest House*
Penwinnick Road, St Agnes
TR5 0PA
t (01872) 552262
e info@penkerris.co.uk
w penkerris.co.uk

## ST AGNES
### Isles of Scilly

**Hellweathers Guest House**
★★★ *Bed & Breakfast*
St Agnes TR22 0PL
t (01720) 422430

## ST AUSTELL
### Cornwall

**Anchorage House** ★★★★★
*Guest Accommodation*
GOLD AWARD
Nettles Corner, Boscundle, St
Austell PL25 3RH
t (01726) 814071
e info@anchoragehouse.co.uk
w anchoragehouse.co.uk

**Cornerways Guesthouse**
★★★ *Guest House*
Penwinnick Road, St Austell
PL25 5DS
t (01726) 61579
e nlosurveys@aol.com

**Crossways** ★★★
*Guest Accommodation*
6 Cromwell Road, St Austell
PL25 4PS
t (01726) 77436
e enquiries@crosswaysbandb.
co.uk
w crosswaysbandb.co.uk

**Greenbank** ★★★★
*Bed & Breakfast*
39 Southbourne Road, St
Austell PL25 4RT
t (01726) 73326
e greenbank@cornish-riviera.
co.uk
w cornish-riviera.co.uk/
greenbank.htm

**Gwyndra House** ★★★
*Bed & Breakfast*
7 Kings Avenue, St Austell
PL25 4TT
t (01726) 73870
e gwyndrahouse@btconnect.
com
w gwyndrahouse.co.uk

**Highland Court Lodge**
★★★★★
*Guest Accommodation*
SILVER AWARD
Biscovey Road, Biscovey
PL24 2HW
t (01726) 813320
e enquiries@highlandcourt.co.
uk
w highlandcourt.co.uk

**Holly House** ★★★★
*Bed & Breakfast*
84 Truro Road, St Austell
PL25 5JS
t (01726) 70022
e penny@holly84.freeserve.
co.uk
w hollyhousecornwall.co.uk

**Little Grey Cottage** ★★★★
*Bed & Breakfast*
Trethurgy, St Austell PL26 8YD
t (01726) 850486
e info@littlegreycottagebb.co.
uk
w littlegreycottagebb.co.uk

**Lowarn** ★★★★
*Bed & Breakfast*
16 Poltair Road, St Austell
PL25 4LT
t (01726) 61669
e lowarne@aol.com

**Lowarth Gwyth** ★★★
*Guest Accommodation*
80 Truro Road, St Austell
PL25 5JS
t (01726) 70513
e ann@lowarthgwyth.co.uk
w lowarthgwyth.co.uk

**Lower Barn Country Escape**
★★★★★ *Guest House*
SILVER AWARD
Bosue, St Ewe, St Austell
PL26 6EU
t (01726) 844881
e janie@bosue.co.uk
w bosue.co.uk

**Mandalay** ★★★ *Guest House*
School Hill, Mevagissey, St
Austell PL26 6TQ
t (01726) 842435
e jill@mandalayhotel.
freeserve.co.uk
w mandalayhotel.freeserve.co.
uk

**Spindrift** ★★★
*Bed & Breakfast*
London Apprentice, St Austell
PL26 7AR
t (01726) 69316

**Tall Ships** ★★★★★
*Bed & Breakfast*
2 Eleven Doors, Charlestown,
St Austell PL25 3NZ
t (01726) 871095
e tallshipscharlestown@tiscali.
co.uk

**Trevu** ★★★ *Bed & Breakfast*
10 Courtney Road, St Austell
PL25 4JF
t (01726) 64480
w trevu.co.uk

## ST BREOCK
### Cornwall

**Pawton Stream** ★★★★
*Bed & Breakfast*
Wadebridge PL27 7LN
t (01208) 814845
e jon.bristow@btopenworld.
com

## ST BREWARD
### Cornwall

**Tarny Bed and Breakfast**
★★★★
*Guest Accommodation*
Row, St Breward, Bodmin
PL30 4LW
t (01208) 851304
e janeattarny@aol.com
w tarny.co.uk

## ST BRIAVELS
### Gloucestershire

**YHA St Briavels Castle** ★★
*Hostel*
St Briavels, Lydney GL15 6RG
t (01594) 530272
e stbriavels@yha.org.uk
w yha.org.uk

## ST BURYAN
### Cornwall

**Boskenna Home Farm**
★★★★
*Guest Accommodation*
SILVER AWARD
St Buryan, Penzance
TR19 6DQ
t (01736) 810705
e julia@boskenna.co.uk
w boskenna.co.uk

**Downs Barn Farm** ★★★★
*Farmhouse*
St Buryan, Penzance TR19 6DG
t (01736) 810295
e carolyn.care@tesco.net

**Tredinney Farm B&B**
★★★★
*Guest Accommodation*
Crows-An-Wra, St Buryan,
Penzance TR19 6HX
t (01736) 810352
e rosemary.warren@
btopenworld.com
w tredinneyfarm.co.uk

**Tregiffian Farm** ★★★★
*Farmhouse*
St Buryan, Penzance TR19 6BG
t (01736) 810243
e vicki.phillips@btclick.com

**Tregurnow Farm** ★★★★
*Guest Accommodation*
St Buryan, Penzance TR19 6BL
t (01736) 810255
e tregurnow@lamorna.biz
w lamorna.biz

**Trelew Farm** ★★★★
*Guest Accommodation*
St Buryan, Penzance TR19 6ED
t (01736) 810308
e info@trelew.co.uk
w trelew.co.uk

## ST COLUMB MAJOR
### Cornwall

**Pennatillie Farm** ★★★★★
*Farmhouse* SILVER AWARD
Talskiddy, St Columb Major
TR9 6EF
t (01637) 880280
e angela@pennatillie.fsnet.co.
uk
w cornish-riviera.co.uk/
pennatilliefarm.htm

## ST ERTH PRAZE
### Cornwall

**Bostrase** ★★★★
*Guest Accommodation*
Tolroy Farm, Off Tolroy Road,
Hayle TR27 6HG
t (01736) 754644
e bostrasecottage@tolroy.
wanadoo.co.uk
w bostraseholidays.co.uk

## ST EVAL
### Cornwall

**Green-Acres** ★★★
*Bed & Breakfast*
Treburrick, St Eval,
Wadebridge PL27 7UR
t (01841) 540671
e greenacres1@hotmail.com

## ST EWE
### Cornwall

**Higher Kestle Farm** ★★★★
*Farmhouse* SILVER AWARD
St Ewe, Nr Mevagissey, St
Austell PL26 6EP
t (01726) 842001
e vicky@higherkestle.
freeserve.co.uk
w higherkestle.co.uk

## ST ISSEY
### Cornwall

**Cannalidgey Villa Farm**
★★★★ *Farmhouse*
Trenance, Wadebridge
PL27 7RB
t (01208) 812276
e cannalidgey@btinternet.com

**Olde Tredore House** ★★★★
*Bed & Breakfast*
St Issey, Wadebridge
PL27 7QS
t (01841) 540291

**Rose Park** ★★★
*Bed & Breakfast*
Penrose Farm, St Issey,
Wadebridge PL27 7RJ
t (01208) 812595

**The White House** ★★★★
*Bed & Breakfast*
St Issey, Wadebridge
PL27 7QE
t (01841) 540884
w whitehousebandb.co.uk

## ST IVES
### Cornwall

**Anchorage Guest House, St
Ives** ★★★★
*Guest Accommodation*
5 Bunkers Hill, St Ives TR26 1LJ
t (01736) 797135
e info@theanchoragebandb.
co.uk
w theanchoragebandb.co.uk

**Blue Hayes Private Hotel**
★★★★★
*Guest Accommodation*
GOLD AWARD
Trelyon Avenue, St Ives
TR26 2AD
t (01736) 797129
e bluehayes@btconnect.com
w bluehayes.co.uk

**Byways** ★★★
*Bed & Breakfast*
22 Steamers Hill, Angarrack,
Hayle TR27 5JB
t (01736) 753463
e bywaysbb@lineone.net
w bywaysbb.co.uk

**Carlill, St Ives** ★★★★
*Guest House*
Porthminster Terrace, St Ives
TR26 2DQ
t (01736) 796738
e lynne@lgpa.freeserve.co.uk

**Carlyon Guest House** ★★★
*Guest House*
18 The Terrace, St Ives
TR26 2BP
t (01736) 795317
e andrea.papworth@
btinternet.com
w carlyon-stives.co.uk

**Chy An Gwedhen** ★★★★
*Guest Accommodation*
St Ives Road, Carbis Bay, St
Ives TR26 2JN
t (01736) 798684
e info@chyangwedhen.com
w chyangwedhen.com

**The Countryman at Trink**
Rating Applied For
*Guest Accommodation*
The Old Coach Road, Trink, St
Ives TR26 3JQ
t (01736) 797571

**Dean Court Guest
Accommodation** ★★★★★
*Guest Accommodation*
SILVER AWARD
Trelyon Avenue, St Ives
TR26 2AD
t (01736) 796023
e info@deancourt.vispa.com
w deancourthotel.com

**The Grey Mullet Guest
House** ★★★★
*Guest Accommodation*
2 Bunkers Hill, St Ives TR26 1LJ
t (01736) 796635
e greymulletguesthouse@
lineone.net
w touristnetuk.com/sw/
greymullet

**Longships Hotel** ★★★★
*Guest Accommodation*
Talland Road, St Ives TR26 2DF
t (01736) 798180
e enquiries@longships-hotel.
co.uk
w longships-hotel.co.uk

**Monterey** ★★★★
*Guest Accommodation*
7 Clodgy View, St Ives
TR26 1JG
t (01736) 794248
e info@monterey-stives.fsnet.
co.uk
w monterey-stives.co.uk

**Sea Breeze** ★★★★
*Guest Accommodation*
SILVER AWARD
5 Higher Trewidden Road, The
Belyars, St Ives TR26 2DP
t (01736) 797549
e jill.yelling@tiscali.co.uk
w seabreeze-stives.co.uk

**Tregony Guest House**
★★★★
*Guest Accommodation*
SILVER AWARD
1 Clodgy View, St Ives
TR26 1JG
t (01736) 795884
e info@tregony.com
w tregony.com

**Treloyhan Manor** ★★★
*Guest Accommodation*
St Ives TR26 2AL
t (01736) 796240
e treloyhan@christianguild.co.
uk
w cgholidays.co.uk

### ST JULIOT
### Cornwall

**The Old Rectory Boscastle**
★★★★★
*Guest Accommodation*
GOLD AWARD
The Old Rectory, St Juliot,
Boscastle PL35 0BT
t (01840) 250225
e sally@stjuliot.com
w stjuliot.com

### ST JUST-IN-PENWITH
### Cornwall

**Bosavern House** ★★★★
*Guest House*
Bosavern, St Just, Penzance
TR19 7RD
t (01736) 788301
e info@bosavern.com
w bosavern.com

**Boswedden House** ★★★
*Guest Accommodation*
Cape Cornwall, St Just,
Penzance TR19 7NJ
t (01736) 788733
e relax@boswedden.org.uk
w boswedden.org.uk

**The Commercial** ★★★
*Guest Accommodation*
Market Square, St Just,
Penzance TR19 7HE
t (01736) 788455
e enquiries@commercial-
hotel.co.uk
w commercial-hotel.co.uk

**Land's End YHA** ★★ *Hostel*
Letcha Vean, Cot Valley, St
Just-in-Penwith TR19 7NT
t (01736) 788437

### ST JUST IN ROSELAND
### Cornwall

**Roundhouse Barns** ★★★★
*Bed & Breakfast*
Truro TR2 5JJ
t (01872) 580038
e info@roundhousebarns.co.
uk
w roundhousebarns.co.uk

### ST KEVERNE
### Cornwall

**Treleague** ★★★★
*Bed & Breakfast*
SILVER AWARD
St Keverne, Helston TR12 6PQ
t (01326) 281500
e mark@treleague.co.uk
w treleague.co.uk

### ST KEW
### Cornwall

**Lane End Farm B&B** ★★★★
*Bed & Breakfast*
Pendoggett, Port Isaac
PL30 3HH
t (01208) 880013
e nabmonk@tiscali.co.uk
w wadebridgelive.com

**Tregellist Farm** ★★★★
*Guest Accommodation*
SILVER AWARD
Tregellist, St Kew PL30 3HG
t (01208) 880537
e jillcleave@tregellist.
fsbusiness.co.uk
w tregellistfarm.co.uk

### ST LEVAN
### Cornwall

**Sea View House** ★★★★
*Guest Accommodation*
Porthcurno, Penzance
TR19 6JX
t (01736) 810638
e seaview.porthcurno@
tinyworld.co.uk
w seaviewhouseporthcurno.
com

### ST MABYN
### Cornwall

**Cles Kernyk** ★★★
*Guest Accommodation*
Wadebridge Rd, St Mabyn,
Bodmin PL30 3BH
t (01208) 841258
e sue@mabyn.freeserve.co.uk
w mabyn.freeserve.co.uk

**Treglown House** ★★★★
*Guest Accommodation*
Haywood Farm, St Mabyn,
Wadebridge PL30 3BU
t (01208) 841896
e treglownhouse@stmabyn.
fsnet.co.uk
w treglownhouse.co.uk

### ST MARY'S
### Isles of Scilly

**Anjeric Guest House** ★★★
*Guest House*
The Strand, St Mary's
TR21 0PS
t (01720) 422700
e judyarcher@yahoo.co.uk
w scillyonline.co.uk/accomm/
anjeric.html

**Annet** ★★★★
*Bed & Breakfast*
SILVER AWARD
St Mary's TR21 0NF
t (01720) 422441
e annet-cottage@lineone.net
w annet-cottage.co.uk

**April Cottage** ★★★★
*Bed & Breakfast*
SILVER AWARD
Church Road, St Mary's
TR21 0NA
t (01720) 422279
e louisehicks@btinternet.com

**Armeria** ★★ *Bed & Breakfast*
1 Porthlo Terrace, St Mary's
TR21 0NF
t (01720) 422961
e dolphindesigns@btinternet.
com

**Auriga Guest House** ★★★★
*Bed & Breakfast*
7 Porthcressa Road, St Mary's
TR21 0JL
t (01720) 422637
e aurigascilly@aol.com

**Beachfield House** ★★★★
*Guest House*
Porthloo TR21 0NE
t (01720) 422463
e whomersley@supanet.com

**Belmont** ★★★ *Guest House*
Church Road, St Mary's
TR21 0NA
t (01720) 423154
e enquiries@the-belmont.
freeserve.co.uk
w the-belmont.freeserve.co.uk

**Blue Carn Cottage** ★★★
*Guest House*
Old Town, St Mary's
TR21 0NH
t (01720) 422309
e philjroberts@tiscali.co.uk

**Broomfields** ★★★★
*Bed & Breakfast*
Church Road, St Mary's
TR21 0NA
t (01720) 422309

**Buckingham House** ★★★
*Guest House*
The Bank, St Mary's TR21 0HY
t (01720) 422543

**Bylet** ★★★ *Guest House*
Church Road, St Mary's
TR21 0NA
t (01720) 422479
e thebylet@bushinternet.com
w byletholidays.com

**Carntop Guest House**
★★★★ *Guest House*
SILVER AWARD
Church Road, St Mary's
TR21 0NA
t (01720) 423763
w carntop.co.uk

**Colossus** ★★★★
*Bed & Breakfast*
Pilot's Retreat, Church Road, St
Mary's TR21 0NA
t (01720) 423631
e enquiries@colossus-scilly.co.
uk
w colossus-scilly.co.uk

**Crebinick House** ★★★★
*Guest House* SILVER AWARD
Church Road, St Mary's
TR21 0JT
t (01720) 422968
e wct@crebinick.co.uk
w crebinick.co.uk

**Eastbank** ★★★★
*Bed & Breakfast*
Porthloo, St Mary's TR21 0NE
t (01720) 423695
w scilly-holidays.co.uk

**Evergreen Cottage Guest
House** ★★★★ *Guest House*
The Parade, Hugh Town
TR21 0LP
t (01720) 422711

**Freesia Guesthouse** ★★★★
*Guest House*
The Parade, St Mary's
TR21 0LP
t (01720) 423676
e freesiaguesthouse@hotmail.
com

**Garrison House** ★★★★
*Bed & Breakfast*
SILVER AWARD
Garrison Hill, St Mary's
TR21 0LS
t (01720) 422972
e garrisonhouse@aol.com
w isles-of-scilly.co.uk/
guesthouses

---

**Kistvaen ★★★★**
*Bed & Breakfast*
Sally Port, St Mary's TR21 0JE
t (01720) 422002
e chivy002@aol.com

**Lynwood ★★★★**
*Bed & Breakfast*
Church Street, St Mary's
TR21 0JT
t (01720) 423313

**Lyonnesse Guest House**
★★★ *Guest House*
Lower Strand, St Mary's
TR21 0PS
t (01720) 422458

**Mincarlo**
Rating Applied For
*Guest House*
Strand, St Mary's TR21 0PT
t (01720) 422513
e manager@mincarlo-ios.co.uk
w mincarlo-ios.co.uk

**Rose Cottage ★★★★**
*Bed & Breakfast*
**SILVER AWARD**
Strand, St Mary's TR21 0PT
t (01720) 422078
e rosecottage@infinnet.co.uk

**St Hellena ★★★**
*Bed & Breakfast*
13 Garrison Lane, St Mary's
TR21 0JD
t (01720) 423231
e mcguiness@st-hellena.fsnet.
co.uk
w http://sthellena.mysite.
freeserve.com

**Santa Maria ★★★★**
*Guest House*
Sallyport, St Mary's TR21 0JE
t (01720) 422687

**Scillonia ★★★**
*Bed & Breakfast*
Bank, St Mary's TR21 0HY
t (01720) 422101

**Shamrock ★★★★**
*Bed & Breakfast*
High Lanes, St Mary's
TR21 0NW
t (01720) 423269

**Shearwater Guest House**
★★★ *Guest House*
The Parade, St Mary's
TR21 0LP
t (01720) 422402
e griswalds00@hotmail.com
w shearwater-guest-house.co.
uk

**Sylina**
Rating Applied For
*Guest House*
Mcfarlands Downs, St Mary's
TR21 0NS
t (01720) 422129

**Tolman House ★★★★**
*Guest Accommodation*
**SILVER AWARD**
Old Town, St Mary's
TR21 0NH
t (01720) 422967
e tolmanhouse@hotmail.co.uk
w scilly-oldtown.com

**Trelawney ★★★**
*Guest House*
Church Street, St Mary's
TR21 0JT
t (01720) 422377
e jharlin@hotmail.com
w trelawney-ios.co.uk

**Veronica Lodge ★★★**
*Bed & Breakfast*
The Garrison, St Mary's
TR21 0LS
t (01720) 422585
e veronicalodge@
freenetname.co.uk

**Westford House ★★★★**
*Guest House*
Church Street, St Mary's
TR21 0JT
t (01720) 422510

**The Wheelhouse ★★★★**
*Guest House*
Little Porth, St Mary's
TR21 0JG
t (01720) 422719

**Wingletang Guest House**
Rating Applied For
*Guest House*
The Parade, St Mary's
TR21 0LP
t (01720) 422381

### ST MAWES
### Cornwall

**Gwelesmor ★★★**
*Bed & Breakfast*
Gwelesmor House, 18 Polvarth
Estate, St Mawes TR2 5AT
t (01326) 270731
e phyllismichell@supanet.com

**Trenestral Farm ★★★**
*Farmhouse*
Ruan High Lanes, Truro
TR2 5LX
t (01872) 501259

### ST MAWGAN
### Cornwall

**Dalswinton House ★★★★**
*Guest Accommodation*
St Mawgan-in-Pydar, Nr
Padstow TR8 4EZ
t (01637) 860385
e dalswintonhouse@tiscali.co.
uk
w dalswinton.com

### ST MERRYN
### Cornwall

**Tregavone Farm ★★★**
*Farmhouse*
St Merryn, Padstow PL28 8JZ
t (01841) 520148

**Trewithen Farmhouse**
★★★★
*Guest Accommodation*
**SILVER AWARD**
St Merryn, Padstow PL28 8JZ
t (01841) 520420

### ST MINVER
### Cornwall

**Tredower Barton ★★★**
*Bed & Breakfast*
St Minver, Wadebridge
PL27 6RG
t (01208) 813501

### ST NEOT
### Cornwall

**Higher Hobbs ★★★★**
*Bed & Breakfast*
Park Farm, St Neot, Liskeard
PL14 6PU
t (01579) 321700
e malcmandy@aol.com

**Higher Searles Down**
★★★★ *Bed & Breakfast*
**SILVER AWARD**
St Neot, Liskeard PL14 6QA
t (01208) 821412
e glen@hsdown.go-plus.net
w hsdown.go-plus.net

**Serena House ★★★**
*Bed & Breakfast*
St Neot, Liskeard PL14 6NG
t (01579) 326079

### ST NEWLYN EAST
### Cornwall

**Trevilson Farm ★★★★**
*Farmhouse*
St Newlyn East, Newquay
TR8 5JF
t (01872) 510391
e trevilson@btconnect.com
w trevilsonfarm.co.uk

**Trewerry Mill ★★★**
*Guest Accommodation*
Trerice, St Newlyn East, Truro
TR8 5GS
t (01872) 510345
e trewerry.mill@which.net
w trewerrymill.co.uk

### ST WENN
### Cornwall

**Trewithian Farm**
Rating Applied For
*Bed & Breakfast*
St Wenn, Bodmin PL30 5PH
t (01208) 895181
e trewithian@hotmail.co.uk
w cornwall-online.co.uk/
trewithianfarm

### SALCOMBE
### Devon

**Burton Farmhouse and
Garden Room Restaurant**
★★★★ *Farmhouse*
Burton Farm, Galmpton,
Kingsbridge TQ7 3EY
t (01548) 561210
e anne@burtonfarm.co.uk
w burtonfarm.co.uk

**Salcombe YHA ★★★** *Hostel*
Overbecks, Sharpitor,
Salcombe TQ8 8LW
t (01548) 842856
e salcombe@yha.org.uk
w yha.org.uk

### SALISBURY
### Wiltshire

**2 Parklane ★★★★**
*Guest Accommodation*
Park Lane, Salisbury SP1 3NP
t (01722) 321001
w 2parklane.co.uk

**78 Belle Vue Road ★★**
*Bed & Breakfast*
Belle Vue Road, Salisbury
SP1 3YD
t (01722) 329477

**94 Milford Hill ★★★**
*Bed & Breakfast*
Milford Hill, Salisbury SP1 2QL
t (01722) 322454

**Alabare House ★★**
*Guest House*
15 Tollgate Road, Salisbury
SP1 2JA
t (01722) 340206
e bookings@alabare.org
w alabare.org

**Avila ★★** *Bed & Breakfast*
130 Exeter Street, Salisbury
SP1 2SG
t (01722) 421093

**Ballantynes ★★★★**
*Bed & Breakfast*
114 Netherhampton Road,
Salisbury SP2 8LZ
t (01722) 325743
e info@ballantynesbandb.com
w ballantynesbandb.com

**The Barford Inn ★★★** *Inn*
Grovely Road, Barford St
Martin, Salisbury SP3 4AB
t (01722) 742242
e info@thebarfordinn.co.uk
w barfordinn.co.uk

**Bridge Farm ★★★★**
*Farmhouse* **SILVER AWARD**
Lower Road, Britford, Salisbury
SP5 4DY
t (01722) 332376
e mail@bridgefarmbb.co.uk
w bridgefarmbb.co.uk

**Burcombe Manor ★★**
*Bed & Breakfast*
Burcombe Lane, Burcombe,
Salisbury SP2 0EJ
t (01722) 744288
e nickatburcombemanor@
btinternet.com
w burcombemanor.co.uk

**Byways House ★★★**
*Guest House*
31 Fowlers Road, Salisbury
SP1 2QP
t (01722) 328364
e info@bywayshouse.co.uk
w bywayshouse.co.uk

**Cawden Cottage ★★★**
*Bed & Breakfast*
Stratford Toney, Salisbury
SP5 4AT
t (01722) 718463
e cawdencottage@yahoo.co.
uk

**The Edwardian Lodge**
★★★★ *Guest House*
59 Castle Road, Salisbury
SP1 3RH
t (01722) 413329
e richardwhite@edlodge.
freeserve.co.uk
w edwardianlodge.co.uk

**Farthings ★★★★**
*Bed & Breakfast*
9 Swaynes Close, Salisbury
SP1 3AE
t (01722) 330749
e farthings@amserve.com
w farthingsbandb.co.uk

**Highveld** ★★★
*Bed & Breakfast*
44 Hulse Road, Salisbury
SP1 3LY
**t** (01722) 338172
**e** y.sfakianos@btopenworld.
com
**w** salisburybedandbreakfast.
com

**Holly Tree House** ★★
*Bed & Breakfast*
53 Wyndham Road, Salisbury
SP1 3AH
**t** (01722) 322955

**Kinvara House** ★★★
*Bed & Breakfast*
28 Castle Road, Salisbury
SP1 3RJ
**t** (01722) 325233
**e** kinvarahouse@aol.com

**Leena's Guest House** ★★★
*Guest House*
50 Castle Road, Salisbury
SP1 3RL
**t** (01722) 335419

**Manor Farm** ★★★★
*Farmhouse*
Burcombe Lane, Burcombe,
Salisbury SP2 0EJ
**t** (01722) 742177
**e** suecombes@
manorfarmburcombe.fsnet.co.
uk
**w** manorfarmburcombebandb.
com

**The Old Post Office Bed &
Breakfast**
Rating Applied For
*Bed & Breakfast*
Lower Road, Salisbury
SP2 9NH
**t** (01722) 501902

**The Old Rectory Bed &
Breakfast** ★★★★
*Bed & Breakfast*
75 Belle Vue Road, Salisbury
SP1 3YE
**t** (01722) 502702
**e** stay@theoldrectory-bb.co.
uk
**w** theoldrectory-bb.co.uk

**Pathways** ★★
*Bed & Breakfast*
41 Shady Bower, Salisbury
SP1 2RG
**t** (01722) 324252

**The Rokeby Guest House**
★★★★ *Guest House*
**SILVER AWARD**
3 Wain-A-Long Road, Salisbury
SP1 1LJ
**t** (01722) 329800
**e** karenrogers@
rokebyguesthouse.co.uk
**w** rokebyguesthouse.co.uk

**Sarum College** ★★
*Guest Accommodation*
19 The Close, Salisbury
SP1 2EE
**t** (01722) 424800
**e** hospitality@sarum.ac.uk
**w** sarum.ac.uk

**Spire House** ★★★★
*Guest Accommodation*
**SILVER AWARD**
84 Exeter Street, Salisbury
SP1 2SE
**t** (01722) 339213
**e** lois.faulkner@talk21.com
**w** salisbury-bedandbreakfast.
com

**Stratford Lodge** ★★
*Guest Accommodation*
4 Park Lane, Salisbury SP1 3NP
**t** (01722) 325177
**e** enquiries@stratfordlodge.
co.uk
**w** stratfordlodge.co.uk

**Swaynes Firs Farm** ★★★
*Bed & Breakfast*
Coombe Bissett, Salisbury
SP5 5RF
**t** (01725) 519240
**e** swaynes.firs@virgin.net
**w** swaynesfirs.co.uk

**Victoria Lodge Guest House**
★★★ *Guest House*
61 Castle Road, Salisbury
SP1 3RH
**t** (01722) 320586
**e** mail@viclodge.co.uk
**w** viclodge.co.uk

**Wyndham Park Lodge**
★★★★
*Guest Accommodation*
51 Wyndham Road, Salisbury
SP1 3AB
**t** (01722) 416517
**e** enquiries@
wyndhamparklodge.co.uk
**w** wyndhamparklodge.co.uk

**YHA Salisbury** ★★★ *Hostel*
Milford Hill House, Milford Hill,
Salisbury SP1 2QW
**t** (01722) 327572
**e** salisbury@yha.org.uk
**w** yha.org.uk

SALTASH
Cornwall

**Kilna House** ★★
*Guest Accommodation*
Tideford, Saltash PL12 5AD
**t** (01752) 851236
**e** kilnahouse01@aol.com
**w** kilnaguesthouse.co.uk

SAMPFORD ARUNDEL
Somerset

**Selby House** ★★★★
*Bed & Breakfast*
**SILVER AWARD**
Brimstone Lane, Nr Wellington
TA21 9QE
**t** (01823) 667384
**e** enquiries@selbyhouse.co.uk
**w** selbyhouse.co.uk

SAMPFORD COURTENAY
Devon

**Langdale** ★★★
*Guest Accommodation*
Sampford Courtenay,
Okehampton EX20 2SY
**t** (01837) 82433
**e** chrisclayton7@lineone.net

SANDFORD
Devon

**Ashridge Farm** ★★★★
*Bed & Breakfast*
Sandford, Crediton EX17 4EN
**t** (01363) 774292
**e** info@ashdridgefarm.co.uk
**w** ashdridgefarm.co.uk

SANDHURST
Gloucestershire

**Brawn Farm** ★★★★
*Farmhouse*
Sandhurst Lane, Sandhurst,
Gloucester GL2 9NR
**t** (01452) 731010
**e** williams.sally@excite.com

SCORRIER
Cornwall

**Whitehall Farm** ★★★★
*Bed & Breakfast*
Whitehall, Scorrier, Redruth
TR16 5BB
**t** (01209) 820333

SEATON
Devon

**Beach End** ★★★★
*Bed & Breakfast*
**SILVER AWARD**
8 Trevelyan Road, Seaton
EX12 2NL
**t** (01297) 23388

**Beaumont** ★★★★
*Guest House*
Castle Hill, Seaton EX12 2QW
**t** (01297) 20832
**e** jane@lymebay.demon.co.uk
**w** smoothhound.co.uk/hotels/
beaumont1.html

**Gatcombe Farm** ★★★★
*Farmhouse*
Seaton EX12 3AA
**t** (01297) 21235
**e** b&b@gatcombefarm.co.uk
**w** gatcombe-farm-devon.co.uk

**Pebbles** ★★★★
*Bed & Breakfast*
**SILVER AWARD**
Sea Hill, Seaton EX12 2QU
**t** (01297) 22678
**e** enquiries@pebbleshouse.co.
uk
**w** pebbleshouse.co.uk

SEEND
Wiltshire

**Malthouse Barn**
Rating Applied For
*Guest Accommodation*
The Malthouse Barn, Baldham,
Melksham SN12 6PW
**t** (01380) 828308
**e** julietreid7@aol.com
**w** themalthousebarn.com

**Rew Farm** ★★★★
*Farmhouse*
Seend Cleeve, Seend,
Melksham SN12 6PS
**t** (01380) 828289

SELSLEY
Gloucestershire

**Little Owl Cottage** ★★★★
*Bed & Breakfast*
Selsey Hill, Selsley, Stroud
GL5 5LN
**t** (01453) 757050
**e** littleowlcottage@btconnect.
com
**w** littleowlcottagebedand
breakfast.co.uk

SEMINGTON
Wiltshire

**Newhouse Farm** ★★★★
*Bed & Breakfast*
Littleton, Semington,
Trowbridge BA14 6LF
**t** (01380) 870349
**e** stay@newhousefarmwilts.
co.uk
**w** newhousefarmwilts.co.uk

SENNEN
Cornwall

**First and Last Cottages –
Treeve Moor** ★★★★
*Guest Accommodation*
Sennen, Penzance TR19 7AE
**t** (01736) 871284
**e** info@firstandlastcottages.co.
uk
**w** firstandlastcottages.co.uk

SHAFTESBURY
Dorset

**3 Ivy Cross** ★★★
*Guest Accommodation*
Ivy Cross, Shaftesbury
SP7 8DW
**t** (01747) 853837
**e** stiktone@aol.com
**w** 3ivycross.co.uk

**The Chalet** ★★★★
*Bed & Breakfast*
**SILVER AWARD**
Christys Lane, Shaftesbury
SP7 8DL
**t** (01747) 853945
**e** enquiries@thechalet.biz
**w** thechalet.biz

**Glebe Farm** ★★★★★
*Bed & Breakfast*
**SILVER AWARD**
High Street, Ashmore,
Salisbury SP5 5AE
**t** (01747) 811974
**e** tmillard@glebe.f9.co.uk

**The Old Forge** ★★★
*Bed & Breakfast*
Compton Abbas, Shaftesbury
SP7 0NQ
**t** (01747) 811881
**e** theoldforge@hotmail.com
**w** theoldforgedorset.co.uk

**The Retreat** ★★★★
*Guest House* **SILVER AWARD**
47 Bell Street, Shaftesbury
SP7 8AE
**t** (01747) 850372
**e** info@the-retreat.org.uk
**w** the-retreat.org.uk

SHAVE CROSS
Dorset

**Shave Cross House Hotel**
★★★★ *Inn* **GOLD AWARD**
Shave Cross Inn, Bridport
DT6 6HW
**t** (01308) 868358
**e** roy.warburton@virgin.net

---

## SHEPTON MALLET
### Somerset

**Belfield House** ★★★
*Guest Accommodation*
34 Charlton Road, Shepton
Mallet BA4 5PA
t (01749) 344353
e info@belfieldhouse.com
w belfieldhouse.com

**Bowlish House** ★★★★
*Restaurant with Rooms*
Wells Road, Bowlish, Shepton
Mallet BA4 5JD
t (01749) 342022
e info@bowlishhouse.com
w bowlishhouse.com

**Littleridge** ★★
*Bed & Breakfast*
46 Compton Road, Shepton
Mallet BA4 5QT
t (01749) 342983

**Maplestone** ★★★★
*Guest Accommodation*
Quarr, Shepton Mallet
BA4 5NP
t (01749) 347979
e gillanddon@hotmail.com

🖼️🚗

**Temple House Farm** ★★★★
*Farmhouse*
Chelynch Rd, Nr Shepton
Mallet BA4 4RQ
t (01749) 880294
e reakesbedbugs@aol.com

## SHERBORNE
### Dorset

**The Alders** ★★★★
*Bed & Breakfast*
Sandford Orcas, Sherborne
DT9 4SB
t (01963) 220666
e jonsue@thealdersbb.com
w thealdersbb.com

**Bridleways** ★★★
*Bed & Breakfast*
Oborne Road, Sherborne
DT9 3RX
t (01935) 814716
e bridleways@tiscali.co.uk

**Cumberland House** ★★★★
*Bed & Breakfast*
**SILVER AWARD**
Green Hill, Sherborne DT9 4EP
t (01935) 817554
e sandie@bandbdorset.co.uk
w bandbdorset.co.uk

**Honeycombe View** ★★★
*Bed & Breakfast*
Lower Clatcombe, Sherborne
DT9 4RH
t (01935) 814644
e honeycombower@talktalk.
net

**The Pheasants B&B** ★★★★
*Bed & Breakfast*
24 Greenhill, Sherborne
DT9 4EW
t (01935) 815252
e info@thepheasants.com
w thepheasants.com

**Village Vacations** ★★★
*Guest Accommodation*
Brookmead, Nr Yeovil
BA22 8AQ
t (01935) 850241
e villagevac@aol.com
w villagevacations.co.uk

## SHIPHAM
### Somerset

**Penscot Inn** ★★★ *Inn*
The Square, Nr Winscombe
BS25 1TW
t (01934) 842659

## SHURDINGTON
### Gloucestershire

**Sundown** ★★★
*Bed & Breakfast*
Whitelands Lane, Little
Shurdington, Shurdington,
Cheltenham GL51 4TX
t (01242) 863353

## SHUTTA
### Cornwall

**Meneglaze Bed & Breakfast**
★★★★ *Guest House*
Shutta, Looe PL13 1LU
t (01503) 269227
e meneglaze@tiscali.co.uk

## SIDBURY
### Devon

**Rose Cottage Sidbury**
★★★★
*Guest Accommodation*
**SILVER AWARD**
Greenhead, Sidbury, Sidmouth
EX10 0RH
t (01395) 597357 &
07891 197218
e roz.kendall@btinternet.com
w rosecottagesidbury.co.uk

## SIDFORD
### Devon

**Core House** ★★★★★
*Bed & Breakfast*
**SILVER AWARD**
Burscombe Lane, Sidford,
Sidmouth EX10 0QA
t (01395) 512255
e burscombe@aol.com
w corehousecottages.co.uk

## SIDMOUTH
### Devon

**Avalon – A haven for non
smokers** ★★★★
*Guest House*
Vicarage Road, Sidmouth
EX10 8UQ
t (01395) 513443
w avalonsidmouth.co.uk

**The Barn And Pinn Cottage
Guest House** ★★★★
*Guest House* **SILVER AWARD**
Bowd Cross, Sidmouth
EX10 0ND
t (01395) 513613
e thebarnandpinncott@
amserve.net
w barnandpinncottage.co.uk/

**Berwick Guest House**
★★★★ *Guest House*
Salcombe Road, Sidmouth
EX10 8PX
t (01395) 513621
e reservations@berwick-
house.co.uk
w berwick-house.co.uk

**Burscombe Farm** ★★★
*Farmhouse*
Burscombe, Sidbury, Sidmouth
EX10 0QB
t (01395) 597648
e burscombefarm@fwi.co.uk
w burscombefarm-devon.co.
uk

**Cheriton Guest House**
★★★★ *Guest House*
Vicarage Road, Sidmouth
EX10 8UQ
t (01395) 513810
e sara.land1@virgin.net
w smoothhound.co.uk/hotels/
cheritong.html

🚗

**Coombe Bank Guest House**
★★★★ *Guest House*
86 Alexandria Road, Sidmouth
EX10 9HG
t (01395) 514843
e info@coombebank.co.uk
w coombebank.co.uk

**Dukes** ★★★
*Guest Accommodation*
The Esplanade, Sidmouth
EX10 8AR
t (01395) 513320
e dukes@hotels-sidmouth.co.
uk
w hotels-sidmouth.co.uk

**Farmhouse Cottage** ★★★★
*Guest Accommodation*
Church Street, Sidford,
Sidmouth EX10 9RE
t (01395) 577682
e farmhousecott@aol.com
w farmhousecottagesidmouth.
co.uk

**Higher Coombe Farm** ★★★
*Farmhouse*
Tipton St John, Sidmouth
EX10 0AX
t (01404) 813385
e kerstinfarmer@farming.co.
uk
w smoothhound.co.uk/hotels/
higherco.html

**Hollies Guest House** ★★★★
*Guest House*
Salcombe Road, Sidmouth
EX10 8PU
t (01395) 514580
e enquiries@
holliesguesthouse.co.uk
w holliesguesthouse.co.uk

**Holmleigh Guest House**
★★★★ *Guest House*
3 Fortfield Place, Sidmouth
EX10 8NX
t (01395) 513580
e holmleigh3@ukonline.co.uk
w holmleigh3.com

**Kyneton Lodge**
Rating Applied For
*Bed & Breakfast*
87 Alexandria Road, Sidmouth
EX10 9HG
t (01395) 513213
e info@kyneton.co.uk

**Larkstone House** ★★
*Bed & Breakfast*
22 Connaught Road, Sidmouth
EX10 8TT
t (01395) 514345

**Lavenders Blue** ★★★★
*Guest House*
33 Sidford High Street, Sidford,
Sidmouth EX10 9SN
t (01395) 576656
e lavendersbluesidmouth@
fsmail.net

**The Long House** ★★★★★
*Bed & Breakfast*
Salcombe Hill Road, Sidmouth
EX10 0NY
t (01395) 577973
e pvcia@aol.com
w holidaysinsidmouth.co.uk

**Lower Pinn Farm** ★★★★
*Farmhouse*
Peak Hill, Sidmouth EX10 0NN
t (01395) 513733
e liz@lowerpinnfarm.co.uk
w lowerpinnfarm.co.uk

**Lynstead** ★★★★
*Guest House*
Vicarage Road, Sidmouth
EX10 8UQ
t (01395) 514635
e info@lynsteadguesthouse.
co.uk
w lynsteadguesthouse.co.uk

**Pinn Barton Farm** ★★★★
*Farmhouse* **SILVER AWARD**
Peak Hill, Pinn, Sidmouth
EX10 0NN
t (01395) 514004
e betty@pinnbartonfarm.co.uk
w pinnbartonfarm.co.uk

**Rose Cottage** ★★★★
*Guest Accommodation*
Coburg Road, Sidmouth
EX10 8NF
t (01395) 577179
e neilsurf@tesco.net

**Ryton Guest House** ★★★
*Guest House*
52-54 Winslade Road,
Sidmouth EX10 9EX
t (01395) 513981
e info@ryton-guest-house.co.
uk
w ryton-guest-house.co.uk

**The Salty Monk** ★★★★★
*Restaurant with Rooms*
**GOLD AWARD**
Church Street, Sidford,
Sidmouth EX10 9QP
t (01395) 513174
e saltymonk@btconnect.com
w saltymonk.co.uk

🖼️🚗

**Sidling Field** ★★
*Bed & Breakfast*
105 Peaslands Road, Sidmouth
EX10 8XE
t (01395) 513859
e shenfield@sidlingfield.co.uk
w sidlingfield.co.uk

**Southcombe Guesthouse**
★★★★ *Guest House*
Vicarage Road, Sidmouth
EX10 8UQ
t (01395) 513861
e mervyn.james@virgin.net

**Southcroft** ★★★★
*Guest Accommodation*
Arcot Road, Sidmouth
EX10 9ES
t (01395) 516903
e southcroft_sidmouth@
yahoo.com
w southcroftsidmouth.co.uk

**Southern Cross Guest House**
★★★ *Guest House*
High Street, Newton
Poppleford, Sidmouth
EX10 0DU
t (01395) 568439
e southerncrossguesthouse@
tesco.net
w southerncrossguesthouse.
co.uk

**Tyrone** ★★★★
*Bed & Breakfast*
Sid Road, Sidmouth EX10 9AL
t (01395) 516753
e tyronehouse@msn.com

**The Willow Bridge** ★★★★
*Guest House*
Millford Road, Sidmouth
EX10 8DR
t (01395) 513599

### SILVERTON
Devon

**Three Tuns Inn** ★★★ *Inn*
14 Exeter Road, Silverton,
Exeter EX5 4HX
t (01392) 860352
w threetuninn.co.uk

### SIMONSBATH
Somerset

**Emmett's Grange** ★★★★
*Bed & Breakfast*
Simonsbath TA24 7LD
t (01643) 831138
e mail@emmettsgrange.co.uk
w emmettsgrange.co.uk

**Exmoor Forest Inn** ★★★★
*Inn*
Simonsbath TA24 7SH
t (01643) 831341
e info@exmoorforestinn.co.uk
w exmoorforestinn.co.uk

### SIXPENNY HANDLEY
Dorset

**Chase House** ★★
*Bed & Breakfast*
Deanland, Sixpenny Handley
SP5 5PD
t (01725) 552829
e chasehouse1@gmail.com

### SLAUGHTERFORD
Wiltshire

**Manor Farm** ★★★
*Farmhouse*
Slaughterford, Chippenham
SN14 8RE
t (01249) 782243
e janmanorfm@hotmail.co.uk

### SLIMBRIDGE
Gloucestershire

**Slimbridge YHA Centre**
★★★ *Hostel*
Shepherd's Patch, Gloucester
GL2 7BP
t (01453) 890275
e slimbridge@yha.org.uk
w yha.org.uk

**Tudor Arms** ★★★ *Inn*
Shepherds Patch, Slimbridge,
Gloucester GL2 7BP
t (01453) 890306
e ritatudorarms@aol.com

### SNOWSHILL HILL
Gloucestershire

**Snowshill Hill Estate**
★★★★★ *Farmhouse*
**SILVER AWARD**
Snowshill Hill, Moreton-in-
Marsh GL56 9TH
t (01386) 853959
e snowshillhill@aol.com
w broadway-cotswolds.co.uk/
snowshillhill.html

### SOMERTON
Somerset

**Fosse House Farm** ★★★
*Bed & Breakfast*
A37, Nr Somerton TA11 7DW
t (01963) 240268
e stay@fossehousefarm.co.uk
w fossehousefarm.co.uk

**Littleton House** ★★★
*Bed & Breakfast*
New Street, Somerton
TA11 7NU
t (01458) 273072

**Mill House** ★★★★★
*Bed & Breakfast*
**SILVER AWARD**
Mill Road, Somerton TA11 6DF
t (01458) 851215
e b&b@millhousebarton.co.uk
w millhousebarton.co.uk

**The Unicorn** ★★★ *Inn*
West Street, Somerton
TA11 7PR
t (01458) 272101
e unicornhotel@virgin.net

### SOUDLEY
Gloucestershire

**White Horse Inn** ★★★ *Inn*
Church Road, Soudley,
Cinderford GL14 2UA
t (01594) 825968

### SOUTH MOLTON
Devon

**Huxtable Farm** ★★★★
*Farmhouse* **SILVER AWARD**
West Buckland, Barnstaple
EX32 0SR
t (01598) 760254
e info@huxtablefarm.co.uk
w huxtablefarm.co.uk

**Kerscott Farm** ★★★★★
*Farmhouse* **SILVER AWARD**
Ash Mill, South Molton
EX36 4QG
t (01769) 550262
e kerscott.farm@virgin.net
w devon-bandb.co.uk

**Old Coaching Inn** ★★★ *Inn*
Queen Street, South Molton
EX36 3BJ
t (01769) 572526

**Townhouse Barton** ★★★
*Farmhouse*
Nadder Lane, South Molton
EX36 4HR
t (01769) 572467
e info@townhousebarton.co.
uk
w townhousebarton.co.uk

### SOUTH NEWTON
Wiltshire

**Salisbury Old Mill House**
★★★★ *Bed & Breakfast*
**SILVER AWARD**
Warminster Road, South
Newton, Salisbury SP2 0QD
t (01722) 742458
e salisburymill@yahoo.com
w smoothhound.co.uk

### SOUTH PETHERTON
Somerset

**Rock House** ★★★★★
*Guest Accommodation*
**SILVER AWARD**
5 Palmer Street, South
Petherton TA13 5DB
t (01460) 241538
e info@stayatrockhouse.co.uk
w stayatrockhouse.co.uk

### SOUTH TEHIDY
Cornwall

**Collingwood** ◆◆◆
*Guest Accommodation*
Mount Whistle, South Tehidy,
Camborne TR14 0HU
t (01209) 7146 9671
e enquiries@accommodation-
in-cornwall.com
w accommodation-in-cornwall.
com

### SOUTHBOURNE
Dorset

**Mory House** ★★★★
*Guest Accommodation*
**SILVER AWARD**
31 Grand Avenue,
Southbourne, Bournemouth
BH6 3SY
t (01202) 433553
e stay@moryhouse.co.uk
w moryhouse.co.uk

### SOUTHVILLE
City of Bristol

**The Greenhouse** ★★★★
*Bed & Breakfast*
61 Greenbank Road,
Southville, Bristol BS3 1RJ
t (0117) 902 9166
e kathy@
thegreenhousebristol.co.uk
w thegreenhousebristol.co.uk

**The White House Guest
Rooms** ★★★
*Guest Accommodation*
28 Dean Lane, Bristol BS3 1DB
t (0117) 953 7725
e info@
thewhitehouseguestrooms.co.
uk
w thewhitehouseguestrooms.
co.uk

### SOUTHWELL
Dorset

**Lobster Farmhouse** ★★★
*Guest Accommodation*
Portland Bill, Portland DT5 2JT
t (01305) 861253

### SPAXTON
Somerset

**Cobb Cottage Bed &
Breakfast** ★★★
*Bed & Breakfast*
Four Forks, Bridgwater
TA5 1BW
t (01278) 671161
w cobbcottage.com

### SPREYTON
Devon

**The Tom Cobley Tavern**
★★★ *Inn*
Spreyton, Crediton EX17 5AL
t (01647) 231314

### STANTON DREW
Somerset

**Greenlands** ★★★★
*Farmhouse*
Stanton Drew, Bristol BS39 4ES
t (01275) 333487

### STANTON WICK
Somerset

**The Carpenters Arms**
★★★★ *Inn*
Stanton Wick, Pensford, Bristol
BS39 4BX
t (01761) 490202
e carpenters@buccaneer.co.
uk
w the-carpenters-arms.co.uk

### STAVERTON
Devon

**Kingston House** ★★★★★
*Guest Accommodation*
**GOLD AWARD**
Staverton, Totnes TQ9 6AR
t (01803) 762235
e info@kingston-estate.co.uk
w kingston-estate.co.uk

### STAVERTON
Gloucestershire

**Staverton House** ★★★★
*Bed & Breakfast*
Cheltenham GL51 0TW
t (01242) 680886

### STEEPLE ASHTON
Wiltshire

**Church Farm** ★★ *Farmhouse*
High Street, Steeple Ashton,
Trowbridge BA14 6EL
t (01380) 870518
e church.farm@farmline.com

**Longs Arms Inn**
Rating Applied For
*Inn*
High Street, Steeple Ashton,
Trowbridge BA14 6EU
t (01380) 870245
e chantal@stayatthepub.
freeserve.co.uk
w stayatthepub.freeserve.co.
uk

### STOGUMBER
Somerset

**Hall Farm** ★★★ *Farmhouse*
Station Road, Stogumber
TA4 3TQ
t (01984) 656321

**Knoll Cottage** ★★★★
*Bed & Breakfast*
Vellow Road, Stogumber
TA4 3TN
t (01984) 656689
e mail@knoll-cottage.co.uk
w knoll-cottage.co.uk

**The White Horse Inn** ★★★
*Inn*
High Street, Stogumber,
Taunton TA4 3TA
t (01984) 656277
w whitehorsestogumber.co.uk

**Wick House ★★★★**
*Guest House*
2 Brook Street, Stogumber,
Taunton TA4 3SZ
t (01984) 656422
e sheila@wickhouse.
fsbusiness.co.uk
w wickhouse.fsbusiness.co.uk

### STOKE ST GREGORY
Somerset

**Meare Green Farm ★★★★**
*Farmhouse*
Meare Green, Nr Taunton
TA3 6HT
t (01823) 490759
e jane.pine@kiteconsulting.
com
w mearegreenfarm.com

### STOKE SUB HAMDON
Somerset

**Castle Farm ★★★★**
*Farmhouse*
North Street, Stoke sub
Hamdon TA14 6QS
t (01935) 822231
e karen@castlefarm.co.uk
w castlefarmaccomodation.
com

**Fleur De Lis ★★★ Inn**
West Street, Stoke-sub-
Hamdon TA14 6PU
t (01935) 822510
e info@thefleur.co.uk
w thefleur.co.uk

### STONEHOUSE
Gloucestershire

**Beacon Inn ★★★ Inn**
Haresfield, Stonehouse
GL10 3DX
t (01452) 728884
e terry@thebeaconinn.co.uk
w thebeaconinn.co.uk

**Merton Lodge ★★**
*Bed & Breakfast*
8 Ebley Road, Stonehouse
GL10 2LQ
t (01453) 822018

### STONEY STRATTON
Somerset

**Stratton Farm ★★★★**
*Farmhouse*
High Street, Nr Shepton Mallet
BA4 6DY
t (01749) 830830
w strattonfarm.co.uk

### STOUR ROW
Dorset

**Woodville Farm ★★★★**
*Bed & Breakfast*
Green Lane, Stour Row,
Shaftesbury SP7 0QD
t (01747) 838241
e woodvillefarm@btconnect.
com
w stonebank-chickerell.com

### STOURTON CAUNDLE
Dorset

**Golden Hill Cottage ★★★★**
*Bed & Breakfast*
Stourton Caundle, Sturminster
Newton DT10 2JW
t (01963) 362109
e anna@goldenhillcottage.co.
uk
w goldenhillcottage.co.uk

### STOW-ON-THE-WOLD
Gloucestershire

**Aston House ★★★★**
*Bed & Breakfast*
Broadwell, Moreton-in-Marsh
GL56 0TJ
t (01451) 830475
e fja@netcomuk.co.uk
w astonhouse.net

**Corsham Field Farmhouse
★★★ Farmhouse**
Bledington Road, Stow-on-the-
Wold, Cheltenham GL54 1JH
t (01451) 831750
e farmhouse@corshamfield.
co.uk
w corshamfield.co.uk

**Crestow House ★★★★**
*Bed & Breakfast*
Fosseway, Stow-on-the-Wold,
Cheltenham GL54 1JX
t (01451) 830969
e fsimonetti@btinternet.com
w crestow.co.uk

**Cross Keys Cottage ★★★**
*Bed & Breakfast*
Park Street, Stow-on-the-Wold,
Cheltenham GL54 1AQ
t (01451) 831128

**Little Broom ★★★★**
*Guest Accommodation*
Maugersbury, Cheltenham
GL54 1HP
t (01451) 830510
w completely-cotswold.com/
maugers/accom/broom/
broom.htm

**Number Nine ★★★★**
*Bed & Breakfast*
SILVER AWARD
Park Street, Stow-on-the-Wold,
Cheltenham GL54 1AQ
t (01451) 870333
e enquiries@number-nine.info
w number-nine.info

**South Hill Farmhouse
★★★★**
*Guest Accommodation*
Station Road, Stow-on-the-
Wold, Cheltenham GL54 1JU
t (01451) 831888
e info@southhill.co.uk
w southhill.co.uk

**Westcote Inn ★★★★ Inn**
Nether Westcote, Chipping
Norton OX7 6SD
t (01993) 830888
e info@westcoteinn.co.uk
w westcoteinn.co.uk

**White Hart Inn ★★★ Inn**
The Square, Stow-on-the-
Wold, Cheltenham GL54 1AF
t (01451) 830674
w whitehartstow.co.uk

**YHA Stow-on-the-Wold
★★★★ Hostel**
The Square, Cheltenham
GL54 1AF
t (01451) 830497
e stow@yha.org.uk
w yha.org.uk

### STRATFORD SUB CASTLE
Wiltshire

**Carp Cottage ★★★**
*Guest Accommodation*
Stratford Road, Stratford sub
Castle, Salisbury SP1 3LH
t (01722) 327219
e bobcurtis@bobcurtis.
wanadoo.co.uk

### STRATTON-ON-THE-FOSSE
Somerset

**Oval House ★★**
*Bed & Breakfast*
Fosse Road, Stratton-on-the-
Fosse BA3 4RB
t (01761) 232183
e mellotte@clara.co.uk
w mellotte.clara.co.uk

### STREET
Somerset

**The Dairy Cottage ★★★**
*Bed & Breakfast*
18 Cranhill Road, Street
BA16 0BY
t (01458) 442992

**The Dorm ♦♦♦**
*Guest Accommodation*
Glaston Road, Street
BA16 0AN
t (01458) 841493
e info@the-dorm.co.uk
w the-dorm.co.uk

**Marshalls Elm Farm ★★★**
*Farmhouse*
B3151, Street BA16 0TZ
t (01458) 442878

**Mullions ★★★**
*Guest Accommodation*
51 High Street, Street
BA16 0EF
t (01458) 445110
e info@
mullionshotelandrestaurant.co.
uk
w mullionshotelandrestaurant.
co.uk

**Old Orchard House ★★★★**
*Bed & Breakfast*
Middle Brooks, Street
BA16 0TU
t (01458) 442212
e old.orchard.house@
amserve.com
w oldorchardhouse.co.uk

**Street YHA ★ Hostel**
The Chalet, Ivythorn Hill, Street
BA16 0TZ
t 0870 770 6056
w yha.org.uk

### STROUD
Gloucestershire

**1 Woodchester Lodge
★★★★ Bed & Breakfast**
Southfield Road, North
Woodchester, Stroud GL5 5PA
t (01453) 872586
e anne@woodchesterlodge.
co.uk
w woodchesterlodge.co.uk

**Hillenvale ★★★★**
*Guest Accommodation*
The Plain, Whiteshill, Stroud
GL6 6AB
t (01453) 753441
e bobsue@hillenvale.co.uk
w hillenvale.co.uk

**Pretoria Villa ★★★★**
*Bed & Breakfast*
SILVER AWARD
Wells Road, Eastcombe, Stroud
GL6 7EE
t (01452) 770435
e glynis@gsolomon.freeserve.
co.uk
w bedandbreakfast-cotswold.
co.uk

**Tiled House Farm ★★★★**
*Farmhouse*
Oxlynch, Stonehouse
GL10 3DF
t (01453) 822363
e tiledhousebb@aol.com
w tiledhousebandb.com

**Valley Views ★★★★**
*Guest Accommodation*
12 Orchard Close, Kings
Stanley, Stonehouse GL10 3QA
t (01453) 827458
w valley-views.co.uk

**The Yew Tree Bed and
Breakfast ★★★★**
*Bed & Breakfast*
Walls Quarry, Brimscombe,
Stroud GL5 2PA
t (01453) 887980
e info@theyewtreestroud.co.
uk
w theyewtreestroud.co.uk

### STUDLAND
Dorset

**The Bankes Arms Hotel
★★★ Inn**
Manor Road, Studland,
Swanage BH19 3AU
t (01929) 450225

**Shell Bay Cottage ★★★★**
*Guest Accommodation*
SILVER AWARD
Glebe Estate, Studland,
Swanage BH19 3AS
t (01929) 450249
e shellbayrose@btinternet.
com

### STURMINSTER NEWTON
Dorset

**Blackmore Farm Cottage
★★★★**
*Guest Accommodation*
Lydlinch, Sturminster Newton
DT10 2HZ
t (01258) 471624
e blackmorefarmcottagebnb@
yahoo.com
w bfcbednbreakfast.co.uk

**Hazeldean Bed & Breakfast
★★★★ Bed & Breakfast**
Bath Road, Sturminster Newton
DT10 1DS
t (01258) 472224
e sarah_grounds@hotmail.
com
w hazeldeanbnb.co.uk

**The Homestead B&B ★★★**
*Guest Accommodation*
Holehouse Lane, Off Glue Hill,
Sturminster Newton DT10 2AA
t (01258) 471390
e townsend@homestead-bb.
co.uk
w homestead-bb.co.uk

**Lower Fifehead Farm**
★★★★ *Farmhouse*
Fifehead St Quintin,
Sturminster Newton DT10 2AP
**t** (01258) 817335

### SWANAGE
#### Dorset

**Amberlea** ★★★ *Guest House*
36 Victoria Avenue, Swanage
BH19 1AP
**t** (01929) 426213
**e** stay@amberleahotel-
swanage.co.uk
**w** amberleahotel-swanage.co.
uk

**Amberlodge** ★★★
*Guest House*
34 Victoria Avenue, Swanage
BH19 1AP
**t** (01929) 426446
**e** amberlodge@onetel.com
**w** amberlodge-swanage.co.uk

**Arbour House** ★★★
*Guest House*
19 Walrond Road, Swanage
BH19 1PB
**t** (01929) 426237
**e** info@arbourhouseswanage.
co.uk
**w** arbourhouseswanage.co.uk

**Bella Vista** ★★★★
*Guest House*
14 Burlington Road, Swanage
BH19 1LS
**t** (01929) 422873
**e** mail@bellavista-swanage.co.
uk
**w** bellavista-swanage.co.uk

**The Castleton** ★★★★
*Guest Accommodation*
**SILVER AWARD**
1 Highcliffe Road, Swanage
BH19 1LW
**t** (01929) 423972
**e** stay@castletonhotel-
swanage.co.uk
**w** castletonhotel-swanage.co.
uk

**Caythorpe House** ★★★
*Guest Accommodation*
7 Rempstone Road, Swanage
BH19 1DN
**t** (01929) 422892
**w** caythorpehouse.co.uk

**Clare House** ★★★★
*Guest House* **SILVER AWARD**
1 Park Road, Swanage
BH19 2AA
**t** (01929) 422855
**e** info@clare-house.com
**w** clare-house.com

**Danesfort** ★★★ *Guest House*
3 Highcliffe Road, Swanage
BH19 1LW
**t** (01929) 424224
**e** reception@danesforthotel.
co.uk
**w** danesforthotel.co.uk

**Easter Cottage** ★★★★
*Bed & Breakfast*
**SILVER AWARD**
9 Eldon Terrace, Swanage
BH19 1HA
**t** (01929) 427782
**e** daveanddiane@
eastercottage.fsbusiness.co.uk
**w** eastercottage.co.uk

**The Fairway** ★★
*Bed & Breakfast*
De Moulham Road, Swanage
BH19 1NR
**t** (01929) 423367
**e** rita@ritawaller.plus.com
**w** swanagefairway.co.uk

**Firswood** ★★★
*Guest Accommodation*
29 Kings Road West, Swanage
BH19 1HF
**t** (01929) 422306
**e** firswood@aol.com
**w** firswoodguesthouse.co.uk

**Glenlee** ★★★★ *Guest House*
6 Cauldon Avenue, Swanage
BH19 1PQ
**t** (01929) 425794
**e** info@glenleehotel.co.uk
**w** glenleehotel.co.uk

**Goodwyns** ★★★★
*Bed & Breakfast*
2 Walrond Road, Swanage
BH19 1PB
**t** (01929) 421088 &
07952 991129
**e** knapman104@btinternet.
com

**Grace Gardens Guest House**
★★★★ *Guest House*
28 Victoria Avenue, Swanage
BH19 1AP
**t** (01929) 422502
**e** enquiries@gracegardens.co.
uk
**w** gracegardens.co.uk

**The Limes** ★★★
*Guest House*
48 Park Road, Swanage
BH19 2AE
**t** (01929) 422664
**e** info@limeshotel.net
**w** limeshotel.net

**Millbrook Guest House**
★★★ *Guest Accommodation*
56 Kings Road West, Swanage
BH19 1HR
**t** (01929) 423443
**e** bob@millbrookswanage.com
**w** millbrookswanage.com

**The Oxford** ★★★
*Guest House*
3-5 Park Road, Swanage
BH19 2AA
**t** (01929) 422247
**e** enquiries@
oxfordhotelswanage.co.uk
**w** theoxfordswanage.co.uk

**Rivendell Guest House**
★★★★ *Guest House*
58 Kings Road West, Swanage
BH19 1HR
**t** (01929) 421383
**e** kevin@rivendell-
guesthouse.co.uk
**w** rivendell-guesthouse.co.uk

**St Michael** ★★★★
*Guest House*
31 Kings Road West, Swanage
BH19 1HF
**t** (01929) 422064

**Sandhaven Guest House**
★★★ *Guest House*
5 Ulwell Road, Swanage
BH19 1LE
**t** (01929) 422322
**e** mail@sandhaven-guest-
house.co.uk
**w** sandhaven-guest-house.co.
uk

**Swanage Haven Boutique**
**Guest House** ★★★
*Guest House*
3 Victoria Road, Swanage
BH19 1LY
**t** (01929) 423088
**e** info@swanagehaven.com
**w** swanagehaven.com

**The White Swan Inn** ★★ *Inn*
31 High Street, The Square,
Swanage BH19 2LJ
**t** (01929) 423804
**e** info@whiteswanswanage.co.
uk
**w** whiteswanswanage.co.uk

**YHA Swanage** ★★★ *Hostel*
Cluny Crescent, Swanage
BH19 2BS
**t** (01929) 422113
**e** swanage@yha.org.uk
**w** yha.org.uk

### SWEETSHOUSE
#### Cornwall

**Rew Farm** ★★★★
*Farmhouse*
Sweetshouse, Nr Lanhydrock,
Bodmin PL30 5AW
**t** (01208) 873798
**e** sue.hopper@btopenworld.
com
**w** rewfarm.co.uk

### SWINDON
#### Wiltshire

**Appletree House** ★★★
*Guest Accommodation*
29 Kingsdown Road, Upper
Stratton, Swindon SN2 7PE
**t** (01793) 829218
**e** tweed_appletree@hotmail.
co.uk

**The Swandown** ★★★
*Guest Accommodation*
36/37 Victoria Road, Swindon
SN1 3AS
**t** (01793) 536695
**e** swandownhotel@gmail.com
**w** s-h-systems.co.uk/hotels/
swandown

**Tap & Barrel**
Rating Applied For
*Guest Accommodation*
115 Manchester Road,
Swindon SN1 2AJ
**t** (01793) 432587

### SYDLING ST NICHOLAS
#### Dorset

**Hazel Cottage** ★★★★
*Bed & Breakfast*
**SILVER AWARD**
1 Waterside Walk, Sydling St
Nicholas, Dorchester DT2 9PJ
**t** (01300) 341618
**e** charlescordy@hazelcottage.
ndo.co.uk
**w** hazelcottagedorset.co.uk

**Magiston Farm** ★★
*Farmhouse*
Sydling St Nicholas, Dorchester
DT2 9NR
**t** (01300) 320295

### TALATON
#### Devon

**Larkbeare Grange** ★★★★★
*Bed & Breakfast*
**GOLD AWARD**
Larkbeare, Talaton, Exeter
EX5 2RY
**t** (01404) 822069
**e** stay@larkbeare.net
**w** larkbeare.net

### TARRANT KEYNESTON
#### Dorset

**The True Lovers Knot** ★★★
*Inn*
Tarrant Keyneston, Blandford
Forum DT11 9JG
**t** (01258) 452209
**e** antony@trueloversknot.co.
uk
**w** trueloversknot.co.uk

### TARRANT LAUNCESTON
#### Dorset

**Ramblers Cottage** ★★★★
*Bed & Breakfast*
Tarrant Launceston, Blandford
Forum DT11 8BY
**t** (01258) 830528
**e** sworrall@ramblerscottage.
co.uk
**w** ramblerscottage.co.uk

### TAUNTON
#### Somerset

**Acorn Lodge** ★★★
*Guest Accommodation*
22 Wellington Road, Taunton
TA1 4EQ
**t** (01823) 337613

**Apple Rydon Bed &**
**Breakfast** ★★★★
*Bed & Breakfast*
Rydon Farm, Nr Taunton
TA7 0BZ
**t** (01278) 663472
**e** info@rydonfarm.com
**w** rydonfarm.com

**The Black Horse Inn** ★★ *Inn*
36 Bridge Street, Taunton
TA1 1UD
**t** (01823) 272151

**Lyngford House** ★★★★
*Guest Accommodation*
Selworthy Road, Taunton
TA2 8HD
**t** (01823) 284649
**e** eldridgek@lyngford-house.
co.uk
**w** lyngford-house.co.uk

**Pyrland Farm** ★★★★
*Farmhouse*
Cheddon Road, Taunton
TA2 7QX
**t** (01823) 334148
**e** reads.pyrland@ukgateway.
net

**Staplegrove Lodge** ★★★★
*Bed & Breakfast*
**SILVER AWARD**
A358, Taunton TA2 6PX
**t** (01823) 331153
**e** staplegrovelodge@onetel.
com
**w** staplegrovelodge.co.uk

**Thatched Country Cottage and Garden B&B** ★★★
*Bed & Breakfast*
Pear Tree Cottage, Nr Taunton
TA3 7QA
t (01823) 601224
e colvin.parry@virgin.net
w smoothhound.co.uk/hotels/thatch.html

**Yallands Farmhouse** ★★★★
*Guest Accommodation*
**SILVER AWARD**
Staplegrove, Taunton TA2 6PZ
t (01823) 278979
e mail@yallands.co.uk
w yallands.co.uk

### TAVISTOCK
Devon

**April Cottage** ★★★★
*Bed & Breakfast*
**SILVER AWARD**
Mount Tavy Road, Tavistock
PL19 9JB
t (01822) 613280

**Beera Farmhouse** ★★★★
*Bed & Breakfast*
**GOLD AWARD**
Milton Abbot, Tavistock
PL19 8PL
t (01822) 870216
e hilary.tucker@farming.co.uk
w beera-farm.co.uk

**Harrabeer Country House** ★★★★
*Guest Accommodation*
Harrowbeer Lane, Yelverton
PL20 6EA
t (01822) 853302
e reception@harrabeer.co.uk
w harrabeer.co.uk

**Higher Woodley Farm** ★★★★ *Farmhouse*
**SILVER AWARD**
Lamerton, Tavistock PL19 8QU
t (01822) 832374
e jablowey@hotmail.com
w woodleybandb.co.uk

**Mallards Guest House** ★★★★ *Guest House*
48 Plymouth Road, Tavistock
PL19 8BU
t (01822) 615171
e mallards-guest-house@tiscali.co.uk
w mallardsoftavistock.co.uk

**Rubbytown Farm** ★★★★
*Farmhouse* **SILVER AWARD**
Gulworthy, Tavistock PL19 8PA
t (01822) 832493

**Tor Cottage** ★★★★★
*Guest Accommodation*
**GOLD AWARD**
Chillaton, Lifton PL16 0JE
t (01822) 860248
e info@torcottage.co.uk
w torcottage.co.uk

### TEDBURN ST MARY
Devon

**Fingle Glen Farm** ★★★
*Farmhouse*
Tedburn St Mary, Exeter
EX6 6AF
t (01647) 61227

**Great Cummins Farm** ★★★★ *Farmhouse*
Tedburn St Mary, Exeter
EX6 6BJ
t (01647) 61696
e davidgaraway@yahoo.co.uk

### TEDDINGTON
Gloucestershire

**Bengrove Farm** ★★★
*Farmhouse*
Bengrove, Teddington,
Tewkesbury GL20 8JB
t (01242) 620332
e libby.hopkins@connectfree.co.uk

### TEIGNMOUTH
Devon

**Britannia House B&B**
★★★★★ *Bed & Breakfast*
**SILVER AWARD**
26 Teign Street, Teignmouth
TQ14 8EG
t (01626) 770051
e gillettbritannia@aol.com
w britanniahouse.org

**The Moorings** ★★★★★
*Guest Accommodation*
**SILVER AWARD**
33 Teignmouth Road,
Teignmouth TQ14 8UR
t (01626) 770400
e mickywaters@aol.com
w visitwestcountry.com/themoorings

**Thomas Luny House**
★★★★★
*Guest Accommodation*
**GOLD AWARD**
Teign Street, Teignmouth
TQ14 8EG
t (01626) 772976
e alisonandjohn@thomas-luny-house.co.uk
w thomas-luny-house.co.uk

**Thornhill Hotel** ★★★★
*Guest Accommodation*
Mere Lane, Teignmouth
TQ14 8TA
t (01626) 773460
e information@thornhillhotelteignmouth.co.uk
w thornhillhotelteignmouth.co.uk

### TETBURY
Gloucestershire

**The Bedlodge** ★★★
*Guest Accommodation*
Long Newnton, Tetbury
GL8 8XA
t (01666) 502475
e info@gtb.co.uk
w gtb.co.uk

### TEWKESBURY
Gloucestershire

**Abbots Court Farm** ★★★
*Farmhouse*
Churchend, Twyning,
Tewkesbury GL20 6DA
t (01684) 292515
e abbotscourt@aol.com

**Corner Cottage** ★★★★
*Bed & Breakfast*
Stow Road, Alderton,
Tewkesbury GL20 8NH
t (01242) 620630
e cornercottagebb@talk21.com

**Gantier** ★★★★
*Bed & Breakfast*
**SILVER AWARD**
Church Road, Alderton,
Tewkesbury GL20 8NR
t (01242) 620343 &
07787 504872
e johnandsueparry@yahoo.co.uk
w gantier.co.uk

**Jessop House** ★★★★
*Guest Accommodation*
65 Church Street, Tewkesbury
GL20 5RZ
t (01684) 292017
e bookings@jessophousehotel.com
w jessophousehotel.com

**Malvern View Guest House**
★★★ *Guest Accommodation*
1 St Marys Road, Tewkesbury
GL20 5SE
t (01684) 292776

### THORNBURY
Devon

**Forda Farm** ★★★★
*Farmhouse*
Thornbury, Holsworthy
EX22 7BS
t (01409) 261369

### THORNDON CROSS
Devon

**Fairway Lodge** ★★★★
*Guest House*
Thorndon Cross, Okehampton
EX20 4NE
t (01837) 55122
e info@fairway-lodge.co.uk
w fairway-lodge.co.uk

### THORNE
Somerset

**Thorne Cottage** ★★★★
*Guest Accommodation*
Thorne, Nr Yeovil BA21 3PZ
t (01935) 421735
e thornecottage@yahoo.co.uk
w thornecottage.co.uk

### THREE LEGGED CROSS
Dorset

**Southview Guest House**
★★★ *Bed & Breakfast*
Ringwood Road, Three Legged
Cross BH21 6QY
t (01202) 813746
e southveiw.guesthouse@btinternet.com
w southview-guest-house.co.uk

**Thatch Cottage** ★★★★
*Guest House*
Ringwood Road, Three Legged
Cross, Wimborne BH21 6QY
t (01202) 822042
e dthatchcottage@aol.com
w thatch-cottage.co.uk

### TIBBERTON
Gloucestershire

**The Laurels** ★★
*Guest Accommodation*
Bovone Lane, Tibberton,
Gloucester GL2 8EA
t (01452) 790300
e henryandchris.rivers@btinternet.com
w newentbedandbreakfast.co.uk

### TIMBERSCOMBE
Somerset

**Knowle Manor and Riding Centre** ★★★ *Guest House*
Knowle Lane, Dunster
TA24 6TZ
t (01643) 841342
e knowlemnr@aol.com
w knowlemanor.co.uk

### TIMSBURY
Somerset

**Pitfour House** ★★★★★
*Guest Accommodation*
**SILVER AWARD**
High Street, Bath BA2 0HT
t (01761) 479554

### TINTAGEL
Cornwall

**The Avalon** ★★★★
*Guest House*
Atlantic Road, Tintagel
PL34 0DD
t (01840) 770116
e avalontintagel@googlemail.com
w avalon-tintagel.co.uk

**Bosayne Guest House** ★★★
*Guest Accommodation*
Atlantic Road, Tintagel
PL34 0DE
t (01840) 770514
e kdjewalker@bosayne.wanadoo.co.uk
w bosayne.co.uk

**Brooklets Cottage B&B**
★★★★ *Bed & Breakfast*
Bossiney Road, Tintagel
PL34 0AE
t (01840) 770395
e brookletscottage@tiscali.co.uk
w brookletscottage.co.uk

**The Cottage Teashop**
★★★★ *Bed & Breakfast*
Bossiney Road, Tintagel
PL34 0AH
t (01840) 770639
e cotteashop@talk21.com

**Four Winds** ★★★★
*Bed & Breakfast*
Knight's Close, Atlantic Road,
Tintagel PL34 0DR
t (01840) 770300
e kay4windsaccom@aol.com

**Lan-Y-Mor** ★★★
*Bed & Breakfast*
Knights Close, Tintagel
PL34 0DR
t (01840) 770933
e dave@dowen20.eclipse.co.uk

**The Mill House** ★★★ *Inn*
Trebarwith Strand, Tintagel
PL34 0HD
t (01840) 770200
e management@themillhouseinn.co.uk
w themillhouseinn.co.uk

**Tintagel YHA** ★★ *Hostel*
Dunderhole Point, Tintagel
PL34 0DW
t (01840) 770334

**TINTINHULL**
Somerset

**Crown and Victoria**
Rating Applied For
*Inn*
14 Farm Street, Yeovil
BA22 8PZ
t (01935) 823341
e info@crownandvictoriainn.
co.uk
w crownandvictoriainn.co.uk

**TIVERTON**
Devon

**Bridge Guest House** ★★★
*Guest House*
23 Angel Hill, Tiverton
EX16 6PE
t (01884) 252804
w smoothhound.co.uk/hotels/
bridgegh.html

**Courtyard Bed and
Breakfast** ★★★★
*Restaurant with Rooms*
19 Fore Street, Bampton,
Tiverton EX16 9ND
t (01398) 331842
e doreen@stonehengeinn.
freeserve.co.uk
w bampton.org.uk/

**Exe-Tor** ★★★
*Bed & Breakfast*
Ashley, Tiverton EX16 5PA
t (01884) 253197

**Great Bradley Farm** ★★★★
*Farmhouse* **SILVER AWARD**
Withleigh, Tiverton EX16 8JL
t (01884) 256946
e hann@agriplus.net
w greatbradleyfarm-devon.co.
uk

**Lower Collipriest Farm**
★★★★ *Farmhouse*
**SILVER AWARD**
Collipriest, Tiverton EX16 4PT
t (01884) 252321
e linda@lowercollipriest.co.uk
w lowercollipriest.co.uk

**TIVINGTON**
Somerset

**Clements Cottage** ★★★★
*Guest Accommodation*
Eight Acre Lane, Nr Minehead
TA24 8SU
t (01643) 703970
e clementscottage@
exmoorbandb.co.uk
w exmoorbandb.co.uk

**TOLLER PORCORUM**
Dorset

**Colesmoor Farm** ★★★★
*Farmhouse*
Toller Porcorum, Dorchester
DT2 0DU
t (01300) 320812
e rachael@colesmoorfarm.co.
uk
w colesmoorfarm.co.uk

**Higher Kingcombe Lodge**
★★★ *Guest Accommodation*
Higher Kingcombe, Dorchester
DT2 0EH
t (01300) 320537
e info@
higherkingcombelodge.co.uk
w higherkingcombelodge.co.
uk

**The Kingcombe Centre**
★★★ *Guest Accommodation*
Lower Kingcombe, Toller
Porcorum, Dorchester
DT2 0EQ
t (01300) 320684
e kingcombe@hotmail.co.uk
w kingcombe-centre.demon.
co.uk

**TOLPUDDLE**
Dorset

**Tolpuddle Hall** ★★★
*Bed & Breakfast*
Main Road, Tolpuddle,
Dorchester DT2 7EW
t (01305) 848986

**TORPOINT**
Cornwall

**Bulland House** ★★★★
*Bed & Breakfast*
Antony Road, Torpoint
PL11 2PE
t (01752) 813823
e info@averywarmwelcome.
co.uk
w averywarmwelcome.co.uk

**TORQUAY**
Devon

**Abingdon House** ★★★★
*Guest Accommodation*
104 Avenue Road, Torquay
TQ2 5LF
t (01803) 201832
e abingdon-house@zen.co.uk
w abingdon-house.co.uk

**Ashurst Lodge** ★★★
*Guest Accommodation*
2-4 St Efrides Road, Torquay
TQ2 5SG
t (01803) 292132
e n.hutch@btopenworld.com

**Ashwood Grange** ★★★★
*Guest Accommodation*
18 Newton Road, Torquay
TQ2 5BZ
t (01803) 212619
e stay@ashwoodgrangehotel.
co.uk
w ashwoodgrangehotel.co.uk

**Avron House** ★★★★
*Guest Accommodation*
70 Windsor Road, Ellacombe,
Torquay TQ1 1SZ
t (01803) 294182
e avronhouse@blueyonder.co.
uk
w avronhouse.co.uk

**Babbacombe Palms** ★★★★
*Guest Accommodation*
2 York Road, Babbacombe,
Torquay TQ1 3SG
t (01803) 327087
e reception@
babbacombepalms.com
w babbacombepalms.com

**Banksea** ★★★
*Guest Accommodation*
51 Avenue Road, Torquay
TQ2 5LG
t (01803) 211501

**The Baytree** ★★★★
*Guest Accommodation*
14 Bridge Road, Torquay
TQ2 5BA
t (01803) 293718
e enquiries@thebaytreehotel.
com
w thebaytreehotel.com

**Beech Close Guest House**
★★★★ *Guest House*
53 Babbacombe Road, Torquay
TQ1 3SN
t (01803) 328071
e beechclose@btconnect.com
w beechclose.co.uk

**Belmont Hotel** ★★★★
*Guest Accommodation*
66 Belgrave Road, Torquay
TQ2 5HY
t (01803) 295028
w belmonthoteltorquay.co.uk

**Bentley Lodge** ★★★★
*Guest Accommodation*
Tor Park Road, Torquay
TQ2 5BQ
t (01803) 290698
e cj@bentleylodge.co.uk
w bentleylodge.co.uk

**Braddon Hall Hotel** ★★★
*Guest Accommodation*
70 Braddons Hill Road East,
Torquay TQ1 1HF
t (01803) 293908
e stay@braddonhallhotel.co.
uk
w braddonhallhotel.co.uk

**Brampton Court Hotel** ★★★
*Guest Accommodation*
St Lukes Road South, Torquay
TQ2 5NZ
t (01803) 294237
e stay@bramptoncourt.co.uk
w bramptoncourt.co.uk

**The Brandize** ★★★★
*Guest Accommodation*
19 Avenue Road, Torquay
TQ2 5LB
t (01803) 297798
e stay@brandize.co.uk
w brandize.co.uk

**Brocklehurst** ★★★
*Guest House*
Rathmore Road, Torquay
TQ2 6NZ
t (01803) 390883
e enquiries@
brocklehursthotel.co.uk
w brocklehursthotel.co.uk

**The Capri** ★★★★
*Guest Accommodation*
12 Torbay Road, Livermead,
Torquay TQ2 6RG
t (01803) 293158
e stay@caprihoteltorquay.co.
uk
w caprihoteltorquay.co.uk

**Cary Court Hotel** ★★★★
*Guest House*
Hunsdon Road, Torquay
TQ1 1QB
t (01803) 209205
e carycourt@aol.com
w carycourthotel.co.uk

**Charterhouse Hotel** ★★★
*Guest Accommodation*
Cockington Lane, Torquay
TQ2 6QT
t (01803) 605804
e charterhousehtl@btconnect.
com
w charterhouse-hotel.co.uk

**Chesterfield** ★★★★
*Guest Accommodation*
62 Belgrave Road, Torquay
TQ2 5HY
t (01803) 292318
e enquiries@
chesterfieldhoteltorquay.co.uk
w chesterfieldhoteltorquay.co.
uk

**Hotel Cimon** ★★★★
*Guest Accommodation*
82 Abbey Road, Torquay
TQ2 5NP
t (01803) 294454
e enquiries@hotelcimon.co.uk
w hotelcimon.co.uk

**Cloudlands** ★★★★
*Guest Accommodation*
St Agnes Lane, Torquay
TQ2 6QD
t (01803) 606550
e info@cloudlands.co.uk
w cloudlands.co.uk

**Cranmore** ★★★★
*Guest Accommodation*
89 Avenue Road, Torquay
TQ2 5LH
t (01803) 298488
e stay@thecranmore.co.uk
w thecranmore.co.uk

**Crimdon Dene** ★★★★
*Guest House*
Falkland Road, Torquay
TQ2 5JP
t (01803) 294651
e marjohn@
crimdondenehotel.co.uk
w crimdondenehotel.co.uk

**Crown Lodge** ★★★★
*Guest Accommodation*
83 Avenue Road, Torquay
TQ2 5LH
t (01803) 298772
e stay@crownlodgehotel.co.
uk
w crownlodgehotel.co.uk

**The Crowndale** ★★★★
*Guest Accommodation*
18 Bridge Road, Torquay
TQ2 5BA
t (01803) 293068
e info@crowndalehotel.co.uk
w crowndalehotel.co.uk

**Daylesford Hotel** ★★★★
*Guest Accommodation*
**SILVER AWARD**
60 Bampfylde Road, Torquay
TQ2 5AY
t (01803) 294435
e info@daylesfordhotel.com
w daylesfordhotel.com

**The Downs**
Rating Applied For
*Guest Accommodation*
43 Babbacombe Downs Road,
Torquay TQ1 3LN
t (01803) 328543
e manager@downshotel.co.uk
w downshotel.co.uk

**Exton Hotel** ★★★★
*Guest Accommodation*
12 Bridge Road, Torquay
TQ2 5BA
t (01803) 293561
e enquiries@extonhotel.co.uk
w extonhotel.co.uk

---

**Fleurie House ★★★★**
*Guest Accommodation*
50 Bampfylde Road, Torquay
TQ2 5AY
t (01803) 294869
e enquiries@fleuriehouse.co.
uk
w fleuriehouse.co.uk

**Gainsboro Guest House
★★★★** *Guest House*
22 Rathmore Road, Torquay
TQ2 6NY
t (01803) 292032
e gainsborohotel@
blueyonder.co.uk
w gainsborohotel.co.uk

**The Garlieston Guest House
★★★** *Guest Accommodation*
Bridge Road, Torquay
TQ2 5BA
t (01803) 294050
e sue@thegarliestoneclipse.
co.uk
w thegarlieston.com

**Garway Lodge ★★★**
*Guest House*
Avenue Road, Torquay
TQ2 5LL
t (01803) 293126
e garwaylodge@hotmail.com
w garwaylodgetorquay.co.uk

**Glendower Hotel ★★★★**
*Guest Accommodation*
Glendower Hotel Falkland
Road, Falkland Road, Torquay
TQ2 5JP
t (01803) 299988
e peter@hoteltorquay.co.uk
w hoteltorquay.co.uk

**Glenross Hotel ★★★★**
*Guest Accommodation*
SILVER AWARD
25 Avenue Road, Torquay
TQ2 5LB
t (01803) 297517
e holiday@glenross-hotel.co.
uk
w glenross-hotel.co.uk

**Glenroy ★★★**
*Guest Accommodation*
10 Bampfylde Road, Torquay
TQ2 5AR
t (01803) 299255
e glenroyhotel@aol.com
w glenroy-hotel.co.uk

**The Glenwood ★★★★**
*Guest Accommodation*
Rowdens Road, Torquay
TQ2 5AZ
t (01803) 296318
e enquiries@glenwood-hotel.
co.uk
w glenwood-hotel.co.uk

**Grosvenor House ★★★★**
*Guest Accommodation*
Falkland Road, Torquay
TQ2 5JP
t (01803) 294110
e etc@grosvenorhousehotel.
co.uk
w grosvenorhousehotel.co.uk

**Haldon Priors ★★★★★**
*Guest Accommodation*
Meadfoot Sea Road, Torquay
TQ1 2LQ
t (01803) 213365
e travelstyle.ltd@talk21.com
w haldonpriors.co.uk

**Haute Epine Guest House
★★★** *Guest Accommodation*
36 Bampfylde Road, Torquay
TQ2 5AR
t (01803) 296359
e hauteepineguesthouse@
hotmail.com

**Haven House ★★★★**
*Guest House*
11 Scarborough Road, Torquay
TQ2 5UJ
t (01803) 293390
e enquiries@havenhotel.biz
w havenhotel.biz

**Heathcliff House ★★★★**
*Guest Accommodation*
16 Newton Road, Torquay
TQ2 5BZ
t (01803) 211580
e heathcliffhouse@btconnect.
com
w heathcliffhousehotel.co.uk

**The Hillcroft ★★★★**
*Guest Accommodation*
Matlock Terrace, 9 St Lukes
Road, Torquay TQ2 5NY
t (01803) 297247
e info@thehillcroft.co.uk
w thehillcroft.co.uk

**Jesmond Dene ★★**
*Guest Accommodation*
85 Abbey Road, Torquay
TQ2 5NN
t (01803) 293062

**Kelvin House ★★★★**
*Guest Accommodation*
46 Bampfylde Road, Torquay
TQ2 5AY
t (01803) 209093
e kelvinhousehotel@amserve.
com
w kelvinhousehotel.co.uk

**Ke'thla House ★★★★**
*Guest Accommodation*
Belgrave Road, Torquay
TQ2 5HX
t (01803) 294995
e stay@kethlahouse.co.uk
w kethlahouse.co.uk

**Kings Lodge ★★★★**
*Guest Accommodation*
44 Bampfylde Road, Torquay
TQ2 5AY
t (01803) 293108
e enquiries@kingshotel-
torquay.co.uk
w kingshoteltorquay.co.uk

**Kingston House ★★★★★**
*Guest Accommodation*
75 Avenue Road, Torquay
TQ2 5LL
t (01803) 212760
e stay@kingstonhousehotel.
co.uk
w kingstonhousehotel.co.uk

**Kingsway Lodge Guest
House ★★★★** *Guest House*
95 Avenue Road, Torquay
TQ2 5LH
t (01803) 295288
e kingswaylodge@onetel.com
w kingswaylodgeguesthouse.
co.uk

**Lanscombe House ★★★★**
*Guest Accommodation*
SILVER AWARD
Cockington Village, Torquay
TQ2 6XA
t (01803) 606938
e enquiries@lanscombehouse.
co.uk
w lanscombehouse.co.uk

**Lawnswood Guest House
★★★★**
*Guest Accommodation*
6 Scarborough Road, Torquay
TQ2 5UJ
t (01803) 292595
e welcome@lawnswood.net
w lawnswood.net

**Lee House ★★★**
*Guest House*
Torbay Road, Torquay
TQ2 6RG
t (01803) 293946
e info@leehotel.co.uk
w leehotel.co.uk

**Lindum Hotel ◆◆◆◆**
*Guest Accommodation*
105 Abbey Road, Torquay
TQ2 5NP
t (01803) 292795
e enquiries@lindum-hotel.co.
uk
w lindum-hotel.co.uk

**Marstan Hotel ◆◆◆◆◆**
*Guest Accommodation*
SILVER AWARD
Meadfoot Sea Road, Torquay
TQ1 2LQ
t (01803) 292837
e enquiries@marstanhotel.co.
uk
w marstanhotel.co.uk

**Melba House Hotel ★★★★**
*Guest House*
62 Bampfylde Road, Torquay
TQ2 5AY
t (01803) 213167
e stay@melbahouse.co.uk
w melbahouse.co.uk

**Moonraker Private Hotel
★★★★** *Guest House*
St Lukes Road, Torquay
TQ2 5NX
t (01803) 297088
e enquiries@moonrakerhotel.
co.uk

**Mount Edgcombe ★★★★**
*Guest Accommodation*
23 Avenue Road, Torquay
TQ2 5LB
t (01803) 292310
e info@mountedgcombe.co.
uk
w mountedgcombe.co.uk

**The Netley ★★★**
*Guest Accommodation*
52 Bampfylde Road, Torquay
TQ2 5AY
t (01803) 295109
e briannetleyhotel@aol.com
w thenetleyhotel.co.uk

**Newlyn House ★★★★**
*Guest Accommodation*
SILVER AWARD
62 Braddons Hill Road East,
Torquay TQ1 1HF
t (01803) 295100
e barbara@newlyn-hotel.co.uk
w newlyn-hotel.co.uk

**The Norwood**
Rating Applied For
*Guest Accommodation*
60 Belgrave Road, Torquay
TQ2 5HY
t (01803) 294236
e enquiries@
norwoodhoteltorquay.co.uk
w norwoodhoteltorquay.co.uk

**The Pines ◆◆◆**
*Guest Accommodation*
19 Newton Road, Torre,
Torquay TQ2 5DB
t (01803) 292882

**Robin Hill International
Hotel ★★★★**
*Guest Accommodation*
74 Braddons Hill Road East,
Torquay TQ1 1HF
t (01803) 214518
e jo@robinhillhotel.co.uk
w robinhillhotel.co.uk

**St Michael's Hotel ★★★★**
*Guest Accommodation*
36 Ash Hill Road, Torquay
TQ1 3JD
t (01803) 297391
e st-michaels@fastnet.co.uk
w st-michaelshotel.co.uk

**The Sandpiper ★★★★**
*Guest Accommodation*
Rowdens Road, Torquay
TQ2 5AZ
t (01803) 292779
e sandpiper57@home13859.
fsnet.co.uk
w sandpiper-hotel.co.uk

**The Sandpiper Lodge ★★★**
*Guest Accommodation*
96 Avenue Road, Torquay
TQ2 5LF
t (01803) 293293
e johnatsandpiper@aol.com
w sandpiperlodgehotel.co.uk

**Sandway House ★★★★**
*Guest Accommodation*
72 Belgrave Road, Torquay
TQ2 5HY
t (01803) 298499
e sandwayhotel@
btopenworld.co.uk

**Sea Point ★★★**
*Guest Accommodation*
Clifton Grove, Old Torwood
Road, Torquay TQ1 1PR
t (01803) 211808
e seapointhotel@hotmail.com
w seapointhotel.co.uk

**The Somerville Hotel ◆◆◆◆**
*Guest Accommodation*
515 Babbacombe Road,
Torquay TQ1 1HJ
t (01803) 294755
e stay@somervillehotel.co.uk
w somervillehotel.co.uk

**South View ★★★★**
*Guest Accommodation*
12 Scarborough Road, Torquay
TQ2 5UJ
t (01803) 296029
e info@thesouthview.com
w thesouthview.com

**The Southbank Hotel**
★★★★
*Guest Accommodation*
15-17 Belgrave Road, Torquay
TQ2 5HU
t (01803) 296701
e stay@southbankhotel.co.uk
w southbankhotel.co.uk

**Suite Dreams Guest House**
★★★★
*Guest Accommodation*
SILVER AWARD
Steep Hill, Maidencombe,
Torquay TQ1 4TS
t (01803) 313900
e mail@suitedreams.co.uk
w suitedreams.co.uk

**Tor Dean Hotel** ★★★★
*Guest Accommodation*
27 Bampfylde Road, Torquay
TQ2 5AY
t (01803) 294669
e stay@tordeanhotel.com
w tordeanhotel.com

**Tower Hall** ★★★★
*Guest Accommodation*
Solsbro Road, Torquay
TQ2 6PF
t (01803) 605292
e john@towerhallhotel.co.uk
w towerhallhotel.co.uk

**Trafalgar House B&B**
★★★★
*Guest Accommodation*
30 Belgrave Road, Torquay
TQ2 5BA
t (01803) 292486
e trafalgar@hotelstorquayuk.
com
w hotelstorquayuk.com

**Trelawney** ★★★★
*Guest Accommodation*
48 Belgrave Road, Torquay
TQ2 5HS
t (01803) 296049
e trelawneyhotel@hotmail.
com
w trelawneyhotel.co.uk

**Trouville** ★★★ *Guest House*
70 Belgrave Road, Torquay
TQ2 5HY
t (01803) 294979
e info@trouville-hotel-torquay.
co.uk

**Villa Marina** ★★★★
*Guest Accommodation*
Tor Park Road, Torquay
TQ2 5BQ
t (01803) 292187
e enquiries@villamarina-
torquay.co.uk
w villamarina-torquay.co.uk

**Walnut Lodge** ★★★★
*Guest Accommodation*
48 Bampfylde Road, Torquay
TQ2 5AY
t (01803) 200471
e stay@walnutlodgetorquay.
co.uk

**The Waters Edge** ★★★
*Guest Accommodation*
Torbay Road, Torquay
TQ2 6QH
t (01803) 293876
e enquiries@waters-edge-
hotel.co.uk
w waters-edge-hotel.co.uk

**The Westbank** ★★★★
*Guest Accommodation*
SILVER AWARD
54 Bampfylde Road, Torquay
TQ2 5AY
t (01803) 295271
e westbankhotel@onetel.com
w thewestbank.co.uk

**The Westbourne** ★★★★
*Guest Accommodation*
106 Avenue Road, Torquay
TQ2 5LQ
t (01803) 292927
e enquiries@
westbournehoteltorquay.co.uk
w westbournehoteltorquay.co.
uk

**The Westbrook** ★★★
*Guest House*
15 Scarborough Road, Torquay
TQ2 5UJ
t (01803) 292559
e westbrookhotel@tesco.net
w westbrookhotel.net

**Westgate Hotel** ★★★★
*Guest Accommodation*
SILVER AWARD
Falkland Road, Torquay
TQ2 5JP
t (01803) 295350
e stay@westgatehotel.co.uk
w westgatehotel.co.uk

**Whitburn Guest House**
★★★ *Guest House*
St Lukes Road North, Torquay
TQ2 5PD
t (01803) 296719
e joe@lazenby15.freeserve.co.
uk
w whitburnguesthouse.co.uk

**Wilsbrook Guest House**
★★★ *Guest House*
77 Avenue Road, Torquay
TQ2 5LL
t (01803) 298413
e thewilsbrook@aol.com
w wilsbrook.co.uk

### TORRINGTON
Devon

**The West Bar – Bistro – B&B**
★★★ *Inn*
18 South Street, Torrington
EX38 8AA
t (01805) 624949
e morrowbrown@btconnect.
com

### TOTNES
Devon

**The Elbow Room** ★★★★★
*Guest Accommodation*
SILVER AWARD
North Street, Totnes TQ9 5NZ
t (01803) 863480
e r.savin@btinternet.com

**Foales Leigh** ★★★★★
*Guest Accommodation*
SILVER AWARD
Harberton, Totnes TQ9 7SS
t (01803) 862365

**Great Court Farm** ★★★★
*Farmhouse* SILVER AWARD
Weston Lane, Totnes TQ9 6LB
t (01803) 862326
e janet.hooper3@btinternet.
com
w greatcourt-totnes.co.uk

**The Great Grubb B&B**
★★★★ *Guest House*
Fallowfields, Plymouth Road,
Totnes TQ9 5LX
t (01803) 849071
e accommodation@
thegreatgrubb.co.uk
w thegreatgrubb.co.uk

**The Old Forge at Totnes**
★★★★ *Guest House*
Seymour Place, Totnes
TQ9 5AY
t (01803) 862174
e enq@oldforgetotnes.com
w oldforgetotnes.com

**Steam Packet Inn** ★★★★
*Inn*
4 St Peters Quay, Totnes
TQ9 5EW
t (01803) 863880
e esther@thesteampacketinn.
co.uk
w thesteampacketinn-totnes.
co.uk

### TREGONY
Cornwall

**Penhesken Farm** ★★
*Farmhouse*
Tregony, Truro TR2 5TG
t (01872) 530629

**Tregonan** ★★★★
*Guest Accommodation*
SILVER AWARD
Tregony, Truro TR2 5SN
t (01872) 530249
e tregonan@fwi.co.uk
w tregonan.co.uk

### TREGREHAN MILLS
Cornwall

**Wisteria Lodge** ★★★★★
*Guest House*
Boscundle, Tregrehan, St
Austell PL25 3RJ
t (01726) 810800
e info@wisteria-lodge.co.uk
w wisterialodgehotel.co.uk

### TRELILL
Cornwall

**Trelulla** ★★★
*Bed & Breakfast*
Trelill, St Kew Highway,
Wadebridge PL30 3HT
t (01208) 850938
e eileenroberts@trelulla.
freeserve.co.uk

### TREMOUGH
Cornwall

**Glasney Parc (Tremough)**
★★★ *Campus*
Tremough Campus, Treliever
Road, Penryn TR10 9EZ
t (01326) 2536 7437
e holidaylets@
tremoughservices.com

### TRENANCE
Cornwall

**Merrymoor Inn** ★★★
*Guest Accommodation*
Mawgan Porth, Newquay
TR8 4BA
t (01637) 860258
e info@merrymoorinn.com
w merrymoorinn.com

### TRESPARRETT
Cornwall

**Oaklands** ★★★★
*Bed & Breakfast*
Tresparrett, Camelford
PL32 9SX
t (01840) 261302

### TREVALGA
Cornwall

**Trehane Farm** ★★★★
*Farmhouse*
Trevalga, Boscastle PL35 0EB
t (01840) 250510
e trehanefarmhouse@virgin.
net
w cornish-farms.co.uk

### TREVELLAS
Cornwall

**Little Trevellas Farm** ★★★
*Farmhouse*
Trevellas, St Agnes TR5 0XX
t (01872) 552945
e velvetcrystal@ukonline.co.
uk

### TREVONE
Cornwall

**Trevone Beach House**
Rating Applied For
*Guest Accommodation*
Trevone Bay, Padstow
PL28 8QX
t (01841) 520469
e trevonebeach@aol.com
w trevonebeach.co.uk

### TREWARMETT
Cornwall

**Melrosa** ★★★★
*Bed & Breakfast*
Trewarmett, Tintagel PL34 0ES
t (01840) 770360
e valerie.stephens@btinternet.
com

### TREWOON
Cornwall

**Cooperage** ★★★★
*Guest House*
37 Cooperage Road, Trewoon,
St Austell PL25 5SJ
t (01726) 70497
e lyn.cooperage@tiscali.co.uk
w cooperagebb.co.uk

### TREYARNON BAY
Cornwall

**Treyarnon Bay Youth Hostel
– AD092** ★★★ *Hostel*
Tregonnan, Treyarnon,
Padstow PL28 8JR
t 0870 770 6076
e treyarnon@yha.org.uk

### TROWBRIDGE
Wiltshire

**62b Paxcroft Cottages**
★★★★ *Bed & Breakfast*
Devizes Road, Paxcroft,
Trowbridge BA14 6JB
t (01225) 765838
e paxcroftcottages@hotmail.
com
w paxcroftcottages.pwp.
blueyonder.co.uk

**Herons Knoll**
Rating Applied For
*Bed & Breakfast*
18 Middle Lane, Trowbridge
BA14 7LG
t (01225) 752593

---

Establishments in bold have a detailed entry in this guide – use the property index to find the page numbers

**Lion and Fiddle** ★★★ *Inn*
Devizes Road, Hilperton,
Trowbridge BA14 7QS
**t** (01225) 776392

**Ring O' Bells** ★★★
*Guest House*
321 Marsh Road, Hilperton
Marsh, Trowbridge BA14 7PL
**t** (01225) 754404
**e** ringobells@blueyonder.co.
uk
**w** ringobells.biz

**Sue's B&B** ★★
*Guest Accommodation*
25 Blair Road, Trowbridge
BA14 9JZ
**t** (01225) 764559
**e** sue_b_n_b@yahoo.com

### TRUDOXHILL
### Somerset

**Trudox Mead Country B&B**
★★★ *Bed & Breakfast*
Foghamshire Lane, Nr Frome
BA11 5DR
**t** (01373) 836387
**e** simon.carewprice@virgin.
net
**w** trudoxmead.co.uk

### TRULL
### Somerset

**Canonsgrove Farm** ★★★
*Farmhouse*
Trull, Taunton TA3 7PD
**t** (01823) 279720
**e** c.ralph57@btinternet.com

**The Winchester Arms** ★★
*Inn*
Church Road, Nr Taunton
TA3 7LG
**t** (01823) 284723

### TRURO
### Cornwall

**The Bay Tree** ★★
*Guest House*
Ferris Town, Truro TR1 3JH
**t** (01872) 240274
**w** baytree-guesthouse.co.uk

**Bissick Old Mill** ★★★★
*Guest House*
Ladock, Truro TR2 4PG
**t** (01726) 882557
**e** enquiries@bissickoldmill.
plus.net
**w** bissickoldmill.co.uk

**Briars** ★★★ *Bed & Breakfast*
14 Blackberry Way,
Beechwood Parc, Truro
TR1 1QX
**t** (01872) 223814
**e** bethinbriars@hotmail.com

**Chy Vista** ★★★★
*Bed & Breakfast*
Higher Penair, St Clement,
Truro TR1 1TD
**t** (01872) 270592

**Hazelnut Cottage** ★★★★
*Bed & Breakfast*
Perranwell Station, Truro
TR4 7PU
**t** (01872) 865082

**Palm Tree House** ★★★★
*Bed & Breakfast*
8 Parkins Terrace, Off St
Clement Street, Truro TR1 1EJ
**t** (01872) 270100
**e** bodybusiness@btconnect.
com

**The Rowan Tree** ★★★
*Bed & Breakfast*
3 Parkvedras Terrace, Truro
TR1 3DF
**t** (01872) 277928
**e** christinecartlidge@freenet.
co.uk

**Stanton House** ★★
*Bed & Breakfast*
11 Ferris Town, Truro TR1 3JG
**t** (01872) 223666
**e** iris@stantons.eclipse.co.uk

**Tregoninny Farm** ★★★★
*Guest Accommodation*
Tresillian, Truro TR2 4AR
**t** (01872) 520145
**w** tregoninny.com

**Treswithian Barn** ★★★★
*Bed & Breakfast*
Ruan High Lanes, Truro
TR2 5JT
**t** (01872) 501274

### TURKDEAN
### Gloucestershire

**Yew Tree Cottage** ★★★★★
*Bed & Breakfast*
SILVER AWARD
Turkdean, Cheltenham
GL54 3NT
**t** (01451) 860222
**e** vivien@bestcotswold.com

### TWO WATERS FOOT
### Cornwall

**Gillwood** ★★★★
*Bed & Breakfast*
Two Waters Foot, Liskeard
PL14 6HR
**t** (01208) 821648
**e** cliffnsheila@tiscali.co.uk
**w** gillwoodbedandbreakfast.
com

**Tithe Hall Farm** ★★★★
*Farmhouse*
Liskeard PL14 6HL
**t** (01208) 872491
**e** tithehall@tesco.net
**w** tithehallfarm.co.uk

**Treverbyn Vean Manor**
★★★★★
*Guest Accommodation*
GOLD AWARD
West Wing, Trevrbyn Vean,
Liskeard PL14 6HN
**t** (01579) 326105
**e** ahindley@mac.com
**w** treverbynvean.co.uk

### TYWARDREATH
### Cornwall

**Morbihan Bed and Breakfast**
★★★★ *Bed & Breakfast*
28 Southpark Road,
Tywardreath, Par PL24 2PT
**t** (01726) 817247
**e** morbihanbandb@yahoo.co.
uk
**w** morbihanguesthouse.co.uk

### UCKINGTON
### Gloucestershire

**Linthwaite** ★★
*Bed & Breakfast*
3 Homecroft Drive, Uckington,
Cheltenham GL51 9SN
**t** (01242) 680146
**e** a.r.marchand@talk21.com

### UPAVON
### Wiltshire

**The Manor** ★★★★
*Bed & Breakfast*
Andover Road, Upavon,
Pewsey SN9 6EB
**t** (01980) 635115
**e** isabelbgreen@hotmail.com
**w** themanorupavon.co.uk

### UPHILL
### Somerset

**The Old Hall** ★★★
*Guest House*
88 Uphill Way, Weston-super-
Mare BS23 4XP
**t** (01934) 629970
**e** oldhallmail@yahoo.co.uk
**w** theoldhalluphill.co.uk

### UPLODERS
### Dorset

**Uploders Farm** ★★★
*Guest Accommodation*
Dorchester Road, Bridport
DT6 4NZ
**t** (01308) 423380

### UPLYME
### Devon

**Elton** ★★★★
*Guest Accommodation*
Lyme Road, Uplyme, Lyme
Regis DT7 3TH
**t** (01297) 445986
**e** mikecawte@aol.com
**w** eltonlymeregis.com

### UPOTTERY
### Devon

**Lower Luxton Farm** ★★★
*Farmhouse*
Honiton EX14 9PB
**t** (01823) 601269
**e** lwrluxtonfm@hotmail.com
**w** lowerluxtonfarm.co.uk

### UPPER ODDINGTON
### Gloucestershire

**Blenheim Cottage** ★★★★★
*Guest Accommodation*
GOLD AWARD
Upper Oddington, Moreton-in-
Marsh GL56 0XG
**t** (01451) 831066
**e** bookings@
cotswoldsoddington.com
**w** cotswoldsoddington.co.uk

**Uphome** ★★★★
*Guest Accommodation*
Upper Oddington, Moreton-in-
Marsh GL56 0XH
**t** (01451) 831284
**e** salgodman@hotmail.com
**w** cotswoldbreaks.co.uk

### UPTON
### Cornwall

**Upton Cross** ★★★
*Guest Accommodation*
Upton, Bude EX23 0LY
**t** (01288) 355310
**e** ramosflav@btinternet.com

### UPTON LOVELL
### Wiltshire

**Prince Leopold Inn** ★★ *Inn*
Upton Lovell, Warminster
BA12 0JP
**t** (01985) 850460
**e** princeleopold@lineone.net
**w** princeleopoldinn.co.uk

### VERYAN
### Cornwall

**Treverbyn House** ★★★★
*Bed & Breakfast*
Pendower Road, Veryan, Truro
TR2 5QL
**t** (01872) 501201
**e** holiday@treverbyn.
fsbusiness.co.uk
**w** cornwall-online.co.uk/
treverbyn/ctb.htm

### WADEBRIDGE
### Cornwall

**Brookdale B&B**
Rating Applied For
*Bed & Breakfast*
Trevanion Road, Wadebridge
PL27 7PA
**t** (01208) 815425
**e** deegrant@freeuk.com

**Brookfields B&B** ★★★★
*Bed & Breakfast*
SILVER AWARD
Hendra Lane, St Kew Highway,
Wadebridge PL30 3EQ
**t** (01208) 841698
**e** robbie@brookfields.info
**w** brookfields.info

**Glenview** ★★★★
*Bed & Breakfast*
Ruthernbridge, Bodmin
PL30 5NP
**t** (01208) 831585
**e** enquiries@glenviewb-b.co.
uk
**w** glenviewb-b.co.uk

**Homebound B&B** ★★★★
*Bed & Breakfast*
Homebound, Gonvena Hill,
Wadebridge PL27 6DH
**t** (01208) 812759
**e** nigelhackling@aol.com
**w** homebound.me.uk

**Monte Gordo** ★★★
*Bed & Breakfast*
Tregonce Farm, St Issey,
Wadebridge PL27 7QJ
**t** (01208) 812082

**Polstags Farmhouse Bed &
Breakfast** ★★★★ *Farmhouse*
Polstags, Amble, Wadebridge
PL27 6EW
**t** (01208) 895134
**e** l.dally@btinternet.com
**w** polstagsfarmhouse.co.uk

**Spring Gardens** ★★★
*Bed & Breakfast*
Bradfords Quay, Wadebridge
PL27 6DB
**t** (01208) 813771
**e** springjen1@aol.co.uk
**w** spring-garden.co.uk

**Tregolls Farm** ★★★★
*Guest Accommodation*
St Wenn, Bodmin PL30 5PG
**t** (01208) 812154
**w** tregollsfarm.co.uk

### WADEFORD
### Somerset

**The Haymaker Inn** ★★★★
*Inn*
Main Road, Nr Chard
TA20 3AP
**t** (01460) 64161
**e** stevetingle11@hotmail.co.uk

Look out for establishments participating in the National Accessible Scheme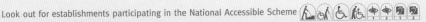

## WAMBROOK
### Somerset

**Woodview** ★★★
*Guest Accommodation*
Wambrook Road, Nr Chard
TA20 3EH
t  (01460) 65368
e  jenny@jsreynolds.fsnet.co.
uk
w  woodview.org.uk

## WAREHAM
### Dorset

**Anglebury House** ★★★
*Guest Accommodation*
15-17 North Street, Wareham
BH20 4AB
t  (01929) 552988
e  info@angleburyhouse.co.uk
w  angleburyhouse.co.uk

**Ashcroft** ★★★★
*Bed & Breakfast*
64 Furzebrook Road, Wareham
BH20 5AX
t  (01929) 552392
e  cake@ashcroft-bb.co.uk
w  ashcroft-bb.co.uk

**Beryl's B&B** ★★
*Bed & Breakfast*
Wareham Road, Sandford,
Wareham BH20 7DF
t  (01929) 550138
e  beryle@homecall.co.uk
w  britainsbestbreaks.co.uk

**Birchfield** ★★★
*Guest Accommodation*
2 Drax Avenue, Wareham
BH20 4DJ
t  (01929) 552462
e  jl.hutton@tiscali.co.uk
w  birchfieldbedandbreakfast.
co.uk

**Blackmanston Farm** ★★★
*Farmhouse*
Blackmanston, Steeple,
Wareham BH20 5NZ
t  (01929) 480743
e  bobbraisby@yahoo.co.uk
w  members.lycos.co.uk/
blackmanstonfarm/

**Primrose Farmhouse**
★★★★
*Guest Accommodation*
East Stoke, Wareham
BH20 6AN
t  (01929) 405691
e  primrosefarmhous@aol.com
w  primrosefarmhouse.co.uk

**Spurwing Guest House**
★★★★ *Guest House*
10 Sandford Road, Wareham
BH20 4DH
t  (01929) 553869
e  spencers@spurwing.info
w  spurwing.info

**Trinity** ★★★★
*Bed & Breakfast*
32 South Street, Wareham
BH20 4LU
t  (01929) 556689
e  enquiries@trinitybnb.co.uk
w  trinitybnb.co.uk

## WARMINSTER
### Wiltshire

**Bugley Barton B&B** ♦♦♦♦♦
*Guest Accommodation*
**GOLD AWARD**
Victoria Road, Warminster
BA12 8HD
t  (01985) 213389
e  bugleybarton@aol.com

**Corner House** ★★★★★
*Guest Accommodation*
The Square, High Street,
Maiden Bradley, Warminster
BA12 7JG
t  (01985) 844629
e  wildlifeinwilts@tiscali.co.uk
w  cornerhousebb.co.uk

**The George Inn** ★★★★ *Inn*
Longbridge Deverill,
Warminster BA12 7DG
t  (01985) 840396
w  thegeorgeinnlongbridge
deverill.co.uk

**Home Farm** ★★★★
*Farmhouse*
221 Boreham Road,
Warminster BA12 9HF
t  (01985) 213266
e  theleggs221@aol.com
w  homefarmboreham.co.uk

**Sturford Mead Farm** ★★★★
*Guest Accommodation*
Warminster BA12 7QU
t  (01373) 832213
e  lynn.stayatsturford@
ntlword.com
w  stayatsturford.co.uk

## WARMLEY
### Gloucestershire

**Ferndale Guest House** ★★★
*Guest House*
Deanery Road, Warmley,
Bristol BS15 9JB
t  (0117) 985 8247
e  alexandmikewake@yahoo.
co.uk
w  ferndaleguesthouse.co.uk

## WASHAWAY
### Cornwall

**Park Farmhouse** ★★★★
*Guest Accommodation*
**SILVER AWARD**
Washaway, Bodmin PL30 3AG
t  (01208) 841277
e  justin897@btinternet.com
w  park-farmhouse.co.uk

**South Tregleath Farm B&B**
★★★★ *Bed & Breakfast*
South Tregleath Farm, Bodmin
PL30 3AA
t  (01208) 72692

## WASHFORD
### Somerset

**Langtry Country House**
★★★★★ *Bed & Breakfast*
A39, Washford TA23 0NT
t  (01984) 641688
e  helga@langtrycountryhouse.
co.uk
w  langtrycountryhouse.co.uk

**Monkscider House** ★★★★
*Guest Accommodation*
**SILVER AWARD**
Main Road, Washford
TA23 0NS
t  (01984) 641055
e  david@netgates.co.uk
w  monksciderhouse.com

## WATCHET
### Somerset

**Esplanade House** ★★★★
*Bed & Breakfast*
Esplanade, Watchet TA23 0AJ
t  (01984) 633444

**Trinity Cottage** ★★★★
*Bed & Breakfast*
Mount Lane, Nr Washford
TA23 0QY
t  (01984) 641676
e  abigailtrin@aol.com
w  trinitycottage.co.uk

## WATERGATE BAY
### Cornwall

**The White House** ★★★★
*Guest Accommodation*
Tregurrian, Newquay TR8 4AD
t  (01637) 860119

## WATERROW
### Somerset

**Handley Farm
Accommodation** ★★★★★
*Farmhouse* **GOLD AWARD**
Waterrow, Taunton TA4 2BE
t  (01398) 361516
e  linda.handleyfarm@
btinternet.com
w  handleyfarm.co.uk

## WELLINGTON
### Somerset

**Backways Farmhouse**
★★★★ *Bed & Breakfast*
Wellington TA21 9RN
t  (01823) 660712
e  info@backways.co.uk
w  backways.co.uk

**Mantle Cottage** ★★★
*Bed & Breakfast*
34 Mantle Street, Wellington
TA21 8AR
t  (01823) 668514
e  dalsod@aol.com
w  mantlecottage.com

## WELLS
### Somerset

**30 Mary Road** ★★★
*Guest Accommodation*
Mary Road, Wells BA5 2NF
t  (01749) 674031
e  triciabailey30@hotmail.com

**55 St Thomas Street** ★★★
*Bed & Breakfast*
46 Church Street, Wells
BA5 2UY
t  (01749) 676522
e  55sttst@fsbdial.co.uk
w  55stthomas.co.uk

**Baytree House** ★★★★
*Guest Accommodation*
85 Portway, Wells BA5 2BJ
t  (01749) 677933
e  baytree.house@ukonline.co.
uk
w  baytree-house.co.uk

**Beryl** ★★★★
*Guest Accommodation*
Off Hawkers Lane, Wells
BA5 3JP
t  (01749) 678738
e  stay@beryl-wells.co.uk
w  beryl-wells.co.uk

**Burcott Mill Historic
Watermill and Guesthouse**
★★★★ *Guest House*
Wookey Road, Wells BA5 1NJ
t  (01749) 673118
e  theburts@burcottmill.com
w  burcottmill.com

**Cadgwith House** ★★★★
*Bed & Breakfast*
Hawkers Lane, Wells BA5 3JH
t  (01749) 677799
e  cadgwith.house@yahoo.co.
uk
w  cadgwithhouse.co.uk

**Canon Grange** ★★★★
*Guest Accommodation*
Cathedral Green, Wells
BA5 2UB
t  (01749) 671800
e  canongrange@email.com
w  canongrange.co.uk

**Carmen B&B** ★★★★
*Bed & Breakfast*
**GOLD AWARD**
Bath Road, Wells BA5 3LQ
t  (01749) 677331
e  carmenb.and.b@
btopenworld.com
w  carmenbandb.co.uk

**Dapa House** ★★★★
*Bed & Breakfast*
62 Bath Road, Wells BA5 3LQ
t  (01749) 689248
e  enquiries@dapahouse.co.uk
w  dapahouse.co.uk

**Islington Farm** ★★★★
*Bed & Breakfast*
Wells BA5 1US
t  (01749) 673445
e  islingtonfarm2004@yahoo.
co.uk
w  islingtonfarmatwells.co.uk

**Mendip House** ★★★
*Guest Accommodation*
46 Portway, Wells BA5 2BN
t  (01749) 679719
e  info@mendiphousewells.co.
uk
w  mendiphousewells.co.uk

**Winston House** ★★★★
*Guest Accommodation*
109 Portway, Wells BA5 2BR
t  (01749) 673087
e  info@winstonhousewells.co.
uk
w  winstonhousewells.co.uk

**Worth House** ★★★
*Guest Accommodation*
Worth, Wookey, Wells
BA5 1LW
t  (01749) 672041
e  margaret@wookey.eclipse.
co.uk

## WELSH BICKNOR
### Gloucestershire

**Welsh Bicknor Youth Hostel**
★★★ *Hostel*
Welsh Bicknor, Ross-on-Wye
HR9 6JJ
t  0870 770 6086
e  welshbicknor@yha.org.uk
w  yha.org.uk

## WEMBWORTHY
### Devon

**Lymington Arms ★★★★**
*Guest Accommodation*
Lama Cross, Wembworthy,
Chulmleigh EX18 7SA
t (01837) 83572
e lymingtonarms@btconnect.
com
w lymingtonarms.co.uk

## WEST BAY
### Dorset

**Beachcroft ★★★★**
*Bed & Breakfast*
23 Forty Foot Way, West Bay,
Bridport DT6 4HD
t (01308) 423604
w beachcroft-westbay.co.uk

**Briarwood House ★★★★**
*Bed & Breakfast*
Old Church Road,
Bothenhampton, Bridport
DT6 4BP
t (01308) 422567
e briarwoodhouse@hotmail.
com
w briarwoodhouse.co.uk

**Bridport Arms ★★★★** *Inn*
West Bay DT6 4EN
t (01308) 422994
e reservations@bridportarms.
com
w bridportarms.com

**Heatherbell Cottage ★★★★**
*Guest Accommodation*
Hill Close, West Bay, Bridport
DT6 4HW
t (01308) 422998
e heatherbell4bnb@onetel.
net.uk
w cu4bnb.com

**Seacroft ★★★★**
*Bed & Breakfast*
24 Forty Foot Way, West Bay,
Bridport DT6 4HD
t (01308) 423407
e seacroft24@btinternet.com
w seacroftbandb.co.uk

## WEST BUCKLAND
### Somerset

**Causeway Cottage ★★★★**
*Bed & Breakfast*
Barbers Lane, Nr Wellington
TA21 9JZ
t (01823) 663458
e causewaybb@aol.com
w causewaycottage.co.uk

## WEST COKER
### Somerset

**Millbrook House ★★★★**
*Guest House*
High Street, Nr Yeovil
BA22 9AU
t (01935) 862840

## WEST COMPTON
### Somerset

**Primrose Hill B&B ★★★★**
*Guest Accommodation*
Knowle Farm Bungalow, Nr
Shepton Mallet BA4 4PD
t (01749) 899279
e mail@primrosehillbb.co.uk
w primrosehillbb.co.uk

## WEST HATCH
### Somerset

**The Farmers Inn ★★★★★**
*Inn*
Slough Hill, Nr Taunton
TA3 5RS
t (01823) 480480
e stay@farmersinnwesthatch.
co.uk
w farmersinnwesthatch.co.uk

## WEST HUNTSPILL
### Somerset

**Ilex House ★★★★**
*Bed & Breakfast*
SILVER AWARD
102 Main Road, Nr Highbridge
TA9 3QZ
t (01278) 783801
e enquiries@ilexhouse.co.uk
w ilexhouse.co.uk

## WEST LOOE
### Cornwall

**The Old Bridge House**
**★★★★** *Guest House*
The Quay, West Looe, Looe
PL13 2BU
t (01503) 263159
e mail@theoldbridgehouse.
com
w theoldbridgehouse.com

**Tidal Court ★★** *Guest House*
Church Street, West Looe,
Looe PL13 2EX
t (01503) 263695

## WEST LULWORTH
### Dorset

**Applegrove ★★★**
*Bed & Breakfast*
West Road, Lulworth Cove,
Wareham BH20 5RY
t (01929) 400592
e jennyandjohn@applegrove-
lulworth.co.uk
w applegrove-lulworth.co.uk

**Gatton House ★★★★**
*Guest House*
Main Road, West Lulworth,
Wareham BH20 5RL
t (01929) 400252
e avril@gattonhouse.co.uk
w gattonhouse.co.uk

**Ivy Cottage**
Rating Applied For
*Bed & Breakfast*
10 Main Road, Wareham
BH20 5RN
t (01929) 400509
e aleigh@fsmail.net
w ivycottage.biz

**Lulworth Cove YHA ★★**
*Hostel*
School Lane, Wareham
BH20 5SA
t (01929) 400564
e lulworth@yha.org.uk
w yha.org.uk

**The Old Barn ★★★**
*Guest Accommodation*
Main Road, West Lulworth,
Wareham BH20 5RL
t (01929) 400305

## WEST DOWN FARM ★★★
*Farmhouse*
West Lulworth, Wareham
BH20 5PU
t (01929) 400308
e sarah@westdownfarm.fsnet.
co.uk
w westdownfarm.co.uk

## WEST MONKTON
### Somerset

**Springfield House ★★★★**
*Guest Accommodation*
A38, Nr Taunton TA2 8QW
t (01823) 412116
e tina.ridout@btopenworld.
com
w springfieldhse.co.uk

## WEST MOORS
### Dorset

**Carey ★★★★**
*Bed & Breakfast*
11 Southern Avenue, West
Moors, Ferndown BH22 0BJ
t (01202) 861159
e russell@lesmor.fsnet.co.uk

## WEST OVERTON
### Wiltshire

**Cairncot ★★★**
*Bed & Breakfast*
West Overton, Marlborough
SN8 4ER
t (01672) 861617 &
07798 603455
e dm.leigh@virgin.net
w cairncot.co.uk

## WEST PORLOCK
### Somerset

**West Porlock House ★★★★**
*Guest Accommodation*
West Porlock, Minehead
TA24 8NX
t (01643) 862880
e westporlockhouse@
amserve.com

## WEST PUTFORD
### Devon

**South Worden ★★★★**
*Bed & Breakfast*
West Putford, Holsworthy
EX22 7LG
t (01409) 261448
e southworden@aol.com
w southworden-holsworthy.co.
uk

## WEST QUANTOXHEAD
### Somerset

**Stilegate Bed and Breakfast**
**★★★★★**
*Guest Accommodation*
Staple Close, Nr Williton
TA4 4DN
t (01984) 639119
e stilegate@aol.com
w stilegate.co.uk

## WEST STAFFORD
### Dorset

**Keepers Cottage ★★★★**
*Bed & Breakfast*
West Stafford, Dorchester
DT2 8AA
t (01305) 264389
e rayandangie@
thekeeperscottage.wanadoo.
co.uk
w keeperscottage.net

## WEST TAPHOUSE
### Cornwall

**Cross Close House B&B**
**★★★★** *Bed & Breakfast*
Cross Close, West Taphouse,
Lostwithiel PL22 0RP
t (01579) 320255
e alex.lister1@tesco.net
w cornwall-online.co.uk/cross-
close

## WEST TOLGUS
### Cornwall

**Solcett ★★★★**
*Bed & Breakfast*
West Tolgus, Redruth
TR15 3TN
t (01209) 218424
e malst@tiscali.co.uk
w visitcornwall.co.uk/solcett

## WESTBURY
### Wiltshire

**Black Dog Farm ★★★★**
*Farmhouse*
Chapmanslade, Westbury
BA13 4AE
t (01373) 832858

## WESTHAY
### Somerset

**New House Farm ★★★★**
*Farmhouse* SILVER AWARD
Shapwick Road, Glastonbury
BA6 9TT
t (01458) 860238
e newhousefarm@
farmersweekly.net
w newhousefarmbandb.co.uk

## WESTON-SUPER-MARE
### Somerset

**The Albany Lodge ★★★**
*Guest House*
9 Clevedon Road, Weston-
super-Mare BS23 1DA
t (01934) 629936
e albany@lodgeguesthouse.
co.uk
w albanylodgeguesthouse.co.
uk

**Cornerways ★★★**
*Guest House*
14 Whitecross Road, Weston-
super-Mare BS23 1EW
t (01934) 623708
e cornerwaysgh@aol.com
w cornerwaysweston.com

**Florence Guest House ★★★**
*Guest House*
32 Upper Church Road,
Weston-super-Mare BS23 2DX
t (01934) 626993
e info@florenceguesthouse.
co.uk
w florenceguesthouse.co.uk

**Grove Lodge ★★★**
*Guest House*
1 Bristol Road Lower, Weston-
super-Mare BS23 2PL
t (01934) 620494
e thegrovelodge@aol.com
w grovelodge.info

**Harmony Poynt ★★★★**
*Guest Accommodation*
Park Place, Weston-super-
Mare BS23 2BA
t (01934) 620258
e enquiries@
harmonypoynthotel.co.uk
w harmonypoynthotel.co.uk

**Lewinsdale Lodge** ★★★
*Guest Accommodation*
5-7 Clevedon Road, Weston-
super-Mare BS23 1DA
t (01934) 632501
e lewinsdale.lodge@virgin.net

**The Lugano** ★★★
*Guest Accommodation*
26 Upper Church Road,
Weston-super-Mare BS23 2DX
t (01934) 628207
e theluganohotel@btinternet.
com
w luganohotel.co.uk

**Milton Lodge Hotel** ★★★
*Guest House*
15 Milton Road, Weston-super-
Mare BS23 2SH
t (01934) 623161

**Moorlands Country House**
★★★ *Bed & Breakfast*
30 Main Road, Hutton,
Weston-super-Mare BS24 9QH
t (01934) 812283
e margaret-holt@hotmail.co.
uk
w guestaccom.co.uk/035.htm

**Orchard House** ★★★★
*Bed & Breakfast*
SILVER AWARD
West Wick, Weston-super-
Mare BS24 7TF
t (01934) 520948

**Richmond** ★★★
*Guest Accommodation*
14 Park Place, Weston-super-
Mare BS23 2BA
t (01934) 644722

**Rosita** ★★★
*Guest Accommodation*
30 Upper Church Road,
Weston-super-Mare BS23 2DX
t (01934) 620823

**Saxonia Guest House** ★★★
*Guest House*
95 Locking Road, Weston-
super-Mare BS23 3EW
t (01934) 424850
e saxoniahotel@btinternet.
com
w saxoniaguesthouse.co.uk

**Hotel Soraya** ★★
*Guest House*
34 Upper Church Road,
Weston-super-Mare BS23 2DX
t (01934) 629043
e enquiries@hotelsoraya.co.uk

**Spreyton Guest House** ★★★
*Guest House*
72 Locking Road, Weston-
super-Mare BS23 3EN
t (01934) 416887
e info@spreytonguesthouse.
fsnet.co.uk
w spreytonguesthouse.com

**Welbeck Hotel** ★★★
*Guest Accommodation*
Knightstone Road, Marine
Parade, Weston-super-Mare
BS23 2BB
t (01934) 621258
e welbeckhotel@aol.com
w weston-welbeck.com

**Hill View** ★★★★
*Bed & Breakfast*
SILVER AWARD
55 Liney Road, Nr Bridgwater
TA7 0EU
t (01278) 699027
e hillview@westonzoyland.
fsbusiness.co.uk
w visit-hillview.co.uk

**Park Farm Barn** ★★★★
*Bed & Breakfast*
Westrop, Corsham SN13 9QF
t (01249) 715911
e parkfarmbarn@btinternet.
com
w parkfarmbarn.co.uk

**Brockenhurst** ★★★★
*Bed & Breakfast*
11 Atlantic Way, Westward Ho,
Bideford EX39 1HX
t (01237) 423346
e petersnowball@btinternet.
com

**Mayfield** ★★★★
*Bed & Breakfast*
Avon Lane, Westward Ho
EX39 1LR
t (01237) 477128
e mayfieldbandb@hotmail.co.
uk
w mayfieldbandb.co.uk

**A Knight's Rest Guest House**
★★★ *Guest Accommodation*
93 Dorchester Road,
Weymouth DT4 7JY
t (01305) 839005
e enquiries@aknightsrest.co.
uk
w aknightsrest.co.uk

**Aaran House** ★★★
*Guest Accommodation*
2 The Esplanade, Weymouth
DT4 8EA
t (01305) 766669

**Albern House** ★★★
*Guest Accommodation*
13 Holland Road, Weymouth
DT4 0AL
t (01305) 783951

**Anchorage** ★★★★
*Guest Accommodation*
7 The Esplanade, Weymouth
DT4 8EB
t (01305) 782542
e info@
anchoragehotelweymouth.co.
uk
w anchoragehotelweymouth.
co.uk

**Arcadia Guest House** ★★★★
*Guest Accommodation*
7 Waterloo Place, Weymouth
DT4 7PA
t (01305) 782458
e roywilcocks@hotmail.com
w arcadiaguesthouse.com

**The Bay Guest House**
★★★★
*Guest Accommodation*
10 Waterloo Place, Weymouth
DT4 7PE
t (01305) 786289

**Bay View Hotel** ★★★★
*Guest Accommodation*
35 The Esplanade, Weymouth
DT4 8DH
t (01305) 782083
e info@bayview-weymouth.
co.uk
w bayview-weymouth.co.uk

**Beach Guest House** ★★★
*Guest House*
34 Lennox Street, Weymouth
DT4 7HD
t (01305) 779212

**Beach View Guest House**
★★★ *Guest House*
3 The Esplanade, Weymouth
DT4 8EA
t (01305) 786528
e beachviewweymouth@
hotmail.com
w beachviewguesthouse.com

**The Bourneville** ★★★
*Guest Accommodation*
31-32 The Esplanade,
Weymouth DT4 8DJ
t (01305) 784784
e enquiries@bournevillehotel.
co.uk
w bournevillehotel.co.uk

**Bridge House** ★★★★
*Bed & Breakfast*
13 Frys Close, Portesham,
Weymouth DT3 4LQ
t (01305) 871685
e thea@theaalexander.co.uk
w bridgehousebandb.co.uk

**Brierley Guest House** ★★★
*Guest House*
6 Lennox Street, Weymouth
DT4 7HD
t (01305) 782050

**Brunswick Guest House**
★★★ *Guest Accommodation*
9 Brunswick Terrace,
Weymouth DT4 7RW
t (01305) 785408
e info@brunswickweymouth.
co.uk
w brunswickweymouth.co.uk

**The Cavendale** ★★★
*Guest Accommodation*
The Esplanade, Weymouth
DT4 8EB
t (01305) 786960
e laraineholder@virgin.net

**Chandlers** ★★★★★
*Guest Accommodation*
GOLD AWARD
4 Westerhall Road, Weymouth
DT4 7SZ
t (01305) 771341
e info@chandlershotel.com
w chandlershotel.com

**The Channel Seafront House**
★★★ *Guest Accommodation*
93 The Esplanade, Weymouth
DT4 7AY
t (01305) 785405
e stay@channelhotel.co.uk
w channelhotel.co.uk

**The Chatsworth** ★★★★
*Guest Accommodation*
SILVER AWARD
14 The Esplanade, Weymouth
DT4 8EB
t (01305) 785012
e david@thechatsworth.co.uk
w thechatsworth.co.uk

**The Clarence** ★★★★
*Guest Accommodation*
20 The Esplanade, Weymouth
DT4 8DN
t (01305) 787573
e clarence.hotel1@btconnect.
com

**Hotel Concorde** ★★★
*Guest Accommodation*
131 The Esplanade, Weymouth
DT4 7EY
t (01305) 776900
w theconcordehotel.co.uk

**Crofton Guest House** ★★★
*Guest Accommodation*
Lennox Street, Weymouth
DT4 7HD
t (01305) 785903
e webber_36-2003@tiscali.co.
uk

**The Cumberland** ★★★★
*Guest Accommodation*
95 The Esplanade, Weymouth
DT4 7AT
t (01305) 785644
w cumberlandhotelweymouth.
co.uk

**The Cunard Guest House**
★★★★
*Guest Accommodation*
45-46 Lennox Street,
Weymouth DT4 7HB
t (01305) 771546
e stay@cunardguesthouse.co.
uk
w cunardguesthouse.co.uk

**Eastney** ★★★★ *Guest House*
15 Longfield Road, Weymouth
DT4 8RQ
t (01305) 771682
e eastneyhotel@aol.com
w eastneyhotel.co.uk

**Flintstones Guest House**
★★★ *Guest House*
10 Carlton Road South,
Weymouth DT4 7PJ
t (01305) 784153

**Florian Guest House**
Rating Applied For
*Guest House*
59 Abbotsbury Road,
Weymouth DT4 0AQ
t (01305) 773836
e clare@florian-guesthouse.
co.uk

**Fosters Guest House** ★★★
*Guest Accommodation*
3 Lennox Street, Weymouth
DT4 7HB
t (01305) 771685

**Gloucester House** ★★★
*Guest Accommodation*
96 The Esplanade, Weymouth
DT4 7AT
t (01305) 785191
e gloucesterwey@aol.com
w gloucesterhouseweymouth.
co.uk

**Green Gables** ★★★★
*Guest Accommodation*
14 Carlton Road South,
Weymouth DT4 7PJ
t  (01305) 774808
e  greengables@w-a-g.co.uk
w  w-a-g.co.uk/greengables

**Gresham Hotel** ★★
*Guest Accommodation*
120 The Esplanade,
Weymouth DT4 7EW
t  (01305) 785897
e  stuart.june@btinternet.com
w  greshamhotel-weymouth.co.
uk

**Harbour Lights** ★★★★
*Guest Accommodation*
20 Buxton Road, Weymouth
DT4 9PJ
t  (01305) 783273
e  harbourlights@btconnect.
com
w  harbourlights-weymouth.co.
uk

**Harlequin House Guest
House** ★★★ *Guest House*
9 Carlton Road South,
Weymouth DT4 7PL
t  (01305) 785598

**High Noon** ★★★
*Guest Accommodation*
12 Holland Road, Weymouth
DT4 0AL
t  (01305) 760587
w  highnoonguesthouse.co.uk

**Horizon Guest House** ★★★
*Guest Accommodation*
16 Brunswick Terrace,
Weymouth DT4 7RW
t  (01305) 784916
e  info@horizonguesthouse.co.
uk
w  horizonguesthouse.co.uk

**Kelston Guesthouse** ★★★
*Guest Accommodation*
1 Lennox Street, Weymouth
DT4 7HB
t  (01305) 780692
e  stay@kelstonguesthouse.co.
uk
w  kelstonguesthouse.co.uk

**The Kinley** ★★★
*Guest Accommodation*
98 The Esplanade, Weymouth
DT4 7AT
t  (01305) 782264
e  hotelkinley@hotmail.com
w  hotelkinley.co.uk

**The Langham** ★★★
*Guest House*
130 The Esplanade, Weymouth
DT4 7EX
t  (01305) 782530
e  enquiries@langham-hotel.
com
w  langham-hotel.com

**Lichfield House** ★★★
*Guest Accommodation*
8 Brunswick Terrace,
Weymouth DT4 7RW
t  (01305) 784112
e  lich.house@virgin.net
w  lichfieldhouse.co.uk

**Lilac Villa Guest House**
★★★★ *Guest House*
124 Dorchester Road,
Weymouth DT4 7LG
t  (01305) 782670
e  lilacvilla@ukonline.co.uk

**Lyndale Guest House** ★★★
*Guest Accommodation*
17 Brunswick Terrace,
Weymouth DT4 7SD
t  (01305) 786275
e  info@lyndaleguesthouse
weymouth.co.uk
w  lyndaleguesthouse
weymouth.co.uk

**Mar June Guest House** ★★★
*Guest House*
32 Lennox Street, Weymouth
DT4 7HD
t  (01305) 761320

**Marina Court** ★★★
*Guest Accommodation*
142 The Esplanade, Weymouth
DT4 7PB
t  (01305) 782146
e  marion@vassie.fsnet.co.uk
w  marinacourt.co.uk

**Mayfair** ★★★
*Guest Accommodation*
The Esplanade, Weymouth
DT4 7BE
t  (01305) 782094
w  mayfairhotelweymouth.co.
uk

**Morven House** ★★★★
*Guest Accommodation*
2 Westerhall Road, Weymouth
DT4 7SZ
t  (01305) 785075
e  matthew.lambley@
btinternet.com
w  morvenweymouth.co.uk

**Oaklands Edwardian
Guesthouse** ★★★★
*Guest Accommodation*
Glendinning Avenue,
Weymouth DT4 7QF
t  (01305) 767081
e  stay@oaklands-guesthouse.
co.uk
w  oaklands-guesthouse.co.uk

**Old Harbour View** ★★★★
*Bed & Breakfast*
12 Trinity Road, Weymouth
DT4 8TJ
t  (01305) 774633 &
07974 422241
e  pv_1st_ind@yahoo.co.uk

**The Pebbles** ★★★★
*Guest Accommodation*
18 Kirtleton Avenue,
Weymouth DT4 7PT
t  (01305) 784331
e  info@pebblesguesthouse.
co.uk
w  pebblesguesthouse.co.uk

**The Redcliff** ★★★
*Guest House*
18/19 Brunswick Terrace,
Weymouth DT4 7RW
t  (01305) 784682
e  contact@redcliffweymouth.
co.uk
w  redcliffweymouth.co.uk

**St John's Guest House** ★★★
*Guest Accommodation*
7 Dorchester Road, Weymouth
DT4 7JR
t  (01305) 775523
e  stayat@stjohnsguesthouse.
fsnet.co.uk
w  stjohnsguesthouse.co.uk

**The Seaham**
Rating Applied For
*Guest Accommodation*
3 Waterloo Place, Weymouth
DT4 7NU
t  (01305) 782010
e  stay@theseaham.co.uk
w  theseaham.co.uk

**Seaways Guesthouse** ★★
*Guest Accommodation*
5 Turton Street, Weymouth
DT4 7DU
t  (01305) 771646
e  seawaysguesthouse@
newsupanet.com

**The Sherborne Hotel** ★★★
*Guest Accommodation*
117 The Esplanade, Weymouth
DT4 7EH
t  (01305) 777888
w  sherbornehotelweymouth.
co.uk

**Spindrift Guest House** ★★★
*Guest Accommodation*
11 Brunswick Terrace,
Weymouth DT4 7RW
t  (01305) 773625
e  stay@spindriftguesthouse.
co.uk
w  spindriftguesthouse.co.uk

**Sunbay** ★★★
*Guest Accommodation*
12 Brunswick Terrace,
Weymouth DT4 7RW
t  (01305) 785992
e  holidays@
sunbayguesthouse.co.uk
w  sunbayguesthouse.co.uk

**Trevann Guest House** ★★★
*Guest House*
28 Lennox Street, Weymouth
DT4 7HE
t  (01305) 782604
e  trevann28@aol.com

**Turks Head** ★★★★
*Guest Accommodation*
SILVER AWARD
8 East Street, Chickerell,
Weymouth DT3 4DS
t  (01305) 783093

**Warwick Court** ★★★
*Guest House*
20 Abbotsbury Road,
Weymouth DT4 0AE
t  (01305) 783261
e  sharon@warwickcourt.co.uk
🏞️ 🖼️

**Weymouth Sands** ★★★
*Guest Accommodation*
5 The Esplanade, Weymouth
DT4 8EA
t  (01305) 839022
e  enquiries@weymouthsands.
co.uk
w  weymouthsands.co.uk

WHEDDON CROSS<br>Somerset

**Exmoor House** ★★★★
*Guest Accommodation*
Wheddon Cross TA24 7DU
t  (01643) 841432
e  info@exmoorhouse.com
w  exmoorhouse.com
🏞️ 🖼️

**Little Brendon Hill Farm**
★★★★★
*Guest Accommodation*
Summerway, Wheddon Cross
TA24 7BG
t  (01643) 841556
e  info@exmoorheaven.co.uk
w  exmoorheaven.co.uk

**Quarme Valley Grange**
★★★★★
*Guest Accommodation*
SILVER AWARD
Wheddon Cross, Minehead
TA24 7EY
t  (01643) 851323
e  stay@quarmevalleygrange.
com

**Sundial** ★★★★ *Guest House*
SILVER AWARD
Sundial Guesthouse, Wheddon
Cross TA24 7DP
t  (01643) 841188
e  admin@sundialguesthouse.
co.uk
w  sundialguesthouse.co.uk

WHILBOROUGH<br>Devon

**Walmer Towers** ★★★★
*Bed & Breakfast*
SILVER AWARD
Moles Lane, Whilborough,
Newton Abbot TQ12 5LS
t  (01803) 872105
e  walmertowers@btinternet.
com
w  walmertowers.co.uk

WHITECROSS<br>Cornwall

**The Old Post Office** ★★★
*Guest Accommodation*
Atlantic Highway, Whitecross,
Wadebridge PL27 7JD
t  (01208) 812620
e  bywaysoldpostoffice@
supanet.com

WHITMINSTER<br>Gloucestershire

**Whitminster Inn** ★★★★ *Inn*
Bristol Road, Gloucester
GL2 7NY
t  (01452) 740234
w  whitminsterinn.co.uk

WHITSTONE<br>Cornwall

**Whiteleigh Cottage** ★★★★
*Bed & Breakfast*
Whitstone, Holsworthy
EX22 6LB
t  (01288) 341082
e  whiteleighcottage@hotmail.
com
w  whiteleighcottage.co.uk

WHITTINGTON<br>Gloucestershire

**Ham Hill Farm** ★★★★
*Guest Accommodation*
SILVER AWARD
Whittington, Cheltenham
GL54 4EZ
t  (01242) 584415
e  hamhillfarm@msn.com

**Whalley Farm House**
★★★★ *Farmhouse*
Whittington, Cheltenham
GL54 4HA
t  (01242) 820213
e  rowefarms@farmline.com
w  whalleyfarm.co.uk

### WIDEMOUTH BAY
Cornwall

**Bay View Inn**
Rating Applied For
*Inn*
Marine Drive, Widemouth Bay,
Bude EX23 0AW
t (01288) 361273
e thebayviewinn@aol.com
w bayviewinn.co.uk

### WILMINGTON
Devon

**The White Hart ★★★★** *Inn*
Wilmington, Honiton EX14 9JQ
t (01404) 831764

### WILTON
Wiltshire

**The Pembroke Arms ★★★★**
*Inn*
Minster Street, Wilton,
Salisbury SP2 0BH
t (01722) 743328
e fleur@pembrokearms.co.uk
w pembrokearms.co.uk

### WIMBORNE MINSTER
Dorset

**96 West Borough ★★**
*Bed & Breakfast*
Wimborne BH21 1NH
t (01202) 884039

**The Albion ★★** *Inn*
High Street, Wimborne Minster
BH21 1HR
t (01202) 882492
e albioninn-wimborne@tiscali.co.uk
w albioninn-wimborne.co.uk

**Homestay ★★★**
*Bed & Breakfast*
22 West Borough, Wimborne
BH21 1NF
t (01202) 849015
e julietridg@onetel.com

**Lantern Lodge ★★★★**
*Bed & Breakfast*
GOLD AWARD
47 Gravel Hill, Merley,
Wimborne BH21 1RW
t (01202) 884183
e pam.munns@amserve.com

**Long Lane Farmhouse
★★★★** *Bed & Breakfast*
SILVER AWARD
Long Lane, Wimborne
BH21 7AQ
t (01202) 887829
e patricksmyth@btinternet.com
w ruraldorset.com

**The Old George ★★★★**
*Bed & Breakfast*
SILVER AWARD
2 Corn Market, Wimborne
BH21 1JL
t (01202) 888510
e chrissie_oldgeorge@yahoo.co.uk

### WINCANTON
Somerset

**Kingwell Lodge ★★★**
*Guest Accommodation*
Old Hill, Wincanton BA9 8BJ
t (01963) 32344
e jackie.may@jockeyclubracecourses.com
w wincantonracecourse.co.uk

### WINCHCOMBE
Gloucestershire

**Cleevely ★★★★**
*Bed & Breakfast*
Wadfield Farm, Winchcombe,
Cheltenham GL54 5AL
t (01242) 602059
e cleevelybxb@hotmail.com
w smoothhound.co.uk/cleevely

**Gaia Cottage ◆◆◆◆**
*Guest Accommodation*
50 Gloucester Street,
Winchcombe, Cheltenham
GL54 5LX
t (01242) 603495
e brian.simmonds@tiscali.co.uk

**Gower House ★★★★**
*Guest Accommodation*
16 North Street, Winchcombe,
Cheltenham GL54 5LH
t (01242) 602616
e gowerhouse16@aol.com.uk

**Manor Farm ★★★★**
*Farmhouse*
Greet, Winchcombe,
Cheltenham GL54 5BJ
t (01242) 602423
e janet@dickandjanet.fsnet.co.uk

**Mercia ★★★★**
*Guest Accommodation*
SILVER AWARD
Hailes Street, Winchcombe,
Cheltenham GL54 5HU
t (01242) 602251
e mercia@uk2.net
w merciaguesthouse.co.uk

**North Farmcote Bed and
Breakfast ★★★★** *Farmhouse*
Winchcombe, Cheltenham
GL54 5AU
t (01242) 602304
e davideayrs@amserve.com

**Oaklands ★★** *Guest House*
16 Gretton Road,
Winchcombe, Cheltenham
GL54 5EG
t (01242) 602272
e pat@oaklands.plus.com

**Old Station House ★★★★**
*Bed & Breakfast*
Greet Road, Winchcombe,
Cheltenham GL54 5LD
t (01242) 602283
e old_station_house@hotmail.com

**One Silk Mill Lane ★★★★**
*Bed & Breakfast*
Silk Mill Lane, Winchcombe,
Cheltenham GL54 5HZ
t (01242) 603952
e jenny.cheshire@virgin.net

**Parks Farm ★★★★**
*Farmhouse*
Sudeley, Winchcombe,
Cheltenham GL54 5JB
t (01242) 603874
e rosemaryawilson@hotmail.com
w parksfarm.co.uk

**Postlip Hall Farm ★★★★**
*Farmhouse* GOLD AWARD
Winchcombe, Cheltenham
GL54 5AQ
t (01242) 603351
e postliphallfarm@tiscali.co.uk
w smoothhound.co.uk/hotels/postlip.html

**Speakers Corner ★★★★**
*Guest Accommodation*
4 Greystones, Gloucester
Street, Winchcombe,
Cheltenham GL54 5NA
t (01242) 602223
e johnwelch@ntlworld.com

**The White Hart Inn and
Restaurant ★★★** *Inn*
High Street, Winchcombe,
Cheltenham GL54 5LJ
t (01242) 602359
e enquiries@the-white-hart-inn.com
w the-white-hart-inn.co.uk

### WINDRUSH
Gloucestershire

**Dellwood ★★★**
*Bed & Breakfast*
Windrush, Burford OX18 4TR
t (01451) 844268
e edwardswindrush@hotmail.com

### WINFRITH NEWBURGH
Dorset

**Wynards Farm ★★★★**
*Bed & Breakfast*
Winfrith Newburgh,
Dorchester DT2 8DQ
t (01305) 852660
e enquiries@wynardsfarm.co.uk
w wynardsfarm.co.uk

### WINKLEIGH
Devon

**The Old Parsonage ★★★★**
*Guest Accommodation*
Court Walk, Winkleigh
EX19 8JA
t (01837) 83772
e tony@lymingtonarms.co.uk

### WINSFORD
Somerset

**Kemps Farm ★★★★**
*Farmhouse*
Kemps Lane, Exford TA24 7HT
t (01643) 851312

### WINSHAM
Somerset

**Fulwood House ★★★★**
*Bed & Breakfast*
Ebben Lane, Chard TA20 4EE
t (01460) 30163
e liz.earl@virgin.net
w fulwoodhouse.co.uk

### WINSLEY
Wiltshire

**Conifers ★★** *Bed & Breakfast*
4 King Alfred Way, Winsley,
Bradford-on-Avon BA15 2NG
t (01225) 722482

**Stillmeadow ★★★★★**
*Bed & Breakfast*
18 Bradford Road, Winsley,
Bradford-on-Avon BA15 2HW
t (01225) 722119
e sue.gilby@btinternet.com
w stillmeadow.co.uk

### WINTERBORNE STICKLAND
Dorset

**Stickland Farmhouse
★★★★** *Bed & Breakfast*
SILVER AWARD
West Farm, Winterborne
Stickland, Blandford Forum
DT11 0NT
t (01258) 880119
e sticklandfarmhouse@sticklanddorset.fsnet.co.uk
w http://mysite.freeserve.com/stickland

### WINTERBORNE ZELSTON
Dorset

**Brook Farm ★★★** *Farmhouse*
Winterborne Zelston,
Blandford Forum DT11 9EU
t (01929) 459267
e kerleybrookfarmzelston@yahoo.co.uk

### WINTERBOURNE ABBAS
Dorset

**The Orchard ★★★★**
*Bed & Breakfast*
Copyhold Lane, Dorchester
DT2 9LT
t (01305) 889025
e godding_1@hotmail.co.uk

### WINTERBOURNE STOKE
Wiltshire

**Scotland Lodge Farm
★★★★** *Bed & Breakfast*
Winterbourne Stoke, Salisbury
SP3 4TF
t (01980) 621199
e william.lockwood@bigwig.net
w smoothhound.co.uk/hotels/scotlandl.html

### WINTERSLOW
Wiltshire

**Shiralee ★★** *Guest House*
Tytherley Road, Winterslow,
Salisbury SP5 1PY
t (01980) 862004
e contact@faisa.co.uk
w faisa.co.uk

### WITCOMBE
Gloucestershire

**Crickley Court ★★★★**
*Guest Accommodation*
SILVER AWARD
Dog Lane, Witcombe,
Gloucester GL3 4UF
t (01452) 863634
e lispilgrimmorris@yahoo.com

### WITHAM FRIARY
Somerset

**Higher West Barn Farm
★★★★** *Farmhouse*
SILVER AWARD
Bindon Lane, Nr Bruton
BA11 5HH
t (01749) 850819
e ea.harrison@tesco.net
w farmstaysomerset.com/farmstaysomerset.htm

### WITHERIDGE
Devon

**Thelbridge Cross Inn
★★★★** *Inn*
Thelbridge, Crediton EX17 4SQ
t (01884) 860316
e admin@thelbridgexinn.co.uk
w westcountry-hotels.co.uk/thelbridgexinn

## WITHINGTON
### Gloucestershire

**Willowside Farm** ★★★
*Guest Accommodation*
Withington, Cheltenham
GL54 4DA
t (01242) 890362
e janeforbes100@hotmail.com

## WITHYPOOL
### Somerset

**Newland House** ★★★★★
*Guest Accommodation*
**SILVER AWARD**
Minehead TA24 7QX
t (01643) 831693
e newlandhousewithypool@
yahoo.com

## WIVELISCOMBE
### Somerset

**Mill Barn** ★★★★
*Bed & Breakfast*
Jews Farm, Nr Wivelscombe
TA4 2HL
t (01984) 624739
e tony&marilyn@mill-barn.
freeserve.co.uk
w mill-barn.freeserve.co.uk

**North Down Farm** ★★★★
*Farmhouse* **SILVER AWARD**
Wiveliscombe TA4 2BL
t (01984) 623730
e jennycope@tiscali.co.uk
w north-down-farm.co.uk

## WOODBOROUGH
### Wiltshire

**Well Cottage** ★★★★
*Bed & Breakfast*
Honeystreet, Pewsey SN9 5PS
t (01672) 851577
e booking@well-cottage.org.
uk

## WOODLEIGH
### Devon

**Higher Hendham House**
★★★★ *Farmhouse*
Woodleigh, Kingsbridge
TQ7 4DP
t (01548) 550015
e higherhendhamhouse@
fsmail.net
w higherheadhamhouse.com

## WOODY BAY
### Devon

**Moorlands** ★★★★
*Guest Accommodation*
Woody Bay, Parracombe,
Barnstaple EX31 4RA
t (01598) 763224
e info@moorlandshotel.co.uk
w moorlandshotel.co.uk

## WOOKEY HOLE
### Somerset

**Whitegate Cottage** ★★
*Bed & Breakfast*
Milton Lane, Nr Wells BA5 1DE
t (01749) 675326
e sueandnic@whitegate.
freeserve.co.uk
w synergynet.co.uk/somerset/
whitegate.htm

## WOOL
### Dorset

**East Burton House** ★★
*Bed & Breakfast*
East Burton Road, Wool
BH20 6HE
t (01929) 462083
e info@eastburtonhouse.com
w eastburtonhouse.com

**The Withies** ★★★
*Guest Accommodation*
16 Colliers Lane, Wool,
Wareham BH20 6DL
t (01929) 405339
e pazwold@btinternet.com

## WOOLACOMBE
### Devon

**Castle Hotel** ★★★★
*Guest Accommodation*
The Esplanade, Woolacombe
EX34 7DJ
t (01271) 870788

**Ossaborough House** ★★★★
*Guest Accommodation*
**SILVER AWARD**
Ossaborough Lane,
Woolacombe EX34 7HJ
t (01271) 870297
e info@ossaboroughhouse.co.
uk
w ossaboroughhouse.co.uk

**Sandunes Guest House**
★★★★ *Guest House*
**SILVER AWARD**
Beach Road, Woolacombe
EX34 7BT
t (01271) 870661
e info@sandwool.fsnet.co.uk
w sandwool.fsnet.co.uk

**Sunny Nook** ★★★★
*Guest Accommodation*
**SILVER AWARD**
Beach Road, Woolacombe
EX34 7AA
t (01271) 870964
e kate@sunnynook.co.uk
w sunnynook.co.uk

## WOOLMINSTONE
### Somerset

**Barn Cottage Bed and
Breakfast** ★★★★
*Bed & Breakfast*
**SILVER AWARD**
Lyminster Farm, Nr Crewkerne
TA18 8QP
t (01460) 75313
e bandbbarncottage@aol.com
w smoothhound.co.uk/hotels/
barncottage

## WOOTTON BASSETT
### Wiltshire

**The Hollies** ★★★
*Bed & Breakfast*
Greenhill, Wootton Bassett,
Swindon SN4 8EH
t (01793) 770795
w bedandbreakfastexplorer.co.
uk

## WOOTTON RIVERS
### Wiltshire

**Royal Oak** ★★★ *Inn*
Wootton Rivers, Marlborough
SN8 4NQ
t (01672) 810322
e royaloak35@hotmail.com
w wiltshire-pubs.com

## WORTH MATRAVERS
### Dorset

**Chiltern Lodge** ★★
*Bed & Breakfast*
8 Newfoundland Close, Worth
Matravers, Swanage BH19 3LX
t (01929) 439337
e densor@btopenworld.com
w chilternlodge.co.uk

## WRAXALL
### Somerset

**Roses Farm** ★★★★
*Farmhouse*
Wraxall Rd, Shepton Mallet
BA4 6RQ
t (01749) 860261
e info@rosesfarm.com
w rosesfarm.com

## YATTON KEYNELL
### Wiltshire

**Combehead Barn** ★★★★
*Bed & Breakfast*
Giddeahall, Yatton Keynell,
Chippenham SN14 7ES
t (01249) 783487
e combe2005@aol.com
w thebarncombehead.co.uk

## YELVERTON
### Devon

**Eggworthy Farm** ★★★
*Farmhouse*
Sampford Spiney, Yelverton
PL20 6LJ
t (01822) 852142
e eggworthyfarm@aol.com

**The Old Orchard** ◆◆◆◆
*Guest Accommodation*
**SILVER AWARD**
Harrowbeer Lane, Yelverton
PL20 6DZ
t (01822) 854310
e babs@baross.demon.co.uk
w baross.demon.co.uk/
theoldorchard

**Overcombe House** ★★★★
*Guest Accommodation*
Old Station Road, Yelverton
PL20 7RA
t (01822) 853501
e enquiries@overcombehotel.
co.uk
w overcombehotel.co.uk

**The Rosemont** ★★★★
*Guest Accommodation*
Greenbank Terrace, Yelverton
PL20 6DR
t (01822) 852175
e office@therosemont.co.uk
w therosemont.co.uk

## YEOVIL
### Somerset

**Greystones Court** ★★★★
*Guest Accommodation*
152 Hendford Hill, Yeovil
BA20 2RG
t (01935) 426124
e peterandsimone.adlam@
btopenworld.com
w greystonescourt.com

**La Oliva** ★★★★
*Restaurant with Rooms*
Forest Hill, Yeovil BA20 2PG
t (01935) 476808
e dan@inntown.net

**Pendomer House** ★★★
*Bed & Breakfast*
Nr Yeovil BA22 9PB
t (01935) 862785
e enquiries@pendomerhouse.
co.uk
w pendomerhouse.co.uk

## YEOVILTON
### Somerset

**Courtry Farm** ★★★
*Farmhouse*
Main Road, Nr Yeovil
BA22 8HF
t (01935) 840327
e courtryfarm@hotmail.com

## YETMINSTER
### Dorset

**Bingers Farm** ★★★★
*Bed & Breakfast*
**SILVER AWARD**
Ryme Road, Yetminster,
Sherborne DT9 6JY
t (01935) 872555
e bingersfarm@talk21.com

## YORKLEY
### Gloucestershire

**Silverdeane** ★★★★
*Bed & Breakfast*
Lower Road, Yorkley, Lydney
GL15 4TQ
t (01594) 560262
e enquiries@silverdeane.co.uk
w silverdeane.co.uk

## ZEALS
### Wiltshire

**Cornerways Cottage** ★★★
*Bed & Breakfast*
Longcross, Zeals, Warminster
BA12 6LL
t (01747) 840477
e cornerways.cottage@
btinternet.com
w cornerwayscottage.co.uk

# Further information

Whitby Abbey,
North Yorkshire

# Enjoy England
# Quality Rose scheme

When you're looking for a place to stay, you need a rating system you can trust. Enjoy England ratings are your clear guide to what to expect, in an easy-to-understand form.

Enjoy England professional assessors pay unannounced visits to establishments that are new to the rating scheme and stay overnight. Once in the scheme establishments receive an annual pre-arranged day visit, with an overnight stay generally every other year. On these occasions the assessors book in anonymously, and test all the facilities and services. So you can be confident that your accommodation has been thoroughly checked and rated for quality before you make a booking.

Based on the internationally recognised rating of stars, the system puts great emphasis on quality, and reflects research which shows exactly what consumers are looking for when choosing bed and breakfast accommodation. Ratings are awarded from one to five stars – the more stars, the higher the quality and the greater the range of facilities and services provided.

Look out, too, for Enjoy England Gold and Silver Awards, which are awarded to properties achieving the highest levels of quality within their star rating. While the overall rating is based on a combination of facilities and quality, the Gold and Silver Awards are based solely on quality.

## Star ratings
Star ratings are your sign of quality assurance, giving you the confidence to book the accommodation that meets your expectations. All bed and breakfast accommodation that is awarded a star rating will meet the minimum standards – so you can be confident that you will find the basic services that you would expect, such as:

- A clear explanation of booking charges, services offered and cancellation terms
- A full cooked breakfast or substantial continental breakfast

- At least one bathroom or shower room for every six guests
- For a stay of more than one night, rooms cleaned and beds made daily
- Printed advice on how to summon emergency assistance at night
- All statutory obligations will be met.

Proprietors of bed and breakfast accommodation have to provide certain additional facilities and services at the higher star levels, some of which may be important to you:

**THREE-STAR accommodation must provide:**
- Private bathroom/shower room (cannot be shared with the owners)
- Bedrooms must have a washbasin if not en suite.

**FOUR-STAR accommodation must provide:**
- 50% of bedrooms en suite or with private bathroom.

**FIVE-STAR accommodation must provide:**
- All bedrooms with en suite or private bathroom.

Sometimes a bed and breakfast establishment has exceptional bedrooms and bathrooms and offers guests a very special welcome, but cannot achieve a higher star rating because, for example, there are no en suite bedrooms, or it is difficult to put washbasins in the bedrooms (three star). This is sometimes the case with period properties.

## Quality
The availability of additional facilities alone is not enough for an establishment to achieve a higher star rating. Bed and breakfast accommodation has to meet exacting standards for quality in critical areas. Consumer research has shown the critical areas to be: cleanliness, bedrooms, bathrooms, hospitality and food.

# Advice and information

## Making a reservation

When enquiring about accommodation, make sure you check prices, the quality rating and other important details. You will also need to state your requirements clearly and precisely, for example:

- Arrival and departure dates, with acceptable alternatives if appropriate
- The type of accommodation you need – for example, room with twin beds, en suite bathroom
- The terms you want – for example, bed and breakfast only; dinner and breakfast (where provided)
- The age of any children with you, whether you want them to share your room or be next door, and any other special requirements, such as a cot
- Any particular requirements you may have, such as a special diet, ground-floor room.

### Confirmation

Misunderstandings can easily happen over the telephone, so do request a written confirmation, together with details of any terms and conditions.

### Deposits

If you make your reservation weeks or months in advance, you will probably be asked for a deposit, which will then be deducted from the final bill when you leave. The amount will vary from establishment to establishment and could be payment in full at peak times.

### Payment on arrival

Some establishments, especially large hotels in big towns, ask you to pay for your room on arrival if you have not booked it in advance. This is especially likely to happen if you arrive late and have little or no luggage.

If you are asked to pay on arrival, it is a good idea to see your room first, to make sure it meets your requirements.

## Cancellations

### Legal contract

When you accept accommodation that is offered to you, by telephone or in writing, you enter a legally binding contract with the proprietor. This means that if you cancel your booking, fail to take up the accommodation or leave early, the proprietor may be entitled to compensation if he or she cannot re-let for all or a good part of the booked period. You will probably forfeit any deposit you have paid, and may well be asked for an additional payment.

At the time of booking you should be advised of what charges would be made in the event of cancelling the accommodation or leaving early. If this is not mentioned you should ask so that future disputes can be avoided. The proprietor cannot make a claim until after the booked period, and during that time he or she should make every effort to re-let the accommodation. If there is a dispute it is sensible for both sides to seek legal advice on the matter. If you do have to change your travel plans, it is in your own interests to let the proprietor know in writing as soon as possible, to give them a chance to re-let your accommodation.

And remember, if you book by telephone and are asked for your credit card number, you should check whether the proprietor intends charging your credit card account should you later cancel your reservation. A proprietor should not be able to charge your credit card account with a cancellation fee unless he or she has made this clear at the time of your booking and you have agreed. However, to avoid later disputes, we suggest you check whether this is the intention.

## Insurance

A travel or holiday insurance policy will safeguard you if you have to cancel or change your holiday plans. You can arrange a policy quite cheaply through your insurance company or travel agent.

## Arriving late

If you know you will be arriving late in the evening, it is a good idea to say so when you book. If you are delayed on your way, a telephone call to say that you will be late would be appreciated.

## Service charges and tipping

These days many places levy service charges automatically. If they do, they must clearly say so in their offer of accommodation, at the time of booking. The service charge then becomes part of the legal contract when you accept the offer of accommodation.

If a service charge is levied automatically, there is no need to tip the staff, unless they provide some exceptional service. The usual tip for meals is 10% of the total bill.

## Telephone charges

Establishments can set their own charges for telephone calls made through their switchboard or from direct-dial telephones in bedrooms. These charges are often much higher than telephone companies' standard charges (to defray the cost of providing the service).

### Comparing costs

It is a condition of Enjoy England Quality Rose assessment scheme that an establishment's unit charges are on display by the telephones or with the room information. It is not always easy to compare these charges with standard rates, so before using a telephone for long-distance calls, you may decide to ask how the charges compare.

## Security of valuables

You can deposit your valuables with the proprietor or manager during your stay, and we recommend you do this as a sensible precaution. Make sure you obtain a receipt for them. Some places do not accept articles for safe custody, and in that case it is wisest to keep your valuables with you.

## Disclaimer

Some proprietors put up a notice that disclaims liability for property brought on to their premises by a guest. In fact, they can only restrict their liability to a minimum laid down by law (The Hotel Proprietors Act 1956). Under that Act, a proprietor is liable for the value of the loss or damage to any property (except a car or its contents) of a guest who has engaged overnight accommodation, but if the proprietor has the notice on display as prescribed under that Act, liability is limited to £50 for one article and a total of £100 for any one guest. The notice must be prominently displayed in the reception area or main entrance. These limits do not apply to valuables you have deposited with the proprietor for safekeeping, or to property lost through the default, neglect or wilful act of the proprietor or his staff.

## Bringing pets to England

Dogs, cats, ferrets and some other pet mammals can be brought into the UK from certain countries without having to undertake six months' quarantine on arrival provided they meet all the rules of the Pet Travel Scheme (PETS).

For full details, visit the PETS website at
**w** defra.gov.uk/animalh/quarantine/index.htm or contact the PETS Helpline
**t** +44 (0)870 241 1710
**e** pets.helpline@defra.gsi.gov.uk
Ask for fact sheets which cover dogs and cats, ferrets or domestic rabbits and rodents.

## What to expect

The proprietor/management is required to undertake the following:

- To maintain standards of guest care, cleanliness and service appropriate to the type of establishment;
- To describe accurately in any advertisement, brochure or other printed or electronic media, the facilities and services provided;
- To make clear to visitors exactly what is included in all prices quoted for accommodation, including taxes, and any other surcharges. Details of charges for additional services/facilities should also be made clear;
- To give a clear statement of the policy on cancellations to guests at the time of booking ie by telephone, fax, email, as well as information given in a printed format;
- To adhere to and not to exceed prices quoted at the time of booking for accommodation and other services;
- To advise visitors at the time of booking, and subsequently if any change, if the accommodation offered is in an unconnected annexe or similar and to indicate the location of such accommodation and any difference in comfort and/or amenities from accommodation in the establishment;
- To register all guests on arrival;
- To give each visitor on request details of payments due and a receipt, if required;
- To deal promptly and courteously with all enquiries, requests, bookings and correspondence from visitors;

- To ensure complaint handling procedures are in place and that complaints received are investigated promptly and courteously and that the outcome is communicated to the visitor;

- To give due consideration to the requirements of visitors with disabilities and visitors with special needs, and to make suitable provision where applicable;

- To provide public liability insurance or comparable arrangements and to comply with all applicable planning, safety and other statutory requirements;

- To allow an Enjoy England assessor reasonable access to the establishment on request, to confirm the VisitBritain Code of Conduct is being observed.

## Comments and complaints

### Bed and breakfast accommodation and the law

Places that offer accommodation have legal and statutory responsibilities to their customers, such as providing information about prices, providing adequate fire precautions and safeguarding valuables. Like other businesses, they must also abide by the Trades Description Acts 1968 and 1972 when they describe their accommodation and facilities. All the places featured in this guide have declared that they do fulfil all applicable statutory obligations.

### Information

The proprietors themselves supply the descriptions of their establishments and other information for the entries, (except Enjoy England ratings and awards). VisitBritain cannot guarantee the accuracy of information in this guide, and accepts no responsibility for any error or misrepresentation. All liability for loss, disappointment, negligence or other damage caused by reliance on the information contained in this guide, or in the event of bankruptcy or liquidation or cessation of trade of any company, individual or firm mentioned, is hereby excluded. We strongly recommend that you carefully check prices and other details when you book your accommodation.

### Quality Rose signage

All establishments displaying a Quality Rose sign have to hold current membership of the Enjoy England Quality Rose assessment scheme. When an establishment is sold the new owner has to reapply and be reassessed.

### Problems

Of course, we hope you will not have cause for complaint, but problems do occur from time to time. If you are dissatisfied with anything, make your complaint to the management immediately. Then the management can take action at once to investigate the matter and put things right. The longer you leave a complaint, the harder it is to deal with it effectively.

In certain circumstances, VisitBritain may look into complaints. However, VisitBritain has no statutory control over establishments or their methods of operating. VisitBritain cannot become involved in legal or contractual matters, nor can they get involved in seeking financial recompense.

If you do have problems that have not been resolved by the proprietor and which you would like to bring to our attention, please write to: Quality in Tourism, Farncombe House, Broadway, Worcestershire WR12 7LJ.

## Help before you go

When it comes to your next English break, the first stage of your journey could be closer than you think.

You've probably got a Tourist Information Centre nearby which is there to serve the local community – as well as visitors. Knowledgeable staff will be happy to help you, wherever you're heading.

Many Tourist Information Centres can provide you with maps and guides, and it's often possible to book accommodation and travel tickets too.

You'll find the address of your nearest centre in your local phone book, or look at the beginning of each regional section in this guide for a list of Official Partner Tourist Information Centres.

# About the guide entries

## Entries

All the accommodation featured in this guide has been assessed or has applied for assessment under the Enjoy England Quality Rose assessment scheme.

Assessment automatically entitles establishments to a listing in this guide. Start your search for a place to stay by looking in the regional sections of this guide where proprietors have paid to have their establishment featured in either a standard entry (includes description, facilities and prices) or an enhanced entry (photograph and extended details). If you can't find what you're looking for, turn to the listing section on the yellow pages for an even wider choice of accommodation.

## Locations

Places to stay are generally listed under the town, city or village where they are located. If a place is in a small village, you may find it listed under a nearby town (providing it is within a seven-mile radius).

Place names are listed alphabetically within each regional section of the guide, along with the name of the ceremonial county they are in and their map reference.

### Map references

These refer to the colour location maps at the front of the guide. The first figure shown is the map number, the following letter and figure indicate the grid reference on the map. Only place names under which standard or enhanced entries (see above) feature appear on the maps. Some entries were included just before the guide went to press, so they do not appear on the maps.

### Addresses

County names, which appear in the place headings, are not repeated in the entries. When you are writing, you should of course make sure you use the full address and postcode.

### Telephone numbers

Telephone numbers are listed below the accommodation address for each entry. Area codes are shown in brackets.

## Prices

The prices shown are only a general guide; they were supplied to us by proprietors in summer 2007. Remember, changes may occur after the guide goes to press, so we strongly advise you to check prices when you book your accommodation.

Prices are shown in pounds sterling and include VAT where applicable. Some places also include a service charge in their standard tariff, so check this when you book.

There are many different ways of quoting prices for accommodation. We use a standardised method in the guide to allow you to compare prices. For example, when we show:

**Bed and breakfast**: the prices shown are per room for overnight accommodation with breakfast. The double room price is for two people. (If a double room is occupied by one person there is sometimes a reduction in price.)

**Evening meal**: the prices shown are per person per night.

Some places only provide a continental breakfast in the set price, and you may have to pay extra if you want a full English breakfast.

### Checking prices

According to the law, establishments with at least four bedrooms or eight beds must display their overnight accommodation charges in the reception area or entrance. In your own interests, do make sure you check prices and what they include.

### Children's rates

You will find that many places charge a reduced rate for children, especially if they share a room with their parents. Some places charge the full rate, however, when a child occupies a room which might otherwise have been let to an adult. The upper age limit for reductions for children varies from one establishment to another, so check this when you book.

**Seasonal packages and special promotions**

Prices often vary through the year and may be significantly lower outside peak holiday weeks. Many places offer special package rates – fully inclusive weekend breaks, for example – in the autumn, winter and spring. A number of establishments taking an enhanced entry have included any special offers, themed breaks etc that are available.

You can get details of other bargain packages that may be available from the establishments themselves, regional tourism organisations or your local Tourist Information Centre (TIC). Your local travel agent may also have information and can help you make reservations.

## Bathrooms

Each accommodation entry shows you the number of en suite and private bathrooms available. En suite bathroom means the bath or shower and wc are contained behind the main door of the bedroom. Private bathroom means a bath or shower and wc solely for the occupants of one bedroom, on the same floor, reasonably close and with a key provided. If the availability of a bath, rather than a shower, is important to you, remember to check when you book.

## Meals

It is advisable to check availability of meals and set times when making your reservation. Some smaller places may ask you at breakfast whether you want an evening meal. The prices shown in each entry are for bed and breakfast and evening meal, but many places also offer lunch.

## Opening period

If an entry does not indicate an opening period, please check directly with the establishment.

## Symbols

The at-a-glance symbols included at the end of each entry show many of the services and facilities available at each establishment. You will find the key to these symbols on the back-cover flap – open it out and check the meanings as you go.

## Smoking

In the UK, it is illegal to smoke in enclosed public spaces and places of work. This means that smoking is banned in the public and communal areas of guesthouses and B&Bs. Some establishments may choose to provide designated smoking bedrooms, and may allow smoking in private areas that are not used by any staff.

If you wish to smoke, it is advisable to check whether it is allowed when you book.

## Alcoholic drinks

Many places listed in the guide are licensed to serve alcohol. The licence may be restricted – to diners only, for example – so you may want to check this when you book. If they have a bar this is shown by the ♀ symbol.

## Pets

Many places accept guests with dogs, but we do advise that you check this when you book, and ask if there are any extra charges or rules about exactly where your pet is allowed. The acceptance of dogs is not always extended to cats and it is strongly advised that cat owners contact the establishment well in advance. Some establishments do not accept pets at all. Pets are welcome by arrangement where you see this symbol ♀.

The quarantine laws have changed in England, and dogs, cats and ferrets are able to come into Britain from over 50 countries. For details of the Pet Travel Scheme (PETS) please turn to page 704.

## Payment accepted

The types of payment accepted by an establishment are listed in the payment accepted section. If you plan to pay by card, check that the establishment will take your particular card before you book. Some proprietors will charge you a higher rate if you pay by credit card rather than cash or cheque. The difference is to cover the percentage paid by the proprietor to the credit card company. When you book by telephone, you may be asked for your credit card number as confirmation. But remember, the proprietor may then charge your credit card account if you cancel your booking. See under Cancellations on page 703.

## Rating Applied For

At the time of going to press some establishments featured in this guide had not yet been assessed and so their new rating could not be included. Rating Applied For indicates this.

## Diamond ratings

Establishments with a diamond rating were awaiting re-assessment under the star-rating scheme at the time of going to press (August 07).

## Property names

Under the Common Standards for assessment, guest accommodation may not include the word 'hotel' in its name. The majority of accommodation in this guide complies with this rule and the national assessing bodies, including VisitBritain, are working towards bringing all guest accommodation in line with this.

# Getting around England

**England is a country of perfect proportions** – big enough to find a new place to discover, yet small enough to guarantee it's within easy reach. Getting from A to B can be easier than you think...

## Planning your journey

Make transportdirect.info your first portal of call! It's the ultimate journey-planning tool to help you find the best way from your home to your destination by car or public transport. Decide on the quickest way to travel by comparing end-to-end journey times and routes. You can even buy train and coach tickets and find out about flights from a selection of airports.

With so many low-cost domestic flights, flying really is an option. Just imagine, you could finish work in Bishop's Stortford and be in Newquay just three hours later for a fun-packed weekend!

You can island hop too, to the Isle of Wight or the Isles of Scilly for a relaxing break. No worries.

If you're travelling by car and want an idea of distances check out the mileage chart overleaf. Or let the train take the strain – the National Rail network is also shown overleaf.

## Think green

If you'd rather leave your car behind and travel by 'green transport' when visiting some of the attractions highlighted in this guide you'll be helping to reduce congestion and pollution as well as supporting conservation charities in their commitment to green travel.

The National Trust encourages visits made by non-car travellers. It offers admission discounts or a voucher for the tea room at a selection of its properties if you arrive on foot, cycle or public transport. (You'll need to produce a valid bus or train ticket if travelling by public transport.)

More information about The National Trust's work to encourage car-free days out can be found at nationaltrust.org.uk. Refer to the section entitled Information for Visitors.

---

**To help you on your way you'll find a list of useful contacts at the end of this section.**

# Counties and regions at-a-glance

If you know what county you wish to visit you'll find it in the regional section shown below.

| County | Region | County | Region |
|---|---|---|---|
| Bedfordshire | East of England | Leicestershire | East Midlands |
| Berkshire | South East England | Lincolnshire | East Midlands |
| Bristol | South West England | Merseyside | England's Northwest |
| Buckinghamshire | South East England | Norfolk | East of England |
| Cambridgeshire | East of England | North Yorkshire | Yorkshire |
| Cheshire | England's Northwest | Northamptonshire | East Midlands |
| Cornwall | South West England | Northumberland | North East England |
| County Durham | North East England | Nottinghamshire | East Midlands |
| Cumbria | England's Northwest | Oxfordshire | South East England |
| Derbyshire | East Midlands | Rutland | East Midlands |
| Devon | South West England | Shropshire | Heart of England |
| Dorset | South West England | Somerset | South West England |
| East Riding of Yorkshire | Yorkshire | South Yorkshire | Yorkshire |
| East Sussex | South East England | Staffordshire | Heart of England |
| Essex | East of England | Suffolk | East of England |
| Gloucestershire | South West England | Surrey | South East England |
| Greater Manchester | England's Northwest | Tees Valley | North East England |
| Hampshire | South East England | Tyne and Wear | North East England |
| Herefordshire | Heart of England | Warwickshire | Heart of England |
| Hertfordshire | East of England | West Midlands | Heart of England |
| Isle of Wight | South East England | West Sussex | South East England |
| Isles of Scilly | South West England | West Yorkshire | Yorkshire |
| Kent | South East England | Wiltshire | South West England |
| Lancashire | England's Northwest | Worcestershire | Heart of England |

To help readers we do not refer to unitary authorities in this guide.

Official tourist board guide **Bed & Breakfast**

# By car and by train

## Distance chart

The distances between towns on the chart below are given to the nearest mile, and are measured along routes based on the quickest travelling time, making maximum use of motorways or dual-carriageway roads. The chart is based upon information supplied by the Automobile Association.

**To calculate the distance in kilometres multiply the mileage by 1.6**

**For example:** Brighton to Dover
82 miles x 1.6 =131.2 kilometres

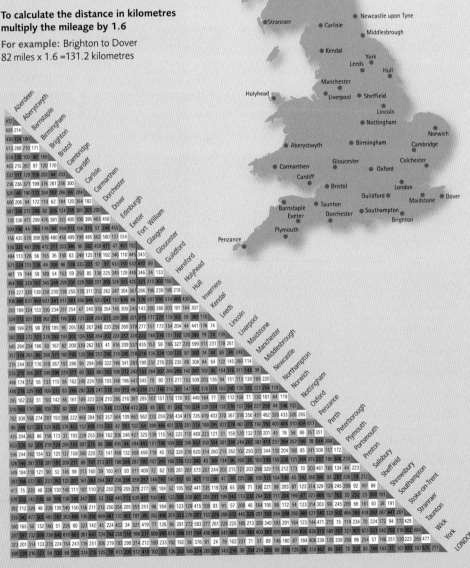

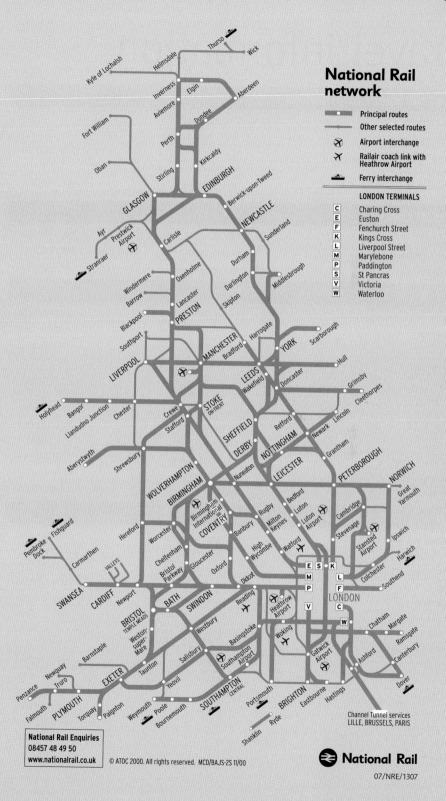

**National Rail network**

- Principal routes
- Other selected routes
- Airport interchange
- Railair coach link with Heathrow Airport
- Ferry interchange

**LONDON TERMINALS**

| | |
|---|---|
| C | Charing Cross |
| E | Euston |
| F | Fenchurch Street |
| K | Kings Cross |
| L | Liverpool Street |
| M | Marylebone |
| P | Paddington |
| S | St Pancras |
| V | Victoria |
| W | Waterloo |

Channel Tunnel services
LILLE, BRUSSELS, PARIS

National Rail Enquiries
08457 48 49 50
www.nationalrail.co.uk

© ATOC 2000. All rights reserved. MCD/BAJS-2S 11/00

**National Rail**

07/NRE/1307

# Travel information

## General travel information

| | | |
|---|---|---|
| Streetmap | streetmap.co.uk | |
| Transport Direct | transportdirect.info | |
| Transport for London | tfl.gov.uk | (020) 7222 1234 |
| Travel Services | departures-arrivals.com | |
| Traveline | traveline.org.uk | 0870 200 2233 |

## Bus & coach

| | | |
|---|---|---|
| Megabus | megabus.com | 0901 331 0031 |
| National Express | nationalexpress.com | 0870 580 8080 |
| WA Shearings | washearings.com | (01942) 824824 |

## Car & car hire

| | | |
|---|---|---|
| AA | theaa.com | 0870 600 0371 |
| Green Flag | greenflag.co.uk | 0845 246 1557 |
| RAC | rac.co.uk | 0870 572 2722 |
| Alamo | alamo.co.uk | 0870 400 4562* |
| Avis | avis.co.uk | 0844 581 0147 |
| Budget | budget.co.uk | 0844 581 2231 |
| Easycar | easycar.com | 0906 333 3333 |
| Enterprise | enterprise.com | 0870 350 3000* |
| Hertz | hertz.co.uk | 0870 844 8844* |
| Holiday Autos | holidayautos.co.uk | 0870 400 4461 |
| National | nationalcar.co.uk | 0870 400 4581 |
| Thrifty | thrifty.co.uk | (01494) 751500 |

## Air

| | | |
|---|---|---|
| Airport information | a2btravel.com/airports | 0870 888 1710 |
| Air Southwest | airsouthwest.com | 0870 043 4553 |
| Blue Islands (Channel Islands) | blueislands.com | 0845 620 2122 |
| BMI | flybmi.com | 0870 607 0555 |
| BMI Baby | bmibaby.com | 0871 224 0224 |
| British Airways | ba.com | 0870 850 9850 |
| British International (Isles of Scilly to Penzance) | islesofscillyhelicopter.com | (01736) 363871* |
| Eastern Airways | easternairways.com | 0870 366 9100* |
| Easyjet | easyjet.com | 0871 244 2366 |
| Flybe | flybe.com | 0871 522 6100 |
| Jet2.com | jet2.com | 0871 226 1737* |
| Ryanair | ryanair.com | 0871 246 0000 |
| Skybus (Isles of Scilly) | islesofscilly-travel.com | 0845 710 5555 |
| VLM | flyvlm.com | 0871 666 5050 |

## Train

| National Rail Enquiries | nationalrail.co.uk | 0845 748 4950 |
|---|---|---|
| The Trainline | trainline.co.uk | |
| UK train operating companies | rail.co.uk | |
| Arriva Trains | arriva.co.uk | 0845 748 4950 |
| c2c | c2c-online.co.uk | 0845 601 4873 |
| Chiltern Railways | chilternrailways.co.uk | 0845 600 5165 |
| CrossCountry | crosscountrytrains.co.uk | 0845 748 4950 |
| East Midlands Trains | eastmidlandstrains.co.uk | 0845 748 4950 |
| First Capital Connect | firstcapitalconnect.co.uk | 0845 748 4950 |
| First Great Western | firstgreatwestern.co.uk | 0845 700 0125 |
| Gatwick Express | gatwickexpress.co.uk | 0845 850 1530 |
| Heathrow Express | heathrowexpress.com | 0845 600 1515 |
| Hull Trains | hulltrains.co.uk | 0845 071 0222 |
| Island Line | island-line.co.uk | 0845 748 4950 |
| London Midland | londonmidland.com | 0845 748 4950 |
| Merseyrail | merseyrail.org | 0845 748 4950 |
| Northern Rail | northernrail.org | 0845 748 4950 |
| One Railway | onerailway.com | 0845 600 7245 |
| South Eastern Trains | southeasternrailway.co.uk | 0845 000 2222 |
| South West Trains | southwesttrains.co.uk | 0845 600 0650 |
| Southern | southernrailway.com | 0845 127 2920 |
| Stansted Express | stanstedexpress.com | 0845 600 7245 |
| Transpennine Express | tpexpress.co.uk | 0845 600 1671 |
| Virgin Trains | virgintrains.co.uk | 0845 722 2333* |

## Ferry

| Ferry information | sailanddrive.com | |
|---|---|---|
| Condor Ferries (Channel Islands) | condorferries.co.uk | 0870 243 5140* |
| Steam Packet Company (Isle of Man) | steam-packet.com | 0871 222 1333 |
| Isles of Scilly Travel | islesofscilly-travel.co.uk | 0845 710 5555 |
| Red Funnel (Isle of Wight) | redfunnel.co.uk | 0870 444 8898 |
| Wight Link (Isle of Wight) | wightlink.co.uk | 0870 582 0202 |

Phone numbers listed are for general enquiries unless otherwise stated.

* Booking line only

# National cycle network

Sections of the National Cycle Network are shown on the maps in this guide. The numbers on the maps will appear on the signs along your route **3**. Here are some tips about finding and using a route.

- **Research and plan your route online**
  Log on to **sustrans.org.uk** and click on 'Get cycling' to find information about routes in this guide or other routes you want to use.

- **Order a route map**
  Useful, easy-to-use maps of many of the most popular routes of the National Cycle Network are available from Sustrans, the charity behind the Network. These can be purchased online or by mail order – visit **sustransshop.co.uk** or call **0845 113 0065.**

- **Order Cycling in the UK**
  The official guide to the National Cycle Network gives details of rides all over the UK, detailing 148 routes and profiles of 43 days rides on traffic-free paths and quiet roads.

| ROUTE NUMBER | ROUTE/MAP NAME | START/END OF ROUTE |
|---|---|---|
| **South West** | | |
| 3 | The West Country Way | Padstow – Bristol/Bath |
| 3 & 32 | The Cornish Way | Land's End – Bude |
| 27 | The Devon Coast to Coast | Ilfracombe – Plymouth |
| **South East** | | |
| 4 & 5 | Thames Valley | London – Oxford via Reading |
| 4 | Kennet & Avon | Reading – Bristol |
| 2, 20 & 21 | Downs & Weald | London – Brighton – Hastings |
| **East of England** | | |
| 1 | East of England | Hull – Fakenham – Harwich |
| **Heart of England** | | |
| 5 & 54 | West Midlands | Oxford – Derby via Birmingham |
| 6 & 51 | South Midlands | Oxford – Derby via Leicester |
| **North East England** | | |
| 1 | Coast & Castles | Newcastle upon Tyne – Berwick-upon-Tweed – Edinburgh |
| 68 | Pennine Cycleway North | Appleby-in-Westmorland/Penrith – Berwick-upon-Tweed |
| 7, 14 & 71 | Sea to Sea (C2C) | Whitehaven/Workington – Sunderland/Newcastle upon Tyne |
| 72 | Hadrian's Cycleway | Ravenglass – South Shields |
| **Yorkshire and North West England** | | |
| 68 | Pennine Cycleway (South Pennines & the Dales) | Holmfirth – Appleby-in-Westmorland/Kendal |
| 1, 14 & 65 | Yorkshire Moors & Coast | Barnard Castle - Whitby & Middlesborough – Thirsk |
| 62 & 65 | Trans Pennine Trail East | Yorkshire – North Sea |
| 62 | Trans Pennine Trail West | Irish Sea – Yorkshire |
| Regional 20 | Walney to Wear (W2W) | Barrow-in-Furness – Sunderland |

# National Accessible Scheme index

Establishments participating in the National Accessible Scheme are listed below – those in colour have a detailed entry in this guide. At the front of the guide you can find information about the scheme. Establishments are listed alphabetically by place name within each region.

## 🦽 Mobility level 1

## Mobility level 1 continued

| | | |
|---|---|---|
| *Holbeach* East Midlands | Ecklinville B&B ★★★★ | 570 |
| *Holbeck* East Midlands | Browns ★★★★★ GOLD | 570 |
| *Skegness* East Midlands | Chatsworth ★★★ | 246 |
| *Skegness* East Midlands | The Sandgate ★★★ | 576 |
| *Wirksworth* East Midlands | The Old Lock-Up ★★★★★ GOLD | 578 |
| *Dereham* East of England | Greenbanks Country Hotel and 3 Palms Leisure Pool ★★★★ | 585 |
| *Halstead* East of England | The White Hart ★★★ | 589 |
| *West Rudham* East of England | Oyster House ★★★★ SILVER | 600 |
| *London SW7* | YHA South Kensington Baden-Powell House ★★★★ | 603 |
| *Abingdon* South East England | Abbey Guest House ★★★★ | 606 |
| *Ducklington* South East England | Ducklington Farm ★★★ | 617 |
| *Folkestone* South East England | Garden Lodge ★★★★ | 347 |
| *Leckhampstead* South East England | Weatherhead Farm ★★★★ | 626 |
| *Marlow* South East England | Granny Anne's ★★★ | 628 |
| *Pulborough* South East England | The Labouring Man ★★★★ | 370 |
| *Sway* South East England | The Nurse's Cottage ★★★★ | 641 |
| *Witney* South East England | Springhill Farm Bed & Breakfast ★★★ | 644 |
| *Bournemouth* South West England | Wood Lodge ★★★★ | 410 |
| *Bratton Fleming* South West England | Bracken House Country Hotel ★★★★★ | 651 |
| *Devizes* South West England | Longwater ★★★ | 660 |
| *Godney* South West England | Double-Gate Farm ★★★★ GOLD | 665 |
| *Lizard* South West England | Lizard Point Youth Hostel ★★★★ | 670 |
| *West Quantoxhead* South West England | Stilegate Bed and Breakfast ★★★★★ | 696 |
| *Weston-super-Mare* South West England | Milton Lodge Hotel ★★★ | 697 |
| *Weston-super-Mare* South West England | Saxonia Guest House ★★★ | 697 |
| *Weston-super-Mare* South West England | Spreyton Guest House ★★★ | 697 |
| *Yelverton* South West England | Overcombe House ★★★★ | 483 |

## Mobility level 2

| | | |
|---|---|---|
| *Carlisle* England's Northwest | Bessiestown Farm Country Guesthouse ★★★★ GOLD | 491 |
| *Ribchester* England's Northwest | Riverside Barn ★★★★★ | 502 |
| *Bardon Mill* North East England | Montcoffer ◆◆◆◆◆ GOLD | 509 |
| *Berwick-upon-Tweed* North East England | Meadow Hill Guest House ★★★★ | 510 |
| *Haydon Bridge* North East England | Grindon Cartshed ★★★★ | 116 |
| *Hesleden* North East England | The Ship Inn ★★★★ SILVER | 513 |
| *Newbrough* North East England | Carr Edge Farm ★★★★ | 515 |
| *Easingwold* Yorkshire | Thornton Lodge Farm ★★★★ | 525 |
| *Helmsley* Yorkshire | Helmsley YHA ★★★ | 529 |
| *Lockton* Yorkshire | YHA Lockton ★★★★ | 532 |
| *Runswick Bay* Yorkshire | Ellerby Hotel ★★★★ SILVER | 535 |
| *Whitby* Yorkshire | Whitby YHA ★★★★ | 542 |
| *Redditch* Heart of England | White Hart Inn ★★★ | 202 |
| *Blaxhall* East of England | Blaxhall YHA ★★★ | 580 |
| *Cheshunt* East of England | YHA Lee Valley Village ★★★★ | 583 |
| *Cromer* East of England | Incleborough House Luxury Bed and Breakfast ★★★★★ | 270 |
| *Sheringham* East of England | Sheringham YHA ★★ | 597 |
| *Walton-on-the-Naze* East of England | Bufo Villae Guest House ★★★★ | 599 |
| *Wangford* East of England | The Plough Inn ★★★★ | 600 |
| *Wells-next-the-Sea* East of England | Wells-next-the-Sea YHA ★★★★ | 600 |
| *London SE16* | YHA London Thameside ★★ | 602 |
| *Heathfield* South East England | Spicers ★★★★ | 623 |
| *Bath* South West England | The Carfax ★★★★★ | 403 |

Establishments in colour have a detailed entry in this guide.

## Mobility level 2 continued

| | | |
|---|---|---|
| *Chedzoy* South West England | Apple View ★★★★ SILVER | 656 |
| *Godney* South West England | Double-Gate Farm ★★★★ GOLD | 665 |
| *Padstow* South West England | Woodlands Country House ★★★★★ SILVER | 447 |
| *Parkend* South West England | The Fountain Inn ★★★ | 678 |
| *Ruan High Lanes* South West England | Trenona Farm Holidays ★★★ | 457 |
| *Sandford* South West England | Ashridge Farm ★★★★ | 685 |
| *Yelverton* South West England | Overcombe House ★★★★ | 483 |

## Mobility level 3 Independent

| | | |
|---|---|---|
| *Longthwaite* England's Northwest | Borrowdale YHA ★★★★ | 499 |
| *Bridlington* Yorkshire | Providence Place ★★★★ | 523 |
| *Harwood Dale* Yorkshire | The Grainary ★★★★ | 528 |
| *Tugford* Heart of England | Tugford Farm B&B ★★★★ | 561 |
| *Skegness* East Midlands | Fountaindale Hotel ★★★★ | 575 |
| *Southwold* East of England | Newlands Country House ★★★★ SILVER | 597 |
| *Cannington* South West England | Blackmore Farm ★★★ | 655 |
| *Colyton* South West England | Smallicombe Farm ★★★★ SILVER | 659 |
| *Godney* South West England | Double-Gate Farm ★★★★ GOLD | 665 |
| *Horsington* South West England | Half Moon Inn ★★★ | 667 |
| *Torquay* South West England | Crown Lodge ★★★★ | 691 |
| *Truro* South West England | Tregoninny Farm ★★★★ | 694 |

## Mobility level 3 Assisted

| | | |
|---|---|---|
| *Stape* Yorkshire | Rawcliffe House Farm ★★★★ SILVER | 539 |
| *Godney* South West England | Double-Gate Farm ★★★★ GOLD | 665 |
| *Truro* South West England | Tregoninny Farm ★★★★ | 694 |

## Access Exceptional Assisted

| | | |
|---|---|---|
| *Tugford* Heart of England | Tugford Farm B&B ★★★★ | 561 |

## Hearing impairment level 1

| | | |
|---|---|---|
| *Blackpool* England's Northwest | The Pembroke ★★★★ | 489 |
| *Whitby* Yorkshire | Whitby YHA ★★★★ | 542 |
| *Holbeach* East Midlands | Ecklinville B&B ★★★★ | 570 |
| *Sway* South East England | The Nurse's Cottage ★★★★ | 641 |
| *Horsington* South West England | Half Moon Inn ★★★ | 667 |

## Visual impairment level 1

| | | |
|---|---|---|
| *Blackpool* England's Northwest | The Pembroke ★★★★ | 489 |
| *Helmsley* Yorkshire | Helmsley YHA ★★★ | 529 |
| *Whitby* Yorkshire | Whitby YHA ★★★★ | 542 |
| *Holbeach* East Midlands | Ecklinville B&B ★★★★ | 570 |
| *Horsington* South West England | Half Moon Inn ★★★ | 667 |

# Gold and Silver Award winners

Establishments that have achieved a Gold or Silver Award in recognition of exceptional quality are listed below – those in colour have a detailed entry in this guide. Establishments are listed alphabetically by place name within each region.

## England's Northwest

### GOLD

| | |
|---|---|
| *Blackpool* **Number One** ★★★★★ | 60 |
| *Borrowdale* **Hazel Bank Country House** ★★★★★ | 63 |
| *Carlisle* **Bessiestown Farm Country Guesthouse** ★★★★★ | 491 |
| *Carlisle* **Number Thirty One** ★★★★★ | 491 |
| *Cartmel* **Hill Farm B&B For Country Lovers** ★★★★★ | 492 |
| *Coniston* **Coniston Lodge** ★★★★★ | 493 |
| *Grasmere* **Lake View Country House** ★★★★ | 495 |
| *Ravenstonedale* **Coldbeck House** ★★★★★ | 502 |
| *Sawrey* **West Vale Country House & Restaurant** ★★★★★ | 503 |
| *Scotby* **Willowbeck Lodge** ★★★★★ | 503 |
| *Stainburn* **Falconwood** ★★★★★ | 504 |
| *Stonyhurst* **Alden Cottage** ★★★★ | 504 |
| *Whitehaven* **Moresby Hall** ★★★★★ | 89 |
| *Whitewell* **The Inn at Whitewell** ★★★★★ | 505 |
| *Windermere* **Beechwood** ★★★★ | 506 |

### SILVER

| | |
|---|---|
| *Accrington* **Norwood Guest House** ★★★★ | 485 |
| *Alston* **Greycroft** ★★★★ | 485 |
| *Ambleside* **Far Nook** ★★★★★ | 485 |
| *Ambleside* **Red Bank** ★★★★★ | 56 |
| *Ambleside* **Amboseli Lodge** ★★★★ | 485 |
| *Ambleside* **Barnes Fell Guest House** ★★★★ | 485 |
| *Ambleside* **Easedale Lodge Guest House** ★★★★ | 485 |
| *Ambleside* **Elder Grove** ★★★★ | 54 |
| *Ambleside* **Fisherbeck** ★★★★ | 485 |
| *Ambleside* **Freshfields Guest House** ★★★★ | 485 |
| *Ambleside* **Kingswood 'Bee & Bee'** ★★★★ | 55 |
| *Ambleside* **Riverside** ★★★★ | 486 |
| *Ambleside* **Stepping Stones** ★★★★ | 57 |
| *Ambleside* **Waterwheel Guesthouse** ★★★★ | 486 |
| *Bassenthwaite* **Herdwick Croft Guest House** ★★★★ | 486 |
| *Bassenthwaite* **Highside Farm** ★★★★ | 486 |
| *Bassenthwaite* **Ravenstone Lodge** ★★★★ | 486 |
| *Blundellsands* **Blundellsands Guesthouse** ★★★★ | 490 |
| *Boltongate* **Boltongate Old Rectory** ★★★★★ | 490 |
| *Brampton* **Vallum Barn** ★★★★ | 490 |
| *Brisco* **Crossroads House** ★★★★ | 490 |
| *Bruera* **Churton Heath Farm Bed & Breakfast** ★★★★ | 490 |
| *Caldbeck* **Swaledale Watch** ★★★★ | 64 |
| *Carleton* **Birklands House** ★★★★ | 491 |
| *Carleton* **River Forge Bed & Breakfast** ★★★★ | 491 |
| *Carlisle* **Cartref Guest House** ★★★★ | 491 |
| *Carlisle* **Courtfield House** ★★★★ | 491 |
| *Carnforth* **Capernwray House** ★★★★ | 491 |
| *Castle Carrock* **The Weary at Castle Carrock** ★★★★ | 65 |
| *Chester* **Mitchell's of Chester Guest House** ★★★★★ | 492 |
| *Chester* **Willow Run Bed & Breakfast** ★★★★ | 492 |
| *Colne* **Blakey Hall Farm** ◆◆◆◆ | 493 |
| *Coniston* **The Old Rectory** ★★★★ | 493 |
| *Dalton-in-Furness* **Park Cottage** ★★★★ | 493 |
| *Dufton* **Brow Farm Bed & Breakfast** ★★★★ | 68 |
| *Far Sawrey* **Fair Rigg at Far Sawrey** ★★★★★ | 494 |
| *Fence* **Grains Barn Farm** ★★★★★ | 494 |
| *Gilsland* **The Hill on the Wall** ★★★★★ | 494 |
| *Gilsland* **Bush Nook** ★★★★ | 494 |
| *Goodshaw* **The Old White Horse** ★★★★ | 494 |
| *Grasmere* **Beck Allans Guest House** ★★★★ | 495 |
| *Grasmere* **Riversdale** ★★★★ | 495 |

Establishments in colour have a detailed entry in this guide.

## England's Northwest continued

## North East England

## North East England continued

### SILVER continued

## Yorkshire

### GOLD

### SILVER

Establishments in colour have a detailed entry in this guide.

## Yorkshire continued

## Yorkshire continued

## Heart of England

Establishments in colour have a detailed entry in this guide.

## Heart of England continued

## East Midlands

## East Midlands continued

## East of England

Establishments in colour have a detailed entry in this guide.

# East of England continued

## East of England continued

Establishments in colour have a detailed entry in this guide.

## South East England continued

## South East England continued

Establishments in colour have a detailed entry in this guide.

## South West England

### GOLD

| | |
|---|---|
| Alderton **Moors Farm House** ★★★★★ | 646 |
| Axminster **Kerrington House Hotel** ★★★★★ | 646 |
| Bath **Athole Guest House** ★★★★★ | 402 |
| Bath **The Ayrlington** ★★★★★ | 647 |
| Bath **The Residence** ★★★★★ | 405 |
| Bibury **Cotteswold House** ★★★★ | 406 |
| Blandford Forum **Farnham Farm House** ★★★★★ | 407 |
| Bourton-on-the-Water **Coombe House** ★★★★ | 651 |
| Bourton-on-the-Water **Meadow View** ★★★★ | 651 |
| Bovey Tracey **Brookfield House** ★★★★★ | 410 |
| Bridport **The Roundham House** ★★★★★ | 413 |
| Bridport **Southcroft** ♦♦♦♦ | 652 |
| Brixham **Brookside Guest House** ★★★★ | 653 |
| Burton Bradstock **Norburton Hall** ★★★★★ | 655 |
| Calne **Queenwood Lodge** ★★★★★ | 655 |
| Cheltenham **Thirty Two** ★★★★★ | 657 |
| Chickerell **Stonebank** ★★★★★ | 657 |
| Chipping Campden **Nineveh Farm** ♦♦♦♦♦ | 657 |
| Christchurch **Seawards** ★★★★★ | 421 |
| Corfe Castle **Bradle Farmhouse** ★★★★ | 659 |
| Corfe Mullen **Elms Lodge** ★★★★ | 659 |
| Corsham **Heatherly Cottage** ★★★★ | 423 |
| Dartmouth **Hill View House** ★★★★ | 660 |
| Dawlish **Lammas Park House** ★★★★★ | 660 |
| Downton **Witherington Farm Bed & Breakfast** ★★★★★ | 661 |
| Dulverton **Three Acres Country House** ★★★★★ | 661 |
| Exeter **The Galley 'Fish and Seafood' Restaurant & Spa with Cabins** ★★★★★ | 428 |
| Falmouth **Dolvean House** ★★★★★ | 430 |
| Godney **Double-Gate Farm** ★★★★ | 665 |
| Hartland **Golden Park** ★★★★★ | 666 |
| Kimmeridge **Kimmeridge Farmhouse** ★★★★ | 668 |
| Landrake **Lantallack Farm** ★★★★★ | 669 |
| Launceston **Wheatley Farm** ★★★★★ | 669 |
| Little Langford **Little Langford Farmhouse** ★★★★★ | 670 |
| Lyme Regis **Clappentail House** ★★★★★ | 670 |
| Lyme Regis **Old Lyme Guest House** ★★★★ | 671 |
| Muchelney **The Parsonage** ★★★★★ | 674 |
| Penzance **Lowenna, Mousehole** ♦♦♦♦♦ | 679 |
| Poole **Danecourt Lodge** ★★★★ | 680 |
| St Austell **Anchorage House** ★★★★★ | 459 |
| St Ives **Blue Hayes Private Hotel** ★★★★★ | 682 |
| St Juliot **The Old Rectory Boscastle** ★★★★★ | 683 |
| Shave Cross **Shave Cross House Hotel** ★★★★ | 685 |
| Sidmouth **The Salty Monk** ★★★★★ | 468 |
| Staverton **Kingston House** ★★★★★ | 687 |
| Talaton **Larkbeare Grange** ★★★★★ | 689 |
| Tavistock **Tor Cottage** ★★★★★ | 690 |
| Tavistock **Beera Farmhouse** ★★★★ | 690 |
| Teignmouth **Thomas Luny House** ★★★★★ | 690 |

| | |
|---|---|
| Two Waters Foot **Treverbyn Vean Manor** ★★★★★ | 694 |
| Upper Oddington **Blenheim Cottage** ★★★★★ | 694 |
| Warminster **Bugley Barton B&B** ♦♦♦♦♦ | 695 |
| Waterrow **Handley Farm Accommodation** ★★★★★ | 695 |
| Wells **Carmen B&B** ★★★★ | 695 |
| Weymouth **Chandlers** ★★★★★ | 697 |
| Wimborne Minster **Lantern Lodge** ★★★★ | 699 |
| Winchcombe **Postlip Hall Farm** ★★★★ | 699 |

### SILVER

| | |
|---|---|
| Alton Pancras **Whiteways Farmhouse Accommodation** ★★★★ | 646 |
| Appledore **West Farm** ★★★★★ | 646 |
| Ashton Keynes **Wheatleys Farm** ★★★★ | 646 |
| Athelhampton **White Cottage** ★★★★ | 401 |
| Axminster **Hedgehog Corner** ★★★★ | 646 |
| Bampton **Lodfin Farm Bed & Breakfast** ★★★★ | 646 |
| Barnstaple **The Spinney** ★★★★ | 401 |
| Bath **Badminton Villa** ★★★★ | 647 |
| Bath **Bay Tree House** ♦♦♦♦ | 647 |
| Bath **Corston Fields Farm** ★★★★ | 647 |
| Bath **The Hollies** ★★★★ | 647 |
| Bath **Ravenscroft (Sydney Road)** ★★★★ | 648 |
| Bath **St Leonards** ★★★★ | 648 |
| Bath **Three Abbey Green** ★★★★ | 648 |
| Bath **Tolley Cottage** ★★★★ | 648 |
| Beaminster **Watermeadow House** ★★★★★ | 648 |
| Berrow **Berrow Links House** ★★★★ | 648 |
| Bideford **Bulworthy Cottage** ★★★★ | 649 |
| Bideford **The Mount** ★★★★ | 649 |
| Bilbrook **The Wayside B&B** ★★★★ | 406 |
| Binegar **Mansefield House** ★★★★ | 649 |
| Bishops Hull **The Old Mill** ★★★★★ | 649 |
| Blockley **Arreton House** ♦♦♦♦ | 649 |
| Blockley **Mill Dene Garden Country Bed & Breakfast** ★★★★ | 649 |
| Bodmin **Bokiddick Farm** ★★★★★ | 649 |
| Bodmin **Bedknobs** ♦♦♦♦ | 649 |
| Boscastle **Reddivallen Farm** ★★★★★ | 650 |
| Boscastle **Home Farm Bed and Breakfast** ♦♦♦♦ | 650 |
| Boscastle **Valency Bed and Breakfast** ★★★★ | 650 |
| Bossington **Tudor Cottage** ★★★★ | 650 |
| Bournemouth **Balincourt Hotel** ★★★★★ | 650 |
| Bourton-on-the-Water **Alderley Guesthouse** ★★★★ | 651 |
| Bourton-on-the-Water **Touchstone** ★★★★ | 651 |
| Bradford-on-Avon **Great Ashley Farm** ★★★★ | 651 |
| Bradford-on-Avon **Honeysuckle Cottage** ★★★★ | 411 |
| Bradpole **Orchard Barn** ★★★★★ | 651 |
| Brentor **Burnville House** ★★★★★ | 652 |
| Bridgwater **Chestnut House** ★★★★★ | 652 |
| Bridport **Highway Farm** ★★★★ | 652 |
| Broadstone **Heathcote House** ★★★★ | 653 |

## South West England continued

Establishments in colour have a detailed entry in this guide.

## South West England continued

## South West England continued

Establishments in colour have a detailed entry in this guide.

# Walkers and cyclists welcome

Establishments participating in the Walkers Welcome and Cyclists Welcome schemes provide special facilities and actively encourage these recreations. Accommodation with a detailed entry in this guide is listed below. Place names are listed alphabetically within each region.

## Walkers Welcome and Cyclists Welcome

## Walkers Welcome and Cyclists Welcome continued

| | | |
|---|---|---|
| Malvern Heart of England | Orchid House ★★★★ SILVER | 200 |
| Pershore Heart of England | Arbour House ★★★★ | 201 |
| Stratford-upon-Avon Heart of England | Broom Hall Inn ★★★ | 206 |
| Chapel-en-le-Frith East Midlands | High Croft ★★★★★ SILVER | 232 |
| Leicester East Midlands | Wondai B&B ★★★ | 239 |
| Lincoln East Midlands | Welbeck Cottage B&B ★★★★ | 240 |
| Mumby East Midlands | Brambles ★★★ | 243 |
| Beccles East of England | Pinetrees ★★★★ | 263 |
| Cavendish East of England | Embleton House ★★★★ SILVER | 268 |
| Diss East of England | Old Rectory Hopton ★★★★★ GOLD | 271 |
| Hickling East of England | The Dairy Barns ★★★★ GOLD | 276 |
| Hunstanton East of England | The King William IV Country Inn & Restaurant ★★★★ SILVER | 277 |
| Norwich East of England | Cavell House ★★★★ | 282 |
| South Walsham East of England | Old Hall Farm ★★★★ | 286 |
| Bognor Regis South East England | White Horses Felpham Bed & Breakfast ★★★★ | 328 |
| Burford South East England | Cotland House B&B ★★★★ | 332 |
| Burley South East England | Wayside Cottage ★★★★ | 333 |
| Chilgrove South East England | Chilgrove Farm ★★★★ | 337 |
| Pulborough South East England | The Labouring Man ★★★★ | 370 |
| Ramsgate South East England | Glendevon Guest House ★★★★ | 370 |
| Rudgwick South East England | Alliblaster House ★★★★★ SILVER | 374 |
| Bath South West England | The Carfax ★★★★★ | 403 |
| Brean South West England | The Old Rectory Motel ★★★★ | 411 |
| Dartmouth South West England | Strete Barton House ★★★★ SILVER | 425 |
| Dinton South West England | Marshwood Farm B&B ★★★★ | 426 |
| Kingsbridge South West England | Ashleigh House ★★★ | 435 |
| Market Lavington South West England | The Green Dragon ★★★ | 441 |
| Martock South West England | The White Hart Hotel ★★★★ | 442 |
| Nether Stowey South West England | Castle of Comfort Country House ★★★★★ SILVER | 445 |
| Padstow South West England | Pendeen House ★★★★ | 447 |
| Pensford South West England | Green Acres ★★ | 449 |
| Penzance South West England | Glencree House ★★★★ | 450 |
| St Just in Roseland South West England | Roundhouse Barns ★★★★ | 461 |
| Sidmouth South West England | The Salty Monk ★★★★★ GOLD | 468 |
| Yelverton South West England | Overcombe House ★★★★ | 483 |

## Walkers Welcome

| | | |
|---|---|---|
| Keswick England's Northwest | Appletrees ★★★★ | 73 |
| Pickering Yorkshire | 17 Burgate ★★★★★ GOLD | 153 |
| Tenbury Wells Heart of England | Millbrook ★★★★ | 210 |
| Hope East Midlands | Underleigh House ★★★★★ GOLD | 236 |
| Rye South East England | Hayden's ★★★★★ | 375 |
| Athelhampton South West England | White Cottage ★★★★ SILVER | 401 |
| Callington South West England | Hampton Manor ★★★★ | 416 |

## Cyclists Welcome

| | | |
|---|---|---|
| Market Weighton Yorkshire | Red House ★★★★ | 152 |
| Sidmouth South West England | Cheriton Guest House ★★★★ | 467 |

Establishments listed here have a detailed entry in this guide.

# Quick reference index

If you're looking for a specific facility use this index to see at-a-glance detailed accommodation entries that match your requirement. Establishments are listed alphabetically by place name within each region.

## 📡 Indoor pool

## 📡 Outdoor pool

## ⇄ Outdoor pool continued

## ✗ Evening meal by arrangement

Establishments listed here have a detailed entry in this guide.

## ✕ Evening meal by arrangement continued

## ✕ Evening meal by arrangement continued

Establishments listed here have a detailed entry in this guide.

## ✕ Evening meal by arrangement continued

| | | |
|---|---|---|
| *Broadway* Heart of England | The Bell at Willersey ★★★★ | 189 |
| *Broadway* Heart of England | Farncombe Estate Centre ★★★★ | 190 |
| *Cheadle* Heart of England | Rakeway House Farm B&B ★★★★ | 191 |
| *Cleobury Mortimer* Heart of England | Broome Park Farm ★★★ | 191 |
| *Colton* Heart of England | Colton House ★★★★★ | 192 |
| *Coventry* Heart of England | Ashleigh House ★★★ | 193 |
| *Coventry* Heart of England | Highcroft Guest House ★★★ | 193 |
| *Hereford* Heart of England | Hedley Lodge ★★★★ | 194 |
| *Lower Loxley* Heart of England | The Grange Applied | 198 |
| *Ludlow* Heart of England | The Clive Bar and Restaurant With Rooms ★★★★★ SILVER | 199 |
| *Ludlow* Heart of England | Cecil Guest House ★★★ | 198 |
| *Minsterley* Heart of England | Holly House B&B ★★★ | 200 |
| *Newport* Heart of England | Norwood House Restaurant with Rooms ★★★ | 201 |
| *Newton St Margarets* Heart of England | Marises Barn ★★★★ | 201 |
| *Redditch* Heart of England | White Hart Inn ★★★ | 202 |
| *Shifnal* Heart of England | Odfellows – The Wine Bar ★★★ | 203 |
| *Stafford* Heart of England | Wyndale Guest House ★★ | 204 |
| *Stratford-upon-Avon* Heart of England | Drybank Farm ★★★★ | 206 |
| *Stratford-upon-Avon* Heart of England | Halford Bridge Inn ★★★★ | 207 |
| *Stratford-upon-Avon* Heart of England | Broom Hall Inn ★★★ | 206 |
| *Stratford-upon-Avon* Heart of England | Quilt and Croissants ★★★ | 208 |
| *Tanworth-in-Arden* Heart of England | Grange Farm ★★★★ SILVER | 209 |
| *Tenbury Wells* Heart of England | Millbrook ★★★★ | 210 |
| *Vowchurch* Heart of England | Yew Tree House ★★★★ SILVER | 210 |
| *Warwick* Heart of England | Longbridge Farm ★★★★ | 211 |
| *Worcester* Heart of England | Holland House ★★★ | 212 |
| *Barrow upon Soar* East Midlands | Hunting Lodge ★★★★ | 226 |
| *Beeley* East Midlands | The Devonshire Arms at Beeley ★★★★ | 227 |
| *Beeston* East Midlands | Hylands ★★★ | 227 |
| *Bradwell* East Midlands | Travellers Rest ★★★ | 228 |
| *Bretby* East Midlands | Bretby Conference Centre ★★★ | 229 |
| *Brigg* East Midlands | Holcombe Guest House ★★★★ | 229 |
| *Buxton* East Midlands | Grendon Guest House ★★★★★ GOLD | 230 |
| *Buxton* East Midlands | Fernydale Farm ★★★★ SILVER | 230 |
| *Buxton* East Midlands | Kingscroft Guest House ★★★★ SILVER | 231 |
| *Buxton* East Midlands | Devonshire Arms ★★★ | 229 |
| *Corby* East Midlands | Manor Farm Guest House ★★★★ | 233 |
| *Creaton* East Midlands | Highgate House – A Sundial Group Venue ★★★★ | 234 |
| *Empingham* East Midlands | Shacklewell Lodge ★★★★ | 236 |
| *Grantham* East Midlands | The Cedars ★★★★ | 236 |
| *Horsley* East Midlands | Horsley Lodge ★★★★ SILVER | 237 |
| *Kettering* East Midlands | Dairy Farm ★★★★ | 237 |
| *King's Cliffe* East Midlands | 19 West Street ★★★★ | 238 |
| *Knipton* East Midlands | Manners Arms ★★★★ | 238 |
| *Laxton* East Midlands | Dovecote Inn | 238 |
| *Lincoln* East Midlands | Damon's Motel ★★★★ | 239 |
| *Lincoln* East Midlands | The Old Bakery Restaurant with Rooms ★★★★ SILVER | 239 |
| *Lincoln* East Midlands | Welbeck Cottage B&B ★★★★ | 240 |
| *Lincoln* East Midlands | Duke William House ★★★ | 239 |

## ✕ Evening meal by arrangement continued

| | | |
|---|---|---|
| *Loughborough* East Midlands | Forest Rise Hotel ★★★ | 241 |
| *Loughborough* East Midlands | Highbury Guest House ★★★ | 241 |
| *Lutterworth* East Midlands | Ashlawn Country Guest House ★★★★ | 242 |
| *Monyash* East Midlands | Arbor Low B&B ★★★ | 243 |
| *Mumby* East Midlands | Brambles ★★★ | 243 |
| *Northampton* East Midlands | The Poplars ★★★★ | 244 |
| *Northampton* East Midlands | The Aarandale Regent ★★ | 244 |
| *Norton Disney* East Midlands | Brills Farm ★★★★ | 245 |
| *Skegness* East Midlands | Chatsworth ★★★ | 246 |
| *Skegness* East Midlands | Grosvenor House Hotel ★★★ | 246 |
| *Skegness* East Midlands | Roosevelt Lodge ★★★ | 246 |
| *Skegness* East Midlands | The Tudor Lodge Guest House ★★★ | 247 |
| *Thornton Curtis* East Midlands | Thornton Hunt Inn ★★★★ | 248 |
| *Uppingham* East Midlands | Spanhoe Lodge ★★★★★ GOLD | 249 |
| *Aldborough* East of England | Butterfly Cottage ★★★★ | 262 |
| *Aylsham* East of England | Old Pump House ★★★★ | 263 |
| *Beetley* East of England | Peacock House ★★★★ SILVER | 263 |
| *Burnham-on-Crouch* East of England | The Railway Hotel ★★★★ SILVER | 264 |
| *Cambridge* East of England | Hamilton Lodge ★★★ | 266 |
| *Cromer* East of England | Incleborough House Luxury Bed and Breakfast ★★★★★ | 270 |
| *Dereham* East of England | Hunters Hall ★★★★ | 270 |
| *Diss* East of England | Old Rectory Hopton ★★★★★ GOLD | 271 |
| *Docking* East of England | Jubilee Lodge ★★★★ | 271 |
| *Fakenham* East of England | Abbott Farm ★★★ | 272 |
| *Freckenham* East of England | The Golden Boar Inn ★★★★ | 273 |
| *Gamlingay* East of England | Emplins ★★★ | 274 |
| *Great Easton* East of England | The Swan Inn ★★★★ | 274 |
| *Great Yarmouth* East of England | Cavendish House ★★★ | 275 |
| *Hevingham* East of England | Marsham Arms Inn ★★★★ | 276 |
| *Hickling* East of England | The Dairy Barns ★★★★ GOLD | 276 |
| *Hunstanton* East of England | The King William IV Country Inn & Restaurant ★★★★ SILVER | 277 |
| *Kettleburgh* East of England | Church Farm ★★★ | 278 |
| *Lowestoft* East of England | Homelea Guest House ★★★ | 279 |
| *Nayland* East of England | White Hart Inn ★★★★★ GOLD | 281 |
| *Norwich* East of England | Cavell House ★★★★ | 282 |
| *Norwich* East of England | Oakbrook House – South Norfolk's Guest House ★★★ | 283 |
| *Saffron Walden* East of England | The Cricketers ★★★★ SILVER | 284 |
| *Shingle Street* East of England | Lark Cottage Applied | 285 |
| *Sibton* East of England | Sibton White Horse Inn ★★★★ | 285 |
| *Stansted* East of England | White House ★★★★ | 287 |
| *Stoke-by-Nayland* East of England | The Angel Inn ★★★★ | 287 |
| *Thompson* East of England | Chequers Inn ★★★★ | 289 |
| *Thornham Magna* East of England | Thornham Hall and Restaurant ★★★★★ SILVER | 289 |
| *Toppesfield* East of England | Harrow Hill Cottage ★★★ | 289 |
| *Woodhurst* East of England | The Raptor Foundation ★★★ | 291 |
| *Wrentham* East of England | Five Bells ★★★ | 291 |
| *London W6* | The Globetrotter Inn London ★★★★ | 309 |
| *Richmond* London | Ivy Cottage ★★★ | 310 |
| *Richmond* London | The Red Cow ★★★ | 310 |

Establishments listed here have a detailed entry in this guide.

## ✕ Evening meal by arrangement continued

| | | |
|---|---|---|
| Surbiton London | The Broadway Lodge ★★ | 310 |
| Adderbury South East England | The Bell Inn ★★★ | 322 |
| Ashford South East England | Dean Court Farm ★★★ | 324 |
| Banbury South East England | St Martins House ★★★★ | 325 |
| Battle South East England | Battle Golf Club ★★★ | 326 |
| Bexhill-on-Sea South East England | Barkers Bed and Breakfast ★★★ | 327 |
| Biddenden South East England | Heron Cottage ★★★★ | 327 |
| Bladbean South East England | Molehills ★★★★ | 327 |
| Brede South East England | 2 Stonelink Cottages ★★★ | 329 |
| Brighton & Hove South East England | The Dove ★★★ | 330 |
| Brize Norton South East England | The Priory ★★★ | 331 |
| Broadstairs South East England | The Bay Tree ★★★★ | 331 |
| Burley South East England | Wayside Cottage ★★★★ | 333 |
| Canterbury South East England | Magnolia House ★★★★★ GOLD | 335 |
| Canterbury South East England | Hornbeams ★★★★ | 335 |
| Canterbury South East England | Anns House ★★★ | 333 |
| Canterbury South East England | Clare Ellen Guest House Applied | 334 |
| Cowes South East England | Anchorage Guest House ★★★★ | 338 |
| Cuckfield South East England | Highbridge Mill ★★★★ SILVER | 339 |
| Dymchurch South East England | Waterside Guest House ★★★★ | 342 |
| East Ashling South East England | Horse & Groom ★★★★ | 342 |
| Eastbourne South East England | Brayscroft House ★★★★ GOLD | 343 |
| Eastbourne South East England | St Omer's ★★★★ | 344 |
| Eastbourne South East England | The Birling Gap ★★★ | 342 |
| Eastbourne South East England | Cambridge House ★★★ | 343 |
| Farnborough South East England | Langfords Bed & Breakfast ★★★ | 345 |
| Fittleworth South East England | Swan Inn ★★★★ | 346 |
| Folkestone South East England | Garden Lodge ★★★★ | 347 |
| Gillingham South East England | King Charles Hotel ★★★ | 349 |
| Guildford South East England | Littlefield Manor ★★★ | 350 |
| Hailsham South East England | Windesworth ★★★★ | 351 |
| Hastings South East England | Swan House ★★★★★ SILVER | 352 |
| High Wycombe South East England | The Three Horseshoes Inn ★★★★ GOLD | 356 |
| Kingston Blount South East England | The Cherry Tree ★★★ | 356 |
| Lamberhurst South East England | Woodpecker Barn ★★★★★ SILVER | 357 |
| Lewes South East England | The Blacksmiths Arms ★★★★ SILVER | 357 |
| Lewes South East England | The Crown Inn ★★★ | 357 |
| Littlehampton South East England | Arun View Inn ★★ | 358 |
| Longfield South East England | The Rising Sun Inn ★★★ | 358 |
| Lymington South East England | Bluebird Restaurant ★★★ | 358 |
| Lymington South East England | Gorse Meadow Guest House ★★★ | 358 |
| Lyndhurst South East England | Rosedale Bed & Breakfast ★★★ | 359 |
| Newbury South East England | East End Farm ★★★★ | 363 |
| Newport Pagnell South East England | Rosemary House ★★★★ | 365 |
| Ockley South East England | The Kings Arms Inn ★★★★ | 365 |
| Pulborough South East England | The Labouring Man ★★★★ | 370 |
| Sandhurst South East England | Lamberden Cottage ★★★★ | 376 |
| Sandhurst South East England | The Wellington Arms ★★★ | 376 |
| Sandown South East England | Rooftree Guesthouse ★★★★ | 377 |
| Sandown South East England | The Philomel ★★★ | 377 |

## ✕ Evening meal by arrangement continued

Establishments listed here have a detailed entry in this guide.

## ✕ Evening meal by arrangement continued

| | | |
|---|---|---|
| Nether Stowey South West England | Castle of Comfort Country House ★★★★★ SILVER | 445 |
| Newent South West England | The George ★★★ | 445 |
| Paignton South West England | Cliveden ★★★★ | 448 |
| Paignton South West England | Sonachan House ★★★★ | 448 |
| Paignton South West England | Benbows ★★★ | 448 |
| Paignton South West England | Rockview Guest House ★★★ | 448 |
| Penzance South West England | Cornerways Guest House ★★★ | 449 |
| Penzance South West England | Harbour Heights Bed and Breakfast ★★★ | 450 |
| Penzance South West England | Menwidden Farm ★★★ | 451 |
| Perranporth South West England | The Whitehouse Inn & Luxury Lodge ★★★★ | 453 |
| Piddletrenthide South West England | The Poachers Inn ★★★★ | 453 |
| Plymouth South West England | Gabber Farm ★★★ | 454 |
| Polzeath South West England | White Heron ★★★★ | 455 |
| Porlock South West England | Rose Bank Guest House ★★★★ SILVER | 456 |
| Port Isaac South West England | The Slipway ★★★★ | 456 |
| Redruth South West England | Goonearl Cottage ★★★★ | 457 |
| Rudford South West England | The Dark Barn Cottages ★★★★ | 458 |
| St Agnes South West England | Penkerris ★★ | 458 |
| St Austell South West England | Anchorage House ★★★★★ GOLD | 459 |
| St Austell South West England | Highland Court Lodge ★★★★★ SILVER | 459 |
| St Columb Major South West England | Pennatillie Farm ★★★★★ SILVER | 460 |
| St Mawgan South West England | Dalswinton House ★★★★ | 462 |
| Salisbury South West England | The Rokeby Guest House ★★★★ SILVER | 465 |
| Salisbury South West England | Alabare House ★★ | 463 |
| Shaftesbury South West England | Glebe Farm ★★★★★ SILVER | 465 |
| Sidmouth South West England | The Salty Monk ★★★★★ GOLD | 468 |
| Slimbridge South West England | Tudor Arms ★★★ | 468 |
| Spreyton South West England | The Tom Cobley Tavern ★★★ | 468 |
| Stogumber South West England | Wick House ★★★★ | 469 |
| Stogumber South West England | The White Horse Inn ★★★ | 469 |
| Stow-on-the-Wold South West England | Westcote Inn ★★★★ | 470 |
| Stroud South West England | 1 Woodchester Lodge ★★★★ | 471 |
| Sydling St Nicholas South West England | Magiston Farm ★★ | 472 |
| Tavistock South West England | Harrabeer Country House ★★★★ | 473 |
| Tintagel South West England | The Mill House ★★★ | 473 |
| Tiverton South West England | Bridge Guest House ★★★ | 474 |
| Torquay South West England | Haldon Priors ★★★★★ | 475 |
| Torquay South West England | Abingdon House ★★★★ | 474 |
| Wadebridge South West England | Tregolls Farm ★★★★ | 478 |
| Warminster South West England | The George Inn ★★★★ | 478 |
| Wells South West England | Worth House ★★★ | 479 |
| Wembworthy South West England | Lymington Arms ★★★★ | 479 |
| Wimborne Minster South West England | The Albion ★★ | 481 |
| Winkleigh South West England | The Old Parsonage ★★★★ | 482 |
| Woolacombe South West England | Sunny Nook ★★★★ SILVER | 482 |

# Hostel and campus accommodation

The following establishments all have a detailed entry in this guide.

# Bank holiday dates for your diary

| holiday | 2008 | 2009 |
|---|---|---|
| **New Year's Day** | 1 January | 1 January |
| **Good Friday** | 21 March | 10 April |
| **Easter Monday** (England & Wales) | 24 March | 13 April |
| **Early May Bank Holiday** | 5 May | 4 May |
| **Spring Bank Holiday** | 26 May | 25 May |
| **Summer Bank Holiday** (England & Wales) | 25 August | 31 August |
| **Christmas Day** | 25 December | 25 December |
| **Boxing Day Holiday** | 26 December | 28 December |

# Index by property name

Accommodation with a detailed entry in this guide is listed below.

# Index by property name

Establishments listed here have a detailed entry in this guide.

Establishments listed here have a detailed entry in this guide.

# Index by property name

Establishments listed here have a detailed entry in this guide.

# Index by place name

The following places all have detailed accommodation entries in this guide. If the place where you wish to stay is not shown, the location maps (starting on page 28) will help you to find somewhere to stay in the area.

Turn to the pages indicated for detailed accommodation entries in these places.

Turn to the pages indicated for detailed accommodation entries in these places.

# 2008 Calendar

## JANUARY

| M | T | W | T | F | S | S |
|---|---|---|---|---|---|---|
|   | 1 | 2 | 3 | 4 | 5 | 6 |
| 7 | 8 | 9 | 10 | 11 | 12 | 13 |
| 14 | 15 | 16 | 17 | 18 | 19 | 20 |
| 21 | 22 | 23 | 24 | 25 | 26 | 27 |
| 28 | 29 | 30 | 31 |   |   |   |

## FEBRUARY

| M | T | W | T | F | S | S |
|---|---|---|---|---|---|---|
|   |   |   |   | 1 | 2 | 3 |
| 4 | 5 | 6 | 7 | 8 | 9 | 10 |
| 11 | 12 | 13 | 14 | 15 | 16 | 17 |
| 18 | 19 | 20 | 21 | 22 | 23 | 24 |
| 25 | 26 | 27 | 28 | 29 |   |   |

## MARCH

| M | T | W | T | F | S | S |
|---|---|---|---|---|---|---|
| 31 |   |   |   |   | 1 | 2 |
| 3 | 4 | 5 | 6 | 7 | 8 | 9 |
| 10 | 11 | 12 | 13 | 14 | 15 | 16 |
| 17 | 18 | 19 | 20 | 21 | 22 | 23 |
| 24 | 25 | 26 | 27 | 28 | 29 | 30 |

## APRIL

| M | T | W | T | F | S | S |
|---|---|---|---|---|---|---|
|   | 1 | 2 | 3 | 4 | 5 | 6 |
| 7 | 8 | 9 | 10 | 11 | 12 | 13 |
| 14 | 15 | 16 | 17 | 18 | 19 | 20 |
| 21 | 22 | 23 | 24 | 25 | 26 | 27 |
| 28 | 29 | 30 |   |   |   |   |

## MAY

| M | T | W | T | F | S | S |
|---|---|---|---|---|---|---|
|   |   |   | 1 | 2 | 3 | 4 |
| 5 | 6 | 7 | 8 | 9 | 10 | 11 |
| 12 | 13 | 14 | 15 | 16 | 17 | 18 |
| 19 | 20 | 21 | 22 | 23 | 24 | 25 |
| 26 | 27 | 28 | 29 | 30 | 31 |   |

## JUNE

| M | T | W | T | F | S | S |
|---|---|---|---|---|---|---|
| 30 |   |   |   |   |   | 1 |
| 2 | 3 | 4 | 5 | 6 | 7 | 8 |
| 9 | 10 | 11 | 12 | 13 | 14 | 15 |
| 16 | 17 | 18 | 19 | 20 | 21 | 22 |
| 23 | 24 | 25 | 26 | 27 | 28 | 29 |

## JULY

| M | T | W | T | F | S | S |
|---|---|---|---|---|---|---|
|   | 1 | 2 | 3 | 4 | 5 | 6 |
| 7 | 8 | 9 | 10 | 11 | 12 | 13 |
| 14 | 15 | 16 | 17 | 18 | 19 | 20 |
| 21 | 22 | 23 | 24 | 25 | 26 | 27 |
| 28 | 29 | 30 | 31 |   |   |   |

## AUGUST

| M | T | W | T | F | S | S |
|---|---|---|---|---|---|---|
|   |   |   |   | 1 | 2 | 3 |
| 4 | 5 | 6 | 7 | 8 | 9 | 10 |
| 11 | 12 | 13 | 14 | 15 | 16 | 17 |
| 18 | 19 | 20 | 21 | 22 | 23 | 24 |
| 25 | 26 | 27 | 28 | 29 | 30 | 31 |

## SEPTEMBER

| M | T | W | T | F | S | S |
|---|---|---|---|---|---|---|
| 1 | 2 | 3 | 4 | 5 | 6 | 7 |
| 8 | 9 | 10 | 11 | 12 | 13 | 14 |
| 15 | 16 | 17 | 18 | 19 | 20 | 21 |
| 22 | 23 | 24 | 25 | 26 | 27 | 28 |
| 29 | 30 |   |   |   |   |   |

## OCTOBER

| M | T | W | T | F | S | S |
|---|---|---|---|---|---|---|
|   |   | 1 | 2 | 3 | 4 | 5 |
| 6 | 7 | 8 | 9 | 10 | 11 | 12 |
| 13 | 14 | 15 | 16 | 17 | 18 | 19 |
| 20 | 21 | 22 | 23 | 24 | 25 | 26 |
| 27 | 28 | 29 | 30 | 31 |   |   |

## NOVEMBER

| M | T | W | T | F | S | S |
|---|---|---|---|---|---|---|
|   |   |   |   |   | 1 | 2 |
| 3 | 4 | 5 | 6 | 7 | 8 | 9 |
| 10 | 11 | 12 | 13 | 14 | 15 | 16 |
| 17 | 18 | 19 | 20 | 21 | 22 | 23 |
| 24 | 25 | 26 | 27 | 28 | 29 | 30 |

## DECEMBER

| M | T | W | T | F | S | S |
|---|---|---|---|---|---|---|
| 1 | 2 | 3 | 4 | 5 | 6 | 7 |
| 8 | 9 | 10 | 11 | 12 | 13 | 14 |
| 15 | 16 | 17 | 18 | 19 | 20 | 21 |
| 22 | 23 | 24 | 25 | 26 | 27 | 28 |
| 29 | 30 | 31 |   |   |   |   |

# enjoy**England** ™

## official tourist board guides

Hotels, including
country house and
town house hotels,
metro and budget
hotels in England 2008

**£10.99**

Guest accommodation,
B&Bs, guest houses,
farmhouses, inns,
restaurants with rooms,
campus and hostel
accommodation in
England 2008

**£11.99**

Self-catering holiday
homes, including
serviced apartments and
approved caravan
holiday homes, boat
accommodation and
holiday cottage agencies
in England 2008

**£11.99**

Touring parks, camping
holidays and holiday
parks and villages in
Britain 2008

**£8.99**

## ...formative, easy to use and great value for money

...s,
...ering

Great ideas for places
to visit, eat and stay
in England

**£10.99**

Places to stay and visit
in South West England

**£9.99**

Places to stay and visit
in Northern England

**£9.99**

Accessible places
to stay in Britain

**£9.99**

Now available in good bookshops.
...ecial offers on VisitBritain publications,
...se visit **enjoyenglanddirect.com**